Behavior Analysis
for Lasting Change

Beth Sulzer-Azaroff

University of Massachusetts
Amherst

G. Roy Mayer

California State University
Los Angeles

WADSWORTH

™

THOMSON LEARNING

Australia • Canada • Mexico • Singapore • Spain • United Kingdom • United States

Publisher   Ted Buchholz
Acquisition Editor   Jo-Anne Weaver
Project Editor   Joyce Jackson
Production Manager   Kenneth A. Dunaway
Cover Design Supervisor   John Ritland
Text Design   Impressions
Cover Design   Patty Potter/Patty Ryan Design
Cover Photos   Susan Lapides, Joel Gordon

Wadsworth/Thomson Learning
10 Davis Drive
Belmont CA 94002-3098
USA

For information about our products, contact us:
Thomson Learning Academic Resource Center
1-800-423-0563
http://www.wadsworth.com

For permission to use material from this text, contact us by
Web:http://www.thomsonrights.com
Fax: 1-800-730-2215
Phone: 1-800-730-2214

Printed in the United States of America

Library of Congress Cataloging-in-Publication Data

Sulzer-Azaroff, Beth.
      Behavior analysis for lasting change / Beth Sulzer-Azaroff,
   G. Roy Mayer.
         p.   cm.
      Rev. ed. of: Applying behavior analysis procedures with children and
   youth. ©1977.
      Includes bibliographical references and index.
      ISBN 0-03-032944-2
      1. Behavior modification. 2. Teaching. I. Mayer, G. Roy, 1940–
   II. Sulzer-Azaroff, Beth. Applying behavior analysis procedures with
   children and youth. III. Title.
   LB1060.2.S85   1991
   371.1'02—dc20   90-24339
                                                         CIP

Dedicated to
B. F. Skinner

—one can picture a good life by analyzing one's feelings, but one can achieve it only by arranging environmental contingencies

from *Notebooks*, p. 127
by B. F. Skinner (1983)

Contents

Preface *xv*
Acknowledgments *xvii*

Chapter 1 **Introduction to Behavior Analysis for Lasting Change**
  Goals *1*
Approaching Behavior Scientifically *2*
What is Behavior Analysis? *3*
Distinguishing Features of Applied Behavior Analysis *4*
  Performance Based *4*
  Analytical *5*
  Technological *5*
  Socially Important *5*
  Contextual *6*
  Accountable *6*
ABA as Science, Technology, and Practice *7*
Applied Behavior Analysis and Behavior Change *7*
  Who Is Concerned with Changing Behavior? *7*
  Addressing Change with ABA *8*
Summary *11*

Section I: Preliminary Steps *13*

Chapter 2 **Goal Selection: Initial Considerations**
  Goals *15*
Is Behavioral Intervention Warranted? *16*
  Realistic Identification of Problems and Goals *17*
  Several Independent Requests for Assistance with the Same Individual *17*
  Functioning Differently from Members of a Comparison Group *18*
  Dramatic Changes in an Individual's Behavior *18*

People Involved in Behavioral Programs and Their Roles *18*
Prior Considerations *19*
  Direct or Informal Solutions *19*
  Priorities and Support *20*
The Behavioral Approach *22*
  Behaviorally Defining Problems and Tentative Goals *24*
Situational Analysis *25*
  Test Scores, Records, and Other Materials *25*
  Narrative Recording and Sequence Analysis *26*
Summary *28*

Chapter 3 **Goal Selection: Guidelines**
  Goals *29*
Choosing from Among Alternative Goals *30*
  General Considerations in Goal Selection *30*
Goal Conflicts *37*
Preventing and Resolving Goal Conflicts *38*
  Participative Goal Setting *38*
  Arranging for Advocacy *39*
  Arranging for Institutional Review *40*
  Behavioral Contracting *40*
Selecting High-Priority Goals *42*
Summary *42*

Chapter 4 **Assessing Behavior and Setting Objectives**
  Goals *43*
Behavioral Assessment *44*
  What Is Behavioral Assessment? *44*
  Behavioral Assessment Justified *45*
  Ecobehavioral Assessment *45*
Specifying the Behavioral Objective *47*

Behavioral Dimensions   47
Context   49
Specifying Criteria   49
Sample Objectives   50
Task Analysis   51
Summary   53

Chapter 5   Behavioral Assessment: Selecting Observational Systems
Goals   55
Observation and Measurement   57
Selecting Valid Measures   58
Factors That Can Influence the Validity of Observations   59
Selecting Reliable Measures   63
Behavioral Recording Techniques   63
Measuring Behavioral Products   63
Measuring Transitory Events   65
Reporting Reliability Data   73
Summary   75

Chapter 6   Behavioral Assessment: Implementing Observational Systems
Goals   77
Behavioral-Recording Staff   79
Clients as Behavior Self-Recorders   79
Contingency Managers as Recorders   80
Automated Recording Systems   81
Training, Calibrating and Supervising Observers   83
Preliminary Steps   83
Training Sites   83
Procedural Clarification   84
Increasing Precision of Observers   84
Recording Independently   85
Maintaining Observational Reliability   85
Observing Behavior in Groups   86
Zone System   86
PLA-Check   86
Ecobehavioral Assessment   87
Graphing Behavioral Data   87
Adaptation   89
Baseline Measurement   91
Graphing Steady State Versus Acquisition Data   92
Summary   93

Chapter 7   Selecting Procedures
Goals   95
Behavior Analysis Procedures   97
What Are Contingencies?   98
Identifying Effective Contingencies   99

Inventories, Interviews, Records, and Checklists   99
Gathering Historical Information About Contingencies   100
Contingency Analyses   100
Selecting Procedural Strategies   101
Controlling Contingencies   101
Behavior Analysis, Procedural Selection, and the Law   103
Professional Ethical Standards   103
Evidence of Procedural Effectiveness   104
Competence of the Behavior Analyst and Contingency Manager   104
Degree of Restrictiveness   106
Positiveness Versus Aversiveness   106
Including Key Individuals in Procedural Selection   108
Contracting for Selection of Procedures   109
Voluntariness Versus Coercion   110
Countercontrol   114
Other Concerns   116
Summary   116

Chapter 8   Implementing Procedures and Monitoring Outcomes
Goals   119
Support for Application of Procedures   120
Identifying Necessary Resources   120
Obtaining Community Support   121
Peer Review   121
Accountability   122
Flexibility   123
Guidelines for Selecting Procedures by Contractual Arrangement   123
Stress the Positive   123
Request and Reinforce Small Improvements   123
Clarify Terms of the Contract   124
Reinforce the Target Behavior Immediately   124
Include an Option to Withdraw or Modify the Terms of the Contract   124
Weigh Costs and Benefits for All Participants   124
Daily Report Cards   125
Self-Management   126
Preparing the Environment   127
Monitoring Procedures   128
Revising Unsuccessful Procedures   129
Terminating Successful Programs   129
Summary   130

Section II: Increasing Behavior   133

Chapter 9   **Increasing Behavior: Reinforcement**
    Goals   137
Reinforcement Defined   138
Positive and Negative Reinforcement   139
    Distinguishing Positive and Negative
        Reinforcement from Other Procedures   141
    Deciding Whether to Apply Negative
        Reinforcement   142
Selecting Appropriate Reinforcers   143
    Unconditioned Reinforcing Stimuli   144
    How Stimuli Acquire Reinforcing Properties   144
    Establishing Conditioned Reinforcers   145
    Matching Reinforcers with Individuals   146
Summary   147

Chapter 10   **Selecting Positive Reinforcers**
    Goals   149
Edible Reinforcers   151
    Examples of the Use of Edible Reinforcers   151
    Factors to Consider in Selecting Edible
        Reinforcers   152
Tangible Reinforcers   153
    Factors to Consider in Selecting Tangible
        Reinforcers   154
Activity Reinforcers   155
    The Premack Principle   158
    The Response Deprivation Hypothesis   159
Social Reinforcers   160
    Examples of Effective Use of Social Reinforcers
        161
    Advantages of Social Reinforcement   161
    Feedback as a Reinforcer   164
    Using Specific or Labeled Praise   165
Generalized Reinforcers   165
Concerns About Contrived Reinforcers   166
    Extrinsic Reinforcers   166
    Bribery   167
    Countercontrol   168
    Treating People Differently   169
    Withholding Reinforcement   169
Summary   170

Chapter 11   **Implementing Effective**
    Reinforcement
    Goals   171
Reinforcing Immediately   173
    Using Supplementary Reinforcers   173
    Teaching Waiting   174
Teaching Discrimination of Contextual Factors   174

Providing an Adequate Amount of Reinforcement
    176
Ensuring Appropriate Reinforcer Quality   176
    Selecting Appropriate Reinforcers   176
    Introducing Variety   180
    Introducing Novelty   180
    Introducing Reinforcer Sampling   181
Assessing For and Overriding Competing
        Contingencies   181
Arranging Supportive Schedules of Reinforcement
    182
    Thinning Reinforcement   183
Identifying Effective Sources of Reinforcer Delivery
    183
    Self-Directed Reinforcement   184
Providing a Reinforcing Environment   186
Summary   187

Chapter 12   **Group and Peer Reinforcement**
    Goals   189
Group Oriented Reinforcing Contingencies   190
    Independent Group Contingencies   190
    Interdependent Group Contingencies   190
    Dependent Group Contingencies   191
    Comparative Effects of Different Group
        Contingencies   191
    Advantages and Disadvantages of Dependent and
        Interdependent Group Contingencies   192
Involving Peers Directly   192
Methods for Training Peers to be Socially Reinforcing
    193
    Teaching Use of Positive Effect   193
    Systematically Involving Peers as Contingency
        Managers   195
    Peers as Tutors and Trainers   198
Summary   203

Chapter 13   **Token Economies**
    Goals   205
Token Economies Defined and Illustrated   207
Token Economies and Effective Reinforcement   208
Designing a System for Supporting Success   209
    Obtaining Approval and Informed Consent   209
    Planning for a Recordkeeping System   211
    Training Staff   211
Implementing Token Economies Effectively   212
    Selecting Tokens   212
    Providing for Minimal Delay   214
    Pairing Token Delivery with Positive Social
        Feedback   216
    Consistent Delivery of Tokens   217

Providing Appropriate Amount   217
Specifying Conditions for Token Reinforcement
   218
Matching Quality and Type of Reinforcers to
   Individual Client Repertoires   218
Marketing and Merchandising Back-Up
   Reinforcers   220
Reducing Behavior Within a Token Economy   220
Response Cost   220
Time Out from Token Spending   221
Maintaining Behavior Changed in Token Economies
   221
Moving from Artificial to Natural Reinforcers   221
Introducing Delay of Token Delivery for Long-
   Range Effectiveness   222
Phasing Out Token Systems   222
Scheduling for Maintenance in the Absence of
   Tokens   223
Summary   224

**Chapter 14   Analyzing Procedures: Withdrawal
and Multiple-Baseline Single-Case Designs
Goals   225**
Evaluating Procedures Experimentally   227
Group Designs   227
Single-Case Designs   228
Advantages of Single-Case Designs   228
Being Accountable   229
Demonstrating Functional Relations   229
Controlling for Extraneous Variables   230
Yielding General Findings   230
Enabling New Discoveries   231
Withdrawal Designs   232
Variations of Withdrawal Design   232
Advantages and Disadvantages of Withdrawal
   Designs   236
Multiple-Baseline Designs   237
Across Behaviors   237
Across Individuals   238
Across Situations   239
Multiple Baselines to Access for Generalization
   241
Summary   242

Section III: Occasioning and Teaching Behaviors
243

**Chapter 15   Stimulus Control: How It Develops
Goals   247**
Stimulus Control   249
Stimulus Generalization and Discrimination   249

Establishing Discriminative Control   251
Differential Reinforcement Defined and Illustrated
   252
Elements of Differential Reinforcement   253
Contextual Variables   254
Setting Events   254
Establishing Operations   255
Stimulus Complexity   256
Antecedent and Response Combinations   256
Discriminating the Presence or Absence of a
   Given Stimulus   257
Discriminating Among Two or More Antecedent
   Stimuli; One Correct Response   257
Two or More Stimuli, Distinct Responses
   Corresponding to Each   260
Complex-Stimulus Control   260
Equivalence Classes   261
Summary   263

**Chapter 16   Promoting and Applying Stimulus
Control
Goals   265**
Using the Stimulus Change Procedure   267
Stimulus Change Procedure Illustrated   268
Advantages of Using Stimulus Change   269
Disadvantages of Using Stimulus Change   270
Using Stimulus Change Effectively   271
When Stimulus Change Fails   272
Is the Response Missing from the Repertoire?
   272
Assessing for the Presence of the Response in the
   Person's Repertoire   272
Is the Stimulus Control Too Weak?   273
Is Stimulus Control Absent?   273
Are There Interfering Stimuli?   273
Effectively Applying Differential-Reinforcement
   Procedures   274
Clearly Identifying Relevant Stimulus Properties
   275
Emphasizing or Enhancing Relevant Antecedent
   Stimulus Properties   276
Using Effective Reinforcement Procedures   277
Prompting   278
Prompting Defined and Illustrated   278
Selecting Prompts   278
Detecting Mysterious S^{D}s   280
Samples as Prompts: Matching-to-Sample   283
Coping with Stimulus Overdependence and
   Overselectivity   284
Summary   285

Chapter 17   **Systematic Prompting Strategies**
  Goals   *287*
Goal-Setting   *288*
  Goal-Setting Defined   *288*
  Goal-Setting Illustrated   *288*
  Goals as Discriminative Stimuli   *290*
  Effective Goal-Setting   *290*
Using Instructional Prompts: The Tell Procedure
    291
  Using the Tell Procedure Effectively   *291*
Providing a Model: The Show Procedure   *294*
  Developing Imitative Prompts as Discriminative
    Stimuli   *294*
  Increasing Generalized Imitative Responding   *295*
  Using Modeling Effectively   *295*
When Telling or Showing Fails: Prompting with
    Physical Guidance   *301*
  Physical Guidance Defined and Illustrated   *301*
  Using Physical Guidance Effectively   *301*
Choosing Among Different Antecedent Prompting
    Strategies   *302*
Summary   *302*

Chapter 18   **Transferring Stimulus Control**
  Goals   *305*
Delayed Prompting   *307*
  Delayed Prompting Defined and Illustrated   *307*
  Advantages of Delayed Prompting   *308*
  Disadvantages of Delayed Prompting   *308*
  Using Delayed Prompting Effectively   *308*
Graduated Prompting   *309*
Fading   *311*
  Fading Defined and Illustrated   *311*
  Using Fading Effectively   *312*
  Fading for Errorless Learning   *314*
  Using Errorless Learning Techniques   *315*
  Disadvantages of Errorless Learning   *320*
Fading Versus Delayed Prompting   *320*
Maintaining Stimulus Control   *320*
Summary   *321*

Chapter 19   **Teaching New Behavior: Shaping**
  Goals   *323*
Shaping Defined and Illustrated   *324*
  Shaping with Groups   *327*
  Shaping and Programmed Instruction   *328*
  Shaping and the Personalized System of
    Instruction (PSI)   *330*
  Shaping and Computer Assisted Instruction   *330*
Using Shaping Effectively   *331*
  Keeping Your Eye on the Goal   *331*

Finding a Starting Point   *332*
Selecting Step Size and Duration of Remaining on
    a Step   *333*
Combining Use of Discriminative Stimuli with
    Shaping   *334*
Strengthening the Newly Acquired Behavior   *336*
Summary   *336*

Chapter 20   **Teaching New Behavior: Chaining**
  Goals   *337*
Chaining Procedure Defined and Illustrated   *338*
  The Formation of Behavioral Chains   *338*
  Composition of Chains   *339*
Forging Behavioral Chains   *341*
  Analyzing the Task Precisely   *341*
  Validating Task Analyses   *342*
  Using Links Already in the Response Repertoire
    343
  Selecting a Starting Point   *344*
  Supplementing Reinforcers   *346*
  Using Discriminative Stimuli   *346*
  Combining Fading with Chaining   *348*
  Combining Shaping with Chaining   *348*
  Strengthening Response Chains   *349*
Summary   *349*

Chapter 21   **Communicative Behavior**
  Goals   *351*
Communicative Behavior Defined and Illustrated
    353
  How Communicative Behavior Is Shaped by the
    Verbal Community   *353*
Rule-Governed Behavior   *354*
  Rule-Governed Behavior Defined   *355*
  Control by Rules   *355*
  Rules and Sensitivity to Contingencies Actually in
    Effect   *356*
Verbal Behavior and Stimulus Equivalence   *356*
Problems in Communicative Behavior   *357*
  Inadequate Verbal Repertoires   *357*
  Maladaptive Verbal Behavior   *357*
  Problematic Speech Topographies   *357*
  Problems in Rule Governance   *357*
Teaching Communicative Skills   *359*
  Promoting Acquisition of Communicative Behavior
    359
  Promoting Generalization of Communicative Skills
    361
  Promoting Acquisition of Manual Communicative
    Behavior   *363*

Modifying Maladaptive Communicative Behavior
363
Cognitive Behavior Modification 364
Remedying Problematic Communicative Topographies
365
Teaching Rule Governance 365
Correspondence Training 366
Breaking Overdependence on Rules 368
Avoiding Use of Rules 368
Summary 368

Chapter 22   Evaluating Behavioral Programs:
Complex Designs and Assessing Significance
of Change
Goals 371
Preliminary Considerations Prior to Adopting
Programs 373
How Internally Valid Is the Program? 373
How Externally Valid Is It? 373
Will Changes in Performance Impact the Bottom
Line? 374
Functionally Analyzing Acquisition of Skills 374
Changing-Criterion Design 374
Multiple Probes 376
Within-Subjects Comparative Designs 378
Intervention Phases as Baselines 379
Withdrawal Comparisons 380
Alternating Treatment (Multielement) Designs
381
Selecting Appropriate Single-Subject Designs 386
Other Considerations with Single-Subject Designs
386
Determining the Significance of a Demonstrated
Functional Relation 389
Experimental Significance 389
Other Forms of Significance 390
Educational and Social Validity 391
Assessing Cost Effectiveness 391
Evaluating the Generality of Findings 392
Evaluating Generality and Long-Term Effects of
Procedural Interventions 393
Summary 393

Section IV: Introduction to Reducing Behavior
395

Chapter 23   Reducing Behavior: Making the
Decision and Using Extinction
Goals 399
Deciding to Target a Behavior for Reduction 401

Procedures for Reducing or Eliminating Behaviors
403
Reducing Behavior with Extinction 405
Extinction Defined and Illustrated 405
Advantages of Extinction 406
Properties of Extinction 407
Disadvantages of Extinction 409
Using Extinction Effectively 409
Summary 415

Chapter 24   Reducing Behavior with Differential
Reinforcement
Goals 417
Differentially Reinforcing Alternative and
Incompatible Behaviors 419
Alt-R and DRI Illustrated 419
Advantages of Alt-R 420
Disadvantages of Alt-R 421
Selecting Replacement Behaviors 421
Using Alt-R Effectively 423
Omission Training 424
DRO Defined and Illustrated 424
Advantages of DRO 425
Disadvantages of DRO 426
Using DRO Effectively 427
Combining With Other Procedures 428
Momentary DRO 428
Whole-Interval Versus Momentary DRO 429
Differentially Reinforcing Low and Diminishing Rates
of Behavior 429
DRL and DRD Defined and Illustrated 429
Advantages of DRL and DRD 430
Disadvantages of DRL and DRD 431
Using DRL and DRD Effectively 431
Summary 433

Chapter 25   Reducing Behavior with Response
Cost and Stimulus Control Procedures
Goals 435
Response Cost 436
Response Cost Defined 436
Response Cost Illustrated 437
Advantages of Response Cost 437
Disadvantages of Response Cost 439
Using Response Cost Effectively 440
Reducing Behavior Through Stimulus Control 443
Stimuli Discriminative for Aversive Consequences
444
Advantages of Developing S^D-s 444
Developing Effective S^D-s 444
Disadvantages of the S^D- 445

Summary   445

Chapter 26   Reducing Behavior with Timeout from Reinforcement
   Goals   447
Timeout Defined   449
Timeout Illustrated   450
Advantages of Timeout   450
   Effectively Reduces Behavior   450
   General Management Procedure   451
   Combines Successfully with Alt-R and DRO   451
Disadvantages of Timeout   452
   Loss of Learning Time   452
   Not Universally Effective   452
   Negative, Nonconstructive Contingency   453
   Legal Restrictions   453
   Potential for Abuse   455
   Public Concern   455
   Suppression of Other Behaviors   456
Using Timeout Effectively   456
   Combining with Other Procedures   456
   Removing as Many Reinforcers Supporting
      Unwanted Behavior as Feasible   456
   Using Variations of Timeout   457
   Making Time-in as Reinforcing as Possible   459
   Avoiding Opportunities for Self-Injury and Self-
      Stimulation   459
   Keeping Duration Relatively Short   460
   Clearly Communicating Conditions for Timeout
      461
   Using Timeout Consistently   461
   Being Able to Implement and Maintain Timeout
      462
   Releasing Client from Timeout Contingent on
      Acceptable Behavior   462
Summary   463

Chapter 27   Reducing Behavior with Aversive Procedures
   Goals   465
Punishment Defined   469
Aversive Stimuli   469
   Unconditioned Aversive Stimuli   469
   Conditioned Aversive Stimuli   470
   Extrinsic and Intrinsic Aversive Stimuli   471
   Aversive Activities   471
Variables Influencing the Effectiveness of Punishment
   474
   Opportunity to Escape   474
   Quality   474
   Schedule and Delay   475

Density   476
Intensity   476
Concurrent Contingencies   477
Contextual Factors   478
Summary   479

Chapter 28   Applying Aversive Procedures
   Goals   481
Advantages of Punishment   482
   Effectively Stopping Behavior   482
   Rapidly and Durably Stopping the Behavior   483
   Facilitating Adaptive Behavior   484
   Instructive to Peers   484
   Possible Convenience to Managers   485
Disadvantages of Punishment   485
   Provoking Withdrawal   485
   Suppressing Responses   486
   Promoting Aggression   486
   Promoting Inappropriate Generalization   486
   Displaying Behavioral Contrast   487
   Modeling Punishment   487
   Influencing Social Status of Recipient   488
   Promoting Negative "Self-Esteem"   488
   Overusing Punishment   489
   Generating Public Antipathy   490
   Difficulty in Selecting Relevant Aversive Activities
      490
   Cost of Managing Aversive Activities   490
Considerations in Electing to use Punishment   490
   Combine Punishment with Reinforcement of
      Alternative Behaviors   493
   Use Effective Stimulus Control Strategies   493
   Program for Generalization and Maintenance
      494
   Obtain Informed Consent   494
   Monitor Continuously   494
Applying Aversive Activities Effectively   494
   Select Activities Relevant to the Misbehavior   494
   Keep Performance of Aversive Activities
      Consistent   495
   Extend Duration of Aversive Activities   495
Summary   496

Section V: Extending and Maintaining Behavior
497

Chapter 29   Extending Behavior: Generalization Training
   Goals   499
Generalization Defined and Illustrated   500

Advantages and Disadvantages of Generalization
     501
Unprogrammed Generalization   502
Establishing the Need to Formally Program for
     Generalization   503
   Assessing for Fluency   504
Assessing for Generalization   504
Programming for Generalization   505
   Reviewing and Refining Behavioral Objectives
     505
   Asking for Generalization   506
   Modifying Behaviors Sequentially   506
   Training to Naturally Supportive Conditions   507
   Modifying Maladaptive Consequences   508
   Training Sufficient Exemplars   508
   Training Loosely   510
   Using Indiscriminable Antecedent and
     Consequential Contingencies   511
   Programming Common Stimuli   512
   Teaching Techniques for Mediating Generalization
     514
   Teaching Generalization as a General Skill   514
Summary   515

Chapter 30   Strategies for Maintaining Behavior
   Goals   517
Factors Impeding Maintenance   518
   Abrupt Cessation of Reinforcement   518
   Continued Reinforcement of the Previous
     Unwanted Behaviors   519
   Punishment of the Modified Behavior   519
   S^{D}s That Prompt Unwanted Behavior   520
Factors Promoting Unprogrammed Maintenance
     520
Deciding to Formally Program Contingencies for
     Maintenance   521
Formal Strategies for Preventing Relapse   522
   Minimize Errors During Acquisition   522
   Build and Sustain Response Fluency   522
   Identify Natural Contingencies of Reinforcement
     524
   Capitalize on Already Existing Natural
     Contingencies   524
   Program Toward Naturally Maintaining Conditions
     525
   Use Correspondence Training   527
   Teaching and Maintaining Self-Management   528

Summary and Conclusions   535

**Chapter 31   Maintaining Behavior: Interval and
   Limited Hold Schedules**
   Goals   537
Interval Schedules Defined and Illustrated   538
Characteristics of Interval-Schedule Performance
     540
   Response Rates   540
   Consistency of Performance   541
   Error Patterns   542
   Responding During Extinction   543
Advantages and Disadvantages of Interval Schedules
     544
Promoting Preferred Rates of Responding Under
     Interval Schedules   545
   Reducing the Length of the Interval   545
   Providing Appropriate History   545
   Using Discriminative Stimuli   546
   Arranging Competition   548
   Capitalizing on Behavioral Contrast   548
   Adding Limited-Hold Schedules   549
Choosing Between Fixed and Variable Schedules
     550
Thinning Reinforcement Under Interval Schedules
     551
Summary   551

**Chapter 32   Maintaining Behavior: Ratio and
   Differential-Reinforcement Schedules**
   Goals   553
Ratio Schedules   554
   Defined and Illustrated   554
   Characteristics of Ratio-Schedule Performance
     554
   Advantages of Ratio Schedules   559
   Using Ratio Schedules Effectively   561
   Disadvantages of Ratio Schedules   563
Differential Reinforcement of High Rates   564
Interactions Among Schedules   565
Summary   568

Epilogue   569

Glossary   583

References   601

Index   645

Preface

During the late 1960s, when behavioral approaches to changing behavior were establishing themselves as useful and accountable, we began to prepare our first collaborative text, *Behavior Modification Procedures for School Personnel* (Sulzer & Mayer, 1972). With professional and research backgrounds in the field of education, we felt that this new scientific form of practice had much to offer students, teachers, and those professional personnel who served them. Behavioral procedures, along with their stunning accomplishments in the fields of mental health, developmental disabilities, and related areas, were beginning to show how behavior analysis could help students improve in academic achievement and conduct.

That initial text drew upon research in education and related areas, but at the time information was relatively sparse. Numerous fundamental principles of behavior had been identified through demonstrated laboratory experimentation, but their application to education was limited. Much of that initial text drew upon those principles, as we extrapolated speculatively as to ways of using them to help solve educational problems.

Soon afterward, behavioral research in education and other fields related to children and youth began to flourish. Major programs, many federally funded, investigated methods for preventing and ameliorating problems among developmentally disabled, deliquent, educationally deficient, and other youngsters. So rapidly did information accrue that within a few years we included those related areas in a revision and expansion of the original text, *Applying Behavior Analysis Procedures with Children and Youth* (Sulzer-Azaroff & Mayer, 1977). Thanks to the ever growing pool of studies, that revision was more data-based and less speculative.

One important repeatedly reproduced finding was that teaching people the rules—principles and procedures—would in no way guarantee they would put them into practice. Supervised applications under simulated and actual field conditions increased the odds. Toward that end, a set of programmed laboratory and field activities was then pooled and published: *Applying Behavior Analysis, A Manual for Developing Professional Competence* (Sulzer-Azaroff & Reese, 1982).

The decade following our first revision in 1977 witnessed a huge expansion of behavior analytic research. Journal reports of behavior analytic studies grew exponentially, as did the areas of application addressed. In addition to the fields of mental health, developmental disabilities, and education—where the methods had been heavily tested—others included families, business, health, recreational, and human-

and community-service organizations. Problems addressed moved beyond those associated with deficit, deficiency, and illness. The thrust began to widen to include prevention or remediation of personal and social difficulties and to ways to foster success in many realms: social skills, nervous habits, job finding, skill mastery, marital interactions, parenting, health maintenance, accident and illness prevention, energy conservation, reduced littering and other environmental areas, organizational functioning, and many more.

The methodological sophistication of the field also continued to evolve. New assessment and analytic approaches eventually were subsumed under the rubric of *behavioral assessment*. The number of books, journals, and papers proliferated to such an extent that by the 1980s no one person any longer could keep abreast of the field. With educators clamoring for ways to improve the discipline, we then decided to emphasize just that area for an original specialty text for educational practices. *Achieving Educational Excellence Using Behavioral Strategies* (Sulzer-Azaroff & Mayer, 1986) focused on basic behavioral methods and principles and how to apply them to improve student achievement in specific skill areas such as reading, arithmetic, writing, and social conduct. That book also considered ways to improve staff performance.

Meanwhile, many of our readers had been encouraging us again to revise the original book, a task we were apprehensive about undertaking. The main challenge of that first book had been to speculate and infer; and for the 1977 revision, to survey the field fairly thoroughly and synthesize the findings. We now knew that this new text would be much more formidable because we would be forced to select from an enormous treasury of fine work.

Our apprehensions have been reinforced during the past five years. Grasping the diversity of topics, methods, and areas of application has been akin to scaling the face of a glass mountain. Only the excellent scholarship of our colleagues, who have synthesized much of their work, has enabled us to gain footholds. They have elucidated many of the highlights of the field, such as the growing emphasis on maintenance and generalization. Inescapably, though, this edition, the title of which reflects that key focus, has had to be selective. Although the list of references exceeds 1300 in number, we have been forced to omit a tremendous number of outstanding sources. We depend on those of you who use this book as an instructional text to supplement with your favorites.

To keep the volume to a reasonable size, we decided to omit study questions from the text itself. Laura Hall has prepared them, though, and they are included in a separate volume. Short essay and multiple-choice quiz items and answer keys also are available in an *Instructor's Manual*. Instructors may obtain these materials directly from the publisher or the authors by requesting them on official letterhead. Permission is granted to instructors to reproduce the quiz materials for instructional purposes.

We hope this book will enable its readers and those they teach or manage to succeed in their efforts to accomplish behavior change that proves enduring. Write and let us hear about your accomplishments.

Beth Sulzer-Azaroff
University of Massachusetts

G. Roy Mayer
California State University at Los Angeles

Acknowledgments

A book of this sort reflects the collaborative efforts of a tremendous number of people. First we must thank the first line contributors to this maturing field, the thousands of scholars and researchers upon whose work we have drawn.

Next, we extend our deep appreciation to our peer reviewers who invested so much effort in helping us to fine tune the content and style of the text: Donald Baer, Wesley Becker, A. Charles Catania, Marjorie Charlop, Walter P. Christian, Harvey Clarizio, Anthony Cuvo, James Fox, Douglas Greer, Tom Haring, Richard Malott, Gale McGee, Donald Pumroy, Julie Vargas, Hill Walker and Paul Ward.

To our students, too numerous to mention by name (but you know who you are) who have provided us with sources, examples, and study and quiz questions, and with constructive and reinforcing feedback, we would like to convey our special thanks. In particular, we owe a debt of gratitude to Brad Meier, Laura Hall, and Camille Ferond for their assistance in the preparation of study and quiz questions.

Now, for the incontestable heroes, our spouses, Jocelyn Mayer and Leonid Azaroff. Both unceasingly and cheerily tolerated the neglect ensuing from our involvement in this mammoth undertaking. Jocelyn Mayer typed the manuscript, and as a committed school psychologist, read and critiqued the material from a consumer's vantage point. She also kept our fictitious characters straight and supported our optimism throughout this arduous process. And Leonid Azaroff—thank goodness he too is a writer who knows what becoming deeply involved in multiyear projects like this is all about. That helped him to support good-naturedly our efforts in many ways—from assuming most of the family chores to providing us with various forms of assistance in the manuscript preparation. Both of us will be eternally grateful to you two.

Beth Sulzer-Azaroff and G. Roy Mayer

Chapter 1

Introduction to Behavior Analysis for Lasting Change

GOALS

After completing this chapter, you should be able to:

1. Define, recognize, and give original illustrations of each of the following terms:
   a. Experimental analysis of behavior
   b. Applied behavior analysis (ABA)
   c. Variable
   d. Operational
   e. Procedures
   f. Replicating
   g. Principles of behavior
   h. Applied behavior analysis program
2. Explain and illustrate what is meant by functional behavior.
3. Illustrate the behavioral model and contrast it with others.
4. List and describe the six distinguishing attributes of applied behavior analysis (ABA).
5. List and illustrate the six ways behavioral procedures can change specific behaviors.[1]
6. Explain how ABA combines science, technology, and professional practice.
7. Tell how everyone stands to benefit from knowing the concepts and skills of applied behavior analysis.
8. Explain why ABA's features tend to minimize exploitation.
9. List and illustrate with original examples, the steps in the ABA model.

---

[1] For simplicity, we have elected to use the term *behaviors* in preference to the more technically correct designation *classes of behavior*.

When was the last time you resolved to change your behavior? On New Year's Eve? Maybe you promised yourself you would begin exercising or become more patient. Perhaps you decided to stop nagging, smoking, biting your nails, or some other nervous habit. How successful were you? Possibly you were. Perchance you weren't.

At some time or another, all of us have failed in our attempts to change. Maybe we got started avoiding sweets or cigarettes for a day or two, or doing calisthenics for a week, only to have our efforts wane. Why do our most earnest resolutions so often disintegrate?

The same sorts of frustrations arise in our relations with others: "Why can't my parents treat me as an adult?" "It wouldn't kill my boss to let me know when I've done a good job!" "Boy, what a spoiled kid. Look how he wraps his parents around his little finger." "My roommate is such a slob. How can he expect me to live in such a mess?" "Anyone who does that (whatever it is) must be crazy!"

Maybe you tried to complain or to ask the person to change, but that didn't help. Why, we all ponder, do people do the things they do? What can be done to change how they behave and to sustain the change?

Dilemmas like these have been posed throughout history, and they continue to concern and fascinate us. Cultures have devised all sorts of fanciful explanations for behaviors that are puzzling or resistant to change: inherent deficiencies or oddities, spirits, demons, altered states of consciousness, and numerous others. Failure to persist toward some goal has been attributed to weak wills, spinelessness, laziness, or inadequate motivation. By agreeing with the presumption that the cause of behavioral difficulties resides within people, the only way to fix them would be to rid them of the cause, as in exorcising demons by burning those in their possession at the stake—a sure-fire method of altering a witch's behavior. Now, thanks to the scientific study of behavior, we are learning a better way.

Approaching Behavior Scientifically

Only within the past century have issues of **behavior** been addressed scientifically. As with other natural phenomena, scholars began to treat the behavior of organisms as a subject worthy of systematic study. In 1897, Wilhelm Wundt organized the first psychological laboratory in Leipzig, Germany. There he began to study the *structure* of the "mind," using a technique called *introspection* to study mental processes. Meanwhile, William James (1890) conjectured that behavior might evolve functionally, that is, in terms of what outcomes it yields for the individual.

From such origins, the study of behavior has evolved over a hundred years into an enormously complex field. Today, scientific investigators generally approach the subject matter from one of several perspectives, using models that are biological, psychodynamic, cognitive, humanistic, or behavioral:

- The biological model views behavior as a function of biological processes.
- The psychodynamic model views it from unconscious determinants.
- The cognitive views it as mediated by thought processes and understanding.
- The humanistic approach focuses on the human desire to achieve its potential.
- The behavioral model views behavior from the functional vantage point (Feldman, 1990).

Analogous to the Darwinian notion of survival of the species by natural selection, the behavioral model—the one we espouse—sees specific **responses** as those "selected" for survival by the function they perform. Behavior is examined objectively and viewed as evolving from people's histories of interactions with their environments.

Beginning in the early twentieth century,

scientific giants like Watson (1924), Pavlov (1927), Thorndike (1932), and Skinner (1953) investigated and interpreted learning and conditioning from the behavioral perspective. Their work has yielded many important findings that have coalesced into a number of general laws and principles. These principles enable us to begin unraveling the mysteries that explain human behavior and ways of changing it—and keeping it changed.

The implications of the findings of a science of behavior can be extended beyond the individual, to society as a whole. Ultimately, world survival may depend on the identification and application of such knowledge. Given the rapid changes in technology, as Bertrand Russell (1955) has argued:

> Whether men will be able to survive the changes of environment that their own skill has brought about is open to question. If the answer is in the affirmative, men will have to apply scientific ways of thinking to themselves and their institutions. They cannot continue to hope, as all politicians hitherto have, that in a world where everything has changed, the political and social habits of the eighteenth century can remain inviolate. Not only will men of science have to grapple with the sciences that deal with man, but—and this is a far more difficult matter—they will have to persuade the world to listen to what they have discovered (p. 7).

What Russell wisely advocates is a science of human behavior, one that not only seeks to discover the laws governing human behavior but also applies these laws to the betterment of humankind. That is the essence of applied behavior analysis.[2]

What Is Behavior Analysis?

Behavior analysis is a field of inquiry devoted to investigating factors that influence behavior in a systematic way—a science of behavior.

There are two forms of behavior analysis: basic, or experimental, and applied. The basic form is usually called the **experimental analysis of behavior**.[3]

Experimental analysis of behavior operates under rigorous laboratory conditions to establish what *systematic relationships* exist between particular conditions of the environment (both outside, such as the rate of receiving food for responding, and inside, such as the amount of a particular stimulant ingested by the organism) and resultant behavior. Notice that the relationships between individuals and their environments are emphasized. Past and present interactions with individuals' environments are what count. The things people do or say to others and themselves are examined not as symptoms but as the main focus of inquiry.

In its applied form, called **applied behavior analysis** (ABA), the investigation moves out into the real-world laboratory, exchanging the more rigorously controlled, enclosed setting for the more representative context within which behavior naturally occurs. There the same kinds of relationships are studied, but the behaviors of interest have much greater social importance. Whereas the applied conditions may be more difficult to experimentally control, the findings can be both informative and readily beneficial. (See Baer, Wolf, & Risley, 1968, 1987.)

Let us describe applied behavior analysis more graphically through a couple of fictitious illustrations.[4] Paula Petworth is employed by the medical claims division at the Purple Triangle Insurance Company. Described by her

---

[2] Refer to the many writings of B. F. Skinner for a thorough discussion of this issue.

[3] Whenever you see a term presented in boldface in this book, it or its variant is defined in the Glossary at the back.

[4] You will encounter many such fanciful illustrations throughout the book. They are intended to help you understand, recognize, or practice applying particular points. You can distinguish the simulated from the true accounts by the fact that citations of authors and dates always will accompany the actual reports.

manager, Angela, as clever, energetic, charming, and ambitious, Paula aspires to progress from her position as claims adjuster to a senior management position. But one roadblock continually obstructs her progress. Each time Paula completes a case, she is expected to write a report that is used by the organization for evaluating the quality of service, accounting, budgeting, and strategic planning. Timely completion of the report is very important. Yet, no matter how hard Paula has tried to make herself fulfill the requirement, she consistently postpones that final task until, with threats and entreaties, Angela eventually bullies her into submitting it. This unfortunate habit of procrastination blocks Paula's planned progress up the organizational ladder.

Lucretia, a student at the Deep Valley School, has acquired a reputation for being unmanageable. Favorite among her antics are pulling chairs out from under the other students while they are sitting down; pushing others as they descend the staircase; and throwing erasers, pinching, poking, and snapping rubber bands at them. Her teachers are distraught and so are her parents, who have witnessed Lucretia's similar misconduct toward her siblings at home.

How might ABA approach situations like these? Directly, by studying the relations between the behaviors of concern and the present and prior environmental conditions influencing them. New knowledge and improved performance should result. An applied behavior analyst might investigate Paula's procrastination (or its converse—performing punctually) by involving Paula and others who share her difficulty in an investigation designed to discover the factors influencing or *controlling* her procrastination. Similarly, events influencing Lucretia's offensive acts could be examined to determine the function they serve for Lucretia, such as getting her attention or removing demands on her.

Following an initial assessment, each different condition, called a **variable**, would be managed systematically to determine what kind of measurable impact it has on the performance. For example, one might alter the *consequences*, such as praise for improvement, and/or the *antecedents*, such as making assignments easier or more interesting or setting a goal of surpassing prior accomplishments. If the investigators design the study with sufficient care to successfully address the particular problem, they may discover the conditions that will influence not only Paula's punctuality or Lucretia's aggression but also ones that work for many other people who exhibit those difficulties.

That is the way ABA studies the variables controlling all sorts of socially important behaviors, such as being altruistic, cooperative, friendly, productive, healthy, skillful, and informed. Discovering and applying these discoveries should permit society and its members to face a brighter future.

Distinguishing Features of Applied Behavior Analysis

ABA has evolved into *a systematic, performance-based, self-evaluative method of studying and changing socially important behavior*. ABA is designed to permit people to understand, prevent, and remedy behavioral problems and to promote learning. The unique contribution of this approach stems from its main attributes: It is performance based, analytical, technological, socially important, contextual, and accountable.

Performance Based

ABA is concerned with investigating people's interactions with their environments. As part of the process, overt behavior is measured, and/or inner events are translated into objectively observable phenomena and then quantified. Vague terms such as *laziness, anger,* and *depression* are redefined into observable and quantifiable behaviors, or stated **operationally**, so their frequency, duration, or other measurable properties (parameters) can be quantified more readily. Instead of trying to treat Paula's laziness or tendency to procrastinate, we would count the number of days, hours, or minutes behind or ahead of deadlines when she turned in her reports. The number of minutes during which Lucretia engaged in her assigned tasks or played with other children without untoward incident and/or the frequency of pushing, throwing objects, and so on, might be measured rather than Lucretia's aggression.

Analytical

ABA uses methods of analysis that yield convincing, reproducible, and conceptually sensible demonstrations of how to accomplish specific behavioral changes (Baer, Wolf, & Risley, 1987). For example, the relation between behavior and the environment frequently is examined to determine the function of an individual's behavior (for example, what events are maintaining the behavior) before the behavior analyst selects a treatment program. If the analysis is valid, the outcomes should be reproducible each time a prescribed set of treatment conditions or **procedures** is repeated or *replicated*, usually according to some conventional experimental design. If investigators could control for irrelevant factors (i.e., extraneous or confounding variables) and if other "procrastinators" were found to profit from the methods used to increase Paula's timely report writing, the investigators would consider the evidence even more powerful. If removing work assignments that proved too difficult for Lucretia were found to reduce her aggressive acts, the same concept might be applied and found general among many other children displaying similar behaviors. Explaining the outcomes on the basis of known principles of behavior would prove especially compelling.

Technological

Replicating, or duplicating a method to demonstrate its consistency in achieving essentially the same results, is the heart of the science of

behavior, because only successful replication can provide convincing evidence of the reliability and significance of the outcomes (see Sidman, 1960). In fact, as Smith (1970) points out, ". . . the neglect of replication must be viewed as scientific irresponsibility" (p. 971). But faithful replications are difficult to achieve without rigorous methods of measurement, procedural intervention, and analysis. Therefore, a technology of behavior analysis has evolved, including tactics of measurement and conventions for their application.

Generally the procedures are founded on fundamental laws or **principles of behavior** that have been derived under scientifically controlled conditions. People in the field also have learned to appreciate the importance of documenting and reporting procedural details explicitly. A behavior analysis of methods to improve Paula's timeliness probably would incorporate principles of effective reinforcement and ways to arrange antecedent events. The procedures applied with Paula or Lucretia also would be verified and described in sufficient detail to permit others to repeat them just as precisely.

Socially Important

To eliminate competing explanations for their results, behavior analysts attempt to hold constant (control) all factors other than the one they are studying. In the experimental laboratory, the behavior being influenced often is kept as uncomplicated as possible for the purpose of accomplishing such experimental control. The rigor of that methodology has permitted the discovery of many dependable findings on which applied behavior analysis procedures have been founded.

By contrast, because applied behavior analysis takes place in real-world settings—businesses, schools, hospitals, homes, the community, and others—the focus often is on altering or preventing problematic behaviors.

Thus, behaviors being affected tend to be socially significant. Additionally, the procedures usually are designed to alter those specific behaviors in one of several ways:

- to *increase* them, such as submitting more reports, or producing more items or words spoken.
- to *teach* new skills and knowledge, such as organizing a complete report, tying a shoe, writing a poem, or using utensils properly.
- to *maintain* the new behavioral patterns, such as continuing to use appropriate grammatical forms or job performance skills.
- to *generalize* or extend them from one situation or response to another, as in transferring the ability to organize a written report effectively to organizing a newsletter article, or from completing many assignments in the resource room to doing just as well in the classroom.
- to *restrict* or narrow the conditions under which a particular response occurs, for instance, limiting running and shouting to the playground or entering only through the door marked "Enter" but not the one marked "Exit."
- to *reduce* such behaviors as looking out the window instead of working, taking overly long coffee breaks, wasting resources, doing injury to oneself, complaining chronically, or fighting.

Contextual

Increasingly, investigators within the field have recognized the importance of the context within which the behavior of concern occurs, including the person's physical condition, the environmental setting, prior and accompanying events, and so on. Context influences how specific variables will affect an individual's behavior at any particular moment in time. We saw how the nature of Lucretia's work assignments might influence her acts of aggression. In Paula's case, timeliness in completing her reports might be influenced by how much sleep she got the night before, how her daughter or husband were feeling, other demands on her time at home and work, adequate supplies and equipment, and so on. For any of us, food is much more reinforcing after we have not eaten for 6 hours than if we just ate 10 minutes ago. Requests from one's superiors in a work setting are likely to carry more weight than a request from strangers on the street.

Accountable

ABA investigators usually continue to address a problem until a solution has been found. However, measured improvement in performance, accomplished under carefully controlled conditions, may be insufficient to "persuade the world to listen," in Bertrand Russell's words. Thanks to the insights of people like Kazdin (1977, 1980a, 1980b, 1984), Elliott (1988), and Wolf (1978), behavior analytic practitioners have begun to assess the value of an intervention in other ways. These practitioners not only analyze how a given approach functions but also ask concerned consumers how acceptable particular procedures are and how satisfied they are with the outcomes. Before practitioners begin a program of setting goals and praising and supplying Paula with feedback for improvements in her punctuality, she and her managers or union representatives might be consulted about Paula's willingness to participate. After the program she also would be asked to evaluate her satisfaction with the program. Lucretia's parents and teachers would be involved in the design, implementation, and evaluation of her program, as well might Lucretia herself. If consumers are to support the continued use of particular procedures, they must find the methods acceptable and be convinced of their efficacy.

ABA as Science, Technology, and Practice

By now you probably realize that ABA is part science, part technology, and part professional practice. It uses the rigor of scientific methods to discover new knowledge, employs technological stratagems to solve practical problems, and typically treats problems identified by organizational or individual clients. As you study this book, you will see these three components illustrated repeatedly.

Scientific method is reflected in ABA's tactics for selecting variables to measure and manage as well as in the various experimental design strategies used. Findings then are more believable, enabling everyone to understand better *why* people behave the way they do. For instance, a professional examination of Paula's procrastination may reveal information on how different schedules of reinforcement (receiving immediate reinforcement from completing smaller, more demanding chores or by chatting with her co-workers) interact with contextual variables, such as day of the week or circumstances in Paula's home.

The technological aspect is reflected by the adaptations of laboratory methods for use in natural settings. These include measurement tools, techniques for changing behavior, and conventions for graphing results and the dissemination of findings. This technological aspect permits discovery of *how* to apply behavioral principles and procedures to change behavior and maintain the change.

Professional aspects are represented in the material dealing with ethics and accountability, such as selecting appropriate goals and procedures and in many of our suggestions for effective intervention. This aspect focuses on the *what*, *who*, and also the *how* aspects of ABA: what behaviors to change, who should undergo the changing, and how they should go about it—notably from ethical, humanitarian, and practical perspectives.

Applied Behavior Analysis and Behavior Change

Now, having acquainted you with the general characteristics of ABA, we turn to a discussion of some provocative issues surrounding the notion of intentionally changing behavior: Who is concerned and how do they address behavior change?

Who Is Concerned with Changing Behavior?

As with all other natural laws, the laws of behavior are always with us, whether or not we are aware of their existence. Whenever we interact with others, for instance, we are influencing one another. Consider the following example.

Bruno and Claud room together. Bruno has installed his electronic keyboard and sound box, which he plays rather loudly every evening until midnight. He relegates studying to the morning and between classes. Bruno's roommate Claud has two different predominant pursuits: his major in foreign languages and his association with women. Most evenings he would prefer to use the room either to study or to entertain his female friends. Claud drops Bruno a few hints like "I'm having a hard time concentrating on this set of idioms," or "I was thinking of inviting Lisa over this evening to help me with my French pronunciation."

But every evening, like clockwork, Bruno is at the keyboard. When Lisa does drop by, the noise interferes with the French tutorial, and Bruno is irritated because he finds himself looking at her instead of concentrating on the music. He is rather ungracious to Lisa the next time she visits and later complains to Claud, "Can't you two study in the lounge?" In obvious and in obscure ways, the roommates are influencing one another's behavior, not just by hinting and complaining, but even in ways they may not be aware of, such as by their facial expressions and body language.

People close to us may powerfully influence our behavior, regardless of our self-acknowledgment of that influence. Say that you bring a friend home to meet your parents. They are cordial and polite, but when you subsequently ask their reaction, they respond "Your friend seems nice enough." Given such faint praise, you may never bring that friend home again.

Even strangers can affect each other's behavior. The cheerful salesperson who reminds you of the special on throw pillows this week encourages your purchase. In turn, the successful sale influences the clerk to smile and recommend the pillows to the next customer. Or you find yourself intimidated as you pass the hangout of the local motorcycle gang. Next time, you choose another route.

The very act of adapting to other human beings—as in establishing and sustaining relationships with friends, colleagues, or lovers—entails behavior change. No person's repertoire of behaviors (except in fairy tales and old Hollywood movies) is perfectly suited to the repertoire of another human being. So individuals in any relationship need to adjust their modes of responding. Such minute habits as patterns of personal care (Where does your spouse place dirty socks? How often does your roommate shower?), participating in particular recreational activities, opening or closing the window, choosing when to go to bed and arise, being punctual or persistently late, and so many others, often need to be modified if people are to reside together in harmony. Whether they are aware of it or not, people continually modify their own and others' behavior. Truax (1966) has shown us that even relatively nondirective client-centered therapists can unwittingly influence the content of their clients' conversations by subtle vocal responses, head nods, and other forms of differential attention.

To nail down the point, during the next few hours see how many instances of interpersonal influence you can observe taking place. Probably you'll witness plenty of them. You will ben-efit by knowing as much as possible about how behavior is affected, because this knowledge will maximize your opportunities and minimize your risks. All of us can profit from learning about how behavior changes.

Parents and people charged with human service and resource responsibilities—teaching, training, managing, and motivating people—have a special responsibility for learning as much as they can about the laws of behavior and how to apply them. Teaching and training entail enabling learners to gain new knowledge and skills. Managing involves encouraging clients, students, or employees to accomplish their tasks successfully by encouraging them to respond more rapidly or frequently. All these are familiar behavior change functions. Practitioners who apply behavior analysis fulfill their roles more responsibly by analyzing as well as by improving the performance of those for whom they are in any way responsible.[5]

Addressing Change with ABA

Is knowing all about ABA necessary for us to change behavior successfully? Certainly not, as any effective teacher, manager, counselor, parent, friend, or self-manager demonstrates. With or without awareness, one can accomplish change by managing behavioral antecedents and/or consequences optimally—that is, according to firmly established **principles**. To illustrate, one commonly used principle is to provide reinforcement immediately following an act that you want to increase. Thus, when Bruno deliberately plans to permit himself to play music *immediately after* completing his homework,

---

[5] The application of behavioral principles and procedures has many names. Educators usually call what they do *behavioral instruction* or *education* or *precision teaching*; therapists often use the term *behavior therapy*; and many managers refer to their efforts in this area as *performance management*. One could equally label these methods as *behavior modification* or *applied behavior analysis*. Over the years subtle differences in practice have evolved, but we shall not attempt to draw such distinctions here. Instead, we use the terms interchangeably.

he is capitalizing on that principle. Similarly, once Polly has learned to ride her bike, her father tends to congratulate her less and less frequently. He is following a different principle, one that is especially suited to *maintaining* behavior.

Our lack of knowledge, however, often can prove counterproductive, as when we inadvertently increase whining, complaining, or crying by acceding to the person's wishes. Additionally, haphazard application of behavioral procedures may cause us to expend more resources than necessary. Quick fixes are rare in behavior modification. The best results are accomplished by taking a more formal approach, by identifying and applying the appropriate rules systematically. An enormous number of reports of the systematic application of behavioral principles, formal *behavioral programs*, have appeared in books and journals. (Well over a thousand are referenced in these pages, and these are just selected illustrations.) The methods have been applied successfully with, among others, "delinquent" youths; students at all educational levels; people with developmental delays or neurological, physical, or sensory impairments; people with emotional difficulties; families; workers; managers; writers; artists; dental and medical patients; personnel who work together in groups; and individuals applying the procedures to others or themselves. People have learned to rid themselves of annoying habits; to improve their health, productivity, and interpersonal relations; and to master many other productive behaviors. As you read on, you will encounter numerous fictitious and actual examples of people who have learned to apply behavior analysis to improve human performance.

Can people be exploited by having their behavior modified without their awareness? Of course—but not in the way ABA is conventionally practiced. ABA generally treats observable behavior directly, using prespecified procedures acceptable to clients or their advocates; nothing is secret or confusing. By openly as-

suming responsibility for improving mutually agreeable personally or socially important behaviors, the approach protects clients from exploitation. Being knowledgeable in ABA would protect them even more.

If promoting beneficial behavior change is your concern, you will profit from learning how to apply behavioral procedures responsibly and effectively. Although complete solutions for many troublesome behavioral problems often remain beyond the practitioner's grasp, in this book we offer the fundamental techniques for devising the most promising behavior change strategies. As a reader, you will begin to view the world and label what you see differently and become more competent as an agent of change, especially if you are able to practice using the methods under supervision (see Sulzer-Azaroff & Reese, 1982, for a source). You also should begin to understand why adhering closely to the procedures is important. The more you learn, the better you will be able to provide people with rationales for your activities, and the more confident you will feel about your ability to perform the interpersonal aspects of your job effectively. Options for you and the people you treat will broaden thereby and, in general, all concerned will become more active participants in designing personal, social, and work environments.

As is true of any human service activity, behavior analysis can be implemented with varying degrees of skill and responsibility. Responsible behavior analysts must know how to select goals, objectives, measures, and procedures ethically and legally and how to use them appropriately. Behavior analysts need to be cognizant of the advantages, limitations, and potential side effects of using particular practices. Practitioners must have mastered the rules and skills for effectively applying the procedures and validly documenting the process and function of the change strategy and results.

This book addresses each of these elements. Ethical, legal, and humanistic considerations in selecting goals and procedures are covered in detail in Section I, as are methods for measuring procedures and behavior. The main body of the text presents behavioral procedures in depth; defining and illustrating them; citing evidence of their effectiveness; offering guidelines for their optimal use; and discussing their strengths, limitations, and possible side effects, according to the current state of our knowledge.[6]

Section II covers ways to increase or strengthen behavior. That section also includes a chapter on basic methods for evaluating programs.

Section III deals with more complex forms of behavior, using antecedents and consequences to refine the circumstances under which given behaviors occur. Material in this section also describes methods of teaching new and complex forms of behavior, such as challenging motor and verbal skills. A chapter on evaluating those more complex programs follows.

Section IV is devoted to methods for reducing unwanted behaviors, and Section V addresses the generalization and maintenance of change.

Figure 1.1 depicts a *model* for conducting an **applied behavior analysis program**, including the set of steps to follow to use the method. The figure also cites what chapters of this book explain the steps in detail. Let us run down these steps together, using procrastinator Paula Petworth as a case in point. The *challenge*: Paula is concerned that her habit of procrastinating will impede her progress up the organizational ladder at Purple Triangle. She and her manager,

Angela, agree that her prior efforts have been ineffectual. So, with the aid of the person charged with managing performance in the company, the Performance Manager, they embark on a program of change.

Preliminary steps include setting the *goal* of increasing Paula's punctuality in meeting deadlines; an *objective* of turning in all reports within 24 hours of their due dates for three months in a row; and an *observational system*, recording all assigned reports, their due dates, and the dates and times on which they actually were submitted. Paula and Angela *implement the observational system* by independently collecting and comparing that information for several weeks, to see what patterns emerge. Having carefully examined the conditions related to the problem, Paula and the Performance Manager *select the procedures* they will use—reinforcement, stimulus control, and shaping. Paula and Angela decide to graph the number and percentage of reports handed in on time, and set weekly goals for increased performance levels. Each time Paula meets a goal, Angela will allow her an extra coffee break as a reinforcer. When the ultimate objective is met, Paula will receive a bonus and a more positive performance rating.

While the *procedures are being applied*, the *change is evaluated* and methods for *extending the change* are considered and possibly implemented. Assuming the objective ultimately is achieved, a structure is put in place to permit the performance *to maintain* and keep being monitored (*follow-up data*). Recording continues; so does feedback, but the graph is discontinued and the extra coffee breaks are provided less frequently. Angela does make a point of praising Paula's continued punctuality, so by the end of the year, Angela, Paula, and the Performance Manager conclude that their *challenge was successfully met!*

Throughout this book you will see the elements of the ABA model discussed in much greater detail. How society could benefit if only everyone were taught ABA methods like these!

---

[6] We have concentrated most heavily on those behavioral procedures that seem to lend themselves most practically to application by human resource and service personnel in educational, business, and service organizations; institutions; and community agencies, as well as by families or individuals, to their own behavior. We have elected to deemphasize procedures directed toward the modification of physiological functioning and those involving covert performance or results. Refer to textbooks and journals on behavioral medicine and cognitive behavior modification for information about such interventions.

Figure 1.1 The Applied Behavior Analysis Model

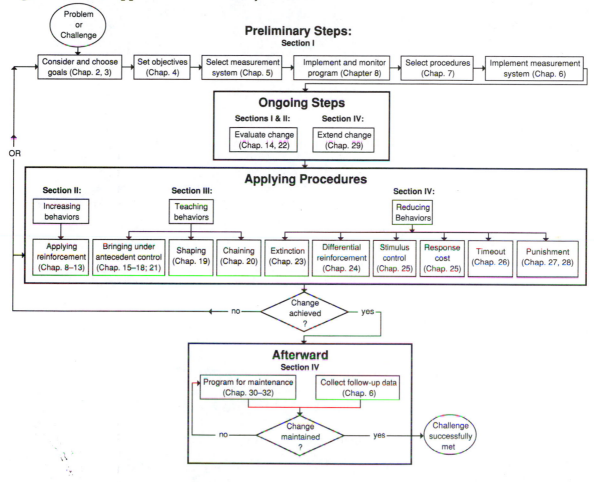

People would become more empowered, more capable of enhancing their own performance and their interactions with others, and more able to recognize and evoke desired or avoid unwanted influences by others.

Summary

The scientific, technological, and professional practice of applied behavior analysis has been discussed in this introductory chapter. The discussion covered the six main characteristics of the field: It is performance based, analytic, technological, socially important, contextual, and accountable. We have discussed issues related to ABA as a science, a technology, and a form of professional practice. The ABA model consists of identifying a challenge or problem; setting goals and objectives; selecting and implementing a measurement and an evaluation system; and procedures for securing, generalizing, and maintaining change. The system incorporates all of the features that constitute a benign, favorable, and accountable approach to behavior change. With this introduction you are ready to embark on a course of learning in detail how to apply behavior analysis procedures for effective and long-lasting change.

Section I

Preliminary Steps

"Did you see that throw? Almost the full length of the court!"

"Yeah. That was something; and with only 6 seconds to play. A great catch and pass over to the forward and swish, in it goes."

"From being one point behind to a 101 to 100 win!"

The town of Deep Valley could not stop talking about the spectacular play of last night's game that catapulted the high school into winning the regional championship.

"Dumb luck," said many.

"No way. Pure skill," contended others.

But when the hero of the evening who made the long throw was questioned, he said "We must have practiced that play at least a hundred times. That's probably why it went off so smoothly."

In any realm of organized activity, success is hardly a result of dumb luck, whether we are talking about sports, business, education, or community or service functions. Acting without careful preparation often means inviting chaos.

This point is just as relevant for the practice of applied behavior analysis as for the strategic planners of industry. Greater accomplishment eventually justifies the time and effort spent up front. So rather than acting impulsively, a series of steps need to be conducted prior to applying any behavior change procedures.

The preliminary steps show us how feasible and justifiable our goals are; who needs to be involved in the program; what kinds of resources and information we require; and how to go about selecting—or, if necessary, negotiating—goals. The steps guide us to view behavior in its context, so when specific behavioral objectives finally are set, they are realistic and have a better chance of being achieved and enduring.

Behavior analysis concerns itself with what people *do*, rather that about what they or others *say* they do, so behavior needs to be monitored closely. Therefore, the next series of preliminary steps describes methods for observing behavior.

Equivalent care must be given to the selection and application of behavioral procedures. Various factors need to be considered, including humanitarian, ethical, practical, methodological, and professional issues. Additionally, sources of support; means for matching proposed procedures against community, professional, and clients' personal standards; techniques for monitoring progress; and guidelines for changing course all require attention.

Just as when you were a child, you couldn't wait for your birthday to arrive, in the practice of behavior analysis, probably you are impatient to get started. Restrain yourself! If you spend the time it takes to master the concepts and methods of behavior analysis initially, you and your clients will profit.

Chapter 2

Goal Selection:
Initial Considerations

GOALS

After completing this chapter, you should be able to:

1. Define, recognize, and give original illustrations of each of the following terms:
   a. Clients
   b. Contingency managers
   c. Behavioral technicians
   d. Applied behavior analysts
   e. Target behavior
   f. Goal
   g. Operational definition or statement
2. Discuss how behavior analysis can contribute to the future of society.
3. Identify and describe three events that signal the probable presence of a behavior problem.
4. Give four illustrations of potential "simple," direct solutions and discuss why each should be considered before implementing an applied behavior analysis program.
5. Identify and discuss what is involved in setting goal priorities for applied behavior analysis programs, mentioning the relevance of each factor.
6. Specify the behavior to be changed for yourself and for each of two clients who wish to change their behavior.
7. Describe the behavioral approach.
8. Describe the role of the behavior analyst in goal selection.
9. Discuss how test scores, records, and other materials are used and the purposes they serve in behavioral programming.
10. Describe and illustrate the purpose of narrative recordings and sequence ABC analyses.
11. Use a sequence analysis to analyze your own behavior and the behavior of others.

That healthy, productive societies depend on effective use of their resources, both material and human, has become increasingly apparent. However, to approach an optimal level, people need to pursue goals that promote effective resource usage and prevent waste over the long range. Prevention of wars; destruction and depletion of our forests, water, and energy resources; clean air; and extinction of our wildlife requires coordinated planning years in advance.

An entire branch of behavior analysis, *behavioral community psychology*, has evolved in recognition of this need for coordinated social planning. Numerous reports of behavioral applications to community issues, such as energy conservation, safety, and litter control, have been reported in the literature (for example, Bacon-Prue, Blount, Pickering, & Drabman, 1980; Geller, Winett, & Everett, 1982; Greene et al., 1987; Kohlenberg, Phillips, & Proctor, 1976).

Our most precious resource, though, is human potential. Who must survive to plan and coordinate activities for the future good of humankind? People. Again, applied behavior analysis has responded to the call. Preventive and therapeutic health practices are being addressed extensively by practitioners of behavioral health (such as Pomerleau, 1979) and safety (examples are Poche, Brouwer, & Swearingen, 1981; Sulzer-Azaroff, 1987). Education (see Sulzer-Azaroff & Mayer, 1986; Sulzer-Azaroff et al., 1988) and the developmentally disabled (Bailey et al., 1987), too, have received major coverage by the field. Yet enormous education and training efforts have been directed toward ameliorating, instead of toward preventing, problems and expanding human potential.

Fortunately, researchers and practitioners have begun to take a more proactive stance by concerning themselves with promoting learner competence (as in Vicci Tucci's [1987] Competent Learner Model, for people with devel-

opmental delays). Yet one potentially very rich resource, gifted students, hardly has been tapped (Belcastro, 1985), except in attempts to remedy underachievement or maladjustment. We call on behavior analysts, whenever permitted by their circumstances of employment, to turn at least a portion of their efforts toward enhancing human competence for the future as well as the present.

Personnel with behavior analysis skills often are employed to help cope with more immediate issues, such as problems of quality, productivity, misconduct, and risks to health and safety. Because time, energy, material, and other resources always are finite, they must be apportioned carefully. You will need to set priorities and distribute your resources sensibly to permit yourself to meet your current job's and your own personal and long-range demands. You will need to decide which challenges to undertake and which to postpone or reject. Certainly, you will want to avoid investing your resources, when a problem is not sufficiently acute to merit a program that includes all the elements of the full behavior analytic model. In this chapter we offer some helpful hints to help guide you through this difficult decision-making process.

Is Behavioral Intervention Warranted?

Returning now to the case of the hard-to-manage Lucretia, the girl's grandmother came to visit. After spending a day with her grandchild, the grandmother chided her daughter, "How can you say that Lucretia is overly aggressive with other children? To me she seems to have improved so much since my last visit. I think you're just expecting too much. All youngsters have occasional squabbles." How accurate is Lucretia's grandmother's assessment? Is Lucretia's behavior so problematic that outside services should be sought? Is this a case for behavioral intervention? What steps would you follow? What information would you collect to guide your decision as to whether to behaviorally intervene, and how would you proceed?

Lucretia's mother pleads, "I'm convinced my child needs help. She is so difficult to manage." Is that information sufficient to prompt initiating a formal behavior analysis program? Many factors enter into the decision. Let us pause and consider some other issues in addition to long-range concerns. These include whether identification of the problem and goals are realistic, designation of those to be involved and their respective roles, and others.

Realistic Identification of Problems and Goals

When serious behavior problems persist, they must be addressed. Taking a realistic view of what constitutes a problem is important, however. Occasionally, people label a pattern of responding as a "problem," when in fact the problem exists only in the eyes of the beholder. Setting unrealistic goals is a case in point. At one time or another all of us have probably set unrealistic goals for ourselves, like aiming to become celebrated concert pianists, Olympic champions, or writers of bestselling novels. When we realized our failure to attain the goals, we may have been tempted to attribute our failures to a fundamental weakness within ourselves or others. Examples of such logic are that we did not work hard enough, office politics worked against us, or we were not appreciated. In the same way, supervisors, parents, and teachers may set unreasonable goals for their subordinates, children, and pupils. When the goals fail to be attained, those individuals are viewed as having problems.

A person may be said to have a behavioral problem on the basis of hearsay evidence. For instance, Timmy's new teacher may have been warned by his previous teacher to watch out for Timmy. The mere fact that Timmy is now

under closer scrutiny may produce heightened reactions to what is normal misbehavior. Or facts may be distorted by irrelevant factors, as in the case of Joyce, who may appear unusually boisterous to the members of the community board simply because she has a particularly loud voice; or the importance of data may be magnified: Jocelyn is convinced that she is fat because she weighs two pounds above her self-designated ideal weight.

What is a reasonable way to decide when a problem is of sufficient severity to justify behavioral programming? Next we discuss several considerations to aid the discussion.

Several Independent Requests for Assistance with the Same Individual

Do requests to help an individual come from multiple sources? Following are a few instances.

Lucretia has been sent home by neighbors numerous times for fighting with the neighborhood children. Her parents observe that other children avoid Lucretia. And the parents freely admit in discussion with a counselor that they have no control over her. They report that she bullies her younger siblings as well as other children in the neighborhood. It is safe to conclude that a problem exists.

Dexter knows that he has ability, because he always scores well above average on ability and achievement tests. However, his schoolwork is poor and his grades are low. Dissatisfied, he goes to the counselor for help. His humanities and science teachers also approach the counselor, convinced that Dexter is functioning below his level of ability. Dexter's mother visits the counselor too, unhappy with his poor progress. It is apparent that Dexter has a problem.

The principal has insisted that Pearl be excluded from regular classes because her behavior is odd. She does not talk like other children do; she neither responds to questions appropriately nor makes "normal" requests. She sings television commercials at unpredictable times and continually flicks her hands before her eyes. Her parents are distraught, and her family physician thinks that referral to a behavioral specialist is in order.

Paula and her supervisor both recognize that she is a severe procrastinator. So do her co-workers. Because Paula wants a promotion but cannot earn it as a result of that habit, the problem is a serious one for her.

Jocelyn's minor concern with her weight is not corroborated by her physician, husband, or friends. She rightly decides this is not a problem worthy of a major investment of resources. In the first four cases, multiple requests should signal a need for a program. Jocelyn's concern, however, does not merit intervention.

Functioning Differently from Members of a Comparison Group

Standardized test scores and the results of other formal evaluations show how the person has performed in comparison with group norms. The more evidence that can be gathered from various independent sources like those and others, the more valid will be the conclusion regarding the existence of a problem.

For example, Charlie scores three years below his grade level on a standardized achievement test, lower than 85 percent of his peers on a mental-maturity test, and several years below his chronological age level on a developmental inventory. Formal and informal observations provide useful data as well. The number of reading tasks he completes compared to those of other members of his group, his poor physical performance in tasks such as throwing a ball, and his erratic social behavior suggest that all is not well with Charlie.

Dramatic Changes in an Individual's Behavior

Again, information from a number of sources helps to confirm the existence of a problem, especially when an individual's behavior ap-

parently has undergone a substantial change. Henrietta usually does well in school. Her grades have been above average, and she has had good relations with her classmates. Within the past month or two, though, she suddenly stopped doing homework and began to develop headaches and stomachaches just before she was to catch the school bus. But by 10:00 A.M. her ailments began to disappear. Henrietta also has been moping around the house on weekends, complaining that she has no one to play with. All of this is a departure from her previous behavior. It is apparent that something is wrong. If atypical behavior continues, something probably should be done to determine the cause and how to deal with this behavior. Assuming medical difficulties are ruled out and the problem is deemed to be sufficiently serious to merit behavioral programming, other issues need to be considered. One of these issues is who else will be affected by the implementation of a behavior analysis program.

People Involved in Behavioral Programs and Their Roles

People play different roles within a behavior analysis program. First are the individuals whose behavior is the subject of the program. Depending on the nature of the relationship, we shall refer to them as **clients**, *participants, subjects, students, subordinates, trainees*, or *patients*. (Recipients of behavioral interventions are not necessarily in positions of lesser power than the change agents, for behavioral procedures may also be applied to supervisors, peers, or oneself.) Second, change agents such as teachers, therapists, volunteers, high-school students (Gladstone & Sherman, 1975), clients themselves, parents, or others who systematically apply the behavioral strategies each day are called **contingency managers**. Third, auxiliary workers, who perform technical aspects of the program, such as observing, recording, or analyzing data, are **behavioral technicians**. Finally, the individuals professionally competent to design, coordinate the implementation of, and experimentally analyze and evaluate the outcomes of the program are **applied behavior analysts**. Frequently, applied behavior analysts are trained psychologists, but they can also be managers, psychiatrists, social workers, nurses, guidance and rehabilitation counselors, parents, teachers, speech therapists, and other change agents who possess the requisite skills or competencies.

Behavior analysts describe to their clients their proposed programs: the probable roles to be played by each participant, the approximate amounts of time and effort that will be required, and the likelihood of success. Candidates should be given time to consider their willingness to become involved as participants. Once all have acquiesced and seem convinced of the feasibility of conducting a program cooperatively, a mutual commitment has been established.

Besides these key people, others may also be affected: additional staff members, relatives, administrators, community members, peers, and those additional people whose lives impinge on those of the clients.

Prior Considerations

Considering all the people who may become involved directly or indirectly, discovering initially whether the problem can be treated in a faster, simpler manner makes sense. Whether the behavior analysis program under consideration has a high enough priority to justify proceeding must also be decided.

Direct or Informal Solutions

Is the problem behavior related to a physical malfunction? For example, Henrietta might be ill. Perhaps she has a vision problem or something more serious. Whenever persistent physical symptoms are reported, the change agent should consult a physician. Perhaps complying with a recommendation for more sleep, a better diet, or eyeglasses might solve Henrietta's problem.

Logistical changes can occasionally accomplish wonders. Sometimes a simple analysis of the sequence of interactions between the child and the physical context (described in Chapters 7 and 8) can help to identify the environmental changes that would produce desired results. Charlie is easily distracted by activities in the classroom. Putting a partition between him and the rest of the class may be just what is needed to help Charlie complete more assignments.

Changes in lighting, furnishings, equipment, room or seating arrangements, or class placements can also provide simple solutions. The importance of having enough materials to occupy all children in a preschool class was demonstrated by Doke and Risley (1972), who showed that only when there were adequate materials did almost all their students participate in activities. Dexter's behavior might improve after a transfer to a different class, to a teacher with whom he has a good relationship. Alternatively, staff assignments can be altered. The manner in which staff responsibilities for students or clients are assigned may affect behavior. LeLaurin and Risley (1972) found that preschool children spent their time more productively when staff members were assigned to supervise children in areas or "zones" of the room, rather than supervising specific children. One of the students in a study reported by Wilczenski, Sulzer-Azaroff, Feldman, and Fajardo (1987) increased his level of participation simply by being assigned to a different work group, and another improved when his seat was changed. Similarly, Rosenfeld, Lambert, and Black (1985) found that students behaved differently as a function of the way their desks were arranged.

The kinds of demands made of people matter, too. Tasks that are challenging but achievable work best, whereas those that are too demanding may evoke problematic responses (Carr & Newsom, 1985; Iwata, Pace, Kalsher, Cowdery, & Cataldo, 1990).

Other obvious attempts hardly seem worthy of mention, but sometimes the obvious is overlooked. One tactic that falls under this heading is to ask the person to change his or her behavior. The teacher and counselor could meet with Dexter and simply request that he try harder. Just knowing that others are showing an interest may be enough to encourage him. It is entirely possible that, in some situations, offenders do not know they are offending. Joyce may not be aware that her voice carries as far as it does. Perhaps taking her aside and quietly asking her to speak more softly will accomplish the purpose.

Often interpersonal problems are resolved by assisting the people involved to identify their goals, priorities, and reinforcers. Various models of family and marital therapy accomplish just that. "I feel tense all the time," complains Joe Duffer to the counselor. They begin to discuss Joe's concerns and the kinds of things Joe finds pleasurable, which include being out of doors, walking, meeting challenges, and so on. Tension, it seems, is integral to his job. Over several sessions, the counselor helps Joe to plan his time differently, setting several blocks aside for him to participate in vigorous exercise. Joe decides to take up golf and swimming and his tension becomes less oppressive.

Cindy and her parents report their home to be a battleground. Cindy stays out too late, deafens them with her favorite music, doesn't do her homework, and never is around to help with household tasks. Cindy protests that her parents are old fashioned and make unreasonable demands on her time. The family therapist helps family members to identify their key concerns, desires, and levels of effort that they are willing to invest. With this clarification of issues and values, all family members understand one

another better and agree to make some concessions. Life becomes more tolerable.

Assuming, however, that solutions such as simple environmental changes, requests, or short-term counseling or therapy do not produce the desired results, we then have to decide whether the problem merits the expenditure of resources required of a behavior analysis program. We need to set our priorities.

Priorities and Support

On what basis do behavior analysts decide which demands take precedence? Unfortunately, there are no hard-and-fast rules, but certain factors may guide the decision-making process: the clients' willingness to participate; the likelihood of success; emergencies and critical events; likelihood of public and supervisory support; control of goals; the behavior analyst's competence; availability of alternative services; and practical considerations, such as funds and personnel.

The clients' willingness to participate. The highest priority status should be accorded to those seeking help. Paula requests assistance from the counselor in overcoming her procrastination. Mr. Grump seeks help in getting his students to like him more. Dexter agrees to join his parents in asking for help from the behavior analyst. Aunt Minerva consents to work to improve her chronic absenteeism, which currently jeopardizes her job. Pearl's parents are desperate for assistance with their daughter. These people probably will try hard, and more likely succeed—in contrast to someone like Harry, who refuses help in dealing with his angry outbursts when things go wrong on the job. (In the next chapter we discuss client voluntariness from an ethical perspective.)

Procedures demonstrated effective. The extensive literature on applied behavior analysis now permits our guesses about the potential of a particular program for success to be more educated. Journals, like the *Journal of Applied*

Behavior Analysis, Behavior Therapy, and others cited in the reference list contain reports of behavior analysis programs that have produced successful results in educational, clinical, institutional, work, community, home, and other settings. The behavior analyst who keeps informed[1] about procedures that have been repeatedly demonstrated to be effective, as well as new and promising ones, is more likely to make wise selections. It is usually a good idea for neophyte behavior analysts initially to repeat (*replicate*) the procedures previously demonstrated to be effective under similar circumstances before they attempt to design new ones.

Emergencies and critical events. A high priority should be given to critical events or emergencies. Imminent danger to clients must be of prime concern. Problems such as extreme aggressive or self-abusive behavior, serious addiction, and exposure to an environmental catastrophe fall into this category. Major life decisions, like dropping out of school, transferring to different training programs, marrying, undergoing an abortion, and so on, may also be placed here. Emergencies may arise among school or community-agency personnel as well: Precipitous decisions to resign, or to request a transfer or reassignment are the types of problems that probably should be given high priority.

Public and supervisory support. Parent groups, boards, committees, and other public organizations often are major determiners of priorities. Such organizations may, for example, urge that primary emphasis be placed on quality assurance, reading achievement, sexually communicated diseases, citizen responsibility, drug abuse, or some other favored issue. Because continued support is so important to the success of any program—particularly one that

departs from traditional practices—this consideration is not trivial. Those served by schools and other community agencies deserve a major say about the nature of those services. Establishing priorities that reflect members' concerns and involving representatives in program planning increase the chances for continuing support. An excellent model for such involvement is the Achievement Place program (Risley & Twardosz, 1974). In that program, people who represent the consumers in the community participate in planning and are consulted regularly by being asked to rate their satisfaction with the program.

Supervisors often manage some of the more satisfying rewards received by personnel: salaries, promotions, assignments, approval, and privileges. Supervisory support, consequently, usually is essential to the continued cooperation of those involved in a behavior analysis program. As with the public, sustained assistance is more probable when supervisors are involved in setting priorities.

Goals under control of those involved. With supportive factors in place, attaining certain goals may seem highly probable. Yet progress bogs down. We cannot fathom why in the world eliminating Lucretia's aggression should be so difficult. Is there any reason why production at Purple Triangle is not improving when the consultant intervenes? We need to ask ourselves "Is the goal we selected beyond our control? Are the important antecedents and consequences of the behavior unavailable to us?"

Perhaps Lucretia's parents and other children unwittingly punish her feeble attempts to play more cooperatively. Proposed rates of increase in production at a manufacturing facility may be unacceptable to the union. When change agents strongly suspect or recognize that a **behavioral goal** will not be supported because outside forces hold greater power over it than they themselves do, they had best seek a substitute outcome (or, as we shall discuss in

---

[1] Readers who master this book will have the necessary knowledge and vocabulary to read and comprehend much of the professional literature.

Chapter 7, identify contingencies of sufficient power to override those impediments). In Lucretia's case, the objective might be limited to her social interactions during school hours; at the manufacturing facility, it might be negotiating with the union to agree on mutually acceptable production rates.

The behavior analyst's competence. Along with their fellow practitioners—physicians, lawyers, teachers, social workers, counselors, and others—applied behavior analysts only institute programs that they are competent to conduct. Preferably, they have mastered their skills through supervised training (a point we discuss at greater length in Chapter 7). So, analysts should assign higher priority to those challenges for which they possess the requisite skills.

Availability of alternative programs. If you work in a school system in a community with an effective drug-treatment program, refer drug-abuse cases there. If a problem seems to arise from family difficulties, local family clinics might be appropriate referral agencies. A personnel manager probably should refer employees having serious adjustment problems to reputable mental health clinics. Within the schools, services may currently be available, such as courses in psychology, parenting or family life, guidance or support groups, and the like. Behavior analysts should acquaint themselves thoroughly with effective programs that their organizations, communities, and schools offer. Other considerations being equal, the primary function of behavior analysts is to fulfill the roles for which they are hired. For example, in a work setting, you probably will be expected to assign top priority to behavioral programs related to satisfactory job performance; in a school, to student adjustment and learning. When you are the only available person capable of providing behavioral services for which a clear need exists, after checking with key people, you may have to expand your sphere of responsibility.

Material and human resources. Funds and the available services, facilities, equipment, and materials certainly must be considered when priorities for behavior analysis programs are being established. If a particular program requires a special facility—for example, a playroom, additional observers and aides, individualized instructional materials, or other costly items—and if funds are unavailable to fulfill the requirement, attempting the program makes little sense. This issue can be placed toward the bottom of the list, however, because lack of resources often can be circumvented. An imaginative and persistent behavior analyst often can tap resources that are not immediately apparent. (Suggestions for free and inexpensive materials and support services are scattered throughout this book.)

The Behavioral Approach

The checklist in Figure 2.1 summarizes the topic of setting priorities. Affirmative responses to most of the items on the checklist suggest that a problem has been identified, so the appropriate decision is to go ahead and begin to select behavioral goals. But first, does the fact that a problem has been recognized mean that it resides in the individual or is his or her fault? The person is not to blame if you take a behavioral perspective. Dexter is not lazy. He frequently fails to do his work. Paula is not a procrastinator; she regularly procrastinates. Bruno is not a prodigy. He plays the piano with exceptional skill. Lucretia is not a rotten little kid. She is a child who hits other children and frequently grabs their toys. By viewing people's problems in terms of what they *do*, rather than what they *are*, we recognize that change is possible. People can't be altered, but their manner of doing things often can.

That is not to say that all are capable of

Figure 2.1 Practical Considerations in Planning an Applied Behavior Analysis Program

Directions: Circle either Y (yes) or N (no) for each question.

1. Does a problem merit a behavioral program?
Y   N   a. Has assistance been sought from several sources?
Y   N   b. Does the behavior of the person or group depart substantially from that "typical" of comparable people or groups?
Y   N   c. Have dramatic behavior changes recently occurred?

2. Have direct or informal solutions been attempted?
Y   N   a. Physical examination?
Y   N   b. Changes in assignments and responsibilities?
Y   N   c. Changes in physical or social environment?
Y   N   d. Direct requests for behavior change?

(If you answered no to any of these questions, consider informal methods before you institute a systematic applied behavior analysis program; but if answers are affirmative or not applicable, feel justified in proceeding.)

3. Does the proposed behavior analysis program have sufficiently high priority and level of support to justify proceeding?
Y   N   a. Is there sufficient evidence that it is likely to succeed?
Y   N   b. Is the problem critical?
Y   N   c. Will the public support the program?
Y   N   d. Will the program receive supervisory support?
Y   N   e. Will the path toward attaining the goal be under the control of those involved?
Y   N   f. Is the behavior analyst competent to conduct the program successfully?
Y   N   g. Are resources adequate?
Y   N   h. Are different organizations unable to handle the problem adequately?

---

acquiring or eliminating every behavior they would wish. That depends on a number of factors, many of which may be beyond their control. Genetic endowment is one, influencing how rapidly and skillfully we learn to do or say different things. Opportunities and traumas are another, because the environment can provide the resources to promote or throw roadblocks in the way of healthy growth and development. Usually the ability to change in a given way depends on prior learning, and when key elements are missing, progress is stymied. Still, one more factor is the set of current circumstances impacting on people's lives, such as the reinforcers, punishers, and contextual conditions within which those consequences are experienced. Thus, people's patterns of performance are a function of the equipment with which they were born, their histories, and their present circumstances.

Where do credit and blame fit in? They don't. *People* are not at fault, because what they do was molded for them by their genetic material and experiences. From the behavioral perspective, "the individual is always right." Notice that we do not say that people don't do things considered wrong according to a set of standards or values. Here we mean simply that the blame for their behavior is not attributable to them or to their ill will or malignancy. Rather, blame must be placed on the factors just discussed. Similarly, change procedures are applied to behaviors, not to people. Dexter is not reinforced. His good work is. Applied behavior analysis is not in the business of changing people, only in changing their behavior.

Also, we are not implying that people have no control over their own behavior. They do, assuming they have experienced an environment that has allowed them to take control over aspects of their own actions. One of the values of learning about behavioral principles is that people can use the rules they learn to govern their own and others' behavior who are influencing them.

We offer one more disclaimer. Whereas a behavioral approach forces us to understand that people are not at fault, we needn't be unfeeling about the things we see them do. The anger, frustration, or delight we experience in response to others' actions is just as faultless as the deeds or misdeeds of the individual producing that reaction in us. Like our clients, we too are human beings with behavioral repertoires shaped by material and experiential factors. But we can learn to modify at least the more distressing of those reactions by acquiring and applying rules to our own responses. That is something else this book should enable you to do.

Behaviorally Defining Problems and Tentative Goals

Now let us return to setting goals. First we shall discuss the process of expressing problems as operations—in behavioral terms. Later, we shall consider steps that should be followed in refining goals and planning the program. Therefore, having determined that a problem is sufficiently deserving of intervention, you must identify clearly the **target behavior**—the behavior to be changed—and the **goals** of the treatment. The goals constitute the desired change in the target behavior: increasing, decreasing, maintaining, acquiring, narrowing, expanding, or extending the rate, duration, and complexity of the target behavior or the conditions under which it occurs.

Dexter is convinced that he needs help. Paula; Mr. Grump; and the parents and teachers of Lucretia, Charlie, Henrietta, and Pearl also recognize their problems. But what needs to be accomplished? Often the problems and goals for people like these are stated rather ambiguously. "Dexter is lazy; he should realize his potential and stop goofing off." "Paula procrastinates. She hopes to rid herself of that nasty habit." "Mr. Grump wants to be more lovable." "Lucretia is hostile; she should learn to get along better with her playmates." "Henrietta is a hypochondriac; she should not be so obsessed with her bodily ills." If only those goals could be reached, the problems would be solved. But first their ambiguity needs to be unraveled.

We already know that the behavioral approach limits itself to the things people do and say; the objectively observable and measurable.[2] This permits change to be more effectively programmed and monitored, and communication to be clearer. So we shall rephrase terms like *lazy, cooperative, lovable, hostile,* and *hypochondriacal,* restating them in terms of behaviors—what we see (or otherwise objectively apprehend) people doing. Such terms are not necessarily irrelevant. Rather, without being stated as observable acts, such terms are not ideally suited to designing programs of change. The terms must be precisely defined.

So, we see that one of the key aspects that distinguishes applied behavior analysis from many other forms of treatment is its precision. Stated in behavioral language, goals are selected on the basis of an analysis of the problem situation and on ethical considerations. Let us look at some of the vague goals mentioned and see how they can be refined.

A good way to approach the task is to ask "What would Dexter *do* (remember the *action orientation* of behavior analysis) if he were to

---

[2] Private events also may be modified, but because precise, valid measurement of changes in private events remains to be perfected, we rarely consider them in this book.

demonstrate greater 'realization of his potential'? Would he complete more assignments accurately, offer more correct answers, or ask to assist others in group activities? Would he read and report on more books, or would he obtain a work-study job and receive satisfactory performance ratings? What would Mr. Grump be doing if he were being more lovable? Would he smile, compliment his students, and otherwise increase his rate of making positive statements; scold, frown, and make negative statements less often; or what?''

When those people concerned with Dexter's behavior are convinced that they are all talking about the same thing, monitoring is easier, because behavior so defined then can be observed. Instead of asking everyone's subjective opinions of Dexter, monitoring specific acts—such as assignments completed, accuracy levels, or instances of volunteering—is far more objective.

When colloquial psychological terms are broken down into measurable components, they are said to be **operationally defined**. An operation is an act that affects the environment. Writing is an operation because it produces assessable changes on paper. Hitting is an operation because it results in a potentially measurable force delivered to a person or object. Screaming is an operation because it raises the level of ambient decibels of noise. "Intelligence," "anxiety," and "hostility" are not operations. Answering questions correctly, tensing one's muscles, or hitting and kicking are operations. *One of the first set of tasks of the behavior analyst is to define vague terms operationally and specify problems and goals in terms of behavior.*

A further caution: Although what people report that they do and their actual performance often match, this is not always the case. Saying and doing are two *different* behaviors. Baer, Wolf, and Risley (1968) noted that, in specifying goals, the issue is what individuals do, not what they say they do, because ABA

. . . usually studies what subjects can be brought to do rather than what they can be brought to say; *unless of course, a verbal response is the behavior of interest.* Accordingly, a subject's description of his own nonverbal behavior usually would not be accepted as a measure of his actual behavior unless it were independently substantiated. Hence, there is little applied value in the demonstration that an impotent man can be made to say that he no longer is impotent. The relevant question is not what he can say but what he can do (Baer et al., 1968, p. 93; italics added).[3]

Situational Analysis

Once the problem and tentative goals have been operationally defined, you will want to do some homework to determine how reasonable and realistic the goals you are considering may be. Review relevant documents such as test scores, records, and other materials, then analyze the current situation. In Chapter 4 we shall consider the way such information and general goals are refined into specific behavioral objectives.

Test Scores, Records, and Other Materials

Standardized test results; records in personnel files or a teacher's gradebook; production, safety, or quality reports; assignment folders; library records; behavior assessment systems (see the journal, *Behavioral Assessment*); and other documents may also provide valuable information of relevance to both general program goals and specific *objectives* as well as to the selection of procedures for given clients. Dexter's school records may show that his intelligence and reading test scores are above average but that he completes very few reading assign-

[3] Reprinted by permission from D. M. Baer, M. M. Wolf, & T. R. Risley. Some current dimensions of applied behavior analysis. *Journal of Applied Behavior Analysis*, 1968, 1, 91–97. Copyright 1968 by the Society for the Experimental Analysis of Behavior, Inc.

ments. His library card may indicate that he has checked out two books on dinosaurs and that the results of an interest inventory peak in the natural sciences area. This hints at a potential goal. Such records and tests furnish general indications of the client's level of functioning and suggest a reasonable starting place for determining the tasks that clients are most likely to attempt and the kinds of materials that are most appropriate.

Be cautious about interpreting the results of standardized tests, though. Scores derived from even the most carefully conceived tests can be influenced by factors stemming from the respondent's history and current circumstances. For instance, the intelligence test scores of children from poverty backgrounds have been improved remarkably by reinforcing correct answers during testing (for examples, see Ayllon & Kelly, 1972; Bradley-Johnson, Graham, & Johnson, 1986; Young, Bradley-Johnson, & Johnson, 1982). Apparently, unlike many middle-class children who work hard just for adult attention, often these children need tangible reinforcers to obtain their optimal IQ scores. When such youngsters are tested under standard conditions, the underestimated quotients they receive may be misleading. Teachers, parents, or other change agents then may expect them to be able to accomplish less than they probably are capable of doing. Those reduced expectations, in turn, may influence the agents to select insufficiently challenging objectives and to provide fewer opportunities for learning.

Clients' case records often contain useful information. Data on physical condition, social and emotional development, and academic or vocational progress may contribute to decisions about goals and procedures. Dexter's records might indicate reasonable progress until ninth grade. Perhaps something about the class, the teacher, the materials, friends, or other events has affected his performance, although such details may not be included in his records. The fact that Dexter has progressed satisfactorily in

the past, however, does say something about his capabilities: Planning a program to help bring his performance up to the level of his classmates would not be totally unreasonable. Yet this sort of information must be augmented with more current and objective evidence. Directly observing and recording the behavior of the person in the natural setting, when feasible, is especially valuable in the goal-setting process. Narrative recordings get you started.

Narrative Recording and Sequence Analysis

A **narrative recording** is a running description of behavior *in progress*. Although these recordings resemble logs or diaries, they are not exactly the same, because logs and diaries generally are recorded following the observation (for example, during a break or at the end of a period). Similar to the systems used by Jean Piaget, Florence Goodenough, and many ethologists, narrative recording involves writing down what is happening in the natural context. No specific behavior is targeted for observation. The recordings just provide a blow-by-blow description of the occurrences during the observational period, which can be used to identify the behaviors and conditions that will be formally measured later on.

Taking the information derived from the narrative recording and using it to try to begin to see how the events interrelate then becomes crucial. Consequently, the events described in the narrative recording are then organized in a **sequence** or **ABC analysis** (Reese, Howard, & Reese, 1977). Categorized are

1. Specific acts (the Behaviors, labeled B) that relate to the goal.
2. Antecedent events (A's) and contextual conditions (time of day, day of week, ongoing activities, others present, tasks, weather, materials, physical surroundings, and so on) that precede and/or accompany those acts.

Table 2.1 Sample sequence analysis

Antecedent Event	Dexter's Behavior	Consequent Event
Teacher asks, "Who will help find information on dinosaurs for a diorama for the science fair?"	Looks out window.	Teacher shrugs shoulders and says, "I'll help you myself as long as no one volunteered."
Teacher says, "Dexter, I know that you have a special interest in dinosaurs. You'd probably be particularly interested in helping. I'd like to count on your participation; may I?"	Replies, "Sure, I have some models I can bring in to school tomorrow."	Teacher says, "Great." John smiles and nods approval.
John moans, scratches his head, and says, "I can't do this geometry problem."	Says, "You're dumb."	Teacher says, "You can hardly afford to call John anything when you don't complete your work either."
Jeanette moans, scratches her head, and says, "I can't do this geometry problem."	Says, "Here, let me help you. Remember the rule about right triangles?"	Teacher ignores Dexter; Jeanette smiles and gives Dexter a grateful "Thanks."

3. The events that follow as Consequences of the act (C's).

Sometimes, several full days of observation are required before we can begin to identify the various conditions most closely connected to the key behaviors. Table 2.1 illustrates what a sequence analysis might look like.

Recording the conditions provides valuable information about where, when, and how to begin formal observation. Dexter may spend more time looking out the window on Friday mornings during math period. If so, then formal observations should include Friday-morning math periods. Paula's downfall seems to be Monday, when she hardly completes anything at all. At the suggestion of the behavior analyst, she decides to observe her Monday activities especially closely.

A sequence analysis can provide quite a bit of information about potential behavioral goals. For example, not offering to participate, look-

ing out the window, agreeing to help, and actually helping all relate to how Dexter offers help. Events that tend to precipitate such behavior include general requests for help and bids for assistance by some particular students. Analyses of consequent events permit us to begin to discern the influence of such events on particular response patterns. Naturally, the four episodes illustrated in the table are insufficient evidence that the patterns exist. Recording 40 or 400 such events might reveal a trend: Dexter does things for people who smile and thank him; he completes more tasks when his teacher mildly reprimands him privately and fewer when he is harshly reprimanded in public.

Another value of a sequence analysis is that it may yield information about the individual's repertoire of behavior and the conditions under which various behaviors tend to occur:

• In 4 full days of observation, Mr. Grump has never once complimented his staff.

Perhaps such behavior is not in his repertoire. He has, however, been seen nodding at a few staff members when they greeted him. Nodding is part of his repertoire.

- Recording the sequence and duration of her activities for a day informs Paula that she spends lots of time filing, sharpening pencils, and daydreaming.
- Watching Lucretia play for several days, the behavior analyst noticed that not once did she ask for a toy but grabbed it instead out of the hands of the other child. Politely requesting a toy seems to be missing from her repertoire.

Figure 2.2 Initial Considerations in Goal Selection

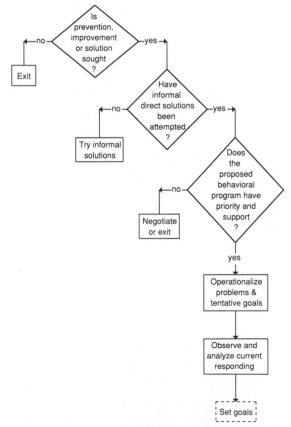

- On no occasion over a week's time was Mel observed to be looking away from the keys as he typed. A reasonable conclusion is that Mel cannot touch-type.

Sequence analyses also permit an estimation of the way people apportion their time, as we saw with Dexter, who spends half his class period looking out the window. Noting her activities for a day, Paula learns how much time she spends sharpening pencils, rereading memos, and daydreaming. Mr. Grump makes many sarcastic remarks and goes for a smoke whenever he has a free moment. Pearl repeats a stereotyped sequence of hand movements during more than 80 percent of the observational session. During her many trips to the coffeepot, Mrs. Kvetch frequently tells her fellow employees how much better her former job was. All this information says something about the seriousness of the problem. Dexter hardly orients toward his work. Paula is off task much of the time. Mr. Grump uses a lot of sarcasm. Mrs. Kvetch does indeed complain. Pearl's stereotypic hand movements occur alarmingly often. Sequence analyses may also help to identify potential reinforcers, as we shall show later in the book.

Summary

This chapter provided guidelines for establishing priorities for behavior analysis programs. A checklist has been included to assist you in this task. Rationales for operationalizing problems and for analyzing the situation before final goal selection have also been presented. Each of these initial considerations is summarized in the flow chart in Figure 2.2; together, they form the first component of the model on which the conduct of applied behavior analysis programs should be based. The broken line around *Set goals* indicates the next main component to be considered. That is the topic to which we turn in Chapter 3.

Chapter 3

Goal Selection: Guidelines

GOALS

After completing this chapter, you should be able to:
1. Discuss how each of the following general considerations enters into goal selection:
   a. Goals achievable yet challenging
   b. Goals constructive and functional
   c. Interventions direct or indirect
   d. Skills foundational or enabling
   e. Beneficiaries of short- and long-term services
   f. Clients age and/or developmental level
   g. Mission of the organization
   h. Goals cooperative, competitive, or individualistic
   i. High priorities
2. Define and discuss the following terms:
   a. Constructional approach
   b. Advocate
   c. Behavioral contract
   d. Voluntary
   e. Informed consent
3. State and explain the advantages of Hawkins' general rules for goal selection.
4. Identify several sources of conflict in goal selection.
5. Discuss how the involvement of each of the following people or methods may help to prevent or resolve goal conflicts:
   a. Client
   b. Behavior analyst
   c. Parent
   d. Staff and administration
   e. Advocates
   f. Institutional review
   g. Behavioral contracting board
6. List at least 10 guidelines for responsible goal selection.

You know from earlier chapters that Dexter is capable of increased accomplishments; Charlie and Fern are deficient in many skills; Mr. Grump has much to learn if the climate of his classroom is to improve; and that something must be done to address turnover in Harry's production unit, complaints about service in the Purple Triangle Health Service, and Pearl and Lucretia's many troublesome acts. As an agent of change, you and your clients need to choose a direction to follow. What is the final destination to be? The choices can be almost infinite. You will want some guidance before proceeding.

The various directions that a behavior analysis program can take are suggested by analysis of the current situation and those aspects of the physical and social environment that operate to support or to interfere with a given behavior. Although as we have seen, test scores, results of surveys, and formal and informal observations also help us to pinpoint behaviors to target for change, human, legal, scientific, practical, and ethical considerations are also critical to responsible goal selection. These latter considerations form the next major component of the applied behavior analysis model and constitute the nucleus of this chapter. First, this chapter helps you deal with selecting from among a variety of potential goals,[1] by offering several rules and guidelines. Next, as different people's choices occasionally conflict, we suggest some methods here for resolving conflicts.

Choosing from Among Alternative Goals

Goals are general statements about the behavior targeted for change and the direction or level that change should take. For instance, goals may be formulated in terms of enabling the person to acquire a behavior, perform it more fre-

---

[1] Goals as "rules" or "instructions" will be discussed in Chapters 15–18 (on stimulus control) and 21 (on verbal behavior).

quently, transfer it into a new context, maintain it over time, or to diminish or stop doing it.

To illustrate, Dexter's goals might be completing increased amounts of work, learning a set of new academic skills, working in the absence of managed reinforcers for increased durations, practicing his new skills elsewhere or adjusting them to meet slightly different requirements, looking out of the window less often or for briefer periods of time, or no longer refusing to perform assignments. Alternatively, the chosen goals may not involve Dexter directly but someone else whose behavior influences his. For instance, the focus could be for the teacher to increase her use of instructional methods built on his interests, to praise and provide him with specific feedback (strengthening behaviors of his teacher), or to rearrange the seating arrangements so he can't look out the window or socialize with others as easily (stimulus change). All of these potential goals have the same general purpose: to improve Dexter's school performance. Which should be selected?

General Considerations in Goal Selection

Ethical, practical, and scientific factors need to be considered when we are selecting goals. It used to be said that "the behavioral approach is a headless technology, having no built-in goals about what should be taught or accomplished." For example, Wilson and O'Leary (1980) stated: "As an applied science, behavior therapy is simply a collection of principles and techniques about how to change behavior, it says nothing about who should modify what behavior, why, or when . . ." (p. 258). During this early phase of applied behavior analysis, change agents often responded to vague complaints by clients or other referring agents with a listing of behaviors to be modified, with no real conception of the process or assumptions involved (Baer, 1982). Frequently, the selection of target behaviors was left to teachers (Winett & Winkler, 1972), parents (Walder, Cohen, & Daston, 1967) or the client: "Choosing therapeutic objectives is a matter of value judgment and ought to be determined primarily by the client" (Wilson & O'Leary, 1980, p. 258).

This orientation is now changing. As Hawkins (1985) contends, goal selection "is as much a scientific question as is the question of effective technique; it is simply a question that behavior therapy and behavior analysis have neglected" (p. 1138). As a case in point, one study revealed that, depending on presenting complaints, behavior therapists varied to a greater or lesser extent in their recommendations for target behaviors and goals (Wilson & Evans, 1983). (For a detailed discussion, see Volume 7, Number 1 of the journal *Behavioral Assessment*, which contains a "miniseries" on target selection.)

In this discussion of general considerations we address ethical, practical, and scientific factors: approaches that are constructive instead of suppressive; direct rather than indirect; foundational or enabling; age and/or developmentally appropriate; and beneficial to the client, significant others, peers, staff, and society. We also note the relation of behavioral **outcomes** to the overall mission of the organization. Additionally, you will see why it is important to focus not only on short-term but also on long-term **outcomes**.

Achievable yet challenging. Paula would like to stop procrastinating immediately. Yet every one of her reports over the past year has been late. Is her goal achievable? How about the one Lucretia's mom requests—that her daughter *never* hit another child or grab another toy? If goals are too difficult to be achieved, everyone involved suffers (Stedry & Kay, 1966). Progress disintegrates and all efforts are fruitless.

The issue of achievability applies to behavior analysts, too. Resist the temptation to collaborate with clients in setting goals that require

you to manage conditions beyond your control. Frustration and failure result when more powerful reinforcement competes from elsewhere. Do not expect to sustain a program directed toward employee satisfaction if an organization is in the process of scaling down and would welcome reductions in its workforce. Recognize the futility of independently competing with peer pressure and the inherent pleasures of such temptations as substance abuse and sexual activity. After all, you cannot act for someone else.

Of course, alternatives exist. You might be able to harness some of the contingencies ordinarily beyond your purview. Working with managers and labor unions may help you adjust the goals of your clients, say to find substitute cost-saving measures. Or you may try to shift peer pressure over toward abstinence from harmful pursuits. Effective leaders have succeeded in supporting programs of that sort.

Reasonable goals have a better chance of being achieved. Paula could aim for handing in one-fourth of her reports on time for several weeks; once that target is accomplished, she could then up the requirement by another one-fourth. Initially, Lucretia might successfully make it through a five-minute play session without hitting. Success is much more likely under those circumstances. So choose goals you have reason to believe are apt to be achieved.

Conversely, some goals can be *too* easy. This situation also can be punishing to clients who see themselves progressing too slowly or who feel insulted by receiving reinforcers for a trivial accomplishment (while their more substantial achievements go unnoticed). Many people find it extremely rewarding to succeed at something difficult (Latham & Baldes, 1975). Unchallenging goals deny people that pleasure. (Later, the discussion about baselines shows how to set achievable yet challenging goals. The chapter on shaping shows how to approach raising goals systematically.)

Constructive and functional. Consider a person who exhibits few adaptive behaviors. If we eliminate all his problems, what will we have? An empty shell, a person with a few desirable behaviors and not much else. What has been accomplished, other than keeping the client out of trouble? Dexter could be taught to stop staring out the window, to stifle his yawns, and to remain silent instead of saying, "I don't feel like doing that." That hardly constitutes an improvement. (As Aubrey Daniels, who teaches organizational managers how to use behavioral methods, contends, goals that can be accomplished by a "dead person" are unworthy!) Similarly, Winett and Winkler (1972) cautioned against using behavioral procedures to promote docility and immobility. Behavior analysts can avoid encouraging docility by helping their clients to set constructive and useful behavioral goals. For example, were Dexter to complete his schoolwork, volunteer frequently, or propose innovative problem solutions, he would be much better off than previously.

You can see why that, whenever possible, goals serving to *construct* repertoires and increase options are preferable to those directed toward eliminating or reducing performance. Try to state goals in terms of what behaviors the person *is*, rather than *is not*, to do: "Be on time" rather than "Don't be late"; "Complete tasks" rather than "Don't waste time"; "Bring work materials" rather than "Don't forget your materials." Use the **constructional approach** (Goldiamond, 1974; Hawkins, 1986).

A constructional approach teaches or builds rather than reduces or eliminates behavior. Specifically, the constructional method (Goldiamond, 1974) involves:

1. Observing or interviewing to determine the desirable outcome or the repertoire to be established.

2. Identifying the current effective repertoires on which to build.

3. Selecting change procedures that will

build on the current effective repertoires in steps that can be accomplished successfully.

4. Selecting and using reinforcers that will maintain the goal behavior throughout the duration of the program and thereafter.

The emphasis is on using reinforcers natural to the environment, such as those that previously reinforced the problem behavior.

A study by Carr and Durand (1985) illustrates the value of the constructional approach. Some of their autistic students were disruptive while working on assigned tasks. The investigators wondered whether the disruption continued because of the attention the students gained or because of the difficulty of the task. The researchers taught one group of these students to say, "How do you like my work?" (which was followed by adult attention and approval); and then later to say, "This is too hard" (which was followed by adult assistance). (They taught the other group in the opposite order.) Some of the students (presumably those seeking attention by disrupting) taught to say "How do you like my work?" disrupted less often; learning the other phrase hardly impacted the frequency of disruption. Similarly, when the other students (presumably those who were disrupting as a way of seeking relief from a task too difficult for them) were taught to obtain attention by saying "How do you like my work?" their rates of disruption continued. Only after learning to say, "This is too hard," did their disruptions decline.

Instead of punishing the disruptive behavior, Carr and Durand (1985) identified the students' *functional* reinforcers (i.e., attention and relief) and taught them alternative, constructive behaviors to produce those reinforcers in that setting. As Hawkins (1986) points out in his discussion of this study, "these researchers circumvented the disruptive behaviors that were immediately costly to the teacher and ultimately costly to the child" (p. 358).

Selecting functional goals that expand

clients' repertoires and yield them reinforcement is critically important. Nevertheless, even though educators may agree that educational activities for severely handicapped students should promote their functioning at home and in their vocational and community settings (e.g., Bates, Renzaglia, & Wehman, 1981; Brown et al., 1979; Burton, 1981; Certo, 1983; Reid et al., 1985), when Green et al. (1986) observed forty-three classrooms of severely handicapped students, they found that about two-thirds of all instructional tasks were nonfunctional. The situation was remedied when Reid et al. (1985) provided consultation and in-service training to these teachers, showing them how to alter their curricula to teach functional tasks.

Sets of behaviors that tend to increase an individual's options have *general utility* and should be given priority. For example, though sometimes situationally specific, skills in decision making, problem solving, time management, generalization, and interpersonal interactions and self-management are useful in many aspects of daily life. If a complaint stems from a deficit in one of these areas, that deficit should be remedied early in the intervention (Hawkins, 1986).

Similarly, potential goals must be analyzed in view of whether they pinpoint for change classes of behaviors that expand or constrain an individual's options, "... behaviors that gain (or deny) the client access to natural environments where a variety of important behaviors will be taught or reinforcers made available" (Hawkins, 1986, p. 375). For example, to survive in school students need to be able to ask questions related to tasks, concentrate on assignments, and follow instructions or directions. Personal cleanliness and social skills are important for permitting access to social groups because such groups can provide rich contexts for learning and reinforcement.

Direct rather than indirect. In a direct approach, we target the behavior of concern, whereas with an indirect approach we try to accomplish the goal by addressing some other behavior that we presume will influence the target. In the past, analysts assumed that if we could just get students to stop disrupting and misbehaving they would automatically learn more; just persuade workers to stop being off task, they would produce more. Now we recognize that these assumptions were naive. Ferritor and his colleagues (1972) reduced disruption, yet their students' school performance did not improve (though conversely, Sulzer and her associates [1971] and Ayllon and Roberts [1974] found that better school performance was accompanied by a reduction in disruptive behavior). For Dexter, selecting goals directly related to improved school performance would be preferable to those focused on eradicating his disruptiveness as the primary goal. Similarly, after extensively reviewing many studies designed to increase educational achievement by enhancing self-concept, Scheirer and Kraut (1979) concluded that improved self-concepts did not necessarily increase school achievement, whereas the opposite did hold: "In this view, self-concept change is likely to be an outcome of increased achievement with accompanying social approval, rather than an intervening variable necessary for achievement to occur" (p. 144). Working with productive performance directly, instead of self-concept, apparently is the most effective and efficient way to go.

Years ago, studies in institutions and clinics also tended to focus on behaviors presumed to interfere with effective performance, such as self-stimulation or disrupting, rather than on remediating clients' behavioral deficits. Although such techniques help a bit, concentrating all one's efforts on reducing aberrant acts does not necessarily lead to optimal performance. By contrast, teaching skills (instead of, or in addition to, working on reducing interfering behaviors, depending on circumstances) provides the client with greater benefits. If readying Helen for community employment is the long-range goal, we would want to be sure to teach her to do her job well, rather than concentrating on eliminating her occasional conversations with imaginary friends. In summary, whenever possible, be direct.

Foundational. When reasonable evidence suggests that higher skills depend upon more basic ones—variously called "keystone," "pivotal," "foundational," or "enabling" skills (Hawkins, 1986)—we must first assess for, and if necessary teach, those fundamental skills. For example, holding the pencil properly, positioning the angle of the paper correctly, and drawing freehand lines and various shapes are enabling skills for handwriting; explaining the functions of each lever and button are enabling skills for operating a cutting machine. You start with those enabling skills if the learners have not yet attained them.

Explicit immediate *and* long-term benefits to client, significant others, staff, and society. Everyone who provides human services probably assumes the recipient will ultimately benefit from the services. Applied behavior analysts, however, require something beyond good faith, especially when it comes to selecting goals whose short- and long-term benefits are neither apparent nor necessarily universally acceptable. Instead, we explicitly state intended outcomes, along with anticipated long- and short-term benefits, enabling all concerned to become aware of the goals and their potential advantages. This permits us as change agents to readily detect which people stand to benefit.

If all the school psychologist needed to state was that she and Dexter would be working on his school problems together, they could be striving toward accomplishing just about anything, including making him compliant or docile, assertive or aggressive, or a better student. Such ambiguity is eliminated with an explicit statement such as "Dexter will complete all the academic requirements for his grade level by the end of the semester."

Educators, clinicians, managers, and direct-service personnel must be able not only to defend the particular goals they select but also to justify their actions related to them.[2] Clearly explicated goals simplify this process by highlighting the relation between methods and anticipated outcomes. Besides defending the importance of helping Dexter to improve his academic performance, his teachers (or counselor or school psychologist) would need to describe how the instructional environment would successfully support the attainment of that goal. (Ecobehavioral analyses [Rogers-Warren, 1984], to be discussed later on, assess the environment to determine environmental supports and impediments.)

Yes, providing for both immediate and long-term benefits to the client is essential, but such benefits may not be apparent. When benefits are not obvious, controversy may erupt. Performance goals composed of stages in learning task hierarchies—holding a pencil, tracing, and writing; setting up, analyzing, and solving an equation; or performing a job skill—usually arouse little contention. In our society acquiring such skills is considered good, and we have established schools and training programs to further those purposes. But what of some of the subtler classes of behaviors: attentional and attitudinal skills, social skills, work habits, responses that may impede growth, and so on? How important are staying on a task for long periods of time, independently seeking more information, volunteering for extra projects, following both simple and complex directions, working without disturbing others, cooperating, organizing activities, and refraining from aggressing or inciting others to engage in disorderly acts? We need to defend the importance of goals based on their pertinence to the de-

---

[2] Justification of procedures will be discussed in Chapter 7.

velopment of other beneficial behaviors: For instance, that paying attention is necessary for learning.

When stated precisely, potentially controversial goals can be scrutinized closely to assess their value to clients and others.[3] The teacher asks: "Here I am, insisting that students request permission to leave the room and punishing those who refuse to comply with the rule. Is the rule imposed because it makes sense or just because that's how my teachers did things when I was a student? How does such a rule benefit my students?" The counselor wonders: "Why did we spend most of our session discussing sports? Did the interchange serve any purpose? Are we wasting time, or did I simply neglect to overtly pinpoint some important goals: to learn to communicate effectively with one another and to make our sessions reinforcing?" The manager questions the ultimate advantage of having her workers punch both in and out on the time clock.

Long-term goals can often be reached by accomplishing a succession of readily accomplished short-term ones. When change agents initiate any complex program of behavior change, if they select initial, rapidly achievable goals, immediate reinforcement will result, not only for the client but also for others directly affected, such as parents, teachers, supervisors, and clients (Krumboltz & Thoresen, 1969; Sulzer-Azaroff & Mayer, 1986).

The goals best defended on ethical grounds are those selected to promote improved adjustment, adaptation, competence, or habilitation; that support the development of a ". . . repertoire that maximizes short- and long-term reinforcers, for the person and for others, and minimizes short- and long-term punishers"

(Hawkins, 1986, p. 351). The adaptiveness of any particular response to the environment is "the degree to which it maximizes the benefits and minimizes the cost" (Hawkins, 1986, p. 351). Notice, despite its parsimony, how flexible and general this rule is. Goals selected according to those strictures are measurable, broadly applicable, individualizable, culturally adaptable, and consistent with the perspective that "adjustment" is a continuous (a question of degree) rather than a dichotomous (either-or) variable. Credit and blame for maladaptive behavior are avoided, yet the impact of the goal is considered in terms not only of its effect on the client but also on the significant others in the client's immediate and broader environment. As Hawkins (1985) points out:

> The scientific question, then, in terms of setting goals for individuals . . . is "what will reduce the costs and/or increase the benefits to this person and/or others?" For an unhappy freshman who is facing vague, existential problems and is questioning the meaning or value of his or her life—a type of problem for which behavior therapists and behavior analysts are least prepared, because no behavior is referred to by the client—one might hypothesize that one or more of several goals is relevant: greater skill at studying or at making new friends, becoming active in an activist organization, setting more realistic academic goals, coming to a decision about tentative career objectives, and so forth. If one or more of those goals is then achieved and it is scientifically demonstrated, by methods such as those suggested by Barlow, Hayes, and Nelson (1984), that the person is no longer unhappy or questioning the value of his or her life, the conclusion suggested is that the goals selected were, indeed, functional for that individual. Similarly, if a clinician teaches a delinquent youth to, for example, carry on conversations effectively with middle-class nondelinquents, to read as well as age peers, and to "read" people's positive and negative social reactions; and if that youth no longer engages in delinquent behaviors (which primarily cost others, at least in the short run), the

---

[3] Budd and Baer (1976) point out that the decision in *Wyatt v. Stickney* (1972) prohibits programs that are designed to extinguish socially appropriate behavior or to develop new behavior patterns that serve only institutional convenience.

conclusion suggested is that these "target behaviors" were functional for this individual and relevant to his or her problem (p. 1138).

Above all, the behavior analyst should be guided by concern for the client. Although teaching Lucretia adaptive and socially constructive modes of responding, such as non-aggressive forms of assertiveness, probably requires considerable time and effort, she will benefit from this investment. Generally, behavior analysts should give precedence to goal behaviors that are most preferred by the clients and/or their advocates, because these people have extensive and intimate experience with the contingencies in their environments (Hawkins, 1986; Nelson & Hayes, 1979).

Age and developmental level. When goals are mission oriented, selected for short- and long-term payoff, functional, and serve as foundations for more advanced performance, they probably are appropriate to the developmental level of, and beneficial for, the client. As Dyer, Santarcangelo, and Luce (1987) have shown, for individuals with developmental delays, selecting goals according to the sequence in which typical children tend to acquire language skills allowed the students to progress more rapidly and accurately than when goals were more developmentally advanced. Generalization, too, has been found to profit from matching goals to children's current language levels (Warren & Rogers-Warren, 1983).

Nevertheless, many instructional activities, justified as being appropriate to the developmental levels of clients, are at odds with their chronological ages. We know of cases in which adult clients with handicapping conditions are taught to string beads, to cut and paste in scrapbooks, or to color. These activities are defended on the grounds of enabling the clients' verbal, cognitive, or motor skills to progress; yet they are hardly age appropriate. Adults in our society usually work at paying jobs to permit the people to live independently. (Supported employment programs that teach developmentally disabled clients marketable skills are much more impressive than programs that teach nonfunctional activities.)

Analysts also need to address how to broaden clients' spectrum of skills to include the wide variety of activities appropriate to their ages and developmental levels. Although playing with puzzles, peg boards and other table toys are age-appropriate skills for primary school aged children, these are not the *only* play skills enjoyed by this population. Watch children during free play, noting how they pretend, playing fantasy games. As Lifter and Bloom (1988) suggest, this type of play is not only reinforcing in its own right, but also serves as a vehicle for learning verbal and other important skills that typify the performance of most children of those ages. (You can see why knowing the typical ways behavior tends to evolve as people develop is essential for practitioners who participate in goal selection.)

Mission oriented. Schools, institutions, agencies, and business organizations each have general purposes. A school's mission may be to enable students to gain the knowledge and skills necessary for functioning independently in society. For a business organization, providing high-quality goods or services at competitive prices may be the mission. Similarly, units within organizations have their own key reasons for existing: The social studies department wants students prepared to participate as responsible members of a democracy; the claims department, to process claims fairly and expediently.

When you affiliate with an organization, in a sense, you buy into its mission. Should the mission be obscure, you should seek to clarify it, permitting you to match your goals with those missions. You will then be able to see whether the group is working together toward a common goal or is at cross purposes. You will have a better idea whether you are being reasonable in anticipating organizational support for your activities. Explicitly matching your goals with organizational mission statements also reveals to your colleagues and supervisors the link between your efforts and the stated direction of the organization. (A missing link between your goals and those of the organization suggests that you need to help reshape the mission or your own goals, or to transfer to a more supportive organization.)

Psychological services in the Deep Valley District have concentrated primarily on conducting assessments of students for special education placement. Mr. Ernest ("Ernie") is more interested in consulting with teachers and has been designing an in-service consultation program. Before beginning this consultation, Ernie presents his plan to his supervisor, and together they review the mission of their unit: "to remediate and prevent students' social, emotional, and academic difficulties." Ernie is able to convince his supervisor that providing consultation to teachers will accomplish their purposes more cost efficiently in the long run. The supervisor becomes Ernie's strongest backer, and the program succeeds.

Cooperative, competitive, or individualistic. Some goals toward which people strive depend only on their own accomplishment, such as operating a mechanical device, caring for themselves, enjoying leisure time alone, and mastering numerous study and work skills; others involve social groupings. This is true of just about any activity in which collective involvement or support is advantageous: group problem solving, many recreational activities, communications, and numerous other sorts of skills, from steering a sailboat to exploring the pros and cons of individual and cooperative learning. When you select a goal, consider the long-range implications along this dimension. Will the person ultimately benefit from being able to perform the behavior totally independently, or will a social milieu be available to support

(or impede) it?

In their book *Learning Together and Alone*, the Johnson brothers (1975) expand upon the themes of building cooperation, competition, and individualization into goals. They cite numerous instances in which cooperation can be more advantageous than either competition or individualization. Should your deliberations convince you that one of these particular goals would best suit your and your clients' purposes, you can select your procedures accordingly. As you study further in this text, you will see many examples of methods supportive of cooperative, individualistic, and even occasionally competitive goals.

Notice that the guidelines we have offered are based on various foundations: practical, empirical, and ethical. Distilling it down to its essence, "The issue is what response at what levels will improve the effectiveness (reinforcer/punisher ratio) of the learner's repertoire" (Hawkins, 1986, p. 358).

Goal Conflicts

Unfortunately, people do not always automatically agree about the priorities they assign to particular goals. Conflicts can arise from many sources. Sometimes an employee's purpose is at odds with the mission of the organization. Short- and long-term goals can conflict with one another, as when a firm strives toward a semiannual profit rather than investing in long-range growth potential. Other conflicts can occur between staff and managers, clients and their change agents, and clients and their significant others. Even when goals do not conflict, perspectives about what constitutes a desirable outcome may vary among concerned individuals. What seems like a beneficial or detrimental outcome to one person may not seem that way to another. To avoid working at cross purposes, we must find ways to resolve these conflicts. Here we offer some measures you might take to avoid and resolve goal conflicts.

Preventing and Resolving Goal Conflicts

Participative Goal Setting

There are no pat solutions to goal conflicts, but some mechanisms prevent them or limit their escalation. These methods include

- participation by clients, parents, and other concerned individuals, such as worker organizations, individual staff and community members
- advocacy
- institutional review
- contracting

The important point is to assess the social context in which your client operates in order to predict whether the anticipated outcome will be disadvantageous to anyone. Only with foresight can you avoid some of the increasingly prevalent social and legal confrontations stemming from controversial methods of providing human services. Such controversies must be ironed out in advance, with the individual concerned receiving the main benefit; otherwise, as Martin has contended, "In the final analysis, if the goal is not to produce a happy functioning person free from state interference, then it will, and should, run into constant legal problems" (1974, p. 11).

Involving the client. Often, conflicts can be avoided and cooperation facilitated when the client is directly involved in selecting goals. For example, the divisional vice president participated in discussions of matching the department's and the organization's missions. Dexter may select writing more and longer book reports because he enjoys reading and writing. But he may be unwilling to complete additional physics assignments, because he is not fond of the subject. Mr. Grump initially may be more amenable to trying to increase his rates of commenting to his students about their specific ac-

complishments (e.g., "You finished this report an hour earlier than the last one.") instead of working on his rates of praising, because he feels so "phony" when he praises.

In addition to the practical advantages of involving clients in setting their goals, ethical and legal factors enter into the situation. This is illustrated by students with special needs who participate in meetings during which their individual educational plans are designed, according to the guidelines of Public Law 94.142 (Pollack & Sulzer-Azaroff, 1981).

> Questions are now arising about how young the consenter might be—the Federal Health, Education and Welfare Department proposed guidelines on experiments with children require consent to be obtained from children nine years old or above. Additional questions are whether an institution can act in the place of a parent and give consent, meaning that a child would have no protection against what the institution has decided to do; and whether there are substantive rights belonging to a child that cannot be waived even with parental consent (Martin, 1974, p. 8).

Involving the behavior analyst. On occasion, the client may select an unrealistic or inappropriate goal. For example, Carmen wants to become the most popular girl in school—an overly ambitious goal, because at the moment she has hardly any friends at all. Instead, Carmen could be offered the opportunity to learn some useful social skills that will enable her to establish a few close friendships. The behavior analyst is responsible for guiding the client to identify an array of potentially attainable goals, but the client should be the one who ultimately selects from among them.

Nevertheless, the client is not always the sole determiner of the goal. Other concerned individuals may have a right to be involved. A transsexual's judgment that a sex-change operation would be the most beneficial outcome for him was not accepted by the behavior an-

alyst (Barlow, Reynolds, & Agras, 1973). Instead, the two compromised on a mutually acceptable outcome: teaching him to behave in a
more masculine manner—thus expanding his
repertoire and augmenting his options. Meanwhile, the client altered his desire for a sex-
change operation. (By contrast, several years
ago, in a presidential address to the Association
for the Advancement of Behavior Therapy, Davidson informed the audience of his decision to
refuse to treat homosexual individuals wanting
to change their sexual orientations.)

Involving parents. Parents of minor children
have legal responsibilities toward their offspring, as well as the "moral obligation" to
bring their children up "properly." Parents also
control many of the contingencies in their
youngsters' lives. A parent has the right to participate in the selection of goals for minor children, particularly when the goals are related to
the parent's responsibilities. Additionally, we
have found that when parents are involved, they
are more supportive of progress.

Older youngsters sometimes select goals
their parents would consider unacceptable.
Carmen may want to join a social group,
whereas her parents want her to spend more
time studying. Henrietta's goal is to quit school
as soon as she is old enough. Her parents want
her to continue her education through college.
Here the behavior analyst might act as an ar-
bitrator, helping each young woman and her
parents to arrive at mutually acceptable goals.

Occasionally, legal minors have problems
that they are unwilling to discuss with their parents, preferring to work in confidence with the
behavior analyst. For example, Henrietta may
want to diminish her smoking and abuse of
drugs and alcohol, which are habits unknown
to her parents. Involving the parents in such a
case might do more harm than good. The behavior analyst must use some subjective standards: Is the client sufficiently mature to know
what he or she wants? Would the goal be ac-

ceptable to the parents if they knew the whole
story? Will the client permit the behavior analyst to discuss the problem with others who
are responsible for him or her—a teacher, the
principal, a doctor? Obviously, solutions are not
simple, so the behavior analyst should consider
the ethics of each situation from as many vantage points as possible. Useful sources are the
American Psychological Association's *Ethical
Principles of Psychologists* (APA, 1981) and the
American Association for Advancement of Behavior Therapy's statement on ethical practice
(AABT, 1977).

Involving other concerned individuals. Particular goals sometimes may impact on teachers,
colleagues, spouses, siblings and other relatives, staff members, or even occasionally close
friends. This influence can be direct, as when
parents accept responsibility for tutoring their
youngster (Broden, Beasley, & Hall, 1978), or
indirect, as when the extra attention given to
one individual causes another to receive less.
Some goals are morally offensive to a person.
For instance, staff members may find themselves philosophically opposed to teaching
methods of AIDS prevention or birth control.

When these concerned individuals are consulted ahead of time, they can express their
opinions and conflicts. Often a minor adjustment in the way a goal is stated will nip potential problems in the bud. Otherwise, if per-
suasion or instruction isn't successful, the
concerned parties may be asked to suggest alternatives as a basis for negotiation.

Arranging for Advocacy

The social movement toward ensuring equal
rights for everyone, regardless of disability or
group affiliation, has accelerated during the past
several decades. Similarly, representatives of
previously powerless groups, like children or
people with severe emotional or developmental
disabilities, increasingly have insisted that the
perspectives of those involved be considered in

decisions affecting members of those groups. This can mean that in addition to their traditional advocates (parents, relatives, or guardians) severely disabled, abused, or very immature clients may be represented by outside advocates.

When a client clearly does not have the capacity to participate in such a decision—for example, when a child lacks speech or an adult totally fails to communicate—an **advocate** may be appointed to represent his or her interests. The appointee, who may be a community representative, like a clergyman, a law student, or even a panel of interested citizens, considers the goal from the point of view of the client (Reynolds, 1973). The advocate is the client's agent, not the agent of an organization or institution. Advocates put themselves in the place of their clients and argue on their behalf. This arrangement makes it more likely that the best interests of the clients are served.

Arranging for Institutional Review

The U.S. government requires that organizations seeking federal funding for research have permanent human subjects' review committees. Their charge is to study research proposals to ensure that the rights of humans research participants[4] are protected. Committees are composed of people from varying backgrounds who are not directly involved professionally in the activity under review. Although the guidelines were developed to protect "experimental subjects" in federally sponsored grant and contract programs, and even though the client in a behavior analysis program may not necessarily be a "subject" in the same sense, the dividing line is a fine one. Some behavior analysis programs have minimal experimental overtones, because they hardly diverge at all from standard operating procedures. Such is the case

for measuring rates of production under regular incentive conditions in a factory or when recognition is the only component added by a teacher who attempts to increase the quality of students' work.

Other outcomes really are experimental, as when the goal is to teach a youth a new way to resist social pressures or counteract depression. Outcomes deviating sharply from those typical of the milieu should also be considered "experimental." We argue, however, that when you are unsure, discretion is the better part of valor. Submit the goals and request committee approval. You probably will be asked to attach an informed consent form that details the purposes and procedures and specifies that the participant may withdraw without penalty at any time.

When constituted to represent the various points of view of the community, institutional review committees can help prevent and resolve conflicts about goals as well as procedures. As "minicommunities" who approve or disapprove planned programs, committees probably reflect the perspectives of the members of the local public. When obvious deviations from policies, laws, or prevailing standards are revealed, the committee's response serves to test public reaction. The behavior analyst then can act accordingly: proceeding as planned, offering further explanations or justifications, or revising the proposal.

Behavioral Contracting

Conflicts in goal selection may arise when benefits and costs affect certain members of a group disproportionately. One way to achieve a more equitable balance is to negotiate a **behavioral contract** (see, for example, Brooks, 1974; Dardig & Heward, 1976; DiRisi & Butz, 1975; Homme, Csanyi, Gonzales, & Rechs, 1970; Krumboltz, 1966; Sulzer, 1962; Sulzer-Azaroff & Reese, 1982). Contracts may stipulate both program goals and procedural details.

---

[4] Similar sets of guidelines for animal research have also been adopted by the American Psychological Association and by the National Institutes of Health.

(The latter type will be discussed and a number of contracts illustrated in Chapter 7.) The former involves consideration of potential goals first by the client and next by others involved. The negotiation should consist of a discussion of the various goals and how their accomplishment might affect, for better or worse, each of the participants. This includes as many short- and long-term benefits and costs as can be anticipated. Benefits could include enhanced personal, social, academic or job skills, or diminished rates of responses that interfere with other desired outcomes. Costs could involve increased expenditures of resources (materials, time, effort); loss of control or power; loss of other social rewards; or increases in unpleasant events, such as delays until clients are dressed, increased noise levels, having to wait patiently, and so on.

When contracts are negotiated noncoercively, we can assume that the participants have entered into the agreement **voluntarily**, and have given **informed consent**. Voluntariness and consent are properties incorporated within a number of ethical and legal codes of conduct, such as the American Psychological Association's *Ethical Principles of Psychologists* (1981), its *Ethical Principles in the Conduct of Research with Human Participants* (1982), and the U.S. Department of Health, Education and Welfare's *Institutional Guide to DHEW Policy on Protection of Human Subjects* (1971). The problem of coercion has been the subject of many court cases ("Connecticut Civil Liberties Newsletter," 1974; Martin, 1974; Schwitzgebel, 1971; Wexler, 1973). Though it may not necessarily be legally binding, a behavioral contract freely negotiated by concerned parties provides evidence that care has been taken to incorporate voluntary informed consent into the program.

Another aspect of ethical goal selection is the client's or appropriate advocate's freedom to terminate the contract. Circumstances under which this is acceptable should be included in any contractual arrangement. For example,

Figure 3.1 Questions for Selecting Goals and Setting Priorities

1. Is the goal
   a. constructive and functional for the client in the short and long run?
   b. likely to be supported in various settings?
   c. likely to be maintained in the natural environment?
   d. mission oriented?
   e. achievable within a reasonable time period?
   f. amenable to direct measurement?
   g. acceptable to everyone involved?
   h. important for the development of other behaviors in a chain or hierarchy of development?
   i. age or developmentally appropriate?
   j. apt to receive a high consumer satisfaction rating?

2. Does the goal
   a. meet multiple needs?
   b. place increasing responsibility on the client?
   c. reduce the likelihood of harm to the client or others?
   d. promote greater flexibility or adaptation to the environment?
   e. require more resources than are apt to be made available?

3. Does the behavior analyst have sufficient
   a. knowledge of the procedure?
   b. skill in applying the procedure?
   c. commitment toward achieving the goal?

4. Can existing programs accomplish the goal more efficiently?

5. What are the benefits and costs for the client, significant others, similar populations, the behavior analyst, and society at large?

6. What resources are available to the behavior analyst?

7. Are goals acceptable to the behavior analyst and significant others in terms of professional and personal ethical values, law, and public policy?

8. What short- and long-term benefits and costs will accrue to the behavior analyst? to significant others?

Dexter and the counselor may specify that if he decides to change his vocational choice, the contract may be renegotiated. All parties to the contract have a right to be informed and consulted about one participant's wish to terminate. Terms, of course, depend on a number of factors, yet with everything spelled out in advance, misunderstandings should be minimized.

Lucretia has a tendency to fly off the handle at the slightest provocation. In a moment of fury, she might decide she wants out of the program immediately. For someone like Lucretia, stipulating a 48-hour cooling-off period prior to withdrawal would be reasonable. Other contracts might require a meeting with a human rights advocate prior to withdrawal.

Selecting High-Priority Goals

That the process of goal selection is developing into a scientific one should be apparent from the preceding discussions. Yet goal setting still remains subjective to a great extent. To assist you, this chapter offered some guidelines for selecting mutually acceptable goals that are meaningful, relevant to clients and others in their lives, and ethically responsible. Once the process has begun and behavioral contracts or other decision-making arrangements have been initiated, consider a variety of alternative goals. After you identify several goals, we suggest you initially give high priority to one that both meets the criteria for acceptability and is likely to be accomplished with relative ease. The rationale for this advice will become clearer in the chapters on reinforcement. For the moment, recognize that success in reaching a goal encourages participants to continue with other goals that may demand more of them.

Figure 3.1 poses a series of questions reflecting the perspectives of clients, the behavior analyst, significant others, and society. Answering these questions may provide you with a more informed and sounder basis from which to set your priorities.

Summary

This chapter emphasized the scientific, ethical, humanitarian, and practical aspects of goal selection. A key theme was the importance of focusing on constructive long-term as well as short-term goals and choosing outcomes likely to maximize reinforcement and minimize punishment for clients and others. We have offered guidelines designed to protect the rights of all involved and to avoid potential goal conflicts. Client, advocate, parent, staff, and community participation, contracting, and institutional review all help to provide such safeguards.

Scientifically sound, practical, and ethically responsible goal selection is not an either/or phenomenon. Rather, goal selection is the result of a skillful balancing act among a variety of considerations. This chapter attempted to guide you to select an optimal mixture.

Chapter 4

Assessing Behavior and Setting Objectives

Goals

After completing this chapter, you should be able to:

1. Define, recognize, and give original illustrations of each of the following terms:
   a. Behavioral assessment
   b. Treatment utility of assessment
   c. Ecobehavioral assessment
   d. Behavioral objective
   e. Criteria
   f. Behavioral dimensions, including:
      i. Frequency
      ii. Rate
      iii. Latency
      iv. Intensity
      v. Topography
      vi. Duration
      vii. Accuracy
   g. Task analysis

2. Discuss the conceptual underpinnings of behavioral assessment.

3. Discuss and illustrate the four basic functions of behavioral assessment.

4. Describe the purpose of ecobehavioral assessment.

5. Develop and specify a single behavioral objective for a client or yourself, following the format provided in this chapter.

6. Describe three methods of generating a task analysis.

7. List three major uses of task analyses.

Recall that Lucretia's mother felt her child was overly aggressive, but her grandmother did not agree. Preliminary analyses indicated that a behavior intervention was merited, and a goal was set. Lucretia was to learn to share more and hit and grab toys less while she played with other children.

Now additional information would be needed to specify the exact objectives of the program. Also, the behavior analyst would need to learn more about Lucretia in order to design an intervention strategy. After the behavior analyst talked further with the concerned parties, she prepared a preliminary case report, based on past and present episodes and conditions in Lucretia's life. Generally, assessments based on the recall of events by clients or people close to them are insufficient because they may be biased to some unknown degree (Kelley, 1950). Therefore, more objective evidence will need to be gathered. Narrative recordings and sequential analyses helped focus on which behaviors need to be addressed: in this case, Lucretia's social interactions at play. But narrations are just the beginning. More specificity is needed.

For this reason, once tentative goals are set, we get down to the business of using the tools of behavioral technology. We begin by ensuring that goals lend themselves eventually to valid measurement, and we consider them from an ecological perspective. (The reasons valid measurement is necessary should become clearer as you read about behavioral assessment. The importance of ecological considerations in setting a course of behavior change also should become more evident.) One way to assure yourself that your goals are measurable is to state them as operationally as possible, preferably in the form of precise behavioral objectives. Valid measurement will enable all involved to be informed about where you are headed and how well you are progressing. The **behavioral assessment** approach is the one we take to valid measurement.

Behavioral Assessment
What Is Behavioral Assessment?
Behavioral assessment is an approach used to depict—as validly, clearly, and objectively as possible—an individual's patterns of behavior, stressing the importance of measuring behaviors "... in and of themselves. Responses are seen as samples of what a person does in a particular interaction, rather than what a person has" (Nelson, 1983, p. 200). Behavioral assessment measures *acts*, like the number or percentage of problems the individual answers correctly within a period of time. This approach does not measure ambiguous terms or labels that are open to a variety of interpretations, such as "IQ": How often Lucretia gets out of her seat and moves around during a series of class sessions would be measured; not her "attention deficit" or "hyperactivity." The type or number of negative statements Henrietta makes about herself or her boss would be quantified rather than classifying her personality type; and a man's **rate** of crying and slowness to respond would be counted instead of measuring his "depression."

Although groups of individuals may be involved, behavioral assessment focuses primarily on the individual level (Nelson, 1983) in that it takes into account the unique context and the clients' repertoires of responses. First, target behaviors are identified and fashioned into objectives. Then, specific measures are selected, based on the behavior and its context, in order to depict clearly the target behavior prior to, during, and after any systematic intervention or treatment. (Methods of evaluating outcomes are described in Chapters 14 and 22.)

Behavioral assessment also recognizes the value of a *multidimensional* approach—"multimethod, multi-informant, and multisetting assessment" (McMahon, 1987, p. 248). Though direct observation is the core of behavioral assessment, additional methods such as interviews, inventories, and checklists also can guide our selection of the most appropriate treatment strategy (Mash, 1987; McMahon, 1987), so gather as much information as you can ethically, by reviewing records, talking to many people, and observing in various settings.

Behavioral Assessment Justified

The "basic justification for assessment is that it provides information of value to the planning, execution and evaluation of treatment" (Korchin & Schuldberg, 1981, p. 1154). Traditional (i.e., nonbehavioral) assessments have seldom altered the diagnostic judgments of clinicians or their treatment plans (Adams, 1972; Hayes, Nelson, & Jarret, 1987). Because psychotherapists have frequently tended to practice according to general schools of psychotherapy, they also have tended to standardize their approaches to assessment. As pointed out by Hayes et al. (1987), "When clinicians apply the same general approach to most clients, assessment data can have few treatment implications" (p. 964). When assessment and treatment are disconnected, ". . . the value of assessment seemingly turns on the question, Is this diagnosis correct? not Is this assessment useful for treatment?" (Hayes et al., 1987, p. 964). Today, however, a large number of specific intervention strategies are available to us, and the need " . . . to identify which treatment works best for whom now carries a sense of contemporary urgency" (Hayes et al., 1987, p. 964).

We have learned that behavioral assessment

- measures behaviors in and of themselves.
- is tailored to individuals (or sometimes groups of individuals) and the context in which their behavior takes place.
- makes use of a multidimensional approach.
- provides information that enables us to better plan, execute, and evaluate treatment.

This last characteristic of behavioral assessment is the component that stresses functionality or treatment utility—"Did the treatment accomplish what it was designed to do?" Hayes et al. (1987) defined the **treatment utility of assessment** as the "degree to which assessment is shown to contribute to beneficial treatment outcomes" (p. 963). Behavioral assessment helps the behavior analyst to select, improve, and evaluate the treatment prescribed for a given client (Nelson, 1983). Such assessment also can inform us about the cost-effectiveness of a program (Yates, 1985), as elaborated in Chapter 22. Further, the data generated by observing the behavior of the client (and later of other clients) under first similar and then experimentally varied conditions often sharpen our ability to predict how these individuals and others will behave in the future. To reiterate this crucial point, *the appropriateness of a selected behavioral assessment strategy should be evaluated functionally* by answering the question "To what degree does it contribute to treatment?" (Nelson, 1983). (Chapters 14 and 22 elaborate on functional analyses.)

Ecobehavioral Assessment

Only in modern times have societies begun to recognize that using resources is not a unidirectional process, but the way they are used impacts the environment. The mine owner no longer just decides to remove minerals from the ground without considering the impact on wildlife, water resources, air quality, and so on. In designing policy, the public, in turn, must consider its mineral needs. Similarly, applied behavior analysts also need to view behavior in terms of its broader context, because as people change their behavior, their social and physical contexts are affected. As behavior analysts, we are also part of the interactive system. "A proper appreciation of context always means we are not merely studying or managing it, but also are part of it and therefore are being managed by it, even down to our studying and managing of it" (Baer et al., 1987, p. 318).

In taking this broader perspective, behavior analysts further recognize that circumstances beyond those directly contiguous with behavior may influence the direction and course of behavior change: our histories of reinforcement for a particular behavior and events like the last time we ate a meal, weather conditions, how much we slept, or an earlier argument with a parent or spouse. In the animal laboratory, circumstances and contiguous events can be known and often may be controlled. In open societies, though, humans have much more complicated histories and live under far more complex networks of contingencies. Ecological factors must be considered during the process of setting objectives and selecting treatments, because they may impede or promote accomplishment of those aims.

Consequently, in fashioning objectives, applied behavior analysts need to deliberate not only about improving a behavior but how it was shaped and is currently being supported. They must try to anticipate how the contemplated change may affect and be affected by current conditions and by any other proposed alterations of the social and physical environment.

Much effort has been invested recently in assessing behavior in relation to its environmental context, to enable beneficial planning, intervening, and support over the long range (e.g., Patterson, 1982; Wahler, 1980). Once achieved, ecologically sound goals and objectives have long-term survival value (a point that will be amplified in the section on maintenance). Those that run counter to natural support systems are less likely to prevail for very long.

Ecobehavioral assessment ". . . incorporates an ecological perspective into the behavior analysis of environment-behavior relationships" (Rogers-Warren, 1984, p. 283). Within ecobehavioral assessment, behavior is examined not only in relation to the social events that immediately precede and follow it but also in terms of its general context of ongoing and prior events and elements of the physical environment.

So, when assessing Lucretia's difficulties, we might consider not only what her playmates, parents, and other adults said and did prior to and following her wanted and unwanted behavior but also other factors like how Lucretia was introduced to the play session; whether she was rested and well fed in advance; what toys, play equipment, and space was available; and so on. We also would examine Lucretia's behavior to see whether the first hit tended to set the stage for her delivering a sequence of blows or kicks or screams. We would study the effect on the other children, the teachers, or her parents, as in the case of their hitting or screaming back.

An example of an ecobehavioral assessment device is a scatter plot that consists of a matrix measuring time of day along the vertical and days across the horizontal, of the type described by Touchette, MacDonald, and Langer (1985).[1] The scatter plot may reveal temporal patterns in Lucretia's outbursts of aggression. By analyzing the results, problematic and nonproblematic times and situations would surface, suggesting strategies to pursue. That is just the way that Touchette and his colleagues used the matrix. They found that one of the clients was particularly disruptive in the afternoon workshop but not in the mornings or on weekends. This information enabled the researchers to plan an alternative schedule of activities, which virtually eliminated the client's troublesome behavior.

A more formal ecobehavioral assessment instrument is one suggested by Rogers-Warren (1984). Included in the matrix she presents are

1. individual initiations and responses ("discrete level").

---

[1] The scatter plot is illustrated in Figures 16.4 and 16.5.

2. initiation-response-reciprocation between two people ("exchange level").

3. events immediately preceding and following the target behavior(s) ("episodes").

4. similar series of events or episodes
("standing patterns").

These four levels of behavior are then analyzed in terms of relations between the behavior
and the environment—whether environmental
events occur along with the behavior and
whether the events facilitate or inhibit it. Next,
relationships are examined to see whether they
might be useful in planning and evaluating the
intervention. At this point, we can recognize
that ecobehavioral assessments can help us to
scrutinize our goals more closely to determine
whether they are valid and ecologically sound.
If so, we are ready to rephrase the goal more
precisely, as a formal behavioral objective.

Specifying the Behavioral Objective

A **behavioral objective** is a *goal* with clear specifications of the *context* within which the behavior is to occur, including the setting, materials, personnel, and so on; and the **criteria**,
or standards for determining when the objective has been accomplished (based on Mager,
1962). These criteria are expressed as **behavioral dimensions** (parameters) that qualify particular aspects of the performance.

Years ago, one of the authors was treating a
child who had essentially no functional speech.
Almost all her spoken language consisted of
"echolalic" repetitions of words or sounds she
had just heard. For example, one parent would
say, "Come here," and, rather than complying,
the child would say, "Come here." Her instructor would ask, "What's your name?" and she
would respond, "What's your name?" The task
was to teach the child to use language functionally, in ways appropriate to her circumstances. Functional language would permit her

to obtain what she needed, accurately describe
and label items and events, supply information
to others, and so forth. As an intervention,
echolalic responses would not be *reinforced*. Instead, such reinforcers as food, attention, and
praise would be withheld following nonfunctional word repetitions. Conversely, any verbal
response that was *not* echolalic would be reinforced immediately every time it occurred.

When, within a few sessions the child had
begun to use many new words and phrases, the
consequences of a crucial tactical error became
apparent. The child began to talk strangely,
often rather bizarrely—repeating portions of
television commercials or discussing plumbing
problems—"Fix the faucet" (although no sink
was located in the room). In effect, she was
being taught to use inappropriate language. After reanalysis, the essential properties of the
desired goal and its context were refined. She
was to acquire noncholalic language that was
relevant to the world about her. What she said
needed to relate to objects, events, or topics
tied to her current, future, or past experiences.
Following this elaboration of the objective, only
those pertinent classes of responses were reinforced. As a result, the child began to approximate using "normal" language.

Behavioral Dimensions

The point of relating this client's experience is
to illustrate why precisely stating the features
of the desired response and the contexts in
which it is and is not to occur is so important.
To accomplish this, we consider the number
and type of features we want the behavior to
possess; that is, its critical behavioral dimensions.

A given performance may vary across a
number of dimensions (or parameters). Table
4.1 lists and illustrates some dimensions frequently represented in behavior analytic work.
Others might include more complex characteristics, such as the consistency with which a

Table 4.1 Behavioral Dimensions Defined

Dimension	Definition	Example
Frequency	The number of times a response occurs	Paula will complete 4 reports thruout Lucretia will ask for toys politely at least 4 times
Rate	The number of times a response occurs within a given period of time or per opportunity	Paula will complete 4 reports per month Lucretia will obtain toys by asking politely at least 4 out of 5 times over 3 play sessions
Latency	The time that elapses between an antecedent (cue, prompt, signal) and a response	Paula will complete her reports within 3 days of gathering all relevant information Lucretia will begin to pick up her toys within 2 minutes of her mother saying "Time to clean up"
Intensity	The force with which a behavior is expressed	Violet will speak loudly enough for all her friends to hear Joe Duffer will hit the golf ball hard enough for it to reach the 100-yard mark
Topography	The form or shape of the response	Sonia's leg will extend straight out at a 45-degree angle Joe will stand with his legs 10 inches apart
Duration	The length of time that passes from onset to offset of a response	Violet will converse audibly for at least 30 seconds at a time Lucretia will play for 30 minutes without grabbing a toy Bruno will practice an hour a day
Accuracy	The extent to which the response meets standards	Dexter will score above 90% on his math quizzes Bruno will play 99 out of 100 notes correctly

behavior is repeated. (Violet's volume is regularly audible; not loud sometimes but soft other times.) Tempo is another: Bruno plays the scherzo movement rapidly, the andante more slowly.

Often measures of these dimensions are indicated on the vertical scale of a graph, and usually they are included within behavioral objectives singly or in combination. For instance, rate and **duration** could be combined into an objective for Lucretia: Lucretia will ask for toys politely at least 4 out of 5 opportunities over five 30-minute play sessions. Criteria like these prevent the intervention from terminating too soon, say after she simply made 4 polite requests. (As we will stress later, occurrence of high and steady rates of the desired behavior is important to achieve sustained change.)

Accuracy, or conforming to a standard, sometimes poses a special problem, because we are uncertain about what specific criteria to apply. Exactly what constitutes a correct response? A full sentence? Phrases identical to those in the book or phrases that incorporate key words? Is an abbreviation acceptable? Are responses considered correct or acceptable if they meet a set of prespecified criteria?

In writing a theme, your students might be expected to include a minimum of five paragraphs, containing a thesis sentence and several examples or other related material; each paragraph following the previous one in a logical sequence; and all sentences complete. For a musical composition, so many bars and harmony conforming to rules indicated in the textbook might be stipulated. For making a telephone call, correct dialing and perhaps an even distribution of talking and listening may be specified.

Note that the examples just given progress from more to less objective criteria. Additional subjectivity intrudes when we try to pinpoint how closely works of art and social behaviors conform to standards of acceptability. This fact makes specification of response properties especially difficult.

In his clever book *Goal Analysis*, Mager (1972) suggests one approach to identifying crucial features on which to base our assessments of the acceptability of a response. Knowledgeable judges are asked to sort a great many response samples into two piles—acceptable and not acceptable—along one dimension related to goals. The dimension may be organization, craftsmanship, politeness, cooperative-

ness, and so on. Then the sorter looks at the two piles and describes how they differ. Well-organized themes may have included clearly specified central topics mentioned in the opening sentences. A well-crafted object may have smooth surfaces and symmetrical components. Once a series of such sorting processes has taken place, the dimensions agreed on by the judges can be listed as the standards of acceptability.

Context

The next essential in selecting the behavioral objective is to specify the context—the conditions and limitations under which the desired response is to occur. If Dexter is to write more reports, is he to do all his preparation during social studies class, other periods, or whenever he wants? To what materials can he have access? If Lucretia is to play cooperatively with other children, sharing materials and not hitting, pushing, or grabbing, how many children is she to play with, where, and with what toys? Obviously, it would not be appropriate for her to share toys during her nap or at mealtimes. What days and times of day will Paula schedule for report writing?

The context delineates any givens or restrictions to be placed on where, with what, when, or how the response is to occur. Referring to Drabman, Hammer, and Rosenbaum's (1979) *generalization map* may remind you to consider categories such as time, settings, behaviors, and subjects. (See our Chapter 29 on generalization for more details.)

Specifying Criteria

The **criterion** is the standard used to determine whether or not the behavioral goal has been reached. We have already seen an example of criteria for Lucretia. Here is another: Preliminary data show that a patient who is seriously asthmatic consistently fails to follow his physician's instructions. The doctor knows that her patient is capable of complying, because he has occasionally done so in the past. The goal for the patient is to comply with instructions for using his inhalation equipment. Must he always use the equipment? If the physician considers that 90 percent compliance would demonstrate success, the criterion is stated as 90 percent of the prescribed number of uses each day. However, is achieving 90 percent usage for one day satisfactory? Of course not. Rate and duration need to be added to indicate over what period of time the behavior should persist before the physician concludes that her patient is complying. The doctor decides that 3 consecutive weeks of compliance would be satisfactory. Also, because correct use of equipment is essential, the doctor might add an accuracy dimension to the criterion.

Above all, the essential standard for determining whether a significant behavioral change has occurred is, according to Baer et al. (1968), its practical importance. If behavior has been altered enough to satisfy significant others like teachers, parents, students, clients, patients, and staff, the criterion can be said to have been achieved. Such a criterion, *which is mutually agreeable to all*, should be established *before* administration of the behavior change program in order to avoid subsequent indecision, disagreement, or bias in determining when the goal has been reached. The criterion level selected should not be the *ideal* level but the minimum that is acceptable to all program participants. Naturally, this choice does not prevent higher levels of performance; it simply serves as a guide to evaluating the effectiveness of the behavior change program.

Sample Objectives

The following illustrations are presented in a format that we have found useful in teaching how to write objectives.[2]

---

[2] Many resources are available to assist designers of behavioral programs to achieve meaningful personal, social, academic, and vocational objectives (e.g., Mager, 1962; Ordione, 1965; Vargas, 1972; and Wheeler & Fox, 1972).

First Illustration:
Problem Behavior: Lucretia does not play cooperatively with other children.
Goal: Lucretia will hand toys to another child on request.
Context/Conditions: Two other children, array of toys.
Criterion Level: At least once in each of 3 out of 4 half-hour blocks of time.
Behavioral Dimensions
    Rate: Every day for 2 weeks.
    Topography: Toy handed (not thrown) to playmate.
Behavioral Objective: Playing with two other children and an array of toys, Lucretia will hand a toy to a playmate on request at least once in each of 3 out of 4 half-hour blocks, each day for 2 weeks.

Many different objectives could have been developed in connection with the problem of uncooperative play. For example, topography could have consisted of Lucretia giving permission for another child to use her toys. But the concerned parties agreed that the dimensions and criterion level chosen were satisfactory.

Second Illustration:
Problem Behavior: Violet does not engage in conversation with her peers.
Goal: Violet will ask her peers questions and respond to theirs.
Context/Conditions: Recreation room, break time.
Criterion Level: At least 1 answer and 1 question.
Behavioral Dimensions
    Rate: At least once a day for 5 consecutive days.
    Intensity: Loudly enough to be clearly heard by the listener.
    Topography: In complete sentences.
Behavioral Objective: Violet will ask and answer questions in complete sentences loudly enough to be heard by the listener at least once daily for 5 consecutive days during break.

Task Analysis

Behavioral objectives may be simple or complex, depending on their components and the repertoires and capabilities of those who are to achieve them. For Aunt Minerva, "Returning to her station each day by 1:10 P.M. for 2 weeks in a row" is a fairly simple behavior. The behavioral requirement probably does not have to be broken down into component tasks. If the objective for Paula, completing reports on time, is too complicated, it should be dissected further, or task analyzed, so each subcomponent is achievable.

A **task analysis** sometimes is referred to synonymously as a **job, conceptual, component, criterion**, or **skills analysis**. The task analysis breaks a complex skill or concept down into smaller, teachable steps or actions. As Axelrod (1983) points out, the task analysis assists the instructor in determining the content, sequence, and starting point of the instruction. Anderson and Faust (1973) describe a task analysis this way:

> A task analysis describes the subskills and subconcepts a student must acquire in order to master a complex skill or an interrelated set of concepts and principles. Such an analysis should be complete, presented in the proper amount of detail, with relationships among component skills and concepts clearly specified. It should identify when and under what circumstances each component skill is to be performed. In short, the task analysis provides a blueprint of the things a student must master if he is to reach the objectives that have been set (p. 82).

Most complex behaviors (e.g., operating a drill press, tying a shoe, solving math problems, washing your hair, using community resources, effectively communicating in marriage, and sharing) are composed of a "chain" of sequentially arranged tasks or response elements. For Paula, the complex behavior of writing a report could be broken down into the following tasks:

1. Gathers information.
2. Places data on file cards.
3. Organizes cards.
4. Obtains writing supplies.
5. Places materials and supplies on desk.
6. Prepares outline.
7. Types draft report, expanding each section contained in outline.
8. Reads and corrects draft report.
9. Submits final report.

Sometimes such behaviors need to be broken down into even finer components. Paula might need to do that with typing or expanding a section of the outline, or even writing the outline itself—depending on her current repertoire. Cutting a piece of cake with a fork would seem to be a very simple behavior, but not for Fern. For her the task must be further analyzed into very tiny components: the position of the cake plate before her, the correct grasp, the proper motion, and so on. You can see that task analyses, then, need to be individualized. Some individuals need smaller steps than others (Tucker & Berry, 1980).

To adjust for individual differences, task analyses frequently are generated and then later revised as they are tested. For example, Foster, Billionis, and Lent (1976) developed a task analysis to teach women with developmental disabilities the appropriate use of sanitary napkins. Their task analysis originally contained 20 steps but was later revised by Foster and Keilitz (1983) to include 35 steps to make it more specific and usable.

Figure 4.1 displays a task analysis developed by Alavosius and Sulzer-Azaroff (1985) for safely transferring patients from bed to wheelchair by health care workers.[3] Notice that the figure includes not only the task analysis, but also columns for checking performance and re-

---

[3] Examples of task analyses for various academic and athletic skills can be found in Sulzer-Azaroff and Mayer (1986). Also, Chapter 20 of this book, which describes chaining, contains several additional illustrations.

Figure 4.1 Positioning a Patient in a Wheelchair

Employee _____   Unit/Ward _____
Date/Time _____   Location _____
Observer _____   Purpose of Lift _____

CHECK			Task Component: One Person Transfer (Total Lift)	Sketch Position:
YES	NO	NA		

YES	NO	NA		
___	___	___	1.	Positions wheelchair near goal (transfer across shortest distance). A 90-degree angle is best.
___	___	___	2.	Explains to client what they are to do (words or gestures).
___	___	___	3.	Locks wheel chair brakes.
___	___	___	4.	Removes adaptive devices:
___	___	___		a. tray.
___	___	___		b. arm rests (if possible).
___	___	___		c. seatbelt(s), other adaptive equipment.
___	___	___	5.	Positions for lift by:
___	___	___		a. Standing at side of chair, at client's hip angle,
___	___	___		b. with feet apart (width of hips, at least).
___	___	___		c. Bending posture, *knees bent, and* spine straight, may be slight bend forward at waist.
___	___	___	6.	Slides client forward on seat, to permit adequate room for step 7.
___	___	___	7.	Supports client for lift:
___	___	___		a. One arm beneath client's arms and shoulders to support head, neck, and upper torso.
___	___	___		b. Other arm beneath client's thighs to support pelvis.
___	___	___	8.	Hugs client (reduces distance between client and staff).
___	___	___	9.	Lifts straight up *by unbending knees* (back remains straight and erect). *Smooth movement.*
___	___	___	10.	Pivots (turns on balls of feet, or short steps, without twisting torso) and aligns client with new surface.
___	___	___	11.	*Bends knees*, lowers client to new surface. Back straight.
___	___	___	12.	Securely positions client on new surface, then releases.
___	___	___	13.	Fastens seatbelts, where appropriate.
___	___	___	TOTAL	

Describe unsafe components, if any: _____

_____

_____

How long did it take to complete this observation? _____

cording other events. As you will learn in Chapter 5, task analyses like these lend themselves readily to measurement functions.

Before you develop your own task analysis for a particular performance, check the literature. Many have been constructed for job (e.g., Bellamy, Horner, & Inman, 1979) and daily living skills (e.g., Wheeler et al., 1987) in sufficient detail to be used with the developmentally disabled. Task analyses continue to be developed for various skills by behavioral programmers for all sorts of client populations: severely and profoundly retarded people, college students, guidance counselors, and even applied behavior analysts (Bernal et al., 1976). Nevertheless, you may find yourself faced with the challenge of needing to construct an original task analysis. How do you proceed?

Original task analyses can be generated in several different ways. Three of the more common methods include

- Performing the behavior yourself and writing down the discrete, observable steps necessary to perform the task. This method has the advantage of acquainting you with the task demands of the sequence (Bellamy et al., 1979).
- Recording the sequence of responses by several individuals who are competent in the skill, as they perform it (Foster & Keilitz, 1983; Horner & Keilitz, 1975; Thompson, Braam, & Fuqua, 1982).
- Consulting with experts on the skill to be taught (e.g., safe job performance, sewing, cooking, leisure skills, eating) in order to identify the steps in the task analysis (Alavosius & Sulzer-Azaroff, 1985; Cronin & Cuvo, 1979; Schleien, Wehman, & Kiernan, 1981; Wilson, Reid, Phillips, & Burgio, 1984).

Regardless of which method or combination of methods you use, the number and order of steps are likely to change depending on the learners' repertoire of skills and/or deficiencies.

One issue is the size of a subcomponent, the component that combines with others to form the more complex task. We know that subcomponents can be further task analyzed, depending on individual learner requirements.

The *completeness* of the task analysis is another issue. An elementary school reading program coordintor used his many talents and skills to design a powerful instructional sequence. His students learned to read many lists of words and stories fluently and errorlessly. But did those students apply their new reading skills elsewhere, such as to read other text books and periodicals? Did they use reading as a medium for interacting more safely and effectively in their environment, by reading signs, instructions, informational items? Did reading serve as an instrument of delight, with students reading for pleasure? The reading coordinator revised his task analysis to include components such as reading more varied materials in an enlarged number of settings, and he added affective targets, such as enjoying the process.

Before finalizing your own task analysis, you too should search for missing elements. Look closely to see whether, among others, you have included

- all necessary skills and concepts.
- any desired extensions or variations in those responses or the circumstances in which they should be emitted.
- easily overlooked features, such as enjoyment.

Once you are satisfied with the task analysis, examine to see if each subcomponent task is adequately worded to meet the requirements for an acceptable objective.

Summary

This chapter described the value, properties, and functions of behavioral assessment, as well as how it is used as a method for designing, applying, and evaluating effective treatment

Figure 4.2 Goals to Objectives

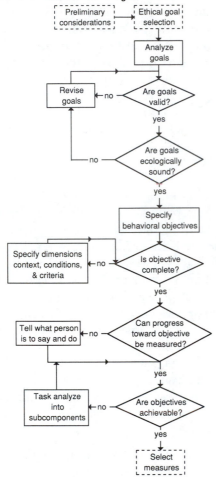

strategies. The ecological validity of selected goals and procedures is ensured when behavior is viewed within its context, according to the ecobehavioral approach. For optimal utility, vague goals need to be respecified precisely as behavioral objectives. Complex, higher-level objectives must be converted into sets of challenging yet readily achievable subobjectives.

Everything the learner needs to know before continuing should be contained in a well-formulated objective: what act is to be changed; within what setting; given what resources and preparation; according to what rate; the duration; and if relevant, topography, **intensity**, and so on. Such precision communicates clear directions to everyone involved and should serve as a basis for valid measurement and effective, efficient instruction.

The utility of task analyses is obvious. They can be used (1) to refine objectives by slicing them into smaller segments that are then converted into behavioral objectives in their own right; (2) to serve as a basis for constructing measurement devices; and (3) as curriculum guidelines. Later, in Chapter 20 on chaining, we return to this topic, discussing tactics for using task analyses as an instructional or training tool.

Figure 4.2 specifies the tasks in the form of a flow chart that you might follow in goal selection as well as some questions to ask yourself as you construct your behavioral objectives. Now you are ready to begin measuring the target behavior, to assess its pattern of occurrence, and then—if supported by the data—to finalize your objective. Turn now to Chapters 5 and 6 and discover the technology for selecting and using behavioral measures.

Chapter 5

Behavioral Assessment: Selecting Measurement Systems

GOALS

After completing this chapter, you should be able to:

1. Define, recognize, and give original illustrations of each of the following terms:
   a. Dependent variable
   b. Independent variable
   c. Collateral measures
   d. Objective measure
   e. Valid measurement
   f. Reliable measurement
   g. Reactivity
   h. Instructional demand
   i. Transitory behaviors
   j. Permanent product recording
   k. Interobserver agreement assessment (IOA)
   l. Event or frequency recording
   m. Discrete behaviors
   n. Behaviorally anchored rating scale (BARS)
   o. Latency recording
   p. Duration recording
   q. Time-sampling: whole-interval; partial-interval; momentary
   r. Coded interval-recording sheet

2. Discuss two key factors the behavior analyst needs to consider when selecting dependent variables.

3. List and define the three features of an acceptable behavioral measure.

4. Identify the factors that can influence the validity of observations and discuss what can be done to minimize their effects.

5. Briefly describe procedures for promoting reliable observational recording and estimating the index of agreement between two or more sets of measures of identical behaviors.

6. List the advantages of being able to measure results or permanent products.

7. Justify why and when each of the following methods is the most appropriate to use:
   a. Event recording
   b. Duration recording

8. Give the formula for calculating an interobserver agreement index for products of behavior.

9. Describe two methods for calculating an interobserver agreement index during event recording. Discuss the pros and cons of each. Present a hypothetical pair of simultaneous recordings and calculate their interobserver agreement index.

10. Give the formula for calculating interobserver agreement for duration recording systems. Offer an illustrative example by providing two sets of scores and calculate the interobserver agreement coefficient.

11. Define interval time-sampling recording and describe an illustrative situation in which it would be the most appropriate observational method. Justify your answer.

12. Describe and justify a situation in which each of the following would be the most appropriate interval time-sampling observational system:
   a. Whole-interval time-sampling
   b. Partial-interval time-sampling
   c. Momentary time-sampling

13. Outline a set of procedures for selecting and obtaining valid and reliable interval-recording data. Construct a pair of illustrative data sets and calculate the interobserver agreement score between the two.

14. Select an observational system for your own or your client's behavior.

15. Explain the circumstances under which only scored intervals should be used in calculating interobserver agreement coefficients.

16. Describe briefly how to report reliability data.

Previous chapters focused on behavioral goals and objectives. Because behavioral objectives include the target performances (the behavior to be altered), the context, and other conditions under which change is to occur as well as the standards by which to assess accomplishment of the objectives, you are already well on your way to developing an effective measurement system. By carefully designating the response properties that constitute the target behavior, you maximize objectivity: "For a period of 10 days in a row Lucretia is not to hit or kick other children," rather than "Lucretia is not to be aggressive or hostile." Lucretia is to share (hand her toy to playmates) at least once each half-hour during free play session for 10 days in a row," rather than "Lucretia will play nicely with her classmates." Directly observable descriptions of acts like hitting, kicking, or sharing are much more objectively stated than terms like *hostile* or *plays nicely*, because the latter are subjective—one observer's impressions may be different from another's. The criteria chosen to judge attainment of the objectives indicates the appropriate measure. "Lucretia is to share her toys at least once each half-hour during free play session. . . ." indicates that "sharing toys" is what must be measured.

When a target behavior like *sharing* is translated into quantifiable terms—"hands toys to others on request within 10 seconds" or "offers a toy to another child even when not asked"—the measure of the event, sharing, (here the frequency) is called the **dependent variable** (i.e., a change in that variable *depends* on a systematic change in another variable—the **independent variable**—the intervention or treatment used). Naturally, the measures of the target behaviors are the key dependent variables.

But measuring other variables (or parameters), whose values may also be altered as a function of the program, can also be important. For instance, suppose you decide to select "increased sharing" as Lucretia's only objective. You may also wish to determine whether any increase in sharing is accompanied by a change in how often she hits or kicks. You would then measure hitting and kicking too. Or the counselor interested in seeing how many tasks Dexter completes may also wish to examine how the teacher interacts with Dexter as his behavior changes. Dexter's completion of tasks and the teacher's attention might be the two dependent variables selected for measurement.

As you decide which variables to measure, start by checking the sequence analysis and identify the target behaviors and the contingencies that appear to suppress, interfere with, or facilitate attaining the objectives. To these, secondarily, add measures of related variables, such as the indirect influence of the anticipated changes on other behaviors, people, outcomes, or in other places. Such **collateral measures** may provide valuable information when you evaluate the effectiveness of your intervention.

Once the dependent variables have been selected, you must choose an appropriate measurement system. This chapter focuses on *selecting* valid measures and methods for constructing measurement systems. Chapter 6 emphasizes how to *implement* those systems. These two chapters will familiarize you with the next several steps in the behavior analysis model: from selecting a valid and reliable recording system to assessing baseline performance.

Observation and Measurement

. . . underlying every science is observation and measurement, providing a description of events and a way of quantifying them so that experimental manipulation may be ordered. The ultimate goal in science is, of course, an ordering of facts into general, consistent laws from which predictions may be made, but it inevitably starts with observation (Bachrach, 1962, pp. 30–31).

Behavioral assessment involves choosing

and using **objective**, **valid**, and **reliable** measures. *Objective* means that the observers who record behavioral data do not allow their own feelings or interpretations to affect their recordings. Consequently, the components of the behaviors targeted for measurement must be specifically defined. *Valid* measures are those that actually *do* directly measure the behavior that they are supposed to be measuring, rather than something else. Counting how long or how often Lucretia hits, teases, or plays cooperatively with her classmates is a more valid measure than the recollections of her parents, grandparents, teacher, or even of Lucretia.

To be valid, measures must be objective, though objective measures are not necessarily valid. For example, suppose you are curious about how parental attention may be influencing Lucretia's aggressiveness. If the observer were objectively to count only the number of words her parents uttered but not the content or other forms of attention such as touching, looking, and so on, the recording could be objective but not valid. Valid measures, however, must objectively measure what they purport to measure.

A *reliable* measure is one that remains standard, or consistent, regardless of who is doing the measuring and on what occasions. Again, measures may be reliable but not necessarily valid. Measures cannot be valid, however, if they are not reliable. You could use a highly reliable method like counting the number of words a person has written (repeated counts by the same or different observers should agree quite closely), but counting reveals little about the quality of the prose. For that assessment you would need to develop sets of criteria that experts agree describe good quality (i.e., valid criteria) as well as determining that all raters use the same criteria in a uniform way (i.e., reliably).[1]

Using objective, valid, and reliable measures provides clear evidence of patterns of performance prior to, during, and following a behavioral intervention. Study of the data gathered permits you to evaluate the effectiveness of a particular program. Because accountability requires valid assessment, applied behavior analytic methods ideally suit the current demands for accountability in management, education, and human services.

Selecting Valid Measures

You would not use a bathroom scale to measure shoe size or a ruler to determine the weight of a barbell. A valid measurement system must be appropriate to the variable it measures. Often people will agree that a particular measure is valid. Tests or interviews are vehicles for assessing a clearly stated memorization objective (e.g., "List three features of an acceptable behavioral measure."). Productivity is determined by counting products that meet given standards of quality. But sometimes discovering valid measures for particular behaviors can be difficult. How do you measure responses characterizing a "patient child," "talented artist," or a "socially effective youth"? If you were to stand on a street corner and ask fifty people at random, you would hear many different answers.

Let us consider "social effectiveness." For one person a valid measure may be the type of clothing the person wears. For another it may be the rate of the person's use of certain language categories. Another observer may emphasize posture or nonverbal communication. Still others may mention the occupations, hobbies, or habits of their friends. Rates of attend-

---

[1] We have been struggling to develop such sets of criteria for students enrolled in a writing course at the university level. The students appear to have improved their use of particular sets of skills, such as organization, sentence structure, phrasing, various stylistic forms, and so on. Now we need to determine whether individual raters will agree in their independent assessments of the same prose passages (reliability) and whether experts of prose writing judge that students have become better writers (validity).

ance, punctuality, or overt or subtle aggression might be valid measures.

In applied behavior analysis, everyone involved must agree that the selected measures are appropriate. Parents may concur that a valid measure of their child's patience is her rate of compliance with their instructions; the group leader, how long she waits quietly for her turn; a behavior analyst, the time interval the child elects to choose between small, immediate and large, delayed reinforcers. Clearly, without prior agreement all these people would be working toward different goals, and very likely not judge the success of the program similarly. Fortunately, when participants share in identifying the problem and selecting the goal, obtaining agreement about the appropriateness of measures is easier.

Wallander, Conger, and Conger (1985) developed an objective standard for measuring components of skills important in male-female social interactions. The measurement system undoubtedly helped to set treatment targets and develop measures for assessing changes in specific heterosocial skills. The social skills the researchers focused on with their abbreviated definitions are included in Table 5.1.

If your program is designed to discover general principles governing the behavior of others who exhibit similar characteristics, you will want to assure yourself that your definitions are valid not only in your setting but elsewhere also. Representative judges may be requested to indicate the extent to which they agree that a given measure is valid. For example, if the goal is to increase creativity in writing style, several possible measures may be listed: use of varied metaphors, descriptive adjectives, verbs depicting sensory impressions, and so on. A number of acknowledged experts may then be asked to select those measures that they believe to be most valid in assessing creativity in writing.

Writing samples from before, during, and after a behavioral intervention can be gathered to demonstrate effectiveness. Presented with these samples in random order, the panel of judges could be asked to sort the samples along the dimension that was to have been measured—in this instance, creativity. If the writing samples judged most creative are the same as those that scored high on the behavioral measures and if those rated least creative by the judges are the same as those that scored low, the **validity** of the measures is supported. (Maloney & Hopkins, 1973, used this kind of method in a program designed to increase creativity in writing.) Furthermore, *consumer satisfaction* data for a particular program (Braukmann et al., 1975), which are based on ratings from the public affected and that match demonstrated changes in observed responses, lend further credence to the validity of the measure.

Factors That Can Influence the Validity of Observations

We mentioned earlier that the purpose of behavioral assessment is to depict, as clearly and objectively as possible, ongoing patterns of behavior as they truly exist. Several factors that can distort the accurate depiction of the behavior therefore need to be carefully avoided.

Reactivity. Reactivity, which describes the effects on the client's behavior produced by assessment procedures themselves (not the treatment), may compromise the validity of the data. For example, when the environment is altered by the presence of live observers or elaborate recording equipment, separating the effects of these changes on the client's behavior from those produced by the behavior change program itself may be difficult. Professor Fogg has presented his multimedia training workshop to impress institutional personnel with the importance of making frequent contacts with clients. The next day the professor visits his trainees' work sites, takes video records of interactions between supervisors and clients, and later counts the number of times the staff has made contact with the clients. He returns on

Table 5.1 BRISS Component Behaviors with Abbreviated Definitions

Category	Definition
Head	The involvement of the head, as a body part, in the interaction, such as its movement and position.
Facial Expression	Involvement of facial expressions in the interaction, such as smiles, animation, and tension.
Eyes	Involvement of the eyes in the interaction, such as eye contact, movement, and characteristics.
Arms and Hands	Involvement of the arms and hands in the interaction, such as their movement and position.
Overall Body and Legs	Involvement of the body trunk and legs in the interaction, such as their movement and position.
Language	Technical quality of the subject's expressions, independent of content, such as vocabulary, grammar, and syntax.
Speech Delivery	Sound of the subject's speech or utterances, independent of content, such as fluency, rate, voice quality, and speech mannerism.
Conversation Structure	Progression of the conversation at a general level, such as its fluency and change between topics.
Conversation Content	Subject matter talked about in the conversation, such as topic interest and substance.
Personal Conversational Style	General communication style of the subject, such as use of humor, self disclosure, and social manners.
Partner Directed Behavior	Verbal behaviors that facilitate the involvement of the partner in the conversation and that are not subsumed elsewhere.

Source: Adapted from Wallander, Conger, and Conger (1985). Reprinted with authors' permission.

two other occasions, each a month apart. Will the data collected validly represent what is happening in the worksite in Professor Fogg's absence? In other words, is it fair to conclude that the data are valid? Probably not. Supervisors may simply be reacting to Professor Fogg's presence—recalling his message that contacts should be increased. Reactivity effects intrude ". . . when the process of observing a subject or subjects alters, either permanently or temporarily, their behavior" (Haynes & Horn, 1982, p. 370).

The presence of reactive effects in obser-

vational data may be suspected, according to Haynes & Horn (1982), when there is

- systematic change in behavior rates, such as increases and decreases in behavior. (A second observer finds that the number of contacts is much lower when Professor Fogg is not present than when he is.)
- increased variability. (The data jump around depending upon who is conducting the observations.)
- self-report by subjects of reactive effects. ("When I saw him come in, that re-

minded me that I needed to increase my contact with clients.")

- any discrepancy among measures of the same behavior. (Fogg's observations and the client's reports of contacts by supervisors bear no relation to one another.)

Such reactive effects appear to increase as the observational environment becomes increasingly more novel or different from the natural environment (e.g., Lipinski & Nelson, 1974). The degree, direction, or rate of occurrence of reactive effects also may vary among subjects as well as behaviors (Haynes, 1978; Haynes & Wilson, 1979).

Haynes and Horn (1982, pp. 381–382) have suggested a number of steps to minimize reactive effects, as paraphrased here:

- involving participant observers or different or supplementary measures (e.g., products or results of behavior).
- observing covertly. For instance, you can record through one-way mirrors, aluminum shadescreens like the inexpensive aluminum shadescreen box (Brechner et al., 1974), or via wall mounted cameras. Videotapes have the advantage of preserving both motor and verbal behavior, and they can be replayed at regular, slow, or rapid speed when the scoring of a behavioral event is questionable.
- minimizing the obtrusiveness of the observers and observational process. For instance, observers should sit in an inconspicuous location. Also, environmental change should be kept to a minimum.
- using telemetry, video cameras, or tape recorders. Contemporary video equipment also permits numerical counts to be superimposed upon the image, easing determining the rate of response. Live observers need not necessarily be involved in order to collect reliable data. Tape recorders and cameras can be programmed

to sample behavior at preselected times. In one study (Sanders, Hopkins, & Walker, 1969) a time-lapse still camera in a classroom obtained permanent photographic records of behavioral samples by automatically exposing the film according to a predetermined schedule. The researchers found that their system had several advantages: It saved observer time, the equipment was easily obtained, and records could be stored easily. The method was inexpensive, and the percentage of agreement among scorers was very high.

- minimizing interactions between the subjects and observers as well as other discriminative (i.e., readily noticeable) properties of the observers.
- instructing subjects to "act natural."
- allowing sufficient time for dissipation of reactive slope and variability in observation data (signifying that subjects have adapted to the measurement system).
- using a number of observers or observation procedures so that differential effects cancel out.

Can reactivity be eliminated entirely? Perhaps it can't. Think about the things you do differently when you know you are being observed versus those you might do when you are alone. Being observed probably alters your performance patterns to some unknown extent. Similarly, the extent of reactive effects with others is difficult to determine without resorting to secrecy or subterfuge—questionable among behavior analysts' tactics. Consequently, the way to deal with reactivity is to try to minimize it to the extent possible and accept the fact that an unknown amount of bias is intruding.

The problem is mitigated to some extent because, as Chapter 6 discusses, we allow for an *adaptation* period during which performance stabilizes. Additionally, most residual reactive effects should persist or diminish, not increase.

Although not always the case, reactivity entails an improvement over typical performance. Workers, students, and self-recorders tend to be more on their toes as they note their performance being observed. When this happens, measures of baseline performance (preintervention) usually inflate. Often, if the effects continue, the influence of reactivity upon the data will remain inflated during intervention, thereby staying relatively constant across conditions. If the effect dissipates (previously unnaturally high baseline measures begin to return to a more natural state during intervention) differences between baseline and intervention measurement would be diminished, thereby introducing a conservative (false negative) bias into the results. Therefore, unless you have good reasons to believe that reactive effects actually worsen behavior, you should feel comfortable about proceeding.

Instructional demand. Variations in the manner of presenting instructions to clients can differentially affect how they behave. For example, Frisch and Higgins (1986) found that variations in instructions (i.e., **instructional demand**) influenced subjects by altering their performance during role playing of social skills. Further, the investigators suggested that by varying instructions, an analyst might be able to optimize the validity of role-play assessments or identify the individuals' response limits or capabilities. This sounds like a good suggestion, provided the analyst takes care to standardize instructions from one observational period to the next, to prevent any observed changes from being a function of the altered instructions.

Behavioral complexity and frequency. Observer accuracy is greater when the behaviors to be observed are not overly complex and their number is limited (Dorsey, Nelson, & Hayes, 1986; Mash & McElwee, 1974). You are more likely to assess three or four behaviors accurately than eight or nine. When we decide that

collecting multiple measures is important (e.g., as in measuring rates, accuracy of academic performance, on-task, other social behaviors by a whole class of students, as well as various teacher behaviors) we use several instruments and multiple observers. In this way the observer can track a smaller, less complex set of behaviors.

Observers' awareness that reliability is being assessed. When observers rated videotapes of parent-child interactions thinking their own scores were being compared to a standard, the ratings agreed much more closely than when observers thought no such comparisons were taking place (Reid, 1970). Other studies have also found that when observers think reliability is being assessed, their agreement level is higher (e.g., Kent, Kanowitz, O'Leary, & Cheiken, 1977; Romanczyk, Kent, Diament, & O'Leary, 1973). We take advantage of this phenomenon to help support accuracy of quiz scoring by using answer sheets that produce duplicates, thereby suggesting that **reliability** scoring may happen anytime. Obviously, frequent reliability checks support accuracy of recording. As O'Leary and Kent (1973) reported, reliability may also be influenced by the experimenter's presence, interestingly, by lowering indexes of agreement. Those authors speculated that observers may have inflated their reliability estimates by communicating about their observations when the experimenter was absent. So periodically dropping in at unpredictable times could increase the accuracy of recording.

Information and feedback. Biasing of observational recording can also result from expecting behavior to change in a particular direction. Especially risky is the situation in which experimenters communicate to observers their satisfaction or disappointment with the way change is progressing (O'Leary, Kent, & Kanowitz, 1975). Being scrupulous to avoid conveying information about anticipated or actual change to observers apparently is essential to reliable recording.

Selecting Reliable Measures

Aunt Minerva has a bathroom scale that responds inconsistently. If she weighs herself once and the scale reads 150 pounds, she steps off and immediately back on. She repeats this process until the scale indicates 145 pounds. At that point she walks away, smiling, and says, "The diet is working." Of course, Minerva's conclusion is erroneous. The scale is not reliable, and she really has no way of knowing whether the diet is working. A reliable scale—one that measures consistently—would provide Minerva with more convincing evidence.

Behavioral measurement requires the same sort of consistency. If the observational system is not reliable, recorded changes in observed behavior may reflect a change in observing and recording responses, rather than in the observed behavior itself (Baer et al., 1968). Consequently, before formal data can be collected, we must ensure that observations can be reliably recorded. We need to avoid inadvertently introducing error into the measurement system.

A major source of error results from not precisely operationalizing—specifying all the acts included in—the target behavior. When broad or general evaluative categories such as *positive*, *negative*, and *neutral* are used, low interobserver agreement tends to result (Stouthamer-Loeber & Peters, 1984).

We can best avoid introducing error into the measurement system by providing precise operational definitions of target behaviors and training, supervising, and, if necessary, retraining the observers in their recording skills. Data become much more believable when at least one regular observer remains totally uninformed about the intervention procedures and expected outcomes. Involving two observers who simultaneously but independently record

identical episodes can also add to the believability of the observational method. This allows us to compare the two recordings on a point-by-point basis to determine how closely they match one another. (Shortly we will describe how we calculate **interobserver agreement indexes**.)

Employees at a paper mill were very eager to reduce their rates of accidents. After the safety staff identified a set of behaviors that had been implicated in accidents in the past, each act was defined as an operation. These definitions were tested first by the experimenter and an assistant, then revised until both found themselves agreeing just about every time about scoring any particular job performance. Then a third observer, who knew nothing other than that the study related to job safety, was given minimal instructions and invited to use the definitions and a recording form to independently record ongoing worker behavior at the same time as the assistant. When evaluations of each separate worker action were compared, both observers agreed almost all the time. The recording system seemed to be quite reliable (Sulzer-Azaroff, Fox, Moss, & Davis, 1990).

Behavioral Recording Techniques

As you can imagine, the validity and reliability of a behavioral measure is influenced by the method used to record it. Some categories of behavior lend themselves to one system of recording; others to another. For instance, when a behavior results in a tangible product, one method of recording is appropriate; when the performance is **transitory**, or fleeting, others are preferred. Here we discuss several recording methods and their suitability for particular purposes.

Measuring Behavioral Products

Some behaviors, like answering quizzes or cleaning tables, leave physical evidence in the form of a result or product that endures more or less permanently beyond the performance. The number of words or sentences written, reports turned in, beds made, items below quality standards, woodworking projects completed, windows broken, and graphs drawn can all be directly counted, either right after they occur or later.

Ongoing data systems like rates of attendance, punctuality, injury, production, quality, waste, or unit costs, profits and losses, and other sorts of results records are indigenous to most organizations. Schools gather standardized test scores from their pupils; institutions, statistics on job and residential placements of clients; advertisers, data about restaurants, hotels, and TV broadcasting stations; service businesses and political organizations survey the public to determine their opinions and satisfaction with the concepts they are trying to promote. Sometimes these ongoing data systems can be used directly as primary measures of behavior change, especially when they closely mirror the behavior of concern. When attendance or punctuality is targeted for improvement, using attendance and time clock records would be suitable measures.

Conversely, many ongoing data systems are impacted by a multiplicity of factors, beyond the focus of the change program. Profits and losses are influenced by the composition of the work force, costs of materials, marketplace conditions, and numerous other variables. People's stated opinions may be slanted by their desire to please interviewers or avoid confrontation; students' test scores by factors other than the teacher's skills—health, home conditions, and so on. Judging the efficacy of any given behavioral intervention on such bottom-line outcome data clearly would be inappropriate in those cases.

However, bottom-line measures may be influenced indirectly by the intervention. If goals are selected in concordance with the mission of the organization, we would anticipate a positive impact on long-range outcome data. Cer-

tainly, such information should be gathered. It may be telling and convincing to the employers of your services. Improvements in safety on the job, for example, eventually should show up in the profit column in the form of reduced medical treatment, staff absenteeism, equipment breakage, insurance and compensation costs, and so on. Application of enhanced teaching skills may well be reflected ultimately in student test scores. But neither are the most valid measures of the efficacy of a behavioral intervention designed to increase safety or teaching skills.

Using **permanent product recording** to measure performance has several advantages. The validity of quantitative or qualitative measures can be demonstrated easily if independent judges are asked to evaluate the products by their own criteria: "Which report is more complete?" Close agreement between the behavioral and judgmental ratings helps to validate the measures.

Permanent product recording can minimize reactivity, because the measures are taken after a passage of time. Observations or changes in the environment do not occur while the behavior is occurring.

Results of behavior also are easier to assess for consistency of measurement.[2] After the work shift, first one observer, then another tours the packaging area to count the number of aisles leading to fire exits that are free of packing cases and other obstacles. The two observers can then compare their totals. A supervisor wants to increase the number of times she jots down a note complimenting subordinates for meeting their goals. The supervisor keeps a log of the notes she sends, specifying dates and times; the recipient saves the notes in a file. With records of this kind, doing an **interobserver agreement assessment** (IOA) is

[2] These scores generally are referred to as *reliability coefficients*. Johnston and Pennypacker (1980) prefer the term "believable" to describe them.

relatively simple. The total indicated by the logged records is compared with the actual notes, according to the formula:

$$\% \text{ agreement} = \frac{\text{Number of agreements (A)}}{\text{Number of agreements (A)} + \text{Number of disagreements (D)}} \times 100$$

Measuring Transitory Events

Many kinds of behavior with which behavior analysts are concerned are transitory and do not yield tangible products. Measuring those ephemeral responses is more difficult. Completing all the steps in sequence in a training trial or a quality audit, sitting quietly and attending to a task, contributing to group discussions, smiling, praising staff members, fighting, tardiness, and the like are impermanent and cannot be assessed accurately after the fact. To measure such behavior, it is necessary to record while the act is going on or to find some method of preserving it. To record transitory behavior usually requires a live observer in the setting. Otherwise, some instrument like an audio- or videotape recorder can be used to preserve the event, or a device like a radio transmitter or a closed-circuit television camera may transfer what is happening. Audiotape recording, for example, has been found to be both cost effective and at least as reliable as direct observation with a variety of behaviors, such as parent-child interactions (Hansen, Tisdelle, & O'Dell, 1985). This section describes a number of specific techniques for recording transitory behaviors.

Event recording. Event or **frequency recording** involves counting the times that a specific behavior occurs within a particular interval: 10 minutes; a session; a class period; a day; the duration of a meal; or a television program.

Event recording is particularly appropriate for measuring **discrete behaviors**, those that have clearly definable beginnings and ends. The numbers of pages read, days present, answers correct, paper airplanes thrown, bites by a sibling, and experiments or tasks successfully completed are all discrete events. However, the behavior must not occur so rapidly that the observer loses count, as in pencil tapping or rapidly repeated forms of self-stimulation. Furthermore, occurrences should be roughly equivalent in duration, or the data could be misleading. For example, suppose you decide to measure the number of times a child cries daily during the hour preceding dinner. The first day 3 brief instances occur. The following day only 1 instance occurs, but it lasts the full hour. Has crying decreased or increased? Your data would erroneously suggest it decreased because the number of episodes of crying dropped from 3 to 1. Here you can see why event recording is not a valid measure unless the instances are roughly equivalent in duration.

Discrete events can be recorded in various ways:

- a check list
- pencil and paper
- a reliable wrist counter (Lindsley, 1968)
- a hand counter (like those used to count the number of people who enter museums or a shopping center)
- electromechanical counters, some of which may be connected to a computer for subsequent analysis.

Chapter 6 suggests additional technological methods of recording behavior. A simple way to count events is to transfer chips, beans, pennies, or some other type of small object from one pocket to another each time the behavior occurs.

Task analyses lend themselves nicely to event recording. The operationalized subcomponents are simply listed with spaces in which presence or absence can be checked off. In Figure 20.2 (Chapter 20), the task of shampooing hair (Gustafson, Hotte, & Carsky, 1976) is easily measured by recording each subtask as a separate event. In finer analyses, the component tasks can be rated on a scale, for example, 1 = none, 2 = some, 3 = all. Figure 5.1 displays a task analysis that Richard Fleming (Fleming & Sulzer-Azaroff, 1989) used for two purposes:

- to *count* the number of subcomponents that a staff member of a residential program for developmentally disabled clients followed in teaching bedmaking and other self-help skills.
- to feed this information back to the staff member afterward. (Feedback like this often produces powerful improvements, as we shall see in Chapters 10 and 11.)

Beware of some pitfalls in analyzing the outcomes of data derived from task analyses, because the simplest method, percentage correct (number of steps correct divided by the total number of steps) may conceal more than it reveals. Also, step sizes may vary in difficulty and complexity, so overall percentage correct may distort estimates of progress. Compare step 1 with step 3 on Figure 5.1, for instance. Trainees rapidly learned step 1, whereas step 3 was far more complicated. (We solved this issue by isolating step 3 results and analyzing them separately.) Haring and Kennedy (1988) offer a number of other suggestions for analyzing the results more meaningfully. One technique is to look at how long it takes to achieve competent performance (trials to criterion); another is to scrutinize the correctness of steps within the task analysis in order to detect and correct error patterns.

Analogous to a task analysis is the **behaviorally anchored rating scale (BARS)**, used frequently within business organizations to rate employee performance. Instead of listing steps in a complex task, you can place descriptive statements of observable behaviors—for example, correct practicing and sequencing of training skills—on a checklist, as in Figure 5.2.

Measurements are then based on the total number scored over several trials. In this case, a score of 25 over 5 training trials represents a perfect score.

A common concern pertinent to event recording is how to count the frequency of a simple response that occurs fairly often, such as number of beard tugs, sneezes, lines written, products checked for quality, utterances of "you know", or of complimentary phrases. When automated devices such as digital wrist counters are beyond your budget, try making your own abacus wrist or watchband (Mahoney, 1974), such as the one illustrated in Figure 5.3. It consists of four or more rows of nine beads attached tautly (to prevent sliding) to a wide band. Each row represents a different place value: ones, tens, hundreds, thousands, and so on. Each time an event occurs, a bead is moved on the ones column of the abacus. When the tenth event occurs, all beads in the ones column are returned to their original position, and one bead in the tens column is shifted. When the 100th event occurs, the beads in the tens column are reset, a bead is shifted in the hundreds column, and so on (see Figure 5.3).

Determining interobserver agreement with event recording. An observer recorded that Lucretia hit Tracy over the head with her plastic sand spade 15 times. What information should convince us that the number of events was recorded accurately? We could position a second observer in close proximity to the first observer (interobserver agreement and accuracy are higher when observers are in close physical proximity [Kapust & Nelson, 1984]) and ask both to record hitting episodes simultaneously. (We must ensure, however, that observers cannot see one another's records or hear what is being written.) Then we could compare the two totals. The formula for estimating interobserver agreement for events is:

$$\% \text{ agreement} = \frac{\text{Smaller total}}{\text{Larger total}} \times 100$$

Figure 5.1 Task Analysis and Feedback Form: Teaching Trainers to Teach Self-Help Skills

Resident:		Trainer:	
Program:	**Location:**	**Date:**	**Time:**
Materials required:			
Program request:			
Rewards:			

1. Materials ready — Prior to giving program request, trainer prepares all materials so that resident does not have to wait more than 10 seconds. `+  −`

2. Correct request to begin program — Trainer uses request specified above (in training area/room). `+  −`

3. Prompts are delivered correctly (by definition) and in proper sequence. Praise/reward provided.

Step	5 sec.	Verb. Instr.	5 sec.	VI & Demo.	5 sec.	VI & Ph. Guid.	Praise/ Reward
_____	`+  −`	`+  −  ○`	`+  −`	`+  −  ○`	`+  −`	`+  −  ○`	`+  ○`
Resident:	I	V		D		PG	
repeated:	`+  −`	`+  −  ○`	`+  −`	`+  −  ○`	`+  −`	`+  −  ○`	`+  ○`
Resident:	I	V		D		PG	

Step	5 sec.	Verb. Instr.	5 sec.	VI & Demo.	5 sec.	VI & Ph. Guid.	Praise/ Reward
_____	`+  −`	`+  −  ○`	`+  −`	`+  −  ○`	`+  −`	`+  −  ○`	`+  ○`
Resident:	I	V		D		PG	
repeated:	`+  −`	`+  −  ○`	`+  −`	`+  −  ○`	`+  −`	`+  −  ○`	`+  ○`
Resident:	I	V		D		PG	

4. Program steps followed in sequence. `+  −`

5. Repeated practice steps completed. `+  −`

6. Rewards resident after last step. — Delivers terminal reward item specified (or tells resident he/she will receive it) paired with praise. `+  −`

7. Records correctly. — Data sheet is filled out completely and correct data are recorded. `+  −`

Comments:

Figure 5.2 Behaviorally Anchored Rating Scale

1	2	3	4	5
Either sequence or steps >80% correct	Sequence >80% proper; steps >80% correct	Sequence followed properly; >80% steps correct	All steps followed correctly; sequence >80% proper	All steps followed correctly in proper sequence

Figure 5.3 Wrist Abacus

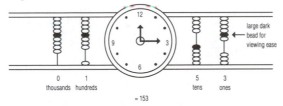

Table 5.2 Event Recording Within Intervals

Observer 1		Observer 2		
Time	Number of Events	Time	Number of Events	Agree-ment
10:00	1111	10:00	111	0.75
10:15	111	10:15	111	1.00
10:30	11111 111	10:30	11111 1	0.75

If the second observer recorded 12 hits, the formula would read 12/15 or 80%. This estimate of interobserver agreement may be inexact, however. It is possible that observer 1 has counted 15 episodes and missed another 10. Observer 2 may have missed several episodes recorded by observer 1 and scored several missed by observer 1. To avoid such inaccuracies, we break observational periods down into intervals, as in Table 5.2. At least with this sort of comparison, when totals within the intervals match, we can feel more confident that both observers have recorded the same events.

Flossie and her mother wanted to record the number of times that Flossie screamed at her older brother. Because the independent recorders were often in different parts of the house, they wanted to be sure that each recorded the same screaming episodes. So they divided their recording sheet into a series of time blocks and marked each screaming event in its time segment (Figure 5.4). Narrowing the field somewhat increased the likelihood that the same events would be recorded. Only scores whose numbers matched within the time block would be counted as agreements. Interobserver agreement could then be estimated by the formula:

$$\% \text{ agreement} = \frac{\text{Agreements}}{\text{Agreements} + \text{Disagreements}} \times 100$$

A dual watch-counter combination described

Figure 5.4 Charts of Flossie's Screaming

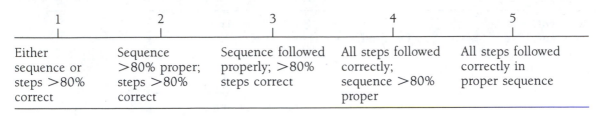

by Katz (1973) is useful for recording both frequency and time. So are some digital alarm watches, because they can be set to repeat their signal following given intervals. A tape recorder with two ear plugs can also be used to signal the end of a recording interval. Be careful, however, that the client's ongoing behavior is not disrupted by the case.

The **coefficient** of interobserver agreement for scoring task analyses and checklists is calculated by comparing the two observers' independent scoring of each item, to see whether they agree or disagree. The same formula as that just given is used to calculate the percentage of agreement.

Flossie and her dad were independently scoring her dressing skills. A low agreement score over a two-week period would mean that the definitions needed further refinements, that both Flossie and her dad needed more practice or training (see Chapter 6), or that accurate scoring would have to be reinforced. To help decide which course to follow, perhaps Flossie's mother could serve as an additional observer for a period of time, during which appropriate refinement might suggest itself (for example, her mother might note that Flossie's scoring is too rigid: that she deserves to be more liberal in evaluating her performance.)

Duration recording. Duration recording is used to measure transitory and discrete behavior when the length of time from the event's beginning to its end is of particular concern or when the occurrences of a behavior vary in duration (as with the earlier crying illustration). A wall clock, stopwatch, or wristwatch can measure the duration of a behavior. Most home computers come equipped with clocks that permit users to record the onset and offset of an event with relative ease.

Suppose Paula is interested in reducing the time it takes her to begin preparing her reports. She can start a stopwatch at the moment that she notes she has collected her last necessary piece of information and stop it when she strikes the first key on her word processor, recording the elapsed time, or technically, her **latency** of responding (the time elapsing from the signal until the response occurs). In one actual case, a youngster complied with the teacher's instructions very slowly. Nancy Fjellstedt (Fjellstedt & Sulzer-Azaroff, 1973) timed how long he took to comply by using a stopwatch. (Later, by rewarding shorter latencies, she was able to teach the child to comply more rapidly.)

The *duration* of the time spent in learning activities is an important consideration in that "academic engaged time is related to student achievement" (Gettinger, 1986, p. 14). Students frequently lose critical instructional time in school because of overly long transitional times as teacher and students settle down to work.

As with event recording, the index of agreement of a latency or duration recording system is estimated by taking the sets of scores obtained by two observers and dividing the shorter duration by the longer duration:

$$\frac{\text{Shorter duration}}{\text{Longer duration}} \times 100 = \% \text{ of agreement}$$

For greater precision, durations can be compared on an interval-by-interval basis.

Interval time-sample recording. Lucretia's parents have decided to observe her closely, noting how cooperatively she plays with other children. They consider counting the frequency of cooperative play episodes. It soon becomes obvious, however, that cooperative play does not lend itself to counting. The behavior analyst informs them that their problem is not unique and that systems of measurement have been devised to solve it. Such systems are called **interval time-sample** systems.

Many kinds of behavior are not clearly discrete but rather **continuous**. Discerning when the responses begin and end is difficult. In such instances, interval time-sampling recording provides the clearest data. For instance, suppose a client makes many loud and disruptive noises, screeching, shouting, hitting furniture, and rattling his chair. Counting each response or measuring its duration would be difficult. When does one episode of chair rattling end and another begin?

As with a stop-action camera or video player, assessing the presence or absence of such responses within brief time frames is possible. That data may then be used as samples of the client's behavior. This process is what is involved in an interval time-sample recording system. The simple presence or absence of given responses in an interval is scored. Systems requiring that the response be emitted throughout the entire interval for its presence to be scored are called **whole-interval time-sampling**. Such systems are used when knowing that the behavior continues without interruption is important. Systems requiring only a single instance of the response within the interval in order to be scored are called **partial-interval time-sampling**.[3] Partial intervals are used to record fleeting nondiscrete behaviors like smiling, praising, communicating with a peer, uttering strings of swear words, or making bizarre gestures. Systems requiring the response be ongoing at the very instant when the interval ends are called **momentary time-sampling** (Powell, Martindale, & Kulp, 1975). Momentary time samples are useful for recording behaviors that are apt to persist for a while, such as Paula's report writing, Pearl's stereotyped hand movements, and Kevin's thumbsucking. Because these behaviors occur so often, the sample should yield a fair representation of their rates of occurrence, assuming the duration of the intervals is sufficiently short.

Lucretia was observed with the same two children for 5 half-hour play periods each week.

Using a partial-interval time-sampling system, an observer watched for 10 seconds to determine whether Lucretia grabbed toys from the other children. If she did, the entire interval was scored minus. If not, the interval was scored plus. The observer recorded the score during the 5 seconds following each 10-second observation period. A similar partial-interval time-sample system was used to score parents' attention to Lucretia. Then the observer scored the interval with a check. Figure 5.5 displays the recording sheet the observer used.

A similar example illustrates the whole-interval time-sampling system. A response is scored only if it occurs throughout the interval. Grabbing toys—a fairly brief response—would not be an appropriate variable to measure with the whole-interval system. However, playing cooperatively (sharing, not grabbing, speaking politely, and so on) with other children would be appropriate for whole-interval recording, because that behavior could persist for some time. In Figure 5.5, any interval throughout which Lucretia continued to play cooperatively was scored.

Sometimes it is necessary to sample several behaviors simultaneously. A **coded interval-recording sheet** can be used for this purpose. A letter is designated for each behavior. The occurrence of a behavior is scored by making a slash mark through its corresponding symbol during the interval. Such a system can be used to take whole-interval, partial-interval, or momentary time-sample measurements of the behaviors of one subject. It can also be used to measure performance by different individuals in a group. A coded interval sheet is appropriate for Dexter, who is concerned about keeping to his tasks. He wants an estimate of the proportion of time during which he engages in activities that interfere with his schoolwork—handling other materials or daydreaming, for example. As his counselor has suggested, Dexter also will record his teacher's behavior—whether the teacher has attended to him pos-

---

[3] Sometimes called *interval spoilage*.

Figure 5.5 Score Sheet for Partial-Interval Time-Sample System

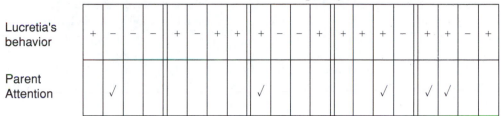

itively, negatively, or not at all. An excerpt from Dexter's coded sheet is shown in Figure 5.6.

The rows of symbols are repeated 5 more times, so the entire school day can be monitored. A very soft click sounds every 10 minutes on a prerecorded audiotape. Dexter then marks the appropriate interval by slashing the code letter: T for on-task, M for handling other materials, D for daydreaming. The teacher's behavior also is scored for positive (+), negative (−), or no (0) attention. Naturally, each of these behaviors has been precisely operationalized. A partial-interval time-sampling system is used: If either M and/or D behavior occurs at *any time during the interval*, its corresponding code letter is slashed. Otherwise, T is slashed. Note that Dexter has scored himself as on-task during the first 2 intervals but as daydreaming in the third. During those same intervals his record shows 1 interval with positive teacher attention and 2 with no teacher attention.

A coded scoring sheet also can be used just as effectively for whole-interval and momentary time-sampling. Its major advantage is that it simplifies the recorder's job, requiring just a slash mark, rather than writing several symbols within a brief time. A light visible only to the aide signals the end of a 2-minute interval, so

at that moment she draws a mark through a plus or a minus to record whether Kevin has his thumb in his mouth at the moment. During baseline, Kevin's thumb is observed to be in his mouth at almost every one of those moments. Later, after the intervention, Kevin's thumb is rarely in his mouth when recording happens—convincing evidence that Kevin's thumb-sucking probably has diminished in that setting. Figure 5.1 uses a similar coded recording system for event recording.

Limitations of interval time-sampling. One limitation of interval time-sampling recording is that it is not practical for studying important but infrequent behavior. Fights between two particular individuals, for example, may occur no more than once a week. Because observations are not continuous, such infrequent events may not be recorded. If such behavior occurs as often as once a week, however, it is probably necessary to do something about it. Arington (1943) suggests as a general rule that if the dependent variable occurs on an average of less than once in 15 minutes, some other way of recording needs to be substituted.

Table 5.3 provides guidelines for selecting observational methods, depending on the characteristics of the behaviors being observed.

Figure 5.6 Coded Interval-Recording Sheet

Dexter	T̸	M	D¹⁰	T̸	M	D²⁰	T	M	D̸³⁰	T	M	D⁴⁰	T	M	D⁵⁰
Teacher	+̸	−	0	+	−	0̸	+	−	0̸	+	−	0	+	−	0
Dexter	T	M	D¹⁰	T	M	D²⁰	T	M	D³⁰	T	M	D⁴⁰	T	M	D⁵⁰
Teacher	+	−	0	+	−	0	+	−	0	+	−	0	+	−	0

Table 5.3 Selecting an Observational Method

| | Select observational method when behavior | | | | |
Observational method	Produces durable product	Is transitory	Is discrete	Is roughly equivalent in duration each time expressed	Is continuous
Permanent product	X				
Event		X	X	X	
Duration		X	X		
Time sampling[a] (whole, partial, and momentary[b])		X			X

[a] The behavior should occur at least once every 15 minutes if time-sampling is to be useful.
[b] In most cases, for teachers to be able to use momentary time-sampling, the behavior needs to occur fairly often, for example, somewhere about 10 percent of the observed time or more. Otherwise, occurrences of the behavior are not likely to be recorded. From Sulzer-Azaroff and Mayer, 1986.

Factors affecting the validity of interval recording. A valid measure of a behavior permits quantification without distortion. Powell et al. (1975) used a stopwatch to continuously measure how long the subject remained seated during thirty 20-minute sessions. These presumably valid data were used as a standard against which the interval-recording data were compared. The researchers found that whole-interval time-sampling consistently *underestimated* the occurrence of the behavior in comparison to the standard. This is understandable, because to be scored the subject had to remain in the seat throughout the observational interval. Partial-interval time-sampling consistently *overestimated* occurrences, in contrast with the standard. This was because any time the behavior was noted within the interval, the whole interval was scored as if sitting had occurred throughout it. Momentary time-sampling was off both ways. When intervals were short, however (80 seconds or less), distortion was minimized. Estimation of a behavior that occurs fairly often but is not amenable to event recording should be possible with brief time-sampling intervals. If an interval is reserved for writing down data, it too should be kept brief, because behavior occurring during the recording interval will not be scored. The longer that recording interval, the more will be missed.

Selecting the most appropriate interval time-sampling system. The purpose of the measurement should determine which of the three interval systems to use in a given situation. Selecting a "conservative" measure as it relates to the intended outcome is preferable. For example, because whole-interval time-sampling slightly underestimates the duration of the response, use the method when striving for an *increase* in the dependent variable. This would tend to bias the outcome by underestimating changes. Suppose the behavioral goal were to increase on-task behavior. A whole 10-second interval time sample should record only those intervals in which on-task responding occurred throughout. Any increases in duration of on-task behavior lasting less than 10 seconds would not be recorded, because the full interval was not spanned. The result would underestimate improvement in on-task behavior. If many intervals were scored positively, however, a substantial change must have occurred—probably greater than reflected by the scores.

Because whole-interval time-sampling

yields an underestimate, it is not appropriate when we are seeking a behavioral reduction, such as less disruptive noise. As noise is not likely to persist unabated throughout an interval, many intervals would remain unscored. A partial-interval system is therefore more appropriate, because it is biased toward overestimation. A convincing presentation of data would show entire intervals free of the undesirable behavior, especially because the inflationary aspect of the recording system is known. An interval scored for an absence of disruptive noises would thus indicate not even a brief episode occurred during that interval.

Partial-interval time-sampling is not the best choice for recording behavioral frequency or duration (Ary, 1984). Instead, use event or duration recording, respectively.

Assessing reliability of interval time-sampling. The method for assessing a percentage of agreement for interval recording is already familiar to you:

$$\frac{\text{Number of agreements}}{\text{Number of agreements} + \text{Number of disagreements}} \times 100$$

In interval time-sampling, though, calculating two separate indexes, rather than a single one is recommended, especially when the target behavior occurs either very frequently or very infrequently (Hawkins & Dotson, 1975). The first would include scored intervals only in the calculations and the second only unscored intervals. Figure 5.7 shows the recording forms of two observers who recorded data on the in-

tervals during which Paula was filing her nails. Notice that observers A and B agreed on the sixth interval, but observer B recorded additional episodes in the fourteenth and fifteenth intervals. Overall agreement was not good. Yet combining all agreements, whether scored or unscored, would yield an inflated index of agreement of 95 percent:

$$\frac{38A}{38A + 2D} \times 100 = 95\%$$

Separate calculations, however, which take into account only the three scored intervals (6, 14, and 15) produce a more conservative figure, revealing that the observational system needs to be refined:

$$\frac{1A}{1A + 2D} \times 100 = 33\%$$

Similarly, when behavior occurs very frequently, calculating the index of agreement for *unscored* intervals permits detection of overly inflated coefficients of agreement.[4]

Table 5.4 offers a guide to the selection of behavior recording techniques for those who are trying to increase their technical competence.

Reporting Reliability Data

To report reliability, you might follow one of the recommendations offered by Morris and Rosen (1982). These include, in order of increasing explicitness: presenting the data in research reports, noting on the graphs days on which reliability was assessed, reporting the reliability data directly on the data figure itself (either globally or preferably for each experi-

Figure 5.7 Two Records of Less Frequent Behavior

---

[4] An alternative is to use Kappa (Hartmann, 1977) or percentage of agreement expected by chance: $(p_1 \times p_2) \times 100$. The p_1 is the proportion of intervals of occurrence for observer one; p_2 for observer two. When nonoccurrence is included, the formula is $([p_1 \times p_2] + [q_1 \times q_2]) \times 100$, where q_1 is the proportion of nonoccurrence intervals scored by observer one, and q_2 for observer two.

Table 5.4 A Guide to Selecting Behavior Recording Techniques

Type of Measure	Definition	Example	Advantages and Disadvantages
1. Permanent Product Recording	Records the enduring outcome of the behavior	Number of completed math problems, windows broken, dresses sewn	Readily assessed for reliability of measurement
2. Event Recording	Records the number of times a specific behavior occurs over a specific interval	Number of books read, paper airplanes thrown, meals eaten	1. Appropriate for behaviors that have clearly definable beginnings and endings 2. May be recorded on a checklist, wrist counter, hand counter, or transfer of objects (e.g., pennies) from one pocket to another
3. Duration Recording	Records the length of time a behavior occurs	Length of time to complete homework	May be recorded with the aid of a wall clock, stopwatch
4. Interval Time-Sampling Recording	Records the presence or absence of a given response within a time interval	Thumb-sucking or sideburn pulling	1. Records behaviors that are not clearly discrete 2. Useful for behaviors that occur at least once every 15 minutes
a. Whole-Interval Time-Sampling	Records the response when it is emitted throughout the entire interval	On-task behavior	1. Tends to under-estimate the occurrences of the behavior 2. Useful when it is important to know that the behavior is not interrupted
b. Partial-Interval Time-Sampling	Records the response when a single instance of the response occurs in the interval	Swearing, bizarre gestures	1. Used to record behaviors that may occur in fleeting moments 2. Tends to overestimate the occurrence of the behavior
c. Momentary Time-Sampling	Records the response if emitted at the moment the interval terminates	In-seat behavior, frequent stereotypic behaviors	Useful to record behaviors that are apt to persist for a while

Source: Prepared by Gregory Ramey.

mental condition, plotting sets of data collected by each observer), and/or presenting reliability bands. Those bands are constructed by connecting a vertical line between the highest and lowest level of behavior scored by the observers or by preparing confidence intervals. (Morris & Rosen, 1982, detail these procedures further.)

Summary

Objective, reliable, and valid measurement is basic to all applied behavior analysis programs. Such a system permits change agents to inform their clients and other consumers of their services' progress and serves as a basis for experimentally studying the impact of the intervention. In this chapter you have become acquainted with the concepts of validity and reliability of measurement and a number of systems for recording behavior. You also learned which measurement systems to select for given purposes, as summarized in Tables 5.3 and 5.4. Now you are ready to discover how to conduct observational recording, including who collects data, who trains the observers, and who uses automated recording devices.

Chapter 6

Behavioral Assessment: Implementing Observational Systems

GOALS

After completing this chapter, you should be able to:

1. Define, recognize, and give original illustrations of each of the following terms:
   a. Criterion observer
   b. Observer drift
   c. Recalibrate
   d. Zone system
   e. PLA-Check
   f. Ordinate or y-axis
   g. Abscissa or x-axis
   h. Adaptation
   i. Baseline

2. List various people who can be trained to collect observational data.

3. Discuss the advantages and disadvantages of having observational data collected by the:
   a. client (self-recording)
   b. contingency manager.

4. List and discuss at least four different methods of cuing an observer.

5. Discuss the advantages and disadvantages of using automated recording systems.

6. Describe various methods of training observers and provide a rationale for each.

7. Describe how reliable data could be obtained for a given situation and how you would train the observers and maintain their high levels of interobserver agreement.

8. List some factors that can reduce interobserver agreement indexes. Specify how to control for, or minimize, each factor listed.

9. Illustrate and discuss the advantages of three different methods of observing behavior in groups.

10. Describe and provide rationales for when it is and is not appropriate for observers to communicate with one another.

11. Collect reliable baseline data and measures of collateral behavior. Graph the data according to standard format.

12. Illustrate and discuss the advantages of a cumulative graph.

13. Differentiate between adaptation and reactivity.

14. Describe how to tell when a representative baseline has been obtained.

15. Describe the major advantages of a baseline.

16. Discuss and illustrate how to graph steady state versus acquisition data.

Having selected appropriate measures, Lucretia's parents and other adults are preparing to record how she behaves in a group. Guided by the school psychologist, Dexter will self-record, and observers have been identified to measure Pearl's behavior in various settings. Paula decides to work on her own. The time has come to proceed with behavioral measurement. Observers and recorders must be selected, trained, and an observation schedule planned. Recording and graphing can begin, progressing through an adaptation period and into a baseline phase. Then behavioral procedures and experimental designs can be selected and implemented.

Behavior-Recording Staff

Organizations that provide human services need people to perform technical functions. A preferred option is to employ *behavioral technicians*. These personnel design and implement observational recording systems, supervise data collection, and design and execute graphing schemes for continual monitoring (see Sulzer-Azaroff, Thaw, & Thomas, 1975). Several state civil-service departments have built that function into their human-services career ladders. At the present writing, however, such staff positions appear to be more the exception than the rule.

When behavioral technicians are not available, other possibilities must be explored. For example, parents, senior citizens, mentally retarded people (Craighead, Mercatoris, & Bellack, 1974), college students on practicum or internship assignments, older children (McLaughlin & Malaby, 1975a), peers, or even clients themselves may serve as observers. In an electronics plant where one of us consulted, a retired manager was rehired on a part-time basis to audit plant safety targets. Some programs require monitoring in many settings around the clock, which may be particularly difficult. Then either the contingency managers

or the clients themselves may have to serve as behavior recorders.

Clients as Behavior Self-Recorders

Engaging clients in observing and recording their own behavior is becoming increasingly popular because, in addition to the bonus of decreasing work loads for behavioral technicians or contingency managers, self-recording frequently results in desired behavior change (Kazdin, 1974a; Harmon, Nelson, & Hayes, 1980; Willis & Nelson, 1982). This happens especially when self-reinforcement is added (Mace & Kratochwill, 1985). Furthermore, as we shall show later on, self-recording is an integral part of self-management or self-control programs. Thoresen and Mahoney (1974), for example, consider it ". . . the life blood of effective self-control methods" (p. 41).

A variety of self-recording systems can be used. Clients may use many of those previously discussed for recording their own behavior. For example, they can transfer objects from one pocket to another, score the frequency of a particular behavior on a card or piece of paper, or use a handheld counter. Paula simply kept a list of the number of pages she completed for her reports each day. Automated recording systems, like videotapes, also have been used to provide observational feedback to students, teachers, counselors, and others (Hosford, Moss, & Morrell, 1976; Kagan, 1972; Walz & Johnson, 1963).

Self-recording has been used with youthful clients—some as young as six years of age (Ballard & Glynn, 1975; Fixsen, Phillips, & Wolf, 1972; Kazdin, 1974a; Thoresen & Mahoney, 1974). Self-recording is not, however, as simple to implement as it may at first appear. Thomas (1976) found that second-grade students varied in accuracy of recording from 56 to 95 percent. Accurate and reliable self-recording, though problematic, is much more likely to occur if reinforced (Broden, Hall, & Mitts, 1971; Fixsen et al.,1972; Kazdin, 1974a).

People seem to be able to more accurately self-record behaviors that they judge as negative than behaviors that they judge as positive (Willis & Nelson, 1982). This is of particular interest ". . . since the target behavior to be assessed in clinical settings is frequently one evaluated negatively by the client" (Willis & Nelson, 1982, p. 410).

Contingency Managers as Recorders

When the contingency manager, who conducts the day-to-day operation of the program, also must record behavioral data, special adjustments are necessary. In a study by Farber and Mayer (1972), the classroom teacher successfully recorded assignments completed. Kubany and Sloggett (1973) have noted, however, that frequently classroom teachers are so involved with instructional activities that they forget to record data from time to time, and their data may be unreliable as a consequence. The same problem occurs with institutional attendants, managers, foremen, supervisors in sheltered workshops, and those who are recording their own behavior as well as that of others: Other activities may demand their attention so that they fail to record all the data. Asking such individuals to record time-sample data in short intervals, like 10-second time blocks, would be unreasonable.

In this predicament some solutions are possible. One alternative is to observe and record intermittently at predetermined random times throughout the time period. Either a momentary sample or a whole or partial measure may be taken during a brief interval (like 5 minutes). Then the observer can return to the regular task until the next predetermined time. In a sheltered-workshop training program, the supervisor wanted to measure the percentage of time several clients remained on-task. Because she was usually occupied directly in activities with the clients, recording their behavior continuously was not feasible. She prepared an audio cuing tape using this process:

1. She placed Bingo numbers ranging from one to ten in a bowl.

2. She drew a number, recorded it, then replaced it in the bowl.

3. She repeated the procedure many times until a long series of numbers had been noted. Each number indicated how many minutes would need to elapse before the gentle sound of a chime would be recorded on the tape.

4. When the tape was completed, she used it to prompt herself to observe and record. At all other times she could go about her usual activities.

The audio signals prevented the supervisor from being prompted to record the behavior only by the disrupting of one of the clients, thereby biasing the data. An alternative would be to enlist the aid of a client whose behavior was not to be recorded. His or her task would be to set a kitchen timer, as recommended by Kubany and Sloggett (1973), for the number of minutes indicated. In either case, at the sound of the timer, the supervisor would stop and record whether the clients were on-task at that moment. In this way, a fairly representative and valid sample of data was collected.

When using a kitchen timer seems inappropriate or inconvenient in a setting, other methods are available for cuing the recording of clearly operationalized behavior within intervals:

- an inexpensive pocket parking-meter reminder, which is a timer that can be set for intervals up to an hour and that then emits a soft buzzing sound at the end of the interval (Foxx & Martin, 1971)
- a recorded click, or chime
- an alarm pocket or wristwatch

If the sound is distracting to clients, observers may use ear buttons, or a small portable cassette player with earphones, so the observers alone hear the signals.

The type of prerecorded cassette tape just

described may also be designed to audibly remind the observer to locate a client ("Find Pearl"), to "observe hand gestures," to record a "score in box 10," and so on. Similarly, the observer can use an earphone to hear a tape-recorded cuing message preprogrammed for interval time sampling like this: "Interval 1: Observe" (followed by a blank interval of 10 seconds); "Record" (then 5 seconds); "Interval 2: Observe" (then 10 seconds); "Record" (then 5 seconds); "Interval 3 . . ."; and so on.

Audiotapes can also be programmed to facilitate recording group behavior ("Scan the group from left to right and count the number of children who are on-task"). Cassette recorders adapted for dual listening can serve to simplify assessments for interobserver agreement. Should you want to collect dual records for purposes of assessing indexes of agreement, two cords—one for each observer—can be connected to the same tape recorder. Just be sure the cords are long enough to allow a sufficient distance between observers to ensure their independence.

You could, additionally, arrange a light cue as an alternative to audible cuing systems. Attach an electrical timer—the type of timer you use to turn on the morning coffee—to a lamp; or use it to activate the audible cuing system (Bernal et al., 1971). For some clients, a system like this might prove less obtrusive than a recorder, and such timers also may be used to cue contingency managers to implement their procedures.

Regardless of the system used, because the contingency manager has a vested interest in the outcome of the program, indexes of agreement must be assessed regularly throughout to ensure that the observer's recording does not begin to drift. Arrange for an observer who is not aware of the exact purpose of the program to enter unobtrusively for unscheduled recording sessions. Close agreement between the two observers would ease the concern that the measures were biased.

Automated Recording Systems

Sometimes having an observer present to record behavior is neither practical nor convenient. Transitory behavioral events then may be preserved on video- or audiotapes at various intervals throughout the day, for subsequent analysis. Video recordings also have the advantages of permitting replay (slowly or rapidly), stopping action, enabling superimposition of time indicators, and other features. We have used video recordings to assess children's social interactions, teachers' applications of particular instructional skills, and for many other purposes. If we are unsure about how to score a given episode, we can replay the segment or slow it down. Interval time-sampling becomes simplified, because a digital presentation of the number of minutes and seconds that have transpired appears directly on the screen, informing us about the beginning of each new interval.

You should recognize, however, that recording from a videotape usually takes at least the same amount of time as actual recording, and when you do slow down or replay an episode, the viewing can take even longer. On the other hand, you also can speed up the playback, permitting certain discrete events to be recorded more rapidly than in real time, such as counting the number of times the foreman pats his workers on the back. Video recorders are ideal for training, calibrating, assessing agreement scores, and collecting highly precise data.

Are you wondering how on earth you might be able to obtain close-up recordings of clients engaging in their usual routines? One method is to use a zoom lens or directional microphone from a distance. Another is to move in closely and follow the person, especially if you want to collect audio records simultaneously. "Isn't that awfully distracting?" you may ask. Our answer: "Sure, in the beginning. But if you do not interact and remain unresponsive to them, your subjects will eventually ignore you.'' That has been the experience with preschoolers and their teachers at the Walden Training Center. In that preschool for both autistic children and children without special needs, each child and teacher is videotaped several times a week, according to a preset schedule. A few weeks into the school term is all it takes for everyone to appear totally oblivious to the recording activities.

Computerized recording systems are being used increasingly to record ongoing behavior. For example, Tyron (1984) discusses methods of mechanically measuring motor behavior and Bernal and colleagues (1971) developed a device for automatically activating an audio recorder at various times in the daily routine of a family. Similarly Gordon Paul has developed a "staff-resident interaction chromograph,[1]" a computerized method for assessing the nature, approximate content, and distribution of interactions between staff and clients. A 12-button keyboard recorder that "writes" on magnetic tape, and at a later time can be fed into a computer, is still one more example. Each button contains a numeral that you would use as a symbol to designate a given behavior, such as 1 = on-task; 2 = self-stimulation; 3 = laughing or smiling; 4 = sneezing; and so on. The key can be pressed momentarily to indicate a single episode like a sneeze (press number 4), or held down for the entire duration of the behavior (press and hold down number 3 until laughing and smiling stops).[2] Others include the more versatile SSR System 7 (Stephenson & Roberts, 1977); the S & K portable, permitting recording of simultaneous events[3]; a

computerized program for calculating frequency, duration, latency, sequence analysis, and statistical analysis (Depaulis, 1983); and several other methods described by Lehner (1979) and Repp, Harman, Felce, Van Acker, and Karsh (1989). Such devices permit data to be analyzed rapidly. For instance, the computer will calculate the relations among behaviors as a function of particular time intervals or events.

Reactivity, you will recall, is atypical behavior because actions are being observed (see Chapter 5). Reactivity may be a problem when automated recording is used. Johnson and Bolstad (1973) compared audiotape recording in the home under two conditions: when an observer was present and when he was absent. They found that the observer's presence apparently had no more effect on family behavior than that of a tape recorder. Both, however, may have had some unknown influence.

Roberts and Renzaglia (1965) found that clients who were receiving counseling and were aware that their words were being recorded behaved differently from clients who were not aware of being recorded. Other investigators also have shown that observers' presence influenced performance (Mercatoris & Craighead, 1974; White, 1973). Yet others (Hagen, Craighead, & Paul, 1975; Johnson & Bolstad, 1973; Wiggins, 1973) have reported no reactivity after extensive habituation to observation when it occurred on unpredictable schedules with delayed feedback and maintained the anonymity of participants so data could not be used to evaluate them. As we shall demonstrate in the discussion of baseline data collection, however, you must provide for a sufficient adaptation period before assuming that recorded behavior reasonably represents the typical performance of the people involved.

The continued development of instruments designed to preserve and analyze transitory behavioral events should result in ever more efficient and reliable recording systems. Because the technology progresses so rapidly, probably

[1] Available from Research Press, 2612 N Mattis, Champaign, Illinois 61821.

[2] Available from: DATAMYTE, Electro/General Corporation, 128 Jackson Ave. North, Hopkins, Minnesota 55343 (or 14960 Industrial Road, Minnetonka, Minnesota 55343.)

[3] S & K Computer Products, P.O. Box 146, Station M, Toronto, Ontario, Canada M6S 4T2.

your best approach is to consult journals such as *Behavior Therapy and Experimental Psychiatry*, *Behavioral Assessment*, and *Research in Developmental Disabilities*, which contain sections on instrumentation.

Training, Calibrating, and Supervising Observers

Many target behaviors are simple and precise, so assessment of interobserver agreement can be done almost routinely with little effort. Multiple-choice or objective questions (like "What is the square root of 16?"), number of buttons buttoned, pages written, objects sorted or assembled, and clear responses like presence or absence in a setting and location in a room are generally scored reliably, and only minimal training is required. But many socially relevant acts, with which applied behavior analysis is particularly concerned, are not so clear-cut. Personal biases can easily confound the measurement of "social isolation," "cooperativeness," "neatness," and other behavior evaluated subjectively, so training, calibration, and supervision are essential. Thus, Thoresen and Mahoney have noted in reference to self-monitoring:

> Training in the discrimination and recording of a behavior is essential. Such training may be enhanced by modeling, immediate accuracy feedback, systematic reinforcement, and graduated transfer of recording responsibilities (external to self). . . . Discrete behaviors and simple recording systems appear to enhance self-monitoring accuracy (1974, p. 63).

Preliminary Steps

Whether by clients themselves or others, ambiguous terms must be operationalized by refining them into component responses before the behaviors can be recorded satisfactorily. Even a response as deceptively simple as "sitting" may be rated differently by different observers. One may define sitting as the child having any part of his body, such as his knees, in contact with the seat, whereas a second may not.

During training, to be certain that a given recording system is sufficiently reliable, independent measurements should be taken by at least two observers several times under the conditions that will prevail throughout the program. If the independent measures do not yield high coefficients of agreement, observational training is essential.

Training Sites

Observational training may occur under supervision on the job or elsewhere when trainees practice under simulated conditions[4]—as we shall soon discuss. As mentioned earlier, during the initial development of a new scoring system, observers often fail to agree as closely as they might. Additional training can occur directly on site, when this is not too disruptive. We were able to do this with our safety work because the plant was so noisy and people so occupied that they hardly noticed our presence. We would observe a performance, check the record sheet, and compare scores, expressing our pleasure when scores agreed and clarifying and modifying definitions when they did not. Eventually, the system worked in essentially the same way for everyone who observed, and we were ready to begin actually collecting our data.

On-site observer training is not always feasible, however. It is not preferable to discuss the intricacies of response definitions with a trainee in a quiet classroom, a patient's private

---

[4] For learning observational training techniques, we suggest intensive reading and practice or participation in "packaged" training workshops like Ellen P. Reese's multimedia workshop "Observing, Defining, and Recording" (Dept. of Psychology, Mount Holyoke College, South Hadley, Mass.). See also Sulzer-Azaroff and Reese (1982), Chapter 4, and Bass (1987), who developed a computer-assisted observer training program to teach college students to use a partial-interval observational recording system.

quarters, or during a social interaction, because the discussion might prove distracting. Instead, you probably would train observers elsewhere, providing them the opportunity to practice with material that simulates the real thing as closely as possible.

Procedural Clarification

Often during observational training, component responses are identified and communicated more precisely, and directions for recording data are clarified, because observers can discuss their recording problems. One effective method for training observers is to use a videotape sample of the behavior to be measured, permitting the same material to be presented repeatedly until all observers' measurements agree. Confusing observational issues can be refined and incorporated in a scoring manual. An outstanding example of a product resulting from this process was a scoring manual for interactions among preschool children (Farmer-Dugan, 1987).

The ultimate demonstration that a scoring system is reliable is when it can be handed to untrained observers, who, after studying the scoring system and independently rating a sample of behavior simultaneously with trained observers, achieve high coefficients of agreement. Eventually, observers should demonstrate that they measure behavior under the conditions that will prevail throughout the program as reliably as the **criterion observer**, the person whose recording serves as a standard against which others are judged.

Increasing Precision of Observers

One way to increase observers' precision is to train them by having the observers record the behavior of collaborators who act out the performances to be scored. If the actors follow a script, they can readily repeat episodes until all observers are closely calibrated to one another (i.e., they agree on a point-by-point basis). In your training, be sure to include behaviors that

occur at different rates. Kapust and Nelson (1984) found that observer accuracy and interobserver agreement vary with the rates of the target behavior. So, to minimize this potential source of error, you will want to include in your films or scripts some behaviors that happen frequently and some that occur rarely.

Another method to increase precision is to videotape several episodes. Ask one observer to score each episode several times in mixed order, then determine how closely the measures of identical episodes match for each scored and each unscored item. Then focus on areas of disagreement. Repeat the procedure with two observers, who record simultaneously but independently, until eventually measures of the identical episodes agree very closely.

While teaching parents how to teach their handicapped children skills such as self-help or language, we designed checklists for observers (Hall & Sulzer-Azaroff, 1987). After the experimenter demonstrated the reliability of her own measurements by repeatedly scoring particular videotaped episodes identically each time, observers were trained to use the checklists to score taped episodes containing varying target rates, until their data agreed very closely with that of the experimenter. (The observers knew nothing about what or when parents were being taught or about the procedural details until the study was over.) Thereafter the observers periodically went to the clients' homes and scored the checklists. Sometimes they went alone and sometimes they were joined by a second observer who recorded independently but in tandem with the first observers or experimenters. Close indexes of agreement assured us that scoring remained consistent. Any time indexes began to diverge (a phenomenon called **observer drift**), we knew it was time to **recalibrate** observers' measurements by retraining them in the same way as previously, thereby permitting interobserver agreement (IOA) scores to remain acceptable.

We have also used similar methods to score

the *results* or *products* of behavior, such as answers to quizzes, or the appearance of a table-top or aisle that is supposed to remain clean. In the Personalized System of Instruction (PSI) courses we teach, students take quizzes on every unit they study. Proctors (students who have already demonstrated mastery of the unit) score the quizzes by referring to an answer key. Because the questions are open ended to some extent, we want to ensure consistency of quiz grading. So we have used special pressure-sensitive paper that produces duplicate copies and ask another proctor or member of the staff to rescore the duplicate copies. (Alternatively, we have also folded down the prior scores or photocopied answer forms with the original scores concealed, with just as much success.) Then we compare how closely the two scores agree on an item-by-item basis (e.g., Johnson & Ruskin, 1977; Ryan, 1974; Sulzer-Azaroff et al., 1976).

To compare ratings of the cleanliness of a tabletop, you could divide the surface into sections and compare scores for each section. In our work in occupational safety, we have observed designated areas such as walkways, then scored the presence of any obstruction. In cases in which no obstructions were found, the walkway was scored as completely safe (e.g., Fellner & Sulzer-Azaroff, 1985).

Recording Independently

Earlier we mentioned that observers can communicate with one another to clarify definitions and recording methods *during observational training*. However, data collected for the purpose of setting behavioral goals (as well as for baseline and treatment) should be collected independently by each observer. Observers must not be able to see what other observers are marking down or to hear their comments. Such communication could contaminate the objectivity of the findings and produce an artificially high reliability estimate. So, to maintain independence of observation, place your observers

equidistant from the people whose behavior they are recording but sufficiently far away from one another to keep recording objective. Observational data must be collected by independent observers.

Once a recording system has been planned and observers trained to implement it, the time has come to begin data collection in earnest. Now we discuss how reliability of scoring, once achieved, can be maintained throughout the program.

Maintaining Observational Reliability

Consistently high levels of accuracy in recording over several sessions is no guarantee that reliability will persist, as demonstrated in two studies (Fixsen et al., 1972; Romanczyk et al., 1973). Romanczyk and colleagues (1973) assessed reliability among observers throughout the course of a classroom investigation. Two assessors recorded data along with the regular observers. One was identified as a reliability assessor; the second was not. The data recorded by the observers more closely matched those of the identified assessor than those of the other. What is more, the data were inflated in the anticipated direction according to the goal of the program. Measurement bias arose from two sources: knowledge that reliability was being assessed and perhaps cues from the identified assessor and expectations of the changes that were supposed to occur.

Knowing that their measures will be assessed for reliability apparently ensures that observers will be scrupulous in their recording (Craighead et al., 1974). Indexes of agreement should be assessed *frequently* throughout the course of a program, and observers should be informed that these assessments will be regularly conducted. Ideally, observers should be unaware of such assessments, though in some situations this ideal is impractical. Because expectations about results may also bias recordings, it is best not to inform observers of the anticipated outcomes. But this course, too, may be impractical, because treatment programs are often very obvious. You can avoid this bias by mixing video recordings of behavior samples taken during various baseline and treatment sessions, so observers can score them without knowing whether the treatment was in progress at the time.

Being informed that regular reliability assessments will be ongoing may help observers to maintain high levels of accuracy. A second method is to reinforce accuracy. Johnson and colleagues (1976) found that accuracy in scoring quizzes increased substantially following administration of a training package. One of the package components was a grade contingency, with "A" grades reserved for those who improved or maintained high accuracy levels. Only when accurate reporting was rewarded did it remain high and stable. Along with all other categories of behavior, reliable observation seems best maintained when observational consistency is reinforced from time to time.

Observing Behavior in Groups

Observing the behavior of people in groups is a special case. Fortunately, a variety of observational systems have been developed for special situations when the behaviors of several individuals are assessed. Here we discuss how three methods—the zone system, PLA-Check, and ecobehavioral assessment—lend themselves to observing the behavior of group members.

Zone System

Observational recording of continuous behavior can prove difficult in large settings when individuals tend to move from one area to another. The **zone system** has been developed for these circumstances. Analogous to the time-sampling system, except rather than (or in ad-

dition to) dividing time up into small intervals, space is divided similarly. The observer sequentially watches all the individuals within one particular area at a time, regardless of how many there are. For example, this system might be appropriate to record behaviors in areas of the school cafeteria and playground and for scoring the degree of safe performance by a large number of factory workers (Sulzer-Azaroff & Fellner, 1984).

To use the zone system,

> Any single instance of a behavior that can be scored is marked when it occurs within the time interval in that particular area. The observer scores behavior within one zone several times in a row before moving on to the next. Naturally, to obtain as representative a picture as possible of what actually is happening, each zone should be relatively small and should provide approximately the same opportunity as the others for the target behaviors to occur. It helps to sketch a map onto the recording sheet to remind observers of the location of each area (Sulzer-Azaroff & Mayer, 1986, p. 29).

PLA-Check

PLA-Check—PLanned Activity Check (Risley & Cataldo, 1973)—is a variant of another well-known time-sampling observational system, momentary time sampling. PLA-Check has been used widely in educational, day care, rest home, and other human-services settings to estimate the extent to which participants are engaged in planned activities. The observer simply counts the number of individuals who are actually engaged in the assigned activity at a particular moment. The sum is divided by the total number of individuals assigned to the activity. Observations are conducted frequently over several days. This result yields an estimate of the proportion of individuals who are on task at various prespecified times. In one study (Wilczenski et al., 1987) teachers used PLA-Check to assess patterns of performance by mainstreamed special education students and their peers. The object was to determine how best to alter the educational environment to promote high levels of productive student engagement. Similarly, managers and administrators could use PLA-Check to determine how effectively different leaders, supervisors, or teachers promoted rates of productive engagement.

Ecobehavioral Assessment

Earlier, we discussed ecobehavioral assessment in general. Here you will see an instance in which the method was used to assess the events and behavior of youngsters using a coded time sampling observation system. The youngsters were from two inner-city schools located in lower socioeconomic areas and from two suburban schools serving middle class populations. Greenwood et al. (1985) included ecological events such as the subject matter, materials or instructions given, the type of peer grouping (e.g., entire group, small groups, or individual), teacher's position, and teacher's behavior in relation to the student being observed. The first three events were recorded in the initial 10-second interval. Next, the other events plus student behavior were coded in six subsequent intervals. They found that students of lower socioeconomic status engaged in significantly less academic behavior in that their teachers "used instructional arrangements which were significantly less related to academic responding" (p. 331). The authors (Greenwood et al., 1985) point out that:

> Research using an eco-behavioral interaction approach in classroom settings offers the potential of studying students' academic achievement or failure in terms of their performance in relation to opportunities to learn, the attempts made to teach them, and the classroom learning interactions in which students engage. This approach to assessment offers enhanced precision by revealing the structure of teaching events in relation to students' behavior. Thus, questions of how instruction affects student behavior from moment to moment, or how teachers may ef-

ficiently alter instruction at specific points in time to obtain desired changes in students' performance, are more likely to be answered with this approach to assessment (p. 332).

Although a complex ecobehavioral assessment system can be a useful way to measure group behavior, you should recognize that the more variables that are observed and recorded, the less accurate the assessment tends to be (Dorsey et al., 1986). Thus, a balance needs to be achieved between the information sought and the complexity of the observational assessment instrument. An alternative would be to record different sets of variables separately. An example is using one pair of observers for social behavior, another for rates of productivity. This, however, might necessitate additional observers (because the data would need to be collected concurrently) unless mechanical means of observation also were used.

Graphing Behavioral Data

After analysts record data, the information should be graphed immediately. The shapes of the curves that are generated by plotting and connecting data points provide information about the changes taking place in the target behaviors. Has the *level* of the performance changed in the intended or the opposite direction? Has the *slope* of the curve altered to show a greater or lesser acceleration? Are the data becoming more *variable* or consistent? For instance, we would want to see the number of pages Paula writes daily; the times Lucretia hits; the intervals during which Dexter remains on-task; the percentage of times that Pearl follows instructions; how many times the supervisor approaches employees; and the number of reservations the agent books or sales he closes.

For clarity of communication, a standard format is used to construct a graph:

1. The **ordinate**, vertical, or **y-axis**, signifies the variables being measured: the fre-

quency, rate, or percentage of the behavior (see [1] in Figures 6.1, 6.2, 6.3, 6.4).

2. The **abscissa**, horizontal, or **x-axis**, indicates the time dimension, usually expressed in days, sessions, weeks (see [2] in Figures 6.1, 6.2, 6.3, and 6.4).

3. Both the ordinate and abscissa are labeled clearly with the measure on the ordinate and a time dimension on the abscissa (see [3], Figures 6.2 and 6.4).

4. Vertical broken or dashed lines indicate changes in conditions or treatment phases (see [4]).

5. Each treatment phase is clearly labeled (5).

6. Data points are discontinued between each phase (6).

7. Usually no more than one set of data is plotted on a graph; when multiple data sets are plotted, different symbols and connecting lines are used for each (see Figures 6.1a and 6.3).

8. "Dead space" is omitted to save space; such an omission is indicated by a break in the axis (see [8] in Figures 6.1a and 6.1d).

9. If many data points fall on the zero line, the ordinate extends below zero (see Figure 6.1b).

10. If data are quite variable but *still experimentally or socially significant,* the ordinate should be contracted (see Figure 6.1c). (Logarithmic scales may also be appropriate here [see Koorland & Martin, 1975]).

11. If data seem extremely stable, *obscuring a socially important change,* expand the ordinate (see Figure 6.1d).

12. Label the graph to describe briefly the data displayed. The labels should make it possible for another person to understand the

Figure 6.1 Variations in Graphic Presentation of Data

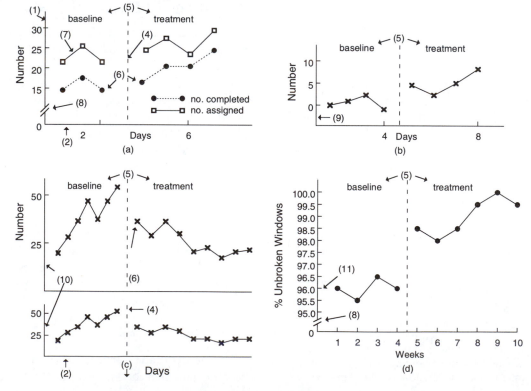

Figure 6.2 Example of a Cumulative Record

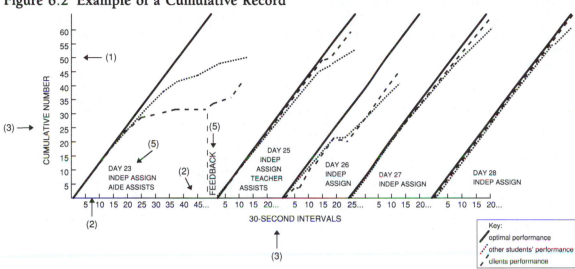

From Wilczenski, F.L. et al (1987). *Feedback to teachers on student engagement as a consultation tool. Professional School Psychology,* 2, 261–272.
Note: Solid line signifies optimal performance; open circle, the other students' cumulative intervals of being engaged; the dashed line, the subject's cumulative intervals of being engaged.

graphed data without needing additional information.

A figure also may present behaviors as *cumulative numbers,* revealing any changes in the slope of the curve. In Figure 6.2 (based on Wilczenski et al., 1987), PLA-Check data have been plotted as cumulative numbers of intervals during which a mainstreamed special student and his classmates remained engaged in classroom activities. On day 23 is the record taken prior to the teacher seeing the data. During days 25-28 she saw it regularly, intervening accordingly. Note the differences in the slope during the prefeedback baseline and treatment with feedback, with the latter showing engagement intervals accumulating at a higher rate.

Cumulative records are particularly useful for plotting acquisition data, like steps accomplished in a shaping program or links or subtasks in a chaining program. They also can display infrequently occurring events clearly. One major advantage of cumulative records is that

they indicate at a glance the total number of responses under each condition. Figure 6.2 indicates that the special education student was engaged during 38 of 60 possible intervals during the one baseline session (depicted by a dashed line) while his classmates (dotted line) were engaged for 48 of 60 intervals. Figure 6.3 displays the cumulative number of quizzes mastered by a student over the course of the semester. The cumulative record also can prove reinforcing to clients. When behaviors such as completing homework or assignments, being punctual, or attending class are graphed "yes" or "no," the downward movement on a regular graph can be discouraging. A cumulative frequency graph, such as in Figure 6.3, avoids this situation.

Adaptation

Watch people entering a room full of strangers, a child joining a new class in the middle of a school year, or patients when an unfamiliar ob-

Figure 6.3 Cumulative Progress Chart. The boxes connected by the solid line indicate the curve that students would need to follow to meet minimal requirements. The open circles connected by the dashed line illustrate one student's actual rate of mastering quizzes.

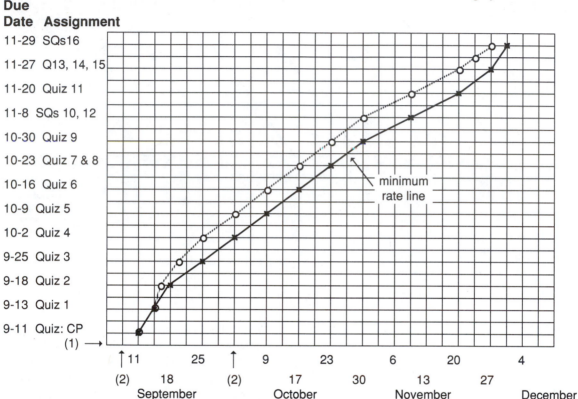

Each time you master a quiz, locate the item on the vertical axis on the graph. With your proctor or instructor, place a circle corresponding to that item on the line indicating the date on which you actually mastered the quiz. The line drawn on the graph, the minimum rate line, indicates the last week during which the quiz can be mastered for full credit. Any time your chart indicates a point above the minimum rate line, you will earn a bonus point.

server visits a ward. Is their initial behavior typical of the way they act at other times? Probably not. Ward staff may interact with patients more pleasantly than usual. When joining an unfamiliar group, newcomers often become quiet for a while and only gradually begin to interact, settling into the situation after a time and eventually falling into their typical patterns. Others cast into unusual circumstances often react similarly. Is it appropriate to assume that initial data validly represent typical performance? Not necessarily. You should not conclude that early measures taken when an observer or client en-

ters a new environment provide an accurate standard against which future change is to be measured; for reactivity (that unnatural response to being observed) must first decline. A period of **adaptation** (or *habituation*) to environmental changes may take a while, and only subsequently should the baseline phase be formally initiated. When performance is relatively stable (say, no new highs or lows for three to five days in a row) it is reasonable to conclude that reactivity has diminished sufficiently for representative behavior to be emerging.

Sometimes, the terms *reactivity* and *adap-*

Figure 6.4 Intervals in Which Dexter Was On-Task

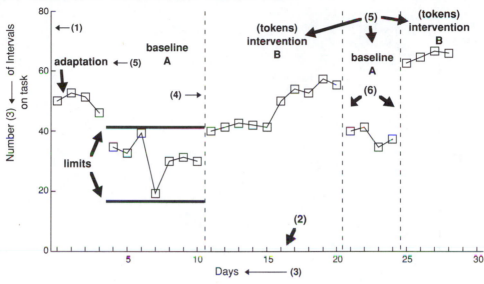

tation are confused. To help you clearly discriminate between the two, remember that reactivity is the individual's *reaction* to being observed. Adaptation is the *return* to typical performance, even though observation is ongoing—a "getting used to it." When adaptation has taken place, reactivity is no longer a threat to the validity of the data. Because applied behavior analysis programs often are carried out in the natural setting, reactivity frequently crops up. Performers need to become accustomed to the presence of strangers who observe and record data. This familiarization process usually can be accomplished quickly by locating observers inconspicuously and requesting that they refrain from interacting with anyone while observations are taking place. The reasons should become clear in our discussion of *social reinforcement* in Chapter 10.

Take a look at the number of intervals during which Dexter remained on-task, as recorded in Figure 6.4. His performance is very high during the first five days of observation. Perhaps he is reacting to the observer's presence, or possibly the novelty of having his be-

havior recorded has facilitated his performance. Such atypical functioning cannot serve as an adequate standard against which to measure change. Notice how after several days the rate drops, showing the importance of awaiting stability, before one concludes justifiably that adaptation has occurred. Only then is Dexter's performance sufficiently representative to constitute a baseline.

Baseline Measurement

When unusual fluctuations begin to diminish, adaptation probably has been accomplished and a **baseline** then can be determined. The baseline phase consists of repeatedly measuring the target behavior over several sessions, days, or even weeks, continuing until the range within which it fluctuates presumably has been identified—no new highs or lows for three days in a row (see Figure 6.4). We note that the boundary within which the number of intervals are scored on-task extends from 19 to 40. The baseline then will serve as a standard against which the effects of the intervention may be compared.

Figure 6.5 Cumulative Number of Skills Acquired

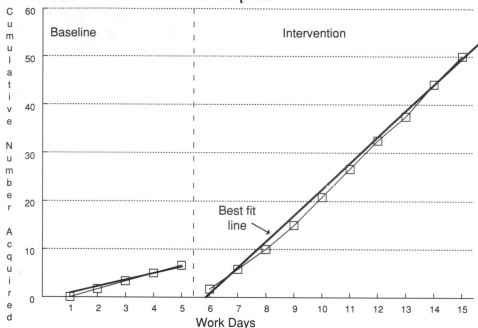

Graphing Steady State Versus Acquisition Data

The foregoing discussion is most applicable to *stable* or *steady state* behaviors—behaviors that are well established response entities, such as sitting, fighting, paying attention, and so on. Many behaviors of concern to behavior analysts, though, are of a different category: those that are being *acquired,* such as learning new or more complex skills. Were you to graph the number of subtasks or subskills mastered over time, the curve would be expected to rise instead of remaining stable, as in Figure 6.5. The way you would use your baseline data as a standard against which to assess change would be to see if the slope of the curve changes as a function of the intervention. Figure 6.5 uses a simple system to help you see the differences in the slope under the two conditions. A line is drawn that fits most closely the direction of the curve, enabling readers to see the change

in rate of acceleration under the two conditions and how variably the individual data points distribute themselves about the line. If the points jump about a whole lot during baseline, measurement probably should continue at least until a stable pattern is established.

After the intervention phase begins, baseline (nontreatment) conditions can be reintroduced periodically for a few days or sessions to see if any changes in the behavioral measure persist beyond intervention. As you will learn in greater detail in Chapter 14, this "ABAB" design (A = baseline, B = treatment) often is used to evaluate the effectiveness of an intervention (as in Figure 6.4). The consistency with which the intervention relates to successful outcomes also may be tested by collecting varying amounts of baseline data on several separate behaviors of one or a group of clients, on a single behavior among a few clients, or on the same behavior of one or a group of clients in different settings. Baselines are maintained for

Figure 6.6 Implementing Measurement Procedures

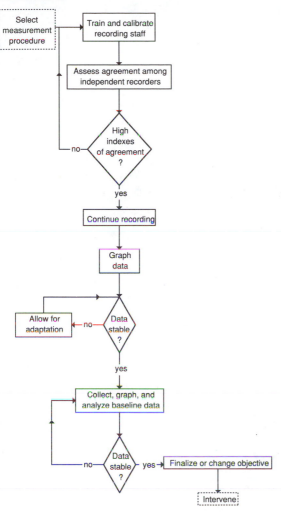

An additional advantage to the collection of baseline data is that it provides an objective measure of a behavior that may have seemed worse than it actually was. For example, suppose a very tall student were seated near the teacher. Although the student does not leave her seat more often than other students, when she does get up, it is more obvious to the teacher. Baseline data can serve as a check on the validity of the selected objective. Had the objective in this illustration been to increase the time the student remained in her seat, that objective would need to be changed. Assuming that baseline data do validate the need for intervention, however, the next step is to select an appropriate procedure—the focus of the next chapter.

Summary

This chapter discussed the implementation of observational systems and graphing of data: who records, what tools they use, and how they become trained and continue to record reliably. Once a measurement system has been demonstrated to be reliable and valid, and once adaptation has taken place, baselines are assessed. Reliable baseline data also can serve as a check on the appropriateness of the selected objective, indicating whether an objective is appropriate or should be discarded in favor of another, more fitting alternative. Assuming that the proper objective is selected, as the baseline progresses, final preparations are made for intervening by selecting an appropriate intervention strategy. Figure 6.6 summarizes the applied behavior analysis model developed so far and highlights major steps in both selecting and implementing observational systems.

different lengths of time to show that *when, and only when* the intervention occurs, does behavior dependably change. This evaluation system, called a *multiple-baseline design*, also will be treated extensively in Chapter 14.

Chapter 7

Selecting Procedures

GOALS

After completing this chapter, you should be able to:

1. Define, recognize, and give original illustrations of each of the following terms:
   a. Behavior analysis procedure
   b. Treatment or intervention phase
   c. Procedural package
   d. Stimulus
   e. Behavioral principle
   f. Contingencies (natural and managed)
   g. Contingent relation
   h. Contingency analysis (A-B-C analysis)
   i. Terminal behavior
   j. Coercion
   k. Countercontrol

2. Explain and illustrate the relations among stimuli and responses within a contingency.

3. List three factors that determine how successful a contingency manager will be in conducting a program of behavior change.

4. Describe the functions of inventories, records, checklists, and interviews in identifying contingencies.

5. Describe the purpose of gathering historical information.

6. Describe how each of the following relates to the selection and implementation of procedures:
   a. Control over contingencies
   b. The law
   c. Ethical standards
   d. Procedural effectiveness

  e. Competence of behavior analysts and contingency managers
  f. Degree of restrictiveness
  g. Positive versus aversive consequences
  h. Informed consent and behavioral contracting
  i. Voluntariness
  j. Countercontrol

7. Describe the conditions under which it is appropriate to use aversive and restrictive interventions.

8. Discuss why involving key individuals in procedural selection is important.

9. Conduct a contingency analysis.

10. Sketch a tentative program plan based on data yielded by a contingency analysis.

11. Identify and respond to three concerns frequently voiced by people who are contemplating using behavioral procedures.

Violet wants to be more outgoing. She and her counselor have agreed on a set of goals for her. She is to engage in conversation with other people by increasing the number of questions she asks and answers. Dexter's counselor, teachers, and parents have agreed that he can and should do better in school. Paula is especially eager to complete her work on time to improve her chances for promotion. The Purple Triangle company wants to improve the quality of its services and the health of its employees. A severely retarded youth, Herbie, will have to stop banging his head and poking his eyes if he is to prevent further brain and eye damage. How these goals are to be accomplished depends very much on the procedures for behavior change that are selected and how effectively they are implemented. In this chapter we shall consider methods of *selecting procedures*; in Chapter 8, we will discuss *implementing procedures* in an ethically responsible manner and monitoring their effects. Factors emphasized here will be the selection of events that function as antecedents and consequences of the target behavior, as well as some of the legal, ethical, and practical aspects of cooperative procedural selection.

Behavior Analysis Procedures

We have mentioned that a **behavior analysis procedure** is an intervention based on principles of behavior and is designed to modify behavior. We shall speak of these procedures as independent variables, because manipulating particular procedures should encourage changes in measured responses—the dependent variables. For example, the application of a given reinforcement system (perhaps Violet's awarding herself with a check mark each time she asks or answers a question) is the **independent variable**. That procedure may change behavior in some measurable fashion (for Violet, initiating a number of questions and answers). The period of time during which the

behavioral procedure is in effect is labeled the **treatment** or **intervention phase**. Multiple procedures can be used in sequence, as when Violet first gives herself checkmarks for answering questions and next for asking them; or procedures can be used in combination, as when Violet gives herself checkmarks and her teacher praises her for asking and answering questions. The terms **treatment** and **procedural package** are used to describe an intervention consisting of a combination of procedures. (The treatment is a major part of a *behavior analysis program*—the full series of steps described in the applied behavior analysis model.)

In the chapters beginning with Chapter 9 many procedures are discussed at length. The operations or activities that constitute each procedure, the rules of effective application, and the advantages and disadvantages of each are considered. The content of those chapters should serve as the basis for informed procedural selection.

A behavioral procedure consists of presenting, withholding, or removing stimuli. A **stimulus** is an object or event that functions to influence an individual's activity by exciting a sensory organ, muscle, or other physical process. Objects or events in the environment that do not have an effect on a person's behavior are not stimuli. Stimuli may derive from outside the individual (the ringing of a bell or a flash of light), or they may be internal (pressure from a full stomach, a pounding heart, or thoughts in the form of the words or images we produce for ourselves). When people sense their own responses (e.g., a pounding heart in reaction to threat or exercise), those responses can also function as stimuli. The types of stimuli that we will emphasize in this book are those that can be observed concurrently by more than one person. Internal stimuli will not be included unless they can be measured with a reliable instrument, as with a thermometer or blood pressure gauge (sphygmomanometer). Overt verbal descriptions of sensations, feelings, or thoughts that can be concurrently observed by others may be considered.

Most stimuli impact on us without a planned design (and often without our awareness), either naturally or through the mediation of others. The warmth of the sunshine; chill of the winter wind; pain of a bee sting; or a pleasant sight, sound, or aroma exemplify natural stimuli. The infant who smiles when her parents enter the room and the boss who frowns when a subordinate fails to turn in a report on time deliver social stimuli, probably without being aware of doing so. Natural physical and social stimuli continually impinge on us, influencing our subsequent performance.

Sometimes, though, stimuli are deliberately arranged for purposes of changing behavior. Supervisors, teachers, counselors, and therapists use stimuli like job descriptions, contracts, school assignments, grades, wages, exercises, and responsive listening to increase particular performances of their subordinates, students, and clients. Parents constantly do the same thing—setting rules, invoking penalties, presenting rewards—to encourage their children to behave as the parents see fit. Parenting, counseling, teaching, managing, and training are all explicitly designed to change behavior by presenting, withholding, or removing stimuli.

Applied behavior analysis (ABA) is also concerned with changing behavior but, as we have been learning, the ABA approach is more systematic and accountable than others. As its name implies, and as Baer et al. (1968) have so eloquently stated, applied behavior analysis is the

> . . . process of applying sometimes tentative principles of behavior to the improvement of specific behaviors, and simultaneously evaluating whether or not any changes noted are indeed attributable to the process of application—and if so, to what parts of that process (p. 91).

Behavioral principles have guided the way we apply procedures toward achieving predetermined goals and objectives. They provide us with suggestions for types of stimuli to select—as well as the timing, frequency, quantity, and context of their delivery or removal—to initiate and maintain change. Our evaluation techniques tell us whether those arrangements are working as hoped and can lead us toward accomplishing increasingly more effective outcomes.

Students, clients, employees, and children may manage the stimuli that influence their own behavior, just as others may who assume the responsibility for accomplishing behavior change. These managers of stimuli (or *contingencies*, as we soon shall learn) are dependent for success on:

- the appropriateness of their objectives to the behavioral repertoire of the person involved.
- a context that will support the application of the procedure(s) and the behavioral change.
- the extent to which they adhere to the guidelines for effectively implementing behavioral procedures.

What Are Contingencies?

Contingencies are *relations* between responses and the events that follow them—their *consequences*—and the events that precede or accompany them—their *antecedents*. In a sense, the consequential events depend on the responses in a probabilistic *if-then* relationship. If a person goes out (the response) into the bright sunshine, he or she will tend to feel warmth (the event)—an example of a *natural* contingency.

Natural contingencies teach us just as *managed* contingencies do. If we go out in the rain, we probably will get wet. If we feel a draft, closing the window is likely to eliminate it. If we run on the ice, we may fall. If we tease an animal, it might growl or bite.

Antecedent stimuli set the stage, conveying

a message about the likelihood that a given behavior will lead to a particular consequence. Hissing cats scratch when petted. Purring cats purr more and cuddle up when petted.

General principles of behavior apply universally. Yet specific contingencies must be arranged to be appropriate to individuals and their current circumstances, because all people are unique and their situations change from moment to moment. Genetic and experiential histories combine with current contingencies to make each person unique. For instance, Sonia's physical endowment, combined with the fact that she grew up in a northern climate and was given skating lessons, permitted her to succeed as a figure skater. For Sonia, ice-skating has become a strong reinforcer. For Juan, who moved north from the Everglades and broke his arm the first time he skated, ice skating has little appeal. Some people find any sort of attention reinforcing; others respond only to attention from particular people. Current circumstances play a role, too. Pearl has just eaten lunch and won't work if food is the reward. After an argument with her boyfriend Sandy, Paula dwells on the episode instead of writing her report.

Identifying Effective Contingencies

Successful programs of behavior change depend on the manner in which contingencies are arranged, as we shall discuss at length throughout the book. Although principles of behavior can guide the arrangement of contingencies in general, at the individual level we need to find the most ideal ways to manage contingencies for each person. This means that we need to

1. identify stimuli and occasions that encourage or discourage that person's performance.

2. determine the specific ways to arrange those contingencies.

Several informal and formal methods exist for accomplishing these purposes: inventories, reviews of records, checklists, narrative recordings analyzed for contingent relations, and the more dependable functional analyses.

Inventories, Interviews, Records, and Checklists

As a starting point, especially when extensive direct observation is impractical, you can begin exploring what consequences may have followed the behaviors of concern (targets); what antecedents may have cued them; and what recent events and personal and contextual conditions may have influenced the behaviors' rates of occurrence. Safety personnel at Purple Triangle examined their records of accidents and noted that many occurred during the summer vacation, just before holidays and during the last hour of the shift. They saw that many accidents happened when workers were not using their protective equipment, such as safety glasses or gloves, and the safety team noted that often employees who did use the equipment were teased by their fellow workers.

"When she has not had enough sleep, just before dinner, and when I have refused a request seem to be the times when Lucretia is at her worst," reports her mother. "I notice that when Herbie hits his head loudly, the staff try to soothe him. As soon as they go away, he bangs his head even harder," comments the residential team leader of Herbie's group home.

Interviews and reviews of records can yield valuable information. So can checklists and forms. Tharp and Wetzel discuss how interviews are frequently used to supplement observation: "Direct observation of target behaviors, while highly desirable, cannot be accomplished for all behaviors. Interview and questionnaire data are valuable elements in the assessment structure" (1969, p. 74). The consulting behavior analyst must, however, remember that interview data are subject to error more often than are direct observations. Having objective observational data on which to base decisions is always preferable.

Ecobehavioral assessments (Rogers-Warren & Warren, 1977), discussed earlier, also can provide useful information about promising behavioral procedures. Often, maladaptive behavior is reinforced inadvertently by providing the individual with attention, assistance, or tangible items. Capitalizing on this fact, Carr and Durand (1985) identified the reinforcers thought to be supporting their clients' maladaptive behaviors (aggression, tantrums, and self-injury) and successfully applied the reinforcers to promote the adaptive behavior of functional communication.

Gathering Historical Information About Contingencies

When behavior analysts attempt to select a procedure for behavior change, they often find it helpful to explore the history of the problem by talking to the client, parents, associates, teachers, supervisors, and other key individuals (with the permission of the client or advocate, naturally). Answers to questions such as the following can be valuable:

- What are the usual antecedents and consequences of the target behavior?
- Under what conditions has the behavior occurred most frequently?
- How does the person spend most of his or her time?
- What has been rewarding to those individuals?
- What do they avoid?
- What other events, privileges, and objects appear to function as reinforcers?
- How do these individuals obtain access to such reinforcers?
- What terminates the occurrence of the behaviors?
- Who exerts control over the consequences of their behavior?

- With what frequency or on what schedule have such negative and positive consequences occurred in the past?
- Who objects to or appreciates these behaviors?
- What reinforcers would be lost or gained if the intervention succeeded?

Answers to these questions could serve as a basis for identifying a hierarchy of potential reinforcers, punishers, and other consequences that occur naturally in the person's environment. Findings also might suggest influential factors to try applying toward achieving the desired behavioral change. Such information can be obtained simultaneously with the collection of baseline data.

Cautela and Kastenbaum (1968) and Sulzer-Azaroff and Reese (1982) have developed questionnaires that clients can use to aid them in identifying effective reinforcing consequences for themselves. In the training workshops that Aubrey Daniels and Associates conduct for performance managers, participants are provided with checklists on which they indicate many items they prefer and events and activities they and their subordinates especially enjoy. These may then be put to the test to see whether those items actually do function as reinforcers. (In the chapters on reinforcement, you will see numerous examples of reinforcers and devices for identifying them.)

Contingency Analyses

Beside their usefulness in goal selection, A-B-C analyses and scatter plots can help to identify **contingent relations**, the contingencies that may influence a person's behavior, revealing information about events that may be increasing, maintaining, expanding, restricting, prompting, interfering with, or reducing specific responses. A-B-C analyses that are used for this purpose are labeled **contingency analyses**. Contingency analyses also suggest substitute antecedents and consequences for individually tailored behavioral interventions.

Table 7.1 illustrates a contingency analysis adapted from a format developed by Goodwin (1969). The information usually is collected through *both* direct observation and interviews with significant others and/or the client. The top half of Table 7.1 is used to specify a particular problem behavior (B) and to approximate its frequency (the second column), the incidents immediately preceding it (A—antecedents, first column), and its consequences (C—third column). The lower half of Table 7.1 uses the same A-B-C analysis as a way to specify goal behavior. If the goal behavior has not occurred, only items 6 and 7 in the third column can be answered. Usually, though, the goal behavior has been observed. Observations of its antecedents and consequences often can help explain some of the reasons the goal behavior is not occurring at the preferred rate and may be useful for planning a subsequent treatment strategy.

The differences in the antecedents of the problem and of goal behaviors illustrated in numbers 2, 3, and 5 and the differences in consequences in number 1 in Table 7.1 are noteworthy. Items 5–7 under the heading General Consequences in the third column are designed to identify consequences (possible reinforcers, punishers, and the like) that will affect the probability of future behavior. Here we notice that the unwanted behaviors lead to immediate positive attention from the teacher and other children. By contrast, the desired goal behavior results in the child's being ignored by the teacher and other children, and reinforcement for completion of work is delayed—inefficient contingencies. No wonder this student disrupts frequently!

Such forms as the one just described have been found helpful not only by educators and clinicians but are also valuable tools for business managers (Daniels, 1989) and consultants to parents. Johnson and Katz (1973) have noted

that training parents to define and record their children's behavior objectively, including correlated antecedent and consequent events, may be clinically useful. Parents can continue to apply the observational skills they have acquired following termination of professional intervention. In addition, such parental observations may facilitate positive contacts between parents and their children because they require that the parent focus not only on the irritating but also on the pleasing conduct of the child.

Selecting Procedural Strategies

A-B-C's, ecobehavioral analyses, and historical investigations via interviews and checklists help us to identify contingencies for managing the behavior of specific persons. Other sources of information are sequence analyses, charts, records, and similar case material. After information has been gathered, the most appropriate procedures must be selected. Our purpose in this section is to guide behavior analysts toward making ethically responsible—as well as legally and functionally sound—selections. We shall consider such factors as **contingency control**, laws, evidence of effectiveness with specific populations, the competence of the behavior analyst and contingency manager, restrictive conditions, environmental support, accountability, flexibility, informed consent, voluntariness, and countercontrol.

Controlling Contingencies

Essential to the success of any behavioral program is the ability of the contingency manager to do what the name implies: manage the contingencies. You can only manage contingencies when they are or can be brought under your **control**. Harry would like to give the members of the claims department a bonus whenever they meet their goals for three months, but the union negotiates all matters related to com-

Table 7.1 Contingency Analysis Chart (The ABC's of Behavior Analysis)

Present *Antecedents* of Problem Behavior (A)	Problem *Behavior* (B): Observable Problem Behavior and Approximate Frequency or Duration of Occurrence	Present *Consequences* of Problem Behavior (C)
1. Activity 　(*All subject matter*) 2. Location of client 　(*Rear of classroom*) 3. Activity of parent or teacher 　(*Working at desk or with other students*) 4. Activity of others 　(*Students and children working on assignments*) 5. At what time of day does the behavior occur most frequently: math class, meal time, ten minutes into lesson, or the like. 　(*Ten minutes into assignments*) 6. Previous experience of the client with activities 　(*Successful completion*) 7. Other _____	Waving hands in front of face and over head while grunting audibly to entire class and teacher. On the average, eight times a day.	1. How do you respond? 　(*Teacher goes to child and talks with him "to calm him down"*) 2. How do others respond? 　(*Students stop work temporarily, then go back to work; generally they ignore it*) 3. What progress is made on the activity or assigned task? 　(*Completion once student is calmed down*) 4. Other _____

Present *Antecedents* of Goal Behavior (A)	Goal *Behavior* (B): In Operational Terms, Giving Approximate Frequency or Duration of Occurrence	Present *Consequences* of Goal Behavior (C)
1. Activity 　(*All*) 2. Location of client 　(*Near teacher's desk*) 3. Activity of parent or teacher 　(*At desk or working with student*) 4. Activity of others 　(*Working on assignments*) 5. At what time of day does the behavior occur most frequently: math class, meal time, ten minutes into lesson, and so on. 　(*Any time*) 6. Previous experience of the client with activity 　(*Success*) 7. Other _____ _____ _____	Complete assignment without waving of hands and grunts. On the average, two full days a week.	1. How do you respond? 　(*Teacher does not*) 2. How do others respond? 　(*No response*) 3. What happens to the activity or assigned task? 　(*Completed*) 4. Other _____ **General Consequences** 5. What does client do when given a free choice (companions, location, activity)? 　(*Reads adventure books alone at table*) 6. What has worked or is working to motivate or reinforce client's behavior? 　(*Praise, pats on shoulder*) 7. What has worked to stop behavior? 　(*A firm "Stop that!"*)

pensation and refuses to permit any deviation from the contract. Despite Ms. Hydra Carbon's efforts to ignore Clyde's use of profanity, the other students gasp and her fellow teachers scold when they hear him swear. Jocelyn plans to remain on her diet by not bringing sweets into the house. Yet when Aunt Minerva drops in for one of her regular visits, she always brings along a box of Jocelyn's favorite pastries or chocolates.

In each of these cases, contingencies are in the hands of someone else. Alternative procedures will have to be selected to ensure success.

Behavior Analysis, Procedural Selection, and the Law

As the systematic application of procedures for behavior change becomes more widespread, litigation keeps pace. Legal challenges often are a healthy sign because they indicate increasing public awareness that clients' rights deserve to be protected. Authority to determine arbitrarily the fate of individuals should not be delegated to any elite group: psychiatrists, correctional officers, managers, supervisors, teachers, school and institutional administrators, or behavior analysts.

Judicial rulings ensure that people with severe disabilities and deficiencies will receive constitutional protection along with all others. For example, a landmark case, *Wyatt* v. *Stickney* (1972), decreed that institutionalized individuals should have private space, not be segregated from the opposite sex, be able to wear their own clothing, not be unnecessarily restricted in their movements, not be deprived in specific ways, and be able to enjoy other "constitutionally guaranteed" rights. Both at the federal and state levels, laws regulating the conduct of human services continually are being decided. It is the responsibility of behavior analysts, as of all other human-services and management personnel, to know the law as it applies to their practice (see Schwitzgebel,

1971; Budd & Baer, 1976; Martin, 1974; Wexler, 1973).

Occasionally the popular press has publicized litigation involving **behavior modification**. Perhaps clearly delineated systematic behavior-change programs are, by their nature, more discernible targets than those methods of intervention that do not spell out their goals and procedures so precisely. Nevertheless, as with other styles of intervention, behavior analytic practice is not immune from errors of omission and commission, and all practitioners need to guard against them.

According to Martin (1974), "the most important reason 'behavior modification' is so much under attack is that the broad label encompasses many techniques that are potentially dangerous, unwarranted and which probably should be inhibited" (p. 3). Included in Martin's list of "behavior modification" techniques are psychosurgery, chemotherapy, neuropharmacology, electroconvulsive treatments, techniques labeled by laymen as "brainwashing," behavioral instrumentation such as implanted electrodes, and genetic screening and manipulation. Setting aside arguments concerning whether such methods are "behavior modification" procedures (we think not) and whether they are effective, physical treatment requires supervision by medical practitioners. Our concern here is with *ethically responsible* behavioral procedures that:

- are based upon the laws of behavior.
- use scientific methods of evaluation.
- improve the quality of peoples' lives and society by helping those persons to enhance their repertoires of constructive and reinforcing behavioral options.

Professional Ethical Standards

Along with the Association for Behavior Analysis (ABA) and regional and local behavior analytic and therapeutic organizations, two of the main professional groups with which behavior analysts have tended to affiliate are the American Psychological Association (APA), especially Division 25—The Division of Experimental Analysis of Behavior—and the Association for Advancement of Behavior Therapy (AABT). The APA (1981) has adopted codes of ethics to which all members are to adhere, plus a set of principles for doing research with humans (1982). AABT handles ethical issues by posing a set of questions, listed in Figure 7.1, that behavior therapists should consider before embarking on a program of intervention. In the interest of consumer protection, all those offering psychological or counseling services, regardless of theoretical orientation, should pose those questions to themselves and be prepared to defend any responses answered in the negative.

Evidence of Procedural Effectiveness

A fundamental guideline for the selection of specific behavior analytic procedures is that they have demonstrated their effectiveness with populations and conditions similar to those of the client. The best way to identify such procedures is to keep abreast of the research literature. The references cited in this book contain reports of many new and refined behavior-change methods. (As you read, you will rapidly learn enough about this subject to comprehend the literature.) As you select given procedures, attend particularly closely to fundamental aspects of method, especially descriptions of subjects, settings, conditions, and staffing, as well as details of the procedural operations. The best tactic is to work under the supervision of or, at least, consult experts and advisory board members before you proceed.

Competence of the Behavior Analyst and Contingency Manager

Behavior analysts should demonstrate their competence in applying a procedure before implementing it.[1] Preferably this competence has been acquired during the apprenticeship period, and/or during in-service training (Baer & Bushell, 1981). For instance, a token economy has many subtle intricacies (see Ayllon & Azrin, 1968). A decision to use a token economy to improve Dexter's academic performance should be undertaken only if the behavior analyst has received formal training *and* supervised practice in using token economies or at least is well informed on the topic.[2] (Of course, we recognize that even after extensive preservice training, not all behavior analysts will have received supervised training for every procedure. Possible alternatives include consultation, intensive study of materials like those presented in this book, observation, filmed instruction, and field-tested program packages [e.g., Risley, 1975]).

This point is also extremely important for the contingency managers who conduct the program on a day-to-day basis, because success depends on implementing procedures precisely. These change agents *must be adequately trained to a predetermined criterion level of performance and must be regularly supervised.* The change agents' training also must extend beyond the instructional or conceptual and should emphasize supervised skill training. Studies repeatedly demonstrate that training alone often is insufficient to guarantee that a procedure will be implemented properly (Cossairt, Hall, & Hopkins, 1973; Maher, 1981/1982; Roffers, Cooper, & Sultanoff, 1988; and others). Consistent supervised feedback; praise; and perhaps other contingency arrangements, like rewards for compliance with procedural instructions, must be programmed. For instance, counselors who received supervised training and feedback demonstrated superior skills and obtained higher client outcome ratings than those who did not receive such training (Roffers et al., 1988). The same principles of behavior

---

[1] See the book by Sulzer-Azaroff and Reese (1982, pp. 401–406) for a list of competencies for applied behavior analysts. Eubanks et al. (1990) have identified a set of behavioral competency requirements for organizational development consultants.

[2] Shapiro and Lentz (1985) have found that practitioners report they are less likely to use a procedure with which they have not received supervised training.

Figure 7.1 AABT Ethical Questions

A. Have the goals of treatment been adequately considered?
   1. To ensure that the goals are explicit, are they written?
   2. Has the client's understanding of the goals been ensured by having the client restate them orally or in writing?
   3. Have the therapist and client agreed on the goals of therapy?
   4. Will serving the client's interests be contrary to the interests of other persons?
   5. Will serving the client's immediate interests be contrary to the client's long term interest?

B. Has the choice of treatment methods been adequately considered?
   1. Does the published literature show the procedure to be the best one available for that problem?
   2. If no literature exists regarding the treatment method, is the method consistent with generally accepted practice?
   3. Has the client been told of alternative procedures that might be preferred by the client on the basis of significant differences in discomfort, treatment time, cost, or degree of demonstrated effectiveness?
   4. If a treatment procedure is publicly, legally, or professionally controversial, has formal professional consultation been obtained, has the reaction of the affected segment of the public been adequately considered, and have the alternative treatment methods been more closely reexamined and reconsidered?

C. Is the client's participation voluntary?
   1. Have possible sources of coercion of the client's participation been considered?
   2. If treatment is legally mandated, has the available range of treatments and therapists been offered?
   3. Can the client withdraw from treatment without a penalty or financial loss that exceeds actual clinical costs?

D. When another person or an agency is empowered to arrange for therapy, have the interests of the subordinated client been sufficiently considered?
   1. Has the subordinated client been informed of the treatment objectives and participated in the choice of treatment procedures?
   2. Where the subordinated client's competence to decide is limited, has the client as well as the guardian participated in the treatment discussions to the extent that the client's abilities permit?
   3. If the interests of the subordinated person and the superordinate persons or agency conflict, have attempts been made to reduce the conflict by dealing with both interests?

E. Has the adequacy of treatment been evaluated?
   1. Have quantitative measures of the problem and its progress been obtained?
   2. Have the measures of the problem and its progress been made available to the client during treatment?

F. Has the confidentiality of the treatment relationship been protected?
   1. Has the client been told who has access to the records?
   2. Are records available only to authorized persons?

G. Does the therapist refer the clients to other therapists when necessary?
   1. If treatment is unsuccessful, is the client referred to other therapists?
   2. Has the client been told that if dissatisfied with the treatment, referral will be made?

H. Is the therapist qualified to provide treatment?
   1. Has the therapist had training or experience in treating problems like the client's?
   2. If deficits exist in the therapist's qualifications, has the client been informed?
   3. If the therapist is not adequately qualified, is the client referred to other therapists, or has supervision by a qualified therapist been provided? Is the client informed of the supervisory relation?
   4. If the treatment is administered by mediators, have the mediators been adequately supervised by a qualified therapist?

Source: Association for Advancement of Behavior Therapy, 1977, pp. 763–764. Reprinted with permission.

apply to increasing, teaching, and maintaining staff behavior as the principles applied to accomplishing client change.

Active supervision is especially important when change agents consider using unprecedented or aversive procedures. Also, unusual and punitive procedures should be approved by clients or their advocates, supervisors, and public representatives. The procedures should reflect a balance between maximum effectiveness and minimum intrusiveness; that is, they should match natural or standard operating procedure as closely as possible. If approval, adequate supervision, and objective monitoring are not feasible, select an alternative. Lovaas and Favell's (1987) comments about using aversive procedures are especially apt:

> . . . rigorous and responsive systems of data review and staff feedback must be in place, and all staff must be equipped to participate in evaluating these data and reaching sound decisions about treatment. In many settings, staff do not have such training or properly supervised experience in measurement, analysis, or clinical use of data, and thus should not employ aversive procedures (p. 316).

Ultimately, though, determining whether a behavior analyst is competent to conduct a particular program depends on objective evidence. We can feel most comfortable about a person's continuing a given practice when data demonstrate that practice's effectiveness and consumers express their satisfaction with its results.

Degree of Restrictiveness

State and federal laws instigated by such court cases as *Wyatt* v. *Stickney* (1972) stipulate that treatment and education should be conducted under the least restrictive conditions possible. Even though monitoring behavior or implementing contingency arrangements may be much simpler in a closed environment, such an environment is probably not ethically defensi-

ble. Similarly, confining school children to isolated or segregated areas is not acceptable unless no other alternatives exist. Given the choice between a procedure that can work only in a restricted setting and one that can work in a mainstreamed environment, the behavior analyst should choose the latter. Although some handicapped youngsters may have a difficult time becoming socially accepted by their nonhandicapped peers (Ray, 1985; Sabornie, 1985), research on mainstreaming indicates that segregation further delays youngsters socially and academically (de Noronha & de Noronha, 1984; Kluwin & Moores, 1985). Were Lucretia to be confined to a room by herself with her own personal change agent, her behavior might come rapidly under control. But a procedure incorporated into her daily routine is more ethically defensible, and, though it may work more slowly, the results will be more readily transferable and easily maintained.

Positiveness Versus Aversiveness

Positive reinforcement is integral to most behavioral procedures, whereas punishment, the application of aversive stimuli, only occasionally is included. Sometimes positive or aversive stimuli are withheld or removed. Each operation defines a different procedure that will be described subsequently in detail. From a functional point of view, each operation has advantages and disadvantages. Other factors being equal, positive approaches are preferable to negative or aversive ones. To increase Dexter's academic productivity, his teacher could scold him or ask him to leave the room whenever he daydreamed; or she could reward him with access to a favorite activity when his academic output improves. Both procedures would likely serve the goal, but the latter is more defensible ethically and, in the long run, functionally as well.

Unfortunately, certain kinds of behavior are extremely resistant to modification by exclusively positive means. If a behavioral goal is considered to be of critical importance to the health or survival of clients or those to whom they relate, temporarily resorting to aversive procedures may be necessary. Be aware, however, that legal restrictions may limit the use of aversive procedures like timeout (*Morales v. Turman*, 1973), restraint (*Wyatt* v. *Stickney*, 1972), and electric shock (*Wyatt* v. *Stickney*, 1972). Roos has argued, however:

> Aversive conditioning has been used primarily to eliminate (or decelerate) behavior which is highly debilitating to the individual and/or his environment. There is now considerable evidence that judicious application of aversive conditioning can be dramatically successful in suppressing long-standing highly incapacitating behaviors (Wolf, Risley, & Mees, 1964; Lovaas, Freitag, Gold, & Kassorla, 1965; Tate & Baroff, 1966; Bucher & Lovaas, 1968). It can be argued, therefore, that selective application of aversive conditioning can be a highly humanitarian procedure. It can free individuals from crippling behavior, enabling them to interact more meaningfully with their environment and thereby enhancing their opportunities to develop their human qualities (1972, p. 146).

What might be the ultimate outcome were Lucretia to continue her aggression against others or Herbie to continue to bang his head intensely against the wall or poke himself in his eyes? Perhaps efforts to block reinforcers for the maladaptive behavior and supply those same reinforcers and others for its adaptive alternative were not successful. In such circumstances, temporarily supplementing reinforcement with an aversive contingency could reasonably be defended on the grounds that children's safety and well-being were being endangered. Paired with reinforcement of adaptive alternative behaviors, punishment in the form of a reprimand or a more intensive stimulus may effectively solve the problem, as we shall see in the section on reducing unwanted behavior.

Once the rate of aggression has been substantially reduced, it should be possible to switch gradually back to reinforcement alone to keep the maladaptive behavior at bay. We advocate that, when an intense, intrusive, unusual, or exotic aversive procedure is under consideration, the following safeguards should be in place:

- informed consent should be obtained
- the human-rights committee should be consulted
- the procedure should be supervised by a professional with demonstrated competence in the safe and responsible application of the procedure
- the target behavior, and relevant collateral behaviors, should be monitored to determine the direct and side effects of the procedure
- at the outset, a reasonable limit should be set on the length of time the procedure is allowed to remain in effect without demonstrable improvement
- the program should include positive reinforcement of desirable behaviors, as well as a mechanism for discontinuing the aversive procedure as soon as feasible.

Lovaas and Favell (1987) summarize their discussion about the use of aversive and restrictive interventions similarly:

> Such techniques are justified only when their effects are rigorously evaluated, caregivers are fully trained and adequately supervised in all dimensions of habilitative services, when a meaningful functional analysis of the child's problem has been conducted, alternative and benign treatments have been considered and are in place, parents and others are fully informed, and there is general agreement that the means justify the ends. The importance of these requirements is matched by the need for increased and refined research in the treatment of behavior disorders, which may one day obviate the need for aversive and restrictive procedures altogether (p. 324).

As you can see, there are many arguments and counterarguments about using aversive procedures. We shall pursue this discussion further in Section IV, which covers reducing unwanted behavior.

Including Key Individuals in Procedural Selection

Many of the conflicts that have arisen out of the application of particular procedures often could have been avoided had key people been involved in selecting them: the client, the contingency manager, and significant others.

Involving the client. Given the large array of available potential procedures, clients may have the option of selecting those to their liking. The behavior analyst assembles the pool of promising procedures for accomplishing the mutually determined goals and discusses with the client (or when appropriate the advocate, parents, or caregivers) the pros and cons of each: implementation methods, speed and durability of effectiveness, risks, positive side effects, and other qualities that we shall discuss later. As trained professionals, behavior analysts should be able to provide guidance in selection. In fact, the Wyatt decision (1972) expressly states that patients have the right not to be submitted to aversive conditioning without "their express and informed consent after consultation with counsel or interested party of the patient's choice" (*Wyatt* v. *Stickney*, 1972).

Several investigators concur about the need to *confer with the client about the contingencies to be used in the program.* Lovitt (1969) and Lovitt and Curtiss (1969) found that children exhibited higher rates of academic behavior (studying, problem solving, and so on) when they were allowed to choose their own reinforcers than when the teacher chose them— even when the reinforcers were identical. Fixsen, Phillips, and Wolf (1973) also reported that, when predelinquents were given complete responsibility for determining the conse-

quences of rule violations, they participated more in the discussion of consequences and reported more of the rule violations than when teachers or parents determined the consequences. Similarly, including workers in the development of pay incentive plans improved their attendance more rapidly than when a similar plan was imposed on workers (Lawler & Hackman, 1969; Scheflen, Lawler, & Hackman, 1971). Besides the ethical aspects, involving clients in procedural selection, therefore, can be advantageous in a variety of ways.

Involving the contingency manager. Unless the client is conducting a self-management program (and self-management procedures are increasingly being used), the people who manage the contingencies must also participate in selecting procedures. Consistent application is then more likely. Contingency managers— teachers, supervisors, counselors, psychologists, parents, or institutional staff members— are aware of the limitations posed by their jobs and are therefore better able to predict whether they will have the time and resources to implement the program.

Involving significant others. As with goal selection, and for reasons similar to those presented in Chapter 3, selection of procedures should include consultation with, and the informed consent of, other people who might be involved directly or indirectly. For example, even when parents are not themselves serving as contingency managers, their informed consent is usually necessary, as is consent from the administrative staff and the human rights committee. Spouses, close friends, relatives, coworkers, and others also may be included when they stand to substantially profit or suffer from the impact of the change procedure. The behavioral contract is probably the best vehicle for recording such consent. If the goal and procedure, anticipated outcomes, and possible benefits and risks are spelled out in detail and

Figure 7.2 Behavioral Contract

NAME: Bill C.

PROBLEM: Excessive period and full-day truancy.

BACKGROUND: Bill has consistently missed part or all of his school day for the past year and one quarter. He has been counseled regarding his truancy, his mother has been contacted, and he has been somewhat restricted at home. His mother seemed to be unable to help him because of her working hours.

BEHAVIORAL IMPLEMENTATION: (1) Bill will attend all classes he is scheduled into every day. (2) Bill will have each of his teachers initial an attendance card at the end of each class period. (3) Bill will have his counselor initial his attendance card at the end of each school day. (4) Bill will exchange the completed attendance card with his mother in accordance with the reward schedule stated below. (5) Bill will chart the cumulative frequency of period attendance on a graph in the counselor's office at the end of each school day. (6) Bill will attend a group rap session once each week.

REWARD SCHEDULE: Successful completion of the above implementation will be rewarded in the following manner:

    1. Bill will exchange the signed attendance card with his mother and will receive ten cents (10¢) for each class attended. This money will be saved for a trip to Disneyland on December 31st. (Note: Bill can hold the money himself or have his mother hold it for him.)

    2. Bill will be allowed to go to Disneyland on December 31st for the New Year's Eve party.

    When school resumes in January, a conference will be held to determine the need for a new contract.

SIGNATURE AND AGREEMENT STATEMENTS:

I agree to follow the provisions of the contract and to dispense the rewards only if the provisions of the contract are met.

_____

                                   Mrs. C.

I agree to follow the provisions of this contract.

_____

                                   Bill C.

I agree to monitor this contract and to make a verbal progress report to Bill and his mother at the end of each week.

_____

                                   Counselor

Source: *Personnel and Guidance Journal, 52,* 3 (1974). Reprinted with permission.

approved ahead of time, all people involved are accorded maximum protection.

Contracting for Selection of Procedures

The behavioral contract, as we have noted previously in Chapter 3, explicitly states the goal, or **terminal behavior**. In addition, the contingencies to be applied can be stipulated in the contract in a manner *mutually* acceptable to the client, contingency manager, staff, parents, significant others, and behavior analyst. For example, that Dexter must stop harassing his brothers has been mutually agreed. A contract is drawn up. The consequences of specific acts are stipulated: His brothers will ignore him for five minutes if he does harass them; his parents will lend him the car if the brothers report no harassing for two days in a row; and so on.

When you select contingencies to include in a contract, use positive and avoid negative or aversive contingencies whenever possible. In addition to the ethical aspects, use of aversive contingencies presents a number of associated problems, as you will discover later. Additionally, they often appear to add nothing to the effectiveness of behavioral contracts. For example, Kidd and Sandargas (1988) found that the "inclusion of a negative component was not necessary and that use of a positive component alone was sufficient to maintain high levels of completion and accuracy in daily math assignments" (p. 118).

Brooks (1974) reported a successful use of contingency contracts with junior high school truants. An example of one of the contracts that he used is shown in Figure 7.2. According to the author,

> Bill did not miss one class for three full weeks, and Mrs. C. followed through on her part of the contract. At the end of the three-week period a conference was held, and Bill decided that he thought he could handle full-time attendance. It was mutually decided by Bill and the counselor that for a three-week period the attendance card previously filled out daily need be filled out only on Friday to cover the entire school week. Bill felt that his presenting the completed card to his mother was sufficient reward. After three weeks Bill was maintaining full attendance, so his behavior modification program was discontinued (1974, pp. 318–319).

Similar contracts were illustrated by Sulzer-Azaroff and Reese (1982) for an adult patient in a state institution (see Figure 7.3) and for a high school student (see Figure 7.4).

Another, simpler contract, illustrated in Figure 7.5 (McGookin and colleagues, 1974), spells out the terms on the front of a card and requires the teachers' signature. On the reverse side, a running record is kept of the progress toward the goal and the reinforcers obtained.

In Chapter 8, we discuss the specifics of behavioral contracting in greater detail and of-fer a set of guidelines for negotiating successful contracts.

Voluntariness Versus Coercion

In addition to informed consent, behavioral contracts usually incorporate the property of *voluntariness*. However, when a behavior analyst speaks of "voluntariness," a conceptual problem may arise: *Webster's New Collegiate Dictionary* defines *voluntary* as "1. Proceeding from the will or from one's own choice or full consent. 2. Unconstrained by interference; self-impelled; freely given, done, etc." (1949, p. 957). Other definitions include nonoperational words like *intent* and *will*. Those definitions are not satisfactory, because as the procedural sections of this book demonstrate repeatedly, all our acts are subject to rewards and constraints. Some are obvious, some subtle: salaries, material gifts, awards, bonuses, eye contact, nods of approval, agreement from some, disagreement from others, privileges, particular activities, observing other people being rewarded, and an endless array of others. The behaviorist argues that a response persists only when it produces at least occasional reinforcement (discussed elsewhere in detail).

Similarly, threats and negative consequences, including withholding, withdrawing, or eliminating reinforcement, also continually operate on behavior. Some constraints are obvious: Speeding over 90 miles an hour may lead to a ticket, arrest, or death on the highway; not fulfilling job responsibilities can lead to dismissal; failing to complete assignments often results in poor grades. Others are far more subtle: inattention to uninteresting conversation; a slight shoulder shrug or a lack of agreement in response to a stated opinion. How long would any of us continue studying if we were not rewarded with grades, increased job options, salary increments, approval from important people in our lives and ourselves, or at least interesting or potentially useful material? Don't

Figure 7.3 Contract in a State Institution

Client: _Jim_	Work Supervisor: _Mrs. Swenson_
Advocate: _Mike Monahan_	Building Supervisor: _Mr. Taylor_
	Psychologist: _Dr. Farmer_

Effective Dates: _Apr. 10_ to _Apr. 24_

Long-term goals: Placement in supervised community residence

Short-term goals: Hold down full-time job within institution; complete one housekeeping job in residence building each day; reduce number of fights and arguments with staff and other residents; keep financial records.

Responsibilities	Positive Ratings	Points/Day
Job: Jim will arrive at work on time.		
Give his job-evaluation form to Mrs. Swenson; Earn positive ratings for attendance, punctuality, and job performance as specified on evaluation form and rated by Mrs. Swenson.	90–100% 80–89 70–79	10 5 2
Residence Building Jim will give his job-evaluation form to Mr. Taylor by 5:30 P.M. each work day;		1
Perform housekeeping job as specified;		0–5
Keep daily records of points earned and spent, and check them with Mr. Taylor		2
Bonus No reported fights or arguments with residents or staff (any disagreement to be settled by Dr. Farmer)		10
Perfect day: 10 job pts; 8 building pts; no fights or arguments		20

Penalty

Fighting or verbal abuse or running away:	loss of 5 pts. and evening's social activities
Argument continuing after a warning:	loss of 1 pt. and evening's social activities
(Points to be exchanged for privileges at the standard rate.)	

_____ Client	_____ Work Supervisor
_____ Advocate	_____ Building Supervisor
	_____ Psychologist

This contract will be reviewed: _April 23_

Source: Based on Sulzer-Azaroff & Reese (1982, p. 23). Reprinted with permission.

Figure 7.4 Contract with a High School Student

Client: _David Jones_   Mother: _Mrs. Jones_
Counselor: _Mrs. Deneau_   Math Teacher: _Mr. Callaway_

Effective Dates: _Feb. 21_ to _Feb. 28_

GOALS
Long-term: _David will graduate from high school_
Short-term: _David will complete his homework assignments in math and earn a grade of C (or better) in the course_

Responsibility (Who, What, When, How well)	Privileges (Who, What, When, How much)
1. David will turn in his completed math assignment to Mr. Callaway at the beginning of class.	David will be excused from the last period of the day (study hall) so he can go to work 1 hour early.
2. Mr. Callaway will correct David's homework and inform Mrs. Deneau of his grade by 1 pm each day.	Mrs. Deneau will thank Mr. Callaway and she will keep all graphs of David's progress.
3. (If the homework does not earn a grade of at least C, this contract will be revised next week.)	

BONUS
If all assignments are turned in for the week, and all are graded C or better, David can leave for work 2 hours early on Friday.

PENALTY
none

Who will monitor the behavior: _Mr. Callaway and Mrs. Deneau_
What records will be kept? _Homework assignments: number turned in and grade_
Who will be responsible for the delivery of reinforcers, privileges? _Mrs. Deneau_

Signed: _David Jones_ Date: _Feb. 17_   _Thomas W. Callaway_ Date: _2/17_
        client   teacher

        Jeanne C. Deneau Date: _Feb. 17_ _Marilyn S. Jones_ Date: _Feb. 18_
        counselor   mother

This contract will be reviewed (date) _Feb. 28_

Source: Based on Sulzer-Azaroff & Reese (1982, p. 22). Reprinted with permission.

Figure 7.5 Sample Contract and Record Form

Goal-Completion Card

Name: *Michael*   **Card:** *I*   **Date:** *3/27/77*

Student Goal: Michael is working on getting along with others.
For each recess without fighting he will receive 10 points to be traded in for 10 minutes of free reading in class.

Teacher	Subject or Behavior	Points	Mon. Yes	Mon. No	Tue. Yes	Tue. No	Wed. Yes	Wed. No	Thurs. Yes	Thurs. No	Fri. Yes	Fri. No
1. *10:00*	*Recess*	*10*	*MJB*		*MJB*							
2. *11:30*	*Recess*	*10*	*MJB*									
3. *1:15*	*Recess*	*10*			*MJB*							
4.												
5.												
6.												
7.												
8.												
9.												
10.												

Front

Assignment	Date	Teacher Initial	Time Earned	Time Left	Time Ret.	Permission to Go/ Teacher Initial	Time Spent	Balance of Time
getting along	*3/27*	*MJB*	*20*				*20*	*0*
	3/28	*MJB*	*10*					*10*

Back

we avoid negative consequences—poverty, loss of prestige, social derision—by remaining in a job, attending school, maintaining a household, and so on? Numerous reinforcers and punishers have been or remain in operation in everyone's lives. Total voluntariness, from the behavioristic point of view, is a myth; positive and negative constraints are never totally absent.

In *Beyond Freedom and Dignity* (1971) B. F. Skinner has encouraged the public to recognize and acknowledge that both obvious and subtle positive and aversive environmental events do affect our behavior. This realization should prompt society and its members to seek ways to maximize positive outcomes through positive means.

This concept of voluntariness is the most suitable for behavior analysts concerned with selecting both goals and procedures ethically. The term is defined to acknowledge the role of past and present events, along with community members' concurrence that a procedure has been "voluntarily" accepted by the client(s) or those representing the client's best interest. Voluntariness can be conceptualized more clearly as the client's voicing agreement with the terms of the behavior-change program in the absence of coercion.

What is **coercion**? Its two forms are oppressive force and disproportionately powerful incentives. If a behavior serves to avoid the former or produce the latter, we cannot speak of voluntariness. Let us consider a couple of examples.

Willie comes to class, takes out his material rapidly, and promptly begins to produce work of excellent quality. When the teacher requests assistance with an exhibit, Willie offers to participate.

First, consider some aspects of Willie's reinforcement history: Willie has received A's for working well in the past. His girlfriend admires his seriousness. His teacher smiles and nods at him from time to time as he works on his assignment and gestures appreciatively when he

offers to participate. Willie looks at his work and sees that he has learned to solve a challenging problem: "That was a tough one, but I did it." Is Willie's performance voluntary? Now suppose that his dad had promised him a motorcycle, car, or trip to Europe if he did well in his studies. Would Willie's behavior still be voluntary?

On the other hand, Willie may have experienced frowns, poor grades, and ridicule from his friends for poor performance in the past. Maybe his dad denied him the use of the car for the remainder of the year if his grades did not improve. Would any of those threatened negative consequences mean that Willie's classroom performance is not voluntary?

Voluntariness is not an absolute but a condition that falls within a range on each of several continua. In Figure 7.6 just how voluntary is Linus's choice not to pelt Lucy with a snowball? Therefore, to meet the ethical requirements for voluntary goal selection, your best approach is to identify clearly any reinforcers and aversive consequences and minimize any that are inordinately powerful.

Figure 7.7 depicts the interaction of factors related to voluntariness. Coercion becomes more pronounced as the power of reinforcers and punishers increases and client involvement with goal selection lessens. In Chapter 8, you will learn how contracting, behavioral report cards, and self-management strategies also help to avoid coerciveness.

Countercontrol

Related to informed consent and involvement in goal and procedure selection is providing people with skills for **countercontrol**: control or influence exerted by the client over the behavior of the contingency manager, with or without the client's awareness. Information about behavior analysis is being disseminated more and more widely through textbooks, workshops, articles, courses, the press, televi-

Figure 7.6 Voluntary Behavior Change?

© 1976 Reprinted by permission of United Feature Syndicate, Inc.

Figure 7.7 Voluntary Goal Specification. The more clients are involved in the selection of goals that yield short- and long-term benefits, the greater the voluntariness. The further out on the limb of aversives and reinforcers, the greater the coercion. Voluntariness almost breaks off completely as goals are selected by others and powerful aversives prevail.

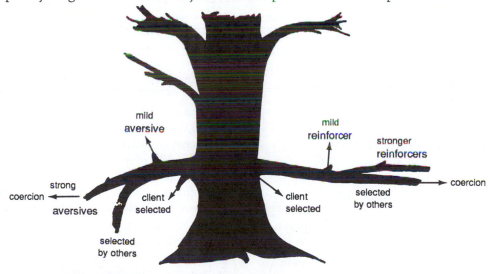

sion "talk shows," and other sources. Provided that clients *control* sufficient contingencies for the contingency manager (e.g., their improved behavior and approval are reinforcing for the manager) such information should provide individuals with the techniques for resisting unwanted controls. As new methods of managing

behavior are developed and communicated, people should become increasingly more capable of countering exploitation.

. . . Just as a professional in behavior modification may use his understanding of behavioral principles in an attempt to alter other persons' behavior, so those other persons can make use of their own understanding and control of themselves and their environment to resist, or indeed to counterinfluence the behavior of the professional. The behavior influence process is always a reciprocal one: The behavior manager attempts to shape the behavior of some other person through changing the consequences of that person's behavior, but, at the same time, the manager's is in turn shaped by the other's response. Control always results in countercontrol (Brown, Wienckowski, & Stolz, 1975, pp. 14–15).

One major purpose of this book is to disseminate information about behavior analysis. As you learn more about behavioral procedures, we believe you will better understand the various factors that influence your own and others' behavior. Such understanding will safeguard you against exploitation.

Other Concerns

When people initially contemplate applying behavioral procedures, sometimes they wonder about the limitations or the scope of applied behavior analysis and the difficulties they might encounter in executing the program.

Individual uniqueness. One frequent issue is whether behavioral principles are universal; if they apply to everyone. The answer is yes, behavioral principles do apply universally. Everyone increases behavior via reinforcement, decreases it via punishment, and so on. Yet because each person is physically unique, has a distinctive learning history, and functions under particular current circumstances, specific procedural applications must suit the individual. Facets of individuals' repertoires and current circumstances may be common, however, such as sharing the same manager or teacher or benefit package. In those cases, a particular contingency arrangement often will operate similarly among all group members. You will see many examples of this phenomenon throughout the pages to come.

Discomfort. "I know I'll feel awkward using praise and acknowledging good behavior. It seems too artificial to me," is another fear we have heard expressed. Our response is that this reaction is not unusual. We all feel peculiar the first time we attempt a new skill, particularly in the presence of others. Recall the first time you recited a poem or speech before a class, hit your first golf ball, or danced your first step. If you are still doing those activities, you have probably overcome at least some of your disquiet, especially if you have been sufficiently successful to begin to find the activity reinforcing.

Using behavioral methods such as praise and recognition usually produces its own reinforcers in the form of positive reactions from the recipients. As we often have witnessed, more than likely you will find yourself enjoying the process after a while.

Personal investment. "This sounds awfully time consuming. Won't it take lots of effort?" Your own personal investment is another understandable concern. We are recommending that you undertake a whole new set of responsibilities. But consider how much time and effort, not to speak of emotional strain, you currently are expending on the problem you are hoping to address. Your up-front investment will begin to pay off as the problem begins to diminish. You also will have learned a number of technical skills to include in your subsequent interventions. Learning to apply behavior analysis is like any other complex skill. It follows a learning curve that is slow at first but begins to accelerate each time you try and succeed. (This is another argument in favor of starting with easily achievable goals and simple procedures.)

Summary

This chapter provided guidelines for structuring responsible and effective behavior analysis programs. Figure 7.8 summarizes the model in a flow chart.

Figure 7.8 Selecting Procedures

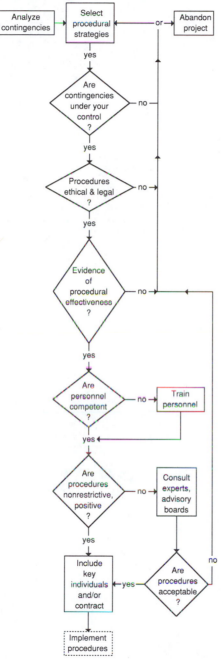

Once an objective has been selected and a measurement system implemented, potential contingencies are identified to serve as components of procedural strategies. But a variety of factors must be considered if ethical, legal, and functionally sound procedures are to be selected. They include laws and ethics regarding treatment, procedural effectiveness, competence of the behavior analyst and contingency manager, conditions and properties of the procedure, informed consent and behavioral contracting, voluntariness, and countercontrol.

In elaborating on ethical aspects of goal and procedural selection, the concept of voluntariness was recast in terms of the intensity of positive and negative consequences and who stands to benefit the most. Voluntariness increases as goals clearly benefit the client and consequences become more positive and natural. It breaks down completely when goals are selected by others for their own benefit and to the detriment of the client, and when consequences are aversive.

This chapter covered several frequently voiced concerns by people contemplating using behavioral procedures. We hope they have addressed any doubts you may be feeling about putting the procedures into operation. Other concerns relating to specific procedures will be discussed within those sections. Now that you have found out how to select mutually satisfactory procedures, turn to the next chapter, where you will encounter general guidelines for implementing them.

Chapter 8

Implementing Procedures and Monitoring Outcomes

GOALS

After completing this chapter, you should be able to:

1. Define, recognize, and give original illustrations of each of the following terms:
   a. Peer review
   b. Accountable
   c. Daily report card
   d. Self-management
2. Describe how each of the following relates to the successful implementation of procedures:
   a. Support for procedural application
   b. Peer review
   c. Accountability
   d. Flexibility
   e. Behavioral contracting and daily report cards
   f. Self-management
   g. Preparing the environment
   h. Monitoring and revising procedures
   i. Providing for generalization and maintenance
3. List, describe, and illustrate six guidelines for effectively implementing behavioral contracts.
4. Discuss the advantages of daily report cards.
5. Describe the importance of monitoring and graphing procedural effects and reliability data.
6. Set up a graph, and include baseline and reliability data on it. (Do not actually attempt to implement a procedure until you have studied the appropriate procedures in subsequent chapters.)
7. Identify several reasons a program might not achieve its stated objective.
8. Outline and discuss the importance of the steps included in the model for behavior change.

You have seen how much preparation and care are expended in designing a behavior-change program. Probably you will find that the more you expend "up front," the less you will need to cope with problems while your program is in progress. Just as in so many other areas of endeavor, "an ounce of prevention equals a pound of cure"; besides, "there ain't no free lunch." Plan and execute your plans with care, and you are likely to be rewarded by success.

In this chapter we consider how behavioral procedures are implemented and monitored for success. A variety of factors need to be considered if selected procedures are to result in effective and enduring behavior change. Factors emphasized here are environmental support, **peer review**, accountability, flexibility, effective contracting, self-management, monitoring and revising procedures, and providing for generalization and maintenance.

Support for Application of Procedures

When you read reports of the successful application of behavioral procedures, they may seem simple and straightforward, yet in all probability considerable effort was invested before and during the implementation of the procedure. Just as the soil must be prepared for crops to flourish, the context in which change is to occur must be ready to support the change. Here we discuss some potential impediments to change and offer ways to overcome them.

Identifying Necessary Resources

Some procedures require more effort, special materials, or facilities than others. Dexter's token system necessitates tokens, charts, material rewards, special activities, the cooperation of other people, additional teacher effort, and the like. To assess the feasibility of meeting requirements like those, as part of your ecological assessment, spend time observing the person's

behavior in the natural setting. Making repeated visits to Dexter's classroom for several hours would inform the behavior analyst about the appropriateness and feasibility of procedures under consideration. First, make sure the procedure is apt to be reinforcing to the user. As Hopkins (1987) has argued,

> . . . The essential ingredient in our producing technology that will be useful is making sure that the technology, in addition to being effective for intended populations, will be reinforcing for all the people who will buy and use it (p. 343).

Occasionally, special environments need to be designed—a costly enterprise. Yet circumstances may justify the decision. The environment simply may not be capable of supporting the behavioral program: Insufficient space, materials, or trained personnel or the interference or apathy of staff or peers may rule out the program in that setting. Then selecting alternative environments temporarily may be justified, provided that long-range plans ultimately are to reintegrate clients into the mainstream of their society.

When clients demand an inordinate amount of attention or care, everyone can suffer. For instance, if a student continually disrupts activities or monopolizes the instructor's time, other members of the group are penalized. Herbie, who is disruptive, violently self-abusive and large for his age, with little functional language and very few academic skills, could not readily be contained in a class of typical peers. Herbie would punch himself in the head, throw other children's materials about, grunt and screech, climb on the furniture, and in general distress everyone. So he was placed in a preacademic group containing just two other children. The goal was to prepare him for a less restrictive environment by teaching him to remain seated and attending to tasks for reasonable lengths of time; to follow simple directions; to eliminate his self-abuse and reduce his noise;

and to use sign language to request materials, attention, and assistance. When those goals had been accomplished, the child could be transferred to a class with more opportunities for mainstreaming.

Obtaining Community Support

Without support from the community, use of particular procedures may be doomed to failure. So procedures need to be adequately explained or justified to the local public and market research must be carefully conducted (Hopkins, 1987). Public policy, laws, or prevailing community standards may make some procedures unacceptable. Consider the following actual episodes.

Depriving residents of meals at the whim of their caretakers was common practice at a public institution for the retarded. Instead, members of the professional staff devised a behavior-change program in which only certain destructive acts would result in briefly postponed access to food. Because the program was explicitly announced, it produced a wave of professional and public outrage. Reliance on food deprivation as an instrument of behavior change was then prohibited altogether. Had a board of community representatives first been asked to scrutinize the behavior-change program, two things would probably have happened:

1. Having been alerted to the prevailing and far more unethical practice of unsystematic food deprivation, the board could have voiced its opposition to ongoing abuse as well as to the proposed program.

2. The behavior-change agents would then have had to devise some other, more acceptable intervention procedure.

The public furor could have been avoided, and the clients would have been more effectively and humanely served.

A second example illustrates how caution helps to avoid roadblocks to procedural intervention. A large city school system had a very high proportion of low-achieving students. A behavior analysis program was discussed with the school committee. Recognizing the need for effective intervention, the committee supported the proposed program, but, reflecting the attitudes of its community, the committee stipulated that neither food nor material rewards be used. After some effort, the behavior analyst was able to marshal an array of powerful reinforcers acceptable to board members, thereby achieving community support throughout the program.

Involving community review boards or human rights committees can serve a number of distinct purposes:

- providing a sounding board for community opinions
- identifying features that require clarification and highlighting aspects needing stronger justification
- providing the impetus to revise or refine goals and procedures in order to promote committee and community support
- bringing questionable prevailing practices to the attention of the community (especially important from a humanitarian point of view)

Unacceptable practices then may be prohibited, thereby ensuring protection of clients' rights.

Peer Review

Committees constituted to represent the perspectives of members of the community, such as human rights groups and school boards, are not necessarily composed of experts in behavior analysis methods. On certain occasions, obtaining the opinion of outside experts can prove valuable. Recognizing this, the Association for Advancement of Behavior Therapy (AABT) designed a peer review process to provide consultation and on-site reviews of treatment programs (Risley & Sheldon-Wildgen, 1982). The purpose of the peer review panel was to provide expert information on behavior therapy, interpret ethical issues as they relate to the program under review, and recommend methods that ensure optimal care and treatment of clients. Assuming that concerned parties agreed to request the review, the AABT committee selected a team to represent a range of expertise in the area of treatment. The committee then reviewed the program and made professional interpretations and recommendations, issuing a report only to the relevant parties.

Peer review can be costly and time consuming, and is not necessarily recommended for evaluating all interventions—behavioral or otherwise. Programs that depart minimally from standard practice within an organization (i.e., regular good teaching or management methods) and for which data documenting success are gathered regularly should be exempt.

When you are considering using procedures that are relatively intrusive, distracting, unusual, exotic or novel, aversive or otherwise potentially controversial, however, contemplate requesting the services of a panel of outside experts. These expert peer reviewers "... should be independent of the program being reviewed, have advanced and recognized expertise in the problem and interventions under consideration, and rotate off the peer review board at regular intervals to provide space for fresh perspectives" (Lovaas & Favell, 1987, p. 316). Such a peer review panel will be advantageous in the long run, not only for the people served by your organization but in terms of preventing potential cost, time, and stress that might be produced by a major confrontation. In several cases, negative press, litigation, disrupted professional relationships, and the necessity for preparing and delivering extensive apologies for controversial procedures could have been avoided by initially obtaining and responding to the opinions of expert peers.

Accountability

Behavior analysis, practiced as we suggest, protects itself from charges that its procedures are ineffective because it holds itself **accountable** for its methods. Accountability is accomplished by collecting data repeatedly over time and demonstrating how behavior change is functionally related to the procedure. These objective measures can yield compelling evidence in support of the utility and fairness of a given procedure.

> Suppose that future courts should decide to employ outcome measures as a means of evaluating treatment adequacy. This approach would imply that initial behavioral assessments would be made of individual treatment needs, the outcomes of different types of treatment programs with various patient populations would be compared over time, and those programs that produce the most favorable results would be implemented on a wide scale. Presumably, the programs would also be subjected to certain basic input criteria, such as those proposed by Wyatt, to protect the basic rights of the residents. What would be the implications of outcome-oriented treatment measures for the field of behavior modification? Experimental analyses of behavior modification techniques have demonstrated repeatedly that environmental contingencies can be arranged to modify deviant behavior patterns and to develop and maintain new skills in persons with behavioral or developmental problems (e.g., *Journal of Applied Behavior Analysis*, 1968–present).
>
> Many of these studies involved classes of persons for whom a right to treatment has been judicially recognized. To the extent that the target behaviors selected for treatment in these studies are considered the relevant outcome variables, behavior modification has demonstrated its effectiveness as a treatment approach (Budd & Baer, 1976, pp. 180–181).

In selecting procedures, behavior analysts choose only those that can be described operationally and the effects of which can be measured validly. Those methods permit users to readily identify sources of failure or breakdowns in effectiveness, comforting them with the knowledge that danger signs will be spotted rapidly. Their willingness to subject their methods to such thorough and continuing scrutiny adds to the ethical responsibility of applied behavior analysts. It is hoped that this aspect of applied behavior analysis will serve as a model for other human-service and management disciplines, thereby enabling the procedures they use to be regularly and precisely evaluated as well.

Flexibility

Accountability goes hand in hand with flexibility in implementing procedures. Should ongoing monitoring indicate a failure to progress as anticipated, the procedures should be modified or discontinued. After a fair try of several days or weeks, alternatives may be attempted either sequentially or in combination, until the desired effect is achieved. Behavior analysts need to guard against the temptation to become so intrigued with a particular procedure that they overuse it despite its ineffectiveness in a particular instance. A *token* program (described fully in Chapter 13) may succeed with Dexter but not Lucretia. *Graduated guidance* (covered in Chapter 18) may be the only effective method of teaching motor skills to youngsters like Charlie, who learns at a much slower rate than his age mates, and Pearl, whose aberrant behavior often interferes with her effective functioning. But graduated guidance may be unnecessary or inappropriate for some high school physical-education students or the service personnel at Purple Triangle. A responsible behavior analyst will be ready to discontinue a procedure by a predetermined date and to substitute another should evidence show that the procedure is not producing the anticipated result.

Guidelines for Selecting Procedures by Contractual Arrangement

Just as contracting provides an opportunity for clients, service providers or managers, and significant others to mutually agree on the objective of a behavioral program, contracts can serve a similar purpose in terms of implementing procedures. If the detailed description of the manner in which contingencies are to be arranged is considered in advance and mutually endorsed, participants should be more consistent and comfortable in following through.

If you include behavioral contracting when you implement your procedure, you will want to know how to maximize its utility. These guidelines, based on a set offered by Sulzer-Azaroff and Mayer (1986), incorporate ethical protection and effective application of behavioral principles. The case of Paula, the office procrastinator, illustrates each guideline.

Stress the Positive

Emphasize actions that *will* be taken, not those that should not: "Angela, the supervisor, will help monitor and deliver feedback and other reinforcers such as praise, notes, and positive ratings punctually at 8:15 A.M." (Do not phrase like this: "Angela will not attend to Paula's failure to hand in her reports on time.")

Request and Reinforce Small Improvements

It is important to succeed regularly, both for the client's sake as well as your own. Starting where the client is and moving forward in small steps is the way to proceed: Paula only handed in 30 percent of her reports on time. The first contract stipulated that during the next week 35% of her reports should be turned in punctually. (Later contracts required 40% per week, 50% per week, and so on.)

Clarify Terms of the Contract

All individuals concerned must know exactly what is required of them within what time period, what consequences each will provide and when, how, and how much they will assist. Whenever Angela asks Paula to prepare a report, Paula and Angela list the key points to be covered, information to be included, other style and format requirements, and the date by which the report should be completed. Each time Paula finishes a report she attaches a self-checked list of the predetermined requirements, date assigned, date to be completed, and date actually completed.

Angela will record this information on a chart and, if merited, will reinforce the quality and timeliness with which the report was completed. Assuming that Paula achieves her weekly goals during at least 20 of 26 weeks, she will earn a rating of satisfactory on her semiannual job evaluation.

Reinforce the Target Behavior Immediately

You will soon learn the importance of immediate reinforcement. Reinforcing immediately is just as important under a contractual arrangement, because it helps the client to discriminate that meeting the terms of the contract is paired with reinforcement. (Note how immediately reinforcing events are used to bridge the time gap between Paula's improved punctuality in report preparation and the reward of a satisfactory job rating.)

Include an Option to Withdraw or Modify the Terms of the Contract

When you negotiate the terms of a contract, you are, after all, collectively making your best guesses about what circumstances are likely to produce success. If your predictions have been imperfect, simply modify the terms of the contract. Perhaps, in Paula's case, one of the goal levels—progressing from 85% to 95%—was overly ambitious. The contract could be renegotiated to enhance chances of success.

Permitting participants to withdraw from contractual arrangements also would be reasonable under certain circumstances, but those circumstances need to be spelled out. Paula or Angela might reach the point when they felt such a contrivance no longer was needed. A clause such as the following would allow for that: "At such a point that 85% of Paula's reports are completed by the preset date for four weeks in a row, except in cases of illness or other serious emergencies, they may opt to discontinue the contractual arrangement for a trial period of one month. Assuming Paula's good rate of progress continues, no further contracts need be negotiated."

Weigh Costs and Benefits for All Participants

When costs are too great or benefits too small for any participants in a contractual arrangement, the program has little chance of long-range success. People will drop out or neglect to meet their obligations. To avoid this problem, pause to inventory. Itemize the immediate and long-range advantages to the client, as well as the benefits to the contingency manager, significant others, and the organization and/or the public. Also list costs in terms of time, money, effort, and even such subtle factors as loss of power or control. If the costs clearly outweigh the benefits, modify the program to make it more practical.

During Angela and Paula's initial conference, Angela asked Paula what sort of reward she felt would be appropriate should she learn to complete her reports punctually. Paula requested a promotion, an action beyond Angela's ability to grant. Instead, they settled on the satisfactory rating, which in turn could improve Paula's competitive edge should a desirable opening occur in the organization.

Daily Report Cards

A **daily report card**, a device sometimes used with school children, is a simplified version of a behavioral contract. The daily report card is simply a contingency arrangement between the key individuals in two settings: the home and the school, the school and the residential cottage, and so on. In one place, a consequence, like a rating or a mark on a checklist or card, is delivered as soon as possible after the target behavior happens. A delayed consequence, like a reinforcing activity, is presented later. The residents of Achievement Place (Bailey, Wolf, & Phillips, 1970) brought home cards from their teachers indicating how well each had performed specific behaviors each day. This procedure, of course, allowed appropriate consequences to be delivered much more frequently than otherwise. Compared to the report cards that public schools typically issue each 6 to 18 weeks, this daily delivery substantially minimized the delay. At Achievement Place, when the youths brought home report cards showing that they had met the criteria for acceptable behavior, they were allowed such privileges as watching television and permission to go places.

In another study (Lahey et al., 1977), daily report cards were sent home to the parents of kindergarten children. The teachers indicated what skill was worked on that day and whether the child followed instructions, rested well, fell asleep, completed assigned work, and got along well with classmates. A survey of parent reactions revealed their uniform support of the daily report card concept. They rated it as improving communication, their understanding of their child's progress, and their child's performance and attitude toward school. They also indicated that the device was a very important part of their child's education and indicated that it resulted in a change of their own use of incentives and rewards. Other teachers in grades 1–5 also voluntarily adopted the system, further attesting to its effectiveness and practicality.

Similarly, investigators (Budd et al., 1981) used daily report cards to reduce preschool and kindergarten children's severe behavior problems, such as aggression and negative statements. Students were each given a brightly colored sticker on a card immediately after each period in which they did not engage in the target behavior. Preestablished numbers of these stickers were exchanged at home for prespecified privileges, such as having a friend visit, watching TV, going swimming, or having a special snack.

A variation of the latter procedure was used by a guidance counselor participating in a workshop conducted by one of the authors. A high school student who completed few assignments was given a card to be signed by each of her several teachers; it indicated whether she had completed the assignment for each period. At-home privileges were provided according to the proportion of "acceptable" marks. Completion of assignments increased substantially. This strategy resembled one followed by Schumaker, Hovell, and Sherman (1977a; 1977b) who implemented an elaborate daily report card system in junior high schools, specifying that home privileges and parent praise would be contingent on improved school conduct. This program resulted in reduced truancy and improvements in class work, daily grades, and teachers' satisfaction with the students' performance.

In each of these examples, the home environment supported progress in another setting. In addition, through the mutual planning integral to the daily report card system, programming between the two was effectively coordinated, thereby increasing the likelihood of consistency in the implementation of the procedures.

The daily report card and other positive messages sent home to parents serve dual functions. As you learn more about reinforcement and stimulus control, you will understand how they can effectively reinforce the students' behavior directly, and function as prompts to parents and contingency managers to deliver reinforcers. Many teachers who have used such notes have reported an improvement in school-home relations. Parents also may begin to seek out school personnel to compliment them for their efforts and cooperate more when the opportunity arises.

Self-Management

Self-management procedures minimize the client's risk of becoming a victim of coercion. Often, too, they can augment the success of the implemented procedure. With self-management, people assume some of the responsibility for changing their own behavior. This responsibility generally may involve some or all of five basic components:

1. Selecting their own goals
2. Monitoring their own behavior
3. Selecting procedures for behavior change
4. Implementing the procedures
5. Evaluating the effectiveness of the procedures

The behavior analyst may function as a consultant, resource person, or coordinator of some aspects of the program, should clients request such assistance or be incapable of managing some aspects by themselves. For instance, Paula and—with his advanced capabilities—Dexter may be able to take full responsibility for managing their own programs. Charlie may be able to place a sticker depicting his self-care accomplishments on a chart but may have a difficult time evaluating the effectiveness of a tooth-brushing program. During the initial stages of the program, Pearl, who has no functional language, will probably be unable to participate initially in any self-control procedures at all.

Used alone, self-monitoring, or self-observation and self-recording, can be problematic. The effects often are temporary: "Unless supplemented by additional behavior change influences (e.g., social reinforcement), self-monitoring does not offer promise in the long-term maintenance of effortful behavior" (Thoresen & Mahoney, 1974, p. 63). Furthermore, self-monitoring may not result in any behavioral change at all unless it is accompanied by reinforcement of the target behavior. For example, Ballard and Glynn found that self-recording of writing by third-grade students "did not increase the number of sentences, number of different action words, or number of different describing words, or improve the quality of the stories" (1975, p. 387). Only after self-selected and self-administered reinforcers were added did rates of response increase substantially and stories receive higher ratings for quality.

A similar effect was shown with three female adolescent offenders (Seymour & Stokes, 1976). Presenting tokens following self-recording of work served as a motivator to increase particular behaviors, which in turn evoked more staff praise.

When Perri and Richards (1977) investigated the effectiveness of college students' self-management programs to curtail overeating or smoking, or to address problems related to dating or studying, they found that using self reinforcement procedures were important elements for success. Komaki and Dore-Boyce (1978) also found level of "motivation" influenced the effectiveness of self-observation and self-recording as a treatment technique for undergraduate college students. Eight students who talked no more than 10% of the time during group discussion sessions participated in a self-observation and self-recording program. Four indicated a repeated desire to verbally participate more; four indicated little interest to change. When those students who expressed their desire to change self-recorded, they talked significantly more often during baseline than those who said they were not interested in changing. Having a vested interest in the progress of the program can, therefore, make a difference for self-recorders. In addition, rigorous training and supervision plus frequent reliability assessments are particularly important.

Epstein and Goss (1978) placed a 10-year-old, highly disruptive boy on a self-management program because it appeared that a positive reinforcement program would be too "burdensome for the teacher to maintain" (p. 111). After training the child in self-evaluation, he was asked to score his own behavior. When the teacher agreed with the score the boy had given himself for the day, his points would double. This aspect was important, for self-reporting by youngsters is more likely to be accurate when accuracy is reinforced (see Broden et al., 1971; Fixsen, Phillips, & Wolf, 1973; and Kazdin, 1974a, for examples of accurate self-recording). Points could be exchanged for time with games and extra recess for the entire class. The student enthusiastically adhered to this program throughout the rest of the school year while maintaining his improved behavior.

Staff members also can learn to manage their own performance, as Kissel, Whitman, and Reid (1983) demonstrated. Through written instructions, videotaped and live modeling, rehearsal and videotaped feedback, institutional staff first acquired skills for teaching their severely developmentally delayed charges. Then, they learned to record, graph, and evaluate the progress of residents. Under those self-management conditions plus only occasional supervision, staff continued to apply their teaching skills. This worked to the ultimate advantage of their clients, whose self-care skills improved.

Actually, many examples of the successful use of self-management have been reported in the behavioral literature. Severely retarded and other developmentally disabled people (e.g., Fowler, Baer, & Stolz, 1984; Shapiro & Klein, 1980), children with a fear of failure (Stamps,

1973), children at risk for school maladjustment and academic failure (Hughes & Hendrickson, 1987), and underachievers (Edgar & Clement, 1980), college students working on study skills (McReynolds & Church, 1973), and teachers trying to enhance their self-esteem (Hannum, Thoresen, & Hubbard, 1974) have all used self-management procedures to improve selected target behaviors. We know several colleagues who have taught high-school-age youngsters behavior principles and supervised as the youths modified their own behavior. We do the same with our own college undergraduate and graduate students. Think about how you would transform Paula's program for promoting her timeliness of report completion, into a self-management program.

Practically everyone can learn to self-manage. Self-management programs are both effective and time saving. While you consider such cost factors as training and managing reinforcing contingencies when you design and implement self-recording systems, recognize that by involving the client, time can be saved while the client is assisted toward greater self-control.

Preparing the Environment

After goals, procedures, participant roles, and functions have been negotiated, you want to assure everyone that the physical and social environment will be as supportive of the program as possible. This may entail changes in staffing patterns and responsibilities (LeLaurin & Risley, 1972), the way work or play areas are physically organized (Twardosz, Cataldo, & Risley, 1974), scheduling of activities (Doke & Risley, 1972; Homme et al., 1963), and the availability of supplies and materials (Hart & Risley, 1974). Sufficient evidence has convinced us that environmental features such as crowding (McAfee, 1987; Paulus, 1980), heat (Anderson & Anderson, 1984), and insufficient (Boe, 1977) or particular toys (Bandura, Ross, & Ross, 1963a) actually set the stage for aggression. Conversely, limited play space has been noted to promote social interactions (Brown, Fox, & Brady, 1987). Examine, too, the sequence in which activities are scheduled, because some—like calming music—may be conducive to subsequent serenity. Other activities, such as competitive or aggressive games, may influence social interactional patterns later on (Murphy, Hutchinson, & Bailey, 1983). (Later, when we discuss antecedents in greater detail, you will understand better the influence of "setting events" like these.) At this point, just review your objectives and contemplate the environmental features and resources you will need, such as:

- personnel and their assignments
- furnishings and their placement
- supplies, equipment, and materials
- schedules and sequences of activities

This sort of forethought undoubtedly will increase your chances of achieving your goals.

Monitoring Procedures

Once ethically and scientifically sound procedures have been selected and the environment prepared, you collect baseline data, as described in Chapter 6. Now you are ready to intervene by applying behavioral procedures. Those are presented in detail in the text to follow. Before you begin to apply a procedure, however, please study it thoroughly. Learn about its strengths and weaknesses, side effects, and methods of application. We also hope you will be fortunate enough to receive competent supervision in your initial efforts. Refer as well to the behavioral journals to help you remain abreast of current developments. Books like ours are not infallible, and because they are based on information available at the time of their publicaton, some of the recommendations they contain may become obsolete.

Remember that during treatment, the effects of procedures should be consistently monitored, and data should be regularly plotted on

a graph and compared against the baseline to permit you to assess progress. When parents, teachers, and other agents can see visual evidence that a procedure *is* bringing about the desired change, they are likely to find the evidence reinforcing. Such reinforcement helps to *maintain* the participation of those people in the treatment program, which is critical if objectives are to be achieved.

Often, during the early phases of a program, small behavioral improvements may be overlooked unless data are collected and graphed, especially when problem behaviors are serious. If vandalism in a school system had decreased, so that the percentage of unbroken windows had increased by only 5%, the improvement might not be instantly apparent. So too with Paula, whose early improvement could readily go undetected, as so large a proportion of her work is still late. Unless data had been collected during the first few days after the behavior-change program had been implemented, the change might have gone unnoticed, and the procedure dropped prematurely.

Graphing methods were discussed in detail in Chapter 6. Figure 8.1 displays a graph of Dexter's task completion. Remember that the ordinate, or y-axis, is labeled with the measure of the behavior to be changed, the dependent variable. The abscissa, or x-axis, is labeled for

Figure 8.1 Dexter's Math Progress

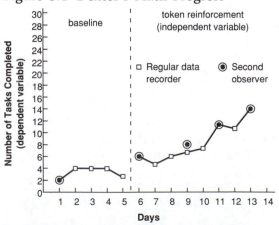

the appropriate time interval—days. Dashed vertical lines indicate changes in procedures. To be confident that the measures in this case were consistent throughout, regular indexes of agreement between observers continued to be calculated as during baseline. The data from these checks were then plotted directly on the graph. If the two points representing measurements of the same dependent variable showed great disparity, the measures would have had to be refined.

Graphing the data also reduces other kinds of misunderstandings. For example, people may be convinced that the client is improving simply because, regardless of its nature, *some* treatment is being provided (a *placebo effect*). One way to correct misconceptions like this, as you will learn in more detail later, is to use a design in which treatment effects are compared against those produced in a baseline phase consisting of the best available treatment alternative.

Graphs function similarly to "fever charts" (Patterson & Gullian, 1968). Plotting data helps to show how much progress actually has been made and how much remains to be accomplished. The data provide regular and rapid feedback on the likely effectiveness of the treatment in progress. If, after a sufficient period of time, an anticipated behavior change has not occurred, the data tell us to stop! We must reevaluate the program and make necessary changes. If change is occurring too slowly, alterations in the program also may be indicated. But if data show that change is occurring at a satisfactory rate, procedures should be continued. Regular collection and graphing of observational data are essential to the efficiency and effectiveness of the treatment program.

Revising Unsuccessful Procedures

The success of a program can be compromised in a number of ways. The objective, contingencies, or selected procedures may be inappropriate and ought to be changed. Often, procedures are not being implemented as originally planned. To avoid this pitfall, in addition to collecting data on the dependent variable (the behavior to be changed), you should also periodically record the accuracy with which the independent variable (the intervention or treatment program) is implemented. Peterson, Homer, and Wonderlich (1982) make a compelling case in favor of safeguarding the integrity of treatment by measuring the independent variable. For example, if Dexter is to be praised at least once every 10 minutes he has remained "on-task" (like doing homework), praise episodes should be sampled from time to time while he is doing his homework to be sure that treatment is happening as agreed.

As we have mentioned previously, consistent monitoring, feedback, and reinforcement are important to contingency managers (see Herbert & Baer, 1972), as well as to clients. Just as prompting during behavioral measurement may be helpful, prompting contingency managers when to act can also serve a useful function and may even be necessary to ensure that procedures are implemented as intended. A variety of prompts will be discussed in Chapters 15–18. Other suggestions have already been provided in Chapter 6. For example, a timer can be set at varying intervals of 5 to 10 minutes whenever Dexter starts his homework. Provided that he has been working continuously, a buzzer signaling the end of the interval cues the parents to praise him. Several investigators (Hallahan, Marshall, & Lloyd, 1981; Hughes & Hendrickson, 1987) have used this sort of procedure quite successfully.

Terminating Successful Programs

Some programs are incorporated in the person's daily home, school, or work routines and remain in effect ever after. Others need to be phased out to enable the client fuller autonomy and/or because the programs demand resources that could be put to better use elsewhere. Although behavior change may have been accomplished with relative ease, transferring the altered performance to new situations and sustaining it may turn out to be another matter entirely. Relapse to previously well-established habit patterns is predictable unless other measures are taken to prepare the individual and the environment to support the change. This can be accomplished by *gradually* altering features of the reinforcing contingencies until they closely approximate those of the supportive environment and by using a number of other tactics (described in later chapters), such as transferring control of the program to the client.

Transfer and maintenance was accomplished for Herbie by gradually reintegrating him into his own class—at first, for only a few minutes a day during periods when his presence would be minimally disruptive; then little by little, for increasingly longer time periods. Although the teacher in the less-restrictive classroom could not conduct the required intensive training, she was able to support the maintenance of behaviors that had been established in the temporarily artificial setting.

Table 8.1 summarizes the manner in which antecedents and consequences can be altered once a behavior becomes well established and fluent. Section V elaborates upon these and other methods for supporting the generalization and maintenance of behavior change.

Summary

This chapter provided guidelines for implementing a behavior analysis program. Figure 8.2 depicts the model in a flow chart.

Several factors must be considered prior to implementing your selected procedure. These include support for application of the procedure, the importance of accountability and flexibility, the utility of behavioral contracting and self-management techniques, and the need to monitor and revise procedures as needed. Monitoring helps to determine whether progress toward the objective is being achieved within a reasonable time period. If so, the program continues until the change is established well enough to shift over to a program of generalization or maintenance. If the objective is not being met, the objective, contingencies, or selected procedures may be inappropriate and in need of revision. Or perhaps behavioral strategies are not being implemented as agreed. Each possibility should be checked until the reason is discovered and appropriate program modifications are made. The next three steps in the model will be discussed in subsequent chapters, but they are included in Figure 8.2 to provide an overview of the complete model.

Throughout this first section of the book, we have detailed the planning and implementation steps in behavioral programming and have suggested methods for resolving some of the major philosophical and ethical issues that are of current concern in our society. As behavior analysis continues to develop, additional issues will

Table 8.1 Altering Antecedents and Consequences to Sustain Change or Prevent Relapse

First, Bring Performance to a High and Steady State, Then Gradually Shift

Consequences

From:	To:
Contrived	Naturally operating
Immediate	Delayed
Continuous	Intermittent
Fixed	Variable
Lots	Some

Gradually Shift Antecedents

From:	To:
Artificial or strong	Natural or subtle

Figure 8.2 Implementing Procedures

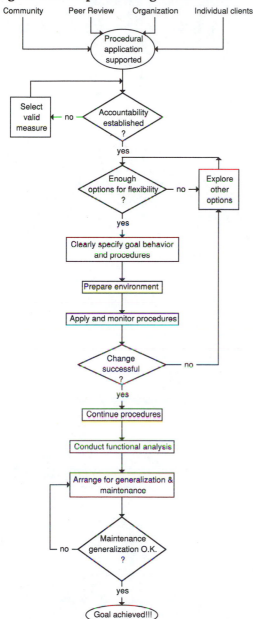

arise. We agree with Brown et al. (1975) that public debate about behavior analysis procedures is bound to continue. Constant professional evaluation and public discussion, however, can help to prevent abuses, as well as to foster greater public understanding and acceptance of the benefits.

> London (1974) contends that ". . . a decent society regulates all technology that is powerful enough to affect the general welfare, at once restricting the technicians as little as possible and as much as necessary." In that context, both continued monitoring of behavior modification by the public and further research on this important technology are needed to serve society and the individuals who make it up (Brown et al., 1975, p.24).

In the next chapters, we present an extensive array of procedures, also providing you with flow diagrams to remind you of the steps to follow in implementing each procedure. Notice, too, that procedures with similar functions generally are grouped together. These include methods for increasing, teaching, and reducing behavior and for promoting generalization and maintenance of change. At the end of each main section we present summary charts defining the operation involved in each procedure, how to use it effectively and its advantages and disadvantages.

Demonstrating your fluency with the knowledge and skills included in this book can be accomplished by meeting mastery criteria on quizzes and by achieving satisfactory performance standards when practicing the skills. You also may want to guide your skill development by participating in workshops and training experiences of the type presented in Sulzer-Azaroff and Reese's 1982 text, *Applying Behavior Analysis: A Program for Developing Professional Competence.*

Section II

Increasing Behavior

Several children, ranging in age from seven to twelve, were patients in a residential treatment center for asthmatics. To avoid more intensive forms of treatment—intravenous-fluid therapy, hospitalization, and drugs with undesirable side effects—the staff repeatedly tried to teach the children how to use inhalation equipment. These attempts were of little avail; the patients seldom used the equipment appropriately. After measuring inappropriate use for several days, the staff chose and set criteria for one subtask—eye fixation—as the target of change. Each time a child met the criteria, he or she received a ticket, 25 of which could be exchanged for a surprise gift. Appropriate eye fixations immediately leaped upward and persisted.

Several days later, the same strategy was initiated in connection with a second subtask: facial posturing. When success with that component was demonstrated, the third and last subtask, diaphragmatic breathing, was targeted and treated similarly. Because the youngsters were to remain at the treatment center for at least six months, determining whether they continued to use the equipment was quite feasible. They did! This meant that drug treatment could be reduced for some patients, because they presumably became healthier and less dependent on intensive medical care (Renne & Creer, 1976).

Fifteen part-time cashiers in a drug store were involved in a study designed to reduce discrepancies between the gross amount of transactions and the amount recorded by the cash register. Punctuality in arriving at work and the manner and the order in which the employees turned in their money at the end of their shifts were also included (Newby & Robinson, 1983). Graphic feedback to individuals produced major progress in each category. When feedback was augmented with rewards[1] (e.g., free movie passes, soft drinks, and candy bars), cash shortages virtually disappeared, and punctuality and checkout proficiency improved substantially.

A second-grade class of disruptive youngsters performing below grade level was observed for 7 days. Then the students were permitted to earn tickets with no redeemable value if they reduced their disruption by 30 percent. Nothing much happened. However, after the tickets could be exchanged for tutoring sessions in reading by either older peers or college students, the children became much less disruptive and improved significantly in word-analysis skills, as measured by a standardized achievement test (Robertson, DeReus, & Drabman, 1976).

Reasoning that the unstructured time young people face once they leave school for the day often serves as an invitation to trouble, a community agency offered a supervised after-school recreational program as a preferable alternative (Pierce & Risley, 1974). To recruit teenagers a membership drive was organized. Members who enlisted others were allowed two opportunities to enter the recreation center an hour ahead of the rest of the crowd. The roster of new members increased substantially during the drive.

Dramatic results like these have been reported for hundreds of categories of behavior. Students are learning more in school (Ayllon, Layman, & Kandel, 1975), developing more effective social skills (Kohler & Fowler, 1985), performing better in sports (McKenzie & Rushall, 1974), increasing their physical activity levels and health fitness (Taggart, Taggart, & Siedentop, 1986), learning to manage their own behavior (Bornstein & Quevillon, 1976), eating more nourishing meals (Madsen, Madsen, & Thompson, 1974), ceasing to suck their thumbs (Knight & McKenzie, 1974), and improving their performance in countless other ways. Their teachers, supervisors, parents, and advisers are also becoming far more effective in fostering and supporting those skills (e.g., Fox & Sulzer-Azaroff, 1982; Harris, Bushell, Sherman, & Kane, 1975; Jones & Eimers, 1975). Other adults in all walks of life are learning to acquire numerous additional types of personal, social, academic, vocational, and professional skills. Many people successfully shed unwanted habits like smoking (Stitzer, Rand, Bigelow, & Mead, 1986) and overeating (Brownell & Jeffery, 1987).

---

[1] Technically, delayed stimuli like these do not "reinforce" behaviors that occurred long ago. Rather, through a process called *conditioned reinforcement*, other stimuli previously reliably paired with preferred items or events—such as statements people say to themselves, images they produce, reactions from others, and additional indicators that the reward will be forthcoming—probably perform the actual immediate reinforcing function. (See Michael, 1980, for an amplification of this point.) Later you will learn more about this issue.

How are such impressive results accomplished? Through the management of contingencies in which reinforcement plays a key role. In this section you will become acquainted with the scientific and technical aspects of reinforcement. You will learn what reinforcement is, how it functions, and how to apply it toward enhancing people's behavior in both individual and group contexts. Table E.1 in the Epilogue displays the features of the two major subcategories: positive and negative reinforcement. Using it as a guide as you begin to analyze people's behavior and to design your own programs of reinforcement may prove beneficial to you.

Chapter 9

Increasing Behavior: Reinforcement

GOALS

After completing this chapter, you should be able to:

1. Define, recognize, and give original illustrations of each of the following terms:
   a. Reinforcement
   b. Reinforcement procedures
   c. Behavioral repertoire
   d. Positive reinforcer
   e. Aversive stimulus (negative reinforcer or punisher)
   f. Avoidance behavior
   g. Escape behavior
   h. Positive reinforcement
   i. Negative reinforcement
   j. Punishment
   k. Recovery
   l. Unconditioned or primary reinforcer
   m. Unconditioned aversive stimuli
   n. Conditioned or secondary reinforcer
   o. Neutral stimulus
2. Describe natural reinforcement and its function.
3. Distinguish and illustrate the differences between the terms *reinforcer* and *reward*.
4. Distinguish negative reinforcement from positive reinforcement and punishment, and describe how each operates.
5. Discuss the pros and cons of using negative reinforcement.
6. Discuss why it is important to determine if the environment is reinforcing undesirable behaviors.
7. Describe and illustrate how to develop conditioned reinforcers.

You are about to become empowered by learning how to analyze, understand, and discover how reinforcement works. You will become capable of using your new competence to understand and eventually to modify behavior. The most fundamental aspects of reinforcement are its properties and function. In this chapter we describe what reinforcement is and does, explain and illustrate the various subcategories of reinforcement, and begin to teach you how to use this basic building block of all behavioral interventions.

Reinforcement Defined

When we speak of **reinforcement**, we refer to a process in which a behavior is *strengthened*. By this we mean the frequency, rate, duration, intensity, and/or other dimension of the behavior increases or persists as a function of an event that occurs *contingent* (or dependent) *on* the response. Reinforcement may occur naturally as people interact with their environments during the normal course of their lives, or according to plan, as in teaching, training, managing, treating, or otherwise modifying behavior.

Instances of *natural*, or *unplanned, reinforcement* include:

- An employee continuing to perform well after receiving recognition for the excellence of a product she has fashioned.
- An infant turning his face toward the bottle because he has gotten milk by turning in that direction in the past.
- A person wearing gloves on a cold day because gloves previously allowed him to avoid getting cold fingers.
- An addict sniffing cocaine as a result of former pleasure.
- A teenager complying with her friends' dares because accepting such challenges previously permitted her to be included in their activities and to avoid their ridicule.

Examples of *planned reinforcement* are:

- A teacher giving a student a gold star for reciting his multiplication tables correctly.
- A salesperson receiving a bonus for closing a large number of sales.
- A mother exclaiming "What a *good* boy!" when her child picks up his toys.

Sometimes, as we have discussed earlier, especially powerful positive reinforcers can increase behaviors that people are ordinarily unlikely to perform. High salaries may encourage workers to continue to carry out boring or unpleasant tasks, and we are all familiar with cases in which consequences like power, wealth, and peer approval have reinforced bullying, stealing, cheating, and even murder.

As you can see, natural reinforcement can operate to the detriment or advantage of an individual or society. A prime example is the "spoiled" child who whines or throws tantrums until he gets his way. Why? Because his tantrums have often provided him what he wanted, and that constitutes reinforcement. From his parents' perspective, giving in to the child's demands is reinforcing because letting the child have his way stops or removes the tantrum they find so upsetting.

Experience teaches people, with or without their awareness, to use reinforcement as a tool for controlling the behavior of others. Claud has learned to scowl or sulk until his roommate stops making demands on him. After reprimanding Kim, an employee who is producing shoddy work, Eduardo observes that Kim's next few products conform better to standards of quality. Consequently Eduardo is likely to rebuke Kim next time Eduardo sees the worker producing substandard products. Someone else might terminate unwanted behavior by physically abusing the person causing the irritation, thereby reinforcing the abuser's response. Complaining is reinforced when a person accedes to demands in order to terminate the griping.

Successful teachers, therapists, and managers often use good reinforcement techniques without their own cognizance. Picture those individuals you admire most for their "people skills"—your most inspirational teachers, human services providers you have seen work wonders with their clients, and managers and "natural leaders" who spur others on to seemingly impossible accomplishments. Maybe you have wondered how they perform the feats they do. As you learn about behavioral principles and procedures, you will begin to understand how. You will realize that those admirable people use effective behavioral procedures all the time.

Continuing to operate without knowledge of principles of reinforcement, though, is chancy for even the most expert. When untrained people using reinforcement techniques meet an insurmountable challenge, they do not know where to turn. In applied behavior analysis, rather than leaving things to chance, reinforcement is *managed* to accomplish intentionally the sorts of beneficial objectives about which you have been reading. Within this framework, **reinforcement procedures** are systematically planned, goal-directed applications of reinforcement principles.

Reinforcement procedures are applied for the purpose of strengthening behaviors that individuals are capable of performing (that is, behaviors that are part of the person's **behavioral repertoire**—behaviors the person has emitted[1] in the past). The procedures also may be used to teach new behaviors and reduce unwanted ones when the procedures are judiciously presented and withheld. This section focuses on the simplest case: strengthening behaviors already in the repertoire. Later sections describe more complex situations. Initially, though, we discuss reinforcement in detail to help you understand how the process works. You will learn how behaviors are strengthened and maintained and how best to arrange reinforcers to achieve given objectives.

Positive and Negative Reinforcement

Did you notice that reinforcement includes two different types of consequences? One category consists of consequences that keep people going, such as **praise**, monetary incentives, food, or symbolic items. The other type of consequences are those people tend to avoid or escape from, such as discomfort, pain, and reprimands. The supportive type is called a **positive reinforcer**, the other, a **negative reinforcer**, punisher, or, the term we favor, **aversive stimulus** (note the word does not contain a *D*). Reinforcing stimuli are events such as receiving a cookie, a dollar bill, a hug (positive for most), or a frown or bitter taste (aversive for most). Assuming we like them, cookies, dollar bills, or hugs—the reinforcers—keep us performing a behavior, while we avoid or escape from noxious or *aversive* circumstances—the frown or bitter taste—the aversive stimulus. (**Avoidance** "refers to cases of negative reinforcement where the reinforced behavior occurs in the absence of the aversive stimulus—thus, to avoid is to prevent or postpone aversive stimulation rather than to remove it" (Hineline, 1981, p. 204). Avoiding a nagging spouse by working late at the office and preventing derision from one's fellow workers by taking a dare are examples. Behavior that reduces or removes aversive stimulation is called **escape behavior**, as when the employee whose boss is constantly "on his case" quits his job.)

---

[1] The verb *to emit* (resembling *to express*) is a technical term used in connection with a certain category of behavior called *operant behavior*, behavior that is modified by its consequences. Unlike *respondent* or *reflexive behavior*, sometimes labeled *involuntary behavior*, operant behavior corresponds closely to that kind of performance colloquially called "voluntary" (Catania, 1968). With respondent behavior, stimuli are said to *elicit* behavior. Because this text is limited to operant behavior, you will see the term *emit* but not the term *elicit*.

In a **positive reinforcement** procedure, a positive reinforcer is presented as a *consequence* of a response for the purpose of strengthening that response. In a **negative reinforcement** procedure, an *aversive stimulus* is set aside, reduced or removed, as the consequence of a response, for the very same purpose: to *strengthen* the response. Whether it is positive or negative, we only can be sure a reinforcer is a reinforcer when its presentation or removal *increases* or *maintains* the behavior it follows. (For reasons that will become clear as you read further, we spend little time teaching you to use negative reinforcement procedures. Consequently, when we use the terms *reinforcer* and *reinforcement*, usually we are referring to positive reinforcement.)

Although similar, the terms *reinforcer* and *reward* are not identical. A reward is a form of recompense—usually an item or maybe an activity, often selected arbitrarily on the assumption that it will get more of a wanted behavior. A reinforcer must have demonstrated its effectiveness as a stimulus for increasing or sustaining a person's behavior in the given context. Frequently rewards do function as reinforcers; occasionally, as you will see, they do not. In applying behavior analysis, you need to be sure any rewards you select indeed are reinforcers.

Let us relate these definitions to the illustrative studies in this section's introduction. When the children in Renne and Creer's study (1976) received tickets for using their inhalation equipment properly, their rates of using the equipment increased dramatically and persisted. We can say that the children's use of the equipment was positively reinforced by the presentation of tickets (the positive reinforcers).

Because rates of nondisruptive behavior increased in Robertson and colleagues' (1976) program, when students earned tickets for tutoring time, receiving the tickets reinforced behaviors other than disruption. So too did reinforcers such as the youths' early access to the recreational center in the Pierce and Risley (1974) study and the movies, candy bars, and soft drinks cashiers earned in the study by Newby and Robinson (1983).

Instances of negative reinforcement have been described in research, particularly studies among populations of children displaying severe behavioral deficits or aberrations. For example, several investigators (e.g., Carr & Durand, 1985; Weeks & Gaylord-Ross, 1981) have found that when assigned difficult tasks, some children increased their rates of self-abuse and aggression, diminishing those rates when task demands were removed. Apparently ridding themselves of the annoying demands (the aversive stimuli) served to reinforce the abusive behaviors. Koegel, Dyer, and Bell (1987) also have suggested that negative reinforcement is responsible for many of the social avoidance behaviors exhibited by learning handicapped individuals, such as gaze aversion, head-hanging, turning or moving away, and blank expressions. Presumably, terminating demanding social situations is negatively reinforcing for those acts of avoidance by individuals whose repeated failure has been paired with a history of nonreinforcement. When teaching activities were modified to permit autistic youngsters to share control, they began to engage successfully in social and learning situations more often. Another study (Carr, Newsom, & Binkoff, 1980) found that boys reduced or eliminated demands by resorting to aggression.

Iwata and his colleagues (1982) have illustrated that sometimes self-injurious behavior has resulted from a history of positive reinforcement in the form of adult attention; at other times it has stemmed from reinforcement in the form of a brief escape from adult demands. Iwata (1987) has urged us to ". . . identify how environments that we create may provide negative reinforcement for undesirable behaviors" (p. 365). He hints that despite our best intentions, inadvertently we may be teaching the very behaviors we are trying to eliminate. Considering whether negative reinforcement is happening because those unwanted behaviors permit the clients to avoid or terminate events aversive to them may help us understand why those behaviors are continuing and what we can do to avoid that trap.

Many of the annoying things that people do are habits that rid them of discomfort that results from unrealistic or unwanted demands. In other words, these habits are often developed through negative reinforcement. Perhaps Oscar has learned to be unfriendly to his boss because when he avoided talking to the boss in the past, he was not given extra assignments.

Distinguishing Positive and Negative Reinforcement from Other Procedures

In the language of the layperson, *negative reinforcement* is often confused with the procedure called *punishment* in behavior analysis. Probably you will find it helpful to be alerted to the differences between those two and among other procedures. Positive reinforcement involves *presenting* a positive consequence; negative reinforcement, *removing* an (ongoing) aversive consequence; **punishment** (see Chapters 27 and 28) consists of *presenting* an aversive consequence.[2] *Extinction* (see Chapter 23) is the label given to the *discontinuation* of reinforcement following a response. **Recovery** (Reese et al., 1977) is the term used to describe the conditions or what happens (i.e., the recurrence of the response that was reduced) when aversive consequences no longer are delivered contingent on a response. For the time being, however, we should concentrate on clarifying the negative reinforcement operation and distinguishing it from all others.

The most common error is to confuse negative reinforcement with punishment. Remember that *punishment decreases behavior*, while *reinforcement*—positive *or* negative—*increases behavior*. Both negative reinforcement and punishment involve aversive stimulus events such as scolding, complaining, disrupting, crying, or other painful or uncomfortable irritants. For example, when a nurse discovered her aide reading a magazine instead of tending to the patients, the nurse began to berate the aide and the aide returned to her assigned task. The nurse's rebuke terminated her aide's magazine reading, qualifying it as a punisher. When a behavior *weakens* (*stops* or *diminishes*) as a function of the addition *or* presentation of a stimulus, we say that the behavior was punished.

By contrast, when a behavior *strengthens* (accelerates or continues) as a function of the *subtraction* or *removal* of a stimulus, we say that behavior was negatively reinforced. What happened when the nurse censured her aide? What consequence followed from it? The irritation of seeing the aide ''goofing off'' disappeared. In other words, chiding the aide worked (at least for the moment). Probably the nurse will rebuke someone again the next time she encounters a similar situation, because her reprimand received negative reinforcement. This will likely happen despite her resolution to try to manage amiably.

Consider one more illustration to ensure that you can discriminate negative reinforcement from punishment and positive reinforcement. Every time Sue passes Harry's desk he pats her on the rear. Sue's protests seem only to encourage him further. So one day Sue ''accidentally'' spills her coffee all over Harry's paperwork just as he reaches up to pat her. Harry withdraws his hand and next time Sue passes with coffee in her hand he resists the temptation to pat her. Why is Sue likely to carry a cup of coffee with her next time she has to pass Harry's desk? Because spilling coffee on his papers was negatively reinforcing; it terminated

---

[2] *Timeout* and *response-cost* procedures (see Chapters 25 and 26) involve the *removal* of positive stimuli (e.g., removing the person from a reinforcing situation or the reinforcing situation from the person, or removing already acquired reinforcers as in response cost) contingent on a response.

the aversive situation. What stopped Harry's unwanted touching? Punishment. In the future he resisted patting Sue.

This last example illustrates the need to carefully observe the actual effects that your intervention may be having, rather than assuming that a given method will work. Sometimes an attempt backfires, the way Sue's protests did. The same sort of thing can happen with intended punishment—reprimanding, for instance. In some cases a public reprimand can be reinforcing; a private one punishing. To illustrate, O'Leary, Kaufman, Kass, and Drabman (1970) observed students disrupting in five classes. They found that when reprimands were loud enough for other students to hear, the rate of disruption *increased*. When reprimands were audible only to the students to whom they were directed, the rate declined. We guess that quiet reprimands served as punishers, whereas the public ones commanded peer attention, sufficiently reinforcing to nullify the punishing aspects of the situation.

Figure 9.1 summarizes each of the procedures we have been discussing; the arrows indicate the direction of the change in positive behavior produced by each.

Figure 9.1 Behavioral Procedures

	Positive Stimulus	Aversive Stimulus
Contingent presentation	positive reinforcement ↑[a]	punishment ↓
Contingent removal	timeout ↓ response cost	negative reinforcement ↑
Contingent discontinuation	extinction ↓	recovery ↑

[a] An arrow pointing up signifies that the behavior increases; an arrow pointing down, that it decreases as a function of the contingency.

Deciding Whether to Apply Negative Reinforcement

If negative reinforcement is an effective method for increasing a behavior, should a change agent select it as a procedure to modify behavior? Look again at the procedure. If negative reinforcement is to be used, *aversive* stimulation must be ongoing. Then the behavior is reinforced by removing the aversive stimulus contingent on the emission of the behavior. As we show in more detail in the chapter on punishment, however, undesirable side effects like escape, avoidance, and aggression are apt to occur when aversive stimuli are used (Azrin & Holz, 1966). Jim stays away from school, and Fred "tunes out" his nagging father by thinking about other things.

Aversive stimuli may also promote aggression. Responding *aggressively* after a person has been scolded, kept after school, isolated in a room at home, teased, or ridiculed is not unusual. Furthermore, often people learn aggressive behaviors because the aggression has worked momentarily to remove an unpleasant stimulus. For example, Lucretia is likely to stop teasing Elmer if she is slapped for doing so. Similarly, Nurse Barton is likely to stop nagging Helen if Helen disrupts the ward by screaming at the nurse when she nags. Elmer's and Helen's aggressive behaviors have been negatively reinforced, because they have terminated the aversive teasing and nagging. Aggression, as well as escape and avoidance, often disrupts social relations and may also promote responses that compete with ongoing programs. A student or subordinate whose stomach is tied up in knots is not in the best condition to profit from instruction.

Recognize, nevertheless, the potential strength of negative reinforcement when you see what people do to avoid or escape peer derision: learning new skills like skiing, jumping into a pool from the high diving board, riding a bicycle or driving, or initiating bad habits or destructive acts like smoking, abusing drugs, and stealing. (Of course, *continuing* bad habits probably derives from both negative and positive reinforcement.) Under rare circumstances, you may need to tap this source. One case is when the most powerful positive reinforcement you can devise is insufficient to produce a crucial change, as in health- and life-threatening situations.

Allen and Stokes (1987) found that "simply providing a prize contingent on cooperative behavior during [dental] treatment was insufficient to reduce the disruptive behavior of children" (p. 388). They taught children to lie still and be quiet by using frequent brief rest periods (escape), plus attention contingent on cooperative behavior. Those interruptions were reduced gradually until the children ultimately experienced the natural escape of the end of the session.

Combining positive with negative reinforcement may accelerate the change process. For example, a junior high school teacher whose class was the first of the day was having difficulties with student tardiness. Students would wander the halls looking for potential "action" before coming to class. According to school rules, tardy marks were indicated on report cards and students receiving five such marks would be expelled. When the teacher realized that many had earned three or four marks within the first quarter of school, he set up a program of negative reinforcement: He removed one tardy mark from his record book for each week in which a student's punctuality was perfect. This he combined with positive reinforcement, complimenting timely arrivals: "I sure am glad to see you make it here on time today"; "You are becoming a responsible class"; "Joe, you have really improved. Let's cross off another of these checks. Soon you won't have any"; "You are doing so well; let's have ten minutes of free time." The program worked successfully. After all the checks had been removed, the students continued to come

to class on time. Being punctual was strengthened initially by the combination of negative and positive reinforcement but appeared to be maintained by social and natural environmental reinforcers.

In most cases, however, positive reinforcement will be sufficient, particularly when you follow established guidelines for its effective application. Should you be tempted to use or find yourself actually using negative reinforcement inadvertently or by design, ask yourself if you have exhausted all possible positive contingency arrangements. Are the reinforcers you are using optimal for the individual and are they being presented according to the rules presented in Chapter 11? Also, review your objectives. Perhaps they are too difficult for the individual or punishing in some other way. Given the choice between using aversive contingencies and adjusting objectives, the latter usually is preferable. Assuming you have selected defensible, reasonable objectives, however, you should be able to depend on positive reinforcement.

Selecting Appropriate Reinforcers

"One man's meat is another man's poison." (See Figure 9.2.) Say you love licorice, and I hate it. You may go out of your way to greet a secretary who has a dish of licorice candies on her desk. I would go out of my way to greet her only if she smiled and addressed me pleasantly in response, my reinforcers. One teacher may find a class of students who are physically active and engaged in animated conversation reinforcing; other teachers are gratified only when all students are quietly working at their desks. The question is "How does one go about selecting the appropriate reinforcer?" To do so rationally, begin by recognizing how stimuli become or fail to become reinforcing for particular individuals.

Figure 9.2 One man's poison is another man's reinforcer.

© 1973 Reprinted by permission of United Features Syndicate, Inc.

Unconditioned Reinforcing Stimuli

Some stimuli are effective reinforcers without the person needing to experience life events in conjunction with those stimuli. The term **unconditioned** (or **primary**) **positive reinforcers** describes them: food for an individual who has not eaten for a while, liquids for one deprived of fluid, warmth to one who is chilled, sexual satisfaction for the healthy adult, and so on. Physical discomfort, hunger pangs, and unpleasant noise exemplify **unconditioned aversive stimuli**, the cessation of which is reinforcing. Contemplate that list of examples and you will see that primary reinforcers probably hold survival value for individuals or the continuation of their species. Organisms who fail to find that nourishment or avoidance of deleterious events are reinforcing would rapidly perish. Were acts of procreation nonreinforcing to members of a species, the species would become extinct. So to endure, organisms must have the capacity to receive reinforcers from key sources, and this tendency is probably inherited.

How Stimuli Acquire Reinforcing Properties

Other stimuli acquire their reinforcing properties only as a function of events in the individual's life. These are called **conditioned**, **secondary**, or **learned reinforcers**. A conditioned reinforcer is a stimulus that, though initially **neutral**, has become reinforcing to the individual by being experienced in conjunction with strong unconditioned or conditioned reinforcers. Therefore, conditioned reinforcers develop as a result of the person's learning history. Once conditioned reinforcers become solidly established, they have the capacity to enhance the behavior on which they are contingent.

Because conditioned reinforcers develop as individuals interact with their environments, the reinforcing value of any particular conditioned reinforcer varies from individual to individual and condition to condition, depending on the reinforcement history of each. Newborn Tina's parents feed, hold, and cuddle her, using certain gestures and vocal tones. When pleased with her actions they praise her: "Good baby." Over a long time, the gestures, tones, words, and other events that have been frequently paired with food and comfort begin to signal that food or comfort is apt to be forthcoming, and eventually the signal itself becomes reinforcing.

Reprimands often are paired with primary aversive stimuli: "No, No Tina, don't touch the stove. It will hurt you." But it's too late and Tina gets hurt. So the "No, No" begins to signal something nasty, ultimately becoming an aversive event in its own right. Finally, attaining or escaping from the once "neutral" events begins to strengthen Tina's behavior, even in the absence of unconditioned reinforcers. The stimuli have become conditioned reinforcers for her as they do for most others. Some children may not have experienced the same verbal or nonverbal pairings with receipt of food. So the stimuli that serve as conditioned reinforcers for Tina remain neutral for them.

A conditioned reinforcer may also consist of the receipt of something tangible. How pennies, gift certificates, or coupons become conditioned reinforcers is easy to understand, because they are linked with highly valued items. But what happens if the objects or events that usually become conditioned reinforcers fail to be paired with unconditioned reinforcers or other effective conditioned reinforcers? Gift certificates (or dollar bills or checks) would have no effect on the behavior of people who had no way to exchange those objects for items of value for them. Growing up without experiencing typical combinations of unconditioned and conditioned reinforcers, like the coupling of food with verbal praise, may explain why some people are less easily influenced by familiar conditioned reinforcers such as approval and good grades.

Establishing Conditioned Reinforcers

When stimuli that typically serve as conditioned reinforcers are not effective for a particular individual in your setting, you may need first to turn to unconditioned reinforcers or more powerful conditioned reinforcers. The latter then can be coupled with the preferred conditioned reinforcers, so that over time they come to assume reinforcing properties for the person.

Mr. Grump learns to accept compliments graciously only after they have been paired repeatedly with supplementary reinforcers, such as preferred assignments and good merit ratings: "Wonderful job, Grumpy. Let me take over while you go on break."

Another example from one of the authors' clinical cases may clarify how a 5-year-old girl was taught to respond to conditioned reinforcers in the natural environment. When she was brought into the clinic, she hardly uttered a word appropriate to her current surroundings, and she would only rarely look at the clinician or respond to her gestures or verbal directions. On those occasions when her behavior approximated a desirable action, the behavior analyst would say "Good" or smile. As this approach had no apparent effect, a more effective reinforcer—food—was used to teach the child to use appropriate language and to follow directions. Lunch was brought to the clinic, and the child was given small bites whenever her speech approximated more functional language or when she followed directions. Within a few months, the youngster was using many appropriate words and complying with a wide array of directions. However, following her around with lunch and a spoon would be impractical for a classroom teacher, so when the child was enrolled in school, a program for developing conditioned reinforcers was instituted. Each time the therapist gave her food, the presentation was paired with a phrase like "good," "fine," "yes," and "you're doing so well," and with an action like smiling, hugging, or nodding. As the child began to master given skills, omitting food reinforcers for those skills became feasible. Soon she was practicing those skills despite receiving only a word like "yes." After completing her third year in school, she was continuing to progress with only the conditioned reinforcers to support her efforts.[3]

Enabling the trainee to attain objectives that are reinforcing in their own right is implicit in many instructional programs. Learning to read; to play a musical instrument; to analyze a story, poem, or problem situation; or to craft an exquisite object are wonderful accomplishments. But of what use are they if the learner fails to derive pleasure (a reinforcer) by exercising the skill? That skill will lie fallow and perhaps deteriorate once external contingency control is discontinued. For this reason, making the practice of the skill as reinforcing as possible is crucial. Links between the new competency and other powerful reinforcers must be strengthened through regular multiple pairings. In plain language: Bombard learners with reinforcers as they progress and achieve!

Accelerating the speed with which a formerly neutral object or event transforms into a reinforcer may be accomplished by using techniques akin to merchandising: Display live or videorecordings of models who obviously are enjoying the reinforcer. If you have influence, talk the reinforcer up and/or have the person's friends and idols do the same. Exhibit prompts as reminders. (And, of course, continue to reinforce as many instances of progress as feasible.)

The mission of the Top Quality Manufacturing Company is—you guessed it—to produce goods of the highest quality. A key goal is for employees to "take pride in their workmanship" (i.e., find excellent workmanship reinforcing). A popular music group records a song on the topic, and the music is played on the loudspeaker periodically. Posters of prestigious employees showing pride in workmanship are displayed every few weeks. Reminders are distributed in memos and the company newsletter about how producing quality goods promotes the reputation of the company, provides job stability, and increases bonuses. Most of all, though, quality is monitored and accomplishments are reinforced.

You should now be able to explain how learning histories affect the manner in which conditioned reinforcers acquire their reinforcing properties. The encouraging aspect of the process is realizing that stimuli indigenous to a setting but currently functionally neutral for some individuals can become reinforcing by being linked with a reinforcer known to be effective for those people.

Matching Reinforcers with Individuals

Although many reinforcers are shared by large numbers of people, notice that each of us has a unique combination of reinforcing stimuli that works for us. So rather than assuming, we need to ensure that the stimuli we select are likely to work for a particular individual. (We return to this topic later on.) To provide you with a pool of potential reinforcers, in the next chapter we present several categories, ranging from those that are artificial in the daily routines of most work settings, homes, schools, institutions, and community agencies to those that are generally indigenous to those settings: tangible, edible, and exchangeable items, activities, and social events.

---

[3] You will want to collect data to ensure that combining two stimuli like food and praise is necessary for producing the intended result. Avoiding nonessential multiple reinforcers can be advantagous because once combined reinforcers are discontinued, the behaviors they were supporting might drop off more rapidly than if a single reinforcer had been applied (Thomas, Faulkner, & Bolt, 1988). Gradually and progressively thinning out the delivery of the stronger reinforcer should help avoid this potential pitfall, as shown in Chapters 30–32 discussion of maintaining behavioral change.

Summary

In this chapter you have learned about unconditioned and conditioned positive reinforcers and aversive stimuli, how they differ from one another and other classes of stimuli, and the way they evolve and function. This information is fundamental to understanding people's behavior and how to change it.

Positive reinforcers enhance behavior by being received as a consequence of the behavior; aversive stimuli, by being removed as a consequence of the behavior. In general, positive reinforcement is preferable to negative, because the latter may promote unwanted collateral effects. Unconditioned reinforcers are almost universally effective, because they evolve as a result of individuals' learning histories and because conditioned reinforcers that function for one individual may not work for the next. Stimuli can be developed into effective reinforcers, however, through repeated pairings with currently effective reinforcers. Discovering stimuli that have reinforcing properties for an individual can be a challenge. So Chapter 10 lists pools of potential reinforcers.

Soon, too, you will encounter some of the key rules for applying reinforcers effectively. By mastering the particulars of effective reinforcement, you will be able to incorporate those rules into procedures designed not only to enhance but also to teach and reduce specific behaviors.

Chapter 10

Selecting Positive Reinforcers

GOALS

After completing this chapter, you should be able to:

1. Define, recognize, and give original illustrations of each of the following terms:
   a. Edible reinforcer
   b. Establishing operation
   c. Satiation
   d. Tangible reinforcer
   e. Activity reinforcer
   f. Premack principle
   g. Response deprivation hypothesis (RDH)
   h. Social reinforcer
   i. Feedback
   j. Specific or labeled praise
   k. Generalized reinforcer
   l. Exchangeable (token) reinforcer
   m. Back-up reinforcer

2. Offer a rationale for using edible or tangible reinforcers.

3. Discuss some of the concerns or problems occasionally encountered when change agents use edible reinforcers in a behavior analysis program. Respond to these concerns.

4. Discuss how to minimize expense and satiation when tangible and edible reinforcers are applied.

5. Compare and contrast the Premack principle and the response deprivation hypothesis as methods of identifying effective reinforcers for an individual.

6. Explain why some people have difficulty using or receiving praise as a reinforcer and describe ways to minimize the difficulty.

7. Discuss the importance of feedback and how to increase its effectiveness.

8. Discuss the advantages and disadvantages of selecting and using effectively each of the varieties of reinforcers discussed in this chapter.

9. Describe the circumstances under which use of extrinsic reinforcers may be justified.

10. Discuss these issues:
    use of extrinsic reinforcers
    bribery versus reinforcement
    what people *should* do versus what they *are* doing
    countercontrol
    treating all people equally

11. Indicate the precautions to be followed when it is necessary to withhold reinforcers.

12. Select an array of reinforcers that would be effective for yourself or a client.

"I use behavior analysis procedures," says Ms. Charming. "We give all the clients in our workshop M&Ms during snack break daily. But," she adds, "sometimes the reinforcement works, and sometimes it doesn't." Ms. Charming is reflecting a common misconception about the application of behavioral procedures—that distributing goodies is all there is to applying behavior analysis. To the contrary, behavior analysts do not select strategies arbitrarily, nor do they assume that a reinforcer effective with most clients works for everyone at all times. Although skilled practitioners may distribute sweets contingently from time to time, they do so according to guidelines based on numerous research findings.

This chapter directs you to methods of reinforcer selection; Chapter 11 covers reinforcer delivery, including such factors as timing, amount, and schedule. Initially, we shall acquaint you with a number of classes of reinforcers: edible, tangible, exchangeable, activity, and social. This extensive pool of potential reinforcers should provide you with numerous alternatives from which to choose, enabling you to select those that are as minimally intrusive (i.e., indigenous to the setting when possible) yet maximally successful as possible in the context in which the performance of concern is to occur.

Edible Reinforcers

Watch recent newborns being fed. Usually as soon as their cheeks are stroked, they turn their heads rapidly—almost frantically—in the direction of the stroking. Interestingly, researchers have found that should food be delivered when the babies' heads are oriented *away* from the stimulus, they rapidly learn to react to the touch by turning their heads in the opposite direction (Siqueland & Lipsett, 1966). Because nourishment is essential to any infant's survival, behaviors instrumental in attaining that consequence rapidly increase in rate. When conditions are

right, access to food tends to strengthen the behavior on which its delivery is contingent. If Flossie receives a peach when, and only when, she includes *please* in her request, *please* will rapidly be incorporated in her requests.

Examples of the Use of Edible Reinforcers

Numerous illustrations of the use of **edible reinforcers** have appeared in the literature. Practitioners have used them to teach language, self-feeding, physical, and social skills to children with severe behavioral deficits. Azrin and Lindsley (1956) reinforced cooperation between children with candy, and Riordan and his colleagues (1984) used preferred food items to reinforce food intake of four hospitalized children who had a history of chronic food refusal. Even more complex skills, like the use of syntactical sentence structures (Wheeler & Sulzer, 1970), have been promoted by means of edible reinforcers.

What are some of the specific types of edibles that behavior analysts use? In one case, to increase academic performance by children in a special class for those with developmental delays, the teacher distributed *extra* milk and cookies after the children had completed more assigned tasks than previously (Campbell & Sulzer, 1971). In a regular public school classroom (Coleman, 1970), when four students earned candy to share with classmates for doing their work, their output increased and disruption decreased. Visual attending increased by more than half after students in three classes for hearing impaired children were signaled with a light flash indicating that they earned M&Ms and cereal bits for visually attending for 10 seconds (Craig & Holland, 1970).

Edible reinforcers need not be limited to children or people with special needs. Ordinary adults can be just as responsive to food. We have seen a number of cases in which behaviors on the job, including producing quality products and reducing scrap, have been enhanced when employees were surprised with treats such as pastries, soft drinks, or luncheons as a consequence of improvement. Similarly, refreshments at parent or staff meetings tend to encourage attendance.

Factors to Consider in Selecting Edible Reinforcers

You will need to weigh a few important factors as you contemplate using edible reinforcers. First if alternatives natural to the context, such as recognition and preferred assignments (and additional possibilities itemized below) are equivalently powerful, avoid depending on food as a prime source of reinforcement. Should such alternatives not prove viable and you conclude that food is the way to go, or when you decide to provide an occasional edible treat, be sure to check for food allergies or other health problems with the clients or their parents, caretakers, or hospital staff. For instance, sweets are harmful to diabetics. Regularly giving children nonnutritious food right before meals may interfere with their appetites and unbalance their diets. Try to select nutritious foods—fruits, vegetables, milk, fruit juices, and such high-protein items as meats and cheeses. Use bits of sweetened cereal, candy, soda, and so on only if the other items do not work. Following are some other suggestions:

extra milk	ice cream or sherbet
apple sauce	potato chips and
baby food	other munchies
canned or fresh fruit	fruit juice
pudding	jam, jelly, peanut
cheese	butter, and crackers
raisins	soft drinks
cupcakes, donuts, or	luncheon meats
pastries	small candies
cookies	"minisandwiches"
dry cereals	second portions of
nuts	lunch or dessert
popcorn	minimarshmallows
yogurt	pickles

Avoid using nuts or popcorn with very young or severely developmentally delayed children, because these foods may cause choking.

The reinforcing value of food and other primary reinforcers can vary from moment to moment, depending on recent historical and contextual events. For instance, conditions such as a period of deprivation from food or drink; an uncomfortably warm, cold, sterile, or crowded environment; or recent exposure to punishment or extinction or other historical or contextual circumstances may alter the reinforcing value of a given stimulus. Michael (1982) uses the term **establishing operation** to describe ". . . any change in the environment which alters the effectiveness of some object or event as reinforcement and simultaneously alters the momentary frequency of the behavior that has been followed by that reinforcement" (pp. 150–151).

Naturally, moving into a room with a temperature of 70 degrees is more reinforcing when the weather outside is extremely hot or cold than when it is mild. Similarly, as you will learn in Chapter 27, delivering a blow may be much more rewarding to a person who has just been hurt than under ordinary circumstances. (Recall your feelings the last time someone stepped on your toe, rebuked you, or dented your car.) Food, too, varies in reinforcer value as a function of preceding events—the time since the last meal, how much of a particular item someone has recently consumed, the person's health status, and so on.

Using edible reinforcers after a person has had a complete meal makes less sense than it would several hours later. The loss of food's reinforcing value after a person has eaten a large meal is an instance of **satiation**, a problem you might encounter if you give someone too much to eat all at once. To postpone satiation, when you need to distribute food items frequently, as in repeated training trials, limit portions, perhaps to a teaspoonful or about a half-ounce. An alternative is to divide regular meals into several minimeals and distribute them throughout the day (Azrin & Armstrong, 1973).

Individuals also develop preferences and aversions for particular foods, probably in good measure as a function of their experiences with the particular items. We may have consumed certain edibles simultaneously with or just before unpleasant events, such as becoming ill, so they have become singularly unappealing to us. Find out what items to select by asking your clients or employees to identify their favorites or offer them pairs of choices and see which ones they select most frequently.

Food grabbing and disruptions in instruction (Thomas, Faulkner, & Bolt, 1988) are problems you might encounter with very young or severely developmentally disabled clients. To avoid this situation, keep the supply beyond reach or out of view, for instance, concealed by furniture or in your pockets. Always pair food delivery with social events like praise, smiles, or gentle caresses to permit those events gradually to begin to acquire a reinforcing function.

Tangible Reinforcers

Just as we work to acquire shelter, clothing, furniture, sports cars, yachts, lakeside cabins, scuba gear, jewelry, antiques, and fine china, most clients will make an effort to earn certain **tangible reinforcers**. Remember our earlier description of the asthmatic patients' efforts to earn surprise gifts? Often people will repeat actions followed by prizes, trinkets, toys, and supplies. A case in point was a safety program with which one of the authors was involved. Customized tape measures, pens, coasters, group photographs, and other items were received with considerable enthusiasm when participants were occasionally awarded them following an especially impressive improvement in their safety performance. Additional illustrative tangible reinforcers in roughly developmentally appropriate order are:

dolls
toy soldiers, Indians
cowboys
clay or nontoxic
    molding materials
jacks
kites
crayons
magic marker
coloring book
puzzles
miniature toys
posters
eraser
note pads
colored pencils
colored paper
whistles or other
    noise makers
jump rope
notebook
playing cards
school decals
tools
paperweight
positive notes home
items from a mail-
    order catalogue
bicycle
toy rings
baseball or football
    cards
models
badges
gold stars
checkers
"tattoo" transfers
musical instrument
teen magazines

car and sports
    magazines
grooming aids
make-up
    combs
    hair cream, after
    shave lotion, and
    so on
pens
felt pens
money
pictures of movie,
    TV, or rock stars
game equipment
pencils
books
paperback books
comic books
calendar
balls
toys for siblings
school pennant
customized shirts or
    jackets
address book
"rental equipment"
cassette players
phonographs,
    television
jewelry
paper dolls
yo-yo
monster books/
    magazines
certificates
frisbees
scout equipment
art supplies
board games

letters of appreciation or commendations,
    copy to supervisors; in personnel file
certificate of accomplishment
letter to family member describing
    accomplishment

collectible objects, such as dishes, glassware, bottle caps, marbles, doll clothes, movie star memorabilia, baseball cards, foreign stamps or coins, stickers, gummed labels, stars, insignia
reserved parking space
sports equipment
instructional supplies
customized patches
plaques, trophies, certificates of achievement
posted compliments
published thanks
merit raise
photographic portrait of group
prize with engraved plate citing accomplishment (e.g., briefcase or tool box)
group reward such as small refrigerator, coffee maker, vending machine
engraved desk items such as pen sets, clocks, schedule books, picture frames
records, audiotapes, videotapes, compact discs

To prevent choking, avoid giving objects small enough to lodge in the windpipes of young or severely developmentally delayed children.

Factors to Consider in Selecting Tangible Reinforcers

Preferences for particular tangible reinforcers usually are shaped by our learning histories in the same manner as for conditioned reinforcers. Objects *per se* have little reinforcing value until they are linked with other strong reinforcers. Owning a sports car increases the likelihood of having good things happen to you. A sports car reflects status and permits access to food, companionship, income, admiration, and so on. Yet some of us prefer full-sized sedans; others a horse and buggy or a sled. The attractiveness of the reinforcer depends on historical and contextual factors: what we have directly or vicariously experienced; the function of the item; its utility under particular cir-

cumstances; and so on. Therefore, as with edibles, you need to preassess the functional effectiveness of any planned tangible reinforcers.

An excellent assessment model is one developed by Mason, McGee, Farmer-Dougan, and Risley (1989). At the beginning and end of the study, the children's preferences were assessed by measuring how each of a pool of items influenced their approach, avoidance, smiling, and compliance with instructions. Additionally, each day, several pairs of preferred items were presented and each child was told to "pick one." Selected items were set aside for use in the subsequent teaching session, and according to the data, functioned very effectively.

Alternatively, although not as valid as providing behavioral choices, you might try direct inquiries. You can also use a reinforcer survey of the type devised by Cautela and Kastenbaum (1968) or Sulzer-Azaroff and Reese (1982).

Establishing operations may make a difference as well, especially for satiation and deprivation. A small trinket is likely to have much more value for an individual who possesses few luxury items than for the "person who has everything." Similarly a new Porsche will have less value for a person who already owns several than for his buddy who is lusting after his first.

Avoiding satiation with tangible rewards is a challenge, because often only one or a few suffice and then the reinforcing value is gone. Most advanced societies have solved that problem by employing symbolic reinforcers instead—exchangeable items, like money, tokens, or checks. Another solution is to loan people the reinforcers temporarily or allot them in small portions: the parts of a model; stamps, coins, or other collectors' items; pieces of sets of china or glassware. Should your financial resources be limited, many free or inexpensive items are available:

factory rejects, seconds
day old baked goods

manufacturers' scraps

bottle and can returns

junk-mail giveaways

promotional items

nature collector items: shells, leaves, fossils

wholesale purchases

plants from cuttings, seeds

white elephants

donations or loans from co-workers, friends, parents

used greeting cards

items obtained from catalogues of free and inexpensive teaching materials

library rentals of books, films, records, videotapes

Satiation for your clients and cost to yourself also may be minimized by awarding the tangible item intermittently rather than every time a behavior is emitted. Television game shows use clever devices for distributing tangible rewards, and you can do something similar. As one example, excitement, surprise, and novelty are incorporated into the "grab bag" game:

- The group and the contingency manager jointly designate behaviors to be accomplished: an improvement in some personal, social, or other skill area (maintaining a health practice, sportsmanship, math scores, housekeeping tasks, contributing to the discussion, helping others, and so on).
- Periodically, when members are seen engaging in one of the desired behaviors, they are permitted to reach into the grab bag and select an item, usually one suggested or contributed by the participants themselves.
- Gift certificates and notes exchangeable for the kinds of activity reinforcers described later may also be included: "You may leave three minutes early for lunch," "You and a friend may have an extra five minutes break," and so on.

Written messages, certificates of achievement, trophies, and other symbolic items can acquire powerful reinforcing properties as people undergo life's experiences. For example, in one study thank you notes to case managers, contingent on visits to their adolescent clients in a residential program, increased the frequency of visits (Clark, Northrop, & Barkshire, 1988). The thank you letters appeared to be a useful tool "for effecting changes in interagency communication and ensuring more personal contact between case managers and their youths" (p. 45). Fortunately, items like these require few resources but can serve a mighty reinforcing function.

Activity Reinforcers

Access to enjoyable activities also can serve as a reinforcer. Planning our schedules so a pleasant activity follows a behavior we are trying to increase illustrates our use of the preferred activity as a reinforcer. "First I'll mow the lawn, then go for a swim." "After I work overtime for a month, I'll go on a trip." A student allows herself to listen to music after finishing her studying. If her rate of studying increases as a function of that arrangement, listening to music is a reinforcer.

Parents often use **activity reinforcers** to teach their children to assume responsibilities or to increase other kinds of behaviors. Dexter's parents let him borrow the car after he has completed all the yard work; his mom teaches him to make pizza after he finishes his homework. After Flossie has picked up her toys, her mother allows her to watch television. Assuming these activities are effective reinforcers for the youngsters, the rates of the responses on which they are made contingent will increase.

In the Achievement Place program (Phillips, Phillips, Fixsen, & Wolf, 1971), such privileges as shopping trips, outings, special assignments, and recreational activities were made available to youths who completed their assigned tasks and met their responsibilities. McEvoy and Brady (1988) permitted autistic and behavior-disordered children access to play materials that were rotated weekly (Legos, dress-up clothes, water colors, a cassette recorder, record player, and a toy kitchen) contingent on correctly completing math problems. Correct responding increased and day-to-day performance variability decreased as a result.

Project 12-Ways is a program designed to improve home conditions of families cited for child neglect (Watson-Perczel, Lutzker, Green, & McGimpsey, 1988). The program uses a combination of tangible and activity reinforcers. The mothers received stickers each time specific areas of the bathroom and kitchen were found to meet standards of cleanliness. When they had accumulated a specific number of stickers, the set could be exchanged for a coveted reinforcing activity, such as cooking a simple side dish, viewing an educational filmstrip, or going on an outing with the contingency manager.

The following lists activities that have been found to be effective reinforcers for children and adults:

jumping down from high place into an adult's arms
listening to self on tape recorder
pushing an adult in swivel chair
being pulled in a wagon
looking out the window
blowing bubbles (soap, gum)
painting with water on chalkboard
cutting with scissors
modeling with clay or putty
throwing a ball or bean bag
turning a flashlight on and off
looking at projected slides
walking around in high heels
carrying a purse or briefcase
popping a balloon, milk carton, or paper bag
playing with a magnet
solving codes and other puzzles

listening to a song
blowing out a match
looking into a mirror
watching the train go around a track
building with blocks
pushing someone in a wagon
playing a short game, like tick-tack-toe
pouring water through a funnel from one container to another
climbing a ladder
sitting in an adult's lap
looking at a Viewmaster™
wearing funny hats
rolling wheeled toy down an incline
stringing beads
operating a jack-in-the-box
singing a song
performing before a group
combing or brushing own or adult's hair
using playground equipment
being pushed on a swing or merry-go-round
playing instrument
drawing and coloring pictures
helping staff
minutes of free play
story time
recess
special playground games
trip to the zoo
private study booth
time in gym
opportunity to stay up later
fishing
swimming
trips to farm, bank, pet shop
class parties
sporting events
recreation program
sharpening pencils
making and playing with puppets
extra recreational time
having copies run off
changing cafeteria table
assisting the teacher
"good letter" sent home

team captain
access to arts and crafts program
writing on chalkboard
special jobs
coming in early
having lunch with teacher
choice from list of activities made up by
    students themselves
running errands
room monitor
cleaning the board
tutoring
grading papers
use of class typewriter
use of piano
field trips
boating
parties
cartoon films
special school events
released time
two-minute break to talk
time to read
access to game room
opportunity to use copy machine
lowest test grade removed
viewing movie
being classroom helper
arranging bulletin board
watching animals
being on committees
listening to records
seeing grade book
doing special projects
time to play with own toys or games from
    home
extra swim period
feeding fish
riding elevator
turning lights on or off
pulling down screen
leading the pledge of allegiance
sitting at the teacher's desk
first in line
help custodian

painting
sandbox
library time
choosing a story
turning filmstrip in projector
distributing milk
first up to bat at playtime
taking care of the calendar
filing for the teacher
passing out paper, other supplies
time in science lab
radio tuned to favorite station
telephone time
relief from assignments
time in class for homework
being excused from a test
leaving class early
using tools
television time
home time
talking to a friend
looking at teen magazine
helping a younger child learn
class debate
time to make cards or presents
services such as house cleaning, yard work,
    auto repair or wash, home repairs, child
    care
paid health club membership
assistance with or relief from assigned duties
a party
a night at a hotel
catered meal
training opportunities
dance lessons
lectures, slide presentations
trips
meal at restaurant
meetings with refreshments, entertainment,
    or prestigious person in attendance

Note that the list items progress in age appropriateness, from young or developmentally delayed children to adults. So consider your clients' chronological ages and developmental levels when selecting from the array. Also, some are very natural to the situations in which they are used, whereas others are less frequently included within the usual routine. For example, free play, recess, and playground games are integral to school programs, whereas private study booths would be unusual. In general, however, activities seem to be regarded by many change agents as less intrusive than edible or tangible reinforcers and may be less costly and more transferable. Satiation is usually less of a problem, because an activity reinforcer is available only for a specific or limited time, and the target behavior must recur before the person again obtains access to it.

Preferences for participating in particular experiences also depend on learning history and current conditions. Therefore, matching reinforcing activities and people is just as important as selecting tangible reinforcers to suit them. To determine what activities are potentially reinforcing for individuals, watch them, provide alternative choices, or simply ask them. As with the other classes of reinforcers, to verify the effectiveness of an activity as a reinforcer, we must test it, determining whether rates of a behavior increase systematically when the activity is made contingently available and/or decrease when contingently withheld.

Should you be searching for mechanisms for providing reinforcing activities for young people, consider an "**activity table**," "**treasure box**," or the "**slot machine game**." The activity table displays an assortment of reinforcing activities—interesting reading materials, checkers and chess sets, cards, a television with headphones, and so on. Whenever they have met predetermined behavioral criteria, participants are permitted a period of time at the table.

A treasure box, which contain toys, games, and arts and crafts materials, and can be exchanged across classes every so often to increase novelty and variety, is a slightly different device that has been used by four teachers at

the Bushard School in Fountain Valley, California (Stansberry, 1973).

Similarly, in a personal communication (July 27, 1976), McGookin described his method: a slot machine—a game-like activity that uses activity and tangible reinforcers. Setting a kitchen timer to signal at random intervals, the contingency manager allows one or more participants, who have been engaging in the desired behavior throughout the interval, to take a chance at the slot machine: four or five inverted paper cups, each of which covers a gift certificate for a reinforcing item or activity.

Each of these schemes lends itself to individualization of activity reinforcers. Yet the analyst still may be at a loss as to what particular event to make available as a reinforcer. Turning to Premack's discovery may solve the quandary.

The Premack Principle

Premack's work (1959) suggests another method for discovering effective reinforcing activities, through identifying an individual's high-probability behaviors. On the basis of a series of laboratory studies involving both animals and humans, Premack demonstrated that those behaviors in which an individual freely engages repeatedly might be used to reinforce low-probability behaviors. This finding, which Lloyd Homme and colleagues (1963) subsequently labeled the **Premack principle**, has been translated into a procedure in which access to high-probability behavior is made contingent on performance of a low-probability behavior. A worker frequently stops and chats with her fellow workers on her way back and forth from breaks and meals. Extra break time with her companions might be a powerful reinforcer for meeting her production quota. If a child frequently plays with a doll but does not do spelling exercises, access to the doll can be made contingent on completion of an exercise.

The Premack principle was applied with impressive effectiveness by Ayllon and Azrin

(1965) with a population of hospitalized, long-term psychiatric patients. In order to engage in high-frequency behaviors—leaving the ward, interacting socially with the staff, playing games, and making commissary purchases—the patients were expected first to perform socially useful work. Similarly, a group of nursery school children had been observed spending considerable time running and screaming, as reported in a study by Homme and his colleagues (1963). By making running and screaming contingent on sitting quietly, the investigators were able to increase the frequency of sitting quietly.

For practitioners, the most appealing aspect of applying the Premack principle probably is the fact that potential reinforcers are already present in their programs. There are always some behaviors in which individuals engage (even if they are sitting and doing "nothing") with greater frequency than others. All that remains is to reorganize the program in such a way that access to those high-frequency behaviors is restricted, making them available only after the target behavior is performed. For example, first- and second-grade students improved the quality and speed of printing and writing when they were allowed access to a playroom after completion and scoring of their papers (Hopkins, Schutte, & Garton, 1971). All the toys, games, and other materials the children were observed using frequently were placed in an "enriched playroom" section of the classroom. These objects included a television set, Lincoln logs, a box, a set of wooden blocks, toys, an old typewriter, a fish tank, dolls, flashcards, checkers, and several picture and story books. In addition, children were allowed to bring objects from home as long as they kept them in the "playroom."

Instead of subjectively judging what people seem to enjoy doing, presuming that an activity is universally reinforcing, or even asking clients what they like to do, the Premack principle requires reinforcing activities to be selected on the basis of formal observation (that is, how often and for how long the person freely engages in the activity in relation to others). Although the three former means of selecting a reinforcing activity may well prove successful, often they fail. Selecting objectively recorded high-probability behaviors may be a preferable alternative.

At this point you may protest that this procedure is hardly new—that managers, parents, teachers, and others frequently use strategies like these. Certainly! A mother says, "First you must clean up your room" (low-probability behavior), "then you may go out and play" (high-probability behavior). Bruno practices his scales (low-probability behavior) before playing his favorite piece (high-probability behavior). A manager says, "After you are attending work regularly, you may select your preferred work schedule." The main difference between these informal applications and the more formal use of the Premack principle is that the Premack principle's foundation is based on objective evidence.

Apparently, applications of the Premack principle can be very effective. What accounts for this? Perhaps response deprivation is responsible. If so, the critical factor may not be that a high-probability behavior is selected as a reinforcer but that restricting access to a response can be sufficient to turn it into a reinforcer.

The Response Deprivation Hypothesis

Sometimes, when access to low-probability behavior has been restricted to below its baseline level, making that *low-probability behavior contingent* on the high-probability one, has *increased* that high rate even further (Konarski, Johnson, Crowell, & Whitman, 1981). In view of this, Timberlake and Allison (1974) have proposed the **response deprivation hypothesis** (**RDH**), ". . . if access to one of a pair of events is restricted below free **operant levels** (baseline), an organism will work to regain access to that activity" (Redmon & Farris, 1987, p. 327). In the human circumstance, then, the person's access to one activity is restricted to below baseline levels. Engaging in the targeted activity at a level exceeding baseline rates is required to gain access to the deprived activity. Therefore, when the Premack principle is being applied an activity is made effective as a reinforcer *not* because of its high probability, "but because when one arranges a contingency, access to one of the events is deprived below its usual level" (Redmon & Farris, 1987, p. 328). "The reinforcement effect will occur only when the condition of response deprivation is present in the contingency" (Konarski et al., 1981, p. 660). Response deprivation apparently is an establishing operation.

Proponents of the RDH would explain the increase in the rates of completed daily copying assignments by the first- and second-grade students in the Hopkins et al. (1971) study by noting that access to the playroom was deprived below its recent baseline level. (Students were not permitted access to the playroom until their daily copying assignments were completed and scored.) The children were working to regain access to their former level. "The deprivation of access to the contingent event and not the probability differential is assumed to be the primary causal variable in the contingency" (Redmon & Farris, 1987, p. 328).

To support the RDH as an explanation for effective applications of the Premack principle, Konarski, Johnson, Crowell, and Whitman (1980) showed that for first-grade children in a special education class, math could act as a reinforcer for coloring only "when the conditions of response deprivation were present even though it was clearly shown in the baseline to be a lower-probability response" (p. 600). They further concluded that "These results support the predictions of the Response Deprivation Hypothesis while being contrary to the notion of probability differential as the critical condition for reinforcement" (p. 606). Similarly,

Konarski, Crowell, and Duggan (1985) showed that, for 7- to 11-year-old EMR (educable mentally retarded) students, feedback with or without the addition of being able to do math had no positive effects on cursive writing, but adding the combination of corrective feedback and the response deprivation contingency for math "resulted in significant increases in the percentage of words written correctly for all of the children" (p. 21). ". . . It appears that the task of establishing effective reinforcement schedules is not limited to finding already potent reinforcers but may be one of simply establishing schedules that produce response deprivation using behaviors already in the student's repertoire" (Konarski et al., 1985, p. 29).

The response deprivation hypothesis provides a means of establishing reinforcers that meet "a person's changing behavioral needs" (Konarski et al., 1985, p. 29), expanding our ability to identify and develop reinforcers beyond the Premack principle. Almost any behavior in which the individual engages is a potentially effective reinforcer, provided access to that response can be restricted. For example, knowing the baseline levels of two important job performances, a manager can establish one as a reinforcer by restricting access to that response for a while, then using it to reinforce the rate of occurrence of the other. Similarly, as Podsakoff (1982) notes,

> . . . almost any response which occurs in an organizational setting may serve to reinforce another response as long as the operant level of the two behaviors exceeds zero and a schedule is imposed which produces a greater disparity from the baseline than is already in effect. If this is a reliable finding, it may eliminate many of the problems managers have in identifying effective reinforcers (p. 346).

Social Reinforcers

Social reinforcers are interpersonal acts that serve a reinforcing function. Examples of common social reinforcers include "attention" (that is, looking at, answering, nodding, and so on), smiling, and statements of recognition or approval. Table 10.1 lists illustrative social reinforcers.

Examples of Effective Use of Social Reinforcers

The literature abounds with demonstrations of the effectiveness of applying social reinforcement. For example, Allen and her colleagues (1964) reported a study of a child who avoided her peers but demanded lots of attention from her teachers. By attending to the girl only while she interacted with other children, the teacher helped her to learn to play more appropriately.

Rates of engaging in assigned tasks is another performance that has been shown to improve via social reinforcement (Allen et al., 1964; Broden et al., 1970; Kennedy & Thompson, 1967). In one study (Broden et al., 1970), two very disruptive second-grade students were seated next to each other. When the teacher systematically increased the amount of attention for appropriate attending to task by one boy, his rate of attending increased. So did the other boy's, although to a lesser degree. When the teacher reinforced the second boy's attending later on, it improved even further. Kazdin (1973a) obtained similar results, while Kazdin and Klock (1973) showed that contingent smiles, patting, and touching increased the attentive behavior of 11 out of 12 mentally retarded school children.

Advantages of Social Reinforcement

Alone or in combination with other reinforcers, social reinforcement also is a *convenient* procedure to use during counseling sessions, as demonstrated by Kennedy and Thompson (1967). In that study, when the child maintained eye contact with the counselor for at least a minute, the counselor gave the child candy, accompanied by praise and smiles. Attending increased during counseling and also in the classroom. Similarly, in group counsel-

ing, contingent comments like "good," "that's wonderful," and "great," as well as smiles, were found to increase the verbal behavior of low-verbalizing sixth- and seventh-grade students (Tosi et al., 1971).

Receiving praise or approval also has been shown to alter individuals' self-reference statements ("self-esteem") for the better, as shown with paper-and-pencil tests. For instance, Ludwig and Maehr (1967) found that when teachers approved students' performance in a physical-education class, their self-reference statements changed in a positive direction. People also have been taught to use praise to effectively reinforce their own accomplishments (Wisocki, 1973), resulting in improved performance and evaluations of their self-worth.

Social reinforcers are practical, because the time required to give recognition, praise, nod, smile, or make eye contact is minor. The only costs are, as we shall see, the discomfort some people feel in delivering these reinforcers (Komaki, 1982) and the effort involved in remembering to deliver them or in devising signaling systems (for example, periodic chimes, light flashes, or cue cards) to prompt their delivery. Most important, because social reinforcers are natural to many social settings, they are unobtrusive. In addition, because they can be used over long time spans, they are particularly suited to supporting recently modified behavior, and can be continued indefinitely to sustain maintenance of well-established performances.

Using praise does not come naturally to all managers, however. In the work setting managers are often reluctant to praise employees because, as Komaki (1982) found, some felt praising was not "macho." Other managers were uncomfortable with or unskilled in using praise. Recipients often have trouble receiving praise gracefully, thereby punishing its delivery. We have found that referring to graphic evidence of improvement makes praise more natural, and the use of specific praise is more easily accepted by recipients. Also, managers can

Table 10.1 Potential Social Reinforcers for Children, Youth, and Adults

Children	Youth and Adults
Nod	Nod
Smile	Smile
Tickle	Laugh (with, not at)
Pat on shoulder, head, back	Wink
Hug	Signal or gesture of approval
Wink	Orienting glance directly toward face
Kiss	Assistance when requested
Signal or gesture to signify approval	Positive comment on appearance
Swing around	Pat on the back
Touch on cheek	Handshake
Holding on lap	Asking client to discuss
Fulfillment of requests	something before group
Eating with children	Asking client about items of
Assistance	interest to individual
Joining class during recess	Asking client to demonstrate
Saying (adding reason)	something
yes	Saying (adding reason)
nice	very good
good	okay
great	beautiful
fine	good for you
very good	exactly
fantastic	thank you
very fine	that's interesting
excellent	_____ is excellent
unbelievable	that's great
marvelous	yeah
atta-girl, atta-boy	great
far out	right
I like that	I agree
right on	good job
right	good idea
that's right	fantastic
correct	fine
_____ is really paying attention	what a clever idea!
wonderful	unbelievable
you really pay attention well	you really are being
you do that well	creative, innovative . . .
I'm pleased with (proud of) you	see how you're improving
that was very nice of you	that looks better than
that's good; great	last time
wow	keep up the good work
oh boy	you've apparently got the idea
very nice	little by little we're getting there
good work	see how _____ has improved
good job	

Table 10.1 Potential Social Reinforcers (continued)

Children	Youth and Adults
great going	you're really becoming an expert at this
good for you	do you see what an effective job ____ has done?
_____ is a hard worker today; good for you	you are very patient
that's the way	that shows a lot of work
that's interesting	you look great today
much better	it really makes me feel good when I see so many of you hard at work
okay	that's the best job I've seen today
you should show this to your parents	you're paying attention so nicely
you're doing better	the interest you are showing is great
that's perfect	it makes me happy to see you working so well
that's another one you got right	that's a thoughtful (courteous) thing to do for _____
you're doing very well	_____ has gotten his materials and has started to work already; good going!
see how well _____ is doing?	_____ is ready to start
look how well he (she) did	you're really very considerate of one another
_____ is really working	
watch what he did; do it again	
show the class your _____	
_____ is really working hard; he is going to be able to _____	
wow, look at _____ work	
you look nice today	
_____ is working nicely, keep up the good work	
I can really tell _____ is thinking by what she just said	
_____ is sitting quietly and doing his work; good for him/her	
_____ is listening with such concentration; that's very polite, _____, thank you	
you should be proud of the way you're sitting quietly and listening to me while I'm giving a lesson	
_____ just earned another point by sitting quietly and listening while I was reading; good job _____	
_____ walked quietly to her seat; thank you	
good, you sharpened your pencil before class; now you're ready to go	
_____ has all of her supplies on her desk and is ready to go; good!	
_____ has gotten his materials and has started to work already; good!	
it's nice to see the way _____ raises his hand when he wants to share	
the whole class is really listening politely to one another	
this whole row is sitting quietly with their chairs on the floor; great!	

profit from seeing and imitating others' delivery of praise. When all else fails, use of praise can be shaped by initially asking the manager simply to describe to the employee what was accomplished. Later on, words of commendation can be added:

1. "Orders are up 2% I see here."
2. "It's good to see that orders are up by 2%."
3. "Your orders are up by 2%. Nice going!"

Because social reinforcers have so much to commend them, they should be included as often as possible within reinforcement programs. Even when tangibles, edibles, activities, or exchangeable reinforcers are necessary because social reinforcers are not sufficiently effective in a given situation, preface the delivery of other types of reinforcers as often as possible with positive social stimuli. In that way, interpersonal acts should begin to assume conditioned reinforcer properties, as described in the previous chapter. Then gradually substituting these newly conditioned social reinforcers for the other nonsocial reinforcers should be possible.

Social reinforcement is just as important for people with sensory impairments as for anyone else, but the medium of delivery may need to be altered for these populations. Oral praise and tactile stimuli—pats, gentle backrubs, and scratching—can communicate social approval to the visually impaired child, whereas visual stimuli—smiles, nods, and gestures of approval—and tactile stimuli are particularly appropriate for those with impaired hearing.

Adults' performance is no exception, because most grown people are responsive to social reinforcement in some form or another. Consider how important recognition, attention, or approval from a parent, spouse, lover, sibling, fellow student, employee, friend, or prestigious person may be to you. This importance reveals the potential utility of social reinforcement for purposes of treating, training, or managing the performance of mature clients, trainees, staff, or ourselves.

Feedback as a Reinforcer

Praise from peers and supervisors, **feedback** in the form of data showing client improvement, or other information about teaching or therapeutic effectiveness, and even feedback derived from self-recordings have been shown to be especially effective reinforcers for many staff. In one instance, nonprofessional institutional personnel increased their daily use of operant training methods when a feedback system, consisting of information about sessions conducted, was publicly disseminated among the staff (Panyan, Boozer, & Morris, 1970). Similarly, Cooper, Thomson, and Baer (1970) found that feedback about staff's definitions of appropriate child responses and their percentages of attending to those responses produced increases in contingent attending. Egan, Luce, and Hall (1988) demonstrated that specific written feedback from peers improved the performance of case managers in organizing and maintaining client records (e.g., program and client descriptions, operational definitions, interobserver agreement, and labeled experimental conditions). Initially, the specific feedback affected only those record keeping components to which it was applied. Later, providing feedback for multiple targets simultaneously was found "to more quickly attain improvement in all standards" (p. 51).

Feedback was found to be one of the most salient features of leadership and supervisory effectiveness, as illustrated in a study of the crew in sailboat racing competitions. Komaki, Desselles, and Bowman (1988) found that approximately 30% of the variability in a skipper's win–loss records could be attributed to two categories of behavior: watching crew members' efforts and letting them know when each was doing something right or wrong. The authors concluded that knowing the frequency with which leaders monitor and provide feedback "gives us a solid foundation on which to predict their success" (p. 19).

Generally, though, compounding feedback with praise or other reinforcers is more effective than feedback alone, as Wikoff, Anderson, and Crowell (1982) demonstrated with work efficiency in a furniture manufacturing company. Crowell, Anderson, Abel, and Sergio (1988) were able to improve the service provided customers by bank tellers by first clearly delineating various goals with specific examples. Desired behaviors quickly increased 12%. The behaviors increased an additional 6% when combined with feedback and even 7% more when praise was added. The effect was reproduced when feedback again was attempted by itself and later with added praise. Similarly, Cossairt et al. (1973) investigated whether feedback to teachers by itself would improve performance. Results were inconclusive, but when praise was combined with the feedback, performance did improve. Feedback also was found to double the productivity of workers in an auto machine shop (Gaetani, Hoxeng, & Austin, 1985). When feedback was accompanied by a commission system in place of traditional wages, dollar gains tripled over the original baseline level.

For analysts concerned with staff, employee, or management training, probably feedback about trainees' and clients' progress, needs to be linked with clear goal setting and praise or some other reinforcer, will be very productive in increasing targeted trainee behavior optimally. Or, as Balcazar, Hopkins, and Suarez (1985–86) point out, feedback "will be effective to the extent that it is related to functional, differential reinforcement" (p. 65).

Using Specific or Labeled Praise

As with feedback, evidence (Bernhardt & Forehand, 1975) suggests that **specific**, or **labeled**, **praise** is a particularly effective way to convey approval and provide a person with rules to guide subsequent response (which is important antecedent control, as we shall see). Specific praise focuses on the meritorious aspect of the behavior. "How wonderful that you remembered to take your medicine without being reminded!" "Congratulations! You integrated the material with examples relevant for you." Specific praise places the emphasis on the behavior, rather than on the person, which is important. When praise then is withheld from inappropriate behavior, people learn to recognize (or discriminate) that it is not they themselves but their actions that are deficient. Specific praise increases the likelihood that the correlated behaviors will be repeated in the future.

You now recognize that social reinforcers are convenient to use, because they can be readily delivered immediately each time a behavior occurs in individual and small-group situations and, very frequently, even in large groups. Because people do not tend to become very quickly sated with social reinforcers, they can function as **generalized reinforcers**.

Generalized Reinforcers

Generalized reinforcers are usually conditioned reinforcers that are effective for a wide range of behaviors as a result of having been paired with a variety of previously established reinforcers. Due to this history, their effectiveness does not depend on any one state of deprivation. Recognition is one form of generalized reinforcer; a token or money is another. Each has been paired frequently with other primary or conditioned reinforcers.

Immediately dispensing tangible and activity reinforcers each time a target behavior occurs is not always feasible. Permitting an assembly line worker an extra break when he meets a goal while the line is moving would interfere with production. In the midst of a spelling test allowing Dexter to leave the room to go shoot baskets as a reward for writing legibly might be disruptive. A solution would be to use another form of generalized reinforcer, an exchangeable reinforcer, such as a **token** that could later be exchanged for access to the reinforcing activity.

Recall that tokens are reinforcers exchangeable for reinforcing objects or events. They share some of the properties of tangible and other more natural reinforcers. Delivering tokens as an immediate consequence of a target behavior permits them to serve as conditioned reinforcers and also to signal that other more powerful reinforcers will be forthcoming.

Token reinforcement systems often are used informally, as when a teacher awards points toward the students' final grades for completing an assignment. The tickets the asthmatic children could exchange for prizes in Renne and Creer's study (1976) and the ones that children used to purchase tutoring in the program described by Robertson et al. (1976) were "tokens." When a mother dispenses check marks or gold stars that can be turned in later for money or special privileges, she is using a token system. Similarly, paychecks, script, vouchers, and even money itself are all forms of tokens. Following are a few other suggestions:

tickets to sports event, concert, theater, or
    film
bonus pay
tuition vouchers
meal tickets
coupons
points or tokens exchangeable for money,
    greens fees or cart costs, or other tangible
    or activity reinforcers
magazine subscriptions
lottery tickets
trading stamps
cash awards
gift certificates for merchandise or service
    such as massage or beauty treatment
memberships in clubs

In and of themselves, tokens reinforce little. The **back-up reinforcers** for which they can be exchanged are what count; but when token systems are used haphazardly, as they often are, their benefit is compromised. By contrast, token systems that incorporate behavioral principles are much more promising (Ayllon & Azrin, 1968).

You already know how important selecting effective tangible and activity reinforcers can be. A well-designed token system includes an assortment of client-tailored items and privileges as back-up rewards. Timing, scheduling, managing the amount to avoid satiation, and pairing token delivery with social reinforcement are also of crucial importance. You will be learning the nuances of these aspects shortly, but now recognize that people often express concerns about using contrived reinforcers.

Concerns About Contrived Reinforcers

Practical, philosophical, and ethical concerns may be voiced when novel reinforcement programs are being introduced. Here we discuss some of these concerns and suggest how you might handle them.

Extrinsic Reinforcers

What does distributing a donut or a trinket have to do with improving performance on the job or in the classroom? Very little. Actually, whenever possible, we try to use reinforcers that are closely tied to the natural function of a behavior, because those conditions tend to support its maintenance. Supplying entertaining reading matter permits skilled readers the reinforcement natural or intrinsic to improved reading proficiency. Obtaining a desired object by describing or asking for it by name is a natural consequence of increased language proficiency. A warm, comfortable shelter is the reinforcer for building a cabin in the woods. A well-manicured landscape is the reward for mowing the lawn. If natural reinforcers are controlling their related performances, introducing contrived extrinsic reinforcers into the system makes little sense. However, Greene and Lepper have stated: "Many important and potentially interesting activities, including, for example, reading, may seem like drudgery rather than fun until one has acquired a few rudimentary skills. There is no question, therefore, that extrinsic motivation is often needed to get people to do things they wouldn't do without it" (1974, p. 50).

Krumboltz and Krumboltz have made a similar point: "For many types of behavior which ultimately bring their own reward, the initial reinforcer is merely a temporary expedient to get the behavior started. Sometimes a shift from a concrete reward to a less tangible one is a step toward gradually helping the child become independent of external rewards" (1972, pp. 111–112). Tharp and Wetzel (1969) have noted that the ultimate aim of all intervention plans is to adjust behavior:

> . . . to make the target eligible for incorporation into the social control (reinforcement) network which shapes us all into Civilization. The aim, then, is to humanize. For some disordered children, it is necessary to begin with candy or money, after all, we all begin with milk (pp. 87–88).

Although reinforcement programs are designed to help individuals become less and less dependent on material or other contrived reinforcers, the reinforcement program must start where individuals are and gradually move toward the place where they should be.

Bribery

What about bribery? Isn't reinforcement a form of bribery? Reinforcement *would* be bribery if the purpose of the reward were to achieve advantage for the person who delivers it instead of for the recipient. The aim of bribery is to corrupt conduct or pervert judgment, or to promote dishonest or immoral behavior. Besides being unscrupulous and exploitive, however, bribes often are tendered before the act, whereas reinforcement can only happen afterward. Behavior analysts attempt to apply reinforcers in as natural a form as feasible. Bribery usually involves more artificial or contrived rewards that bear little relation to the act. Bribery has no place in behavior analytic practice.

Even though reinforcement isn't bribery, sometimes people object to the notion of "paying" individuals to behave properly. But let us look at the behavior of most adults. No matter how strongly people are dedicated to their professions, how long would most adults continue at their jobs in the absence of a contingent paycheck, which could later be exchanged for many other tangible reinforcers? Probably not indefinitely, especially with other options available for pay. "Then," we might continue, "adults work for paychecks, but children don't earn money for learning and behaving acceptably. Why not limit reinforcers for youngsters' behavior to traditional ones, like grades and praise, which educators and change agents have always used with relatively good effects?" The answer to this question, as we have seen, is simple: Traditional reinforcers do not work well with some youngsters, and they fail completely with others. We assume that readers of this book are seeking alternative solutions for clients who are not responding as desired to traditional reinforcers. Ask yourself too, why *should* people necessarily be expected to work hard for minimal reinforcers when we earn substantial incentives to perform our jobs?

We must concern ourselves more with what *is* rather than what *should be*, within, of course, ethical and humanitarian constraints. If, for example, our clients are performing satisfactorily and their progress seems to be supported adequately by the natural consequences of success, arranging formal reinforcing events is not necessary. Instead, we would continue to praise and recognize their accomplishments intermittently as merited.

If, on the other hand, our clients are not performing satisfactorily, the responsibility for attempting to remedy the situation is ours. Collaboratively, where possible, we need to try to rearrange the environment—turn things around to promote success. This may be accomplished by providing support services, transferring clients to different settings, or modifying their current environments. In many cases, we will need to manage the very same reinforcing consequences that we already are dispensing unsystematically (e.g., attention, assistance, and privileges) and begin to deliver them according to a more precise plan. In other circumstances, as encouragement we may need to augment the natural reinforcing events with other, more powerful ones for the individual. (Later you will learn that when progress is well established, we begin gradually to dispense with those artificial supports, using the individual's patterns of behavior to guide our actions.)

Countercontrol

When you worry about bribery, recognize also that although contingency managers may be trying to influence their client's behavior, their clients probably also are controlling powerful reciprocal social reinforcing contingencies. Clients' reactions can reinforce (smiles, compliance with suggestions) or punish (frowns, refusal to comply, grumbles). (Remember the Brown et al., 1975, quotation from Chapter 7: "Control always results in countercontrol.")

Rather than leaving countercontrol up to chance, several investigators (Graubard, Rosenberg, & Miller, 1971; Polirstok & Greer, 1977; Sherman & Cormier, 1974) purposely trained students to reinforce their teachers' use of effective procedures. Graubard and his colleagues astutely noted that

1. Children spend more time with classroom teachers than they do with professional consultants or administrators.

2. Students have the greatest personal interest in changing their teachers.

3. "The positive use of power leads to self-enhancement and positive feelings about the self" (1971, p. 83).

To manage this countercontrol, each student was given the responsibility for accelerating praise rates and decelerating negative comments by the teachers. The behavioral investigators noted, "The children's labor contributing to effective change was free; and it is certainly less costly to employ pupils using reinforcement readily available in the classroom, than it is to pay clinical personnel within the traditional medical model, to change behavior" (p.89).

Similarly, Polirstok and Greer (1977) worked with an eighth grader from a low socioeconomic area who was described as exhibiting extreme behavioral problems. She had been referred to the dean of students for disciplinary action five to six times a week for using verbally abusive language and for more serious offenses. Her counselor successfully taught the girl to socially reinforce her teachers' interactions when disapproval was absent with statements such as "fine," "right," "I appreciate that," "thank you," "beautiful," "neat," "super," "cool," and "right-on." Nonverbal approval consisted of smiles, pats, head nods, looking at the teacher when the teacher was talking, hand-raising when appropriate, and other behaviors indicating praise or attentiveness. When four of her teachers were observed (in math, social studies, science, and Spanish classes), three of the four increased their use of approval and decreased disapproval as a function of the student's countercontrol. A follow-up evaluation 6 weeks later showed that these results were maintained for the teachers and student. Further, the teachers indicated that they were pleased with the student's remarkable socialization and newfound "maturity." More importantly, she was referred to the dean of students only once after the training was terminated. The student also frequently commented on "how much nicer she thought her teachers had become" (p. 715). Perhaps one day people, including children, will be formally taught to effectively reinforce the behaviors they prefer from those controlling important contingencies for them, such as employers, parents, teachers, and spouses, to everyone's mutual benefit.

Treating People Differently

If each person's learning history dictates distinctive reinforcing contingencies, won't it occasionally be necessary to treat some differently from others? Certainly, especially if you are unable to identify a common reinforcer of sufficient potency for the whole group. Realize, though, that we already do treat people differently when we attend to troublesome behavior. Also, because everyone possesses unique genetic and learning histories, some individuals may respond idiosyncratically to given events. Consequently, treating everyone the same is not necessarily uniformly beneficial.

Still, many potential consumers remain concerned with the question, "Won't the others become jealous or angered if someone else is receiving special reinforcers they themselves are denied?" That is a reasonable issue, but, because each group is different, there is no simple answer. One possibility is to explain to those involved that each of us is unique and that each has special interests, skills, and areas of weakness (yourself included). Often clients and patients will understand that focusing on different behaviors to change and using different methods makes sense.

Surprisingly, knowing that help is finally on the way can be a source of relief to peers who may have been suffering from the individual's performance difficulties. Peers also may recognize that they stand to benefit indirectly from the intervention. Sometimes pointing this benefit out to them and reinforcing their supportive efforts helps, enabling the performance of the whole group to improve as a result. This is what Christy (1975) found in working with two classes of children, aged 3½ to 6 years.

Sometimes peers have been seen to applaud the successes of their fellows. In this way the reinforcement program causes the environment to become more pleasant and rewarding for everyone.

Nevertheless, should you or others involved continue to be concerned about apparent inequities, other options remain open. If ignoring peers' expressions of dissatisfaction (Christy, 1975) is ineffective, you could point out that the person is receiving the special privileges, objects, or access to activities for making *progress*. Inviting others to design programs for themselves in areas in which *they* need to improve is also possible. Emphasis is placed on each individual's progress, *not* on competitive comparisons. Another alternative is to change the program so that the client earns reinforcers not only for himself or herself but also for the whole group. This alternative will be elaborated on later in Chapter 12.

Accepting the fact of individual uniqueness underscores our presumption that "nothing is more inequitable than the equal treatment of unequals." Providing students with different learning materials suitable to their current levels of functioning is standard for teachers. Similarly, appropriate reinforcers must be provided for each person if optimal results are to be achieved. Remember that there are "Different strokes for different folks!"

Withholding Reinforcement

Conversely, should an analyst deprive a client of unearned reinforcers, such as food, while others are enthusiastically consuming their goodies? Such incidents do cause concern among personnel and observers (not to mention the deprived client)—and rightly so. Our response is that if goals and procedures are selected carefully, nonreinforcement should rarely occur.

In the unusual situation in which contingency rules dictate that reinforcers must be withheld, we avoid severe repercussions by using a system resembling that applied in many organizations. Just as companies often provide regular increases in compensation for satisfactory performances—adding "merit pay" or bonuses for extra accomplishments—we have distributed base portions of reinforcers "noncontingently" (i.e., the base portion is not made contingent on any particular response). For instance, children may be provided freely with milk and one cookie but must earn additional portions. Although one does trade off some effectiveness (see Amount of Reinforcement in Chapter 11), enhancing consumer satisfaction more than compensates for the concession. Actually, legal interpretations have supported this approach among children having special needs (e.g., *Wyatt* v. *Stickney*, 1972), again underscoring the advisability of providing your clients with all minimum needs noncontingently while programming extras as contingent reinforcers.

Summary

In this chapter we have presented a very broad array of potential reinforcers: tangible, consumable, activity, social, and exchangeable. They provide you with an extensive list from which to select. Sometimes, locating an effective reinforcer is tricky, demanding added imagination, flexibility, creativity, and time. Initially, selecting reinforcers that are somewhat intrusive or contrived may be necessary when the reinforcers more natural to the environment are ineffective. As soon as the behavior of concern begins to change in the desired direction, however, gradually introducing less-intrusive reinforcers, while replacing them with reinforcers indigenous to the situation, should be possible. Remember, if progress begins to wane, the fault lies neither with behavior analysis nor the client. Rather, the selection of objectives and reinforcing contingencies requires examination. In this chapter you have learned how to select effective reinforcers. In the next, we explore the variables that influence the reinforcement process.

Chapter 11

Implementing Reinforcement Effectively

GOALS

After completing this chapter, you should be able to:

1. List and describe the optimal application of each of the features that influence the effectiveness of reinforcement.

2. Explain why immediacy of reinforcement is so important during the initial stages of a program. Provide illustrations showing how immediacy can be incorporated within programs.

3. Describe four methods of introducing delay of reinforcement.

4. Define, recognize, and give original illustrations of each of the following terms:
   a. Supplementary reinforcers
   b. Discrimination
   c. Deprivation
   d. Reinforcer survey
   e. Reinforcer menu
   f. Intrinsic motivation
   g. Reinforcer sampling
   h. Continuous reinforcement (CRF)
   i. Intermittent reinforcement
   j. Schedules of reinforcement

5. Discuss how contextual conditions may influence the effectiveness of a reinforcement procedure.

6. Describe how the quantity of a reinforcer may influence its effectiveness and how to determine when the quantity is sufficient.

7. Describe and illustrate four objective means of identifying reinforcers.

8. Discuss why matching reinforcers to individuals rather than selecting reinforcers based on their success with others is important.

9. List and discuss the advantages of using (a) natural reinforcers and (b) a variety of reinforcers.

10. Discuss and illustrate how establishing operations can influence the effectiveness of a selected reinforcer.

11. Discuss how novelty influences the effectiveness of reinforcers and how it might be used in a specific program.

12. Design a plan for using reinforcer sampling in a behavioral program.

13. Discuss the role of competing contingencies in a reinforcement program.

14. Discuss when using the following is best: (a) continuous reinforcement, (b) intermittent reinforcement. Predict the outcome when each schedule is not used appropriately.

15. Discuss how the source of reinforcement can influence its effectiveness.

16. Discuss the advantages of teaching people to reinforce their own behavior.

17. Describe how to teach clients to reinforce their own behavior.

18. Discuss the factors that appear to make self-monitoring and self-reinforcement effective sometimes and ineffective at other times, and when self-directed strategies might prove most useful.

19. Describe the importance of a reinforcing environment.

20. Design a reinforcement program that includes all of the methods for maximizing the effective use of reinforcement and explain the influence of each method.

"Aha," says Ms. Charming. "Now I have some ideas about new reinforcers to try in the workshop. In addition to M&Ms, I can try social, activity, exchangeable, tangible, or other edible reinforcers." Selecting appropriate reinforcers, however, is only part of the process of effective reinforcement. Once those consequences have been chosen, several other factors must be considered. These include timing of presentation, context, amount of reinforcement, appropriateness, novelty, variety, competing contingencies, scheduling, and others. In this chapter we explain and discuss each of these factors.

Reinforcing Immediately

One basic principle of behavior is that *immediate is more effective than delayed reinforcement* (Skinner, 1938). One of the main reasons why is discussed by Reynolds (1968):

> . . . Delayed reinforcement is not as effective as immediate reinforcement, partially because it allows the organism to emit additional behavior between the response we wish to reinforce and the actual occurrence of the reinforcer; thus, the intervening behavior is also reinforced, with the result that what is reinforced is the response followed by some other behavior rather than just the response alone (p. 29).

His supervisor has decided to give Charlie a positive rating when he performs well in his vocational training program. But suppose Charlie is horsing around just as the rating forms are delivered. The positive rating may well reinforce horsing around. Immediate reinforcement would have avoided that problem.

People with reasonable skills in verbal comprehension can sometimes still profit from delayed outcomes, because immediate statements from others or themselves may support the behavior: "Charlie, you are going to get a high mark because you learned how to put the new kits together so well." However, evidence seems to suggest that the lower people's meas-

ured IQ, the less likely it is that their actions will be influenced by delayed consequences (Herrnstein, 1989), unless steps are taken to teach waiting (as described later).

Young children and those deficient in verbal comprehension have an especially difficult time with delayed reinforcement, because the relation between the response and the reinforcer is unclear. When reinforcement delay is at issue, signaling precisely what is being done correctly at the moment becomes particularly crucial. Nods, winks, smiles, a "V for victory" sign, and enthusiastic "okays" and "all rights" suit that purpose well. These signals can function just as well with other clients whose skills are advanced, including adults, as we have found in teaching nursing staff to lift safely (Alavosius & Sulzer-Azaroff, 1986, 1990). Using supplementary reinforcers is another way to cope with necessary delay.

Using Supplementary Reinforcers

Applying reinforcers immediately may prove unwieldy for managers who supervise large groups of people, for instance when the group is striving to earn a powerful incentive that entails a delay. Ms. Feeney has decided to take her class on a field trip to reinforce the students' correct completion of the week's assignments. Naturally, delivering the trip to each student immediately, contingent on the completion of an assignment, would be impossible. Fortunately, an alternative exists: the use of **supplementary**, conditioned **reinforcers**. The contingency manager can use a signal to indicate that a stronger reinforcer will be presented: "Good, I see you are getting your work finished. This way you'll be able to go on the trip Friday." If a verbal statement is not effective, a token system might be. She could give tokens to the students as soon as each one completes a subsection of work; a specific number of tokens can be required for each to go on the trip. That is essentially how the delay was bridged for students who earned tickets exchangeable for subsequent tutoring (Robertson, DeReus, & Drabman, 1976).

Teaching Waiting

Another way to deal with the issue of timing of reinforcement is to systematically teach people to wait patiently during delays of increasing duration. One method is to program delay into the routine gradually. When Charlie persists in pestering his supervisor to look at his work or constantly asks to have his accomplishments praised, it is probably because he has not learned this type of patience. The supervisor then may set up a program with Charlie to help him bridge the time gap. For a while, the supervisor may try to check the work on request. Little by little he can begin to delay for a moment or two, simultaneously using verbal prompts: "I'll be over to check your work in a couple of minutes." After many instances of brief delay, he can gradually lengthen the interval.

Recognize that people generally tend to maximize the overall amount of reinforcers that they receive (King & Logue, 1987; Logue, Pena-Correal, Rodriguez, & Kabela, 1986). Therefore, try to arrange to make your delayed reinforcers stronger than more immediate ones. Schweitzer and Sulzer-Azaroff (1988) taught several hyperactive preschoolers to elect larger delayed reinforcers over smaller, immediate reinforcers by increasing the length of the delay periods very gradually.

Another method used to help some clients begin to wait for their reinforcers is to introduce distracting stimuli while the clients wait. For example, Volpe, King, and Logue (1988) found that radio music decreased impulsiveness in situations in which adults were otherwise found to act quickly rather than making the most advantageous choices. The investigators pointed out that distracting stimuli can diminish the aversiveness of delay periods. Other investiga-

tors have posited that teaching people coping strategies for managing waiting—such as singing songs, counting, practicing relaxation exercises, playing games, and so on—also supports patient waiting. Therefore, you might consider combining strategies like these while you gradually lengthen the intervals between a behavior and its contingent reinforcer.

All of us need to be able to wait for reinforcers in order to continue learning and to function successfully in society. Because this skill is so important, we will return to this topic again in our section on maintaining behaviors.

Teaching Discrimination of Contextual Factors

Immediate reinforcement helps people to discern or **discriminate** the basis on which reinforcers have been dispensed—*to identify which of their behaviors lead to reinforcement and which do not.* Another way to facilitate such discriminative learning is to specify clearly the context, or stimulus conditions, under which a given response will be reinforced. Although situational conditions were elaborated on in Chapters 3 and 4, we will briefly review them here because they are critically important to the effective use of reinforcers.

If Kevin must complete all his chores before 9:00 A.M. in order to receive his allowance, his parents should stipulate these conditions. If you were a teacher, you would specify the circumstances under which hand-raising is to be reinforced, such as during study time, but not during recess or discussion time when spontaneous participation is acceptable. Tell your employees where, when, and how they must perform their jobs if they are to earn bonuses or positive evaluations. Prepare a precise job description. By clearly specifying the context and/or the qualities a behavior should possess for it to merit reinforcement, you are more likely to see your expectations met. This is one reason why educators in effective schools clearly specify classroom and school disciplinary rules, and successful organizations prepare precise policies and procedures.

Because *behavior tends to increase more rapidly when the conditions under which it will be reinforced are communicated clearly*, many successful behavioral programs incorporate this feature. Actually, the conditions signaling the probability of receiving reinforcement for a specific response can be communicated in different ways. In addition to instructions, objectives, promises, rules, guidelines, policies, and so on, clients may observe others receiving reinforcers following the targeted response (i.e., *modeling* or, as some label the event, *vicarious reinforcement*), or their performance can be prompted or guided.

Verbal prompts are often used to cue a verbal response, such as a word or concept. "If you want to be able to discriminate between the terms *ordinate* and *abscissa* (the vertical and horizontal axes of a graph, respectively), remember that the word '*abscissa*' has a *b*, and *b* stands for *bottom*." This sort of a prompt will help you to respond *abscissa* next time someone asks you about labeling the horizontal axis of a graph; the condition, a horizontal line, begins to signal that the response, *abscissa*, will be reinforced. A gesture or verbal reminder also can help us to perform a nonverbal response correctly—like showing the motions to be imitated or telling the person how to do it (e.g., "Keep your eye on the ball!").

Physically guiding a movement, such as a tennis swing or soccer kick, helps communicate exactly how a particular body movement should be executed so that reinforcers will result. Self-monitoring—observing and recording one's own behavior—also can facilitate discrimination. For example, Mace and his colleagues (1986) found that although reinforcers alone increased the productivity of retarded adults employed in a sheltered workshop, adding self-monitoring reduced variability and increased productivity even more. Self-monitoring without reinforcement, however, was insufficient to maintain the improvement over baseline levels. Therefore, the effectiveness of self-monitoring appeared to depend on reinforcement, with self-monitoring seeming to facilitate discrimination of the circumstances under which the reinforcers would be forthcoming.

Contractual arrangements are another device for signaling the conditions for reinforcement: for example, establishing weight goals or caloric intake for control of obesity or setting goal levels for the number of times a supervisor, teacher, or parent is to apply specific management techniques each week. Setting group goals and objectives, such as weekly departmental performance-improvement goal levels, can promote social support for the desired behavior change (Hayes et al., 1988). So can publicly monitored self-management goals.

Prompts, goals, criteria, and contextual conditions will soon come to cue (set the occasion for) the occurrence of the behavior, as long as these stimuli are consistently paired with reinforcement of the response: The hands on the clock approaching the hour of nine will begin to signal Kevin that his chores must be completed if he is to earn his allowance. Passing the plant entrance cues Larry to don his hard hat so he can avoid being chewed out by the boss.

These examples show us how important it is to specify clearly the conditions under which reinforcement will occur, as well as applying it optimally when the behavior occurs under those conditions. What you are trying to accomplish, as implied previously, is to teach the learner to *discriminate* the conditions under which a particular behavior will be reinforced. Later in Chapters 15–18 we discuss other strategies for teaching more complex discriminations.

Providing an Adequate Amount of Reinforcement

The decision about the quantity—*how much* reinforcement to deliver following the target behavior—depends on a number of factors: (1) the type of reinforcer used; (2) the deprivation conditions; (3) whether or not reinforcement is externally managed, and (4) the cost (time, effort, and additional resources required to make the response). Recall that people satiate more rapidly on food than on other reinforcers. In general, with negative reinforcement, the more aversive the stimulus is to the client, the greater is its power. For positive reinforcement, the more deprived the client is of the stimulus, the more likely it will function as a reinforcer. An empirical approach, however, is the best way to find out how much is enough: Try it out and see. Count the number of hours since the client has eaten. See how long the target behaviors continue when reinforced with small amounts of given foods.

Deprivation (the absence or reduction of a reinforcer for a period of time) and satiation probably play a lesser role with social reinforcers. A smile or saying "good boy" may be effective, even though the child has received several such reinforcers in the recent past.

All other factors being equal, responses requiring considerably more effort or cost require more reinforcement than easier tasks or than those that are "intrinsically" reinforcing (i.e., "maintained by consequences that are natural and automatic results of responding," Dickinson, 1989, p.2). Ask yourself which course you would take, assuming both courses taught you the same amount and provided you with the same number of credits: one that required a reasonable amount of work or one requiring twice as much?

Parents, teachers, employers, and other managers often find it difficult to alter their social-interactional habits and to reinforce good performance, rather than criticize poor performance. In order to teach themselves or one another more effectively to increase their rates of reinforcement—the more effortful responses—they may need additional incentives (for example, reinforcing feedback about client success, praise from peers or supervisors, release from duties, extra free time, easier assignments).

Generalized reinforcers that can be exchanged for others, like tokens, money, coupons, trading stamps, or credits, are only minimally affected by satiation. Even individuals with a large bank account usually continue to strive to increase their funds. The same is true of events that signal forthcoming reinforcers, like a smile or a promise. By now, it should be apparent that no simple formula exists for determining what quantity of reinforcers to deliver. The final judgment must be made on the basis of empirical data.

Ensuring Appropriate Reinforcer Quality

We have already discussed the importance of carefully selecting a reinforcing item or event of a particular quality. Here we consider some factors that may influence the reinforcing value of any given type of reinforcer: appropriateness, variety, novelty, and other contingencies in operation.

Selecting Appropriate Reinforcers

You don't only select reinforcers because they increase or maintain just anybody's behavior, but because you have evidence that they maintain or increase the behavior of the specific person involved. Before any potential reinforcer is adopted for a behavioral program, you must demonstrate that it is effective with the individual under the circumstances in which it is to be applied. Little Elroy's teacher discovered the value of hugs and pats for him by first counting the proportion of directions he followed without hugging or patting him for compliance for several days. Then for another few days she hugged or patted Elroy each time he followed a direction, and his rate of compliance increased. To establish the extent to which compliance was dependent on those consequences, she discontinued them for a few days, noting a drop in Elroy's rate of compliance. Only when hugs and pats were reintroduced did he again begin to follow directions. Having demonstrated the reinforcing properties of hugs and pats for Elroy, the teacher could now use them to promote other behaviors and eventually to develop other conditioned reinforcers.

Although following such an elaborate routine may not always be necessary to demonstrate the effectiveness of reinforcers, successful programming demands that *individuals and reinforcers be matched on the basis of objective observation*. If the rate of a behavior does not increase or sustain when a particular stimulus is delivered contingent on the behavior, one possible explanation is that the stimulus is not sufficiently reinforcing for the client in that context. Other reinforcers should be attempted until one is demonstrated to be effective.

To further complicate matters, we have already pointed out that the effectiveness of a particular reinforcer can vary. In fact, Mason, and colleagues (1989) found that preferences do change not only from month to month but also from session to session. It was not surprising, then, that when children's preference for reinforcers was assessed daily, the researchers found that nontargeted maladaptive behaviors were virtually eliminated, and the accuracy with which the children identified their body parts increased. Thus, constantly check on the effectiveness of your selected reinforcers and be prepared to vary them frequently.

If you are having difficulty identifying promising reinforcers, especially for verbally delayed clients, offer choices in pairs to the person and observe which is selected most often. By sequentially presenting different combinations of objects so that each eventually is matched with every other, you can establish a hierarchy of preference. A variation of this method has been described and evaluated by Green and her colleagues (1988). They first asked direct care and professional staff to rank stimuli (i.e., hugs, vibrator, verbal interaction, pudding, juice, rock or soft music, mechanical toy, hand-held toy, hand clap, light board, tactile mitt) that their 12- to 34-year-old profoundly handicapped clients preferred. The stimuli then were presented in groups of three to discover which the clients would either approach or maintain contact with for at least 3 seconds, smile at, or make positive vocalizations toward, and which ones they would avoid by pushing or turning away. These choices were offered repeatedly over a period of 5 weeks. The stimuli determined in this systematic way were assumed to represent the individual's preferred reinforcers. Interestingly, ". . . there were no statistically significant correlations between any student's preferences based on the systematically assessed ranking and the preferences based on the staff opinion ranking" (p. 34). Apparently, the judgments of those who worked with the clients differed from the results of the direct assessment. That the stimuli selected by the caregivers "did not function as reinforcers unless those stimuli were also preferred on the systematic assessment" (p. 31) should come as no surprise. When you hear people protest, "I tried reinforcement but it didn't work," suspect that the stimuli they applied did not function as reinforcers for the individual at that time. Again, as this study illustrates, basing reinforcer selection on objective data is preferable to relying on subjective opinion. Opinions must be verified.

Another way to identify appropriate reinforcers is to ask people to select their own; but they must know themselves very well. Verifying the accuracy of their judgment is usually a good idea. For example, if the consequence is withheld contingently, does the behavior decrease? Does contingent presentation increase it? A student may say that he would love a volume of Shakespeare's plays as a reward for turning in his English assignments. However, the reward may not actually be a reinforcer. He may make this request because he wants to please his teacher, not because he really likes Shakespeare. One way to check the validity of his statement would be to look at his library card to see what books he has taken out lately. That information might hint that a good collection of science-fiction stories would be a far more powerful reinforcer.

Durand and his colleagues have been developing a promising instrument for assessing the functional (i.e., reinforcing) value of maladaptive behavior, including self-injury, aggression, and tantrums. The Motivation Assessment Scale (MAS) asks when, where, and under what circumstances the behaviors occur, and what the consequences of those behaviors are. Motivational or maintaining variables specifically probed for are (1) social attention, (2) tangible consequences, (3) reinforcing sensory feedback, and/or (4) escape from demands or other aversive situations. Through repeated testing of the scale, the authors have commented that its results correlate highly with other forms of contingency analyses, and it appears to be very user-friendly.[1]

Verbally skilled people can respond to a **reinforcer survey**. Actual questions would depend on the client's developmental level and social-cultural environment. However, typical questions included on reinforcement surveys include:

1. What are your favorite foods?
2. If you had _____ dollars to buy whatever you wanted, what would you buy?

[1] Research recently completed suggests that further refinement of the scale may be necessary to enhance its reliability. (Rourke, Dorsey, Geren, Barry, & Kimball, 1990).

3. If you had 30 minutes of free time at _____ (school, work, home), what would you really like to do?
4. What are three of your favorite things to do _____ (at work, at home, at school, with friends)?
5. Who are the people you prefer doing things with at _____ (home, school, work)?

The information obtained from these questions can suggest consequences to test to determine whether items or events actually function as reinforcers.

You now know of several ways to identify promising reinforcers:

- Observe to determine what consequence increases the occurrence of a behavior.
- Present several stimuli or a **reinforcer menu** (a list of possible reinforcers) and determine which the individual selects or approaches repeatedly.
- Withdraw or withhold access to suspected reinforcers as a consequence of a behavior, and determine whether the behavior does decrease.
- Measure "free operant" baseline levels (described in Chapter 10). Then make the activities or items available contingent on a behavior to see the impact.

As each of these four methods is based on objective observation rather than just on someone's subjective reporting, you can feel reasonably confident about using the reinforcers under similar circumstances.

Deciding to systematically manage external reinforcement. A very important decision, not to be overlooked when you choose reinforcers, is whether you really need to plan a systematic program of external reinforcement for a particular circumstance. For example, in an arithmetic class, consumable reinforcers appear essential for keeping one student working, whereas for another student social reinforcement is sufficient. A third works in the absence of any formal delivery of reinforcers, reputedly "**intrinsically motivated**." Of course, he still receives reinforcers, but on a thin, not-very-obvious schedule. Even though all three students enthusiastically consume yogurt-covered peanuts whenever given the opportunity, would you involve all three in a system of regular reinforcement with peanuts for completion of their daily math assignments? No; only the first student!

Greene and Lepper and others have worried that perhaps "the use of extrinsic rewards . . . can undermine the intrinsic interest of a child in the activities for which he received a reward" (1974, p. 54). Students were told that they would receive and did receive "extrinsic" rewards or access to special activities for engaging in classroom activities they already did without further encouragement. These activities, playing with markers and solving puzzles, presumably were "intrinsically reinforcing." Once the extrinsic rewards were terminated, the children decreased the amount of time they spent on those activities.

An overview of the extensive literature on this topic suggests that any post-reward decrease in behavior following delivery of rewards for working at preferred activities is transient and limited (Dickinson, 1989). Nevertheless, some reward procedures can be aversive. (Of course, by our definition, they would not be reinforcers, then, but punishers.) Might you not find it distressing if your parents gave you a special prize for spending time with your favorite friend? To avoid problems with using extrinsic reward systems, the research suggests that "rewards should be noncompetitive, *reinforcing*, and contingent upon performance standards rather than task engagement; and standards should be objective and attainable" (Dickinson, 1989, p. 13) (italics added). We also suggest that if a person works at a desired task at a high rate in the absence of any regularly dispensed reinforcers (other than those

given as an occasional surprise) you avoid using an extrinsic reward system with the person. If peers are receiving rewards for performing that task, and you are concerned with being equitable, find a more appropriate task to reinforce for this person.

Natural versus artificial reinforcers. Your systematic search for individually effective reinforcers should begin with those that are most natural or indigenous to a situation and, if necessary, progress gradually toward more **artificial** or intrusive ones. If praise or attention are the consequences most frequently applied in a situation, attempt those first. If job ratings, incentive plans, gold stars, grades, or happy faces are natural to the setting, begin with those. Then, assuming that all the other techniques for effective reinforcement are followed consistently for a reasonable period of time and the anticipated rate increase has not occurred, begin your search for alternatives. Progress from the indigenous to those stimuli that are slightly more artificial or intrusive in the situation. If attention, praise, smiles, favorite school activities, pats, and hugs did not work with Elroy, then the teacher could progress toward trying objects exchangeable for normally enjoyable activities, such as music, special games, picnics, and so on. If those also proved ineffective, toys, trinkets, nutritionable edibles, or sweets could be attempted next. Assuming a strong reinforcer eventually were discovered, it could be used initially to increase the rate of the target behavior. Later it could be gradually shifted back to more natural reinforcers. (We shall discuss this procedure in detail in the chapters that describe maintenance.)

The following are among the advantages of attempting natural reinforcers:

- People are practiced in and usually comfortable with applying them.
- The use of natural reinforcers makes it easier to shift back to normal routines.

- Natural reinforcers are less likely to arouse the concern of staff, parents, and the public because they are unobtrusive.
- They do not set the recipient apart from others.

If Sloppy Smith were the only employee in his unit who received a soft drink each time he straightened up his workstation, his fellow workers would surely notice, and Sloppy might resent being treated differently from the others. Although such problems are not insurmountable (as you saw in Chapter 10), avoiding them in the first place whenever feasible is preferable.

Establishing operations. Recall that an establishing operation (Michael, 1982) is an event that strengthens or reduces the reinforcing value of a stimulus and increases or decreases the rates of behaviors that produce that reinforcer. Familiarize yourself with those sorts of recent events in the client's life, such as how long it has been since the person has eaten or had something to drink or been physically active, for these events will affect the value of food, liquids, or exercise for a while. Remember that conditions like those may explain why stimuli found to be effective under some circumstances may not be under others.

Of course, establishing operations often are manageable. You could withhold reinforcers for a while to make them more powerful or alter conditions to enhance the probability of certain behaviors. Recognize, however, that depriving a person of food far beyond regular mealtimes is ethically questionable and in some cases illegal. To take advantage of the establishing operation of food deprivation, plan instead to conduct your teaching sessions just prior to the client's next meal, perhaps dispensing portions of the next meal (or, as Azrin and Armstrong [1973] refer to them, "minimeals"). Once your intructional session is over, you can permit free access to the remainder of a meal. (We return to this topic in Chapter 15.)

Introducing Variety

Rather than depending on a single reinforcer to maintain the effectiveness of a behavior analysis program, use a variety. Varying reinforcers not only introduces novelty, a factor we shall consider soon, but also decreases the likelihood of satiation. Additionally, as just shown, establishing operations and other factors can influence the effectiveness of any reinforcer at a given time. So if one reinforcer doesn't work momentarily, another might. Mr. Goforth, the physical education instructor, offers choices to his students: "Do you want to play soccer or baseball, or have an indoor track meet after calisthenics?" Tiny Tina's mom gives her carrots, applesauce, and pudding, Tina's favorites, rather than just one food, to encourage the child to feed herself. Angela, the supervisor, changes her praise statements from one time to the next—"Nice going," "Good job," "All right"—instead of sounding like a broken record. Plan to vary your reinforcers because your program is likely to be much more effective if it includes an array of *different* types of reinforcers rather than just one or two. Exchangeable reinforcers lend themselves especially well to this.

Introducing Novelty

"Other things being equal, organisms will often prefer to put themselves in novel situations" (Millenson, 1967, p. 397). This conclusion, based on the results of a number of studies, is one that contingency managers should find illuminating. They will frequently find that capitalizing on this principle pays. Some illustrations follow.

A teacher we know prepared a surprise box containing slips of paper on which all sorts of different directions were written: Draw a picture of a cow; wash the blackboard; get a drink of water; write a paragraph describing your pet; take five minutes of free time; tutor a friend in reading; and so on. Students drew slips from the box after completing their assignments. Not knowing what the slip might contain added lots of excitement.

The "job jar" is a closely related idea. Coveted assignments are listed on slips of paper, placed in a jar, and drawn at random following the wanted behavior. Similarly, Chinese restaurants help to reinforce their customers' patronage by providing cookies containing novel fortunes. Sometimes performance managers distribute surprise treats or gifts, such as donuts and coffee or tangible rewards (which often—but not always—function as reinforcers) when their subordinates have met their goals several times in a row—another way of taking advantage of the reinforcing quality of novelty. The most successful teachers continually seek new activities to stimulate and excite their students.

In the community and in schools, special activity centers often provide original learning experiences to students and local residents. For example, the activity center in a school familiar to us schedules instructional activities, such as woodworking, baking, construction, macramé, and other crafts. Students completing their assigned work may visit the activity center for a set period of time. Another high school reported how parents and students participated by offering instruction in their own areas of expertise, such as tie dyeing, guitar playing, calligraphy, auto engine repair, model building, sculpture, kite building, social dancing, ceramics, identification of edible wild plants, natural foods cookery, and other workshops of particular interest to teenagers as reinforcers for assignment completion.

Introducing Reinforcer Sampling

Although variety and novelty may enhance the reinforcing aspects of a stimulus, people might be hesitant to sample something new. They don't know what fun they're missing until they try. Shirley was hesitant the first time she went water skiing, rode a roller coaster, and performed before an audience; but afterward she really began to enjoy these activities.

Before a person has had experience with a potentially reinforcing stimulus, its appeal may be minimal. Holz, Azrin, and Ayllon (1963) found that when psychiatric patients were persuaded to try new things, like certain foods, subsequently the patients would work to acquire those foods. Consequently, Ayllon and Azrin (1968) suggested a **reinforcer-sampling** rule: "Before using an event or stimulus as a reinforcer, require sampling of the reinforcer in the situation in which it is to be used" (p. 91).

Organizations using incentive programs often display prizes conspicuously, just as consumer goods are shown to their best advantage in catalogues and store windows. Similarly, cable TV companies allow viewers to see HBO for several days at no charge. Teachers and parents learn "intuitively" to make use of reinforcer sampling—displaying a new book, reading the beginning of a fascinating story, teaching a new game, organizing a new project, and otherwise exposing youngsters to novel events or objects. Once the youngsters begin to enjoy an experience, it is transformed into a reinforcer that can then be presented contingent on the performance of a targeted task: "As soon as we finish our reading, we will use the remainder of the period to play the new game we learned yesterday."

Assessing for and Overriding Competing Contingencies

Human environments teem with a complexity of contingencies, all impinging simultaneously. Think about the reinforcing and punishing contingencies operating on your behavior at any one time:

- Rewards for your performance of assigned educational or job tasks; punishment for nonperformance.
- Attention from friends—or perhaps their neglect in social settings.
- Consequences from parents, spouses, or

roommates for the chores you do or don't do at home: some good, some bad, some nonexistent.

Various contextual stimuli guide your choice of activities outside the home, like shopping, recreation, traveling, and just about all of your other actions. Some environmental reactions are stronger and exert greater influence than others, and sometimes alternative contingencies directly compete with one another. In all likelihood, responses that support your survival and that of the species, like food, clothing, shelter, and procreation, are stronger than those that provide weaker reinforcers, like approval from someone you do not know very well or do not particularly like.

The path people follow depends in good measure on which particular contingencies are or have been most powerful. Alone with his teacher, Elmer's completion of his tasks might be sustained just by her approval. But as 1 of 28 children in her class, Elmer is rarely alone with his teacher. Instead his milieu consists of a network of contingencies. For instance, Elmer may find Jane's giggling at his grimaces far more reinforcing than the teacher's attention to his academic performance, or avoiding his buddies' ridicule more appealing than avoiding a scolding by conforming to school rules. From his teacher's perspective, in a one-to-one setting, any slight improvement in Elmer's performance could be reinforcing; but in the class setting, the relief she experiences by ejecting Elmer from the room and no longer having to contend with his antics probably would be far more reinforcing.

So you see why successful programs depend on an assessment of contingencies currently in operation in the person's life via A-B-C analyses, scatter plots, and so on. When natural contingencies support competing behaviors, managed contingencies must be powerful enough to override the former, or the entire effort will be of no avail. For example, Elmer's

teacher would need to heavily reinforce both Elmer's remaining on-task and the other students' ignoring of his disruptive behavior. The teacher might arrange things so that Elmer's progress earned *extra* minutes of recess or free time for the whole class. To avoid too much pressure on Elmer, by ignoring his misbehavior, the class could continue to earn its basic reinforcers even when Elmer did not.

The teacher who finds removing Elmer from the room more reinforcing than witnessing his marginal progress might be furnished with supplementary reinforcers for keeping him in class and coping with the problem. Approval from supervisors and consultants for improvements in Elmer's behavior, changes in responsibilities more to the teacher's liking, and encouragement from peers might combine to shift the balance of power.

Arranging Supportive Schedules of Reinforcement

The "rule followed by the environment in determining which among the many occurrences of a response will be reinforced" (Reynolds, 1968, p. 60) is what is meant by a reinforcement schedule. If every time Oscar follows safe lifting procedures, he is praised by his supervisor, safe lifting is being continually reinforced—it is said to be on a **continuous reinforcement schedule** (CRF). More than likely, however, workers are only occasionally complimented for lifting safely, so the behavior is on an **intermittent reinforcement schedule**.

Many different **schedules of reinforcement** have been identified, and each has its distinct properties and produces reasonably predictable effects. Although schedules may be geared to procedures designed to shape, increase, maintain, or decrease behavior, the issue of increasing behavior is the primary focus of the present discussion. How scheduling affects other behavioral aspects will be considered in detail later.

When the goal of a program is to *increase* or *stabilize* behavior, use a very dense or continuous schedule of reinforcement. For example, if parents are trying to teach their children a new routine, the more often they reinforce exercise of the routine, the better. The Hendricks decide that the time has come for Flossie and her brothers to put their dirty dishes in the sink. Every time the children do so, their parents should pour on the praise. After the behavior has been pretty well established (is occurring very consistently—at a *high and steady rate*), fortunately, they can reduce the frequency and regularity of reinforcer delivery.[2] Reinforcing every occurrence of all desired behavior is impossible for a parent, teacher, employer, or anyone else to do. Indeed, as shown later on, established behaviors will better withstand conditions of nonreinforcement (extinction) after the individual has been exposed first to noncontinuous reinforcement for a while. CRF is reserved for increasing and stabilizing a behavior.

Adults also need to receive frequent reinforcement during initial efforts to change their behavior. If you are working as a trainer, supervisor, or consultant to employees, management, or staff, your success will depend in large measure on the extent to which your trainees receive regular and frequent reinforcement. Indeed, consistent use of reinforcement may well prevent staff burnout. The value of frequent reinforcing feedback has been borne out in many studies. In one paper, Balcazar, Hopkins, and Suarez (1985–86) examined 126 reports of the use of feedback[3] as a management tool. Those studies reporting the most improvement in their subjects' performance included use of regular feedback (paired with other reinforcers and/or goal setting).

Thinning Reinforcement

Is the notion of continuous reinforcement totally impractical? Not if you plan your solutions creatively. Often, reinforcing feedback is given in person, but adequate support can be provided via charts and graphs, telephone calls, and notes, and also by encouraging peers to supply positive recognition of the newly acquired skills. Dustin (1974) commented that if institutional change is to persist, change agents need to ". . . possess tenacity to follow through and to return to the same tasks and the same individuals time and again" (pp. 423–424).

Once change is well established, you may be able to gradually reduce the frequency of praise, phone calls, charts, and graphs to a comfortable, workable level. This occasional intermittent reinforcement and the ongoing social support should enable you to diminish the amount of time you need to devote to the program without compromising the durability of change. In their study on principals as agents of change for teacher performance, Cossairt, Hall, and Hopkins (1973) found that praise by teachers maintained and even increased when they themselves were praised intermittently for using it. They concluded that: ". . . the excuse that principals and supportive staff do not have time for the social reinforcement of teacher behavior is invalid" (p. 100). Thus, steps must be taken to ensure that staff is *trained* to an acceptable level of competence and regularly *supervised* in the use of reinforcement or in any other procedure that they may apply.

Identifying Effective Sources of Reinforcer Delivery

The role of those who dispense reinforcers probably influences the success of the outcome of a program, as Fairbank and Prue (1982) have

---

[2] Such a switch to an intermittent schedule of reinforcement appears to facilitate the occurrence of behaviors that occur in more than one setting (generalization). This point will be elaborated upon later in the text.

[3] Although feedback is *not* identical to a reinforcer, as you shall see, it often serves that function in practice.

posited in relation to feedback. Receiving a compliment from the big boss probably goes a lot further with Paula than when one of her co-workers compliments her work. We are shattered when certain people are critical of our actions, whereas the same criticism from others might bounce off our backs. Unfortunately, little research has been done on the impact of reinforcers, although, in one case (Fox & Sulzer-Azaroff, 1989), feedback from direct line supervisors and from safety specialists was compared. Neither proved more powerful in general, but some individual employees responded differentially to one or the other.

People occupying different roles within organizations have, to varying extents, been effective delivery agents of reinforcers and feedback: parents, managers, teachers, supervisors, consultants, peers, subordinates, and others. We suspect that selecting people who are in control of many powerful social or material reinforcers (the rich, famous, powerful, charming, lovable, and/or entertaining) would be good choices. So would close friends, popular peers, supervisors responsible for making personnel decisions, and clients (whose improvement or satisfaction means so much to us).

Should you encounter difficulty in identifying a promising source of reinforcer delivery, teach candidates the skills it takes to perform the function satisfactorily. Help candidates to enhance their social skills and to capitalize on opportunities to become "generalized reinforcers" by learning how to be reinforcing to be with. Nice guys can win ball games!

Self-Directed Reinforcement

Relying on others to furnish reinforcers has limitations, because the other people may be absent or attending to other things. An alternative is to arrange for people to reinforce their own behavior.

Harry and Larry were fifth-grade students in an "open classroom" containing 30 children (Szykula, Saudargas, & Wahler, 1981). Neither performed well in arithmetic, producing many errors and rarely completing assignments. With so many students, the teacher was unable to readily supply the attention required for the boys to progress. So they were taught to record their own arithmetic performance. On 3-inch-by-5-inch cards Harry and Larry noted the number of problems assigned to them, how many they completed, and how many were correct. After recording as instructed for several days, each boy was awarded a prize. The boys then were asked to select as a goal the percentage correct they would try to achieve each day. Larry selected 80 percent, and his performance improved accordingly. Harry, who selected 60 percent, did not progress. So a reinforcement condition was added. When Harry met his goal for the day, he earned pieces to a model van that he eventually could assemble. Harry himself indicated whether he had met his goal and went to the cabinet to select the parts of the model he had earned. That method was successful, and Harry's accuracy began to improve. After a while the boys stopped self-recording, yet they continued to perform well. Then their teacher took a leave of absence, and performance rapidly deteriorated with the new teacher. So the previously effective conditions again were implemented, with the same happy results.

An aide taught a fifth grader through role playing, practice, and earned praise to manage his own behavior in math (Stevenson & Fantuzzo, 1984) by

1. setting a goal for the number of problems he wanted to complete accurately.

2. counting and recording on a chart the number of problems he correctly completed.

3. comparing the number with the predetermined daily goal.

4. awarding himself a gold star if he achieved his goal.

5. exchanging the gold stars for various

items from a self-determined menu of reinforcers.

Weekly meetings with the aide who provided intermittent reinforcement prevented his self-management skills from deteriorating. Not only did the boy do better in math performance, but so did the boy next to him, who was not trained in self-management. (This carryover was probably due to modeling effects—see Chapter 17—and fewer distractions.) Also, the deportment of both students improved in school and at home.

The efficacy of self-administered reinforcement has been demonstrated by Perri, Richards, and Schultheis (1977) who discovered that a major difference between college students who were successful in reducing their smoking rates and those who were not was that the former reported that they used more self-reinforcement. Similarly, Heffernan and Richards (1981) found that college students who used more self-reinforcement and self-monitoring had better study habits and grades.

These examples show that individuals can learn to reinforce their own behavior, and those who do use self-reinforcement appear to be able to produce the changes more readily than those who do not. Actually, many examples of the successful use of self-reinforcement have been reported in the behavioral literature. Severely retarded and other developmentally disabled people (e.g., Fowler, Baer, & Stolz, 1984; Shapiro & Klein, 1980), children with a fear of failure (Stamps, 1973), underachieving children (Edgar & Clement, 1980), college students working on study skills (McReynolds & Church, 1973), teachers trying to enhance their self-esteem (Hannum et al., 1974), and many other populations of children and adults have used self-reinforcement procedures to improve their targeted behaviors.

What factors make self-reinforcement successful? Sufficient research has not been conducted to enable us to respond definitively to that question, but conjectures posited by Jones, Nelson, and Kazdin (1977) and ourselves (Sulzer-Azaroff & Mayer, 1986) include several external variables: history, criteria setting, self-monitoring, surveillance, and external consequences for self-reinforcement and for the target behavior.

History. The individual's prior involvement in a program of training to learn self-administration of reinforcers as well as the length of time the target behavior has been treated by external contingencies can be influential, because they help determine how durable the change may be. That is why you first will need to provide an intensive program of *training* in self-administration of reinforcers. Then continue to apply external contingencies for a long time to establish a firm history sufficient to support the behavioral change and the use of self-reinforcement prior to shifting primary control over to the individual.

Setting criteria. Criteria for assessing success can be imposed externally or set by those involved. Depending on whether goals are lenient or stringent, different outcomes may be achieved. The results of several studies on goal-setting suggest that the most promising approach is to have individuals set fairly challenging though achievable criterion levels *themselves*.

Self-monitoring. A system that incorporates self-reinforcement usually also includes self-monitoring—observing and recording one's own behavior. As we learned previously, the very act of observing and recording has been found to influence performance. Yet separating self-monitoring from self-reinforcement is not always possible, so the degree to which the two factors interact remains unclear. Richards (1981) concluded that with individuals "motivated to self-monitor and change their behavior . . . self-reinforcement may occur naturally" (p. 163). How motivated individuals are, though, appears to depend on how supportive their environment is of the change. For example, Mace and his colleagues (1986) found that productivity rates by retarded adults in a sheltered workshop increased only when self-monitoring was combined with reinforcement from others. Yet, they also discovered that external reinforcement alone was less effective than external reinforcement combined with self-monitoring. Similarly, Hayes et al. (1988) demonstrated that self-reinforcement needed to be combined with external feedback for the study skills of college students to improve. Hence, self-monitoring and self-reinforcement appear to be dependent, at least to some extent, on a supportive environment. We also suggest that self-reinforcement and self-monitoring be used in *combination*, particularly when natural reinforcers are delayed or presented infrequently.

Surveillance and quality assurance. The presence of an external agent—a teacher, employer, peer, consultant, or someone else—who monitors how people self-reinforce may encourage people to be more scrupulous in conducting their programs. Even if the external agent is not intentionally monitoring the self-administration of reinforcers, subjects may be influenced by the person's presence. Whether to arrange for surveillance will depend on your own circumstances, but the data you collect will indicate which kind of surveillance helps.

You may also need to externally reinforce accurate reporting or penalize inaccurate reporting, as Speidel and Tharp (1980) discovered when they saw subjects award themselves undeserved reinforcers. Plan to use a system to reinforce or penalize accurate or inaccurate self-reinforcement from the very beginning, not as difficulties arise. We have found that if we made a big deal of praising honesty during initial phases of a program, accuracy tended to persist.

Supplemental consequences. As we mentioned previously, *a supportive environment is necessary for effective reinforcement,* because both deliberately arranged and unintended contingencies may be in operation. For example, sometimes publicly announcing the number of reinforcers particular people earn can generate negative reactions by others, causing the plan to backfire. (Other times the method works very successfully.)

If a target behavior has changed and sustains satisfactorily for an extended time period, then avoiding highly contrived external reinforcing methods is probably best, because apparently the environment is being sufficiently supportive. But if, as in the study by Szykula et al. (1981), self-reinforcement alone fails to produce the intended results, turning to some supplemental reinforcing contingencies may be judicious. Eventually, you might try to remove the external reinforcers gradually to see if self-reinforcement has assumed sufficient control to permit the improvement to persist.

Providing a Reinforcing Environment

Throughout this section on increasing target behavior we have emphasized the crucial importance of delivering *reinforcers* contingent on selected behaviors. Probably you will find that elevating the overall level of reinforcement in your setting will pay off in the long run as well. We all seek reinforcing environments and attempt to escape from nonreinforcing or punishing surroundings. Ask yourself and others what sort of steps you can take to augment reinforcement in general, because as Nevin (1988) has found, even a certain amount of "noncontingent" reinforcement (reinforcers not systematically presented as a consequence of any particular response) can help to support lasting change.

Consider some of the following activities:

- Making tasks intrinsically more enjoyable by setting attainable but challenging goals; providing more appealing, interesting, and novel activities; supplying new or better tools, supplies, or materials, and trying other techniques.

- Providing pleasant physical surroundings.
- Being friendly—greeting people cordially, getting to know them well enough to converse about the things that interest them.
- Soliciting, listening to and acting on useful suggestions.
- Commenting on and praising peoples' accomplishments, even those they are expected to perform.
- Playing preferred nondistracting background music when feasible.
- Arranging space to people's preference.
- Providing preventive programs for health and safety (e.g., exercise facilities, protective equipment, and consultation).
- Rolling up your sleeves and helping people out in a pinch.
- Being regularly present and visible.
- Joining in organizational recreational activities, such as attending parties, playing sports with the clients, and so on.
- Surprising folks occasionally—inviting an entertainer, giving time off, developing flextime, trying role reversals, hosting parties, holding lotteries, awarding prizes or bonuses, or holding games.

You and the setting will become imbued with reinforcing qualities. People will like to be there with you and all of you will find the quality of your lives improved. Fewer problems will arise, and those that do can be handled more satisfactorily. In summary—*up your reinforcement!*

Summary

Several guidelines for maximizing the effectiveness of reinforcement procedures have been presented. Usually, when a program does not work, one or more guidelines have been overlooked. Therefore, when you set up a reinforcement program, arrange to:

- Reinforce immediately until the behavior is occurring at a high and steady rate, then gradually introduce delay.
- Reinforce every response initially until the behavior is well established, and then gradually introduce intermittent reinforcement.
- Specify the conditions under which reinforcers will be delivered and incorporate other antecedent conditions, and consider establishing operations in effect and the source of reinforcer delivery.
- Deliver a quantity of reinforcers sufficient to maintain the behavior without causing rapid satiation.
- Select reinforcers appropriate to the individual, using those as closely indigenous to the situation as possible.
- Use a variety of reinforcers and reinforcing situations.
- Try to include novel and generalized reinforcers.
- Provide opportunities for reinforcer sampling.
- Eliminate, reduce, or override competing contingencies.

Self-reinforcement is one method that permits reinforcers to be dispensed immediately after each occurrence of the target behavior. With conditions clearly specified and supervised, self-reinforcement programs permit greater independence from external sources of influence. Lastly, do what you can to raise the general level of reinforcement in your setting.

In subsequent chapters, you will learn more about increasing target behaviors, such as the importance of combining reinforcement with modeling and other "discriminative stimuli," and planning for generalization and maintenance once the behavior has been well established.

Peers can also play an important role in determining the success or failure of reinforcement programs. The next chapter focuses on this aspect.

Chapter 12

Group and Peer Reinforcement

GOALS

After completing this chapter, you should be able to:

1. Define, recognize, and give original illustrations of each of the following terms:
   a. Independent group contingencies
   b. Cooperative learning
   c. Interdependent group contingencies
   d. Dependent group contingencies
   e. Peer-mediated strategies
   f. Personalized system of instruction (PSI)

2. List the advantages and disadvantages of interdependent and dependent group contingencies.

3. Describe at least four programs designed to encourage participants to increase their use of social reinforcement.

4. List and illustrate seven reasons why peers should be involved in behavior change programs.

5. List the advantages of peer tutoring.

6. Discuss several possible reasons peer tutoring has been shown to be so effective.

7. List the steps to follow in organizing a peer tutoring program.

8. Discuss the pros and cons of various methods of tutor selection.

9. List the factors to consider in training tutors.

10. Discuss the factors to consider to help ensure that the tutor (not just the tutee) will continue to benefit from the program.

The context in which we live, work, and learn influences the form of our interactions with others. A reinforcing atmosphere promotes an agreeable social community, whereas, as we will show in the chapter on punishment, punitive surroundings evoke escape and aggression—reactions that impede learning, productive performance, or harmonious social relations. Peers can have an enormous impact on the social milieu. They are in control of so many aversive stimuli—threats, coercion, criticism and "put-downs"—and of positive stimuli—approval, praise, and other forms of support. Peer reactions have been shown to prompt and/or reinforce such welcome behaviors as *social effectiveness* (e.g., Strain, Cooke, & Apolloni, 1976; Hendrickson, Strain, Tremblay, & Shores, 1982), *academic skills* (e.g., Egel, Richman, & Koegel, 1981; Trovato & Bucher, 1980), and unwanted acts such as *disruption* (e.g., Soloman & Whaler, 1973), *noncompliance, complaining, and fighting* (e.g., Christy, 1975).

Group Oriented Reinforcing Contingencies

Peer reactions often depend upon the way contingencies are arranged. Group oriented contingencies can be categorized into three types of arrangements: independent, interdependent, and dependent (Litow & Pumroy, 1975). This discussion examines each to discover the nature of the peer reactions each tends to evoke.

Independent Group Contingencies

Independent group contingencies involve setting the *same* response contingencies for all group members but applying them to performances on an individual basis. The criterion level can be *the same* for each group member, as when each individual member of the group earns reinforcers as a consequence of reaching the criterion level. (For example, "Each worker who

meets the production quota will earn a bonus." "You must have 9 out of 10 correct to earn two tokens." "When you correctly complete today's assignment, you may have free time."). Or the criterion can *vary* to allow for individual differences, as when one child has to complete 10 arithmetic problems and another, 20. Because any worker or student failing to achieve the standard loses access to the reinforcer, reinforcement for one member is *not* dependent on the performances of others in the group.

Commonly used in education, this type of **group contingency** also appears generally acceptable to group members. Shapiro and Goldberg (1986), for example, found that a group of 53 sixth-grade students rated the acceptability of this contingency significantly higher than that of the other two methods. (Perhaps the size of the group accounted for this outcome.)

Because independent group contingencies permit each individual to profit, regardless of the performance of other members in the group, peers have no incentive to try to influence one another by such tactics as tutoring or reinforcement. That contrasts with interdependent and dependent group contingencies, which *do* promote **peer influence** because the group members are working to achieve a common goal or reinforcer. Illustrative are **cooperative learning** or cooperative reward structures (Johnson, Maruyama, Johnson, Nelson, & Skon, 1981), which rely on dependent and interdependent group contingencies. In those arrangements, group members share their reinforcers.

Interdependent Group Contingencies

Interdependent group contingencies involve treating the members of a *group* (class, row of students, sales division, personnel in a particular production unit, and so on) as if they were a single behaving *individual*. Here is a hypothetical example. After the nine-member plating division of Top Quality Corporation has met its goal of fewer than 1% defects, the company president visits and presents the group with an award and a new coffeemaker. In one phase of an actual study (Ulman & Sulzer-Azaroff, 1975)—the interdependent or "collective" phase—pennies earned by group members were divided equally among all members of a group of retarded young adults. In that case, compared with an independent group contingency, the collective condition was found to be as effective and a lot less time consuming for the contingency managers.

The noise in a public school class was diminished by using a decibel meter to monitor the sound level (Schmidt & Ulrich, 1969). Any noises, regardless of source, would be registered. So for the class to earn extra gym time, everyone had to cooperate to keep the noise level below a preset criterion. A similar procedure was applied effectively in a school cafeteria (Michelson, Dilorenzo, Calpin, & Williamson, 1981).

Interdependent group contingencies have been found to promote relatively higher rates of academic achievement and cooperation than individual and competitive contingencies (Hamblin, Hathaway, & Wodarski, 1974; Johnson et al., 1981; Slavin, 1983), including among students in classes for emotionally disturbed adolescents (Salend & Sonnenschein, 1989). In the cooperative learning approach, students working in small groups give each other help and suggestions and produce a single final product. This product is graded and each member receives the composite grade. Slavin (1983) also found that the greatest academic productivity by those in the interdependent group arrangement was achieved when the performance of each group member was clearly visible, quantifiable, and accountable to the other group members.

Dependent Group Contingencies

Dependent group contingencies make access to reinforcers by the group members contingent on the behavior of a *selected* group member or *subgroup* of members. Reinforcement does *not* depend on the entire group's performance, as

with interdependent group contingencies. In the Hamblin et al. (1974) program, the group received reinforcers dependent on improvement in the level of the lowest three scores in the class. This arrangement seemed to encourage the more able to tutor the less advanced students, raising the achievement level for the group as a whole.

Sometimes the reinforcers that an individual student earns are shared among the whole group (Walker & Buckley, 1972). For example, a teacher we know made a "work-meter" for her class, onto which she added five points when a target child completed his assignment. When the meter reached a certain level, the whole class received a treat. In another instance, Kazdin and Geesey (1977) found that when, as a consequence of paying attention, two retarded children earned tokens that could be used to purchase back-up events for the entire class, the group paid more attention than when they earned tokens only for themselves.

Comparative Effects of Different Group Contingencies

Do different group arragements function differently? Speltz and his colleagues (Speltz, Shimamura, & McReynolds, 1982) were curious about the direct and indirect effects of different group contingencies on the arithmetic and social performance of twelve 7- to 10-year-old students in a learning disabilities class. The students could earn points for correctly answered problems to trade for a variety of privileges, activities, and games. Contingencies specified that points be dependent on one of the following:

- the average of each student's individual scores.
- the average score of the class.
- the performance of an identified class member.
- performance of an unidentified student.

The number of problems completed correctly using each of those conditions rose significantly above baseline levels. Positive social interactions also rose significantly, primarily during the last (unidentified student) condition.

In another educational study conducted by Van Houten and Van Houten (1977), students were divided into two teams during reading class. In one phase, each student's accomplishments were posted publicly; in another, the scores of the team as a whole were posted as well. Although rates of lesson completion increased during the individual phase, the increase was far greater during the "team" phase. Peer comments increased substantially for the team, probably contributing to the differential effect. When the researchers capitalized on their findings by formally teaching peers how to comment positively on achievement, rates rose even further. Similarly, in a study by Frankowsky and Sulzer-Azaroff (1975), interdependent group contingencies generated more collateral positive verbal and nonverbal social behaviors than did individual contingencies.

Advantages and Disadvantages of Dependent and Interdependent Group Contingencies

People working for individual reinforcement tend to be concerned primarily with their own performance, but when reinforcers depend on the accomplishments of others, people often try to boost one another's performance by prompting, reminding, encouraging, and helping one another. When the situation permits, specific group members may "perform the various task components at which they are most skilled, leading to a group product or outcome" (Greenwood, Carta, & Hall, 1988, p. 261). In several cases, group contingencies like these have prompted peer tutoring and a consequent increase in student academic accomplishment (Hamblin et al., 1974; Speltz et al., 1982).

However, a drawback to group contingencies is that sometimes group members threaten or punish the peers upon whose performance their own reinforcers may depend (Axelrod, 1973). Although this is no certainty (e.g., Speltz et al., 1982, noted an increase in positive interactions), to avoid those undesirable side effects, be sure all members can do the work and the criteria for reinforcement are set at achievable levels. Also, teach participants how to prompt and praise through instruction and modeling and be careful to monitor peer reactions throughout.

Involving Peers Directly

Some group arrangements produce peer cooperation and assistance indirectly. Another tactic is to design your behavior change program to promote direct peer participation. Greenwood et al. (1988) call this approach a **peer-mediated strategy**. Peer-mediated strategies involve peers as "cotherapists" in directly delivering services. Peers may deliver reinforcers or other elements of a planned behavior change program and are directly trained, supervised, and monitored (Greenwood et al., 1988).

A peer contingency manager may, for example, initiate play (Strain & Fox, 1981) or some other social interaction (James & Egel, 1986), deliver points within a token economy (Greenwood, Baskin, & Sloane, 1974), contingently withhold attention (Fowler, Dougherty, Kirby, & Kohler, 1986; Goldstein & Wickstrom, 1986), or provide reinforcing feedback (Fleming & Sulzer-Azaroff, 1990). Similarly, peer tutors present learning tasks, monitoring and responding contingently to the academic performance of their tutees. In both the cotherapist and tutor roles, peer contingency managers are trained, supervised, and monitored by a teacher, counselor, psychologist, consultant, supervisor, or employer.

Approval, recognition of accomplishments, and statements of caring are among the most powerful reinforcers known, but applying these reinforcers optimally is a skill only acquired by means of a fortuitous learning history. Therefore, using effective prompting and reinforcement techniques does not necessarily come naturally to peer trainers. To promote competence, a number of schemes have been devised. Some techniques are informal, designed to heighten the level of social reinforcement in general. We will first discuss them. Then we will examine some more systematic approaches to involving peers as contingency managers.

Methods for Training Peers to Be Socially Reinforcing

Teaching Use of Positive Effect

You may be surprised to discover that the ability to show affection is by no means universal. This inability can create problems in more ways than you might imagine, because expressing affection is often a way of communicating a variety of rich messages. A light touch on the arm, a hug, or a kiss on the cheek can signify "I like you; I feel comfortable with you." A hearty handshake, a broad smile, a pat on the back, or a grasp of the shoulders can mean "Nice going; I'm proud of you." By now you recognize that messages like these can serve as powerful social reinforcers. So people who fail to express affection are handicapped in their ability to deliver social reinforcement. Contingency managers who are capable of dispensing reinforcers readily are more likely to succeed.

Can people learn to show affection? Of course. Consider an extreme case, that of people labeled "autistic." Autism is a condition characterized by multiple cognitive and social deficits, especially the ability to relate or express affection to peers (Rutter, 1978; Wing, 1976). Yet McEvoy et al. (1988) successfully helped young autistic and nonhandicapped children learn to show affection to one another through songs and games (e.g., to pat their friends on the back, to hug their friends, and

to give their neighbors a "high five"). With a bit of prompting by the teacher, the autistic children's reciprocal peer interactions increased afterward, during free play, and the nonhandicapped peers responded much more favorably to those initiations than they had during the baseline period.

Environments rich in social reinforcement may not only strengthen desired behaviors but also may enhance students' self-esteem (i.e., their overt or covert self-evaluative comments). As a result, many efforts have been directed toward devising ways to promote delivery of lots of social reinforcement. One way is to introduce activities that encourage peers to compliment each other's achievements.

In a workshop one of us attended for business and service organizational managers, participants selected distinctive stickers, such as a frog, a star, and so on (to allow them to remain anonymous if they wished), and received a pad of forms on which they could indicate how any of the other members in the group helped them. A posted chart listed the name of each participant. When participants detected an action worthy of their expression of appreciation, they filled out the form citing the pertinent action, and delivered it to the relevant individual. Typical comments included:

- "I found your case example about the incentive system intriguing. I'm thinking about trying it."
- "I never realized that quality assurance could be treated that way. Thanks for the idea."
- "By explaining the concept of a discriminative stimulus, you taught me why antecedent events work the way they do."

At the same time, the commender placed his or her distinctive sticker on the chart next to the name of the recipient.

In this way the chart displayed episodes of participants' praiseworthy acts and the number of compliments delivered by the holders of each distinctive sticker. Trainees selected a series of goals for the total number of stickers to be displayed by a given date, and they set a reward they would earn when the goal was met, such as having the workshop coordinator confess his middle name, schedule an outing, or host dinner out. Not only were goals met and exceeded, but adults who had rarely noted and/or conveyed positive recognition began to generate very specific praise statements frequently. In many cases the experience enabled trainees to apply this new, heavily practiced and reinforced skill to their home organizations with relative ease.

Jackson (1974) has described similar practices used by several teachers with children in her school district to enrich the reinforcing quality of the social environment. Some used "fuzzy-grams"; others "compliment meters":

> . . . On the bulletin boards of several schools in the Fountain Valley School District are the words: "Send a fuzzy-gram to a friend." [A fuzzy-gram is shown in Figure 12.1.] Fuzzy-grams are in a pocket on the board and members of the class may write a note on them to someone in the class. Only positive statements may be written on the fuzzy-grams, and the message should make the recipient "feel warm and fuzzy inside." They may be delivered to the person or put up on the board.
>
> Another idea that helps children focus on the positive is the "compliment meter." The meter looks like a thermometer and can be drawn on the chalkboard or be on a chart. Children write compliments to other members of the class and put them in a gaily decorated box: "I liked the way you helped Jeff," or, "Your book report was very good." At the end of each day, the number of compliments are counted and the notes passed out. The total is added to the meter. When the class reaches a predetermined goal, they [students] may go on a picnic, have a popcorn party, have an extra twenty minutes for games or some such treat. If a class is difficult to motivate, the teacher may give small rewards at increments along the way to the final goal.
>
> The "compliment meter" can be used for an individual as well as a total group. This can be a massive self-esteem builder when all the class members reinforce good behavior with their positive notes. [An example of the compliment meter appears in Figure 12.2] (1974, p.3).

The "Secret Pal Game" (Smith & Mayer, 1978), a variation on this theme, ensures that all children receive compliments. Each week every child draws the name of a secret pal whom he or she is to observe doing "something

Figure 12.1 A Fuzzy-Gram

Figure 12.2 A Compliment Meter

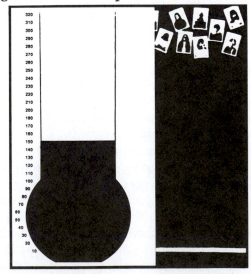

nice." Children then write a description of their observations on forms, and deposit them in their pal's envelope. The teacher helps initially by showing the children some illustrative messages and prompting when necessary, so that by the week's end each child has received at least one message. A compliment meter, showing a weekly count of the messages delivered, supports the activity temporarily, but after several weeks the activity can continue on its own, sustained only by the natural positive reactions of recipients.

Similar methods have been used successfully by teachers at the upper elementary, junior high, and secondary school levels and by counselors with small groups. Adult staff and supervisors also have used games like these to promote positive feedback within their own peer groups. In one case, the "I Spy" activity, participants filled out a form like that shown in Figure 12.3.

As a fund raising effort at Charter Oak High School, a service organization sold "telegrams," consisting of a carnation plus a personal positive note. Elsewhere, staff, employers, and managers send one another "Success-O-Grams." (See Figure 12.4.)

Reinforcement bombardment is another way to teach staff or management to increase its use of praise. In a group of six or fewer people, each member talks for about 2 minutes on a topic about which he or she is excited, such as a student's or employee's recent success. Meanwhile, the other group members record commendable aspects of the content and style of the presentation, conveying their observations to each speaker at the end of the talk. A "Warm Fuzzy" or "Thank You Board" located in a central location, such as a lounge or break area, serves a similar purpose (see Figure 12.5).

Activities like these are flexible enough to be used in almost any group setting and appear to foster pleasant, cooperative group interactions. Each activity represents an attempt to

harness the powerful reinforcing properties that peers are capable of delivering to one another for their accomplishments. Now let us look at a number of ways peers can be involved more integrally in behavior analysis programs.

Systematically Involving Peers as Contingency Managers

Peers can have a powerful influence on group members' performance, as we have shown. This especially occurs when the peers are facile in applying social reinforcement. In the previous description you saw how that ability can be taught and supported. Now consider why and how to involve peers more formally in behavioral programs.

Reasons to Use Peers as Contingency Managers. Why are peers such a good choice for involvement in programs of behavior change?

- Because of their frequent, daily contact, peers are usually in an excellent position to continuously *monitor and respond regularly and rapidly* when target behaviors occur (Strain et al., 1976).
- Peers provide the *natural context* for teaching social skills.
- Peer-managed intervention is often *preferred* by the clients (Phillips, Phillips, Wolf, & Fixsen, 1973).
- Peer involvement more readily promotes *generalization and maintenance* across settings, times of day, and following program termination (Kohler & Greenwood, 1986; Smith & Fowler, 1984; Strain, 1981) than when others manage the contingencies.
- The presence of a peer who has served as a contingency manager is likely to *cue* the client to engage in the desired behavior following program termination (Smith & Fowler, 1984).
- ". . . Peer-mediated intervention programs present clear benefits both for the children receiving intervention and the

Figure 12.3 Form

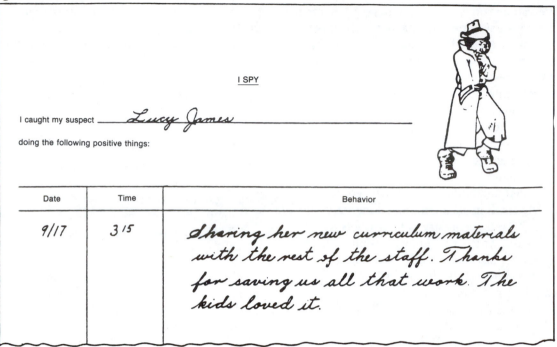

Figure 12.4 "Success-O-Gram" for Staff and Students

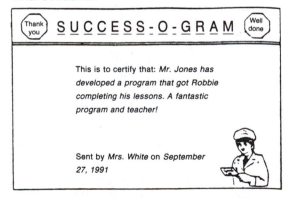

children providing intervention" (Smith & Fowler, 1984, p. 214). Not only do the clients benefit from learning the social, work, or academic skills being taught, but the *contingency managers* often learn the skills better [sometimes improving almost

as much as their clients do (Dineen, Clark, & Risley, 1977)].

• The peer managers' *social status* is often enhanced.

Let us see these advantages illustrated.

Illustrative studies. By involving fifth-grade students with behavior problems in a peer monitoring program, Stern, Fowler, and Kohler (1988) were able to reduce rapidly pupils' off-task and disruptive behavior. As monitors, the students were trained to deliver points to a peer by checking off specific activities they saw the student perform (e.g., such as sitting in chair; working on an assignment; being quiet; putting name, date, page, and problem number on assignment; erasing neatly; writing legibly; and completing work), or the students earned points for displaying those accomplishments themselves. The points the youngsters earned

Figure 12.5 Thank You Board

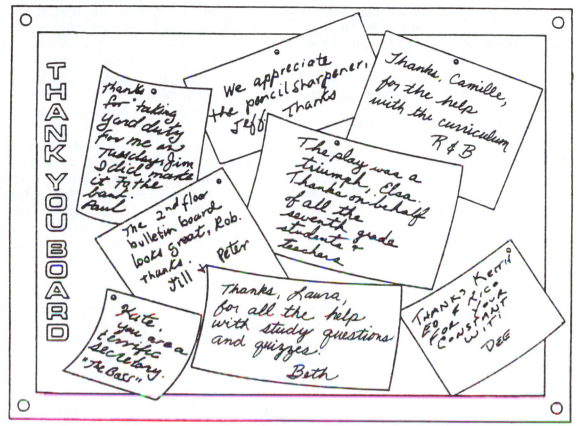

could be exchanged for a class reward, such as a movie (a dependent group contingency). As the researchers pointed out, despite the 45 minutes that training took and the occasional corrective feedback that needed to be provided, the procedure was an attractive and cost-effective solution for reducing inappropriate behavior during independent work time.

In several studies, interdependent group reward contingencies were combined with peer management procedures to decrease disruption and increase academic performance of underachieving students (Pigott, Fantuzzo, Heggie, & Clement, 1984; Wolfe, Fantuzzo, & Wolfe, 1986; Wolfe, Fantuzzo, & Wolter, 1984; Wolter, Pigott, Fantuzzo, & Clement, 1984).

Fifth- and sixth-grade underachieving stu-

dents with behavior problems were assigned separate peer management roles, such as coach (peer instructor), scorekeeper (peer observer), referee (peer evaluator), and manager (reinforcer of peer behavior) (Wolfe et al., 1986). Each was made individually accountable to the group (Slavin, 1983). After receiving training in the use of the reciprocal peer-management program during three 45-minute sessions, the students selected both the number of arithmetic problems their group needed to answer correctly and what person would perform what role. If the team met or exceeded the goal, it earned a group reinforcer.

The program resulted in effective increases in the number of accurately completed arithmetic problems and decreases in disruption.

Further, the group that had chosen the most stringent goals improved and generalized its skills more than the group that chose the most lenient performance criterion. Also, the latter group failed to maintain or consistently generalize the skills. These findings further support the importance of selecting stringent or challenging criteria for goals.

Sainato, Maheady, and Shook (1986) assigned the classroom manager's role to three withdrawn kindergarten students, each of whom served for three weeks. Provided with a large "manager" button, the student led the class in highly preferred activities, including ". . . directing the feeding of the class guinea pig, collecting milk money and taking lunch count, ringing the bell for clean-up time, and handing out the 'keys' to the barber shop and shoe store [play] areas" (p. 190). As a result, all three children initiated and received more positive social interactions and were rated more positively by their peers. Follow-up data also showed partial maintenance of these gains a month after each student served as manager.

What explains this success? Placing people in leadership positions in which they control other people's access to positive reinforcing consequences can promote interpersonal attractiveness (Strain, 1981). Perhaps the leader becomes a cue or "discriminative stimulus" for reinforcement, and/or what Baer and Wolf (1970) call the "natural community of reinforcement." As Sainato et al. (1986) point out: "As a result of having their initiations responded to favorably, they may have increased the rate at which they approached their classmates. This may account for the fact that social interaction rates remained above baseline levels even though subjects no longer occupied manager positions" (p. 194).

The two previous examples illustrated involved peers in programs designed to improve conduct and interpersonal skills. Yet peers may also participate in instruction of language and other academic subjects. For instance, Goldstein and Wickstrom (1986) taught two non-handicapped preschoolers strategies to promote communicative interactions with three preschool children whose language was delayed. The strategies included obtaining eye contact by saying the child's name or tapping the child's arm, asking the child to look at something, suggesting a joint activity, describing one's own play or that of others, prompting requests, and restating or adding to what the child said or requesting clarification. Noting the improved interaction among all three handicapped children, the researchers pointed out that peers may promote the generalization and maintenance of the skills, because the interactions are naturally reinforcing and peers can move from place to place with one another.

Sasso and Rude (1987) taught both high- and low-status nonhandicapped primary school students to initiate positive social interactions with severely handicapped students during recess. The researchers found that involving high-status nonhandicapped students prompted their nonhandicapped peers to initiate increased levels of positive interactions with the handicapped children to a greater extent than involving low-status nonhandicapped students as confederates.

Those results were consistent with earlier findings that peers are more likely to imitate when the model is prestigious (e.g., Bandura, Ross, & Ross, 1963b). Chapter 17 further discusses this subject. However, one highly aggressive and disruptive handicapped student profited only marginally from the program, probably due to the aversiveness of his noxious behavior to the peer. Consequently, to encourage peers to initiate social interchanges with a person with serious misbehaviors, you may first need to address those misbehaviors.

Peers as Tutors and Trainers

Involving peers in a teaching capacity is broadly practiced in educational organizations and in job settings. One survey found that peer training is the most frequent method used to orient co-workers to new job functions. Peers also act as tutors from the preschool level to the university level:

- in preschools, to teach colors and shapes to learning-handicapped children (Kohler, 1987) and to enhance language in other ways (McGee, Almeida, Sulzer-Azaroff, & Feldman, 1990).
- with youngsters with severe handicaps, to teach self-help and prevocational skills (Walker, 1985; Young, 1981).
- at the elementary school and junior high levels, to teach sight words, letter names (Heron, Heward, Cooke, & Hill, 1983; Heward, Heron, Ellis, & Cooke, 1986), math facts, word meaning, oral reading (Dinwiddie, 1986; Greenwood, Delquadri, & Hall, 1984), reading comprehension (Polirstok & Greer, 1986), and spelling (Greenwood et al., 1987; Maheady & Harper, 1987).
- at the high school level, probability, cartography (Bloom, 1984), and social studies (Maheady, Sacca, & Harper, 1988).
- in higher education, in calculus, physics, psychology, engineering, and many other course topics, within a PSI format.

In the **Personalized system of instruction (PSI)**, students demonstrate mastery of small units of material via frequent quizzing and immediate feedback from a proctor, retaking the quizzes as often as necessary to achieve the preset criterion level and progressing at their own rates.

Reasons to use peers as tutors and trainers. Recall how peer-mediated strategies help overcome logistical difficulties that change agents often face in attempting to reinforce frequently, consistently, and immediately; to promote generalization and maintenance; and to provide both peer trainers and trainees with augmented opportunities for reinforced practice, thereby

increasing the skill of all participants (Cohen, Kulik, & Kulik, 1982; Polirstok & Greer, 1986). Peer tutoring has been shown to be similarly beneficial in the following ways:

- reducing classroom behavior problems (Greenwood et al., 1984; Kohler, 1986; Wolfe et al., 1984).
- increasing social interactions between autistic and typical preschoolers within a play context (McGee et al., 1990).
- improving interpersonal relations between racially or ethnically different students (Johnson & Johnson, 1983; Sharan, 1980) and persons with and without disabilities (Anderson, 1985; Johnson, Johnson, Warring, & Maruyama, 1986; Wilcox, Sbardellati, & Nevin, 1987).
- improving peer affiliation, self-concepts, and attitudes (Maheady & Sainato, 1985; Pigott, Fantuzzo, & Clement, 1986).

Peer tutoring also has been shown to be more cost effective than computer-assisted instruction, reducing class size, or increasing learning time (Levin, Glass, & Meister, 1984). Also, use of peer tutors has proven more effective than conventional instruction (Bloom, 1984). Whorton, Walker, Locke, Delquadri, and Hall (1987) have noted that students in peer tutoring programs for at least one academic year perform considerably better than the peers who have not participated. Those who serve as one-to-one peer tutors to students with severe disabilities have been demonstrated to be as effective as teachers working with individuals or in small groups.

Reasons for success of peer tutors. A likely reason for such effectiveness is that classwide peer tutoring increases student engaged time (Bloom, 1980) and the opportunity to respond orally and in writing to academic material (Hall, Delquadri, Greenwood, & Thurston, 1982). These are necessary conditions for academic achievement (Delquadri, Greenwood, Whorton, Carta, & Hall, 1986). Without a doubt, peer tutoring can produce "powerful and practically important academic and social effects" (Greenwood et al., 1988, p. 262).

Organizing a peer tutoring program. If you want to set up a successful peer tutoring program, consider the following important components. First, *work out the routine clearly in advance* so all participants know who is to do what, where, with whom, using what materials for how long, what to expect, and to what end. Such details help organize the program and provide the necessary facts for obtaining participants' informed consent. Preparing tutors to anticipate potential problems, such as the fact that many of their initiations might be ignored (Strain & Fox, 1981; Strain, Kerr, & Ragland, 1981), helps the tutors to persist in the face of such difficulties.

Program supervisors and teachers also need briefing in advance. For example, teachers should be prepared to accept an increase in noise and activity levels within the classroom, and occasional tutor-tutee disputes in the beginning.

As you review the routine and expectations, you might list each step on a wall chart and provide tutors with individual checklists that they could mark as they complete each step, while verifying their activities from time to time. For example, Ramey and Sulzer-Azaroff (1979) used the peer tutoring checklist in Figure 12.6.

Greenwood and colleagues (1988) summarize how to instruct peers to tutor as follows:

Most systematic peer tutoring programs provide the tutee (a) repeated opportunities to respond (e.g., task trials presented by tutors), (b) immediate feedback and consequences (e.g., placing a flash card on a pile or verbal praise), (c) remedial prompts for incorrect responses (e.g., No, the word is spelled C A T, write it three times), and (d) tutor collected data (e.g., number of points earned by the tutee). These events comply with generally accepted principles of effective instruction, time allocated to instruction in the classroom (Bloom, 1980), opportunity to respond (Greenwood, Delquadri, & Hall, 1984), rapid pacing (Carnine, 1976), feedback and immediate error correction (Rosenshine & Stevens, 1986), and content coverage with mastery (Borg, 1979; Bloom, 1984) (Greenwood et al., 1988, p. 266).

Selecting and training tutors. In our PSI courses (Keller, 1968), students become proctors once they master the material and demonstrate friendliness, patience, and ability to follow instructions well. We want to be certain that tutors refer their students to the appropriate resources for further study and that they do not overprompt students. (We return to PSI in Chapter 19.) In the Greenwood et al. (1988) program, systematic tutoring "has been developed far beyond the simple assignment of an advanced student to teach a less skilled student" (p. 268). Because everyone participates and consequently benefits, tutors are not imported from elsewhere. One way that peer tutors are selected in classes in which all students participate involves random pairing weekly to prevent student boredom (Delquadri, Greenwood, Stretton, & Hall, 1983). Adults who are beyond formal schooling can serve as tutors, too. In a management training workshop, tutors-in-training were asked to master the answers to a set of questions printed on cards (with the correct answers on the reverse side). They took turns asking and answering questions until both certified that the other successfully had defined all the concepts, and solved all the problems presented on the cards.

Tutoring also may be conducted within teams, and tutors may be selected by first testing everyone on the content to be learned and then developing groups consisting of members with heterogeneous skills. For example, Slavin (1983) formed four heterogeneous groups by assigning the four highest-scoring students, one

Figure 12.6 Peer Tutoring Checklist

Remember to . . .

____ 1. Have the lesson ready.

____ 2. Talk clearly.

____ 3. Be friendly.

____ 4. Tell the student when he is right.

____ 5. Correct mistakes. STOP! Give the right answer. Have the student do it.

____ 6. Praise good work!

____ 7. Make the lesson fun.

____ 8. Do not give TOO MUCH help.

____ 9. Fill out the daily sheet.

____ 10.

(Source: Ramey and Sulzer-Azaroff, 1979.) Permission to reprint the figure granted by the authors.

to each team; the next four highest, one to each team; and so on. This method of distributing skill levels across teams increased the potential for help and error corrections within each team.

Selecting peer tutors for disabled students presents special challenges. These procedures are not yet well developed, nor do educators have a firm understanding of their benefits to the tutors. Current work hints that when provided adequate training and reinforcement, tutors of handicapped children find the responsibility rewarding, and the experience helps them feel good about themselves.

Selecting and training developmentally delayed children to serve as tutors may be far more complicated, depending on their individual repertoires. It does appear that although nonhandicapped tutors may be trained in a few hours, to train handicapped tutors successfully may take much, much longer (up to 30 hours according to Young, 1981). Nevertheless, both autistic (Whorton et al., 1987) and nonhandicapped students (Young & West, 1983) have been successful in tutoring their handicapped peers. In fact, Young and West (1983) reported not only increases in target skills but also increased integration, friendship, and improved attitudes.

For peer tutoring programs to succeed, tutors need to be *carefully trained and supervised* in and receive reinforcement for carrying out their roles as designed. They also have to be familiar with the content and to use correctly selected materials and instructional techniques. A task analysis usually is constructed to form the tutor training curriculum, including:

- cuing or instructing without overprompting, by not providing extraneous hints.
- assessing and scoring performance accurately.
- role playing and modeling.
- being friendly.
- praising, delivering rewards, and correcting errors appropriately (Delquadri et al.,

1986; Heward et al., 1986; Ramey & Sulzer-Azaroff, 1979).

Written rules for conducting specific tutoring sessions and self-checks can help, but they usually are not sufficient.

Proctors in our PSI courses participate in a series of workshops in which they are provided with guidelines, engage in practice, and receive feedback on accuracy of scoring, administrative skills, proper prompting, and social effectiveness. Checklists based on these skill areas are used later to provide periodic feedback and reinforcers following sessions observed by supervisors. It pays to observe the first several sessions that tutors conduct. Adults (Greenwood et al., 1987) or students (Pigott et al., 1986) can observe the tutoring sessions and provide reinforcers and corrective feedback as merited. Throughout the tutoring sessions, supervisors must be available to respond to questions and provide direct instructions. If necessary, trainers can reinforce tutors' compliance with the routine with privileges, tokens, or points, as Greer and Polirstok (1982) did to increase tutors' rates of approval and as McGee et al. (1990) did by permitting their preschool tutors a break in the teachers' room to reinforce their tutoring initially.

Sometimes, reinforcing the tutor's rates of reinforcing tutee responses can influence how well the tutee learns. In fact, Polirstok and Greer (1986) found that such tutor points (for teaching reading comprehension in junior high school and exchangeable for tangible or activity reinforcers) were "the most important component of the tutoring package for both tutee and tutor" (p. 101). At other times, just the prestige accorded to a tutor appears sufficient, because the feedback tutors give themselves (or may receive from the tutees, observers, or teacher) sustains their levels of performance.

In summary, to set up a tutoring program you follow these steps:

1. Plan the program.

2. Train tutors.
3. Select and adapt curricula and materials.
4. Supervise tutoring sessions.
5. Reinforce tutoring.
6. Evaluate progress.
7. Revise procedures as necessary.

You may wish to refer to model manuals, such as one that describes a competitive game format for teaching spelling, reading, and math (Carta, Greenwood, Dinwiddie, Kohler, & Delquadri, 1987). If it is feasible, also try to obtain formal training in running programs like these, review some of the studies cited in this chapter, and, under qualified supervision, adapt those strategies to your own needs.

Evaluate progress of tutors and tutees regularly to monitor their gains. If progress is slower than anticipated, attempt to identify the trouble spots. Ask these questions:

- Is the content too challenging or simple?
- Are materials appropriate to the objectives?
- Is the instructional environment conducive to instruction and learning? (Is it too noisy? Too crowded? Can space be divided differently?)
- Are tutors and tutees well matched—are their social repertoires compatible?
- Are the gaps between the level of content being taught too wide to justify any benefit to the tutor?
- Are tutors using reinforcers effectively?

Resist the temptation to involve students as tutors when the activity can no longer be justified as educationally advantageous for them, as in the case of too many repetitions of instruction in the same content. Once tutors have become very fluent with and have sufficiently generalized concepts and skills, they deserve to progress to material more advanced for them.

Summary

Peers have considerable power over one another's actions. They also have the advantage of being readily available to provide immediate and frequent feedback and reinforcers. Peers also can serve as effective role models. Harnessing peer power, therefore, can prove an invaluable aid to promoting and sustaining behavior change. One natural way to accomplish this purpose, although indirect, is through interdependent group contingency arrangements. These are particularly well suited to prompting peer support, because under those conditions the performance of individual members impacts upon the reinforcers received by other group participants. As a consequence, peers are energized to encourage and assist one another.

Alone, however, group arrangements are not necessarily the most direct strategy for ensuring that peers perform specific functions as agents of change. A more straightforward approach is to teach, monitor, and supervise tutors operating in that specific role within interdependent groups. Then, tutors are more likely to be successful and to benefit by gaining enhanced leadership skills and status, additional fluency with the skills they are promoting, and improved self-esteem.

Chapter 13

Token Economies

GOALS

After completing this chapter, you should be able to:

1. Discuss the circumstances under which one should and should not consider instituting a token economy.

2. Define, recognize, and give an original illustration of a token economy.

3. Describe the characteristics of a well-designed token economy.

4. List the factors to consider in advance of designing a successful token economy.

5. List several fundamental privileges to which dependent clients should have noncontingent access.

6. List and discuss the purpose and advantages of obtaining approval and informed consent.

7. List and discuss the purposes of recordkeeping, staff training, and providing reinforcing consequences for staff participation.

8. List and describe the contribution of each factor that can influence the effectiveness of a token economy.

9. Provide a rationale for selecting a particular type of token to use in a setting familiar to you.

10. Describe a token economy that is both logistically sound and instructive.

11. Explain the purpose of pairing positive social feedback with token delivery.

12. Identify and discuss the factors to consider in selecting back-up reinforcers.

13. Identify two problems that might occur when you use tangible back-ups and describe how to avoid them.

14. Describe methods of marketing and merchandising back-up reinforcers.

15. Describe two basic methods for reducing behaviors within a token economy.

16. Specify four reasons why token systems should be phased out gradually.

17. Describe a situation in which a token economy should remain in effect indefinitely and one in which it should not.

18. Describe two ways in which a delay of token delivery may be introduced into a token economy and the purpose that delay serves.

19. Describe how delay is interposed between token accumulation and token exchange.

20. Describe how the "tiered" or "level" system can be used to integrate delay of reinforcement into a token economy.

21. Describe a strategy for moving from artificial to more natural reinforcers within a token economy.

22. Develop a program for the gradual removal of a token economy system. Be sure to include methods of incorporating delay and intermittent reinforcement.

When you are responsible for people, each of whom has multiple educational, training, and/or management needs, your best bet may be a token economy. In the four previous chapters, you have become acquainted with the process by which reinforcement operates and the procedures to follow in applying it effectively. In this chapter, you will learn how the token economy incorporates ideally all those features. Carefully designed token economies have demonstrated their success among numerous populations. A sample list of clients includes:

- *psychiatric patients* (Paul & Lentz, 1977; Nelson & Cone, 1979).
- *delinquents* (Wood & Flynn, 1978).
- *parents* (Muir & Milan, 1982).
- *miners* (Fox, Hopkins, & Anger, 1987).
- *college students* (Jacobs, Fairbanks, Poche, & Bailey, 1982).
- *other educational populations* (Fantuzzo & Clement, 1981; Carden Smith & Fowler, 1984; Jason, 1985; Kistner, Hammer, Wolfe, Rothblum, & Drabman, 1982; Robinson, Newby, & Ganzell, 1981; Saigh & Umar, 1983; Speltz, Shimamura, & McReynolds, 1982; Van Houten & Nau, 1980).
- *ordinary citizens in ancient Greece* (Paschalis, 1987).
- *contemporary students in third world countries* (Saigh & Umar, 1983).

However, before you launch such a program, reconsider for a moment, because token economies are artificial and sometimes contribute little beyond results achievable in less complicated programs (Howie & Woods, 1982; Manos, 1983). For motivated clients, developing an elaborate token economy is like trying to kill a fly with an elephant gun. As Howie and Woods (1982) found with their program serving adult stutterers, a simpler procedure can suit the purpose just as well.

When *should* you consider instituting a token economy?

- When the natural methods and other good teaching and training methods prove unsatisfactory.
- When you have tried matching tasks and materials to the interests and abilities of the people involved.
- When scheduling, group arrangements, interesting activities, and other less-complex but optimally arranged contingencies have not worked.
- When you wish to avoid depending on strong aversive contingencies.

This chapter presents many examples of token economies and describes various strategies for effectively implementing them with groups. Because token economies can be intrusive, preliminary planning is crucial, and extra precautions need to be heeded. These are considered along with some legal and ethical issues. We also discuss how tokens are eventually phased out and supplanted by reinforcers natural to the environment.

Token Economies Defined and Illustrated

A **token economy** is a system that consists of a combination or "package" of contingencies incorporating many effective behavioral procedures—primarily, powerful reinforcement contingencies. (See Ayllon & Azrin, 1968, for a full treatment of this topic.) You already are familiar with the concept of a token as an exchangeable reinforcer. Tokens are delivered shortly after a target response occurs and are exchangeable at a later time for a reinforcing object or event, fulfilling thereby one key rule for reinforcement effectiveness: immediacy. Token economies also lend themselves ideally to the other rules of effective reinforcement that you have learned, as will become apparent as this chapter progresses.

Most cultures have developed token-like systems of reinforcement to strengthen and maintain the productivity of their members. In advanced societies, the system is called "wage earning." Production is compensated regularly with an exchangeable reinforcer called money. Money actually is a form of token, because it functions as a tangible item that can be exchanged for other reinforcers. However, not all modern compensation systems are as effectively designed as they might be, whereas a well-planned token economy that incorporates all the essentials of good behavioral programming can function extremely well.

Numerous reports of precisely and effectively planned token economies have appeared in the literature. They have been used to assist psychiatric patients to develop much more adaptive skills and habits (Ayllon & Azrin, 1968; Nelson & Cone, 1979; Paul & Lentz, 1977; Schaefer & Martin, 1969) and to aid people with serious developmental delays, educational handicaps, and maladaptive behaviors to develop more adaptive, functional, and constructive response repertoires (e.g., Cohen & Filipczak, 1971; Walker & Buckley, 1975; Wood & Flynn, 1978; and others). Token economies have helped in some of the following ways:

- Preschoolers have improved their social skills (e.g., Odom, Hoyson, Jamieson, & Strain, 1985; Wolfe, Boyd, & Wolfe, 1983).
- Children, delinquents, and predelinquent youths have improved their academic, social, and personal skills (e.g., Bijou, Birnbrauer, Kidder, & Tague, 1967; Cohen & Filipczak, 1971; Kistner et al., 1982; Manos, 1983; Phillips, Phillips, Fixsen, & Wolf, 1972; Speltz et al., 1982; Sulzer, Hunt, Ashby, Koniarski, & Krams, 1971; Wolf, Giles, & Hall, 1968).
- Developmentally delayed young women have learned daily living skills (Thomas, Sulzer-Azaroff, Lukeris, & Palmer, 1977).
- Children have improved their deportment (Carden Smith & Fowler, 1984; Saigh &

Umar, 1983; Van Houten & Nau, 1980; Wolfe et al., 1983) and compliance with various health regimens (Claerhout & Lutzker, 1981; Lowe & Lutzker, 1979).

Token systems have enabled youths in trouble with their societies to return to the mainstream; retarded children to care for themselves and their surroundings and to become participating members of their communities; academically delayed students to catch up with or even surpass their age mates; and "normal" children to function more positively as family members.

Token systems have been used to improve the performance of adults too, such as parents (Muir & Milan, 1982; Watson-Perczel, Lutzker, Greene, & McGimsey, 1988), college students (Jacobs et al., 1982), and mine workers (Fox et al., 1987). In the latter case, for instance, mine employees received trading stamps each month if they did not lose any time from work due to injuries during that month. They could exchange the stamps for items from a pool of hundreds of back-up items.

What constitutes a well-designed token economy? Why are they so successful? What are some of the legal and practical limitations of token economies? What problems may be encountered in using them, and how may those problems be avoided? How are token economies planned for immediate and long-range effectiveness? The following material is directed toward answering these and related questions.

Token Economies and Effective Reinforcement

A well-designed token economy incorporates all the essential aspects of an effective reinforcement program. Targeted behaviors, or approximations to them, are immediately and consistently reinforced by delivery of a sufficient number of tokens. The token, you will recall, is any object or symbol that can be exchanged for a back-up reinforcer—usually one of an array of tangible objects or events. The conditions for token delivery are clearly described, and various methods are included to make back-up reinforcers attractive, such as sampling and novelty.

After the target behavior is occurring at a high and consistent rate, intermittent delivery of tokens begins, while delivery of the back-up reinforcers is delayed progressively longer. The number or value of tokens delivered also may be gradually phased out, consonant with the principles of effective behavioral maintenance (described in Chapters 30–32). Because tokens may be used to purchase an almost infinite variety of reinforcing objects or events, satiation is generally avoided.

Here is an illustration of an actual token program used to increase a family's enjoyment of its summer vacation. Nine-year-old Flossie, her parents, and her older brother were going on a long trip. Although all the family members looked forward to it, Flossie feared that she might periodically become bored and tired. Her parents also worried that the excitement and the irregular schedule might make her irritable. So Flossie and her parents sat down together and discussed the kinds of behaviors that would be acceptable and would ensure a pleasurable experience for everyone: being pleasant (no whining and complaining), trying new foods without negative comments, using reasonable table manners (operationalized in detail), and a few others.

Flossie thought that her performance should be evaluated three times a day: at lunch for the morning, at dinner for the afternoon, and at bedtime for the evening. She elected a self-recording system. A scorecard was prepared with several boxes for each day of the vacation. If Flossie judged that the targets for that time segment had been met, she would award herself a point for each. A bonus was included for marking the card on time. A system of bonuses for accurate scoring was also planned.

Flossie's father was to check the card from time to time, at random. If he agreed that the scoring was accurate, bonus points would be awarded. If there was a disagreement, Flossie's mother would be consulted, and if both parents agreed that some points were undeserved, they would be removed. A simple rejoinder by Flossie would be acceptable, but a heated argument would be penalized by a point loss.

More than anything else, Flossie wanted a multibladed camping knife. The token system enabled her to earn a maximum of about 15 points a day, and it was decided that for each 50 points she would earn a camping-knife "blade." Under optimal conditions, she would earn about eight blades during the trip. Once the system was instituted, Flossie worked hard to earn her points and marked them down faithfully. By the end of the trip she had received an eight-bladed Swiss army knife. Needless to say, all enjoyed themselves, and (after careful safety instruction) Flossie was the heroine of the neighborhood as she proudly displayed the scissors, fish scaler, and tweezers her knife contained.

Designing a System for Supporting Success

Before you implement a token economy, you need to take several steps. These include obtaining approval and informed consent, preparing to keep appropriate records, and training and supervising staff.

Obtaining Approval and Informed Consent

Token economies are relatively intrusive, because they introduce many novel and artificial stimuli into a situation. Consequently, obtain approval before implementing the program. First, though, familiarize yourself with any related legal issues. Then, once you have done your homework, you will be in a better position to respond to questions and concerns, as you obtain the approval and informed consent from those who will be directly and indirectly involved: administrators, supervisors, and/or employers, parents, and naturally the participating clients.

Legal issues. Become familiar with laws delineating fundamental privileges to which dependent clients (such as those residing in institutions) should have noncontingent access (Wyatt, 1972, pp. 379–386, 395–407). They include communication—that is, mail and some telephone privileges; meals, including access to nutritionally adequate food in the dining room; the privilege of wearing their own clean clothing; space in specified areas; heating, air conditioning, ventilation, and hot water; specified furnishings for the residence unit and day room; bathrooms with clean, safe equipment and supplies; housekeeping and maintenance by the staff; and various clearly specified privileges connected with religion, exercise, medical care, grooming, education, and interaction. (This list is discussed in more detail in Budd & Baer, 1976.) Naturally, laws change and differ between communities and states, so you must periodically relearn those currently in effect that affect your clients. If you have any question about the legality of withholding or using a particular reward or privilege, obtain legal advice.

Administrative approval. First and foremost (after doing your homework), you should check the plan out with the clients' employers or administrators and supervisors. Occasionally, some people find token economies objectionable, at least until they realize that a token economy is no different from any system for reinforcing productive activity (just as they are compensated for doing their own jobs). So to be prudent, first obtain formal approval for undertaking the program in that particular setting. It is wise to talk to administrators and supervisors and to present data on the intended participants' prior performances, showing that despite all the methods tried, progress remains unsatisfactory. Then describe the details of the token program. Negotiating may be necessary, for instance, coming to terms about a set of mutually agreeable back-up reinforcers.

Parental approval. Next, if minors or dependent people are involved, talk to all parents or their surrogates or advocates, explain the proposal, and obtain their informed consent. Use simple language to explain how the program can help the participants. When parents or guardians are presented with this sort of program, most are enthusiastic; usually those whose children have not been succeeding in school or in a group program are very aware of and unhappy about it, preferring not to let their children fail. In one of our classroom token programs, to be sure all parents were fully apprised, we contacted parents by telephone and/or visited them at home. By answering any questions posed, we almost always were able to obtain parents' informed consent and cooperation. If personal meetings or telephone calls are not feasible, notes or letters may suffice.

Describe the exciting data on token economies and the promise the system holds for enabling their children to improve their learning and enjoyment. Allay occasional anxieties about reinforcers such as trips or certain foods. These questions can be discussed, and, if necessary, the program should be flexible enough to adjust to any concerns, such as offering to provide substitutes like raisins or cereal bits for candy.

Participants' approval and cooperation. Talking to the participants or their advocates and obtaining their consent also is important. You should explain the plan and rationale for the program. There is no substitute for openness and honesty with people who know they need to improve their performance. Explain how all people concerned can mutually assist each other. Participants can help in selecting reinforcers, according to the suggestions given in Chapter 10, or they can assist in reinforcer selection in some other way. For a token program in a fifth-grade class, for instance, the children nominated five of their classmates to shop for back-up reinforcers. They selected various inexpensive items, such as modeling clay, beads, little toys, and pencils. Participants can also share in planning assignments, selecting materials, recording systems, and other aspects of the program. As other organizations have found, encouraging participation in the development and implementation of programs promotes cooperation.

When participants or advocates consent to a particular program, chances of inadvertent exploitation are diminished. A great temptation is to use a token economy for the convenience of staff, rather than to the long-range advantage of the clients served. For instance, using tokens to deter swearing, noise, or disorder may make supervisors' jobs easier, but do the clients benefit in the long run? Referring back to participants' long-range goals and to data about the natural setting to which they will return is advised.

Planning for a Recordkeeping System

We have repeatedly suggested that continuous records of program effectiveness be kept. Besides the usual records you will keep on changes in target responses, also plan to record token exchanges to determine high- and low-preference items, in order to set token prices. It also is helpful to collect data on numbers of tokens earned and conditions under which they have been delivered.

The conventional measures of the key dependent variables inform us about how effectively the system is working. The other records provide useful information for staff on how closely procedures are adhered to and signal

when to alter the price of a back-up, vary response requirements, begin to phase out the economy, and so forth. Seeing data indicating improvement in targeted responses also can be reinforcing to the staff and participants who are able to comprehend the results.

Training Staff

The success or failure of a token program rests upon the precision with which it is implemented: the care with which it is monitored, how tokens are delivered, and how consistently other logistical aspects are implemented. Success is best accomplished by training and supervising the staff, a point emphasized by Atthowe (1973). Training may consist of lectures, discussions, reading assignments, modeling, and role playing. Evidence suggests that the more closely training is tied to the target performance, the more likely trainees are to comply with performance instructions (Gladstone & Sherman, 1975). Lectures, discussions, or other oral or written instructions should be supplemented with some direct practice. For instance, participants in a staff-training workshop may see a videotape of someone modeling delivery of a token. Next, some participants can be assigned to play the roles of staff members and clients, while others observe and offer feedback. We have tried this sort of system many times and have found that trainees and trainers both enjoy and learn from the experience.

As we have repeatedly suggested in this book, instruction alone is often insufficient. Reinforcing consequences should follow practice, at least intermittently, if newly acquired skills are to persist over time. The principle also applies to implementation of contingency packages, particularly complex ones like token economies. As staff members carry out their roles as designed, reinforcing consequences must be delivered for adequate performances. In a school or community facility, a supervisor may provide those consequences, perhaps in the form of written or oral feedback or some other reinforcing contingency. In homes, relatives often perform that function. Alternatively, a system for self-monitoring and self-reinforcement can be adopted (Thoresen & Mahoney, 1974). Even clients can be trained to reinforce behaviors of staff, as was done in a program by Graubard et al. (1971). Like all others, staff members tend to sustain a response only as long as the contingencies support its continuation.

Implementing Token Economies Effectively

Once you have obtained approval and informed consent, have developed a recordkeeping system, and have trained and supervised your staff, you are ready to review the factors that influence the effectiveness of a token economy. This discussion first details using token systems to increase behavior. Next, we *briefly* refer to methods for using tokens to decrease unwanted behavior. Finally, again briefly (because the decrease and maintenance of behaviors are emphasized more heavily in subsequent chapters), we describe factors that will assist us in maintaining behavior. At this point we begin with methods for selecting tokens.

Selecting Tokens

What kinds of tokens should be used? Among those familiar to us are plastic chips, "bankbooks" (Bucher & Reaume, 1979), trading stamps (Fox et al., 1987), poker chips, points, stars (Claerhout & Lutzker, 1981), stickers, foreign coins, play money, beads, and other similar objects. Robinson et al. (1981) used metal tokens that could be used to operate video and pinball games. Within your setting, staff or clients will have suggestions.

One of the easiest systems we have used is a sheet of paper onto which in each quadrant a box of 100 squares was drawn. (See Figure 13.1.) Folding the sheet into quarters produced a little booklet with 100 boxes on each page. An "X" in a box, marked with a distinctively colored felt-tipped pen, signified 10 points, a diagonal mark, 5 points. One point was indicated by a hatch mark. The booklet was identified with the participant's name, and marks were made in such a way that they could not readily be forged. Expenditures were indicated by striking through the box with a horizontal line. If the possibility of counterfeiting concerns you, purchase a personalized rubber stamp, or sign your initials or name instead of using a mark.

In general, tokens should be suited to the population with whom you are working. Small metal or plastic objects may be fine for normal children over 6 or 7 years old but not for young or severely retarded clients, who may swallow or choke on them. Paper or cardboard tokens may be appropriate for most youngsters but not for those who tend to be destructive.

A paper token that we have found particularly useful is a construction-paper coin. You can obtain commercial rubber-stamp impressions of 1-cent, 5-cent, and 10-cent coins at teacher supply stores. These can be stamped on squares cut from construction paper and then laminated. Such tokens serve a dual function—as exchangeable reinforcers and for teaching coin equivalence and computational skills. One teacher of a combined second- and third-grade class set up a program in which students could earn "1 cent" by engaging in behaviors like getting their work card, "5 cents" for following directions, and "10 cents" for choosing an activity. Class members could earn five minutes of free time for "$1.50," the opportunity to be cashier for "$1.00," the chance to be first out for recess for "$1.00," writing on the blackboard for "$1.85," or helping the teacher for "$1.75."

Another way to meet both logistical and instructional purposes with tokens is to try the method that Kincaid and Weisberg (1978) used

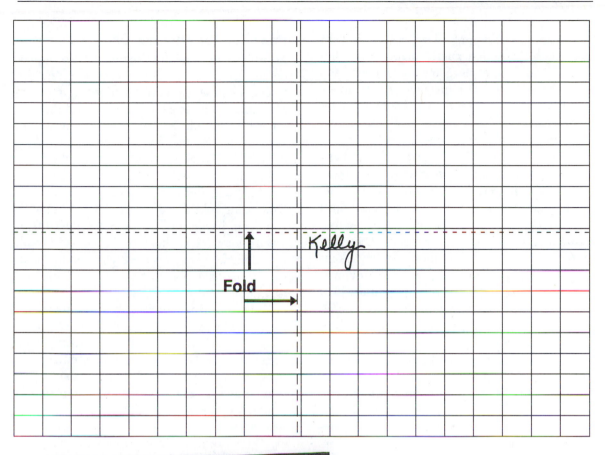

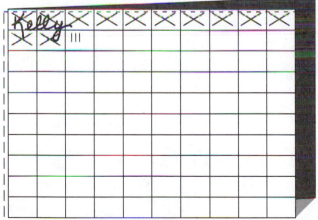

Figure 13.1 Point Booklet Fashioned on a Sheet of 8½″ × 11″ Paper. Each quadrant contains 100 boxes. By folding the paper twice (step two), you produce a booklet. Dispense points by marking a box with an X (10 points) or hatch marks (1 point each).

to teach preschoolers to discriminate and name the letters of the alphabet. Tokens were chips on which letters were superimposed. Before being allowed to exchange a token for a back-up, the children were required to label the letter it contained. No wonder the children rapidly learned the letters of the alphabet!

In another case of multiple functions (Ford,

McClure, & Haring-McClure, 1979), tokens consisted of wooden puzzle pieces. The children could fit the piece into a template and exchange it for snack items when the template was filled. This apparently more reinforcing token system promoted greater resistance to extinction than round wooden tokens. In the study by Thomas and colleagues (1977), many of the clients could neither write nor count. They could, however, figure out the price of an object from the "price tag." The tag was a sheet of cardboard on which the outlines of the requisite number of tokens were drawn. The client only had to fill in the outlines with her tokens to pay the correct amount, also teaching one-to-one correspondence as a by-product. For other young or developmentally delayed children, pictorial representations of the cost may be used (see Figure 13.2).

So, you can see that the form of a token may range from points in a grade book or on a chart or marks on a blackboard to much more elaborate objects, like play money, puzzle pieces, trading stamps, or instructional materials. Try simple systems first, using the more elaborate ones only if they suit your purposes more effectively.

Providing for Minimal Delay

As briefly mentioned in Chapter 10, tokens can be delivered readily after *minimum delay* to bridge the time gap until functional reinforcers are available. Flossie checked her card right after each time block. The bonus-point system saw to that. Had the reward been scheduled for delivery at the end of the long trip, the delay would have probably been too extended for a child her age. Remember your own childhood? How being told that if you did such and such you could have a bicycle or some other major reward for your birthday or Christmas? Recall how difficult it was? Maybe the possibility of an end-of-the-year bonus is both tantalizing and frustrating you the same way now.

Having learned previously the importance of minimal delay and achievability of challenging goals, perhaps you already have formulated the solution: When behavioral requirements are delayed and seemingly insurmountable, break them into a series of components, immediately reinforcing the accomplishment of each phase with a token.

The work done by Phillips and colleagues (1972) at Achievement Place also nicely illustrates how token systems permit rapid reinfor-

Figure 13.2 "Price Tags" for Young Children with Developmental Disabilities

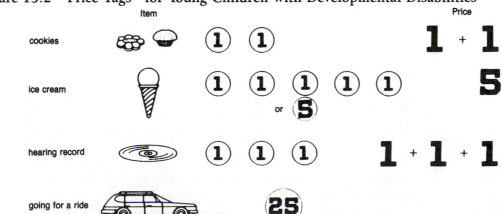

cer delivery. Achievement Place is a "... group living environment designed to provide the socializing influences of models, values, and contingencies that facilitate redirection for youths whose behavior has caused them serious trouble" (Wolf, Braukmann, & Ramp, 1987, p. 347). The youths are responsible for caring for themselves and for performing duties necessary to the effective functioning of a group home—dressing, grooming, cleaning up their own rooms, and participating in household activities. There are also requirements necessary to reasonable social functioning—cooperation, leadership, and other prosocial behaviors.

Because the Achievement Place program has been striving to develop leadership qualities in the youths that it serves, it also allows program participants to take part in delivering points, with supervision and self-evaluation. Initially, youths receive points very soon after completing their required jobs; delay in delivery of reinforcers is built into the program at a later phase.

Illustrative studies. Many other examples illustrate how tokens can be used to bridge delay in reinforcer delivery. Following are a few summaries.

- Institutionalized, developmentally disabled women being prepared for community placement (Thomas et al, 1977) were awarded tokens as they performed their tasks. For instance, as they learned to fold their clothing after it came from the dryer, each fold was rewarded with a cardboard token. Later on, combining series of folds was possible before delivering tokens.
- A thirteen-year-old boy whose parents felt he watched television excessively and to the detriment of other important activities earned tokens to activate a timer permitting the television to operate by doing homework; extracurricular reading; and playing sports, musical instruments, and with his friends (Jason, 1985).

- College students sharing a house were concerned that housekeeping and other responsibilities be accomplished (Miller & Feallock, 1975). A system was designed to provide daily reinforcers for job completion with credit toward eventual rent reduction. Jobs included sweeping floors, straightening the group living area, preparing food, and others.
- With feedback to maintain their accuracy, elementary school students awarded kindergartners points for cleaning up, proper deportment in the bathroom, and waiting patiently. The points could be used subsequently toward voting on and participating in outdoor activities (Carden Smith & Fowler, 1984).
- Mothers referred to an agency due to child neglect earned stickers later exchangeable for extra time with and instruction (e.g., how to bake a pie) by the behavior analyst for performing specific cleaning chores in their bathrooms and kitchens (Watson-Perczel et al., 1988).
- For delivering reinforcers, as stipulated, to their tutees, peer tutors earned points they could exchange later on for extra gym time, fast-food certificates, films, audiocassettes, and letters to their parents (Polirstok & Greer, 1986).
- Parents of handicapped children earned lottery tickets that could ultimately win them toys, household merchandise, discounts, or complimentary restaurant meals for teaching and demonstrating progress by their children (Muir & Milan, 1982).
- Each time college students car pooled, they received a coupon good for 25 cents worth of merchandise at local stores (Jacobs et al., 1982).
- Psychiatric inpatients earned tokens for personal hygiene, personal management, ward work, and social skills, all necessary for their transfer into open wards. Tokens

could be used in the future to purchase beverages, fruit, to buy or rent records, and other items and privileges (Nelson & Cone, 1979).

Teaching nonverbal clients the function of a token. The best way to teach a young or severely delayed child the function of a token is to assemble an array of powerful reinforcers, like ice cream and fruit juice, along with the tokens. Storing the chips in an apron pocket, the contingency manager instructs the child to do something he or she is fairly certain to comply with: "Look at me," or "Put your hand on your head." Following the response, small amounts of the reinforcer are delivered. When the response rate is high and steady, the manager smiles, praises the child, and hands him or her a token immediately following each response. Then, almost simultaneously, the back-up reinforcer is delivered as the token is retrieved. Little by little, a few seconds delay is introduced between delivery of the token and the back-up reinforcer, and the token is retrieved just as the reinforcer is being offered. Later on, when the child appears to be tolerating a delay of a minute or so, the manager delivers first one token for one response and then another for a second. Then the manager retrieves both tokens in exchange for the powerful reinforcer. Bit by bit, the token takes on its reinforcing value. Usually it is best to plan a few such sessions over several days, always dropping back a few steps at the beginning of each session before progressing farther, because such clients have difficulty duplicating the newly acquired patterns after long intervals.

Pairing Token Delivery with Positive Social Feedback

If positive feedback, like praise or approval, were sufficient reinforcers for a given target response, there would be little need for a token economy. Only when such feedback is not suf-

ficiently reinforcing do token systems make sense. Nevertheless, in the natural environment a desired response is much more likely to be followed by social feedback than by contrived reinforcers like tokens. Some form of positive feedback is predictable, at least occasionally: a smile, a nod, an "okay," a "good job," or a comment like "Having that file available really came in handy during the conference." So, as discussed earlier, participants in many token economies would be helped by enabling social feedback to become effectively reinforcing for them.

Promoting praise as a conditional reinforcer. To accomplish this, the analyst precedes delivery of tokens with positive social feedback. The tokens, which derive their power from their back-up reinforcers, are paired with the less potent social feedback: "How terrific. You've done a beautiful job of making your bed. Here's your token." Not wishing to interrupt a client working in a sheltered workshop, the supervisor pats him on the shoulder, smiles, and places a token on his board.

Using tokens to cue praising. Actually, an additional advantage of a token economy is that tokens may begin to prompt the contingency manager's delivery of more frequent social feedback (Breyer & Allen, 1975; Mandelker, Brigham, & Bushell, 1970; Trudel et al., 1974). Breyer and Allen (1975) adopted a token economy as a "last resort" to increase a first-grade teacher's positive responses. Instituting the token system produced an increase in verbal praise *and* a decrease in aversive comments. The tokens appeared to remind the teacher to look for and reinforce positive behavior.

A couple of approaches you might try, should your managers not distribute sufficient tokens, is to assign the managers a goal or provide them with a set token supply to be dispensed by a given date or time. You also might mention to them that in a study by Kistner et al. (1982), teachers who delivered tokens were rated more highly by their students than teachers who did not.

Promoting peer feedback by involving the group. Chapter 12 discussed various group reinforcing activities. Token programs are particularly well suited to group contingency arrangements, because tokens may be retained by individuals, or they may be shared, divided, or exchanged. Assume that group cooperation is a goal. Under an interdependent group contingency, all members can work toward a common goal, such as a trip, dance, game, musical program, puppet show, or play. As soon as each member earns a particular number of tokens, the activity is awarded and shared by the entire group. Lectures on interesting topics like politics, ecology, natural foods, adventure, sexual practices, child rearing, auto repairs, or whatever is intriguing can also be shared by the group. When access to such activities depends on the performance of each individual, group members tend to help and encourage one another (Speltz et al., 1982). If one or two members fail to earn the requisite number, it is possible to adopt a *collective* system [Ulman & Sulzer-Azaroff, 1975], in which all tokens are pooled until the total required is earned. (Or the noncooperating members may be assigned to a separate activity elsewhere.) The point is, use the group arrangement as a vehicle for inducing positive peer feedback.

Consistent Delivery of Tokens

Another major principle of effective reinforcement can be recognized in the illustration of Flossie's summer vacation: the principle of consistency. *Every time* Flossie met requirements, she could award herself points. Certainly, delivering a knife blade to her each time that she had met a criterion would not have been possible. But the points served to reinforce the target behaviors consistently until the multibladed camping knife had been earned. In each of the programs cited, delivering tokens was possible after *each* instance of the requisite behavior. In the Achievement Place program, privileges could not easily be delivered every time, but the tokens that earned the privileges could. In a series of classroom studies (Campbell & Sulzer, 1971; Sulzer et al., 1971; Sulzer-Azaroff, Hunt, & Loving, 1972), tokens in the form of points were delivered to students on completion of short academic tasks, such as problem sets. Back-up reinforcers of privileges, educational games, and enjoyable group activities surely could not have been delivered every time the students completed a daily assignment in arithmetic, spelling, or the like. However, point delivery was no problem at all.

Providing Appropriate Amount

Token economies also are ideally suited to delivery of appropriate amounts of reinforcers. Careful planning should ensure that back-up reinforcers are delivered in sufficient quantity to maintain performance, yet sparsely enough to prevent satiation. If Flossie had received an eight-bladed camping knife after every period of good behavior, she would have accumulated a closet full of camping knives; certainly they would have lost their reinforcing value early on. Similarly, in the Achievement Place and classroom programs described, students could have easily become sated by some of the activities earned; instead, reinforcers were earned in more modest measure through the use of tokens.

As in all other aspects of applied behavior analysis, data-based decision making is crucial in choosing the quantity of reinforcers to deliver. If clients are responding at an acceptable rate, you can assume the amount is adequate. If the rate begins to diminish, question whether the clients have obtained enough or too many back-up reinforcers or points. Maybe deprivation or satiation is responsible.

An abrupt cessation or evidence of "ratio

strain'' may be seen right after the person receives a long-awaited, costly back-up reinforcer. For instance, employees at Top Quality had spent many weeks being careful about the quality of their product, enabling them finally to earn the required 500 points for a group picnic. After the picnic, the next event on the agenda was a party that would require another 500 points. In this instance, a deceleration in product quality was no doubt a function of the renewal of a very demanding response requirement.

Again, clever planning of the economy can help avoid ratio strain. In the school study by Wolf et al. (1968), a system was designed to avoid both satiation and ratio strain. Points were recorded on one of several pages, with each page representing a separate account. One account allowed the participant to spend points frequently, for small tangible rewards; another served as a savings record for larger tangible rewards; another was used for long-range group activity reinforcers. Points were evenly distributed across the various accounts as they were earned. Therefore, even when a large quantity of points was invested in a back-up reinforcer, a sufficient amount remained on deposit in the other accounts. Participants never needed to suffer the discouragement of being broke. Sulzer and her colleagues (1971) and Sulzer-Azaroff et al. (1972) used a similar procedure in their classroom programs. Points were distributed evenly between each of two of the four pages of their booklets; one for short-range back-up reinforcers; the other for long-range reinforcers.

Regardless of the savings system used, designing it to minimize the likelihood that participants will spend all their points at once probably is a good idea. Adjust prices so participants can afford their back-up reinforcers and still have some points left over. Otherwise, it is preferable to develop some sort of insured-savings system and/or pay interest on savings to avoid bankruptcy and its unwanted conse-

quences—cessation of responding or misbehavior (Hogan & Johnson, 1985).

Specifying Conditions for Token Reinforcement

When the rules of the game are clearly specified, they are more likely to be followed; this applies to token economies as well. Because Flossie participated in defining the rules under which she could earn her tokens, she was well aware of the contingencies in operation. When some minor interpretive misunderstanding occurred, the system permitted clarification. The Achievement Place program also sees to it that rules are clearly specified by the youths and house parents. See an example of the definitions used in one case to measure room cleanliness in Figure 13.3 (Wood & Flynn, 1978). Rules can be publicly displayed on pictorial or written charts (as in Wood & Flynn, 1978), and/or they can be reviewed orally. In Campbell and Sulzer's program (1971), the rules for earning points with the Sullivan reading workbooks were reviewed at the beginning of each period. A student would remind the class: "First we read; then we mark; then we check."

Matching Quality and Type of Reinforcers to Individual Client Repertoires

Token systems are ideally suited to matching reinforcer quality to participants' preferences. The only limitation is the imagination of those involved. Back-up reinforcers may include an infinite variety of objects and activities, both *natural* and *artificial*. For reasons elaborated earlier, natural back-up reinforcers generally are preferable. As in all other aspects of applied behavior analysis, however, "the participant is always right." If a selected back-up reinforcer is not working, the data will inform us that other back-ups need to be tried, until eventually an array that produces the desired response is identified. Review Chapter 10 for ideas and

Figure 13.3 The Definitions Used to Measure the Cleanliness of Each Boy's Room

1. The bed should be made with two sheets, one pillow with case, and the bedspread. (NOTE: there should be no additional blankets on top of the bed.)
2. None of these objects should be visible except the bedspread while looking at the level of the steel frame that runs around the lower edge of the bed or while looking down at either end of the bed.
3. There should be no objects greater than 0.25 by 0.25 by 0.25 in. on the bedspread (this includes blankets).
4. The bedspread should be tucked in under the mattress completely around the bed, and no part of the bedspread should hang through the bed springs longer than 2 in., which is the level of the steel frame.
5. The pillow must be within 6 in. of the head of the bed and centered within 6 in. of the center of the mattress.
6. The bedspread must be tucked at least one inch under the pillow so that it makes a straight line across the bed. The line should not be more than 3 in. from a 90-degree angle with the edge of the bed.
7. There should be no wrinkles greater than 6 in. long, 1 in. wide, and 0.5 in. high on the entire bedspread including the sides.
8. All the hangers should be in the closet and hanging on the cross bar, and all nonfolded clothes should be in the closet on hangers, and shelf straight.
9. Shoes should be on the closet floor with the toes or heels touching a wall and the sides of a pair of shoes touching in one place. All shoes must face the same direction.
10. Objects greater than 0.25 by 0.25 by 0.25 in. should not be on the closet floor without permission.
11. All clean clothes that are folded should be put away in the drawers properly. All other objects in the drawers must be arranged in an orderly fashion.
12. The dresser top must be clear of all objects greater than 0.25 by 0.25 by 0.25 in. except for lamps, clocks, and other objects that have permission to be left out and be dusted.
13. All of these objects must not be within 2 in. of the edge of the dresser top and must not extend out over the edge.
14. The back of the dresser must be within 6 in. of the wall and one end should not deviate from the other more than 3 in. The head of the bed should be at least 6 in. but not more than 18 in. from the wall.
15. No clothes or personal objects may be laying on the floor or placed inappropriately on any furniture.

Wood & Flynn (1978), p. 505. Permission is granted to reprint from the Society for the Experimental Analysis of Behavior.

consider one additional technique: the opportunity to earn oneself off the token system, an effective back-up for students in a study by Kazdin and Mascitelli (1980).

The records you have kept of items purchased can also provide valuable information for making future selections. Ruskin and Maley (1972) found that for schizophrenic patients, edible reinforcers were by far the most powerful of the array available in their token store. (The records also showed some valuable information about program effectiveness, as well as the rate of purchasing grooming items, reflecting clients' increasing interest in their appearance.)

Remember, too, the empirical choice strategies suggested in Chapter 11.

Sometimes problems arise when tangible back-up reinforcers are used. Excitement reigns, generating noise, confusion, and perhaps pushing, when it is time for children to trade in their tokens. Our solution: use order blanks. Deliver these to the customers, who either write or check off their orders. Distribute the order blanks only when the customers are behaving acceptably, and before long serenity will prevail. To minimize jealousy and stealing, after collecting tokens, package items in opaque bags, staple the order form to the top, label the bag with the customer's name, and deliver it at departure time.

Marketing and Merchandising Back-Up Reinforcers

Kagel and Winkler (1972) have compared the token economy with a "closed economic system." They argue that the fields of economics and of applied behavior analysis have much to learn from each other. Surely those who conduct token economies may learn from both business and economics ways of enhancing the effectiveness of their systems. (Ayllon & Azrin, 1968, have incorporated many economic principles in their token systems.)

One basic consideration—the law of supply and demand—is certainly important in designing a token system. Atthowe (1973) reported that patients' activity diminished when either savings or debts accumulated, and Hogan and Johnson (1985) found that incidents of misbehavior increased with loss of tokens. Prices should reflect this law, with high-demand items costing more and low-demand items less. When demands change, as in Ruskin and Maley's study (1972), prices can be adjusted accordingly. To avoid the problems that may accrue from changing prices at arbitrary times, Campbell and Sulzer (1971) and Sulzer et al. (1971) adjusted prices regularly. Students knew that every few weeks prices would be altered according to supply and demand.

An effective token system requires demand to be kept high. A sufficient array of appealing reinforcers needs to be on hand, as Fox et al. (1987) showed by using trading stamps exchangeable for any of hundreds of items. Sometimes you may want to use activities or items with which participants are not familiar. One technique for encouraging people to sample novel reinforcers within token economies is to make only a few items available at any one time. When the array of choices is narrow, any single item is in greater demand than it would be if many choices had been available.

As marketing experts have long known, novelty and change play a great part in the desirability of an object of merchandise. Window displays are changed frequently to capitalize on this effect. In our token economies, we shifted the back-up reinforcers each week or two, so that some novel items were always available. The value of any single back-up reinforcer can also be heightened if students are allowed to sample it briefly, or if they see prestigious peers consuming it. Then, it can be displayed attractively or depicted on the price chart. For some of our nonreading consumers, price charts included a color picture of each object and outlines of the number of tokens required. To keep the object in view of their young subjects, Staats and colleagues (1962) taped it to the top of a clear cylinder, in which marble tokens were placed. When the cylinder was filled, the object had been earned. To advertise, we have kept objects on display shelves or have attached them to plastic containers.

As in business, *bonus tokens* may enhance productivity (Rickard, Melvin, Creel, & Creel, 1973). Children in a summer-camp remedial program increased their academic productivity when bonus tokens were delivered contingent on increases over their best previous three-day records. Bonuses of this sort may be particularly useful when behavior appears to have reached a plateau.

Reducing Behavior Within a Token Economy

Response Cost

Response cost, described fully in Chapter 25, is a procedure used to manage inappropriate behavior and, provided the person has a store of accumulated tokens, readily lends itself to inclusion within a token economy. Costs for particular undesirable behaviors may be negotiated in advance by staff and clients. For instance, in the Achievement Place program, specific penalties are levied for behaviors like fighting and using unacceptable language. In one study, a "violation ticket" system, detailing the offenses and the fines, was given to any patient who violated ward rules (Upper, 1973). Fines were subtracted from a 15-token reward that each patient received daily, resulting in a reduction in violations. But in a token program with emotionally disturbed adolescents, response cost was eliminated (Hogan & Johnson, 1985). Because the cost system provoked, rather than lessened, misbehavior, an all-positive program was instituted instead.

Time Out from Token Spending

Response cost requires tokens to be surrendered following an infraction; a relatively simple, straightforward measure, especially if further penalties or fines are levied should the tokens not be surrendered immediately. With very young, retarded, or socially disturbed persons, however, attempting to recover penalty tokens may precipitate a crisis, as Hogan and Johnson (1985) found.

To prevent clients from becoming aggressive or resistant, an alternative approach is to invoke a penalty called "time out from token spending."[1] In this procedure, exchanging tokens is prohibited for a specific time period, such as a half day, following an infraction. Of course, tokens may be earned during that time, but they may not be spent.

Should you consider using response cost, time out from token spending, or other penalty variations, you should first study the procedure in detail. Ways to glean information you need are contained in Chapter 25.

Maintaining Behavior Changed in Token Economies

Moving from Artificial to Natural Reinforcers

Although one can readily argue in support of token systems on the basis of their potential effectiveness and feasibility, in many cases they

should be gradually phased out and replaced by more naturally reinforcing contingencies. Several arguments support this position. First, token systems do take time and require additional resources; they also require careful planning and monitoring. One needs to gather evidence favoring the need for this system over a well-structured program involving instant feedback and frequent success. If, as Howie and Woods (1982) found with stutterers, you find that tokens make no appreciable difference, then they are superfluous.

Second, the argument, addressed in Chapter 11, that superimposing rewards upon behavior already occurring at high rate might be aversive, also should alert us to this possible—albeit unlikely—problem. (Who would go to the trouble of devising and running a token system if wanted behaviors were occurring at high rates?) Therefore, if a preferred behavior has continued at a high and steady rate for a long time without any systematic external reinforcement, using other than sporadic tangible reinforcers makes little sense.

Third, some people are outraged at the idea of children and other dependent individuals with problems receiving tangible rewards for behaving as they are "supposed" to behave. That argument has little justification from our point of view. Those critics should ask themselves how long they would remain at the repetitive, difficult, or demanding occupational tasks they are required to perform were they not to receive tangible rewards in exchange. Why should clients experiencing serious difficulties be expected to accomplish what the critics themselves would not? Nevertheless, trouble can be avoided from such sources if a plan for shifting back to more natural contingencies is incorporated into the overall program.

Another argument concerns the potential for abuse. Gagnon and Davison (1976) have questioned using token economies in mental hospitals, because most such programs fail to represent the demands of nonhospital life. This argument further underscores the need to assess the participant's home-based ecology and plan the system accordingly. For instance, grades, work ratings, daily report cards, or self-checks might be substituted for the tokens while the program is being phased out.

The last, and most compelling, reason to switch, from our point of view, is that most employment settings, schools, and human-service programs do not normally use token systems. Clients need to be prepared to function in absence of such reinforcers in order to move more freely within the larger system. Consequently, before an analyst shifts clients to those environments, they need to be weaned off the system. Suggestions follow.

Introducing Delay of Token Delivery for Long-Range Effectiveness

One of the prime advantages of token systems is that they permit the immediate delivery of conditioned reinforcers as soon as the target response occurs. After the objective has been met, however, introducing delay is reasonable because immediate reinforcement is not characteristic of the real-world contingencies. As in the instance provided earlier (Thomas et al., 1977), developmentally disabled women learning to fold clothing were given tokens immediately following each correct fold, then after a few garments, and so on. In a sense, increasing the size or complexity of the response introduces a delay factor. Token delivery recedes farther and farther in time as the behavioral requirements are enlarged. Another example of delay is provided by a classroom study (Sulzer et al., 1971). Students were initially assigned a few pages in a workbook. Once they completed their assignment, tokens were awarded. Later, more pages were added gradually to the assignments, with a delay in the time when the tokens would be delivered.

Besides increasing the size of the response requirement, delay can be introduced into the program in another way—through addition of a time interval between the response and delivery of the token. For instance, points can be delivered 5 minutes after a set of problems has been completed or after the stack of clothes has been folded. Then, over time and dictated by the data, token delivery may be delayed even longer, say, 10 minutes, and so on.

Another important temporal aspect of a token economy is the time between token accumulation and token exchange. Again the decision is based on the data. For very young children or those with serious deficits, permitting tokens to be exchanged frequently is crucial at the beginning of the program. Later, the time between receipt and exchange can be lengthened.

In their evaluative review of the token economy, Kazdin and Bootzin (1972) suggested that building delay into token systems probably increases resistance to extinction. So introducing delay between token receipt and exchange into the later phases of a token economy seems reasonable.

The *tiered* and *level* systems used in some well-established token economies illustrate how delay can be incorporated. In the Achievement Place program (Phillips et al., 1972), when youths begin the program, they enter a very highly structured "earn and lose" exchange system. Points are earned or lost almost moment by moment. Exchanges occur each couple of hours. As the youths progress toward developing acceptable social, academic, and maintenance behaviors, they move into a daily, then a weekly, then a merit, then a homebound system. By the time participants are ready to return home, they have had a prolonged experience with self-managed delayed-reinforcement contingencies.

Phasing Out Token Systems

Despite our earlier contentions, not all token programs need to be adjusted. Sometimes they can remain intact. Just as providing wages to workers is permanently incorporated within our economic system, in many situations there is no reason why token economies cannot remain in effect indefinitely. The mining company interested in minimizing lost time injuries (Fox et al., 1987) continued to reward absence of accidents monthly over a 4-year period, and in light of its success would have little reason for ever discontinuing the use of trading stamps as token reinforcers. (And in fact, the authors reported that the owners instituted the program in two other strip mines.)

More temporary enterprises have a different agenda, however, especially if participants will eventually shift to a milieu devoid of token reinforcement. Examples are

- criminals with limited sentences.
- juvenile offenders assigned to group homes for a period of time.
- abused, neglected, or acutely disturbed clients in emergency placement.
- people in comprehensive training or treatment programs, such as for weight loss; anorexia; regulation of a medical condition like asthma, diabetes, or addictions.
- temporary special class placements.
- intensive workshops for managers or staff.

In each of these cases, the people involved will move or return to settings lacking the optimal contingencies or reinforcement accorded by token systems. To avoid total regression to pretreatment habits, members need to be weaned gradually off the system, with contingencies substituted that resemble, as closely as possible, those of the environment set to receive them. Even this may prove unsatisfactory in some circumstances, as Wolf et al. (1987) discussed in their plea for continuing services to severely chronic juvenile offenders.

How is this return to natural reinforcement accomplished within a token economy? Here is a system we have followed:

1. Back-up reinforcers were replaced on a periodic basis.

2. As responding reached and sustained its intended rate and tempo, we continued praising and giving other forms of recognition but began to substitute activities and privileges for the tangible rewards.

3. Next, we shifted to certificates, transferable for time to be spent at high-interest educational or otherwise relevant activities. Little by little, in this manner, phasing out the tangible and artificial activity reinforcers became possible.

The scheme for moving from artificial to natural reinforcers is discussed in Chapters 29–32 in much greater detail, along with various methods for extending and maintaining behavior.

In their token economy, Jones and Kazdin (1975) were able to program response maintenance by substituting social events for tokens. They also supplemented the shift of tokens with a peer support phase, in which peers earned reinforcers at the end of the day if target students had met their goals.

Scheduling for Maintenance in the Absence of Tokens

Two important steps toward behavioral maintenance in the absence of tokens have already been discussed: moving from artificial to natural back-up reinforcers and building in delay. The next step is to gradually reduce the amount and/or frequency with which tokens are delivered, according to the behavior maintenance guidelines presented in greater detail in Chapters 30–32. Using intermittent reinforcement schedules is one strategy. For example, Kazdin and Polster (1973) used tokens to reinforce conversation between pairs of developmentally delayed adults. Conversation was reinforced either continuously or intermittently with tokens. The subject who received intermittent reinforcement for initiating conversation persisted in the behavior when tokens were removed, but the client whose behavior was continuously reinforced did not. A similar outcome was found in a study of tooth brushing (Fisher, 1979). Brushing maintained better during periods of nonreinforcement after periods of few token awards than after periods of high token awards.

Rather than relying solely on a gradual thinning of tokens to achieve behavioral maintenance, however, we can adopt some shortcuts. As you saw earlier, token delivery usually is paired with more natural stimuli, like praise. Later, praise can gradually be substituted for some of the tokens. The next step, after the switch to an intermittent schedule, is gradually to shift from the tokens to direct reinforcers by contingently providing activities and other more natural reinforcers that have been used as back-up reinforcers. Here is a case in point: Three preschoolers were referred to a parent and child training project for noncompliance, crying, cursing, and aggression. They were placed in a token program to promote cooperative play (Wolfe et al., 1983). Earning ''happy face'' stickers for each minute of playing cooperatively, they could later exchange a set number of those tokens to be permitted to play outside. After achieving an 80% level for 3 sessions, the requisite interval of cooperative play was lengthened gradually to 5 minutes. By the time the children achieved 80% at that new requirement, the stickers were discontinued altogether. Playing outside then became contingent upon an 80% rate of cooperative play alone. The token system was no longer needed.

Summary

A multitude of consumers have found token economies effective and acceptable. Nevertheless, they require considerable planning and care. Well-designed token systems incorporate all the features of effective reinforcement, including immediate and consistent delivery of an adequate amount of individually effective reinforcers.

Generally, a token economy is best reserved for instances in which less-intrusive contingency arrangements have not been effective. Then, after proper clearance and planning, the token system can be implemented. Logistic, economic, legal, and other issues must be considered, and when appropriate, plans for the eventual phasing out of the system devised. This is accomplished by shifting from artificial to natural back-up reinforcers, by programming in delay of tokens delivery and back-ups, and by gradually reducing the amount and/or frequency of token delivery, and by gradually switching from tokens to contingencies natural to the context.

Chapter 14

Analyzing Procedures: Withdrawal and Multiple-Baseline Single-Case Designs

GOALS

After completing this chapter, you should be able to:

1. Define, recognize and give original illustrations of each of the following terms:
   a. Confounding (extraneous) variables
   b. Single-case (subject) experimental design
   c. Accountability
   d. Functional relation
   e. Withdrawal (ABAB) design
   f. Reversal
   g. Probe
   h. Multiple-baseline across behaviors
   i. Multiple-baseline across individuals
   j. Multiple-baseline across situations

2. Compare and discuss group versus single-subject designs, explaining the conditions under which each is useful.

3. Specify and discuss the common advantages and purposes of single-case designs.

4. Discuss the conditions under which it is appropriate and inappropriate to move from one experimental phase to another.

5. List and illustrate several variations of the withdrawal design and discuss when each is applicable.

6. List and describe the advantages and possible disadvantages of the withdrawal designs.

7. Offer tactics for minimizing the possible disadvantages of using withdrawal designs.

8. List and describe the advantages and disadvantages of each variation of the multiple-baseline design.

9. Describe a situation for each of the four designs that would make that specific design the best possible one to use. Be sure to justify your selection clearly, pointing out why other designs would not be as appropriate in each situation.

Jocelyn was concerned about her lack of pep and weight gain. So she consulted her physician, who prescribed a particular self-management behavioral routine of exercises, diet, and medication. On Jocelyn's return visit several weeks later, she was found to be in excellent condition. Duly impressed, her doctor speculated, "Maybe I should assign that program to all my patients!" A moment later, though, she was seized by a gnawing doubt: "Perhaps Jocelyn's improvement is just a happy coincidence, and the procedure had nothing to do with it." How could she overcome her suspicions? She would need to discover whether the technique would continue to work reliably with Jocelyn and other patients also, or if its effectiveness was just a chance event, influenced by unidentified factors.

All responsible applied scientists and practitioners must ask themselves questions like these, and now that you have learned the basics for increasing the desired behavior, so must you. If you select a given procedural arrangement, you need to be as certain as possible that (1) it is producing change in the desired direction, and (2) the procedures you set in motion and not some other conditions are responsible for the change. Otherwise, you might neglect more effective strategies while wasting your own, your clients', and perhaps the public's resources.

Notice that evaluation of programmatic effectiveness is not delayed until the end of treatment. Behavior analysis is ongoing, permitting the impact of any changes occurring as a function of systematic interventions to be revealed while the program is in progress. Specific strategies for conducting functional analyses of programs that increase behavior are presented in this chapter. In Chapter 22, after you learn about more complicated methods of intervention, other designs capable of handling those situations will be described. Depending on the purposes and methods of any behavior analytic program, the designs presented in either Chapter 14 or 22 may be suitable. Otherwise, we refer you to texts devoted specifically to the topic of applied behavior analytic methodology (e.g., Barlow & Hersen, 1984; Johnston & Pennypacker, 1980; Kazdin & Wilson, 1978).

Evaluating Procedures Experimentally

Group Designs

One way Dr. Daring could resolve her dilemma would be to do an experiment—that is, systematically to vary some conditions while holding others constant to determine objectively measurable changes. She could ask the nurse to use the procedure with one randomly assigned group of her patients and not with another, and then statistically analyze the changes in data, describing the patients' well-being. Group experimental designs like these have been used for many years as standard research tools in the behavioral sciences. When appropriately conceived, such designs minimize the effects of **confounding** or **extraneous variables**. (Variables, other than the ones you are managing, that may confuse or confound the findings. For elaboration of confounding variables, see any one of the many current textbooks on psychological, educational, or mathematical statistics.)

In group experimental comparisons, subjects presumably are assigned randomly to their groups. Interpretations of results rest on the assumption that measures of central tendency (the averages) within each group and the amount of variability with which the scores are distributed about that average represent those of the larger group from which the random sample was drawn. Therefore, they may prove especially practical in drawing conclusions and making predictions and recommendations for the population that the sample represents. Results of a group design might assist a textbook purchaser to select a book likely to benefit a group of students in general, an architect to design senior citizen housing units of particular sizes and layouts, or a public health official to decide whether to inoculate a population at large.

Group designs do permit us to draw inferences for the larger group from which the test samples have been drawn. However, because they are based on combined scores, they do not permit extension to any individual member of the group. We have no way of knowing whether a particular textbook will do a better job of teaching any particular student, only a suggestion that students on the average probably will perform better. Actually, some students may achieve less. Who they are will be lost with the group design.

Another potential difficulty with the group design is that positive effects for some individuals may be camouflaged, especially when others showed neutral or negative effects. In such cases, comparisons might indicate nonsignificant results and the method might be discarded. An instance here might be investigating whether a new method of teaching language— say using manual signs—is better than the standard practice of presenting the word aloud. Some students might learn better with the new method; others with the standard one. If so, the effects for each of the two subgroups of students would cancel one another out and the results would be discarded as nonsignificant. (Barlow & Hersen, 1984, and others discuss in detail the limitations of group designs for individual decision making.)

Single-Case Designs

Dr. Daring wants to know whether the fact that Jocelyn recorded her adherence to her medical regimen was responsible for the young woman's improvement and whether the same technique would work for some or all of her other patients. Tricia's teacher wonders what would be the best way to select reinforcers for the child and the other students in her class so they will learn more rapidly and engage in lower rates of self-stimulation. The owners of a chain of restaurants are curious about the impact upon sales of a novel method of employee compensation. Questions like those are the kind asked by managers of performance in service, business, educational, and other organizations. Managers want to know not only the impact of a procedure on the group as a whole but also how reliable the effect is for individuals or small groups; that is, whether repeating or replicating the procedure will reproduce the same effects within a single individual or across other individuals or groups. If managers are concerned with ruling out whether the improvements are a function of conditions other than those they have identified, though, the managers will need to conduct their evaluations under *controlled conditions*. **Single-case experimental designs** (also referred to as **intensive** [Thoresen & Anton, 1974], *within-subject*, *single-subject*,[1] *repeated measures*, and *time-series* experimental designs) can provide the necessary control conditions free of the limitations of group designs.

Advantages of Single-Case Designs

Single-case designs serve a number of the same controlling functions as group designs do, and then some. Perhaps their most important attribute is their ability to go beyond demonstrating correlations to revealing functional relations. Correlations only show that different values of two sets of scores vary in tandem. They indicate nothing about whether these variations influence one another directly; for this information you must demonstrate **functional relations**. Using single-case designs to demonstrate functional relations promotes **accountability**. Let us examine more closely how such accountability is achieved.

---

[1] See Barlow & Hersen (1984) for an extensive treatment of single-case experimental designs.

Being Accountable

Instead of being based on faith, applied behavior analysis qualifies as an accountable, data-based, scientific approach. By collecting data objectively and analyzing the function of procedural effects rigorously, behavior analysts become accountable for their results. Many consumers no longer are content to accept methods simply because practitioners are trained to use them or "intuitively feel" that they will work, or because former clients or onlookers attest to their success. Clients and the professionals serving them want and deserve confirmation that given methods are effective. Beyond asking the consumers of the behavior analytic services how satisfied they were—how socially important and appropriate the changes were (Wolf, 1978), the most convincing way to accomplish this is by demonstrating functional relations.

Demonstrating Functional Relations

As introduced in Chapter 6, the behavior analysis model provides for evaluating the effectiveness of particular interventions, usually at an individual but sometimes at a group level. This is accomplished by demonstrating functional relations between the measures of the *dependent variables*, which normally are the behavior of concern (e.g., health status, rate of language acquisition, or sales), and the *independent variables*, commonly the behavioral procedures (particular self-monitoring, reinforcement systems, or other procedures found throughout this book). Demonstrating a functional relation between a procedure and behavior indicates that the method, and not some extraneous event, is associated systematically with the change in behavior.

Functional relations are confirmed by showing that the dependent variables change reliably *when and only when* the treatment is in place. Phases prior to treatment (baseline), during treatment (intervention), and afterward (follow-up) include collection of sufficient repeated measures to enable the behavior of concern to be revealed validly. The extent of the change is assessed by noting any marked alterations in the following:

- the *level* of the data—how high data have climbed or low they have dropped.
- their *rate of change*[2]—how rapidly they have been modified over time.
- their *variability*—the extent to which the data points have bounced about the new level or trend.

Numerous conventions have evolved for assessing the significance of the change, including how closely the new pattern matches a preset criterion level, noting data points that generally fall outside of the range of those in other phases, and various statistical tests, such as time-series analyses. (See texts like Barlow, Hayes, & Nelson, 1984; Barlow & Hersen, 1984; Drew & Hardman, 1985; Johnston & Pennypacker, 1980; for elaboration of this topic.)

In group designs, the power of the tests derives in large part from the number of subjects in relation to the variability of measures; in the single-subject design, number and stability of data points per individual or within the group are what analysts calculate. Just as you would want to measure the number of calories you consume not only on one day but for each day over a few weeks to accurately describe your eating habits, the more data points (behavioral measures) that fall within a given range, the more convinced we are that the emerging picture depicts what is truly happening. The extent to which a set of measures actually represents what it professes to measure indicates its validity. So to the extent that the series of measures collected during any phase of the study truly represents how the person behaves under those circumstances, those particular measures are valid.

---

[2] Depicted by the *slope* of the curve—the angle it forms from the horizontal.

So you collect data that you and any skeptic would agree adequately depict performance during the phase. That means the measures include several instances of any circumstances suspected of influencing them, such as days of the week, activities, personnel changes, or types of tasks.

You must be careful *not* to introduce a new phase simultaneously with any event that might also produce systematic change. For instance, were you studying the influence of an intervention on employee attendance, you would avoid introducing treatment on the day new personnel join the group, on school holidays that affect attendance of employees with school-age children, on the last day of the fiscal year, or during the World Series or a snow storm.

One rule of thumb for deciding you have collected sufficient data during a phase is the absence of any new high or low points *three times in a row*. As Gelfand and Hartmann (1984) note, beyond those three successive stable measurements you need an additional session of data collection for each 10% of variability (with variability determined by subtracting the lowest point from the highest and dividing that by the highest point). Also, avoid introducing any new phase when the data points show a trend in the direction expected for that next phase (Gelfand & Hartmann, 1984). Therefore, do not introduce interventions when baselines are moving in the desired direction, although if they are trending in the opposite way, that is a good time to begin. Extremely high baselines (presuming high performance levels are what you are after) or low ones (when reducing behavior is of concern) suggest any improvements you might add will not look very compelling and that you might question the sense of trying to improve the behavior anyway.

A series of physiological measures prior to treatment constitute Jocelyn's baseline. Her doctor would consider that baseline reasonably representative of her "true" functioning, because it did not vary much from one time to the next. Then during treatment, if the scores improved and remained consistently higher, her doctor could begin to assume they validly represented what was happening with Jocelyn during the treatment. To establish the *function* of the procedure, the doctor could determine whether improvement occurred *when and only when* the treatment was put into effect, with another patient, then another, and so on, following baselines of different lengths.

Controlling for Extraneous Variables

Experimenters and evaluators want to be sure that the method they employed, rather than some other factor (confounding variable), has been responsible for changes they observe. Single-case designs include a screening process that enables the experimenter to discard competing explanations of results. For example, say that after baselines of varying lengths are obtained, an intervention is introduced that duplicates its results when applied with different people. In such a case, external events like holidays, day of the week, seasonal factors, maturation of the subject, and passage of time alone can be discarded as alternative explanations. Similarly, if ongoing measurement, tasks, and other contextual factors are kept constant throughout baseline and treatment, those factors can be dismissed as rival explanations of any noted improvement. Because individuals serve as their own controls, that is, measured changes are contrasted against their own baseline performance, individual differences do not affect or confound the results.

Yielding General Findings

Single-case research can help analysts discover findings that are applicable to a particular individual or even across a number of individuals. Dexter's completion of arithmetic problems increased as a function of praise from his parents, teachers, the guidance counselor, and others, suggesting that adult approval could serve a reinforcing function for his behavior under other circumstances. The more frequently the intervention that was used with Jocelyn was found to reproduce its success among other patients, the more generally applicable it could be assumed to be.

Enabling New Discoveries

The following comment by Eaton, Gentry, Haring, and Lovitt (1972) on applied research in education is just as relevant to other human services:

> An educational system based on expediency without a concomitant research program would be analogous to a medical treatment program based only on the use of currently available drugs and procedures, without research programs to develop new and better medical treatments. As an ongoing commitment to research is vital to progress in medicine, so a systematic and applied program of educational research is vital for extending our knowledge of teaching procedures and learning processes (pp. 1–2).

Integral to behavior analysis is a system for discovering new and better ways to modify behavior. For instance, when procedural replications fail to duplicate results across people, contexts, or behavior, behavior analysts do not discard an intervention. Instead, they continue to investigate the sources of the variation by trying different procedural arrangements, until success is achieved (or the method is abandoned as too expensive or unlikely to pay off) (Michael, 1974). Say that Jocelyn's success with her self-management strategies was not achieved by the other patients. On inquiry, the behavior analyst working with the doctor discovered that those other patients stopped applying the procedures after a few weeks. So, to encourage them to continue, the analyst began to call a few of them weekly and visit them monthly to ask about their data, congratulating them for self-recording and reinforcing any improvements they reported. Results were much

better, so she tried the same technique with a few others, who improved similarly. In this way a better method was discovered.

Additionally, ways that experimenters have to change their experimental technique to reproduce the results across subjects may provide information about a person's prior history (Bijou & Baer, 1960). That information also may help experimenters identify confounding variables that must eventually be controlled if outcomes are to be optimized for that individual under other circumstances. Were praise from men but not women found to work best with Dexter, arranging for males to provide him with approbation would be most beneficial.

With experimental analysis[3] an essential component of applied behavior analysis (ABA), every behavior analytic program is, in essence, also an experiment. Like the basic laboratory researcher, the applied behavior analyst is concerned with discovering factors that affect behavior lawfully. But rather than experimenting with convenient responses in the laboratory, the primary concern is with improving the effectiveness of socially important behavior in natural settings (Baer et al., 1968).

The main advantages here are that the behavioral changes accomplished through behavior analysis have social value and validity—they improve performance in the context in which they will be applied. By contrast, though, applied behavior analysis has its costs. Seldom is the natural setting ideal for conducting research. "The analysis of socially important behavior becomes experimental only with difficulty" (Baer et al., 1968, p. 92). Structuring the situation carefully, that is, using adequate controls, becomes very important. For this reason, we now elaborate upon some single-subject experimental designs that are particularly useful in analyzing behavioral interventions in applied settings.

---

[3] Sometimes called "functional analysis."

Withdrawal Designs

As described earlier, the term *functional relation* means that changes in the independent variable reliably produce corresponding changes in the dependent variable(s). If a particular independent variable (e.g., praise) is functionally related to a particular individual's behavior (e.g., rate of answering questions), the contingent presentation of the independent variable will affect that behavior systematically (increasing the rate of answering questions). If, instead, praise is an aversive stimulus, the rate should decrease; but if praise is indeed a reinforcer, *withholding* it following answers to questions also should have a systematic effect (after an extinction burst)—causing the rate to decrease. So, systematic changes in the dependent variable as a function of whether the independent variable is being presented increases our confidence in the functionality of the relation. We conclude that our procedure, rather than some extraneous variables, accounts for the changes in behavior. This logic is the basis for the **withdrawal design**.

Recall the characteristics of the withdrawal design (Chapter 6). First, baseline performance was measured. Next, the independent variable was introduced. Then the independent variable was removed until performance began to return to its baseline levels and lastly the independent variable was reintroduced. The first baseline was identified as the A phase; the experimental condition, in which the independent variable was introduced, the B phase. The return to baseline conditions was the withdrawal phase (a second A), and the replication of the procedure was labeled "B." For obvious reasons, withdrawal designs are often called "ABAB designs."

Figure 14.1 shows how completely supervisors filled out accident report forms as a function of feedback and praise from the researchers (Fox & Sulzer-Azaroff, 1987). Apparently, feedback had a considerable impact, and when it was withdrawn during the follow-up period the behavior returned to its previous baseline level.

Figure 14.2 illustrates an autistic child's percentage of correct verbal responses as a function of whether a "normal" boy of his age gave him small portions of his favorite food contingent on correct responses or not (Schram & Sulzer-Azaroff, 1972).

Withdrawal designs need not be limited to instances of reinforcement. They can be used to analyze the influence of any manipulatable independent variable, such as teaching a response that competes with an eye-blink tic (see Figure 14.3; Azrin & Peterson, 1989) or any of the other procedures presented in this book. One proviso is essential: The measured performance must be sufficiently flexible to move up and down. Otherwise, the measure cannot show how performance shifts systematically as a function of the independent variable.

The withdrawal design can inform us not only about the functional relation between the independent and dependent variables but also about the durability of change. (See Rusch & Kazdin, 1981, for elaboration of this point.) In cases of *rate* changes alone, ABAB designs often reveal that the change depends on the continuation of the B condition, as in the feedback for completing safety reports. However, when the design is used to analyze the acquisition of *new* behavior, the design is more apt to demonstrate that the change maintains at near optimal levels.

Variations of Withdrawal Design

Baselines with reinforcement not contingent on the dependent variable. Should you be concerned with testing the effectiveness of a particular set of reinforcers on a given behavior, you may want to be sure that it is the *contingency* you arrange that is responsible, not just the influx of reinforcement into the situation. If so, keep the overall level of reinforcement relatively

Figure 14.1 Average Number of the 14 Feedback Items Completed for Each Set of 10 Accident Reports During Each Phase of the Study

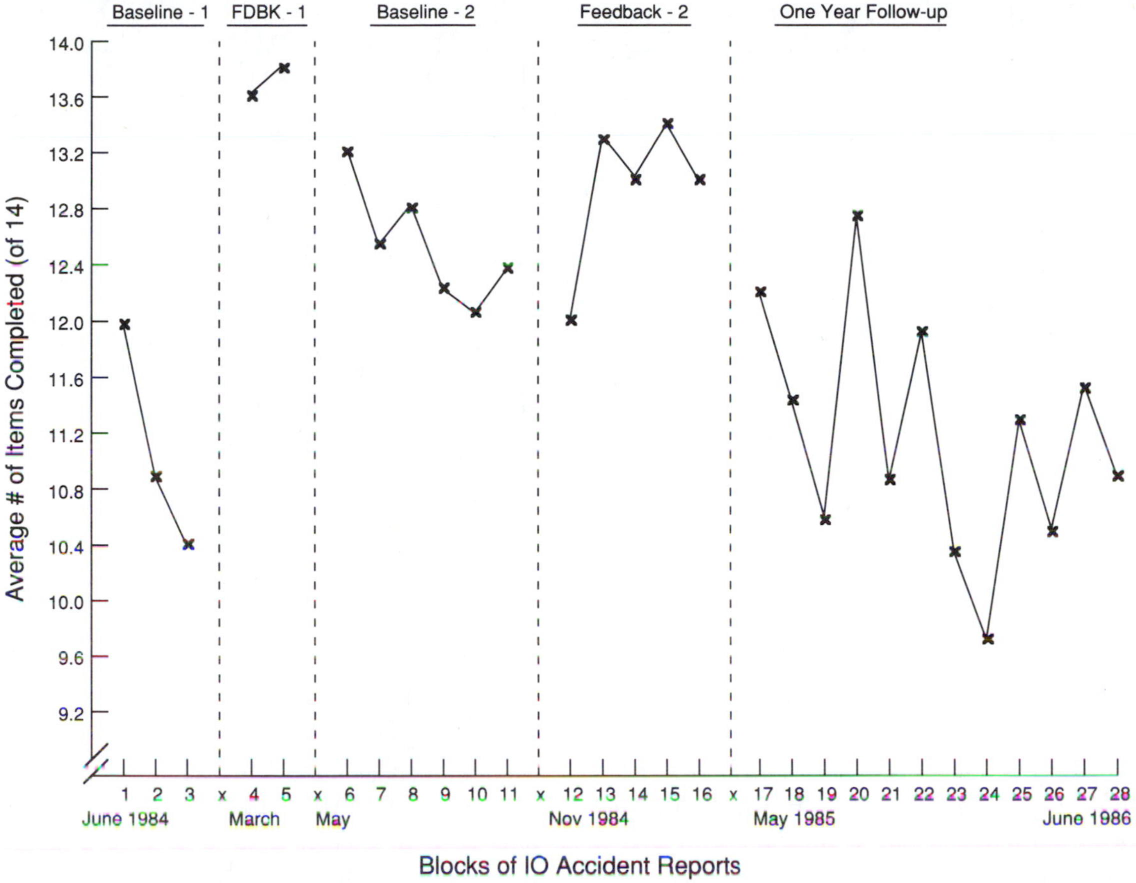

Reprinted with permission from the *Journal of Safety Research, 18,* C. J. Fox & B. Sulzer-Azaroff, "Increasing completion of accident reports," copyright, 1987, Pergamon Press, Inc.

constant during all phases, but make it contingent upon the behavior only during the B phases.

For instance, one study we conducted involved a tutoring program with a group of 9- and 10-year-old students (Sulzer-Azaroff et al., 1972). The treatment consisted of delivering points, backed up by access to preferred activities like games, crafts projects, films, and trips, contingent on performance in academic assignments (number completed and percentage correct) in reading and arithmetic workbooks. Besides worrying about whether the students would remain in the study due to an insuffi-

ciency of reinforcement, we wanted to ensure that any changes were a function of the intervention and not just the addition of those reinforcers. Therefore, during the baseline phase we made the reinforcing activities available to the students "noncontingently," permitting them to participate in the activities regardless of their performance on academic tasks. Then, once the experimental phase was in effect, access to the activities had to be earned. Although the difference in performance between the A and the B conditions was not as dramatic as it probably would have been had reinforcement been totally

Figure 14.2 Verbal Responses as a Function of Treatment

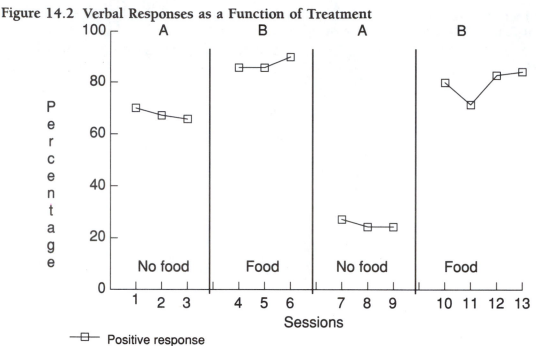

Adapted from Schram & Sulzer-Azaroff (1972).

absent during A, further improvement was demonstrated during B. Of practical importance was the fact that, except for one student who left, all the students opted to continue attendance at sessions throughout the year.

Intervention phases as baselines. Sometimes we want to find out whether we can get behavior to change with only a minor change in contingencies. So we begin with minimal contingencies, augmenting them only if necessary. That strategy was followed in a study that investigated the simplest contingencies possible to encourage nurses' aides to use infection control procedures in a head injury clinic (Babcock, Sulzer-Azaroff, & Sanderson, 1989). Following a baseline in which the aides were observed for handwashing and use of gloves (A), we provided simple forms and asked the nurses who supervised the aides to check the forms and give them to their aides, praising improvement as merited (B). Little change occurred, because the nurses only fol-

lowed through minimally. We then instituted several procedures contingent on the nurse's delivery of feedback and reinforcement, including feedback and praise by the researchers and letters of commendation (C). The nurses increased their follow-through in implementing the feedback and reinforcement, and their aides began to improve their infection control practices. From a design perspective, the B phase served as a new baseline on which the C phase was imposed. The B phase remained in effect, whereas the C phase could be implemented or withdrawn as desired.

Brief baseline phase. Another variation of the ABAB design involves a brief baseline phase. This variation is used most frequently when many repeated baseline measurements would be patently absurd. A case is when the individual has either never or hardly ever been seen emitting the target behavior, so repeated baseline measurement makes no sense. Specific examples in-

Figure 14.3 Frequency of Eye Tics Per Minute in the Clinic from Direct Observation Measurements During Baseline and Competing Response Phases

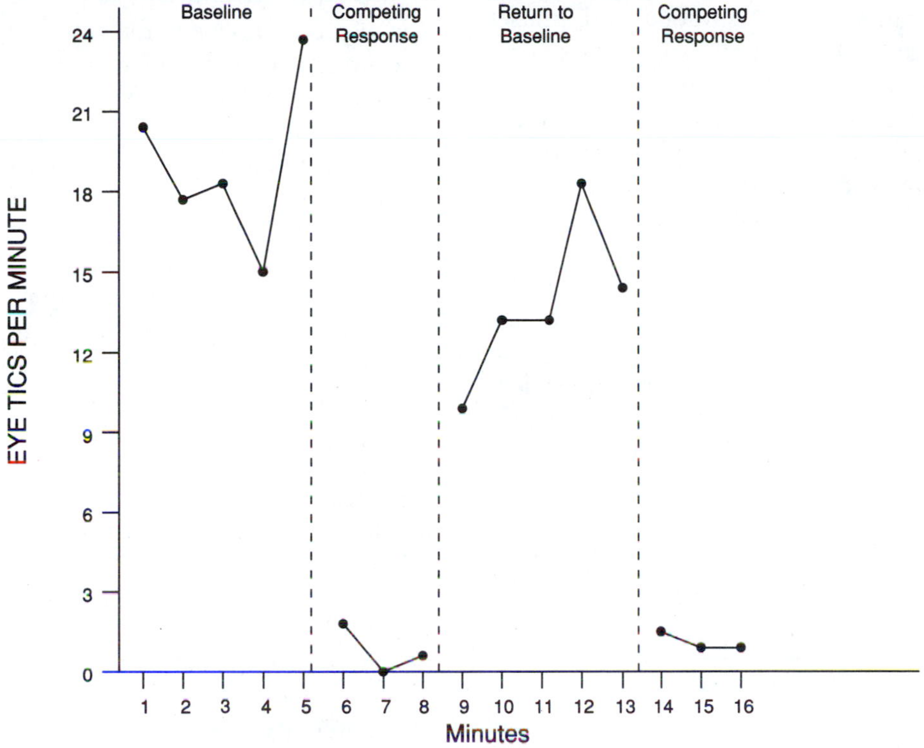

Source: Azrin & Peterson (1989), p. 469. Reprinted with permission from the Association for the Advancement of Behavior Therapy and the authors.

clude assessing the number of printed words a first grader reads when he has never shown any evidence of reading in the past, or measuring the time a woman spends on a task when she has never had an opportunity to perform that task before. The latter occurred in a study that assessed the effects of a token system on the job performance of patients in a psychiatric ward (Ayllon & Azrin, 1968). The jobs had not been available to the patients before, so taking repeated measures of typical performance made little sense. The baseline that is available, however, should be used. In these cases, it is zero. However, recording at least a few initial baseline measures can't hurt. (Chapter 22 returns to methods for functionally analyzing acquisition data.)

Differential reinforcement reversal. When time is of the essence, you may wish to demonstrate the function of the independent variable by applying it contingent on different classes of behavior during different phases of the study. This variation is called the **reversal design**. If those behaviors shift up and down in relation to the intervention, you will have powerfully demonstrated the function of the intervention.

In 1967, Baer, Peterson, and Sherman taught profoundly retarded children to imitate certain behavior. First, the children received food and praise for imitating, thereby substantially increasing the frequency of that response class. To demonstrate that the reinforcing contingencies were responsible for the change, for a time food and praise were delivered after an interval during which imitative behavior was *not* emitted, causing the rate of the behavior to plunge rapidly. When imitation-contingent food and praise were reinstated, the children again began to imitate the behavior at a high rate.

A similar reversal design was used by Wheeler and Sulzer (1970) in a language-training program. The percentage of sentences correctly used by a speech-deficient child is plotted across sessions in Figure 14.4. The label "training form I" represents an experimental phase in which the child's approximations to full sentences were reinforced with small snacks and praise. The return to baseline conditions yielded only minor effects. When a different form was reinforced (training form II), and the child's incomplete sentence productions were also reinforced, the percentage of his correct responses dropped substantially. After a return to the first experimental condition, a high rate of correct responses quickly returned. The functional relation between the behavior and the contingent reinforcers was demonstrated.

Figure 14.4 Percentages of Form-1 Responding in Six Experimental Conditions

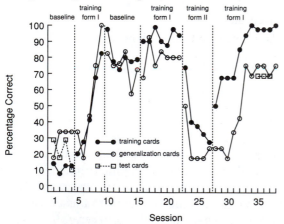

Adapted by permission from A. J. Wheeler and B. Sulzer. Operant training and generalization of a verbal response form in a speech deficient child. *Journal of Applied Behavior Analysis.* 1970. 3. Fig. 1. Copyright 1970 by the Society for the Experimental Analysis of Behavior, Inc. Reprinted with permission from the Society for the Experimental Analysis of Behavior and the authors.

Advantages and Disadvantages of Withdrawal Designs

The major advantage of the withdrawal design, of course, is that it demonstrates a functional relation between the dependent behavior and the intervention, thereby providing a major basis for accountability. In addition, withdrawal designs can be used to determine how successfully the modified behavior persists in the absence of the arranged contingencies. Also, in conjunction with arranged contingencies as a teaching tool, the withdrawal design can demonstrate to contingency managers and consumers just how effective and necessary continuing the new procedures might be.

The few disadvantages of withdrawal designs relate to the need to establish baselines and fear of recovery of unwanted behavior during the withdrawal phase. Establishing and measuring baseline conditions takes time, and unless the performers react positively just to being observed (which also distorts the depiction of ongoing preintervention performance), the conditions themselves do not contribute to the actual behavioral change. Baselines that faithfully represent current behavior are essential, however, as a basis for assessing subsequent change. How could the influence of the intervention be determined without knowledge of the pattern of the behavior before that phase was introduced?

In addition to the time problem, practitioners often fear that the modified behavior may not recover after the return to baseline conditions. The only reply to that argument is evidence that once behavior has been acquired initially, it is reacquired more rapidly (Keller & Schoenfeld, 1950). Sometimes contingency managers are unwilling to institute a withdrawal, regardless of how instructive it may be, because they don't want to jeopardize the improvement. Informing contingency managers that it is not necessary for behavior to return completely to its baseline level may be helpful.

A substantial shift back toward baseline is sufficient to convince most skeptics. Nevertheless, withdrawal designs do introduce temporary disruptions in progress.

We might question the **ethics** of implementing even brief withdrawals (often called **probes**) on ethical grounds. Withdrawals may be justified ethically because they provide information about how independently the client is able to function in the absence of the behavioral program. If the behavioral program is not permanent, responsible professionalism demands that the potential for independence from the program be determined by removing it from time to time. The probe fulfills this requirement nicely. Advance negotiation of plans to assess for persistence of change, as discussed earlier in relation to Figures 14.1 and 14.2, probably is a good strategy. Chapter 22 discusses multiple probes (Horner & Baer, 1978) as a technique for functionally analyzing the relation between an intervention and the acquisition of untreated responses.

Multiple-Baseline Designs

A multiple-baseline design offers an alternative to the withdrawal design. This tactic uses baselines of differing lengths to control for time-dependent extraneous variables, such as history, maturation, time of year, reaction to being measured for longer or shorter periods, seasonal influences, and so on. The functional relation between the independent and dependent variables is demonstrated by showing that substantial change in level, slope, or variability happens *when, and only when*, the independent variable is introduced. The three frequently used variations of the multiple-baseline design are across behaviors, across individuals, and across situations.

Across Behaviors

Multiple-baselines across behaviors are composed of a series of several responses that are identified and measured to provide a baseline against which change can be measured. Once the baselines are established, an intervention is applied to one of those behaviors but not to the others that remain under baseline conditions. Then, rather than withdrawing the intervention, it is applied to the second, presumably unchanged, response. Changes in the pattern of performance at that point provide evidence that the treatment was responsible and not just coincidental. Applying the treatment to a third response and achieving similarly reliable changes adds further to the evidence in favor of a functional relation between the treatment and the behavior. (See Baer et al., 1968.)

Across-behaviors multiple baselines illustrated. McAllister and colleagues (1969) used this form of the multiple-baseline research design to demonstrate the effect of the teacher's praise and disapproval on several target behaviors in two high school classrooms. Following baseline assessments for all of the target behaviors, praise and disapproval were based first on inappropriate talking, whereas baseline conditions were maintained for inappropriate turning around. Inappropriate talking diminished during that phase, and turning around remained relatively stable. Next, the same contingencies were applied to turning around, leading to a rapid decrease in that behavior, thereby demonstrating the effectiveness of the contingencies.

Schmidt (1974) also used this design to evaluate his effectiveness in counseling a client. An 18-year-old woman wished to increase her verbal skills. After a week of collecting baseline data about her speaking at work, speaking loudly, and initiating conversations, he told her "that for each time she spoke to someone at work during any given day she could have two minutes that same day with her counselor, talking about anything she wished." Speaking at work increased from the baseline of 1.0 to 8.2 times a day. Speaking loudly and initiating conversations remained near baseline levels of 1.6 and 0.6 times a day, respectively. At the beginning of the third week, the client was told "that she could now have only one minute of counselor time per day for each time she engaged in desirable verbal behavior but that she could now combine categories one and two—speaking at work and speaking loudly." The mean frequency for speaking at work increased to 15.8 times a day, and the count for speaking loudly increased to 5.2 times a day while initiating conversation remained near baseline level (0.8). Finally, at the beginning of the fourth week one minute of counselor time was made contingent on any of the three target behaviors. By the end of that week, speaking at work had increased to 14.6 times a day, speaking loudly to 12.2 a day, and the mean count of initiating conversations to 7.4 a day. This design offered two major advantages for Schmidt: "First, working on one behavior at a time ensured that the number of tasks would not be overwhelming to the client. Second, the multiple baseline design sorted out the importance of counselor time as a contingency" (1974, p. 204).

Selection considerations. A major consideration in using the multiple baseline design to demonstrate experimental control is that one must be reasonably assured beforehand that the dependent variables or target behaviors are not interdependent or highly interrelated. If they are, a change in one can also be expected to change the others. Although the ripple effect can be a welcome occurrence, because you have gotten something for nothing, the power of the demonstration will be lost. Significant change has not coincided with the implementation of the intervention in that situation. For example, if smiles are associated with eye contact and answering questions, then an increase in any one of these target behaviors probably will be associated with similar increases in the others. Avoid this situation through careful observation. Ask yourself if you saw smiling associated with eye contact or answering questions. If not, applying a multiple-baseline design across those

behaviors may be appropriate; but if they tend to *covary*—to change in tandem—choose an alternative design. Also, the less equivalent the structure or function of the behaviors, the less likely they are to covary. So, when you enlist this design, try to select behaviors as dissimilar from one another as possible.

Should unplanned generalization occur with any of the multiple-baseline arrangements, you always have the option of nesting a withdrawal within one or more of the baselines. Farnum and Brigham (1978) were interested in determining how helpful study guides were for students, so after instituting baselines for both, they supplied the guides first to one group, then another, for two different books. Then they removed the study guides for one book from one of the two groups, and from the other group for the other book. (Study guides made a big difference! We hope you have discovered the value of using the study guide that accompanies this text.)

Across Individuals
Instead of introducing the intervention across a sequence of *behaviors*, the **multiple-baseline across individuals** involves collecting baselines on the *same behavior* of *several persons*, preferably in different settings. The effects of the intervention are tested first with one person while baseline conditions are continued with the others; later the intervention is introduced with the others in sequence. The object is to show that—regardless of time, specific subject, and environmental factors—each individual's behavior (or that of a composite group) changes with the intervention. In one case, Cossairt et al. (1973) investigated the effects of an experimenter's instructions, feedback, and feedback combined with social praise on three elementary school teachers' use of praise for students' paying attention to their math tasks. The last method, the combined "package," was more effective across each of the teachers.

Figure 14.5 illustrates this design across

Figure 14.5 Proportion of Work Hours Spent in Direct Contact with Clients by Three Groups of Clinicians Under Baseline, Self-Monitoring, and Self-Monitoring Plus Assigned Goal Conditions

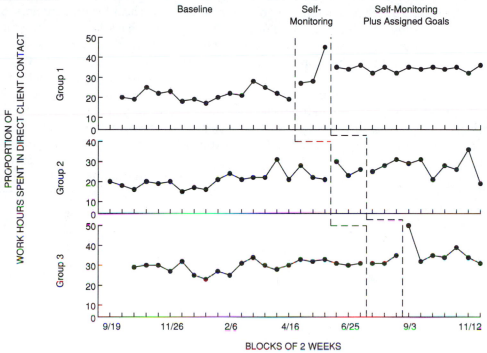

Reprinted with permission of the Haworth Press, Inc.

groups of five or six professionals in different counties (Calpin, Edelstein, & Redmon, 1988). Self-monitoring and then a combination of goal-setting and feedback were used to increase the group's proportion of work hours spent in direct client contact. The results speak for themselves!

Because the intervention lags across time, this design is especially handy for analysts serving people in multiple settings; they do not have to intervene everywhere at once. Instead, as some individuals are treated, others are waiting in the wings while their baseline performance continues to be assessed. The major difficulty is preventing those who received treatment from influencing the behavior of others who have not yet received treatment. Otherwise, the supposedly untreated baseline data will change,

and the demonstration of control will be lost. Avoid this by choosing people who do not interact or, if necessary, requesting that the subjects avoid discussing the treatment with others. If communication is likely across individuals whose performance measures constitute different baselines, selecting another design is recommended. Also recognize that some recipients must await treatment longer than others, so that this design is best for behavior that does not require immediate action.

Across Situations

The third variation of the **multiple-baseline** design is **across situations or settings**. In this design "data are collected for a target behavior for one or more subjects across different circumstances or situations" (Kazdin, 1973b, p.

521). Alan and Brian regularly ground their teeth, a habit occasionally associated with damage to teeth, gums, and facial bone structure (Bebko & Lennox, 1988). A combination of praise for not grinding his teeth and a cuing procedure was instituted with each boy, first in one setting, and then another (shown in Figures 14.6 and 14.7).

Long and Williams (1973) also used this design, combined with others, for an inner city seventh-grade class, in order to assess the effects of contingent free time on student conduct. Baselines were taken both in the students' math and in their geography classes. Appropriate behavior improved maximally in each class only when strategy of contingent free time was used.

As with the across-individuals variation, this design has the advantage of permitting the program to be implemented sequentially, which is especially practical for practitioners. Similarly, the major drawback is that unanticipated generalization from one locale to the other thwarts the strength of the demonstration. If you suspect that changing a client's behavior in one situation will lead to corresponding modifications in others, you should select another design. For instance, being the clever young woman that she is, Jocelyn might well decide to use her self-recording method to manage her time and responsibilities, without anyone's direction. Some people quickly transfer their new skills to other situations, whereas others do not. Such generalization appears to depend on past

Figure 14.6 Rates of Bruxism (in % of time samples) for Alan Across Two School Situations. The less structured is represented in the upper panel, the most structured in the lower.

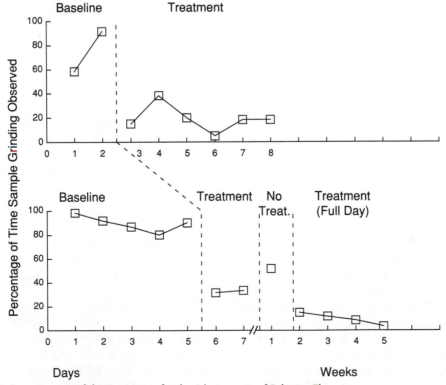

Reprinted with the permission of the Association for the Advancement of Behavior Therapy.

Figure 14.7 Rates of Bruxism (in % of time samples) for Brian Across Two School Situations. The less structured is represented in the upper panel, the more structured in the lower.

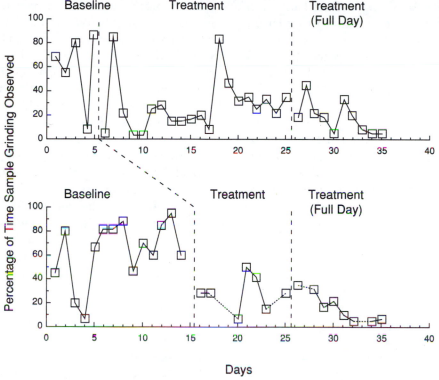

Reprinted with the permission of the Association for the Advancement of Behavior Therapy.

experiences and on other factors described in greater detail in Chapter 29. Before you use this design, try to estimate the likelihood that the effects will transfer across situations. Also select contexts for the other baselines that are sufficiently dissimilar from one another to minimize such unplanned transfer of the behavior from one situation to the others.

Multiple Baselines to Assess for Generalization

Perhaps you have recognized the value of assessing baselines for all the behaviors, individuals, or situations across which you hope the influence of the intervention will or will not spread. As you will learn in Chapter 29, which discusses generalization, the greater the num-

ber of examples or settings, the more likely that the desired transfer will take place. So if you are teaching a strategy you hope will generalize to new responses or contexts, collect the data for as many of those behaviors or settings as practically feasible. As you introduce the intervention sequentially, transfer eventually may begin to occur in the untreated baseline, and all you will need to do is to intermittently reinforce instead of instituting the full-blown intervention.

As an example, perhaps Jocelyn originally failed to self-record her food intake on weekends, when away from home, during vacations, holidays, and on other occasions. By sequentially intervening for each of those circumstances, while monitoring all, she and the behavior analyst could judge if and when the time came when further interventions were no longer necessary, because the young woman had begun to self-record in the new settings without direction from anyone else.

Use multiple baselines as an ecological tool when you want to assess the broad impact of an intervention. Peck, Killen, and Baumgart (1989) asked teachers to view videotapes and generate ideas for embedding instruction related to their students' individual educational plans. They wondered if their advice might have an impact not only in the planned setting but elsewhere as well. For this reason the investigators observed the teachers at work with the students in those other settings. The data showed that following the consultation, two of the three teachers used the instructional methods in the new contexts, too.

George and Hopkins (1989) used the same design strategy to demonstrate the multiple effects of compensating food servers for productivity—amount of food sales. The baselines revealed that production increased along with take-home pay for the servers, whereas owners' labor costs were shown *not* to improve, revealing a potential stumbling block to the continued use of the method.

Summary

This chapter introduced some of the underlying assumptions and strategies for choosing and applying withdrawal and multiple-baseline ex-perimental designs. These designs are well suited to assessing the functional relations between performance and strategies for increasing or decreasing behavioral rates. Chapter 22 continues the discussion of experimental analyses, focusing on methods for evaluating response acquisition and comparing different independent variables. Keep in mind, though, as Johnston and Pennypacker (1980) caution, that we need to be sensitive to the many subtleties and complexities of the decisions we make in selecting a particular design strategy. We should avoid adhering rigidly to any particular structure, because "the particular manipulations within each experiment [must] be viewed from a *dynamic* rather than a static perspective" (p. 251). We need to leave room for modifying our planned tactics and following the hunches that are suggested by serendipitous findings. "Any story of scientific achievement has as its subtheme the sensitive flexibility characterizing the investigator's style of scientific inquiry" (p. 251). In other words, suit the design to the question, rather than the other way around. Just be certain to control your experimental analysis as you remain watchful for interesting or puzzling occurrences, then pursue those paths that seem most promising.

The designs we have presented here and later do suit admirably many problems of evaluation. To assist your selection of those that best suit your purposes, we summarize the advantages and limitations of each design in Table 22.1 (Chapter 22).

Section III

Occasioning and Teaching Behaviors

An aircraft filled with vacationing families approaches its destination through a densely overcast sky. Guided only by instruments, the pilot makes a perfect landing.

Ms. Ophelia, Shakespearean scholar, selects a passage from *Twelfth Night* and renders an extraordinarily perceptive interpretation.

In the small hours of the morning, an ambulance siren wails as a stricken patient is rushed to City Hospital. Dr. Daring's rapid diagnosis allows a miraculous cure for the illness.

How do these people become so accomplished? Not just by means of simple reinforcement. Control by antecedents plays an essential part, as do more specialized forms of reinforcer delivery.

You already recognize from your earlier exposure to the sequence (ABC) analysis in Chapter 2, just how powerful antecedent events can be. Here the focus is on a more technical analysis of antecedents and their application as well as on complex reinforcement contingencies. The thrust is to promote classes of behavior often labeled in everyday language as knowledge, proficiency, sophistication, culture, sensitivity, and creativity.

When an antecedent stimulus, like the position of a dial on an aircraft flight panel, a script, or a set of symptoms, is observed to increase the probability of a given response—landing, interpreting, diagnosing—we say that the response is "under the control" of that antecedent stimulus. The technical term for a response under antecedent or **stimulus control** is **discriminated operant**, because the operant (i.e., "voluntary") response occurs only under particular conditions, which the individual detects, or "discriminates," from others.

Reflect on antecedent control; you will recognize how critical it is to our personal and societal survival. If everyone freely responded anywhere at any time, chaos would prevail. People would wake and sleep, eat and mate, say and do anything they chose to do, regardless of circumstances. Continued existence requires that we select carefully the items we consume, choose clothing and shelter appropriate to climatic conditions, and avoid dangerous situations. Social order dictates that we sleep only in certain places, such as at home or in a tent; that we mate in private; and that we speak when others are present and actively listening—or into a telephone, dictaphone, or recording device. We had better not enter the ladies room if we are male, drive through a red light, ignore a police officer's instructions, or give someone a hundred dollar bill for a $1 charge. If we break these norms we will be in trouble, or labeled strange, criminal, stupid, or incompetent.

Natural experience teaches us which foods will taste good or make us sick, that cats generally purr when we pet them and scratch when we pull their tails, which flowers smell sweet or unpleasant, and countless other discriminations. Child-rearing practices, formal education, training, management, counseling, and therapy further the process. Parents instruct their children where and when particular acts are acceptable; teachers, what terms, concepts, and skills apply in given instances; job trainers and managers, what to do how, where, when, and with what; counselors and therapists, what responses are cued by what circumstances and how to alter those relations. Whether everyone performing those functions recognizes it or not, each is concerned with bringing given responses under stimulus control.

Suppose, though, that the person is not capable of performing the response in the first place. Antecedents will not be able to evoke it until the individual acquires the behavior. Analysts guide clients in acquiring the behavior by using reinforcement in special ways; by reserving delivery of reinforcers for steps in the right direction, via a method called **shaping**, or for new combinations of responses, as in **chaining**.

The principal advantage of becoming skilled in using stimulus control, shaping, and chaining procedures is that you will increase your proficiency as a manager, teacher, or trainer. So in this section we will tell you about various ways[1] to teach behavior by bringing it under the control of antecedents, including verbal stimuli, and

---

[1] Negative (aversive) procedures, like the punishment of a response emitted in the presence of a given stimulus, will not be elaborated on here. After mastering the material on punishment (see Chapters 27 and 28), you should be able to design such a procedure. At this point, be aware that using punishment is risky, even when punishment is for the purpose of promoting control by antecedents.

how to skillfully deliver reinforcers as a consequence of behaviors of increasing complexity or sophistication. For your convenience, Table 2 in the Epilogue summarizes the key features of each of these procedures.

Chapter 15

Stimulus Control: How It Develops

GOALS

After completing this chapter, you should be able to:

1. Define, recognize, and give original illustrations of each of the following terms:
   a. Stimulus control
   b. Discriminated operant
   c. Occasion
   d. Discrimination
   e. Generalization
   f. Stimulus generalization
   g. Overgeneralization
   h. Discriminative stimulus (S^D)
   i. Three-term contingency
   j. S^+
   k. S^-
   l. Differential reinforcement
   m. Four-term contingency
   n. Setting events
   o. Establishing stimulus (S^E)
   p. Matching-to-sample
   q. S-delta (S^Δ)
   r. Stimulus equivalence
   s. Concept
   t. Equivalence class

2. Differentiate between antecedent and consequential control.

3. Differentiate among generalization, overgeneralization, and discrimination.

4. Describe how a stimulus develops into an S^D.

5. Discuss and illustrate with an example how stimulus control is developed.

6. Identify and discuss the difficulties associated with implementing the three elements of differential reinforcement to achieve stimulus control.

7. Differentiate between the contextual variables of setting events and establishing operations, and describe how each can influence the frequency of a behavior.

8. Illustrate and differentiate among three antecedent and response combinations.

9. List and illustrate four reasons why a particular antecedent may not evoke a specific response.

10. Describe and illustrate with an example the importance of stimulus control in concept formation.

11. Explain and illustrate how an S^D for one response is often an S^Δ for another.

12. List the advantages of the phenomenon called stimulus equivalence.

Dr. Daring, our fictitious physician, is admired by her colleagues and the community she serves. Why? Because she is an expert diagnostician. Diagnostic expertise (like any sort of expertise) means that the person accurately responds to the presence or absence of a particular combination of stimuli.

Can such expert ability be trained by applying behavioral procedures? Indeed. In an actual case, doctors at the Fargo Clinic who specialized in pediatrics, internal medicine, family practice, orthopedics, and neurosurgery improved the accuracy of their diagnoses along with other important skills when they participated in a behavioral training program (Snyder, 1989). A major aspect of the program involved methods for promoting stimulus control.

Stimulus Control

Stimulus control describes behavior governed by stimuli that precede a behavior—antecedent stimuli. Examples of behavior under stimulus control (technically called **discriminated operants**) are shown in Table 15.1. In each of the instances listed, an antecedent stimulus event (the signal, cue, prompt, instruction, or sample) set the **occasion** for (occasioned, triggered, or evoked) the specific response. Stimulus control was demonstrated because given responses were more probable—or we can say "occasioned" reliably—by specific antecedent stimuli. (The word *control* has many meanings. In this instance it simply describes a highly predictable relation between a stimulus and a response. The term does not imply control of a self-serving nature or a coercive restriction on an individual's options.)

Note that the relations between stimuli and responses differ between antecedent stimulus control and consequential control. In reinforcement and punishment—both consequential events—stimulus events occur as a consequence of, that is, *following* a response. Reinforcement increases or maintains the rate of the response.

Punishment reduces or eliminates the response. In stimulus control, the response rate is influenced by the stimuli that *precede* or accompany that response. The individual's previous history of reinforcement (or punishment) in the presence of those antecedent stimuli determines, in great measure, whether or not the response will occur. Why?

When a response is reinforced repeatedly in the presence of a stimulus (or combination of stimuli), the stimulus begins to occasion the response because reinforcement is highly probable under those circumstances. Answering the phone when it rings has usually resulted in hearing someone's voice, but not when it hasn't rung first. Jumping into the cool ocean has been reinforced during hot weather but not during cold.

Stimulus Generalization and Discrimination

If we are to concern ourselves with antecedent stimuli and the roles they play in controlling behavior, we must distinguish between **discrimination** and **generalization**. Discrimination involves restricting the range of stimuli that evoke a given behavior. With generalization, a variety of stimuli evokes the behavior—the range of stimuli that evoke the behavior is broader. The same behavior may occur in response to different stimuli, such as other forms, sounds, times, places, in the presence of other people, and so on. "When an individual responds in the presence of a new stimulus in the same way as to a previously taught stimulus having some of the same characteristics, the event is called **stimulus generalization**" (Becker, Engelmann, & Thomas, 1975, p. 145).

When Baby Bonnie's parents cue her to say "red" when she is asked the color of an apple, a strawberry, and her brother's wagon, and she does, her parents lavish praise upon her. Now

Table 15.1 Examples of Behavior Under Stimulus Control

Antecedent(s) SDs Setting the Occasion for:	Behavior
Instructions from air traffic controller	Comes in for a landing.
Telephone rings	Penny picks it up and says, "Hello."
A sample of floor covering	Quality assurance technician rejects the whole lot as substandard.
The computer screen flashes "5×4"	The students answer "20."
Study questions asking for definition and example of stimulus control	Student provides acceptable definition and illustration.
Clyde's father asks if eating a candy bar without permission is honest	Clyde says "no."
A particular musical selection	Paula and Sandy get up and dance.
Consultant suggests managers use labeled praise	Paula's supervisor compliments her for reporting all the essential points in her memo.
The coach instructs, "Watch Jerome's position."	Members of the team imitate Jerome's stance.
"Here is a letter used in German: ü. Say its sound."	Students correctly say the sound that matches the umlauted letter.
Families use "Table-Talk" placemats containing colorfully illustrated games and conversational topics (Green, Hardison, & Greene, 1984).	Family interactions increase.

when, for the first time, she sees a fire engine, she also says "red." The antecedent-response relation is generalizing. During training, Dr. Daring accurately discriminated various symptoms to diagnose a difficult adult case, receiving the congratulations of her supervising physician. Now in practice, when she sees a child with similar symptoms, she makes the same diagnosis.

Generalizations may be appropriate by social convention or not, though. Baby Bonnie gave the correct color name to the fire engine but also called her pink dress "red," an incorrect generalization. Besides imitating his expert moves on the ice, Jerome's teammates imitated his penchant for attacking members of the opposing team, also an inappropriate generalization. Inappropriate generalizations are called **overgeneralizations**. Racial or gender bias is an instance of overgeneralization. Here, the person

might respond to an irrelevant stimulus, such as a person's skin color or gender, as if it were the equivalent of some sort of threatening stimulus.

Making a correct discrimination is the opposite of overgeneralizing. Through her parents' tutelage, Bonnie learns to label pink correctly, no longer confusing it with red. She "discriminates" between pink and red. Dr. Daring bases her diagnoses on subtle differences in symptoms, differences that control her behavior. We may say she discriminates accurately among the sets of symptoms.

Contestants in a race must wait for the signal "Go!" before starting in order to be eligible to win. Those who wait to hear "Go!" are discriminating the critical stimulus "Go" from other sounds they hear. Said a different way, the starter's stimulus "Go" is a discriminative stimulus for running. That is why a stimulus that occasions a response is called a **discriminative stimulus**—abbreviated S^D—S for *stimulus;* ^{D} for *discriminative.* One might say that a discriminative stimulus signals that a response probably will be reinforced.

Sometimes generalizing—responding the same way to similar but not identical stimuli—is just what we want to accomplish. A student is taught that the symbol R is pronounced "rrr," so responding with that sound to variations of the printed R—R, r, $\mathcal{R}$, $\imath$—would be appropriate. A counselor teaches a shy young woman to look at him while they converse, in the hope that the control exercised over this response by that set of circumstances will generalize to her conversations with other people. Chapter 29 discusses more extensively how to promote wanted generalization of newly acquired or strengthened behavior to novel contexts. The emphasis in this section, however, will be on how people learn to discriminate; how the S^+, *the stimulus designated ultimately to become the controlling or "discriminative" stimulus* (S^D), does become the S^D. It begins to evoke particular responses and not others, because in the presence of that stimulus the response is more likely to be reinforced. (Table 15.2 summarizes the various abbreviations we shall be using in this section.)

Establishing Discriminative Control

Unlike the power of unlearned antecedent stimuli (unconditioned stimuli, UCSs), such as the meat powder that caused Pavlov's dog to salivate or a puff of air that elicits an eye blink, antecedent stimuli must be reliably present when a response is reinforced before the stimuli become discriminative.[1] Just as many reinforcers acquire their influence through condition-

ing, conditioning is necessary for stimulus control to develop. (The difference is that a conditioned reinforcer comes *after* the behavior, deriving its governing properties from being paired with a powerful reinforcer—no specific antecedents need be involved—whereas an S^D comes *before* [or accompanies] the behavior and receives its control from the reinforcer that follows the behavior when it occurs in the presence of the antecedents.)

In the simplest instance of the development of stimulus control, a selected response (the behavior, B) occurs. When that behavior occurs under specific stimulus conditions (the antecedents, A), it is reinforced (the consequences, C). If those antecedents are not present, the behavior is not reinforced. The phrase **three-term contingency** often is used to describe this interrelation between antecedents, behavior, and consequences: A-B-Cs. (Remember the term *contingency* refers to the *relation* between stimuli and responses.)

A caller's voice is heard *only* if the phone is picked up when it is ringing, so the ring of the phone establishes stimulus control over the response of answering it. This difference in reinforcement conditions, the differential-reinforcement operation (defined below), establishes stimulus control. People learn to emit a given behavior more frequently in the presence of S^+s—stimuli that eventually are to become the S^Ds—and not others, the S^-s—*the stimuli that are not to become S^Ds but are to become S^Δs or S^{D-}s.*

The basic operation is identical for developing simple as well as complex stimulus control, as you will see. For the sake of clarity, however, we shall start the discussion by using a few relatively elementary situations, like the one illustrated in Table 15.3. Then, we shall show that more complex learning, such as the type of skills often labeled "cognitive" (communicating, problem solving, applying moral concepts, and so on), develops similarly.

[1] The application of respondent-conditioning principles to alter physiological responding is a major topic in many books on behavior therapy.

Table 15.2 Stimulus Terminology

Abbre-viation	Term Denoted	Definition	Examples
S	Stimulus	A stimulus:	A light, a smile
Consequential Stimuli			
S^R	Primary Reinforcing Stimulus	reinforcing in absence of a prior learning history	Fluids, when deprived of liquids
S^P	Primary Aversive Stimulus	aversive in absence of prior learning history	The burning heat of a stove
S^r	Conditioned Reinforcing Stimulus	initially had no reinforcing properties but does now through conditioning	A gold star on a paper
S^p	Conditioned Aversive Stimulus	initially had no aversive properties but does now through conditioning	"No. Bad boy!"
Antecedent Stimuli			
S^+	Neutral Stimulus	designated to become a discriminative stimulus (S^D)	The word *water* before the student learns to read it
S^-	Neutral Stimulus	designated to become an S^Δ or S^{D-}	The word *wader* before the student learns to read *water*.
S^D	Discriminative Stimulus	in the presence of which a given response is likely to be reinforced	The picture sets the occasion for → parking
S^{D-}	Negative Discriminative Stimulus	in the presence of which a given response is likely to be punished	The picture inhibits → drinking
S^Δ	S-Delta	in the presence of which a given response is unlikely to be reinforced	Gas gauge reads "empty."
S^E	Establishing Stimulus	upon which reinforcement of an S^D–R relation depends	Car keys need to be found (to permit placing them in the ignition to start the car)

Differential Reinforcement Defined and Illustrated

Differential reinforcement consists of two basic operations: reinforcing a given response, and not reinforcing a response (i.e., placing it on extinction). Discriminative control is established as a given response is reinforced when it occurs in the presence of, or follows, one or more particular stimuli. The response also is extinguished when it occurs in the absence of

Table 15.3 Development of Stimulus Control

Antecedent Stimulus Conditions	Response	Consequence
Telephone rings	Picks up telephone, says "Hello"	"Hello"
In the absence of a ring	Picks up telephone, says "Hello"	No "Hello"

that particular stimulus or group of stimuli. As the response is reinforced repeatedly, with the reinforcement only conditional on the presence of these distinctive stimuli, these antecedent stimuli begin to assume control. Eventually, the response will be evoked only in the presence of the stimuli, even if the response is no longer reinforced every time.

Consider an illustration from a study by Kazdin and Erickson (1975). A group of severely retarded children failed to follow instructions like "Sit down"; "Catch the ball"; "Roll it to me." During training, each time a child followed an instruction correctly, he or she received food and praise. If the instructions were not correctly followed, initially the child was physically guided to complete the response correctly and then given food and praise. Later, the reinforcers were given only for unguided correct responses; incorrect responses were extinguished. Eventually the children attended to instructions without any guidance. Their behavior came under the control of that set of verbal stimuli.

Elements of Differential Reinforcement

Although differential reinforcement seems easy to accomplish, that appearance can be deceptive. Producing perfect stimulus control may prove to be quite a challenge for

- those attempting to teach a job or social skill, a language, dance, science, or any academic subject matter.
- the therapist who is trying to remediate deficiencies or to assist a teacher or parent

to use effective but unfamiliar behavior management techniques.
- the parent who struggles to teach a child the subtleties of appropriate moral and social behavior.
- individuals who want to alter their own habitual patterns of reacting to certain situations.
- essentially everyone concerned with changing performance.

Much more may be required in this process than initially meets the eye:

1. The appropriate response must occur, and for this to happen, it or its component parts must be present in the person's repertoire.
2. The learner must detect the antecedent stimuli.
3. Responding to the stimuli must be reinforced frequently enough to establish the relationship.

Note how those three features are represented in the following example.

A tape-recorded click that occurred every 20 seconds was used to prompt a class of 14 preschool children to pick up 50 large hollow blocks quickly at the end of free-play (Goetz, Ayala, Hatfield, Marshall, & Etzel, 1983). The click was paired with the request, "It's time to pick up the blocks." Only after teachers began to praise compliance did pick-up time decrease substantially. Further, after the click "had been paired with praise, the auditory stimulus alone maintained a shorter pick-up time" (p. 251). Teacher praise was necessary to get the click to function as a stimulus for picking up the blocks efficiently. Once the click functioned to signal the children to pick up the blocks, however, intermittent praise was sufficient.

Contextual Variables

Almost every time you meet a group of your friends, you greet them and have a lively exchange of conversation, reinforced by your friends' reactions. We could depict the learning history like this:

$$S^+ \longrightarrow B \longrightarrow S^r$$
See friends   Greet and   Friends
               converse   converse
                            and smile

After many such pairings, the S^D evokes the behavior:

$$S^D \longrightarrow B$$
See friends   Regularly greet
               and converse

Undoubtedly, though, you have noted that a response may fail to occur even though all the conditions of the three-term contingency have been met: The individual is known to have had an adequate history of reinforcement for an established response in the presence of the antecedent stimulus-response pairing. You hear an excellent speech and do not applaud. You open a book and look at the pages but do not read them. You run into your friends, and other than briefly waving, you do not talk to them. Why? Contextual variables may be at work, creating a **four-term contingency**.

Setting Events

One type of contextual variable is the presence or absence of an S^D that alters the function of any other S^D in a general way.[2] Perhaps your

[2] The technical term for this set of circumstances is *conditional discrimination* (Catania, 1984; Sidman & Tailby, 1982).

friends tend not to respond when you talk to them during a movie:

$$S \longrightarrow B \longrightarrow\!\!\!/ \ \ \cancel{S^r}$$
Friends   Converse

So, in the context of the movie theater, you minimize your conversations, as diagrammed in Figure 15.1.

You usually speak casually, feeling no compunctions about throwing in a colorful four-letter word periodically, and act "naturally" in other ways—that is, at home or school or with your friends or family. But how about when you are at a job interview, religious ceremony, or meeting your fiancé's boss? All sorts of response patterns change. The term **setting events** could be used to describe the contextual stimuli of the kind just mentioned because they alter the function of the S^D: people available for conversation. Setting events occur temporally and interact with the current S^D, resulting in a different behavior than that usually occasioned by the current S^D. (See Wahler & Fox, 1981).

Recognize that setting events acquire their function through a history of differential reinforcement, just as any other sort of discriminative stimulus does. Baby Bonnie might cry or speak loudly at a wedding ceremony, because the S^D of being with her family is in control and being quiet at ceremonies with them has not been sufficiently reinforced. You might blow it with your fiancé's boss because your learning history has failed to permit discriminative con-

Figure 15.1 An Illustration of the Influence of Context on Behavior

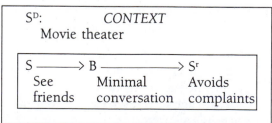

trol to develop over your topics of conversation with potential bosses.

A contextual event, the size of the work units, has been shown to influence employee absenteeism (Durand, 1985). Atwater and Morris (1988) have identified a general classroom context for student compliance. It consists of a setting in which teachers provide a high degree of structure, deliver positively phrased direct imperatives and high rates of approval to individual students, and the pupils engage in appropriate activities rather than being disruptive or off-task.

Mace et al. (1988) found that by getting students to comply over and over again through presenting requests to which they were very likely to acquiesce, compliance persevered despite a subsequent shift to requests to which the child previously was not likely to accede. So if you are attempting to attain a person's compliance with a particular instruction, embed it in a series of instructions with which his or her compliance is highly probable (the setting event) and distribute generous doses of reinforcers along the way.

Many other contextual stimuli related to classroom performance have been discovered. For example, faster rates of presentations of instructional stimuli are associated with both lower rates of disruption (e.g., out of seat, hitting, yelling, throwing objects) and higher rates of correct responses than are slower-paced presentations (Carnine, 1976, 1981; West & Sloane, 1986). So too are frequent praise, clear signals, consistency within a setting, and immediate feedback (Carnine, 1981).

Establishing Operations

Establishing operations, as you will recall from Chapter 10, are specific contextual or setting events that impact on a stimulus's reinforcing (or punishing) function and therefore the behavior that leads up to it. Your brother invites you out to dinner. You refuse, which is way out of keeping with your character. Why? You just indulged yourself in an ice cream sundae; or, you aren't feeling well; or, you just had a knockdown drag-out fight with your fiance. In other words, food simply is not reinforcing at the moment. So any behavior that has been reinforced by food in the past is less likely to occur. Notice that establishing operations resemble events that other learning theorists might have labeled "drives" or "motivational" variables.

Other examples of establishing operations are running five miles in the heat, consuming lots of salty foods, or having a fever. Those events increase the frequency of behavior reinforced by consumption of fluids, like going to a water fountain or to a soda machine. Behavior that permits aggression might increase after a person has experienced an aversive event, such as having a new car dented, losing a job or lover, or being called a particularly nasty name. These sorts of establishing operations (along with learning history) probably play an important role in instances of spouse and child abuse. Perhaps, too, they help explain why vandalism rates in schools have been found to be higher where there is a heavy reliance on punitive disciplinary techniques (Mayer, Butterworth, Nafpaktitis, & Sulzer-Azaroff, 1983).

Various drugs or chemicals in the body also can serve as establishing operations. For example, Ritalin and other drugs are still used to control hyperactive behavior (Rapport, Murphy, & Bailey, 1982). Perhaps they reduce or block the reinforcing value of excessive movement or enhance the reinforcer value of certain environmental stimuli, or maybe the excessive movement now requires such additional effort that it has become aversive.

Establishing operations can impact fulfillment of work duties, as well. Characteristics of on-the-job performance have been analyzed as a function of differences between work and nonwork environments (Redmon & Lockwood, 1986).

A history of differential reinforcement is

much less relevant with establishing operations. The first time a baby is nauseated, he or she will refuse food. The baby doesn't have to have learned previously that eating will be punished. Regardless of whether injury of an adversary has been differentially reinforced, when hurt an animal will attack any nearby creature (Ulrich & Azrin, 1962). So, the establishing operation is not the same as a discriminative stimulus and does not obtain its controlling properties in the same way.

Michael (1982) does describe one form of conditioning that produces an evocative relation similar to that of an establishing operation. That is the instance in which a response cannot occur unless some stimulus change enables it to happen. For example, you cannot drive your car unless you have the key, but you have misplaced it. So you look in all the familiar places until you find it. Locating the key is a conditioned reinforcing event, whereas hunting for it was evoked by the stimulus event—no key. Michael (1982) has proposed the term **establishing stimulus (S^E)** to describe this antecedent-response relation between when you find yourself "desperately seeking" or "needing" an item or event, person, tool, or different environment and when you respond according to your prior experiences (i.e., your learning history). The circumstance that evoked your behavior is an establishing stimulus.

The establishing operation and S^E influence other behaviors under stimulus control (i.e., discriminated operants), often in rather dramatic ways. For this reason, human service or resource personnel need to consider this kind of variable to analyze puzzling behavior. So when you find someone acting out of character, you might attempt to determine whether some physical condition or some other overarching evocative event, like a family crisis, is distorting the person's typical performance.

Stimulus Complexity

One of the most critical challenges to bringing behavior under the control of antecedent stimuli, however, is the subtlety and *complexity* of those antecedent stimuli. Identifying and distinguishing a glass of milk from a glass of orange juice is rather straightforward (unless the responder is an infant, speaks a different language, or is impeded from the identification by a disability). However, distinguishing the health of a body organ by its color, size, shape, or other vague features, or a slight deflection on a dial among an array of many dials, or the significance of a metaphor in a line of a Shakespearean drama would be a major obstacle for many people. The person would have needed to receive differential reinforcement for identifying the critical features of those stimuli and discriminating those features from ones characterizing other sets of stimuli to achieve such expertise.

Chapter 17 returns to this topic and provides some hints on how to zero in on critical features to assist you in teaching difficult discriminations. At this point, we shall discuss a series of different antecedent and response combinations.

Antecedent and Response Combinations

Stimulus control is at the foundation of all behavior we call informed, skilled, logical, rational, conceptual, civilized, and creative. From the perspective of operant psychology, the class of behavior called "cognition" ("thinking," "reasoning," "remembering," "classifying," and so on) depends on stimulus control. Numerous instances of this control will be cited in the pages to come, enabling you to see how different combinations of antecedents and responses may combine either simultaneously or sequentially to promote those higher-order skills.

Discriminating the Presence or Absence of a Given Stimulus

As has already been illustrated, the sound of a click signals clean-up time. (Technically, the person is discriminating the presence of a stimulus from its absence.) A few new instances include *locating* a red block on request or identifying a mechanical or an anatomical part. All of these examples represent one type of stimulus control that fits this category.

Numerous other examples abound in the literature, as well. (Many involve rule governance, a concept you will learn about in Chapters 17 and 21.) For instance, to increase use of safety belts, several investigators (Rogers, Rogers, Bailey, Runkle, & Moore, 1988; Thyer & Geller, 1987; Weinstein, Grubb, & Vautier, 1986) have used small dashboard stickers displaying a message such as "Safety Belt Use Required of All Vehicle Occupants," as an S^D for fastening seat belts. Presumably some self-delivered reinforcers maintained compliance with the instructions.

Van Houten, Malenfant, and Rolider (1985) used a sign plus feedback to encourage pedestrians to signal drivers their intention to cross the street. The pedestrian sign stated:

"TO CROSS THE STREET—
1. EXTEND ARM—
2. PLACE FOOT ON STREET—
3. WAIT UNTIL CAR STOPS—
4. THANK DRIVER WITH A WAVE AND SMILE" (p. 105).

Also, at both ends of the crosswalks, the instruction "EXTEND ARM TO CROSS" was painted on the street. These procedures were effective in getting cars to stop for the pedestrians.

The paradigm for this type of discrimination looks like this:

$$S^+ \longrightarrow B \longrightarrow S^r$$

"Extend arm"	Extends arm	Traffic stops

In many instances using signs, prompts, instructions, models, signals, directives, assistance, goals, guidelines, and policies exemplifies this category, because particular antecedents are supposed to evoke specific responses. When the response fails to happen, usually one of several conditions has not been met:

- The behavior or its prerequisite components are not in the person's repertoire.
- The person has not attended to the antecedent stimulus.
- The person has not had a sufficient history of reinforcement for the S^+_ response combination or, as you will see, a *functionally equivalent* combination of the S^+ and the response (i.e., the requirements of the three-term contingency) has not been experienced.
- Other circumstances, such as contextual variables or establishing operations, are interfering with the response.

Discriminating Among Two or More Antecedent Stimuli; One Correct Response

If we are to be convinced that a given response is under proper stimulus control, it must occur under specific circumstances but *not* under irrelevant stimulus conditions. Ms. Charming wants to know whether Fern can distinguish boxes of particular sizes, so she asks her to get the 24-inch-by-24-inch box. Fern complies. Does this guarantee that Fern is discriminating that box from the others? It does only if she consistently demonstrates the behavior while boxes of other dimensions are present.

The child who is developing social skills must discriminate relatives from strangers. Hugging relatives is reinforced, but hugging strangers is not. (In fact, it may be punished.) Bonnie had better not call strange men "Daddy." Being naked is acceptable only at home. Running and screaming in the gymnasium or playground is permissible, but not in the library or during a chamber music concert. Of the multiple choices in your exams, you need to select the one correct answer to the question. Given a set of words, Marjorie is to identify the one that means "horse." From an array of flasks, Dexter is to select the one that contains ammonia. After noting the price tags on two blouses, Fern is to select the one she can afford. From the set of drawings that he has produced, Pablo is to choose the one that he thinks is best to submit to the art fair. Of a variety of social events, Clyde is to learn those under which swearing will be condoned.

Table 15.4 depicts the differential reinforcement operation that would teach Penny to distinguish between the sound of the doorbell and of the telephone.

Only picking up the telephone when it rings will be reinforced by hearing someone speaking. Consequently, over many trials of reinforced responding in the presence of the telephone ring, that ring will become discriminative for answering the phone. With the passage of time, this ring will evoke answering, even though occasionally no one answers the "Hello" (see Table 15.5).

How do pictorial signs develop controlling properties? Requesting an ice cream cone at a window displaying a picture of an ice cream cone will be reinforced with receipt of the ice cream, while the request will not be reinforced when the picture looks like a mug of root beer.

Matching-to-sample is another skill that belongs under this heading. This skill entails presenting the responder with an array of two or more stimuli, such as objects, figures, letters, or sounds. Given a variety of possible choices,

such as a set of picture cards of different machine parts, the task is to take a single sample, such as a card with a picture of a gear, and match it against the gear in the array (see Figure 15.2). The sample picture may be presented while the choices are exposed, as in *simultaneous matching-to-sample*, or removed prior to the choices, as in *delayed matching-to-sample*.

A sample size 24-inch-by-24-inch box is used to teach Fern which size to select for a particular packing operation. Ms. Charming holds up the box and says "Use one like this." In this simultaneous matching-to-sample task, the sample box remains displayed while Fern chooses a box. If her choice is correct, the supervisor praises her. Otherwise, she doesn't. Had the sample box been removed in advance of Fern's selection, the task would have been delayed matching-to-sample.

Another class of responses that fits this category is forming **concepts**: redness, elegance, honesty, and many more. A concept is one or a set of abstract critical properties common among a number of antecedent stimuli, much the same as the features that permit classifying. That critical property, technically labeled an *abstraction*, exerts stimulus control over a particular response.

Consider the concept of "dog." Among the features common among dogs (with unusual minor exceptions) are that they have hair, tails, and four legs; they bark; and they are readily domesticated. That lets out rodents, raccoons, and cats, who don't bark, and seals, who don't have four legs, and turtles, who don't have hair.

Again, the learning history for this form of stimulus control remains the same: differential

Table 15.4 Differential Reinforcement with Several Stimuli

Antecedent	Behavior	Consequence
S telephone rings ⟶	B "Hello" into telephone ⟶	S "Hello"
S doorbell ring ⟶	B "Hello" into telephone ⟶/	No answer

Table 15.5 Occasioning a Behavior

Antecedent	Behavior	Consequence
S^D telephone rings ⟶ S^Δ doorbell ring ⟶	B "Hello" into telephone ⟶	Sr Voice usually responds

Figure 15.2 Match the Choice Gear to the Sample Gear

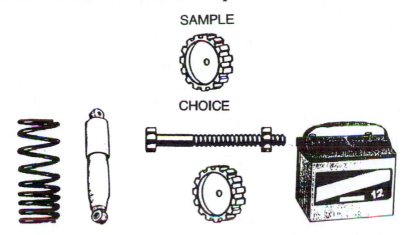

SAMPLE

CHOICE

reinforcement. In this instance, however, the response is reinforced in the presence of any of a variety of antecedent stimuli possessing those *abstract properties*; the response is not reinforced in the presence of stimuli that do not contain that property. If Bonnie identified a seal as a dog, her parents would not reinforce that response.

Differential reinforcement in these situations consists of reinforcement of the "correct" response and extinction or punishment of the "incorrect" response. (Chapter 16 returns to this point, because punishing wrong responses has both advantages and disadvantages.) This

history causes the probability of responding in the presence of the S^- to diminish. If Fern never received approval when she selected the incorrect size box, eventually she would learn not to get the wrong size in response to the request. Stimuli in the presence of which particular responses have a low probability of occurring are **S deltas (S^Δs)**[3]. (See Table 15.6). Next look at a more complicated form of discrimination.

[3] The designations S^D and S^Δ are defined differently by different authors (for example, Reynolds, 1968; White, 1971).

Table 15.6 Discrimination of Antecedent Stimuli

Antecedent	Behavior	Consequence
S_2^D ⟶	"two" ⟶	S^r "good"
S_7^Δ ⟶	"two" ⟶	

Two or More Stimuli, Distinct Responses Corresponding to Each

Can Fern reliably distinguish between one box and others half or twice as large? She would convince us that she could were she to select correctly the small, medium, or large boxes from the array when she was so instructed. Somewhere along the way, as we have considered stimulus control, you have probably realized that an S^Δ for one response often is an S^D for another. Learning to read is an example of this sort of multiple-stimulus control situation. When seeing the *p*, the student must pronounce the label "p"; when seeing *q* the student is to say "q." A 2 is "two," and a 7 is "seven," which produce the consequences listed in Table 15.7. Almost imperceptible cues like turned-down lips and knitted eyebrows are discriminative for nonreinforcement, whereas turned-up lips and eyes crinkled at the corners suggest that reinforcement may be on its way. What events account for the acquisition of those discriminations? After a while, 7 becomes discriminative for saying "seven" and 2 for saying "two."

As time passes, Bonnie only approaches her Dad for a hug when he smiles, a process shown in Table 15.8. In each of these instances, differential reinforcement has occurred: One particular response, but not others, was reinforced in the presence of a specific stimulus. Other responses are reinforced only in the presence of their own corresponding antecedent stimuli.

Many cognitive skills are developed in this manner, like the ability to sort, or *classify*. Items with an exclusive property are placed in one group; those with another into a different one; and so on: "The perfect products go in this box; defective ones in that"; or "Identify the poems that illustrate epic and those that illustrate romantic genre."

Comprehension may be assessed by giving several different instructions and evaluating the responses. Translating a series of phrases written in a foreign language is an obvious example. A person takes a set of instructions, like a recipe or a list of steps to follow in assembling a tool or implementing a given behavioral procedure, and follows through successfully. Apparently an adequate history of differential reinforcement has been at work.

Complex-Stimulus Control

The marvelous aspect of stimulus control is that it serves as the foundation of all sorts of complex human behavior—solving problems, understanding concepts, behavior in private and in public—indeed the wide array of behaviors involved in most instances of "thinking" and doing. Understand how stimulus control operates, and you will begin to realize its role in the most subtle and sophisticated nuances of your behavior. At issue is just one key element: that of stimulus features that reliably set the occasion for reinforcement, extinction, or punishment.

Identifying simple concepts like *members of the immediate family* or complicated ones such as *beauty* or *gracefulness* happens in exactly the same way. Admissible stimulus features are isolated (e.g., a parent, sibling, or offspring in the

Table 15.7 Developing Multiple Stimulus Control

Antecedent	Behavior	Consequence
S_7 ⟶	"seven" ⟶	"right"
S_2 ⟶	"seven" ⟶/	
S_2 ⟶	"two" ⟶	"right"
S_7 ⟶	"two" ⟶/	

Table 15.8 How Facial Expressions Develop Discriminative Properties

Antecedent	Behavior	Consequence
☻ ──────────────→	reach for hug ──────────────→	hugged
☹ ──────────────→	reach for hug ─────────/───→	

case of immediate family; maybe "attracting prolonged attending; producing a positive emotional reaction; approaching"; and so on, in the case of beauty), and in their presence stating the given label is reinforced. Stimulus control functions similarly to guide rational thought, as in using covert cues to set the occasion for sequences of self-statements; to guide complex sequences of overt responding, as in reciting to oneself the rules for performing a particular surgical procedure or for flying a plane under adverse weather conditions. Stimulus control permits people to distinguish right from wrong, whether solving school problems or moral dilemmas. Although a thorough treatment of this key aspect of human performance is beyond the scope of this text, you will see numerous instances of the way stimulus control operates as you proceed in your reading. Go beyond these pages, though, and watch yourself and others in action. See how pervasive a role stimulus control plays in just about every aspect of human existence.

Equivalence Classes

Must every single antecedent stimulus-response combination be adequately differentially reinforced for the response to become a discriminated operant? Fortunately not, because of a phenomenon called **stimulus** or **functional equivalence**.

When humans are taught a series of distinctive discriminations, the stimuli involved in these discriminations may begin to function in ways not explicitly taught. This phenomenon, stimulus equivalence, which parents or caregivers probably take advantage of without formal design, typically has been investigated experimentally in a matching-to-sample format.

A1, B1, and C1 might be varieties of the same tool, like a wrench, diverse ways of representing the same number, or different examples of the same concept. Suppose, as in Figure 15.3, the person learns "given the word 'THREE' (A1), to pick the number 3" (B1). The person then is taught to select another unfamiliar visual form from another array of forms in response to one of the previously learned stimuli. For example, "given THREE, pick ***" (C1). (To control for a history of reinforcement for selecting particular stimuli, the incorrect comparison forms are correct in the presence of different samples.) With this kind of training, it is likely that, without additional instruction, the person will select THREE from an array of comparisons, when shown 3 or given *** as samples. The person is also likely to select B1, given C1 as a sample, and C1, given B1 as a sample (e.g., Sidman, 1971; Sidman, Cresson, & Willson-Morris, 1974).

In a similar case, say that through differential reinforcement, one stimulus, the spoken word *cat*, becomes discriminative for choosing the picture of a cat from an array of pictures of other animals. In other words, when the responder hears the word *cat* he selects the picture of the cat. Additionally, he learns to select the written word C-A-T from an array of cards on which other words are written, such as C-O-T, C-O-A-T, or B-A-T. Now the responder is given the two assortments of cards: the written words and the pictures. Lo and behold, he matches the written word C-A-T with

Figure 15.3 Stimulus Equivalence in Operation

STIMULUS EQUIVALENCE IN OPERATION

THREE   SAMPLE

MATCHING RESPONSE

2   3

SELECTING 3 IS REINFORCED
SELECTING 2 IS NOT

THREE   SAMPLE

MATCHING RESPONSE

***   **

SELECTING *** IS REINFORCED
SELECTING ** IS NOT

THEN WITH NO PRIOR TRAINING GIVEN *** OR 3,
THE PERSON WILL SELECT THE WORD THREE AND
NOT TWO

the picture, despite a lack of direct differential reinforcement for doing so. Each of the stimuli is discriminative for each of the others, so all fuse together into a class of equivalent stimuli.

When stimuli assume equivalent functions, they can be grouped together into complex sets called **equivalence classes**.[4] What happens

---

[4] To merit the label "equivalence class," the three defining relations of *reflexivity* (e.g., A1 = A1; and B1 = B1); *symmetry*, (A1 = B1 and B1 = A1), where the relation between A and B can go in either direction); and *transitivity* (if A1 = B1 and B1 = C1, then A1 = C1) must be present (Sidman & Tailby, 1982; Sidman, Wynne, Maguire, & Barnes, 1989).

when someone learns an equivalent relation is that when one relation is learned, its corollary is also, without any further training. So once Baby Bonnie learns that her dog is "Tiger," without further explicit training, she now knows that Tiger is her dog.

Stimulus equivalence probably is at play when people learn to "decode" or give the "meaning" of new words as in reading, language comprehension, and other conceptual and language skills. For instance, when a child is taught to point to a particular object given a particular written word, the child may point to the word given the object without specific training to do so. Naming tasks like these have been used by many investigators to study language empirically (e.g., Sidman & Tailby, 1982; Sidman, Kirk, & Willson-Morris, 1985; Spradlin & Dixon, 1976).

Stimulus equivalence has been demonstrated among a wide variety of human subject populations using a broad array of stimulus materials (Dixon, 1976; Gast, VanBiervliet, & Spradlin, 1979; Hayes, Tilley, & Hayes, 1988; Mackay & Sidman, 1984; Sidman & Tailby, 1982; Spradlin & Dixon, 1976; Wulfert & Hayes, 1988). Even children as young as 2 years old will display such effects (Devany, Hayes, & Nelson, 1986). Children without spontaneous productive use of signs or speech, however, have yet to be found to show equivalence (Devany et al., 1986), nor have animals.

Now you recognize that a combination of operations—reinforcement and extinction—is the fundamental source of all sorts of classes of orderly human performance. Behaviors ranging from moving when the light turns green to interpreting poetry, diagnosing illnesses, and flying airplanes safely under adverse circumstances all originate from stimulus control. In the next chapter you will learn what you can do to facilitate the process, as we show how to promote discrimination learning.

Summary

This chapter introduced stimulus control. The concept has been defined and illustrated, and its development discussed. Unlike the procedures discussed in the previous chapters, antecedent stimuli are essential to the development of the process. Stimulus control is said to exist when specific antecedents set the occasion for responses. As we shall show later, stimulus control may also operate to suppress responses. Antecedent stimuli that evoke given responses are called discriminative stimuli, or S^Ds, and stimuli that signal nonreinforcement, S^Δs. Differential reinforcement of the antecedent stimulus-response combination or a functionally equivalent stimulus is essential for stimulus control to be established. Contextual factors can influence the rate with which a particular discriminated operant occurs.

Behavioral complexity depends in large measure on the relations between S^D and responses. The least-complex arrangement is one in which a single antecedent stimulus evokes a specific response. Other arrangements include two antecedent stimuli and a single correct response; two S^Ds that control two different responses; many varied S^Ds that control a single response; and an array of others. Fortunately, frequently paired stimuli can develop equivalent functions, enabling discrimination learning to proceed more efficiently. When reliable control by given antecedent stimuli is essential but has not been achieved, however, procedures can be applied to increase its strength. The next two chapters describe such methods. As a person concerned with effective behavior change, you should find those strategies to be valuable tools.

Chapter 16

Promoting and Applying Stimulus Control

GOALS

After completing this chapter, you should be able to:

1. Define, recognize, and give original illustrations of each of the following terms:
   a. Stimulus change
   b. Strong or complete stimulus control
   c. S^{D-}
   d. Elicit
   e. Prompts
   f. Incomplete stimulus control
   g. Scatter plot

2. Provide two reasons why it is important to provide assistance before the response occurs.

3. Define, illustrate, and differentiate among the influences of S^D, S^A, S^E, and S^{D-}s.

4. List two advantages of using stimulus change.

5. List and discuss the disadvantages of stimulus change.

6. Differentiate between stimulus control and respondent conditioning.

7. List and discuss what can be done to use stimulus change effectively.

8. Provide two reasons why stimulus change might fail to occasion a response.

9. Describe and illustrate how to assess the presence of a given response in a person's repertoire.

10. Describe what would need to be done to develop strong stimulus control when it is (a) weak or (b) absent.

11. List possible types of stimuli that can interfere with stimulus control and discuss what might be done to remedy each situation.

12. List, discuss, and illustrate what should be done to effectively use differential reinforcement in developing stimulus control.

13. Illustrate and discuss how the system of "least prompts" can be used to identify the most natural prompts.

14. Illustrate and compare the minimum-to-maximum and maximum-to-minimum methods in using prompts to train behavior.

15. Discuss and illustrate when and how contrived prompts can be used to promote the development of stimulus control.

16. Describe and illustrate the value of a scatter plot.

17. Discuss and illustrate various uses to which matching-to-sample can be put.

18. Explain why a response might become overly dependent on a nonrelevant prompt and discuss methods of minimizing such occurrences.

Discouraged by the fact that the housekeeping department failed to perform its job adequately, the manager sat down with the departmental supervisor and sketched out a checklist identifying each task to be accomplished daily, weekly, and monthly. Performance improved when weekly meetings were scheduled to provide feedback and praise accomplishments and to set goals for the next week.

To cure the monotony of his students' material written in a creative writing course, Professor Fogg listed a set of guidelines, such as varying sentence length and word choice, then distributed the list to the class. The students' writing became more imaginative.

A client requested help in controlling his temper. The young man was taught to recognize subtle cues, such as clenching fists and rapid breathing, that were indicative of his beginning to "lose it." Subsequently his rates of emotional outbursts diminished.

In each instance, the system was fairly straightforward. The relevant stimulus properties were identified and introduced; targeted behaviors thereby increased and were differentially reinforced in the presence of those stimuli.

The situations just described illustrate the value of being capable of promoting stimulus control,[1] that is, managing antecedents effectively. That skill permits behavior to be evoked rapidly and readily, when and where needed. Stimulus control procedures are especially useful when clients are not likely to respond independently in exactly the desired manner because ". . . research suggests that assistance before the response rather than correction after the response accelerates acquisitions of skills

(Walls, Zane, & Thvedt, 1980; Zane, Walls, & Thvedt, 1981)" (Schoen, 1986, p. 62). Likewise, LeBlanc and Ruggles (1982) point out that stimulus control procedures need to be used to reduce errors from the outset of the learning process. Errors committed during learning produce extinction and punishment ". . . which in turn could lead to response reduction and possible resistance to future responding . . ." (p. 130).

This chapter and the next look at ways to use and promote stimulus control. Initially we concentrate on using stimulus change. Subsequently, the focus will be on ways of arranging antecedent stimuli and differential reinforcement to convert neutral antecedent stimuli (S^+s) into discriminative stimuli (S^Ds).

Using the Stimulus Change Procedure

The **stimulus change** procedure involves either *presenting or removing* antecedent stimuli, such as discriminative or establishing stimuli and others.[2] When a particular response is tightly controlled by antecedent stimuli, increasing or decreasing its probability becomes feasible simply by presenting or withdrawing the discriminative stimulus. (We shall use terms like strong, tight, powerful, or **complete stimulus control** when a given response occurs at a much higher or lower frequency in the presence of the identified S^D or S^Δ than in its absence.) This strategy is tremendously useful in teaching, training, and consulting activities. When managers present instructions to encourage behavior they are using stimulus change procedures. The textbook you are reading is a collection of antecedent stimuli that we hope serve as S^Ds for you. We anticipate that if you learn the rules for analyzing and applying behavioral proce-

---

[1] Discriminative stimuli that effectively control behavior that is remote in time, as in these instances, may be mediated by other events, such as covertly stating rules to oneself or possibly imagining the stimulus-response relations.

[2] Antecedent stimuli that abolish or inhibit responses—S^Δs and S^{D-}s—are discussed later on.

dures, you will be more likely to use them to guide your own practice. (Readers of previous texts often tell us they refer to the text when they implement particular behavioral procedures, as in designing an effective reinforcement strategy.) Sample rules (S^{D}s) for successfully obtaining your objectives are illustrated below:

S^D ⟶ R ⟶ S^r
(Illustrative Rules: Conduct Achieve
"Consequence has program objectives
had to be effective
formerly with person
in that context;
amount sufficient;
delay minimal")

Stimulus Change Procedure Illustrated

Any time we present or withdraw an antecedent stimulus for the purpose of changing the frequency of a behavior, we are using a stimulus change procedure. The antecedents may include physical, social, verbal, gestural, textual, pictorial, or other classes of stimuli. Altering the physical environment is a very familiar example of stimulus change, as when we play soothing background music to induce relaxation.

Numerous illustrations of the influence of altering antecedents—discriminative (S^D) or **establishing (S^E) stimuli**—can be found in the research literature: After furniture was rearranged (Melin & Gotestam, 1981), patients diagnosed as suffering from senile dementia conversed and ate more. Perhaps facing one another eased conversation, because they could hear better, see their companions' reactions, and therefore receive more reinforcement. Similarly, when elderly residents were notified of availability of free coffee and cookies in a lounge area of a nursing home, they increased attendance and interactions, and decreased their television watching (Quattrochi-Tubin & Jason, 1980). Those kinds of minor changes in elderly patients' physical surroundings helped to ". . .

promote therapeutic changes" (Melin & Gotestam, 1981, p. 47).

Self-injury is another example of a class of behavior that often has been found sensitive to changes in the physical environment, because investigators have found that certain conditions, such as availability of toys, seem to be less conducive to injuring oneself than other conditions, like sterile surroundings (Favell et al., 1982; Mulick, Hoyt, Rojahn, & Schroeder, 1978). Sometimes self-injurious clients manage their own antecedents to keep from hurting themselves—using objects like rigid tubes to constrain their arm movements or putting their hands in their pockets (Pace, Iwata, Edwards, & McCosh, 1986).

Numerous other conditions of the physical and social context can set the occasion for or evoke different classes of behavior. Besides abundant instances in the behavior analytic literature, look to social psychology and human ecology to identify other circumstances that correlate with favored and unwanted behaviors: size of groups, crowding, furnishings, noise level, exposure to aggression on television, and so on. According to Evans (1979), crowding causes increases in heart rate and blood pressure, whereas Paulus and Matthews (1980) found that crowding has a negative impact on task performance. A number of investigators have noted the relation between aggression and antecedent events, such as viewing television violence (e.g., Eron, 1982), heat (Anderson & Anderson, 1984), and noise (Donnerstein & Wilson, 1976).

Antecedent stimuli also can be used to *deter* behavior. Remember the other sort of discriminative stimulus, the S-delta (S$^\Delta$) from the last chapter? S-deltas set the occasion for the nonreinforcement of a response. Recall that the person who discriminates that given responses are not likely to be reinforced in the presence of the antecedents is *less* likely to emit those behaviors in that context. Having experienced the lovely fragrance of a rose and the lack of aroma of a buttercup, we are much more likely to sniff roses than buttercups. Buttercups are an S^Δ for sniffing.

The following is a slightly more complicated case of a *conditional discrimination*. The behavior is reinforced under most but not all circumstances. Paula enjoys talking to her boyfriend Sandy on the telephone and calls him every day after 6 P.M. She has learned to call Sandy at home and not at work, because he will converse at length only when he is at home.

$$S^D \longrightarrow B \longrightarrow S^r$$

| After 6 P.M. | Calling boyfriend | Long, relaxed conversation |

Under most circumstances, calling her boyfriend has been reinforced.

But:

$$S^\Delta \longrightarrow B \not\longrightarrow$$

| Before 5 P.M. present | Talking to boyfriend | Pleasant conversation ✗ |

During work hours, calling her boyfriend is not reinforced.

Paula's use of the telephone to call Sandy is under the control of the time of day. The form of control is deterring or constraining the frequency of the behavior.

Just as well-established S^Ds can be used to promote the frequency of a behavior, strong S-deltas can be used to curb it. Paula's work time conversations with Sandy have not been reinforced, so work time becomes an S^Δ for calling him.

Another variation is the S^{D-}, *the antecedent that is discriminative for punishment*. Ragweed makes you sneeze, so you hardly ever sniff it.

$$S^{D-} \xrightarrow{\quad/\quad} B$$

| Ragweed | Does not lead to | Sniffing ✗ |

Because in the past:

$$S \longrightarrow B \longrightarrow S^P$$

| Ragweed | Sniffing | Sneezing |

When Bruno plays the piano in the lounge, his friends gather round and smile admiringly. Yet when their favorite TV program is being broadcast, they shout "Not now, Bruno!" (a punishing event) and other more colorful epithets, when Bruno begins to play.

Usually,

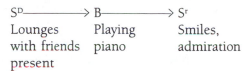

$$S^D \longrightarrow B \longrightarrow S^r$$

| Lounges with friends present | Playing piano | Smiles, admiration |

But when friends' favorite TV program is on:

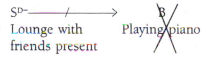

$$S^{D-} \xrightarrow{\quad/\quad} B$$

| Lounge with friends present | Playing piano ✗ |

Consequently, when that TV program is on, Bruno no longer plays the piano.

You can see that as long as a behavior is tightly controlled by an antecedent stimulus, whether an S^D, an S^E, an S^Δ, or an S^{D-}, its frequency can be increased (as in the first case) or decreased (with the last two) by presenting that discriminative stimulus.

Removing a discriminative stimulus can have the opposite effect, especially in the case of conditional discriminations. In the latter case, the individual has experienced receiving reinforcers (or punishers) in the presence of some antecedents and not in the presence of others. Take away the due date for the paper, and you very likely will return to your favorite Wednesday night program. When Paula knows that Sandy is home with a cold, she might place several calls to him during working hours. (Henceforth, the main emphasis in this section of the book will be on using antecedent stimuli to evoke, not to deter, behavior. Section IV returns to the latter topic.)

Advantages of Using Stimulus Change

The most apparent advantage of using stimulus control is that when behavior is under the strong control of an antecedent stimulus (the antecedent is *discriminative* for a particular behavior) the rate of the behavior can be managed by presenting or withdrawing the stimulus. Often, presenting antecedents is much easier than using other methods of behavior management.

Stimulus change also is an especially useful adjunct to other procedures, because it can evoke or suppress a behavior temporarily, whereas other methods are applied toward producing a more lasting change. You have seen how reinforcement can be combined with stimulus control procedures. Similarly, stimulus control procedures may enhance the effectiveness of other behavior modification procedures including shaping, chaining, and the many procedures for reducing, extending, and maintaining behavior change.

Disadvantages of Using Stimulus Change

Not dependable. The main problem with depending on stimulus change is that it may not necessarily function on any particular occasion. When stimulus control is well established for a given response, the observer may assume, erroneously, that presenting or withdrawing the antecedent stimulus will turn the behavior on or off every time; that the antecedent stimulus will "cause" the behavior to happen. Remember, however, that we are describing a probabilistic relation between the antecedent stimulus and the response that follows it: No one-to-one relation exists between the stimulus and the response, as in **respondent** or reflexive behavior. For instance, crowding, seeing televised acts of aggression, and hot weather appear to produce violence. Violence, however, is not guaranteed under these establishing conditions. In respondent conditioning, a bright light **elicits** a pupillary reflex, but S^{D}s simply *set the occasion for* the response. The governing function of the antecedent derives its strength from a prior history of reinforcement (or extinction or punishment)

when the response was emitted in the presence of that stimulus.

Whereas a bright light always elicits a pupillary reflex, discriminative stimuli like ringing telephones do not cause the same reaction every time. While a person is in the shower, bathing the baby, or making love, the ringing telephone may go unanswered, just as Desmond may continue working during a fire drill. Although our trainees have shown their capabilities in following policies and procedures, they may not do so on any given occasion.

The form of the response can vary as well. Errors and mistakes can be committed, as when Clyde mistakenly confuses the definition of stimulus control with that of respondent conditioning. A football play could be identified incorrectly, and Twinkle Toes Smith could twirl instead of leap as directed during the third scene of the ballet.

In those instances, stimulus control is incomplete or weak or possibly under the influence of unusual contextual variables.

S^{D}s not always manageable. Stimulus change depends entirely on one's ability to manage the S^{D}s. S^{D}s beyond our control make the procedure useless. No amount of encouraging production workers to meet their quotas will work if the essential S^{D}s—available materials are not being delivered. Despite whatever parents tell their adolescent children, the conflicting urgings of their peers often take precedence.

Even when we are attempting to manage antecedents for ourselves, our ability to control them may be limited. Physiological events, such as feeling hungry, sleepy, ill, or tense, are one type of circumstance that can evoke crabbiness or depression. Other circumstances are obsessively repeating covert statements or images. In such cases the best we can do is to obtain help to self-manage the stimuli. Behavior therapists often are concerned with these sorts of issues as they attempt to help people to manage their own antecedents and consequences, to take more charge of their bodies and their behavior.

Using Stimulus Change Effectively

Determining that stimulus control is well established. Clearly, using stimulus change requires strong stimulus control; otherwise, S^{D}s like signs, signals, cues, demonstrations, or instructions will fail to evoke the desired response. Therefore, before attempting to use the method in a particular situation, you will need to determine whether the antecedent has the function of evoking the response.

Determining whether antecedents are manageable. Once you recognize that competing antecedent stimuli controlling a response are beyond your control, seek some other way to diminish their effects or provide strong enough contingencies to override them. Establishing operations that occur away from your setting or are internal to the individual—such as psychological abuse or biochemical signals—are illustrative. (Another option is to try to enlist the aid of specialists like social workers or neurophysiologists, who sometimes help.) Peer modeling might be another instance of a stimulus beyond your control. Rules from parents that conflict with those of the teacher are another. If we fail to gain control of the functional antecedents we may need to substitute others we are capable of managing, condition the antecedents more powerfully, or change our objectives or the procedures by which we hope to achieve them.

Choosing S^{D}s. Often a number of different S^{D}s will evoke the same response, but one antecedent may work more effectively than another. So you may find it helpful to compare, in advance, the relative success with which various stimuli set the occasion for the selected response. In one illustrative case, Bunck and Iwata (1978) compared four different **prompts** for getting elderly citizens to participate in a nutritious meal program:

> (1) public service radio announcements for four weeks to advertise the meal program and the availability of free transportation, (2) a home visit that served as a personal invitation and a second prompt for participation, (3) a follow-up telephone call, and (4) an incentive menu for participation, which was sent through the mail (p. 75).

(The incentive menu contained a variety of activities, items, and services that the people could select after participating in the meal program: trips, movies, state lottery tickets, games, housecleaning, yard work, and car washing.) Both the home visits and the incentive menu promoted participation and were superior to the other two conditions. The incentive menu, however, was the most cost-effective intervention of the two. Such a comparison revealed that the widely used public service announcement appeared not to be all that effective an S^D for prompting participation by the elderly.

Combining stimulus change with other procedures. Stimulus change can be augmented by combining it with other procedures, such as those designed to increase rates of behaviors, teach new ones, or to reduce, expand, and/or maintain given forms of responding. Beware though, because antecedent control will eventually deteriorate in the absence of any differential reinforcement.

Watching for intensifying antecedent stimuli. One warning signal is finding yourself repeating an antecedent several times, or presenting it louder, faster, or harder. If the individual has the sensory apparatus and has received your input, intensifying the stimulus will accomplish little. Your S$^+$ has not been established as a strong enough S^D. Joe swings his club in too wide an arc. "Follow through, follow through, follow through!" advises the pro, to no avail. "Be more creative," urges the professor. Yet no matter how loudly or long he delivers that message, the students continue to deliver their hackneyed prose. Nagging of that sort is a sign of weak or missing stimulus control. What is the alternative? To teach the response, strengthen the relation between the S⁺ and the response, or eliminate interfering conditions.

When Stimulus Change Fails

Should you observe that a particular antecedent event fails to occasion a designated response, try to determine the reasons for this failure. Is it because the response is missing from the person's repertoire or because stimulus control is weak or absent altogether?

Is the Response Missing from the Repertoire?

Here we are concerned about whether the response alone, regardless of antecedent stimuli, is in the individual's repertoire. No matter how logically and precisely we instruct Claude to maneuver a soccer ball as he runs, it is a lost cause. He has yet to acquire the skill. Using instructions to facilitate a complex response is not feasible if the person has failed to acquire the response or at least its critical components. How can you instruct yourself to paint a masterpiece, write a Pulitzer Prize-winning book, or win at the Olympics? All your self-instructions probably are a waste of time, for you probably do not have the requisite component responses in your repertoire.

Similarly, no antecedents will be effective if an employee, student, or client has not learned the requisite performance. A first grader cannot respond to a request to tie his shoe because he is not skilled in holding the string, looping it, pushing it, pulling it, holding onto looped strings, and so on. A brilliant student of chemistry may not be able to conduct an experiment according to instructions because she failed to learn one of the component tasks involved—how to use a certain instrument. Antecedent stimuli (S^+s) can become discriminative stimuli only if the person is able to perform the response. (Do not despair: You still may paint your masterpiece, write your prize-winning book, or win the Olympics. Just turn to the

chapters on shaping and chaining and learn how to augment your response repertoire!)

Assessing for the Presence of the Response in the Person's Repertoire

To discover whether your employees, students, or clients are capable of performing the response—that is, possess the response in their repertoires—apply alternative antecedents or try to identify and eliminate interfering conditions. Perhaps Paula would get her report in on time if she were allowed to use a quiet office or were relieved of all other responsibilities for a day.

What do instructors do when they want to determine whether a student has already acquired some verbal knowledge? They give tests. Human resources staff often request samples or demonstrations of skills from job applicants. The psychologist wishing to assess the self-care repertoire of a client presents a series of tasks and completes a corresponding checklist. Paula's supervisor, Angela, might examine Paula's component writing skills. Informal tests and probes of this sort, as well as more formal behavioral inventories, often are used to determine whether specific responses are within the responder's repertoire and/or are emitted reliably in the presence of a given stimulus.

Should the S^+ fail to occasion the appropriate response, probe further before you conclude that the response is absent from the repertoire; try other instructions, **prompts**, or demonstrations. When Desmond fails to respond to the fire bell, the supervisor can present a rationale or emphasize the fact that everyone else, including the chief executive officer, is evacuating the building. That may work. Suppose, though, that the appropriate response does not result when suspected interfering stimuli are removed, or other S^Ds, instructions, or demonstrations are presented. If modeling and gentle physical guidance fail too, the behavior must be taught, as described in Chapters

19 and 20. Conversely, if supplements do evoke the response, realize that the task will be that of transferring control over to the S⁺, rather than one of teaching the response *per se*.

Is the Stimulus Control Too Weak?

Perhaps Desmond evacuated the building in response to the fire alarm on some occasions but not on others. This is an example of **incomplete stimulus control**. So much of the frustration in human relationships arises from inadequate control by antecedents, especially by spoken or printed words. You arrange to meet a friend at 1:00 P.M. You arrive on time but your friend is 45 minutes late. The verbal agreement did not exert tight enough control over your friend's response. "Be sure to check the time clock records every month and show them to me," says the supervisor, but the records are not presented monthly. When the supervisor insists on seeing them, she finds them incomplete. "Now put your books and notes away for this quiz," directs the teacher, but two students are seen peeking at their texts and the teacher disciplines them harshly.

When stimulus control is weak, the manager's ability to increase or decrease the frequency of the response is compromised. The challenge then becomes one of strengthening the relationship. This can be accomplished by applying differential reinforcement systematically.

Is Stimulus Control Absent?

Consider the situation in which a particular S⁺ fails to evoke a designated response altogether. For example, suppose Desmond never responded to a fire bell. Apparently the bell was not governing Desmond's evacuating the building—a potentially life-threatening situation. Why? Either the bell had not developed discriminative properties for Desmond, or other conditions interfered. If the bell had no S^D properties, stimulus control would need to be established, possibly by using a different prompt

like a buzzer or flashing light. That would be comparable to the tactic Etzel (1969) used in changing the instructions from asking students to sort items according to whether they were the "same" and "different" (which did not work) to whether they were "like" and "not like," (which did evoke correct responses) in a discrimination learning situation. Or maybe verbal instructions or modeling works initially. (The next two chapters are devoted, respectively, to ways to prompt responses systematically and transfer that influence over to the S⁺s—the critical antecedent stimuli.) If interfering conditions were operating, a different strategy would need to be invoked: identifying and removing them.

Are There Interfering Stimuli?

Avoid concluding too hastily that stimulus control is absent, because interfering contingencies may be to blame. Suppose Desmond were fully aware of the meaning of the bell, but his peers were providing him with subtle social reinforcement for his *machismo* in defying the rules. For safety's sake, those impediments would need to be curtailed. Perhaps an ecological rearrangement could solve the problem: appointing prestigious peers to be fire-evacuation patrol leaders. In an analogous situation, peer-mediated instruction was found superior to teacher-mediated education in improving students' weekly academic test scores (Greenwood et al., 1984).

In another hypothetical case, a young girl is brought to a speech clinic for an articulation assessment. The speech therapist asks her a number of questions. Instead of responding, the child looks about the room, at the pictures, toys, and faces of strange adults. Those stimuli could be occasioning competing responses. Earlier we recommended that the setting be carefully selected and that an adaptation phase be provided prior to collection of any formal assessment data. So, to determine whether the little girl is reacting to the interfering stimuli, the speech therapist provides an adaptation phase, allowing the child to become acquainted with her and the new surroundings.

Other *contextual variables*, as described in the previous chapter, can interfere with or block the occurrence of the behavior. The client might be tired or under the influence of drugs or alcohol; a close relative may be seriously ill; he may not have had any breakfast; or a variety of other such contextual variables could be operating. Identifying and treating those factors, if feasible, would alleviate the situation.

Occasionally the individual's *sensory or motor* deficits impede the development of stimulus control. Auditory, visual, or motor limitations sometimes make it impossible for an individual to respond to a particular S^D. Either the person fails to detect the signal or is physically incapable of responding as desired. In such cases, find auxiliary antecedents with the guidance of professional specialists (e.g., physical or occupational therapists, or special educators). When the person has an auditory deficit, combine oral instructions with gestures, demonstrations, written instructions, changes in illumination, or physical guidance. For the individual with visual limitations, employ auditory or tactile stimuli in place of visual ones. When motoric impairments interfere, supplement with prosthetic devices, such as a brace, wheelchair, or specially designed eating utensils.

Often a breakdown in stimulus control is traceable to an *absence of reinforcement* for the combination of the S^+ and the response, at least in that context. A universal complaint is "I asked _____ to _____. They did for a while and then just stopped." Say a staff member in a community residence for youthful offenders has been asked to keep records of the youths' school attendance and completion of household chores. He fails to maintain the records, complaining that he is too busy with other more important matters. He was trained to keep the records, so we can assume that recordkeeping

is not missing from his repertoire. Because reinforcement does not derive from the record-keeping activity itself, there is a dearth of reinforcers for the time-consuming activity. By recognizing this paucity of reinforcement, the creative manager will arrange to make the task less punishing by simplifying it as much as possible and adding positive consequences. Possibly the manager could regularly review and compliment the staff member's completion of the records.

A failure to respond to an S^D also could be traceable to a *history of punishment* for the S^+-response combination. Perhaps once upon a time, Desmond was severely rebuked for getting out of his seat while he was supposed to be working on an assigned task. So, when the fire bell sounds, he remains seated. If you suspect a history of punishment might be responsible for an antecedent's failure to induce a person to respond, you will have to override that effect by finding an effective supplementary prompt, such as gentle guidance, or reinforcing an approximation toward the behavior with especially powerful consequences. If those methods prove ineffective, you will need to either employ more systematic prompting and fading strategies or shape the response anew in the context, as described in Chapters 17–19. Regardless of how you begin to initiate your attempts to establish stimulus control, though, remember that differential reinforcement is essential to success.

Effectively Applying Differential-Reinforcement Procedures

A number of factors should be considered in planning a differential-reinforcement procedure for supporting the development of stimulus control. Some factors relate to the discriminative and reinforcing aspects of the stimulus.

Clearly Identifying Relevant Stimulus Properties

Because the procedure for developing stimulus control requires that reinforcement either be delivered or withheld contingent on the emission of a specific behavior in the presence of certain stimuli, it is crucial for the contingency manager to be clear about the exact properties of these stimulus conditions. Depending on the types of stimuli involved, one should specify such properties of the S^{D}s as their form, position, or size, and other relevant stimulus dimensions. As with the response specifications discussed in Chapter 4 (size, shape, color, texture, pitch, volume, and so on), the program designer must ask, "Under what very specific circumstances will the target response be reinforced? Under what specific circumstances will it not?" Clyde's father clearly classifies *all* instances of taking property belonging to others without permission as "dishonest." That allows him to be consistent in differentially reinforcing his son's judgments.

Now take a look at a published example: In a successful attempt to teach creativity, Glover and Gary (1976) focused on four properties: fluency, flexibility, elaboration, and originality. Each property was defined as a specific set of responses, and the students were instructed that team points exchangeable for extra recess time, milk, and cookies would be contingent on corresponding increases in those response categories. When students earned points for increasing numbers of responses, fluency increased; when the students earned points for novel responses, originality climbed; and so on. Apparently, stimulus control can work as a method for promoting creativity. (Refer to this example when a naive critic accuses behavior analysis of encouraging conformity.)

Probably the most challenging aspect of teaching such complex behaviors as creativity, concept formation, problem solving, and analytic evaluation is specifying relevant stimulus properties. Before you instruct an individual in a concept like "zero defects," "friendliness," or "ethnicity," the critical features of the property need to be identified—those that are common among the various instances of the concept. To teach problem-solving skills or evaluation techniques, the strategies or criteria first must be pinpointed, so the occasion for delivering reinforcers is clear. As we continue to discuss teaching complex behavior, from time to time we refer to examples of this kind. Remember, though, that regardless of the intricacy of the relevant stimulus properties, the differential reinforcement procedure is fundamental to the process. Beyond that, program designers either need to be adept at discriminating those S$^+$s that need to be developed into S^{D}s or must seek consultation.

Think about it for a moment, realizing that it is at this point that the subject-matter expert or specialist comes into the picture. The masterful wine taster is distinguished by the ability to discriminate between examples of excellent and of reasonably tasty wine. The proficient coach discriminates between acceptable and unacceptable movements or team plays. The respected critic distinguishes among poor, average, and great productions. The master teacher is able to judge exactly when a student is improving.

When Alavosius and Sulzer-Azaroff (1985) wanted to develop a program to prevent nursing staff from suffering back injuries, they called on the expertise of ergonomists and orthopedic specialists to find out exactly which rules are supposed to guide safe lifting and transferring of patients. (Refer back to Figure 4.1 for a task analysis of a safe one-person transfer.) Applied behavior analysts cannot be expected to become competent in every content area with which they deal. Instead, they should recognize their own limited repertoires and refer to experts when necessary.

What the behavior analyst *should* be able to do is to translate information obtained from informed sources into behavioral terms, so that contingency managers will know under what antecedent conditions given types of behavior should be reinforced. This is pretty much what Glover and Gary (1976) did. They read about creativity, found that it consisted of certain identified qualities, and asked "What do people *do* when they are being fluent, flexible, original, and so on?" The answer was rephrased as a set of response definitions, and instructional stimuli were prepared. At that point, it became possible to use those definitions to guide their teaching of each of the "creative" responses.

Specifying the S⁺s can prove troublesome sometimes. One way to identify elusive distinctions between those antecedent stimuli to be developed into S^Ds and those into S^Δs is by carefully observing ongoing responding or audio or video recordings of acceptable and unacceptable performance. For instance, a client and speech therapist could listen to brief speech samples and decide which should be reinforced. The youth counselor and client could view a tape of a modeled situation displaying an episode apt to provoke anger. While viewing, they could distinguish key features of the interaction. "See, when George annoys Charlie, Charlie begins to lose it. Does that sort of hassling bother you too? How can you be more sensitive to the cues that hint you are beginning to feel irritated? Let's play that sequence again and think how you'd feel. When you think you're about to become angry, let's stop and consider alternative ways of handling the situation." Refer to the earlier material on behavioral objectives and task analyses (in Chapter 4) and note how clearly stated objectives serve this purpose.

Emphasizing or Enhancing Relevant Antecedent Stimulus Properties

Just because the contingency manager has identified the relevant properties of the S⁺, that does not guarantee that all learners will be equally aware of those essential features. The features may not be sufficiently *salient* or obvious to the learners. Consider the instance of five minimally literate juvenile offenders (Murph & McCormick, 1985) who were learning to read road signs. The instructors showed the boys each sign, discussed its type (e.g., warning, yield, road construction, pedestrian crossing, bike crossing, and merge left), and pointed out each crucial feature and its specific meaning (e.g., shape, color, location, and what to do). After requesting each student to identify the type of sign, its meaning, and what to do, in his own words, they taught the student to discriminate each separate sign, rewarding correct answers with checks, stars, and praise and incorrect ones with minus signs and no praise. All five boys learned and maintained this skill during 1- to 8-month follow-ups and correctly identified the signs in the driver's-license manual.

Consider a couple of other examples to understand the importance of this point. A teacher of art appreciation wants to illustrate how paintings can induce different reactions by viewers. First, she shows a reproduction of Monet's *Water Lilies* and asks the class members to describe how the painting makes them feel. One student mentions "peaceful," another "serene." Then she displays Duchamp's abstract, *Nude Descending a Staircase*, and a student says that it conveys a sense of "movement." The teacher and some of the other students agree. Apparently, however, the majority of the students are reticent about offering their impressions and appear to be at a loss. At this point, the teacher decides to help the students focus on the distinctive aspects of the two works and generate some rules.

"What are some of the distinctive qualities of each?"

"In the *Water Lilies* the edges are blurred," says one student.

"The pastel colors—especially the soft blues and purples—blend into one another, whereas in the Duchamp painting, the parallel dark lines vividly contrast with the white; the lines are sharp; the diagonal angles distinct," comments another.

Now, when another example is displayed, the students focus their attention on the relevant properties and are able to express themselves more knowledgeably and confidently. As peers and the teacher concur, their responses are reinforced.

A father complains to a therapist that his teenage son is rude and leaves a mess in his wake wherever he goes. An in-home observation suggests that the parents focus most of their attention on the disruptive behavior, ignoring acceptable instances. To help the parents scan for the positive, the therapist asks the family to audiotape dinner-time conversations for a few days. Afterward, they identify instances of politeness or cooperation together. After discovering enough examples, the parents are ready to reinforce those classes of behavior, now depending only on periodic prompts from the course being served to seize the next opportunity to "catch their son being good" and reinforce with attention and approval.

Using Effective Reinforcement Procedures

Applying differential reinforcement to promote stimulus control requires that we follow the same rules as those noted in the early section on reinforcement. To increase responding in the presence of S⁺s, we must reinforce the response under those conditions, as soon and as often as possible with an adequate amount of a suitable object or event. Then, once responding in the presence of the antecedent stimulus has reached a high, consistent rate, gradually building in a delay and switching over to intermittent reinforcement and less powerful reinforcers should become possible. (A more extensive discussion of how to accomplish this changeover occurs in Chapters 30–32.)

In the initial stages of coaching a golfer to discriminate the correct from the incorrect swing, the pro should either arrange conditions to permit the golfer to imitate successfully—that is to attain reinforcement each time as a result of duplicating the correct move—and/or deliver extrinsic reinforcement immediately. O'Brien and Simek (1978) accomplished this with novice adult golfers. Once shown the correct putting swing, they were instructed to try it out by standing very close to the cup. Naturally, the swing succeeded. Then bit by bit they moved farther and farther away from the target, until eventually they were continuing to practice the discriminated operant flawlessly, performing significantly better than members of a control group.

When Clyde correctly labels a behavior "honest," his dad should reinforce the labeling until the concept appears to be firmly established. Only later would it be advisable to reinforce less often or to use a less-powerful reinforcer. When Granny's rule of child rearing, "Be consistent," is implemented, behavior comes more readily under stimulus control.

Do not confuse consistency of reinforcement of the S⁺-response combination with endless repetition of the task itself. Research shows that learners are more responsive when tasks are varied periodically than when they are kept constant (e.g., Bilsky & Heal, 1969; Cantor & Cantor, 1964; Fantz, 1964; Hutt, 1975). Stipulating that a task must be practiced repeatedly without relief can result in "boredom" (Dunlap & Koegel, 1980; Ross, 1977) or a decrease in the response rate. For example, Dunlap and Koegel (1980) found that autistic children's responses declined during a repetitive task condition, but "the introduction of task variation during the second condition served to restore the children's responsiveness, produce high levels of correct responding, and, perhaps, delay the adverse effects of boredom" (p. 626). The practicing golfer probably would diminish his rate of putting after the hundredth putt in a row, but keep going longer if the pro had him switch from putts to drives to escaping sand-traps every once in a while.

Suppose, however, that the S⁺s have been identified, and their critical features made as salient as possible. Yet differential reinforcement is not feasible because the associated behavior fails to be emitted. Where do you turn? To prompting.

Prompting

Prompting Defined and Illustrated

"Prompting is the substitution of an effective but inappropriate stimulus for an ineffective but appropriate stimulus. Prompts are stimuli that control the desired behavior but that are not functionally related to the task" (Touchette & Howard, 1984, p. 175). Synonyms for prompts are "hints" or "cues," concepts with which you surely are familiar. All of us have used and experienced prompts on numerous occasions—usually when we attempted to evoke a response. "Don't tell me. Just give me the first letter." "Remember what you do with the clutch." "Say 'pl____' if you want your juice." "Don't forget to turn in your paper before you leave."

Formal prompting strategies are used in management, training, therapy, counseling, and instruction for the very same purpose—to promote wanted responses. Figure 16.1 shows how prompting was used to help a youngster deal with teasing from his peers. The prompts consisted of the counselor showing and coaching the youth to change his activity, to relax, and to praise himself for doing so when the other kids teased him. Given those prompts, the antecedent of peers teasing (Sᴾ) no longer evokes an aggressive reaction. Eventually, the function of the stimulus transfers over to an Sᴰ, so now the boy reliably changes his activity, relaxes, and congratulates himself any time the others tease him. (Transferring from a prompt to the critical Sᴰ may or may not occur auto-

matically. Chapter 18 emphasizes procedures for promoting transfer of stimulus control.)

Selecting Prompts

Any stimulus that evokes the wanted behavior—instructions, rules, demonstrations, gestures, pictures, goals, guidance, and so on—can work. How do you decide which prompts, though, to start with? To answer this question, first assess the person's behavioral repertoire to determine which Sᴰs currently control the wanted response. From this array, to facilitate learning and eventual transfer to natural Sᴰs, order each stimulus in a hierarchy from the *most natural* (the one most closely resembling the relevant S⁺) to the *most artificial* (the one that bears the least resemblance to the S⁺).

Suppose you are trying to teach a student to identify the Hebrew letter *aleph*. Various alternative prompting strategies are available. Some relate to the inherent characteristics of the stimulus, for instance, the size of the *aleph* can be enlarged or its hue intensified. These are *within-stimulus prompts*. Otherwise, you can use a prompt external to the stimulus—an *extra-stimulus* prompt. It can be embellished with a pattern, a light can be focused on it, it can be cut out of sandpaper to have its own unique texture, and so on. Of all the possible alternatives, probably a prompt that draws the learner's attention to the configuration of the letter by magnifying its critical features is best, whereas a prompt that distracts the learner from attending to the letter's configuration is highly artificial. So, to *identify* (although not necessarily to *train*) an appropriate prompt, use this system of "least prompts."

For *training*, in many situations you also will want to use the minimum-to-maximum prompting strategy, so you supply no more support than is necessary. For skills, the hierarchy usually (though not always) progresses from instructions or simple communicative gestures to imitative to physical prompts. (See Chapter

Figure 16.1 The Prompting Process

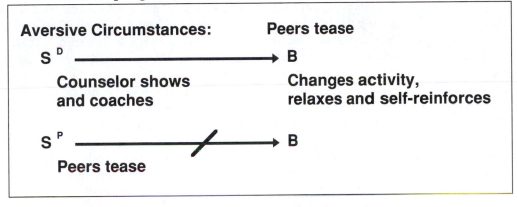

17.) For verbal behavior, the level frequently progresses from minimally informative instructional prompts through the array of artificial or intrusive prompts that culminate in a "give-away" prompt. Instruction, then, proceeds by beginning with the prompt that most naturally occasions the target behavior. Assuming any contrived prompts are necessary, teaching begins there, with those supportive prompts gradually replaced until the critical features of the stimulus alone are sufficient to prompt the correct response.

Sometimes you may want to take the opposite approach, however: moving from the maximum to the minimum prompt level. Although that approach may involve unnecessary training steps, it virtually guarantees success, as Luyben, Funk, Morgan, Clark, and Delulio (1986) found. Their students—three mentally retarded male adults—were taught a 9-component soccer pass via a hierarchy beginning with instructions combined with a strong physical prompt, then continuing on to a mild phys-ical prompt, an imitative prompt, and then a gestural and verbal cue. Balance prompts also were provided and gradually withdrawn, such as a walker, to a quad cane to a standard cane, to no support. The main advantage seen by the researchers was that the players were successful almost every time (96.7%), a reinforcing event rarely experienced in the past. (Later you will recognize this method as a standard "fading" procedure.)

Numerous classes of S^Ds, such as extrasensory prompts, can be used temporarily to evoke responses not yet under the control of S^+s. Bruno uses a musical score while memorizing a concerto, and the coach diagrams plays in advance. Instructional manuals and operating guides use sketches, whereas pictures can be especially helpful for nonreaders or for those who have difficulty following written instructions. For instance, pictorial images were useful adjuncts to teaching mildly handicapped youngsters how to access and exit a microcomputer program (Frank, Wacker, Berg, &

McMahon, 1985). More severely impaired adolescents saw the steps to follow in performing daily living tasks such as dusting tables, folding laundry, and stuffing envelopes (Wacker, Berg, Perrie, & Swatta, 1985). Pictures also helped developmentally delayed adults to prepare complicated meals (Martin, Rusch, James, Decker, & Trtol, 1982). Tactile prompts (e.g., sandpaper-covered numerals) aided a deaf and blind student to learn how to package and to stuff envelopes (Berg & Wacker, 1989).

Color prompts can be especially beneficial instructional aids. Four girls and two boys, ranging in age from 6 to 18 and classified as severely retarded, matched colors correctly but did not climb stairs one foot at a time (Fowler, Rowbury, Nordyke, & Baer, 1976). They learned the skill via temporary color prompts: red or yellow tape was affixed to alternating steps and also to the youngsters' shoes. Except for one student who needed physical guidance, all the youngsters needed to do was to place their shoes sequentially on the steps containing their corresponding colors. After considerable reinforced practice, it was possible gradually to remove the tape from either stairs or shoes and for the teacher to begin to distance herself, while the students continued to climb the steps in the newly acquired alternating pattern.

Good results were obtained when trainers pointed to their mouths, then paused, during language instruction, to increase the stimulus control exerted by spoken words (Foxx, McMorrow, Faw, Kyle, & Bittle, 1987). Pointing to the correct choice in a visual/auditory discrimination task was less effective, though, with several autistic children, who became overly dependent on the prompt (Schreibman, 1975). It should come as no surprise that only when the *critical component* of the discrimination was isolated and enlarged to maximize its discriminative properties were the children able to use the prompt effectively.

To illustrate, in a basic experiment on errorless discrimination learning, Schreibman (1975) isolated the correct and incorrect aspects of sets of the antecedent stimuli. These were isolated and taught in a series of fading steps (see Chapter 18). The stimulus designated as correct (S^+) contained a stick figure with arms stretched in a diagonal direction, and the incorrect stimulus (S^-) contained arms set at an angle to one another. Only later were the components shared redundantly by both figures reintroduced as shown in Figure 16.2. Analogous results were produced with contrived auditory stimuli, which either were irrelevant (a buzzer) or relevant (the sound of the syllable).

To highlight the appropriate arithmetic operation, pictures, such as a multiplication sign, were embedded in a picture depicting multiple quantities of objects. Those prompts enabled developmentally disabled Dutch students to perform better in arithmetic (Lancioni, Smeets, & Oliva, 1987). Hoogeveen, Smeets, and Lancioni (1989) also used pictorial prompts to teach four children to match the shape of a letter (grapheme) with the sound the letter made (phoneme) by embedding it in a picture of an object beginning with the sound of the letter. An English-language example would be a picture of an ice cream cone that contained a highlighted vertical line as in Figure 16.3.

Numerous other methods have been developed to emphasize the relevant properties of an antecedent stimulus. When acquiring form-discrimination—numbers, letters, shapes, and the like—students may be asked to trace distinctive parts of each stimulus with their fingers. Yarn, clay, and other textures may be added temporarily to magnify the salience of the critical features (see, for example, Fauke, Burnett, Powers, & Sulzer, 1973).

Detecting Mysterious S^Ds

Occasionally contingency managers are puzzled by inexplicable behavior. What is cuing it? We would like to know because we may wish to present that stimulus to evoke the behavior

Figure 16.2 Fading Steps for the Within-Stimulus Prompt Procedure on the Visual Discrimination Tasks

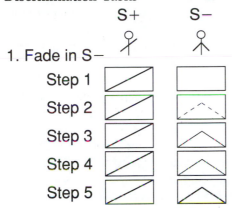

Source: Schreibman (1975), p. 98. Reprinted with the permission of the Society for the Experimental Analysis of Behavior and the author.

Figure 16.3 Emphasizing Critical Features: Embedding Letter in Picture

**Emphasizing Critical Features
Embedding Letter in Picture**

o

See the **I** *in the ice cream cone*

crastinates when the job is too difficult for her. By changing the circumstances—when or how the toy is removed or the difficulty of the job—the problem often can be eliminated.

Sometimes, however, interfering conditions are elusive, and informal observation fails to reveal where the fault lies. In such circumstances, carry out an ecobehavioral assessment (Rogers-Warren, 1984) by conducting sequence and contingency analyses. You might use a scatter plot, to help you locate factors that are contributing to the difficulty. Because we have discussed sequence and contingency analyses previously (see Chapters 2, 4, and 7, respectively), here we focus specifically on scatter plots. However, we do encourage you to review that earlier material.

Scatter plots can reveal interfering conditions, in that they "display periods during which problem responding virtually never occurs or occurs with near certainty" (Touchette et al., 1985, p. 343). A scatter plot usually displays frequency counts in half-hour intervals or less. Figure 16.4 illustrates a sample scatter plot. The time of day is indicated in half-hour intervals on the ordinate; the days on the abscissa. Each box on the grid identifies a specific time interval on a given day that can be filled with an X indicating more than one occurrence or a / indicating a single occurrence. Blank cells indicate no occurrence. As noted by Touchette

or, perhaps, remove it to suppress the response. Sometimes antecedent events are easy to identify, as when a child stops playing cooperatively and starts throwing a tantrum because a toy was taken from him; or when an employee pro-

Figure 16.4 Sample Scatter Plot Form

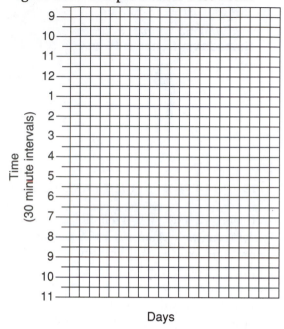

Days

et al. (1985), ''problem behavior may be highly correlated with a time of day, the presence or absence of certain people, a social setting, a class of activities, a contingency of reinforcement, a physical environment, and combinations of these and other variables'' (p. 345).

Figure 16.5 is based on data collected by Touchette et al. (1985). The case concerned Joan, a 14-year-old institutionalized, multihandicapped, highly aggressive young woman. As you can see from the scatter plot, aggressive incidents were most frequent between 1:00 and 4:00 P.M., on Monday through Thursday, during prevocational and community living classes. On Friday, field trips or swimming were scheduled at those times. During the morning when Joan was involved in one-to-one instruction, she was not assaultive, ''. . . suggesting that demands and training alone did not provoke assaults. Uneventful group activities in the community and at the gym suggested that simply being in a group was not the provocation'' (p. 346). The intervention, then, consisted of replacing the

conditions associated with the filled cells with those associated with the empty cells. This stimulus change brought about an immediate decrease in the assaults. Then, starting with the fifth week, her original training programs were reintroduced very gradually by returning her to a classroom for short periods and by slowly increasing demands in those situations. By the end of the year, Joan was participating in group instruction for 3 to 4 hours daily, and assaults hardly ever occurred.

As you can see, ecobehavioral assessments of this type can help you to identify functional S^Ds and S^Δs. Once the mystery is solved, you then may be in a position to select a functional prompt to initiate your program of developing stimulus control.

Regardless of which method is used to select prompts—contingency analyses, scatter plots, sequence analyses, or systematic comparisons—take care to select S^Ds that are as natural as feasible. Those not integral to the usual context are artificial and of relatively lesser value. ''Who is buried in Grant's Tomb'' is a ''dead giveaway'' (Oops!). You also want to avoid overly ''gimmicky'' or contrived ones that provide too many hints: ''When did Columbus discover America?'' Don't provide a picture of a boat with 1492 stamped on its side.

Occasionally you may be stymied by trying to magnify only the relevant and critical features of the S^+s. Irrelevant cues can be better than nothing. The important thing is to evoke and reinforce the response in the presence of the relevant stimuli, even when the stimuli are artificially contrived. Developers of programmed instruction occasionally have used contrived S^Ds to prompt *initial responses* in a series (e.g., Skinner, 1958; Taber, Glaser, & Schaefer, 1965). You too might consider using these temporary expedients to get appropriate behavior started, provided you select the S^Ds judiciously and transfer control back to the appropriate S^+ as soon as possible. You will learn more about this topic in Chapter 18.

Figure 16.5 Scatter Plot of Joan's Assaults. Filled circles indicate 30-minute intervals during which more than one assault occurred. Open boxes represent intervals with only one assault.

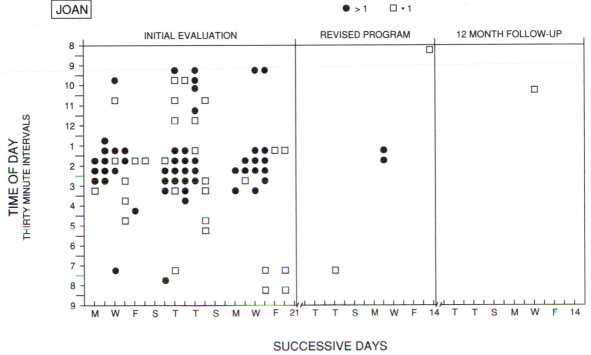

Source: Touchette et al. (1985). p. 347. Reprinted with the permission of the Society for the Experimental Analysis of Behavior and the author.

Instructors must be very sensitive to any verbal or nonverbal hints that people display in response to a prompt, however, because over-prompting can be punishing for the learner. None of us likes to be told how to do something we feel we have already mastered. A frown, a change of topic, or a move toward leaving may tell us that the prompt is aversive rather than helpful. Under such circumstances, terminate the selected prompt and, if necessary, choose an alternative, nonaversive one.

Samples as Prompts: Matching-to-Sample

Matching-to-sample is a technique, as described in Chapter 15, that can be used to bring complex behavior, such as concepts and verbal skills, under stimulus control (e.g., Sidman, 1969; 1977; Sidman & Cresson, 1973). Stimuli with which the individual is familiar are matched or paired with stimuli that are to acquire functional equivalence for the learner. For instance, a student may be able to identify a picture of a doctor but may not know how to read the word "doctor." The learner may be capable of identifying an egg beater but not know its function. The matching-to-sample method teaches the student to match the picture with the word and not some other word (and/or the word with the picture of the doctor and not with a picture of a plumber, carpenter, or astronaut).

Akin to matching the picture of the doctor with its corresponding printed word, Sidman (1977) has used the match-to-sample method to teach developmentally delayed students words like car or boy. The samples were three-letter words projected onto a center window, surrounded by nine windows on which different pictures were projected. If the student touched the picture matching the central word, a reinforcer was delivered. Otherwise, nothing happened. Naturally the student would continue trying until the reinforcer was received. To test whether the student actually had learned to "decode" the word, the instructor dictated it and had the student select the printed word from several available choices. Remarkably, many students were successful in learning the spoken and printed words and pictures as a class of functionally equivalent S^{D}s. They could select any one of the three correctly when either of the other two was presented.

The technique also can be used to teach uses or meanings, such as the purpose of an eggbeater, except instead of printed words as the set of choices, they might include pictures of tools being used, such as an eggbeater mixing eggs, a hammer hitting a nail, a spatula spreading frosting, or knife slicing a turkey. Other arrays could include similar pictures, including, perhaps, a knife carving a roast, so sufficient exemplars of a carving knife's functions could be displayed as the student correctly paired the tool with pictures of many of its applications.

The match-to-sample method lends itself nicely to teaching discriminations errorlessly. That is especially advantageous for people with histories of failure with respect to such discriminations. The basic approach is to ensure correct choices all along the way, by beginning with very easy tasks, such as touching the only window or picture displayed before the choices are displayed. Progressively other (incorrect) choices are introduced, whereas correct matches continue unabated.

Evidently many adjuncts for producing suitable stimulus control stand ready. In deciding which to choose, you first see which currently are operative. Then usually you select those most natural and *relevant* to the ultimate S^D and that direct the learner's attention to the critical features of the natural stimulus. In Chapter 17 we discuss in greater detail systematic prompting strategies designed to minimize errors during the learning process. For purposes of the moment, though, always ensure that the student or trainee is aware of the features that distinguish one antecedent stimulus from another.

Coping with Stimulus Overdependence and Overselectivity

Sometimes a response is overly dependent on an irrelevant stimulus, such as an extraneous aspect of the antecedent stimulus configuration or of the artificial prompt. This may happen because a contrived cue is kept in place too long; the response has been "overprompted" by an S^D other than the critical feature(s) of the stimulus (i.e., those that should be exerting control). Even though completely capable of playing his concerto music by memory, Bruno does not unless the score rests before him.

Figure 16.6 shows another example. Underline the Hebrew letter *aleph*.

You probably correctly selected the second character from the right. But the basis for your selection most likely was an irrelevant cue: the distinctive size or shading of the letter. To test yourself, don't study the shape of the letter and in an hour or so, turn to your dictionary's Hebrew alphabet. Cover up the transliterations

Figure 16.6 Prompting the Selection of the Hebrew Letter *aleph* with Two Irrelevant Cues: Size and Shading

(the phonetic names written in latin letters) and try to locate the *aleph*. Did you?

By contrast, here is another example in which the prompt included a magnification of the *critical features*—a strategy we now know to be more effective because it focuses the learner's attention *on* the *relevant* properties of the numerals 2 and 7 (Figure 16.7). Note that the distinctive stimulus properties are highlighted.

Now consider this example:

> Roses are red, violets are blue,
> Twenty-one and one are twenty-_____?

You probably supplied the correct word two, but the response was occasioned by a feature other than a relevant one. The rhyming properties of *blue* and *two* probably acted as a control, rather than the appropriate S^D: "Twenty-one and one equal what?"

Young and autistic children may respond "overselectively" to one or a few cues instead of the full complement of multiple cues; that is, their behavior is controlled by a limited number, or even just one—often a nonrelevant stimulus—of the complex. Instances are giving an answer based on the placement of an object, its color, or the persons doing the teaching (Lovaas, Schreibman, Koegel, & Rehm, 1971). The placement of the object, not the object itself, cues the student to label it correctly. Naturally, generalization of the stimulus-response relation to other locations is compromised. A familiar example for instructors is when they recall someone's name because of the seat he sits in and not because they recognize him. Pass the person on the street, and you're in trouble.

Correcting overselectivity requires reasonable technical skill, because control has to be transferred over to the critical aspects of the S$^+$. Several tactics seem to have been helpful in this regard. One is to alternate trials involving single components of the complex stimulus with trials containing the intact complex stimulus (Schreibman, Koegel, & Craig, 1977). Another is to use intermittent schedules of reinforcement. As an example, Koegel, Schreibman, Britten, and Laitinen (1979) taught 12 children with autism to choose correctly from pairs of cards displaying multiple stimuli. After reaching a criterion of correct responses 10 times in a row, they were presented 100 additional trials with reinforcers occurring for either every correct response for one set or for an average of every third correct response for the other set. Surprisingly, the intermittent reinforcement condition produced much lower rates of overselectivity. Perhaps, as the investigators posit, because they may have responded as if they had committed an error, the irregular reinforcement caused the children to attend more closely to the subsequent stimuli. (We return to the topic of transferring stimulus control in Chapter 18.)

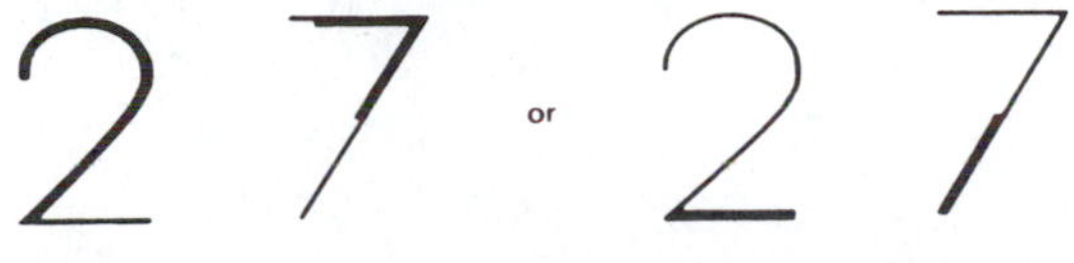

Summary

You have now seen how stimulus change can be used when S^{D}s strongly control a behavior and otherwise how that missing control can be achieved. Procedures are available for developing stimulus control for purposes of teaching simple and complex motor, cognitive, social, personal, and vocational skills. To enable S$^+$s to acquire sufficient strength to reliably occasion the appropriate response, along with others, be sure to do the following: (1) Clearly identify relevant stimulus properties; (2) Emphasize the relevant stimulus properties so they are readily detected; and (3) use effective reinforcement procedures.

Often the wanted response occurs when we use prompts to evoke it under particular circumstances. But first, the analyst needs to know

Figure 16.7 Magnifying Critical Features of the Numerals 2 and 7

why it is not happening in the absence of the prompt. Is the response absent from the repertoire or is stimulus control just insufficiently developed? In this chapter we have discussed ways to attempt to answer those questions and if needed, to prompt the response. But if relatively direct prompting strategies suggested here fail, you can turn to one of two general strategies: (1) using more systematic prompting methods, such as instructions, modeling, or guidance (Chapter 17), or (2) teaching the behavior as a new skill or concept by using shaping (Chapter 19) or chaining (Chapter 20).

In either case, once the response is acquired and/or brought under the control of the critical stimuli, before it can be said to be occurring independently, usually contrived prompts will need to be removed, preferably by *fading* (Chapter 18). As rules are one type of antecedent readily available to almost everyone, though, often rules can be kept in place. By learning about how verbal behavior is developed and influenced (Chapter 21), we can help ourselves and others to apply rules to guide their performance as preferred. Let us progress on to those topics.

Chapter 17

Systematic Prompting Strategies

GOALS

After completing this chapter, you should be able to:
1. Define, recognize, and give original illustrations of each of the following terms:
   a. Goal-setting
   b. The instruction or "tell" procedure
   c. Rule-governed behavior
   d. Critical stimuli
   e. The modeling, or "show," procedure
   f. Imitation
   g. Generalized imitation
   h. Self-modeling
   i. Physical guidance
2. Discuss the purpose of goal-setting; why a goal may fail to function as an S^D; and what should be done to maximize the effectiveness of goal-setting.
3. Illustrate and discuss the importance of eight suggestions for using the tell procedure effectively.
4. Describe and illustrate how to develop imitative prompts as discriminative stimuli.
5. Describe how to strengthen imitative responding.
6. List and discuss the importance of the factors that should be considered when an analyst selects a model.
7. List and discuss what can be done, in addition to selecting effective models, to increase the likelihood that the model's behavior will be imitated.
8. Describe and illustrate how to use physical guidance effectively.
9. Present a general guideline for selecting a prompting strategy, and discuss when using that guideline would not be appropriate.

Despite urging, cajoling, hinting, and promising all sorts of captivating incentives (or, heaven help us, dire threats), you will find that some responses simply do not happen. "Look, Joe, if you don't follow through, the ball is not going to land on the green!" warns the pro. "Thunk" it goes, into the sand trap. No matter how sweetly Ms. Charming asks Fern to sort boxes according to size, the task is not accomplished. "Go on. Don't be afraid," coaxes Violet's teacher. But Violet refuses to ask the other children if she may play with them.

What happens when you fail to bring a behavior under stimulus control by prompting it informally? Such situations often are encountered in educational and training programs, as in teaching difficult physical, social, communicative, cognitive, and vocational skills. Take heart. Considerable progress has been made in the area of systematic prompting.

Formal prompting strategies have aided in successfully establishing stimulus control in the face of exactly those sorts of challenges. In just one illustrative category of instances, the methods to be described have helped adults with developmental disabilities to acquire the following community survival skills:

- *grocery shopping* (Heal, Colson, & Gross, 1984; Matson, 1981).
- *fire safety* (Fox & Sulzer-Azaroff, 1989; Haney & Jones, 1982; Katz & Singh, 1986).
- *housekeeping* (Bauman & Iwata, 1977).
- *transport skills* (Coon, Vogelsberg, & Williams, 1981).
- *ordering meals* (Marholin, O'Toole, Touchette, Berger, & Doyle, 1979).
- *telephone usage* (Risley & Cuvo, 1980).
- *meal preparation* (Martin et al., 1982; Sanders & Parr, 1989).
- *leisure skills* (Johnson & Bailey, 1977).
- *eating nutritionally balanced meals* (Reitz, 1984).

If populations like those can succeed, just think what prompting methods can do for individuals with more advanced repertoires! In this chapter we present a number of tactics for evoking responses so they can be brought under the control of the designated S⁺s. These include using goal-setting and other verbal, imitative, and physical prompts.

Goal-Setting

Goal-Setting Defined

Goal-setting refers to specifying a standard or level of performance to be attained. Goals may refer to

- *ultimate* long-range outcomes, such as the mission of an organization (e.g., to enhance the quality of life of people with developmental disabilities in the state).
- bottomline results (e.g., increasing yearly profits by a certain percentage).
- *intermediate or enabling* objectives that permit the ultimate ones to be achieved, such as behaviors (X rate of delivering praise) or results (Y amount of profits each month).
- *initial or logistical* objectives (Z projects designed of A quality).

See Malott and Garcia (1987) for an elaboration of this topic. Then there are *subgoals*, usually numerical quantities designating the next level of accomplishment toward any of the former.

Goal-Setting Illustrated

To provide an illustrative case (Sulzer-Azaroff, Loafman, Merante, & Hlavacek, 1990) a large telecommunications company included the well-being of employees in its *mission statement*. That implied an *enabling objective* of reducing accidents on the job. To reduce accidents, an assessment was conducted and acts that had contributed to accidents in the past were identified for each of several departments. Safe alternatives were specified, and tasks were analyzed and placed on a checklist for purposes of measurement.

Now a *logistical objective* of 100% safe performance for at least three weeks in a row on each of the safe alternatives was specified. Meeting those criteria would be the occasion for a major departmental celebration. Achieving that objective rapidly, however, was judged overly ambitious, so *subgoals* were specified. These were selected by examining prior performance patterns and choosing a level toward the upper portion of the existing distribution. In Figure 17.1, the horizontal lines depict each subgoal level to be achieved. When workers achieved a subgoal a few times in a row they

were presented with a small item, such as a tape measure or a pen. In contrast to 13 lost-time injuries plus "recordable accidents" during the previous 6-month *preintervention* period in 1 work unit, over a 6-month period the number dropped to only 1.

Goal-setting like this can be used for any performance: reports, projects, to-do items completed on time; percentages of top quality products; number of interactions with clients; and so on. In our own regular activities we use goal-setting with our graduate students (to help them progress toward completion of their major tasks, such as review papers and dissertations); with our clients (who provide services to or-

Figure 17.1 Safety Performance as a Function of Levels of Subgoals

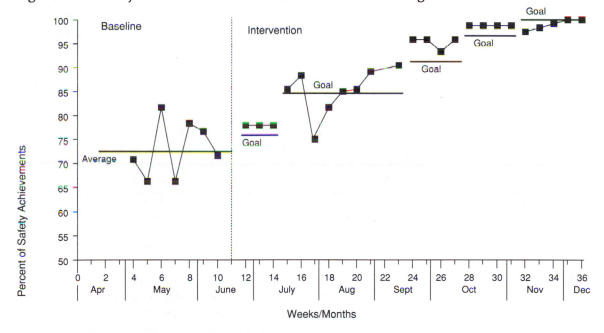

January through June		July through December	
OSHA recordable accidents	11	OSHA recordable accidents	1
Lost-time accidents	2	Lost-time accidents	0

Source: Sulzer-Azaroff, Loafman, Merante, and Hlavacek (1990), p. 112. Permission to reprint from *The Journal of Organizational Behavior Management* and the authors.

ganizations); with our employees; and for ourselves in our writing. Numerous organizations recently have discovered the value of including goal-setting within their management systems, because, as Balcazar et al. (1985–1986) have discovered, goals combine well with feedback and/or other reinforcers to improve performance of personnel.

Goals as Discriminative Stimuli

The purpose of any goal is to govern the quality or amount of performance accomplished; goals, such as the lines displayed on the posted chart in Figure 17.1, are supposed to operate as discriminative stimuli. (See Fellner & Sulzer-Azaroff [1984] for a behavior analytic account of goal-setting.) Often, goals do function as S^{D}s; sometimes they do not. When they do not, it is probably because accomplishment of the goals has not produced reinforcement. Maybe nothing good happened, or reinforcers were too delayed after the goals were reached.

Negative results also can happen when the goals are too *challenging* or too *easy*. In the first case, reinforcers that should have been forthcoming as a consequence of achievement are not received sufficiently often. In the second, participants may find accomplishing so little to be punishing, or become satiated with them.

Effective Goal-Setting

A well-specified goal is stated as a full behavioral objective, including the acts to be performed, the conditions, and the standards or levels of accomplishment. Such specificity makes the critical aspects of the antecedent conditions clear to everyone—to those striving to achieve the goal and to those who are to deliver consequences contingent on its accomplishment.

One possible way to make the most of goal-setting is to invite the people concerned to participate in setting the goal levels for themselves. Of course, you may need to provide some guidelines to prevent them from choosing outlan-

dishly easy or difficult subgoals. On the several occasions when we have used *participative goal-setting*, we noted a slight superiority of effects and a general preference for the approach (e.g., Fellner & Sulzer-Azaroff, 1985). This resembled findings by Cotton et al. (1988), who identified 11 of 15 cases in which workers' participation in work decisions impacted positively on productivity.

If you are working in organizations with large groups of employees, we suggest you break down the groups into *smaller sized* units. Then even if you wish to keep people's specific contributions confidential, the impact of their participation still can be felt by everyone. Otherwise, individual members may see their responsibility as diffused, with any consequences shared by the others (a theory promoted by Wallach, Kogan, & Burt, 1967). From a behavioral viewpoint, the issue becomes one of the extent to which each individual's efforts are reinforced as a function of the size of the group.

Naturally, *differential reinforcement* is the foundation of a successful goal-setting program. Achieving a goal or subgoal should always be reinforced. The reinforcer need not be extremely powerful. Often, especially with typical adults, feedback plus a bit of approval will be sufficient, just as long as the accomplishment is recognized in some way. Intermittently, though, particularly when an especially challenging goal is met, or when improved performance has persisted for several occasions in a row, surprise them with more powerful reinforcers (such as letters of commendation to the boss, a treat, or whatever turns them on). For major goal achievements, seize the opportunity to mount a big celebration, such as a feature article in the organizational newsletter, or present some other highly visible and valued object or event. The accomplishment will be reinforced and perhaps serve as an incentive to others in similar circumstances to continue pressing forward. The participants in the safety program cited earlier were delighted by the fancy luncheon given in their honor for achieving such an outstanding safety record. (So were their supervisors, who stood to earn bonuses for improved safety, and top managers, who recognized the enormous value of preventing the human suffering and financial expenditures entailed by accidents.)

Goals may be stated as verbal descriptions or numerical values. They are, in a sense, a subset of verbal antecedents. Instructions are another. Let us now therefore turn to the topic of using instructions to prompt behavior.

Using Instructional Prompts: The Tell Procedure

Instructions generally are among the least intrusive and most efficient kinds of prompts you can use. All you have to do is *talk* (or *write*). "Aim to the left rear of the court; keep the ball low . . ." coaches the tennis instructor. "Remember the sign for the interrogative that preceded a question in Spanish?" reminds the romance language teacher. "See," guides the consultant, "this is the moment to catch the child being good." "Now check the pressure and temperature so the mixture doesn't thicken too much," drills the supervisor.

Instructional prompts are used freely by coaches, consultants, clinicians, teachers, and parents—and for good reason. Instructions may readily summon the response when the natural antecedents fail to, thereby providing an opportunity to reinforce the response. Eventually, of course, the instructions may be eliminated; but even as temporary stopgaps, they can be extremely helpful. Illustrations abound in the research literature, as in the following instance.

Nonhandicapped preschool children are more accepting of their developmentally delayed peers who respond to the children's social initiations than they are to the delayed peers who do not respond to their overtures. To en-

courage interacting, teachers used instructions to prompt both autistic preschoolers and non-disabled confederates to "be good teachers"—that is, to play with particular children (Strain, Odom, & McConnell, 1984). Prompting the autistic children to initiate playing with the confederates increased not only their rates of initiating play but also their rates of responding to the confederates' initiations (Odom & Strain, 1986).

Using the Tell Procedure Effectively

The **tell procedure** has been applied universally by managers, teachers, parents, and consultants from time immemorial. Even nonhumans appear to use the method, as the dance of the honey bee is thought to prompt the others in the hive to locate nectar. Why, then, does this topic need to be considered at all? Because a number of variables have been identified that can influence success with the procedure. In the last two chapters, you became familiar with several of those variables, such as being certain the response is in the person's repertoire, that optimal reinforcement methods are being employed, and that the context is supportive. Others include determining

- whether the person's responding in general is **rule-governed**—controlled by verbal antecedents—or if rule governance needs to be developed.
- whether the verbal stimuli are prompts or the actual critical variables of concern—the S^+s.
- whether the stimuli serving as prompts are known to the performer (i.e., can be pointed to on request).
- the rates at which instruction is presented.
- whether instructions should be combined with modeling.

Chapter 21 returns to the topic of rule-governed behavior, as it relates to verbal behavior as the topic of direct interest. Here we emphasize how rule-governance relates to instructional prompts, where a class other than verbal behavior is to be the end-product.

Ensuring that rules govern the individual's behavior in general. Rules or instructions begin to exert control early in people's lives. Infants rapidly learn to look, wave "bye-bye," lie down, and play "peek-a-boo" in response to cues from their parents. Later on, phrases like "Come here," "Give me," "Pick up," and so on, begin reliably to evoke the matching responses. How is the generalized control by verbal antecedents—*rule-governed behavior*—achieved? You guessed it. By getting the many responses out by whatever it takes—guidance, demonstrations, or whatever—and then differentially reinforcing them. Mom picks up Baby Bonnie's hand and helps her wave it back and forth, cooing her approval and hugging her all the while. Something similar happens with peek-a-boo, and so on. When she responds to Mom's and Dad's instructional prompts, good things happen (and when she fails to, the outcome is less favorable). So she learns to comply.

How precisely a given set of rules governs any particular person's behavior depends upon the subtleties of physical status, learning history, and current circumstances, just as all other forms of stimulus control do. So you cannot take for granted that just because you tell people to do something, they will react as you think they should. They may follow or make use of rules under some conditions but not others; adhere to certain ones more meticulously than to alternatives; and be inconsistent in other ways.

Some people have extremely low rates of complying with certain rule categories, such as a rebellious adolescent who consistently fails to do what his parents ask. For others, particular types of verbal antecedents exert hardly any control at all, even in cases when the verbal sequences describe operative contingencies: "If you get your toys picked up before five o'clock, I'll give you a cookie," but Junior keeps playing beyond the deadline.

At one extreme, people for whom verbal antecedents exert little or no control often are labeled as highly independent, creative, or self-reliant, especially when their actions are socially valued. At the other extreme, these people may be perceived as immature, foolish, delayed, psychopathic, delinquent, or emotionally disturbed, when their actions are aversive to others. The issue, however, is not what they *are*, but what they *do* or fail to do under what conditions—and what can be done to rectify the situation.

Sometimes, as we know, a skill deficit may be at fault. People with severely delayed receptive language abilities frequently fail to profit from instructional prompts due to that skill deficit. So, before rules can be brought to exert control, the person must be taught the "meaning" of the instructions. By contrast, people with adequate repertoires of the targeted skills, but who are unresponsive to verbal antecedents because current contingencies are not sufficiently supportive, would profit from a rearrangement of contingencies. Then the words will begin to function by specifying that a given response is likely to be reinforced.[1]

Developing instructions as discriminative stimuli. Instructions become discriminative for specific responses in exactly the same manner as do other stimuli. In fact, one example that we used in Chapter 12 (Kazdin & Erickson, 1975) illustrates this. When children failed to follow instructions, the response was guided and reinforced directly after instructions were delivered. In another situation, Fjellstedt and Sulzer-Azaroff (1973) taught a student to comply with instructions. In this instance, the youngster actually did follow instructions—but later, rather than sooner. Stimulus control was incomplete. When asked to take out his work

---

[1] Some, for instance Blakely and Schlinger (1987), prefer to apply the term "function-altering contingency specifying stimuli" to rules, instead of labeling them S^Ds, because their effects often are delayed.

and start, he dawdled and took many minutes to respond. A requirement was added to the procedure: For the response to be reinforced, it had to follow the instruction within a preset period of time.

Having seen how verbal instructions can evoke a response in the presence of the **critical stimuli** that are eventually to control it, you now probably recognize that using verbal instructions can be an effective and expedient way to prompt behavior. That is why books, lectures, seminars, discussions, and workshops are so heavily relied on as instructional media.

Using stimuli known to the learner. You may remember that when Clarke, Remington, and Light (1986) were teaching total communication words to educationally handicapped children, the youngsters more rapidly acquired the words they knew than those with which they were unfamiliar. Correspondingly, when Etzel (1969) substituted the familiar words *like* and *not like* for the unfamiliar *same* and *different*, their students learned the selected discriminations more rapidly. One reason why chapter goals suggest you define terms in this text is to permit you to use the concepts appropriately. Analogously, before you attempt teaching a complicated discrimination, be sure the stimuli are known to the student.

Using a rapid rate of presentation. Recall that rapidly paced instructions have been associated with lower rates of disruption and superior comprehension (Carnine, 1976; West & Sloane, 1986). Therefore, when you are teaching a skill (e.g., to discriminate, label, sequence, or imitate), see to it that the elapsed time is brief between the delivery of the reinforcer for success in one trial and the initiation of the next. In a specific case, Koegel, Dunlap, and Dyer (1980) found that when the S^D for each subsequent trial was presented about 1 second following the end of the previous trial, their autistic students answered more accurately and

learned more rapidly than when intervals were 4 seconds or longer. As the investigators note, "it seems increasingly important to examine characteristics of the learning situation which occur between trials. The present results show that such variables can have a relatively large influence on teaching these children" (p. 98).

Combining instructions with modeling. Sometimes, despite the best efforts of the contingency manager, verbal instructions fail to accomplish their purpose. The responder appears unable to act according to a particular set of verbal guidelines and no amount of telling, training, or consulting bears fruit: "Clean up your room, Joey." But on inspection, his room resembles the aftermath of Hurricane Hannah. "I shall munch on carrots, not on potato chips for the rest of the year," says Diligent Dottie, whereas Mr. Novice vows he will scold less and praise more; however, neither follows through on the resolutions. The teacher announces, "Look, more new books for you to read!" and only two of eight children respond by reading (Haskett & Lenfestey, 1974). Obviously, the rules fail to govern the desired responses.

Occasionally, specific instances of rule governance are nonfunctional, and repeated attempts to bring the behavior under the control of designated verbal S^+s have been unsuccessful, too difficult or time consuming. One solution is to try an alternative method, such as **modeling** (the **"show"** procedure), or physical guidance, the description of which we give shortly.

Adding modeling to instructions can produce better results than just using instructions alone (LeBlanc & Ruggles, 1982), especially when you are requesting the performance of a skill, such as pointing, donning a life jacket, or operating a piece of equipment. Snell (1982) taught developmentally delayed adults how to make their beds by supplying verbal prompts while demonstrating how to complete a sequence of tasks. So begin with tell *and* show. Then, after the response is well established, gradually remove the "show" prompt, retaining the instructions for a bit longer.

Providing a Model: The Show Procedure

Often, though, just *seeing* someone performing, demonstrating, or modeling behavior is sufficient to prompt its **imitation**. When the students in the study by Haskett and Lenfestey (1974) failed to read their new books, even when encouraged, tutors began to pick up the books and read aloud. The students soon began following suit, substantially increasing their reading and related responses. Similarly, modeling was more effective than direct instructions or group discussions in rapidly changing parental behavior (Johnson & Brown, 1969). Modeling and role playing also were superior to written instructions or lectures in teaching parents to use timeout appropriately (Flanagan, Adams, & Forehand, 1979), perhaps because the procedures both promote discriminating between more and less optimal performance and increase the likelihood that matching the behavior will be reinforced.

Modeling has been shown to facilitate the acquisition of a variety of responses, both simple and complex, such as socially appropriate conduct (Bandura, 1969; 1977; 1986. Similarly, the method has been successful in teaching acceptable alternatives to behavioral problems, including:

- *fears* (Bandura & Menlove, 1968; Downs, Rosenthal, & Lichstein, 1988).
- *anxiety and skill deficiencies in job interviews* (Hall, Sheldon-Wildgen, & Sherman, 1980; Hollandsworth, Glazeski, & Dressel, 1978; Schloss, Schloss, & Smith, 1988).
- *inadequate athletic skills* (Shapiro & Shapiro, 1985).
- *inappropriate food purchases* (Winett, Kramer, Walker, Malone, & Lane, 1988).

- *social withdrawal* (O'Conner, 1972).
- *uncooperative behavior during dental treatment* (Stokes & Kennedy, 1980).
- *excessive alcohol consumption* (Caudill & Lipscomb, 1980; DeRicco & Niemann, 1980).
- *language deficits* (Brody & Brody, 1976; Brody, Lahey, & Combs, 1978; Goldstein & Brown, 1989; Heward & Eachus, 1979).

Perhaps modeling operates so effectively because words cannot adequately describe the nuances of certain responses. Sometimes, providing a demonstration is much more efficient. Occasionally, trainees are incapable of comprehending verbal descriptions of the response. A mother hardly would be successful just by using words to teach her infant to play peek-a-boo. Nor do successful physical education, art, or music teachers rely entirely on rules. Instead they reinforce close matches in responding after demonstrating what to do: "Serve the ball like this." "Listen to the melody while Bruno plays it." Ultimately, the demonstration can be eliminated; controlled either by generic instructions ("Show how you throw the ball") or the critical S^{D}s (the musical score) and their natural reinforcing consequences. As with verbal instructions, the instructor needs to sequence the demonstration carefully and, when necessary, apply effective techniques for transferring stimulus control (discussed in the next chapter).

Developing Imitative Prompts as Discriminative Stimuli

From the earliest months of an infant's life, imitative behavior is taught through reinforcement. "Peek-a-boo" says Mama, covering her eyes, smiling, and laughing. If baby doesn't initially match Mama's behavior by bringing his hands to his eyes, Mama assists by guiding them. When baby responds to "peek-a-boo" with an approximation of his own, bells ring, fireworks explode, and trumpets blare: "Look! He's playing peek-a-boo!" Baby's imitation of Mama is reinforced heavily. Junior rubs cream over his face, pretending to shave. Daddy says, "You're a big man, just like me!" Imitative responses are prompted and socially reinforced similarly throughout childhood: "See how Penny picks up her toys. I bet you can do that."

Differential reinforcement also is integral to many children's games, like "Simon Says" and "Follow the Leader." Research with pigeons (Epstein, Lanza, & Skinner, 1980) and rats (Hake, Donaldson, & Hyten, 1983) have demonstrated that exactly this sort of differential reinforcement can teach animals to imitate one another successfully.

Eventually, after numerous instances of imitation are reinforced within varied contexts, children begin to acquire **generalized imitation**, as a response class, using the skill not only in response to familiar examples but in novel contexts as well. Although it is usually adaptive, though, sometimes generalized imitation leads to trouble. Observe children engrossed in fantasy play to see what we mean. Junior picks up Dad's briefcase, pretends to head out the door, and says, "Bye, Honey, see you tonight," in a deep voice, just like Daddy's. The adoring parents beam and congratulate his cleverness. But when Junior makes believe he is arguing with his wife—"Shut up, you #!*#!"—his accurate portrayal lands him a scolding. Junior must learn to discriminate when imitating is and is not appropriate.

Increasing Generalized Imitative Responding

Although most people acquire generalized imitation in their early years, some may be deficient in this skill. Because well-established imitative responding is essential to the rapid acquisition of many types of behavior, the generalized skill may need to be trained intentionally. Imagine trying to teach someone incapable of imitating to knit; solder; slam a Ping-Pong ball; pronounce a word in a foreign language; shuffle cards; or stop, look, and listen. Actually, the person with underdeveloped imitative skills is in serious jeopardy. Learning to speak, socialize, or acquire complicated physical or cognitive skills—like orienting toward instructional materials—would be compromised, because acquiring all these behaviors depends to a great extent on being able to imitate.

Generalized imitation is taught by heavily reinforcing the imitative response class as often and under as many circumstances as possible. For example, several investigators (Baer et al., 1967; Lovaas, Berberich, Perloff, & Schaeffer, 1966) taught initially nonresponsive, autistic, and severely retarded individuals to imitate by pairing instructions (for example, "Touch your head") with a demonstration of the act. Any imitative reaction then was reinforced with praise, small bits of food, and so on. (Ultimately, the demonstrations were faded, as verbal instructions began to serve as adequate prompts. See Chapter 18's section on fading prompts.) These same techniques also have been used to teach sign language to people lacking or deficient in language due to hearing impairments, retardation, and socioemotional difficulties, thereby enabling them to communicate at last (e.g., Barrera, Lobato-Barrera, & Sulzer-Azaroff, 1980).

Using Modeling Effectively

In addition to generalized imitation, other variables have been found frequently to influence the probability of a given imitative response; depending, of course, on the individual's history. Included as variables are the people serving as models and whether other strategies are applied during training.

Selecting models. Five basic factors are worthy of consideration when an analyst selects models. These include:

- the models' similarity to the observer.

- the models' competence.
- the observer's previous experience with the models.
- the models' prestige.
- the use of multiple models.

Similarity refers to the characteristics shared commonly by the models and individuals who observe them (for example, sociocultural background, job roles, age, grade, interests, physical appearance, and experiences). People are more likely to imitate someone whom they know shares attributes, talents, or deficiencies with themselves (Bandura, 1968; Byrne, 1969; Byrne & Griffitt, 1969; Kazdin, 1974b; Kornhaber & Schroeder, 1975; Rosekrans, 1967; Statland, Zander, & Natsoulas, 1961; Statland & Hillmer, 1962). However, the particular types of attributes that serve as S^{D}s for imitation can vary among individuals. For example, Kevin may mimic people who resemble him physically, whereas Pete may not.

Children's peers, particularly friends, are more readily imitated than adults (Barry & Overman, 1977; Hicks, 1965; Kazdin, 1974b; Kornhaber & Schroeder, 1975). Presumably, adults may serve as especially effective models for one another. Probably this happens because friendships often are based on shared skills and interests, and it could be one reason why friends tend to mimic one another's dress, social deportment, and activities. You can capitalize on this likelihood by selecting as a model a friend who is competent in the behavior to be performed. Whether they are friends or just co-workers, though, peers can serve as extremely effective models for on-the-job training and other essential skills (Jones, Fremouw, & Carples, 1977; Fleming & Sulzer-Azaroff, 1990).

This emphasis on similarity does not, however, imply that no differences should exist between models and observers. *Similar* is not to be confused with *identical*. Differences are unavoidable and actually may be helpful. In fact,

too much behavioral similarity can handicap a group's ability to change for the better. For example, Mayer and Kahn (1976) caution against forming extremely homogeneous counseling groups: ''. . . if the group members all engage in the same problem behavior (stealing, classroom disruption, drugs, etc.) they will tend to reinforce one another's problem behavior . . .'' (pp. 2–3). Just as variability of responding is essential to shaping, diversity of performance of group members must exist if appropriate behaviors are to be selected for modeling and reinforcement. Group members should not share identical behavioral problems (deficits or excesses), only features with which they can identify readily.

No one, of course, is more similar than individual clients are to themselves. Capitalizing on this fact, several investigators (Dowrick & Dove, 1980; Hosford, 1980) have used a **self-modeling** procedure to teach a variety of professional, social and physical skills.

> Self-modeling works like this: the student is videotaped while performing a particular skill. The tape then is edited to remove weak performance and external prompts. Only the exemplary performance is retained. (This differentiates *self-modeling* from *self-observation*.) The taped performance then is shown to the student to prompt imitation (Sulzer-Azaroff & Mayer, 1986, p. 118).

We have used self-modeling to train teachers to use particular instructional strategies and to teach children safety skills. So consider using a playback of the client's own exemplary performance as the imitative prompt.

A second factor to consider when an analyst selects models is the *competence* of the model. In other words, people who are seen to accomplish what they set about to do are the most likely to be imitated (Croner & Willis, 1961; Kanareff & Lanzetta, 1960; Rosenbaum, Chalmers, & Horne, 1962; Thomas, Due, & Wigger, 1987). In fact, the functional value of the modeled behavior (i.e., its proficiency in producing consequences) outweighs age and other characteristics of the model (Schunk, 1987). The *functional value* of the modeled behavior, then, appears to be a powerful determinant of modeling (Bandura, 1986). While similarity suggests an answer to the question, "Can *I* do it?" model competence helps provide answers to the question, "Will it get me what I want?" (i.e., reinforcement), and of course, if the act doesn't lead to reinforcement, "Why should I bother doing it even if I can?"

Suppose you were organizing a counseling group to increase socially acceptable responses to difficult situations, such as refusing offers of drugs. You would be certain to include some peers with shared characteristics—ethnic or cultural—but who also were highly effective and whose avoidance of pressure to abuse drugs was heavily reinforced.

Generally, *coping models*—those who begin with some difficulty or are known to have experienced difficulty—have proven more effective than "mastery models"—those who portray complete competence from the onset (Bandura, 1986; Rosenthal & Bandura, 1978). Many modeling programs capitalize on this technique. When peers are selected as models, similarity can be enhanced by selecting those who have "experienced the same type of problems. Their growth in this area allows them to demonstrate approximations to the desired behavior that are not too complex or unrealistic for the other clients to imitate" (Mayer & Kahn, 1976, p. 3). For example, Warner and Swisher (1976) used audiotaped models of youths who were former drug users as a component of their group-counseling program with adolescent drug abusers. The goal of such groups was to teach "alternative ways of experiencing life without the use of artificial aids like drugs" (p. 511). Highly competent colleagues, too, can teach one another effectively by demonstrating skills and explaining facts. In one study (Jones et al., 1977), not only did teachers successfully instruct their colleagues in strategies of classroom management, but maybe because their own skills continued to improve correspondingly, disruptions decreased even further than previously in their own classrooms as well.

The importance of exposing learners to peers with more advanced competence has been used as an argument in support of "mainstreaming" youngsters with special educational needs by integrating them among contemporaries (Mann, 1975). Several studies support this concept. For example, Egel et al. (1981) found that autistic youngsters with IQ's ranging from 50 to 87 evidenced very low levels of correct responding when prompted by the therapist, but when "normal peers modeled correct responses, the autistic children's correct responding increased dramatically" (p. 9), and these increases were maintained after the peer models were removed. Normal peer models also have had similar effects on the performance of retarded children (e.g., Apolloni, Cooke, & Cooke, 1976; Barry & Overman, 1977; Rauer, Cooke, & Apolloni, 1978). It is well substantiated that learning is enhanced by the availability of peers competent in the behavior to be modeled.

A third model selection factor consists of several components having to do with *previous experience*. One is the observer's success or failure on a prior task. Those who have failed previously are more likely to imitate a modeled behavior (Gelfand, 1962; Mausner, 1954). Another related facilitative factor is the person's previously having participated in a cooperative experience with the model (Mausner & Block, 1957). Perhaps this latter factor may help explain why participant modeling generally is more effective than filmed modeling (Bandura, 1986; Downs et al., 1988). (Another reason might be that participant modeling offers more multisensory input than filmed modeling [Rosenthal & Downs, 1985]). These factors—past failure and previous cooperative experiences with the model—frequently serve to foster imitative behavior.

Prestige is a fourth factor analysts consider when selecting models. Natural group leaders usually are those who are seen to receive a variety of coveted reinforcers, particularly from the peer group. For example, Thomas et al. (1987) found that the model's prior success influenced the degree to which behavior was imitated on a subsequent task for which the observer had not achieved competence. Ernie's friendliness, athletic prowess, good looks, and cheerfulness have gained him lots of attention, particularly from attractive women. Observing this, other youths would be more likely to imitate Ernie's behavior, rather than the behavior of someone who is ignored (Bandura et al., 1963b; Mayer, Rohen, & Whitley, 1969; Thomas et al., 1987). Remember, though, to ensure that the models share sufficient attributes with the observers; otherwise, imitation is less likely.

A fifth point is to select *multiple models,* because several models exert more influence than a single one (Barton & Bevirt, 1981; DeRicco & Niemann, 1980). Also, choosing the same individuals too often may alienate them from the group, causing them to be designated as the "teacher's pets," or by some other colorful label.

Promoting imitation of the model's behavior. Beyond care in model selection, several other tactics can promote effective modeling. These include:

- highlighting the similarity between observers and models.
- encouraging behavioral rehearsal.
- providing instructions, rules, and rationales.
- ensuring simplicity of the modeled behavior.
- reinforcing the modeled behavior.
- reinforcing acts of imitation.

You now know the importance of a resemblance between models and observers, but points of similarity are not always apparent. What you might do in such cases to enhance success is to *highlight the resemblance between the model and the observer* (Bandura, 1968; Byrne, 1969; Byrne & Griffitt, 1969; McCullagh, 1987). You could indicate shared enjoyment of activities, common heritage, or prior experiences. Have you noticed how commercial advertisements often select models resembling the intended consumers and try to communicate this resemblance? "Mrs. Blue, a cat lover like you uses Farfel Cat Food."

Encourage rehearsal of imitative behavior. Imitation will not necessarily occur spontaneously. Despite modeling to facilitate sharing, Rogers-Warren, Warren, and Baer (1977) found that preschool children did not share. Similarly, Barton (1981) found that the children needed to be shown and told how to share and then requested to rehearse or practice the skills in order to accomplish the goal. Once the children began to increase their rates of sharing, prompting and praising sharing in the natural group setting accomplished even more. Also, Blew, Schwartz, and Luce (1985) found that involving normal peers in a program of modeling functional skills for autistic children was not successful until the models tutored and helped (modeled and instructed) the autistic children to practice the functional skills in the community.

Verbal instructions and rules also may augment the effectiveness of modeling. For example, novel and relatively stable abstract performances, like the Piagetian concept of "conservation" can be taught. Modeling may be combined with verbal instructions and rules to guide the model's behavior (Zimmerman & Rosenthal, 1974).

When you provide a *rationale* or explain why a particular action of the model's is appropriate in the presence of the observer, not only imitation but also generalization and retention may increase (Braukmann, Maloney, Fixsen, Phillips, & Wolf, 1974; Poche et al.,

1981; Zimmerman & Rosenthal, 1974). We have been applying this rule throughout the book. For example, we just provided a series of rationales for following specific methods to promote imitation (e.g., why you should use multiple models). We hope you are reciting to yourself a rule like "I will maximize my reinforcers and minimize my aversives, if I imitate the exemplary performance of those I've been reading about."

Ensure simplicity of the modeled behavior. Sometimes a modeled behavior is too complex for the observer to imitate. Try to imitate operating a complicated instrument; or watch a star ballet dancer or athletic performer and attempt to duplicate his or her actions. You will see what we mean. According to Bandura (1965a), an imitative behavior is likely to be acquired more rapidly if it includes some components that the individual previously has learned and if the complexity of the stimulus is neither too great nor presented too rapidly. When a behavior is too complex for the imitator to mimic successfully, however, it must be broken down into its components. Then it needs to be explained, modeled, and role-played.

Suppose Ms. Charming is orienting Fern to her new work assignment. She selects a worker who she thinks will provide an appropriate model to demonstrate the job skill for Fern. This procedure will work well if Fern has had prior experience with similar tasks. But suppose this is her first workshop experience. The complex behavioral sequence may be too much for her. Simply requesting the behavior and providing a good model probably will be insufficient. Fern may first have to practice imitating each component behavior separately before attempting the complete task. As each part is imitated competently, it can be joined with the next until the full pattern is smoothly executed. (See Chapter 20 for guidelines in breaking down complex behavior for more effective instruction.)

Think what you would do as a counselor trying to teach a student how to refuse, firmly but politely, an offer of drugs. If directly modeling a fully competent response failed to evoke the desired reaction, you might break the response down into its parts: effective use of eye contact, gestures, tone of voice, verbal statements, and so on. Video recording equipment can be especially helpful here, permitting replay as often as necessary, possibly in slow motion.

Reinforce the model's behavior. Reinforcing the modeled performance has been found to increase imitation (Bandura & Kupers, 1964; Bandura et al., 1963a; 1963b). As we have mentioned previously, this technique offers one way to promote model "prestige." For example, children who saw a model's choice of one particular picture from a pair reinforced were more likely to imitate that choice than if the choice had been punished or received neutral consequences (Levy, McClinton, Rabinowitz, & Wolkin, 1974). Similarly, high school juniors learned information-seeking behaviors like talking, reading, listening, writing, visiting, and observing by listening to the audiotapes of other high school juniors handling the process of deciding on their careers and receiving reinforcers from peers and a counselor (Stewart, 1969). This combination of modeling and reinforcement (i.e., vicarious reinforcement) has been shown to be effective in increasing the information-seeking behaviors of youth in other studies as well (Krumboltz & Thoresen, 1964; Lafleur & Johnson, 1972).

The following episode illustrates alternative ways in which imitative S^Ds may be used in the classroom. Dexter seems to understand how to solve algebraic equations, on one occasion correctly stating the series of steps to follow. Yet the next day he omits a crucial element. The teacher can handle such a situation either by modeling the appropriate behavior in order to prompt Dexter to give the correct response, or she can call on another child, Tim. Assuming that Tim gives the appropriate response, it can be reinforced, and Dexter then asked to solve the problem again. Hearing Tim praised for the correct answer, Dexter is more likely to be correct, thereby enabling his response to be reinforced. In the future Dexter will be more apt to solve equations correctly. Procedures like those can be used to increase all sorts of performances, such as doing a competent job, hanging up one's coat, paying attention, or even bringing berries (see Figure 17.2). Reinforcing the model's behavior is a good teaching strategy.

Reinforce acts of imitation. Reinforcing the particular act of imitating a model would seem obvious, particularly in light of the message throughout this book: If you want a behavior to increase, reinforce it! Yet, we have found that reinforcing imitation in general has proven difficult for many contingency managers. Having seen the client misbehave recently, for instance, the managers have a hard time presenting reinforcers for designated meritorious acts, like imitating desired behavior. However, if the imitative act is not reinforced, imitation will not continue. Barton (1981) found that

when children who shared well were praised, the others in the group did not necessarily copy them. Later on, though, when the nonsharing children in the group did share and were praised for doing so, their rates increased. A similar discovery was made by Ollendick, Dailey, and Shapiro (1983). While working on puzzles, some children were praised; others were not. For a while the "observing" children increased their performance just as the models did. But after a time, the number of puzzles correctly placed by the observers began to drop back. When observers received intermittent praise for puzzle placement, though, they performed as well as the models.

As always, you need to examine the environment to assess whether the natural context will provide sufficient reinforcement for the behavior. If it does not, you need to provide supportive contingencies. Observers have to obtain frequent reinforcement and feedback for practicing and/or role playing the modeled skill until a mastery criterion is achieved (Rickert et al., 1988), after which reinforcers can be gradually thinned.

Figure 17.2 Reinforcing the Model's Act to Promote Imitation

Reprinted with special permission of North American Syndicate, Inc.

Be careful, though, about what imitative acts you reinforce, because *saying* and *doing* are not the same. In one case (Rogers-Warren et al., 1977), preschoolers shared more only after reinforcement was limited to their *accurately* reporting that they had shared. You may be able to promote imitation by reinforcing verbal reports of imitation, but first you must be sure that what the reporter says *corresponds* to what the reporter does. In the absence of accurate information on correspondence between saying and doing, we suggest that you stick to reinforcing deeds rather than words.

When Telling or Showing Fails: Prompting with Physical Guidance

Generally, instructions, modeling, or a combination of the two can be used to prompt a response. Sometimes, however, none of these approaches suffices to evoke the desired response. "When you hit the ball, you must follow through," instructs the golf pro; then he demonstrates. Despite seeing experts perform many times and hearing and reading the instructions, the duffer fails to follow through appropriately. The pro then may provide **physical guidance** by actually performing the movements with the novice, who eventually gets the feel of the motion. Ultimately, the instructions no longer need to be supplemented by physical prompting.

Physical Guidance Defined and Illustrated

Physical guidance can be a particularly useful way to teach young, inexperienced, or developmentally delayed people new skills and to correct bad habits. Striefel and Wetherby (1973) taught a profoundly retarded nonverbal boy to follow instructions, such as "nod your head yes (or no)," "drink from the glass," and others, by using a "putting through" or physical-guidance procedure. Guidance was paired initially with the verbal instructions, in a series of steps, eventually terminating in the appropriate responses independent of any physical guidance. Physical guidance also has been used to help severely handicapped youngsters learn to communicate by signing (Barrera & Sulzer-Azaroff, 1983; Clarke et al., 1986). Parents use similar methods to teach youngsters to dress, as in helping them to put a sweater over their heads. Conscientious teachers correct mistakes, such as inappropriate pencil holding, by guiding the correct grasp, and the sailing instructor guides the novice sailor's steering, before gradually lessening his assistance, while imitative and instructional prompts begin to gain stimulus control.

Using Physical Guidance Effectively

When using physical guidance to prompt a response, you need to follow several guidelines: First, arrange conditions so the learner will be likely to attend to the appropriate proprioceptive cues—the bodily sensations the person has while engaging in the response. Second, gradually transfer stimulus control from the physical prompt to another discriminative stimulus to permit the child to eventually follow instructions, the driver to respond to road conditions, and the writer to see and feel how to position the pencil properly.

Securing the client's cooperation and guiding minimally. Relaxed learners can focus on the way their performance looks and feels while being guided through a motion, so they need to be comfortable with the contingency manager's touch. Tension or resistance will cause them to miss those essential cues. Resist the temptation to use force, because that could incite the individual to become increasingly agitated, evoking interfering reactions like struggling to escape, fighting, or crying. Besides being an establishing operation for competing emotional behaviors, using undue pressure is ethically questionable; excessive force is dangerous! This general admonition is especially important for physical guidance, because the ultimate objective is for individuals eventually to respond independently, after trainers have gradually diminished their assistance.

The contingency manager needs to speak calmly and the setting should be pleasant and comfortable. Providing a few reinforcers non-contingently at the beginning of a training session and/or interspersing easier tasks throughout the session can be helpful. Typical mature learners should adapt rapidly, permitting training to progress with ease.

Tips for physical guidance of special-needs clients. Proceed cautiously with people with special needs when they are resisting or appear anxious or fearful. Use the following techniques:

- Wait patiently for them to calm down before you take each new step.
- Maintain physical contact and move passively with the client if necessary until the struggling ceases and you are able to guide the movements gently.
- Keep the amount of pressure exerted to the minimum required to guide the movement properly.
- Consider providing preliminary relaxation training. It may help especially anxious clients (see Cautela & Groden, 1978, for a relaxation training manual for adults and children, and children with special needs; also Paul, 1966; Bernstein & Borkovec, 1973; and other sources on relaxation therapy).

Choosing Among Different Antecedent Prompting Strategies

We have implied that given the choice, your best option is to adhere to the sequence of least intrusiveness in selecting your prompting strat-egy. Yet that depends on your ultimate purpose. Do you want your students to learn from the actual contingencies in place, or would you prefer that they imitate the model's behavior? In one instance, Bondy (1982) compared the effects of explicit training—physical prompts and praise versus modeling. In that context, when new patterns were modeled, those in the physical prompt and praise group adhered much more closely to their previously trained patterns of responding, whereas the modeling group shifted to the new pattern. So if you want a response pattern to endure in the face of novel modeling conditions, you might be well advised to use explicit training; otherwise, begin with modeling.

How about modeling versus vocal prompts? Again, that depends on the situation and the purpose. One approach is to take each of your optimally developed methods and compare them systematically by using a design of the kind you will read about in Chapter 22. Espin and Deno (1989) did this with two approaches to teaching children to read sets of words. One set was presented by using initial phonetic prompts in sequence (e.g., "dr-dri-"), waiting 3 seconds after each prompt, and moving on to the next word if the child failed to read it; the other by modeling the complete word (e.g., "drink") if necessary, and requiring that it be repeated before moving on. In this case, most of the students learned and retained the words better when the complete word was modeled.

Summary

Several specific prompting procedures were presented in this chapter: goal-setting and the tell, show, and guide procedures. Before you select one, be sure a prompt is necessary. Then decide which to use. Begin by presenting the S+ just before the response. If the response is not evoked, use goal-setting, instructions, modeling, or physical guidance, whichever is most relevant and least contrived or intrusive.

If prompting is not effective, perhaps the person must first be trained to follow instructions, to imitate, or to move under guidance; or, as with imitation, perhaps you need a more appropriate model to perform and receive reinforcement for the behavior. Whichever procedure you select, always consider the factors that influence its effectiveness. Once the response does occur reliably, then you can begin to transfer or fade control from one of the auxiliary, or artificial, S^Ds—the guidance, show, or tell prompts—to the appropriate S^D, as we shall describe next. Heavy reinforcement of the critical S^+ plus response combination should continue until the behavior is established firmly. Afterward, deliver reinforcers less and less frequently, but always contingent on the specific S^+ and response combination.

Chapter 18

Transferring Stimulus Control

GOALS

After completing this chapter, you should be able to:

1. Define, recognize, and give original illustrations of each of the following terms:
   a. Delayed prompting
   b. Moment of transfer
   c. Graduated prompting or increasing assistance
   d. Fading
   e. Graduated guidance
   f. Errorless learning
   g. Stimulus equalization
   h. Response delay

2. List the advantages and possible disadvantages of delayed prompting.

3. List and discuss factors that may influence the effectiveness of delayed prompting.

4. Compare the use of graduated prompting with maximum to minimum prompt reduction. Describe a context for each prompting style in which it might be the best procedure to use.

5. List and give illustrations of the major variables that facilitate fading.

6. Discuss and illustrate how fading can be used to help develop an S^- into an S^{Δ}.

7. Discuss the pros and cons of minimizing errors during response acquisition (learning).

8. Discuss and compare how fading, response delay, and delayed prompting can be used to minimize errors.

Helen takes her medication on time without being reminded and Tiny Tina uses a utensil, rather than digging in to her food with her hands. The workers at Top Quality no longer need to refer to their checklists to perform their jobs safely. Performance is under proper stimulus control, having shifted or *transferred* from the prompts over to the critical stimuli that are supposed to control them—the time of day, food on the plate, and a potentially risky task.

In everyday life, no formal planning is required to transfer control from artificial to natural antecedent stimuli. Nor is the individual necessarily aware that the transfer is taking place. One day Joe just will get the "feel" of how to swing his club, and his putt will sink into the cup. Tina pushes her Mom's hand away and insists on feeding herself. The workers recite the rules to themselves or just continue without any assistance to conduct their tasks safely.

Because unprompted performance usually is more efficient, society tends to reinforce independence from contrived supplementary cues. People described as being independent or having expertise require few prompts. While performing a difficult operation, the expert surgeon no longer needs to rely on directions or reminders. Neither does the master photographer, who invests considerable solitary time taking, developing, and printing excellent photographs. Only when supplemental prompts are completely eliminated and just the natural discriminative stimulus sets the occasion for a response can a person be said to be functioning independently (Schoen, 1986).

Beyond efficiency and independence, unnecessary prompting, as previously mentioned, can be punishing. How do you feel when your parent reminds you to button your coat, wear your overshoes, or call home; or when someone provides you with detailed directions for carrying out a task you feel you have mastered?

As Krumboltz and Krumboltz have noted:

. . .[M]ost people do not like to depend on others to give them cues. They want to be independent and will readily interpret someone else's deliberate cue as an effort to control. Adolescents, in their strenuous effort to achieve an independent identity, are particularly sensitive to cues which they may perceive as a challenge to their own good judgment (1972, p. 76).

Sadly, though, we dare not presume that transfer always will occur spontaneously. Just "training and hoping" for unprogrammed generalization (Stokes & Baer, 1977) often fails. Frequently, control never does shift away from a reliance on prompts. Although an adult, Mel still counts on his fingers. The only time Dexter opens a book is when his teacher instructs him to. Unless Joyce's husband signals her to calm down during the community board meeting, she becomes obnoxiously boisterous. Pearl can label a picture of an apple but not the actual fruit, and Leroy only stops hitting his head briefly when told to stop.

Whether due to a change agent's failure to avoid fostering overdependence on prompts, or because circumstances failed to support transfer of stimulus control to natural cues, the dependency exists. Dependence like this impairs performance, and something must be done. This chapter addresses ways to prevent or remedy such difficulties by applying instructional strategies to evoke a given behavior when and where needed, in the absence of artificial external support. First we will define, illustrate, and discuss *delayed prompting*, a method for removing prompts altogether by interposing time delays. Next we present *graduated prompting*, a technique that usually involves shifting from one class of prompts to another, as in moving from instructions to demonstrations. Finally, we describe *fading*, a procedure for shifting control, often within a given prompt category, such as from one visual or tactile stimulus to another.

Delayed Prompting

Delayed Prompting Defined and Illustrated

Delayed prompting accomplishes the transfer of control from the prompt—the controlling S^D—to the S^+, the stimulus designated to evoke the behavior. This is accomplished by interposing a period of time between that stimulus, the S^+, and the prompt, which ultimately permits the prompt to be discarded altogether. Various researchers have labeled the procedure by different names: *time-delayed prompting* and *progressive delay* (e.g., Bradley-Johnson, Sunderman, & Johnson, 1983; Touchette, 1971; Touchette & Howard, 1984), as well as *time delay* (e.g., Browder, Morris, & Snell, 1981; Halle, Marshall, & Spradlin, 1979; McDonnell & Ferguson, 1989). We have elected to use the simple, specific term, *delayed prompting*.

In delayed prompting, the particular prompt remains constant, but a time period—constant or graduated—is introduced to separate the natural S^+ from the prompt. When **graduated (or progressive)** delayed prompting is used, first the S^+, such as a request, is presented. This is followed by the prompt that is as minimally obtrusive as possible yet that reliably occasions the response: a demonstration, gesture, a verbal cue, a correct answer to a problem, or gentle guidance. After it is evident that the individual is responding correctly (e.g., after two consecutive correct trials), the S^+ is presented and a brief delay interposed before the artificial S^D—the prompt—is presented again. The prompt continues to be delayed, a bit longer following several correct trials in a row, or a shorter delay after incorrect responses. Eventually, the person begins to respond *before* the prompt. The point at which this happens is called the *moment of transfer*.

According to Handen and Zane (1987), who reviewed 26 studies of the procedure, delayed prompting has been used successfully to teach people aged from 3 to 60: subjects of normal intelligence and those with developmental or sensory disabilities. Tasks have included:

- discriminating easily confused letters and numbers (Bradley-Johnson et al., 1983).
- purchasing objects (McDonnell, 1987).
- distinguishing different orientations of the letter *E* (Touchette, 1971).
- distinguishing difficult numerals, letters, and words (Touchette & Howard, 1984).
- following simple motor instructions (Striefel, Bryan, & Aikins, 1974).
- using sign language (Browder et al., 1981).
- performing practical assembly tasks (Walls, Haught, & Dowler, 1982).
- making beds (Snell, 1982).

After a peer modeling procedure had proven unsuccessful, Charlop and Walsh (1986) used a graduated delayed prompting strategy to teach four autistic boys to verbalize affection spontaneously while being hugged; to say things like "I like you" or "I love you." Prompted or not, whenever the child said those words of affection, he was praised and given a preferred food. After the child correctly imitated the phrases twice in a row, a 2-second delay was added between the S^+, the hug, and the modeled phrases. Eventually, after further training by peers and parents in the home, modeling and reinforcing the words became unnecessary. As a result of the treatment, parents and siblings reported that the autistic children were more socially responsive, loved them more, and that they themselves had begun to spend more time interacting with the children. Figure 18.1 illustrates the delayed prompting process.

Striefel et al. (1974) have demonstrated the transfer of stimulus control from guidance to verbal stimuli. First, clients were physically guided to imitate a series of movements, such as "Raise your hand," "Nod your head 'no,'" "Eat with a spoon," and so on. During the

Figure 18.1 Using Graduated Delayed Prompting

	Designated Natural Stimulus		Effective Prompt	Wanted Behavior	Reinforcement

INCREASING TIME DELAY

S^+ ———————————————$\rightarrow S^D$ ————$\rightarrow$ B ————————$\rightarrow$ S^r

Hug   "I Like You"   "I Like You"   Food and
                                                            Modeled   Imitated   Praise

Eventually,

S^D ———————————————————$\rightarrow$ B

Hug   "I Like You"

transfer phase, a verbal instruction was presented immediately before a behavior was modeled. Correct responses were reinforced, but on subsequent trials the delay between the verbal instruction and the modeled behavior was extended. Eventually, the client "anticipated" the modeled behavior, responding before the response was modeled. The fact that the delay was introduced gradually and that the method provided maximum opportunities for reinforcement surely facilitated the transfer.

Teachers learned to use a fixed time delay of 5 seconds before offering to help their retarded, language-delayed students (Halle, Baer, & Spradlin, 1981). If the child did not initiate during the delay, after modeling the appropriate response, the teacher waited for imitation before fulfilling the child's request. Halle et al. (1981) found this procedure "quick to teach and simple to implement" (p. 389). The delays also increased the students' verbal initiations by helping "those who live and work with them to provide appropriate demands, expectations and opportunities for effective language performance" (p. 406).

Advantages of Delayed Prompting

Delayed prompting increases the learners' opportunity to respond independently, perhaps because the best way to obtain the reinforcer

in a hurry is to skip waiting for the prompt, or maybe because the delay permits the learners extra time to respond. Carefully programmed, the method also can enable discrimination learning with few or essentially no errors (Touchette & Howard, 1984). The same authors have suggested other advantages:

- The subject is less likely to attend to an irrelevant prompt.
- Training stimuli do not need to be modified, as necessitated with fading (discussed later).
- The trainer will know the exact moment of transfer—the moment when the S^+ takes over control—thereby avoiding unnecessary training trials.

Disadvantages of Delayed Prompting

Striefel and Owens (1980) have noted that delayed prompting requires that the response already be in the person's repertoire; otherwise, it first must be taught. Additionally, they note, some students may never emit the response unassisted, regardless of how long a delay is interposed, or in acting before the prompt is presented, many respond incorrectly.

Using Delayed Prompting Effectively

No single variation appears best for everyone, for as Handen and Zane (1987) have commented, ". . . variables that proved to be advantageous within one category of comparison were often found to be a hindrance in another" (p. 321). Whether the time delay should be lengthened gradually or remain constant awaits further research. Both methods have proved successful, to date. Our guess is that people who have had long histories of failure and dependence on others would profit most from a progressive increase in the delay, beginning with a very short interval of a second or less. Nevertheless, many have learned well with fixed delays ranging from 4 to 15 seconds. To decide on the specific arrangements you want to use, consider clients' repertoires of skills and their ability to respond independently, to wait patiently when necessary, and to experience failure. Then examine the task closely to see how it matches those characteristics.

Suppose, however, the learner gives an incorrect response during the time delay procedure. What might you do? Several methods have been used: prompting the correct response, removing your attention, as in turning away briefly, or in a matching (pointing) task—removing the client's hand from the stimulus and presenting the next trial, modeling the response, and repeating or terminating the trial (Handen & Zane, 1987). Again, the method you select will depend on the client.

Several experimenters have used "random sequence" trials following each training session as a check on acquisition and as a device for providing additional practice (Handen & Zane, 1987). Naturally, these test probes and refresher trials only are conducted with responses that have met some criterion for acquisition already, such as responding correctly in advance of the prompt 5 times in a row.

Delayed prompting lends itself nicely to inclusion within more complex teaching programs. Several developmentally delayed women were taught daily living skills, such as turning on a faucet, tooth brushing, bed making, and hand washing, through a prompt sequence that included successively: verbal instructions, dem-

onstrations, and physical guidance. A delay of approximately 5 seconds was interposed prior to delivering each prompt (Fleming & Sulzer-Azaroff, 1989).

Delayed prompting, then, can be an effective strategy for teaching independence from supplementary prompts. For if people are capable of performing the instructed behavior, the delay seems to set the occasion for the performance (Halle et al., 1981). Should the method fail to evoke the desired response, you can always attempt to teach it, perhaps by substituting a different and progressively more natural series of prompting categories, as in moving from guided to modeled prompts.

Graduated Prompting

Graduated prompting (Correa, Poulson, & Salzberg, 1984), or **increasing assistance** (Gaul, Nietupski, & Certo, 1985; Schoen, 1986), is a method that begins with the natural classes of S⁺ and progresses from the *least-to-most* intrusive sequence, such as from verbal to gestural to guided prompt categories. The rationale for following this sequence is similar to that of delayed prompting, in that it offers the learner the opportunity to respond in advance of more intrusive prompts.

To visualize the procedure in action, consider how four profoundly retarded youths were taught to make toast and popcorn and to operate a washing machine and dryer (Steege, Wacker, & McMahon, 1987). First, a naturally occurring prompt ("Let's make popcorn") was presented. Assuming the appropriate sequence of responses failed to follow, the instructor applied increasingly more restrictive prompts in sequence until success was achieved:

1. A nonspecific verbal prompt (e.g., "Gather the things you need").
2. A specific verbal prompt ("Open the package").
3. A gesture plus a verbal prompt ("Open

the package," while the demonstrator opened a package).

4. A verbal prompt plus a partial physical prompt (assisting the student to open the package).

5. If need be, a total physical and verbal prompt (fully guiding and instructing the student's opening of the package).

Graduated prompting has been used to teach community living (Sanders & Parr, 1989; Steege et al., 1987) as well as a host of other skills. For example, Tucker and Berry (1980) used graduated prompting in association with a time delay of 5 seconds to teach severely multihandicapped youngsters to put on their hearing aids independently. The task was broken down into a sequence of 31 steps, from opening the container to setting the gain control. Following a request to put on his hearing aid, the student was allowed 5 seconds to complete each step independently. Correctly completed steps were praised, while incorrect steps were followed by verbal instructions. If the step then was performed correctly, praise was given; if not, a 5-second delay was interposed, and then the skill was demonstrated and verbal instruction provided. If that did not achieve the goal, instructions and physical guidance were used after another 5-second interval. Unnecessary prompts were dropped as no longer needed. The task was presumed to have been learned when performance was 100% correct for all steps without any prompting, for two consecutive sessions.

Correa et al. (1984) also used a similar graduated prompting procedure containing a 10-second delay interposed among increasingly intrusive prompts to teach young blind or severely or profoundly handicapped children to reach for and grasp toys that made a sound (the natural S^D), or to reach and grasp when instructed to for toys that made no sound. Again, the more intrusive prompts were dropped as soon as feasible.

Reinforcement plus graduated prompting were applied to increase two severely handicapped, partially deaf-blind young adult males' time on-task (playing a game) and their social interactions (Van Hasselt, Hersen, Egan, McKelvey, & Sisson, 1989). The 3-step procedure they used involved the following: When the client was off-task for 20 seconds, the trainer prompted him by pointing. If this was ineffective, the trainer tapped his arm. If that prompt didn't work, he used physical guidance. Reinforcement, in the form of tokens exchangeable for soda, was first provided for 10 to 20 consecutive seconds of remaining on-task. Later the requirement shifted to 25 to 30 seconds. Not only did the clients increase the time they spent on-task and interacting socially, but their hand flapping, mouthing, and rocking decreased.

Graduated prompting strategies consisting of three prompt levels—verbal, modeling, and guidance—also have been used to teach grocery-purchasing skills to adults within the moderate to severe range of developmental disability (Gaul et al., 1985), and tooth brushing, hand washing, and deodorant use to severely and profoundly handicapped youths (Freagon & Rotatori, 1982). In another case, a fourth prompt level, gesturing, was added to instruct a severely handicapped individual to take photographs (Giangreco, 1983).

In the study described earlier, Steege et al. (1987) compared the relative effectiveness of "least-to-most" graduated prompting to a *prescriptive variation* that was used as an assessment tool. The prescriptive variation involved the trainer sequentially initiating more restrictive levels of prompting until the functional S^D was found. Once that S^D was determined, however, rather than sequentially initiating the more restrictive levels each time the student did not respond to the naturally occurring prompt, the trainer provided a prompt within the category just below (less restrictive than) the functional one. So, if the student reliably responded to partial guidance, training trials began with a gesture plus a verbal prompt. If the student was unsuccessful at this level, the functional S^D (e.g., partial guidance) was provided. This variation was no more effective than the basic graduated prompting procedure in teaching the skill, but it did help speed up the process. The reason for the greater efficiency is probably due to the fact that ". . . the prescriptive method provided for a more precise selection of prompts, thus dispensing with unnecessary errors or failures to respond" (p. 299).

Presuming that students eventually begin to respond in advance of progressively less intrusive prompt levels, eventually natural or minimally intrusive circumstances should assume stimulus control. Suppose, however, a person remains overly dependent on a given prompt. How might responding be shifted over to the control of those stimuli that are supposed to evoke it? Fading may be the answer.

Fading

Fading Defined and Illustrated

Fading is the systematic, gradual removal of artificial or intrusive prompts to enable control to transfer to the antecedent stimuli that are supposed to evoke the response naturally. Fading begins initially by providing whatever prompts a person needs to succeed, but those prompts then are gradually removed (Becker et al., 1975; Hively, 1962) while the designated S$^+$ may gradually be introduced (Deitz & Malone, 1985; Rilling, 1977). Often the shift occurs *within* a prompt category, as in substituting one visual (or auditory or tactile) stimulus for another. At other times control transfers *across* one prompt category to another, as from physical guidance to instructions. Either way, *prompts are reduced by moving from maximal toward minimal assistance*, until stimulus control transfers to the more natural or appropriate S$^+$. To summarize, "In fading, a property of a stimulus is gradually changed on successive trials to transfer control of responding from one property of a stimulus to another" (Rilling, 1977, p. 466) or, we might add, from one stimulus—the prompt—to another—the S$^+$.

During fading, the response and reinforcement usually remain constant, while the S^{D}s that have temporarily served to cue these behaviors are slowly and progressively removed or substituted by stimuli resembling the S$^+$s more and more closely. Fading does not necessarily involve interposing a time delay between the prompt and the S$^+$ (although such a method also may be used to supplement the procedure). Rather, the prompt changes across sessions or trials. Fading does resemble the other procedures used to transfer stimulus control because *it is designed to evoke a given behavior reliably* in response to the S$^+$, independently of other supportive prompts.

You will notice that most of our cited examples of prompt reduction strategies involve developmentally delayed clients. Probably this is because others often learn despite less-than-optimal instructional methods, whereas the developmentally delayed may require precision of this kind. Does this mean that the method is applicable only to this group? Not at all. Coaches, job trainers, family therapists, self-managers, parents, counselors, supervisors, teachers, and others use methods like these that help their trainees to learn successfully and ultimately to perform the skills independently. Observe your own instructional and training activities carefully and you should be able to improve your methods by using techniques like these to reduce prompts.

Fading can be used with diverse classes of responding, including language, motor, social, and other skills. Suppose a teacher is instructing a student to translate the Spanish word *gato* into the English word *cat*. She could use numerous prompts to evoke the English translation: a picture of a cat, the sound "meow," a purring sound, the initial "ka" sound, and so on, to enable the student to give the right answer. But to obtain a fully independent response, she would have to fade those prompts, perhaps by saying them more softly or gradually removing aspects of the pictorial cue until all elements were gone.

As the instructor teaches motor skills, such as assembling equipment, he or she might describe each step as the trainees progress through the task. After performing the job successfully several times with the aid of the verbal guidance, the instructor can then gradually fade out the supplementary verbal prompts while acceptable performance continues. Parallels to these examples can also be found in physical education, language, and music training (Carlson & Mayer, 1971; Greer, 1980; 1981).

Abundant illustrations of fading have appeared in the literature. In one case, an enuresis control device was deactivated after a boy with a history of bed-wetting achieved 30 consecutive dry nights (Hansen, 1979). First one pad, then another pad, then the control device was gradually faded. Yet the boy remained continent.

Restraints or protective equipment that help prevent self-injurious behavior also can be faded to some degree. Several investigators (Pace et al., 1986) used pneumatic devices (air splints) for patients who engaged in head or face hitting "because the air pressure can be easily monitored and gradually decreased to allow full mobility" (p. 387). In one of their cases, tennis wristbands eventually could be substituted for the deflated air splints. This air-pressure fading combined with differential reinforcement for alternative behaviors allowed the boy complete mobility, and his appropriate behaviors increased and self-injury became very infrequent.

Fading often plays an important part in counseling and therapy. In the initial stages of role playing, the role often is clearly delineated and the setting carefully arranged. This specification is necessary because usually many of the role-playing responses are not within the client's repertoire. The prompts gradually are withdrawn, though, as the client's sophistication in role playing increases.

Similarly, in directing counseling interviews, counselors find that initially they must assume much more responsibility with elementary than with secondary school age children (Carlson & Mayer, 1971). We also have used verbally directed role playing, gradually fading the verbal instructions, to teach proctors in a course on personalized systems of instruction (PSI) to use appropriate prompting and correction procedures (Johnson & Sulzer-Azaroff, 1977). To teach Helen to take her medication on time, the nurse or her parents would fade out their verbal reminders, shifting control to the S^+, the clock.

Dan, Dave, and Roger, three developmentally disabled men with limited vocabularies and motor abilities, were taught several soccer skills, such as looking at the ball, turning, picking up the ball, pushing it with their feet, and so on, via a "maximum to minimum" prompt reduction method (Luyben et al., 1986). The authors reasoned that the method would maximize success and would be easy for the direct care staff to implement. Training began with instructions and a "strong physical prompt," plus praise and approval. After three consecutive correct responses the prompt level was advanced one step up the hierarchy—a mild physical prompt. This progression continued, through imitative, gestural, and verbal prompt levels. In the event that two consecutive errors were committed, the trainers gave a "descriptive correction" and dropped back one prompt level, until the three-in-a-row criterion again was reached. This technique helped avoid errors, and the successful results maintained and generalized across settings.

Using Fading Effectively

Supplementary prompts can be smoothly and effectively shifted over to natural stimuli, with minimal disruption. This end is best accomplished by removing prompts gradually and by progressing toward those more natural. Subtle skills are involved in transferring stimulus control from physically guided to self-guided motor behaviors, from demonstrations to instructions, and from irrelevant prompt to relevant S^+s. Some of those skills are described in the following sections, along with several methods for avoiding or minimizing errors.

Gradually removing prompts. Once the desired response has been occasioned reliably by prompts, those prompts should be removed gradually. Corey and Shamow (1972) used a fading procedure to teach reading to nursery school children aged 4 to 5.8 years. Words first were illustrated with pictures. Gradually, the pictures became progressively darker while the words remained at full strength. This method appeared to reduce early reading errors and to result in high retention of oral reading skills. Similarly, Haupt, Van Kirk, and Terraciano (1975) taught 9- and 10-year-old children number facts (addition, subtraction, and multiplication) by gradually covering the answer to a number fact with layers of cellophane or tracing paper. This fading procedure produced fewer errors and better retention than regular drill for those children who had had long histories of unsuccessful experience with typical number-fact drill procedures.

Earlier you saw how handicapped male adults were trained to execute a soccer pass by using the following maximum-to-minimum prompt reduction strategy (Luyben et al., 1986). After the pass had been performed three times at criterion, fading was then employed to eliminate the walker that had been used as a prompt. The walker was replaced by a quad cane, then a standard cane, and eventually that too was withdrawn. Prompts on the floor that had cued the foot positions for getting set and stepping forward were gradually repositioned, while the amount of tape visible was reduced and ultimately removed completely.

Inhibiting unwanted responses. Fading also can be used to transfer S^- into S-deltas in order to inhibit unwanted responses. The procedure begins by presenting antecedents that currently impede responding and progressing back to the natural S^-. A child's thumb should be an S^Δ for the response of placing it in his mouth. To prevent nocturnal thumbsucking, Van Houten and Rolider (1984) began by placing a boxing glove on a child's hand when he went to bed. Later this was faded progressively to absorbent cotton over the thumb, to a fingertip bandage over the thumb, to no prevention at all. They found that the fading procedure combined with daily feedback and other reinforcers for not sucking his thumb were crucial to the overall effectiveness of the program.

Preventing overdependence on physical prompts. *Physical prompts* also need to be faded as soon as possible to prevent overdependence on them. If Dad had insisted in hanging on to the wheel whenever he took his son out to practice driving, the boy might never have learned to drive independently. Physical prompts like those should be presented with demonstrations, instructions, or both. Then as mentioned earlier, the physical guidance can be removed gradually while the demonstration or instructions remain. Little by little, instructions alone should come to suffice.

Ultimately, instructions are also faded. The critical stimuli and the kinesthetic (how the clients' bodies feel to them) and visual cues should assume full control.

Graduated-guidance procedure. Sometimes simply reinforcing a few guided trials is sufficient, and individuals take over movements on their own. For others, the abrupt transfer from physical guidance to no physical guidance is too large a step, and a few intervening ones must be added. The **graduated-guidance** procedure (formally described by Foxx & Azrin, 1972) is particularly appropriate for those who are cooperative. Graduated guidance begins with as much assistance as necessary; the contingency manager uses the minimum amount of pressure essential to complete the motion.

Guidance is first focused on the body part that is the locus of action, for example, the hand in spoon feeding. Little by little, the pressure is reduced, and the locus of the guidance becomes more remote.

Here is an example: Joe Duffer fails to follow through with his swing. Instructions, modeling, and even some guidance have been insufficient to prompt the appropriate motions. The pro places his hand directly on Joe's hands and exerts enough pressure to promote the follow-through. As the pro begins to feel Joe responding appropriately, he gradually diminishes his pressure on Joe's hands. As Joe's movements gradually approximate the proper follow-through, the pro continues to reduce the pressure, moves the locus of the contact to Joe's wrists, then his lower arm, and elbow—and ultimately moves away from the arm altogether. Control has shifted over to Joe slowly enough so that errors have not been allowed to emerge.

Combined with verbal prompting, graduated guidance has been used to teach many complex responses, including:

- self-care and vocational skills to developmentally delayed women (Thomas et al., 1977).
- independent and social play skills to profoundly retarded adults (Singh & Millichamp, 1987).
- self-dressing to a variety of handicapped individuals (Azrin, Shaeffer, & Wesolowski, 1976; Sisson, Kilwein, & Van Hasselt, 1988; Young, West, Howard, & Whitney, 1986).

We advise against using graduated guidance with severely resistant or uncooperative clients. To do so may be ethically questionable, as well as counterproductive, a point to which we shall

return when discussing overcorrection in Chapters 27 and 28.

Modeled and instructional prompts. The basic system just described is analogous for *modeled and instructional prompts*. Unless the response occurs in advance of the prompt, you will need to fade that prompt. Demonstrations consist first of the fully modeled target behavior, diminishing into more subtle gestures and eventually vanishing altogether. Tiny Tina's mom prompts her to wave bye-bye by modeling the response herself. As Tina becomes progressively more adept at waving bye-bye, her mom will not fully model the behavior. Eventually, Tina will wave bye-bye when verbally prompted. Ultimately, the words "Bye-bye Tina," the stimulus that should naturally cue her response, will assume control.

One of the self-care skills taught in the study by Thomas and colleagues (1977) was folding clothing after it was removed from the dryer. First, the response was fully guided with an accompanying instructional narrative. Next, the guidance was faded, and demonstrations substituted. Demonstrations were then gradually faded; gestures, like pantomimes of holding the corners, were supplied when necessary. Eventually, the gestures became superfluous, and little by little, instructional prompts were also withdrawn. By the end of the training, the clients needed only to be presented with bundles of their clothes in order to fold them appropriately. Helen's mom could fade her reminder to take medication by pointing to the clock for a few days until the behavior was well established.

Fading for Errorless Learning

When the removal of prompts is so carefully engineered that errors fall essentially to zero, the system is called fading for **errorless learning.** An error or inappropriate response is one that fails to conform to the specifications of a behavioral objective. Suppose the objective is for the client to point to five specific body parts when so instructed, three times in a row. Failing to respond would constitute an error of omission. Pointing to his foot when instructed to point to his head would constitute an error of commission. Shaking his head, rather than pointing to it, would also constitute an error of omission. The primary problem with errors is that once they have occurred, they are much more likely to recur (McCandless, 1967; Terrace, 1963). Each time the client points to the wrong part, the probability that he will repeat the error increases. Throughout this chapter we have presented methods for minimizing errors. Prompts supporting correct responding are maintained for a sufficient period to prevent errors of commission.

Regardless of how carefully instruction is programmed, however, errors are bound to occur from time to time. Sometimes an inappropriate stimulus occasions the desired response; sometimes the appropriate stimulus occasions an inappropriate response. Behavior analysts should therefore be aware of procedures that will, first, assist them to avoid situations that promote errors and, second, reduce the probability that an error once committed will reoccur. If errors are apt to be committed because of irrelevant stimuli, or because the differences between S+s and S−s are very subtle, steps can be taken to avoid the likelihood that the wrong stimulus will occasion the response—primarily by being careful about the way the prompts are introduced.

Using Errorless Learning Techniques

Fading techniques lend themselves to strategies designed to promote errorless learning. Within instruction using matching-to-sample, stimuli may be systematically programmed to accomplish shifts of stimulus control from irrelevant to relevant stimuli in much the same way as we have described. Recall from Chapter 15 that an S+ is presented, and the task is for the student to respond by selecting a matching stimulus from among several alternatives. The situation can be arranged so that initial responding allows for matching to the controlling stimuli, such as those of larger size, and gradually shifting to the relevant stimuli.

Errorless learning illustrated. A program demonstrated by Ellen Reese and her students in the film *Skills Training for the Special Child* (1971) provides an elegant illustration of this application of matching-to-sample. Reese and Werden (1970) designed the program used in the film to teach number concepts to severely retarded children; size fading was used to help the children discriminate one numeral from another. In one part of the program, for example, each child was shown five sets of objects that differed in number and was asked to select the set that corresponded to a particular numeral (see Figure 18.2). Before the program, most of the children could recognize some numerals, and some of them could recite the words "one, two, three" in order. But they could not match or pair either numerals or names with actual numbers of objects, nor could they match two

Figure 18.2 Matching a Numeral with Corresponding Number of Items Assisted by Size Prompts

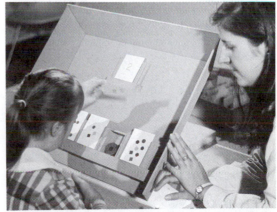

Source: Film *Skills Training for the Special Child*. Distributed by Ellen P. Reese.

sets of objects on the basis of number. If they were shown a set containing three objects, they could not select from five alternatives another set that contained three objects.

The first training program was therefore designed to teach matching sets of objects on the basis of number. Because the children had no difficulty discriminating difference in size, the objects in the sample set and in the correct alternative were very large, whereas the objects in all the incorrect alternatives were very small.

Initially, the children could select the correct set on the basis of size alone. As the program progressed, the size of the object in the incorrect alternatives was gradually increased. By the end of the program, all the objects were of uniform dimension, and the correct choice depended on number alone. (See Figures 18.2 and 18.3.)

In approximately 3.5 hours (spread over several weeks), all the children learned to match as many as four objects; then they were taught to match numbers of objects to numerals. This second fading program took even less time (approximately 2 hours) than the first. Training was transferred from these two matching tasks to seven other tasks, including two

that did not involve matching: counting a given number of objects when they were handed to the child and counting out a requested number of objects from a set of 30 and handing them over to the experimenter. Reese later reported that these gains were maintained a year later and that most of the children had acquired further skills with numbers. Most could tell time on the hour and some could exchange 5 pennies for a nickel (Reese et al., 1977).

An alternative to the size prompt would be to start with a different irrelevant stimulus property, such as color, pictorial cues, intensity, and texture. The relevant stimulus features would be introduced gradually, whereas the irrelevant one would be faded. Figure 18.4 illustrates this alternative. The sample card might then go through the sequence shown in Figure 18.5.

Alternatively, an audio stimulus could be superimposed, activated as the student presses the choice button, shown in Figure 18.6. In this instance, the volume of the audio cue would be gradually reduced once the response had been established (McDowell, 1968; McDowell, Nunn, & McCutcheon, 1969).

Focusing on critical stimuli. Special caution must be taken in promoting conditional discriminations via errorless methods, where ultimately the individual will need to respond one way in the presence of a stimulus and in a different way in the presence of an often subtly different stimulus. Examples are distinguishing and/or correctly labeling sensory stimuli such as letters, words, pictures, tastes, and sounds. Unless the prompt relates to the critical or relevant property of the stimulus during training, superimposing cues on the stimuli may impede transfer of control, as Koegel and Rincover (1976) and Schilmoeller and Etzel (1977) discovered. The irrelevant stimulus must not distract the individual's attention from the critical properties of the S⁺. Such a result could occur if the audio mechanism were operated in some manner other than the student pushing the

Figure 18.3 Size and Intensity Prompts

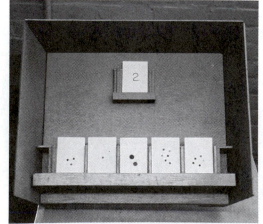

Source: Film *Skills Training for the Special Child*. Distributed by Ellen P. Reese.

Figure 18.4 Early and Middle Phases of Training Using Matching-to-Sample Errorless Teaching Methods

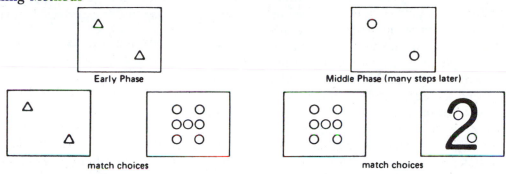

Figure 18.5 Late Phase of Training Using Matching-to-Sample Errorless Teaching Methods

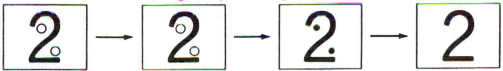

Figure 18.6 Superimposing an Auditory Prompt

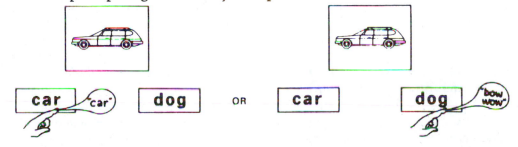

word panel. The student might attend to the manipulandum (mechanism) or to the speaker, rather than to the critical feature, the word. Then the rate of responding in the presence of the S⁺ would decrease rapidly when the irrelevant stimulus was no longer present (Anderson, 1967; Terrace, 1966).

In a clever demonstration of how an analyst can sustain focus on the critical stimuli during a conditional discrimination training procedure, Schilmoeller, Schilmoeller, Etzel, and LeBlanc (1979) used prompts based on topographical features of the stimuli to teach typical four- and five-year-old children to match geometric forms correctly. For instance, the children learned that a triangle with lines behind it represented the S⁻, by first seeing those features embedded in a picture of a witch. The children learned the discriminations far more effectively that way than by trial and error, or when the S⁻ form was faded in by increasing the darkness of the lines with which it was printed. That probably was because when boldness of lines was used, the children continued "to attend to the light-dark differences between the S⁺ and S⁻ stimuli rather than to shift their attention to the critical form-background dimensions" (p. 418).

Removing irrelevant stimuli. Irrelevant stimuli can prevent desired responses from occurring. For example, Dixon (1981) found that severely handicapped, nonverbal adolescents were unable to match a photo with its object until the figures in the photos were cut out. Removing the rectangular shape and background of the photo allowed the edge of the photo and the shape to be the same.

Similarly, Hoko and LeBlanc (1988) used a procedure they called **stimulus equalization** to eliminate differences in the irrelevant dimensions of stimuli. To facilitate discrimination, they temporarily reduced the complexity of a stimulus by eliminating irrelevant dimensions so that only the critical dimensions were left. To understand this concept, consider the case of a student having difficulty picking out the turtles with pointed heads (snapping turtles) from a varied array of harmless mud turtles. First, make all the figures the same size and color with the same size feet, and so on, so that they differ only in the slope of their heads. Once you have developed correct responding, gradually reinstate the differences. Correct responding probably will continue while the differences in size, color, and shape of the mud turtles are reintroduced.

The reinforcer you select also can serve as an irrelevant cue if you use only one reinforcer to teach one form of conditional discrimination and another to teach a different form. Should the reinforcer shift under natural circumstances, the match may be disrupted, as Dube, McIlvane, Maguire, Mackay, and Stoddard (1989) discovered. Therefore, unless the reinforcer has a natural tie to the stimulus, such as its picture, name, and so on, you had best vary the reinforcers when you teach these sorts of discriminations.

The duration of the delay between the presentation of the sample stimulus and the choice stimuli—those from which the participant is to select the correct match—may be increased as a fading tactic. You need to be careful and proceed slowly, though; as Sidman (1969) found with his neurological patient-subjects, the longer the delay, the less correct the match.

Initially introducing S⁻s very different from S⁺s. I was quite familiar with the word *hyperbola*, having become initially acquainted with the term in a geometry class. One day a friend used the word *hyperbole*, and I corrected his use and pronunciation of the term. He told me that I should look up the term in the dictionary, which I did. Sure enough, there was *hyperbole*. I had committed an error. With all your knowledge of stimulus control, you will recognize this example as one of incomplete stimulus control. My response was under the control of only the first eight of nine letters. Had I never seen or heard the word *hyperbola* I might never have acquired the discrimination between the two. *Hyperbole* was bound to come along, however. When a functionally different stimulus with a very close resemblance to the S⁺ is likely to make its appearance in the natural environment, you can minimize errors by preparing the person not to emit the particular response in the presence of the inappropriate antecedent stimulus. One way to do this is to highlight the differences initially, as you progressively diminish those exaggerated differences, as Schilmoeller et al. (1979) did.

The major advantage of initially presenting S⁻s that are quite different from the S⁺ is that the learner is much more likely to be correct. Consequently, the ratio of reinforced responses to nonreinforced responses is going to be much greater. Although later it will be possible to introduce S⁻s that are more and more similar to the S⁺, during initial instruction, this sort of procedure minimizes the negative side effects that frequently accompany extinction.

Initially introducing S⁻s briefly and at weak intensity. Again we must thank the laboratory investigator for discovering methods of improving correctness in making *simple* discriminations (two or more stimuli; one correct choice). A pigeon's responses, fortunately for our purposes, do not easily come under the control of verbal instructions, so other techniques have had to be devised to help it learn to discriminate. But then those methods can be easily adapted to teaching human beings who experience difficulty in making verbal discriminations. Terrace (1966) and his colleagues are among those investigators who have developed the method of initially presenting S−s only briefly and at weak intensities. By doing so, they have been able to teach their subjects to make some extremely fine visual discriminations. In one sequence with human subjects, their techniques were used to teach the discrimination of 2 from 7 by means of flash cards: In each instance the student was asked to select the 2. At first only one card with a 2 was presented. After several correct responses, a second card was paired briefly with the card showing the 2. On the second card, a 7 was very lightly introduced. Because the 2 card was presented for a longer period of time and was much more clearly visible, students were more apt to select it. As long as few or no errors occurred, the sequence continued, with 7 presented for longer and longer time periods and more and more clearly drawn until both numerals were of the same intensity and were presented for equal periods.

The technique described here may be used with a wide variety of stimuli: visual, audio, tactile, and others. It may also be used in combination with the technique of starting first with topographically different stimuli; for example, rather than introducing a 2 as the S+, a very dissimilar visual stimulus could have been used. Such "errorless learning" procedures have been successfully used with students who have failed to learn under more traditional trial-and-error procedures: persons with delayed development and those who appear to have perceptual handicaps (Sidman & Stoddard, 1967). The amount of effort involved in programming stimuli is more than compensated for when students with long histories of failure finally succeed.

Response delay. Another method of antecedent control you can use to reduce the likelihood that errors will occur is the **response delay** procedure. Very simply, this entails *preventing the student from responding too quickly* by requiring a preset time delay between the S+ and the response (Dyer, Christian, & Luce, 1982). The technique was used to teach receptive and expressive language to 3 residents of a facility for autistic children. In 2 of the cases, the child was to point to an object according to its proper pronoun reference or to its function. In the third case, the child was to follow a motor instruction, such as "Raise your right hand." The response delay aspect was managed by holding the child's hand for a 3-to-5-second interval before permitting the response. For these three children at least, the delay procedure appeared to evoke better performance than the no-delay condition. The authors suggested that because having their hands held seemed to have been aversive to the children, the delay might be introduced instead by removing the stimuli to be touched from the child's reach during the interval.

Several investigators (McMorrow, Foxx, Faw, & Bittle, 1987) combined a 2-second response delay following object identification questions (e.g., "What do you use to clean your teeth?" while pointing to a photo of the correct object [e.g., toothbrush]). The method was used to help handicapped echolalic patients, who were previously taught to label objects, to answer questions correctly in both trained and novel situations. After several correct responses, the picture was covered, but if necessary, still signaled, and the student asked, "What is this?" Eventually, the pointing and verbal cues also were no longer needed. This combined cue-pause-point procedure appears to hold considerable promise in helping children who echo what they hear in a nonfunctional way to begin to use language more appropriately.

In essence, the response delay procedure appears to inhibit impulsiveness by supplying an interval during which the student can overtly or covertly apply self-prompting strategies, such as verbal instructions or images. This is what we do when we stop and wait for a few moments to remind ourselves of the bidding in a hand of bridge or covertly rehearse the sequence of steps we should follow in preparing to taxi our plane down the runway or to execute a complex dance routine. (Some of our best friends call those behaviors "thinking"; many of our close colleagues would label them "cognitive processing.") At any rate, the procedure is worth applying when your students or trainees tend to commit errors by responding too rapidly.

Disadvantages of Errorless Learning

Although minimizing errors has obvious advantages, the question of whether or not consistent, error-free responding is desirable has yet to be resolved. Terrace has raised one issue, that a lack of frustration tolerance might ". . . result from a steady diet of errorless discrimination learning" (1966, p. 335). Krumboltz and Krumboltz (1972) echo that concern. We are not worried about that issue because we presume that no one can successfully avoid all mistakes completely. Despite the best of planning, failure is bound to occur sufficiently often to teach the person in even the most carefully programmed environment to persist in the face of failure.

Programming for errorless learning also requires a considerable time investment—one that might be nonessential. The student may be able to proceed with minimal errors despite an absence of fading or graduated or delayed prompting. In fact, the slow pace dictated by instruction for errorless learning may be aversively boring. The frequency of mistakes is one way to tell whether a curriculum has been programmed well enough. Before jumping to the conclusion that the errors mandate errorless programming, though, be sure they are not being committed due to inattentiveness caused by too simple or unchallenging a task.

Fading Versus Delayed Prompting

How do you decide whether to use a delayed prompting or a fading procedure? That depends on the features of each procedure. McDonnell and Ferguson (1989) taught four moderately handicapped adolescents to use an automatic teller machine and to cash checks through either fading or delayed prompting. The researchers found that both procedures taught the skills, but that fading taught them more rapidly than did delayed prompting. However, the researchers used a two-step delayed prompting procedure in which the delay period was increased from 0 seconds to 3 seconds.

Because others had found that time delays that were increased in 1-second intervals *across multiple training steps* were much more efficient than those augmenting by 3-second or 5-second intervals (Walls et al., 1982), McDonnell and Ferguson (1989) concluded that the lack of a *gradual* progressive delay may have resulted in their delayed prompting strategy being less efficient. Also, even though they used a simplified version of delayed prompting, the undergraduate student trainers found the strategy more difficult to implement than fading by gradually reducing prompts within each step of the task.

Maintaining Stimulus Control

The original objective of the various methods for developing and transferring stimulus control was eventually to enable behavior to come under the control of appropriate antecedents. Once it does, the control needs to be firmly established. At least occasionally the S+ response combination still needs to be reinforced to permit use of a stimulus change procedure alone. The optimal arrangement is to reduce the quantity of reinforcers gradually, to shift their quality to more natural ones, and to introduce a delay period gradually before delivery of the reinforcers. Chapters 30 through 32 discuss at length suggested guidelines for maintenance of behavioral change. Here suffice it to say that the reinforcer would need to be delivered less and less frequently until a point is reached at which the behavior is emitted reliably in the presence of the stimulus, with only an occasional presentation of the reinforcer.

By now the primary school child's correct labeling of 2 and 7 would be reinforced only occasionally and probably with weaker reinforcers like "Uh huh" and a nod. The youth counselor can arrange meetings with his client, during which he can give the young man feedback about the apparent control demonstrated earlier, rather than reinforcing (the control) immediately. The crucial point to remember in initiating such a change in quantity or density, immediacy, and quality of reinforcement is that if stimulus control appears to be disintegrating, the shift has been too abrupt. At that point, back up to a more optimal reinforcement strategy to reestablish the S⁺-response combination, then begin once again to thin out the reinforcers, but at a slower pace.

Summary

Several procedures can be used to transfer stimulus control from prompts to S⁺s. These include delayed prompting, graduated prompting, and fading. Delayed prompting interposes a time period—constant or graduated—between the S⁺ and prompt. Graduated prompting begins with the natural S⁺ and progresses to more intrusive prompts until the person exhibits the desired behavior. This latter method, though, does not prevent all possible errors, because sufficient prompts are not presented until less-restrictive prompts have failed. The maximum to minimum prompt reduction procedure does a better job of preventing the occurrence of errors, but risks overprompting, which can be aversive for the client. When possible, it is best to start with the currently functional prompt and gradually progress to the S⁺.

Fading is the gradual removal of a prompt combined with, when appropriate, the gradual introduction of the S⁺, as illustrated by the errorless learning method. Although often used in conjunction with other methods of transferring stimulus control, fading does not necessarily involve interposing a delay between the S⁺ and the prompt.

All these techniques for transferring stimulus control are designed to enable a behavior to occur independently of extra prompts. Apparently, though, no one strategy for transferring control to the natural S⁺ is ideal for everybody. So to achieve transfer of stimulus control, consider each person's repertoire of skills, ability to respond independently, to wait patiently, and to experience failure. Then, examine the task or procedure to see how closely it matches those characteristics.

Regardless of the approach taken to promote transfer of stimulus control, however, the S⁺-response relation needs to be strengthened and maintained, by at least occasional reinforcement. (See Chapters 30–32 for discussions of ways to maintain behavioral change.)

Prompting and fading are methods for bringing behavior under appropriate stimulus control. But to prompt a response, the behavior must already be incorporated within the person's repertoire. Otherwise, it will have to be taught. Shaping and chaining accomplish that purpose, so we turn to these two procedures next.

Chapter 19

Teaching New Behavior: Shaping

GOALS

After completing this chapter, you should be able to:

1. Define, recognize, and give original illustrations of each of the following terms:
   a. Shaping
   b. Successive approximations
   c. Programmed instruction
   d. A frame
   e. Personalized System of Instruction (PSI)
   f. Computer assisted instruction

2. Explain how the phenomenon of response induction or response generalization can facilitate your ability to conduct a shaping program.

3. List the advantages of teaching by means of programmed instruction and describe how it incorporates shaping.

4. Describe how PSI incorporates principles of effective shaping.

5. List and illustrate the major variables that facilitate shaping.

6. Give an example of combining (a) instructions, (b) imitative prompts, (c) physical guidance, and (d) fading with shaping.

7. Design a shaping program for a particular student, trainee, or client, and provide the details of its implementation.

Penny, a 4½-year-old with cerebral palsy, had been walking only since she was 3 and needed to learn numerous other motor skills: step walking, sliding, rolling, and so on (Hardiman, Goetz, Reuter, & LeBlanc, 1975). In contrast to our earlier examples, in which behavior was increased through simple or differential reinforcement, those contingencies were insufficient here. The behavior was not part of her repertoire. First she had to acquire the skills before they could be strengthened through reinforcement. In this chapter we focus upon **shaping**, a procedure that may be used for teaching new verbal, motor, social, personal, and other classes of behavior. Here and in the next chapter you will learn how shaping and chaining can be used to teach new skills, such as being neater or more punctual; supplying better service; giving and receiving compliments graciously; and other social, academic, vocational, motor, and self-care skills.

Shaping Defined and Illustrated

Shaping is used to guide the formation of a behavior that does not already exist in the individual's repertoire or that occurs so infrequently that little opportunity presents itself to reinforce the behavior. Simply reinforcing the behavior or prompting it is not feasible because it never, or rarely, has been emitted. Reinforcing an infant's language is impossible if the infant has never said something resembling a comprehensible word. No amount of instruction or prompting will occasion the complete response. Neither will a young child write numbers or letters if such a behavior or its components are not in his or her repertoire. Expecting Mr. Grump to accept a compliment graciously is unreasonable. He has never been noted doing that before. First, the behavior or its components must be emitted; then, and only then, can it be strengthened. Once a new or

very low-frequency behavior has been shaped, it can then be strengthened with reinforcement, using the methods already known to you.

The procedure for shaping new behavior begins with a response as it exists in the repertoire. Slight changes in form or rate of the behavior are reinforced until it gradually approaches the target. Elements, or subsets of behavior that increasingly *resemble* or *approximate* the desired behavior are differentially reinforced.

Leroy has never made a mark that approximates a straight line, but the teacher wants him to learn to write the number 1. On occasion, Leroy has drawn something that looked like a curvy line. If the teacher selectively reinforces the production of that kind of line, Leroy will write those lines more often. But something else probably will happen: Some of the lines will be curvy, but others will be a little straighter. Reinforced responses are not repeated identically; often their form varies slightly from one emission to the next, a phenomenon labeled response induction (Catania, 1984) or response generalization (Reynolds, 1968). So whenever Leroy makes a slightly straighter line, the teacher will then be in a position to reinforce selectively that subset of responses (drawing straighter lines) and can continue in this manner until Leroy consistently produces an acceptable line. At the same time, old responses or inappropriately directed changes (curvier lines) will not be reinforced. The process also could be applied to firmer lines, or those drawn at a given rate, and so on.

The series of slight changes, or subsets that are reinforced because they are increasingly more similar to the ultimate objective are called, technically, **successive approximations**. Shaping, then, is a procedure in which successive approximations to a behavioral goal are reinforced.

As another illustration of the shaping procedure, consider how Pearl could be taught to attend to the therapist when so requested. At first, any attending in the direction of the therapist, in response to the request "Look at me," would be accepted (reinforced). Once such orienting (body angle no more than 45 degrees away from the therapist) was well established (in more than 90 percent of trials over 3 days), the next step could be to make reinforcement contingent on closing the angle to no more than 25 degrees. After that, the criterion for acceptance gradually could be raised until Pearl consistently turned her body toward the therapist when asked to look at her. Then the focus could shift to Pearl's orienting her head so that she was apt to see the therapist's face, an essential requirement if Pearl were to learn functional language and many other skills. If approximations of orienting toward the therapist did not occur, they could be prompted or physically guided. Shaping has been used in this way to teach many youngsters deficient in attending to a teacher or therapist to acquire this essential prerequisite behavior.

Suppose you wanted to teach Mr. Grump to accept a compliment or Paula to be punctual in handing in her reports. Whenever Mr. Grump acknowledged a compliment, whether graciously or not, you would smile at him or pat him on the back (reinforcers you know to work with him). At the slightest hint of a smile or a more pleasant word from him, you would deliver the reinforcers. Eventually, you might work up to a point where you sincerely can comment "Gosh, George, your saying you appreciate my remarks really makes me feel good!" Similarly, although eventually Paula finishes her reports, she consistently completes and turns them in late. One day she hands in a report that although not on time is less late than before. That permits her supervisor, Angela, the opportunity to praise the improvement. Any time the reports are written and submitted even earlier, Angela praises Paula liberally. Little by little, Paula begins to be more timely in writing and submitting her reports.

Most textbooks, workbooks, teachers' guides, and training manuals are organized according to the assumption that in order to acquire new skills, one must gradually move from previously acquired toward more advanced instructional objectives. One set of responses is acceptable at one level, but a different set is required at more sophisticated levels—a strategy akin to shaping. A handwriting workbook, for instance, can be designed along such lines. At first, letters easily discriminated from others are presented. Then the student is guided through a series of steps in which more and more precision is required.[1] In this instance, reinforcement might take the form of teacher approval, or perhaps the gradually increasing similarity of the letters to the model or sample letters printed in the book, or both.

Shaping frequently is used in combination with other procedures to develop all sorts of objectives, such as:

- motor skills (Fitterling & Ayllon, 1983; Hardiman et al., 1975; O'Brien, Azrin, & Bugle, 1972).
- social behaviors like assertiveness (Bloomfield, 1973; Gross, Heimann, Shapiro, & Schultz, 1983).
- conversational skills (Minkin et al., 1976).
- sharing and smiling (Cooke & Apolloni, 1976).

Foxx has used a card game to teach social skills to emotionally disturbed adolescents (Foxx & McMorrow, 1985; Foxx, McMorrow, Hernandez, Kyle, & Bittle, 1987) and to mentally retarded adults (Foxx, McMorrow, Bittle, & Ness, 1986). Latchkey children have learned to respond appropriately to strangers, deal with emergency situations, and select nutritious snacks (Peterson, 1984), whereas blind adolescents have acquired multicomponent safety skills (Jones, Van Hasselt, & Sisson, 1984). Par-

---

[1] B. F. Skinner and S. A. Krakower (1968) designed a series of writing workbooks that rely on a shaping procedure.

ents and direct care staff also have learned to apply shaping plus other procedures to teach skills such as self-help (Heifetz, 1977) and pre-reading (Wedel & Fowler, 1984).

A study by Harris, Wolf, and Baer (1967) provides an excellent example. A little boy was observed to spend almost no time on the climbing frame while he was in the school playground. His teachers decided that climbing on the frame was the sort of vigorous activity that would further his physical development, and their attention was selected as the contingent reinforcer: "The teachers attended at first to the child's proximity to the frame. As he came closer, they progressed to attending only to his touching it, climbing up a little, and finally to extensive climbing. Technically, this was reinforcement of successive approximations to climbing behavior" (1967, p.154). By means of this procedure, the boy ultimately came to spend more than half of each recess on the climbing frame.

Shaping procedures also have been found to reduce social and personal problem behaviors effectively, as in the studies reported by Carr et al. (1980), who arranged to shape adaptive behaviors as substitutes for problematic ones. Similarly, college students who were rated high in performance anxiety successfully overcame their "stage fright" by proceeding through a series of graded tasks (Kirsch, Wolpin, & Knutson, 1975). These progressed from reading lists of unrelated words through reading another student's speech, writing an original speech, delivering the speech from notes, to delivering the speech from note cards.

A related procedure was used to reduce avoidance responses among snake-phobic students (Barlow, Agras, Leitenberg, & Wincze, 1970). In this study, closer approaches to the snake were socially reinforced. When a therapist modeled the successive approximations himself, the rate of approaching increased even more rapidly.

We have also heard of instances in which shaping procedures have been used to teach young people how to behave during job interviews, on dates, and while proctoring peers. Similarly, dining skills have been taught as well as many other functional personal and social behaviors. Seigel (1988) has outlined the steps a child should follow when threatened by a bully. When steps are specified clearly, as in cases like these, approximations are more apparent and easier to reinforce.

Shaping often is practiced by parents and society in general, without their awareness. Language development is a case in point. Although language is acquired by means of imitative, chained (complex combinations of simple responses), differentiated, and generalized responses, shaping is a critical aspect of the process. If, for instance, the person has not learned to imitate verbal samples adequately or has some well-practiced but inappropriate speech patterns, proper speech may have to be shaped.

An illustration is the early verbal learning of the infant. When the infant babbles, the parents reinforce any similarities between the baby's speech and acceptable words. At first, they reinforce production of sounds that are distant approximations to real words, like "ook" or "kuk" for *cookie*. Later, closer approximations are required for reinforcement. As the child grows older, other individuals also reinforce improved speech patterns and help to extinguish the poor ones. Nonfamily members are more likely to reinforce statements and requests that communicate successfully than poorly and inappropriately enunciated words.

Related to this concept is work done to improve the speech fluency of stutterers. In one case (Howie & Woods, 1982), shaping consisted of reinforcing fluent speech, beginning with a very slow pace and then reserving reinforcement for increasingly more rapid rates. As you might imagine, shaping requires considerable attentiveness and diligence. Fortunately though, the process can be made more manageable, because the successive approximations can be incorporated directly within group, textbook, and computerized instruction. Next, we describe those approaches.

Shaping with Groups

Shaping need not be restricted to individuals, because approximations accomplished by groups of people can be reinforced in the same way as with other group arrangements (refer back to Chapter 12). The students in Ms. Hydra Carbon's chemistry class at Deep Valley High have been lax about completing their assignments, so the school psychologist, Mr. Ernie, helps the teacher design a shaping program. A center has been organized where students can participate in popular group activities like photography, guitar, and dance workshops. To shape assignment completion, the baseline (average percentage of assignments completed by the whole group) is calculated for a few weeks: approximately 52%. Ms. Carbon and the class jointly set a goal for the following week: 60%. Because the class average reaches 62% that next week, on Friday the whole class is excused to attend the activity center during the regular chemistry period. Then, the requirement is raised little by little, every few weeks. Whenever weekly goals are met, the group contingencies are provided.

Group programs like these, adjusted for different performances and reinforcement contingencies, can be and have been implemented successfully in all sorts of organizations: schools, institutions, business and industrial organizations, summer camps, sports teams, volunteer groups, and just about anywhere groups of people function. We have used group goal-setting and shaping to improve occupational safety (Fellner & Sulzer-Azaroff, 1984) and numerous other performances. One example shows how the method can be applied in a setting in which participants each have *different* functions and objectives.

Improving the quality of services was the key objective of the Psychology Department of a residential school for the developmentally disabled. To accomplish this, individual members pinpointed performances they wanted to improve, such as the number of in-service training programs conducted, times they visited and provided feedback to staff in cottages, assessments completed, programs designed and implemented, reports written, and so on. Weekly, participants selected their own challenging and achievable individual goals for the next week, based on their prior performance, marking the goals on their graphs. To protect the identity of actual participants, Figure 19.1 displays fictitious data for one psychologist who wanted to complete an average of 7 assessments a week but who had only been doing 3 or 4.

For the first 2 weeks following baseline, she decided to work toward 5 and was successful. Encouraged by her achievement, the next week

Figure 19.1 Number of Assessments Conducted (fictitious data)

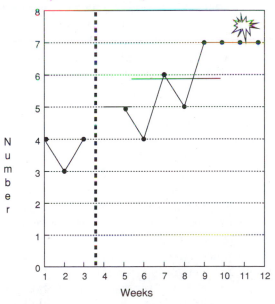

Horizontal line = goal

she selected 6, but only did 4. That prompted her to continue to set goals of 6 for the next 3 weeks. Not only did she achieve the 6 for 2 weeks but by the following week, the number had increased to 7. Sustaining this level for 3 weeks in a row permitted her and the supervisor to conclude that this psychologist's goal had been achieved, as indicated by the sun blaze on the graph. She then could initiate working on another pinpoint while continuing to chart and receive reinforcers for completing an optimal number of assessments. Another member who completed 3 in-service training sessions the previous week might set a goal of 4 for the following week, and so on for each participant.

Regardless of whether individual participants did or did not achieve their weekly (sub)goals, a composite percentage of goal attainment was calculated for the group by dividing the number of participants who reached their goals by the total number present and multiplying by 100. This figure was plotted on the graph, as in Figure 19.2. Based on that percentage, a new group goal was set for the following week. When weekly goals were reached, members cheered and their supervisor complimented the achievement. When the goal achievement reached 100%, a special event was scheduled, such as refreshments, a visit, or a letter of commendation from the superintendent. Although the data displayed here are fictitious, we have carried out an almost identical program (Pollack, Fleming, & Sulzer-Azaroff, 1990).

Systems like this probably would function well for patients in hospital wards, who are supposed to complete assigned exercises or other individual health routines. When all group members reach their weekly subgoals—the stepping stones toward the ultimate long-range goals—a group-reinforcing activity could be delivered. Surely you can think of other potential applications. Methods of this kind actually have succeeded with workers at com-

munity service facilities (e.g., Calpin et al., 1988), employees at retail establishments (e.g., Anderson, Crowell, Hantula, & Siroky, 1988), and in many other settings. (See the *Journal of Organizational Behavior Management* for numerous other examples.)

One caution: In assigning tasks to individuals, guide participants to select *achievable* interim goals. If some are given too difficult an assignment, all the others will be penalized. This situation can be avoided through the use of a collective contingency of the kind discussed in Chapter 12, and by keeping the size of the group relatively small. Should the group be too large, you can subdivide it into separate noncompeting teams, as we have done with large production units in factories.

The previous examples illustrated performances of a fairly complex nature. The same method of reinforcing successive approximations can be applied to behaviors of a much simpler variety, as with the very discrete concepts found in programmed instruction.

Shaping and Programmed Instruction

Programmed instruction epitomizes an educational application of the shaping procedure. Derived directly from behavioral methods developed in the laboratory, B. F. Skinner described this approach in detail in a paper published in 1958. In that paper, Skinner discussed using shaping to teach academic skills, emphasizing the importance of reinforcement, primarily confirmation of correct responses, as the student progresses in steps from one academic level to the next. Usually, an instructional program starts with questions that can be answered easily by the student and increases gradually in difficulty to ensure that each correct response is reinforced. The steps in an instructional program are arranged to maximize success via various prompting and fading strategies, and by gradually increasing degrees of difficulty. Because being correct can be a powerful reinforcer

Figure 19.2 Percentage of Weekly Goals Achieved (fictional data)

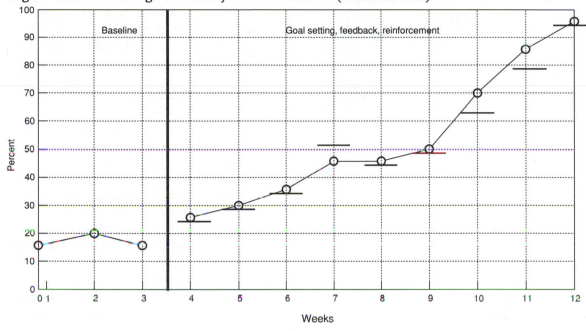

Horizontal line = goal

for many students, reinforcement continues to be attained at a fairly constant rate.

Instructional programs may assume many forms: books, tapes, strips of paper, computer programs, video disks, or microfilmed slides. Teaching segments generally consist of a series of finely graded steps, called **frames**. The content of the frames proceeds in graduated steps from the simple to the more complex. This gradual, cumulative progression helps the student to be correct and receive confirmation as often as possible.

The advantages of shaping concepts through programmed instruction are numerous:

- The material is organized and presented in a logical sequence.
- Frequent and active responding is required of the student, which, in turn, expedites learning.
- The student receives immediate feedback.
- Students can begin at their own levels, move at their own rates, and not be held up or forced ahead by classmates.

The approach to developing an effective program is empirical. Students work on an initial draft, and their performance on each frame is evaluated. If a student fails to learn, it is the fault of the program, not of the student. Items or frames may be revised, reorganized, expanded, or reduced until most students progress without error. If the programmer or teacher suspects that the problem is motivational, supplementary reinforcers may be added temporarily. In a classroom program conducted by Sulzer and her colleagues (1971), when points exchangeable for tangible and activity reinforcers were delivered contingent on correct answers in a Sullivan workbook (1965), performance improved markedly.

Shaping and the Personalized System of Instruction (PSI)

Flora approaches a young woman about her own age, Gwen, who is seated at a table working as a "Course Manager." "Hi, Gwen. I'm ready for the study questions for Chapter 19 on shaping." Gwen rummages through the files and locates a set of pages, entitled "Chapter 19. Shaping." It contains the reading assignment, and approximately 40 "study questions," each followed by sufficient empty space to accommodate a written response. "Thanks, Gwen. See you on Tuesday, when I plan to take the Chapter Mastery Quiz."

Flora returns to her room and reads the assigned pages through once. Then she takes the study questions and, rereading the material, writes her answer. After a few hours of reading, answering, checking, and studying, she feels that she has mastered the chapter. On Tuesday she goes to a separate study area near the quiz room to review her material briefly one more time.

Then, returning to Gwen, she announces, "I'm ready for the quiz on Chapter 19."

"Here you are, Chapter 19, form B."

Flora signs for the quiz form and proceeds to respond on a separate answer sheet. The quiz contains a series of questions, requiring short answers and/or brief essays based upon the study questions. All essential points of the chapter are probed, with some questions requiring integration of several concepts. When Flora completes the quiz to her satisfaction, she returns the quiz form and gives her answer sheet to a *proctor*. Her proctor, Virgil, a more advanced student, takes her answer sheet and checks it against his key. "Questions 1–7 and 9–12 are fine, but number 8 is unclear. Could you say more about why you think this illustrates the concept of 'reinforcing successive approximations'?" Flora responds, apparently to Virgil's satisfaction. He asks her to write down her clarification. "Fine. You've mastered this chapter." Virgil records Flora's "pass" on her folder, and Flora returns to Gwen for the next set of study questions.[2]

You have just read a description of a **personalized system of instruction (PSI)** course in operation. Notice how closely PSI resembles programmed instruction, in the sense that objectives are clearly defined, step sizes relatively small, correct responses prompted via study questions, and feedback and reinforcement delivered consistently and with minimal delay. Because PSI is directed toward a different population of students who are more advanced and mature, it permits the students to work more independently and progress in larger steps than they would with programmed instruction. In his classic article "Goodbye Teacher," Keller (1968) used a similar illustration to introduce the system. PSI has been used in thousands of classes and training groups at all levels to teach many subjects: basic and applied sciences, humanities, and many other disciplines. Research (Johnson & Ruskin, 1977) has shown that PSI helps students to learn and retain their material better than conventional instruction and has many other advantages. One key reason why PSI is so effective is because it incorporates the principles of effective shaping. Approximations consist of mastering the concepts included in short prose passages. Achievement is reinforced consistently and with minimal delay. After explaining more about using shaping effectively, we return to this topic to illustrate how well PSI incorporates principles of effective shaping.

Shaping and Computer Assisted Instruction

Today, the availability of inexpensive computers provides the opportunity for well-conceived programmed instruction to be disseminated

[2] In our PSI courses, we only permit clarifications for one answer, provided that would allow the student to achieve the mastery level of 90% or above, given with a satisfactory explanation. We have found that allowing multiple clarifications tends to encourage sloppy preparation.

broadly. In fact, **computer assisted** or **aided instruction** has evolved into a field of its own. Although not always done as a matter of course, it now is possible for computer programs to capitalize on our knowledge of effective instruction by designing them to permit, among others:

- a multitude of stimulus forms and response modalities
- student responses to be analyzed immediately.
- feedback and reinforcement to be provided as merited.
- branching into remedial or advanced instruction where appropriate.

Although most programmed or computerized instruction has been designed to diagnose and teach conceptual skills, such as math (Bitter, 1987; Bruno, 1987), reading (Wepner & Kramer, 1987), writing (Cullen, 1988; Troutner, 1988), foreign language (Garrett & Hart, 1988), and identifying or defining terms (Strang, 1988), new software capabilities allow other classes of skills to be taught. For instance, studying has been improved via the computer (Grabe, 1988), and programs have been developed to educate people with mild handicaps (Woodward, Carnine, & Collins, 1988). Graphic displays have been used to teach art (D'Angelo, 1988), engineering design (Hodgson, 1988), anatomy (Richards, 1987), new ways of solving mathematical problems (Demana & Waits, 1987), and methods of discriminating or reproducing visual forms, such as how to perform differential dental and medical diagnoses (Watt & Watt, 1987), draw a blueprint, operate a control panel, and discover a glitch in a system.

Because an instructional or training program is attractively or impressively packaged, however, does not necessarily guarantee that it will teach effectively. Instructional programs must be based on the rules for effective shaping

if they are to demonstrate their value. A well-developed program usually is accompanied by data on its utility for the students for whom it was developed. If the population of learners is adequately described, teachers or trainers should feel reasonably safe using the material among similar populations.

Educators need to be sensitive to both group and individual performance with any particular instructional program. If students commit too many errors or become bored and distracted, the program is not performing its intended function. Instead, it needs to be limited to that subpopulation of students for whom it operates effectively, and/or be revised further, or replaced. In fact, seldom is a program successful among all students in a group. Careful monitoring and supervision are necessary to identify the particular subpopulation for which the material is appropriate.

Using Shaping Effectively

Keeping Your Eye on the Goal

As with other behavior analysis procedures, the first step in shaping is to specify (or "pinpoint") the instructional objective clearly. Other requirements for using behavior analysis procedures, such as selecting and testing reliable and valid performance measures, also should be met (see Chapters 2–6). Additionally, you will want to identify criteria for any subgoals or approximations, including such dimensions as the number, topography, intensity, or other performance features for which reinforcers will be delivered along the way. Precise pinpointing reduces the likelihood of strengthening irrelevant responses and increases the probability that appropriate approximations will be reinforced.

Suppose that Violet almost never has responded to a question in an audible voice when adults were present. Were the terminal and subgoals vaguely stated (e.g., "decreasing Violet's elective mutism"), contingency managers might overlook and fail to reinforce some approximations to the desired behavior. Violet, for instance, may speak loudly and shout when playing with friends. In the absence of an objective such as "speaking without the listener needing to say 'What?' at least once a day for 5 days," any approximations such as her speaking audibly to peers may well be overlooked or possibly even punished. With the specific objective in mind, however, the adult is more likely to reinforce any audible vocalizations, no matter where emitted, as the first step toward the terminal goal.

Finding a Starting Point

Just as a ceramic vase must be shaped from a lump of clay, so must new behavior be shaped from existing behavior, through reinforcement of successive approximations. A starting point has to be found, even when the initial behavior bears little or no apparent resemblance to the final performance. For this reason, observing the person in the natural setting becomes very important. Through observation, behavior can be identified in which the client engages at a fairly frequent rate and that may bear at least some resemblance to the final objective.

Consider shaping completion of assigned arithmetic papers. Observation over a period of a few days indicates that Bobby usually attempts the first problem, and failing to devise a solution, gives up and either scribbles on or crumples his paper. But once, when a review sheet of simple problems was handed out, Bobby completed about half the assignment before crumpling up his paper.

Alternative starting points are suggested in this situation:

- The teacher can start with the regular arithmetic assignment and can shape from the partial completion of one problem.

- The teacher can start with problems similar to those found on the review sheet.
- The teacher could combine both.

This decision might be based on a number of factors: practical considerations, like access to prepared materials; the time available for preparation of new individualized assignments; or the similarity between the initial and the terminal behavior. If the review sheet contains simple multiplication problems and the terminal goal is the solution of 10 multiplication problems involving 2 decimal places, the terminal and starting behaviors bear a substantial resemblance to each other. Dropping back then to the simpler review items may be preferable. On the other hand, the review sheet may contain verbal problems that require simple computations and that bear little resemblance to the 2-place multiplication problems. Selecting the alternative task, which bears a closer resemblance to the goal, then would be more advisable.

The way to determine the starting point in this particular situation is to have Bobby engage in a set of graded tasks in arithmetic. When he reaches a point at which he begins to perform poorly and fails to complete a problem, he has undoubtedly passed the optimal starting point. Shaping should begin at the place where he had last achieved success.

Arithmetic is a subject that is generally taught in graded sequences of difficulty. Many behaviors, however, are not arranged in a logical order. Again, consider Violet, who fails to speak aloud in the presence of adults. We have already suggested one starting point: clearly audible speech in the presence of peers. But suppose that Violet has not been observed speaking aloud so that others can clearly hear her. Some other starting point must be identified.

Violet can be seated close to an adult who will reinforce any approximations to speech: facial expressions, gestures, sighs, grunts, whispered words, and other rudimentary behaviors resembling attempts to communicate. By reinforcing the entire range of such behaviors over many trials, their frequency should increase. For instance, if Violet's whispering could be heard fairly consistently, *it* would be selectively reinforced, whereas reinforcement would be withheld for gestures and other forms of nonverbal communication. A starting point for shaping audible speech would have been established.

Van Der Kooy and Webster (1975) taught an "electively mute" 6-year-old child who did not speak at all outside the home by starting with an avoidance response. After trying various positive approaches to helping him talk, they occasioned an early approximation by splashing him during swimming period. The splashing was terminated when the child said "No" or "Go away." Once this approximation to conversational speech was being uttered regularly and negatively reinforced, prompting and positively reinforcing other similar approximations were possible.

Selecting Step Size and Duration of Remaining on a Step

We already have discussed the stepwise progression of shaping and recognize that the responses that intervene between the starting point and the terminal goal are broken down into a set of steps, or successive approximations. Now we need to consider how *large* each step (approximation/subgoal) should be and how *long* a client needs to remain at each step before proceeding to the next. What should be done in the event that the client's behavior begins to disintegrate? Unfortunately, no hard and fast rules exist, so we extrapolate from what we know about training and instruction in general.

First, observe the individual's behavior closely. If progress is consistent and satisfactory, we can assume that the step size and duration of remaining at each step have been appropriately selected. If, on the other hand,

progress begins to level off, falter, or deteriorate, then the choices should be reexamined.

Let us refer again to Bobby, who was having trouble with arithmetic. Suppose his teacher has decided to increase by one the number of problems required for completion each day. On the first day, Bobby receives reinforcement for completing 1 problem. On the second, for 2. He finishes the first and starts the second; but because he fails to complete it, reinforcement is withheld. On the third day, Bobby fails even to tackle the first problem for that day. Quite possibly the teacher has set the requirements too high. A more successful sequence might be completing 1 problem within a given time limit each day for 5 days, then finishing one and starting a second each day for 5 days, then completing 2 problems on each of 5 days, and so on. (*Precision teaching*, such as McGreevy's [1983] English instructional program, incorporates this sort of *fluency building* within its methodology.)

The same sort of repeated trial and success procedure seems applicable to goal-setting programs with adults, for if goal levels are increased too rapidly, the failure to earn reinforcement will cause progress to deteriorate. The situation should be arranged so participants are able to succeed much more often than they fail. At some later time, the step size can be increased. Were Bobby consistently completing 5 problems a day correctly, the next requirement could be completion of 6 problems for only 3, rather than 5, days. This interval might continue until the terminal goal of 10 completed problems were reached. (Notice in Figure 19.2 how a goal level was dropped for week 8 following participants' prior failure on week 7 to achieve too ambitious a goal.)

Let us consider now the selection of step size and the number of trials at a particular level for Violet. The starting point has been selected: Violet's whispering in the proximity of an adult. Next, the sequence of steps to be followed is planned. First, Violet remains next to the adult until she whispers loudly enough to be clearly understood for 5 consecutive statements. Naturally she will receive reinforcers for each of these utterances. The adult may say, "Violet, you've made an interesting point" and repeat it to others, or she may agree, smile, allow Violet access to a favorite activity, or use any of the other reinforcers that have been determined to be effective for Violet.

Once the criteria for success in the first step have been met, the second can be taken: Violet's chair is moved back about a foot. The same criteria and procedures as in step 1 can be employed again. The process continues little by little until Violet is seated across the room from the adult. Again, her behavior must be carefully observed. If the new behavior progresses consistently, it can be safely assumed that appropriate criteria for practice and success at each level have been selected. To repeat, any disintegration of the behavior suggests the need for smaller steps and more repeated practice of mastered steps.

Sometimes the step sizes originally selected are too small or the learner is required to remain at one particular level for too long a time. Inattention and boredom can result. Put the issue to an empirical test. Increase the size of the steps to determine whether performance begins to improve. If it does, obviously the altered conditions should remain in effect.

The same situation may occur in the shaping of new behavior in large group settings. Because the group contains many members, steps often are selected to meet the requirements of the majority. Along with those who can't keep up with the pace, the few who are capable of acquiring the new behavior in larger units and with less practice may become inattentive or turn to nonassigned activities. As an alternative, either form subgroups of members with roughly equivalent repertoires or substitute different materials for those individuals, eliminate some of the steps or practice items, and either replace

them with more challenging assignments or permit peers to tutor one another.

Occasionally, just as progress seems to be moving smoothly, the student suddenly reaches a "plateau" and appears to be stalled. Maybe too much reinforced practice has occurred at that level, establishing the approximation too firmly at that spot. To reinstate progress, make the next approximation very easy and allow a few trials of several small steps. Suppose, for example, that Violet was given too many reinforced opportunities to whisper at one particular distance from the adult, firmly establishing whispering from that distance. An appropriate modification might be to move her a couple of inches back every few days, rather than a foot at a time. Under such circumstances, she might be forced to whisper more and more loudly and ultimately begin to combine more audible sounds with the whispers.

Combining Use of Discriminative Stimuli with Shaping

If the individual has not learned a complex behavior or its components, prompting that behavior with discriminative stimuli (S^Ds), like instructions or gestures, will not be possible. Such stimuli, however, may be used to help occasion *approximations* to that response. Returning to Violet, who failed to speak aloud, let us consider this procedure: Assuming that Violet has begun to whisper to the adult next to her, the teacher could use S^Ds to cue repetitions of that response. For instance, she could say, "Good; I like the point you made" (reinforcement) and then, "Would you please say it again?" (S^D). Other whispering responses could be occasioned by asking Violet other questions, nodding expectantly toward her, or gesturing. Prompts like those were used by Van Der Kooy and Webster (1975) to teach their "electively mute" client to speak.

Combining modeling with shaping. Recall that modeling involves presenting an S^D in the form of showing someone what to do. Modeling may occasion imitation, especially if the client's repertoire approximates the demonstrated behavior and if that person has received reinforcement previously for responses resembling those of the model. Just as other S^Ds tend to occasion approximations, modeling may prompt an approximation to a behavior that is too complex for direct imitation. Rather than simply waiting for the approximation of the desired behavior to happen, the change agent can demonstrate it to the client.

This procedure often is used by speech therapists in attempting to shape the proper enunciation of a word. Suppose a client is able to enunciate only one or two components of a complex word. When presented with a picture of a ball of string, he may pronounce "fing," the "str" combination being absent from his repertoire. The components of "str" are presented as models for the client to imitate. The *s* sound is modeled, and the client is asked to repeat it a number of times; then the *t* is presented repeatedly and then *st*. The procedure is continued until the response is shaped; the client combines and properly enunciates first the single sound, then the 2-letter blends, then finally, the whole word.

Teachers and parents use similar procedures to shape the components of numerous academic tasks (e.g., handwriting, computation, and reading), or self-help skills (e.g., dressing, washing, and eating). Supervisors use modeling in on-the-job training. In fact, the show and tell methods probably are the most prevalent job training strategies used, even for executive skills (Dingman, 1978). Modeling has been used to teach communicative skills to autistic children (Carr et al., 1980), and social skills to mentally retarded (Foxx et al., 1987) and hearing impaired clients (Lemanek, Williamson, Gersham, & Jensen, 1986).

Combining physical guidance with shaping. Physical guidance, another form of S^D, often is

used to prompt approximations of motor skills. Hardiman and colleagues (1975) guided Penny's successive approximations as she learned to climb, reinforcing her progress: "Good Penny, you put a different foot on each step" (p. 405), and Thomas and colleagues (1977) helped several community-bound young retarded women to acquire housekeeping skills— folding clothes, mopping floors, and washing tables—by guiding and reinforcing approximations of the skills. Skidgell and Bryant (1975) have recommended the same approach for teaching dining skills, whereas Ayllon and colleagues have used physical guidance as an aspect of their training programs in football and ballet (e.g., Fitterling & Ayllon, 1983).

Combining fading with shaping. We have discussed how shaping can be expedited by using instructions, imitative prompts, and physical guidance to prompt approximations. Those S^Ds eventually will need to be removed if the terminal goal is to be firmly established within the learner's repertoire. As Bruno acquires virtuosity in the performance of his scherzo, he must become less dependent on the coaching of his teacher and the notations in the score, so those S^Ds gradually must be faded.

In one inventive application of this concept, O'Brien et al. (1972) used graduated guidance to reduce developmentally disabled children's dependence on physical assistance while learning approximations to walking. A thick, taut rope attached to the ceiling with a pulley was substituted for an adult's hand. Gradually the rope was loosened and ultimately detached from the ceiling. Next, portions of the rope gradually were removed until it became very short in length. Eventually, the children discarded the rope altogether, walking independently. In each instance, cues and prompts to approximations were faded.

Fading and shaping procedures frequently are combined in the development of programmed instructional materials. Programmers often find that fading reduces errors, so mistakes are less likely to recur.

Skinner and Krakower's "Write and See" instructional handwriting program (1968) illustrated how fading could be a useful tool in the hands of the educator. Reese has described the program lucidly:

> The handwriting program shapes successively closer approximations of writing by immediate differential reinforcement of the correct response and by gradual attenuation of the controlling stimulus. The controlling stimulus is a letter which the child traces. Portions of the letter are gradually faded out, and the child composes increasingly more of the letter freehand until he is writing the whole letter himself. Immediate differential reinforcement is provided by a special ink and a chemical treatment of the paper. The child writes with a pen which makes a black mark when the letter is properly formed, but which turns the paper orange when the pen moves from the prescribed pattern. The child thus *knows* as he is *writing* whether or not he is drawing the letter correctly, and he can immediately correct a response by moving the pen so that it makes a black mark. Under these conditions, the children learn quickly; they learn to write well; and they love it (1966, p. 57).

Strengthening the Newly Acquired Behavior

Shaping a new behavior does not guarantee that it will remain firmly established. Submitting the newly achieved performance to the same type of strengthening procedures that were described in Chapters 9 to 13 is very important.

Reaching the goal is not sufficient. Violet quickly will revert to whispering if her audible talking is not immediately and consistently reinforced. Once a behavior is well established, procedures can be designed to maintain and, if necessary, assist its generalization to new contexts. (See Section V.)

Summary

Shaping is a procedure used to form behavior that is not present in the repertoires of individuals or that occurs very infrequently. Well-designed training and teaching methods, and programmed, computer-assisted, and personalized systems of instruction incorporate the features of effective shaping. Because shaping operates by reinforcing successively closer approximations to the desired terminal behavior, clearly specifying the objective is necessary. In addition, the shaping procedure requires careful observation to determine how large each step size should be and how long the learner performs at each step or successive approximation.

Combining shaping with discriminative stimuli such as instructions, demonstrations, and physical guidance can expedite the process. Naturally, any artificial or intrusive S^Ds must be faded before the objective can be said to have been achieved. Essential, too, is the application of the principles for effectively strengthening, maintaining, and promoting generalization. Only then will shaping be complete.

Chapter 20

Teaching New Behavior: Chaining

GOALS

After completing this chapter, you should be able to:

1. Define, recognize, and give original illustrations of each of the following terms:
   a. Links
   b. Chain
   c. Chaining procedure
   d. Rational task analysis
   e. Empirical task analysis
   f. Chaining (forward *and* backward)
   g. Concurrent (total or whole task method of teaching)
2. Describe and illustrate the dual-stimulus function played by each behavior in a chain.
3. List seven dimensions of a chain and discuss how each can influence how rapidly and accurately the complex behavior is learned and retained.
4. Discuss and illustrate how chaining incorporates a task analysis.
5. Describe how to develop and validate a task analysis.
6. Describe how using existing links and carefully selecting a starting point can improve the effectiveness of chaining.
7. Differentiate by discussion and illustration between serial and simultaneous (concurrent, whole, or total task) methods of teaching chains.
8. Describe how and why backward chaining works.
9. Discuss why and how reinforcement is delivered during the development of a chain, and explain why interim reinforcement shouldn't be overdone.
10. Give an example of combining chaining with S^Ds, fading, and shaping.
11. Describe how to strengthen a chain once it occurs.

As Flossie was learning to play tennis, her instructor showed her the steps in serving:

1. Place your feet so they are at a 45-degree angle to the net.
2. Hold the racket down over your shoulder.
3. Grasp the ball toward the tips of your fingers.
4. Position your hand over the foot closest to the net.
5. Toss the ball up gently.
6. Swing the racket counterclockwise over your shoulder.
7. Strike the ball with the racket.

The tennis serve had to be analyzed and broken down into its component tasks, because it was too difficult for Flossie to learn the serve as a cohesive unit. Once the sequence was broken down, each of the subtasks could be performed in sequence and Flossie was able to serve the ball properly. Causing the ball to land in the proper place was reinforcing to Flossie.

In behavioral language, the component tasks (subskills) within the sequence are called **links**. Links are joined together in a series called a **chain**. The technique used to teach people ultimately to perform the sequence as a cohesive performance is called a **chaining procedure**.

Chaining Procedure Defined and Illustrated

The formal definition of the *chaining procedure* is the reinforcement of a specified sequence of relatively simpler behaviors already in the repertoire of the individual to form a more **complex behavior**. To teach him to brush his teeth, Charlie's mother may be able to help him combine several instances of behaviors that he has already demonstrated he is capable of doing in a more complex chain. Charlie already may know how to put paste on a brush, place the

brush against his teeth, move the brush up and down, and so forth. When these separate behaviors are combined in proper sequence, the complex behavior of tooth brushing will have been established.

The Formation of Behavioral Chains

How can a series of previously learned responses be combined and strengthened when reinforcement appears to occur only at the end of the behavioral chain? Charlie's mom reads him a story only after he has brushed his teeth. Flossie receives reinforcement when her tennis serve is well placed. Paula's completion of her reports is complimented only after she has engaged in a long series of behaviors. The whole sequence of tasks that Harry must perform to produce a circuit board is reinforced only by seeing the finished product. Solving a challenging arithmetic problem will be reinforced only after a solution has been obtained. Asthmatic children only achieved relief from their symptoms (negative reinforcement) after they properly used a complicated device that delivered bronchodilator medication to the lungs (Renne & Creer, 1976). Unless we are fortunate enough to have someone else complete the chain for us, we usually need to progress through a series of steps before we feel comfortably sated: preparing a meal or going to a restaurant, and ordering, then consuming the food we receive.

Considering our previous discussion of the need for immediate reinforcement in strengthening behavior, such delays in reinforcement pose an enigma. How can chains become established, often in the absence of planned intervention? The answer lies in conditioned reinforcement.

Earlier you saw that when a stimulus or event is paired with or directly precedes reinforcement, eventually it will begin to acquire reinforcing properties of its own. The stimuli that acquire such reinforcing properties serve to forge the links of the chain into a complex response that can be strengthened or maintained by a single reinforcing event.

The skillfully placed final serve in a game of tennis and the last expert roll of a bowling ball each signals to the player that a victory or a good score is at hand. The feel of the racket as it makes perfect contact with the ball becomes reinforcing in itself. Such stimuli reinforce the immediately prior responses, for example, the stance, or position of the player. Over time, that stance will begin to set the occasion for the skillful swing or throw. We begin to see that the components of a complex behavioral chain operate in dual fashion. By this we mean that each link operates both as a discriminative stimulus, which occasions the subsequent link, and as a reinforcing stimulus, which reinforces the link that occurs immediately before it.

For an illustration of the same phenomenon, consider the complex behavior of brushing one's teeth, as it is broken down into its subtasks, or links: taking the brush, applying paste, turning on the water, wetting the brush, applying it to the teeth, moving it up and down in various positions, rinsing the mouth and the brush, putting away the brush, and putting away the paste. If putting the brush and paste away has in the past been paired consistently with a reinforcing stimulus (S^r) in the form of approval from mother and a story, the brush and paste in their proper place become a signal that reinforcement is imminent; that event will evolve into a *discriminative stimulus* (S^D).

Through further pairings with reinforcement (S^r), the discriminative stimulus (S^D) itself (putting the brush and paste away) will begin to reinforce (S^r) the *previous* link in the chain (rinsing the brush). Following a similar process, rinsing the brush will become both an S^D that sets the occasion for putting the brush and paste away and also a conditioned reinforcer (S^r) for the prior link in the chain, rinsing the

mouth. This process is illustrated in Figure 20.1.

Each link in an established chain, therefore, performs a *dual-stimulus function*: reinforcing the behavior it follows, and setting the occasion for the behavior that it precedes.

Composition of Chains

In considering sequences of responses that hold together to form a cohesive complex behavior, you need to recognize that chains can vary on numerous dimensions. Those features may make a difference in terms of how rapidly and accurately the behavior is learned and retained.

Length. Some chains are relatively short, such as opening a door with a key. Others are much longer, like doing the laundry. Naturally, short chains are easier to learn correctly than longer ones. As you add segments to a chain, errors might crop up, although this effect may be attenuated by providing feedback on accuracy (Richardson & Warzak, 1981).

Another choice is to break the task into clusters representing natural breaks in the task, as Snell (1982) did when teaching bed making. She was able to teach and reinforce the accomplishment of each cluster, in sequence.

Complexity. A chain can be **homogeneous**, in the sense that each component response is almost identical to the next, as in hammering a nail or doing a set of exercises, or it can be **heterogeneous**, with component responses differing from one another, as in playing a football game or assembling a wheel barrow or an outdoor barbecue grill. Presumably, a string consisting of the same responses is easier to acquire than one composed of different components.

Difficulty. Wexley and Yukl (1984) contend that in deciding what trainees need to be taught to perform their jobs efficiently, not only complexity but also difficulty needs to be taken into consideration. A long ground ball requires a more powerful swing than a bunt; lifting a heavy

Figure 20.1 Example of Hold Stimulus Components of a Complex Behavioral Chain Operating in a Dual Fashion

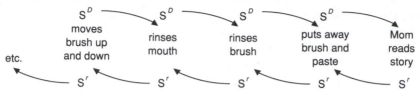

object necessitates much more exertion than lifting a light one. The extra effort required may impair the firmness with which the sequence is joined together. How well established the link is in the person's repertoire also influences its level of difficulty. Chains containing links that cannot be expressed fluently may be in jeopardy of deterioration.

Interdependence among links. According to Catania (1984),

> . . . Some sequences can be put together in such a way that each response produces stimulus conditions that set the occasion for the next, whereas others must be integrated in such a way that the responses appear in the proper order without each depending on the consequences of the last. For any given behavior the issue is deciding which sequence it is (p. 122).

Lifting the tennis racket clearly is a prerequisite for hitting the ball, whereas setting a screw does not necessarily depend on the prior installation of a washer. In cases in which one link is not necessarily dependent on the prior one, you will have to be especially careful to include each essential part of the chain as you train.

Task organization. Another factor identified by Wexley and Yukl (1984) is the degree of interrelationship among the parts of the complex task. All the aspects of a tennis serve are closely interrelated, whereas the separate subtasks involved in assembling a barbecue grill are not essentially tied to one another. Wexley and Yukl (1984) conclude that highly organized tasks are best taught by the "whole method" (discussed later).

Discriminative features. Some links of a chain are paired with readily discriminable properties, like the different sizes and shapes in an assembly kit or the diverse responses in completing a gymnastics routine. Other links bear close resemblance to one another, such as the minor (but significant) variations between one batting swing and the next. Readily discriminable links probably will be simpler to keep in proper sequence than those that are difficult to discriminate from one another.

S^Ds also can serve a time-marking function, indicating that the ultimate reinforcer is approaching. Driving home from work consists of taking particular turns in the road. Each landmark signals increasing proximity to the final destination.

Intrinsic reinforcers. Just as the crowd roars its approval for a well-placed ball in a tennis match or the scoreboard displays two additional points for a ball sunk in a basketball game, responses in some complex chains produce conditioned reinforcers supplemental to the ultimate reinforcer, like winning the game. Some responses in a chain feel good. Tasting your favorite flavor of ice cream compounds with satisfying your hunger. Other responses contain few supportive auxiliary reinforcers. Few reinforcers are integral to buttoning one's shirt or making the bed. Undoubtedly, chains that include intrinsic reinforcers should be acquired more readily than those that do not.

Probably other features of the complex behavior's topography and the functions of its constituent components impact upon the rate and accuracy with which a given complex behavior is mastered and maintained. In planning to apply a chaining procedure, you should examine such factors carefully to determine how to proceed optimally.

Forging Behavioral Chains

You now know that simple responses are capable of being forged together into chains, even without careful arrangement. You also know that the features of the task and the capabilities of the person who is to perform it bear careful scrutiny. To guide your design of any chaining procedures, first recognize the importance of a precise task analysis, then forge complex behaviors, when possible, from behavioral links already in the client's repertoire. Then consider the direction to pursue, such as backward chaining—starting with the final link—forward—beginning with the initial link—or at other points. Finally, consider the value of using multiple procedures in combination, like chaining combined with the presentation of various types of discriminative stimuli, fading, and shaping. This discussion covers each element in implementing chaining.

Analyzing the Task Precisely

As with shaping, having a clear description of the steps to be followed in a chaining procedure is vital. Because the sequence of component behaviors is so crucial to the development of the appropriate target behavior, each component and its place in the sequence must be precisely specified. Yet, analyzing a task is not always simple. Nor are all task analyses performed on simple tasks. Resnick and Ford (1978) have reported on task analyses of reading, mathematics, and other academic subject matter. In industry, job task analyses (Ross, 1982) have been developed for all sorts of operations, ranging widely from those performed

by "information desk clerks" (Wexley & Yukl, 1984) to nuclear power plant operators.

Figure 20.2 diagrams a task analysis of the chain "washing hair at the sink," one of several target behaviors that were selected for a group of community-bound, developmentally delayed women (Gustafson, Hotte, & Carsky, 1976). As in the tooth-brushing illustration, the sequence of behaviors must follow the specified order for hair washing to be considered correct. What if step 8 (rinsing hair thoroughly) were omitted? The client would hardly have clean hair.

Sometimes chaining procedures are selected to teach a substitute for an inaccurate or undesirable behavior. For example, if Charlie had rinsed his mouth without moving the brush up and down, the appropriate chain, as shown in Figure 20.1, would not have occurred. If, after rinsing his brush, Charlie threw it at another person before putting it away, the desired chain would also not have occurred. *Each link must occur in succession* without any omissions or intervening occurrences in order to form the target chain. Different terminal behavior is produced when links are omitted or interpolated.

So you see, in chaining, you need to describe the task completely, along with the necessary sequence of responses, because omitting or inadequately describing links crucial to an accurate chain can lead to disaster. You know what happens when a chain has a weak link! In a bow-tying task analysis, we neglected to include tightening the bow after it was formed, and naturally the bow came apart. As a demonstration, try to do an "armchair analysis" of a task very familiar to you, like washing dishes, putting on an article of clothing, or boarding a public bus. Then try asking a cooperative friend to follow it exactly as written to see whether you have actually included all the links in the chain.

Our advanced students have undertaken an assignment similar over the years using the Sulzer-Azaroff and Reese (1982) text as a guide. They are asked to identify and teach the group a skill that they but none of the other students

Figure 20.2 Task Analysis of the Chain "Washing Hair at the Sink"

Name: _____

Washing Hair at Sink

Date:								
1. Collect shampoo, towel, comb								
2. Remove blouse or shirt								
3. Place shampoo, towel, comb near sink								
4. Adjust water to lukewarm								
5. Wet hair thoroughly								
6. Apply shampoo to hair								
7. Rub into hair and scalp to form suds								
8. Rinse hair thoroughly								
9. Towel dry hair								
10. Place cap on shampoo								
11. Comb out hair								
12. Put clothing back on								
13. Return shampoo, towel, comb to respective places								

Source: Gustafson, Hotte, & Carsky (1976). Reproduced with permission of the author.

possess (e.g., a magic trick or a special sports skill like paddling a kayak, juggling, identifying different trees from twig samples, and so on). The results often are hilarious as these teachers discover the key links they have omitted in their task analyses. Not long ago, a student-instructor needed to add about a dozen steps to his task analysis before his professor (one of us) successfully performed what appeared to be an extremely elementary magic trick.

Validating Task Analyses
Armchair task analyses have their shortcomings, the most serious of which might be compromising the validity of the description. Imag-

ine, for a moment, how you might feel about a surgeon practicing a technique that was erroneously detailed by her trainer while they conversed during a flight to a conference. What other methods are available to ensure that a task analysis is complete, with each component in the proper sequence? Cooper, Heron, and Heward (1987) suggest four other methods applicable to a chaining procedure.

1. Observe competent individuals performing the task.

In some of our research on teacher training we have watched our most effective teachers at work. Horner and Keilitz (1975) based their task analysis of tooth brushing on the performance of staff.

2. Consult with experts.

The task analysis for the positioning of wheelchair-bound patients, shown in Figure 4.1 (Alavosius & Sulzer-Azaroff, 1986), was based on input from ergonomists, physical therapists, and other specialists in prevention of back injury.

3. Perform the behavior yourself repeatedly (presuming you are highly competent in doing the task), revising and refining it as you go along. Then pilot test it with others, continuing to refine and revise as necessary.

This is the tactic usually followed by authors of cookbooks. (Unfortunately, not all the authors are quite so scrupulous, as we have found to our chagrin when attempting an untried recipe for a dinner party.)

4. Consider the temporal order of the skills to be mastered.

List and shape the responses in the order in which they are to be performed. In the task analysis in Figure 4.1, setting the brakes on the wheelchair *after* transferring the patient would be both silly and dangerous.

In Resnick and Ford's (1978) extensive discussion of task analyses, they draw a distinction between **"rational"** and **"empirical" task analyses**. The rational type is "an attempt to specify processes or procedures that would be used in highly efficient performance of some task" (p. 385) and is derived rationally from the structure of the subject matter. Empirical task analyses are based on data obtained by systematically observing the learner in action. Resnick and Ford have described how they used the empirical approach to identify preferable methods for teaching various mathematical skills.

Anthony Cuvo and his collaborators have developed and experimentally analyzed numerous task analyses to assist disabled clients to function more successfully in the commu-

nity. Cuvo (1978) recommends that tasks be validated by using skill experts, and experts in the particular area of disability of concern. To this list might be added social, developmental, and educational validity (Voeltz & Evans, 1983); cost effectiveness; and other considerations we have discussed in Chapters 2–4 on selecting goals and objectives.

You now see again how important constructing valid task analyses can be for effective instruction, in this case in relation to chaining. Should you be heavily involved in teaching and training, you would be well advised to hone your expertise in this area by consulting materials devoted specifically to this topic, such as those by Resnick and Ford (1978).

Using Links Already in the Response Repertoire

A fairly basic principle for establishing chains efficiently—one that should be obvious by now—is to try to form the chain from behavior that is already well established in the individual's repertoire. Teaching children to write their names if they can already write each of the component letters is simpler than shaping the writing of each letter as part of the instructional procedure. Training a clerk to file is easier if he is already familiar with the various classification schemes important to the operation of the office. Standing up and speaking before a large audience for the first time probably would progress much more smoothly for the young professional woman who already has the behaviors of looking at people when speaking to them, organizing materials, speaking distinctly and loudly enough to be heard at a distance, and using appropriate gestures.

Sometimes equivalent complex tasks can consist of different response components. Teaching someone to wash her hair in the shower, rather than at the sink, is an example. Giving an effective speech before a large audience may include some behaviors different from those just specified: using an informal, conversational style rather than a formal, tightly organized style; showing slides instead of using gestures; and so on.

When there is a close resemblance between two acceptable complex terminal behaviors, the alternative that includes components well established in the person's repertoire is probably the one that will be acquired more easily. Fern can snap but not tie. In teaching her to dress herself, her teacher should provide clothing with snaps and not ribbons or strings, if possible.

Selecting a Starting Point

Given the intricacy of most complex skills, instructors will need to decide where to begin. Should teaching be initiated with the first link, the last, or somewhere in between? Should responses be joined one at a time or as groupings of subtasks? A distinction may be made between two *serial* methods, **forward** and **backward chaining**, and a *simultaneous* teaching method called **concurrent** (McDonnell & McFarland, 1988), **total** (Schuster, Gast, Wolery, & Guiltinan, 1988), or **whole task** (Wexley & Yukl, 1984), depending on the approach to connecting the links.

Coaching a tennis serve can be used to exemplify a forward chain, when training starts with the link that occurs first in the sequence: positioning the feet. This link is then joined with holding the racket over the shoulder (the second link), and so on. To learn family style dining skills, a group of profoundly retarded clients were instructed via a forward chaining method, beginning with gathering their eating utensils and progressing until they had served themselves appropriately and were ready to eat their meal (Wilson et al., 1984). The same sort of approach was used to teach developmentally delayed adults to make their beds (Snell, 1982).

Backward chaining progresses in the opposite direction, starting with the last link. Gruber, Reeser, and Reid (1979) applied this method to help their profoundly retarded students to walk unassisted from their residences to school, whereas Walls, Zane, and Ellis (1981) used all three techniques to teach assembly tasks, such as putting a circuit board or bicycle brake together. The whole or total task method involves training all the subgroups, or all the tasks concurrently, rather than joining or adding one link at a time.

How and Why Backward Chaining Works. Chapter 9 discussed the development of stimuli as conditioned reinforcers. You saw that stimuli may take on conditioned-reinforcing properties as a function of being paired with either unconditioned or other conditioned reinforcers. The discussion emphasized that many pairings between a stimulus and a reinforcer are needed before the stimulus itself will assume reinforcing properties.

In the tooth-brushing example discussed in this chapter, which link in the chain is paired most frequently with mother's reading a story—that is, the reinforcer? The behavior of putting the brush and paste away, because it is the one that is emitted with the closest proximity to and with the shortest delay before the reinforcer—the story. Putting the brush and paste away under these circumstances should, in time, come to operate as a reinforcing event in itself. It will be a stronger reinforcer than the previous link in the chain: rinsing the brush. We have learned that the shorter the delay between the response and the reinforcer, the more effective the reinforcer is. From the point of view of immediate reinforcement, use backward chains by initiating the training with the final link instead of with the first.

First, mother could read her son the story after the brush and paste were put away. Next, the reinforcer would be made contingent on rinsing the brush and putting it and the paste away. Once this chain had occurred fairly frequently, the reinforcer could be made contingent on rinsing the mouth, and so on, until the entire chain had solidified into a complex behavior.

The way this strategy was applied in the study by Gruber et al. (1979) to teach independent walking skills, was as follows: Once the students experienced an overview of the course they would need to travel, they received intensive training, which began very close to the school, with later steps progressing farther and farther away, until ultimately they completed the entire route autonomously. Backward chaining functioned well in this particular instance.

Backward chaining can also be applied to teach cognitive ("thinking") skills, such as computation, as described by Benoit (1972). A sixth-grade teacher wanted to help a student, Igor, switch from working multiplication problems by the method illustrated in Part A of Figure 20.3 to solving them by the method illustrated in Part B, as a preliminary to learning to multiply two-digit numbers, as in Part C.

The teacher had been using forward chaining for months without success and so decided to try backward chaining. The major steps for multiplying 2-digit numbers by 2-digit numbers were outlined:

1. Multiply the 1s times the 1s.
2. Multiply the 1s times the 10s.
3. Leave a place for the zero.
4. Multiply the 10s times the 1s.
5. Multiply the 10s times the 10s.
6. Add partial products.

The last step resulted in the correct answer

Figure 20.3 Three Steps in Learning to Multiply

	A			B	C
478	$8 \times$	$8 =$	64	478	23
$\times 8$	$8 \times$	$70 =$	560	$\times 8$	$\times 43$
	$8 \times$	$400 =$	3,200	3,824	69
			3,824		92
					989

and social reinforcers from the teacher. Figure 20.4 illustrates the actual steps taken.

Several practice trials were given at each step. Within 30 minutes, Igor was multiplying appropriately.

We have tried backward chaining to train staff supervisors to use behavioral procedures, with excellent results. The reinforcer, evidence of effective client training, was achieved first by implementing "prepackaged" training programs. Then, little by little, the supervisor-trainees assumed more and more of the responsibility for formulating programs, always terminating the sequence with effective procedural outcomes.

A question that may be asked about the advisability or necessity of teaching a complex behavior by means of a backward chaining procedure is, "What evidence is there that the approach is any better than teaching by adding behavioral components from the beginning?" The answer remains ambiguous. One comparison study (Walls et al., 1981) showed that both forward and backward chaining resulted in far fewer errors than a whole-task method when they taught vocational assembly tasks. Conversely, Spooner, Weber, and Spooner (1983) discovered that a total-task method required

Figure 20.4 Backward Chaining in Teaching Multiplication

Printing = steps by teacher
Handwriting = steps by Igor

1.	94		2.	73	
	$\times 57$			$\times 67$	
	658			511	
	4700			4380	
	5358	(step 6)		4891	(steps 4–6)
3.	40		4.	23	
	$\times 19$			$\times 43$	
	360			69	
	400			920	
	760	(steps 3–6)		989	(steps 1–6)

fewer trials to criterion and was associated with fewer errors than backward chaining.

What accounts for the disparity? Perhaps backward chaining operates more effectively with some complex behaviors than others. Maybe the opportunity for an interim reinforcer or the size or difficulty of the task makes a difference. In most of the studies of whole task and forward chaining, opportunity existed to reinforce links of the chain externally as they were expressed.

Sometimes this is not feasible, as in situations demanding independence. The trainer can't readily provide a sky diver with supplemental reinforcers for pulling his rip cord at the right moment. Only the ultimate reinforcer, a safe landing, can be delivered. Additionally, backward chaining might be the only option when clients with no receptive language are involved, because the S^{D}s that usually accompany forward chaining procedures would not be functional for them. Another possibility is that backward chaining is most successful when the completion of the chain entails a reinforcer especially powerful for the individual: reaching a destination, obtaining a tasty meal, or constructing a useful object. Only future research will permit this dilemma to be solved.

In the meantime, try various approaches. If you want to use the total-task method with an especially long or complex sequence, though, try using small groupings of responses first, then combining them.

Supplementing Reinforcers

Although the ultimate reinforcer for learning a complex behavior is supposed to be completing it independently, you may be able to speed up the process by reinforcing the correct components as they are expressed along the way. Praise or even stronger reinforcers have been used in many of the programs already cited. This was one of the aspects of McDonnell and McFarland's (1988) curriculum in teaching laundromat skills to students with severe handicaps. Similarly, continuous praise was combined with pennies for clusters of bed-making skills completed correctly in Snell's (1982) study.

Be especially careful not to overdo interim reinforcement during a chaining procedure; try to save the most powerful reinforcers until the end. Evidence from the study of responses by pigeons, at least suggests that interim reinforcers may block the effect of subsequent reinforcers, including the ultimate one (Catania, Sagvolden, & Keller, 1988). Too much reinforcement during the training of a daily living skill might block the student's experiencing the ultimate reinforcing value of having clean clothes or a well-made bed. Diminish your supplementary reinforcers as quickly as feasible, permitting the subsequent link in the chain to assume conditioned reinforcing properties.

Using Discriminative Stimuli

In addition to the discriminative stimuli that are integral to the response chain, supplementary S^{D}s may be used to facilitate forging of specific links in the chain. Verbal directions, gestures, written instructions, and similar prompts may effectively shorten the time needed to establish a fairly simple behavioral chain. For example, Renne and Creer (1976) taught asthmatic children to use the intermittent positive-pressure breathing (IPPB) device by prompting the links of eye fixation, facial posturing (keeping the mouth firmly around the mouthpiece while not puffing the cheeks and while breathing through the nose), and diaphragmatic breathing. Prompting of the last link consisted of ''pushing in on the abdomen of the subjects while, at the same time, instructing them to breathe out as fully as possible from their mouths. They were then told to use their stomachs to push the experimenter's hand away while breathing in as deeply as possible through their mouths'' (1976, p.4). Proper responses were rewarded with tickets (accompanied by social praise) that could later be exchanged for surprise gifts.

Similarly, in our tooth-brushing illustration, if Charlie's mother had said, "Remember to rinse your brush and to put the toothbrush and toothpaste away" and had consistently reinforced the emission of those links, they might have been acquired more rapidly than if she had simply waited for them to be emitted spontaneously.

Should you decide to break your terminal goal into subgoals, certainly you could use the description of each to serve as an S^D to encourage the approximation. Suppose you are training an employee how to instruct developmentally delayed clients. You could first hand the trainee a checklist containing the steps, such as readying materials, attaining eye contact, orally instructing the client; then, if necessary, you could show or guide the response; then you could reinforce the completion of the response, as was done in a study by Fleming and Sulzer-Azaroff (1989). Your staff trainee could use the checklist as a set of guidelines or you could orally prompt and reinforce performance of the correct step to maximize success.

Many studies cited earlier in the chapter did use these and other sorts of prompts to occasion correct approximations. Snell (1982) used verbal prompts in teaching developmentally delayed adults to make their beds. So did Schuster et al. (1988), when instructing their clients to prepare their meals; Cronin and Cuvo (1979) during instruction in mending skills; and Spooner et al. (1983) in training assembly tasks.

People frequently imitate complex behavior that is novel for them—printing Chinese characters, repeating lines of poetry, doing homework and craft projects, and so forth—as long as the behavior modeled is not too complicated and the learners are capable of performing the components. Modeling is also used as an adjunct to formal chaining procedures and indeed was also used in each of the studies just cited.

Much elaborate language probably is learned in this manner, as demonstrated in a series of studies with language-deficient normal children (Guess et al., 1968; Wheeler & Sulzer, 1970; Whitehurst, 1971; Lutzker & Sherman, 1974; Clark & Sherman, 1975).

With more intricate behavior, however, accomplishing the goal directly via imitation may be tricky. Acquiring the proper sequence of responses in a more complex chain may prove too difficult if the entire sequence is presented all at once. In the tooth-brushing illustration, even though allowing an older brother to model the entire sequence might have been sufficient to occasion the chain for his little sister, with longer or more complex chains, like organizing and conducting a debate, modeling the whole process would be less likely to work. One might have more success if the chain were broken down into shorter sequences, with each sequence modeled. The clients could then first imitate each link in the chain. Then the chain could be gradually unified in the manner previously described, and the segment prompts could be phased out. That is exactly how hair washing and other everyday living skills were taught to the community-bound clients described by Gustafson et al. (1976). When necessary, each link in the chain was occasioned by some form of prompt—a tell, a show, or a guide prompt.

Physical guidance usually will prompt a correct motor response when all else fails. When necessary, mending was physically guided in Cronin and Cuvo's (1979) study, as was bed making in Snell's (1982) instructional program in bed making.

At this point you may ask. "Why not simply use prompts such as directions or models to teach all complex behavioral chains?" The answer lies partially in the fact that directions or imitative prompts are not always adequate S^Ds for all clients. They may not reliably occasion the desired response. Similarly, locating effective models may be difficult for the person who fails to follow directions. In addition, many instructional and behavioral goals are much more intricate than those we have illustrated, and the components of the particular chain may not be in the individual's response repertoire. Furthermore, too much prompting, as you know, may make the person overly dependent on those artificial supports. Fading those prompts as rapidly as possible becomes critically important.

Combining Fading with Chaining

Prompts for each of the links of the chain must be removed before one can assert that the behavioral goal has been achieved. In the solution of long-division problems, for instance, the ultimate goal would be for the students to carry out the entire process without any external prompts. Suppose the teacher said, "First compare the divisor and the dividend to see which is larger," and waited for the students to do so; then said, "Now place a decimal point to the right of the dividend," and waited for them to do so, and so on. Few would agree that the terminal behavior (being able to solve long-division problems) had been acquired. The criterion for acceptable acquisition of the response chain probably would be correctly solving a number of long-division problems independently.

As with shaping, gradually fading the intermediate prompts in a complex chain of behaviors is obviously essential if the complex skill is to be expressed accurately and fluently. Too abrupt a removal of these prompts would probably result in the breakdown of the behavioral chain. The prompting described for the asthmatic clients was faded by first gradually eliminating the "hand-against-the-abdomen," followed by verbal instructions, as appropriate responding increased. Similarly, those links in the hair washing chain that were occasioned by either a guided, modeled, or verbal prompt were faded gradually, moving from the most intrusive to the most natural, as covered in Chapter 18.

"At which link should we begin to fade prompts?" Again, this is an empirical question awaiting an answer. Your best bet is to begin with the most well-established link. In backward chaining, the link that probably has the greatest strength is the last one. So remove your prompt for the last link first. In the example of long division, the instruction to reduce the fraction to the smallest common denominator should be removed first. As that final link and the one immediately before it become fairly well joined, the S^D for the preceding link (the instruction to place the remainder over the divisor) may then be eliminated, and so on, until the entire chain is performed with perhaps only a single S^D at the beginning, like the instruction to divide 987 by 31.

Alternatively, you can fade S^Ds on all links simultaneously by using a time-delay procedure. Snell (1982) used time delays progressing from 0 to 8 seconds, as a fading strategy while teaching bed making, and Schuster et al. (1988) introduced a constant time delay of 5 seconds as a fading method during instruction in food preparation.

Combining Shaping with Chaining

Certainly chaining will take place more rapidly if all the behavioral links of the chain have already been developed. Occasionally, however, one or two of the links are weak or missing from the individual's repertoire. For instance, Fern may have a difficult time rinsing the shampoo out of her hair, or Flora, the student in the college PSI course, may be unable to fill out her study guide in sufficient detail. Each missing or weak link can be shaped and then strengthened through reinforcement. Once that has been accomplished, the chain can be developed more readily. If most links in a chain are absent from the repertoire, however, seriously reconsider teaching the selected target behavior. In all likelihood it is overly ambitious for the individual learner, and an alternative, probably a more basic behavioral objective, should be sought.

Strengthening Response Chains

The first time Charlie brushes his teeth or Flora fills in her study guide in sufficient detail, the response is still rather weak, for unless it is strengthened, the chain can easily snap apart. Components still may be omitted, their order confused, or inappropriate components added. Charlie may take his brush, wet it, and replace it; Flora may again answer her questions too sketchily. If a complex behavioral chain is to persist intact, *reinforce the fully correct chain*, as often as possible, with minimal delay and adequate amounts of reinforcers known to be effective for the individual.

Mother would therefore have to observe Charlie's tooth brushing to be sure that it was correctly carried out, then follow immediately with a favorite story. Flora's instructor should check her study guide several times and comment positively when it has been completed in sufficient detail. (In this instance, a slightly more delayed reinforcer, demonstrating mastery of the material by passing the unit quiz, will support the behavior in a more natural fashion, once it becomes better established.)

Safely transferring disabled patients from one location to another was reinforced repeatedly as a cohesive performance until it was expressed at a high and steady rate (Alavosius & Sulzer-Azaroff, 1986), resulting in persistence over the seven-month follow-up period. As in all instances in which behaviors are at low strength, these optimal conditions must be continued until fluency is achieved. Eventually, shifting to the sorts of procedures described in Chapters 29–32 for maintaining and generalizing well-established behavior will be advisable.

Summary

The chaining procedure is a method devised to produce a cohesive complex behavior from components the performer already is capable of expressing. Chains of behavior derive their ability to aggregate from the fact that links begin to acquire both discriminative and conditioned reinforcing functions during the learning process. Chains vary from one another in terms of their length, complexity, and difficulty for the individual; interdependence among links; task organization; discriminative features; the reinforcers intrinsic to their expression; and perhaps in other ways.

Effectively forging a behavioral chain depends on a precise task analysis, validated as accurate through observation by competent individuals, consultation with experts, pilot testing, and careful planning of the temporal order of the links. Chains can be forged by joining one link to the next in a forward or backward direction or by presenting the whole task and prompting and reinforcing correctly performed links. Although not always practical or feasible, the backward chaining method has the advantage of capitalizing on the reinforcing properties inherent in the completion of the chain. Forward and whole task chaining must depend on external prompting and reinforcement, but interim prompts need to be faded and reinforcers thinned out completely before the behavior can be said to have been mastered. Occasionally a weak link may require further instruction through shaping.

When the sequence eventually is emitted as an accurate cohesive unit, it must be strengthened, just like any other behavior whose rate needs to be increased. Only when the performance occurs at a high and steady rate in its appropriate context can one assume the purpose has been achieved.

You have seen how verbal prompts may be used to promote stimulus control, shaping, and chaining. Indeed, communicative stimuli—language—may facilitate human performance in numerous ways, probably accounting in great measure for the special complexity and sophistication of human behavioral repertoires. The next chapter devotes itself to this topic.

Chapter 21

Communicative Behavior

By Linda J. Hayes, Matthew J. Aguiar, and Steven C. Hayes

GOALS

After completing this chapter, you should be able to:

1. Define, recognize, and give original illustrations of each of the following terms:
   a. Communicative (verbal) behavior
   b. Contingency shaped behavior
   c. Incidental teaching
   d. Correspondence training

2. Explain the relationship that contingency-specifying stimuli have to rule governed behavior.

3. Explain why inaccurate rules that lead to ineffectual behavior are followed.

4. Discuss the difference in responding to unannounced changes in contingencies between those whose behavior was acquired through contingency shaping versus rule governance.

5. Discuss the relevance of stimulus equivalence to the development and teaching of language.

6. List what circumstances might cause an inadequate communicative repertoire, and discuss the problems resulting from such an inadequacy.

7. Illustrate both maladaptive communicative behavior and disfluent speaking. Discuss likely consequences of such behavior.

8. Differentiate between rules stated by others and self-rules, and discuss the relevance of self-rules and their relationship to cognitive and insight-oriented therapies.

9. Identify and discuss the relevance of each type of problem that can occur related to rule governance.

10. Identify at least three types of basic and complex communicative repertoires and describe how each can be taught.

11. Describe how incidental teaching can facilitate generalization of communicative skills.

12. Identify at least three important factors for teaching signing.

13. Describe what can be done when strongly established rules block an individual's learning from the contingencies.

14. Describe cognitive behavior modification from the perspective of a behavior analyst and point out the contributions that cognitive behavior modification makes.

15. Discuss the social importance of correspondence between a person's statements and deeds.

16. Describe what would be the most effective approach for developing say/do and do/say correspondence.

17. Discuss when the use of rules can be avoided.

Humans differ from nonhumans in countless ways, but no distinction is as significant as the human capacity for language. The development of human civilization appears to have coincided with the development of complex language. A question that experimental and applied behavior analysts have increasingly asked is "What is it about verbal behavior[1] that might enable individual and social functioning to become so complex?"

We are learning more and more about the influence of language on behavior. As you know, verbal behavior influences the effectiveness of simple and complex behavioral procedures, from the most basic reinforcement strategies to those involved in high-level instruction. Examples of the uses of communicating include to:

- get someone (ourselves included) to do something for us.
- provide rules by which to guide our actions.
- enable us to increase reinforcement for ourselves and others.
- help us to tolerate time delays to reinforcers.

Communicative behavior can also sometimes impair our functioning, as in the case of following inaccurate rules.

Communicative Behavior Defined and Illustrated

We may view language according to its form or structure, as many linguists do, or in terms of its function, as Skinner (1957) and other behavior analysts prefer. According to Skinner, the term **verbal behavior**, or as we often refer to it, **communicative behavior**, is behavior reinforced through the mediation of other persons. In plain language, verbal behavior helps you get what you want and avoid what you don't want more efficiently.[2] Skinner's definition broadens the act beyond vocal speech, to include "any movement capable of affecting another organism" (p. 14). Admissible, then, are gestures and other forms of "nonverbal" (i.e., nonvocal) communication—writing, typing, signing, and so on.

Reinforcement of verbal behavior derives from that special function of influencing others but not from that alone. Skinner contends that verbal behavior ". . . has a special character only because it is reinforced by its effects on people—at first other people, but eventually . . ." (1974, pp. 88–89) speakers themselves. Communicative events may function as antecedent stimuli that prompt others (or ourselves) to behave in a way that reinforces our verbal behavior and may include simple or complex spoken or written utterances, rules, instructions, demonstrations, gestures, signs, and so on.

How Communicative Behavior Is Shaped by the Verbal Community

As a newborn infant, little Leroy awakened and began to squeal. Mom came in and fed, changed, or cuddled him. Before long, Leroy began to squeal, cry, or vocalize in other ways when he was wet, hungry, cold, or deprived of stimulation. Rates of vocalizing increased, as any operant would when reinforced. After many months, Mom or Dad responded faster or more positively when Leroy's vocalizations began to sound like "Ma" or "Da," differentially reinforcing those particular sounds, especially as they successively approximated conventionally sounding "Mommy" or "Daddy."

---

[1] Numerous texts are devoted to the elaboration of this important aspect of human performance, and we refer the interested reader to them (e.g., Hayes, 1989; Skinner, 1957; Sundberg, 1987).

[2] Here and elsewhere in the chapter, operationally define *want* as behaving in a way that gained the person a given reinforcer in the past and *don't want* as behaving in a way that permitted the person to avoid a given aversive stimulus in the past.

As time passed and Leroy reached unsuccessfully for his bottle, his Mom gave it to him. That reach eventually was shaped into a pointing motion. Simultaneously, his parents probably commented "You want your bottle," which Leroy began to imitate. Eventually the word "bottle" would be shaped, as his progressive approximations were reinforced. Leroy was beginning to be able to prompt others to deliver particular reinforcers to him.

Leroy often received an item by pointing to or naming it; but life is more complicated than that. Sometimes the reinforcers that are especially potent at the moment are not as obvious. Maybe he wants one particular toy, food item, or activity or to rid himself of a specific discomfort. Pointing or naming is insufficient, because although his parents try to figure out what he wants, Leroy's reinforcement is delayed. His parents begin to offer and label first one, then another, item or event. "What do you want, darling, the brown bear? The white bear?" "Are you cold?" Ultimately, they earn the reinforcer of Leroy's contented smile by delivering the appropriate reinforcers to him. Again, via imitation of verbal or auditory stimuli, Leroy learns to say the more complex or subtle words, discovering too that some **verbal stimuli** share equivalent functions.

By now, Leroy's parents have experienced that teaching him to label his wants more precisely results in his smiling more often (and screaming less), so they apply tactics now familiar to you, such as delayed prompting. As soon as Leroy yells or points at an object, they prompt "Do you want the (*pause*) brown bear?" Eventually Leroy uses the descriptive adjective in advance of the prompt. Leroy now is beginning to name things, actions, and relations.

As time passes, Leroy produces progressively more sophisticated responses, such as increasingly elaborate communication—utterances, writing, and gestures—because those responses are differentially reinforced according to the context in which they occur (conditional discriminations) by the verbal community. Regardless of the topographic features of the communicative behavior, its evolution can be traced to reinforcement based on "selection" by the community. This chapter examines communicative behavior in much finer detail, describing how language can influence our overt actions and how both adaptive and problematic verbal behaviors are acquired and maintained.

Rule-Governed Behavior

People learn well by experiencing contingencies directly, and healthy development involves allowing children to make contact with natural reinforcers and mild (not dangerous) punishers. Letting an infant struggle to get from place to place by crawling or toddling permits the child to obtain a reinforcer—the item the infant is trying to get—and will enhance the child's mobility and independence. (In fact, blocking an organism's ability to influence the environment can lead to a condition called "learned helplessness" [Maier, Seligman, & Solomon, 1969]). Allowing a child to taste a spicy food will be a more powerful learning experience for him than any words of advice you could offer.

Verbal behavior, though, often simplifies the process. When we wish to influence the behavior of others, we generally start with what is perhaps the dominant form of social influence: We tell the person what to do. We may describe when they should do it, why, and what will happen if they do or do not. This is so commonplace that we may fail to notice its extraordinary qualities. You can be told to do things you have never done before, provided only that you understand the components of the request and have developed the skills to do it. You can be promised consequences you have never actually received for similar actions. You may be told to do things at times and in places that you have never even seen before. And yet, you may be able to follow such instructions.

Rule-Governed Behavior Defined

In behavioral terms, as you know from Chapter 17, instructions of this kind are called *rules*. According to Skinner (1966, 1969) and Brownstein and Shull (1985), *rule-governed behavior* is operant behavior occurring under the discriminative control of *contingency-specifying stimuli*. The words function as S^{D}s, describing the relations between the response and its consequences and antecedents. It is not behavior that has been shaped by direct exposure to the contingencies specified. You need not have experienced the alarm going off to avoid exiting a building through a door marked: "Emergency exit only. Opening door will activate alarm." Furthermore, rules do not have to specify explicitly all the terms of the contingency, because one or more of the three terms of the contingency may be clearly implied. For example, "Don't walk on thin ice" may be conceptualized as a rule even though a *consequence* is not specified. "Dangerous curve" may be thought of as a rule, even though the *behavior* is not specified.

Knowing about the conditions under which rules acquire their ability to control responding is especially important for the manager of behavior. As you shall see, rules can lead people in directions that may be either advantageous or detrimental for them. You want those near and dear to you to behave according to the rules that will keep them healthy and safe and allow them to realize long-term rewards for their efforts. We may want to prevent people from skating on thin ice (literally or metaphorically) or encourage them to respond in other ways beneficial to them or society, in the absence of a direct experience. Parents, for instance, attempt to teach their children rules of conduct before the youngsters actually come in contact with the reinforcer or punisher. ("Do your homework and you will be admitted into the college of your choice." "Avoid drugs. They will fry your brain.")

We need to use rules to enhance our opportunities, avoid trouble, and attain reinforcement. Meanwhile, though, we still need to remain sensitive to contingencies actually in operation so we are not misled into following rules disadvantageous to us. Unfortunately, not all rules presented by others accurately describe the contingencies in operation. Our boss may tell us that hard work pays off, but being charming and friendly is actually what counts. That's important to discover.

Control by Rules

Just because people can explain a rule does not necessarily mean they will adhere to the rule. One possible reason, alluded to earlier, is that rules may not assume discriminative control. Galizio (1979) has argued that if instruction-following is an operant, it should be maintained only when instructions are accurate, because only under these conditions will it be reinforced. He found that subjects followed instructions when they were accurate and not when they were known to be inaccurate; and that subjects would work to produce access to accurate instructions.

Unfortunately, people may fail to discriminate between accurate and inaccurate rules, to their detriment. Merely telling people that they would receive reinforcement for an average number of responses (a variable ratio schedule) was sufficient to maintain their responses for up to 3 hours when conditions of complete extinction actually were in effect (Kaufman et al., 1966; see also Weiner, 1970). To the degree that we follow rules, we may become relatively less sensitive to the contingencies of reinforcement actually operating in the situation. For example, suppose a slot machine has broken in a Reno gambling casino. An otherwise intelligent person might continue pouring money into the machine all night despite the fact that it never delivers even a small jackpot as the other machines do. This behavior may not be under the control of the direct consequences (in this case, extinction) but rather a rule, such as "it has been so long since this slot machine paid off, it surely must be due for a big hit."

For instance, subjects may lose out on potential reinforcers by following inaccurate rules, like telling themselves that one reinforcement schedule is in effect despite experiencing contingencies in the form of a different schedule (Hayes et al., 1985, Exp. 2). In cases like these, you would need to take steps to help the participant obtain maximal payoff by providing more accurate instructions and/or more salient contingencies.

Rules and Sensitivity to Contingencies Actually in Effect

Much is being learned about sensitivity to contingencies actually in effect through studies of the effects of *unannounced changes in contingencies*, as when college student subjects' original performances either have or have not been instructed (Shimoff, Catania, & Matthews, 1981). In one case (Matthews, Shimoff, Catania, & Sagvolden, 1977), *instructed* subjects were told to push a button to receive points, whereas other subjects had this performance *shaped* through reinforcement of successive approximations. Those in the latter group, the **contingency shaped** group, switched from low rates to high rates of response when the reinforcement contingencies shifted correspondingly. By contrast, only 4 of the 10 instructed subjects showed increased rates under these conditions. Similar results were obtained with a different form of communication—a demonstration. Subjects were taught to press a telegraph key either by a shaping procedure or by the experimenters demonstrating a key press; those subjects who learned via demonstration were less sensitive to changes in the contingencies than those whose form of response was shaped.

Verbal Behavior and Stimulus Equivalence

If each different communicative response had to be learned by differential reinforcement and shaping, our language repertoires would be far more limited. Fortunately, through processes like functional or stimulus equivalence, we learn to generalize from one verbal stimulus to another of equivalent function. (See Chapter 15.) For instance, equivalence relations can be capitalized on efficiently to teach severely disabled students comprehension and reading tasks (Mackay & Sidman, 1984; Sidman, 1977; 1987). (Hayes & Hayes, 1989, also propose that stimulus equivalence probably is a by-product of language training.)

Knowing about **functional equivalence** can also help us understand why certain training programs work in some instances and not in others. Clarke, Remington, and Light (1986) analyzed differences in rates of acquisition of vocabulary words acquired in a total communication speech training program. They trained severely educationally handicapped children to physically imitate the language sign denoting various objects and to form the sign for the object's name when presented with its picture and name. "Signs corresponding to known words were generally acquired faster and retained better than signs corresponding to unknown words" (p. 231).

These results could be explained on the basis of functional equivalence. Probably because the children could identify pictures of the words, the words and their pictorial representations were functionally equivalent. So when the children were taught to form a manual sign in response to the oral instruction, they could do the same thing in response to the presentation of the picture, without further training. This was not the case with "unknown" words, because the picture and its spoken label did not hold discriminative control over one another.

Further training would have been required (preferably beginning by teaching the children to identify the pictures in response to their spoken labels).

Given the complexity of language learning and communication, all sorts of things can go amiss along the way. In the next section we describe a few of the more troublesome of these problems, particularly those that have been addressed effectively by applying behavior analysis.

Problems in Communicative Behavior

Just as difficulties may be encountered with other classes of behavior, communicative behavior also may be problematic. So the people involved in the verbal interchange may fail to get what they want and avoid what they don't want as effectively and efficiently as they might otherwise. Among the troubles you might encounter in this domain are inadequacy of a person's verbal repertoire, maladaptive verbal behaviors, disfluencies, and problems of rule governance.

Inadequate Verbal Repertoires

Many people suffer from inadequate verbal repertoires. As a result they miss opportunities for reinforcement and probably experience relatively more aversive consequences than their more verbally skilled peers. Children who lack the ability to request reinforcing items or to rid themselves of aversive stimuli surely suffer more than others. An extreme instance is the self-injury that some language-deficient people inflict on themselves as a way of escaping demanding situations (e.g., Iwata, Pace, Kalsher, Cowdery, & Cataldo, 1990).

Maladaptive Verbal Behavior

Saying inappropriate things to others or oneself can lead to all sorts of trouble. This extends from mild rudeness, which may cause people to respond with irritation, to threatening statements, which may result in counteraggression or arrest. Natives of a community who say words totally out of context, or use language not shared by or generally reinforced by other members, often are labeled "strange" or schizophrenic. Relationships, jobs, freedom of movement, and other major sources of reinforcement may be denied them as a consequence.

Problematic Speech Topographies

The form with which words are delivered, rather than the content, may prove problematic. Inserting extra syllables or pauses within one's oral speech can cause difficulties for both the speaker and the listener. Both find the unnecessary delay punishing—the speaker who is eager to complete the statement, and the listener who awaits the message. Additional difficulties of this nature include loss of voice (aphonia), mutism, poor articulation, and other forms of communication disorders.

Problems in Rule Governance

How sensitive one is to the rules in effect and how accurately those rules describe contingencies actually in operation may have wide reaching implications for successful human functioning. Many clinical disorders involve problems in communicative control of one kind or another: problems in self-rule formulation or in rule formulation by the community; failure to follow rules; and indiscriminate rule following. For example, people whose behavior is not governed by the rules imposed by others often get into trouble with the law, their neighbors, or their families. Others whose behavior is not well governed by rules need to rely more heavily on contact with actual contingencies, which may be inefficient, costly, or painful. Reciting incorrect rules to oneself also can lead to no good for the individual, as in the case of a "paranoic" man who tells himself that people are out to get him, thereby setting the occasion for interacting aggressively with others.

Problems in self-rule formulation. A verbally competent person is both a speaker and a listener. Listening to your own talk enables you to participate in the control of your actions. Harry says, "Today is the day to clean out the garage," and he does.

The social contingencies for following self-rules and rules stated by others, of course, differ. Nevertheless, formulating self-rules is one way of controlling impulsive acts and other behaviors controlled by direct contingencies.

Disorders of self-rule formulation might occur in at least two basic ways: First, a person fails to formulate worthwhile rules. Not specifying an important rule like the following could well be disadvantageous to the worker: "If I remember to do my job well and smile and not complain when the boss visits, I'll be more likely to get my promotion." Second, a person formulates inaccurate or unrealistic rules. "*All we have to do around here is ingratiate ourselves with the boss to get a promotion.*"

Much of the cognitive therapy literature can be interpreted as an attempt to train individuals in proper rule formulation to replace irrational or nonexistent rules (Zettle & Hayes, 1982). An emphasis on developing accurate self-rules also can be discerned in insight-oriented therapy. In this case, a relationship is structured in which the client is encouraged to bring verbal behavior under the control of direct contact with experienced events, rather than hopes or fears or audience control (e.g., attempting to please others). Instead of "If I call her for a date, she'll probably say no," the young man is encouraged to try and see what actually happens.

Problems in rule formulation of the verbal community. Many of the rules that guide our behavior are learned from others. In much the same manner that self-rule formulation can cause problems, problems can occur in the rule formulation practices of the larger verbal community. Particular cultures and subcultures may fail to develop adequate rules or may fashion inaccurate ones. For example, one subculture might develop rules that discourage members from seeking medical attention for life-threatening diseases; another may generate rules about the futility of working for a living.

A failure to follow rules. Rules often are devised to compete with the destructive effects of some kinds of immediate contingency control, such as the immediate reinforcement of stealing, raping, consuming dangerous substances, and so on. For example, a father may have presented his teenage son with the rule "Don't take addictive drugs; they are likely to lead to undesirable ends." Without a sufficiently strong pattern of following his father's rules, the immediate reinforcers of peer approval may draw the teenager into a habit of abusing drugs.

Rule following in this sense involves three distinguishable aspects:

- being able to describe accurately the function of the rules to oneself or others (in lay terms, to "understand" the rule)—a setting event.
- labeling circumstances (S^Ds) for which a particular rule applies.
- following the rule (the response).

Some clinical techniques have been oriented toward increased understanding, and almost all assume that the person can recognize the conditions under which rule following is prescribed. The focus of most clinical psychotherapeutic interventions, therefore, is establishing rule following *per se*.

Some of the techniques used with people who act impulsively, dangerously, or antisocially can be understood as an attempt to establish a greater degree of rule following. For example, drug treatment programs such as Synanon are highly regimented, with many clearly stated rules of conduct. Compliance is promoted through group meetings during which members' infractions are the focus of attention.

Excessive rule following. Rule-governed behavior can never capture completely the subtlety of behavior shaped directly by experience. Driving a car after having read a manual is not the same as driving after months of practice. Hearing a lecture on harmonious courtship would hardly substitute for many successful experiences in dating. Learning from direct consequences is necessary for one to achieve goals in one's occupational and interpersonal life and in the daily performance of routines, for that is the form of learning that permits fluent (i.e., smooth and rapid) responses to relevant cues. If pilots or surgeons needed to recite rules to themselves continuously we hardly would consider them experts.

Sometimes, though, certain rules may be supported so pervasively by the verbal community that direct experience cannot overcome the effects of the rule. (An old adage warns that "Only bad things happen on Friday the 13th.") In other cases, the previous use of a rule may interfere with the control by direct experience, to the extent that the benefits of subsequent direct experience are attenuated. Convinced by his buddies to pilfer a candy bar, yet brought up with the rule that stealing is wrong, Randy finds little joy in eating the candy.

As previously indicated, people often become insensitive to direct contingencies when verbal control is well established. Perhaps this explains why therapies that attempt to bring the person in direct contact with contingencies sometimes fail. The person goes through the experience, reinforcers are presented, but the rules the individual recites to himself interfere with reinforcement: "Yeah. My boss was fair this time, but I know he has it in for me. So, I'm not going to finish this job on time."

Difficulty in rule specification. Some classes of behavior are so extensive, complicated, and dependent on subtle contextual factors that adequately specifying the rules becomes next to impossible. "Social skills" are a case in point, because they are so numerous and so dependent on contextual factors. Preferably the antecedents and responses need to be specified very precisely, as in teaching someone how to answer an office telephone or greet a customer of the shop. It is possible to avoid many of these problems by avoiding verbal control as a means of therapeutic change, a point to which we shall return.

Teaching Communicative Skills

One major advantage of viewing verbal behavior from a functional perspective is that we then may assume it is amenable to change through managing contingencies. Inadequate, inefficient, or maladaptive repertoires should be capable of remediation through the application of the kinds of behavioral procedures included in this book. A considerable body of research, conducted over the past three decades, has demonstrated the utility of behavior analysis in improving limited, maladaptive, and/or dysfunctional communicative behavior. Numerous examples follow.

Promoting Acquisition of Communicative Behavior

Within normal adult, adolescent, and child populations, behavioral procedures have been used both to increase fluency and to train the acquisition of parts of speech. For example, various combinations of behavioral procedures have been employed to help people.

- identify the major ideas in prose text (Glover, Zimmer, Filbeck, & Plake, 1980).
- correct articulation errors (Bailey, Timbers, Phillips, & Wolf, 1971).
- enhance conversational (Minkin et al., 1976) and reading skills (Schwartz, 1977; Corey & Shamow, 1972).
- increase spontaneous (Reynolds & Risley,

1968) and productive speech (Mann & Baer, 1971).

- improve handwriting (Brigham, Finfrock, Breuning, & Bushell, 1972).
- increase creative verbalizations (Glover & Gary, 1976) and class discussion (Smith, Schumaker, Schaeffer, & Sherman, 1982).

Similarly, prompts, modeling, stimulus control, and contingent reinforcement have been employed to facilitate the acquisition of descriptive adjectives (Lahey, 1971); letter discrimination (Tawney, 1972); adjective-noun combinations (Neville & Shemberg, 1978); sight-word vocabulary (Lahey & Drabman, 1974; Kirby, Holborn, & Bushby, 1981); and compound sentences (Risley & Reynolds, 1970).

Basic repertoires. Numerous programs based on the principles of behavior have been successful in teaching expressive object naming. For example, Luiselli and Donellon (1980) used a fading procedure to teach color names, and McGee, Krantz, Mason, and McClannahan (1983) applied an incidental teaching procedure, modified to suit the repertoires of autistic youth, to increase those students' vocabularies.

Much of the work on naming has emphasized conditions under which the skill may be generalized, including the types of training materials used, schedules of reinforcement employed, and the contributions of other already established repertoires. Labeling has generalized to nontraining circumstances more successfully when real objects rather than pictures are used in training (Welch & Pear, 1980; Salmon, Pear, & Kuhn, 1986), and when reinforcement for correct labeling is provided intermittently rather than continuously (Stephens, Pear, Wray, & Jackson, 1975; Olenick & Pear, 1980).

An interesting finding having to do with the contributions of other repertoires on naming

has been reported by Charlop (1983). Charlop found that capitalizing on a repertoire of echolalic speech facilitated autistic children's acquisition and generalization of receptive labeling tasks. This finding is particularly interesting because echolalia typically is targeted for change as an inappropriate behavior. Verbal imitation or echoic behavior (Butz & Hasazi, 1973) and responses to questions (Handleman, 1979; Clark & Sherman, 1986; McMorrow et al., 1987) are among other classes of communicative behavior that have been shaped by behavior analytic training procedures.

Asking questions (Charlop, Schreibman, & Thibodeau, 1985; Halle et al., 1981; Yamamoto & Mochizuki, 1988) also has been established through reinforcement procedures. Of particular interest was the use of delay. When delay was imposed between the opportunity to engage in a certain task and the essential assistance of the teacher (as in the other time-delay procedures discussed in Chapter 18) students eventually asked questions to enlist the rapid assistance of the teacher (Charlop et al., 1985; Halle et al., 1981).

Teaching **stimulus equivalence** requires that the stimuli to be taught possess the features of symmetry, reflexivity, and transitivity (see footnote 4, Chapter 15). The match-to-sample method (Chapter 18) can be applied to teach students to match names, numbers, definitions, or other functionally equivalent discriminative stimuli conditional upon their relations to one another. The basic methodology includes teaching conditional discriminations among stimuli (when you see *two*, selecting 2 is reinforced, and vice versa) by reinforcing matches for some but not all combinations and permutations of the stimuli within the functional class. This is the way a normal adult and a teenager with autism were taught, in a basic laboratory study, to match numerals with Greek letters (Sidman, Wynne, Maguire, & Barnes, 1989), and developmentally disabled participants learned to match colors or numerals with their names (Mackay & Sidman, 1984).

More elaborate forms of verbal behavior, including sustained conversation, also have been taught to retarded subjects (Haring, Roger, Lee, Breen, & Gaylord-Ross, 1986; Kleitsch, Whitman, & Santos, 1983). By arranging conditions in which participants needed to complete tasks requiring cooperation and interdependence, Mithaug and Wolfe (1976) fostered conversational interactions—a technique of particular value when extrinsic consequences are difficult to deliver. The procedure takes advantage of the contingencies arising out of the task itself.

Finally, reading or "textual" behavior (Singh & Singh, 1984) and composition or written intraverbal behavior (Brigham, Graubard, & Stans, 1972) have been amenable to behavior analytic interventions. By manipulating consequences, for example, Brigham et al. (1972) increased the total words, the number of different words, and the number of new words written by students in a remedial fifth-grade class.

Complex repertoires. Behavior analytic procedures also have been used to expand language repertoires, such as various parts of speech and the construction of sentences. Among the grammatical elements amplified by behavioral training programs are plural morphemes (Schumaker & Sherman, 1970; Guess & Baer, 1973); prepositions (Frisch & Schumaker, 1974); articles and auxiliary verbs (Wheeler & Sulzer, 1970); adjectives (Martin, 1975); pronouns (Rubin & Stolz, 1974); and comparative and superlative suffixes (Baer & Guess, 1971).

The construction and use of simple singular and plural declarative sentences with subject-verb agreement have been accomplished using modeling, imitation, and reinforcement procedures for retarded subjects, normal toddlers, and autistic subjects (Campbell & Stremel-Campbell, 1982; Lutzker & Sherman, 1974; Stevens-Long & Rasmussen, 1974). Autistic

students also have been taught compound sentence structure (Stevens-Long, Schwartz, & Blis, 1976.) Campbell and Stremel-Campbell (1982) attribute the success of their program to what they call a "loose training" strategy (a method for promoting generalization, as you will see in Chapter 29). This strategy involved conducting language training in the context of other academic tasks so the student was able to initiate language related to a wide array of naturally occurring stimulus events.

Provided you pinpoint and task analyze the skills you are attempting to teach, these methods can be applied to instruction in all realms of verbal learning. This includes the stimulus-response combinations of the type often subsumed under the category of cognitive processes. Recognize that they may be learned in the same way as other forms of behavior, and that instructional prompts may support their development.

Promoting Generalization of Communicative Skills

We know not to anticipate that newly acquired skills will spontaneously generalize beyond tightly controlled training settings without special programming. Numerous methods will be discussed in Chapter 29, but one is especially relevant to the promotion of complex language in the natural environment: **incidental teaching** (Hart & Risley, 1968; 1974; 1975; 1980). The following prototypic case describes how incidental teaching works.

Children in a preschool serving lower-income families were observed to speak and use elaborate language markedly less often than their more privileged peers. Time in school, intermittent teacher praise, and social and intellectual stimulation were insufficient to remedy the problem. Although formal group instruction effectively increased the children's rates of using color-noun and number-noun combinations in that context, they did not initiate such behavior spontaneously elsewhere.

Incidental teaching then was employed during free-play activities. Whenever the children seemed to want to play with a particular item (toy, game, and so on), they were prompted and required to ask for it, first by name (noun), then by name plus a word that described the material (adjective-noun combination), and finally by requesting the material and stating how they were going to use it (compound sentence). After incidental teaching of compound sentences, increases in unprompted use of compound sentences were seen for all the children. First the sentences were directed to teachers, and then to children, according to who attended to the children's requests for play materials. By the end of the preschool year, the rate of speaking and degree of elaboration of the children's unprompted words equaled that of other more affluent preschool children, regardless of whether the response had been specifically trained or not.

In this example, both prompting and contingent reinforcement were used to evoke the desired verbalizations. However, the increase in language elaboration probably was traceable to the incidental teaching. Hart and Risley (1980) have described and discussed the features of the incidental teaching procedure they assumed were responsible for the positive results obtained as follows:

> First, incidental teaching is conducted within the very setting conditions that naturally maintain language use. That is, incidental teaching is conducted in a richly varied stimulus environment, full of people, things, and activities to be accessed and manipulated through language use. . . .
>
> Second, incidental teaching is conducted casually throughout the child's day, at various times, in various contexts, in relation to whatever aspect of a varied stimulus environment the child selects as a momentarily prepotent reinforcer. As the child initiates with language related to many different aspects of his environment, many different elaborations are requested. . . .
>
> Third, incidental teaching is by its nature

> "loose training" (Stokes & Baer, 1977). Adults arrange the context for incidental teaching, but they have little control over the particular stimulus a child will select to initiate about at any given moment. The child in fact controls the incidental teaching interaction because he or she initiates it, specifying a reinforcer an adult can deliver. . . . Therefore, the adult must focus on keeping the child initiating rather than on a criterion for a specific response topography. This means keeping the incidental teaching interaction brief, positive, and focused on the child-selected reinforcer. . . .
>
> Fourth, the conditions of incidental teaching are such that the actual contingencies of reinforcement are likely to be much less discriminable than those in a one-to-one training situation. The adult conducts incidental teaching only when he or she has both the time and an appropriate, reinforcer-related prompt for elaboration. Therefore, the adult sometimes delivers a child-requested reinforcer without asking for language elaboration; sometimes he or she prompts once, sometimes more than once. Over time, merely the focus of close adult attention when the child initiates is likely to become a discriminative stimulus for elaboration, such that the adult does not have to prompt at all.
>
> Perhaps most importantly, incidental teaching establishes a class of behavior, language use, which is likely to be generalized by stimulus similarity across settings and occasions. Not only does language function differentially to gain access to reinforcers, but language initiation is followed, on an intermittent schedule, by close, receptive adult attention; focus on the reinforcer the child has selected; and often a request for more of the behavior, language. A response class, language *use*, is reinforced in a wide variety of stimulus conditions (pp. 409–410).

Regardless of the class of communication being learned, incidental teaching provides an excellent opportunity for aiding transfer of verbal skills into the everyday environment. Whether a disfluency, an elaboration, practice of a verbal skill or whatever, access to natural reinforcers—audience reaction, access to items, or whatever—may be withheld until the skill is appropriate.

Promoting Acquisition of Manual Communicative Behavior

The same strategies that have been employed to teach people "higher mental processes" can work just as well in an entirely different problem area: teaching people who lack functional speech to use manual or sign language. Recent work has focused on how specific aspects of the training procedures may contribute. One facet has been the extent to which concurrent auditory stimuli facilitate normal hearing students' acquisition of signing skills. Apparently, total communication approaches, in which both visual and auditory stimuli are employed, produce results superior to those achieved with auditory stimuli alone, even among developmentally disabled children with limited vocal repertoires (Sisson & Barrett, 1984) and echolalic autistic children (Barrera & Sulzer-Azaroff, 1983; Remington & Clarke, 1983). Interestingly, auditory stimuli controlled the behavior of hearing children, whereas visual stimuli controlled the behavior of a mute child. Carr, Binkoff, Kologinsky, and Eddy (1978), on the other hand, found that stimulus control was occurring by way of the visual rather than the auditory stimuli for autistic children in their study. The work of Schepis et al. (1982) is relevant here. The researchers discovered that when incidental teaching strategies were used to teach signing, vocalizations increased as well.

Other factors found to be important in teaching signing have included the student's previously established verbal repertoire and the context in which signing is taught. For example, Clarke et al. (1986) found that expressive sign acquisition was facilitated when the words involved in sign training were already available in the subject's receptive language repertoires. With regard to contextual variables, Carr and Kologinsky (1983) found greater spontaneity and generalization of signing when many people and objects were involved in the training.

Modifying Maladaptive Communicative Behavior

Maladaptive communication of the sort observed in schizophrenics is amenable to behavior modification, as typified in the following hypothetical case.

Robert, age 32, had a 12-year history of frequent admissions to an inpatient mental health facility and had been diagnosed as schizophrenic, either catatonic or undifferentiated. Nursing staff, some of whom had known him for years, commented that his condition had deteriorated progressively, especially over the past 5 years. On the inpatient unit, Robert withdrew socially (i.e., failed to initiate conversations with others) and made grandiose ("delusional") statements when engaged by others in conversation (e.g., "I am a four-star general appointed by the president," "I am an emissary of the Pope," and "I am going to practice medicine when I get out of here.")

The team responsible for Robert's treatment targeted both his failure to initiate conversations and his delusional speech for modification. To increase Robert's initiating conversations, a staff member would prompt him by holding a reinforcer before Robert and saying "Say 'Hello!' " If he greeted the person, he was given the item. If he failed to do so within 30 seconds, the staff member walked away. When Robert began to greet the staff member consistently, verbal prompts gradually were faded. The staff member then progressively faded the visual prompt (display of the reinforcer) by holding the item farther and farther away until it remained in his pocket.

Next, reinforcement was gradually delivered progressively less often until Robert consistently greeted people without receiving any tangible reinforcers. Finally, this procedure was repeated with additional staff members until Robert consistently greeted anyone who would approach him.

To reduce Robert's delusional and increase his rational speech, staff members conducted 10-minute daytime interviews after Robert greeted them. These were terminated prematurely any time he spoke grandiosely, whereas he could earn time toward a 30-minute informal evening chat with the staff, during which coffee and snacks were available, by talking rationally during the daytime interviews. Under this procedure, Robert's percentage of rational talk increased markedly and persisted even when the amount of reinforcement was diminished by half.

That hypothetical case illustrates results actually obtained by Kale, Kaye, Whelan, and Hopkins (1968) and Liberman, Teigen, Patterson, and Baker (1973) with different groups of schizophrenic inpatients. As in modifying other classes of maladaptive behavior, the procedures (i.e., prompts, fading, contingent reinforcement, generalization training, and differential reinforcement) work just as well with communicative behavior. Such approaches have been employed successfully in various clinical populations, including the chronically mentally ill (e.g., Wong et al., 1987); elderly with impaired functioning (e.g. Praderas & MacDonald, 1986; Green, Linsk, & Pinkston, 1986); hearing-impaired (e.g., Heward & Eachus, 1979); and brain-injured (Lewis, Nelson, Nelson, & Reusink, 1988).

Cognitive Behavior Modification

In earlier chapters you learned about the potential usefulness of self-instructions or self-statements. You know, then, that the things people say or fail to say to themselves can influence what they do. The degree of influence, though, depends upon the nature of the strength of rule governance over those behaviors. For instance, labeling herself as obese, even though the rest of the world views her as thin, may cause Jocelyn to restrict her intake of food to detrimental levels. Failing to deliberate adequately in advance describes impulsiveness, a response pattern in which persons respond too rapidly, to their disadvantage. Even the way we talk to ourselves about pain can influence how severely we experience it. Cognitive behavior modification is a strategy designed to modify what people do by altering what they say to themselves.

Countless articles and books (e.g., Beck & Emery, 1985; Craighead, Kazdin, & Mahoney, 1981; Kendall & Hollon, 1979; M. J. Mahoney, 1974; Meichenbaum, 1974) have been written on the topic of cognitive behavior modification. Recognize that if a person lacks a particular verbal repertoire to recite to himself or herself, this repertoire can be shaped. A classic method to combat impulsiveness (Meichenbaum & Goodman, 1971) involved teaching a general series of self-instructions, including questions to identify the task, answers, and related plans, plus self-guidance and reinforcement. These self-instructions were shaped in a series of steps beginning with the teacher modeling the behavior and the self-instruction, then gradually shifting control over to the child. Elements of that basic format have been included in and combined with methods for managing hyperactivity, conduct disorders, social withdrawal, and numerous other behavioral problems of childhood.

Cognitive behavior modification also has been used to treat adults for all sorts of difficulties, including obsessions and compulsions; fears; social inadequacies, such as dating difficulties; and numerous others. One instance is that of correcting negative body images (Rosen, Saltzberg, & Srebnik, 1989). The young women who participated were taught to substitute accurate descriptions and positive self-statements for their irrational negative ones, a strategy that was reflected in improved scores on several scales and questionnaires.

As in many of the case reports of the use of this type of treatment, transfer into the real world and everyday life was not monitored directly, to see how the presumed changes in self-statements related to alterations in patterns of eating. In all likelihood, generalization and maintenance methods need to be combined with the cognitive behavior modification methods, if significant change is to transfer to other contexts and persist. One means of accomplishing this is through correspondence training, discussed later. Others are delineated in the last part of this text in the section on maintenance and generalization.

How successful might you expect to be in teaching clients to use coping self-statements to guide their future performance? One important factor on which the answer depends is whether the self-statements are made in *private or public*.

Speech-anxious college students showed significantly greater improvement when their coping self-statements were public than when they were not (Zettle & Hayes, 1982). Similarly, coping self-statements can increase pain tolerance (Hayes & Wolf, 1984). Subjects who voiced their self-coping skills aloud before a group were able to experience an uncomfortable task—keeping their hands immersed in cold water—longer than subjects in an attention-only placebo group. The same holds for children (Rosenfarb & Hayes, 1984) fearful of the dark. Coping self-statements and modeling were found to be equally effective in increasing dark tolerance but only when presented in a public context.

Remedying Problematic Communicative Topographies

Behavior analytic procedures have also been used to modify problems not with content but with speech forms, including disfluencies (Seigel, Lenske, & Broen, 1969); lengthy pausing

(Singer, Pasnak, Drash, & Baer, 1978); poor articulation (Murdock, Garcia, & Hardman, 1977); and aphonia (Jackson & Wallace, 1974). One instance (Singer et al., 1978) involved a procedure to reduce pausing by presenting food intermittently, contingent on participants' rapid vocalizations and briefly darkening the room following long pauses. Journals on communication disorders have published numerous other examples of how stuttering, "elective mutism," and other difficulties of oral speaking have been modified successfully.

Teaching Rule Governance

As in all other circumstances, you need to know the nature of the difficulty if you are to attempt to rectify a problem in the domain of rule-governed behavior. Is failure to apply rules to oneself the problem, or is the issue one of complying with inappropriate rules or failing to comply with beneficial ones specified by oneself or by the community? Do strongly established rules block the impact of actual consequences or interfere with response fluency?

Task analyses and the other techniques for targeting or pinpointing behavior might enable you to detail the essential elements of the rules you are trying to fashion, so they can be modified and applied effectively. When strongly established rules block an individual's learning from the contingencies actually in operation (e.g., stating "Safety glasses are for sissies," but if he were to wear them his work unit would get a better safety score), the rules can be made more salient by emphasizing their various parameters: arranging more timely and frequent delivery of reinforcers; heightening their discriminability and value; and so on.

To teach compliance with specific rules for self-application or use with others, you use differential reinforcement, as suggested in Chapter 16. Tell the rule and immediately reinforce compliance with it. Repeat the sequence frequently under all the circumstances in which it is to gain control, until the relation is high and steady. To promote more general rule following in particular settings, such as at work or in school, repeat the same sort of sequence for *all* essential rules. After a while, even new rules may take hold in the absence of the specific strategy or reinforcement. For example, the safety director at Top Quality is trying to achieve perfect compliance with his employees' adherence to safety rules. He teaches all the foremen to post and explain each rule (e.g., "Wear hard hats and safety glasses at all times" plus a number of others) and to immediately and consistently comment positively on adherence to each rule. Once all workers are regularly complying with all the posted rules, when a new one is added, workers adhere to that one as well.

Correspondence training also can be extremely useful when the concern is one of teaching compliance of a more general sort. Once established, a high degree of correspondence can permit you to modify behavior by altering the rules people generate for themselves rather than treating the behavior directly.

Correspondence Training

Rule governance is a powerful form of behavioral control. It does not, however, simply emerge full-blown once the child acquires a basic communicative repertoire. Children may know many words and still not accurately say what they did this morning or accurately report what they will do this afternoon. Correspondence research addresses how we learn to say what we do or to do what we say.

Correspondence defined. In general terms, correspondence between a person's oral and overt behavior occurs when his or her oral statement accurately describes the function, form, or topography of the related noncommunicative behavior (i.e., telling the truth).[3] The presumed correspondence between an individual's state-

ment and deed plays an important role in social mechanisms used to shape behavior. For example, educators strive to foster social attitudes by shaping statements about the standards of society and the role the individual plays in that society. This process is expected to lead to corresponding actions (e.g., obeying the law). Similarly, many forms of psychotherapy deal most directly with a client's verbalizations, presumably with the view that verbal changes will be associated with changes in their overt actions (e.g., "I will go to the store even though I'm afraid to go outside—I can be afraid and still do it").

Teaching correspondence. The social importance of the correspondence between saying and doing has led to a significant body of research concerned with training and maintaining that correspondence. **Correspondence training** teaches children to produce their own verbal cues and enhances the controlling function of such cues. As you will see in Chapter 29, such training has considerable potential for generalization to other situations, because the child can generate those verbal S^Ds in novel situations. Maintenance of behavior change (Chapters 30–32) also may be enhanced by teaching people to produce verbal cues for themselves when no one is there to do that for them.

Reinforcing correspondence. Many researchers have found that reinforcing modifications in what children said often influenced what they did subsequently (Lovaas, 1964; Rogers-Warren & Baer, 1976; Williams & Stokes, 1982). In all of these studies, however, the degree of correspondence was limited and its maintenance transitory. Reinforcement of statements of intentions or true or untrue descriptions of prior performance alone did not necessarily lead to changes in corresponding performance.

---

[3] Equivalence relations, discussed in Chapter 15, may be the basis for correspondence (Matthews et al., 1987).

In a pioneering study, when Risley and Hart (1968) made reinforcement contingent on the actual *correspondence* between saying and doing, that made a difference! Initially, preschool children received reinforcement for any true or untrue report of prior use of a specific preschool material. Reinforcement then was made contingent on reports that corresponded with actual use of the material (i.e., true reports). *Afterward*, reinforcing the childrens' statements of what they intended to do was sufficient to get them to follow through with their stated intentions.

Israel and O'Leary (1973) trained preschoolers to say what toy they were going to play with. Then they reinforced the childrens' actual follow-through with their stated intentions. That "say then do" training sequence produced better correspondence than just asking the children to say what they had done and reinforcing true reports (do/say), without any previous statements of intent. Similar results were obtained by Karoly and Dirks (1977). In fact, some research suggests that reinforcing verbalizations prior to the correspondence training may not be necessary to the effectiveness of the procedure (Baer, Detrich, & Weninger, 1988; Israel & Brown, 1977). But Baer et al. (1988) showed that prior verbalizations by either a teacher or the child helped. Presumably the verbalizations served as S^{D}s, setting the occasion for following through with the behavior described.

Train the form of correspondence you are looking for. Is your objective to teach people to do what they promise, to report honestly about what they did, or both? Apparently, you will need to teach each of these specific cases separately, because generalization has been found to be limited to the specific correspondence sequence trained (Israel, 1978). If the student says she will play with a particular friend and does, reinforce the deed. If the student said she played with a particular friend and she did, reinforce the statement.

You also might consider using functional equivalence training to facilitate the acquisition of correspondence. Functional equivalence is the foundation both for reliably doing what we say and saying what we do. Using the methods for teaching functional equivalence, then, may help to produce say/do and do/say correspondence through matching the tasks of saying and doing.

Use modeling and chaining procedures to teach correspondence. To heighten correspondence, try reinforcing models' honest reporting of their prosocial behaviors, such as sharing and praising (Rogers-Warren & Baer, 1976), and/or break the behavior down into its components and use chaining procedures. Paniagua and Baer (1982) have identified two possible chains. The first consists of the following steps:

1. A promise to perform a behavior.
2. Intermediate behaviors (i.e., behaviors enabling the promised behavior, such as asking for a toy before playing with it as promised).
3. Fulfilling the promise.
4. Reporting subsequently about the fulfillment of the promise.

The second consists of:

1. Preceding behaviors (i.e., behaviors that necessarily must be performed before a later-reported activity).
2. Participation in the later-reported activity.
3. A subsequent report about participation.

Reinforce correspondence as a response class; then provide for generalization and maintenance. As pointed out by Matthews, Shimoff, and Catania (1987), single instances of saying followed by doing are insufficient to permit us to conclude that correspondence has been trained. What you need to do is to watch to see correspondence with *promising* to do something and doing it and correspondence with *not* promising to do something and then not doing it. Only when each of the two matches closely can you feel fairly certain that correspondence does exist as a response class for that person in that context.

To broaden the class, you will need to train many instances of correspondence, under many sets of circumstances, until correspondence is achieved within those general conditions. As always, correspondence needs to be programmed for maintenance and generalization; not left to chance. (See Chapters 29–32.)

Breaking Overdependence on Rules

Some rules are foolish, dangerous, counterproductive, inefficient, or just downright wrong. Going a mile out of your way because if you don't the black cat that crossed your path will bring you bad luck is an instance of a rule better off broken. Urgings to do illegal or unhealthy things, or fallacious reasoning are other instances. Breaking overdependence on well-established rules can be difficult, but you can help clients accomplish the break in one of two ways:

- By differentially reinforcing adherence to more sound competing rules ("That's a silly superstition. I'll just continue on my way.").
- By applying any of the methods for reducing unwanted behavior (e.g., the superstitious self-statements), as described in Section IV.

Avoiding Use of Rules

Sometimes the exact elements of complex behaviors, such as social interactions on a date or at work (e.g., topics of conversation, vocal tone, and body language), might be so elusive that you risk targeting inappropriate or trivial skills instead of those most essential. If you find the validity of your set of target behaviors questionable, bypass the rules and find a way to expose the clients to the experience directly. Azrin and Hayes (1984) used this approach, reasoning that if subjects could know when they were having a positive or negative impact on others, then they would be able to learn by direct experience which social behaviors produced these effects.

Male participants viewed videotapes of interactions between males and females, judging the females' interest in the males with whom they conversed. Information based on criteria generated by the filmed subjects, on how interested those females actually were, was then given to the male viewers without any further instructions. The male viewers' ability to discriminate interest improved and generalized to previously unviewed females, and in subsequent social skills role-play situations. Apparently, a social skill could be assessed and trained without having to determine the components of the skill, and without using any instructions about such components.

Similar results were obtained in a later study of assertiveness (Rosenfarb, Hayes, & Linehan, 1989) in which the experimenter used his "gut reaction" to provide global feedback on socially effective or ineffective performances. Social skills were assessed and treated effectively but without first having to identify the particular subcomponents of the social skills needing to be improved.

Summary

The ability to use language has allowed humans to develop highly sophisticated behaviors. Verbal skills enable people to influence their own actions and those of others. As with any other class of behavior, language is learned via the interplay of intricate contingencies of reinforcement. Rules, a critical feature of language, are words that inform people about the relations between responses and their antecedents and consequences. Rules can abet or may interfere with people's receipt of reinforcers, depending on the match between the rules and actual contingencies in operation.

As with any category of learned behavior, people can experience problems with communicative behavior. Inadequate or maladaptive repertoires, problematic speech topographies, difficulties in rule formulation for oneself or by the community, failure to follow rules or adhering to them too slavishly, and difficulty in rule specification are illustrative.

Various tactics have been devised for teaching and managing communicative behavior: reinforcement, stimulus control, shaping, and other standard behavioral procedures to promote acquisition of simple and complex communication. Functional equivalence training can be used to teach the "meaning" of words and expand the repertoire without necessarily having to train every instance of a stimulus plus verbal response relationship. Generalization and maintenance of verbal behavior do not necessarily happen spontaneously. Procedures like incidental teaching and other methods that are described in Section V of this book should be useful for practitioners concerned with this issue.

Problems with language have been dealt with similarly. Contingencies of reinforcement have been arranged successfully to teach manual language, modify maladaptive repertoires, and enable people to overcome disfluencies and other topographical difficulties. Rule governance can be promoted through differential reinforcement and correspondence training. The latter is accomplished by reinforcing correspondence between what people do and say according to the needed form, using modeling and chaining, reinforcing correspondence as a response class and providing for generalization and maintenance. People also can be taught to break their overdependence on rules or to avoid or alter those that are inaccurate.

At this point you have learned a great deal about teaching simple and complex behaviors, including the things that people do and say aloud and to themselves—thinking. But you never can be confident that your procedures were responsible for any changes accomplished unless you functionally analyze the treatment. The next chapter covers several experimental methods especially well suited to the analysis of complex behavior.

Chapter 22

Evaluating Behavioral Programs: Complex Designs and Assessing Significance of Change

GOALS

After completing this chapter, you should be able to:

1. List and discuss three questions that can be raised legitimately before a behavioral program is adopted on a broad scale.

2. Define, recognize, and give original illustrations for each of the following terms:
   a. Internal validity
   b. External validity
   c. Changing-criterion design
   d. Multiple probes
   e. Multiple treatment interference
   f. Sequential withdrawal design
   g. Alternating (multielement) treatment design
   h. Sequence effects
   i. Experimental significance
   j. Clinical (social, personal) significance
   k. Educational significance
   l. Social validity
   m. Direct replication
   n. Principles of behavior
   o. Systematic replication
   p. Behavioral laws

3. In your own words, identify and describe the advantages and possible limitations of the changing-criterion design, and discuss how to minimize each possible disadvantage.

4. Describe the purpose and advantage of using multiple probes intermittently, and differentiate between using multiple probes and intermittent sampling.

5. Discuss and illustrate how an intervention phase can be used as a baseline phase for another treatment.

6. Describe how withdrawal methods can be used for comparing treatments and in assessing for maintenance.

7. List, describe, and illustrate with a new example the advantages and possible limitations of the alternating treatment design, and discuss how to minimize each possible disadvantage.

8. Discuss why it usually is not possible to conclude that one generic procedure is better than another.

9. Describe a novel situation for each of the designs compared in Table 22.1 for which that specific design would be the most appropriate. Be sure to justify your selection clearly. (Use your response to Goal 9 in Chapter 14 for part of your answer.)

10. Summarize the advantages, strengths, and weaknesses common among single-subject designs. (Use your response to Goal 3 in Chapter 14 as part of your answer.)

11. Discuss how to determine the significance of a demonstrated functional relation. Include a list of criteria.

12. Explain how to determine cost effectiveness and discuss its importance.

13. Discuss the importance that replication plays in developing behavioral laws and in establishing generality of findings.

14. Discuss the importance of conducting preplanned probes of generality and maintenance.

15. Conduct a single-subject research experiment.

How many areas of human performance have you seen illustrated in the multitude of examples presented thus far? Surely you are convinced that behavioral procedures lend themselves to application essentially anywhere humans reside. Success stories in the behavior analytic journals have spanned numerous settings: on the job; in the open community; at home, school, or summer camp; on the golf links; at the swimming pool; in nursing homes, hospitals, community clinics; and many other locations. The categories of behaviors addressed are even more extensive: from classroom deportment to rate and quality of production, energy conservation, skills in sports, academics, social interactions, self-management, oral and written communication, rule governance, problem solving, and on and on.

All right, you're convinced. Behavior analysis has lots to offer, plus a technology for discovering more. Then why is the approach not embraced more universally? Not because people are evil or naive, but for the same reasons why anyone does or fails to do anything. Perhaps they lack essential knowledge or skills, or their learning histories have generated competing behavior, or current contingencies fail to uphold the practice. If a manager has not learned the rules for using differential reinforcement optimally or gained skill in applying them, she will be unlikely to achieve her goals through stimulus control, shaping, chaining, or use of instructions. Perhaps, even if she has acquired such expertise, previously well-established rules or patterns may compete, such as habitually correcting errors instead of reinforcing progress. Alternatively, maybe her efforts have been insufficiently reinforced or possibly punished.

Preliminary Considerations Prior to Adopting Programs

Certainly people who are unaware of the accomplishments of behavior analysis cannot be expected to embrace its methods; nor can skeptics who, reasonably, demand evidence of effectiveness of particular procedures. Their hesitancy is not necessarily misguided. Following is a set of questions any of us might legitimately raise before adopting any broad-scale program, including a behavioral one:

How Internally Valid Is the Program?

Questions of **internal validity** are concerned with ". . . whether there is a causal relationship from one variable to another in the form in which the variables were manipulated or measured" (Cook & Campbell, 1979, p. 38). For behavioral programs, the question is how convincingly can the procedures be shown to relate functionally to changes in behavior? As we already have learned, single-case designs are eminently well suited to this concern because they eliminate competing explanations for the findings.

How Externally Valid Is It?

Cook and Campbell use **external validity** to refer to the ". . . approximate validity with which conclusions are drawn about generalizability of a causal relationship to and across populations of persons, settings, and times" (p. 39). In behavior analysis we want to know whether the procedures have generality beyond the original set of cases, to other people, behaviors, or settings. The investment in an expensive curriculum designed to train managerial skills may be justifiable only if the program would be exportable to other units of the organization. We also want to be able to predict how enduring the effects are likely to be. Will improvement disappear along with the behavior analyst?

The designs described in this book meet this requirement. As you saw in Chapter 14, multiple baselines conducted across settings, tasks, or people permit such generality to be tested. The strategy of collecting measures repeatedly prior to, during, and following intervention informs us about the durability of effect.

Will Changes in Performance Impact the Bottom Line?

If Mel learns a set of dating skills, will he get more dates and will they be more satisfactory? If safe practices are increased, will accidents drop? When students remain on-task, do they necessarily learn more? If managers use more praise and recognition, will their subordinates be more productive? Additionally, analysts should consider what the net benefit of the methods in producing change are apt to be in contrast with the regular ongoing methods or alternative possibilities, or in terms of achieving predetermined goals or standards, or per dollar costs versus expenses. By collecting data on performance and outcome results, behavior analysts also can satisfactorily address these concerns.

The most stringent forms of program evaluation methods use scientific methods to address these questions of validity. In behavior analysis that means conducting careful within-subject (or single-case) functional analyses. These tactics permit us to begin rejecting competing explanations of results as well as to examine the impact on the general ecology of the context in which the change takes place. Both the withdrawal and multiple-baseline designs presented in Chapter 14 permit internal validity to be assessed, whereas the multiple baseline may lend itself to evaluating external validity. This chapter presents additional methods for functionally analyzing the relation between treatments and behavior when more complex behaviors or comparisons are involved. Included are ways to experimentally evaluate people's progress in acquiring and/or maintaining new skills, in the comparative effects of different strategies of change, and in the significance of the changes achieved.

Functionally Analyzing Acquisition of Skills

Ms. Charming decided to evaluate the functional effectiveness of the methods she wanted to use to shape Fern's acquisition of skills as a box packer. Mr. Ernie, the psychologist, is attempting to help his client, Helen, to learn a set of effective social coping skills. Paula's boss, Angela, needs to teach Paula a new system of accounting and decides to try a backward chaining approach. How could the relation between those treatment methods and the performances of concern be evaluated?

As discussed in Chapter 14, although increases in response levels may be revealed during the treatment phase, using a withdrawal design would not be a suitable tool for functionally analyzing nonreversible patterns of behavior. Measures of successfully acquired skills would not tend to return to baseline levels during the withdrawal phase. Just as we don't forget our proficiency in riding a bicycle or reading, Fern, Helen, and Paula would not be expected to forget the skills they had mastered.

Also recall from Chapter 14 that multiple baselines can reveal changes in levels of responding as a function of treatment, without necessitating a reversal in the level of performance as evidence of success. The strength of the demonstration lies in showing that change only occurs reliably when the intervention is put into effect for each particular baseline. But what do you do when no other behaviors, settings, or people are available? Also, you may want to shape a behavior by steps, according to preset levels, and would like to see if your treatment is in control. One alternative is the changing-criterion design.

Changing-Criterion Design

Hall has described the **changing-criterion design** as follows:

> In using the changing criterion design, the experimenter successively changes the criterion or consequation, usually in graduated steps, from baseline levels to a desired terminal level. If the behavior changes successively at or close to the set criterion levels, experimental control can be demonstrated (1971a, p. 24).

Shaping and differential reinforcement of low or diminishing rates (see Chapters 19 and 24) and progressive or adjusting schedules (Chapter 30) involve successively changing the criterion levels; consequently the changing criterion design is especially well suited for analysis of those techniques. Hall (1971b) illustrated this design by citing a study of smoking reduction. A 23-year-old male graduate student who had smoked 20 to 30 cigarettes a day for several years, wanted to quit. The program was first set up so that if he smoked more than 15 cigarettes in a day, he would tear a dollar bill into tiny pieces and throw it away. This criterion of 15 cigarettes remained in effect for 5 days; then it was changed to 13 cigarettes for 5 days, and so on. In discussing the study, Hall noted that "the systematic stairstep ceiling was never exceeded and in most cases was closely approximated. . . . Each 5-day phase acted as a baseline for the next 5-day phase and demonstrated that the self-imposition of the consequence of having to tear up a dollar bill was effective in keeping smoking below the criterion level" (1971b, p. 55).

In a very similar case—this one designed to reduce caffeine intake in a more positive fashion (Foxx & Rubinoff, 1979)—participants received partial refunds of money they had deposited for achieving criterion levels. (See Figure 22.1. Also, refer back to Figure 17.1 to see how workers' performance of safe job skills adhered closely to the levels set as goals for any particular week.)

The changing-criterion design also was used to demonstrate the control of reinforcement over the number of correct answers in math (Hall, 1971a, Figure 22.2). Note that for criterion 8, the number of days was greater. For experimental purposes, *varying the number of sessions* among criterion levels is best, in order to illustrate more clearly that the behavior remains at, or close to, the criterion level until the level is changed. (Even more compelling would be a "reversal" in an occasional step

level, to show the adherence of the level of the performance to the preset criterion step.) A replication across subjects, as actually was done in the Sulzer-Azaroff et al. (1990) safety study, again with varying time spans for each criterion level, would provide still more supportive evidence.

Because the changing-criterion design depends on the match between the value of the dependent variable and the preestablished criterion level, change agents must be cautious in setting those levels. If they are too close together, the behavior may "run away with itself," and control over extraneous variables will be lost. If set too far apart, the criterion levels may never be reached.

Aunt Minerva decides to use a point system to help her to lose weight, and she wants to find out whether the points, exchangeable for a bikini and a trip to the south of France, closely influence her eating habits. She sets the criterion for receipt of points for the next week at a level of intake that is 20 calories below that set during the previous week. The following week, she sets the criterion 20 calories lower, and so on. Yet the data show that her intake is reduced far more substantially than the preset average of 20 calories each week. She loses weight, but also experimental control. Because the calorie-intake level does not match the preestablished criteria, any possibly controlling function of the point system is obscured. Maybe other unidentified factors were at work, and she doesn't know whether or not the point system had any influence at all. Had Aunt Minerva set the criteria at a more challenging level, she might have been able to demonstrate experimental control.

Similarly, applied researchers who are considering a changing-criterion design should select each criterion level with care, so the measures of the dependent variable are likely to match it. In the event that the behavior appears to run away from the criterion level, the latter

376 Evaluating Behavioral Programs

Figure 22.1 Subject's Daily Caffeine Intake (mg) During Baseline, Treatment, and Follow-Up. The criterion level for each treatment phase was 102 mg of caffeine less than the previous treatment phase. Solid horizontal lines indicate the criterion level for each phase. Broken horizontal lines indicate the mean for each condition.

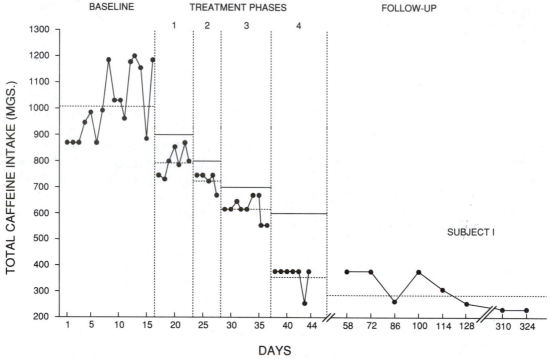

Source: Foxx & Rubinoff (1979), p. 339. Reprinted with the permission of the Society for the Experimental Analysis of Behavior.

can be made more stringent, thereby allowing control to be reestablished.

Multiple Probes

With the changing-criterion design, we might lose the opportunity to see whether any sub-component or related behaviors could have been improving simultaneously, or if change might be achieved more rapidly. Maybe setting a 90% criterion level at the onset would have boosted safety performance immediately to that level, obviating any need to shape gradual improvement. Chapter 14 described one possible alternative: using multiple baselines to determine whether responding has generalized from

one baseline to another. (You might review that design at this point.)

To assess progress in shaping or chaining, you could take the skill you are teaching, break it down to its separate elements, collect baseline measures, and apply the intervention sequentially to each element's baseline to see whether change depends on the intervention or if elements change regardless. Maybe acquiring one segment of a chain immediately produces mastery of another element, as in the case of any reasonably proficient typist's being able to begin to compose on a word processing program after learning to access the program.

The same logic can apply to assessing whether intervention with one element of a task analysis or performance level influences per-

Figure 22.2   Results of a Changing-Criterion Design for Placing Numbers of Correct Answers in Math Under Control of Reinforcement

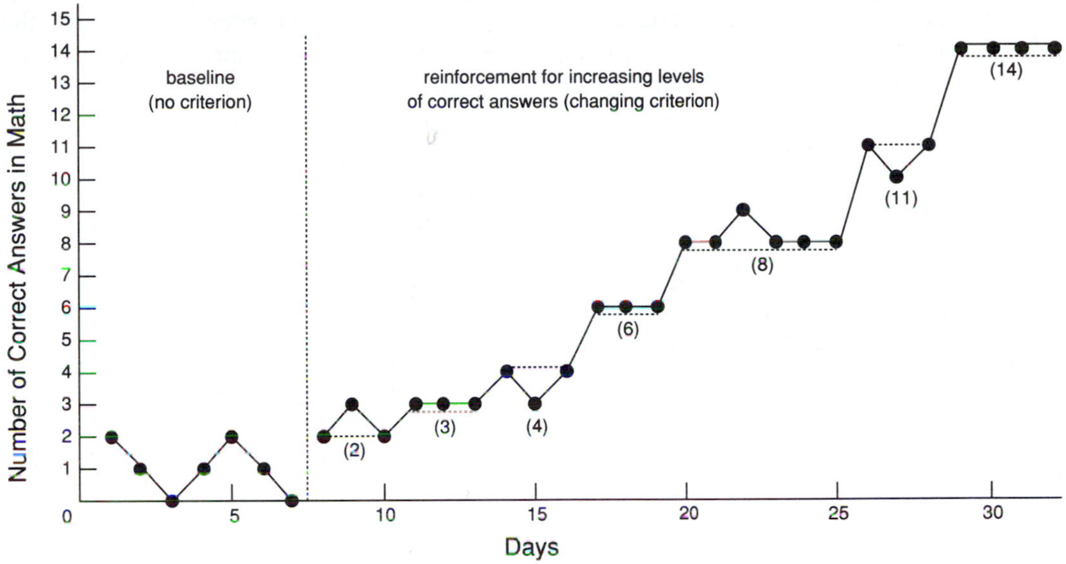

Source: Hall (1971a), p. 25. Permission to reprint by R. Vance Hall, Ph.D., H&H Enterprises, Inc.

formance on another. Intervene with one skill or rate and watch what happens with the others, in multiple-baseline fashion. Horner and Baer (1978) supply the example of a student learning to do long division. Learning to multiply, one of the steps in the chain, could influence success with other untutored steps.

Consider this tactic for a moment, though, and you will realize that taking continuous baselines for unlearned segments occasionally may be impractical or punishing for the evaluator and the learner. Asking someone unfamiliar with word processing commands to format documents throughout repeated baseline trials would be foolish and maybe sufficiently punishing to cause the student subsequently to avoid the program altogether.

Just as a nurse does not take a person's temperature continuously but instead probes the temperature occasionally, a preferable approach here is to "probe" the untreated baselines intermittently (Horner & Baer, 1978). In **multiple-probe** fashion, once in a while you

would provide the learner with an opportunity to perform the untrained responses, just to ascertain whether they were being acquired adventitiously (i.e., as a function of some unidentified conditions). Horner and Baer suggest that this opportunity be presented and the probe conducted:

1. initially on each of the training steps.
2. again "on every step in the training sequence after criterion is reached on any training step" (p. 190).
3. then in a series just prior to teaching a particular step.

To illustrate, consider the steps in teaching an abbreviated word processing operation:

1. Turn on the computer.
2. Access the word processing program.
3. Open a file.
4. Type a paragraph.
5. Save the file.
6. Print the file.

Instead of asking the student to perform each step repeatedly, you might ask the student to perform each step just once. Next, take a few baseline measures on Step 1; then train that step by telling, showing, and reinforcing. Once Step 1 is learned, you would again assess Steps 2 through 6; then you would probe Step 2 in a series, followed by training in a similar manner. Again you would probe the remaining steps and take a series of measures for Step 3, and so on. Perhaps you would see performance was beginning to improve at the more advanced levels, in the absence of instruction. So further teaching would not be necessary.

Figure 22.3 displays probe data for one of three developmentally delayed young men learning laundry skills (Thompson et al., 1982). The probes measured each response in the entire chain right before baseline and training of each component. No reinforcers were delivered during probes. The baseline data only measured components previously trained plus the component to be trained next. As the data indicate, Chester did *know* how to do some of the untrained steps prior to the intervention.

Avoid confusing the multiple probe method of experimental analysis with intermittent sampling of skill acquisition in general, though, if you want to be able to assess learning trends. Multiple probes do include closely repeated measures of performance at the step being taught. That is not the same thing as quizzing weekly, monthly, or twice a semester—an all-too-familiar practice. One of several disadvantages of infrequent assessments is, as shown by Munger, Snell, and Loyd (1989), that except when graphed data showed systematic improvement in performance, the instructor's judgment of students' variable, stable, or decreasing performance trends may be distorted. Unwise program recommendations could result.

The design strategies presented to this point permit behavior analysts to assess the functional relation between a given intervention and performance by revealing patterns of responding prior to and during the intervention. Suppose your concern goes beyond that, though, because some interventions might promise to work more rapidly, or be more durable, costlier, or more or less practical or acceptable to consumers than others. You want to know which among a number of alternative strategies is preferable. Maybe you are wondering whether oral instructions are sufficient to teach word processing or if modeling might speed up the process. Perhaps you wish to analyze the effects of three contingencies on schoolchildren's completion of tasks: no extra recess (treatment A), extra recess time with planned activities (treatment B), and extra recess time with free play (treatment C). In these circumstances you might compare the different contingencies by selecting a design strategy based on repeatedly measuring their various impacts within individual subjects.

Within-Subjects Comparative Designs

Often change agents are concerned about which among a set of possible procedural arrangements will accomplish their purposes best. Will providing staff with an instructional manual be sufficient, or will feedback be necessary to maintain their correct implementation of a peer review system (Eagen, Luce, & Hall, 1988)? Will autistic children learn to communicate more rapidly with oral or total communication training (Barrera & Sulzer-Azaroff, 1983; Barrett & Sisson, 1987)? Will students perform better when working for themselves or for the entire group (Kazdin & Geesey, 1977; Ulman & Sulzer-Azaroff, 1975)? In selecting instructional targets for developmentally disabled students, does it matter whether the skills are age or developmentally appropriate (Dyer et al., 1987; Lifter, Sulzer-Azaroff, Anderson, & Edwards, 1989)? Will students learn

Figure 22.3 Percent Correct Responses for Each Trial on Each Component of the Laundry Chain. Heavy vertical lines on the horizontal axis represent successive training sessions. Shorter vertical lines along the horizontal axis indicate trials within a session.

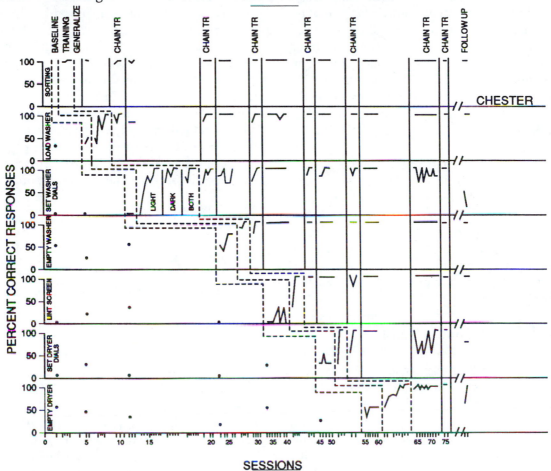

Source: Thompson et al. (1982), p. 180. Reprinted with the permission of the Society for the Experimental Analysis of Behavior.

to spell more rapidly when positive practice is added to positive reinforcement (Ollendick, Matson, Esveldt-Dawson, & Shapiro, 1980)?

Intervention Phases as Baselines

When you pause to consider, you will realize that in applied research, "no-treatment" baselines do not exist. Antecedent and consequential contingencies of various kinds are embedded in every context in which people find themselves. At issue only is whether the con-

tingencies are administered according to plan or exist by happenstance. Regardless, baselines do not occur in a vacuum. So, in a sense, when we contrast the effects of a formal treatment with those under "baseline conditions," we are examining the influence of superimposing the new treatment component on or exchanging it for the contingencies previously in operation.

Given this line of reasoning, one treatment phase should be able to serve as a baseline condition for another. Presuming care has been taken to equalize the size and difficulty of each step, in an approach derived from a study by Jones, Ollendick, and Shinske (1989), try teaching fire evacuation skills via behavioral rehearsal alone, as a baseline condition, then add a cognitive component—elaborative training with questions and answers about the components, to see whether or to what extent the rate of progress speeds up. If it does, apply the elaborative training sequentially to the other baselines generated by teaching skills with behavioral rehearsal alone.

Recognize, though, that this tactic says nothing about what would happen were elaborative training used in the absence of behavioral rehearsal. To discover that relationship, you would need to train other skills of a similar nature, beginning with an elaborative training baseline and superimposing the behavioral rehearsal phase on *it* later on, as described previously.

Withdrawal Comparisons

Another way of attempting to answer the questions raised in this discussion is to use a withdrawal design consisting of a baseline followed by one treatment, followed by a return to baseline, then the same or a different treatment, randomizing the order of the various interventions, and usually separating them by baseline phases (e.g., A-B-A-C-A-C-A-B-A-C, and so on) continuing across different tasks or materials. This is a popular method for comparing the influence of short-acting drugs and/or of different strategies that presumably temporarily influence maladaptive behavior. (See Burgio, Page, & Capriotti, 1985, for an example.)

A history of one treatment condition might influence performance on a subsequent treatment. That would be a case of **multiple treatment interference**—a situation in which an observed change under one condition actually is due to the influence of prior treatment variables. To rule out this potential confound the

order of treatments could be reversed on replication (e.g., A-C-A-B) within, preferably, or across subjects.

That was the strategy followed by Dyer et al. (1987) and Lifter et al. (1989). In both cases individual children were taught either age or developmentally appropriate tasks—language in the former, play in the latter—in different intervention phases, demonstrating that they learned the developmentally appropriate tasks more rapidly than the age appropriate actions, regardless of the treatment order. (See Higgins Hains and Baer, 1989, for further discussion of the strengths and weakness of this approach.)

Assessing for maintenance with withdrawal designs. What if your concern is whether some particular element of the treatment is still essential to the maintenance of performance? According to Rusch and Kazdin (1981) "In the **sequential-withdrawal design**, one component is withdrawn initially, then a second, and so on until all components have been withdrawn" (p. 132). This format permits an assessment of whether any single component is essential to the *maintenance* of the behavior change. After you have learned how to operate the word processor, removing each instructional element in turn should reveal how durable the skill has become in the absence of any prompt.

A related method is to partially withdraw elements by removing one element at a time from each baseline of a multiple-baseline design. Joe Duffer has learned to drive, putt, and escape from sand traps via a combination of modeling, instructions, graduated guidance, and praise for improvements. The pro takes away one of those elements at a time from the putting, leaving the elements in place with the other skills. When no deterioration follows, the elements are removed from the next skill, and so on. Martin and Rusch (1987) used this tactic successfully to determine which instructional components might be dispensed with after a group of mentally retarded adults had acquired meal preparation skills. So if you are concerned about the advisability of whether to keep an intervention intact, try one of these withdrawal methods alone or in combination. (To learn more about these methods of evaluation, see Rusch and Kazdin, 1981, who discuss these and other variations and the advantages and disadvantages of each.)

Disadvantages of withdrawal comparisons. Wondering how long to sustain a treatment phase may be of concern, though, especially if one procedure seems to be taking forever to show any effect. Long exposures to particular treatments may impact positively or negatively on performance during the subsequent treatment, and this multiple-treatment interference might introduce ambiguity into the situation. Wouldn't the opportunity to test both interventions simultaneously be an advantage? Provided you were working with "sensitive" responses capable of shifting their rates readily, you could randomly alternate conditions rapidly within or across sessions or days. Then, by examining any differences in rate emerging as a function of each intervention, you would be able to discover which produced superior effects as soon as those differences clearly emerged. This is what the designs to be described next are intended to accomplish.

Alternating Treatment (Multielement) Designs

Experimental designs operating on the principles just described have been called by different names, including **alternating treatment**, (Barlow & Hersen, 1984), **simultaneous treatment** (Kazdin & Hartmann, 1978), **multielement** (Bittle & Hake, 1977; Sidman, 1960; Ulman & Sulzer-Azaroff, 1975), or **multiple schedule** (Leitenberg, 1973). (See Barlow & Hayes, 1979, and Kazdin & Hartmann, 1978, for fine distinctions.) Alternating treatment designs involve rapidly—within or between observational sessions—alternating two or more

treatments or conditions with the same person (Barlow & Hersen, 1984). To illustrate, Harris and Sherman (1973a) wanted to assess how valuable peer tutoring might be for their students' math performance. They compared tutoring and nontutoring conditions by separating math assignments into 2 daily sessions with equivalent problem types and difficulty levels. Peer tutoring occurred before only 1 of 2 sessions: during some phases before the morning session, or during others before the afternoon sessions. Pairing each of the 2 different contingencies with particular sessions permitted the 2 elements to be analyzed separately, revealing the superiority of the peer tutoring condition.

Alternating treatment designs also have been used to compare the effectiveness of different teaching methods. Three autistic children had very limited language skills beyond echolalia (nonfunctionally imitating verbal stimuli they heard) (Barrera & Sulzer-Azaroff, 1983). On the basis of earlier work, the authors suspected that the youngsters would learn more rapidly to label objects functionally with total communication, rather than by using an oral-only training method. So objects whose labels were of relatively equivalent difficulty were selected and the children were taught to name some of the objects via one of the techniques and the others with the alternative. Notice in Figure 22.4 how the authors' suspicions were confirmed.

To add strength to findings revealed by an alternating treatment design, take the intervention that has proven most successful and apply it to the behaviors that have not yet been acquired by the less-successful method. Note how Ollendick et al. (1980) used this tactic to produce compelling results. (See Figure 22.5.)

If you want the curves to separate more rapidly or you intend to see how a given intervention functions within contexts, pair distinctive S^Ds with each intervention. Then, if different response patterns develop that are unique to each particular experimental condition, exper-

Figure 22.4 Word-Acquisition Comparisons Across Categories for Three Children

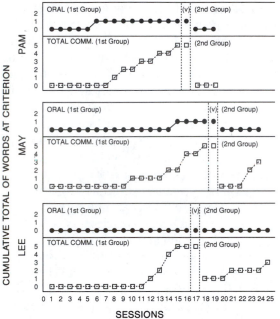

(v) - verification test conducted

Source: Barrera & Sulzer-Azaroff (1983), p. 386. Reprinted with the permission of the Society for the Experimental Analysis of Behavior.

imental control has been demonstrated (Sidman, 1960; Ulman & Sulzer-Azaroff, 1975).

Each of three different adults was assigned to 1 of 3 different contingency conditions in an attempt to determine whether or not the adults would acquire differential stimulus control functions over the cooperative play behavior of 2 severely retarded boys (Redd, 1969). Each session was divided among 4 conditions, each with a specific stimulus. The first condition was baseline, in which no adult, and consequently no programmed contingencies, was present. Second, adult 1 was paired with a mixed schedule of reinforcement contingent on cooperative play, and, at other times, reinforcement was delivered regardless of whether the response was emitted ("noncontingently"). Third, adult 2 was paired with contingent reinforcement

Figure 22.5 The Number of Words Spelled Correctly During Three Experimental Phases for Three Sets of Words.
During the alternating treatments phase, words from Set A were assigned to a positive practice plus positive reinforcement condition; words from Set B were assigned to the traditional "Study the words you get wrong" plus positive reinforcement condition; and words from Set C were assigned to the traditional alone condition. During the last phase, positive practice plus positive reinforcement were used with all three sets of words.

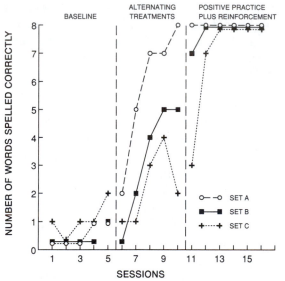

Source: Ollendick et al. (1980), p. 651. Reprinted with the permission of the Society for the Experimental Analysis of Behavior.

only. And, finally, adult 3 was paired with "noncontingent" reinforcement. As all four conditions occurred in random order during each session, it was possible to minimize sequence effects and to monitor the evolution of stimulus control over time, thus supporting the hypothesis that different adults can acquire discriminable stimulus properties, depending on the contingencies they use.

Lloyd and colleagues (1972) used an alternating treatment design to investigate the reinforcing properties of university lectures. When different days of the week were paired with different contingency arrangements, each day developed discriminative properties for class attendance.

Advantages of alternating treatment designs. Alternating treatment designs are especially useful for analyzing complex behaviors. They permit the effects of one or more independent variables to be compared. For example, no treatment might be compared with 1 or 2 different treatments; or the impact of 1 treatment under 1 set of antecedent conditions contrasted with another, such as types of study questions (Semb, Hopkins, & Hursh, 1973) or different contingencies for cooperative play (Redd, 1969).

The design is especially well suited to studying the influences of different contexts (Higgins Hains & Baer, 1989, p. 58). One instance was the effect of an observer's presence on students' classroom behavior (Weinrott, Garrett, & Todd, 1978). Additionally, alternating treatment designs sometimes may reveal differences rapidly and they do not require protracted baseline phases. Instead, following a brief original baseline period, subsequent baseline conditions can be interspersed among alternating treatment conditions throughout the program. Although the conditions do not eliminate multiple-treatment interference, they may reduce the extent of such interference, because the orders of the different treatments are varied and exposures to each of the different interventions are short (rather than extended, as in the withdrawal or multiple-baseline designs).

Another advantage is that these designs permit the variables to be compared against the context of more slowly changing background variables, thereby minimizing the impact of such uncontrolled slow-moving events as seasonal variations in available materials, and so on. Suppose you wanted to know whether hourly or daily supervisory feedback made any difference in product quality. Were you to use an A-B-A-C design, in which each phase lasted several weeks, it would be impossible to prove whether orders for goods might also be shifting in tandem with the phase changes. You wouldn't know whether any distinctive effects were a function of the two different schedules or of the numbers of orders being filled. By contrast, the alternating treatment design would enable you to shift conditions far more rapidly and reveal any differences while patterns of orders remained relatively stable.

The design possesses other distinct advantages (Ulman & Sulzer-Azaroff, 1975), including:

- its appropriateness for studying dependent variables whose rates are less likely to be reversed following protracted presentations of the independent variable.
- the possibility that differential effects may emerge rapidly, thus allowing early termination of the evaluation if necessary.
- its utility when baselines are apt to be variable.
- its more ready acceptance by human-services personnel.

As Higgins Hains and Baer (1989) indicate, by elaborating on the design (and, unfortunately, losing the advantages of simplicity and rapidity), alternating treatment designs are suited to studying the interactions of contextual effects (e.g., whether some treatments function more effectively in some particular contexts than in others).

The alternating treatment design generally is not best used for analysis of simple operant behaviors, because it requires fairly elaborate scheduling of the different conditions and careful monitoring to see that each condition is implemented exactly as planned. This presents a challenging task for the contingency managers involved. The design does, however, open avenues to more sophisticated analyses of complex behaviors in applied settings.

Disadvantages of the alternating treatment design. A major disadvantage of the design has to do with sequencing effects, a form of the more general multiple-treatment interference. **Sequence effects** or **carryover** or **alternation effects** all refer to situations in which one experimental treatment influences behavior within other treatment phases (Barlow & Hersen, 1984).

Two major sources of confounding may be produced by sequence effects. One has to do with the *order* of treatments. For example, if one treatment (*G*) always precedes another (*H*), what happens during *H* actually may be a function of its *G* history. For instance, Theobald and Paul (1976) demonstrated that a history of experiencing tangible reinforcers paired with praise affected the subsequent responses of patients to praise alone. Would treatment *H* have a different effect if not preceded by *G*? To help minimize (though not eliminate entirely) this sequence effect, the order of presentation of treatments is counterbalanced and delivered for only brief periods of time. The sequence might be *A* (baseline), *A, A, G, H, A, H, H, G, A, G, H*. Also, different sequences may be used within the same subjects for different behaviors.

The other sequence effect has to do with the influence of the treatments on one another, irrespective of which one came first. For example, if you compared the motivational effects of $5 to $10 for doing the same task, the $5 might lose its value. (Why should I do it for $5 when I've gotten $10 for doing it?) In contrast, if the $5 was used by itself, it might have maintained its reinforcing value.

This disadvantage may be turned into an advantage, however, as Higgens Hains and Baer (1989) indicate. Sometimes the alternating treatment design is applied with sets of variables that must naturally interact with one another. (For example, contextual variations, such as the deprivation and nondeprivation inherent in daily meal scheduling. The schedules would influence the effect of contingent and noncon-tingent delivery of food). Here the design may reveal the interactional effects of different influences on a treatment. As Higgins Hains and Baer (1989) contend, that feature permits single-subject designs to more efficiently examine interactive effects and, by so doing, to begin to determine the degree to which currently understood behavioral phenomena are general or limited.

Using alternating treatment designs for comparative purposes. You now have seen that when order effects are assumed to be of minor concern, basic alternating treatment designs can reveal the influences of different conditions. You proceed by establishing a baseline, then introducing the treatments in rapid alternation, either within or between observational sessions, to analyze differences apparently influenced by each condition in the separate elements. This can be accomplished by plotting a separate curve of the behavior under each element on your graph and determining whether the curves separate reliably. If and when they do separate, you select the superior condition and apply it to all elements. Thus you can feel even more confident of the impact of that condition when the other elements improve correspondingly.

Watch out for the conclusions you draw from your results, though. Remember that you may only generalize from the specific conditions you used. Don't make the mistake of going beyond your data. An investigator poses the question "Does treatment 1 do a better job than treatment 2?" with treatment 1 assigned a generic procedural label, such as "reinforcement," "punishment," "timeout," or whatever. Then a particular instance of the procedure, say reinforcement—contingent praise—is arranged and counterpoised with a different arrangement of another procedure, say timeout—contingently removing the person from the environment for a specific time period.

Suppose that one of the two appears to produce better results. Can we say that the generic procedure is superior? No! We don't know if the differential results are a function of the generic procedure *per se* or of the specific way the key variables (parameters) of each are arranged (sequence effects aside). Enhance the value of the reinforcing contingencies, and the scale may be tipped in that direction. Use more optimal arrangements of the parameters of the timeout method (e.g., specify the rules clearly or make time-in more reinforcing), and the balance may shift in the other direction. (See Van Houten, 1987, for further discussion of this issue.)

Frequently, the impetus for these kinds of comparisons derives from political, philosophical, or economic rather than scientific agendas. Adherents of particular viewpoints, such as those who espouse being tough (believing that punishment pays), want to show their approach is superior to another's, such as being gentle (an all-positive approach), or vice versa. Just as statisticians may select their tools according to their predispositions, so may behavior analysts. Learn to beware of analyses that purport to prove the superiority of generic procedures. Instead, examine how critical parameters, such as amount, schedule, intensity, delay, type, context, rules, establishing operations, and other antecedents and consequences are arranged.

Nevertheless, under some circumstances, generic procedural comparisons may be justified. One is when the procedures are highly standardized, as various aversive or intrusive methods have been by public policy. Key parameters then are recognized. Another is when the baseline consists of the best available alternative (again, clearly delineated). Another, and this is the most difficult one to achieve because we may be unaware of the importance of some key parameters, is when all those variables are equivalent. An instance would be comparing the impact of two schedules of reinforcement in which number and quality of reinforcers, immediacy of delivery, task complexity and difficulty, accompanying stimuli,

Figure 22.6 Percent Intervals of Timeout (TO)-Producing Behaviors Plotted Across Baseline, TO With Delay, and TO Without Delay Conditions

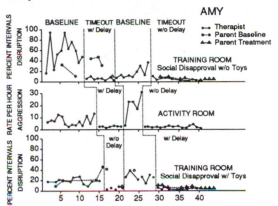

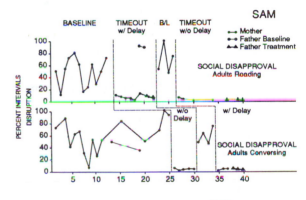

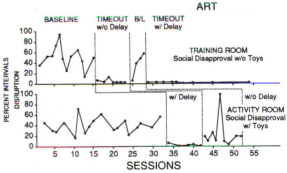

Source: Mace, Page, Ivancic, & O'Brien (1986), p. 82. Reprinted with the permission of the Society for the Experimental Analysis of Behavior.

and so on, were all kept constant. Be sure, though, if you do pursue this direction, that in reporting you carefully justify and identify any limitations (and there are always limitations) to the generality of your findings.

Selecting Appropriate Single-Subject Designs

Our discussion of functional designs in applied behavior analysis research has by no means been exhaustive. In addition to several others that are used in complex research (see Hersen & Barlow, 1976), all the designs discussed in Chapters 14 and 22 can be combined in various ways. Figure 22.6 illustrates the use of a combined multiple-baseline-and-reversal (ABAC) design (Mace, Page, Ivancic, & O'Brien, 1986).

Study the figure closely to determine the rationale for using such a combination. An examination reveals a very important point: Experimental designs should be used to facilitate functional analyses of experimental questions. Experimental questions should not be altered to "fit" existing designs. The question always comes first!

To increase further the probability that we shall select the most appropriate general type of design to provide the most functional answer to our experimental questions, we have included Table 22.1, which compares design types, conditions for selecting and avoiding them, and other advantages.

Other Considerations with Single-Subject Designs

A few other issues related to single-subject designs are worthy of consideration. First, there are no hard-and-fast rules about the number of withdrawals, multiple baselines, criteria, or alternating conditions that are necessary to show the unquestionable effects of the experimental variable. When, however, a statistical analysis is employed, as in group designs, the suitability of the chosen inferential statistic must also be judged. In either single-subject or group designs, "the judgments required are highly qualitative, and rules cannot always be stated profitably" (Baer et al., 1968, p. 95). The question remains open.

Another consideration has been implied previously: The single-subject design is not necessarily the most practical way to arrive at normative group decisions. Instead, group experimental-research designs may be more expedient. Suppose a state education department needs to decide whether to adopt a new set of programmed materials. A group comparison of gains from pretest to postest between the group who received the materials and the control group (a sample of clients who did not use the materials) could provide valuable information. If, however, the behavior analyst, clinician, nurse, counselor, psychologist, teacher, or parent wants to know whether the new materials will help a particular client or what kind of individual it works best with, a single-subject design is in order.

We know that certain interventions may promote irreversible behaviors. Once Chuck has received reinforcement for correctly reading certain words, those responses usually will not diminish when reinforcement is withdrawn. Other sequences, as you saw, forcefully influence subsequent performance. When circumstances require comparison of the effects of two or more intervention conditions upon irreversible responses and/or when multiple-baseline or multielement designs are rejected because of powerful sequence effects, a group statistical design may be the most suitable choice for initially investigating the problem. Jones et al. (1989) found it more expedient to use a group design to compare different methods of teaching clients the skills involved in evacuating a building during a fire. Of course, afterward, the most promising method could be applied subsequently to other individuals in multiple-base-

Table 22.1 Functional Analysis Designs

Design	Operation	Select When	Avoid When	Other Advantages
Withdrawal (ABAB)	Measure baseline (A); apply procedure (B); return to baseline conditions (A); repeat procedure (B)	Extended baseline conditions can be tolerated before and during intervention	Behaviors not reversible; rapid results required; reversal of specific target behavior ethically irresponsible	Alternating A and B conditions may facilitate client's discrimination of relevant stimuli in the situation and transfer from CRF to intermittent schedules
Withdrawal (with reinforcement not contingent on target behavior during A condition)	Same as ABAB, except reinforcers not contingent on the targeted behavior during A and contingent on the targeted behavior during B	Comparing effects of noncontingent with contingent reinforcement; when overall level of reinforcement needs to be maintained	Same as ABAB; independent variable expected to produce only slight effect	Same as ABAB; reinforcers available throughout
Reversal	Following intervention (B), apply contingencies to ommision of target or to alternatives to target behavior during reversal phase (A)	Target behavior resistent to reversal; rapid demonstration of control desirable	Same as ABAB; "other" behaviors may be dangerous or otherwise undesirable	Same as ABAB; reinforcers available throughout
Multiple-baseline (General)	Measure baselines of several behaviors; apply procedure to one behavior, continuing baseline measures of other behaviors; apply procedure to second behavior; continue measuring treated and untreated behaviors; and so on	Target behavior is nonreversible or reversal is undesirable	All behaviors require rapid change	Intervention not interrupted once instituted, consequently more acceptable to clients and staff than reversals or withdrawals
Multiple-baseline across behaviors	Apply procedure to different behaviors one at a time with the same individual	Same as multiple-baseline design; several behaviors of one individual targeted for change and independent of one another; demonstrating control of procedure across behaviors	Same as multiple-baseline design; effects of procedure may spread to baselines of other behaviors	Same as multiple-baseline design

Table 22.1 Functional Analysis Designs (continued)

Design	Operation	Select When	Avoid When	Other Advantages
Multiple-baseline across situations	Apply procedure to behaviors of one or more subjects across situations and at different times	Same as multiple-baseline design; same behaviors of one or more individuals are targeted for change in more than one setting; demonstrating control of procedures across situations	Same as multiple-baseline design; behavior change in one situation may spread to baselines in other situations	Same as multiple-baseline design
Multiple-baseline across individuals	Apply procedure to same behavior of different individuals at different times	Same as multiple-baseline design; same behavior targeted for change among several individuals; demonstrating control of procedure across individuals	Same as multiple-baseline design; changes in one individual's behavior may affect other individuals' baselines	Same as multiple-baseline design
Changing criterion	Apply intervention when behavior meets criterion level; change value of criterion at irregular intervals	Teaching new behaviors; intervention consists of graduated steps (as with DRL, and *progressive* or adjusting schedule changes)	Responding is likely to exceed the criterion	May ideally serve programming needs when criteria are changed gradually and progressively
Multiple probes	Probe performance intermittently prior to intervention (and more regularly during intervention)	To assess acquisition of skills; more frequent assessments would interfere with learning or are difficult practically	More frequent data required	May use to assess for steps acquired without formal training
Alternating treatment	Successively apply different interventions under distinctive stimulus conditions in rapid alternation with equivalent behaviors	Evaluating one or more different procedures; targeting behaviors unlikely to be reversed; stable baseline difficult to achieve; sequence and contrast effects minor or the subject of analysis	Unwilling or unable to continue alternating conditions until clear differences are manifest	More acceptable than reversals in applied settings; can show rapid effects over a limited time

line fashion. Baer, Wolf, and Risley (1987) eloquently summarize the issue of selecting experimental designs: ". . . a good design is one that answers the question convincingly . . . and needs to be constructed in reaction to the question and then tested through argument in that context . . . rather than imitated from a textbook" (p. 319).

Determining the Significance of a Demonstrated Functional Relation

Applied behavior analysis meets concerns of internal validity through the use of single-case designs. Those presented in this text provide reasonable control over external sources of variability. The designs permit reliable differences between levels, trends, and/or variability of behaviors to be demonstrated between baseline and one or more intervention conditions. Now we switch the focus primarily to issues of external validity. A key question is "Of what significance is any given functional relation that may have been demonstrated?"

One traditional approach has been to base interpretations of significance on probability theory, asking "What is the likelihood that these results could have been obtained by chance alone?" If the numbers convince us that the results we obtained were very unlikely to have been produced solely by chance, we are more likely to accept the findings as "statistically significant." In applied behavior analysis, however, the emphasis is more on experimental, social, personal, educational, or clinical than on statistical significance.

Experimental Significance

Experimental significance may be determined by asking what the behavior is now and what the behavior would be if the experimental intervention had not occurred (Risley, 1970). According to Kazdin (1976), there are a few ways

in which results clearly meet the criterion for experimental significance.

The first way results meet the criterion is when plotted performance data during the intervention rarely overlap with performance during baseline, especially when the treatment is replicated within subjects over time, or across subjects, settings, or behaviors. Figure 22.7, displaying the results of a token program designed to encourage asthmatic children to use

Figure 22.7 The Mean Number of Inappropriate Events Recorded by the Experimenters over a Series of 26 Trials with 4 Subjects on Three Target Responses: Eye Fixation, Facial Posturing, and Diaphragmatic Breathing. The maximum number of inappropriate responses per trial was 15 for each behavior.

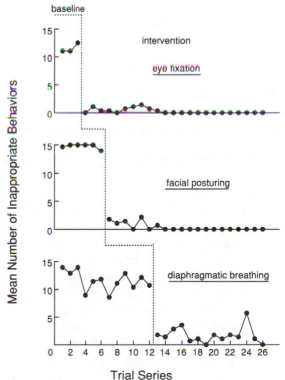

Source: Renne & Creer (1976), p. 6. Reprinted with the permission of the Society for the Experimental Analysis of Behavior.

inhalation equipment correctly, illustrates this point. Looking at the mean number of inappropriate behaviors during baseline and comparing it with performance during intervention, we note that there is no overlap in the distribution of measures.

Another way results meet the criterion is when systematic changes in the trend occur as a function of treatment conditions. Figure 14.3 illustrates this point. The trend toward reduced eye ticks in phase B was reversed in phase A2, when competing responses were removed.

A third way to meet the criterion is through statistical significance based on time-series analyses of the patterns of repeated measures of individuals' performance under each experimental condition. This situation applies especially when visual displays are insufficiently convincing or when measures are not independent of one another (serial dependence) (Hartmann et al., 1980). Data might be so variable that the actual magnitude of an effect is obscured, causing important results inadvertently to be discarded as insignificant. Various statistical methods have been devised to assess the significance of change in single cases (see Cook & Campbell, 1979; Kazdin, 1976; Tryon, 1982; the series of articles in the *Journal of Applied Behavior Analysis,* 7, 1974, 627–653; and others).

For those of us whose primary concern is the enhancement of personally, educationally, and socially important behavior, however, another approach is available. For example, when the goal is to increase a behavior and data show lots of variability, with many overlapping data points (lots of "high" days during baseline and lots of "low" days during treatment), the program should be modified, rather than trying to tease out the subtle effects of the data. In general, we concur with Michael's recommendation:

> When a dependent variable is not under good control—when there is considerable

unexplained variability even though the independent variable being studied is at a constant value—it is not usually necessary to go ahead with other planned manipulations. Further efforts can be made to obtain a more stable dependent variable or to discover and eliminate some of the sources of uncontrolled variation (1974, p. 651).

Other Forms of Significance

In addition to the significance of the functional relation between the behavior and treatment(s), the applied behavior analyst also asks about the importance of the outcome for particular individuals and/or their society (Risley, 1970).

Some program evaluation models are based on the discrepancy between expected and actually achieved outcomes. This same approach can be used to assess the value of change achieved through the application of behavioral procedures. Chapter 4 discussed specification of behavioral objectives. Beyond the statement describing the response, and the conditions under which it is to occur, a behavioral objective includes a standard or criterion for determining its attainment. According to a series of papers on the topic of **clinical significance** in the journal *Behavioral Assessment* (Number 2, 1988), these criteria may derive from normative studies, meta-analyses, clarification of goals, statistical significance, social evaluation, termination of the complaints of the clinician and client, and other sources. Should the intervention be functionally related to an improvement in the behavior to the preestablished criterion level, we must certainly conclude that the outcome is "significant," for the achievement of the objective has been demonstrated.

Alternatively, the social, personal, or clinical significance of an outcome may be determined following intervention by assessing changes in the individual's ecological context. Determine whether the behavior change has spurred correlated beneficial or detrimental changes for the participants, and their physical and social environments. Enabling a person to be more productive may be of benefit to a worker by increasing her wages, yet simultaneously threatening to her or her co-workers because her rate is too rapid to maintain adequate safety. Helping someone to be more innovative may be advantageous for him but cause difficulties in his organization.

Educational and Social Validity

How do you determine whether the work you have done is educationally or socially valid? **Educational significance**, according to Voeltz and Evans (1983), depends not only on whether change has occurred as a function of the program but also whether the intervention was implemented as specified and beneficial to the student and those in his or her environment. Regarding **social validity**, Wolf (1978) has suggested that three factors be considered:

- the social significance of the goals.
- the social appropriateness of the procedures.
- the social importance of the effects.

The first two issues were discussed in the chapters on goal and procedural selection. In terms of social importance, Wolf suggests that we find out whether consumers are satisfied with the results, both planned and unplanned. No matter how effective an intervention may be shown to be experimentally, what is the use if consumers do not like what it accomplished? They will not continue to use the treatment. Perhaps the behaviors are too costly, bothersome, intrusive, or unpalatable.

One way to shed some light on this aspect is to ask people about results objectively. Use well-designed questionnaires or structured interview formats—such strategies are being used increasingly by behavior analysts. In one case (Greenwood et al., 1979), extensive satisfaction measures of a school consultation program package included obtaining ratings from students, teachers, and consultants. In another

case (Alavosius & Sulzer-Azaroff, 1990), we asked nurses a series of consumer satisfaction questions about the value of the training they had received in safely lifting and transferring clients. All agreed that the methods were helpful and acceptable. Maybe that is why some participants reported that they had initiated teaching the techniques to their fellow workers. The findings also have encouraged us to continue further work along these lines.

A different approach is to ask uninformed judges to make global assessments of change, as Schreibman, Koegel, Mills, and Burke (1981) did to socially validate change among their autistic clients. Judges were able to distinguish those children whose behavior had been shown experimentally to have improved from children whose behavior had not.

Subjectivity always is an issue of concern in using measures such as human opinion. Often respondents are concerned about supplying the answer they think the inquirer wants to hear. An alternative, when feasible, is to provide opportunities for consumers to make *behavioral choices*. After the program has been completed, offer to repeat it or to conduct other viable alternatives (such as prior methods) with other behaviors, other people, or in other settings. See which, if any, they select.

Assessing Cost Effectiveness

Beneficial or detrimental outcomes to people and their environments are primary considerations when you evaluate the value of an intervention program. So is consumer satisfaction. Yet no matter how pleased any constituencies may be with the outcome, their enthusiasm will be offset by the expenses involved. Practitioners, as well, should be aware of the costs they themselves incur if they are to charge reasonably for their services.

Brian Yates (1985) has offered a useful strategy that science/practitioners may use to determine cost effectiveness. Basic steps involve:

1. Decide which program or technique to analyze.

2. Use experimental analyses.

3. Decide how to assess costs and benefits in advance.

4. Use multiple measures and comparison procedures.

Costs may be assessed by identifying the necessary resources for a program (personnel, materials, facilities, equipment, and so on) and determining the value of each. The total then may be contrasted with the costs of putting the resources to the best alternative use. Additionally, clients' and staff time and the psychological cost to them, volunteer time, inflationary adjustments, and other expenses suggested by interested parties may be included in the list. Besides effectiveness and satisfaction, value of interventions may be assessed in terms of actual cost savings, present and future income by the agency and clients, and others. Yates has provided far more detail, including methods for assessing the relationship between costs and effectiveness.

Regardless of which formulae you select, be sure to contrast the various immediate and long-term outcomes of this particular program with results that have been or might be achieved by others, such as previous interventions. Perhaps despite the costs, you will conclude that on balance, the intervention you have evaluated is preferable.

Evaluating the Generality of Findings

Once a conclusion about the experimental and social significance of a finding can be defended, you may wish to ask how general this finding is. Replications establish ''the generality of phenomena among members of a species, . . . and at the same time extend its generality over a wide range of situations'' (Sidman, 1960, p. 111). Recall that earlier, when single-subject designs were discussed, we mentioned that those designs allow for generation of principles of behavior for particular individuals. When **directly replicating**, an experimenter repeats a procedure intact; when results reproduce themselves across more and more behaviors, individuals, or settings sharing similar characteristics, the experimenter begins to see how generally the procedure applies. Examples are presented repeatedly throughout this book. Rules describing such reliable effects are called **principles of behavior**.

An even stronger case in favor of the generality of the principle is made when results are reproduced despite allowing a number of conditions to vary, such as the task, setting, or other parameters of the basic procedure, as in the **systematic replication** tactic. A couple of illustrations follow.

The CLASS (Contingencies for Learning Academic and Social Skills) program was developed by Walker and his colleagues (e.g., Walker & Hops, 1979) to remediate the opposition and acting out of pupils in the primary grades. The clearly delineated package of components, including teacher praise, individual and group contingencies, school and home rewards, contracting, and response cost, had been applied successfully in numerous students, classrooms, and schools. Then Walker, Retana, and Gersten (1988) decided to try out the program in Costa Rica, where many environmental variables, such as class size and parental involvement, differ from those in the United States. Results achieved by this systematic replication were similar to those achieved previously (although not quite as dramatic), lending credence to the hardiness and generality of the CLASS package.

The fundamental elements of a program designed by Sulzer-Azaroff and her colleagues to prevent on-the-job injury include pinpointing behavioral targets related to previous injuries or ''near misses'' in particular settings, devising valid measures of those performances, assessing baseline performance, then regularly feeding back the results of those and subsequent assessments to the workers and/or their supervisors. A series of systematic replications demonstrated the general effectiveness of the package across numerous conditions: different safety targets, job settings, augmented rewards and social events, schedules of feedback, group size, and others (Sulzer-Azaroff, 1989).

Principles of behavior that have been demonstrated to possess very broad generality may be referred to as **behavioral laws**. The frequently cited parametric arrangements related to immediacy, sufficiency, type, and schedule of reinforcement recommended as optimal in this text have repeatedly demonstrated their effectiveness among numerous populations, over wide classes of behavior and under varied conditions. They can, therefore, be designated as laws of behavior. Remember, however, that laws have their exceptions—and it is from these exceptions we learn how the laws need to be refined. Only continuing research allows us to keep elaborating upon fundamental laws of behavior.

Evaluating Generality and Long-Term Effects of Procedural Interventions

Experimental analyses and replications permit the function and generality of intervention programs to be assessed. Other measures allow us to evaluate their social importance and cost effectiveness. Evaluation is not complete, however, until periodic preplanned probes of generality and persistence have been conducted while the intervention is in effect, and afterward. This measurement will inform us about whether the natural community of contingencies has assumed sufficient control over the change or whether further environmental arrangements must be structured to cause it to

generalize and to maintain the behavior change (see Chapters 29–32).

Summary

Any human service program should be evaluated for its validity and significance. Single-case designs lend themselves especially well to the requirements of rigorous research methodology, permitting internal validity, an essential of program evaluation, to be addressed. Chapter 14 began with the less-complex designs that are especially useful for analyzing the influence of "motivational factors."

In this chapter the more complex changing-criterion and alternating treatment designs have been described, illustrated, and discussed. These designs, along with reversal and multiple-baseline designs, have been compared in a table specifying the operation, conditions for selection and avoidance, and other advantages of each design. To establish functional relations, use withdrawal and multiple baseline designs when extended phases can be tolerated. If the target behavior is capable of readily changing direction, the withdrawal design may be selected. Changing criterion and multiple-probe designs are especially well suited to demonstrating experimental control over skill acquisition, whereas the alternating treatment methodology serves to compare different treatments along with any interactions between treatments and contexts. Experimental strategies, though, must be adjusted to the particular question being posed, and not the other way around.

Questions of significance, generality, and of cost/benefit also have been considered. In applied behavior analysis, significance is judged primarily on the basis of the social importance of results. Finally, the need for follow-up to evaluate or provide for maintenance and generalization has been emphasized.

Section IV

Introduction to Reducing Behavior

"How are things going at the plant?" asked Barney's buddy, Art, the school principal.

"Pretty well," replied Barney. "We're making our production quota and the boss is pretty satisfied. But you remember Clarence, the guy we call 'Sloppy Smith'? He gives me a royal pain."

"Why? What's he done lately?"

"It's not what he does. It's what he doesn't do. If I ask him to do something that is not in his job description, he gives me a big hassle. For instance, the other day I asked him nicely to clean up his work area, because I'm embarrassed by the mess when people come through the unit. He said, 'I do what I'm supposed to do, don't I? The union says as long as I get my assigned job done, I'm not required to do anything else. My job description doesn't include janitorial work!' Can you imagine?"

"I'd fire the bum," Art said.

"That's easier said than done. Besides, he's really good technically and I wouldn't want to lose him—although at times like these I'm sorely tempted. But even if I wanted to, his job is protected and he makes sure not to step across the line."

"I know what you mean. A couple of teachers on my staff give me the same kind of difficulty," replied Art. "They argue whenever I ask them to do something out of the ordinary, like chaperoning the dance, helping with graduation, or attending in-service sessions after school. Of course, some of our students are even worse. I wish I were able to deal better with that kind of lack of cooperation."

Lack of cooperation, noncompliance, and outright misconduct are familiar problems to everyone. Unfortunately, so are more serious difficulties, such as aggression toward others or oneself, destroying property, risking one's health and safety, being absent excessively, and a long list of other noxious behaviors. Obviously, not every troublesome act is a candidate for a behavioral reduction program. Limited resources don't permit that. In addition, behaviors troublesome to you may not be to someone else. How is the decision made to proceed, and if so, what can be done to reduce or eliminate unwanted responses? This section helps you to decide whether to select a method for reducing behavior and provides you with a set of alternatives.

When a behavior is a nuisance, it doesn't necessarily have to be targeted for reduction. Perhaps the manager needs instead to take a more constructional approach. If after careful analysis, reducing a particular performance is deemed essential, follow this sequence of actions:

1. Assess the function of the problem, and if feasible, alter conditions to allow the individual access to the same or added reinforcing contingencies by means of a more acceptable action.

2. If that solution proves unworkable, before proceeding, consult laws and policies.

3. Select the least restrictive method supported by research to promote optimal results with the client.

Although on a descriptive basis, different reductive methods can be ordered in terms of levels of restrictiveness and intrusiveness, each needs to be examined in terms of the value of its parameters, the recipient, and the context. For instance, punishment—the seemingly most restrictive procedure—can in some forms (such as a horizontal head shake) be less restrictive than an extended phase of differential reinforcement. Quality or type and amount of stimuli, temporal, contextual, and schedule factors may vary widely, thereby influencing eventual outcome.

The chapters covering the different categories of **reductive procedures** begin with those that avoid applying aversive stimuli: extinction and differential reinforcement. Next are two—response cost and timeout—that involve contingently subtracting the reinforcers the individual receives, by a given amount or for a given time, respectively. Then are the methods that do involve presenting punishing stimuli or events: overcorrection, contingent exertion, and punishment. Learn what it takes to use these procedures humanely and effectively.

Only a holistic analysis addresses the issue of whether to choose a reductive procedure. To prepare you to deal with these numerous factors, in Table 1 we have supplied a list of defined and illustrated reductive procedures. Table E.3 in the Epilogue summarizes the main features of the various reductive procedures for you. In this section's chapters, you will learn about each approach in detail.

Table 1

- Antecedent: Barney makes a request of Sloppy.
- Unwanted behavior: noncompliance.
- Definition: Sloppy says "No" or argues in response to a request to do anything beyond his formal job description.
- Effective reinforcers for Sloppy include attention, subtle forms of approval, (such as smiles and head nods), plus coffee and soft drinks.

Procedure	Operation	Example
Extinction	Withhold reinforcer following response $R \xrightarrow{\quad / \quad} S^r$ refuses attention	Whenever Sloppy refuses, Barney withholds reinforcement (e.g., attention).
Reinforce alternative behavior (Alt-R) OR Differential reinforcement of alternative behavior (DRA)	Present reinforcer following any specific behaviors except refusing $R \xrightarrow{\quad} S^r$ any except refusing	Barney reinforces whenever Sloppy agrees to do the task following a request.
Differentially reinforce incompatible behavior (DRI)	Present reinforcer following response incompatible with refusing $R \xrightarrow{\quad} S^r$ complying	Barney reinforces whenever Sloppy agrees to or actually complies with request.
Differentially reinforce absence (zero responding) of behavior during an interval of time; often called differential reinforcement of other behavior (DRO) or omission training	Present reinforcer following time period in which no refusals occurred (e.g., an hour) $\left[\begin{array}{l} \text{S: After } x \text{ time} \\ R \xrightarrow{\quad} S^r \\ \text{all but} \\ \text{refusals} \end{array}\right.$	Every hour Barney stops by Sloppy's desk and delivers reinforcers provided Sloppy has not refused to clean up during the past hour.
Differentially reinforce low rates of behavior (DRL)	Present reinforcer for response after x interval $R \xrightarrow{\quad} S^r$ After x time	Barney reinforces Sloppy's refusal to clean the work area, provided that Sloppy has not refused during the previous x time period.
Differentially reinforce diminishing rates of behavior (DRD)	Positive reinforcement at the end of intervals containing reduced rates of the response	Barney positively reinforces at the end of intervals for reduced rates of refusals (i.e., the interval gradually increases, and/or the frequency of refusing gradually decreases).

Table 1 (continued)

Procedure	Operation	Example
Timeout	Following unwanted behavior, all manageable sources of reinforcement withdrawn for x time $\text{R}_{\text{refusal}} \longrightarrow \text{loss of access to reinforcement for } x \text{ time}$	Barney totally ignores Sloppy and removes access to soft drinks, coffee, and peer interactions for a half hour after Sloppy refuses to comply.
Response cost (S^{rc})	Following unwanted behavior, reinforcers are subtracted $\text{R}_{\text{refusal}} \longrightarrow \text{loss of } x \text{ number of reinforcers}$	Barney places a canned soft drink on Sloppy's desk. When Sloppy refuses a request, Barney takes the can and drinks it himself.
Stimulus discriminative for aversive consequences	$\left[\begin{array}{l} S^{D-} \\ \text{R}_{\text{refusal}} \longrightarrow S^{p} \end{array}\right.$	In the presence of the big boss, if Sloppy refuses to comply, the boss reprimands him severely.
Overcorrection	Following unwanted behavior, person required to practice the positive behavior and provide restitution $\text{R}_{\text{refusal}} \longrightarrow \text{positive practice and restitution}$	When Sloppy refuses to clean up the mess around his desk, the debris causes a co-worker to slip and fall. Barney tells Sloppy to take her to the infirmary, then return and clean up not only his own mess but any other items on the office floor.
Contingent exertion	Same as above except consequence requires effort not necessarily related to unwanted behavior	When Sloppy refuses to comply, Barney assigns him additional work that falls within his job description but that requires extra effort.
Punishment	An aversive stimulus follows the unwanted behavior $\text{R}_{\text{refusal}} \longrightarrow S^{p}$	Barney chews out Sloppy in the presence of his co-workers.

Key:
S^{r} = reinforcing stimulus.
[= indicates "in the context of"—in this case, in the context of the passage of a particular time period or in the presence of an S^{D-}.
S^{p} = punisher (aversive stimulus).

Chapter 23

Reducing Behavior: Making the Decision and Using Extinction

GOALS

After completing this chapter, you should be able to:

1. Discuss considerations in deciding whether to target a behavior for reduction.

2. List helpful information to gather when assessing the function of a problem behavior and explain the value of such an assessment.

3. Discuss the importance of checking laws and policies prior to selecting a punitive procedure.

4. Explain when a slow-acting nonrestrictive procedure could be judged more restrictive than a faster-acting, more restrictive procedure.

5. Explain each of the reasons for using the least restrictive consequence and explain why restrictive procedures should be phased out as soon as possible.

6. Define, recognize, and give original illustrations of each of the following terms:
   a. Parameter
   b. Extinction
   c. Extinction burst
   d. Extinction-induced aggression
   e. Spontaneous recovery or resurgence
   f. Positive scanning

7. List and discuss the importance of a procedure's parameters in judging the acceptability of a reductive procedure.

8. List and explain each of the advantages of using extinction.

9. List and provide illustrations of the predictable properties of a behavior undergoing extinction, and discuss the value of being prepared for them.

10. List and illustrate the factors known to influence how rapidly a behavior is eliminated through extinction.

11. List the disadvantages of using extinction and discuss their ramifications.

12. Cite and illustrate the variables that help maximize the effectiveness of extinction.

13. Describe specific situations in which extinction would and would not be the behavioral procedure of choice; justify your position in each case.

14. Discuss what can be done to minimize the negative side effects of extinction.

Before yielding to the temptation to use a reductive procedure, you need to give the matter serious consideration. Does the target behavior really merit the treatment? What factors impact that decision? This chapter reviews those aspects with you. Next, we help you begin to select from the array of available choices. Then we move on to using extinction, the first reductive procedure presented in detail.

Deciding to Target a Behavior for Reduction

Should just any behavior be targeted for reduction? Ask yourself first whether the problem belongs to you or to the person who is disturbing you. Will remedying the difficulty benefit you, your organization, or that individual now and in the future? Refer back to Chapters 2 and 3 to remind yourself of the guidelines for selecting sound behavioral objectives and the value of the constructional approach. Ethically, developing new productive behaviors is more to people's advantage than simply eliminating behaviors from their repertoires. Pragmatically, focusing on the development of new behavior tends to produce positive spin-offs, such as people seeing themselves in a more positive light, becoming more cheerful, remaining in the situation, and continuing to progress.

Despite everyone's combined best efforts, however, sometimes the focus must shift to behavioral reduction. This approach is appropriate when people's behavior is dangerous or destructive, or when their actions seriously impede their own or others' ability to function adequately. (See Stolz, 1976, for an extensive discussion of this and related issues.)

When clients or their advocates and society agree that a goal is to their mutual benefit, using reductive procedures may be defensible. Consider a few examples. Lucretia's aggression toward the other children endangers them and interferes with their ability to play in peace.

Fern's disruption in the workshop is an impediment to her own and her fellow workers' wage earning and progress. Pearl's stereotypic hand motions command her constant attention and screen out learning opportunities from the environment. (Lovaas, Litrownik, & Mann, 1971, found that autistic children engaging in self-stimulatory behavior were less responsive than others to environmental stimuli.) Paula's procrastination prevents her from receiving her coveted promotion. Mr. Grump's sarcasm compromises his students' progress by reducing their performance rates and their satisfaction with school, and Sloppy's carelessness places himself and his coworkers at risk.

Angela's habit of twirling her hair, however, is a different story. The habit is neither harmful nor disruptive. In her case, using reductive procedures would not be justified (unless, of course, Angela herself wants to do something about it).

Once an ethically responsible decision has been made to target a behavior for reduction, first you need to try to discover what is keeping it going by using assessment of the kind discussed in Chapter 7. Often, for example, severe behavioral disorders are maintained because they function to rid the person of difficult or demanding tasks, or they help the person to obtain attention (Carr & Durand, 1985b). Next you should check laws and policies and consider those procedures that are least intrusive (most natural) and benign. Involve trained and competent personnel at this point. Finally, be sure the selected procedure has previous empirical support for its use with the type of client and behavior being targeted.

To begin to determine the function of a problem behavior, you might try the assessment method advocated by Groden (1989). Included are an indication of the day, date, time, and location of each problematic episode, a description of the episode, the immediate antecedents, such as the ongoing activity, social-interpersonal events, information about what the client was saying to himself or herself or was imagining (obtained by listening or questioning), organismic/affective signs (bodily/emotional signs), distant antecedents, and programmed and other environmental consequences. That information is then collated and analyzed to help explain the problem behavior and to suggest what measures would be most appropriate for remeding it.

Should the functional assessment strongly suggest the root of the problem, you may be in a position to remove the antecedents that set the occasion for its occurrence and/or teach a new, socially desirable response that yields the same reinforcers. Resorting to a punitive method may not be necessary if the frequency of the unwanted behavior declines correspondingly. (See Carr & Durand, 1985a; 1985b; Durand & Carr, 1987; Durand & Kishi, 1987; Horner & Budd, 1985.) When the strategy is not sufficient, you may decide to consider using a reductive procedure.

Next, as mentioned, *check federal, state, and local laws, and organizational policies.* With developmentally disabled children you will need to abide by the guidelines for Public Law 94–142 and other more recent legislation. In general, you will be required to provide free appropriate education under the least restrictive conditions feasible. The latter has been defined in detail by various state and local agencies. In Massachusetts, for example (Commissioner of Mental Retardation, 104, CMR 20.15), state policy regulates three different levels of intrusiveness. The first requires only supervisory approval; the second, fairly elaborate human rights, and professional and advocate reviews and approvals; and the third, court approval. State educational policies regulate disciplinary practices by teachers, and labor departments and/or union agreements often govern disciplinary practices in work settings.

Choose the *most constructive, least restrictive and intrusive* procedures feasible. This means you begin by selecting positive approaches first,

and only if those fail should you consider more negative or intrusive methods like withholding reinforcers (extinction), removing reinforcers (response cost), removing the opportunity to earn reinforcers (timeout), requiring that behavior be corrected (overcorrection), or presenting aversive stimuli contingent on the behavior (punishment).

If you must select aversive stimuli, select those intrinsic to the context, such as reprimands, demerits, or penalties. If those are not effective with the individual, you might then need to consider others of a more contrived nature, such as other social events or aversive activities. Finally, give some thought to using unconditioned physical aversives, with painful stimulation, such as electric shock, as a last resort, for such a method "... is generally ranked highest in terms of its aversiveness, intrusiveness and/or restrictiveness" (Foxx, McMorrow, Bittle, Bechtel, 1986a, pp. 170–171).

What is most restrictive can be a matter of judgment. Some may find protracted extinction conditions far more aversive than a brief slap or sharp reprimand. ("Go ahead, spank me so we can get it over with!" pleads Charlie, fearing his parents will give him the cold treatment instead for days.) As Van Houten et al. (1988a) point out:

Consistent with the philosophy of least restrictive yet effective treatment, exposure of an individual to restrictive procedures is unacceptable unless it can be shown that such procedures are necessary to produce safe and clinically significant behavior change. It is equally unacceptable to expose an individual to a nonrestrictive intervention (or a series of such interventions) if assessment results or available research indicate that other procedures would be more effective. Indeed, a slow-acting but nonrestrictive procedure could be considered highly restrictive if prolonged treatment increases risk, significantly inhibits or prevents participation in needed training programs, delays entry into a more optimal social or living environment, or leads to adaptation and the eventual use of a more restrictive procedure. Thus, in some cases, a client's right to effective treatment may dictate the immediate use of quicker acting, but temporarily more restrictive, procedures (p. 383).

Note the emphasis is on the *temporary* use of restrictive procedures. Another reason for stressing using the least restrictive consequence (in addition to ethical and humane concerns) is that severe punishment is

> usually incompatible with the placement of retarded persons in least restrictive living environments (community living arrangement, foster home). Regulations of many publicly supported community service facilities in the United States prohibit the use of behavioral treatments considered aversive (Dixon, Helsel, Rojahn, Cipollone, & Lubetsky, 1989, p. 92).

In other words, when care givers rely on delivering severe punitive consequences, they are restricting *severely* the types of environments in which their clients can live or work. If you use a highly restrictive procedure, carefully monitor its effects and phase out its use as soon as feasible.

Procedures for Reducing or Eliminating Behaviors

Many behavioral procedures have been devised for the very purpose of reducing or eliminating problematic deportment: extinction, differential reinforcement, timeout, response cost, contingent exertion, overcorrection, and punishment. This section's chapters present each of these in turn. Critical properties are reviewed, effective application described, advantages and disadvantages discussed, and numerous fictitious and actual illustrations offered. By the time you complete your study of this provocative topic, you will have various options available from which to select. Choose the ones that

promote the most advantageous and lasting changes for the people you serve.

To provide you with a general overview, Table 1 in the section introduction defined and illustrated the procedures covered. Use this table to help you distinguish each procedure and to understand not only the apparent but the subtle differences between the various approaches.

Being able to define a procedure is just one aspect of understanding reductive methodology. Another is knowing how parametric adjustments in the procedures, such as timing, intensity, schedule, quantity and quality of reinforcers, frequency, and so on, are apt to influence the outcomes. Shifting **parameters** influence the speed, effectiveness, safety, constructiveness, legality, ethics, ecological impact, acceptability, and other outcomes. In fact, whole books (Axelrod & Apsche, 1983; Lavigna & Donnellan, 1986; Sidman, 1989) and many papers (e.g., Homer & Peterson, 1980) have been devoted to this knotty topic. Realize, then, that any particular procedure will produce different outcomes depending on the individuals involved, situational factors, and the values of particular procedural parameters.

In other words, it is not the generic procedures *per se* that must be judged, but the *details* of their application with that person within a given context. Value judgments need to be based on weighing the costs and benefits, primarily to the client but also to the other concerned people as well. Perhaps as you become more familiar with the intricacies of reductive procedures, you too will recognize that to outlaw a general procedure, such as reinforcement or punishment, on the basis of its topographic description may be less constructive and humane than examining the functional relation between clients' repertoires, environmental contexts, safeguards in place, and the values of parameters used within the procedures. The focus of concern should be on a broad perspective of how the procedure works and what it *does*, as applied, not what it sounds or looks like.

To illustrate this point further, here we review a few of the variables that have been studied fairly extensively. Some examples also are supplied to help you distinguish between a topographical and a functional perspective:

- *Quality or type* of reinforcers and aversive stimuli: Reinforcers vary from those that are natural to the individual's setting, such as smiles and signals of approval, to those that are quite contrived, such as sweets, tangible rewards, and money. Aversive stimuli, too, can run the gamut from a raised eyebrow or expression of displeasure to a facial screen or electric shock. The strength of any given stimulus depends on the person's physical idiosyncrasies, learning history, and contextual factors.
- *Amount or intensity* of reinforcing and aversive stimuli: Reinforcers range from the miniscule, such as the wink of an eye, to the gargantuan—maybe a Porsche or multimillion dollar lottery prize. So too with aversive stimuli, say from a slight horizontal side to side shift of the head to an intense spank or very distasteful substance placed on the tongue. The amount of effort the individual expends when involved in a contingent exercise routine or the loudness of a reprimand would also fit here.
- *Temporal factors*, such as the time required to perform a routine, the delay between responses and reinforcers or aversive stimuli, the duration of onset to offset of reinforcers or punishers (how long music is broadcasted, free time scheduled or scolding continued), the pacing of prompts, and others.
- *Contextual factors*, such as setting events, establishing operations, and discriminative stimuli. Relevant examples are the

size and arrangement of the physical environment; amount and type of tasks, materials, and supplies; knowledge, skills, and other characteristics of personnel; the health condition of the client; types of instructions or prompts; and the characteristics of other contingencies in operation currently, and in the recent and distant past. [Haring and Kennedy (1988) discovered that their two subjects were less disruptive when a differential reinforcement of zero responding (DRO) procedure was used during instruction, but not during leisure time, whereas timeout was effective only during leisure activities.]

- *Schedules*, or presentation of antecedents and consequences. These can range from response-contingent to time-based, from every time the response occurs (continuous) to sometimes (intermittent) to very rarely; from regularly—a fixed schedule—to inconsistently—a variable schedule.

Let us look at a few examples.

In conference with Mr. Ernie, the school psychologist, Charlie's parents complain that he refuses to obey them. "He doesn't come home when he's supposed to, his chores are never done, and we don't ever see him do homework. When we try to get him to do what he's supposed to, he just sasses us back."

"How have you tried handling it?"

"Well, when I get home from work I just take off my belt and give him what's coming."

"What happens then? Any improvement?"

"Nah. He just gets meaner and more hateful than ever. Disappears for hours and only comes home when he's good and hungry."

"Have you tried anything else?"

"We already took away his allowance and wouldn't let him listen to his radio for a month, but that didn't do any good either. He just played it anyway, as soon as we were gone."

Violet's parents confer with Mr. Ernie and her teacher over a very different concern. Their daughter returned from school yesterday, went to her room, and burst into tears without saying a word.

"I asked her what was wrong. Finally she sobbed that her teacher doesn't like her."

"Did you ask her why she felt that way?" inquired the worried teacher.

"She said that you seemed so disappointed that she only got a grade of 92 on her test."

"Heavens. I can't imagine why she thought that. A 92 is fantastic. Most of the other kids flunked. Maybe I looked out of sorts over that and poor little Violet thought I was directing my displeasure at her. Please tell her I wasn't annoyed with her at all. I know how sensitive she is. I'll have to be more careful."

You get the picture. What looks like intense punishment in Charlie's case isn't punishment at all, because the behavior on which it is contingent does not diminish. Also, the various consequences are delivered inconsistently and fail to include the many strategies for optimizing the effectiveness and humaneness of the procedures. Charlie's parents are using procedures that could be labeled topographically as "punishment" and "timeout," but functionally they are neither.

With Violet, punishment probably did happen, despite her teacher's failure to recognize what was taking place. (We're assuming this on the basis of Violet's description and her emotional reaction—a typical adjunct to punishment.) The episode was a fleeting one-time event and hardly anyone would describe the topography of the teacher's slight frown as a punisher, but for Violet it functioned that way.

Practitioners, consumers, policymakers, and the public need to be apprised of these distinctions, so that instead of attributing malignant or benign qualities to given procedural descriptors, they can see the picture from a broadened perspective. By weighing all the factors, advisory and policy boards, the courts, parents, advocates, and others will be better able to draw conclusions about the acceptability

of a given intervention with each particular client.

We hope you retain this holistic perspective while you study the specific reductive procedures we describe. For practical reasons we shall often speak in generalities; but remember that each case and context is different. What applies in each case is for one client at one time and place.

Reducing Behavior with Extinction

Swinging her feet from the shopping cart, Baby Bonnie points to the cookies. "Want that!"—the maraschino cherries—"Want that," pointing to six or seven candy bars pleading "Daddy, want that." Daddy does not appear to hear her until they reach the fruit stand. "Want that," says Bonnie, reaching for an orange. "All right—but hold it, and you can eat it when we get home." Technically, Bonnie's "Want that"s, often reinforced in the past, are being placed on extinction except when the little girl's request is for a nutritious item.

Earlier, extinction was presented as one of the two operations involved in promoting stimulus control, and you know it to be a condition that explains the drop in rate of a behavior. In this chapter, we discuss extinction as a management procedure applied intentionally to reduce annoying, functionless, maladaptive, or other unwanted behavior.

Extinction Defined and Illustrated

Conceptually, extinction is simple and straightforward, but as a reductive method it is not necessarily the easiest procedure to implement. Recall that **extinction** is a procedure in which *reinforcement is withheld* from or no longer follows a previously reinforced behavior. Ultimately, extinction leads to a reduction in the rate of that behavior to its prereinforcement level. For instance, if Bonnie is never given candy, she will eventually stop asking for it.

Intentionally or inadvertently, most of us use extinction as a tool, especially when we attempt to manage people's behavior. Parents, teachers, behavior analysts, employers, and even partners within interpersonal relationships may apply extinction to reduce or eliminate unwanted behaviors. You can be sure that management at Purple Triangle withholds merit raises from employees whose performance fails to meet job requirements.

Henrietta tells Mr. Ernie about all her current aches and pains. Her foot hurts; she has a headache. And last night she really felt dizzy just when it was time to clear the table. Assured by the doctor that Henrietta's complaints have no organic basis, the school psychologist averts his gaze and makes no response while Henrietta is on that particular subject. When she mentions that she has received an "A" on a spelling paper or the fun she had at the game, he reacts with enthusiasm. The unfounded somatic complaints have been placed on extinction, whereas other specific categories of verbal behavior are reinforced.

Extensive research on the topic of extinction has revealed much about its properties. Therefore, after discussing the procedure's advantages, prior to talking about its disadvantages, we emphasize those properties. A number of variables known to influence the effective application of extinction will be considered as well. Recognizing those factors should help you use extinction beneficially and provide you with a basis for deciding when extinction is and is not a method of choice.

Advantages of Extinction

Effectively reducing behavior. Usually applied in combination with other procedures, such as reinforcement of preferred alternatives, extinction has been found to be an effective strategy for reducing many classes of unwanted behaviors, including, among others:

- crying (Hart et al., 1964);

- throwing one's eye glasses (Wolf et al., 1964);
- whining (Hall et al., 1972);
- disruptive classroom behavior (Thomas, Nielsen, Kuypers, & Becker, 1969; Zimmerman & Zimmerman, 1962; O'Leary & Becker, 1967);
- aggression (Carr et al., 1980; Scott, Burton, & Yarrow, 1967; Brown & Elliot, 1965);
- tantrums in the classroom (Carlson, Arnold, Becker, & Madsen, 1968);
- nonstudying (Thomas, Becker, & Armstrong, 1968; Hall, Lund, & Jackson, 1968);
- excessive classroom noise (Wilson & Hopkins, 1973);
- deviant sexual arousal (Alford, Morin, Atkins, & Schoen, 1987);
- fear of snakes (Kaloupek, Peterson, Boyd, & Levis, 1981).

One instance, among many combinations of extinction and reinforcement, was described in a report by Wilson and Hopkins (1973). Reasonable levels of noise in a junior high school class were determined via an automated sensing device. Students learned to modulate the volume of the noise they produced because an electronic device activated a popular radio music broadcast when the sound level fell below 70 decibels, but interrupted it above that level.

School counselors used extinction procedures to weaken or eliminate deviant behaviors (Krumboltz & Hosford, 1967) p. 33 by withholding reinforcement (usually attention) for certain classes of verbalizations or other undesired behaviors. For example, in one case, increased verbal participation was the goal of a counseling group. Whenever clients left the counseling table or failed otherwise to participate, the counselor discontinued paying attention to them.

Extinction can help distraught and demoralized parents, teachers, and managers to boost their self-respect. Recognizing the control their children or subordinates have been exerting on them, these people can reestablish some degree of their own sense of control by using extinction successfully.

Long-lasting. If the extinction procedure is used optimally, its results can persist, a finding discovered by Skinner, in 1938, and supported by the findings in the many studies cited in this chapter. Here and in the section on maintenance, you will learn how to use extinction to help promote lasting change.

Aversive stimuli not required. Extinction simply involves the nondelivery of reinforcement. Aversive consequences need not be presented, permitting the procedure to avoid some of the ethical and legal problems entailed in using aversive control.

Properties of Extinction

When all reinforcement is permanently withheld contingent on a behavior, that behavior should gradually diminish to its prereinforcement level and perhaps ultimately cease altogether. As it is undergoing extinction, however, the behavior often is characterized by predictable patterns. Included are temporal features, initial increases in response rates and intensities, extinction-induced aggression, and spontaneous recovery (sometimes called *resurgence*).

Gradual behavioral reduction. Once its reinforcing consequences are removed, a behavior continues for some indeterminate amount of time before stopping (Skinner, 1953). The whining child or nagging spouse continue to whine or nag for a while, even when those behaviors yield them no further satisfaction.

Several factors are known to influence how rapidly a behavior is reduced through extinction:

- the number of previously reinforced trials.
- the schedules on which the response previously has been reinforced.
- contextual factors, such as the deprivation

level of the individual and other establishing operations and setting events.
- the effort needed to make the response.
- other contingencies currently operating (Millenson, 1967).

In general, behavior that has received optimal reinforcement, and is occurring at a high, steady rate, is much more resistant to extinction than one weakly established and practiced and reinforced only rarely. Also, a response previously reinforced on an intermittent (especially variable) reinforcement *schedule* is more resistant to extinction than one that has been continuously reinforced. Had Mrs. Hendricks laughed at her husband's tactless jokes every time she heard them, rather than inconsistently, the behavior would probably have disappeared sooner after she ceased laughing at the jokes altogether.

The more *deprived* of a given reinforcer a person is, the longer the behavior that previously functioned to secure that reinforcer will continue under extinction conditions. This factor is especially important when the behavior has been maintained by unconditioned reinforcers (Holland & Skinner, 1961). A hungry child will whine for a cookie at a higher rate, although whining has produced no cookies for months, than the same child would after having completed a big meal.

A response that requires considerable *effort* will extinguish more rapidly than an easy one. Mrs. Kvetch's complaining will disappear much more quickly if she has to climb three flights of stairs to air her grievances than if she only had to step next door to visit her formerly sympathetic boss.

When extinction is combined with *reinforcement of an alternative or incompatible behavior*, the response will diminish more rapidly, a point emphasized in the next chapter. Reese, Howard, and Rosenberger (1974) found that institutionalized retarded males produced far fewer errors when an alternative, reinforceable response was available to them than when errors were placed only under extinction. The same is true of applying extinction in combination with other reductive procedures, such as response cost, timeout, punishment, and contingent effort, about which you will learn shortly. Were Mrs. Hendricks not only to stop laughing at his jokes but also privately rebuke her husband (aversive to him) for their tastelessness, he might stop joke-telling sooner than if all she did was to ignore them.

Increases in rate and intensity of responding. Temporary increases in the rate and intensity of responding have been observed in both animals (Millenson, 1967) and humans (Kelly, 1969) immediately after the cessation of reinforcement, especially when a large proportion of the previous responses have been reinforced. What do you do when a vending machine fails to deliver? Pull the plunger more and more frequently and with greater vigor before you give up and go away. The infant whose crying is ignored for the first time may continue to scream with increasing intensity before the crying eventually subsides. Some behavior analysts label this predictable reaction an **extinction burst**.

Inducing aggression. Related to the behavior's temporary increase in rate and intensity is the aggression that sometimes accompanies the early stages of extinction (Skinner, 1953) (also considered an aspect of the extinction burst). Discontinuing positive reinforcement has been found to produce aggression in pigeons (Azrin, Hutchinson, & Hake, 1966) and in squirrel monkeys (Hutchinson, Azrin, & Hunt, 1968). Kelly (1969) has demonstrated a similar response in human males. In the latter study, subjects received money for pulling a knob. When money was discontinued, several subjects forcibly hit the apparatus, just as some do to the vending machine that fails to deliver.

Numerous examples of this reaction are seen in the natural setting. The top student who cries in exasperation when he does not receive a high enough grade; the employee who, suddenly deprived of an anticipated promotion, picks a fight with one of his co-workers; and students who don't succeed in school and turn to violence and vandalism probably are exhibiting **extinction-induced aggression**.

Spontaneous recovery. Another phenomenon that has been observed in connection with extinction is the reappearance of the "extinguished" response after a while despite no resumption of reinforcement. This phenomenon is called **spontaneous recovery** (Skinner, 1953) or **resurgence** (Epstein & Skinner, 1980). Although this phenomenon is transitory, recognizing its existence can save contingency managers from making a tactical error.

Consider this example: Thanks to his older brother, Reggie came to school with a vocabulary of off-color words that would make a turnip blush. The behavior analyst, to whom the problem was referred, observed that Reggie's colorful vocabulary seemed to be strongly maintained by his social environment. The teacher frowned and scolded him; classmates giggled and gasped; the principal lectured. Perhaps because Reggie had a history of being deprived of attention, the quantity he received from the teacher, peers, and principal served as a powerful reinforcer. Recognizing what was happening, the analyst suggested that a full-scale extinction program be put into effect. The teacher began to turn away when Reggie swore, and discretely praised the students when they ignored the swearing and ultimately stopped attending to the swearing. The principal no longer discussed the topic with Reggie. Reggie's swearing gradually subsided and seemed to have been eliminated.

Then, one day Reggie uttered a choice four-letter word and the moment of truth was at hand. How people responded was critical. Were his teacher to have scolded him even once, or the other students to have gasped, the behavior might have recovered its former strength. But fortunately, the teacher and students were prepared for that predictable resurgence and were able to sustain extinction until the recovery again dissipated. (Had the swearing been reinforced, eliminating it once again by using extinction would still have been possible, just more difficult.)

Disadvantages of Extinction

Many of the disadvantages of the extinction procedure have been covered in our discussion of its properties. Consider their ramifications.

Delayed effects. The delay involved in the time it takes to reduce behavior with extinction could pose a serious problem. Although a youngster's rudeness may be tolerable for a while, running out into a street full of traffic is not. Ignoring that would be absurd and dangerous: The child himself may be extinguished before the response is eliminated. Therefore, dangerous acts demand that extinction be combined with procedures producing more immediate effects, such as punishment or response cost.

Extinction bursts. Recognizing that extinction bursts are temporary is a consolation; even so they can be troublesome. Instituting an extinction program on a day when the school board is making its annual visit would not be a clever move for the teacher. Nor would the morning after a big party be the best time to begin applying extinction to your roommate's gripes about your housekeeping practices. The patience required during the early stages of the extinction program can be compromised by personal pressures, so plan with care and prepare to endure until the extinction bursts dissipate.

Imitation of inappropriate behavior. Unconsequated noxious acts like aggression often are imitated by peers, especially when adult supervisors ignore them (Bandura & Walters, 1963; Bandura, 1965b). Managers who remove reinforcing attention by ignoring aggression need to be aware of this potential trap and may want to opt for an alternative procedure. Additionally, they need to realize that total extinction would be very difficult to accomplish in a group setting, because victims and peers are almost certain to react.

Reinforcers may be uncontrollable. Sometimes eliminating the reinforcing consequences of unwanted behaviors is impossible, because the natural function of many behaviors is very reinforcing. As long as thieves are not caught, stealing is reinforced by the goods attained. Removing the reinforcing consequences of speeding in a car (getting there faster); cheating on examinations (earning higher grades); consuming drugs, alcohol, or sweets; experimenting with sex, masturbation, rocking, or some forms of self-injurious behavior would be pretty difficult. In fact, researchers have been discovering numerous physiological reinforcers for various substances (e.g., nicotine, Pomerleau & Pomerleau, 1984) and certain forms of self-abuse (Barrett, McGonigle, Ackles, & Burkhart, 1987).

Peer reactions pose a major challenge too. When either the identification or the control of the reinforcing contingencies is very difficult or impossible, you will need to do something about it, or select a different procedure. Often, though, extinction is the method of choice, so learn how to use it effectively—the focus of the next discussion.

Using Extinction Effectively

Identifying and controlling sources of reinforcement. Sometimes reinforcing consequences are fairly obvious; at other times, they are not. Considerable painstaking investigation may be required to discover what reinforcers are maintaining the behaviors (e.g., Carr & Durand, 1985a; Durand & Crimmins, 1988; Iwata et al.,

1990; Zarcone et al., 1990). Identifying reinforcement can be particularly difficult when it happens so infrequently that the observer fails to notice it.

Does Harry gripe angrily because it upsets his boss, produces peer support, relieves tension, or produces all these and/or other reinforcers? Does Jack take money from the petty cash drawer because he needs it for food or items that he cannot afford? Or is obtaining the money this way just easier than cashing a check? Does Mincrva frequently leave her work station because her job is boring, she likes to talk to her friends, and/or because her supervisor is sure to notice?

Effective extinction requires that *all* reinforcers be withheld contingent on the target response. Again, the method for determining which reinforcers are maintaining the behavior is based on formal observation. An A-B-C analysis or scattergram can be used once the response has been operationally defined. Or the probable reinforcing object or event can be systematically withheld and presented for periods of time. If the behavior subsequently declines when the reinforcer is withheld and increases when it is presented, one reinforcing contingency has probably been identified. This procedure can be repeated for each of the suspected reinforcers. Carr and his colleagues (Carr & Durand, 1985a; Carr et al., 1980) and Iwata et al. (1990) provide excellent examples of ways to attempt identifying reinforcers for certain self-injurious acts.

Withholding reinforcement from the unwanted behavior. Once the reinforcers maintaining a particular undesirable behavior have been identified, those consequences should be permanently removed if possible. Suppose in Harry's case, his boss's and peers' reactions were demonstrated to be supporting his griping. After the boss and peers (prompted by their boss's example) decided to ignore it, the behavior diminished to a tolerable level.

The importance of determining empirically the functional properties of a presumed reinforcer is underscored by an example from the classroom literature. O'Leary and his colleagues (1969) tried to reduce the disruptive behaviors of seven second-graders by ignoring disruptive and praising desirable behaviors, an approach they knew to have been successful with other populations. In this instance, however, the procedure was not effective. Apparently, attention had not been the key reinforcer. The investigators were forced to try an alternative approach. Success was finally accomplished by using a stronger reinforcer—a token system.

In terms of peer management, though, you do have some recourse. One of the most obvious strategies is to reinforce when peers withhold attention from disruptive behavior. For example, when a worker indulges in foolishness like turning an air hose toward an associate, the manager can praise a model, such as a popular co-worker who ignores the risky antics.

Patterson (1965) found a way to recruit support toward reducing the hyperactive behavior of a 9-year-old boy. Patterson's approach was to permit Earl and his classmates to obtain candy or pennies from a "magic teaching machine" whenever Earl attended for 10 seconds. His classmates were also rewarded for withholding their attention during his antics. Extinction conditions were rapidly obtained, and the teacher himself found the more favorable classroom environment very reinforcing. (See if you can solve the dilemma posed in Figure 23.1.)

When Solomon and Wahler (1973) discovered that peers continually paid attention to the disruptive behavior (talking, being out of seat, and classroom play) of 5 sixth-grade boys, they selected 5 cooperative high-status peers who were then trained in extinction and reinforcement techniques. The application of these behavioral procedures by the high-status peers met with remarkable success, and the "problem" children produced less deviant and more prosocial behaviors.

Figure 23.1 What's Happening? What Should the Teacher Do?

Yet no matter how hard we try, certain irritating behaviors are nearly impossible to ignore. The consequence is that we don't attend to those irritants for a while but ultimately cave in, reacting with a barrage of criticism. "The way you crack your knuckles drives me nuts. For heaven's sake stop it!" (Sound familiar? It's part of the human condition.) Assuming the attention is a potent reinforcer, that could make the matter worse because this intermittent schedule of reinforcement is ideally suited to long-term maintenance of behavior. What is to be done? You have a few choices:

- Select a different reductive procedure—fortunately, we present a number of these alternatives for you to consider.
- Head off the irritating behavior at the pass, by redirecting the individual into a different activity. If you are studying and your roommate approaches the stereo to play a selection you can't stand, you ask him to help you rearrange the sofa at that moment, thanking him profusely afterward. He will be less likely to want to get your goat right after you have been so appreciative.
- You get yourself out of the situation before your resolve is broken. For example, as your roommate moves in the direction of the stereo you decide the time has come for you to study in your room.
- Try giving out tokens (along with behavior-specific praise) for the desired behavior. Often, as described in the chapter on token economies, token delivery can increase attention to the positive behavior, which can help you to ignore the negative.

This last suggestion encourages you to use **positive scanning**, because the tokens remind you to catch people being good. With positive scanning you direct your attention to positive behaviors to such an extent that you begin to fail to notice the negative, which in turn helps you to ignore the latter (e.g., McFall, 1970). A couple of true illustrative episodes follow. (Recognize, though, that these reports were not based on hard, experimentally controlled data; the utility of "positive scanning" awaits additional experimental verification.)

One incident involved a family with a 15-year-old son whose conduct was totally out of control. Truancy, experimentation with drugs, sexual misconduct, remaining out all night without permission, failure to comply with other parental requests, and hostile confrontations with them were among their complaints. Sessions were attempted with the entire family, but after one visit the boy refused to return. So helping the parents to cope with the situation until the boy reached his majority was emphasized instead.

That the parents were incredibly upset was apparent; and this was causing them enormous stress and discomfort. The mother was very depressed, and the father seethed with anger. Meanwhile, their other child, a daughter, was being adversely affected by the tension in the home. A promising goal was to try to help them to shift their focus to the good things their son did. For a homework assignment, they were asked to list at least three positive things the boy did each day.

"What good things? He doesn't do any!" they protested.

After pursuing the topic extensively, it turned out that their son had cleared his dishes from the table, brought in the newspaper, and had returned home at the appointed time one day. Little by little, the parents began to be able to discover more laudable acts, and after several weeks the list began to expand. Therapy sessions were devoted increasingly more to noting and discussing those progressively more detectable commendable acts and less to the son's problems. After a few months passed, the mother's depression seemed to be lifting and the father appeared more relaxed. From their reports, the boy was becoming more responsible and conciliatory, and was easier to live with. Because the problems were hardly discussed any more, what happened to them is not known, but presumably they must have diminished in intensity.

A second case concerned a couple married many years. Their relationship seemed to be eroding day by day, and complaining and bickering characterized their daily interactions. Being in their presence was becoming unpleasant. No matter what viewpoint one expressed, the other spouse took the opposite position. This produced anger, arguing, and criticizing. All the nasty things the other recently had done and said were rehashed. (Could all this attention have been reinforcing?) So fluent was the recitation that one had the sense that they rehearsed covertly the list of complaints in readiness for the first provocation. Neither one had any interest in terminating the relationship, and the wife asked the consultant to help. Positive scanning was suggested.

As in the previous case, the wife needed some assistance to get started.

"He does make breakfast, doesn't he?" inquired the consultant.

"Yes, but he always does, so why count that?"

"Is that nice for you? Or would you rather do it yourself?"

"Oh no. It's just fine the way it is."

"So count it. Now find two more."

After several sessions of coaching, the list of three good deeds a day began to be produced regularly. At that point, the goal level was raised to four.

"Forget it, I'll never find another."

But with additional coaching, she finally did.

"Can't I list the bad things too? That only seems fair."

"No way. Remember, our task is to find the good. In fact, I don't want to hear about the others. You want to stay married to him so make the best of it by accentuating the positive. Now that you've found four items a day for a few weeks, let's try for five."

"I suppose I could, but it will be almost impossible."

"You like a challenge. Go for it!" And she did.

As the cold weather approached, the couple went south for several months.

"Call me when you reach six," instructed the consultant.

A couple of weeks later the phone rang.

"You won't believe it. Today we reached six," the wife laughed, "and we seem to be getting along so much better."

"Great. Stay with it and keep me posted from time to time."

Several months later a bonanza report came in.

"These days we're up to 9 or 10. Yesterday was a 12. I can't get over it. Life is beautiful. Your system of 'accentuating the positive' is a real winner. You'd better put it in one of your books."

So we did!

Specifying clearly the conditions for extinction. Mom told Flossie that when Mom was working at her desk, she would not respond to Flossie's pestering for snacks. Flossie quickly learned that Mom-at-the-desk meant that pestering would not work. Had no information been exchanged about the conditions under which extinction would occur, eventually Flossie would learn not to interrupt her mother while she worked at her desk, but it might take much longer.

"Remember, a story, a drink, and a trip to the potty, that's all," Dad reminds Baby Bonnie as he puts her to bed and holds to the contingencies. Bonnie learns to acquiesce reasonably rapidly.

The earlier discussion of stimulus control, you'll recall, elaborated on the importance of specifying conditions under which extinction and reinforcement occur. Stimulus control was used there for the purpose of instruction. Here, stimulus control is used to aid the extinction process, so the important point to note is that the conditions should be communicated *before* the event of concern. Avoid lengthy *post hoc* explanations, for such attention may serve as a reinforcer: "I told you not to bother me at my desk. I have work to do. You know how mommy needs to work. . . ."

Naturally, however, at the appropriate time you would reinforce the absence of the undesirable behavior. When Mom leaves her desk she tells Flossie how she has appreciated her not interrupting, offers her a snack, and offers to play Flossie's favorite game with her.

Maintaining extinction conditions for a sufficient time. Extinction bursts can be very distressing. The first time the teacher ignored Reggie's colorful language, he responded by bursting forth with a hair-raising stream of epithets. The teacher might well have branded the technique of ignoring undesirable behavior a failure. But was it? The only way the teacher could find out was to ride the crest of the wave for a while (and hope the other students were no more sophisticated than the teacher himself had been at their age) and to see if it would begin to subside. Assuming that the teacher's frowning and scolding were the reinforcing events, the behavior would ultimately diminish. At such times, data collection can be a tremendous asset. The number of class periods during which Reggie did *not*

swear could be tallied, perhaps with the help of a wrist counter. If the data showed a small but steady increase, there would then be room for optimism. Sometimes improvement is so gradual that in the absence of graphed data, improvement remains undetected. The point is, you need to prepare yourself for extinction bursts, and plan to hang on long enough—at least a few weeks—to give the procedure a fair try.

Combining extinction with other procedures. Although extinction can be effective on its own, we strongly recommend you combine it with other procedures, especially reinforcing acceptable alternatives. The reasons are probably apparent to you now. One concerns the tendency for everyone to continue responding until some reinforcing consequence occurs. The other has to do with "killing two birds with one stone."

Because extinction implies discontinuation, or withholding, of reinforcers contingent on a particular response, determining whether individuals have "sufficient" reinforcement available from other sources is critical. When Harry's temperamental responses were no longer yielding him the attention he sought, his manager would have to make sure that Harry did not lose out on receiving his attention altogether. If Harry could find no constructive way to make the boss notice him, he would probably continue trying different, perhaps even more troublesome, behaviors, until one succeeded. Consequently, plan to deliver lots of reinforcers for desirable behaviors to the individual whose specific unwanted behavior is undergoing extinction. His boss could comment on the apparent care with which Harry performed his job assignments, smile at any friendly overtures, and so on.

In large, understaffed institutions serving severely developmentally delayed people, residents often repeat puzzling behaviors—stereotypic responses like head weaving, repetitive hand movements, rocking, and pacing a given area over and over. What explains the development and maintenance of such seemingly

Figure 23.2 Deciding Whether to Use Extinction

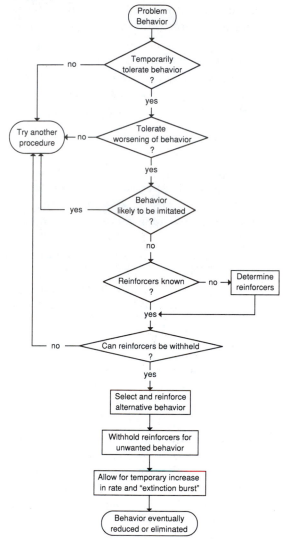

auditory patterns—or in the form of social attention from peers or staff members, who inadvertently reinforce through attention. Alternatively, they may give up altogether, having no way of controlling their world, and curl up in bed or in a corner. Such a response to the environment is labeled "learned helplessness" (Seligman, 1975).

These adverse reactions do not happen when the environment is structured to maximize reinforcement for adaptive behaviors, as effective programs do. A case in point is the program at the Walden Learning Center, a preschool serving typical and autistic children; it conveys a very different picture. Children are busily engaged in arts and crafts, dramatic play, singing, having snacks, playing with toys or on outdoor exercise equipment, and receiving lots of special attention for making progress in areas designated in their individual educational plans. The stereotypic and self-abusive behavior so characteristic of many autistic children is rarely seen. Additionally, the dense reinforcement makes the children, like everyone else, feel good as well as more positive about themselves (Ludwig & Maehr, 1967; Wisocki, 1973).

Besides the inexcusable omission of all sources of programmed reinforcement, the main problem with using extinction alone is that no alternative constructive behaviors are designated to replace those to be eliminated. For these reasons, you will always want to select and reinforce other *preferred* performances in concert with extinction. That combination constitutes, as you already know, differential reinforcement. Supplementing extinction with differential reinforcement has the added advantage of attenuating the negative side effects, such as the extinction bursts that often accompany the procedure. Now the individual has a reliable source of reinforcement for engaging in alternative behaviors. In the next chapter we elaborate on the latter procedure.

functionless acts? Perhaps extinction is the answer. When members of a large group lack adaptive behaviors sufficient to permit them to capture natural reinforcers (such as attention, affection, material goods, and so on) many will continue to express functionless or maladaptive behaviors for the meager reinforcement they yield. The reinforcement may be in the form of sensory stimulation—changing visual, tactile, or

Summary

Assuming, based on considerations presented early in the chapter, a decision has been made to select a reductive procedure, the behavior analyst needs to select those to apply. Various methods are available, including extinction, various differential reinforcement techniques, response cost, timeout, and punishment. Each has advantages and limitations. In this chapter we began with the conceptually (though not necessarily the most procedurally) simple alternative: extinction.

By itself or in combination with other procedures and in various situations, extinction effectively can reduce undesirable behaviors. Figure 23.2 is intended to assist you in deciding whether extinction is an appropriate procedure in a given situation. Appropriate responses to the questions posed should be obtained before extinction is selected.

Extinction takes time. In fact, the behavior may get worse before it gets better. One must be able to tolerate this temporary setback. As a general rule, extinction should not be used as the sole method of dealing with destructive or dangerous behaviors, especially in social settings.

Efficient use of extinction requires identifying and withholding all reinforcing consequences for the undesirable behavior. If it is not possible to remove the reinforcing contingencies for a specific response, an alternative reductive technique should be used.

In situations in which the behavior to be reduced is not serious, temporary setbacks can be tolerated, and all the reinforcers for the behavior can be withheld over an extended period of time (including during spontaneous recovery), extinction is a reasonable choice. Its effectiveness will be further enhanced when desirable behaviors are reinforced simultaneously. Generally, any reductive procedure is more effective when desirable behaviors simultaneously are reinforced.

Chapter 24

Reducing Behavior with Differential Reinforcement

GOALS

After completing this chapter, you should be able to:

1. Define, recognize, and give original illustrations of each of the following terms:
   a. Differential reinforcement of alternative behavior (Alt-R or DRA)
   b. Incompatible behavior
   c. Differential reinforcement of incompatible behavior (DRI)
   d. Differential reinforcement of the nonoccurrence (or of zero rate) of a behavior (whole-interval DRO)
   e. Behavioral contrast
   f. Momentary DRO
   g. Differential reinforcement of low rates (DRL)
   h. Differential reinforcement of diminishing rates (DRD)
   i. Good Behavior Game

2. List, discuss, and illustrate the four major advantages of using Alt-R and DRI procedures.

3. List, discuss, and illustrate two major disadvantages of using differential reinforcement to reduce behavior.

4. Provide four guidelines for selecting alternative target behaviors.

5. Enumerate, discuss, and illustrate the factors that influence the effectiveness of the Alt-R procedure.

6. Compose an example of the use of modeling as an adjunct to Alt-R for reducing behavior.

7. Describe a technique to help youself increase your use of modeling.

8. Carry out an effective Alt-R procedure.

9. List and discuss the advantages and disadvantages of DRO.

10. List, discuss, and illustrate the factors that influence the effectiveness of a DRO procedure.

11. Discuss under what condition momentary DRO may be just as effective as whole-interval DRO.

12. Carry out an effective DRO procedure.

13. List and discuss the advantages and disadvantages of methods of differentially reinforcing low or diminishing rates of behavior.

14. List, discuss, and illustrate the factors that influence the effectiveness of DRL and DRD procedures.

15. Describe the Good Behavior Game, including steps that can be taken to minimize its disadvantages.

16. Carry out effective DRL and DRD procedures.

17. Describe when a punitive rather than a positive procedure should be used to reduce behavior.

18. Complete Table 24.1.

Henrietta's somatic complaints and Harry's tempermental outbursts are no longer gaining them reinforcers. There we see the most unfortunate aspect of using extinction alone: the absence of reinforcement. Differential reinforcement remedies that deficiency. Chapter 15 discussed using differential reinforcement for purposes of bringing behavior under stimulus control. Here the same basic procedure is used to achieve behavioral reductions, with slight variations, as you saw by looking at Table 1 in the section introduction. After discussing the distinctions among **differential reinforcement of alternative behaviors** (Alt-R or DRA) and differential reinforcement of incompatible behaviors (DRI), we shall consider each in turn. Then we shall turn to three other differential reinforcement operations: DRO, DRL, and DRD.

Differentially Reinforcing Alternative and Incompatible Behaviors

Skim Table 1 in the section introduction again to refresh yourself about the examples. Notice that in the case of **Alt-R or DRA**, *any* specific alternative to the unwanted response is reinforced while the unwanted behavior is placed on extinction. As Barney ignores Sloppy's refusals, he will deliver reinforcement any time Sloppy agrees to comply, nods acquiescence, says he'll think about it, or any other acceptable alternatives to refusing.

With **differential reinforcement of incompatible behaviors (DRI)**, a behavior **incompatible** with the unwanted one is selected for reinforcement. Sloppy will obtain Barney's approval, or a cup of coffee or a soda, only when Sloppy complies with requests; failure to comply will be ignored, as will smiling or saying he will do it soon. *DRI*, then, is a subclass of the Alt-R or DRA procedure in which a behavior *incompatible with* the unwanted behavior is selected as the alternative response to reinforce.

Alt-R and DRI Illustrated

Take a look at a few more examples of these differential reinforcement procedures: Violet quietly isolates herself in a corner during lunch time. Targeting goals such as turning one end of a jump rope, conversing, sitting with peers, and playing a group game or other activities incompatible with social isolation would be a good choice. Strengthening those behaviors should reduce the frequency of Violet's moments alone.

Vernon is frequently in trouble with the police, breaking windows, pilfering from stores, spraying paint on walls, and shooting BBs at passers-by, all during school hours while he is truant. Attending school is incompatible with those behaviors. If Vernon's school attendance is the alternative to be strengthened, his lawless behavior should decrease.

Allen and colleagues (1964) worked with a preschooler who seldom played with other children. Rather than punishing or ignoring the isolate behavior, or inadvertently reinforcing it by trying to cajole her into playing, they decided to pay attention to her whenever she was seen interacting with other children (an alternative to isolate behavior). As a result, the child became more gregarious. A similar approach was used to diminish a preschooler's hyperactivity (Allen et al., 1967). Flitting from one activity to another brought the child no reinforcement, but engaging in one activity for specific periods of time was socially reinforced, and hyperactivity was reduced.

You can use DRI to achieve clinical objectives as well. For phobic behaviors, DRI is used to help shape approximations toward the phobic object or event (Kaloupek et al., 1981). For sexual deviance, responsiveness to appropriate stimuli can be achieved via DRI (Alford et al., 1987). For loneliness and depression, you could target dating (Goldstein, Sprafkin, Gershaw, & Klein, 1980), social interactional skills (Blom & Zimmerman, 1981; Bornstein, Bellack, & Hersen, 1977; Gottman, Gonso, & Rasmussen, 1975) or recreational participation (Goldstein et al., 1980). (See numerous cases in the *Journal of Consulting and Clinical Psychology, Behavior Therapy, Behavior Research and Experimental Psychiatry, Behaviour Research and Therapy,* and other journals.)

An actual client, like Pearl, stereotypically wove her hands before her face. Because this and several other behaviors interfered with her attending to relevant environmental stimuli, these were targeted for reduction by her therapist. DRI was used by selecting and reinforcing a large group of hand-involved instructional and play behaviors: using the sand table; assembling puzzles; piling blocks; painting; and so on. With sufficient reinforcement, she began to engage in those constructive play activities much more often. Stereotypic hand movements were never attended to, either positively or punitively, yet because they could not coexist with the more constructive behaviors, they gradually diminished. When her teacher used a similar approach, parallel results were achieved in school.

Advantages of Alt-R

Constructive. In selecting alternative behaviors, identifying one or more beneficial alternatives usually is possible. In the illustrations cited, increased social interactions, task completion, and participation in group play undoubtedly contributed to the individuals' progress personally, educationally, and socially, because they learned what *to do* instead of what *not* to do. This advantage contrasts with other reductive procedures, such as extinction, punishment, response cost, and timeout that focus primarily on eliminating behavior. Eliminating behavior enhances neither learning nor development.

Benign. Extinction, response cost, timeout, and

punishment all have negative qualities, requiring either that reinforcers be withheld or withdrawn or that aversive consequences be presented. With Alt-R, reinforcement continues, so a carefully planned program will yield regular reinforcement and all the good things that go along with it. Any generalized responding to stimuli in the setting is likely to be positive. People also are more likely to remain in situations in which reinforcement is delivered. In our clinical illustration, the child who learned to use her hands in useful ways always attended sessions willingly and never attempted to leave. Had we scolded, slapped, or withheld attention whenever the stereotypic hand movements occurred, she may have found the situation aversive and tried to leave or, at least, refused to cooperate in the program.

Acceptable. Practitioners who see the purpose of their jobs as helping individuals to develop to their fullest possible potential often are unwilling to use aversive contingencies. Many prefer not to spend their time scolding, punishing, threatening, or intentionally ignoring clients, choosing instead to help them acquire beneficial skills (e.g., see Kazdin, 1980a; 1980b; Kazdin, French, & Sherick, 1981; Elliot, Witt, Galvin, & Peterson, 1984; Singh & Katz, 1985). Reinforcing a productive, desirable alternative to an unwanted behavior is well suited to those ideals. Additionally, both parents and children appear to prefer DRI to other procedures (Kazdin, 1981).

Lasting change. Once the alternative behavior occurs at a rate high and steadily enough to block the occurrence of the unwanted behavior, the latter is, at least temporarily, eliminated. As long as the alternative behavior is *maintained* at a similar rate, the behavior it replaced is not apt to return. Foxx et al. (1986) found this to be the case when they reinforced an alternative behavior, to replace public masturbation by a 16-year-old severely retarded male. Therefore, by following the rules for maintaining high rates of behavior (detailed in Chapter 32), we can achieve an enduring reduction of the undesirable behavior.

Disadvantages of Alt-R

Effect may be delayed. Reinforcement procedures may take time to achieve their results, particularly if the alternative response is not well established in the client's repertoire. Unless the replacement behavior occurs at a fairly high and steady rate, time remains to permit the undesirable one to be expressed. Until Violet interacts with others frequently, she still has lots of opportunity to remain alone. While Desmond's rate of remaining on-task increases, he can continue to disrupt. By combining Alt-R with other procedures, you may be able to speed up the process somewhat. While reinforcing its replacement, using response cost or stimulus change to reduce the undesirable behavior more rapidly may reduce the time lag. But again, once an aversive consequence like response cost is introduced, some of the major advantages of DRI—that it is a positive and constructive approach—are lost.

Mixed evidence of effectiveness. A given Alt-R procedure does not guarantee that the unwanted target behavior will decrease (Young & Wincze, 1974). For example, Ferritor et al. (1972) attempted unsuccessfully to increase the academic performance of third-grade students indirectly by presenting or withholding their attention for engagement. Only when contingencies were placed directly on math performance did the students increase their percentages of problems completed correctly; but then, student inattention increased.

In contrast with the experience of Ferritor and colleagues (1972), when Eggelston and Mayer (1976) reinforced paying attention, not only did attention increase but the number and percentage of math problems completed also increased. Similarly, others (Sulzer et al., 1971;

Ayllon & Roberts, 1974) found that when reading performance was reinforced, disruptive behavior decreased. In Ayllon and Roberts' study (1974), those students who received tokens for reading achievement dramatically reduced their rates of disruption. In the study by Sulzer and colleagues (1971), the students doubled or tripled their rates of progress in reading and spelling over those of the previous year, while at the same time attending to task more regularly. What's more, students often were overheard to voice their pleasure with school. All this was achieved with practically no negative consequences.

Fortunately, these studies do agree in one respect. All found that when *both* paying attention and performing math were reinforced, both increased maximally. Consequently, if the goal is to increase Desmond's (or anyone else's) attending *plus* production, both should be reinforced. This combined approach will help you achieve these multiple goals.

Selecting Replacement Behaviors

The selection of goals was discussed at considerable length in Chapter 3. To review, the targets you select to replace the unwanted behavior should be constructive, likely to be supported in the natural environment, readily achievable, acceptable to all concerned, and functional, in the sense that they enable the person to earn the same (or better) reinforcers than those previously obtained by means of the unwanted behavior. (Figure 3.1 summarizes many of these factors.) Here we elaborate on several of those aspects that are especially relevant to this topic.

Striving for behavioral incompatibility. When you select responses to reinforce, be careful to emphasize alternatives that are not apt to occur simultaneously with the unwanted behavior (although as Young and Wincze, 1974, have shown, even this is no guarantee of success). If both can occur simultaneously, the unwanted one may be strengthened inadvertently. Suppose Vernon not only gets into trouble during school hours while he is truant but also manages to steal and destroy property in school. Simply reinforcing school attendance will not reduce his misbehavior but may even accidentally strengthen it in the school setting. So you have to be very specific about the alternative reinforceable behaviors you select. Doing schoolwork at his desk, participating in group activities, or engaging in wood working and art projects may not be compatible with stealing and destruction. Strengthening other activities, such as allowing Vernon to go on errands, remain alone without supervision, or have access to free and unstructured time, would be avoided, because these are not incompatible with theft and vandalism. Vernon could conceivably write on walls while on an errand, rifle students' desks while alone in the room, and so on. Therefore, whenever feasible, select as a replacement behavior one that is fully incompatible with the undesired behavior. Then you will be using DRI.

Selecting a behavior already in the response repertoire. Given a set of alternative responses among which to choose, if all other factors are equal, selecting one that is already present in the repertoire of the client is a good idea. The goal should be accomplished more quickly if the alternative behavior is already occurring at some rate above zero, because shaping a new behavior may involve considerable delay.

"Can't you do something with that guy?" pleads the storeroom supervisor to Barney, Sloppy Smith's manager. "Every time he borrows a tool, it disappears for months afterward. When I ask him for it back, he protests he returned it; and he probably did—but always to the wrong place."

"Does he know where it belongs?" asks Barney.

"Darned if I know."

"Well, we could teach him, but that would take so long. Suppose, instead of asking Sloppy to return the tools to the place where they belong, we put a box near the door with a sign saying 'Return tools here'—something we know he's capable of doing. That will make returning tools easier for him and replacing them in their proper locations simpler for you."

"Great idea. I'll do it!"

Selecting behavior likely to be supported by the broader environment. Practitioners cannot remain with their clients constantly, so preferably the alternative behavior should be one that other people will tend to support. Polite, well-modulated speech; no speech; minimal speech; whispered words; incomprehensible words; and others are all incompatible with using abusive language. But some of these would yield the client reinforcers in the outside world. Not speaking, whispering, and uttering incomprehensibly probably would undergo extinction. Conversely, friends and strangers probably will naturally reinforce polite, well-modulated speech.

Calling an activity "practical" usually implies that it readily accomplishes something—that it is functional. For instance, teaching polite, well-modulated speech is likely to result in environmental support because it is functional. Whenever feasible, then, *select practical, incompatible behaviors*, because they usually are socially important and apt to be maintained through "natural" consequences.

Selecting behavior that serves an equivalent function. Try your best to select a behavior that at a minimum serves the *same function* (i.e., yields the same reinforcers) as the unwanted behavior. Mrs. Kvetch's complaining gets her lots of attention. Saying pleasant things to her co-workers will yield her attention also, justifying making positive statements as functionally equivalent replacement behaviors. In the past, because Pearl's mother offered her daughter food to distract the child from her stereotypic finger flicking, Pearl flicked her fingers especially intensely when she was hungry. After Pearl was taught to form the sign for food and was no longer fed for flicking her fingers, she began to use the sign instead.

Several studies have supported the importance of discovering the function of a maladaptive behavior in order to select an appropriate replacement response. Carr and Newsom (1985) found that three developmentally disabled children used tantrums in an equivalent way: to obtain relief from demands being placed on them. When the demanding instructional process was made more reinforcing by augmenting praise with food for correct answers, the children no longer tantrumed to avoid the situation. In an analogous case, Carr and Durand (1985a) found that four children engaged in aggression, tantrums, and self-injury when presented with high levels of task difficulty and low levels of adult attention. After the children learned to ask for help or attention, their inappropriate behaviors diminished considerably, because the latter were replaced by socially acceptable alternatives that produced the same result: either relief from a difficult situation or attention. Consequently, before intervening to reduce a behavior, try to identify the function it is serving and substitute a response of *equivalent functions*. Such responses also are more likely to be supported by the broader environment.

Using Alt-R Effectively

In addition to the factors to be considered as you select replacement behaviors and use reinforcement and extinction, recognize that supplementing differential reinforcement with other behavioral procedures can increase the effectiveness of the Alt-R procedure. Alt-R can be combined with most of the other procedures for reducing behavior described in this and subsequent chapters. Such procedural combinations usually produce more rapid results than either alone, as will be illustrated later.

If a promising alternative behavior is not present in the person's repertoire, *differential reinforcement, shaping, or chaining* can be used to promote its development, as you saw in the example of the child with the stereotypic hand movements. If the behavior is under *stimulus control*, the practitioner may model the behavior, give verbal directions, and present other S^Ds to occasion and subsequently strengthen the response. If, for instance, a youngster who seems to have a difficult time sticking to one activity for very long responds correctly to the direction "Please, do your work," giving that instruction while reinforcing increasingly longer periods of staying on-task would make sense.

As always, the change agent must be very sensitive to the effects of instructions like those. Do they just occasion the desired behavior, or do they also reinforce unwanted behavior by providing contingent attention? In order to find out, you can try instructions for a few days and observe their effects on the frequency or duration of the unwanted behavior. If the attention is reinforcing, the behavior will increase. Waiting for the wanted behavior to occur by itself or prompting and reinforcing a nearby peer's performance to occasion it would then be preferable to the directive. Then, following with reinforcement should boost the rate.

The following case (Fowler et al., 1986) illustrates several of the aforementioned points. Three seven-year-old boys, Chuck, Bob, and Adam, frequently misbehaved during recess. Then they were trained and appointed as peer monitors. Their job was to award or subtract points, depending on their assigned buddies' conduct on the playground. The monitors recorded the points by moving beads on a string and received feedback on the quality of their monitoring and their own deportment during play. Monitors and the rest of the class shared in the back-up activities earned by the buddies they supervised. The three monitors' own negative interactions diminished substantially during the recess periods in which they served as monitors, but not during other recess periods. Notice how the Alt-R, being a monitor, tended to be incompatible with misbehaving, and how the reinforcement associated with that role supported the children's job performance.

Modeling can be an especially helpful adjunct to Alt-R as well as other reductive procedures. While other people are misbehaving, a model's exemplary deportment can serve as an imitative prompt. "Ebenezer, I sure am pleased to see you working quietly"; "Wow, Clyde is really getting down to work now, too." Comments like these may set the occasion for peers to imitate the behavior, thereby providing the peers the opportunity to receive reinforcement. Kazdin, Silverman, and Sittler (1975) delivered a verbal prompt—"Dave, look at Ted [the target subject]"—and immediately nodded approval to Ted, the target subject, whose attentive behavior was featured as a model. Under those conditions both children improved.

Notice how modeling, paired with Alt-R, accelerated the rate of behavioral reduction. Another key advantage of combining modeling with Alt-R is that it prompts positive scanning, modulating the natural inclination to respond disproportionately to negative behavior: "Roberto, sit down!" "Eric, be quiet!" "Stop that!" "Don't you know any better?" "Get back to work!" Using modeling helps to turn the tables so the individuals who are behaving well obtain their share of recognition.

In case you find it difficult to notice and point out models of good behavior, you might try this strategy: Use the minor misbehaviors you do notice to cue yourself to find several individuals who are engaging in *constructive alternatives*, and reinforce their actions (Becker, Madsen, Arnold, & Thomas, 1967). For example, when her supervisor notices Minerva filing her nails instead of completing her job assignment, the supervisor could use this as a cue to voice her pleasure to those nearby who are working appropriately.

"Jim, I'm so pleased to see you're getting your work done. I see you're almost finished too Mary. That's going to help us meet the deadline."

Then, hopefully, Minerva will get the message and start working, shortly providing her boss the opportunity to reinforce Minerva's industry.

Take care, however, when you put this suggestion into practice. Just as reinforcing a model's desired behavior can prompt others to imitate, reinforcing unwanted behavior can do the same. Although the caution may seem obvious to you, it is worth emphasizing, because all of us inadvertently reinforce behavior we would prefer not to see repeated. For example, Witt and Adams (1980) showed that observers would imitate either appropriate or inappropriate behavior, like playing with a pencil, if their teacher paid attention to that behavior.

Omission Training

Omission training, sometimes called **differential reinforcement of zero rates of the behavior (DRO)** (i.e., during a prespecified period of time), is an especially popular method for reducing behavior. While still benign, the method does not require the same degree of vigilance as does reinforcing specific alternative behaviors (Alt-R and DRI). Because DRO is a time rather than a response-dependent schedule for applying differential reinforcement, parents, teachers, managers, and care givers are not required to monitor everything the individual does from moment to moment. Instead, they only need to note the absence of the unwanted behavior. Let us examine this procedure more closely to help you see what we mean.

DRO Defined and Illustrated

Conceptually, the notion of differentially reinforcing the absence of a response makes no sense. Reinforcement is an operation that involves a response-contingent consequence leading to an increase in the rate of that response. A nonresponse can't be reinforced. Yet, *procedurally*, a reinforcer can be delivered following a period of time during which a given response has *not* occurred. (Presumably, whatever behavior is ongoing at the time will be reinforced.) This situation describes the DRO procedure. A time period passes. Assuming the target response does not occur in the interim, a reinforcer is delivered. The rule stipulates that the unwanted behavior must be absent. Because the behavior cannot be reinforced, its rate begins to diminish.

During math and language arts, the children in a third-grade class frequently disrupted by running around the room, making noise, or disturbing other children or their property in numerous other ways (Allen, Gottselig, & Boylan, 1982). The teacher used a clever DRO procedure to eliminate the difficulties almost completely. After explaining and posting rules, she set a kitchen timer for 5 minutes. When the timer signaled the end of the interval, if the children had not disrupted, the teacher flipped over a card displaying the numeral 1, indicating that the class had earned a minute of free play. Subsequently, for each 5-minute period during which the class did not disrupt, the next numeral in the sequence was displayed. This continued until the period ended and the class was able to cash in its points for the free time. The teacher reported that besides disrupting less, the children actually increased the number of assignments they completed, despite the shortened period required to allow for the free time reward. Presumably, when the students no longer were disrupting, they kept to task and received reinforcement for that activity. In this case, although not so stipulated, the DRO may have functioned as a DRI.

Often DRO is used as the primary (although not necessarily only) procedure, especially when highly interfering, dangerous, or disruptive behaviors are the targets of change. Examples are self-stimulation (Harris & Wolchik,

1979), public masturbation (Foxx et al., 1986), ". . . repetitive vocalizations in the form of meaningless sounds, shrieks, and incoherent statements" (Luiselli & Reisman, 1980, p. 279), hyperactivity (Patterson, Jones, Whittier, & Wright, 1965), vomiting and spitting (Garcia & DeHaven, 1974), and many more.

Advantages of DRO

Widely applicable. You have been alerted already to the fact that DRO is benign and relatively easy to use, at least when compared to the dense reinforcement required of DRI. In addition to the list just mentioned, Homer and Peterson (1980) have reported that the method has been used successfully to reduce a wide spectrum of behaviors, including vomiting, spitting, self-injury, disruption, aggression, hyperactivity, stereotypy, thumb sucking, and sibling conflict. With appropriate training, both sophisticated and naive change agents have been able to carry out the procedure successfully. DRO schedules alert managers to dispense reinforcers regularly, reminding them to monitor for and act on the omission of unwanted behavior.

Relatively rapid. In several instances, DRO has produced substantial decrements in behavior within a few or even a single session (Homer & Peterson, 1980). Those authors provide evidence suggesting that although slower acting than punishment and overcorrection, DRO may function more rapidly than extinction. (Remember to be cautious, however, in interpreting the results of such comparisons, because as mentioned previously, outcomes vary depending on the values of the variables applied within each procedure. As Van Houten [1987] cautions, "Unless we know how to make each treatment optimally effective, it will be pointless in many cases to compare techniques" [p. 109]. If the most optimal arrangements are unknown, any comparisons between different procedural techniques should at least use the arrangement known to be the best currently available.)

Often durable and general. Numerous instances have been reported in which DRO apparently produced lasting response suppression. Many of these, however, have actually combined DRO with other procedures, such as timeout (Bostow & Bailey, 1969; Iwata & Lorentzson, 1976; Repp & Deitz, 1974). Generality of effect, with DRO alone, was achieved in at least one case with thumb sucking (Lowitz & Suib, 1978). An eight-year-old girl and her mother were trained initially in the laboratory. Later the mother implemented the procedure at home, while the child listened to a story record, watched television, or slept. Here, of course, generality was programmed, rather than left to chance, because the child earned pennies or stars under each of those circumstances. Apparently, results were so successful and long lasting that a follow-up call a year later indicated that the child's dentist no longer planned to prescribe braces to straighten the previously evolving malocclusion of her teeth.

Disadvantages of DRO

Fails "dead man's test." Though reinforcement is the main application in DRO, the procedure is not necessarily a constructive one, as we have seen. As Axelrod (1987) contends, DRO fails the dead man's test, because it neglects targeting a constructive replacement behavior. (A dead person can omit just about any behavior you can name.) This is one reason why, as you will see, we recommend that you combine DRO with Alt-R or DRI, especially DRI.

This point has been dramatically supported in a study by Leitenberg, Burchard, Burchard, Fuller, and Lysaght (1977). Six families with 16 children aged 2 to 10 participated in a study that compared the effectiveness of Alt-R and DRO in reducing conflict. Sibling conflict was defined as physical and verbal attacks—hitting, pushing, throwing objects, taking another's belongings, making threats, name calling, and so on. During the DRO phase, children were praised and given a penny following each 1-minute interval in which there was no conflict. Instances of conflict were neither reinforced nor criticized; they were ignored. During Alt-R, praise and pennies were distributed following episodes of appropriate interactions, such as playing, helping, or sharing. Both procedures were equally effective in reducing sibling conflict, but only during Alt-R did the children increase their appropriate interactions. The point is, if you elect to use a DRO procedure, don't assume that other behavior will necessarily improve.

Accentuates attending to the negative. Using DRO requires that the unwanted behavior be kept under surveillance, thereby riveting the manager's attention to the problem. The observer might inadvertently begin to reinforce the behavior through their increase in attending. You saw several instances in the section on *positive scanning* in the previous chapter.

Also, McFall (1970) found that smokers who counted the number of cigarettes they smoked *increased* their smoking rates, whereas those who recorded the number of urges *not followed* by smoking decreased their rates. Therefore, be sensitized to the possibility of reactivity with DRO. Watch carefully for any sign of a worsening of the target behavior that could be traceable to increased attending to it. If that happens, either switch the observational recording function to an instrument or person outside of the client's normal social network or shift over to Alt-R or DRI.

Other behavior possibly worse. All behaviors, other than the one to be eliminated, are equally eligible for reinforcement under DRO conditions. This arrangement could conceivably mean that you could find yourself in the position of reinforcing a behavior that was just as bad as, or perhaps even worse than, the behavior to be eliminated. Pearl is given a small piece of fruit or a raisin every 5 minutes, provided that she has not been flicking her fingers. It just so happens that she is rocking at the end of 5 minutes when the fruit is given to her. Rocking may increase as a result. This sort of problem is more apt to happen to people with lots of unsuitable behaviors in their repertoires. When working with these clients, turn to one of two alternatives: either apply DRO to several of the most serious unwanted behaviors (provided that a sufficient number of reinforceable intervals will be available to allow the program a chance to work) or elect another reductive procedure.

Behavioral contrast. When using DRO or any other reductive procedure to reduce a specific behavior, you must ensure that the behavior does not receive reinforcement at other times. Otherwise, if the behavior is placed on a DRO in some contexts, although it decreases in those contexts, it may *increase* in the contexts in which reinforcement continues. Support for this contention derives from a study performed by Reynolds (1961). Pigeons' key pecking continued to be reinforced under one discriminative stimulus (S^D), whereas nonkey pecking was reinforced under a different S^D. Although the rate of key pecking under the DRO-correlated stimulus was practically eliminated, responding under the non-DRO stimulus conditions increased to a level higher than previously. Reynolds (1961) labeled this phenomenon **behavioral contrast**, defining it as a "change in rate of behavior during the presentation of another stimulus" (p. 57). Although data on this phenomenon in human subjects are largely anecdotal, watching for the possible occurrence of a contrast effect during the use of DRO seems advisable. For instance, Pearl's hand stereotypy should be measured when the contingency manager is in *and* out of the room. An increase while the contingency manager is out of the room over the rate while she is present suggests a contrast effect.

Using DRO Effectively
Maximizing opportunities for reinforcement. Because DRO is a differential reinforcement procedure, all the methods for using differential re-

inforcement effectively hold here as well. To maximize the person's opportunity for reinforcement, look closely at the baseline performance. Determine the average period of time the individual successfully omits the unwanted behavior and set the DRO interval just below that.

Pearl's caregivers are convinced that hardly a moment goes by without her flicking her fingers. Yet when the data are studied closely, Pearl actually spends an average of 2.7 minutes between bursts of that form of stereotypy. Beginning with a DRO interval of 2.5 minutes would permit Pearl to receive reinforcement frequently.

Another way to increase reinforcement is to reset the time period immediately following the target behavior, rather than waiting for the entire interval to expire. This will provide more opportunity for reinforcers to be earned.

Adjusting schedule gradually. After the objectionable behavior has begun to diminish in rate, the intervals can be gradually extended. For example, Herbie bites his nails, a habit that has caused him distress for many years. He decides to use a DRO procedure to rid himself of the behavior. He sets his wrist alarm to sound every 10 minutes while he is reading, studying, and watching TV (peak nail-biting times). When the timer sounds, he records whether his fingers touched his teeth in the interim. If not, he awards a token to and praises himself. Tokens are exchanged for the opportunity to read his girlfriend's letters, to call her, or to take photographs (his hobby). When the frequency of nail biting has diminished by perhaps 50% for a few days in a row, he lengthens the interval to 20 minutes. This pattern continues until Herbie's nails remain unbitten for 3 months. The same "adjusting DRO" tactic could be used with Pearl or with any client who wants to eliminate an unwanted behavior.

Evidence in favor of this sort of "graduated omission training" was presented by Cross, Dickson, and Sisemore (1978), who found that

moderately retarded males decelerated their
rates of lever pressing much more rapidly and
effectively when the DRO interval began at 2
seconds, and gradually increased in 2-second
increments to 8 seconds, than when the 8-sec-
ond interval was introduced initially. In an applied example to eliminate stealing, Rosen and
Rosen (1983) gradually reduced the frequency
with which they checked the items a child had
stored in his desk to see whether any were
marked (indicating they were not his). Initially
they checked every 15 minutes; ultimately, every
two hours.

Combining With Other Procedures

The way to make the most of DRO, as you have
already seen, is to combine it with other procedures, especially Alt-R or DRI. While continuing the DRO, reinforce desired alternative behaviors when they occur, particularly those
clearly incompatible with the target for reduction. You can do this, for instance, by complimenting the person not only at the end of the
interval for omitting a response but for the desired responses as they do occur.

Unfortunately, this tactic may not accomplish the purpose either, so then consider
"shaping" the reduction in response rate by
interposing a differential reinforcement of low
rates (DRL) procedure (described next), and
analyze each of the variables in your program.
See whether the reinforcers can be made more
powerful by checking their quality, adequacy,
amount, and intensity; try reducing the size of
the DRO and/or DRI interval; and examine setting events, establishing operations and schedules of reinforcement. Give the most feasibly
optimal arrangements a reasonable chance.
Then, provided that the unwanted behavior is
sufficiently objectionable, consider adding another reductive method such as a reprimand
(Luiselli, 1980; Rolider & Van Houten, 1984),
timeout (Vukelich & Hake, 1971), overcorrection (Gross, Farrar, & Liner, 1982; Harris &

Wolchik, 1979), contingent exercise (Luce &
Hall, 1981), or punishment (Young & Wincze,
1974). Recognize, though, that at this point,
the prime advantage of depending solely upon
differential reinforcement will have been lost.
Additionally, you will require special knowledge and skill to apply each of these other reductive methods ethically and successfully.

Momentary DRO

Switching to momentary DRO. After the unwanted behavior has been reduced to close to
zero for several observational sessions, you can
then consider using a method that Repp and
Deitz (1974) have called **momentary DRO**.
With this procedure, the change agent observes
the individual only at the end, not throughout
the interval, as is required by the standard
whole-interval DRO method. In the Lowitz and
Suib (1978) case, the mother did not stay awake
all night to determine whether her child's thumb
was in her mouth. Instead, she was instructed
to spot-check the child 10 times before she herself retired. Actually, Rosen and Rosen (1983)
also were using a momentary DRO when they
checked the child's items, because they were not
watching him throughout the interval.

Advantages of momentary DRO. The advantage
of using a momentary DRO should be obvious.
It is a boon to busy people. When signaled to
observe, you stop for a moment to note the presence or absence of the unwanted behavior and
provide reinforcers if merited. Then you continue your activities. Suppose you are trying to
eliminate a nervous habit, like tugging on your
sideburns, twirling your hair, or sucking your
fingers while studying. You could set your wrist
timer to sound every X number of seconds. At
the sound, you would determine whether you
were displaying your nervous habit and give
yourself a reward if you deserved it. Then you
could return to your studies. That's much easier
than trying to concentrate on both at once, as
Herbie had to do.

Disadvantages of momentary DRO. Like other things in life, it seems, the good of a technique may be counterbalanced by the not so good. This is true of momentary DRO; for, when reinforcement is contingent on only the omission of the response at the moment when the interval terminates, the unwanted behavior still can continue during the interval. Were he to have used a momentary DRO, Herbie could still bite his nails, as long as his fingers were not in contact with his teeth at the precise moment his wrist alarm sounded. The same would be true for hair tugging. By contrast, the whole-interval DRO schedule does not permit any nail biting during the interval, allowing the behavior to subside more rapidly.

Whole-Interval Versus Momentary DRO

This phenomenon may have explained their findings when Repp, Barton, and Brulle (1983) compared whole-interval and momentary DRO to determine which was most effective. As you probably anticipated, the whole-interval DRO was more effective. Yet, interestingly, when the momentary DRO had been preceded by a phase of whole-interval DRO, during which the rate of the unwanted response had diminished sizably, the momentary approach functioned quite well, a result that Barton, Brulle, and Repp (1986) later replicated. These findings may well have been the result of the history provided during the first phase in each study, because the initial reduction in rate minimized the likelihood of reinforcement being associated with the problem behavior once momentary DRO was activated.

For this reason, if you are contemplating switching to a momentary DRO, we advise that you begin with whole-interval DRO. After the rate has subsided substantially, choose as the size of the initial momentary interval one during which you can reasonably expect the unwanted behavior hardly ever to occur. As the response continues to diminish, begin to lengthen the size of that interval until it is large enough for you to manage without undue distraction. (Later, in the sections on maintaining behavior, you will learn about other techniques for sustaining long-lasting change.)

Differentially Reinforcing Low and Diminishing Rates of Behavior

A behavior that may not need to be eliminated rapidly or completely can be gradually reduced. Consuming small quantities of alcohol may not be deleterious, whereas too much can be. Ludwig, the student who writes too quickly and ends up handing in a sloppy paper, the swimmer who needs work to perfect a stroke, the ballet dancer who performs more rapidly than called for by the musical score—all must be slowed down. Ralph's tendency to dominate group discussions, Desmond's distraction of other workshop members, and Mrs. Kvetch's complaining are examples of behaviors that should be reduced but not necessarily eliminated. It is okay for Ralph to participate and Desmond to distract—but not as often. The reductive procedures best suited for this change are schedules of differential reinforcement of low and of diminishing rates.

DRL and DRD Defined and Illustrated

The **differential reinforcement of low rates (DRL)** procedure, as used in the laboratory, states that reinforcement is contingent on responses that are being emitted at low rates—responses that are spaced relatively far apart. In the DRL procedure, a behavior is reinforced *only* if it occurs following a specific period of time during which it did not occur (Ferster & Skinner, 1957). A monkey will receive a banana pellet for pulling a chain only if he has not pulled that particular chain for *T* moments previously. If he should pull the chain too soon, a new interval of *T* moments is initiated. In other words, *T* moments must elapse before chain pulling will produce reinforcement.

Ralph and Mrs. Olsen agree that if he waits 3 minutes after participating, she will call on him at the next opportunity. If not, she will ignore what he says and require him to wait 3 more minutes for his next opportunity. Additional examples of using the DRL procedure would include permitting workers to take a break only when they hadn't had a break during a specific intervening time period; or permitting rapid eaters to take a bite only after a 15-second pause (Lennox, Miltenberger, & Donnelly, 1987).

Notice that the DRL schedule is designed to reduce a behavior by reinforcing the target behavior (*not* an alternative) when a specific time interval has passed without its occurrence. Eventually, the rate of responding should drop to that set by the rules of the contingency.

A variation on this theme changes the contingency arrangement slightly. In this instance, reinforcement is delivered at the end of the interval, "when the number of responses (n) in a specified period of time is less than, or equal to, a prescribed limit" (Deitz & Repp, 1973, p. 457). In the laboratory analogue of this variation, the monkey would automatically receive a banana pellet at the end of a preset interval (whether he pulled the chain or not), as long as he had pulled the chain fewer than *n* times during the interval, and reinforcement would not necessarily be contingent on a chain pull. This schedule may be easier to use with groups of people, because all that is required is counting responses up to *N* number within an interval. If the number is exceeded before the end of the interval, reinforcement is withheld when the interval is over. Otherwise, reinforcement is delivered, whether the particular target behavior is occurring at the moment or not.

Another variation is analogous to shaping in the sense that the size of the interval between responses lengthens gradually, or the maximum number of acceptable responses within an interval decreases gradually. These variations are called **differential reinforcement of diminishing rates (DRD)**. Two more examples, one of each procedure, should help to clarify the distinction between DRL and DRD.

Ralph's excessive talking during group counseling is becoming a pain in the ear. The counselor decides that it is only fair to allow the other youths a chance to participate, too; but Ralph dominates the discussion. Because the goal is to diminish—not eliminate—Ralph's contributions, a DRL procedure is selected. Ralph is called to contribute only after he has been silent during a specified period of time.

Harry wants to stop smoking, so he and his wife contract that she will make him his favorite dinner on Friday night if the number of cigarettes he has smoked during the week is 5 less than the previous week. This DRD procedure is relatively painless for Harry, weaning him gradually off his nicotine dependence over several months.

Advantages of DRL and DRD

Benign. Both DRL and DRD provide for regular reinforcement and therefore offer many of the same advantages as other positive procedures: Good things still continue to happen! Certainly it would be possible to slow response rates in other ways: to reprimand people when they hurry, to ignore them altogether, to keep reminding them to slow down, to feed them tranquilizing drugs, and all kinds of other possibilities. But here is a situation in which reinforcement continues as people go merrily on their way. When you want a nonaversive method for reducing the rate of a behavior, consider DRD or DRL.

Tolerant. DRL and DRD reflect a built-in tolerance for the target behavior, communicating the message, "What you're doing is okay, as long as it's not done to excess." The procedures foster moderation. Although too much clowning is a nuisance, an occasional antic can relieve the monotony. Dominating the conversation is boorish, but contributing to it from time to time is socially appropriate. Everyone complains once in a while. That is okay. Mrs. Kvetch just should not complain all the time. DRD and DRL are the procedures of choice when an individual wishes to moderate, but not necessarily eliminate, habits like eating junk food, consuming alcohol, talking on the phone, watching television, or procrastinating. Fortunately, the techniques are particularly amenable to self-management.

Convenient and effective. DRD has been shown to be effective with an assortment of populations. For example, Deitz and Repp (1973) described their experience with a group of 10 noisy, trainable, mentally handicapped (TMH) children who talked, sang, or hummed without the teacher's permission, and with an office-procedure class of 15 "normal" high school senior girls who frequently wasted time discussing social topics in class. Given a baseline of 32.7 "talk outs" per 50-minute session, the contingency was set so that, when the TMH children produced 5 or fewer talkouts in 50 minutes, each member would be allowed to select two pieces of candy. The TMH children's rate of talking out immediately declined to an average of 3.13 instances per session.

The senior girls had averaged 6.6 social discussions per 50-minute session. For them the DRD procedure was instituted in a series of phases: Initially, when fewer than 6 social discussions occurred during the period for each of the first 4 days of the week, the Friday class would be a "free" period. Next, fewer than 3 discussions were allowed. Eventually the criterion was reduced to 0 (technically evolving into a DRO schedule). In addition to finding the DRD procedure very easy to use, the high school teacher reported that the "free time" worked well as a reinforcer. "She found it more useful to have four days in which the students are not disruptive and are working than to have five rel-

atively disruptive days" (Deitz & Repp, 1973, p. 462).

DRD also successfully reduced an 11-year-old fifth-grade boy's rate of talking out and a sixth-grader's rate of leaving her seat (Deitz & Repp, 1974). In each instance the behavior was reduced when 2 or fewer responses per period earned them gold stars. Differential reinforcement with either gold stars or access to a sand table (Deitz et al., 1978) was applied in a learning disabilities class to reduce a number of a seven-year-old's inappropriate behaviors and a group of five-year-old handicapped children's unpermitted talk outs.

Disadvantages of DRL and DRD

Time. Compared to the more rapid acting reductive procedures to be discussed later (e.g., punishment, response cost), DRD and DRL procedures take time. The change agent would not select a DRL or DRD procedure to reduce a strong person's violent assaults, nor even tolerate their diminished rates. A speedier procedure would be more appropriate.

Focus on undesirable behavior. As with DRO, and by their nature, DRL and DRD procedures require negative scanning by the contingency manager and program recipient. Preferred behaviors tend thereby to be overlooked or unwanted ones unduly attended to. A strategy that added Alt-R and modeling procedures and/or stipulated that a minimum of three positive comments be delivered per hour for desirable behaviors might help to counteract this potential hazard.

Using DRL and DRD Effectively

The effective application of DRL and DRD is very much the same as for DRO. Use optimal reinforcing contingencies and base the sizes of intervals on baseline performance. Additionally, you will want to increase the size of the interval gradually. Too abrupt an extension will produce the same sort of disruption as selecting too large a step in shaping. Proceeding gradually by increasing the length of the interval very slowly is far more preferable. The individual's behavior will provide information about the appropriateness of the change, because serious regression mandates a rapid retreat to a shorter interval.

In addition to using S^{D}s like models, rules, and explanations of the program and its contingencies, some investigators (e.g., Brockman & Leibowitz, 1982) have successfully used DRD and DRL in combination with other reductive procedures to obtain faster results. The **Good Behavior Game** (Barrish, Saunders, & Wolf, 1969; Harris & Sherman, 1973b) is an example of such a combination. In the Barrish et al. (1969) study, a fourth-grade teacher divided her class into two groups and listed several rules:

- Students were not to be out of their seats or to talk with their classmates without permission during specific class times.
- If any member of a team violated the rules, that team received a mark next to its name.
- The team or teams with fewer than a criterion number of marks or the fewest marks by the end of the day "won" the game.

All members of the winning team(s) were allowed special privileges: first position in line for lunch, extra recess, special time for projects, victory tags, and so on. Later Harris and Sherman (1973b) used the game in a fifth-grade class and in a sixth-grade class to reduce various disruptive behaviors: throwing objects, whistling, talking out, and so on. The rules were written on the chalkboard. As in the study by Barrish et al. (1969), the team with the fewest marks or the team or teams that obtained below a certain criterion number of marks would win the game. "Each member of the winning team(s) was allowed to leave school 10 minutes

early at the end of the day. Members of the losing team were required to remain in the classroom working on assignments until the regular dismissal time for the school" (Harris & Sherman, 1973b, p. 408). The Good Behavior Game significantly and reliably reduced disruptive student behaviors in each study.

Most children seem to enjoy the game and it is easy to implement, usually not requiring the contingency manager to deal with members individually. Should a member or two decide not to play, place the dissenters on teams of their own, rather than penalizing other teammates, as Harris and Sherman (1973b) did. In that case the same consequences continued for each team but with one addition: Each check over criterion equaled 5 minutes after school. This procedure produced an effect within a few days. The investigators reported that "after the fifth day of this condition the students on the third team asked to be returned to their former teams; the teacher allowed them to do so" (p. 416). Both teams involved went on to win the game on subsequent days.

Similarly, Butterworth and Vogler (1975) placed any fifth-grade child who committed two violations (only the first would count against his team) in a timeout room. The child was excluded from the special privileges if his or her team won and had to make up the lost time after school.

One successful adaptation of this game for school classes and other groups has been to divide each group into 6 or 8 teams. The group designates 5 to 7 positive behaviors for which points can be earned and 5 to 7 negative behaviors for which points can be lost. Before the last half-hour of the day, negative team marks are subtracted from the positive points of each team. Any team that receives no negative marks receives bonus points. The other portions of the game remain the same.

Another successful variation used an Alt-R version of the game rather than a DRD to reduce fourth-graders' disruptive library behavior

(Fishbein & Wasik, 1981). The children were noisy, failed to use the library as intended for reading or reference, pushed one another, and playfully shocked each other after rubbing their shoes on the carpeted floor. Together, the librarian and the class developed a set of rules for appropriate conduct in the library:

> (a) If you talk, talk quietly. (b) Choose a library book or look at library materials during the library period. (c) When walking, be very careful not to shock one another. (d) Treat one another with respect at all times, being careful not to push or fight (p. 91).

The class was divided randomly into two teams. The librarian looked up several times during the period and awarded a team a point only if all its members were following the rules, or specified desired alternative behaviors (Alt-R). To win the game, a team needed to obtain three out of four possible points. The winning team(s) could choose between working on an art project or hearing a story read by the regular classroom teacher during the last 10 minutes of the afternoon. Any losing team would continue with its regular classroom work. Both teams usually won the game, and there was no report of students who didn't play the game. Perhaps the more positive thrust of this variation of the Good Behavior Game, plus the greater involvement of the students in establishing the rules, resulted in "increased student motivation to behave appropriately" (Fishbein & Wasik, 1981, p. 93).

The Good Behavior Game is strictly a group-management game. We encourage those who plan to use the game to combine it with other procedures directed toward task accomplishment. Remember that a reduction in disruption is no guarantee that more task-relevant or adaptive behaviors will emerge.

Summary

This chapter has presented several differential reinforcement techniques for reducing behavior that are constructive alternatives to punishment: Alt-R (DRA) and DRI and various ways of reinforcing zero, low, and diminishing rates of behavior. To help you distinguish the subtle differences between the various positive reductive procedures, refer back to Table 1 in the introduction to Section IV, and read and complete Table 24.1. Note that each differential reinforcement procedure includes extinction, or the nonreinforcement of the undesired behavior.

When carefully selected alternatives are reinforced, not only does the undesirable behavior rapidly diminish in rate but the individual is also taught how to behave more appropriately. The Alt-R procedure, therefore, brings about behavioral reduction indirectly. A constructive behavior interferes with the occurrence of an unwanted one. If the preferred alternatives are properly strengthened and maintained, the Alt-R procedure can produce long-lasting results. Because the approach is positive, practitioners can use it with comfort. Appropriate reinforcement techniques, total incompatibility with the unwanted target, and combined use with other procedures—particularly extinction of the undesirable behavior—should accomplish behavioral reduction with maximum effectiveness. Although slower than some reductive procedures, Alt-R or DRA has many advantages that make it worthy of regular selection as a management procedure.

By using modeling to prompt the preferred alternative, the process can be hastened. Also, combining modeling and Alt-R permits attention and recognition to be distributed for positive and constructive, not problematic, performances.

Differential reinforcement of the nonoccurrence (zero-occurrence or omission) of a behavior (DRO) can be a rapid and effective method of reducing undesirable behaviors, provided that reinforcers are withheld under all conditions following each occurrence of the undesirable behavior and that, at least initially, programming reinforcement for the nonoccurrence of the target behavior is possible to

Table 24.1 A Comparison of Positive Reductive Procedures

Procedure	Illustrative Behavior		
	Criticizing	Leaving the work station	One of interest to you _____
Alt-R (DRA)	Positive reinforcement for complimenting someone	Positive reinforcement for doing work	
DRL	Positive reinforcement of criticizing after an interval of not criticizing	Positive reinforcement of leaving the work station after an interval of not leaving	
DRD	Positive reinforcement at the end of intervals containing reduced rates of criticism	Positive reinforcement at the end of intervals containing reduced rates of leaving the work station	
Whole-Interval DRO	Positive reinforcement following intervals of not criticizing	Positive reinforcement following intervals of not leaving the work station	
Momentary DRO	Positive reinforcement for not criticizing at the moment the person is observed	Positive reinforcement for not being away from the work station at the moment the person is observed	

do very frequently. Although requiring close monitoring, the whole-interval DRO is a particularly powerful reductive procedure. DRO is probably best reserved for use with individuals with few other unwanted behaviors.

Reinforcing low and diminishing rates of a behavior differentially through DRL and DRD is an excellent method of decelerating high rate behaviors. These methods are easily adapted for use with groups and can be combined with other procedures to reduce unwanted behavior rapidly.

As with the Alt-R and modeling, each method relies on positive reinforcement to reduce inappropriate behavior. However, Alt-R and modeling teach individuals what they should be doing, whereas DRD, DRL, and the various forms of DROs teach how not to behave. For this reason, the DRD, DRL, and DROs

should be combined with Alt-R and modeling whenever possible.

Although convenient and effective, because these procedures do not necessarily provide immediate relief, they should be reserved for reducing behavior that can be tolerated temporarily. Due to the problems associated with punitive procedures, these constructive alternatives are generally preferred. Turn to punishment only for dangerous or extremely objectionable responses.

Each of the positive reductive methods can be combined with one another. Selecting them in preference to punishment permits your behavior management methods to be more positive, constructive, and usable in a broader array of situations. Using them will also help you feel better about yourself and your work.

Chapter 25

Reducing Behavior with Response Cost and Stimulus Control Procedures

GOALS

After completing this chapter, you should be able to:

1. Define, recognize, and give original illustrations of each of the following terms:
   a. Response cost
   b. Bonus response cost
   c. S^{D-}
2. Define, recogni_·, and illustrate the differences among extinction, punishment, and response cost.
3. List and discuss the advantages and disadvantages of response cost.
4. Tell how to use response cost effectively.
5. Describe specific situations in which response cost would and would not be the best behavioral procedure; justify your position.
6. Describe and illustrate how antecedent stimuli can be developed to "inhibit" behavior by means of extinction, punishment, and response cost.
7. Summarize the advantages and disadvantages of different inhibiting stimuli.

Response Cost

Increased knowledge of current national and world events was selected as a goal for residents of Achievement Place (Phillips et al., 1971), because of its relevance to their academic performance in school and its suitability for promoting conversational skills. After the boys watched an evening news broadcast, they were asked questions about its content. Initially, they answered a few correctly. Then points exchangeable for various back-up reinforcers were awarded for correct answers. The number of questions correctly answered increased slightly. Next, when points could be earned only if 40% or more of the answers were correct, and a point penalty was added for failing to meet the 40% criterion, correctness increased substantially. The threat of the point loss provided a powerful contingency for reducing errors.

The point-penalty system is called **response cost**, a reductive procedure consisting of the removal or withdrawal of a *quantity of reinforcers* contingent on a response. Incorporated into many behavioral programs, response cost often has produced impressive results. Nevertheless, response cost is an aversive procedure. As such, it is often nonconstructive and may promote countercontrol responses from recipients and those representing their interests. As with other aversive procedures, the use of response costs may raise ethical and legal issues. Consequently, before the change agent implements intensive formal response cost procedures, institutional review, contracting, and a review of governmental policy and law should be undertaken. However, compared with the other aversive procedures to be presented in this book (timeout, contingent effort, overcorrection, and punishment), response cost is relatively benign and minimally intrusive. Using it to reduce actions dangerous or destructive to individuals or society should not be too difficult to justify.

Another relatively benign aversive procedure is the presentation of antecedent stimuli (S^D-s) discriminative for aversive consequences (i.e., unpleasant consequences, that one works to avoid, reduce, or escape from). They develop their capability of inhibiting behavior by being paired with a given response that is followed by an aversive consequence. Thus, they function as warning signals: If you engage in a certain behavior, an aversive consequence probably will occur. Consider next how these procedures are designed to operate as effective components of behavioral programs.

Response Cost Defined

Response cost, as described earlier, is the withdrawal of specific quantities of reinforcers contingent on a response. Sometimes, it is called "contingent reinforcement loss" (Luce, Christian, Lipsker, & Hall, 1981) or "negative punishment" (Catania, 1984). Removal of a certain number of tokens, the imposition of a fine, and a cut in salary as a penalty for an unwanted behavior illustrate response cost. A traffic fine for speeding, a familiar example of response cost, would be diagrammed this way:

Response Cost:

R————————————————→ S^{rc}
(speeding)   ($75 fine)

A *quantity* of reinforcers is withdrawn.

Technically, response cost differs from punishment in that punishment involves *presenting* an aversive stimulus contingent on a response, rather than *withdrawing* a certain amount of reinforcers, as in response cost. Fining a person 10 points or confiscating his radio for fighting is a response cost procedure. Reprimanding him for fighting is punishment, if it reduces the rate of fighting (see Chapter 27). Contrast the operations of response cost and punishment by examining these diagrams:

Response Cost

R————————————————→ S^{rc}
(fighting)   (10-point fine)

A quantity of reinforcers is withdrawn.

Punishment
R ——————————————→ S^P
(clowning, fighting)   (reprimand)

An aversive stimulus is presented.

Response cost may be applied to tangible as well as symbolic reinforcers. For instance, a parent may remove a child's dessert from the table contingent on some misbehavior. However, when used systematically in applied settings, response cost usually is limited to the withdrawal of symbolic or other conditioned reinforcers like grades, points, and tokens. In order to remove specified amounts of a reinforcer, the individual must have "some level of positive reinforcement . . . available in order to provide the opportunity for . . . withdrawing that reinforcement" (Azrin & Holz, 1966, p. 392). Little would be accomplished by imposing a fine on someone who had no money, and removing an edible reinforcer that had already been consumed would be impossible.

Response Cost Illustrated

A yardage penalty in football is also a form of response cost, as are breakage costs charged to college-dormitory residents. In schools, a familiar response cost practice is removing points toward, or lowering, a grade contingent on some unacceptable performance. Within token systems, response cost is illustrated by the removal of a set number of tokens as a consequence of particular unwanted acts. In a classroom token economy program (Sulzer et al., 1971), fixed fines were levied for certain disruptive behaviors, such as throwing objects.

Switzer, Deal, and Bailey (1977) used a response cost contingency to reduce stealing in three second-grade classrooms. They compared the effects of an antistealing lecture with no specific contingency implied with those of an interdependent group response cost program that combined (1) loss of free time for the entire class if items were not returned, (2) access to regular free time if stolen items were returned,

and (3) extra free time for no thefts. The antistealing lecture was found ineffective, whereas the group response cost contingency effectively reduced the stealing.

Just as inflated prices alienate potential customers, response cost also can suppress desirable behavior inadvertently. Under such circumstances, identifying and removing the cost can reverse the situation. For example, noting that "lost ads" greatly outnumbered "found ads" in classified sections of newspapers, a group of investigators (Goldstein, Minkin, Minkin, & Baer, 1978) arranged to remove the fee for the found ads in three newspapers, and discovered that the found ads increased in each. More personal property was returned as a result.

Advantages of Response Cost

Strong and rapid behavioral reduction. Weiner (1964a; 1969) discovered some time ago in the laboratory that, for many subjects, response cost usually reduced responses fairly rapidly. In applied settings, contingency managers appreciate the way response cost rapidly suppresses problem behaviors, such as

- violence by psychiatric patients (Winkler, 1970).
- aggression and classroom disruptions by elementary school students (Foreman, 1980).
- aggressive statements and tardiness by predelinquent boys (Phillips, 1968; Phillips et al., 1971).
- off-task and rule violation in classrooms (Iwata & Bailey, 1974; Rapport et al., 1982).
- excessive local directory-assistance phone calls (McSweeny, 1978).
- many other unwanted or maladaptive behaviors (see Kazdin, 1972; 1975, for excellent integrated reviews of the procedure).

Two seven-year-old boys were diagnosed as

having "attentional deficit disorder with hyperactivity" and spent excessive time off-task (Rapport et al., 1982). A program was instituted allowing each youngster to earn up to 20 minutes of free time for working during the period. Any time the child was not working during the period for more than 2 seconds, he would lose 1 minute of free time. The investigators reported that response cost was more effective than Ritalin in reducing time spent off-task. Such findings are important, as the authors point out, because "medicated children continue to experience academic difficulty (Riddle & Rapoport, 1976; Weiss, Kruger, Danielson, & Elman, 1975) and that many do not respond positively to psychostimulant medication" (p. 215).

Mine workers (Fox et al., 1987) could earn trading stamps for not suffering lost time from injuries. However, as a consequence of an injury, they not only lost the stamp bonus for themselves but for their work groups as well. The investigators reported that accidents plummeted rapidly as a result of this combined positive reinforcement and response cost program.

Reiser (1984) found that response cost could significantly reduce procrastination in an introductory speech communications class using a personalized system of instruction (PSI) format. Students were randomly assigned to a penalty group (i.e., a loss of 2 points for each instructional unit they failed to master by the deadline), a reward group (i.e., a gain of 2 points were awarded for each instructional unit mastered by the deadline), and a no-treatment control group. The results showed that students in the penalty group proceeded through the course at a significantly more rapid pace than the control group. Despite no significant differences between the groups in students withdrawing from the class, their final examination performances, and measured attitudes toward the class, the penalty group met 61.6% of its deadlines; the reward group 43.8%; and the control 22.2%.

Some variability in the effectiveness of response cost seems to occur, probably as a result of individual histories (Weiner, 1969). A response cost system was designed to suppress such maladaptive behaviors as personal assaults, swearing, and property destruction among institutionalized retarded adolescents (Burchard & Barrera, 1972). The investigators found that even fairly steep fines reduced those behaviors for only 5 of the 6 youths, while for the latter youth, the results were opposite. This finding suggests the necessity of determining empirically whether a particular cost technique can indeed reduce a given individual's performance in a given context.

Promotes discrimination. Response cost can promote discrimination learning. For instance, Trent (1983) found that the combination of response cost and reinforcement taught adults to discriminate a single light switch problem (i.e., which "of six opaque buttons was connected to each of six red lights" [p. 209]) faster than feedback, reinforcement, or response cost alone.

Schnake (1986) used response cost to help workers discriminate job expectancies. A confederate was told her output was significantly lower than her co-workers' in the presence of a group of temporary clerical employees (undergraduates) at a university and was either given a pay cut from $5 an hour to $3.50 an hour or, in the presence of a similar group, a threat of such a cut. These two conditions were compared to one another and to a group witnessing no aversive consequence. "Subjects who observed a co-worker receiving a reduction in pay produced significantly more output than subjects who observed a threat of a reduction in pay or subjects in the control group. . . . Further, subjects across groups did not differ in levels of job satisfaction" (p. 343). Apparently, combining response cost with reinforcement is a useful way to promote rapid discriminations and behavior change. It also may help people learn rules more rapidly.

Possible long-lasting effects. Several studies

have found that response cost has produced persistent suppression of unwanted behaviors, such as speech disfluencies (Kazdin, 1973c; Siegel et al., 1969) and weight gain (Harmatz & Lapuc, 1968). Others, however, have noted the recovery of responses when response cost was removed (Birnbrauer et al., 1965; Iwata & Bailey, 1974). Although the explanations for the differences remain to be determined, it is our guess that the reinforcement histories associated with response cost are critical variables in determining the persistence of behavioral suppression. Particularly relevant would be the presence or absence of internal or covert reinforcement and S^Ds (i.e., the person's "motivational level"), magnitude of the fine, length of time that contingencies remain in effect, and the schedule for removing contingencies. (Chapters 30–32 elaborate on maintenance of change.)

Convenient. Response cost can be very convenient, especially in conjunction with point and token systems. As soon as the unwanted behavior is emitted, a token or point is removed usually quietly and effortlessly. In fact, because response cost is easy to use, it may be tempting to apply it more often than one should. George insults Jennifer, and the contingency manager says: "Okay, George. You're teasing. That will cost you 100 points! You're scowling. Another hundred." Similarly, it is not unusual to find a token economy system set up so that *all* infractions (major and minor) have a penalty or fine attached to them, which in turn produces continual negative scanning.

When used with discretion, though, response cost can help eliminate behaviors very efficiently without disrupting ongoing activities. Subtracting a few of George's points as a consequence of a major disruption is much easier than removing him from the room (timeout), scolding him (punishment), or changing his seat (stimulus change). Perhaps this is why Frentz and Kelley (1986) found that 82 mothers from a variety of settings rated response cost (i.e., taking away privileges) significantly more acceptable as a method of treating behavior problems than differential attention, timeout, spanking, or timeout combined with spanking. Similarly, Heffer and Kelley (1987) reported that both lower- and middle-upper-income parents rated response cost (loss of privileges) and positive reinforcement (praise and privileges) significantly more acceptable than timeout (10 minutes of isolation), spanking, or medication. Also, teachers have rated response cost higher than other aversive reductive procedures (Elliott, Witt, Peterson, & Galvin, 1983). Response cost, then, seems to be a socially accepted procedure.

Disadvantages of Response Cost

One disadvantage of response cost has already been suggested in the foregoing discussion: the fact that it cannot be depended on to produce lasting response suppression. The danger of using it too often and using overly harsh and unjustified penalties has also been mentioned. Why this temptation to abuse response cost exists is not difficult to understand. The ease of application keeps the "cost" (i.e., effort) low for the managers and the rapid effects provide them with immediate (negative) reinforcement.

An unfortunate outcome of such abuse is that program participants then need to exert inordinate effort to recoup their losses, and may give up—victims of "ratio strain." Only careful planning and close supervision can prevent this kind of misapplication. Another deficiency is the need for a reserve of conditioned reinforcers, as elaborated later.

Response cost, like other aversive contingencies, also may provoke escape and aggression. When Mom takes Baby Bonnie's dessert away because she is throwing her peas on the floor, the child throws a tantrum. Boren and Colman (1970) found that when they used a fine system with a group of delinquent soldiers the men rebelled and stayed away from meetings. Similarly, Hogan and Johnson (1985) reported that they eliminated the response cost facet of a token economy for emotionally disturbed adolescents because the cost promoted rather than lessened aggression. Their elimination of response cost resulted in "declines in the frequency of misbehavior reports, use of the timeout room, and number of episodes involving violence" (p. 87). Other investigators (Doty, McInnis, & Paul, 1974) have reported emotional reactions of a similar kind when extremely aggressive residents have refused to pay their fines.

Conversely, others have not encountered such problems (Bucher & Hawkins, 1971; Reiser, 1984; Schnake, 1986). Reiser (1984) informed the college students in his PSI course of the importance of meeting deadlines and provided frequent reminders. In Schnake's study (1986), the participants, also college students, were not acquainted with the confederate receiving the fine; she simply acknowledged the pay cut and continued working. If response cost were (1) responded to more "emotionally" by those receiving it, as is more likely with disturbed or younger individuals, (2) applied without explaining the program and its costs to the participants, (3) to occur to a close friend, and/or (4) to appear unfair, our guess is that emotional reactions similar to the above studies also might have occurred.

Using Response Cost Effectively

Allowing for build-up of reinforcement reserve. For a response cost system to function, we mentioned that participants need to build up a reserve of reinforcers. This usually happens as a matter of course when a token system is first introduced, because token systems typically are instituted to strengthen weak behaviors. Consequently reinforcement would be more frequent in the beginning. After participants accumulate a reserve, penalizing transgressions becomes feasible.

Response cost probably has its strongest impact after people have had an opportunity to sample their reinforcers. They know what they will be missing, and work to avoid loss of the reinforcers. Whatever the response cost system employed, this practice of permitting a reserve of reinforcers to accumulate should hold. If, for instance, reinforcers consist of points toward a grade, permit students the opportunity to earn a sufficient number of points before withdrawing any.

Determining response cost magnitude empirically. Response cost, as suggested by Azrin and Holz (1966), has much in common with punishment. Both are aversive contingencies—one because positive reinforcers are removed, the other because aversive consequences are delivered. Both produce rapid and often permanent response suppression as a partial function of the intensity of the aversive consequences. Azrin and Holz (1966) discovered that the more intense the aversive stimulus, the more effective the response suppression.

With response cost, intensity is represented by the size of the penalty. Indeed, Burchard and Barrera (1972) found that more severe costs, a 30- as opposed to a 5-token fine, suppressed maladaptive behaviors much more effectively. Such findings hint that, if we impose a fine, it should be a whopping one. Yet, fortunately, for the reasons mentioned earlier, there is a rub to this logic. Numerous studies have also reported success despite minimal fines, as low as 1 cent (Siegel and colleagues, 1969). Similarly, Sanok and Striefel (1979) combined awarding a penny and praise for understandable verbal responses and a 1-cent fine for either nonverbal responses (e.g., gestures) or no speaking to teach an 11-year-old elective mute girl to talk.

History probably plays an important part in determining whether a fine of a given size will be sufficient to diminish the rate of a behavior. *If the individual has a recent history of experiencing heavy fines, a small cost will have little effect. Otherwise, a minor fine may be sufficient. In* fact, in Burchard and Barrera's study (1972), the clients had histories with contingencies that combined a 5-token penalty with 5 minutes of isolation (timeout) for serious infractions. Yet, when results of *either* 5 minutes of timeout or a 5-token response cost were compared to those of either 30 minutes of timeout or a 30-token response cost, the separate and smaller contingencies had weaker effects. Because the clients had already experienced the stronger combined contingency, the 5-token fine seemed weaker by contrast. It is not surprising, then, that the 5-token fine had little effect in comparison with the much heavier 30-token fine.

The way to select the proper price to levy is to approach the problem empirically. The unwanted behavior must be monitored and various cost magnitudes attempted until the desired response reduction is reliably achieved. One word of caution, though: *Do not increase the cost in small increments*, because the client may adapt to the gradual increase (just as individuals have been noted to adapt to gradually increasing intensities of punishment). Instead, return to baseline conditions for a protracted time and then implement the selected response cost magnitude; or implement a much stronger cost abruptly and maintain it for several days and monitor the effects.

Here is an example: Clyde loves to shock the other members of the group and the counselor by shouting obscenities—a very distracting habit. Extinction and other positive procedures are rejected, because everyone concurs that too much of the group's time already has been wasted. The group has been operating on a system that permits individuals to earn points redeemable for optional activities, so the contingency manager decides to try a response cost of one point for each episode; but that accomplishes little. The expletives continue. Would a harsher fine, say, 10 points, work better? That notion is rejected as excessively punitive. So the cost contingency is dropped altogether for a while, and then a 3-point fine is successfully instituted. Here adaptation to aversive consequences is avoided by making the contrast sharper; rather than following 1 point directly by 3 points, the sequence is 1 point, no points, 3 points, making the latter more salient.

An otherwise-valued employee, Gregory, has discovered what fun he can have frightening the young women on his shift by speeding toward them in his forklift. Several of his buddies usually join in the laughter, probably maintaining this dangerous behavior. The first few times he sees Greg pulling this stunt, his supervisor reprimands Greg and deducts $1 from his paycheck. Nevertheless, the behavior persists. The supervisor then has the option of increasing the fine to $2 or to some other level. Returning to a no-fine contingency is too risky, because the victims are in danger of being seriously hurt. The supervisor decides to implement a $10 fine for "reckless driving." Greg halts the behavior.

Several other arguments for minimizing the magnitude of response cost should be taken into account in the decision-making process. Very heavy costs may suppress not only the behavior of concern but others as well. If Clyde is charged 10 points every time he utters an epithet, he will soon be bankrupt, with no chance of being able to earn an optional activity. He may then give up performing altogether, for what is the use? Then, of course, there is the humane concern about avoiding excessive harshness and the increased likelihood that the procedure will promote aggression (Hogan & Johnson, 1985). Finally, as Doty et al. (1974) found, sometimes collecting fines can be problematic. Those authors needed to develop some fairly elaborate accounting procedures in order to reduce refusals to pay fines.

Avoiding emotional outbursts. We have found that aggression, escape, and other emotional reactions can be kept at a reasonable level by clearly communicating the cost rules, keeping fines moderate, imposing them without fanfare, and ignoring or fining emotional outbursts. One particularly successful strategy in elementary school classes was to display the cost of violations on the token price chart, as if they too were back-up rewards. For instance, participants might have been able to purchase time to play a game for 20 points and the opportunity to throw things about the room for 100 points. When an object was thrown, we simply remarked: "Oh, I see you just purchased the opportunity to throw something. I'll collect the 100 points." The dazed student surrendered the points but was not eager to repeat such an expensive purchase in the future.

Another method that works well is to return part of the fine if the client responds "responsibly," for example, paying the fine immediately and returning to work right away. This procedure has the added advantage of reinforcing responses incompatible with escape or aggression.

Some managers have described how they use a **bonus response cost** system to avoid aggressive reactions when people are fined. Rather than points or tokens that a client has earned being taken away, they are subtracted from a pool of potential bonus reinforcers. For example, Ms. Charming awards tokens to her workshop clients who perform their job tasks correctly. Additionally, clients begin each day with 10 bonus tokens held in reserve for them. When a client misbehaves, bonus tokens are subtracted from the reserve. Should no penalties be necessary, the client receives all 10 bonus tokens at the end of the day.

In an actual investigation, children's behavior during family shopping trips was managed in a similar way (Clark et al., 1977). Each child was allotted a 50-cent allowance at the outset of the shopping trip. Four good shopping guidelines, or S^Ds, were communicated to the child:

- Stay close so we can talk to one another (within touching distance).
- Do not touch objects for sale.
- Don't make distracting comments such as "I want . . . ," or "Johnie did . . . ."

- Do not run, fight, or generally roughhouse.

Each time a child violated a guideline, a nickel would be withheld from that child's shopping allowance. After a total of 32 minutes of shopping, the child was given 10 minutes to spend whatever money remained in the shopping allowance. Money withheld on one trip could be spent on the next trip if the child qualified as a "good shopper." To qualify as a good shopper, no more than two violations could occur during that shopping period. In addition, while the children behaved properly, the parent engaged them in relevant conversation (e.g., "Where can I find a potholder? What things can be found in this department?"). The program successfully reduced children's disruptions and increased positive interactions between the parents and children.

Such bonus response cost systems are worth trying when regular response cost is chancy. Combine bonus response cost with a regular reinforcement program, because the reinforcement in this modified system is much too delayed for many clients. Avoid using bonus response cost alone. Combine it with Alt-R or some other procedure that includes reinforcement.

Communicating the rules of the game. As with all behavioral procedures, individuals who are informed of the specific contingencies in operation become more active participants in the contingency system. Role-playing or guided practice sessions can help people better understand "the rules of the game."

Sometimes members can share in setting the response cost penalties or even impose contingencies on themselves in order to achieve the goals they seek. Shirley was very eager to attend the college of her choice, so she imposed response cost contingencies on her procrastination in studying to help her achieve the necessary grade point average. For every hour she watched television beyond the first 2, she donated $1 to charity.

As with any self-administered contingency, however, there is always the temptation not to apply it or to cheat. To overcome this problem, some managers have found it helpful to return a portion of the fine for administering the penalty to oneself correctly. Another way is to make public the commitment and/or self-statements the persons apply to themselves (e.g., Rosenfarb & Hayes, 1984). Self-management like this is a step toward self-control.[1]

Consistently implemented cost rules begin to serve as discriminative stimuli. Such and such behaviors will be penalized (S^{D-}s); others will be rewarded (S^Ds). People can learn to discriminate more rapidly when the rules are available to them. The rules function as other cues do in the development of conditional discriminations. Therefore, rules related to costs and earnings are usually posted publicly for all participants to review. They serve as reminders that certain behaviors will lead to specific quantities of losses and gains. Used in this manner, S^{D-}s begin to inhibit (occasion low rates of) undesirable behaviors.

Combining response cost with other procedures. Response cost, like other reductive procedures, is not used in isolation but is combined with reinforcement of desired alternative behaviors. For example, Dougherty, Fowler, and Paine (1985) combined response cost with time-out, Alt-R, and a dependent group contingency to reduce aggressive behaviors (e.g., hitting, pushing, threats, offensive gestures, property destruction) and playground rule infractions by two 9- and 10-year-old boys. Starting recess with 4 to 6 bonus points, points were removed for aggression and rule infractions. Other points were awarded for positive behavior (e.g., cooperative play, refusal to fight). If all points were lost, the child was placed in timeout for the remainder of the recess. At the end of the recess,

points could be exchanged for a 5-minute game with 2 or 3 chosen peers. In addition, points were accumulated toward a special class reward (e.g., popcorn, field trip, film) selected weekly by the class—an excellent way to garner social support.

Because response cost can conveniently and rapidly reduce unwanted behaviors, it is a good temporary expedient to apply while alternatives are being strengthened. The procedure may suppress undesirable behaviors long enough to permit the person to begin to approximate more preferred conduct, which then can be reinforced. Ultimately, as the desirable behavior increases in strength, dropping the cost contingency should be possible. The opportunity to frequently engage in undesirable behaviors will have been minimized.

Reducing Behavior Through Stimulus Control

Occasionally a situation arises in which it is important not only to reduce but also actually to inhibit or suppress a behavior that appears imminent. We shall use the term "inhibit"[2] to signify that the presence or presentation of a particular antecedent stimulus (S^{D-}) sets the occasion for the absence or low rate of a particular behavior. This S^{D-} functions in that manner because it has acquired discriminative properties that connote the behavior is likely to be punished under those circumstances (or consequated by timeout, contingent effort, or response cost). It serves as a warning signal. As Tiny Tina reaches for something on the hot stove, the act must be inhibited. This discussion covers how these discriminative stimuli are de-

---

[1] Skinner, in Part I of *Cumulative Record* (1961), and in *Beyond Freedom and Dignity* (1971), deals with such philosophical issues as freedom and self-control.

[2] Other learning theorists (for example, Hull) have used this term differently to denote an internal state. *Signaled avoidance* is a term behavior analysts use to describe behavior controlled by stimuli paired previously with punishment. The definition offered here is intended simply to describe an event under discriminative control.

veloped and describes some of their advantages and disadvantages.

Stimuli Discriminative for Aversive Consequences

We have discussed how stimuli that precede or are presented simultaneously with response cost and/or other aversive consequences may acquire discriminative properties (S^D⁻s). This happens in a manner comparable to the way stimuli discriminative for reinforcement (S^Ds) develop. In the case of the S^D⁻, however, the discriminative stimulus serves not to occasion but in a sense to *inhibit* responding. Consider this illustration: While traveling at 67 MPH you pass a sign reading "Speed Limit 55 MPH," at a certain place on the highway. Within moments your rear view mirror reflects the flashing lights of the highway patrol. Yes, you receive a costly speeding ticket. Guess what you do the next time you pass that particular spot on the highway? Suppose the whole experience were repeated? See Figure 25.1 for a diagram of the event.

If Greg's boss wanted to remind Greg, and any other drivers of small vehicles in the plant, to suppress any temptation to be reckless, he might post a warning sign saying: *"Reckless*

Driving Fined $10." But then, of course, instances of reckless driving would have to be clearly defined, closely monitored, and systematically penalized any time they were detected. Otherwise, the sign rapidly would lose its ability to influence the behavior.

Advantages of Developing S^D⁻s

Although we prefer not to emphasize negative contingencies, developing stimuli that inhibit responding has some very clear advantages. Such signals may protect young children and dependent persons from danger, as when a parent shakes his head "no" as a youngster approaches an electrical outlet with a metal tool in hand. That S^D⁻ may help the child to avoid the far more punishing contingency of an electric shock. Managers who are responsible for people's safety and well-being need to know how to develop S^D⁻s effectively.

Developing Effective S^D⁻s

The S^D⁻ is developed in the same manner as is the S^D (see Chapters 15–18), except that the consequence is aversive. Unwanted target responses emitted in the presence of the selected S^D⁻s consistently are followed by effective aversive consequences. (We recommend the use of

Figure 25.1

A (Antecedent)	B (Behavior)	C (Consequence)
"Speed Limit 55 MPH" at given place ⟶	Drive at 67 MPH ⟶	Receive ticket

Next time or after a repetition of the above:

A (Antecedent)	B (Behavior)	C (Consequence)
"Speed Limit 55 MPH" at given place ⟶	Does not drive above 55 MPH ⟶	Does not receive ticket

Figure 25.2 Reducing Behavior with Response Cost

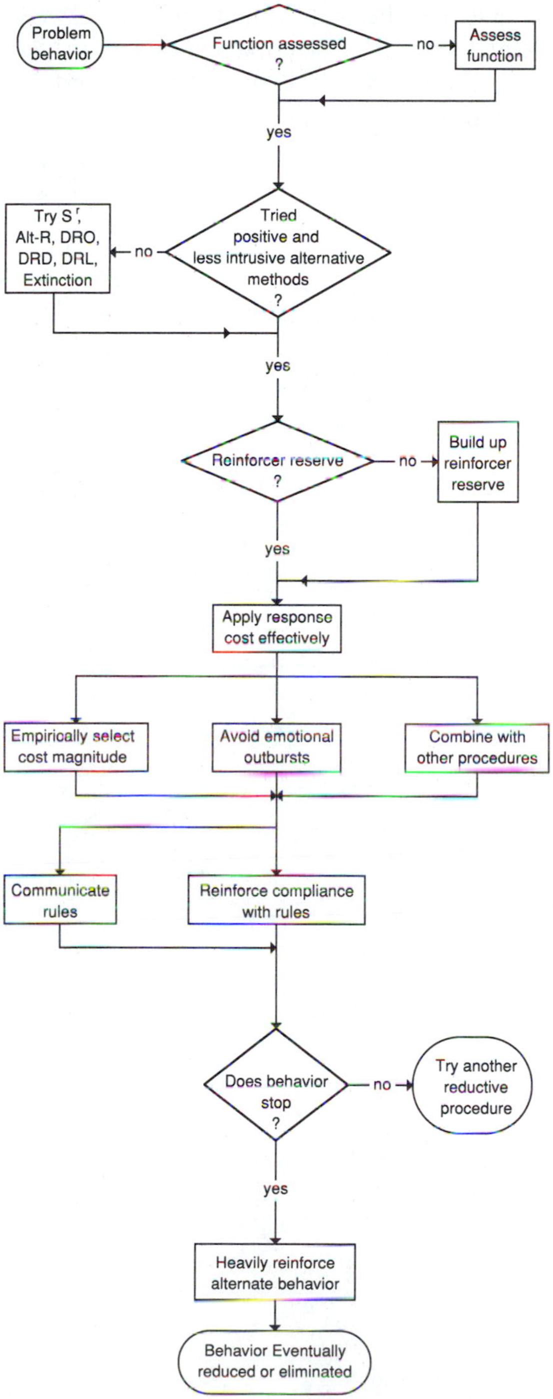

```
Problem      →  Function assessed  — no →  Assess
behavior           ?                        function
                    |
                   yes
                    ↓
Try S⁻,         Tried
Alt-R, DRO,  ← no — positive and
DRD, DRL,         less intrusive alternative
Extinction         methods
                    ?
                    |
                   yes
                    ↓
              Reinforcer reserve  — no →  Build up
                    ?                      reinforcer
                    |                      reserve
                   yes
                    ↓
              Apply response
              cost effectively
                    |
Empirically select   Avoid emotional   Combine with
cost magnitude       outbursts         other procedures
                    |
Communicate      Reinforce compliance
rules            with rules
                    |
              Does behavior  — no →  Try another
                 stop                reductive
                  ?                  procedure
                  |
                 yes
                  ↓
              Heavily reinforce
              alternate behavior
                  |
              Behavior Eventually
              reduced or eliminated
```

strong conditioned aversive stimuli, timeout, or response cost, rather than unconditioned aversive stimuli, whenever possible. Ethical considerations generally contraindicate the latter.) Clearly identifying the relevant stimulus properties is also important. That is why ''recklessness'' would need to be defined for Greg, the forklift driver: Driving more than x MPH; turning corners at y MPH; not stopping at striped lines; and so on.

Disadvantages of the S^{D-}

The S^{D-} requires that responding be paired with unpleasant consequences. As we frequently have cautioned, such stimuli may generate aggression, avoidance, and escape, so the procedure should be reserved for very serious cases. Because S^Δs, the stimuli that signal nonreinforcement, also serve to *inhibit* behaviors, they are preferable whenever there is a choice (see Chapter 15 for review of the means by which S^Δs are developed through pairing with nonreinforcement). A frown will begin to serve a suppressive function, if consistently paired with nonreinforcement, just as a frown paired with punishment does. While S^Δs may take longer to develop than S^{D-}s, S^Δs are more benign.

Summary

Although the effects of response cost may differ from individual to individual, the procedure has often been found to reduce unwanted behaviors quickly and conveniently. If this procedure is to be used effectively, participants must have a reinforcement reserve, as illustrated in Figure 25.2. Otherwise, the response cost penalty will be meaningless, as will the use of the procedure in general. An option is to use the bonus response cost strategy instead. Once a decision has been made to implement response cost, communicate the rules of the game; keep costs to a minimum; and continue permitting reinforcers like points to be earned contingent upon desirable behaviors. Because it is an aversive approach, response cost may promote aggression, avoidance, and escape. For that reason, use it sparingly and only as a temporary expedient.

Pairing antecedent stimuli with response costs or other aversive consequences, such as timeout and punishment, results in discriminative control by the S^D-s. Those antecedent stimuli then begin to inhibit given behaviors. Before developing or implementing S^D-s, however, carefully review their advantages and disadvantages.

Chapter 26

Reducing Behavior with Timeout from Reinforcement

GOALS

After completing this chapter, you should be able to:

1. Define, recognize, and give original illustrations of each of the following terms:
   a. Timeout
   b. Seclusion
   c. Planned ignoring
   d. Contingent observation
   e. Timeout ribbon
   f. Facial screening
   g. Required relaxation
   h. Movement suppression timeout
   i. Contingent delay

2. Define and illustrate how timeout differs from response cost, extinction, and punishment.

3. List, illustrate, and discuss the advantages and disadvantages of timeout.

4. Discuss the policy of the least restrictive environment in relation to timeout.

5. List and illustrate the various categories or levels of restrictiveness of timeout.

6. Differentiate between exclusionary and nonexclusionary timeout, providing illustrations of each; Compare and contrast their advantages and disadvantages.

7. List and describe the safeguards to include in a timeout program.

8. List what informed consent involves.

9. List and illustrate the factors that influence the effectiveness of a timeout procedure.

10. Differentiate by explanation and examples between planned ignoring and extinction.

11. Discuss why determining what is reinforcing and maintaining the unwanted behavior is important before a timeout program is implemented.

12. Describe the use of the timeout ribbon as a form of nonexclusionary timeout.

13. Comment on how learning history can influence the effectiveness of a selected timeout duration and discuss the problems associated with long timeout periods.

14. Explain the purpose of including a provision for contingent delay in a timeout program and why the authors maintain that it should be used cautiously.

15. Describe specific situations in which timeout used alone and combined with other behavioral procedures would and would not be the procedure of choice; justify your position.

Seymour, Jacqueline, Esmerelda, and Fred form the "Hard-Core Four" of a group of academic losers. Despite his extensive collection of excellent instructional materials, their new teacher, Mr. F. R. Vescent, is rapidly becoming discouraged. Although the other students staunchly attempt to complete their assignments, the Hard-Core Four continually interfere. Egged on by each other, one or another of them is perpetually disruptive, stealing pencils, hiding work, telling jokes, clowning, ganging up during recess on peers who have "ratted" to the teacher, and in general impairing the learning atmosphere. Well aware of the long histories of punishment shared by these four students, Mr. Vescent is reluctant to repeat the practice. But he finally realizes that if the rest of his students are to learn, some reductive procedures will have to be implemented. Besides response cost, timeout from reinforcement is a procedure worthy of his consideration. Like response cost and punishment, timeout can effectively reduce unwanted behavior and may be appropriate to such a group. Learn here about timeout to see what sort of program might be recommended to Mr. Vescent.

Timeout Defined

Timeout describes a procedure in which access to varied sources of reinforcement is reduced for a particular time period, contingent upon a response.[1] Similar to response cost, in that both procedures involve the contingent withdrawal of reinforcement, timeout does not require withdrawing specific *amounts* of reinforcers as response cost does. Rather, the requirement is for reinforcement to be contingently withdrawn for a specified period of *time*. Like extinction, timeout also involves nonreinforcement. In extinction, however, the stimuli that previously

---

[1] This definition is a variation of one offered by Reese (1966) combined with Ferster and Skinner's laboratory-derived definition (1957).

reinforced the target behavior are no longer delivered, contingent on a response. Clarissa's suitor stops calling her because she never comes to the telephone anymore when he calls. Tracy no longer receives a cookie when she cries. Crying and demanding lead to no change in the environment, because no cookies are delivered. Extinction can be diagrammed:

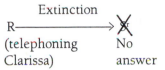

Telephoning Clarissa leads to no change in the environment.

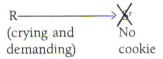

Crying and demanding lead to no change in the environment.

In timeout, however, something does occur. The environment does change, contingent on the response: The opportunity to receive reinforcement is reduced. Either the individual is removed from the reinforcing environment (as in isolation, or the placement in a nonreinforcing location) or the reinforcers or reinforcing environment is removed from the individual for some stipulated duration (e.g., Forehand et al., 1976; Scarboro & Forehand, 1975). Time out from token earning is one example (Winkler, 1971).

Removing Tracy from the kitchen for a specific time (t) contingent on crying for cookies illustrates timeout. The opportunity to receive cookies or almost any other reinforcer is unavailable for 10 minutes. (Alternatively, Tracy's mother might have contingently removed herself and the box of cookies from the kitchen for a few minutes, leaving the child in the now nonreinforcing environment.) Timeout can be diagrammed in this way:

$$\text{R} \xrightarrow{\hspace{1cm}\text{Timeout}\hspace{1cm}} \text{S}^{to}$$

(crying, demanding)   (removal from room
                            for 10 minutes)

The reinforcing environment is removed for 10 minutes contingent upon crying or demanding.

Timeout also differs from punishment in that the latter includes *presenting* an aversive stimulus to reduce the rate of a behavior, rather than, as with timeout, *removing* the opportunity for reinforcement. Verbally reprimanding Seymour for clowning can be called "punishment" if it results in the *reduction* of the clowning, whereas removing Seymour for 5 minutes for clowning during an enjoyable (reinforcing) school play is timeout. The operations that identify timeout and punishment are diagrammed this way:

$$\text{R} \xrightarrow{\hspace{1cm}\text{Punishment}\hspace{1cm}} \text{S}^p$$

(clowning)   ("No")

An aversive stimulus is presented.

$$\text{R} \xrightarrow{\hspace{1cm}\text{Timeout}\hspace{1cm}} \text{S}^{to}$$

(clowning)   (5 minutes
                       out of room)

Seymour is removed from the room, depriving him of the reinforcing environment for 5 minutes.

Timeout Illustrated

When Kevin pushes Debbie into the pool, his dad orders him to sit on a bench for 10 minutes instead of swimming. Sally is rude to her mother; she is sent to her room until it's time to practice the piano. Esmerelda throws a paper clip; Mr. Vescent instructs her to stand in a secluded part of the room for 2 minutes. The entire class becomes rowdy; the children are all instructed to put their heads down briefly. A group of students in the senior class paint anatomical parts on a statue of the school's namesake and are suspended from school for a week. Jacqueline is caught in the act of taking money from another girl's coat pocket; she is required to stay at home for the weekend. A 45-year-old schizophrenic woman who talked to herself, quietly or loudly, is socially isolated for 10 minutes each time the behavior happens (Haynes & Geddy, 1973). These episodes illustrate both informal and planned timeout contingencies. You probably can provide further illustrations, for timeout is a commonly used disciplinary technique. (Did prison sentences occur to you?)

Advantages of Timeout

Effectively Reduces Behavior

The main benefit of timeout is that it can be a powerful method that does not require directly presenting aversive consequences; only removing positive ones. Support for the effectiveness of the procedure is based on numerous published studies.[2] Here we describe instances in which timeout was reported to control disruption, aggression, tantrums, tics, noncompliance, stuttering, seizure-like behavior, complaints of pain, and many other unwanted behaviors.

To reduce aggression Olson and Roberts (1987) found that having siblings sit facing a wall contingent on each fighting episode effectively reduced their fighting with one another. Timeout in the form of a 5-minute isolation in a small open booth that blocked the youngster's view of the other students effectively reduced a kindergarten child's hitting, kicking, tripping, and throwing, as well as the aggression of his classmates (Wilson, Robertson, Herlong, & Haynes, 1979). After careful analysis of their data, the authors concluded that reductions also

---

[2] See Johnston and Pennypacker's (1980) survey of timeout for an extensive review of the evolution of research on the procedure.

obtained in the peers' aggressive behaviors appeared to be due to modeling effects, commenting that modeling effects as a result of using timeout ". . . can be a useful vehicle for the teacher in her efforts to reduce aggressive behavior in the classroom" (p. 108).

Wolf, Risley, and Mees (1964) reported success with a timeout procedure to diminish an autistic boy's temper tantrums. As soon as he began to tantrum, the child was isolated from his peers and aides by being placed in a room for a few moments beyond the duration of the tantrum. As his temper tantrums were virtually eliminated, a similar procedure was used effectively with the same child to reduce tantrums and pinching in school (Wolf, Risley, Johnson, Harris, & Allen, 1967).

Satiation having failed, Lahey, McNees, and McNees (1973) were able to almost eliminate a 10-year-old student's "verbal tic" (obscene vocalizations accompanied by facial twitches) by using timeout. After each tic, the teacher removed the student from the classroom for a short period of time, placing him in an adjacent unfurnished well-lighted 4 × 10-foot room that had originally been used for typing instruction. Timeout "was quickly effective in this case" (p. 104).

Unable to control the disruptive behavior of delinquent boys around a pool table by means of other techniques, Tyler and Brown (1967) reported that brief confinement in a **timeout room** was useful in reducing the misbehavior.

Timeout has been used to support home accident prevention programs with year-old infants (Mathews, Friman, Barone, Ross, & Christopherson, 1987). Mothers were taught to attend positively to safe behavior, to childproof their home, and to say "No," picking up the infants so they faced away from their mothers and placing them in a playpen immediately contingent on dangerous behaviors. The infants remained in the playpen timeout until they were quiet for 5 to 10 seconds. As a result, all infants decreased their risky behaviors, which

". . . remained at near-zero levels at a 71-month follow-up" (p. 168).

Karen, a 10-year-old girl, complained about stomachaches and was kept home from school frequently as a result. Physical causes were eliminated by the doctors, and timeout was applied. Whenever Karen complained of a stomachache, she was restricted to her room where she could rest, provided only with her meals and a book or two. Complaints diminished rapidly at home and school (Miller & Kratochwill, 1979).

Zeilberger, Sampen, and Sloane (1968) reported using a timeout procedure successfully with a four-and-a-half-year-old child for screaming, fighting, disobeying, and bossing at home. To remedy the situation, the behavior analyst provided the parents with detailed instructions and follow-up consultation as to how to implement the procedure effectively. In a like manner, timeout often is used as a component of parent and teacher training packages for managing children's *noncompliance* (e.g., Forehand & King, 1977; Roberts, McMahon, Forehand, & Humphreys, 1978; Wahler, 1969) and *disruption* (Colter, Applegate, King, & Kristal, 1972).

General Management Procedure

Timeout also has been used effectively as a *general management procedure* to control aggression on the playground (Murphy, Hutchinson, & Bailey, 1983), just as it is used in competitive sporting events like ice hockey. Aggressive acts during organized games were treated with a 2-minute timeout on the bench for the offender.

Combines Successfully with Alt-R and DRO

Roberts, Halzenbuehler, and Bean (1981) compared four treatment conditions to determine their differential effects on the noncompliance of 32 clinic-referred preschool children: praise for compliance, timeout (i.e., sitting on a chair in a corner for 2 minutes), praise for compliance combined with timeout for noncompliance, and a no-treatment control group. As you might expect, the praise combined with the timeout condition was the most effective. However, "the absence of a timeout contingency was associated with decreasing compliance ratios" (p. 98). In other words, using only praise for compliance resulted in an *increase* in noncompliance. The authors concluded, "Programs limited to training parents in attending to 'good' behavior and ignoring 'bad' behavior will probably not be effective in increasing compliance ratios" (p. 98). (Our comment is that whether to ignore or consequate bad behavior with timeout probably depends on the child's reinforcement history and the context.) In a related case, Wahler and Fox (1980) found that four young children's extreme misconduct and noncompliance, although not durably suppressed by means of a contract, were successfully reduced when parents began to use a timeout contingency.

Jim, a 10-year-old, had an average of nearly 30 body sores resulting from scratching or picking his skin. A DRO procedure (a special weekly outing contingent on achieving a specific reduction in number of sores) was combined with isolation for 20 minutes after scratching. The combination produced a substantial reduction in the number of sores (Carr & McDowell, 1980). A similar amalgam of DRO and timeout (resting in his curtained cubicle until the episode passed) plus an enriched living environment nearly eliminated nonepileptic "seizure-like" responses by an institutionalized 41-year-old mentally retarded man (Iwata & Lorentzson, 1976).

Given all these promising results, timeout can be a very appealing and reinforcing strategy for caregivers, managers, parents, and clients to apply. Yet, timeout is not without its limitations, as we shall see next.

Disadvantages of Timeout

Among the list of the disadvantages of using timeout is that it is not universally effective. Also, it is nonconstructive, may raise ethical and legal concerns, and has a potential for abusive overuse. Additionally, timeout sometimes causes suppression of other client behaviors and negative public reactions.

Loss of Learning Time

Depending on the form of timeout used, the procedure may interfere with learning opportunities to a greater or lesser extent. Students or trainees removed from classrooms obviously miss out on ongoing instruction. Those who remain in a modified timeout arrangement may lose access to active involvement in instruction or to reinforcement for their progress. Contingent observation, for instance, limits learning to the "vicarious" form.

Not Universally Effective

You cannot assume that using a timeout procedure will always be successful. As you will see, the effectiveness of the method depends on the availability of a heavily reinforcing ambience, a fortuitous learning history, the managers' ability to control reinforcers, and many other factors. Sometimes the reason why a given timeout method fails remains obscured. Escorting five-year-old Wesley to a timeout room where he remained for 2 minutes after leaving his seat actually appeared to *increase* the rate of the unwanted behavior (Bitgood, Peters, Jones, & Hathorn, 1982). Satisfactory results were achieved only when the instructor immobilized the boy for 15 seconds whenever he raised himself from his chair. Steeves, Martin, and Pear (1970) found that timeout from instruction, in the form of withdrawal of the teachers' attention, functioned as a reinforcer for an autistic student. One could speculate that the instruction was not particularly reinforcing for him.

Negative, Nonconstructive Contingency

Because the timeout procedure involves the withdrawal of a reinforcing environment, it is a nonconstructive contingency. Timeout for noncompliance is no guarantee that compliance will result, however, as several investigators (Doleys, Wells, Hobbs, Roberts, & Cartelli, 1976) discovered. The developmentally handicapped students with whom they worked improved only slightly or actually worsened their noncompliance when they were required to sit in the corner for 40 seconds as a consequence of those acts. Only firm reprimands accomplished the purpose.

Stimuli paired with timeout, like the person administering timeout, may acquire aversive properties. Many years ago, Ferster and Skinner (1957) showed how a stimulus correlated with timeout can function as a punishing (i.e., aversive) stimulus. Organisms usually will work to avoid or escape from and may even become aggressive in response to such stimuli (Oliver, West, & Sloan, 1974). Most managers, educators, and clinicians prefer that clients be motivated toward achieving positive goals such as social effectiveness, knowledge, skills, and other forms of achievement or productivity, rather than away from aversive circumstances like nonreinforcing environments.

Legal Restrictions

From a legal perspective, removing a client to an isolated room, constitutes **seclusion**, so case law related to seclusion often applies. Ennis and Friedman (1973) have cited judicial decisions establishing that adults, including those in seclusion, are entitled to adequate food, heat, light, ventilation, bedding, hygiene supplies, and clothing. Budd and Baer (1976) reported several juvenile cases in which solitary confinement has been held unconstitutional, singling out one case in particular, *Morales* v. *Turman* (1973), as applying to timeout procedures. Budd and Baer interpret specifications about

dormitory confinement, placing a juvenile inmate alone in a locked room within his own dormitory, as timeout. The *Morales* standard for the maximum duration of dormitory confinement is 50 minutes.

In discussing school expulsions, which also might be considered instances of timeout, Singer and Irvin (1987), have pointed out:

> Several recent court decisions have interpreted P.L. 94–142 in such a way as to limit the school's power to remove severely disordered students. Courts have ordered due process proceedings before a handicapped child could be expelled, and warned that expulsion could not be used if it circumvented the right to an education in the least restrictive environment (*Doe* v. *Koger,* 1979; *S-1* v. *Turlington,* 1981; *Sherry* v. *N.Y. State Education Dept.*, 1979; *Stuart* v. *Nappi,* 1978) (p. 46).

The *Wyatt* decision (1972) established legal protections connected with seclusion of institutionalized mentally handicapped residents. Emergency isolation of patients who harm themselves or others is limited to no longer than 1 hour. A qualified mental health professional must give the appropriate order in writing, and it must be put into effect within 24 hours or not at all. During each hour in seclusion, the patient's physical and psychiatric condition is charted, and bathroom privileges must be allowed.

For the mentally retarded, seclusion is *prohibited* by the *Wyatt* decision, but "legitimate," professionally supervised timeout may be used in "behavior-shaping programs" (a term not defined in the decision). Another decision, *New York State Association for Retarded Children* v. *Rockefeller* (1973), prohibits seclusion of mentally retarded residents. In *Welsch* v. *Likins* (1974) a baseline is required before timeout or seclusion are used, and the frequency of the objectionable behavior must be shown to have decreased after the intervention. Otherwise, timeout must be stopped. Similarly, after reviewing a large number of court decisions, Singer and Irvin (1987) concluded that: "For intrusive or restrictive procedures to be used, they must be aimed at educational objectives and must clearly be the least restrictive alternatives" (p. 51).

Because of the confusion between the terms *timeout* and *seclusion,* Budd and Baer (1976)[3] offer an important distinction:

> The decisions in the *Wyatt, Carey*, and *Horacek* cases have direct implications for behavior modification. By outlawing or severely restricting seclusion as a treatment technique, the cases could well be interpreted as prohibiting a room-timeout procedure. This would seem to be a serious mistake, because timeout is one of the mildest aversive procedures available for handling undesirable behavior and has repeatedly been demonstrated to be a highly effective control technique (e.g., Bostow and Bailey, 1969; Clark, Rowbury, Baer, and Baer, 1973; Wolf, Risley, and Mees, 1964). When it is employed properly, timeout has three features which distinguish it from the usual seclusion, solitary confinement, or segregation practices. First, timeout is consistently administered contingent on occurrences of an undesirable behavior. Second, it is a brief procedure, often lasting between one and five minutes and rarely extending longer than 15 minutes (cf., Clark, Rowbury, Baer, and Baer, 1973; Risley and Twardosz, 1974). Third, the use of timeout is coupled with objective observation of whether or not it is fruitful in remediating the problem behavior. By contrast, traditional seclusion or solitary confinement procedures are usually employed on an unsystematic basis and, when used contingently, they are probably used for only extreme examples of the behavior. They are typically lengthy procedures, lasting hours or even several days, and with little or no monitoring of their effectiveness in modifying the undesirable behavior. Because of these important differences between the correct use of

timeout and use of other seclusion practices, timeout would seem to be a humane and acceptable treatment procedure. It is to be hoped that future courts will recognize this distinction and, in so doing, specifically authorize room-timeout as a legitimate treatment procedure under the conditions outlined above (pp. 214–215).

In 1975 a special task force for the state of Florida (May et al., 1976) prepared a report containing a set of procedural guidelines, including those related to timeout. This included the policy of the *least restrictive environment* (Ennis & Friedman, 1973) that mandates confinement be in the most minimally restrictive form that will permit treatment purposes to be met.

To enable policy makers and practitioners to judge the "level of restrictiveness" of any given timeout strategy, the procedure has been classified into various categories (Brantner & Doherty, 1983) with *contingent observation* (sit and watch) and other *nonexclusionary* methods (e.g., the timeout ribbon, described later in this chapter) considered the least restrictive, **exclusionary timeout** the next least intrusive (moving the individual to another part of the room or area), and *seclusion* or *isolation* (placing the person in a separate room or behind a physical barrier), especially "locked timeout," being the most restrictive. The latter is covered in a resolution by the Executive Committee and Behavior Modification Special Interest Group of Division 33 (Mental Retardation and Developmental Disabilities) of the American Psychological Association (1989), which includes the following statement:

> Highly restrictive procedures shall not be employed until there has been sufficient determination that the use of less restrictive procedures was or would be ineffective or harm would come to the client because of gradual change in the client's particular problematic behavior (p. 3).

Other guidelines have been included in state

---

[3] Reprinted by permission of Federal Legal Publications, Inc., and the authors, from *The Journal of Psychiatry and Law*, Vol. 4, no. 2 (1976). © 1976 by Federal Legal Publications, Inc. 95 Morton St., New York, N.Y. 10014.

standards (e.g., for California, Loberg, 1980), have been suggested by individuals (e.g., Gast & Nelson, 1977) and in other professional organizational policies (the AABT Task Force Report on the Treatment of Self-Injurious Behavior, 1982).

Potential for Abuse

Like response cost, timeout is easy to abuse. Caregivers sometimes are tempted to apply it more often or more restrictively than necessary. Why? Not only does timeout rapidly reduce unwanted behavior, but by isolating offenders, their aversive behavior is removed immediately—providing optimal negative reinforcement for the contingency manager's use of timeout. To avoid becoming overreliant on timeout, restrict its application to severe circumstances when constructive, or less aversive, optimally applied procedures have failed. Additionally, even though more difficult for caregivers, see to it that the doctrine of least restrictiveness is adhered to.

Public Concern

Timeout has been known to cause public controversy. The public probably reacts differently depending on the form of timeout that is applied. For example, Kazdin (1980a) found that respondents rated nonexclusionary timeout as more acceptable than exclusionary timeout, and less aversive and more acceptable than drug or shock therapy (Kazdin, 1980b).

A visitor who has not been briefed adequately passes a cubicle labeled "timeout booth" and recoils in horror. Concluding that some poor child is being kept in solitary confinement, the visitor raises a ruckus, thereby threatening the viability of the program along with improvement in the client's behavior. These reactions happen. We too might respond similarly to seeing seclusion timeout without knowing that it was being used on severely dangerous, destructive, disruptive, or unhealthy acts. A number of *safeguards* will help to min-

imize adverse public reactions like these to the use of seclusion timeout:

- Ensure adequate lighting and carpeting. Placing a client in a dark room devoid of furniture with nothing but a cold floor on which to sit is unnecessarily harsh.
- Remove all potentially dangerous objects, such as items that can be torn from walls, objects with sharp corners, and anything that can be thrown or swallowed.
- To prevent injury, be sure clients can be observed. Remain just outside the timeout area (e.g., Harris, Hershfield, Kaffashan, & Romanczyk, 1974) and/or set a timer to remind yourself when the timeout period has expired.
- Obtain the clients' or their advocates', parents', or guardians' informed consent, as well as permission from supervisors, before using the procedure. Obtaining informed consent involves:

  Detailed description of problem behaviors; previously attempted treatment(s); proposed treatment(s); risks and expected outcomes; data collection procedures; alternative treatments; and statements of consent including the right to withdraw consent at any time (Irvin & Singer, 1985) (Singer & Irvin, 1987, p. 48).

- Check current policies and laws regulating the use of timeout and seclusion procedures.
- Use a neutral descriptor for the timeout area, such as "quiet area" or "relaxation room" rather than "timeout booth," a rather mechanical sounding term. Timeout areas do serve the purpose of quieting and relaxing people whose behavior is out of control.
- Brief visitors before they enter the setting. Mention all the safeguards that have been instituted, and show and interpret the baseline and intervention data that document the effectiveness of the procedure.

- Consider forming a Human Rights Committee (some schools have expanded their IEP [Individual Education Planning] procedures to include this responsibility [Brakman, 1985; Irvin & Singer, 1984]) to review the treatment program. The function of the committee is to: (a) provide due process and safeguards for clients, (b) ensure appropriate educational treatment, and (c) protect staff (Singer & Irvin, 1987). Minimally, as Brantner and Doherty (1983) recommend, determine the acceptability of your timeout procedure to the concerned public prior to implementing exclusionary timeout. This can help avoid reactions that might affect adversely the program's survival.
- Above all, continually monitor and make available summaries of the effects of the program.

Suppression of Other Behaviors

In addition to the problematic acts, timeout may lead to the suppression of other acceptable responses. This is more likely to happen when the client has few S^Ds, or cues for discriminating the specific conditions under which timeout is instituted. Perhaps rules were not clearly and consistently delineated: "You may not bite." In other cases, clients may be so disabled as to be incapable of making appropriate discriminations ("It's okay to talk here but not to bite people"). Such failure to discriminate was demonstrated in a study by Pendergrass (1972). Two severely retarded children were isolated for persistent misbehavior. According to the frequency records of misbehaviors and social interactions, while the timeout was in effect, the misbehavior diminished, but so did social interactions.

Nevertheless, when less restrictive, more benign methods are given a fair try and found wanting, timeout may present a viable alternative approach to eliminating severe behavioral difficulties. To assist you, next we offer a set of guidelines for using the procedure effectively.

Using Timeout Effectively
Combining with Other Procedures

Undoubtedly, at this point you recognize that procedures need not be applied in their "pure form," but can be combined to yield greater success. For instance, timeout paired with reinforcement of correct responding facilitated the imitation training of a four-year-old retarded child over just using extinction combined with reinforcement (Parsons & Davey, 1978).

A laboratory study (Holz et al., 1963) demonstrated a similar outcome. When just a single response was available to the people serving as subjects, timeout was only minimally effective, whereas the availability of a second alternative caused the response treated with periodic contingent timeout to be almost immediately eliminated. In another instance, timeout was insufficient to reduce dangerous aggression like choking and grabbing people, until lots of attention, hugs, and treats were added contingent on the absence of aggression (Vukelich & Hake, 1971).

Naturally, the unwanted behavior must be placed completely on extinction when any reductive method, including timeout, is applied. Yet sometimes sources of reinforcement are elusive, requiring skillful detection, as you shall see in the next discussion.

Removing as Many Reinforcers Supporting Unwanted Behavior as Feasible

Mr. Vescent decided to try timeout with Esmerelda. Whenever she pushed or hit another child, she was told simply but firmly: "You cannot push. You must leave." Nothing more was said. (Further conversation might be reinforcing.) Esmerelda was immediately placed on a chair in the hall outside the classroom for 5 minutes. Things went along fine for some time, and Esmerelda's rate of pushing and hitting began to subside. But then the improvement seemed to stop. When the teacher investigated, he found that the principal had come by on several occasions and asked Esmerelda why she was out in the hall, giving her a sympathetic pep talk on the importance of getting along well with other children. This unprecedented attention from the principal probably reinforced her undesirable behavior. A conference between the teacher and the principal cleared up the situation, and the principal no longer attended to the child when she was seated in the hall. Pushing and hitting began to subside once more, and timeout was again in effect and performing its function.

One of the authors had a similar experience while teaching in an inner-city school. Children who misbehaved while preparing for dismissal were told to return to their classroom to remain after school. Although this approach proved effective with some, other students actually appeared to solicit the timeout. A retrospective analysis suggested that remaining while the teacher decorated the room and performed other duties, actually may have been reinforcing. A switch in procedure showed that it was probably so. For these students, the teacher used staying after school and helping the teacher as a reinforcer for meritorious performance. The approach proved to be a powerful incentive for several students.

Identifying and removing *all* reinforcers in a situation may be impossible; but identifying and contingently removing access to powerful reinforcers that sustain the unwanted behavior may be sufficient. McReynolds (1969) used ice cream as a reinforcer to facilitate a child's speech development. When the child lapsed into meaningless jargon (presumably rein-

forced in the past by attention), a timeout was instituted consisting of the experimenter's taking the ice cream and turning her chair away from the child. This timeout signaled nonreinforcement and produced a reduction of the jargon.

Using Variations of Timeout

Planned Ignoring. Many teachers of young or developmentally delayed children have learned the value of a similar procedure—dropping their heads and remaining motionless briefly—as a timeout consequence for whining, self-stimulation, and other events that interfere with instruction. This variation of timeout, in which usual attention, physical contact, and any verbal interactions are removed for a short duration contingent upon the occurrence of the unwanted behavior, has been labeled **planned ignoring** (Nelson & Rutherford, 1983).

Planned ignoring is different from extinction in that with extinction essentially all reinforcers are withheld from a *particular previously reinforced behavior* and no time element is involved. Planned ignoring is a form of timeout, however, because the opportunity to obtain various types of reinforcers is removed for a period of time. Planned ignoring, like contingent observation (described later), is a relatively nonintrusive timeout procedure that can be quickly and conveniently applied, but its broad-ranging effectiveness remains to be conclusively demonstrated (Nelson & Rutherford, 1983).

Contingent Observation. A procedure called **contingent observation** (Porterfield et al., 1976) is another relatively benign form of timeout. A child who misbehaves while working in a group is relocated a few feet away from the table, where the opportunity to observe is available but not to participate in reinforceable activities. This variation is less restrictive than seclusion timeout and certainly is preferable. Nevertheless, clients may refuse to remain in their chairs. This situation may be handled by arranging a room timeout for a minute or two as a consequence of failing to remain in the timeout chair, a method that Roberts (1988) found to be equally as effective as a spank.

Timeout Ribbon. Another relatively benign form of timeout involves removing the reinforcing environment from the clients. Foxx and Shapiro (1978) accomplished this timeout by providing each of their severely retarded students a ribbon (sometimes referred to as the **timeout ribbon**) to use as a necktie. If a child engaged in one of any specifically designated set of misbehaviors, the tie was removed for 3 minutes or longer, if necessary, until the misbehavior stopped. Treats and praise were delivered to the children every few minutes, provided they wore their ties.

Facial Screening. Facial screening is a more restrictive form of timeout. "Facial screening involves the contingent application of a face cover, usually a soft cloth (e.g., a terry-cloth bib)" (Horton, 1987, p. 53), a blindfold (Murphy, Ruprecht, & Nunes, 1979), or the contingency manager's hands (McGonigle, Duncan, Cordisco, & Barrett, 1982). To be effective, the visual input must be contingently blocked for about 5 to 15 seconds (Demetral & Lutzker, 1980; Gross, Farrar, & Liner, 1982; Horton, 1987; Singh, Beale, & Dawson, 1981; Winston, Singh, & Dawson, 1984), following each occurrence of the unwanted behavior. The procedure should be combined with a differential reinforcement procedure such as Alt-R and/or DRO (Gross et al., 1982). Attempts to remove the facial screen have been handled successfully with a stern "No" followed by physically guiding the client's hands down to his or her side (Gross et al., 1982).

Facial screening has proven very successful with a variety of self-injurious behaviors: among others, slapping, hitting, or scratching the head or face (Demetral & Lutzker, 1980; Lutzker,

1978; Singh et al., 1981; Winston, Singh, & Dawson, 1984; Zegiob, Alford, & House, 1978), chronic hand or thumb biting (Demetral & Lutzker, 1980; Singh, 1980), and trichotillomania (chronic hair pulling that results in spotty baldness) (Gross et al., 1982); stereotypy, such as hand clapping (Zegiob, Jenkins, Becker, & Bristow, 1976), spoon banging during mealtime at school (Horton, 1987), tongue clicking, repetitive fabric pulling, visual fixation on finger movements (McGonigle et al., 1982); and excessive screaming (Singh, Winton, & Dawson, 1982). Facial screening also was found more effective than water mist spray and forced arm exercise with two profoundly retarded 17-year-old girls for self-injurious finger-licking and excessive ear-rubbing (Singh, Watson, & Winton, 1986). Seeing the screening procedure in operation may upset unprepared visitors, though, and colleagues tell us that it doesn't work universally. So use it with caution.

Required relaxation. Sometimes a person is so out of control that implementing the milder timeout methods described earlier is not feasible. Often trying to contain the person in the situation is fruitless. Seclusion timeout, in the form of placing the person in a secluded "quiet area," could help. As all parents know, one such place is the child's bed—a place to calm down and relax.

Required relaxation (i.e., requiring that the individual lie on the bed) was successfully used as an alternative to a timeout room to reduce adult men's rates of severe violence and/or destructiveness (Webster & Azrin, 1973). Alternatively, an empty room, an area behind a screen, or an alcove may suit this purpose. For persons with histories of extreme violence, rooms without furniture or breakable windows have been used. Such isolation areas are best reserved for those who are dangerously out of control[4] (see "Legal Sanctions," discussed earlier in this chapter).

Movement suppression timeout. In cases of severe self-injury, an option is **movement-suppression timeout** (Rolider & Van Houten, 1985a). Seriously dangerous behaviors, such as ingesting nonedible objects like rocks, poking one's eyes, or hitting one's head against the wall, were rapidly suppressed by having the person remain totally immobile in a corner for a few minutes. By requiring her seven-year-old boy to sit on his hands when he violently waved and flapped them, and by using DRO for nonflapping, Carl's mother helped the boy to reduce his self-stimulation to very low levels (Hanley, Perelman, & Homan, 1979). (This movement suppression method resembles the "freeze" technique that Allison and Ayllon [1980] successfully used to coach football, tennis and gymnastics skills. In commenting on the technique, which required instant immobility to permit their errors to be analyzed, trainees said, "It was uncomfortable in the 'frozen' position, but it helped me learn a lot" [p. 313].)

Making Time-in as Reinforcing as Possible

Timeout from positive reinforcement can effectively reduce a behavior optimally *only if the* individual's "time-in" environment is rich in reinforcement. The procedure will not work effectively if the person moves from a time-in

environment devoid of reinforcers or replete with aversive stimuli to one from which aversive stimuli have been removed, or differences in density of reinforcement hardly are discernible. Esmerelda, who violently dislikes social studies, soon finds that causing a disturbance during that class results in her being asked to leave the classroom. In doing so, Mr. Vescent inadvertently is negatively reinforcing Esmerelda's disruptive behavior.

Solnick, Rincover, and Peterson (1977) reported timeout to be ineffective initially in reducing a 16-year-old retarded boy's spitting and self-injurious behavior. Only after the regular environment was made reinforcing by introducing new toys, verbal prompts, and praise was the timeout procedure effective. Consequently, if the natural time-in environment fails to offer sufficient reinforcement, you will need to increase its density if timeout is to be effective.

Avoiding Opportunities for Self-Injury and Self-Stimulation

Using a mild form of timeout, like withholding all attention for a period of time, as Harris and Wolchik (1979) did, may be insufficient—especially with people who do not find attention reinforcing in the first place. Nor is it wise to seclude a client in timeout who frequently engages in self-injury or self-stimulation. This point is especially crucial when the performance targeted for reduction is being maintained by negative reinforcement (escape-avoidance), as mentioned earlier, or reinforced by sensory stimulation (e.g., rocking, eye poking, head banging, throwing oneself on the floor, masturbating, or daydreaming) (Lovaas & Favell, 1987).

The requisite nonreinforcing environment required for timeout conditions cannot be readily achieved with clients who use the occasion to engage in an orgy of the self-reinforcing activity. Such powerful reinforcement will cause

---

[4] An alternative is to restrain dangerous behavior by means of camisoles or other devices. From a behavior analysis point of view, the attention connected with implementation of such procedures may provide lots of inadvertent reinforcement for maladaptive behaviors, and they are advisable only when no other alternatives are available. Various legal decisions on restraint have been handed down. At this writing, it is probably legally acceptable for a qualified professional to give written orders for the brief use (a few hours or less) of safe restraints, provided that there is a written check each half-hour and that 10 minutes of exercise are allowed each 2 hours. Behavior analysts should study current law, administrative policies, and ethical standards when considering this procedure.

the unwanted behavior to increase rather than decrease. For example, timeout was attempted in order to reduce a six-year-old autistic girl's tantrums; but the child frequently engaged in self-stimulation (Solnick et al., 1977). Instead of being reduced, the tantrums increased. Apparently timeout conditions were not achieved, because the isolation provided her with an opportunity to engage in self-stimulation to her heart's content.

However, timeout *can* work to reduce self-injury that is maintained by positive social reinforcement. Therefore, before implementing a timeout program for self-injury or self-stimulation, you need to try to determine what events are supporting and maintaining the behavior. Is it negative reinforcement (escape-avoidance from an aversive situation, such as excessive demands [Carr, Newsom, & Binkoff, 1976])? Is it reinforcement obtained through sensory stimuli for engaging in the act itself? Or, is the behavior reinforced by social attention? Obviously, different treatment strategies would be mandated depending on the function of the self-injury (Lovaas & Favell, 1987; Repp, Felce, & Barton, 1988).

If you suspect that self-injury is being sustained by tactile stimulation, try using protective equipment, such as a padded helmet for head hitting or padded gloves for hand biting while the timeout is in effect (Dorsey, Iwata, Reid, & Davis, 1982). Another alternative is to remove access to a reinforcer, such as a hand-held vibrator, contingent on self-injury (Nunes, Murphy, & Ruprecht, 1977).

Keeping Duration Relatively Short

Logic may tell us that if a little timeout works pretty well, a lot of timeout will work very well. But evidence defies this conclusion (Zimmerman & Baydan, 1963; Zimmerman & Ferster, 1963). With few exceptions, longer timeouts appear to provide no further reductive effect and sometimes even seem to disrupt behavior

in other ways. In addition, some evidence suggests that short timeouts generally have proven quite successful (e.g., Clark et al., 1973; Risley & Twardosz, 1974).

In a study by Tyler (1965), a youth's outbursts resulted in a timeout period that lasted 15 minutes; in two others (Wolf et al., 1964; Wolf et al., 1967) an autistic boy was isolated for brief periods of time, usually for a few minutes longer than the duration of any tantrum. In each instance, the undesirable behavior was reduced significantly. In another study (Bostow & Bailey, 1969), two hospitalized retarded adults' severe disruption and aggression were reduced through use of a procedural package. One component was a 2-minute timeout; the other was differential reinforcement of acceptable alternatives. Rolider and Van Houten (1985a) used a duration of 1 to 3 minutes of movement suppression timeout.

As with response cost, an individual's experience with timeout may influence the suppressive effects of various durations. To determine whether the rate of suppression of severely disruptive behaviors by 20 institutionalized retarded persons was differentially affected by these various durations, White, Nielsen, and Johnson (1972) compared three different lengths: 1 minute, 15 minutes, and 30 minutes. On the average, both the 15- and 30-minute timeout periods produced greater suppression than the 1-minute duration. But the 1-minute duration did suppress behaviors effectively among 5 of 6 subjects for whom it was the first duration encountered. For the other subjects who had already experienced longer durations, the 1-minute duration had hardly any effect.

Essentially the same outcomes were discovered when 5- and 30-minute timeout durations were compared. A 5-minute timeout phase that preceded a 30-minute timeout phase for instances of delinquent youths' aggression resulted in the rates being diminished; but when the 5-minute timeout followed the 30-minute timeout phase, the shorter duration was almost completely ineffectual. In fact, physical aggression was worse than during baseline (Kendall, Nay, & Jeffers, 1975).

In a study by Burchard and Barrera (1972), the maladaptive behavior of a group of mildly retarded adolescent boys was contingently treated with a 5-minute timeout plus a 5-token fine over a 2-year period. Then the authors decided to compare the efficacy of the 5-minute timeout *versus* the 5-token fine. The maladaptive behavior increased under each separate contingency. Apparently, the separate contingencies were weaker than the two combined, producing less suppression. Only either a 30-minute timeout *or* a 30-token fine suppressed the behaviors appreciably.

The moral is that contingency managers need to be cognizant of *each* individual's history with timeout in a given context, and if the managers plan to use a brief timeout, they should not maintain a client under timeout conditions for a period longer than intended. Otherwise, the contingency manager builds in a history of longer durations, and shorter ones may lose their effectiveness. A signaling system, like a kitchen timer, can remind us that the time has expired; better still, assign a staff person, a friend, or another client to monitor the timeout from a vantage point invisible to the client. The monitor can also ensure that the client is not in any danger. (A notable exception to the rule of keeping timeout durations brief was reported by Foxx and colleagues, 1980).

Long timeouts may teach clients new ways to obtain reinforcers for themselves via self-stimulation, fantasizing, and so forth. Long timeout periods also present other risks. Care givers may hesitate to enforce extended periods of timeout, producing a situation in which the timeout procedure is undermined by being inconsistently implemented.

Long timeouts also interfere with a clients' productivity to a greater extent than shorter ones. Suppose every time Seymour throws anything, he is sent to the principal's office for 2 hours. He would miss the lessons given during that time. Because short timeout periods can be effective, there is no need to adopt long and potentially disruptive ones.

Clearly Communicating Conditions for Timeout

Clearly describing the rules covering the conditions under which timeout will be invoked may help clients discriminate acceptable from unacceptable behaviors more rapidly, and to act accordingly (although not necessarily reducing resistance to timeout [Roberts, 1984]). When Giselle and Griselda become embroiled in a fist fight, each is sent to a quiet place to calm down. When Dad hears the twins just beginning to become upset with each other, he warns them, "Remember, if you can't play nicely with each other, you'll each have to go to your rooms for awhile." That warning, assuming that it has been regularly paired with the fighting ——→ timeout contingency in the past, should inhibit the fighting. Kendall et al. (1975) used that type of warning in their successful timeout program.

Data seem to suggest that explanations do little to augment the value of timeout *while it is in the process of being implemented* (Alevizos & Alevizos, 1975; Gast & Nelson, 1977). In fact, care givers who yield to the temptation to lecture clients in route to timeout inadvertently may be reinforcing those acts. To avoid such a situation, rules of conduct should be reviewed regularly at other times, especially when participants are calm and attentive, such as during opening exercises or weekly meetings.

Using Timeout Consistently

Most experienced practitioners know the importance of consistency. We have already discussed the need for consistently maintaining reinforcement and extinction conditions. The same holds for timeout (Zimmerman & Baydan, 1963). To reduce a behavior, timeout should be applied initially as regularly as possible. Once the reduction has been accomplished (to a predetermined criterion of no more than N responses per T time period), however, shifting to an intermittent schedule may be possible.

Such a shift was accomplished effectively in a study by Clark and colleagues (1973). An eight-year-old retarded child displayed behaviors that were considered disruptive and dangerous to other children, such as choking, attacking people, and destroying materials. Timeout was instituted consistently in sequential order for each category of behavior. Following substantial reductions in each of the behaviors, various timeout schedules were attempted. Low levels of the behaviors were maintained when the child was placed in timeout an average of each third response but not when the rate averaged only one in eight responses.

Being Able to Implement and Maintain Timeout

Certain skills are involved in applying timeout effectively, including clear rules, appropriate warning techniques, detecting and following through when circumstances call for invoking timeout, and the other suggestions given earlier. This requires careful training and supervision of contingency managers. When Flanagan et al. (1979) compared four different techniques for teaching parents to use the skills appropriately, role playing proved superior during rehearsal while modeling did the best job of promoting generalization into the home. Lectures and written instructions were less effective under both situations. Don't be misled into assuming that because people can describe how to use timeout (or any other procedure) effectively, they actually will implement and maintain it optimally. Instead, verify the user's skills and when necessary train, preferably in the natural setting, using modeling or behavior rehearsal.

Timeout is not a logical choice when clients are so resistant that timeout conditions cannot be sustained (e.g., Azrin & Wesolowski, 1975). For large children or handicapped adults, this factor must be considered before the procedure is selected. Usually, individuals will obey an authority figure and remain in timeout for the required duration. Some, however, may balk, as reported in one case (Foxx, Foxx, Jones, & Kiely, 1980). If two attendants had not been available to escort the enraged client to social isolation, the program could not have been accomplished.

Avoid becoming embroiled in a physical altercation with a wrongdoer (Benoit & Mayer, 1975). First of all, you can get hurt. Secondly, struggling with an authority figure in the presence of one's peers actually may contribute to the person's social status. If the resistance can be overcome readily, without causing undue commotion, however, timeout still may prove effective.

Resistance has been overcome by holding or locking the door while maintaining proper supervision, placing the individual in a more restrictive timeout (Roberts, 1988), using physical restraint (Foxx et al., 1980) or some form of punishment (Roberts, 1988), and by using contingent delay (illustrated below). Corporal punishment, such as a spanking, probably is the most aversive and therefore used as the last resort. A sharp verbal "No!" may work for some individuals. (See Chapter 27 for considerations in using punishment.)

Releasing Client from Timeout Contingent on Acceptable Behavior

Escape from an aversive situation, such as timeout, can be very reinforcing. Therefore be certain that release from timeout is not contingent upon a maladaptive response; otherwise, you might inadvertently reinforce it, as Harris and Ersner-Hershfield (1978) have posited.

Contingent delay might help you avoid that

Figure 26.1 Selecting and Using Timeout

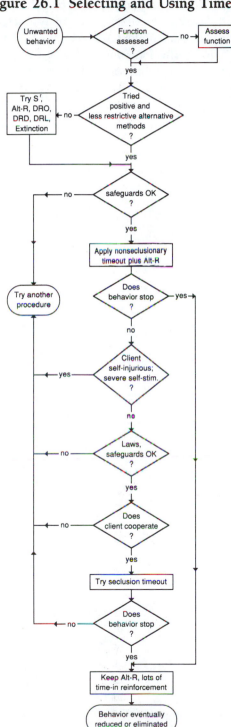

pitfall. The technique involves extending the timeout interval contingent on inappropriate behavior that occurs during timeout (Bostow & Bailey, 1969). Thus, an individual would not be permitted to leave timeout until his or her behavior was acceptable. The data available indicate that adding contingent delay does reduce inappropriate behavior during timeout, but findings are mixed as to whether it enhances timeout's effectiveness in reducing the target behavior (Hobbs & Forehand, 1975; Mace et al., 1986). In addition to its inconclusive effectiveness, several possible liabilities are associated with the use of contingent delay:

- Clients are likely to be retained in timeout for minor offenses that would not normally result in timeout, such as crying or getting out of their seats (Mace et al., 1986).
- More demands, time, training, and supervision are required of contingency managers to ensure correct application (Mace et al., 1986).
- The situation could "result in a control-countercontrol struggle between the child and caretaker" (Mace et al., 1986, p. 83).
- Individuals, particularly those who are highly resistant, may be kept in timeout for periods beyond that necessary for effectiveness (Hobbs, Forehand, & Murray, 1978; Mace et al., 1986).

We recommend that contingent delay only be applied when its necessity and utility can be justified on the basis of objective evidence with the particular client.

Summary

Timeout from positive reinforcement has frequently demonstrated its effectiveness in reducing objectionable behavior. When opportunities to obtain reinforcement are completely and consistently removed contingent on a maladaptive behavior, while alternative adaptive behaviors are reinforced simultaneously, time-out can be very effective. Used alone, however, it is neither positive nor constructive. For those reasons and because the procedure has the potential for being abused, timeout probably should be limited to serious situations in which more benign, less restrictive reductive techniques would not be effective. The flow chart in Figure 26.1 summarizes the key points that should be considered *before* an analyst selects and implements timeout. Overlooking such factors reduces the likelihood of successful rate reduction. Now, what suggestions do you have for Mr. Vescent's use of timeout? Do you have an inkling why our system of jailing miscreants functions less than optimally?

Chapter 27

Reducing Behavior with Aversive Procedures

GOALS

After completing this chapter, you should be able to:

1. Discuss why the use of punishment is so prevalent.

2. Discuss why understanding punishment is important even though it should be used infrequently.

3. Define, recognize, and give original illustrations for each of the following terms:
   a. Punishment
   b. Aversive stimulus
   c. Unconditioned aversive (punishing) stimulus (S^P)
   d. Conditioned aversive (punishing) stimulus (S^p)
   e. Extrinsic aversive stimuli
   f. Intrinsic aversive stimuli
   g. Contingent exertion
   h. Restitution training
   i. Overcorrection
   j. Positive practice
   k. Negative practice

4. Compare and contrast the various types of aversive stimuli listed in 3c and d.

5. Describe the similarities and differences between contingent exertion and overcorrection.

6. Explain why immobilization and the freeze technique are aversive.

7. List, discuss, and illustrate the factors that influence the impact of punishment.

8. Describe what can be done when administering punishment consistently and immediately is not feasible.

9. List the advantages of re-creating-the-scene as an adjunct to punishment.
10. Specify and discuss the dangers of using punishment inconsistently.
11. Discuss why habituation can be minimized by varying aversive stimuli.
12. List and discuss the conditions under which mild punishment can be used.
13. Discuss how masochism may develop.
14. List and discuss the similarities between maximizing the effectiveness of punishment and reinforcement.

Work at Top Quality is progressing as usual, when suddenly a scream pierces the air. Barney rushes over to find Sloppy Smith writhing in pain, with several fingers bleeding and one bent at a weird angle. The offending machine that Sloppy had been repairing continues to chug away.

"You dumb ————," shouts Barney. "Don't you know enough to turn off a machine before trying to repair it?"

Sure, Sloppy knew that he was supposed to "lock out" machines before working on them. Yet he didn't! The consequences were severe: besides his own pain and suffering, Sloppy required costly medical care, and would lose several weeks of work at company expense. Production also was halted temporarily, as concerned onlookers paused to survey the crisis. The time supervisors and medical personnel would have to spend preparing reports and meeting with insurance investigators certainly could be put to better use. The plant manager was furious because the accident meant a sure loss in the bonus he would have collected had the plant maintained its excellent record of accident-free days. The prominently placed sign proudly announcing "150 days without an accident," would be supplanted by an empty space—a grim reminder of the tragedy.

Here is a situation in which a dangerous behavior occurred despite the victim's "knowing better." Using the proper "lock-out" procedure was in Sloppy's repertoire. He just didn't exercise his ability. Apparently plant policy has had little impact on Sloppy.

In a contrasting example, let us suppose that Pearl, who spends so much of her day repetitiously flapping and twisting her hands, or slapping her own face, has been treated with both Alt-R and DRO procedures to remove those impediments to learning. But self-stimulation occurs at such a high rate that catching an adaptive alternative response or any intervals without the hand movements to reinforce has been almost impossible. Response cost has done lit-

tle good, because few effective reinforcers have been discovered to remove, and timeout would make no sense, for the behavior could continue easily while Pearl was isolated. In this instance, alternative strategies need to be invoked.

Faced with circumstances such as these, many in positions of responsibility would elect immediately to punish, wanting to eliminate the offensive behaviors as fast as possible, because that is what punishment is supposed to accomplish. *Yet punishment rarely is the best answer.* Often it is applied too frequently, indiscriminately, counterproductively, and with neither documentation nor simultaneous programming of constructive techniques.

Decrying punishment's widespread use in schools, Skinner (1968) graphically has illustrated the point:

> The cane is still with us, and efforts to abolish it are vigorously opposed. In Great Britain a split leather strap for whipping students called a taws can be obtained from suppliers who advertise in educational journals, one of whom is said to sell three thousand annually. (The taws has the advantage, shared by the rubber truncheon, of leaving no incriminating marks.) (p. 96)

In the United States, too, corporal punishment is condoned in schools by the vast majority of the states, and officially across the globe as a treatment for criminals. Aversive stimuli are applied in many forms world wide, by just about everyone, at one time or another.

Undoubtedly you have thought of numerous other examples; history is replete with instances. Bullies and the power hungry often are experts in the selection and application of aversive stimuli, with some, like the Marquis de Sade, developing the practice to a state of high art. But punishment also takes place in everyday life as an aspect of management, family relations, classroom and military discipline, law enforcement, and in all other social organizations (with the exception of Utopian societies like *Walden Two*, Skinner, 1948). We need to learn about punishment, whether or not we intend to use it, so we can be sensitive to its impact, as well as to its use and abuse by others.

Why is punishment so prevalent? Probably because at some level it has survival value, and because it permits individuals to control their environments. Even the gentlest animals reliably react to aversive stimulation by attacking, which helps ensure their viability. The tiniest infant rapidly learns to get what it needs (positive reinforcement) by screaming—an aversive stimulus for parents. Hastily the parents learn to terminate the event (negative reinforcement) by supplying nourishment or comfort to the infant.

Although *delivering* aversive stimuli sometimes may be punishing to the agent, as in the case of a parent who finds that disciplining his child "hurts himself more than the child," using punishment also can be very reinforcing. Mrs. Kvetch finds that her complaining pays off, because "the squeaky wheel gets the grease." Bullies in the fifth grade can get the younger kids to knuckle under and do their bidding just by dispensing a threat or two.

As Hutchinson (1977) and numerous other investigators have found, reacting by attacking is highly probable immediately after the individuals themselves have been punished. So *being punished* can function as an establishing operation, turning the opportunity to deliver punishment (i.e., the reaction to aggression) into a reinforcer. Remember the last time someone banged into your car? What was your initial impulse? Probably to lash out somehow. Aggression in reaction to punishment is a lawful phenomenon. (Fortunately, our culture teaches us more civilized alternatives to this primitive response. Otherwise, the law of the jungle would prevail universally.)

So we see that punishment is an aspect of the human condition, with aversive stimuli experienced and delivered naturally and by design. As you may already have concluded, though, along with Skinner (1968), we gener-

ally oppose its planned application. Some of our reasons are clear to you by now; others will emerge in these chapters. Why, then, should we even discuss the topic? For a few purposes:

- to alert you to the fact that you and others do use punishment, with or without awareness, which may produce short-term but not long-term advantages.
- to help you recognize how ineptly punishment frequently is applied.
- by teaching you about its predictable disadvantages, we hope to discourage you from using it except when justified by special circumstances.
- given the latter justification, to help you to use the procedure as benignly and constructively as possible.

Learning about the many facets of punishment also will broaden your understanding of some of life's most perplexing problems: why violence and aggression prevail and what might be done to mitigate them.

Sometimes, mild punishment clearly is warranted, such as indicating that an answer is incorrect or reprimanding someone caught in the act of doing something reprehensible. Otherwise, clients might conclude that their actions were acceptable. Barney would be justified in sharply rebuking anyone he notices preparing to repair a machine without first locking it out. Pearl might benefit from a requirement that she engage in a mildly unpleasant activity contingent on the self-stimulation, such as contingent exertion and/or positive practice (because if her rate of stereotypy can be reduced sufficiently, she could be taught some adaptive behaviors, thereby allowing Alt-R or DRO to succeed). Later, we shall offer a more detailed discussion of the advantages and disadvantages of using punishment. At this point, we proceed by reviewing its definition.

Punishment Defined

The term *punishment* has many connotations. Some people see it as inflicting physical pain, as when a mother, wishing to convince her son not to pull the tablecloth off the table, slaps his hands hard enough to hurt. Others view punishment as a symbolic or "psychological" wound, for instance, the teacher who ridicules a student before the class. Many people view an event as punishing when they recognize that they themselves would be, or have seen others, actually or metaphorically bruised by the event. (A spanking would often be identified as a punishing activity, even though a particular youngster actually may solicit spankings because of the attention they yield. In this situation, spanking is not punishing for the child.)

Because of its ambiguity, the term *punishment* must be clarified prior to any meaningful discussion on the topic. To review, **punishment** is a procedure in which the presentation of a stimulus contingent on a behavior reduces the subsequent rate of the behavior (Azrin & Holz, 1966). Punishment can be said to have occurred only if the person's rate of emitting the treated behavior has been demonstrably reduced. Like reinforcement, punishment is defined solely by its effect on behavior. Any procedure is therefore identified as punishing if it involves presenting a contingent stimulus event that reduces the subsequent rate of the behavior it has followed.

If a father reprimands his child for interrupting, and the interruptions then cease, the reprimand has been punishing. If, however, interrupting continues unabated, the reprimand has not been punishing. In fact, if the interrupting behavior *increases* in rate, the reprimand has been *reinforcing*, rather than punishing. (Reprimands, verbal or nonverbal expressions of disapproval, are the most common form of punishment used by parents, teachers, employers, and peers [Van Houten & Doleys, 1983]).

Aversive Stimuli

The stimulus that functions as a punisher may be labeled an **aversive stimulus**.[1] In most instances, stimuli that operate as punishers also are rigorously avoided by the individual. Although that rule has occasional exceptions (Church, 1963; Solomon, 1964), we have elected to use the term *aversive stimulus* to apply to stimuli variously labeled *reductive* or *punishing*, inhibiting or to those whose termination is *negatively reinforcing*.

Unconditioned Aversive Stimuli

Some types of stimuli are punishing to just about everyone, even in the absence of conditioning. Forceful blows, intense electric shocks, noxious odors, and sudden exposure to overly brilliant lights and deafening sounds are examples. Should those stimuli consistently be experienced contingent on a specific behavior, the rate of the behavior usually diminishes (unless, through one's learning history, those intense stimuli lose their aversiveness, as in learning to enjoy listening to loud rock music). A small child who is harshly spanked for dashing out into the street will be less likely to repeat the act in the future. Like many of us, you may have learned to avoid touching a frayed electric cord the hard way—by getting shocked. The same principle applies to a child who was burned by touching a hot stove. Probably next time he goes to repair a machine, Sloppy will deactivate it first. In general, a stimulus that is aversive in the absence of any prior learning history is called an **unconditioned aversive** or **punishing stimulus**, abbreviated S^P in this book.

The human services literature is replete with examples of this type:

- *Contingent darkness* was used by Hewitt

---

[1] The spelling of *aversive* is frequently confused with that of *adverse*. Be sure to note this distinction.

(1965) in conjunction with a speech program for an autistic child.

- *Aversive tickling* (Greene & Hoats, 1971) was tried to reduce destructive head banging.
- *Lemon juice* was squirted into the mouth to treat arm biting and eye poking (Favell, McGimsey, & Jones, 1978), screaming, self-hitting, and hitting a body part against a hard object (Mayhew & Harris, 1979), and chronic rumination (i.e., "voluntary" or operant regurgitation of food) (Becker, Turner, & Sajwaj, 1978).
- A *cube of ice* was placed briefly on the cheeks, chin, and under the chin of profoundly retarded individuals to help diminish audible teeth grinding (bruxism) (Blount, Drabman, Wilson, & Stewart, 1982).
- *Aromatic ammonia* inhalants were presented under the nostrils to stop self-injury (Altman, Haavik, & Cook, 1978; Baumeister & Baumeister, 1978; Tanner & Zeiler, 1975) and aggression (Doke, Wolery, & Sumberg, 1983).
- *Water mist* has been sprayed at people to suppress pica (the persistent eating of nonnutritive substances such as flakes of paint, tacks, staples, crayons, strings, woven material, and cigarette butts) (Dorsey, Iwata, Ong, & McSween, 1980; Jenson, Rovner, Cameron, Petersen, & Kesler, 1985; Rojahn, McGonigle, Crucio, & Dixon, 1987).

Applying unconditioned aversive stimuli with dependent clients in places like schools, hospitals, clinics, or institutions, raises numerous legal, ethical, and practical issues, to be discussed in Chapter 28.

Conditioned Aversive Stimuli

Stimuli previously paired with powerful aversive events. Much in the same way that a formerly neutral stimulus acquires reinforcing properties (see Chapter 9), some stimuli may be conditioned as a result of being presented just before or along with powerful aversive stimuli. A good example of a **conditioned aversive (punishing) stimulus (S^P)** is the word "No," spoken in a loud, sharp tone. For most individuals this "No" has, in all likelihood, been paired with the delivery of another strongly aversive stimulus. Baby Bonnie's mother shouts "No!" as the child touches the hot stove. Both the loudness of the sound and the pain of the burn contribute to the child's learning the "meaning" of "No" (i.e., it has become a conditioned aversive stimulus for Baby Bonnie).

Any behavior followed by a loud, sharp "No" probably will diminish, at least temporarily, as long as it is paired occasionally with more powerful aversive stimuli. Other examples of conditioned aversive stimuli include frowns; gestures, like shaking a finger; or motions, like clenching a fist or swinging a hand as if preparing delivery of a spanking or a blow. Stimuli, like warnings and threats (S^D-s), presented repeatedly just before timeout, response cost, or other aversive events also may become conditioned aversive stimuli. Hineline (1984) informs us, as well, that depending on the prior history of the individual, particular reinforcement schedules can be aversive.

Stimuli paired with nonreinforcement. Frequently, punishment is paired with nonreinforcement. Marks in the Good Behavior Game, for instance, have accompanied loss of recreational time. That is how such previously neutral stimuli, like marks on a board, can acquire conditioned aversive properties. The stimuli are associated with a period of nonreinforcement. Recall how antecedent or contextual stimuli that have been paired with extinction begin to acquire aversive properties (S-deltas or S^Δs) (Azrin & Holz, 1966).

Clyde's mom asks him to go to his room to do his homework, where receiving attention or other reinforcers from friends and family is unlikely. The instruction to go to his room becomes aversive under those circumstances.

Ms. Charming repeatedly has requested that her superior, Ann Thrope, provide funds for tokens, back-up reinforcers, and recording equipment for her workshop program. Ms. Thrope never delivers. After a while, Ms. Charming begins to dislike Ms. Thrope and avoids joining her for lunch. Ms. Thrope's presence has become aversive.

Extrinsic and Intrinsic Aversive Stimuli

So far, the examples we have presented have been of the **extrinsic** type. The stimuli were *delivered socially or physically by an external agent*, as with reprimands from the boss, or painful shocks or burns from an electrical cord or hot stove. Intentionally designed punishment programs often involve managing stimuli of the "extrinsic" variety, for example, reprimanding any worker seen violating a safety practice or delivering a warning to a client who obviously is beginning to lose control.

Yet, just as reinforcers may be intrinsic to an act, so may aversive stimuli. Difficult or highly repetitive motions fit this category, as does total inaction, especially when no reinforcement follows, and when the rate of the behavior is obliged to occur far beyond its typical baseline range. (See Morse & Kelleher, 1977, for a discussion of this aspect.) Try doing a hundred push-ups, and unless you are in superb physical condition, you will understand the concept of **intrinsic aversiveness**. You will see several illustrations of the management of these types of aversive activities next, when we describe positive and negative practice, restitution, contingent effort, and response suppression procedures.

Aversive Activities

Contingent exertion is a procedure in which the individual is required to perform effortful exercises as a consequence of a targeted behavior (e.g., Luce et al., 1981). This exertion may take various forms. For instance, arm and hand exercises have been used to reduce inappropriate foot movements and vocalizations (Epstein, Doke, Sajwaj, Sorrell, & Rimmer, 1974); 10 minutes of window washing to decrease swearing (Fischer & Nehs, 1978); standing up and sitting down 10 times to eliminate aggressive acts and comments, such as "I'm going to step on your face" or "I'm going to kill you" (Luce, Delquadri, & Hall, 1980).

Probably you are acquainted with the procedure and may have used it as a disciplinary tool. That is what a coach is doing when he requires team members to run laps or do push-ups or sit-ups following transgressions. Military sergeants are notorious for ordering disciplinary routines such as trench digging, forced hikes, potato peeling, and sets of push-ups in order to turn their rookies into compliant soldiers. Probably everyone is familiar with teachers who require students to write "I will not...." or the correct form of misspelled words several hundred times. Many parents have been known to insist that their youngsters clean their rooms, do dishes, or do yard work as punishment. Judges have sentenced violators to make restitution by performing public service, cleaning streets, parks, or removing graffiti from walls.

Restitution training is a formal application of such recompense, with an added feature. It requires that offenders restore the environment to a condition the same as or better than before the misbehavior was committed, and the approach is a key element of a procedural package called **overcorrection** (Foxx & Azrin, 1972; 1973). For example, a student who has overturned his desk would first be told "No!" (a conditioned aversive stimulus), "You overturned your desk" (a specification of the behavior), immediately after which he would be required not only to put it back in its correct upright position but also to dust and clean it. A youth who marks up a wall is instructed not only to erase the marks but also to clean the entire wall.

Positive practice, the second component of overcorrection, stipulates that the miscreant *repeatedly practice* an acceptable alternative behavior. For example, the student who has overturned the desk would also be told to straighten, dust, and clean other desks in the room in addition to his own. The youth who has marked the wall additionally may be required to practice writing on appropriate materials, such as copying patterns or words onto a piece of paper. Any employee caught attempting to repair a machine without first deactivating it might be required to spend extra hours without compensation practicing the appropriate lock-out procedure and carrying out preventive maintenance procedures with several machines. Positive practice is intended to reeducate. In our examples the offenders are taught positive or correct ways of treating desks; where and how to use pencils, crayons, or markers; and how to follow the appropriate safety practices.

Foxx and Azrin (1973) have described a case with a girl, Tricia, in which they used positive practice but not restitution to treat her head-weaving. They reasoned that since head-weaving creates no environmental disruption, a restitutional overcorrection procedure would not be applicable as a treatment, whereas positive practice overcorrection could teach and motivate the girl to move her head only for functional reasons:

> Any time that Tricia began head-weaving, she was immediately given Functional Movement Training for five minutes. In beginning the training, the teacher used her hands to restrain Tricia's head. The teacher then instructed Tricia to move her head in one of three positions, up, down, or straight by stating, for example: "Tricia, head up." If Tricia did not immediately move her head in the desired direction, the teacher manually guided Tricia's head. Eventually, Tricia should respond to the verbal instructions

alone in order to avoid the trainer's guidance as in conditioned avoidance (Azrin, Holz, & Hake, 1963). Tricia was required to hold her head stationary for 15 seconds, at the end of which another instruction was given. If Tricia moved her head during the 15-second period, the trainer immediately restrained her head. As Tricia began following the directions, the teacher faded out the manual guidance, but continued to "shadow" Tricia's head with her hands. The instructions were given randomly to ensure that Tricia was learning each individual instruction and not a sequence of instructions (p. 7).

Work requirements like those have reduced many kinds of unwanted behavior, as reviewed by Foxx and Bechtel (1982) and Miltenberger and Fuqua (1981). The latter authors cited close to 100 studies in which rates of aggressive-disruptive, self-stimulatory, self-injurious, toileting, oral, and undesired educational-social behaviors were reduced with contingent exertion. To illustrate, in one study, clients involved in toilet training cleaned up traces of their accidents, washed their soiled clothing, showered themselves, and dressed in fresh clothing (Azrin & Foxx, 1971). In another, by having the participants both return the snacks they pirated and practice the positive action of giving their own snacks to their victims, institutionalized retarded adults were taught not to steal one another's food (Azrin & Wesolowski, 1974).

At one time, **negative practice** involved requiring the individual to engage in massed practice of the unwanted behavior noncontingently (Dunlap, 1928; 1930). In that form it was both successful (Yates, 1958) and unsuccessful (Feldman & Werry, 1966) in reducing tics, and either partially successful or unsuccessful in attempting to reduce chronic bruxism (grinding of teeth) (Ayer, 1976; Glaros & Rao, 1977; Heller & Forgione, 1975). Nevertheless, using a longer practice regimen (15 seconds followed by 15 seconds of rest, repeated 10 times immediately before going to bed as opposed to 5-second intervals repeated 6 times during the day) Vasta and Wortman (1988) were successful in using negative practice to treat chronic nocturnal bruxism of a 22-year-old female college student.

Probably you recognize one reason for these mixed results: the nature of the contingency arrangements. If an activity is to operate as an effective punisher, it needs to occur as a direct consequence of the offense (Azrin, 1956; Azrin et al., 1963; Van Houten, 1983). Therefore, Foxx (1982) and Secan and Egel (1986) suggested that the use of negative practice should occur contingent on the unwanted behavior. In light of this, we offer a revised definition of negative practice: *requiring the individual repeatedly to practice the unwanted target behavior for a predetermined time period contingent upon the emission of that behavior.*

Secan and Egel (1986) implemented negative practice contingently on three developmentally handicapped students' self-stimulatory hand-clapping. As soon as a youngster's hands made contact, a staff member would say, "If you want to clap, you will clap" (p. 33), and the youngster was instructed to clap until he had clapped 60 times. If he did not comply, clapping was physically guided until 60 claps were completed. Teachers reported advantages ". . . that the procedure was implemented throughout the day with success, took very little time to implement (approximately 45–60 seconds), and, with these students, did not result in side effects such as aggression or resistance" (p. 36).

In addition, a reduction in the self-stimulatory hand-clapping provided greater access to reinforcing activities such as catching, rolling, and throwing a ball. (As mentioned elsewhere in the text, providing a reinforcing milieu is essential for maintenance of behavioral change.)

Naturally, negative practice would not be used for dangerous behaviors, only for those that can be tolerated at lower rates. Our parents applied the procedure for swearing and door slamming. Negative practice probably works for a couple of reasons: extinction and satiation. The response occurs repeatedly without extrinsic reinforcement, and the person begins to satiate on whatever conditioned intrinsic reinforcement it contains. Hearing yourself say "Damn" or slamming the door a hundred times does begin to get old.

Another aversive activity (or technically, nonactivity) involves *immobilization.* For example, Bitgood, Crowe, Suarez, and Peters (1980) successfully used immobilization to reduce stereotyped or self-stimulatory behaviors of four retarded, autistic children. The procedure consisted of grasping the child's forearms from behind and holding them at his or her side for 15 seconds. No prompts or verbal cautions preceded the immobilization, and the force used was only that necessary to keep the arms touching the side of the body.

The "freeze" technique also fits under this category. Ayllon and his colleagues (e.g., Allison & Ayllon, 1980) have applied the method to coach football, gymnastics, and tennis. Essentially, trainees are instructed to "freeze" during their execution of a play, holding the position long enough to receive necessary corrective feedback. This immobility probably was aversive to some extent, as suggested by the negative comments of the players, but it also had the advantage of allowing the correction to occur at the right place in the chain.

Notice that immobilization, a form of restraint, differs from the way restraint typically is used to manage violence. The former occurs briefly and contingent upon an unwanted behavior, whereas the latter, whether physical (e.g., camisoles or "straitjackets") or chemical (e.g., tranquilizing drugs), incapacitates the person for prolonged time periods. Immobilization is designed to be educative; noncontingent restraint is a control device, not a behavior analytic procedure.

On analysis, single instances of any of the

activities described in this section would not be aversive in and of themselves. The aversiveness derives from the fact that they are required to occur at a rate or in a form that differs markedly from that typical of the individual. With **contingent exercise** and positive and negative practice, the required rate is higher; with immobilization the rate is much lower. Restitution and positive practice involve encouraging behaviors rarely exhibited by the person; immobilization prevents the occurrence of behaviors expressed too often. So again we see the value of assessing baseline performance. Without that information, success may be compromised.

Variables Influencing the Effectiveness of Punishment

This discussion concerns a number of variables that have been identified as influencing the impact of punishment. They include escape opportunities; temporal and scheduling properties; intensity of the stimulus; and the effect of combining punishment with other operations, like reinforcement, extinction, and stimulus control, among others.

Opportunity to Escape

Escape is a natural reaction to aversive stimuli. If the individual succeeds in leaving the situation, the contingency manager loses the opportunity to apply any procedure, of course. The effect of punishment is more acute when escape is blocked (Azrin, Hake, Holz, Hutchinson, 1965; Dinsmoor & Campbell, 1956). If Pearl runs out of the room instead of participating in an overcorrection routine for self-stimulation, the procedure can have no effect; were escape prevented, the procedure would have a good chance of working.

Some escape behaviors merit encouragement, however, because they are acceptable alternatives to the unwanted target behavior. Permitting Lucretia to escape from contingent

observation, when she has been compliant and indicates her readiness to play nicely, is one example. An appropriate way for Pearl to escape overcorrection would be by cooperating in the positive-practice routine and returning to active participation in instructional tasks, rather than to self-stimulation. Such situations actually are episodes of negative reinforcement (the removal of aversive stimuli contingent on the behavior). Naturally, when appropriate escape behaviors are emitted for a time, they should be positively reinforced. (Guard against making acceptable escape behaviors the only occasion for reinforcement, though. Shortly you will see why.)

Quality

In reading about the various classes of aversive stimuli, you learned about many types. Yet, just the way reinforcing stimuli are idiosyncratic to individuals, so are aversives. Additionally, as we mention later on, whether a given aversive stimulus will be effective at any one time can depend on the context in which it is delivered. Probably you have anticipated at least one of the reasons why different stimuli influence people distinctively: their learning histories. Conditioning makes the difference in terms of whether any particular formerly neutral event (or sometimes, even a primary aversive, like hitting one's head or being restrained) begins to acquire reinforcing properties. The same is true of conditioned aversive stimuli. In some households, arguing is considered terribly noxious; in others, it is an activity enthusiastically embraced. Some children respond to reprimands by melting, whereas others appear oblivious to scolding, no matter how harsh.

The individual nature of aversive stimuli poses a problem for policymakers attempting to restrict their use. The temptation is to categorize such stimuli according to their apparent degrees of intrusiveness or restrictiveness. Yet for any singular person, such arbitrary designations may be inappropriate. For instance, Favell et al. (1978) found that physically restraining some profoundly retarded persons for self-injurious behavior functioned not as a punisher but as a positive reinforcer. Only the functional effect on a given individual's behavior within a particular context permits the term "punishing" to be applied.

Schedule and Delay

Like reinforcement, punishment is more effective when the aversive stimulus is applied every time the offense occurs (Acker & O'Leary, 1988) and as soon as possible afterward (Azrin, 1956; Azrin et al., 1963; Zimmerman & Ferster, 1963). For example, punishment should be applied consistently and immediately whenever an employee is seen acting recklessly. Such a procedure should reduce the behavior quickly and help the person to discriminate more rapidly the types of risk-taking that are not acceptable. Suppose a toddler has run into the street.

> To teach him the danger associated with being in the street, the child's parent might give the child one sharp spank as he picks the child up out of the street. This spanking would teach the child to associate the middle of the street with danger, but a spanking after he is safely back in the curb is poor timing. The child should associate the street with danger; the curb, with safety. (Krumboltz & Krumboltz, 1972, p.206)

Administering punishment consistently and immediately may not always be feasible. When confronted with such a situation, consider *recreating the episode*, so at a latter time the early links in the undesired chain of behaviors are paired with the punisher, as in two successful studies with developmentally delayed and psychotic children (Rolider & Van Houten, 1985b; Van Houten & Rolider, 1988). This procedure was used with a 17-year-old developmentally delayed girl to reduce her compulsive stealing and hoarding. Planted and stolen items that

were found during a check were returned and the scene re-created and followed by punitive consequences. Each behavior was suppressed after 2 to 4 sessions.

Rolider and Van Houten (1985b) used a similar procedure to diminish children's tantrums successfully in public places. The tantrum was tape recorded, an illustrative segment of about 1 minute extracted, and several hours later their parents replayed the recording at home. A timeout procedure was implemented following each of 4 repetitions. Van Houten and Rolider (1988) have concluded that using this type of punishment procedure has several advantages: rapid behavioral reduction, enabling punishment of behaviors that are not easily detected or dealt with when they occur; and permitting the behavior analyst or someone trained in the use of the procedure to apply it reliably and safely.

Be alert to the dangers of using punishment belatedly and inconsistently within a given context though. Regarding inconsistency, recognize that each time the individual gets away with the infraction, both positive and negative reinforcement are the likely consequences—and that will encourage a repetition of the misbehavior. Sloppy had gotten into the habit of not bothering to deactivate machinery before he serviced it, because he had many successful experiences in taking that sort of shortcut. In the absence of other benign programming, such as reinforcing consistent compliance with lockout routines (Sulzer-Azaroff et al., 1990), or aversive programming, such as a costly penalty, only a very intense punishing episode, like an injury, has a chance of overriding the weakness of the punishing contingency. (Even so, we know of several carpenters who have lost fingers not only once but on several occasions. The negative reinforcement of taking the easy route must have overshadowed the impact of the intermittent injuries.)

Delayed punishment, too, has its pitfalls. When the aversive stimuli are delivered at a different time, the behavior immediately preceding the punishment, rather than the unwanted one, may be impacted. When Timmy's dad returns from work, the boy's mother regales her husband with tales of the child's misdeeds, insisting that dad discipline the child. The main effect of dad's disciplining is to prompt Timmy to avoid his dad. Of course, rules can aid in bridging the gap, "Wait till your father gets home and he hears what you've done. He'll let you have it." But, as we have seen, contingencies tend to be more powerful than rules in governing behavior. So the moral of the story is, if you are unable to use it every time and immediately after the unwanted behavior occurs (or find a way to bridge the gap), don't use punishment. Otherwise you might cause more difficulties than you solve.

Density

Just as the reinforcing value of a stimulus will lessen with overuse, so will the suppressive value of an aversive stimulus that is experienced too often. The person begins to adapt or *habituate* to the stimulus. Consequently, you need to avoid extended periods of punishment (Azrin, 1956). For example, people eventually learn to tune out constant nagging. Similarly, children become insensitive to overly frequent spankings or reprimands unless the aversive stimuli become extremely harsh. This is the sort of phenomenon that leads to physical or psychological abuse—one more reason why punishment is best reserved for only the most serious infractions.

To some extent, habituation can be avoided by varying the aversive stimuli. For example, one study (Charlop, Burgio, Iwata, & Ivancic, 1988) found that developmentally delayed children engaged in inappropriate behaviors less frequently when varied punishers were presented, such as overcorrection, timeout, or the word "No," instead of a single punisher. The authors postulated several reasons for this effect:

- Individuals might adapt to the repeated presentation of a single punisher.
- Perhaps the use of multiple punishers increased the salience of the consequences.
- The literature on avoidance behavior (e.g., Dunlap & Johnson, 1985; Sidman, 1953) indicates that "unpredictable contingencies promote a more steady rate of avoidance behavior" (p. 94).

"The varied-punisher condition may be viewed as a combination of a continuous schedule of punishment with the unpredictability of specific punishers, thus maximizing the effect" (p. 95).

Intensity

One property of aversive stimulation makes it all the more dangerous—that all other factors being equal, the more intense the aversive stimulus, the more powerful its effect. A sharp retort is more influential than a mild one; so is a harder blow or a longer regimen of effortful exercises. Depending on the learning history of the individual, low-intensity aversive stimuli may or may not be effective. Those who have rarely experienced that particular form of punishment in that particular context may be influenced by the mildest of aversives, whereas those with long histories of punishment in a setting hardly may be affected by the harshest of aversive stimuli, due to habituation. In general, though, all else being equal, mild punishment produces a less durable effect than the more severe variety.

Organisms adapt easily to repetitions of mild aversive stimuli and to those that gradually increase in intensity (as many teen-agers adapt to loud music), whereas strong aversive stimuli can produce enduring effects (Azrin & Holtz, 1966; Boe & Church, 1967). In a specific instance, a strong admonition may stop a particular behavior for a longer period of time than would several mild, weak rebukes or several of increasing potency. A firmly stated "No" usually is more effective than a shake of the head followed by increasingly stronger head shakes and an ever-louder "No." So the least effective approach is to increase the severity of the stimulus gradually, instead of presenting it at an intensity strong enough to permit it to produce durable suppression.

Milder punishment works better with behaviors not well established in the person's behavioral repertoire. As mentioned earlier, the frequency and schedule with which the behavior has been reinforced influences its strength. A behavior that is not well established obviously is easier to eliminate, so mild punishment should be sufficient to eliminate weak behaviors. Conversely, probably more intense punishment would be required to reduce well-established performances or to override their reinforcing effects. For example, when little Bonnie reaches to grab the tail of her dog, Tiger, for the first time, mild punishment, like a simple "No" or head shake, probably would successfully eliminate the behavior. If Bonnie habitually torments her reinforcingly responsive Tiger, however, mild punishment probably will be insufficient to override the effects of the reinforcer.

Another way to avoid resorting to an intense aversive stimulus is periodically to pair the mild one with an unconditioned punisher. For example, visual screening used to reduce a severely retarded child's aggression, destructiveness, and loud screeching, became more effective after it occasionally was paired with aromatic ammonia (Dixon et al., 1989).

Concurrent Contingencies

Combining punishment and extinction. Punishment works more rapidly in combination with *extinction* than when applied alone (Azrin & Holz, 1961; 1966). Rapid results dictate that reinforcers maintaining behavior be removed and made contingent on only desirable alternative behaviors. Recall that a stimulus acquires conditioned aversive properties when it signals that no reinforcement is forthcoming. Such conditioning would be delayed or prevented if the behavior received reinforcement simultaneously from some other source, such as peer approval or speeding up the completion of the task.

Similarly, the effectiveness of a punishing event will be diluted if the behavior is followed by both aversive and reinforcing stimuli. Investigators have found that under such circumstances offenses like blurting out (Acker & O'Leary, 1988) or aggression (Deur & Parke, 1970; Sawin & Parke, 1979) tend to persist rather than decline, and become more resistant to extinction. Long verbal reprimands yield adult attention that might serve as a reinforcer for some children. Perhaps this is why Abramowitz, O'Leary, and Futtersak (1988) found that for 7 hyperactive second and third graders, "short reprimands resulted in significantly lower rates of off-task behavior than did long reprimands" (p. 243).

The person whose disruptive behavior provokes not only an aversive scolding but also the approval of peers will be more likely to disrupt in the future than if peer approval was lacking. Sometimes, however, removing reinforcement for engaging in a specific behavior is extremely difficult, especially when the act itself provides immediate reinforcement. In such cases, externally delivered punishment will contribute little other than to teach the person to be more discreet. Circumstances like these probably are at the root of many of our most serious social problems, such as theft, rape, child molestation, unsafe sex, substance abuse, and some forms of self-injury. Behaviors of this variety can yield the individual rapid and powerful reinforcement, whereas any punishment that others administer is usually delayed and intermittent—and, as a result, not too effective. This partially explains why recidivism rates are so high.

Combining punishment with Alt-R. For behaviors of this nature, alternative reductive methods are preferable, especially when opportunities are provided for the individual to achieve equivalent or stronger reinforcement from more acceptable sources. In the example of stealing, this goal might be accomplished by offering alternative socially desirable behaviors through, say, training in a skill that is both intrinsically reinforcing and highly remunerative. As long as successful thieves have no socially acceptable way to earn the coveted things in life, they probably will continue to steal. Only if thieves escape from punishment *and* engage in heavily reinforced acceptable alternative behaviors will they likely cease stealing. Behavior therapy journals (see, for example, *Behavior Therapy*, *Behavior Therapy and Experimental Psychiatry*, and *Behaviour Research and Therapy*) have published some very promising experimental and case reports of procedural combinations effective in changing antisocial sexual and drug-abuse behaviors. Many of the procedures promote alternative or incompatible behaviors or both—sometimes in conjunction with even more effective reductive procedures.

Alt-R also can enhance the effect of mild punishment. We have already mentioned that very intense punishment will reduce well-established undesirable behaviors more effectively than milder intensities of punishment, whereas milder punishment generally reduces well-established behavior only temporarily. Milder punishment does produce a more *lasting* reduction of the behavior, however, if the individual simultaneously is given access to an alternative reinforceable behavior (Azrin & Holz, 1966). Mild aversive stimuli, like a ''No,'' a frown, or a head shake, may be sufficient to stop the occurrence of a behavior, provided that the individuals already have desirable alternatives in their repertoires and the environment offers them access to, and reinforcement for, engaging in those behaviors.

Developing Masochism. How can events that are almost universally aversive become reinforcers? Some people fail to receive sufficient reinforcement in the more usual ways for accomplishments, work, and so forth. Instead, reinforcement occurs only after they engage in and are punished for a particular act. Tim's mother is frequently occupied with other things and tends to ignore him except when he hurts himself or his younger brother, or does some damage. The ensuing spanking or scolding imbues her with remorse, so she cuddles him and says that she is sorry for punishing him. Just as even moderately strong shocks can begin to serve a reinforcing function under laboratory conditions (Holz & Azrin, 1961), Tim soon learns that hurting himself is one sure way to obtain affection from his mother.

Youngsters with preoccupied parents, teachers, or care givers often do similar types of things as attention-getting devices. Though punished, the misbehavior will persist if it is the primary way in which they can receive reinforcement.

These examples illustrate how difficult removing all sources of reinforcement for a punished behavior can be. As long as such sources of reinforcement remain, the effectiveness of the punishment will be limited.

Contextual Factors

Earlier you saw how receiving punishment temporarily can turn the opportunity to deliver punishment into a reinforcer for the recipient. Now, we need to consider establishing operations as they impact on the extent to which punishment works. Probably the person's physical state, such as duration of sleep or food deprivation might make a difference, especially when reinforcers for the unwanted response are influenced by those circumstances. Many of us have had the experience of seeing a tired child respond to a reprimand with a tantrum, instead of meekly obeying in his typical way.

Discriminative stimuli, such as the time, setting, agent, rules, and so on, can make a big difference too in how successfully punishment works. Close proximity appears to increase the effectiveness of reprimands (Van Houten, Nau, MacKenzie-Keating, Sameoto, & Colavecchia, 1982), as does a fixed stare and a firm grasp of the child's upper arm (Van Houten et al., 1982). (Similarly, smiling and giving a pat on the back have been shown to increase the effectiveness of praise [Kazdin & Klock, 1973; Kazdin et al., 1975]). Also, as Van Houten and Doleys (1983) speculate, using specific reprimands probably increases the effectiveness of punishment, just as specifying the desired behavior while praising increases the effectiveness of praise (Bernhardt & Forehand, 1975; Goetz & Salmonson, 1972).

As with other procedures, when the conditions under which punishment will be delivered are explicitly clear, its effectiveness is more powerful: "Do not smoke. Violators will be prosecuted" functions as an S^{D-}, informing people that smoking in that situation will probably be punished. Phrases like "Falling rock zone," "High voltage lines—danger"; symbols like those in Figure 27.1; and the sound so familiar to dwellers in tornado county—the tornado warning siren—have a similar function. As we described in Chapter 16, the S^{D-} develops in almost exactly the same manner as the S^{Δ}, by being consistently present when certain consequences follow a behavior. Here a given response is consistently punished when those stimuli are present.

The impact of a given episode of punishment also may depend on the *agent* delivering it. In the opera *Boris Godounov,* in response to Tsar Boris' threat: ". . . But should you lie to me, I promise you a death so terrible, so frightful, that Tsar Ivan himself will shudder in his grave in horror! . . ." Prince Schuisky replies "I fear no death—but fear [only] *your* displeasure" (Moussorgsky, 1874).

Each of us has people in our lives whose approbation or disapproval is terribly important; others' opinions matter hardly at all. Just a hint of dissatisfaction from the former can be more punishing than a severe reaction from the latter. In all likelihood, those whose reactions count are people who are in control of many important reinforcing contingencies in our lives: our spouses, parents, children, bosses, and close friends. Although experimental evidence regarding this parameter of punishment remains to be studied, the results of the few experiments known to us on source of feedback (e.g., Fox & Sulzer-Azaroff, 1989) hint that the agent who delivers punishment could make a difference.

Summary

Punishment is an integral part of everyone's lives, but it is used more frequently and less effectively than it should be. One reason is that using punishment can be reinforcing to the agent because of its rapid results and the intrinsically rewarding value of lashing out when the agent has just been the recipient of punishment himself or herself. By definition, punishment reduces behavior, and the aversive stimuli integral to punishment come in many forms, including unconditioned, conditioned, intrinsic, and extrinsic physical events and activities. Contingent exertion, an aversive activity, is a key property of the overcorrection procedure, whereas negative practice and immobilization are other aversive activities.

To understand the impact of punishment, become familiar with the variables that are

Figure 27.1

known to influence the effectiveness of the procedure. Such variables are the opportunity to escape; appropriate quality for the individual; schedule; delay; density; intensity; concurrent contingencies in effect, including availability of reinforcement for alternative behaviors; con-

textual factors, such as establishing operations, setting events, and agent; and others.

Applying punishment in a structured way, however, needs to be reserved, until you are familiar with its advantages and pitfalls. The next chapter addresses those issues.

Chapter 28

Applying Aversive Procedures

GOALS

After completing this chapter, you should be able to:

1. Identify the advantages of using punishment.
2. List, compare, and contrast the advantages of overcorrection with other forms of punishment.
3. Specify the disadvantages of punishment and discuss their implications for using the procedure.
4. List the specific disadvantages of aversive activities and comment on the implications.
5. Describe the circumstances under which punishment might be defensible. Justify your position.
6. List and discuss the importance of the "considerations in applying aversive stimuli effectively."
7. Discuss the pros and cons of applying highly aversive stimuli, such as electric shock, and the precautions that should be associated with their use.
8. Explain why it is important to consider the characteristics of punishment in designing and conducting the program.
9. Explain why punitive procedures should not be used unless combined with reinforcement of alternative behaviors.
10. Discuss the importance of continuously monitoring a range of behaviors while punishment is being used, and why programming for generalization and maintenance is essential.
11. Define and illustrate reinforced positive practice, and discuss the pros and cons of using it.

In the past several years advocates and opponents of aversive procedures have stirred a great deal of debate about whether the technique should be used. The controversy probably is motivated by sensational media coverage of several cases in which extraordinary aversive methods were used to reduce the severely maladaptive behaviors of developmentally delayed clients. Advocacy groups for the developmentally disabled, such as the Association for Retarded Citizens and the Association for Persons with Severe Handicaps, have taken a position opposed to the use of *any* aversive behavioral methods. Other groups have argued just as fervently that aversives need to be included among the alternatives for providing dependent people with their reasonable rights to effective treatment.

From our point of view, however, whether aversive stimuli should be used is not the question, because they are an integral part of human existence. No policies or edicts can remove the aversive qualities inherent in failure or disappointment, having one's options blocked by a limited or inappropriate repertoire of responses, or receiving disapproval or cues that extinction or other less preferred consequences are on the way. Nor, apparently, is our society ready to dispense with its systems of punishing criminal, dangerous, or disruptive behavior. Mechanisms in place for maintaining reasonable discipline in work and educational settings will not be discarded.

Instead, the main point at issue is how the *purposeful* application of aversive stimuli needs to be governed, especially with dependent and/or nonconsenting people. As we proceed toward that objective, first we shall outline the general advantages and disadvantages of aversive procedures. Next, we summarize a set of guidelines for effectively implementing these procedures, including recommendations for preserving clients' human and legal rights.

Advantages of Punishment

Effectively Stopping Behavior

Numerous cases have been reported in the human and animal literature to demonstrate that the presentation of aversive stimuli can effectively stop behavior—which is no surprise, because the punishment procedure is defined by its successful reduction in rates of the treated behavior. (See Azrin & Holz, 1966; Forehand & Baumeister, 1976; Hineline, 1984; Kazdin & Wilson, 1978; Guess, Helmstetter, Turnbull, & Knowlton, 1987; Matson & Taras, 1989, for reviews.) The kinds of target behaviors diminished by punishment have included stereotypy, self-injury, aggression toward others or the environment, and disruption. The procedure also has been used to supplement development of adaptive behaviors such as discrimination, attention, and word recognition (Guess et al, 1987).

Not every report cites success, however. According to Guess et al. (1987), a substantial number of clients' behaviors worsened. How is that possible, given the definition of punishment? As we already have seen, sometimes what appears to us to be a punishing stimulus may not actually serve that function with a given individual in a particular context; or the aversive stimulus may not be powerful enough to overcome the countervailing reinforcement for the same behavior.

By recognizing that punishment effectively reduces the rate of a behavior, you should begin to understand why sometimes a person fails to express a desired response you know he is capable of emitting. Punishment may be the culprit. Sloppy Smith knows how to wear his hard hat and safety glasses, but he doesn't because wearing them is punishing. They are a nuisance and whenever he does use them, his fellow workers razz him. Shrinking Violet used to volunteer to read to the class, but she doesn't any more. Did she have some sort of "traumatic" experience, such as her teacher embarrassing her before her friends? In those cases, heavy doses of reinforcement of successive approximations may be the best recourse, as demonstrated in several safety studies (e.g., Hopkins et al., 1986; Sulzer-Azaroff, 1982; 1987). Reinforcement of safe practices obviated the need for using any punishment, because workers complied with safety practices increasingly.

Rapidly and Durably Stopping the Behavior

Occasionally, you need to change dangerous behavior rapidly—to stop a child from running into a busy street or maneuvering to push another child over a guard rail. In addition to restraining the individual, an intense punishing stimulus, like a loud, sharp verbal reprimand or a slap, may be appropriate because *optimal* application of punishment offers the advantage of rapidly and durably halting the behavior (Azrin, 1960). In their review of 20 years of literature on punishment and other methods for reducing the problem behaviors of developmentally delayed persons, Matson and Taras (1989) concluded that aversive procedures produced rapid and significant maintenance of treatment over a month's span or longer. Some examples follow:

- A five-year-old retarded client was inducing hundreds of damaging epileptic seizures daily by blinking and moving his hands rapidly before his eyes. Aversive consequences rapidly reduced those behaviors (Wright, 1973).
- Dangerously malnourished patients' persistent vomiting (Kohlenberg, 1970) and ruminating (Cunningham & Linscheid, 1976) and clients' violent aggression (Foxx et al., 1986a) have been reduced rapidly by means of electric shock.

Later, the ethical and legal aspects of using

stimuli of this sort will be discussed. In a number of cases, response suppression has taken considerably longer, some up to 176 hours (Guess et al., 1987).

Overcorrection procedures can produce very rapid and long-lasting effects. In one report, Foxx and Azrin commented that "Overcorrection procedures reduced self-stimulation substantially on the first day and to a near zero level by the end of ten days and sometimes sooner" (1973, p. 11). They also found that aggression, disruption (1972), and self-stimulation (1973) were reduced more rapidly, completely, and durably with overcorrection than with timeout, social or physical punishment (disapproval or slaps), or reinforcement of competing behavior.

Those findings probably result from the fact that the overcorrection procedure exchanged the maladaptive behaviors for new adaptive responses apt to be supported by the natural environment. However, Foxx and Livesay (1984) have pointed out that in contrast to most individuals, the reductive effects of overcorrection are not likely to be long-lasting for very "low-functioning" people. They offer several possible reasons: First, due to their severely limited behavioral repertoires, low-functioning individuals tend to express fewer competing reinforceable behaviors, so adequate naturally occurring environmental support is lacking. Additionally, should the person's maladaptive behavior have returned after a period of time, staff may fail to reimplement the complex and time-consuming overcorrection procedure, reverting instead to less demanding (and less effective) methods used previously, such as timeout or physical restraint (Foxx & Livesay, 1984).

Nevertheless, according to studies reviewed by Guess et al. (1987), 71% reported durable effects of punishment in reducing self-injury. But some of the follow-up assessments were carried out for less than a year, so this issue is far from resolved.

Facilitating Adaptive Behavior

Can punishment promote constructive outcomes, either directly or collaterally? According to Marshall (1965) punishment can inform students about the acceptability of their conduct, and deportment often improves when objectionable behavior is punished and preferred behavior reinforced. For example, Pfiffner and O'Leary (1987) found that following a period of enhanced positive consequences, students who received firm, brief, specific reprimands contingent on off task behavior rapidly began to increase their time on-task and improve the accuracy of their academic performance. Once these gains were established, *gradually* (not abruptly) shifting over to a primarily positive approach permitted the improvement to maintain successfully.

Overcorrection is designed specifically to be educative by including the restitutional and positive practice elements. The literature, however, is mixed on the extent to which this purpose has been achieved (Carey & Bucher, 1986; Foxx & Bechtel, 1982; Miltenberger & Fuqua, 1981). Successful examples include:

- Normal, retarded, and severely learning-disabled children and adolescents who improved their spelling (Foxx & Jones, 1978; Ollendick et al., 1980; Stewart & Singh, 1986).
- Developmentally delayed adult clients learning vocational and self-care skills (Carey & Bucher, 1981; 1983; 1986).
- Delayed children improving oral reading proficiency (Singh, 1987; Singh & Singh, 1986; Singh, Singh, & Winton, 1984).
- Autistic children learning appropriate toy play (Wells, Forehand, Hickey, & Green, 1977).
- Hearing-impaired and multiply handicapped kindergarten and normal preschool children sharing materials more frequently (Barton & Osborn, 1978).

Perhaps because overcorrection is explicitly designed to have an educative component, school personnel, administrators, parents, the public, and subjects prefer it to other aversive activities (Foxx & Bechtel, 1982; Foxx & Jones, 1978; Matson, Stephens, & Horne, 1978; Matson, Horne, Ollendick, & Ollendick, 1979; Ollendick et al., 1980; Polvinale & Lutzker, 1980; Webster & Azrin, 1973).

Unlike other forms of punishment, neither restitution nor positive practice model delivery of aversive stimuli. Rather, the behavior modeled is positive and constructive. For instance, practicing being polite as a consequence of rudeness might also be instructive to peer observers.

Sometimes anecdotal or experimental evidence indicates that recipients of punishment have collaterally improved adaptive skills, such as appropriate play and improved attending to environmental events. Newsom, Favell, and Rincover (1983) have described a number of instances in which developmentally disabled children's toy play increased in conjunction with a reduction in their rates of self-stimulation. Similarly, they reported that eye contact, attention to task, and attention to peers and surroundings in general have improved as a side effect of punishment. Facilitation of social interactions and cooperation is, according to Newsom et al. (1983), ". . . the most frequently noted side effect of punishment" (p. 302). Cases cited included those of clients whose reduced aggression, destructiveness, self-injury, and rumination was followed by enhanced social responsiveness or cooperation. Of the 25 studies with aversive components they reviewed, Matson and Taras (1989) cited that 96% resulted in positive side effects, such as weight gain, improved self-help, social interactions, and responsiveness to the environment, plus reduced crying and disrupting.

Instructive to Peers

A behavior is more likely to be imitated in a situation in which it is followed either by no consequences or by reinforcement (Bandura,

1965a; 1965b). When a misbehavior is punished, however, others are less likely to copy the unwanted act in that context. As a case in point, when some students were reprimanded for being disruptive, others disrupted less (Van Houten et al., 1982).

After witnessing his accident, you can wager that Sloppy's co-workers will be sure to abide by proper lock-out procedures, for a while at least. Seeing the behavior punished causes the others to be less apt to commit similar transgressions. They learn the conditions under which punishment is likely to be forthcoming, and those stimuli develop discriminative properties that inhibit the behavior under those circumstances.

Possible Convenience to Managers

Results can be accomplished quickly and with little effort using tactile aversive stimuli, such as shock, ammonia inhalants, water mist, lemon juice, or tickling (Guess et al, 1987). On the other hand, contingent exercise, positive or negative practice, and restitution activities require much more of an investment.

Imagine why many staff prefer to use the former types!

Disadvantages of Punishment

In a series of elegant studies, Hutchinson (1977) and his colleagues have demonstrated the predictable sequence of side effects to punishment. Besides suppressing the punished response, other reactions occur reliably when aversive stimuli are delivered. This course of reactions has been found to repeat itself across many species, including volunteer human subjects, when escape is blocked:

1. When the delivery of punishment is signaled in advance, the individual accelerates its rates of scanning the environment, manipulating objects, and locomoting.

2. Immediately prior to and during the delivery of the aversive stimulus, the organism "freezes," ceasing to respond altogether.

3. Immediately afterward, biting or other forms of aggression occur; otherwise, manual manipulations and drinking elevate.

This information helps us to understand why, in addition to its apparent benefits, punishment can have serious disadvantages,[1] especially withdrawal, general response suppression, and aggression. While Matson and Taras (1989) argue that their review of 382 applied studies with the developmentally disabled does not support the contention that side effects frequently accompany aversive methods, a number of instances have been documented, including stimulus generalization and behavioral contrast. Analysts also worry about imitation; peer reactions; negative "self-esteem"; risk of abuse through overuse by staff; and a variety of social concerns such as ethical, safety, and legal issues. These factors combine to make punishment the most controversial of all behavior modification procedures.

Provoking Withdrawal

Generally, individuals will attempt to withdraw in response to punishment. The literature has indicated repeatedly that an organism will escape from a punishing situation if possible (Azrin et al., 1965; Hutchinson, 1977). You probably have seen exaggerated instances of this phenomenon illustrated in cartoons and situation comedies: The victim of a nagging spouse stomping out of the house; the severely rebuked child heading around the corner carrying his hobo pack; the employee who quits after being chewed out by the boss. Examples from everyday life are just as common: the staff member whose efforts are regularly criticized is often absent or late and may eventually resign; the student who is repeatedly repri-

---

[1] For an amusing set of illustrations of punishment in the course of daily life, see R. Mager's film: *Who Did What to Whom?*, issued by Research Press, Champaign, Illinois.

manded develops feigned or actual illnesses, cuts class, or drops out of school altogether. Children avoid adults who rely on punitive methods of control (Morris & Redd, 1975; Redd, Morris, & Martin, 1975). Escape also may be symbolic or indirect, rather than literal. For example, the student may doodle or hum, or the spouse turn away and sulk in response to criticism. In all cases, the social process is disrupted, and communication breaks down.

Suppressing Responses

A woman whose close relative is gravely ill waits agitatedly. When the phone rings, she stiffens. After discouraging news, she puts the phone down, and instead of returning to her normal daily routine, sits and stares out the window. The aversiveness of the circumstances immobilizes her. Yes, ongoing aversive circumstances can suppress responding. Jones, Simmons, and Frankel (1974) reported that while an autistic girl was undergoing a shock regimen for self-injury, she stopped eating. So when you see a student, employee, patient, or client being immobile, try to detect whether aversive stimuli are in operation.

Promoting Aggression

Extinction already is known to us to be a precursor to aggression. Punishment is another. Identifying factors that promote aggression is critical to our understanding of the world and to our control over our own lives, to the fulfillment of our responsibilities and protection of society. Young children who are aggressive have an increased likelihood of " . . . criminal behavior, number of moving traffic violations, convictions for driving while intoxicated, aggressiveness toward spouses" (Eron, 1987, p. 439) and punishing their own children.

Both people and animals tend to become aggressive in response to aversive stimulation, especially when escape is blocked (Hutchinson, 1977). In laboratory studies, Azrin, Hutchinson, and Hake (1963) have shown that, on de-

livery of shock, normally friendly monkeys will begin to fight fiercely, and Azrin (1964) has demonstrated similar responses to aversive stimulation by a wide range of animals. Oliver, West, and Sloane (1974) discovered that when volunteer human subjects were shocked, their rates of aggression increased ninefold over baseline. Hutchinson (1977) found that human subjects reacted to shock with biting or jaw clenching, just like members of other species.

Eron (1987) has noted that in the natural home environment, low levels of reinforcement and high levels of punishment have been related to excessive proportions of aggression in school by eight-year-olds, whereas Mayer and his colleagues (Mayer & Butterworth, 1979; 1981; Mayer et al., 1983; Mayer, Nafpaktitis, Butterworth, & Hollingsworth, 1987; Mayer & Sulzer-Azaroff, 1990) have discovered that vandalism rates in schools have corelated positively with a heavy reliance on punitive disciplinary techniques and with unsuitable academic assignments. Presumably the latter are punishing because they either are insufficiently or overly challenging. Similarly, Carr, Newsom, and Binkoff (1980) established that people often use counteraggression to terminate the aversive stimuli inflicted by others, and Berkowitz and his colleagues (Berkowitz, 1983; Berkowitz, Cochran, & Embree, 1981) have found that aversive stimulation induces the victim to harm others. Numerous instances of "punishment-induced aggression" also emerge in our normal daily lives.

Promoting Inappropriate Generalization

Stimulus generalization is a risk with punishment. As you saw in Chapters 15 and 16, people respond to stimuli that resemble or contain properties of those present when the behavior was being conditioned. When a stimulus shares properties with those present during punishment, it may evoke the same sorts of reactions as those that happened during the punishment, at least temporarily. In one classic study (Watson & Rayner, 1920), an 11-month-old child's conditioned fear of a rat generalized to all furry objects. If the objective is to accomplish generalized suppression, as with self-injury or acts of violence, such a spread of effect can be advantageous. As Newsom et al. (1983) have noted, however, the effects tend to dissipate "as the subject has additional opportunities to discriminate the actual contingencies of punishment in force" (p. 299).

Generalization to stimuli related to punishment can be problematic. Unintended reactions to the stimuli, such as the inclination to escape or retaliate, or worse yet, to become immobile, can spread to the punishing agents themselves, such as the manager who rebukes his employees, or the teacher or parents who discipline the child. Or they may transfer to the context—the job or school setting. For example, a student scolded for speaking out of turn may respond with aggression toward, or withdrawal from the teacher, the principal, the subject he is studying, the school, and so forth. Or a student might stop responding altogether in school, not speaking, writing, reading, or working for a time due to punishment by another school authority, a parent, or a peer.

Another danger is *learned helplessness* (Maier et al., 1969). Rats who received inescapable shock in one situation failed to take advantage of the available opportunity to escape in other situations. When you are perplexed by a person who has real options and yet does nothing to rid himself of aversive circumstances—such as an abusive partner or punishing job—recognize that this sort of overgeneralization may be at work.

Ultimately, the fact that the punishment is delivered for a specific behavior tends to be discriminated, as in a number of cases cited by Newsom et al. (1983). Sometimes this is detrimental, as when you would prefer to see a behavior disappear across all contexts. Otherwise, when a behavior only is unwanted under particular circumstances, learning the discrimination is beneficial. You can't count on the discrimination happening spontaneously, though. So to ensure that it is acquired you need to inform clients that they have been punished for *specific acts*. Clear antecedents for the desired alternative behavior followed by lavish reinforcement for compliance should help them make the necessary distinctions.

Displaying Behavioral Contrast

We discussed behavioral contrast previously in association with other procedures. To review, behavioral contrast describes a change in the rate of an untreated behavior as a function of a change in a treated behavior. The phenomenon also has been noted in conjunction with punishment.

Behavioral contrast has been observed when punitive procedures have been used in applied settings. For example, Risley (1968) noted that while an autistic child's climbing on a bookcase was being reduced by electric shock, climbing on a chair increased. When Foxx and Azrin (1973) used overcorrection to reduce one of their subject's mouthing of objects in a daycare center, they found that though the behavior decreased in that location, the problem increased at home. Similarly, self-injury decreased by electric shock in school was noted to increase slightly at home (Merbaum, 1973).

Because behavioral contrast appears more likely to occur when the individual is obtaining insufficient reinforcement for constructive alternative behaviors, all reductive procedures should be combined with Alt-R. Nevertheless, given the potential for behavioral contrast, you also need to concurrently assess other situations and classes of problematic behavior whenever you use an aversive procedure.

Modeling Punishment

In our discussion of the advantages of punishment, we mentioned that clients are less likely to imitate a punished behavior. What they may imitate, however, is the *act of delivering punishment* (Bandura & Walters, 1963; Bandura, 1965c).

Peer aggression, in particular, tends to be imitated (Kniveton, 1986a; Ling & Thomas, 1986), especially by youngsters having three or more siblings (Kniveton, 1986b). For example, youngsters who viewed videotapes of aggressive and nonaggressive play behavior by children similar to themselves became more aggressive only after viewing the aggressive models. Extrapolating further, Eron (1987) found that youngsters who were exposed to aggressive models at age 8 tended to be more aggressive 10 and 22 years later. In addition, he found that: "One of the best predictors of how aggressive a young man would be at age 19 was the violence of the television programs he preferred when he was 8 years old" (p. 438). Apparently, young children's television viewing does need to be monitored and managed to avoid repeatedly exposing them to undue aggression.

Chapter 17 discussed how people tend to imitate the behaviors of prestigious persons, especially when those behaviors are reinforced. Unintentional teaching of that kind can take place in any sort of a work, educational, or community setting where use of punishment is reinforced by the immediate cessation of aversive events—that is, by negative reinforcement. How do many managers learn to be cruel toward their employees? By watching their own supervisors receive reinforcement that way. Several studies have shown that individuals often imitate the kind of punishment that they have experienced themselves (Gelfand et al., 1974; Mischel & Grusec, 1966).

By now, you can begin to understand why violence is so widespread, for in addition to extinction and punishment-induced aggression, here is another to add to the list: People with prestige and power (those in control of contingencies) may actually be teaching aggression by modeling it! If you want to avoid be-

coming an unwitting trainer of violence, then, be sure you avoid punishing whenever possible, especially in the presence of those who admire and respect you.

Influencing Social Status of Recipient

Aggressive children account for a high proportion of those who are rejected by their peers (Waas, 1987). One possible reason for this rejection is the frequency with which aggressive children receive punishment from their teachers. Those who are continually singled out for punishment may risk becoming conditioned aversive stimuli, avoided or stigmatized by their peers. Such adverse effects may be mitigated by giving the recipients of punishment an opportunity to make restitution for their misbehavior or by providing and liberally reinforcing acceptable alternatives. Such opportunities should help reinstate the children socially. For example, following a particularly cooperative act, the person can be asked to help perform some prestigious task, like reporting the results of a group project, gathering or handing out materials, or being placed in charge of a group activity or event.

Under other circumstances, punishment also may occasion peer support or sympathy for the punished individual—the "underdog" effect. This sort of reinforcement by peers might counteract the effects of the punishment, perhaps even resulting in an eventual *increase*, rather than a decrease, in the misconduct. When you observe such an effect, change the approach: use another reductive procedure and/or discuss the rationale with the group and obtain its cooperation.

Promoting Negative "Self-Esteem"

Being the frequent brunt of punishment may negatively influence the clients' views of themselves or their surroundings, as measured by responses on paper-and-pencil tests of self-esteem. The things people say to or about themselves or about their environments after they have been punished are more likely to be negative, particularly if the aversive stimuli were directed at them as people, rather than at the behavior ("You're a bad boy." "Jim is immature. Sometimes he acts like a two-year-old." "Clarence is irresponsible."). The importance of this point cannot be overlooked. Studies like one by Wattenberg and Clifford (1964) have indicated that what clients say about themselves is related to school achievement. Other studies (Flanders, 1965; Ludwig & Maehr, 1967; Staines, 1958) also have indicated that teachers' comments directed to the child, rather than to the behavior, modified students' self-reports or self-concepts in the direction of the comments. If aversive stimuli must be used, they should never be directed at the individual ("You're a bad boy") but at the behavior ("No, don't hit Jane"). This approach helps people to recognize that it is a specific behavior that is unacceptable and not everything about themselves.

Again, encouraging alternative reinforceable behaviors can help clients to discriminate which specific behaviors will and will not be tolerated. Furthermore, reinforcement in the form of praise is likely not only to occasion and strengthen desired behaviors but also to enhance people's statements about themselves and their surroundings (Bandura, Grusec, & Menlove, 1967; Brehm & Cohen, 1962; Davidson & Lang, 1960; Flanders, 1965).

Overusing Punishment

Why do people continue to use punishment more than necessary? Now we know many of the reasons: Because their behavior is maintained through the positive reinforcement of getting them what they want, and through the negative reinforcement of eliminating aversive stimuli; because if their behavior recently was punished, they briefly will find the opportunity to aggress reinforcing (Azrin, Hutchinson & Hake, 1963); or because they have observed

others using and/or receiving reinforcement for applying punishment. Even mild aversive contingencies often produce rapid (but not necessarily enduring) cessation of an offensive behavior (Azrin & Holz, 1966).

A study by Martin (1974) illustrates this effect. A group of young children sometimes was praised for staying on-task when requested to play with objects like beads or blocks, and at other times they were reprimanded for being off-task. When reprimanded, their rates of staying on-task were higher than they were under the praise for the on-task condition. This result would undoubtedly reinforce the contingency manager's use of reprimands.

The negative side effects that might serve as a deterrent may be delayed or obscure. In the Martin study (1974), though, a generalization phase demonstrated that despite their working faster when reprimanded, the children later avoided using the objects with which they had been playing while being reprimanded. The punishing agent might not observe such an example of avoidance learning right away—if ever. That is why people naive about the principles of behavior may continue to dispense punishment. Perhaps this is why many teachers rely very heavily on reprimands or disapproving comments (Heller & White, 1975; Thomas, Presland, Grant, & Glynn, 1978; White, 1975).

So we can see that natural and historical contingencies may heavily support the use of punishment. And because of the rapid reinforcement for the use of punishment procedures by managers, alternative practices might not be researched. Probably public policy restrictions on the use of punishment have been partially responsible for the upsurge in research on alternatives to punishment.

To prevent abusing the punishment procedure, we need to provide managers with reinforceable alternatives, many of which have been presented already in this book.[2] Additionally,

---

[2] For an excellent training text for organizational managers, see Daniels (1989).

further work needs to be done to promote a greater reliance on reinforcing and less on punitive methods of behavior management.

Generating Public Antipathy

Many people oppose punishment in some or all of its facets. The reasons for such antipathy are many:

- Press coverage of misapplications of punishment.
- Attributing their own perspectives to others.
- Actual personal experience.
- Legal, professional, or ethical considerations.
- Objective evidence.

Undoubtedly those who have spearheaded the antiaversive movements within professional organizations and governmental agencies represent that viewpoint. According to Elliott (1988), "people generally rate positive treatment procedures as more acceptable than negative procedures for changing children's behavior" (p. 72).

Nevertheless, this opposition is by no means universal, and often respondents will endorse using more intrusive or restrictive methods to treat severe problems (e.g., Elliott, 1988; Elliott et al., 1984; Kazdin, 1980a), especially when given information about treatment effectiveness (Von Brock & Elliott, 1987). The attitudes of the public, professional, and paraprofessional employees and clients, can be assessed by checking with community representatives. Informing the public about problem severity and treatment effectiveness also should help.

Difficulty in Selecting Relevant Aversive Activities

To be educative, aversive activities such as the restitution aspect of overcorrection must be relevant to the misbehavior. Sometimes, figuring out just what the activity should be may be difficult. (What would be an appropriate restitution procedure for the behavior of peeking under a woman's skirt?) When immediate action is called for, identifying an appropriately relevant aversive activity on the spot can pose a problem. Perhaps further research and experience with overcorrection will help to resolve such difficulties.

Cost of Managing Aversive Activities

To be effective, aversive activities must be instituted immediately and for a given duration, therefore requiring the undivided attention of a staff member. Often, too, they must be maintained over long time spans, because if they are discontinued before eliminating the behavior altogether, it may recover or go beyond its previous baseline rate. Although conceivably a group manager could oversee such activities, often that would not be feasible. If a restitution activity requires that a student right all the desks he has overturned, someone must watch to see that he does so. If he encounters difficulty in righting the desks, physical guidance may have to be used, requiring further staff time and effort.

To encourage staff to follow through, the cost to them must be reduced. This could be accomplished by enabling them to obtain more immediate natural reinforcement by planning initial interventions with more capable clients with lesser problems (Foxx & Livesay, 1984) and by providing supplementary reinforcement for consistently implementing the overcorrection procedure.

Before electing to employ overcorrection, therefore, you need to consider in detail both the client and the activities and decide whether sufficient reinforcement and adequately trained staff will be available for the anticipated duration of the procedure.

Considerations in Electing to use Punishment

By now you are familiar with classes of aversive stimuli, the characteristics of punishment as a behavioral procedure, and its main advantages and disadvantages. Would you be justified in applying the method? If so, under what circumstances? Possibly you might be swayed by such compelling arguments as those posed by the Association for Behavior Analysis Task Force on the Right to Effective Treatment, that recipients

> . . . of treatment designed to change their behavior have the right to: (1) a therapeutic environment, (2) services whose overriding goal is personal welfare, (3) treatment by a competent behavior analyst, (4) programs that teach functional skills, (5) behavioral assessment and ongoing evaluation, and (6) the most effective treatment procedures available (Van Houten et al., 1988b, p. 111).

Or you might concur with Matson and Taras (1989), who conclude:

> The issue then should be proper regulation and peer review to insure that where very severe problems exist (e.g., biting off fingers, blinding oneself) that treatments to curb such problems including punishment methods be available and implemented by trained professionals. This, in our view, is a moral issue. Parent and patient consent, properly qualified professionals, and peer reviews should be included with aversives being a last resort, *but an available one* (p. 99).

Maybe data on the efficacy of mild or educative aversive methods, such as reprimands or restitution and positive practice, have convinced you that is the way to go, when conditions merit. Or perhaps you have found an "all-positive approach" not practically feasible. If so, you will want to make the ultimate decision based on a case-by-case review and be sure to protect the recipient's legal and human rights along with your own.

Should policies, or regulations, or your own ethical and moral perspective force you totally to reject applying aversives within your formal programming, you still need to know about their application. Such knowledge will enable you to be more vigilant about your own interpersonal interactions and to recognize when aversives are being applied counter to policy, unethically, ineffectively, or counterproductively in your setting.

Assuming you have attempted to analyze and correct the function of the problematic performance, considered less restrictive methods, and checked out legal and ethical factors, begin with the least intrusive aversive stimulus. If (after a fair trial of several weeks) those are not effective, you might put others to the test. In the most extreme case, an uncomfortable stimulus, like electric shock, might be the only answer.

Because it is so aversive, intrusive, and restrictive, shock generally is limited to instances in which clients engage in severe self-injurious, aggressive, or life-threatening situations, such as rumination (Foxx, Plaska, & Bittle, 1986c). Even in such situations, therapist and staff accountability regarding its use is of paramount concern. To help ensure accurate program implementation and avoid staff misuse of a small hand-held electrical shock device the shock device was modified so it would "automatically record the number of shocks delivered and when the first shock in a particular time period was administered" (Foxx, McMorrow, Rendleman, & Bittle, 1986b, p. 187). The modification also permitted increased accuracy of data collection and reliability checks. This device, combined with heavy reinforcement for appropriate behavior, reduced the severely aggressive behavior of a 20-year-old retarded, deaf male after all previous interventions had been ineffective (Foxx et al., 1986a). Not only was the aggressive behavior reduced to zero or near zero levels, and maintained by nonprofessionals, but the client was able to begin working all day in the vocational workshop and make home visits.

Of course, such an aversive program was not implemented without a detailed informed-consent document (see Foxx et al., 1986c, for illustrative informed consent documents). The document was sent to and approved by the institution's superintendent and Human Rights and Behavior Management Committees, the client's parents, and the director of the state's Department of Mental Health and Developmental Disabilities. If such a program were not permitted, what would have happened to the client? Perhaps, as the authors noted, "to not have attempted the program could have been tantamount to relegating Jack to a lifetime of restrictive, yet ineffective, interventions" (p. 182).

A potential dilemma is raised by federal guidelines for the use of shock with the retarded based on the Wyatt (1972) decision. According to Budd and Baer (1976), the Wyatt decision limits the use of electric-shock devices with mentally retarded residents to "extraordinary circumstances, to prevent self-mutilation leading to repeated and possibly permanent physical damage to the resident and only after alternative techniques have failed" (p. 218). Shock treatments may be administered only after approval of the institution's human-rights committee; with the express and informed consent of the resident or, if he is incapacitated, the next of kin; and under the direct and specific order of the superintendent (Budd & Baer, 1976). Budd and Baer have commented that the dilemma:

> . . . concerns the ruling that shock can be employed with the retarded "only after alternative techniques have failed." (344 F. Supp. at 401.) It could be argued that this requirement conflicts with another Wyatt standard, which directs staff workers to employ the least restrictive alternative in providing treatment. More specifically, it could be considered more restrictive to delay the use of, a powerful, but (presumably) effective technique—shock—while exhausting all milder but (presumably) less effective alternatives than to provide shock treatment at the outset. As Baer (1970) noted in his discussion of the choice of punishment techniques:

> That question, How long will it take? is the morally critical question, in my opinion. For as time goes by while the

therapist tries his hopefully more benevolent or more basic methods, the patient still undergoes punishment while he waits for a good outcome. In effect, the therapist has assigned the patient to a punishment condition from which he might have long since removed him (p. 246).

Thus, for behavior problems as serious as mutilating one's body, it would seem most humane for the courts to allow early use of shock treatment in special cases, rather than reserving this technique until all possible alternatives have been exhausted. In place of a general court ruling, the decision of if and when to prescribe shock treatment for particular cases might best be made by an institution's advocacy committee in consultation with staff personnel. In this way, residents with serious problems which require a very powerful therapy technique such as shock punishment would have an opportunity to receive more efficient treatment than is presently permitted by Wyatt's ruling (1976, pp. 219–220).[3]

Other safeguards might include consultation by specialists and/or external review committees composed of impartial experts. In cases of aversive procedures whose effectiveness has not been assessed and documented to be effective with a like population, adhering to the American Psychological Association's *Guidelines for Clinical Practice* and for *Research with Human Subjects,* including informed consent, cost/benefit, free access to data, and other provisions for protection of subjects' human rights must be met in all such cases. Unusual or exotic aversive procedures not adhering to those ethical requirements should not be permitted.

A final consideration is to *acknowledge the characteristics of punishment* in designing and conducting the program. See whether the person is likely to escape the situation, and if es-

---

[3] Reprinted from *The Journal of Psychiatry & Law,* vol. 4, no. 2. (1976). *Wyatt* v. *Stickney.* © 1976 by Federal Legal Publications, Inc. 95 Morton St., New York, NY 10014.

sential, make appropriate provisions to block that eventuality. To whatever extent possible, curtail any reinforcement of the performance. Apply individually effective aversive stimuli of sufficient intensity, immediately, every time the episode happens, and pair it with a brief reprimand (e.g., "no biting"). Avoid the temptation to deliver lengthy harangues or rationales. Save the latter for calmer moments. Be prepared for agitation following a sign that punishment is imminent, immobility during punishment, and punishment-induced aggression afterward; also be ready for behavioral contrast.

In an example of retarded adults, who stole snacks from one another (Azrin & Wesolowski, 1974), reinforcers were rapidly curtailed by requiring that the stolen food be returned immediately. This exchanged the reinforcement the culprit apparently had been gaining (by obtaining more food and annoying the victim) to reinforcement for the victim. Similarly, after unsuccessfully trying an Alt-R procedure, investigators (Luiselli, Helfen, Pemberton, & Reisman, 1977) used an overcorrection procedure to reduce public masturbation. The procedure consisted of having the child move his arms in one of four positions and hold them there for 3 seconds immediately on touching the zipper area of his pants. Public masturbation stopped after 9 days and maintained over a year.

Combine Punishment with Reinforcement of Alternative Behaviors

You have learned that mild punishment can be effective if the person simultaneously has access to an alternative reinforceable behavior (Azrin & Holz, 1966). That is fortunate, because punishment intense enough to override powerful reinforcers frequently is neither feasible nor ethical. This combined procedure should, however, prove attractive to practitioners who seek the rapid and long-lasting effects of punishment but who are unwilling or unable to use strong

aversive stimuli. Because of this, "it is universally acknowledged that aversive procedures should only be employed in the context of the development of alternative appropriate behavior" (Lovaas & Favell, 1987, pp. 316–317). Further,

> . . . if a program cannot conduct alternative interventions in a high quality fashion, then it should not employ aversive procedures. It is perhaps less obvious, that if a program cannot ensure the necessary degree of quality in the use of alternative treatments, then the facility or agency should not purport or attempt to treat severe problem behavior at all (Lovaas & Favell, 1987, p. 320).

Numerous investigators have combined punishment successfully with reinforcement of alternative behaviors. For example, in the Secan and Egel (1986) study described previously, negative practice was combined with DRO and Alt-R to reduce self-stimulatory clapping. The authors pointed out that once the clapping diminished, the clients had more opportunity to play ball—an activity they apparently enjoyed.

Use Effective Stimulus Control Strategies

To teach that under specific conditions a given act is unacceptable, it should be immediately punished every time that act is emitted under those conditions by a strong aversive stimulus. If Clyde steps out into traffic when the traffic light is red and the sign says "Wait," he is immediately scolded—a powerful aversive for Clyde. "Don't pull Tiger's tail" should function as an S^{D-} when Baby Bonnie reaches for the dog's tail. Should she proceed, she would be punished by Mother and perhaps by Tiger's snarling, growling, or taking a nip at her. The same sort of consistency should be followed in any organization.

So people need to be clearly *informed about the conditions* under which given acts will be punished: "Hurting others and destroying or taking other people's materials will be punished by . . ." In a group situation, especially with older children and adults, it makes sense to *involve clients in specifying the rules*, and *provide a rationale or reason* for not engaging in the behavior (Parke, 1969). For, as we have mentioned (Chapter 16), they will then be more aware of those rules, and peer support will be more likely. In addition, providing a rationale for the punishment appears to help lessen the occurrence of emotional reactions and a deterioration of the relationship between the supervisor and the subordinate in the work place (Greer & Labig, 1987), and is related to lower aggression toward family members in the home (Larzelere, 1986). In fact, frequency of spankings in the absence of a rationale is related to very high rates of physical aggression by youngsters (ages 3–17) (Larzelere, 1986).

Occasionally, staff rules also have to be clarified. Again, involving staff in setting and clarifying rules that affect their performance and explaining the underlying reasons are good ideas. Organizational policies often fulfill that function, for example, clarifying the conditions for dismissal: "In other than cases of imminent danger (specified in detail), hitting clients or fellow workers will be grounds for immediate dismissal." Assuming rules have been previously enforced, such clear explication will reduce the likelihood that specific acts will occur under given circumstances.

Program for Generalization and Maintenance

Generalization of the effects of punishment is by no means a foregone conclusion; nor is maintenance. In fact, sparse research is available on this topic, and what little there is seems to be based on case reports. Rather than risk too narrow a spread of effect of the outcome or rapid resurgence of the problem performance, conduct the program in all settings in which the response reduction is desired and design a tech-

nique to prevent relapse. (Section V details such methods.) At the minimum, train and supervise all managers, staff, parents, peers, clients, and others who control contingencies to properly implement the methodology.

Obtain Informed Consent

If the individual involved is judged sufficiently capable of understanding and providing it, obtain *informed consent* when feasible. Otherwise seek consent of parents, guardians, or advocates. As you know, the change process may be facilitated by involving the person in the process and clearly delineating the rules of the game. If a reasonable contract is negotiated that includes powerful reinforcers for alternative acceptable behaviors, you are even more likely to achieve success.

Monitor Continuously

Records need to be kept to document the integrity with which the procedure is implemented; naturally, the rate of the target behavior must be recorded and graphed daily, and matched against the baseline. This will permit regular assessments of change in order to decide whether to continue, revise, or discontinue the procedure. Because punishment may generate various side effects, other problematic and adaptive behaviors need to be measured as well. Evidence of behavioral contrast, suppression of other behaviors, attempts to withdraw from the situation, severely aggressive responses, detrimental peer reactions, and diminished self-esteem all should be measured. Data suggestive of marked increases in those side effects—or evidence of their absence—will be useful in assessing the utility of the program.

Applying Aversive Activities Effectively

Select Activities Relevant to the Misbehavior

When you use aversive activities, as with overcorrection, try to select those that are relevant to the misbehavior. Foxx and Bechtel (1982) argue that procedures that use irrelevant responses do not constitute overcorrection even if they share common characteristics with overcorrection. In addition, as Foxx and Azrin have noted, "This characteristic of relevance should also motivate the educator to apply the restitution procedure since the educator would otherwise be forced to correct the general disturbance himself" (1972, p. 16).

The misbehaving client should directly experience the effort normally required by others to undo the damage created by the client's misbehavior. For example, the person who overturns the desk is instructed to set it upright and to dust and clean it. Clients who frequently had their hands in their mouths (Foxx & Azrin, 1973) or bit their hands, which resulted in formation of calluses that were then irritated, reddened, and torn open (Barnard, Christophersen, Altman, & Wolf, 1974) were required to brush their gums and teeth with a toothbrush that had been partially immersed in a container of oral antiseptic (mouthwash) and to wipe their outer lips with a washcloth that had been dampened with the antiseptic. This restitutional activity was initially selected by Foxx and Azrin because "mouthing of objects or parts of one's body results in exposure to potentially harmful microorganisms through unhygienic oral contact. The Restitutional Overcorrection rationale suggests that this possibility of self-infection be eliminated" (1973, p. 4). In addition to the 2-minute oral-hygiene procedure, the clients in the study by Barnard and colleagues (1974) were required to engage in 2 minutes of washing the affected areas, using a cotton swab and mild soap; one minute of hand drying; and 2 minutes of rubbing hand cream into the affected area. (A kitchen timer was used to determine the time.) Mouthing or biting hands was substantially reduced among all children in both studies.

Keep Performance of Aversive Activities Consistent

As already implied, aversive activities need to be performed without pause. Furthermore, additional work and effort are included, for as Foxx and Azrin have indicated in relation to overcorrection, "an increased work or effort requirement is known to be annoying and serves as an inhibitory event" (1972, p. 16). However, ethical considerations demand that *excessive force be avoided*, because injuries could result. Wait patiently until strong resistance subsides; being emotionally distraught interferes with learning.

Extend Duration of Aversive Activities

While clients are engaged in an aversive activity, their access to reinforcement is removed (that is, a timeout condition is in effect). Consequently, its duration should be longer than that needed simply to correct a wrong (for example, setting a chair upright) and to restore the environment. As pointed out in Chapter 26, this period *should not*, however, be excessively long. Depending on the behavior, 2 to 10 minutes beyond the time needed to restore the disrupted environment is usually plenty.

To ensure that timeout conditions are approximated during an aversive activity, keep reinforcement to a minimum and avoid giving undue attention, praise, and approval. In working with brain-damaged individuals who demonstrated aggressive-disruptive behaviors, Foxx and Azrin (1972) confronted the problem of how to occasion the aversive activity without using reinforcement. They considered verbal instructions as one such alternative. Another was physical guidance using just enough pressure to sustain the desired rate.

Foxx and Azrin (1972) and Foxx and Bechtel (1982) also have cautioned against using reinforcement during positive practice because they were concerned that the maladaptive behavior might increase elsewhere. This risk would be most likely if the client received more reinforcement for constructive alternative behaviors during positive practice than at other times, especially in an impoverished environment devoid of reinforcement for correct practice. However, Carey and Bucher (1986) compared the relative effectiveness of the standard positive practice, without reinforcement, with positive practice that included reinforcement for correct practice. (The outside environment in their case did provide reinforcement for correct performance.) Carey and Bucher found that reinforcing the correct positive practice of retarded adults yielded faster training of motor tasks and equivalent reductions of stereotypic behavior. They concluded that in situations containing outside environments in which correct practices are positively reinforced, ''the use of reinforcement for positive practice would appear to be the treatment to be tried in preference to the traditional version'' (p. 90). Other examples of **reinforced positive practice** might include reinforcing Tricia's moving her head as instructed, or repeated practice of correctly written previously misspelled words.

A combination of positive practice plus reinforcement provides you another constructive option (along with Alt-R, modeling, DRL, DRD, and DRO) as an alternative to punishment. The procedure even may act more rapidly than DRO.

Summary

Should punishment be applied systematically to modify behavior? The answer to this question needs to be made on a case-by-case basis and after a functional assessment has been conducted to attempt to identify and control the cause of the problem performance. The advantages and disadvantages, and various ethical, legal, and human considerations of the procedure will need to be taken into account. Punishment can curtail behavior rapidly and perhaps durably and may facilitate people's acquisition of preferred alternatives. Peers tend to be less likely to imitate behaviors they observe being punished, and some aversive procedures are easy for staff to apply. By contrast, though, punishment can produce numerous, generally detrimental, side effects, such as withdrawal, immobility, aggression, inappropriate generalization, behavioral contrast, imitative delivery of punishment, lowered social status and self-esteem by recipients, risk of overuse, and negative responses from members of the community. Relevant aversive activities may be difficult to identify, and costly to implement.

The issues of least restrictiveness and right to effective treatment can serve as a basis on which to decide whether to use a particular punishment procedure, but at times the two conflict. Such conflicts can be resolved by inviting individual specialists or committees of impartial outside experts to review the program. Only procedures well documented to be effective with like populations should be considered. Otherwise, ethical guidelines for research with human subjects need to be followed.

If a judgment has been reached that the person ultimately will benefit from a punishment procedure, the specific strategy is best fashioned by incorporating current knowledge of effective methods of punishment. Sufficiently intense aversive stimuli that are individually effective in the particular context need to be applied consistently and immediately. While the punishment procedure is in effect, heavy doses of reinforcement need to be delivered for acceptable alternatives, stimulus control strategies need to be applied, generalization and maintenance should be programmed, and performance of the problem and other behaviors should be monitored continuously. If the aversive event is an activity, it should, when feasible, relate to the misbehavior and be performed without pause over an extended duration. In the absence of evidence of progress after a few weeks, the program should be revised or discontinued.

Section V

Extending and Maintaining Behavior

Finally, we address the fundamental premise of this book: that modified behavior often can be extended beyond the circumstances of its original modification and helped to persist. That is, given sufficient skill and control over contingencies, time, and resources (no small qualifiers) that objective lies within the realm of possibility.

No, we are not asserting that all people's behavior can be generally and durably changed in the way they would prefer; only that a reasonable possibility exists if analysts are willing to invest sufficiently in the enterprise. The days of naively assuming that change spontaneously would spread and last are long gone, and now we recognize that in behavior analysis as elsewhere, usually we need to pay for what we get. (By the same token, we also have learned that if flexibility or restricted responding are wanted, these too need to be programmed, not left to chance.)

Fortunately, during its maturation process, the field of behavior analysis has been addressing the difficult challenge of promoting generality and durability, and slowly we are seeing the evolution of a dependable technology of generalization and maintenance. That technology is heavily ecological, founded on viewing behavior in relation to its context. Many of the strategies for generalization and maintenance, such as identifying contingencies standing ready to support or impede the change, require a thorough familiarity with ongoing contingencies within the individuals' natural surroundings. Knowing about and capitalizing on the formal and informal contingency networks operating within the companies, schools, families, treatment facilities, and communities in which our clients work and reside is essential if change is to persist.

Increasingly, applied behavior analytic researchers are assessing for generality and durability and addressing strategies for accomplishing extended and lasting change. Collecting follow-up data over months or years no longer is unusual; nor is assessing for generality across behaviors, settings, or people.

Basic experimental analyses also continue to contribute to the evolving methodology. Beyond the extensive set of findings on how simple schedules of reinforcement influence subsequent performance, laboratory researchers are adding to our knowledge about the impact of verbal behavior, the contingencies that affect choice, and many other areas of particular relevance to the topic at hand.

Probably you have been wondering about how the actual and hypothetical behavior changes about which you have been reading might be nurtured to expand and persist. Surely those concerns must extend to those you actually are planning or conducting. The next set of chapters should prove valuable in this regard. We recommend that anyone contemplating applying behavior analysis master the concepts these chapters contain and keep abreast of the literature as it continues to reveal new findings. For purposes of distilling the material covered in this section, though, we have devised Table 5 in the Epilogue.

Chapter 29

Extending Behavior: Generalization Training

GOALS

After completing this chapter, you should be able to:

1. Define, recognize, differentiate between, and give original illustrations of each of the following terms:
   a. Stimulus generalization
   b. Response induction or response generalization
   c. Exemplar
   d. Stimulus change decrement

2. List and discuss the advantages of stimulus and response generalization.

3. List and discuss the disadvantages of stimulus and response induction.

4. Describe how to determine when and why it is necessary to program for generalization.

5. State and illustrate what factors need to be included as part of a behavioral objective to promote attention to generalization and discrimination training.

6. List and discuss the variables that promote generalization.

7. Differentiate between an exemplar and a nonexample.

8. Review the definitions of and illustrate:
   a. Incidental teaching
   b. Correspondence training

9. Use generalization training to occasion a behavior in more than one setting, across behaviors, or with other people.

Working in cooperation with a behavior analyst, Ms. Charming, the workshop supervisor, has taught her client Fern to attend to tasks and to complete her work assignments acceptably. Fern is now ready to seek employment in a community workshop. Will her recently acquired skills be extended and maintained in the new setting? Paula regularly submits her reports in time, but will she now be punctual in her other activities? Sloppy Smith's work bench is neat. How about his desk and the rest of the shop? Mr. Grump has begun to praise his students' accomplishments; but will he persist while the students adjust to his altered style? Lucretia has learned to play cooperatively with a particular group of children. What will happen when she finds herself in a different group? Dexter completes his math and science work satisfactorily and is now concerned about social studies. What does applied behavior analysis have to offer to assist in extending a behavior across behaviors or into new situations?

The various procedures that have been discussed in the preceding chapters are designed to increase, establish, and reduce specific behaviors. They serve, in essence, as the major focus of applied behavior analysis programs. Let us recall, however, that the full behavior analysis model includes a series of essential components: preliminary steps, goal selection, specification of objectives, selection of measures and contingencies, a series of procedural steps—plus evaluation, maintenance, generalization, and communication (see Chapter 8). Consequently, even though the effectiveness of a behavioral procedure may have been demonstrated, the job is not yet complete. Evaluation, maintenance, generalization, and communication remain. Evaluation, as discussed earlier (Chapters 14 and 22), is planned before implementation of procedures and is carried out during the program. In this section of four chapters, we examine behavioral principles and procedures that help behavior change to expand and last: generalization and maintenance.

Dexter and his teacher had negotiated a contract earlier in the year. One provision allowed him to earn points that could be exchanged for special privileges. It is late in the semester, and a plan for next year must be considered. Dexter does not want to depend on the point system forever and would like to terminate it. Yet he, his teacher, and the school psychologist are all afraid that the recently acquired study behaviors may not persist in the new situation. What kind of programming will help Dexter to sustain his newfound gains when he shifts to a new environment? Generalization and maintenance strategies emphasize such goals. We turn first to generalization.

Generalization Defined and Illustrated

When behaviors learned under one set of circumstances occur at other times and places and/or in the presence of other people, or the change in one behavior occurs with a second, or form of a response shifts, we call the spread of effect *generalization*.[1] Note that generalization usually takes two different forms: stimulus generalization and induction (response generalization). With **stimulus generalization**, as discussed in Chapter 15, the same response occurs in the presence of different stimuli, such as in other contexts, at other times, or in the presence of other people. Ms. Charming uses her newly acquired management skills to help her other workshop clients. Baby Bonnie says "Da-da" to all males who have beards like her father's. Dexter designs a contract to use by himself. Ms. Feeney's sixth graders use proper capitalization and punctuation in writing complete sentences, not only to prepare compositions (the medium through which they were taught) but also when they write letters. Mr.

---

[1] Cognitive psychologists tend to use the term *transfer* to describe this phenomenon. In this chapter we interchange those terms simply for purposes of variety.

Grump comments approvingly when his wife reports an accomplishment at work. These are instances of stimulus generalization for behaviors learned under one set of stimuli occur in the presence of different stimuli.

In the second form of generalization, **response induction** (e.g., Catania, 1984) or **response generalization** (Skinner, 1953), the behavior does not remain intact, as it did with stimulus generalization, but it begins to shift its form or topography. After reading his book on perfect golfing techniques, Joe Duffer tries out his new swing. The first time his club connects with the ball beautifully, but afterward he misses more often than he connects. The form of his response has varied from the initially successful swing. Sometimes Mr. Grump praises with moderate enthusiasm, sometimes with a flat tone, and once in a while quite heartily. Willie has been taught to follow a given strategy for solving scientific problems. On occasion, he modifies the strategy by eliminating or adding steps.

Advantages and Disadvantages of Generalization

Generalization, whether of the stimulus or the response variety, can prove valuable or detrimental, depending on the circumstances. Repetition of certain behaviors under a variety of stimulus conditions is often highly advantageous. Vocabulary taught in school is useful there as well as at home, on the job, and in the community; so is the transfer of Mr. Grump's use of praise. From a pragmatic perspective, we can view desirable generalization, whether planned or not, as a way of obtaining behavior change in contexts other than the original training conditions for less cost—in terms of time, effort, and material resources (or by "lesser means," as Stokes & Baer, 1977, have called it). Initially, teaching customer service personnel to smile, greet people by name, and look

at the customers directly may take the training staff considerable time in the first setting. If the personnel only require occasional minimal prompting for them to behave similarly under new conditions, the cost will be far less. Although generalization usually does not give us something for nothing, it may provide it at bargain prices.

Conversely, stimulus generalization may be problematic, as when we use our native language in a country where a different tongue is spoken. Baby Bonnie's mom blushes with embarrassment whenever her little one calls a bearded stranger "Da-da." Making eye contact and smiling serve us well in many social circumstances, but can you think of cases where doing that might prove disadvantageous? (How about a threatening-looking person on a dark street? In Japan, a child who looks an adult authority figure directly in the eye is considered rude.) We know of an instance in which a group of developmentally delayed youngsters was taken on a field trip to a department store. Seeing a display toilet, one of the boys began to unhitch his pants. A lesson in discrimination training was needed on the spot. Remember, when the objective is for a behavior to occur under only some circumstances but not others, we need to focus on teaching tight stimulus control. Remedying unwanted generalization adds to the cost of changing behavior, because we then need to teach new discriminations. So, it is best prevented in the first place. (Refer back to Chapter 15 to remind yourself how discrimination training is accomplished.) But when expanding the scope of the behavior beyond a training setting is the goal, generalization is what we are after.

Response induction also can come in handy or cause difficulties. The primary advantages of this approach are that minor variations of a behavior don't have to be taught completely from scratch, and the variations expressed in response induction permit a behavior to be shaped. The tennis coach can capitalize on his trainee's skill in badminton to teach an appropriate tennis swing. All she has to do is teach a modification of the swing, rather than starting from the very beginning. Heavy reinforcement can be presented when Willie uses an especially fruitful problem solving strategy or Mr. Grump uses hearty praise. There is no need to teach those particular response topographies as separate new behaviors.

Shaping, as you recall, depends on the variations that occur through response variation. We scrutinize carefully to reinforce those variations that more closely approximate the goal behavior. Listening to Claud attempting to imitate a proper "eu" sound, his teacher nods and smiles following those that more and more closely resemble an ideal French pronunciation. As the principal and Mr. Grump have agreed, she will wink, smile, nod, and signal "Okay" from the back of the room each time she notices successively more enthusiastic variations in Mr. Grump's use of praise. With response induction, Claud now is more quickly able to learn a different but related sound, "Ü." Mr. Grump more readily increases his ability to give behavior-specific feedback—a related but different behavior.

Sometimes, however, unwanted response induction can bring us grief. Behavioral variation in landing an airplane or performing brain surgery could lead to disaster. Willie may try a few shortcut variations that impair his solutions to problems. Practitioners have failed to achieve their purposes because their application of a behavioral procedure has drifted from the standard: A teacher skipping the step of identifying and using individually effective reinforcers or a caregiver using overly long timeout intervals are some examples.

Unprogrammed Generalization

What would happen if the change in our clients' or students' behavior were restricted to a single form, occurring only when we were there and in the setting in which it was taught? The task would be monumental. The learner would need to acquire each target behavior in every setting in which it was supposed to occur and in the presence of all the people who would be expected to be present there. Time and resources would be insufficient to permit anyone to function adequately in society.

Although parents, teachers, and other change agents often tend to assume it will happen, only occasionally does generalization take place without formal programming. For instance, Kennedy and Thompson (1967) described how a first-grade child who learned to increase attending in a counseling session also increased attending in arithmetic class, despite no arranged contingencies in the latter setting.

An experimental group of paraprofessional and clerical staff employed in a community social service agency participated in a behavioral training condition. They were taught such interpersonal skills as eye contact, body and facial expression, and speech duration (Schinke, Gilchrist, Smith, & Wong, 1979). Using a vignette as a focal point, participants then had an opportunity to practice receiving continual coaching, feedback, and praise until they mastered the skills. The treatment for the control group consisted of films and discussions of past and present interpersonal difficulties. During a generalization assessment—role playing with different vignettes—experimental group members expressed more of the skills than control group members.

You also may have noticed that contingencies were carefully arranged in our examples in which shaping was assisted by capitalizing on response induction (Chapter 19). Yet variations in responding often are shaped naturally, without any planned management. When he varies his sales pitch slightly, Rick closes a difficult sale. He probably will repeat that variation. When Shirley smiles a bit more broadly than usual, Willie asks her for a date. Flashing her best smile at Willie becomes habitual, even though Shirley may not realize what she is doing or why.

Sometimes, as we have seen earlier in this chapter as well as in Chapter 15, unprogrammed generalization may produce undesirable responding. How many of us are afraid of harmless spiders and snakes? Did you ever find yourself jamming on the brake instead of tapping it gently during a skid?

As you recall, inappropriate generalization is corrected via discrimination training. Critical features are isolated and the individual is taught to respond differently under each situation. Baby Bonnie's mom explains, "Our daddy is Bill. He lives with us. Our daddy, Bill, hugs you and plays with you. . . . That man is not daddy Bill because he does not live with us, hug you, or play with you."

In this chapter, however, our concern is the opposite, because the objective is to *encourage* a response to transfer across situations or to adjust its form to new requirements. As you will see, unless your planning has been designed to allow the natural community of reinforcers to assume control, you will have to program specific steps to achieve generalization. Desired generalization usually does not just occur by itself.[2]

Establishing the Need to Formally Program for Generalization

You probably can think of lots of occasions when the generalization you expect to naturally occur does not. Your students correctly solve a problem on their worksheets about the amount of lumber they would need to build a set of book ends. Yet when they attempt similar calculations in shop, their incorrect calculations

cause them to waste too many materials. Hours are spent in the youth group discussing why members tend to lose their tempers in certain situations and how to stay in control in the future. Sometimes practice in role-play situations is provided, but fights on the playground continue unabated. We spend months listening to tapes and practicing phrases in Italian. Yet, as soon as we arrive in Rome, and attempt asking directions to our hotel, we realize by the puzzled expression on our listener's face that we're saying "Where is the bathroom?" instead. When Lucretia joins a new group of children, she reverts to her earlier antisocial behavior. The skills the staff learns during in-service training are not applied on the job. Being able to recite rules of acceptable performance is no guarantee that the rules will transfer into practice. Our "train and hope" technique (Stokes & Baer, 1977) has not panned out.

The following set of circumstances occurs frequently enough to remind us that generalization must usually be programmed, rather than left to chance: Parents of seriously disabled children find it very difficult to get away from home for very long, particularly if the child requires specialized care, such as for frequent epileptic seizures. One potential solution is to hire a trained respite care worker who can come into the home and take over the parents' child care responsibilities. But are all such respite care workers necessarily competent to provide adequate care? According to Upshur (1982), parents most frequently cited inadequate training of the respite care worker as a reason for dissatisfaction. They probably meant that the workers failed to practice appropriate skills with the children; that is, they failed to *transfer* or *generalize* practices from the training to the actual home site.

In another instance, despite having learned to follow instructions for safely lifting and transferring their patients, three of four care givers did not spontaneously transfer the skills to other job skills, even when they were supplied

---

[2] Practitioners working with students with severe handicaps should find Haring's (1988) text especially helpful in teaching skill generalization.

with a written task analysis (Alavosius & Sulzer-Azaroff, 1990). The point is that we cannot risk taking generalization for granted but must demonstrate its occurrence by collecting data, as Schinke et al. (1979) did. Hard data showed that members of Schinke and colleagues' experimental group did increase their practice of their recently improved interpersonal skills while performing on the job. Data tells us when generalization needs to be programmed.

Possible explanations abound for a failure of a trained behavior to generalize. Perhaps the person has not learned it fluently enough, so the response is difficult to express. (Recall that activities that require extra effort can be punishing.) It took Ms. Charming many, many successful trials before she felt comfortable addressing a large audience. At first, you might have to work hard to withhold attention from a complaining employee and to respond enthusiastically when the employee is saying pleasant things. Conversely, previously learned undesired competing behaviors require little effort. So the increased cost of expressing the new behavior beyond the circumstances existing during training can undermine its expression in favor of a previously learned competing behavior. Additionally, stimulus conditions in the new situation may set the occasion for a well-practiced competing behavior. For instance, surroundings, people, and/or their actions may differ; sometimes establishing operations activate changes (e.g., Harry was well fed and rested when he practiced remaining calm while being teased; now when he is tired and hungry, under the very same circumstances he becomes agitated).

Assessing for Fluency

You need to determine whether the behavior is being expressed fluently. Is it being repeated smoothly and with apparent ease? Just as the coach repeatedly checks to see if a preferred way of tossing a forward pass has been well

established, you probe for generalization. If the behavior is not occurring fluently, provide lots of opportunities for reinforced practice by asking the trainee to execute the response so often and reinforcing it so often that it appears to become "second nature." If desired generalization still does not seem to be happening, you should verify this and conduct a more formal assessment to investigate the contingencies at work. (An analogous method is the multiple probe technique, Chapter 22.)

Assessing for Generalization

As we have said, data provide the basis for deciding whether to design an explicit program for generalization. We collect and examine measures of responses or of intended variations of the responses emitted under the conditions to which we hoped they would generalize. You can use a "generalization map" (Drabman et al., 1979) to ensure that you plan and assess for generalization along the dimensions of relevance, such as setting, behavior, people, time, and so on. (See Chapter 5 for an example.) A thorough ecobehavioral assessment (Rogers-Warren & Warren, 1977) will assist you in identifying stimulus factors within generalization settings that may potentially interfere with or support the hoped-for spread of effect. For example, see how a scatter plot was used to assess influences on self-injury by referring to the paper by Touchette et al. (1985), and look at the report by Vyse, Mulick, and Thayer (1984) to find out how they conducted an ecobehavioral assessment in a classroom to examine stimuli affecting aggressive and other problem behaviors.

In case you are investigating generalization of easily measured response classes, such as how readily written solutions to arithmetic problems solved on worksheets in class transfer to solutions of homework problems, you can just collect, record, and plot both sets of data on a graph. Should frequently measuring the behavior you want to see transfer be impractical, you could take periodic samples (say, weekly). This strategy can be particularly handy with labor-intensive measurement. For example, to assess the transfer of behavior taught outside of class to the natural social milieu, you could count the number of social initiations made by the adolescent toward all classmates, some of whom have, and some of whom have not participated in a social-skills training program. Rather than all day, every day, those data could be collected during a randomly selected period each week.

To assess how well parents functioned as therapists for their children's stuttering after the youngsters were trained in the clinical setting, Budd and colleagues (1986) measured disfluencies during parent-child interactions at home. Data were recorded for one to four baseline sessions and during five post-training sessions 1 or 2 months apart. (Data demonstrated parental effectiveness in that therapeutic role.)

Three multiply disabled young men volunteered to participate in a program designed to teach them restaurant skills (Van den Pol et al., 1981). A classroom was arranged to resemble a fast food restaurant. Photographs, instruction, and role playing were used to help the students learn to order, pay the bill, eat, and clear their tables. Transfer of training was probed periodically at actual Burger King and McDonald's restaurants, demonstrating the effectiveness of the program. The point of both of these examples is that *objective documentation of generalization is necessary*. We need to collect data in both the training and the real-life settings in order to determine whether effective transfer has indeed taken place.

Programming for Generalization

When the data verify our concerns that training is not transferring "automatically," the solution is to program deliberately for generalization; that is, to arrange contingencies that prompt and reinforce the target behaviors under the critical circumstances. As the field of applied behavior analysis progresses, a growing number of strategies for programming contingencies in support of generalization are being identified. Many of these have been summarized in three review papers (Baer & Stokes, 1977; Stokes & Baer, 1977; and Stokes & Osnes, 1989). Besides the sort of *training and hoping* that we have seen meets with limited success, they include the following:

- Sequential modification.
- Introduction to natural maintaining conditions.
- Training sufficient exemplars.
- Training loosely.
- Using indiscriminable contingencies.
- Training for correspondence.
- Programming common stimuli.
- Mediating generalization.
- Training "to generalize."

In the remainder of this chapter, we shall first review why it is so important to fashion complete and precise behavioral objectives. Next, we elaborate on a number of the techniques that have been used to promote generalization successfully.

Reviewing and Refining Behavioral Objectives

By now you should recognize that generalization and discrimination are an important component of behavioral objectives. Earlier examples may have helped you recognize that even some relatively innocuous behavioral objectives, like speaking and smiling, need to be restricted to particular stimulus conditions. Maybe you are beginning to realize how broadly you had hoped the effect of your training would spread while you neglected to explicitly identify all the circumstances under which the behavior should and should not occur. That is the function of the "situations" portion of a complete behavioral objective. When you state the context or conditions under which the behavior should and should not be emitted, you indicate the line where generalization is supposed to stop and discrimination begin.

Instead of stating simply, "The trainee will be able to pilot the plane to a safe landing," the objective might be expanded to "Under all atmospheric conditions—including snow, sleet, rain, darkness, or heavy winds—the trainee will be able to pilot the plane to a safe landing." By stipulating all the relevant conditions, the trainer and student know where the skill needs to be monitored, demonstrated, and (if necessary) trained. In your own case, you assess the extent of generalization in all the pertinent situations you have identified, and if performance is acceptable in each one, fine! You are home free. If not, you now know the subsequent step is to implement **generalization training**.

Once you have determined the need to promote generalization, a number of options are available. We start with the simplest generalization technique of all—asking for generalization.

Asking for Generalization

The most direct generalization programming technique to try first is to ask for generalization: "Why don't you try the skill that you learned during the in-service here on the job?" You might just get the response, "Oh, yeah! I could do that! I never thought of that!" However, if asking doesn't work, you need to be prepared to use a more systematic technique to assure that the altered behavior occurs under all conditions. One is sequential modification.

Modifying Behaviors Sequentially

Three little girls attending a public preschool were referred for help with their gross and fine motor skills (Kirby & Holborn, 1986). Instructions consisted of the teacher and child describing the critical features of the task, mod-

eling, and practice reinforced with descriptive praise. The first skills trained were balance-standing and walking. In some circumstances, collateral changes were noted, such as improvements in compliance with instructions. Learning how to balance-stand and walk, however, did little to improve other sets of gross motor skills such as rolling, hopping and crawling, bouncing, catching and throwing a ball, and running and jumping, until each of those sets of skills was taught separately in sequence. You too may find that when you want a behavior to transfer over to other related behaviors (you are hoping for response induction), and it doesn't occur automatically, you will need to identify each of the behaviors specifically and train each one.

Nine parents of toddlers deemed to be at risk for developmental delay were taught to use four different behavioral techniques to instruct their children (Bruder, 1986). Measures indicated some transfer across one skill area, such as from using consequences to arranging antecedents or from choosing targets to collecting data. Those specific skills that the parents were observed to apply most successfully, however, were the ones that were directly trained in more than one setting. Discovering those sorts of minor improvements in a second (or more) skill concurrent with a given intervention is not unusual, but often the transfer is insufficient. (Interestingly, Shapiro and Lentz [1985] also found that despite having been exposed to many behavior modification procedures, school psychologists tend to rely most heavily on those in which they have received supervised practice.)

In another case, two retarded children learned to use complex sentences containing five-word chains to orally describe a series of pictures (Garcia, Bullet, & Rust, 1977). The skill did not transfer to the classroom and home, however, until some of the instances were actually trained in those settings. Consequently, when generalization does not occur spontaneously, it can be accomplished by a "systematic sequential modification in every nongeneralized condition, i.e., across responses, subjects, settings, or experimenters" (Stokes & Baer, 1977 p. 352).

Training to Naturally Supportive Conditions

If you carefully assess the relation between the behavior and the environment in which a selected target is to be expressed, you may note conditions that stand ready to support it. Otherwise, contingencies in the transfer setting will need to be arranged to reinforce a modified form of the response. (See Chapter 4 to review ecobehavioral assessment and Chapter 11 for ways to identify effective reinforcers.) In a separate setting, you might teach a child the skills for gaining entry into a group of children playing together: by standing and waiting, mimicking the peer group's activity, then saying something about the group or activity. You are fairly confident that those skills will be sustained in the child's natural play situation, because those are the tactics that other children have used successfully to be admitted into a play group (Dodge, Schlundt, Schocken, & Delugach, 1983).

Naturally supportive conditions were identified in an actual study. Participants were three moderately handicapped students, a 10-year-old girl, Ann, and two 13-year-old children, Mark and Kim (Haring et al., 1986). Appropriate conversational skills were identified (1) by interviewing first graders and (2) by asking fifth graders to interview their friends and write down their friends' responses. The teacher then used the typical conversational patterns to teach the three subjects to initiate and extend conversations. Data collected in other locales, such as unsupervised eating and working situations, indicated that the skills did generalize and that nonhandicapped peers did respond and expand conversations with the subjects.

The authors posited that the teaching of language natural to the situation may have contributed to the more effective generalization obtained in their study than other investigators were able to demonstrate. We agree that the careful assessment of conversational content used naturally by others probably was crucial for success.

A new employee, Alvin, has joined your staff. Despite his apparent expertise in the field, within a couple of days, veteran staff members are becoming very annoyed with him. "What a pompous ##!**#!" "Boy, does he think he's something else!" are their comments. Observing the setting closely, you note that advice is most readily accepted when it is requested, but not otherwise. Alvin has been offering all sorts of unsolicited suggestions. You and Alvin have a long talk and together you identify, role play, and practice the way that peers help each other to solve their problems in your organization. For instance, Alvin practices saying, "I heard of someone who had a similar experience. Let me know whether you'd like me to tell you about it sometime," in place of "Well, I've read every issue of the *Journal of Quick and Dirty Behavior Change* for the past 10 years and you're doing it all wrong!" When he tries the new approach on the job, he finds that once in a while someone takes him up on his offer. You have helped Alvin to adjust the behavior of offering advice so it is no longer punished and is at least intermittently reinforced by his coworkers. In this case, the form of a complex behavior was modified so natural reinforcement would be more likely than punishment.

Finding ways to encourage participation in activities among physically frail residents of nursing homes can be quite difficult. Yet, several investigators (Powell, Felce, Jenkins, & Lunt, 1979) found a way by assessing the residents' interests. In addition to making other forms of recreation available, they introduced a gardening program and trained a volunteer to coordinate it. A number of skills were addressed:

making pictorial calendars with dried flowers and grasses, flower arranging, writing and decorating labels, tending house plants, taking cuttings, and planting seeds. Participation was much higher during gardening sessions than at other times and this level was maintained beyond a 4-month follow-up assessment. The authors posited that reinforcement arose naturally from the gardening activity, in the form of crafts, objects, and produce to support the generalization of their participation to many different activities. (As you shall see in the next chapter, natural reinforcement like this is one way that maintenance can be supported.)

Modifying Maladaptive Consequences

Behavioral problems persist because they are maintained by inauspiciously placed consequences. So to encourage an alternative adaptive behavior to generalize, the misplaced consequences need to be terminated. That is the objective of many staff and parent training programs. Care givers are taught not to attend to unwanted behavior but to provide lots of reinforcers for desired performance. Chapter 24 contains several examples from the literature.

Training Sufficient Exemplars

When many stimulus or response variations are appropriate to a newly modified behavior, train and reinforce the behavior under some of the stimulus situations in which it is supposed to be expressed, or in some of its forms. Presumably, the more exemplars—examples containing the critical stimulus or response features—that are provided, the more likely induction or generalization will occur without specific instruction in the presence of new variants. As new exemplars are added, the individual should become increasingly capable of *generalizing* to others containing the same critical features, in the absence of formal programming.

For instance, you are learning a foreign language in which both familiar and formal types of address are used. You read and practice suf-

ficient exemplars in conversation using both the familiar and the formal form. You learn to use the familiar form with subordinates, close friends, and little boys. Similarly, when your instructor asks you to translate "How are you feeling, little girl?" you automatically (and correctly) use the familiar form. (The "critical feature" here is that the little girl is in a socially subordinate position.) But when you address the instructor, you use the formal construction.

Say that your physics professor demonstrates a formula for solving several problems related to energy. You practice solving a few more problems on the topic for homework and receive reinforcing and corrective feedback as to when and when not to use the formula. Then you are able, when appropriate, to apply the formula with novel examples.

You help your niece to ride a two-wheel bicycle by steadying it, then gradually diminishing your assistance. Once she learns to ride that bike independently, she is able to ride other two-wheeled bikes using the same braking system and needs only a little help to get the hang of a bike with a different braking system.

In each of these illustrations, generalization to untrained stimulus conditions or to untrained responses was taught by "training of sufficient exemplars (rather than all) of these stimulus conditions or responses" (Stokes & Baer, 1977, p. 355). (Can you describe sets of the features that are critical or essential characteristics of the physics problems or the bicycles?)

Earlier we talked about a safety program in which four hospital caregivers learned to adhere to a task analysis for transferring and positioning patients (Alavosius & Sulzer-Azaroff, 1990). Without further intervention, one of the four began successfully adhering to another task analysis, one for safely feeding patients. (The other three participants did not.) Presumably, for the first individual, the two examples were sufficient to enable her to transfer across response classes. For the other three, two were not enough. Perhaps formal interventions would need to be carried out on a third, fourth, or maybe even more classes, before generalization occurred "spontaneously."

Other investigators (Haring, Kennedy, Adams, & Pitts-Conway, 1987) taught sufficient exemplars by using videotaped models. After finding that the three autistic youths who learned to purchase items in one setting failed to generalize their new skills to different settings, the investigators played videotapes of same-aged, nonhandicapped peers demonstrating each of the tasks in the sequence in varied settings. While the youths viewed the tapes, the instructor asked the youths questions, stopping to model the relevant response when questions were answered incorrectly. Generalization probes showed that the *simulation* procedure was sufficient to induce and sustain near-perfect performance in the novel settings.

Despite what one might assume, not all children know how to use toys appropriately. Haring (1985) wanted to teach four handicapped students to play with toys like their nonhandicapped peers did. So he gathered sets of toys, each of which contained many exemplars, like sets of boats, bugs, and airplanes. He taught the children to use first one, then another within a set by demonstrating, guiding, and praising the correct responses. Meanwhile, generalized play with other untrained toys from the set were probed. Eventually the children began to use the untrained toys appropriately. What's more, each time the children mastered playing with all the members of a set (e.g., every boat) and moved on to the next set, they began to generalize earlier than previously.

After a young autistic boy had begun to acquire a reasonably extensive vocabulary, the time came for him to learn how to use familiar words in full sentences (Wheeler & Sulzer, 1970). Prompting, fading, and reinforcement, were used to teach him to describe a set of pictures using the sentence form "The (subject) is (verb in present participial form) the (ob-

ject)" (e.g., "The boy is throwing the ball"). When probed for generalization with cards not used directly in training, the youngster continued to use the correct form.

Here is an illustration from a university setting (Chase, Johnson, & Sulzer-Azaroff, 1985). The objective was to teach undergraduates a set of complex concepts, like "constructional approach," "tau effect," and "abulia." During training, they were supplied with many, many examples of one of the concepts. When tested later on each, with novel questions about each of the concepts, the students were better able to identify novel examples of that particular concept. But they were less successful with the other two concepts for which they had received different kinds of training (i.e., to generate examples on their own or provide definitions). For instance if the students were given many examples of the tau effect, they were better at selecting examples of the tau effect from a list containing examples of the other concepts as well. The trained skill appeared to transfer better, probably because the right kinds of exemplars had been provided.

Besides illustrating how using sufficient exemplars helps to promote generalization, the Chase et al. (1985) study teaches us another important lesson: One gets what one gives. If you want your students to be able to define terms, give them lots of opportunities to define words. But if you want them to identify or produce examples, they need plenty of practice in doing so.

Selecting the right kind of exemplars is done by analyzing the task: identifying the critical features of the stimulus, or those that must be present if the example is to belong to the general stimulus class. (Abulia's five critical features were: first a high rate of behavior; high ratio of reinforcer to behavior at first; ratio of reinforcer decreases; rate of behavior decreases; and decrement in reinforcer/behavior ratio is abrupt.) The critical features of a bus are: transports more than six people on the ground, has wheels and an engine. Exemplars might be school buses, public buses, and airport buses. Assure yourself that wrong examples are not included by generating a separate list of "nonexamples" that contain most but not all the critical features—taxis, pedal bikes, boats, planes, and so on.

Stop and think for a moment about how this book is organized. Refer to the goals at the beginning of each chapter. Can you guess what kinds of skills we are hoping you acquire in dealing with the many concepts contained herein? Notice that most key concepts are illustrated several times. Why do you think we rejected the notion of limiting the presentation to abstract definitions and elaborations? Do you find yourself analyzing or interpreting the things you see people do in behavior analytic terms? If so, you are generalizing beyond your formal instructional experience. Good for you! (And good for us, because that's what we were hoping you would do.) Sufficient exemplars were provided.

Training Loosely

Another way to promote generalization is by doing the opposite of what you do in discrimination training. Instead of using a precisely repeated set of stimuli or formats, Stokes and Baer (1977) suggest that transfer can be encouraged by conducting teaching ". . . with relatively little control over the stimuli presented and the correct responses allowed, so as to maximize sampling of relevant dimensions for transfer to other situations and other forms of the behavior" (p. 357).

The purpose of training loosely is to prevent irrelevant stimulus controls (e.g., overselectivity) that would inhibit or suppress generalization. Thus, a teacher of autistic children would train loosely—would take pains to wear different clothes on different teaching days; to sometimes stand and sometimes sit during teaching; to sometimes face the student and sometimes

be behind the student during teaching; to sometimes use one tone of voice and sometimes another; to sometimes use one form of requesting the response and sometimes another (e.g., "What's this?" "Tell me about this," "Tell me," "What's the answer?" "Next!"); to vary the reinforcer and its schedule; to sometimes have another teacher substitute; to teach sometimes in one locale, sometimes in another; etc. That prevents accidental correlations of the correct response with any stimulus that is fortuitously but not meaningfully paired with the target stimulus, such as teacher's face, voice, position, clothes, and the room.

Many opportunities are available for training loosely. For example, you can capitalize on teaching opportunities that occur at unanticipated times and places. Say that you are trying to help your preschool students increase their use of descriptive adjectives. Many instructional options are available:

- You could set up formal lessons: selecting a set of pictures and asking for a description of each one, reinforcing those responses that contain descriptive adjectives.
- You could make lots of enticing toys available and watch the children at play, instructing as opportunities present themselves. "I see you're playing with the big, green cement truck. Which one do you want to drive? The little yellow one or the big brown one?" Next, after prompting, if necessary, you could reinforce by praising responses containing combinations of adjectives.
- You could wait for the child to initiate an interaction, capturing that teachable moment. It is free play period and Sammy tugs at your skirt and asks, "Teacher, can I have that truck?" "Which truck do you want? Do you want the big, green cement truck or the little red fire truck?" "The big, green cement truck." "OK. here you are." Receiving the truck is the natural reinforcer.

The last situation illustrates *incidental teaching* (about which you read earlier) and resembles an approach used on several occasions by Hart and Risley (e.g., 1975). You teach toward a specific, predetermined objective, yet you capitalize on natural unplanned opportunities (beyond providing enticing objects just out of reach). Probably you would find, as McGee, Krantz, and McClannahan (1985) did with incidental teaching to encourage use of prepositions, that your students generalize to a greater extent than with more formalized methods. Perhaps one reason why incidental teaching so successfully promotes generalization is because it incorporates the elements of loose training by permitting students many opportunities to sample relevant dimensions of various stimulus situations (e.g., green cars, green trucks, green apples, and green books).

Were you to learn all your behavior analytic concepts by only identifying sets of examples that we present, you would have a difficult time transferring the concepts to new situations. That is why the study questions in the study guide for this text (Hall & Sulzer-Azaroff, 1991) ask you to generate original examples and to apply what you learn beyond the classroom door. Probably your teacher, fellow students, and you yourself attempt to capitalize on natural opportunities to help you transfer concepts to novel cases. Interesting current events can provide productive opportunities for doing this. Intriguing court cases, racial strife, wars, murders, suicides, or acts of heroism or altruism (on the rare occasion when the latter two are reported in the press) have stimulated animated discussion in our classes and have provided opportunities to "loosely train" important concepts.

Using Indiscriminable Antecedent and Consequential Contingencies

You are driving along the highway on a sunny day, at eight miles over the speed limit. Several cars coming toward you are blinking their headlights. "Why?" you wonder. "Is it foggy ahead? Is there an accident? Is a police car poised beyond the next bend?" You slow down. You also reduce your speed at a point on the road where you've seen a police car previously and where you have noticed someone receiving a ticket. The response of driving within the speed limit transfers across all those situations, even though you yourself may have only received one speeding ticket and that was years ago. Why? Because you are unable to discriminate the contingencies in effect at any particular moment in time, and you respond to only loosely related cues. Indiscriminable contingencies promote *generalization;* clear, situation specific stimuli promote *discrimination.*

Diane, a typical four-year-old girl, hardly ever played with crayons, beads, or books, or in the kitchen area (Baer, Williams, Osnes, & Stokes, 1985). So a program was designed to promote such play activities. If the child said "yes," when asked if she planned to play with the crayons, beads, or books, she was praised and given a token. Her rate of using those increased, but just temporarily. So a *correspondence training* program (see Chapter 21) was implemented. Diane received reinforcement only after she actually played with the crayons when she had previously said she would. Crayon play increased. Interestingly, just reinforcing verbal statements of *intent* to play with the other play materials resulted in her actually following through, although correspondence was not reinforced for those other activities. Apparently, correspondence between saying and doing generalized from crayon play to the three other behaviors. Perhaps reinforcing correspondence at times and reinforcing only stated intentions at other times created an ambiguous situation; Diane may not have been able to discriminate which contingencies would be in effect at any given time, so she responded as if correspondence were being reinforced.

If your work involves teaching or managing a group of people, you can make use of this tactic to encourage effective participation among all group members. First, establish correspondence between stating an intent to carry out a particular responsibility and actually executing the action, and reinforce following the action when it matches the stated intent. Then, across different people and at random times, you can vary your reinforcement of either actual accomplishments or of statements of intention to accomplish something in particular. Reports of previous accomplishments or of correspondence between verbal statements and actual performance can also be reinforced intermittently. Because it will be difficult for group members to discriminate the contingencies in effect at any one time, generalization of correspondence will be more likely. You will have taught the group members to make and keep promises.

Programming Common Stimuli

Lathes, saws, presses, and other manufacturing equipment furnish the laboratory for the training of safety personnel at the headquarters of a major industry. As you enter, you feel as if you are inside an actual plant. Operators of atomic energy plants are trained similarly. Room-sized control boards including meters, blinking lights, levers, buttons, and all the other paraphernalia reproduce in perfect detail actual operational control rooms. Simulators of this type are used to train pilots, tank operators, and many other trainees for occupational tasks that require error-free performance. Chemistry labs, woodworking shops, cooking classrooms, and other laboratories in schools are also designed with the same concept in mind: Learning is best promoted in a setting that resembles as closely as possible the conditions under which skills will be practiced.

When training includes as many physical and social elements as possible that are common to the setting in which skills are to be practiced, you are using a sound instructional method. From laboratory experiments, we know that the more closely a test stimulus resembles a training stimulus, the more likely generalization is to happen (Rilling, 1977), and that the greater the stimulus difference, the less likely stimulus generalization is to happen (Michael, 1985). This decrease in responding as a function of a change in stimuli is called **stimulus change decrement**. It may occur because the different conditions contain few elements in common with the training condition.

When several discriminative stimuli combine to set the occasion for the occurrence of the behavior, it is even more likely to be emitted. Which doctor would you prefer to perform surgery on you: one who only has listened to lectures from an inspirational surgeon and memorized the textbook, or one who not only knows facts on the topic but has practiced on inanimate and animate patients in an actual amphitheater under the guidance of the super-surgeon?

Social dancing is a popular community group activity, so 5 mentally retarded teenagers who were scheduled to move from an institution to a group home were given dance instruction (Lagomarcino, Reid, Ivancic, & Faw, 1984). Trainers found that they needed to supervise the youths if they were to apply the steps learned in class. Trainers also taught the staff who would be present during actual dances to supervise in the same way. Consequently, most elements (SDs) of the supervisory procedures were *common across settings*, assisting the youngsters to generalize from one dance location to the next.

Effective teachers make frequent use of methods for facilitating generalization training, though they may not be aware of doing so. Such teaching goes on all the time. For example, a teacher says:

You know the word b*all*.
Now we are going to learn the word f*all*.
Notice the a-l-l at the end of the word b*all*.

It says *all*.
The word *fall* also ends in *all*, and it is pronounced f-*all*.
Now, how do you pronounce t-a-l-l?

The teacher is selecting the common elements among the words *ball, fall,* and *tall,* emphasizing those elements that tend to facilitate learning. Of course, the teacher presents nonexamples as well, such as *fell* and *talk,* to prevent overgeneralization.

Social stimuli can be very powerful, producing alterations in even very well-established behaviors. Because peers can be readily transported from place to place along with clients, they can participate even when a behavioral program is conducted in a special location, such as during a counseling session or in a resource room. The peer present during training also can return with the trainee to the natural setting to increase the commonalty of S^{D}s. Several cases have been reported in which peers were deliberately involved in promoting generalization. In one, by Stokes and Baer (1976), a student's generalization was increased when a peer tutor was brought into a setting in which the tutor usually was not present. Similar transfer is often reported when peers participate in tutoring and training. (See Dineen et al., 1977; Greer & Polirstok, 1982; and Jones et al., 1977, for examples.)

You even have to be careful to match schedules of reinforcement across the various settings. You should not be surprised that research (Koegel & Rincover, 1977) has shown that even if a behavior does generalize, maintenance is not likely in the generalization environment when the reinforcement schedule there differs from the original. Suppose a youth is taught in the clinic how to express his anger in a socially acceptable manner, on a rich intermittent schedule of reinforcement. Yet, when he returns to his home, the behavior is only reinforced sparingly. At home, the new skill probably will rapidly extinguish.

Behavior analysts have a responsibility for helping other practitioners and the public realize how important generalization from special and remedial to regular programs is. Unless generalization training is planned to accompany procedures in special settings, behaviors learned in such programs are not likely to transfer to natural settings (Walker & Buckley, 1972; Walker, Hops, & Johnson, 1975). For example, special classrooms have been set up for "handicapped" children and youths in many school districts. Frequently, each class has small numbers of students and at least one teacher with trained aides. Materials used are different from those in regular classrooms. In such an environment, many students learn appropriate academic and social behaviors, but when the students are mainstreamed into regular classrooms, the gains made in the special classroom do not carry over. A major reason is that conditions have not been arranged to facilitate generalization.

The special and regular classroom situations are too dissimilar. There are differences in the numbers of students and teachers and in the types of materials and tasks requested of students. Also, changes in the frequency of reinforcement encountered in moving from the special classroom to the regular classroom may almost resemble extinction conditions. If generalization is to occur, discriminative stimuli—similar rules, instructional materials, and schedules of activities—must be provided, and no abrupt change in reinforcement schedules should take place. A few school districts have set up "halfway" classes to help bridge the gap between the two very different types of classrooms. Others gradually introduce students into regular classroom settings or train "regular" classroom teachers in the procedures used by special education teachers. For example, Walker and colleagues (1975) developed an elaborate program for training regular classroom teachers in many of the behavioral strategies used in experimental classrooms.

Sheltered workshops for developmentally

delayed or disabled persons help to smooth the transition to regular vocational positions. Halfway houses perform similar functions for youths moving back to the community from correction facilities or for retarded citizens moving toward full community placement.

Do you understand why, in study after study, findings show that job skills trained in one setting fail to transfer to the location in which they are supposed to be practiced? Too often, no provisions have been made to promote generalization. People then are dismayed when it does not occur. As Haring (1988) suggests, behavior analysts must include generalization criteria in the standards for judging achievement of objectives.

Teaching Techniques for Mediating Generalization

People can learn to help themselves transfer their responding across conditions or behaviors by instructing themselves (aloud or covertly), arranging physical cues, or by using other self-management techniques. In the following illustrations, note how mediating responses are behaviors just like any others. Their generalization and maintenance are just as problematic and as needy of correct programming as are the target behaviors that they are supposed to mediate. Also, programming the generalization and maintenance of these mediating skills is often easier than for the original target behaviors.

"Now, I must remember to keep my eye on the ball and follow through with my swing," says Joe Duffer, as he practices the drive techniques he learned during his session with the golf pro.

Training in *self-instruction* has often been found to effectively mediate generalization by enabling people to control their own rates of disruption, aggression, cheating, and other maladaptive behaviors, but the training has not been successful at other times (Bornstein, 1985).

Correspondence training, is one technique for bringing overt behavior under the control of rules. Teach people to match reports of their performance with what they actually do or did (e.g., Israel & O'Leary, 1973), and the verbal statements can begin to be used to promote generalization.

A different procedure for mediating generalization is to teach people to *record* their own behavior. "Nice work, Harry. Your department handled more claims this week than during any previous week this year," says Sally.

Sandy checks her "praise card," noting that she is praising much more than criticizing on the job, just as the consultant suggested.

As with self-instruction, people's faithfulness and accuracy of self-recording may be inconsistent, depending on a number of factors. Both aspects of self-recording have a good chance of sustaining if each continues to be reinforced by other people or by strong evidence of improvement in the target performances. Otherwise, the consistency and accuracy of self-recording may drop off because it does take time and concentration.

Teaching Generalization as a General Skill

Whenever you learn a new principle in behavior analysis or in other subjects, apply it to your own work, school, and home life. You will learn it better and be able to use it in novel situations. By following this advice, you will more likely learn how to generalize principles. But this is not an especially easy skill. You probably will become proficient at doing this (or teach the general skill to others) by using sufficient exemplars.

That is what happened in the Haring (1985) toy study: Children began to generalize not only within but across toy sets. Eventually, some children only needed to be taught how to play with a single exemplar in a set before they spontaneously used the same play technique

Figure 29.1 Generalization Strategies

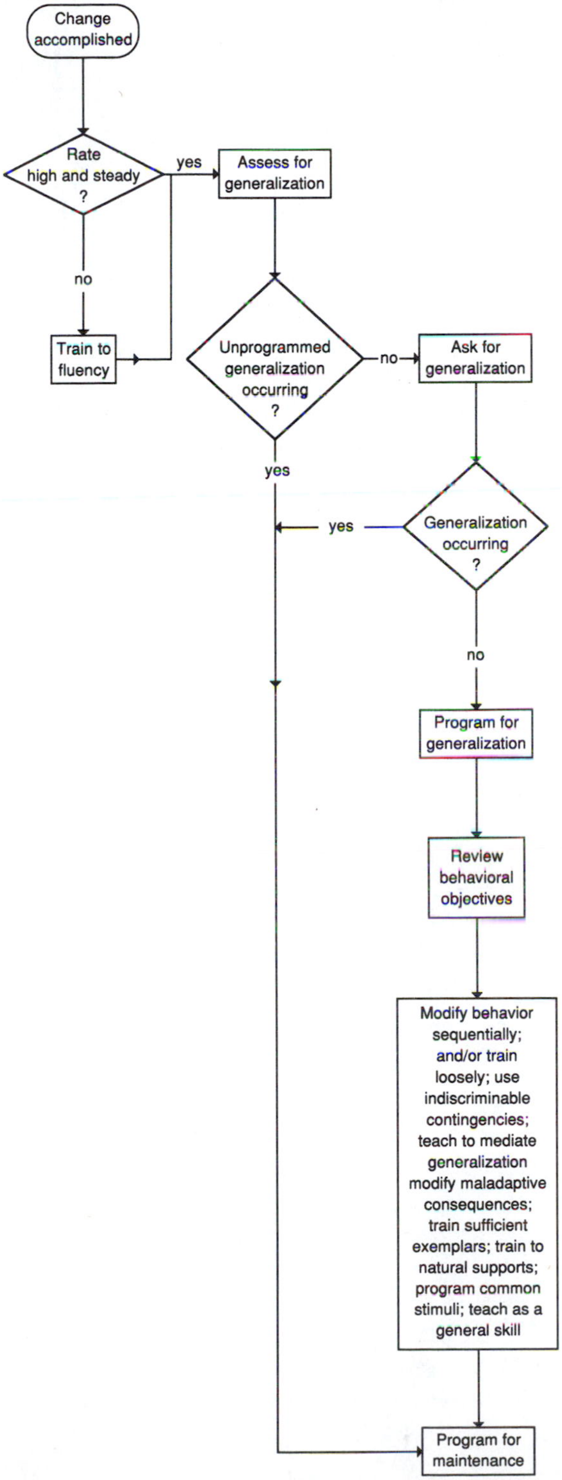

with the untrained exemplars in the set. Apparently, the children learned generalizing (at least within toy groups) as a response class in and of itself.

Summary

Only under the most fortuitous circumstances will generalization take place naturally. Prudent behavior analysts, therefore, plan and assess for generalization as an integral part of their programs. An extensive set of methods to achieve that goal has been presented in this chapter: asking for generalization, modifying behaviors sequentially, training to naturally supportive conditions, eliminating maladaptive consequences, training sufficient exemplars, training loosely, using indiscriminable contingencies, programming common stimuli, and teaching techniques for mediating generalization. (Figure 29.1 summarizes these strategies for promoting generalization.) Assuming that generalization is of concern, while the behavior change program is ongoing, probe for generalization regularly (Chapter 22). Avoid the temptation to take for granted that the natural community of reinforcers will take control automatically. Your data will tell you where and how intensively you need to intervene.

Generalization is one concern. Another is how to keep a modified behavior going after it is regularly occurring wherever it is supposed to. The next series of chapters addresses strategies for achieving lasting change.

Chapter 30

Strategies for Maintaining Behavior

GOALS

After completing this chapter, you should be able to:

1. List the factors affecting relapse and discuss how each contributes to relapse.

2. List the factors that naturally maintain altered or new behavior and discuss how each helps to maintain behavior.

3. Discuss when contingencies need and need not be programmed for maintenance.

4. List the strategies that can be used to prevent relapse and discuss why each can be used to maintain behavior.

5. Illustrate how each relapse prevention strategy can be used on a newly learned behavior.

6. Define, recognize, and illustrate response fluency.

7. Describe a time management program and its components.

8. List the factors to consider in arranging for naturally maintaining conditions.

9. Explain the Relapse Prevention Model and compare and contrast it with other behavioral strategies for promoting enduring change.

10. Use relapse prevention strategies on newly learned behavior.

"What is the greatest challenge in changing human behavior?" Ask this of any group of teachers, parents, human service workers, or managers; inquire of people trying to modify their own habits. Almost as a single voice they will respond: "Keeping it changed." Examples are easy to generate:

"Seeing my clients continue to use the social skills I've helped them learn."

"Teaching my students rules for proper sentence construction has been no problem. They all can recite the rules perfectly and apply them in their workbooks. But getting them to follow those rules consistently in their writing is another matter entirely."

"I thought I had it licked. I started praising more and scolding less. Now I seem to be back in the same old rut."

"That happened to me with my own eating habits. The new diet worked just fine for a couple of weeks and then just fell to pieces. I've actually gained back more than I lost."

Factors Impeding Maintenance

Why is it so difficult to get performance to stay modified and what can we do to prevent relapse? (Although the term usually is reserved for a return to unwanted habits, here *relapse* describes the recovery of baseline levels of any class of performance.) To begin to address questions of maintenance, or generalization over time, let us recall two key conditions that influence people's behavior: (1) their prior conditioning histories and (2) the contingencies currently in effect.

Throughout life, our behavior is continually being influenced by a multitude of different contingencies—reinforcement, extinction, punishment, S^Ds, and so on—within a variety of contexts. Some of these contingencies are supportive of enduring change; others are not. Fundamentally, though, modified behavior tends to persist when conditions (described later in detail) have allowed them to be firmly established in the first place; then supported. Otherwise relapse is predictable. Let us look at relapse as affected by:

- An abrupt cessation of reinforcement.
- Continued reinforcement for the previous unwanted behavior.
- Punishment of the modified behavior.
- S^Ds that set the occasion for the interfering or unwanted behavior.

Abrupt Cessation of Reinforcement

You have already seen that the best way for a behavior to become well established is for that behavior to be reinforced effectively—rapidly, frequently, with the kinds and amounts of reinforcers functional for that person at that time, and within a supportive context. Firmly establishing a behavior is important but not necessarily sufficient to guarantee that it will stay changed. Only if contingencies supportive of maintenance are in place is it reasonable to anticipate that the change will persist. Otherwise, disintegration is likely, especially when reinforcers are withdrawn abruptly. Here is an example:

"Okay, Fern. You are sorting the dishes and packing them in boxes pretty quickly, and you haven't broken anything in weeks. That's great. Keep up the good work." Satisfied with Fern's progress, the workshop supervisor, , turns her attention to her other clients.

But Fern gradually slows down, until the supervisor wonders if she might need to send her back for more training. Why has this happened?

Analyzing the situation, we conclude that the supervisor's praise probably was a very effective reinforcer. Fern really responded well to Ms. Charming's words of encouragement. In fact, the client's correct performances were on a rich schedule of reinforcement, because she was finally responding correctly almost every time. The problem was that although the supervisor waited until Fern's rates of careful sorting and packing reached an acceptable level, she then withdrew the praise abruptly. Had she gradually switched to a reasonable intermittent schedule, extinction might well have been delayed. As it was, though, extinction replaced reinforcement. Even though her shaping and chaining procedures had been carried out successfully, she neglected to see to it that the change was maintained.

Continued Reinforcement of the Previous Unwanted Behaviors

A major challenge to response maintenance is the likelihood that the person's previous unwanted habits will continue to be reinforced. Students' misbehavior often receives all sorts of reinforcement, in the form of peer and teacher attention. Sometimes we inadvertently teach people to do the opposite of what we intend by providing just what they want. "From here on," the teacher says, "I am only going to recognize those children who raise their hands." Yet, Ebenezer and Ralph keep calling out and the teacher can't seem to restrain herself from congratulating them when they offer good answers. Naturally, they keep calling out their answers.

A group of institutionalized delinquent girls was taught to comply with instructions (Buehler, Patterson, & Furniss, 1966). Yet their peers reserved their (primarily nonverbal) reinforcement for delinquent behavior, undoubtedly compromising the durability of improvement.

An example with which you probably are familiar is the New Year's resolution. We promise to watch our diets, exercise more often, stop smoking, drink less alcohol, be more patient with the children, practice playing musical instruments, learn a new language, and so on. For a short period we keep to our resolve but, more often than not, we begin to return to our old habits.

What explains this tendency to relapse? Put simply, our unwanted behaviors continue to receive reinforcement, thereby competing with those we would prefer to establish. Also, in contrast with the selected replacements, those prior behaviors may have been more firmly established. In that case, even occasional intermittent reinforcement can sustain the old ways. The foods we shouldn't be eating rapidly assuage our hunger and consistently taste good. Where is the equivalent reinforcement for abstaining from those foods?

The same can be true for alcohol or smoking, depending on one's constitution and reinforcement history. Research findings (e.g., Pomerleau & Rodin, 1986) inform us that within moments of beginning to inhale a cigarette, many smokers experience all sorts of pleasures: relaxation, enhanced alertness, and a sense of well-being, directly traceable to identifiable chemical changes. If it weren't for the immediately noxious effects that nonsmokers experience the first few times they try to smoke or reminders of the long-term punishment, probably many more people would indulge in smoking.

Losing our tempers can function similarly. Suddenly shouting or loudly slamming objects often produces rapid compliance. Remaining calm may pay off in the long run, but not immediately.

Reinforcement for the time and effort involved in attaining new skills is often delayed, whereas established unwanted behaviors continue to receive immediate reinforcement. That too is why so many of our resolutions fail.

Punishment of the Modified Behavior

After several weeks of participation in a training program in performance improvement, Charlie has learned how to convey his appreciation when his supervisor, Barry, notices his accomplishments.

"Hey, Charlie, I see your unit processed more claims last week than ever before."

"Thanks for noticing and letting me know, Barry. Maybe next week we'll do even better."

Barry departs with a smile.

Meanwhile, emerging from behind the water cooler, Cliff, the manager of the adjoining department, approaches Charlie.

"Hi guy! I see you're getting good at buttering up the boss. Bucking for a raise or what?"

A few days later, when Barry praises Charlie's unit for improving even more than previously, Charlie ignores the compliment. If those sorts of interchanges persist, Barry's compliments will slowly evaporate.

In a parallel situation, the delinquent girls of whom we spoke a little earlier (Buehler et al., 1966) punished their peers' compliance with institutional rules in addition to reinforcing noncompliance. Long-term maintenance of improved behavior by juvenile delinquents is extremely difficult to accomplish once the youngsters return to their original living situations (Kirigen, Braukmann, Atwater, & Wolf, 1982). Peer punishment is probably at least partially responsible. (Other related variables, such as constitutional plus environmental factors, are discussed in detail by Wolf et al., 1987.)

The following example illustrates a situation in which engaging in a newly acquired behavior can be intrinsically punished: Early in June, Polly suddenly realizes that she and her friends will be going to the beach soon. Studying her reflection carefully, she resolves to rid herself of a few unsightly bulges. The next morning she dons her leotards and joins in a televised exercise program. By the following day, she is so sore, she can hardly move. So much for her good intentions!

In each of these cases, even though reinforcement stood ready, the change was unexpectedly punished, causing the behavior change to deteriorate. You can probably think of numerous other examples. One we have experienced concerned a staff's failure to continue using an elaborate observational system.

The required time and effort apparently was too punishing. Another is promoting workers' use of troublesome protective equipment. We have learned to try to assess the setting and the task to predict any potential sources of punishment for the desired behavior. Sometimes this sends us back to the drawing board to alter either the target behavior or the contingencies. For instance, especially powerful reinforcers might need to be added to override possible punishing influences. The precaution is worth it, though, because it allows us to avoid wasting our resources needlessly.

S^Ds That Prompt Unwanted Behavior

The situation can be complicated further when powerful antecedent events are present to set the occasion for the unwanted behaviors that interfere with lasting change. Walking home in the early evening, you pass a pastry shop. First, the aroma of warm, freshly baked goods assaults your nose. Your stomach growls. You look toward the window, and the sight of your favorite chocolate eclairs is just too much. You succumb, seduced by all those powerful discriminative stimuli. The same sort of conditions operate when our faint-hearted friends yield to cues to smoke: exsmokers succumb to the presence of others smoking or the conditions paired with smoking in the past—a cup of coffee, the end of a meal, feeling anxious.

How about sexual practices? Think about how powerful the S^Ds can be and how they might cue one to respond without taking appropriate health precautions. Or, maybe losing your temper was paired with a release of tension in the past: powerful negative reinforcement! So when you feel tense, you yell. You probably can supply numerous other examples.

Factors Promoting Unprogrammed Maintenance

You may be beginning to conclude that accomplishing enduring behavior change is a lost cause, particularly when habits are well entrenched. But does relapse always happen? No. We all know of instances in which people have conquered the odds: a friend who has succeeded in attaining a new, slim figure; the reformed smoker, or drug or alcohol abuser; the person whose laziness has been replaced by ambition; the intemperate youth who has developed into a patient adult. Also, aren't some things learned and never forgotten, like writing, reading, or riding a bike? Don't children who learn to tie their shoes or dress themselves continue without any further assistance or arranged reinforcement?

Of course, people often *do* sustain their altered behavior. But how? Let us look more closely at the classes of modified behaviors that do tend to persist in the absence of formal programming. In many situations, reinforcement is still at work, although a different set of reinforcers may now be supporting the change, or the source of reinforcement may not be external any longer. Sue's husband, children, colleagues, and friends may lavish praise upon her for abstaining from smoking. Mr. Grump may congratulate and remind himself how much better his relationship will be with his students each time he successfully counts to ten and calms down instead of exploding. Sometimes the reinforcement derives from the very act itself or from its natural effect on the environment. Effective writing generates a product that evokes the desired response from readers; reading conveys information or a story; riding a bike takes you somewhere in a hurry. Being dressed and having shoes tied are prerequisites to going out. When tied, shoes are less likely to be lost or cause one to trip.

In a program on preventing back injuries (Alavosius & Sulzer-Azaroff, 1986), direct care workers learned how to safely transfer adult clients from their beds to their wheelchairs and back again. To everyone's pleasant surprise the new skills persisted after the intervention was discontinued totally. Previously, different classes of trained safety practices had not en-

dured as well following the termination of formal programming. When asked why they continued to practice the skills, workers replied that the new methods were easier for them. In contrast, the other safety practices, such as using protective equipment or putting things away, had required added effort. When reinforcement had been withdrawn from the effortful precautionary actions, workers reverted to previous levels. In other words, the safe transfer skills provided reinforcement by reducing the cost (i.e., effort) of doing the job, while the other practices had increased the cost making them more punishing.

Deciding to Formally Program Contingencies for Maintenance

Preliminary and ongoing ecological assessments may have convinced you that a newly established behavior will be naturally reinforced, at least intermittently, and that formally programming contingencies is unnecessary. However, reconsider. As always, the individual's performance must provide the cue. Suppose observing the environment's positive reactions to a child's behavior, such as Violet's speaking loud enough to be heard, convinces you that the behavior is being reinforced naturally. You also note that the child is maintaining her response rate over time and appears to be enjoying herself. You may be relatively safe in suspending intensive formal programming, but you should keep collecting follow-up data to be certain that your assumptions are correct. Even when your data corroborate the change's permanence, we would advise you to distribute an occasional reinforcer at unpredictable times after the response has occurred. That probably won't hurt, and just possibly could help prevent relapse. If data are not sufficiently compelling to convince you that the change will be supported naturally, you will want to design and implement a formal program to accomplish that purpose.

Formal Strategies for Preventing Relapse

Except in the face of incontrovertible evidence that a modified behavior indeed is persisting over time, your best option is to undertake a formal program. Otherwise, your efforts may have gone for naught. We suggest that first you ensure that the behavior is well established. Then you can select from a number of available strategies. These include some already discussed in Chapter 29 in the context of generalization: training toward naturally supportive contingencies; using indiscriminable contingencies and stimuli common to both the training and maintenance settings, correspondence training, and "self-reinforcement" techniques. In this chapter, we shall elaborate on these as they relate to maintenance. Later chapters focus on schedules of reinforcement to show how histories with different schedules may affect subsequent response patterns. Familiarity with these concepts can increase your success in promoting enduring change.

Minimize Errors During Acquisition

One way to increase behavioral durability is to minimize practice and reinforcement of unwanted competing behaviors during acquisition of a novel behavior. The errorless training paradigms you learned about in Chapter 18 discourage unwanted responses from occurring in the first place. Because those errors are rarely committed under the particular stimulus arrangement, they are unlikely to recur—even when the acquired behavior no longer results in reinforcement.

Hildegarde, who studied English as a second language in her native Germany, learned from the beginning to use pronouns correctly (i.e., errorlessly). Years later, as an adult now living in the United States, she still doesn't make the types of grammatical mistakes the rest of us often do. Her correct usage is reinforced; it works for her because she gets understood.

When errors are kept to a minimum from the beginning, new skills should endure intact. As you learned earlier, some findings show that *trial and success* produces more durable learning than trial and error, so attempt to minimize errors from the outset.

Build and Sustain Response Fluency

One way to help prevent a behavior from rapidly deteriorating once it is no longer regularly reinforced is to ensure that it is well established in the first place. Seeing the behavioral goal achieved only one time is insufficient; it must occur repeatedly. Just as making one perfect tennis swing, fly cast, or cheese souffle does not qualify you as an expert, concluding that your trainees or students are expert may be premature when they correctly perform a job operation, repeat a flawlessly accented phrase in French, correctly solve an algebra problem on the board, or effectively refuse an invitation to join a pot party in a role-play situation. Rather, they need to demonstrate the skill repeatedly, under both similar and varied conditions. The terms used by educators to describe this step are *overlearning* (Liebert & Poulos, 1973) or *overtraining*. You require multiple repetitions, conduct many conversations incorporating the phraseology, assign lots of different algebra problems related to the same basic concept, and set up a variety of role-play episodes on similar themes. You watch to see that the target behavior is consistently performed until it matches the criterion level (i.e., its frequency, duration, and so on) that you set in your objective.

Once the response is well established through frequent reinforcement, the fluency with which it is expressed is also very important. By performing *fluently*, we mean repeating it smoothly and rapidly with short latencies between any S^Ds and the responses, and with little apparent effort. To develop fluency, sequences of repetitions need to be reinforced. Bobby should be able to add *rapidly* and *correctly* his columns of numbers, without pausing after the S^Ds (a short latency period) or looking troubled. When operating the computer, Sara strikes the keys at a *high and steady rate*, hardly needing to correct herself. While in the past he needed all sorts of assistance, Frank now *regularly* puts on and buttons his shirt in just a few minutes. Similarly, reading needs to be accomplished *fluently* before the student is said to have mastered the skills. For example, children who can only slowly read a given vocabulary list at 100%-correct levels probably will not get any natural reinforcement from reading material with content that interests them. By contrast, children who have been taught sufficiently to read the same words as quickly as their eyes can scan them, and at the same 100%-correct level, probably will find reading stories to be fun and interesting, that is, reinforcing.

Support for the need to establish **response fluency** can be found in a number of studies. Literature from basic research (e.g., Weiner, 1964b), applied research (e.g., Young et al., 1986), and program evaluation (Becker & Carnine, 1981) has emphasized how important fluency training is for relapse prevention. In one laboratory study, Weiner used money to reward a simple button-pressing response. Some subjects received the money for pressing the button slowly; others for working rapidly. Later on, when the schedule of payoff switched so that button presses were reinforced no longer on the basis of rate but only for responses after a period of time passed (on an interval schedule), subjects continued to display patterns that resembled those expressed during the former phase. Subjects who had received reinforcement for high rates continued to respond rapidly; subjects who were rewarded for the low rates continued at their low rates. Therefore, if you want high rates to be firmly established *and* sustained, you should repeatedly reinforce responses occurring in rapid sequence before progressing to a more easily manageable reinforcement schedule. (Later you will recognize this strategy as a *differential reinforcement of high rates* [DRH] schedule.)

In the Young et al. (1986) study, two developmentally disabled preschoolers were taught to dress themselves by means of instructions, gestures, and graduated guidance. Although they gradually improved, the skills continued to be expressed somewhat variably in the training setting and irregularly elsewhere. A new phase was then introduced: fluency training. This consisted of identifying responses in the chain with which the children were experiencing difficulty and providing 10 trials of repeated practice on that response. During this phase, the children's accuracy and rates of responding increased substantially and generalized to other settings as well.

Fluency training is also a component of the Direct Instruction model (Becker & Carnine, 1981). Students not only must show that they are capable of reading particular words or performing arithmetic computations but are also required to achieve high rates of accurate performance. It seems reasonable to presume that one of the factors that accounts for the broadly documented success of Direct Instruction is this emphasis on fluency training.

Fluent performances generally require less effort than those not so thoroughly mastered. Watch any expert—a bowler, pianist, gymnast, surgeon, typist, linguist—and you'll be impressed with the apparent ease with which the skill is executed. When you initially try to imitate them, you wonder why you feel so awkward and ill at ease. Only with effort are you able to progress. By the time your own performance becomes smooth and fluent, though, you find you don't have to work so hard. The inherent cost diminishes, reducing punishment and thereby the likelihood of relapse.

Once response fluency is established, arranged reinforcement should be thinned out. After all, continuing to deliver very heavy reinforcement is neither practical nor feasible. Whether to plan to stop delivering reinforcement altogether depends on the availability of other contingencies ready to take over. If so, just fade over to those natural events. If not, thin out the rates of reinforcement slowly and gradually, watching your data for any deterioration of performance, until it reaches a level you can easily sustain indefinitely. Regardless of where you stop, though, you want the transition to be as smooth and free of disruption as possible. Later, we discuss how to accomplish smooth transitions for reinforcement schedules.

Identify Natural Contingencies of Reinforcement:

As you have learned, knowing about natural contingencies of reinforcement will enhance your ability to program maintenance successfully. Peer reactions are one potentially very powerful source of natural reinforcement. Kohler and Greenwood (1986) offer five methods for identifying natural contingencies of peer reinforcement:

- See whether the new behavior has generalized across settings or other conditions. Peer reinforcement may be a plausible explanation.
- See whether the behavior maintains ". . . after the original training stimuli have been removed from all other settings and behaviors" (p. 21). Data on long-term maintenance are more convincing than on shorter durations.
- Note any data that demonstrate that natural social stimuli consistently precede and/or follow behavior, appearing to influence its rate of occurrence.
- Conduct a functional analysis in the form of a reversal design, to show that peer

reinforcement is naturally operating. (To accomplish such a reversal, the peers would have to present or withhold their approval according to schedule as they did in a study of peer tutoring conducted by Kohler, Greenwood, & Baer, 1985.)
- Conduct a systematic replication: reproducing the results by applying the same peer stimuli contingent on other behavior within various settings.

Peer reactions, however, are not the only source of natural reinforcement. Others include the ongoing feedback systems within the organization, such as report cards and teacher approval in schools, job performance reviews, statistical reports, debriefings, and figures from the bottom line. Seeing improvements in the profit and loss statements at the end of the week or month, for instance, can be a major reinforcer, particularly when such improvements are tied to raises or bonuses. Job functions that minimize stress or effort, or maximize novelty or opportunities for socializing or for creativity (depending on the preferences of the employee) are all potentially reinforcing. Also, try to identify all the ongoing feedback systems, because they can prove to be a gold mine of potential reinforcement. (You may wish to review the section on ecobehavioral assessment in Chapter 6.)

Capitalize on Already Existing Natural Contingencies

After identifying the potential natural reinforcers, plan to capitalize on them. Recall the example of likely intrinsically reinforcing natural contingencies (reduced effort required) in the case of teaching care givers more efficient patient lifting and transferring techniques. You can do something similar. Suppose you identify a target to teach. Before initiating instruction, consider the reinforcers that are potentially integral to the behavior or currently available in the environment. Also, try to determine whether the student is already receiving reinforcement for expressing a variant of the behavior. That may help you to select an altered version to teach, one that is even more reinforcing.

Although a beginner, Sara loved to play her violin, even during vacations when she was not having her regular lessons. Her teacher purposely identified some of Sara's favorite songs and taught her to play them. Just hearing the music she produced seemed to be sufficient reinforcement to keep Sara going.

"Why didn't I think of that. It's so much easier this way," exclaimed Joe as the consultant showed him how to use a computer pad, not only to record but also to analyze his observational data. This enabled Joe to note subtle changes in his workers' behavior each day. Joe continues to collect the data, despite a general lack of support from his manager. (See Repp, Harman, Felce, VanAcker, and Karsh, 1989, for an actual computer-based data collection system.)

Program Toward Naturally Maintaining Conditions

When a target behavior fails to maintain on its own because the individual's learning history has not permitted natural ongoing contingencies to take control, you may be able to supply the necessary history via careful programming. The quality of antecedents and the quality, quantity, regularity and timing of reinforcement can be altered gradually, until each aspect resembles closely those of the natural environment. Also, relating contingencies to the performance of the group rather than the individual can set the stage for peer support, and various forms of self-management can also aid the process.

Fading antecedents. One feature on which to concentrate is the quality of the controlling antecedent stimuli. If a newly acquired behavior is to persist when you no longer keep an explicit intervention in place, natural antecedents must exert functional control, not prompts. In the beginning, using one's fingers to help oneself count, reciting the rules for shifting the car, or responding to the trainer's step-by-step instructions, orders, threats, or promises may be all right. Eventually, however, the responses should be controlled by the demands of the situation, without any intervening mediation.

The main challenge is identifying the natural antecedents. In the case of counting, that's easy. The numbers are the natural S^Ds. Often the links of a chain constitute the natural antecedents, each of which is supposed to set the occasion for the next link, as in shifting the car. Once you have identified the appropriate S^D, though, all you have to do is to apply a fading technology, such as progressively delayed prompting (Chapter 18), a relatively straightforward task.

Adjusting timing, regularity, quantity, and quality of reinforcement. Henrietta's academic performance began to improve when she participated in a program that allowed her to exchange her tokens for tangible rewards and extracurricular activities. (So did her headaches and stomachaches.) At first, after acceptably completing each assignment, Henrietta was given tokens and allowed to exchange them immediately for her preferred rewards. Eventually she began to produce at a rate similar to that of the other high achievers in the class.

At that point, instead of dispensing with the system, her teacher began to program for maintenance: Watching the data for any signs of relapse, the teacher began to *delay* the times for token exchanges to only twice daily, and back-up rewards were shifted away from tangibles to activities. The nature of the activities on the reinforcing menu also gradually changed, from extracurricular to preferred academic assignments.

Simultaneously, the teacher began to send home a card each day, reporting on Henrietta's accomplishments. The parents were instructed to praise these accomplishments and provide occasional rewards for series of good reports. Token exchanges continued to be delayed longer and longer, until they happened only biweekly. At that point, Henrietta and her teacher agreed that tokens were no longer necessary. Instead, the whole class would receive a special treat, like a party or a trip, when everyone performed at a given level for a number of days. Of course, praise continued intermittently. Meanwhile, reports gradually were sent home less often, until the schedule was the same as that for the other children. The only card Henrietta now received was the same one as her peers. Because her grades had improved and because her parents had learned to reinforce her accomplishments, she needed no additional incentives to keep her going.

Lest you doubt that little children can be taught to tolerate delays in reinforcement, consider the findings of a study conducted with preschoolers identified by their teachers as "impulsive" (Schweitzer & Sulzer-Azaroff, 1988). The children seemed to respond before considering the consequences of their actions. For instance, when offered a choice between a small immediate reward or a large one for which they would have to wait, any time the wait was more than a few seconds, the children would choose the smaller, immediate reward. (Familiar adult examples include: electing to eat a candy bar immediately instead of waiting for a more nutritious meal later on; spending one's whole paycheck on small unimportant items rather than saving for larger more meaningful ones; and stealing rather than taking the time to earn reinforcers.) Training the "impulsive" preschoolers started by arranging almost no difference in the reinforcement delay between the two choices. As you'd expect, the children preferred the large rewards. Then delays of a few seconds were slowly introduced for the larger choice, whereas the alternative small choice was always presented immedi-

ately. Little by little, over a series of sessions, the children began patiently to wait much longer than they had previously for the larger rewards—some for more than a full minute. (Sit and concentrate on watching the second hand sweep around until a minute elapses to see how long that can be.)

Parents, teachers, trainers, and managers also teach people to accept delay and changes in the quality, quantity, and regularity of reinforcement, usually without being aware of doing so. "Let's take turns, children. I'll call on you one at a time." "Can we meet at the end of the day, instead of now? I have an appointment with someone else." "Eat your vegetables. Then you can have your dessert." Mom and Dad give Flossie a prize the first time she behaves well at the dentist. The second time they limit themselves to congratulating her cooperativeness. What is different in this formal training for maintenance is that we proceed *systematically;* continuing to collect data to guide us to decide whether and when we should extend the delay period or, if necessary, back up a bit because performance shows signs of deteriorating.

Tightening criteria for reinforcement. A fairly straightforward way to reduce the amount and/or to increase the delay of reinforcement to "thin" reinforcement is to alter the criterion level for reinforcement. For instance, to earn the opportunity to participate in a special group activity, members are required to achieve at $X\%$ higher than the previous day or sustain performance at an optimal level, such as 80%. When Greenwood and colleagues (Greenwood, Hops, Delquardi, & Guild, 1974) used that kind of strategy, improvement in students' deportment persisted over more than 20 sessions. Ultimately, a group activity could be built into the schedule as a natural reinforcer when members complete their assignments acceptably by a given time.

Use care, though, when you increase criteria

for earning reinforcement. Too large or too rapid a shift might well cause a disruption in performance. (Chapter 32 describes such disruption as a case of "ratio strain.") For several weeks, to earn tokens Henrietta has had to score at least 60% on her spelling paper. Abruptly her teacher changes the minimum criterion to 90% for the following week. Henrietta refuses to do her spelling assignment, scowls, stamps her feet, and mumbles a string of unflattering remarks about her teacher (an extinction burst) and complains of a headache. Elevating the criterion to 70% rather than 90% might have avoided the entire scene.

Setting up peer support as a naturally maintaining contingency. If you teach certain categories of skills such as positive social interactions or affective (i.e., emotional) responses, they are likely to evoke positive reactions from others. "Spontaneous" peer support has been reported by Kohler and Fowler (1985), who taught elementary school aged girls prosocial skills, and Hopkins (1968), who taught a retarded child to smile.

Sometimes group contingencies will serve as setting events for peer support. In one of our studies (Frankowsky & Sulzer-Azaroff, 1978), developmentally delayed teenage boys worked on a prevocational sorting task. They could receive rewards either for the work they did individually or for the collective effort of three youths working together. Although both contingencies produced similar output, during the collective arrangement peers encouraged one another. This mutual support even spilled over to situations later on. Be certain though that all group members are capable of performing at similar levels when you plan group contingencies like these. Otherwise, peers may begin to coerce or punish one another.

You can arrange group contingencies in your organization as a device for evoking peer support. Suppose you are interested in increasing the productivity of your staff or students; to increase educational plans written or implemented, assignments completed, and so on. With the group, you might plan to divide people into cohesive "support groups," to whom feedback and occasionally special rewards are delivered as a consequence of meeting collective production goals. For instance, the average number of completed assignments could be posted for each unit. At various times, when things were going particularly well, the company could arrange some special event, like a recognition luncheon.

Evidence for the effectiveness of the type of strategy just described is provided by results of a study conducted by Greenwood and colleagues (1974). Children in first-, second-, and third-grade classes participated in a program in which rules for proper classroom deportment were presented, and then feedback was provided along with the rules. Behavior improved somewhat. Yet progress was far more substantial when an additional condition was implemented: teacher praise plus permitting pupils access to special group activities, contingent on meeting a preset performance criterion for the group. In cases like this, children usually spontaneously dispense social reinforcement to their classmates by cheering, smiling, or otherwise expressing their delight when the group is informed that it has earned its reward. (See Chapter 12 for additional strategies for obtaining peer support.)

Use Correspondence Training

Maintenance also has been shown to be helped by means of correspondence training. In correspondence training, as you learned earlier, people are taught to match statements describing their behavior with the corresponding act. Correspondence training *requires*, that you have accurate, complete information on the person's performance in order to reinforce only corresponding reports and withhold reinforcement from noncorresponding reports. A toddler is observed sharing a toy with her friend Willie. Afterward, the teacher asks, "Did you share your toys?" If the response is "Yes, I shared a toy with Willie," we can say that the verbal statement corresponded to the act. Children (not to speak of adults) do not necessarily act as they report or promise, so we need to teach them to describe their behavior accurately. This is important not only because honesty is moral but also because when verbal reports consistently correspond to behavior, it may be possible eventually to change behavior by differentially reinforcing the promises or reports rather than the actions themselves. When that happens, you can occasion a statement of intention to follow through later on—to promote maintenance of performance.

"What kind of snack will you take today? Fruit or chips?"

"Fruit."

Then later—"What snack did you take?"

"Fruit"

"That's great. You did. And the fruit tasted good, didn't it? And it is so good for you."

Next time the child is asked and promises to choose fruit, he is more apt to choose the fruit rather than the chips. The advantage of achieving reliable correspondence is that you don't always have to be present when the behavior is actually expressed. Moreover, once correspondence is well established, you might promote successful maintenance in some cases by reinforcing statements of intention sometimes, performance of the target behavior at other times, and accurate correspondence of verbal reports following the behavior. Perhaps you will be fortunate enough to find, as Guevremont et al. (1986) did with the classroom deportment of two preschoolers, that the behavior tends to endure.

Teaching and Maintaining Self-Management

Under ideal conditions, clients assume major responsibility for preventing relapse of their own altered behaviors, freeing the change agent to concentrate on other activities. Through careful observation, identifying, teaching, and maintaining promising self-management strategies usually is possible. Among them are time management, self-recording, self-reinforcement arranging one's own environment, lifestyle changes and others. One important trick is to discover effective reinforcers that the client can readily manipulate, and to supervise and occasionally reinforce their application. Familiar examples of self-management strategies include self-recording (Chapter 6), self-reinforcement (Chapter 11), and arranging one's own social and/or physical environment so that the target response tends to receive reinforcement intermittently. Here the discussion begins with helping clients to find the time to carry out their self-management programs.

Teaching time management. "I'd love to do it but I don't have time." How often have you heard or expressed that protest? The fact is that all of us have the same amount of time in a day. What people generally mean when they say they don't have time is that they are busy doing other things: tasks demanded by their jobs, families, or their own bodies (like sleeping, eating, mating, exercising, relaxing) plus various social, recreational, and other activities.

Few of us analyze the patterns of our use of time. (We are too busy!) If you do stop for a while to perform such an analysis, though, you may be surprised and find the investment worthwhile. Record your activities for a week or two, using a prepared daily schedule form and abbreviations or codes to simplify the recording task. Then classify what you do in terms of how essential each activity is for your physical survival and economic and familial well-being. Regard your other doings as optional. By examining the latter list, you will begin to see that you engage in some activities in response to unanticipated antecedent stimuli: A friend calls and you spend 45 minutes discussing old times. Your roommate turns on the television and you get hooked into watching a 2-hour ball game. A brightly colored bird flies past the window, and you run for the binoculars. An advertisement seduces you into purchasing concert tickets or to shop for an item you are now convinced you need.

The availability of immediate reinforcement, often of a lesser value, will also tempt you to act now, despite the likelihood of receiving a more valuable reinforcer for postponing that action. Come on, confess. How often have you postponed studying in order to have a good time with your friends? How many times have you pleaded insufficient time to help your kids with their hobbies because you had to finish a report so the boss wouldn't get angry? (Completing the report is negatively reinforced when you avoid the aversive consequences.)

The point is that just as other aspects of our behavior are controlled by contingencies, so is our allocation of time. When we take responsibility for managing time, we, not life's vagaries, are in control. Thus, request your clients to ask themselves if they are doing the things that are of highest priority. If so, they should congratulate themselves and forget about the rest. More than likely, though, a certain amount of their time is wasted in unimportant or even counterproductive activities. If so, help them to identify their goals and their most preferred activities, then to set priorities and decide what and what not to do.

Next help them to arrange their schedules to accommodate the activities highest on the list, so more reinforcing events follow closely in time those that are less reinforcing. They might plan to go out with friends (or have time to themselves—depending on their reinforcers) *after* they have studied for a given number of minutes. Assuming that anticipating their boss's or instructor's ire consistently has been sufficient to cause them to submit reports on time regularly, they could schedule writing their reports after they have spent a half hour working with their youngster on her soccer kick. When

time is allocated in advance, they can relax and forget about what else needs to be done until the time comes. You or your client can also let other people know, so they will more readily relinquish their company and remind your client to move on to the next event. If forgetting to switch activities is a problem, suggest to your clients that they use a timer or wrist alarm to signal the approach of the end of the interval.

Time-management programs have been used to help people increase the amount of time they devote to instructional activities. In one case, parents learned to schedule and incorporate teaching sessions with their retarded children within their daily routines (Hall & Sulzer-Azaroff, 1987). One mother elected to read her child a bedtime story nightly, including language training trials within the activity (pointing to pictures, asking questions, and so on). Another taught language while bathing her child. On inquiry, several months following the termination of the formal parent training intervention, the parents reported continuing to teach their children, and the data on the children's continued progress supported their claim.

Nine resource teachers, three in each of three junior high schools, participated in a time management program (Maher, 1982). Observers used a 10-second interval scoring procedure to record three categories of instructional and three categories of noninstructional teacher behavior during baselines lasting from 1 to 3 months. During a 50-minute period, each teacher was found to spend an average of about 39% of the period carrying out instruction.

Then the teachers participated in a time management program consisting of the following:

1. *Time management problem analysis*: recording the amount of time spent on various professional activities and comparing the results against priorities or predetermined standards to determine nonessential work, unnecessary activities, and other time wasters.

2. *Plan development and implementation*: determining daily and weekly priorities, distribution of activities, and schedule changes. The methods designed to help ensure productive activity included (a) setting weekly goals, (b) identifying behaviors necessary to achieve the goals, (c) specifying time wasters, and (d) environmental cues.

3. *Plan evaluation phase*: obtaining and analyzing information about the extent to which their plan was being implemented as intended.

4. *Monthly social support meetings*: discussing with the supervisor and group time management problems, plans and methods to address problems, and results of their evaluations.

Results were powerful, with the mean percentage of instructional times in each school rising to between 80% and 88% after training.

Time management permits natural stimuli such as time of the day and day of the week to become the S^Ds for priority activities. So, assuming that time is allocated to practicing and reinforcing newly acquired behaviors, you can see how time management can be used to support enduring change.

Think about how you or your clients can plan when, for how long, and how often recently acquired skills will be practiced. Try to incorporate the practice within the daily routines so the events that regularly precede that practice should begin to prompt it. Stop off at the gym Mondays, Wednesdays, and Fridays on the way home from work. Shop for low-calorie foods Saturdays just after lunch, and so on.

Before we leave time management, though, a caution is in order. Time management can be dangerous if carried to an extreme, as when "low-level" classes of reinforcing events (e.g., discussing old times and watching T.V.) are scheduled out of your life entirely. The result can be burnout, as reflected by expressed dissatisfactions with your job, spouse, and life. Instead, try occasionally to balance your activities, following those of greater importance with

these "low-level" reinforcing events. All work and no play can do more than make "Jack a dull boy." It can make him depressed.

Teaching self-recording. Now that they have set time aside to conduct programs, clients can begin to carry out the technical aspects of self-management. Self-recording is an element of many self-control programs, such as management of obesity (Epstein, Wing, Koeske, Ossip, & Beck, 1982), depression (Roth, Bielski, Jones, Parker, & Osborn, 1982), high blood pressure (Jacob, Fortmann, Kraemer, Farquhar, & Agras, 1985), and many others. This procedure can be especially helpful in preventing relapse of modified habits.

A group of clients who stuttered learned to speak fluently by being trained to slow down their rates of talking (Craig & Andrews, 1985). Once stuttering no longer occurred at that slow pace, they were taught to accelerate their rates of fluent speech to resemble a typical tempo. Ten months later, some had relapsed. These clients then were retrained and provided with a set of self-control methods, including monitoring and counting stuttering, rating the quality of their fluency skills each half hour, and rewarding themselves with money. Further relapse was prevented for almost all of the subjects. Additionally, most reported via a Locus of Control Scale (Rotter, 1966) that they felt more in control of themselves.

As part of the requirement for a laboratory project in self-management, students in our courses in applied behavior analysis must modify a behavior of their own and supply a plan to sustain the change. (See Sulzer-Azaroff & Reese, 1982, for details.) Self-recording is usually an element of the change, as well as the maintenance strategy. For instance, our students have recorded the number of sweets they have ingested, cigarettes smoked, miles jogged, sit-ups performed, pages written or read, and many other classes of performance. After reaching their goals, some continue to monitor the behavior and display graphs of their records. Often these people are the most successful in preventing relapse.

As you can imagine, it isn't easy for most parents to fulfill a complex teaching function with their severely retarded youngsters. They may lack requisite instructional skills, and other demands vie competitively for their time and energy. Accordingly, the series of home-based training programs of which we spoke earlier (Hall & Sulzer-Azaroff, 1987) was designed to teach parents skills for instructing their children. Besides scheduling and managing their time, parents also rewarded themselves for doing so. One aspect of the program was to self-record the results of the training trials they conducted in a simple plus or minus fashion. This way, they could see even subtle progress as it occurred. These strategies appeared to help the parents to continue instructing their children.

Service personnel should be able to use similar methods to support their own programs of relapse prevention. For instance, teachers might record whether they provided feedback to specific students within a given block of time, such as 15 minutes. A director of a clinic who wishes to continue visiting his staff might check the names of the people he visited each day or week. A direct care worker could write down and chart the number of times he solicited and reinforced merited praise from his supervisor.

Self-recording need not be limited to adults. Children are capable of checking their own performance also. Using checklists or graphs, students of all ages have been able to record their scores for assignments, pages read, problems solved, tasks completed; to record time blocks during which they performed a target behavior like sharing toys or contributing to the group discussion, or during which they successfully avoided sucking their thumbs, or misbehaving in particular ways. In a specific case, Heins, Lloyd, and Hallahan (1986) taught 4 boys in a class for children with learning disabilities to record their own instances of attending to task. Attending did increase under those conditions. Results were even more impressive when the boys learned to observe and record at the moment they heard an audio cue instead of when left on their own recognizance. In another case (Ridley, 1986), Aaron, a six-year-old, functioning at about a level of 4 years, only ate pureed foods. After he learned to eat solids, his teacher taught him to record his own successes. While self-recording, he continued to consume the solids consistently.

Teaching reinforcing one's own behavior. People are capable of administering reinforcement to their own behavior, and the procedure has been used often within self-management packages. One example was a study involving second graders (Glynn, Thomas, & Shee, 1973). Those children assessed and recorded their own performance, determined whether they had earned reinforcement, and administered reinforcement for their behaviors. Using the combined set of procedures, the students remained on-task at higher rates than they had under two different forms of group contingencies.

Our own students usually choose activities or rewards to deliver to themselves as a consequence of meeting set criteria. These reinforcers are determined via reinforcement surveys and self-recordings of how they spend their time. They use the latter information to identify high-frequency behaviors according to the Premack principle. Favorite activities include writing letters, making or receiving telephone calls, going dancing, and buying jewelry or items of clothing. In the Hall and Sulzer-Azaroff study (1987), each parent chose items and events to dispense to themselves contingent on their adhering to their weekly tasks. The kinds of activities chosen included time alone, working at a part-time job, recreation like bowling with spouses, or going out to dinner.

Interestingly, we have found that despite earning reinforcers, students and clients often fail to deliver the rewards to themselves. They posit that seeing evidence of improvement and the feedback from peers and the instructor is more powerful than the self-reward. (Just as Nyborg and Nevid [1986] found, Spouse involvement helped marital partners who smoked to abstain from smoking more successfully than when the couples tried initially on their own.) Perhaps, as with self-instructional training (Bornstein, 1985), self-reinforcement produces variable outcomes, depending on a number of other factors: learning history, social support, cultural factors, and so on. Nevertheless, rewards do seem to help people initiate and express more satisfaction with their programs. You could try self-recording alone and see whether that works sufficiently well. If not, adding a self-reward component might help your clients over the initial hump.

Teaching people to arrange the social and/or physical environment. In discussing self-control, Skinner (1953) talked about modulating the variables that control one's own response to increase or decrease the probability of that response. One way to help people guard against relapse is to teach them to arrange environmental stimuli to support the behavior. Suppose your client found it difficult to keep working on a long writing task. Despite his firmest resolve that today would be the day to return to his writing, he found himself doing all sorts of other, "more demanding" activities, like preparing other assignments, making phone calls, answering mail, filling out forms, planning the menu for dinner, and removing the dead leaves from the plants. One solution: Suggest he find a place away from all potentially distracting stimuli (the telephone, the papers, the plants). A library carrel is a good place to work. Suggest he go there at a prescheduled time, bringing only the material he needs for the writing assignment and not telling his friends where to

find him. If possible, he might arrange return transportation for a particular time to be less tempted to leave the library early. He may find that all choices but working on the writing task are eliminated. Seeing progress, perhaps by self-recording, may help make the activity more reinforcing. If he is fortunate enough to have a computer available, he could chart number of bytes he produces daily or weekly.

To help forgetful clients remember to record daily data, suggest they place a large calendar where they will be sure to see it (over the sink) and to check it each day. In his book, *Enjoy Old Age,* Skinner (1983) suggests many hints like these. If consistently practicing your guitar is your goal, put the guitar where you spend your unstructured time, and you can't fail to notice it—maybe in front of the unplugged television set. To help your staff continue to provide feedback to their students or clients, provide them with timers or pocket or wrist counters to cue the behavior. Another suggestion is to implement a token economy. As Breyer and Allen (1975) found, dispensing the tokens reminded the staff member to attend to the recipient. You could use the system to set the occasion for distributing feedback.

Some of our students arrange their environment so that social reinforcement is regularly forthcoming to support their altered behavioral patterns. A couple have posted their records of writing products or weight loss over their office desks. Their friends often notice the charts and compliment their success in sustaining change. Other students broadcast to all their friends and acquaintances what they have accomplished and plan to accomplish, requesting that those folks comment positively when they observe continuing success. They do! Peers also have been shown to be able to function in the role of contingency managers in programs of occupational safety (Sulzer-Azaroff, Fox, Moss, & Davis, 1990) and in quality of instruction (Fleming & Sulzer-Azaroff, 1990).

A variety of ways can be used to evoke social

reinforcement. These include: providing opportunities for staff, students, or clients to meet and share their accomplishments; reporting their successes in the organizational newsletter or public press; arranging exchange visits, open houses (say, from class to class or ward to ward), or traveling performances or exhibits (skits, craft displays, or other events); and supporting staff attendance at a national or regional conference where they report on a successful new teaching or training technique. With the right kind of preparation and planning, a positive response from the audience is almost guaranteed.

Teaching people to change their lifestyles. Changing one's lifestyle is an especially promising self-management technique for encouraging durable change. As suggested with time management, what you do is help people to modify the way they do things and sustain the changes by incorporating the activities into their daily routine. Events that follow these behaviors serve as reinforcers; events that precede them function as discriminative stimuli.

An example: You want to increase the time you spend exercising. Find a time of day and something that is a well-established part of your routine, and sandwich the exercises in, not permitting yourself to progress on to the next activity until you complete your exercise requirement. The night before, you set the alarm to awaken you 2 minutes early. When it rings, you arise and begin some aspects of your morning routine, but stop before showering, brushing your teeth, giving the kids breakfast, or whatever you usually do every day, and couldn't bear to skip. For 2 minutes, do your exercises. Then continue with the regular routine. Keep this up for a week or so, allowing yourself a preset number of days off. Then turn the alarm back another minute. Exercise for 3 minutes. Keep this up until you have reached your optimal amount of exercise time, such as a half-hour. Within a half a year or so, the behavior will be well established within your lifestyle, without your even suffering the jolt of suddenly losing a half hour's sleep or any muscle pains.

Is this a realistic suggestion? Well, what you just read describes exactly what one of us did—and has continued to do for 18 years (with a bit of cheating during illnesses, trips, vacations, and under other circumstances when discriminative stimuli are altered).

Lifestyle changes like these are incorporated in many habit change programs. Alcohol abusers are taught to substitute alternative regular group recreational activities instead of visiting bars; smokers, to avoid stimuli that cue smoking; overeaters to take small bites, to chew completely, and to pause between mouthfuls. Epstein et al. (1982) described how lifestyle changes could be incorporated within an exercise program for obese children. These changes included asking the children to earn aerobic points (determined by time × intensity) by climbing the stairs instead of taking the elevator; walking instead of riding; and otherwise minimizing the use of energy-saving devices instead of performing aerobic exercises at scheduled times. Whereas children who did scheduled exercises lost as much weight as those who used the lifestyle change, the latter group was outperforming the former during follow-up assessments after 6 and 17 months. As with most lifestyle changes, the children changed their targeted habits and probably no longer needed extraneous prompts or reinforcers to keep them going.

The Relapse Prevention Model (Marlatt & Gordon, 1985) addresses the extremely high relapse rate—50% to 90% (Brownell, Marlatt, Lichtenstein, & Wilson, 1986)—found among those patients who had been "successfully" treated for abusing nicotine, alcohol, or drugs, and for eating disorders. Three stages are included in the model presented by Brownell et al. (1986):

1. Motivation and commitment.

2. Initial change.
3. Maintenance of change.

Motivation may be assessed by screening, and possibly enhanced through education on the dangers of addiction, encouragement from the therapist, public campaigns, and so on. (However, data are not yet available to support these presumptions.) To prevent dropout, studies have shown that monetary incentives, in the form of deposits refunded for attendance and follow-through, often operate effectively. Initial change is accomplished in various ways that are now familiar to you for modifying behavior, plus others, such as a number of cognitive-behavioral strategies. In one example, treating obesity (Perri et al., 1984), clients learned self-monitoring, stimulus control strategies, self-reinforcement, relaxation training, procedures to slow the pace of eating, and suggestions for exercise management. Then a group of the clients was taught and practiced skills to prevent relapse:

- To recognize and identify situations posing a high risk of relapse.
- Problem-solving techniques for meeting the challenges of high risk situations.
- *In vivo* practice of coping with high risk situations.
- Cognitive strategies (verbal statements to oneself) to cope with feelings of guilt and failure in reaction to slips (e.g., labeling a slip as an opportunity to intervene and to practice a self-control skill).

In the Perri et al. (1984) study, some of the clients remained in contact with the therapist by mail and telephone relaying information on their weight and practice of skills. Although all the clients had lost weight 12 months later, the relapse prevention group experienced the most weight loss and the least relapse.

Notice how many of the strategies previously discussed in this chapter are included within the Relapse Prevention Model. As with

Figure 30.1 Maintaining Behavior

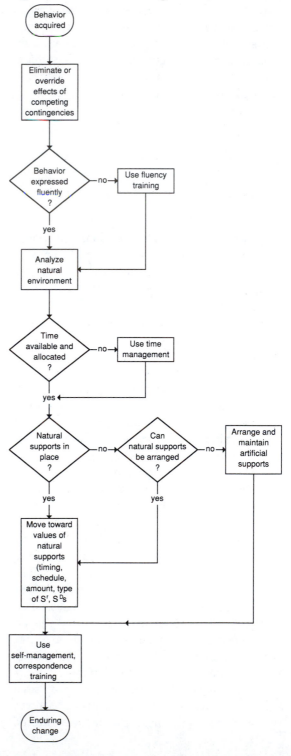

reinforcement "packages," maintenance packages like these hold great promise for the successful long-term treatment of behaviors, especially those prone to relapse.

Summary and Conclusions

You have seen how the presence or absence of current and prior reinforcing contingencies can influence maintenance of change as well as the manner in which behavior alters under extinction conditions. Unless modified performance is supported by natural reinforcers, once arranged reinforcement is terminated, change is unlikely to maintain "spontaneously." Consequently, in the absence of follow-up data demonstrating enduring change, you will need to program for maintenance (see steps in flowchart, Figure 30.1). In this chapter, you have encountered a number of strategies for preventing relapse. While adhering to these and the subsequent suggestions is no guarantee that wanted behavior will persist, surely you and your clients will find them helpful in many instances. Additional research continues to be needed in this critical area. Next, we elaborate on one particularly well established technique for sustaining performance: intermittent reinforcement.

Chapter 31

Maintaining Behavior: Interval and Limited Hold Schedules

GOALS

After completing this chapter, you should be able to:

1. Define, recognize, and give original illustrations for each of the following terms:
   a. Interval schedules
   b. Fixed-interval (FI) schedules
   c. Fixed-time (FT) schedules
   d. Variable-time (VT) schedules
   e. Variable-interval (VI) schedules
   f. Behavioral contrast or contrast phenomenon (positive and negative)
   g. Limited-hold schedules
2. Compare and contrast fixed- and variable-interval schedules.
3. List and describe the characteristics typifying performance under interval schedules of reinforcement.
4. Discuss the differences between animal and human responses under FI schedules.
5. Discuss the advantages and disadvantages of using interval schedules.
6. Discuss how (a) interval length, (b) history, (c) presence of discriminative stimuli, (d) competitive contingencies, (e) behavioral contrast, and (f) limited-hold restrictions can influence rates of performance under interval schedules.
7. Describe under what conditions a fixed versus a variable interval schedule should be selected.
8. List and explain two ways to thin reinforcement when interval schedules are in effect.
9. Implement interval schedules to maintain a behavior at a high, steady rate.

After the behavior change you have been seeking has been well established by using a rich schedule of reinforcement, you may begin to diminish the frequency of reinforcement by making the schedule more intermittent. Recall that a schedule states the conditions that must be in effect for reinforcers to be delivered (Zeiler, 1977). Usually these conditions relate to passage of time or completion of numbers of responses. We also know that intermittent reinforcement serves to maintain behavior in applied settings. In these next two chapters, however, we shall examine schedules of reinforcement much more closely, to discover the sorts of performance patterns that tend to be generated by particular schedules. As a behavioral practitioner, whenever response patterns are important, you will find it advantagous to use your knowledge of how schedules of reinforcement are likely to influence the rate and consistency with which a behavior is repeated.

You also will find it helpful to know the extent to which these schedules provide opportunities for competing behaviors to occur, both *while* the schedule is in effect and *after* reinforcement has been discontinued. This chapter will be directed toward the simpler interval and limited-hold schedules. In Chapter 32, we introduce ratio and differential reinforcement of high rates of behavior.[1]

Interval Schedules Defined and Illustrated

Interval schedules are dependent on the passage of specific periods of time. Ratio schedules, to be discussed in Chapter 32, depend on numbers of responses. When a particular response is scheduled for reinforcement following the passage of time and that time requirement is held constant, the schedule is a **fixed-interval (FI) schedule**. For example, Chuck and his teacher have agreed that he should volunteer to speak in class more regularly during social studies discussion. After defining *volunteering* as "raising his hand and responding with a novel comment directly relevant to the topic," his teacher activates an audiotape that sounds an unobtrusive click that only she can hear. The first time Chuck volunteers following the sound of the click, his teacher makes a check mark next to his name in her record book. At the end of the week the check marks are tallied and Chuck can exchange them for earned activities from his "reinforcement menu." Fixed-interval schedules are abbreviated "FI," and the schedule in this illustration would be called an "FI 5 min." a fixed-interval 5-minute schedule.

Every 2 hours Angela, the manager, circulates about the office, complimenting clerks who are hard at work. She waits for those who are not at work to return and engage in their tasks before complimenting them.

You have to be careful not to assume that an FI schedule is in operation just because reinforcers are dispensed at regular times. For a schedule to qualify as FI, reinforcement must be *contingent on* the occurrence of a particular response following a fixed interval of time, not just delivered regardless of what's going on. Notice the behavior that is reinforced in the example just presented. In the case of the office worker, it is being busily working, not performing a particular job. Suppose the supervisor stopped by all clerks' desks every 2 hours and complimented them on their work, whether or not they were doing their assigned tasks at the time. Technically, that schedule would not be a fixed interval; rather it more properly would be labeled a **fixed-time (FT) schedule**. The passage of time is the only condition stipulated for reinforcement to occur. When reinforce-

[1] Much more is known about the the behavior of organisms under complex schedule arrangements, but a treatment of such combinations transcends the scope of this book. Instead, we limit our presentation to relatively simple arrangements, because we feel those are most pertinent to practical application. Readers wishing more complete discussions of specific simple and complex reinforcement schedules should see Ferster and Skinner (1957), Catania (1984), and Zeiler (1977).

ment is dispensed according to a fixed-time schedule, the recipient may develop superstitious behavior (Ono, 1987), repeating acts contiguous with reinforcement but not at all relevant to appropriate performance.

Similarly, you want to be very clear about the *features* of a response that are to be reinforced. Mr. Goforth, the physical education instructor, might assume that if he delivers reinforcement every 5 minutes, all of his students will continue their exercising. When he tries that approach, all the students exercise but some work vigorously and consistently, and others pause and slow down following reinforcement. That is exactly what DeLuca and Holborn (1985) discovered. Each minute, contingent on the boys' pedaling a stationary bicycle, the experimenters dispensed tokens exchangeable for preferred arts and crafts items or games to their 4 male subjects. Interestingly, 2 of the boys, who were slim, pedaled at a high, consistent rate during the token phase as well as afterward. The other 2, who were obese, slowed down or paused at various times during the interval, dropping even lower in rate when tokens were no longer delivered. In this case, pedaling alone, not a high rate of pedaling, had been identified as a necessary feature of the response.

In group programs for children and youths, many events are scheduled regularly: recreation and lunch periods, evaluations, delivery of progress reports, classes in specific subjects, and many others. At home, too, various events are scheduled at relatively fixed times: meals, chores, music practice, radio and television shows, and so on. Notice that some of the happenings generally would be considered target responses, whereas others probably function as reinforcing events. Can you differentiate these 2 classes? For the latter, what additional information would you need to help you decide whether you think they are operating on FI or FT schedules?

Distinguishing between the two schedules

is critical for the practitioner because FI and FT produce very different outcomes. With FI, you have a regular contingent relationship between the target response and a reinforcer. With FT, because the reinforcer is received regardless of what is going on at the time, the target response is much less likely to be reinforced unless it is occurring at a sufficiently high and steady rate.

Suppose grooming skills have been selected as a target behavior for residents in a group home. Lunch is served at noon. If access to lunch is contingent on the youths meeting the standards for acceptable grooming (such as clean hands, nails, and combed hair), the schedule would be fixed interval. If lunch were served regardless of whether or not grooming standards were met, the schedule would be fixed time.

An actual example of a successful application of both FT and **variable-time (VT)** techniques can be found in a study by Saudergas, Madsen, and Scott (1977). Schoolchildren were given reports to take home to their parents weekly, either on the same day each week or on variable days of the week. During the variable-time condition, 7 to 9 students out of 26 were randomly selected each day to receive a home report, with the stipulation that each student receive at least 1 report each week. The children's production rates improved, especially during the VT schedule. Presumably a richer schedule was not necessary as their levels of production were occurring sufficiently often to permit the schedule to take hold.

Variable-interval (VI) schedules operate similar to fixed interval schedules, except that the time interval varies about some average time span. Chuck's teacher could have varied the length of time from 0 to 10 minutes when she prepared the audio-recording of clicks to signal the end of the interval. Eventually the span of the intervals would average about 5 minutes. Such a schedule would be called a VI 5 min. or "variable-interval 5-minute" schedule. On the average of every 2 weeks, the elected manager of the community group home makes a tour of inspection. Those residents who have met their responsibilities are invited to participate in a special reinforcing activity that evening—perhaps making popcorn or fudge, listening to favorite records, or the like. The inspections are on a VI schedule. Under VI scheduling, some reinforcers may be delivered very close together and others very far apart. Inspections can occur as closely spaced as 2 days in a row or as widely spaced as once in 4 weeks. This characteristic of VI schedules may generate performances different from those of FI schedules. In the following discussion, we will examine those differences, along with some of the general properties of interval-schedule performance and their relevance for practical application.

Characteristics of Interval-Schedule Performance

The bulk of our knowledge of the characteristics of performance under different schedules of reinforcement derives from laboratory work with animals. This has proven to be somewhat problematic, especially in relation to interval schedules, because, "Unlike nonhuman animal performance on FI schedules, human responding has been shown to be highly variable across subjects" (Buskist & Miller, 1986). Nevertheless, a number of general characteristics do appear to apply to humans. Because designing and providing a particular reinforcement schedule history for a given response is possible at the individual level, we can obtain fairly tight control of subsequent interval-schedule performance (Weiner, 1969). For instance, either very rapid or very slow rates of responding can be promoted under VI schedules, depending on what schedules have been used previously with the same response. How this goal may be achieved will be discussed later. Here we shall

survey such VI characteristics as rate, consistency of responding, error patterns, and maintenance of performance during extinction.

Response Rates

Desired rate of responding during the maintenance phase is an important consideration in planning applied behavior analysis programs. If a relatively low rate is tolerable, an interval schedule may be the best solution, because it carries only the simple requirement that the specific response occur at least 1 time following the completion of the interval. A pigeon can peck a disk once at the end of a required interval and receive its grain. Chuck, who works on a fixed-interval 5-minute schedule (FI 5 min.), can technically receive his token as long as he contributes just once after each 5-minute interval. (In contrast, a ratio schedule requires that the individual emit a particular number of responses as a condition for reinforcement.)

Single responses per interval are not typical under FI schedules, however. As discovered in the laboratory, animals tend to pause following reinforcement when FI's are in effect. Then, as the interval progresses, they begin to accelerate their rates of responding. This pattern is so predictable that it has been aptly labeled a "fixed-interval scallop," a phenomenon we discuss shortly in greater detail.

With the time-based FI schedule in effect, responders are not penalized by postponement of reinforcement if they stop the behavior for a while, as they would be under the response-based ratio schedule. The only time reinforcement is postponed under an FI schedule is when the individual fails to respond at the completion of the interval. Chuck would begin to miss out on receiving tokens only if he did not contribute to the discussion when the 5-minute interval terminated. The clerks not busily occupied would have to get back to work to receive a compliment. So FI schedules tend to generate lower response rates than ratio schedules, though, over time, responding does usually maintain at a rate sufficient to allow individuals to maximize the reinforcers they earn when they do become accessible.

In general, responding is more rapid under VI than under FI schedules. The variable nature of the VI schedule allows responding to be reinforced at unpredictable times. This unpredictability appears to keep the individual emitting responses at a fairly constant rate, thereby producing more responses per time period. If the office clerks had no way of anticipating when Angela, the supervisor, would stop by, they would be more likely to keep working just on the chance that Angela might come along. But still there is a limit, imposed by the scheduled interval, on the number of responses that can be reinforced under VI. Very high rates of responding contribute nothing to the amount of reinforcement received. Rates are therefore more likely to be lower than those based on response frequency.

One feature that influences rate of responding during interval reinforcement is the *size* of the interval. Why the size of the required interval has an effect on the overall rate of performance should be fairly apparent. As the individual is required to make at least one response per designated time interval in order to receive maximum reinforcement, the shorter the required time interval, the higher the rate. If Chuck were working on an FI 2 min. schedule, he would have to contribute at least once each 2 minutes to earn the maximum number of tokens. In an FI 9 min. schedule, a single contribution each 9 minutes would suffice for maximum payoff. If room inspection were hourly, rather than on alternate days, much more tidying would be going on. As Lowe, Harzem, & Bagshaw (1978), have shown response rates may be manipulated by shortening or extending the length of the interval in an FI schedule.

Consistency of Performance

As we have seen among laboratory animals, fixed-interval responding is usually characterized by a fixed-interval scallop. Because of the nature of the FI schedule, the animal does not need to continue to emit the target response throughout the interval. What frequently happens is that immediately following FI reinforcement, the pigeon (or other animal) tends to do other things. As grain has never been delivered immediately following a previously reinforced peck, it does not "pay" for the pigeon to resume pecking right away. Instead, it pauses, struts, coos, preens, and flaps its wings before accelerating its rate of disk pecking again toward the end of the interval. Occasionally, under laboratory conditions, human adults (Lowe et al., 1978) or infants (Lowe, Beasty, & Bentall, 1983) have generated the same kinds of FI performance patterns as those of (other) animals (e.g., Ferster & Skinner, 1957). Often, however, adult people have not. Sometimes they consistently perform at high rates throughout the interval instead of stopping or slowing down following reinforcement (Weiner, 1964b). At other times, they may stop responding altogether for a while, then abruptly shift to a high rate pattern (Buskist & Morgan, 1987; Lowe et al., 1978). Presumably, accounting for differences are such factors as:

- Rules (Matthews, Catania, & Shimoff, 1985; Vaughan, 1985).
- Instructions (Lippman & Meyer, 1967).
- Other schedules currently in effect (Buskist & Morgan, 1987; McSweeney, 1983).
- Schedules that operated in the past (Dougan, McSweeney, & Farmer, 1985; Weiner, 1964b).

Yet in the natural setting, analogues of instances of post-reinforcement pauses can occasionally be identified. Figure 31.1 illustrates the FI scallop generated by the U.S. Congress, showing accelerated responding before adjournment.

Figure 31.1 Cumulative Numbers of Bills Passed During the Legislative Sessions of Congress from January 1961 to October 1968

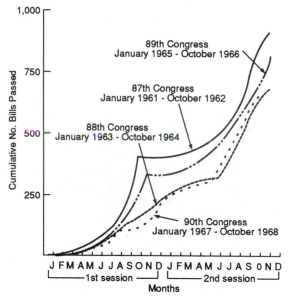

(Weisberg & Waldrup, 1972, p. 95.) Reprinted with permission of the Society for the Experimental Analysis of Behavior and the author.

In another analogous situation, students who are quizzed or graded at regular intervals (technically a *limited hold schedule*) often tend to delay studying until just before the event. As the interval progresses, the studying behavior accelerates. While study behavior is low, other response rates are higher: playing, working on other assignments, and so on. Mawhinney and colleagues (1971) measured minutes of studying per day by college students under daily and 3 weekly quiz conditions. (Quizzes probably consist of both positively and negatively reinforcing contingencies.) Figure 31.2 indicates that studying was relatively consistent under the daily schedule, but it was slow at first, then accelerated during the three-week schedule.

During social studies class, Chuck could conceivably look out the window, disrupt, get a drink, doodle, or do lots of other things in the early phases of each 5-minute interval. Yet he could still remain eligible for and receive maximum token reinforcement as long as he contributed to the discussion at least one work response following each 5 minutes. How do you think the group home residents' rooms might look on the day between fixed alternate-day inspections?

Such inconsistency does not usually occur under variable interval schedules. As reinforceable responses cannot be predicted—some occur close together, others farther apart—the individual tends to maintain a steady pace of responding, except when reinforcement occurs too often at the extremes of the interval. Two successive pecks sometimes yield grain to the pigeon, so it continues to peck following reinforcement. Students whose instructors give "pop" quizzes also tend to keep up better with their assignments. Whether the function is to avoid failure or to seek success, studying is maintained, and students are less likely to engage in competing activities. Following a spot inspection by the elected manager, residents would probably continue to meet their responsibilities at a pretty constant rate, just in case there might be an inspection the next day. Because variable-interval performance is typified by consistency, whereas fixed-interval performance may not be, it is a good idea ultimately to switch from FI to VI when consistency of performance is desired.

Error Patterns

Different patterns of error production may emerge under some interval schedules. In a study of matching-to-sample performance under fixed-interval schedules, children produced the largest number of errors in the second quarter of each interval (Davidson & Osborne, 1974). Those operating under variable-interval schedules distributed errors more evenly within the interval.

Figure 31.2 Average Minutes Studied Per Session by All Subjects During Alternating Daily and Three-Week Testing Conditions

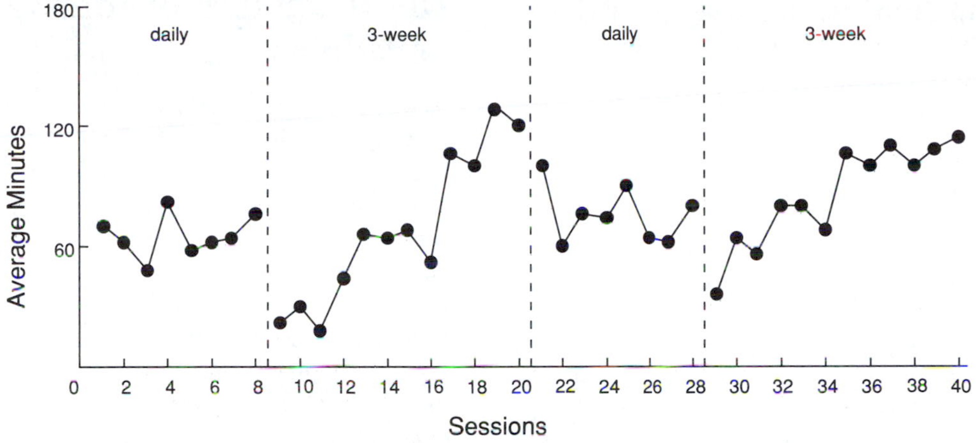

(Mawhinney et al., 1971, p. 262.) Reprinted with permission of the Society for the Experimental Analysis of Behavior and the author.

Responding During Extinction

Chapter 30 discussed the issue of maintenance, mentioning that intermittent reinforcement encourages responding to persist during extinction, when reinforcement no longer is being delivered (Ferster & Skinner, 1957). (Remember, intermittent reinforcement may happen whether you want a behavior to sustain or not, as in the case of negative behaviors like complaining or disruption. A little reinforcement goes a long way.) The schedule has taught the individual that not all responses are followed by reinforcement, and in the case of VI, the time for reinforcement for any given response is unpredictable.

Lucretia's teacher will praise her occasionally when she is playing nicely with the other children. The boss drops by and comments on the fine quality of your work. No one knows when. So when reinforcement is discontinued altogether, it takes quite a while for the altered condition to be discriminated, especially when the interval has been long. Naturally, sooner or later, if no form of reinforcement is forthcoming, the response probably will return to its baseline level. Even here, we still don't get something for nothing.

In contrast with continuous reinforcement (CRF), interval schedules tend to generate responding that maintains longer during extinction. In general, if a particular response has been maintained on a schedule with a very long interval requirement, the response will probably maintain longer than if the interval has been fairly short (Reynolds, 1968). This tendency again underscores the importance of using a program that progressively extends the interval before reinforcement. It would be premature to terminate the reinforcement program when Chuck was functioning on either an FI 5 min. or a VI 5 min. schedule, just because he had achieved the terminal goal—contributing to the social studies discussion. A sudden withdrawal of the reinforcing contingencies might result in disruption of the response before much time had passed. It would probably be preferable to "thin" the schedule by lengthening the required interval gradually until token delivery was made contingent on continuing to contribute over days or perhaps even weeks. By that time, removal of the tokens hardly would be noticed.

If the intention of the practitioner is to design a program to yield consistent responding once the reinforcing contingencies have been removed, a variable-interval schedule would probably be the training schedule of choice. The regular responding that is characteristic of performance under VI-reinforcement schedules appears to maintain itself under extinction. Laboratory animals that have been trained on VI schedules have continued to respond in similar fashion under extinction conditions. Responding maintains without pausing; though, of course, over extended periods of time the rate diminishes and ultimately ceases. On the other hand, performance under extinction following FI training tends to be interspersed with numerous periods without responding, before ultimately ceasing. In the event that a fixed-interval training schedule is selected, for practicality or convenience, switching eventually to a variable schedule before removing all reinforcing contingencies usually is possible. The group-home manager could switch from alternate days to a VI 3 day schedule, then continue progressively to alter the schedule in the direction of a sparse VI schedule.

To reduce a student's thumb-sucking, a special education teacher gave him a token each time the bell on a kitchen timer rang, and his thumb was not in his mouth. During the first phase, the timer was set at regular intervals. In the next phase, numbers from 1 to 20 were selected at random: Numbered paper slips were drawn from a bowl, noted down, and replaced. The timer was then set according to the size of the interval indicated on the slip. The random selection of intervals from 1 to 20 provided a schedule that operated on a variable interval averaging 10 minutes (VI 10 min.). Later on, as thumb-sucking disappeared for longer and longer time periods, the average interval length was expanded, until ultimately the timer no longer rang. Henceforth, the teacher occasionally complimented the boy for keeping his thumb away from his mouth. That was sufficient. Thumb-sucking was conquered!

Advantages and Disadvantages of Interval Schedules

In addition to their utility as a method for promoting maintained responding—not only during reinforcement but during extinction as well—the primary advantage of using interval schedules is their ease of implementation. Because they are time-based, rather than counting responses, one simply has periodically to check a clock, timer, or calendar, or respond to a visual or auditory signal. When there are competing demands on the time and attention of contingency managers, the interval schedule is particularly appealing.

Still one more advantage of interval schedules, as with other intermittent schedules of reinforcement, is that they help to delay satiation. This probably is responsible to some degree for maintained responding during reinforcement. Too much of a good thing—whether banana splits or pats on the back—is still too much. When they are received too often, you stop working for them. With the reinforcers only delivered every once in a while, under interval schedules, such satiation is forestalled.

You should be able to promote consistent responding while reinforcement is ongoing, through the use of a variable-interval schedule. As we have noted, however, you need to be cautious about selecting a fixed-interval schedule if consistency is desired during reinforcement and afterward. You also have seen that interval schedules may tend to support low rates of responding. It should be possible to avoid this problem, however, by means of careful programming, as we discuss shortly.

One other difficulty that might arise is excessive displays of unrelated behaviors (i.e., to fill the time during the interval), such as drinking, moving, self-stimulating, and so on (Granger, Porter, & Christoph, 1984). We guess those behaviors happen when other reinforceable activities are not available during the time between reinforcements ("interreinforcement interval"). Prudence dictates that you avoid FI's with children who are hyperactive or who frequently engage in destructive or abusive behaviors, unless the interim between availability of the FI reinforcer is structured to permit other constructive activities to be reinforced.

Promoting Preferred Rates of Responding Under Interval Schedules

The available information on interval schedules can guide you to apply them effectively. In brief, if you would find a low-to-moderate rate of responding acceptable, you can schedule reinforcement following a moderate interval size. To increase the response rate, start with a shorter interval and gradually increase it.

When we talk about effective use of interval or, for that matter, other schedules, we must ask ourselves, "Effective for what purpose?" Are we just looking for a modified behavior to persist at some moderate level, as with a reasonable amount of volunteering to do extra jobs or initiate social interactions; at a high rate, as in completing many training tasks or rapidly producing answers to problems; or at a low rate, as in slowly forming handwritten letters or being "it" in a group game? Or are we hoping that the behavior will cease being expressed altogether, as with using abusive language or biting one's nails?

You also need to consider the patterns of performance. Is consistency critical, or can abrupt bursts and long pauses be tolerated? Once you are clear about the rates and patterns you are looking for, during reinforcement and after its termination, you can select the schedule. By judiciously combining it with other elements, such as instructions or supplementary discriminative stimuli (e.g., a clock or calendar), you can plan how to apply it best. So, let us turn

to the factors that are known to influence interval schedule performance and see what they do.

As we noted earlier, fixed-interval schedules are frequently used on the job, probably due to their ease of application. Wouldn't you find it a lot simpler to rely on the clock or calendar or on your wristwatch alarm to prompt you to deliver a reinforcer than to keep a continual count of a particular response? We sure would. But the low response rates that sometimes happen under interval schedules can be problematic. Fortunately, a number of strategies are available to promote high (or low) rates under these schedules. These include:

- Reducing the size of the interval for a while.
- Providing a history of reinforcement for high (or low) rates of the response.
- Using instructions or rules.
- Taking advantage of contrast effects.
- Considering competitive contingencies.
- Adding a limited-hold component to the schedule requirement.

Reducing the Length of the Interval

In general, the shorter the interval, the more rapid the rate of responding. If not too difficult logistically, that is one factor you can use to your advantage. You want to speed up the rate of productivity in your classroom or plant. Circulate and frequently compliment students or employees for working rapidly. (If you have read Peters and Austin's book, *A Passion for Excellence,* published in 1985, you might recognize this strategy as "Management by Walking Around.")

Providing Appropriate History

The schedule that has operated on a particular response in the past can influence the rate of performance subsequently under a different schedule; and "the more a subject's history resembles current conditions in terms of temporal proximity and other common elements, the more likely it (*i.e. the subject's history*) is to persist to affect current responding" (Weiner, 1983, p. 522).

With both human and nonhuman subjects, Weiner (1964b) found that if high rates were generated over time via a different schedule, such as a differential reinforcement of high rates (DRH) or a variable ratio schedule (to be discussed later), those high rate patterns would tend to persist despite a shift to an interval schedule. Similarly, histories promoting low rates of responding were followed by low response rates during interval schedules. The way instructions influence patterns of responding under reinforcement schedules has also been attributed to reinforcement history (Baron & Galizio, 1983).

You can take advantage of your knowledge of the influence of recent schedule histories by temporarily instituting methods for rate-building (or lowering) under the conditions that will prevail when the interval schedule is to be in effect. Say that you and your staff of managers have pinpointed increasing the time they spend out on the floor (i.e., with clients, students, or subordinates) as a key goal. Initially you provide reinforcement, in the form of written or personally delivered praise, occasionally paired with something more powerful, like a treat or time off, contingent on number of minutes they spend out on the floor. When the rate has increased to a high and stable level over many days, you begin to present the reinforcers several times a day (about as many times as you did previously, but no longer depending on the high rate; instead, you make reinforcement contingent on the performance at those times). Then, you gradually thin the schedule by extending the reinforcement intervals, until they reach a length with which you can comfortably function. Carefully watch the response rate, though. If it begins to lag, you may need to reapply the rate-building temporarily, later shifting back to the interval schedule again.

Using Discriminative Stimuli

Various types of verbal stimuli have been shown to exert a powerful influence over behavior while interval reinforcement schedules are in effect. Generating verbal discriminative stimuli for oneself, receiving instructions, describing the contingencies and self-instructions are examples. Lowe and colleagues (1978), for instance, found that subjects reported counting to themselves as a method of estimating when to respond under a fixed-interval schedule.

Many investigators have studied how and why instructions sometimes override contingency effects. (See Baron & Galizio, 1983, for a review.) Under particular reinforcement schedules, people respond rapidly when instructed to do so and their response rates often are more powerfully affected by instructions than by weak consequences. In a study by Buskist and Miller (1986), when college students were left to their own devices (i.e., without instructions), after they had experienced an FI 30 sec. schedule long enough, their rates of operating a manipulandum that dispensed pennies tended to match the schedule. That is, they would wait about 30 seconds before responding, a pattern that allowed them to minimize effort and maximize payoff. The same sort of thing happened with members of another group who were informed that obtaining the pennies would be possible every 30 seconds. However, the response patterns of the latter group matched the contingency from the beginning. Learning to pace their responses to approximately one each 30 seconds took hardly any time. Another group was misinformed. They were told they could obtain the pennies each 15 seconds. Within a few sessions, however, they learned to match the contingencies, responding in intervals of 30, not 15, seconds. But for the last group, informed that the schedule was an FI 60 sec., responding was slower than the 30 sec. optimal rate. In that case, instructions actually overrode the contingencies in effect, producing longer pauses following reinforcement. (Whether the behavior of these college student subjects would come under better contingency control if the reinforcers were more powerful remains to be explored.)

Even young children's response rates can be modified by instructions when FI schedules are in effect (Bentall & Lowe, 1987). The children responded either rapidly or slowly when intervals were of identical size, depending on instructions from the experimenter or self-instructions.

Research has begun to show that if you shape how people describe a given contingency under which they are functioning, their patterns of responding may adjust to those descriptions regardless of whether the verbal description accurately characterizes the contingency actually in effect (e.g., Catania, Matthews, & Shimoff, 1982). Presumably, rates of responding under interval schedules may be modifiable in either an upward or downward direction. Try this by asking the responder to describe the schedule and reinforce statements that successively approximate the description of a contingency that would support a given rate.

Although we would not encourage you to misinform anyone, you can begin to see how people might misinform themselves under ambiguous circumstances. They could generate hypotheses about contingencies and then begin to act as if those contingencies actually were operating. Convinced that the things one says to oneself can have an especially powerful impact on patterns of responding under various reinforcement schedules, many researchers posit that such self-statements may account for the differences in response patterns between humans and animals. Although Weiner (1983) convincingly has argued that this is an oversimplification, it does seem clear that instructions about contingencies can influence performance patterns, particularly when weak reinforcers are used.

The main point is that under ambiguous situations, people may behave differently from one another due to instructions they give themselves. So if you want to establish a pattern that matches the contingencies in effect, you should provide very clear and accurate descriptions of the reinforcement schedule in effect. (For example, "If you turn in your report at the end of every pay period, I will read and give you feedback on it.") If, instead, you would like to shift over to an interval schedule from one that has been supporting a high (or low) rate and you want the ongoing rate to persist, saying nothing may be best. The change may go unnoticed as folks continue as previously.

You already know that rules and instructions can influence performance patterns under interval schedules. Instructions can be in the form of demonstrations as well as in words, as when the experimenter rapidly or slowly presses a button to show how an apparatus works. "Watch Willie," his teacher directs, as Willie dribbles the basketball. The others pick up the tempo.

Other S^Ds can influence response rates or tempos, too. We are told that some restaurants play music with a fast beat, ostensibly to encourage their patrons to eat rapidly. Perhaps that is true. Try applauding in a usual random pattern while others in the audience are clapping in unison to a set beat. Attempt talking rapidly when everyone else is enunciating slowly. You may find it difficult. When rates of responding are influenced by the performance patterns of others, we can say that *social facilitation* is at work (Hake & Laws, 1967).[2]

While much needs to be learned about the fine details of control exerted by social stimuli (Hake, Donaldson, & Hyten, 1983), social facilitation may make a big difference when you want to alter rates of responding within groups.

---

[2] A similar phenomenon may be at work with "group conformity," a concept studied extensively by social psychologists. (See Feldman, 1985, pp. 334–346.)

Our guess is that social facilitation will most likely influence rates when many members of the group, especially prestigious leaders, support the pace. An interesting example is an episode that occurred in a noisy manufacturing plant in Israel (Zohar, Cohen, & Azar, 1980). Because workers generally failed to use ear plugs, the objective was to increase their rates of using the protective devices. Regular feedback was supplied, indicating the amount of temporary hearing loss they suffered each day without using ear plugs. Eventually, most of the work force used the protection. This effect then carried over to new employees, who never received the feedback but who did see most of their co-workers using the protectors. (Some would say the *corporate culture* had been modified.)

You see the same sort of thing happening when you feel yourself compelled to conform because the audience hushes in preparation for the opening of the curtain, or shouts and cheers as the quarterback reaches the end zone. Generate a few examples of your own. The moral: Find a way to encourage many members of the group to meet a standard of performance (in this case, a rate standard), and the others may fall in line. Then grab opportunities to reinforce the group as a whole. ("Everyone is working hard. That will give us time to have an extra break today.") Ergo, even though reinforcement operates primarily on an interval schedule, rates will be where you want them to be.

Arranging Competition

Competition describes a situation in which reinforcers are limited to only one individual or group among several. Only one team can win the game; just one student wins the spelling bee. What does a competitive contingency do for response rates supported by fixed-interval reinforcement? Buskist, Morgan, and Rossi (1984) conducted an experiment in which two individuals either worked alone or competed

for points during FI 30 sec. schedule. Regardless of whether subjects were informed of the competitive contingency, their rates of responding increased substantially under the competitive arrangement. Subjects who were told about the competition in effect increased their rates rapidly; those left to discover the competitive contingencies for themselves took a while to accelerate their responses.

Personally, we are not strong advocates of competition, because winning (obtaining reinforcement) for some means losing (extinction) for others. Nevertheless, many competitive circumstances permit each member to gain sufficient reinforcers along the way, if not ultimately. The points for each exercise in a gymnastics competition or for each hand in a bridge game, offers of particular jobs when plenty are available, and being the winning team in the Good Behavior Game (Barrish et al., 1969) are examples, because if each team achieves a given criterion, each can win. So if you want to increase response rates under FI schedules, consider adding a competitive aspect—make a game of it—and you may find the rates increasing over those that would be generated by the FI schedule alone.

Capitalizing on Behavioral Contrast

Another way you might be able to alter the rate of a response, at least temporarily, is to take advantage of the **contrast phenomenon** (McSweeney, 1982). Recall that this phenomenon is seen when two (or more) different schedules are simultaneously in operation and reinforcement then changes in one of the schedules. Despite no change in the schedule of reinforcement for the other, performance on that other schedule may increase when the first schedule has supported a decrease in responding (*positive* **behavioral contrast**). Or, conversely, when reinforcement is increased in one schedule, performance may decrease in the other (*negative behavioral contrast*).

You might take advantage of the contrast phenomenon when direct strategies are impractical. Say that your unit is being audited later in the day. You want to make sure performance is exemplary. You discontinue any approval until that time. Your sparse words of approval during the audit go much further.

Sometimes, when the situation dictates, you can focus on altering a second reinforcement schedule with the intention of causing an indirect change in the first. While his teacher has been too occupied with other students to notice him, Timmy increasingly has been causing disturbances in the class by drawing unflattering caricatures of the principal and teachers. Several of his classmates signal their approval by giggling, pointing, and poking one another amiably—delicious reinforcers for Timmy. His teacher decides to enlist the help of several prestigious classmates, who agree to ignore Timmy's disruptive actions, and the rest follow suit. Simultaneously, while Timmy is behaving nicely, as soon as the teacher has the opportunity, he gives Timmy lots of positive attention.

The contrast between the extinction schedule for disrupting and the intermittent reinforcement schedule for acceptable conduct briefly promotes an unusually high rate of the latter. The teacher knows how to capitalize on this effect by providing heavy reinforcement as soon as he can. He invites Timmy to become the official class artist as a reward for his good behavior. For each day he continues to behave well, Timmy is allowed to do something he enjoys, like designing the class logo, preparing signs, and planning the scenery for the class play. This sustains the high rate of good conduct. The teacher then can then begin to capitalize on this improvement by shifting over to an interval schedule. This is convenient because even when occupied with other students, he can look up from time to time to attend positively to Timmy (and others), provided the boy's behavior is acceptable.

In any event, as Redmon and Farris (1987) advise:

> . . . if a change in the schedule of reinforcement in one situation or setting is likely to have effects on behavior in other settings, then coordinated intervention is a necessity. Thus, in the case where children move from one environment to another or from activity to activity, program changes in one component should be coordinated with conditions in other components (p. 331).

You may not want to overly depend on generating contrast effects as a method for altering rates because they are not necessarily reliable. Probably this is a result of differences in the histories and current contingencies in each person's life. Nevertheless, when other alternatives are unavailable, they just might provide an opportunity to change a rate temporarily. Consider capitalizing on contrast effects, particularly when you recognize that circumstances will interfere with your own control over the contingencies for a while.

Adding Limited-Hold Schedules

Still one more way to influence the rate of responding under an interval schedule is to impose an additional restriction on performance. That restriction, the **limited hold**, requires that a primed response (the first response following termination of the required interval) must occur within a specific time limit following the interval if reinforcement is to be made available (see Figure 31.3).

Under a limited-hold schedule, individuals must hurry in order not to lose the opportunity for reinforcement, whereas under a simple interval schedule they can afford to delay responding. That is, reinforcement is available only temporarily under a limited-hold schedule. This type of schedule is one that many of us have probably learned to use without awareness. You receive approval or avoid criticism if your monthly reports are submitted on the appropriate date (the FI), not afterward (the lim-

Figure 31.3 The Fixed-Interval and Limited-Hold Schedules Compared

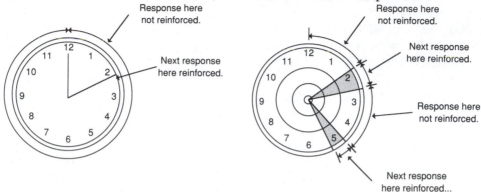

Fixed interval of 10 minutes; the first response following termination of the interval is reinforced.

The limit is 2 minutes following the 10-minute interval; if no response occurs during those 2 minutes, reinforcement will no longer be available.

ited hold). Teachers give grades only when an assignment is completed within a certain time. The group is dismissed for recreation as soon as the members come to order (VI); but if they fail to come to order within a certain number of minutes, recreation time will be over and the opportunity will be lost (limited hold). Grungy George never combs his hair or cleans his fingernails. He agrees that Dad will check his appearance before dinner each day. If George looks neat and clean he will receive his allowance. If not, there will be no allowance, and he will have to wait until the next day. The limited-hold contingency increases George's neatness.

The teacher assigned a project in a seventh-grade social studies class. Each student was to bring in 10 newspaper clippings. The students would present their current-events items to the class and would receive credit toward their grades. The teacher did not specify a time by which the clippings were due. Some students went for several weeks without doing the assignment and then, toward the end of the marking period, began to bring in reams of clippings. The last week before report cards were to be distributed, the class was overloaded with current-events presentations. The teacher was forced to postpone presentation of the next planned subject unit, and some of the students

never did complete the assignment. In order to avoid such a situation in the next marking period, the teacher added a restriction: Credit would be given only once a week, on Friday. The students had only one week in which to collect and present the news clippings. They would receive no credit if they brought the clippings in on the following Monday. The opportunity for reinforcement was available for only a brief period.

Laboratory studies demonstrate that the imposition of a short limited hold has the effect of increasing response rates (Reynolds, 1968). In the situation just described, the new policy had a similar effect. In order to avoid losing the opportunity to earn credits, the students brought in the clippings regularly and more often. One way, therefore, to speed up responding under interval schedules is to restrict the time during which reinforcement is available to a brief period—to use a limited-hold contingency. Using ratio schedules, another way to promote rate, will be discussed in Chapter 32.

Choosing Between Fixed and Variable Schedules

Consistency of performance can be very important, as in exercising, practicing a musical instrument, or logging job activities daily for a short period rather than waiting and spending many hours on the chore once at the end of the week. If consistency is your concern, you will want to avoid a fixed-interval schedule. As we have seen, FI schedules sometimes promote scalloping patterns, with pauses following reinforcement. (Is that the way you prepare for quizzes, or do you study consistently?) Select a VI schedule instead. When pauses and bursts are irrelevant, either FI or VI will do, and you have the luxury of choosing the most convenient one. Weekly progress reports can be written anytime, provided they are turned in by Monday morning. You don't care whether they are prepared on Friday or Sunday at 4 in the morning. The FI schedule is acceptable.

Thinning Reinforcement Under Interval Schedules

Despite the convenience of using interval schedules, short intervals can be a nuisance. Should you wish to reduce the frequency with which you deliver reinforcement, you can choose one of these alternatives: lengthen the interval gradually or withhold reinforcement at the end of some of the intervals.

You have been increasing your staff's productivity by checking and complimenting their work products following a given time period. When the rate reaches an acceptable level, you can begin to thin reinforcement *slowly*, by gradually expanding the length of the interval. This strategy frequently is followed.

The initial signaling tape used in the "Practice Skills Mastery Program" (Erken & Henderson, 1976), a classroom token economy program, emits a beep on the average of every minute or two. The beep cues the teacher to scan the classroom and call out the names of the individuals or groups of students who are observed to be on-task and the number of points they are to record for themselves. (The teacher also records the names of students who were not awarded points to verify records later

on.) As on-task performance improves, the lengths of the intervals are extended as a "thinning" device. Five other signaling tapes are used in sequence, each containing fewer beeps per time period, with the last containing only three, a variable interval of approximately 15 minutes. As Henderson, Jenson, and Erken (1986) contend, the schedule is easy for teachers to use for a continuous behavior like on-task. They also have demonstrated, in three different experiments, how effectively the program promotes classroom productivity. A very similar method of extending intervals was used to increase the length of time a hyperactive boy paid attention in class (Alabiso, 1975).

A related technique is to withhold reinforcers at the end of an occasional interval. Best substitute a conditioned reinforcer instead, at least in the beginning. Instead of giving Tracy a spoonful of pudding every 2 minutes for playing nicely with toys, once in a while, say "Nice playing" instead. Provided that her performance persists, you can gradually substitute the conditioned reinforcer for the food.

Watch for deterioration, though. It will signal that you are thinning too fast. Return to a denser schedule of the reinforcement (shorten the interval and/or replace the stronger reinforcer) until the desired rate recovers and then proceed to thin once more, very carefully. If you do your job well and reinforcement concurrently is available for other responses, you may find the target performance persisting for extended durations with very little reinforcement.

Summary

Interval schedules probably are the most convenient ones to use in applied settings because they do not require constant vigilance. Instead, reinforcers are delivered based on the passage of fixed or variable periods of time. Sometimes this can lead inadvertently to a failure to reinforce *contingent on* the target response. In that event, the schedule is transformed into a fixed or variable *time*, rather than a fixed or variable *interval*, posing the risk that unwanted behaviors may be reinforced inadvertently. Another potential problem with interval schedules is that they often generate low rates of responding, but this can be remedied by shortening the length of the interval.

In the case of fixed-interval schedules, inconsistency can result as well. Responses that have been supported by interval schedules tend to continue longer than those that have been continually reinforced, an advantage or a disadvantage, depending on the nature of the behavior. Interval schedules permit other behaviors to occur without reducing the rate of payoff, again a phenomenon that can be for the better or worse. Lastly, variable-interval schedules are more likely to produce consistency of responding than fixed-interval schedules.

To increase the rate of responding while interval schedules are in effect, you can shorten the length of the interval. Other methods are available for influencing rate patterns under interval schedules as well. These include providing the right history; using a variety of discriminative stimuli, such as instructions and models; and arranging competition. Social facilitation and contrast effects can also set the occasion for increased (or decreased) rates under interval schedules, and adding a limited-hold provision can also speed things along.

Interval-schedule performance rates may be sustained by carefully "thinning" reinforcement. One way to accomplish this is to gradually expand the size of the interval. Another is to withhold reinforcement at the end of some intervals, perhaps filling in with conditioned reinforcers. Ultimately, performance may persist despite very infrequent reinforcement.

Chapter 32

Maintaining Behavior: Ratio and Differential-Reinforcement Schedules

GOALS

After mastering the material in this chapter, you should be able to:

1. Define, recognize, and give original illustrations for each of the following terms:
   a. Ratio schedules
   b. Fixed-ratio (FR) schedules
   c. Variable-ratio (VR) schedules
   d. Ratio strain
   e. Adjusting schedule
   f. Differential reinforcement of high rates (DRH)
   g. Matching Law

2. List and describe the typical characteristics of variable and fixed ratio-schedule performance.

3. Identify and discuss several factors that influence response-rate characteristics, for example, consistency, under ratio-schedule performance.

4. Discuss the advantages and disadvantages of ratio schedules.

5. Describe and illustrate how ratio and DRH schedules can increase response rates under interval scheduling, and outline the steps to follow for accomplishing a smooth transition from a ratio to an interval schedule.

6. Give several examples of ways that different schedules can interact to influence performance.

7. Maintain a selected target behavior at a high, steady rate.

Many individuals and organizations are interested in promoting high performance rates: increased productivity; high levels of compliance with policies and regulations; frequent application of good practices and skills. Chapter 31 showed that interval schedules tend to generate low or moderate response rates. Yet when high rates are desired, alternatives are available. We now turn our attention to two schedules that promote high response rates: ratio and differential reinforcement of high rates (DRH) schedules.

Ratio Schedules

Defined and Illustrated

We have learned in Chapter 31 that *interval schedules* are dependent on the passage of specific periods of time. When reinforcement is made contingent on *a given number of responses*, the schedule is called a **ratio schedule**. Sometimes a *fixed number* of responses is required before the response is reinforced. Then the schedule is called a **fixed-ratio (FR) schedule**. The classic illustration of an FR schedule comes from industry; it is called "piecework." When each twentieth piece of equipment is assembled, the worker is credited with $5. In school, an FR schedule might involve giving a student a certain number of points upon completion of 3 pages of a workbook. (The term *fixed-ratio schedule* is often abbreviated FR for the sake of convenience. In the last illustration, for example, reinforcement would be delivered at the ratio of 3 page units to 1 reinforcer, and the schedule could be abbreviated FR 3.)

More typical of reinforcement schedules in applied settings, however, is the **variable-ratio (VR) schedule**. Although reinforcement in the VR schedule is also contingent on number of responses, *the number of required responses varies about an average*. Typically, a VR schedule in the laboratory is programmed for a mean number of required responses. For example, a pigeon's disk-pecking is to be reinforced on the average of once for each 50 responses. (In this instance the schedule would be abbreviated VR 50.) Suppose that Fern is packing items in boxes with sections that vary from 4 to 8 with an average of 6. If reinforcement in the form of points toward her paycheck was delivered after she packed each box, she would be working on a VR 6 schedule.[1]

Characteristics of Ratio-Schedule Performance

Ratio schedules tend to generate distinctive performance characteristics, both while they are in effect and during extinction conditions. Given experimental arrangements in the laboratory, animals perform under different ratio schedules in quite distinct and predictable ways (Ferster & Skinner, 1957); but among human beings who function in the real world, such characteristics cannot be predicted as precisely. One reason is that studying schedules with humans is difficult because we don't have complete control over their chief contingencies of reinforcement.

Nonetheless, general patterns of performance have been found to emerge in studies in which simple (Hutchinson & Azrin, 1961), as well as complex (Bijou & Orlando, 1961; Long, 1962; 1963; Davidson & Osborne, 1974), schedules of ratio reinforcement have been tested with human subjects. Among the predictable characteristics of responding under ratio schedules are high and fairly consistent rates of behavior while the schedule is in effect and continued responding when extinction is introduced initially. These performance characteristics will be examined in more detail so the factors that appear to influence each one can be identified.

---

[1] In reality, any one individual is usually operating under many different, complex schedules simultaneously, and the various schedules can interact with one another and influence behavior correspondingly. We have simplified the material for purposes of this discussion.

High rates of responding. Although rare exceptions have been noted (Yukl & Latham, 1975; Yukl, Latham, & Pursell, 1976), ratio schedules tend to promote high performance rates. With ratio schedules, because reinforcement is contingent on a number of responses, the more rapidly one responds, the sooner reinforcers are received. Unless the reinforcement pool is limited, rapid responding also allows the accumulation of more reinforcers within a given time period. Naturally, individuals tend to work more rapidly under ratio schedules than under interval schedules. Typists being paid by the page will be likely to work as quickly as possible: The faster they type, the more pages they can complete within a given period, and the more money they can consequently make. Similarly, a client who is allowed out to play on completion of a number of assigned homework pages will probably hasten to finish. In this case, the client has earned no more reinforcers than the total pool available but finishes faster and receives the reinforcement of additional play time.

Part-time examination graders worked faster under VR 2 than CRF schedules, with amount of reinforcement held constant (Yukl, Wexley, & Seymour, 1972). Students instructed to increase or lower their heart rates were provided with feedback on different schedules: none, continuous, or fixed ratio (Hatch, 1980). Those in the latter group learned to increase their rates more than the other groups. Experienced trappers working for a lumber company worked more rapidly when they earned equivalent amounts on a VR 4 schedule than they had on a CRF schedule (Latham & Dossett, 1978).

Several specific factors have been found to affect rates of responding on a single task. Among those are the ratio of nonreinforced to reinforced responses (e.g., Everett, Studer, & Douglas, 1978), reinforcement history (Chappell & Leibowitz, 1982; Weiner, 1981a; 1981b), age (Lamal, 1978), and the gradual-

ness with which the reinforcement schedule is phased out. We also have surmised that the fluency with which the response is being emitted is important (Young et al., 1986).

A number of investigators have studied the effects of the size of the ratio requirement upon the response rate. Hutchinson and Azrin (1961) and Weiner (1980) demonstrated that human responding was comparable to animal responding under ratio schedules (Boren, 1956; Skinner, 1938). Their general finding was that, to some maximum level, the larger the response requirement, the more rapid the response rate. Beyond that level, the rate of responding drops (Everett et al., 1978). This finding has been further supported by applied behavior analysts. Stephens et al. (1975) compared various schedules of reinforcement to determine the effects of ratio size on the rate at which retarded children learned picture names. Various schedules of contingent candy delivery operated during different phases. Both continuous and very infrequent candy delivery (FR 25) generated low response rates. The children responded much faster on intermediate schedules (e.g., FI 5).

If Fern packs 2 boxes of uniform size under an FR reinforcement schedule within a specified time period, she can be expected to pack more boxes in proportionally less time. For instance, we would expect that a 10-box requirement (FR 10) would take five times as long as a 2-box requirement, yet the experimental findings suggest that 10 boxes would be packed in less than 5 times the time required for 2 boxes. All other factors being equal, the rate per box would be higher if reinforcement were made contingent on a 10-box requirement than on a 2-box requirement.

It seems logical to conclude, then, that high ratio requirements are to be preferred. But individuals and tasks vary, and predicting exactly when this principle may break down is not possible. At some point the ratio requirement becomes too large, and the individual may begin to pause at unpredictable times. The person is then said to be suffering from **ratio strain**. By failing to deliver reinforcement frequently enough, the schedule, in a sense, has introduced extinction conditions. The avoidance and aggression that are often associated with abrupt increases in ratio requirements (Hutchinson, Azrin, & Hunt, 1968) certainly resemble the reactions we know to frequently accompany extinction. Ultimately, as we indicated previously, responding can disintegrate altogether.

Of course, increasing the ratio gradually will delay such effects. Kirby and Shields (1972) programmed an **adjusting** FR **schedule** for a student who seldom completed his math assignments. (An adjusting schedule gradually alters the time or ratio requirement of the response.) Starting with praising and marks of "correct" for each two problems completed correctly, the FR schedule was gradually increased to 4, then to 8, and so on until 20 problems had to be completed correctly before praise would be given. Achievement remained high throughout. Eventually, however, a point can be reached at which the steady high rate begins to slow down, as in Stephens and colleagues' picture-naming study (1975). When this occurs, the ratio can be reduced to the level at which rapid responding resumes. Then the requirement can be increased even more gradually.

Similarly, improving the handwriting legibility of a group of special education students was the goal of a study that employed an adjusting fixed-ratio schedule (McLaughlin, 1981). To receive points exchangeable for privileges in an ongoing token economy, the students needed to write *one additional* (the *adjusting* aspect of the schedule requirement) legible letter on each successive trial. Students in the FR adjusting schedule group improved significantly—from 35 at the pretest to 63.8 at the posttest. A no-token control group only improved from 31.1 at pretest to 41.1 at posttesting.

Let us suppose that the training staff at Pur-

ple Triangle is trying to increase its rate of completing assignments. The supervisor begins complimenting and writing notes to staff members each time they complete an assignment. This reinforcement has the effect of increasing the rate of completion. Gradually the notes are written less often, but compliments continue as staff members complete their assignments. As time goes by, reinforcement diminishes, but the response rate keeps rising. Eventually, weeks go by without delivery of any contingent reinforcers. Then the rate of completing assignments begins to decline sporadically, so the reinforcers are reinstated occasionally. The high rate of completion of assignments is then restored and remains at its high level.[2]

A generalization can be extracted from this discussion: If the goal for a particular program is a high response rate, use an *adjusting schedule* to increase the ratio requirement gradually until the behavior reaches its peak or the increase stops and the rate levels off and remains steady. If the rate of responding begins to disintegrate, temporarily reduce the ratio requirement to solve the problem.

Consistency of performance. Animal studies (Reynolds, 1968) have shown that a subject may tend to pause immediately after reinforcement under large FR requirements. This post-reinforcement pause is not, however, consistently observed in human FR performance. Generally, performance is less variable under fixed-ratio than under fixed-interval schedules. The individual assigned a fixed number of pages to complete before receiving bonus points may or may not stop working for a while after receiving the points. If the required number of

---

[2] Companies using goal-setting among groups of employees are doing something directly analogous. In coordination with their supervisors, the group jointly specifies a level of performance—often number of accomplishments—to be achieved by the next meeting. Naturally, reinforcement is delivered whenever the goals are met. (See Daniels 1989 and *Performance Management Magazine* for numerous examples.)

pages is very large, pausing may be more likely after the points are received than when a few pages are required. At least the possibility of a pause before the next response exists, potentially disrupting the consistency of responding. During the pause the individual may engage in unwanted behaviors such as doodling, leaving the room, daydreaming, and so on.

Variable-ratio (VR) performance, however, is almost never characterized by *postreinforcement pauses*. Let us look at an illustration of a VR reinforcement schedule. Fern is receiving reinforcement on a VR 6 schedule. Bonus points are delivered on the average of every 6 boxes packed. The actual reinforcement program can be diagrammed, as in Figure 32.1.

Each R represents the response of packing a box. By looking at the way the responses are distributed just before reinforcement, we can see that in some instances reinforcement follows a fairly large number of responses (10R), whereas in other instances it follows just a few responses (2R). The client has no way of anticipating when the next reinforcer will be delivered. It can be after 2 boxes are packed or after 10 boxes are packed. Because reinforcement may be imminent, work is quickly resumed with hardly a pause. This is exactly what Miltenberger and Fuqua (1983) found with a retarded male working on a folder assembly task—a higher response rate with VR than FR.

Analogous is the situation in which the teacher collects written assignments at random, spot checking on an average of every fifth page completed by each student. Some students could conceivably complete 10 pages before the teacher checked and praised them for their performances. Others might have 2 pages in a row checked. When the objective is to maintain a high and consistent performance rate, VR schedules are preferred. This is because VR schedules do not tend to generate pauses in performance, whereas FR schedules, particularly those with high ratio requirements, may.

Evidence in favor of using a variable ratio in preference to a fixed-ratio schedule resulted from a study conducted by Van Houten and Nau (1980). In an adjustment class for deaf children, a buzzer would sound every 5 minutes. If the 5 students were attentive and not disruptive when the buzzer sounded, they earned checks for an opportunity to win a prize. During the FR condition, checks were displayed on a chart. Whenever students earned 8 checks, they could reach into a grab bag for a prize. When they met appropriate behavioral standards in the VR condition, rather than receiving a check each time the buzzer sounded, they could draw a block from a bag containing 7 brown blocks and 1 blue block (a VR 8 schedule). Were they lucky enough to draw the blue block, they would win a prize. Attentiveness increased and disruptiveness decreased during both reinforcement conditions, but the level of each was better and more stable under the VR condition. Although a number of problems solved were not reinforced, each child performed better during reinforcement phases. The VR condition, however, produced the highest rates of production.

Continued responding in extinction. Ratio schedules, like interval schedules, have been shown to provide reinforcement histories that tend to support sustained performance once reinforcement has been terminated (e.g., Beaman, Stoffer, Woods, & Stoffer, 1983). Dis-

Figure 32.1

7R⟶ S^r	5R⟶ S^r	10R⟶ S^r	2R⟶ S^r
(RRRRRRR)⟶ S^r	(RRRRR)⟶ S^r	(RRRRRRRRRR)⟶ S^r	(RR)⟶ S^r

tinctive performance patterns generally emerge following the termination of different kinds of ratio schedules, and some of their important characteristics have been identified. You will find it helpful to become familiar with those characteristics.

Performance following the termination of an FR schedule is often characterized by bursts of responding at the same high rates that were emitted when the schedule was in effect (Reynolds, 1968). The problem is that between the bursts of high responding, the periods of non-responding become longer and longer. Eventually, the frequency of the response bursts diminishes to almost nothing, and the frequency of the periods of nonresponding increases. Ultimately the behavior may cease completely.

Cindy's mother usually refused her daughter's initial requests for money, figuring that if Cindy really needed it she would ask again. Cindy had learned that money was usually forthcoming after her third request (an FR 3 schedule). On Cindy's 13th birthday her mother decided that Cindy should earn her own spending money. The next time Cindy came with a request for funds, her mother told her to find a baby-sitting job. Cindy continued to plead, but to no avail. She went away for a while and then returned—it always worked before. The pleading resumed. But her mother was steadfast, and the requests for money stopped eventually. (Had her mother relented, Cindy's requests for money probably would have returned to their former level almost immediately.)

Another illustration of this phenomenon can be taken from a work setting. Every Friday the staff in the billing office at Purple Triangle was provided with donuts or cookies during its break, provided that the department processed a given number of bills for the week. When petty cash funds were used up, the treats were discontinued, and no alternative special privileges were substituted. Processing of bills continued at a high rate, but occasionally a few workers began to work more slowly. After a while several others were noted to be slowing down. The point here is that, after an FR schedule has been discontinued, responding may maintain for a short while during extinction. But, assuming that no other contingencies have taken control, the overall rate of responding will eventually approach its prereinforcement level.

Nevertheless, a VR schedule tends to sustain behavior for a long time under extinction conditions. One example is the rates of sharing by young children who had received reinforcers; on a VR schedule but when they no longer received candy rewards for sharing they still continued to share (Beamon et al., 1983).

The extent of a person's history of continuous reinforcement may well make a difference, though. Apparently, the longer the individual is exposed to continuous reinforcement prior to partial reinforcement, the less resistant to extinction responding will be (Nation & Boyajian, 1980).

By contrast, a history of a VR schedule with a very high ratio requirement (that is, very thin **reinforcement density**) for a particular response can yield an exceedingly high and persistent performance pattern under extinction conditions. For example, Professor Fogg gave a few spot quizzes during the first half of the semester, then stopped giving them. His students did their assignments religiously "just in case." Out of approximately 20 entries, Uncle Herman won a trip to Florida in one contest, a $5 gift certificate in another, and a case of dog food in a third. Although Uncle Herman has not won a thing for many years after his streak of luck, he still spends all his spare time entering contests. Once Jocelyn had taken her medication regularly for several weeks, her lab results improved and her doctor and nurse occasionally complimented her. Later in the year such compliments were no longer delivered, but Jocelyn continued to take her medication regularly for a fairly long time.

Despite thorough medical examinations and

a variety of physical treatments, 10-year-old Josh continued either to retain his feces or soil himself (Bornstein et al., 1983). A simple daily point card, backed up by money, for nonsoiling and proper elimination rapidly "cured" the problem. Beginning in the 11th week, the schedule was "thinned out" gradually, so that by the 17th week the point card was no longer used. Praise from the therapist continued, but also was thinned gradually until the 28th week, when contact with the therapist was terminated altogether. A year later the problem had not reappeared. Similarly, relapses in bedwetting occurred less frequently when children were signaled by an alarm bell on a partial (70% schedule) rather than on a continuous schedule (Finley & Wansley, 1976).

In most instances, no matter what the schedule history, a response will diminish and eventually return to its preintervention level when extinction conditions are maintained completely, that is, when previously arranged reinforcers are discontinued and no natural reinforcers take over. Under VR histories, recovery of baseline performance simply takes much longer.

Typical performance following the termination of VR reinforcement consists of very long, sustained, and rapid bursts of responses, interspersed with gradually increasing periods of nonresponding similar to those following termination of an FR schedule. But in VR performance, the periods of nonresponding usually begin later and occur less frequently than in FR performance. If Cindy's mother had given her money after an irregular number of requests, the requests would probably have persisted much longer. If the cookies or donuts had been delivered irregularly, rather than regularly, the workers would probably have sustained their high billing rates for a longer period of time after the treats had been terminated.

Two important practical conclusions can be drawn from the fact that a well-established history of a thin VR schedule of reinforcement tends to generate very persistent performance under extinction conditions. First, if the terminal goal of a program of behavior change or of an instructional sequence is maintenance of the response once contingencies are removed, a variable-ratio schedule of reinforcement that has been gradually thinned should best suit the purpose. Second, conversely, an unwanted behavior should *never*, if possible, be maintained by such a schedule. As the schedule tends to make behavior very resistant to extinction, eliminating the problematic performance will prove very difficult.

Advantages of Ratio Schedules

Beyond its practical features, the main advantage of intermittent reinforcement is its promotion of maintained responding. The reinforcement schedule that is based on the number of responses, the ratio schedule, offers a few specific advantages. The first and most obvious is that it tends to generate high response rates—a point that probably does not have to be reiterated at this time. A second advantage, related to the first, is that given an initial phase of ratio reinforcement, the high rates initially generated may continue under interval schedules.

Weiner (1964b) found that the rate of keypressing responses by humans on FI schedules was markedly affected by their previous experience on the apparatus. Those subjects who had histories of receiving FR reinforcement performed on an FI schedule at rates that were quite high—similar to their FR schedule performance. Other subjects who had histories of receiving reinforcement only when they responded very slowly continued to perform slowly when the schedule was switched to FI. Over a great many sessions, the rates among some of the subjects who responded at high FI rates began to diminish but never to the low levels of their more slowly responding counterparts. The significance of this point for practitioners is that achieving a reasonably high rate of performance under interval scheduling is possible.

Let us say that Fern's supervisor prefers to use FI reinforcement for convenience's sake. In order to avoid the potentially low rates that are known sometimes to characterize FI performance, she plans an initial phase of FR reinforcement. After all, she does not want Fern to work only toward the end of each interval. An aide agrees to help. They start with a fairly low ratio requirement, FR 5: after every fifth item packed they give Fern a token. The ratio of required responses is gradually increased to about FR 30. Then, when Fern is spending most of the time working on her assignment, they switch over to an FI schedule. Ultimately, the supervisor can take over contingency control without assistance and remain fairly confident that the high rate of responding will maintain for quite a while. A periodic shift back to an FR schedule, with the assistance of the aide, could further ensure the maintenance of the high rate of response.

A third advantage of ratio schedules is that they are particularly easy to use when the target response results in a permanent product. Products can simply be counted as they are produced, and reinforcers can be presented as scheduled: after so many boxes packed, problems solved, answers to questions written, buttons buttoned, tables cleaned, beds made, pages typed, complimentary notes sent, and so on. (Recall that determining the reliability of measurement is also simplified through the use of permanent-product data.)

Fourth, ratio schedules may be used to facilitate the transition from artificial to natural reinforcement. This goal is accomplished through scheduling two sets of consequences for the target response: The weaker but more natural consequences are provided with increased frequency; the more powerful artificial consequences are provided less often. As long as a stronger reinforcer is continually paired

with a weaker one, the latter should begin to acquire its own reinforcing properties.

Lucretia is observed to share a toy on the request of a playmate. Her mother smiles, nods "Um-hum," and gives her daughter a hug, a powerful reinforcer for Lucretia. As the rate of sharing increases, her mother continues to smile and hug, but the ratio of hugs begins to diminish to about every other sharing response, then to about every third one, and so on. The smiling and nodding contingent upon sharing seem to maintain the response successfully, and hugs have been reduced to a ratio that Lucretia's mother can easily manage. (Much later, when the rate of sharing is sufficiently high and stable, even the contingent smiles and nods may be presented intermittently; the rate is still likely to persist.)

Another advantage of ratio schedules is that they can help avoid problems like "learned helplessness" and "stimulus overselectivity." Undergraduates were given a pattern completion task designed to evoke "learned helplessness" (giving up). One group was "inoculated" against learned helplessness in an escape task. Members were told they were trying, and received ". . . the partial reinforcement schedule containing consecutive failures" (Stein, 1980, p. 1148). Results showed this group performed better than those who were told they weren't trying or who had experienced continuous reinforcement. It seems that experiencing failure from time to time permitted participants in the first group to deal more effectively with the failure. Stimulus overselectivity (responding exclusively to just one among a complex set of stimuli), an impediment to discrimination learning among many autistic people, has also been found to be more effectively modified when training involves a phase of variable ratio rather than continuous reinforcement (Koegel et al., 1979).

Using Ratio Schedules Effectively

In our discussion of ratio schedules we have attempted to identify several response characteristics that should have direct bearing on programming for maintained responding. You have seen how ratio schedules promote high response rates. If consistency of responding is an issue, however, the ratio schedule should have a variable base.

Individual variability in rates of responding under ratio schedules is not unusual. Various factors have been identified as influencing these rates, including instructions, models, and history (Chappell & Leibowitz, 1982; Weiner, 1981a; 1981b; 1982). If response rates under fixed ratio schedules are not as high as you would prefer, there are a few things you can do. As Weiner (1981a; 1981b) did with his schizophrenic participants, you might provide clear instructions, such as "The machine is set so that you will earn a penny every time you press the button 40 times. The faster you press, the more pennies you will earn." (Weiner, 1981a, pp. 452–453).

An alternative is the method Weiner (1982b) found to be even more successful than instructions: Ask the client to imitate the rate of responding of someone else shown earning a reinforcer. Bruno is having great difficulty playing his scherzo movement rapidly enough. The maestro demonstrates the correct tempo, asks Bruno to do the same, and praises when Bruno's rate matches his own. Or, "Look, Paula. Notice how rapidly Sal fills out her claims reports. You try to work at that pace, and soon you will earn your raise."

If you prefer a slower rate during an FR schedule, provide a history by making reinforcement contingent on temporally spaced responding ("Good, Bruno, you've extended the time between your notes in this adagio movement"), or use other standard ways of slowing response rates (Weiner, 1982). Continue this pretraining until the ideally slow rate is stable and then shift over to the FR.

You will need to consider each individual separately, however, if you want optimal performance from all. Some people require dense reinforcement schedules; others appear to need hardly any reinforcers at all for given performances. For this reason, Platt, Harris, and Clements (1980) developed a method for determining the ideal level of reinforcement for each student. They gradually thinned the ratio of reinforcement while monitoring performance to determine when the accuracy of math assignments completed by their behaviorally disordered students began to fall below 90%. That was judged to indicate that the density of reinforcement had fallen just below its optimal level. The best part here was that the method permitted students to receive no more extrinsic reward than necessary to encourage their high-quality performance.

Clients can apply variable-ratio schedules for self-reinforcement too. For instance, Dexter may want to use a variable-ratio schedule for problems completed; Bruno for scales practiced; Paula for claims processed; Mr. Grump for praise statements delivered. Here are a few clever, convenient techniques that have been devised to simplify variable-ratio reinforcement delivery to oneself or others.

- Use a spinner of the type used in board games. Only if the pointer comes to rest in a designated segment is a reinforcer earned (Pawlicki & Morey, 1976).
- Instead of a spinner, use a watch with a sweep second hand. Look at it immediately on completion of the performance. If it is in the predesignated segment, award a reinforcer (Dorsel et al., 1980).
- Place hard candies, marbles, or other small items, all except one of the same color, into a container. Or mark one of the items—analogous to choosing straws. When the distinctive item is drawn from a container (the short straw), award a reinforcer (Dorsel, 1977; Latham & Dossett; 1978).

- Use a card or checklist and star just some of the blanks. Deliver rewards only for checks in the starred blanks (Bornstein et al., 1983).
- Try the drawing game in which dots are connected in numerical sequence. Dots, covered by scratch-off ink or bits of stickers, are revealed each time the child emits a given response. Some of the dots are large, signaling reinforcement. So the child is permitted to take a turn with a spinner, the face of which is divided into segments, *each one of which* indicates a distinctive reinforcer, such as a 5-minute back scratch or being leader in a recess game (Jenson, Neville, Sloane, & Morgan, 1982).

Here is another system devised by Jenson (1980): Each student received a card listing specific, pinpointed chores or "continuous" behaviors—those with no clear beginning or end (e.g., being polite), plus a row of nine 5s next to each item. As clients completed their chores, they could request points. Assuming the completion of the chore fell within a time limit and met a preset standard of performance, the staff member would circle the appropriate number of 5s. Staff could also award points when they caught the client emitting the desired continuous behaviors. Each evening, points were exchanged for back-up reinforcers or the points were banked.

You can guess how the density of the ratio schedule was selected in each case. All they had to do was to designate an area of proper proportion on the watch face or spinner. For a 1:2 ratio (VR 2), one half the spinner or watch face circle would be designated; for a 1:3, a third of the circle; for a 1:12, each 5-minute mark or 1/12 of the spinner face. If you would like to set up a VR 6 schedule, have the client toss a die. If a preset number comes up, the person receives the reinforcer.

With a ratio schedule, thin or lean the den-sity gradually.[3] You may wish to select a given criterion for each thinning step, such as a minimum of 80% over 20 trials, before moving to the next less dense schedule. (See Deckner, Deckner, & Blanton, 1982, for an example of using this approach with young psychotic children.) For the checklists, just diminish the number of starred blanks each week. Similarly, modify the number of items in the container or proportion of large to small dots according to the schedule you want to use: To shift from a 1:5 ratio (VR 5) to a 1:8, add three more items identical to the original set of four and the one distinctive item.

Because the same sort of disruption in responding (ratio strain) that tends to accompany extinction happens when a schedule requirement shifts too abruptly to a much higher ratio, it is best to adjust the ratio requirement gradually. Along the way, supplement the schedule with other, perhaps less powerful, reinforcers such as praise or other social events. Then continue increasing the ratio requirement until it reaches its limit and the rate no longer increases (technically, its *asymptote*). Determining whether a "true" limit has been reached may be difficult, however, for ratio strain may be operating. A temporary reduction in the ratio requirement, followed by perhaps an even more gradual increase, may provide the evidence by which to judge whether the absolute limit has been reached.

Dexter has made very satisfactory progress with his studying. He is managing his own contingencies, using a point system. He has designed a reinforcement menu for himself, with a number of preferred activities costing specific numbers of points. He can go to the science museum for 50 points, read a chapter in his science-fiction book for 25 points, call his

---

[3] To avoid confusion, we prefer the term *thin* rather than *fade*, as *fade* conventionally is the word used to describe when prompts are diminished for the purpose of producing stimulus control.

friend for 10 points, and visit a pal in another community for 500 points. During the first week the system is in operation he assigns himself 1 point for each paragraph that he reads and is able to summarize to himself in 1 sentence. The next week he increases the requirement to 2 paragraphs per point; the next, to a page. Eventually he requires 2 pages, then 5, then a chapter for a single point.

But Dexter notes that his studying has begun to fall off precipitously. He is finding all sorts of excuses for not working. One day he has a headache. He accidentally leaves his books at school a couple of times. His friends keep calling him, and he just cannot seem to end the conversations. Is it possible that the ratio requirement has something to do with the disruption? What he should try to do is to drop back a few steps, perhaps to the requirement of 2 pages per point, and to reestablish his previous high rate. Then he can proceed more cautiously—from 2 pages to 3, 4, 6, and so on. If the more gradual progression does not promote a breakdown in rate, fine. But, if disruption occurs again, perhaps he should just drop back a little bit and stay there.

Disadvantages of Ratio Schedules

The ratio-strain problem that may be encountered during too rapid an increase in a ratio requirement has already been discussed, and some possible solutions have been offered. An additional problem in the implementation of ratio schedules is that the topography (or quality) of the response may begin to disintegrate at very high rates. Davidson and Osborne (1974) found that children produced a high proportion of errors immediately after reinforcement in an FR matching-to-sample task. Using a ratio schedule to maintain adequate amounts of practicing scales on the piano, Bruno von Burn awards himself a point for every 10 scales that he practices. The points can then be exchanged for minutes during which he allows himself to

play current hit tunes. His rate of practicing scales increases, but his technique begins to deteriorate. This sort of problem appeared when McLaughlin and Malaby (1975b) examined the effects of awarding points to fifth- and sixth-grade students for completion, rather than for accuracy, of math assignments. Rates of solving problems increased, but accuracy deteriorated.

If Bruno wanted to be sure that his technique would not disintegrate, he would have to define the response more carefully. Just completing scales would not be adequate. Only scales meeting a predetermined standard of acceptability would count toward the ratio. Consequently, to avoid the deterioration in response topography that might accompany the high rates promoted by ratio schedules, it is particularly important that the standards for acceptable quality be established beforehand. Then deliver reinforcement only contingent on the topographically correct number of responses required to complete the ratio. If errors persist, the ratio requirement can be reduced until the appropriate quality occurs reliably or an additional rule can be appended to the contingency arrangement: All responses in the series must be topographically correct, or no more than X% error will be allowed.

The mastery requirement in Personalized Systems of Instruction (PSI) illustrates one way that inaccuracy of responding can be minimized. Students must complete a predetermined number of units to earn a grade; quizzes must be passed at 90% level of correctness or better if the student is to be allowed to proceed. In this manner, students are prevented from committing too many errors while rushing through the material in the course.

Sometimes using ratio schedules can be inconvenient or impractical because we need to count responses. This requirement can present a problem if clients cannot keep reliable track of their own rates of responding or if no support staff or costly instruments are available to accomplish this task. Many alternatives may be considered in those circumstances: peers, volunteers, inexpensive instruments like shopping counters, and others (see Chapter 6).

As maintained responding in the total absence of contingent reinforcement is very improbable, some provision must be made for intermittent reinforcement to occur either naturally or as part of the program. Managers of programs probably find interval schedules easier to implement than ratio schedules. Clients, too, may prefer interval schedules. When rates of payoff are kept essentially equal, humans and other species appear to prefer time-dependent (interval) to response-dependent (ratio) schedules (Schaeffer, 1979). College students who could earn about the same number of points under either schedule generally chose the interval schedule. Only when payoff was substantially higher for the ratio schedules did they shift to the latter. (One might conclude that this preference for interval schedules is based on the fact that interval schedules require comparatively less responding than ratio schedules, thereby minimizing effort. Nevertheless, in this latter case, relative response rates were not significantly lower during the time-dependent schedule.)

Additionally, interval schedules usually are much easier than ratio schedules to implement, but, as previously indicated, they are not conducive to high rates. When keeping count of a response is not difficult and high rates are desired, starting with a ratio schedule is most practical. As you discovered in Chapter 31, once responding has been established, you can switch to an interval schedule. The following material on differential reinforcement of high rates illustrates a different way to provide that history.

Differential Reinforcement of High Rates

Another method for producing high rates of responding is a schedule of **differential reinforcement of high rates (DRH)**. In establishing a

DRH schedule, observe sequences of responses very closely. Deliver reinforcement only when several responses occur in rapid succession; at or above a preestablished rate. When pauses are interspersed, postpone reinforcement. You will be reinforcing high rates in preference to low rates. This schedule is the opposite of the DRL schedule discussed in Chapter 24. (You may wish to review that material.) When the mile runner completes his run in less than 4 minutes, the crowd cheers. Times over 4 minutes are not cheered. When Chuck correctly finishes all the problems in his workbook within a week, he is given an ''A.'' If he takes longer, the grade is a ''B.'' Returning to the illustration of Grungy George, let us suppose that he combs his hair and cleans his nails only once a week. Then a friend visits, and George combs his hair and cleans his nails 4 days in a row. The sequence is reinforced, not only by his allowance but also by social reinforcers and perhaps some extra money to entertain his friend. Such powerful contingencies are repeated with George each time he looks neat and clean for several days in a row. In this manner, the response rate is more likely to increase. Once the rate reaches an acceptable level, it will be possible to switch from that particular DRH schedule to a more demanding one or to an interval schedule.

Sometimes the DRH schedule is combined with other schedules in order to achieve a rapid rate of responding, particularly when we seek to provide the kind of history that will promote a rapid rate of responding under a variable-interval schedule. For illustrative purposes, consider Desmond, who has been participating in a vocational workshop. The supervisor knows that Desmond can do the sorting work, because when the supervisor sits down with Desmond on a one-to-one basis, he completes it correctly. In a group setting, however, Desmond never finishes his work and is labeled ''lazy'' and ''obstinate.'' Rather than working, he wanders around the room and earns another label: "hyperactive."

After careful observation, however, Desmond is found to have been functioning on a CRF schedule. His work is completed if, after completing each task, he receives reinforcement in the form of attention from the supervisor. The average assignment is about 25 sorting tasks (VR 25). The supervisor thinks that he would be able to attend to Desmond about once an hour under ordinary circumstances. Placing Desmond's responding on a VI of 1 hour at this time is, however, apparently like placing his performance under extinction conditions. The staff decides to return to a CRF, to provide a brief interval of attention each time Desmond completes a sorting task.

To facilitate this plan, Desmond is asked to raise his hand whenever he finishes a sorting task. This requirement is soon changed to an FR 2: After the completion of every two tasks, he raises his hand for recognition and reinforcement. The schedule is then changed to a VR 3; the number of tasks Desmond is asked to complete before raising his hand varies among 2, 4, and 3. This schedule is very soon changed to VR 5. During this phase of providing a history of ratio reinforcement, the amount of time taken to complete several tasks is also noted. If the specified number of tasks is completed correctly within less time than average, he earns a bonus reinforcement (for example, an extra coffee break). In this manner, the DRH is combined with the variable-ratio schedule.

Soon the staff decides to change over to a VI schedule of reinforcement. The supervisor tells Desmond that he wants to see how many tasks he can complete before the supervisor returns shortly. A VI schedule of 5 minutes is selected, because that is the average time it takes Desmond to complete 5 tasks under the VR 5 schedule. The change will thus go practically unnoticed by Desmond. After approximately 5 minutes, then, the supervisor checks back. If Desmond is working on his task, the supervisor provides reinforcement. If he has completed more problems than usual in the amount of time that has elapsed, the supervisor differentially reinforces this high rate of behavior (DRH) with extra praise, recognition, or some sort of bonus.

The VI 5 is then gradually adjusted to VI 8, VI 15, VI 30, and VI 60 (one hour). Throughout the variable-interval schedules, a limited hold is also used. If a specific number of sorting tasks is not completed, no reinforcement is delivered for that interval. This combination of a ratio history, DRH, and limited hold helps Desmond to work quickly and for extended periods, thereby enhancing his eligibility for actual competitive employment.

Interactions Among Schedules

Knowing about the characteristics of behavior that tend to be generated by particular schedules of reinforcement should help you to understand and manage current performance and anticipate future patterns. You would expect, for example, highly consistent rates when a response has been reinforced on a variable-ratio schedule and persistence for quite a while during extinction. You would not be surprised to see a response pattern deteriorate rapidly when extinction conditions follow an extended phase of continuous reinforcement.

Nevertheless, many factors complicate our ability to understand, manage, and predict response patterns on the basis of one particular schedule. The picture is far more complex. We have already learned about individual variations in terms of schedule effectiveness and the influence of history and social (e.g., models) variables. Another powerful influence is *other schedules* very recently or currently in effect.

People don't spend their entire day doing the same thing. One reason is because the value of reinforcers alters from one time to another (food is more reinforcing at some times of the day than others; so is engaging in social interactions, job, or recreational activities). Another reason is that different schedules of reinforcement are concurrently available, operating either at the same time (simultaneously) or one after the other (sequentially).

These complex schedule arrangements interact with one another to influence response distributions and patterns. If two fixed-interval schedules, one short and one long, are in effect at the same time, animals are apt to emit the response required by the short requirement, rather than that by the longer (Catania et al., 1988). So if you want responding to continue throughout a fixed-interval, try to avoid adding a shorter fixed-interval reinforcement schedule on top of it. If you are hoping your staff will keep working at one task until break time, it is better to avoid giving them a different, shorter task to complete until afterward.

When two different schedules with different proportions of payoff are operating simultaneously, you may see responding distributed between the two schedules. Bruno delivers reinforcement to himself for practicing scales. His mother praises his performance of her favorite pieces. Certain pieces have passages that Bruno loves to hear; others contain parts he doesn't like at all. Bruno distributes his practicing, rather than sticking with one category.

If you skim the journals publishing reports of schedule performance, such as those mentioned in our reference list, you will see that nonhuman organisms ("animals" for convenience sake) also tend to distribute their responding across the various options available to them. In fact, when all other potentially confounding factors are controlled (a rare situation with humans living in open societies), animals have a propensity for distributing their responses according to the proportion of payoff. If pecking one disk yields a pigeon grain 40% of the time and pecking the other yields the grain 60% of the time, the pigeon will tend to peck the first disk about 40% of the time and the second about 60%. This phenomenon has been labeled the **matching law** (Herrnstein, 1970).

Many years of follow-up research, however, have shown that the ways animals, including humans, distribute their responding under different schedules are influenced by a number of other schedule factors. These factors include whether it is a variable or fixed schedule (pigeons prefer variable schedules) (Herrnstein, 1964), antecedent stimulus factors (they "like" informative stimuli), freedom (preferred) or constrained choice, and many more. Also, as we mentioned earlier, people and other organisms tend to "maximize"—usually responding most heavily, often exclusively—to choices that yield the highest ultimate payoff. (See Chapter 7 of Catania, 1984, for an extensive discussion of this topic.)

Different people's sensitivity to particular schedules may vary. Some respond as though unaware of the nature of an even fairly obvious schedule currently in effect. This seems to be the case particularly with autistic youngsters, who have been found to fail to *maximize* (i.e., select the choice with the richest payoff) and also to be less responsive to extinction conditions than their typical peers (Mullins & Rincover, 1985).

When maximizing is important, as it is in many situations in life, such as choosing activities that will yield lots of reinforcement (the best job, most supportive social group, and so on), you can see what kinds of problems might arise when people are insensitive to schedule variations. Conversely, a failure to detect differences in schedules sometimes can be an advantage, as when they are undergoing a transition from the managed reinforcement for adaptive behavior within the school or work environment to the sporadic schedules of less structured settings.

Recall our discussion of contrast effects from Chapter 31. You may see instances of the way a schedule change affects unrelated performance in your own behavior, such as when your rates of studying your text books drop while you are attending a stimulating professional meeting (presumably a reinforcer for you). We have seen instances of negative behavioral contract with developmentally disabled clients. Despite an unchanging reinforcement schedule associated with progress in one area, say, practicing self-help skills, the clients' progress began to fall off because they began to receive extra helpings of reinforcement for progress in other areas.

Examples of positive behavioral contrast also may be found. Seven hearing-impaired middle school students rotated from among 3 work stations: applied math, programmed instruction, and computation (Simon, Ayllon, & Milan, 1982). When they began to receive tokens exchangeable for prizes and candy at each station, their rates of accuracy increased (and disruption decreased) over baseline. Subsequently, tokens were discontinued for performance at the programmed instruction and computation stations but held constant for applied math. You can imagine what happened. Rates *increased* for applied math (positive contrast) and dropped for the other 2. Reinstating tokens for all three resulted in performance eventually recovering at the other 2 stations, while the rate in applied math began to drop off somewhat (and disruption increased). You may notice children inexplicably misbehaving. Perhaps attention for their socially acceptable acts has been discontinued.

Changes in *density* of reinforcement probably function similarly to changes from no reinforcement to some or vice versa. Discriminating different magnitudes of reinforcement seems to influence performance with some degree of predictability. You are dieting to try to lose weight. The first week you lose 4 pounds. The second week, you lose only 1 and experience an ''extinction burst''—you feel angry and give up on the diet. Your specific reaction

probably depends upon many factors, including your own self-reinforcement schedule. (Yes! Self-reinforcement operates on lean, dense, regular, irregular, and other variations in schedules, too.)

Elaine Heiby (1983) studied this type of phenomenon. She determined whether her subjects tended to deliver reinforcers to themselves frequently or infrequently. Then she gave them an anagram task and provided first lots (80%) of ''extrinsic'' reinforcement, then a little reinforcement (20%) for some participants. (Others received proportions of reinforcement in the opposite order, or in unchanging amounts.) She found that those students who reinforced their own behavior infrequently reported a greater depression in the 80% to 20% drop in reinforcement than in the other groups. Apparently, those individuals who reinforced their own behavior often were less dependent on the external reinforcement. The contrast resulting from the sequence of changing from a very dense to a lean schedule may have been mitigated by the availability of their own self-administered reinforcement.

Are you holding your head and saying, ''Why bother? The tangle of interacting schedules is so complicated, I might as well forget it.'' Don't do that! Instead, use this information to help yourself:

1. Try to understand mysterious changes in behavioral patterns.

2. Alter rates indirectly by capitalizing on contrast effects (pour on the reinforcement for making acceptable choices or withhold it from all but the one you want to see increased).

3. Find ways to override the influence exerted by schedules over which you have little or no control. Despite ongoing competing schedules, you may well achieve your objective by powerfully reinforcing the target behavior on a CRF or dense VR schedule. Look. You have just about finished reading this book. Consider the schedules that have sustained your diligence!

Summary

Ratio and DRH schedules have been defined and discussed as procedures for maintaining behaviors at high rates. Ratio schedules generally produce higher rates of responding than do interval schedules even under subsequent extinction. This is especially true of their VR schedules.

When your goal is to maintain a behavior at a high rate while avoiding the necessity of counting responses before the delivery of reinforcement, you can plan an interval schedule. Providing a ratio- or DRH-schedule history and a limited-hold requirement should increase the rate of performance under interval scheduling.

Arrange the initial switch from continuous to ratio schedules so that progressive increments in ratio requirements are implemented gradually. By supplementing the gradual progression of ratio requirements with less powerful reinforcers, you may avoid ratio strain.

Finally, understand that people's histories with regard to schedules tend to vary and that a multiplicity of schedules are in effect within human societies. Realize that management of many of these will be outside of your control. If you are fortunate, though, you can make use of those that are manageable to accomplish the purposes you and your clients elect to pursue.

Epilogue

Are you ready to tackle your New Year's resolution? How about the behavioral problems and challenges of your job or family life? At this point, you should be equipped to begin addressing them, especially if you are fortunate enough to have received expert supervision as you practiced using the concepts and skills presented in this book. Otherwise, struggle on alone, as many of us had to do, providing your own rules, feedback, and reinforcement and/or enlisting support from others.

Predicting how successful you are apt to be in any given instance can be accomplished by referring to the model we presented at the end of the introductory chapter. Ask yourself whether the problems you have chosen to address are defensible and can be validly and reliably measured, and whether you have sufficient control of the right contingencies to implement the most promising procedures. Determine whether supports are in place or can be established to assist the altered behavior to spread across appropriate contexts and to endure. Be cautious, though. Do not rely simply on the conviction that your strategies are working. Measure progress and functionally analyze results.

To help you decide which procedures to apply, how to go about using them effectively, and ways to anticipate any positive or negative side-effects, we present Tables E.1 through E.4 for your convenience. Remain skeptical, though, as you refer to them. The information they contain is based on our understanding of the state of the art of applied behavior analysis. But research findings are in a constant state of flux. Today's theories may be fiction tomorrow. Your best recourse is to remain abreast of the literature.

As the twentieth century draws to a close we have cause for rejoicing. Along with other physical and natural sciences, the science of human behavior advances in scope and sophistication. This evolution permits increasingly improved technological application. Although much remains to be discovered in the vast unknown territory of the whys and wherefores of human performance, achieving lasting behavioral change becomes progressively more attainable.

Table E.1 Procedures for Increasing Behavior

Procedure	Operation	Maximizing Effectiveness	Temporal Characteristics[a]	Duration of Effect[a]	Other Characteristics[a]
Positive reinforcement	Positive reinforcer presented as consequence of response	1. Reinforce immediately 2. Specify conditions under which reinforcement will be delivered 3. Deliver sufficient quantity to maintain behavior without rapid satiation 4. Select reinforcer appropriate to individual in that context 5. Use variety of conditioned, unconditioned, and generalized reinforcers and reinforcing situations 6. Try to use as reinforcers high-frequency behaviors, behaviors restricted to below their baseline levels, and others natural to the environment 7. Provide opportunity for reinforcer sampling 8. Eliminate or reduce competing contingencies 9. Reinforce every response initially 10. Combine with modeling or other prompts, if needed 11. Label or describe the behavior being reinforced 12. Combine reinforcement with positive social events (praise, smile, etc.)	Gradual	Long-lasting	1. Positive (possible positive generalization) 2. Constructive 3. Occasions positive self-statements

		13. If using groups, keep size small; provide feedback and reinforcement to individuals and to group		
		14. Plan for intermittency, delay, reduction in size or value of reinforcer, and generalization, once behavior is high and steady		
Negative reinforcement	Aversive stimulus removed contingent on response	1. Remove aversive stimulus immediately 2. Select stimulus aversive to individual 3. Apply every time 4. Specify act being reinforced 5. Combine with positive reinforcement, following guidelines listed in steps 1–4	Gradual	1. Possible negative generalization
			May be long lasting in context if aversive stimuli available	1. Aversive stimulus occasions avoidance, escape, aggression
				2. Behavior increase may be restricted to teaching context

ª Assuming optimal use of the procedure

Table E.2 Procedures for Occasioning and Teaching New Behavior

Procedure	Operation	Maximizing Effectiveness[a]	Temporal Aspects	Duration of Effect	Other Characteristics
Stimulus change	Presenting or removing a discriminative stimulus	1. S^Ds & S^Δs manageable 2. Stimulus control well established 3. Select most powerful S^Ds 4. Combine with other procedures, especially differential reinforcement	Immediate	Continues as long as S^Ds present	May be influenced by competing contingencies
Differential reinforcement for stimulus control	Reinforcing responses only in presence of S^Ds; withholding reinforcement in the presence of S^Δs	1. Identify relevant stimulus properties 2. Emphasize relevant stimulus properties 3. Use differential reinforcement consistently 4. Apply, then fade prompts 5. Identify & manage interfering S^Ds	Gradual	Temporary until stimulus control firmly established; then long-lasting, given intermittent differential reinforcement	Risk of over-dependence on supplemental prompts or over selectivity
Prompting	Substituting an effective but inappropriate stimulus for an ineffective but appropriate stimulus (e.g. goal setting; rules; models; physical guidance)	For *Goal setting:* 1. Select challenging but achievable goals 2. Keep group size small 3. Reinforce goal attainment 4. Increase goal levels by challenging but attainable steps 5. Involve participants For *Instructions or rules:* 1. Ensure rule governance in repertoire or teach 2. Use stimuli familiar to learner 3. Present fast 4. Combine with differential reinforcement, other prompts if needed	Rapid	Lasts as long as prompt present	May create overdependence on prompts

		Guidelines		
		For *Modeling:* 1. Teach generalized imitation if not in repertoire 2. Select models similar to client; competent; who share positive prior experiences with client; prestigious 3. Highlight similarities between client and model 4. Encourage rehearsal of modeled behavior 5. Provide rules 6. Keep behavior simple 7. Reinforce model's behavior 8. Reinforce imitative acts For *Physical Guidance:* 1. Secure client's cooperation 2. Guide minimally For *All:* 1. Fade as rapidly as feasible		
Delayed prompting	Interposing a delay between S+ and prompt	1. Increase delay gradually 2. Assess for acquisition with random sequence trials 3. Include in more complex teaching	As delay increases, time to evoke response also increases until *moment of transfer*	Depends on how firmly established S+ control has become	Increases opportunity for independence; may permit errorless learning; *moment of transfer* immediately known
Graduated prompting	Sequentially applying prompts of increasing intrusiveness	1. Give less intrusive prompts fair try 2. Assess by locating functional S^D and begin there	Time consuming, depending on level of initial instruction	Depends on how firmly established S+ control has become	Maximizes success; unless prompt levels faded may cause overdependence or very intrusive prompts

(continued)

Table E.2 Procedures for Occasioning and Teaching New Behavior (continued)

Procedure	Operation	Maximizing Effectiveness[a]	Temporal Aspects	Duration of Effect	Other Characteristics
Fading	Systematic, gradual removal of prompts until S⁺ takes control	1. Progress to less intrusive prompt levels or to more appropriate stimulus property 2. Remove prompts gradually 3. To remove physical prompts, try graduated guidance 4. For visual discriminations, try fading in a match-to-sample paradigm 5. To minimize errors: Select S⁺'s very different from S⁻'s; introduce S⁻'s briefly and at weak intensity at first 6. Consider using response delay 7. Reinforce S⁺ — R combination heavily until firmly established; then thin schedule of reinforcement	Slow	Depends on how firmly established S⁺ control has become	Essential for independence from artificial supports; when done with care, can establish powerful stimulus control
Shaping	Reinforcing successive approximations to goal	1. Keep your eye on goal 2. Start with behaviors in individual's repertoire 3. Start with behaviors that most closely resemble goal behavior 4. Select challenging but achievable step size 5. Remain at a given step only long enough to incorporate it within individual's repertoire	Gradual	Long-lasting	Positive, constructive approach; requires careful planning

Chaining	Reinforcing combinations of more than one response link or behavioral component to form a complex behavior	1. Do careful task analysis 2. Validate task analysis 3. Select links in individual's repertoire 4. Shape components if necessary 5. Consider starting with final link 6. Occasion response combinations with prompts; then fade 7. Use effective reinforcement during teaching and to consolidate ultimate complex behavior	Gradual; if links already in repertoire, may be faster than shaping	Long-lasting if optimally reinforced	Positive, constructive approach
Teaching rule governance	Reinforce responses conforming to contingencies specified	1. Use effective stimulus control methods 2. Target essential elements of rules 3. Use correspondence training when appropriate 4. Break overdependence on incorrect rules 5. Avoid using nonvalidated rules 6. Promote generalization and maintenance	Can be rapid; depends on repertoire; history of reinforcement for rule governance	Depends on prior and current s^R contingencies, especially competing contingencies	Important adjunct to other procedures; essence of cognitive behavior

[a] Assuming optimal use of the procedure.

Table E.3 Procedures for Reducing Behavior

Procedure	Operation	Maximizing Effectiveness	Temporal Aspects	Duration of Effect	Other Characteristics
Extinction	Withholding reinforcers as a consequence of a behavior	1. Identify all reinforcers for particular behavior and withhold completely 2. Maintain procedure long enough to begin to show effect 3. Reinforce alternative behaviors 4. Specify conditions under which extinction conditions are in effect and follow through	Gradual	If maintained permanently can be long-lasting	Aversive stimuli not required; may be temporary increase in response rate, aggression, escape (extinction burst); may be difficult to identify and withhold all reinforcers; unwanted behaviors may be imitated
Reinforcing alternative behaviors (Alt-R)	Reinforcing any alternative to unwanted behavior	1. Use effective reinforcement and extinction 2. Avoid reinforcing other unwanted behavior 3. Combine with other procedures	Gradual	Can be long-lasting	Positive, constructive, requires less vigilance than DRI
Differential reinforcement of incompatible behavior (DRI)	Reinforcing behavior not compatible with unwanted behavior	1. Same as for Alt-R, plus: 2. Ensure chosen behavior not compatible with unwanted response; in repertoire; likely to be naturally supported	Faster than Alt-R	Once incompatible behavior firmly established can be long-lasting	Positive, constructive; need to watch for and reinforce incompatible act

Technique	Description	Guidelines	Speed	Durability	Comments
Differential reinforcement of other (zero) behavior (omission training)	Reinforce as a consequence of a time period without unwanted response	1. Same as above, plus: 2. Begin with short intervals; increase size gradually 3. When unwanted behavior no longer occurring, shift to momentary DRO	Gradual	Provided intermittent reinforcment continues, can be long-lasting	Relatively easy to use; fails "dead man's test"; other behaviors could be worse; increases monitoring for unwanted behavior; possible behavioral contrast
Differential reinforcement of low rates (DRL)	Reinforce behavior when occurs after x amount of time without that behavior	1. Use effective reinforcement procedures; 2. Extend interval gradually 3. Combine with other procedures, like stimulus control	Gradual	May be long-lasting	Benign, tolerant convenient; focus on unwanted behavior
Differential reinforcement of diminishing rates (DRD)	Reinforce at the end of intervals containing diminishing rates	1. Same as above	Gradual	May be long-lasting	Same as above
Response cost[a]	Withdrawing n reinforcers contingent on response	1. Allow for buildup of reinforcement reserve 2. Determine effective magnitude of response cost empirically 3. Communicate rules of game 4. Apply every time 5. Combine with reinforcement of alternative behaviors 6. Consider 'bonus response cost'	Rapid	Long-lasting, particularly when combined with Alt-R	Negative; Learning promotes discrimination; convenient; effect depends on reinforcement history of individual; may occasion aggression and escape; associated stimuli may become aversive

(continued)

Table E.3 Procedures for Reducing Behavior (continued)

Procedure	Operation	Maximizing Effectiveness	Temporal Aspects	Duration of Effect	Other Characteristics
Timeout[a]	Withdrawing reinforcement for *t* time, contingent on response	1. Remove all reinforcers during timeout 2. Make time-in as reinforcing as possible 3. Avoid providing opportunity for self-generated reinforcers 4. Be able to maintain timeout conditions 5. Keep duration relatively short 6. Apply consistently 7. Communicate conditions for invoking timeout prior to unwanted behavior 8. Combine with reinforcement of alternative behaviors 9. Remove timeout contingent on acceptable behavior	Rapid	Long-lasting	Negative; stimuli paired with timeout become aversive; not constructive; may occasion aggression and escape; loss of learning time; not universally effective; may be legally restricted, readily abused; public concern; may generalize to wanted behaviors
Overcorrection[a]	Overcorrecting environmental effects and requiring positive practice of correct behavior	1. Make relevant to misbehavior 2. Apply consistently 3. Apply immediately 4. Arrange environment to block escape 5. Combine with extinction and timeout conditions 6. Keep performance consistent during procedure 7. Combine with reinforcement of alternative behaviors 8. Avoid excessive force	Rapid	Long-lasting	Minimizes disadvantages of punishment but still aversive; educative

Technique	Definition	Guidelines		
Punishment[a]	Presenting an aversive stimulus, contingent on a response	1. Arrange environment to block escape except via acceptable alternative behavior 2. Apply stimulus aversive to individual in that context 3. Apply consistently 4. Apply immediately 5. Maximize intensity of stimulus 6. Combine with extinction 7. Avoid applying with too many unwanted behaviors simultaneously 8. Combine with reinforcement of alternative behaviors 9. Communicate the rules of the punishment contingency in advance. 10. Use safety, other ethical precautions	Can stop behavior immediately, if concurrent reinforcement for act does not override effect	Long-lasting; may be permanent in that context	Facilitates discrimination; may occasion negative generalization, avoidance, escape, and aggressive behavior; may occasion the punished response or the act of punishment by observers under other conditions; may occasion negative statements about self, lower social status; public, legal concerns; may be costly

[a] Use only with informed consent of client, parent, advocate, and/or agency human rights committee.

Table E.4a Procedures for Promoting Transfer and Maintenance of Behavior

Procedure	Operation	Maximizing Effectiveness	Reinforcement in Effect	Reinforcement Removed
Generalization training	Reinforce response in other contexts	1. Train to fluency 2. Review behavioral objectives 3. Reinforce sequentially in other contexts 4. Use many exemplars 5. Train to natural supportive contingencies 6. Train loosely 7. Use indiscriminable contingencies 8. Teach generalization as a general skill 9. Teach to mediate generalization 10. Remove blocks to maintenance 11. Program common stimuli	Continues in context in which trained	Should continue but will diminish unless maintenance strategies in place
General maintenance procedures	(Varied)	1. Minimize errors during acquisition 2. Promote response fluency 3. Identify and capitalize on natural reinforcement contingencies and contextual supports 4. Use peers, self, time management, correspondence training, life style changes 5. Progressively lengthen delay, vary frequency of reinforcement; reduce value of reinforcers, and thin reinforcers	Low error rates High, steady rates	Low error rates; rates may gradually diminish, especially in novel contexts, unless maintenance procedures in place

Table E.4b Procedures for Maintaining Behavior

Procedure or Schedule	Operation	Maximizing Effectiveness	Response Characteristics		Other Characteristics
			Reinforcement in Effect	Reinforcement Removed	
Intermittent reinforcement (in general)	Reinforcing some but not all emissions of a specific behavior	1. Switch gradually and progressively from continuous to intermittent reinforcement 2. Supplement change with S^Ds 3. Supplement change with other reinforcers, especially those found in natural environment	Maintains performance; topography may be irregular at first	Performance maintains longer than under CRF	Delays satiation; efficient; convenient; facilitates development of "intrinsic motivation"
Fixed-interval schedule (FI)	Reinforcing the response after t amount of time	1. Start with short intervals; increase gradually and progressively 2. Temporarily shorten interval requirement if responding begins to disintegrate 3. For high response rate, provide ratio, limited-hold, and/or DRH history	Lower response rates possible, accelerating toward end of interval ("FI Scallop"); post-reinforcement pause in some instances	Scallop pattern: gradually accelerating rates, followed by gradually longer pauses; responding ultimately ceases	Much opportunity for competing responses; easy to implement
Variable-interval (VI)	Reinforce response following an average of t time	1. Start with short intervals; increase gradually and progressively 2. Temporarily shorten interval requirement if responding begins to disintegrate 3. For higher response rate, provide ratio, limited-hold, and/or DRH history	Moderate response rate; consistent responding	Consistent, moderate responding continues; slowly levels off	More closely approximates contingencies of natural environment
Limited-hold	Reinforcing responses emitted following t_1 time but no later than t_2 time	1. Select time unit on basis of observational records	Rate higher than interval performance	High for a while	

(continued)

Table E.4b Procedures for Maintaining Behavior (continued)

Procedure or Schedule	Operation	Maximizing Effectiveness	Response Characteristics			Other Characteristics
			Reinforcement in Effect	Reinforcement Removed		
Fixed-ratio (FR)	Reinforcing every nth emission of the behavior	1. Start with low ratios; increase gradually and progressively 2. Temporarily reduce ratio requirement if responding begins to disintegrate	High response rates; post-reinforcement pause following high-ratio requirements; otherwise generally consistent pattern of responding	Responding ceases over time, especially with low ratio histories; bursts of responding followed by pauses		Easy to program; requires continuous counting
Variable-ratio (VR)	Reinforcing the response following an average of n responses	1. Start with low ratios; increase gradually and progressively 2. Temporarily reduce ratio requirements if responding begins to disintegrate	High response rates; consistent responding	Longer responding than under FR but will ultimately cease; long bursts of responding followed by pauses		More closely approximates contingencies of natural environment; requires counting responses
Differential reinforcement of high rates (DRH)	Reinforcing only bursts of responses emitted with less than t time between each response or with more than n responses within t time	1. Increase rate requirement gradually 2. Lower rate requirement temporarily if rate begins to disintegrate	Very high response rate	High for a while		

Glossary

(Note: Numerals indicate the chapter(s) in which the term was introduced.)

A-B-C Analysis. Viewing behavior (B) as a function of its consequences (C) and its antecedents (A). 2

Abscissa. The horizontal or x-axis on a graph. In applied behavior analysis, the abscissa usually depicts successive trials or the passage of time, such as days. 6

Accountability. Objective demonstration and communication of the effectiveness of a given program: functional relations, behavioral outcomes, cost benefit, consumer satisfaction, and so on. 8, 14

Accuracy. The extent to which the response meets standards or is correct. 4

Across-behavior multiple-baseline design. A single-subject or intensive experimental design that involves: (1) Obtaining pretreatment measures (baseline) of several *different behaviors*; (2) applying the intervention or experimental procedure to *one* of the behaviors until it is changed substantially while continuing to record the baseline measures of the other behaviors; (3) applying the intervention to a second behavior as in item 2, and so on. This procedure is continued until it becomes apparent that each behavior changes concurrently with the intervention. 14

Across-individuals multiple-baseline design. A single-subject or intensive experimental design that involves: (1) collecting baselines on the same behavior of several *different individuals*; (2) applying the intervention first with one individual while the baseline conditions are continued with the other individuals; and (3) applying the intervention to the second individual's behavior as in item 2. This procedure is continued until it becomes apparent that each individual's behavior changes current with the intervention. 14

Across-situations multiple-baseline design. A single-subject or intensive experimental design that involves: (1) Collecting baselines on a behavior of one or more individuals across *different situations*; (2) testing the effects of the intervention (*independent variable*) first in one situation while the baseline conditions are continued through the other situations; and (3) applying the intervention in the second situation as in item 2. This procedure is continued until it becomes apparent that behavior changes systematically only in the situation in which the intervention is applied. 14

Activity reinforcer. Contingent access to activities (watching TV, skating, playing, and so on) that increase or maintain the occurrence of the target behavior. 10

Activity table. A table displaying a variety of reinforcing activities. Individuals earn access to time at the table for accomplishments, such as completing their work or following various classroom rules. 10

Adaptation. The gradual change in behavior that often occurs after an individual moves to a new environment or when novel stimuli are introduced into a familiar environment. When the rate of the behavior has stabilized, adaptation is assumed to have been accomplished. 6

Adaptation period. The phase in a behavior analysis program during which *adaptation* takes place. This can be assumed when behavioral patterns stabilize. 6

Adjusting schedule. A schedule that changes according to some feature of the subject's performance. For example, a ratio requirement might be raised gradually as long as the ratio was completed within a given period of time. However, if pausing exceeded a given duration, the ratio would be reduced. This procedure is continued until the behavior reaches some predetermined criterion. 32

Advocate. A person or group serving to protect a client's interests; not one who is employed as an agent of other individuals, an organization, or institution. Advocates, who may be community representatives such as clergymen, law students, or a panel of interested citizens, consider a program's goals and procedures in terms of what they believe is best for the *individual client* and argue on the client's behalf. 3

Alternating-treatment design. A within-subject or intensive experimental design consisting of alternating presentations of two or more independent variable arrangements, each of which is correlated with a distinctive stimulus. The differential effects then are observed by comparing performance under each of the variables. 22

Alternation effects. *See* Sequence effects. 22

Alt-R. *See* Differential reinforcement of alternative behaviors, reinforcement of incompatible behaviors. 24

Antecedent stimulus. A stimulus that precedes or accompanies a behavior and may exert discriminative control over that behavior. 1

Applied behavior analysis. A behavior analytic system designed to examine or change behavior in a precisely measurable and accountable manner; restricted to those interventions that include an experimental design to assess their effects. *See also* Behavior modification. 1

Applied behavior analysis program. A systematic approach to analyzing and changing behavior. The program essentially incorporates the full behavior analysis model (see Figure 1.1). It entails establishment of behavioral objectives; selection and application of valid and reliable measures; regular recording; consistent application of selected procedures based upon principles of behavior; plus an experimental evaluation of results. An applied behavior analysis program sometimes is referred to as a *behavior analysis program, behavioral program*, or a *behavior modification* or *therapy program*. 1

Applied behavior analyst. An individual who has demonstrated mastery of the professional competencies involved in assessing behavior and designing, implementing, evaluating, and communicating the results of an applied behavior analysis program. 2

Applied research. Research directed toward an analysis of the variables that can be effective in improving the behavior under study (Baer et al., 1968). In applied behavior analysis, research involves examining socially important behaviors. Applied research usually is conducted in a natural setting rather than in the laboratory.

Artificial discriminative stimulus. A prompt or discriminative stimulus that is not usually present in the environment. Because an artificial stimulus is intrusive, it should be faded or gradually eliminated before the learner has been judged to have achieved of the goal. (E.g., verbal instructions serve as artificial stimuli as a student learns a new motor skill and are faded as the skill is refined.) 15

Artificial reinforcer. A reinforcer not usually present in the natural setting or not a natural consequence of the behavior. For example, trinket rewards serve as artificial reinforcers in many school programs. 11

Aversive stimulus. A stimulus, also called a *punisher*, that has the effect of decreasing the strength (e.g., rate) of a behavior when it is presented as a consequence of (is contingent on) that behavior; a stimulus that the individual will actively work to avoid. A stimulus, also called a *negative reinforcer*, the contingent *removal* of which results in an *increase* in the rate of the behavior. Organisms will work to avoid aversive stimuli. Nontechnically: A noxious object or event. Note: There is

no *d* in the word *aversive*. *See also* Negative reinforcer; Punisher. 9, 27

Avoidance behavior. A case of negative reinforcement in which the behavior increases in rate when it postpones or avoids completely an aversive stimulus. (Avoidance does not remove that aversive stimulus, because it has not yet occurred.) Nontechnically: Staying away from or doing something to keep from getting punished. 9

Back-up reinforcer. An object or event that already has demonstrated its capability to reinforce an individual's behavior. It is received in exchange for a specific number of tokens, points, or other exchangeable reinforcers. For example, points might be exchanged for the back-up reinforcer of free time. 10

Backward chaining procedure. Effecting the development of a behavioral chain of responses by reinforcing the last response, element, or link in the chain first; the last two next; and so on, until the entire chain is emitted as a single complex behavior. 20

Baseline. Repeated measures of the strength or level (e.g., frequency, intensity, rate, duration, or latency) of behavior before an experimental variable (treatment, intervention, or procedure) is introduced. Baseline measurements are continued until performance has stabilized and can be used as a basis for assessing the effects of the experimental variable. 6

Behavior. Any directly measurable thing an organism does. Included are saying and doing, including physically functioning. In this book we use the term *behavior* synonymously with *response* and *performance*, and the term *behaviors* as an abbreviated way of saying "classes of behavior." 1

Behavior analysis procedures or strategies. Interventions or treatments used to induce behavioral change. Behavioral procedures, or strategies, are used to occasion, teach, maintain, increase, extend, restrict, inhibit, or reduce behaviors. They are the core of most applied behavior analysis programs. 7

Behavior modification. Interventions that are designed to change behavior in a precisely measurable manner. Often used interchangeably with the terms *applied behavior analysis* and *behavior therapy*. However, applied behavior analysis is restricted to those interventions that also include an experimental analytic design to assess treatment effects. When respondent (i.e., "Pavlovian") procedures are emphasized, the term *behavior therapy* tends to be used. Treatment involving modification of self-communication ("thoughts" and "images") usually is labeled "Cognitive Behavior Therapy." 7

Behavioral assessment. Behavioral assessment is used to depict, as validly, clearly, and objectively as possible, an individual's patterns of behavior. Specific measures are selected based on the behavior and its context in order to depict clearly the target behavior prior to, during, and after any systematic intervention or treatment. This information is used for the planning, execution, and evaluation of treatment. Though direct observation forms the core of behavioral assessment, indirect methods also are used at times to supplement information for guiding our selection of the most appropriate treatment strategy. 4

Behavioral contract. The negotiated goals and procedures of a behavior analysis program, mutually agreed on by the client or advocate and other involved persons, and modifiable by joint agreement. Also called a *contingency contract*. 3

Behavioral contrast. If behavior has been maintained in two (or more) contexts, and a procedure that decreases behavior (e.g., DRO, extinction, or punishment) is introduced into one of these contexts, the behavior may increase in the other, despite no other change in contingencies. This increase is called *positive behavioral contrast*. Behavioral contrast also has been observed when the schedule of reinforcement has been increased in one situation while remaining constant in the other. In this case performance may *decrease* in the constant situation producing a *negative behavioral contrast*. 24, 31

Behavioral dimensions. Measurable descriptive characteristics (parameters) that qualify particular aspects of the performance, such as frequency, rate, intensity, duration, topography, and accuracy. 4

Behavioral goal. *See* Goal. 2

Behavioral laws. Principles of behavior that have been demonstrated to possess very broad generality. Immediacy and schedule of reinforcement are examples. 22

Behavioral measurement. *See* Precise behavioral measurement. 5

Behavioral objective. Precise specification of a goal behavior, including three essential elements: (1) Behavior; (2) the givens, situations, context, or conditions under which the behavior is to occur; and (3) the standard of acceptability or *criterion* level of performance. When the objective is related to formal instruction, it is called an *instructional objective*. 4

Behavioral principles. Lawful relations between behavior and the variables that control it, discovered through experimental analyses of behavior. Behavioral principles may help to explain prior and present performance and to predict future behavior, because the relations have been found to apply across responses, people, and contexts. 7, 22

Behavioral rehearsal. Reinforced practice of a complex skill under simulated conditions. Role playing is one form of behavioral rehearsal.

Behavioral repertoire. Behavior that a particular person has emitted in the past. It has been shaped, or, if it has been extinguished, it may be rapidly reconditioned (Catania, 1968). 9

Behavioral technicians. Auxiliary workers, such as observers and data recorders, whose services may be required to conduct some of the technical aspects of a behavior analysis program. 2

Behaviorally anchored rating scale (BARS). A method of assessing performance by assigning a numerical value to one's judgments. Each number on the scale represents a specific set of observable behaviors, such as steps, tasks, or skills involved in a complex task. These numbers and their corresponding behaviors are located on a rating scale. 5

Bonus response cost. *See* Response cost. 25

Carry-over effects. *See* Sequence effects. 22

Chain. A complex behavior consisting of two or more response segments that occur in a definite order. A chain can be homogeneous or heterogeneous. Homogeneous chains consist of responses that are similar to one another, as in lifting or throwing. Heterogeneous chains consist of responses that differ from one another, as in playing football or assembling a barbecue. 20

Chaining. A procedure in which intact responses are reinforced in sequence to form more complex behaviors that ultimately occur as a single cohesive performance. *See also* Backward chaining procedure and Forward chaining. 20

Changing criterion design. An applied behavior analysis design that involves successively changing the criterion for delivering consequences, usually in graduated steps from baseline levels to a desired terminal goal. Experimental control is demonstrated if the behavior changes to meet or approximate each successively set criterion level. 22

Client. The person who hires the services of the behavior analyst, such as an agency or organization, or the person whose behavior is targeted for change. Often, the subject of the behavior analysis program. The terms *subjects*, *students*, *learners*, and *patients* are used interchangeably with clients. 2

Clinical significance. The change is considered clinically significant if the pre-stated objective is obtained, and/or when the behavior change has spurred correlated (ecological) changes for the participants, and their physical and social environments. 22

Coded interval-recording sheet. An observation form with letter codes for each behavior of concern designated on it, permitting simultaneous recording of several responses of one or more subjects. The presence or absence of each behavior is scored by making a slash mark through the letter that stands for that behavior. 5

Coefficient of agreement. *See* Reliability. 5

Coercion. Inducing a behavioral change toward an objective not wanted by the client through the use of threats, severely punitive contingencies, or disproportionately powerful incentives. As the value of incentives and threats increase beyond socially or personally acceptable norms and the client becomes progressively less involved with goal selection, coercion can be said to be at work. 7

Collateral behaviors. Behaviors not treated directly, yet whose rates may change as another behavior is directly treated. Also, behaviors, other than those intentionally treated, that might be influenced by the treatment. (Sometimes labeled *adjunctive behaviors*.) 14

Collateral measures. Measures of variables that relate indirectly to changes in the target behavior. Included would be the impact on the "bottom line" as well as the unprogrammed spread of effect to other people, places or behaviors. 5

Communicative behavior. Behavior reinforced through the mediation of other people. Using words and other forms of symbolic communication enables us to attain reinforcement more efficiently. A term used in place of Skinner's term *verbal behavior*. *See also* Verbal behavior. 21

Communicative stimuli. *See* Verbal stimuli. 21

Complete stimulus control. *See* Stimulus control, complete. 16

Complex behavior. Behavior consisting of two or more subsets of responses. (Almost all the kinds of behavior with which applied behavior analysts are concerned are complex.) 20

Component analysis. *See* Task analysis. 4

Computer assisted or aided instruction (CAI). Instruction aided by computer technology. Computers may present curriculum, request student responses and provide feedback and reinforcement. They may permit responses to be analyzed immediately, and material to branch into remedial or advanced instruction depending on the learner's performance. 19

Concept. One or a set of abstract critical properties common among a number of antecedent stimuli.

Conceptual analysis. *See* Task analysis. 4

Concurrent task method of teaching. A simultaneous teaching method in which all or many subgroups, or tasks are taught concurrently, rather than joining or adding one link at a time, as in the serial methods of forward and backward chaining. 20

Conditional discriminations. A discrimination in which the role of one discriminative stimulus is conditional on the presence of other discriminative stimuli. *See also* Setting events. 15

Conditioned aversive stimulus. A stimulus that initially has no aversive properties but acquires them as a result of repeatedly accompanying or occurring just prior to (1) the withdrawal or absence of reinforcers or (2) the delivery of unconditioned or other conditioned aversive stimuli. (Abbreviated S^p.) 27

Conditioned reinforcer (S^r). A stimulus that initially has no reinforcing properties but, through occurring simultaneously with unconditioned or strongly conditioned reinforcers, acquires reinforcing properties. Also called *secondary, learned reinforcer*. 9

Confounding variables. Uncontrolled variables that influence the outcome of an experiment to an unknown extent, making precise evaluation of the effects of the independent variable impossible. 14

Constructional approach. An approach to changing behavior that places an emphasis on building behaviors rather than reducing or eliminating them. It involves (1) observing or interviewing to determine the goal; (2) identifying the current repertoires on which to build; (3) selecting change procedures to build on current repertoires in accomplishable steps; and, (4) selecting and using natural reinforcers that will maintain the goal behavior. 3

Contingencies. The specified dependencies between behavior and its antecedents and consequences. Contingencies can occur naturally or can be managed intentionally by presenting, withdrawing, or withholding stimuli to affect either people's own behavior or that of others. 7

Contingency analysis. A description of an individual's goal and/or problem behavior and the events that appear to precede and follow those behaviors. Used to begin to identify contingencies that may be functionally related to goal and problem behaviors. 7

Contingency control. Effectively managing the functional antecedents and consequences of given responses. 7

Contingency managers. Individuals—parents, nurses, teachers, counselors, therapists, and/or the clients themselves—who conduct the day-to-day operation of a behavioral program by systematically applying behavioral strategies or procedures. 2

Contingency-shaped behavior. Behavior that has been learned by experiencing the consequences directly. 21

Contingent delay. A technique involving extending the timeout interval by a couple of minutes contingent on inappropriate behavior that occurs during timeout. *See also* Timeout (TO). 26

Contingent exertion. Physical exertion or effort required as a consequence of a misbehavior. An aspect of certain reductive procedures, such as overcorrection and contingent exercise. 27

Contingent exercise. A contingent exertion procedure

in which the individual is required to perform an exercise routine such as standing up and sitting down rapidly 10 times following each occurrence of the unwanted response. 27

Contingent observation. A reductive procedure that contains elements of timeout. The individual, located few feet away from the reinforcing activity is close enough to observe the activity, but not to participate in it. Used as a mild form of timeout. *See also* Timeout (TO). 26

Contingent relation. The relation between a behavior and its antecedents and/or consequences. 7, 8

Continuous behavior. A response that does not have a clearly discriminable beginning or end. Pouting, smiling, eye contact, and other behaviors often are treated as continuous responses because determining when the behavior begins and terminates is difficult. 5

Continuous reinforcement (CRF). A schedule of reinforcement in which each occurrence of a response is reinforced. 11

Contrast phenomenon. *See* Behavioral contrast. 31

Control. (1) The condition that exists when there is a *functional relation* between a performance and a particular event or independent variable. For example, if a child usually or consistently asks for ice cream while driving past the local ice cream stand, the response, requesting ice cream, is "controlled" by the antecedent event, passing the ice cream stand. (2) Control, as in *experimental control*: to have eliminated alternative explanations for the results of an experiment by eliminating or holding constant extraneous or confounding variables. 7

Cooperative learning. *Interdependent* and/or *dependent* group contingencies arranged to promote peer influence. Group members share their reinforcers. 12

Correspondence training. Delivering reinforcers contingent on correspondence or agreement between verbal reports (saying) and actions (doing). For example, the teacher praised Diane only after she actually played with the crayons when she had previously said she would. Mother loaned Bob the car when he said that he helped Jan with her math, because she saw that he did actually help her with her math. 21, 29

Countercontrol. The action taken by an individual in response to often powerful or perhaps troublesome control by another. When both individuals are able to arrange contingencies that strongly affect each other's behavior, reciprocity may develop. However, when contingency control is primarily available to only one member of the pair, countercontrol will be weak and coercion or exploitation may occur. In such instances, social regulations may be necessary to protect the rights of individuals. 7

Criteria. *See* Criterion. 4

Criterion analysis. *See* Task analysis 4

Criterion. The standard used to indicate when a behavioral goal has been reached; or the specification of an acceptable level of performance that a person is to achieve. Criteria are composed of *behavioral dimensions* and are used to evaluate the success of a given behavior analysis program. 4

Criterion observer. The person whose recording serves as a standard against which other observers' are judged, especially during training technicians to become reliable data recorders. 6

Critical features of stimuli. The distinctive properties of stimuli, such as size, shape, position, and color, that enable one stimulus class to be discriminated from another. Stimuli that share a number of critical features often can be grouped to characterize a particular concept. For example, stimuli sharing the features of being alive—having fur, a backbone, and a spinal chord; or suckling young—characterize the concept "mammal." Yet other critical features shared only among subsets of the stimuli, such as particular shapes, habits, genetic qualities, and so on, distinguish one subclass of stimuli from another, as with different species of mammals. 17

Daily report card. A contingency arrangement among the educational personnel, students, and their families, and designed to coordinate the contingencies across settings. In one setting (usually the school), the teacher marks a card contingent on the presence or absence of the target behavior and sends it each day to the other setting (usually the home), where a delayed consequence is presented. 8

Delayed prompting. When the natural antecedent stimulus (S^+) fails to evoke a given response, an artificial S^D (prompt), usually the correct answer, is inserted to occasion the behavior so it can then be reinforced. Teaching usually progresses by gradually delaying the time between the S^+ (e.g., a math problem) and the prompt (the answer), until the student emits the correct response reliably in advance of the prompt. *See also* Transfer of stimulus control. 18

Delphi method. A strategy for identifying the best examples of any particular class of items is to ask a panel of experts independently to suggest an optimal list. By pooling the items and sometimes repeatedly having each member independently rank order them, a select set rises clearly to the top. The Delphi method can be used to identify high-priority goals and objectives, lists of recommended readings, "key" examination items, and so on. 7

Dependent group contingency. A contingency arrangement in which the performance of an individual or several members of a group determines the group's access to reinforcement. For example, everyone in the class receives reinforcers dependent on improvement of the lowest three student scores. 12

Dependent variable. A variable that is measured while another variable (the *independent variable*) is changed in a systematic way. When systematic changes in the independent variable are accompanied by changes in the dependent variable, we say that the two are *functionally related*—that the level or value of the dependent variable is in fact *dependent* on the level or value of the independent variable. In applied behavior analysis, the dependent variable usually is behavior; the independent variable some condition or treatment that may affect the level of that behavior. 5

Deprivation. The absence or reduction of a reinforcer for a period of time. Deprivation is an establishing operation that increases the effectiveness of the reinforcer and the rate of behavior that produced that reinforcer in the past. 11

Differential reinforcement. (1) The reinforcement of one class (or form, or topography) of behavior and not another. (2) In producing stimulus control, reinforcement of a behavior under one stimulus condition but not under another stimulus condition. Also, reinforcing one behavior under one stimulus condition as other behaviors are reinforced under different stimulus conditions. 15

Differential reinforcement of alternative behavior (ALT-R or DRA). A reinforcement procedure usually designed to reduce a given behavior by increasing alternative behavior while withholding reinforcement for the unwanted response. 24

Differential reinforcement of diminishing rates (DRD). A schedule according to which a sequence of responses repeated below a series of gradually diminishing preset rates is reinforced. (E.g., reinforcers followed when a student talked out no more than 5 times during the period; then no more than 4; then no more than 3; and so on.) 24

Differential reinforcement of high rates (DRH). A schedule that specifies reinforcement of a sequence of responses only when they occur in rapid succession (i.e., above a preset rate). 32

Differential reinforcement of incompatible behaviors (DRI). A particular ALT-R or DRA procedure designed to increase the rate of a behavior or a set of behaviors that cannot coexist with the one targeted for reduction. (E.g., reinforcing completion of work reduces those forms of disruption that are incompatible with working.) 24

Differential reinforcement of low rates (DRL). A behavior is reinforced only if it is expressed after a preset interval of time but has not been emitted *during* that interval. Example: A teacher compliments and calls on a student who waits 3 minutes before participating again. 24

Differential reinforcement of other behaviors (DRO). A reductive procedure in which reinforcers are delivered contingent on the nonoccurrence of a response for a given time interval. Sometimes called *omission training*. See also Momentary DRO. 24

Direct instruction. A teaching method that involves using a prepared curriculum (i.e., DISTAR™): (1) following a very carefully organized and detailed sequence of instruction; (2) teaching skillfully in small groups when appropriate; (3) evoking unison responses; (4) using signals to encourage all students to participate; (5) pacing presentations quickly; (6) applying specific techniques for correcting and preventing errors; and (7) using praise.

Direct observational recording. A method, sometimes called *observational recording*, in which a human observer objectively records ongoing behavior. Event and time sampling are both direct observational recording methods.

Direct replication. *See* Replicate. 14, 22

Discrete behavior. A behavior that has a clearly discriminable beginning and end. Lever presses, sneezes, and writing answers to addition problems are examples of discrete responses. 5

Discriminated operant. A response under stimulus control The response occurs only when the particular S^D is present. 15

Discrimination. The restriction of responding to certain stimulus situations and not others. Discrimination may be established by *differentially reinforcing* responding in one stimulus situation and extinguishing or punishing that response in other situations, or by reinforcing other behavior in the other situations. 11, 15

Discriminative stimuli. Stimuli are said to be discriminative when, after they have been present reliably when a response has been reinforced, their presence or absence systematically alters the probability of the rate of response. Discriminative stimuli influence given subsequent behavior. Three types of discriminative stimuli include: 15

S^Ds—A stimulus in the presence of which a given response is likely to be reinforced. An S^D occasions a particular response in that reinforcement is likely to follow it. 15

S^Δs (S-deltas)—A stimulus in the presence of which a given response is not likely to be reinforced. An S^Δ inhibits or suppresses the response in that reinforcement of the response is not likely in its presence. 15

S^{D-}s—A stimulus in the presence of which a given response is likely to produce aversive consequences, such as punishment, timeout, or response cost. An S^{D-} reduces the rate of the response in that the response is likely to lead to aversive consequences. 16

DISTAR™. *See* Direct Instruction.

DRA. *See* Differential reinforcement of alternative behaviors. 24

DRD. *See* Differential reinforcement of diminishing rates. 24

DRH. *See* Differential reinforcement of high rates. 32

DRI. *See* Differential reinforcement of incompatible behaviors. 24

DRL. *See* Differential reinforcement of low rates. 24

DRO. *See* Differential reinforcement of other behaviors. 24

Duration. The length of time that passes from onset to offset of a behavior or a stimulus. 4

Duration recording. Recording the time that elapses from the onset to the offset of a response (e.g., the length of time a person spends talking on the phone). 5

Ecobehavioral assessment. Studying behavior in relation to its context—ongoing and previous contingencies. Ecobehavioral assessment considers how a behavior change may affect *and* be affected by contextual conditions as well as by changes in the social and physical environment. 4

Edible reinforcer. Food with a reinforcing function. 10

Educational significance. An assessment that considers whether change occurred as a function of the program, the intervention was implemented as specified, and if the intervention was beneficial to the student and those in his or her environment. 22

Elicit. A verb used to denote the effect of an antecedent conditioned or unconditioned stimulus on a conditioned or unconditioned response in respondent or classical conditioning of reflexes. In describing the salivary reflex of a dog, we would say that meat *elicits* salivation. Following conditioning, another stimulus, such as a tone, also might elicit salivation. *See also* Respondent behavior. 16

Emit. A term that describes the occurrence of operant behavior. In this text, familiar verbs such as *express, perform, respond,* and *behave* are used as equivalents. *See also* Operant behavior. 9

Empirical task analysis. *See* Task analysis. 20

Equivalence class. Complex behavior that consists of three defining relations of reflexivity, symmetry, and transitivity. *Reflexivity* refers to identity matching (e.g., Daddy is a specific man, 9 is a specific numeral); *symmetry* refers to functional reversibility (e.g., given a picture of a dog, select the word dog, and given the word dog, the picture of the dog is selected); and, *transitivity* refers to the equivalence of three stimuli. 15

Errorless learning. Acquiring particular discriminations by means of instruction designed to prevent errors. Sequences of artificial discriminative stimuli are arranged carefully and faded slowly and systematically so that control eventually shifts to the natural stimuli identified ultimately to evoke the response. 18

Escape behavior. Behavior that reduces or removes aversive stimulation, thereby producing negative reinforcement. *See also* Negative reinforcement. 9

Establishing operation. An antecedent event or change in the environment that alters the effectiveness of the reinforcer and the rates of the responses that have produced that reinforcer previously. Having just eaten a large meal will diminish the effectiveness of edible reinforcers. Similarly, deprivation will increase the effectiveness of reinforcers. 10

Establishing stimulus (S^E). A stimulus that gets paired with an establishing operation, and the response or stimulus change it evokes becomes a conditioned stimulus for that operation. It cues or prompts the occurrence of the establishing operation. 16

Ethics. Operating according to ethical precepts: providing for voluntariness and/or informed consent by clients or advocates; arranging the least intrusive or restrictive and most benign yet effective procedures; being accountable; obtaining, maintaining, and continuing development of competence, and so on. 14

Event recording. An observational recording procedure in which the number of occurrences of a given discrete behavior are counted—number of times correct answers are given, blows delivered, and so on—over a specified period of time. The interval may be, for instance, a classroom period, a day, or the duration of a meal or of a TV program. 5

Exchangeable reinforcers. *See* Token Reinforcers. 10

Exclusionary timeout. *See* Timeout. 26

Exemplars. Examples containing the critical stimulus or response features. For example, the critical features of a bus are that it transports more than six people on the ground, has wheels and an engine. Exemplars would include public busses, school busses and airport busses. Non-exemplars would be pedal boats, airplanes and horse drawn wagons. 29

Experimental analysis of behavior. A scientific method designed to discover the functional relation between behavior and the variables that control it. 1, 14

Experimental design. An aspect of an experiment directed toward establishing experimental control unambiguously to demonstrate a functional relation. Experimental designs control for extraneous influences such as placebo and Hawthorne effects, passage of time, and other subject, task and environmental confounding variables. *See also* Withdrawal design, Multiple baseline design, Alternating-treatment design, and other specific design strategies. 14

Experimental significance. In determining experimental significance we ask what the behavior would be if the experimental intervention had not occurred. Did the treatment result in a meaningful change in the behavior? 22

External validity. The correctness or validity of conclusions about the generalizability of a functional relationship to and across other people, behaviors, or settings. 22

Extinction. A procedure in which the reinforcement of a previously reinforced behavior is discontinued. Also may be used to describe the "process" by which a previously learned behavior disappears as a result of nonreinforcement. 23

Extinction burst. A temporary increase in the rate and intensity of various responses (the target behavior, aggression, crying, and or other more primitive behavior previously followed by the reinforcer) immediately after the cessation of reinforcement or the introduction of extinction. 23

Extinction-induced aggression. Aggressive behavior that often accompanies extinction in its early phases, in the absence of any other identifiable precipitating events. 23

Extraneous variables. See Confounding variables. 14

Extrinsic aversive stimuli. Aversive stimuli delivered by an external agent. 27

Facial screening. A timeout procedure; visual stimuli are contingently blocked by a face cover, such as a cloth, blindfold or hands for a given duration. See also Timeout. 26

Fading. The systematic, gradual removal of usually artificial or intrusive prompts, or discriminative stimuli such as directions, imitative prompts, physical guidance, and other cues. Used to foster independence from supplemental prompts, and/or to shift control over to the stimuli designated to evoke the response. 18

Feedback. Information transmitted back to the responder following a particular performance: seeing or hearing about specific features of the results. Feedback may function as a reinforcer or punisher; and/or may serve a discriminative function. 10

Fixed interval (FI). See Interval schedules of reinforcement. 31

Fixed ratio (FR). See Ratio schedules of reinforcement. 32

Fixed time (FT) schedule. A schedule of reinforcement in which reinforcers are delivered following the passage of a specific amount of time and not dependent on a particular response. 31

Forward chaining. Effecting the development of a chain of responses by training the first response or link in the chain initially; the second next; and so on, joining the series of links together, until the entire chain is emitted as a unitary complex behavior. 20

Four-term contingency. A phrase used to describe the interrelationship among contextual variables, antecedents, behavior and consequences. 15

Frame. A finely graded instructional step. Part of a teaching segment in programmed instruction. Reinforcement is used as confirmation for correctly responding to each step. See also Programmed instruction. 19

Frequency. The number of times a behavior occurs. Often expressed as rate—that is, in relation to a given period of time. 4

Frequency recording. See Event recording. 5

Freeze technique. Instructing individuals to become immobile while maintaining the current topography of their behavior. Used to teach people to discriminate positive and negative examples of particular motoric forms.

Functional analysis. See Experimental analysis of behavior.

Functional equivalence. "When changes in the contingencies controlled by one pair of stimuli are sufficient to change the subject's behavior with respect to other pairs" (Sidman et al., 1989, p. 272). 15, 21

Functional relation. A lawful relation between values of two variables. In behavior analysis, a *dependent variable* (treated behavior) and a given *independent variable* (intervention or treatment procedure) are *functionally related* if the behavior changes systematically with changes in the value of the independent variable or treatment. For example, the greater the intensity of an aversive stimulus, the greater the response suppression. 14

Functional skill. A skill that enables the individual to obtain reinforcement. Usually it is age or at least developmentally appropriate, socially significant, and likely to be reinforced or supported by the natural environment in both the short *and* long run.

Generalization. See Generalization, response and Generalization, stimulus. 15

Generalization, response. (Induction) The spread of effects to other classes of behavior when one class of behavior is modified by reinforcement, extinction, and so on. For instance, the way a particular letter is shaped or formed may vary in ways that are similar but not identical to the formation of the letter as it was originally reinforced. 29

Generalization, stimulus. The spread of effects to other stimulus situations when behavior is modified in the presence of one stimulus situation. Generalization occurs when stimulus control is absent or incomplete. (The child who calls all quadrupeds "doggie" is generalizing.) The same response occurs at other times, in other places, or in the presence of other people. 15, 29

Generalization training. A method designed to occasion in another stimulus situation a behavior emitted in one stimulus situation; programming for stimulus generalization. For instance, students who learned skills in one setting (i.e., the resource room) may be taught to apply those skills in other settings (i.e., the classroom). 29

Generalized imitation. Duplicating modeled behavior in novel instances beyond those explicitly taught. 17

Generalized reinforcer. A conditioned reinforcer effective for a wide range of behaviors as a result of pairing with a variety of previously established reinforcers. Due to this history, the effectiveness of a generalized reinforcer tends not to depend on any one state of deprivation. Money is a prime example of a generalized reinforcer. It has been paired with and can be exchanged for a variety of other reinforcers. 10

Goal. The intended outcome of an intervention. *Behavioral goals* usually are presented as a statement of the direction and extent to which the target behavior is to be changed: Increased, decreased, maintained, developed, expanded, or restricted. A behavioral goal should be translated into a set of behavioral objectives prior to designing a program. *Goal levels* refer to a preset value of performance to be reached at a given time. *See also* Goal-setting. 2

Goal, outcome. A specification of the end product or behavior sought as a result of the treatment program. Examples include decreases in vandalism cost or reductions in the number of absences. 2

Goal, process (or treatment). A target, the accomplishment of which enables the achievement of an outcome goal. For example, increasing a teacher's rates of giving approval might be a *process goal* enabling the *outcome goal* of improving students' scholastic achievement.

Goal-setting. Identification in advance of values or levels to be reached, often by a particular time. A goal might be set at a certain number of accomplishments, level of quality, percentage of correct answers, and so forth. A term often used in organizational management. 17

Good behavior game. A group management package in which the group is divided into two or more teams, and rules are specified. In its original form, a team received a check against it if a member violated one of the rules. Reinforcers were provided for each team with fewer than the criterion number of marks or for the team with the fewest marks at the end of a preset period. Now its use frequently involves reinforcing consequences as well as punishment, such as providing points exchangeable for reinforcers for a team when its members act according to the rules. 24

Graduated guidance. The combined use of physical guidance and fading, resulting in a systematic gradual reduction of the intensity of physical guidance. 18

Graduated prompting. A stimulus control method that begins with the natural S^+ and progresses from the least-to-most artificial or restrictive prompts until the desired behavior occurs. 18

Group contingencies. Arrangements in which consequences are delivered to some or all members of a group as a function of the performance of one, several, or all of its members. *See also* Interdependent, dependent, and independent group contingencies. 12

Guiding. *See* Physical guidance. 17

Imitation. Matching the behavior of a model, or engaging in a behavior similar to that observed. 17

Imitative prompt. A discriminative stimulus consisting of a behavior that is modeled in order to occasion an imitative response. 17

Incidental teaching. Teaching toward specific, predetermined objectives, by capitalizing on natural unplanned opportunities, as in temporarily blocking a child's access to an item until particular adjectives are used to request the object. 21, 29

Incompatible behavior. A specific alternative response (Alt-R) or behavior incapable of being emitted simultaneously with another behavior; behavior that interferes with specific other behavior. 24

Incomplete stimulus control. *See* Stimulus control, incomplete. 16

Increasing assistance. *See* Graduated prompting. 18

Independent group contingency Applying the same consequences to the same or different behavior of each member of a group. The reinforcement for one member's behavior does not depend upon the performance of others. 12

Independent variable. The variable that is managed or manipulated. In behavior analysis, the independent variable often is a behavioral procedure, package, or other intervention or treatment program. 5, 7

Informed consent. Clients (or their advocates) and/or parents and caretakers have the right to be informed about proposed experimental or programmatic outcomes and procedures and their advantages and disadvantages, and to participate in the selection or rejection of specific goals and procedures. This information must be communicated at a level that will be understood by the client or advocate if consent or rejection is to be considered "informed." 3, 7

Instructional demand. An unintended alteration in behavior as a function of variations in the way instructions are delivered in an experiment. 5

Instructional objective. *See* Behavioral objective. 4

Intensity. The strength or force with which a stimulus is delivered or a behavior is expressed. Sounds, lights, and physical blows can vary in intensity. 4

Intensive designs. *See* Within-subject experimental designs. 14

Interdependent group contingencies. Contingency arrangement in which members of the group are treated as if they were a single behaving individual. The group's performance determines the reinforcer each member receives. For example, "If the group averages 90% on the test, everyone will have free time." 12

Intermittent reinforcement. A schedule of reinforcement in which some, but not all, of the occurrences of a response are reinforced. 11

Internal validity. A feature that describes how correct or valid conclusions are about the functionality of a relationship between two variables, such as a procedure and changes in behavior. Internal validity, then, addresses the validity of the answer to the question, "did the treatment bring about the behavior change?" 22

Interobserver agreement assessment (IOA). A method for estimating the reliability of a behavioral observation system. A coefficient of agreement is calculated by comparing scores obtained by two or more independent observers and determining the number of times they agreed (and/or disagreed) in proportion to the number of observations scored. *See also* Reliability. 5

Interval spoilage. See Partial interval time sampling. 5

Interval schedules of reinforcement. A schedule in which reinforcement is made contingent on the passage of a particular duration of *time* before the response is reinforced. (a) *Fixed interval (FI)* schedule—a schedule in which the duration is always the same. (b) *Variable interval (VI)* schedule—a schedule in which the time interval varies about a given average duration. 31

Interval time-sampling. *See* Time sampling. 5

Intervention. *See* Treatment. 7

Intrinsic aversive stimuli. Aversive properties integral or natural to particular acts, such as doing excessive exercise, being totally inactive, or repeating the same movement excessively. 27

Intrinsic motivation. A hypothesized state inferred by observing an individual expressing a particular behavior at high rates in the absence of any identifiable external reinforcing consequences; presumably, emitting the behavior is itself reinforcing. Behavior controlled by a very thin schedule of reinforcement. 11

IOA. *See* Interobserver agreement assessment. 5

Isolation. *See* Timeout. 26

Job analysis. *See* Task analysis. 4

Labeled praise. *See* Specific praise. 10

Latency. The elapsed time from the presentation of an antecedent stimulus (cue, prompt, signal) and the response. 5

Learned reinforcer. *See* Conditioned reinforcer. 9

Learning. Any enduring change in behavior produced as a function of the interaction between the behavior and the environment. Often used to describe motor or cognitive skills, but term also may refer to social, affective, personal, and other classes of behavior.

Learning history. The sum of an individual's behaviors that have been conditioned or modified as a function of his or her interaction with environmental events.

Limited hold. A restriction placed on an interval schedule requiring that the response occur within a particular time limit following the interval to be eligible for reinforcement, or the reinforcer is lost. 31

Link. An intact response, or performance, that is combined with others in the formation of a behavioral chain. 20

Maintenance procedures. Strategies used to promote the persistence of behaviors under natural environmental conditions, such as alterations in reinforcing contingencies, fading prompts, and teaching self-management.

Matching law. A description of a phenomenon according to which organisms tend proportionally to match their responses during choice situations to the rates of reinforcement for each choice (i.e., if a behavior is reinforced about 60% of the time in one situation and 40% in another, that behavior tends to occur about 60% of the time in the first situation, and 40% in the second). 32

Match-to-sample method. A task in which a student selects from two or more alternatives the stimulus that matches or corresponds to a standard or sample. 15

Model. A person whose behavior is imitated. 17

Modeling procedure. A stimulus control procedure that uses demonstrations or modeling to prompt an imitative response; colloquially, a *show procedure*. 17

Momentary DRO. A variation of the DRO procedure. Reinforcers are delivered at a particular preset moment, provided a particular behavior is *not* being expressed at that moment—best reserved for *maintaining* rather than for initially reducing rates of responding. 24

Momentary time-sampling. A time-sampling procedure in which a response is recorded only if it is occurring at the point in time at which the interval terminates. For example, a timer goes off at the end of a 10-minute interval, and the observer checks to see whether the youngster has his thumb in his mouth *at that moment.* 5

Movement suppression timeout. A form of timeout in

which movement is contingently restricted for a period of time. *See also* Timeout. 26

Multielement design. *See* Alternating treatment design. 22

Multiple-baseline designs. A within-subject or intensive experimental design that attempts to replicate the effects of a procedure (treatment or intervention) across (1) different subjects, (2) different settings, or (3) different classes of behavior. The intervention is introduced independently to each subject (or setting or class of behavior) in succession. *See also* Across-behaviors multiple-baseline; Across-subjects multiple-baseline; Across-situations multiple-baseline; Within-subject experimental design. 14

Multiple probes. Probing or measuring untreated responses intermittently to assess any variations in those responses due to unidentified condition(s). *See also* Probe. 22

Multiple-schedule design. *See* Alternating treatment design. 22

Multiple-treatment interference. A condition in which one treatment's *history* influences the performance under a subsequent treatment. Observed changes in the dependent variable (the behavior receiving treatment) then would be confounded by the prior treatment, rather than being a function of the designated independent variable. 22

Narrative recording. A written description of behavior in progress. The recorded events then can be ordered into a *sequence analysis* that specifies a behavior, its antecedents, and its consequences. 2

Natural discriminative stimulus. A discriminative stimulus indigenous to the natural environment, not one artificially introduced. The printed word is a natural S^D for reading the word; a hint is not. The hour that marks the beginning of the work day is a natural S^D for starting to work. 15

Natural reinforcer. A reinforcer indigenous to the natural environment. A good mark is usually a natural reinforcer in a school setting as is pay for a worker. 9

Needs assessment. A systematic method for identifying goals to target for programmatic change. Needs assessment may include observations, tests, interviews, questionnaires, and other sources of input. 4

Negative practice. A punishment procedure that requires the client to practice repeatedly the target behavior for a predetermined time period contingent on the occurrence of the unwanted behavior. 27

Negative reinforcement. Removing an aversive stimulus as a consequence of a response resulting in the maintenance of or an increase in rate of the behavior. A behavior has been negatively reinforced if it *increases* or is *maintained* as a function of the contingent *removal*

or *reduction* of a stimulus. This procedure sometimes is referred to as *escape conditioning.* 9

Negative reinforcer. An aversive stimulus; a stimulus that, when removed or reduced as a consequence of a response, results in an *increase* in or *maintenance* of that response. *See also* Aversive stimulus. 9

Neutral stimulus. An object or event that is neutral with respect to some property that it later may acquire. A neutral stimulus does not affect behavior reliably in a particular context until it has been paired sufficiently, often with some event that does have controlling properties (i.e., it has not yet developed into an S^D, reinforcer, and so on). 9

Objective measurement. Recording behavioral data unbiased by the observer's feelings, interpretations, or other extraneous factors. 5

Observational recording. *See* Direct observational recording.

Observer drift. A point at which indexes of agreement between observers begin to diverge. 6

Occasion. To increase the likelihood of the emission of a response by arranging prior stimulus conditions. Also used as an action verb in reference to operant behavior, where the response bears a probabilistic relationship (not a one-to-one relationship, as with *elicit*) to the occurrence of the S^D. The terms *set the occasion for, evoke, promote, cue,* and *signal* may serve as synonyms. 15

Omission training. *See* Differential reinforcement of other behaviors (DRO).

Operant behavior. That class of behavior controlled (at least in part) by its consequences. 3, 9

Operant level. The strength (e.g., rate or duration) of behavior prior to any known conditioning. (*Baseline*, which subsumes operant level, refers to the strength of behavior before the introduction of an experimental variable but does not preclude earlier conditioning.) 10

Operationally defined. Colloquial psychological terms that are broken down into measurable components. 2

Operational statement. The product of breaking down a broad concept, such as "aggressiveness," into its *observable* and reliably *measurable* component behaviors (frequency of hitting or biting others, duration of scream, and so on). Sometimes referred to as a *pinpointed* or *targeted behavior.* 1

Ordinate. The vertical or y-axis on a graph. In behavior analysis, the response measure (e.g., frequency) usually is plotted on the ordinate. 6

Outcome goal. *See* Goal, outcome. 3

Outcome variables. Those "bottomline" measurable factors that characterize the outcome goal, such as annual profit, and improved academic and social performance.

Overcorrection. A reductive procedure that is a sub-category of contingent exertion. Overcorrection consists of one or both of two basic components: (1) *Restitutional training* (or restitutional overcorrection), which requires the individual to restore the environment to a state substantially improved from that which existed prior to the act; and (2) *positive-practice* (or positive-practice overcorrection), which requires the individual repeatedly to practice a positive alternative behavior. When no environmental disruption occurs, only the positive-practice procedure is used. 27

Overgeneralization. Emitting a response appropriate to some contexts in an inappropriate context. For example, calling all men "dada." 15, 29

Package. *See* Treatment.

Parameter. Any of a set of physical properties whose values determine the characteristics of a behavior, such as schedule and quantity or quality of reinforcers. Differences in parametric values may influence how rapidly, effectively, safely, constructively, durably, and so on, that a given behavior changes. 23

Partial-interval time-sampling. A time-sampling procedure whereby a response is recorded if it occurs at any time(s)—even momentarily—during the interval, and not necessarily throughout the interval, as in *whole-interval* time-sampling. Sometimes it is called *interval spoilage*, because any instance of the behavior (especially an unwanted behavior) "spoils" the interval. 5

Peer influence strategies. Arrangements of group contingencies that promote peer influence (e.g., peer tutoring and peer reinforcement). Illustrative are cooperative learning structures that rely on *dependent* and *interdependent* group contingencies in which group members share reinforcers. 12

Peer-mediated strategy. Method of training, supervising, and monitoring peers to serve as contingency managers, cotherapists, or tutors. Peers provide services directly. 12

Peer review. A panel of unbiased professional colleagues that reviews issues and methods related to programs under review, and recommends any changes to enhance the quality of care and treatment of clients. 8

Performance feedback. *See* Feedback. 10

Permanent product recording. A behavioral recording method in which durable products of a behavior—such as the number of windows broken, widgets produced, homework problems handed in, rejects, percentage of test questions correct, and so on—are assessed. Not suited to measuring *transitory behaviors.* 5

Personalized system of instruction (PSI). A method of teaching that usually is characterized by: (1) The go-at-your-own-pace feature, which permits a student to move through the course at a speed commensurate with his ability and other demands upon his time. (2) The

unit-perfection requirement for advance, which lets the student go ahead to new material only after demonstrating mastery of that which preceded. (3) The use of lectures and demonstrations as vehicles of motivation, *rather than sources of critical information.* (4) The *related* stress upon the written word *in teacher-student communication;* and, finally: (5) The use of proctors, *which permits repeated testing, immediate scoring, almost unavoidable tutoring, and a marked enhancement of the personal-social aspect of the educational process* (Keller, 1968, p. 83). Also known as the "Keller Plan," after its originator. 12, 19

Physical guidance. A form of response priming in which the appropriate body part or parts are physically guided through the proper motion by another person. For example, a swimming coach guiding the movement of a youth's arm to demonstrate the proper stroke uses the physical guidance procedure. 17

PLA-Check (Planned Activity Check). An observational recording system in which, according to a preset schedule, the observer counts the number of individuals engaged in the assigned task at that moment. *See also* Momentary time sampling. 6

Planned ignoring. Deliberate withholding of attention, verbal interaction, and physical contact for a short duration as a consequence of an infraction. A mild form of timeout in that the opportunity to obtain various types of reinforcers is removed for a brief period of time. 26

Positive practice (overcorrection). *See* Overcorrection. 27

Positive reinforcement. A procedure whereby the rate of a response maintains or increases as a function of the contingent presentation of a stimulus (a positive reinforcer) following the response. 9

Positive reinforcer. A *stimulus,* such as an object or event, that follows or is presented as a consequence of a response and results in the rate of that response increasing or maintaining. Food, praise, attention, recognition of achievement and effort, special events, and activities often serve as positive reinforcers. Nontechnical terms for positive reinforcers include *incentives, rewards,* and *strokes.* 9

Positive scanning. Focusing one's attention on desirable rather than unwanted behavior, often by recording it. The positive scanners tend to "notice" and hence reinforce positive behaviors more and negative behaviors less. 23

Praise. *See* Positive reinforcer; Specific praise. 9

Precise behavioral measurement. The selection and implementation of accurate, clearly defined operations for recording and quantifying behavior. Precise measurement allows change to be measured and evaluated unambiguously. 5

Premack principle. A principle that states that contingent access to high-frequency behaviors ("preferred" activities) serves as a reinforcer for the performance of low-frequency behaviors. *See also* Response deprivation hypothesis. 10

Principles of behavior. *See* Behavioral principles. 1, 7, 22

Primary reinforcer. *See* Unconditioned reinforcer. 9

Probe. A brief phase in a behavior analysis experiment designed to test the effect of a given intervention. A short *withdrawal* phase is a probe, because the intervention is removed for a period of time to assess some aspect(s) of the behavior in the absence of the intervention. 14

Procedural package. *See* Treatment. 7

Process goal. *See* Goal, process.

Programmed instruction. The selection and arrangement of educational content based on principles of human learning (Taber et al., 1965). The student progresses in steps from one level of difficulty to the next. Reinforcement is primarily in the form of confirmation of correct responses. 19

Progressive delay procedure. *See* Time delay procedure. 18

Prompt. An auxiliary discriminative stimulus presented in order to occasion a given response. Prompts usually are faded before the terminal goal is judged to have been achieved. (For example, the *f* sound serves as a prompt in "2 + 2 are f ____ ." The *f* sound must be faded completely to conclude that the student has achieved the goal of knowing how to add 2 + 2.) 16

PSI. *See* Personalized system of instruction (PSI). 12, 19

Punisher. A stimulus that, when presented immediately following a response, effects a *reduction* in the rate of the response. This text uses the term *aversive stimulus* interchangeably with *punisher* or *punishing stimulus*. 9, 27

Punishment. A procedure in which a punisher or aversive stimulus is presented immediately following a response, resulting in a reduction in the rate of the response. 9, 27

Qualitative praise. *See* Specific praise. 10

Rate. The average frequency of behavior emitted during a standard unit of time. Formula: Number of responses divided by the number of time units. For example, if 20 responses occur in 5 minutes, the rate is 4 responses per minute. 4

Rational task analysis. *See* Task analysis. 20

Ratio schedules of reinforcement. A schedule in which reinforcement is delivered contingent on the last of a *number* of responses. (a) *Fixed ratio (FR) schedule*—A reinforcement schedule in which a constant number of

responses must occur prior to the reinforced response. For example, an FR 3 schedule indicates that each third response is reinforced. (b) *Variable ratio (VR) schedule*—A schedule in which a variable number of responses must occur prior to the reinforced response. The number of responses usually varies around a specified average. For example, a VR 6 means that an average of one of six performances is reinforced. 32

Ratio strain. A disruption in performance when ratio requirements are very high or are raised abruptly. An individual is said to be suffering from "ratio strain" when previously high rates of responding disintegrate. Ratio strain is avoided by increasing ratio requirements very gradually. It is treated by temporarily reducing the ratio requirement. 32

Reactivity. An artificial effect produced by the assessment or experimental activities other than the selected independent (treatment) variable. For example, just the presence of an observer in the classroom may influence the dependent variable(s) or distort the validity of the data, as when a teacher uses more verbal praise than usual in the observer's presence. 5

Recalibrate. Retraining observers to improve interobserver agreement scores, or to maintain their performance at acceptably high levels. 6

Recovery. The recurrence of the rate of a response that had been reduced when aversive stimuli no longer are present or delivered contingent on the response. 9

Reductive procedure. A procedure, such as *Alt-R, DRL, punishment, response cost*, and *timeout*, used to reduce the rate of a behavior. Section IV

Reinforced positive practice. A positive practice procedure in which the positive practice activity is reinforced. *See also* Overcorrection. 28

Reinforcement. A process in which a behavior is strengthened (i.e., the behavior's frequency, rate, duration, intensity, or other dimensions increase or persist) as a function of an event that occurs as a consequence of, or contingent on, the response. Reinforcement may occur naturally or be planned. It is defined solely by its function of increasing or maintaining behavior. Two basic reinforcement procedures are discussed in this book: *positive reinforcement* and *negative reinforcement*. Both increase or maintain behavior. 9

Reinforcement density. Frequency or rate at which responses are reinforced or the quantity of reinforcers delivered per presentation. The lower the ratio or shorter the interval required by a given reinforcement schedule, the denser the reinforcement. 32

Reinforcement history. *See* Learning history.

Reinforcement procedure. Systematically planned, goal-directed applications of principles of effective reinforcement. 9

Reinforcement reserve. The unconsumed quantity of reinforcers in the possession of an individual or group. This term frequently refers to a number of tokens or other exchangeable reinforcers. 13

Reinforcement schedule. *See* Schedule of reinforcement. 11

Reinforcer. A consequential stimulus occurring contingent on a behavior that increases or maintains the strength (rate, duration, and so on) of the behavior. A reinforcer is defined solely by the fact that it increases or maintains the behavior on which it is contingent. *See also* Positive; Negative; Conditioned; Edible; Tangible; Unconditioned; and other classes of reinforcers. 11

Reinforcer menu. A list of stimuli from which responders may select those they prefer to be awarded as a consequence of a unit of work. 11

Reinforcer sampling. A procedure that enables an individual to come in contact with a potential reinforcer to experience the positive characteristics of the stimulus. The procedure is useful in developing new reinforcing consequences for a given individual. 11

Reinforcer survey. A set of questions designed to identify an array of reinforcers effective for a particular individual. 11

Reliable measurement. Measurement that remains consistent regardless of who does it and what conditions prevail when it is conducted. *See also* Reliability. 5

Reliability. Consistency of measurement. In applied behavior analysis, preferably, different observers estimate reliability by assessing the interobserver agreement, or coefficient of agreement between two or more independently scored records of data in the same episodes. The coefficient of agreement often is calculated as a percentage by dividing the number of agreements by the number of agreements plus disagreements, then multiplying the fraction by one hundred. Agreement measures should be reported for each phase of a within-subject design when feasible. When estimating reliability of interval recording systems, if there are many unscored intervals, only *scored* intervals should be included in the calculations. Or two separate percentages of agreement can calculated—one for scored, one for unscored intervals. 5

Repertoire, behavioral. *See* Behavioral repertoire. 9

Replicate. To repeat or duplicate an experimental procedure, usually to demonstrate its reliability by reproducing the results. *See also* Systematic replication. 14

Required relaxation. A form of timeout in which the person is required to rest (e.g., lie on a bed) contingent on misbehavior. *See also* Timeout. 26

Respondent behavior. A response that is lawfully elicited by antecedent stimuli. Also, reflexive behavior. Unconditioned respondent behavior is an autonomic response that requires no previous learning. Other respondent behavior may be conditioned, as in Pavlov's famous experiments with the conditioning of dogs' salivation responses. *See also* Elicit. 16

Response. A directly measurable behavior. Used interchangeably in this book with *behavior* and *performance*. 1

Response cost. A reductive procedure in which a specified amount of available reinforcers are contingently withdrawn following the response. Usually these reinforcers are withdrawn from the client's reserve, as with loss of points or yardage, or fines. However, in a modification of this procedure, *bonus response cost*, the reinforcers are taken away from a reserved pool of potential bonus reinforcers. 25

Response delay. A procedure in which the reinforcer is delivered contingent on a preset time intervening between the S^D and the response. Response delay helps to manage impulsiveness (e.g., S^D = "Keep working"— 10 minutes later, "Nice work!"). 18

Response deprivation hypothesis. A hypothesis that states when access to one activity is restricted to below baseline levels, the person will engage in the targeted activity at a level exceeding baseline rates in order to gain access to the deprived activity. Restricting access to below baseline levels, then, serves as an establishing operation. 10

Response fluency. A state achieved when a client's targeted behavior occurs smoothly, rapidly, and with little apparent effort; a condition that facilitates generalization and maintenance and helps prevent relapse. 30

Response generalization. *See* Generalization, response. 29

Response induction. *See* Generalization, response. 29

Restitutional training. *See* Overcorrection. 27

Resurgence. *See* Spontaneous recovery. 23

Reversal design. An experimental design in which the effects of the *independent variable* are tested by introducing a phase (e.g., an Alt-R or DRO treatment phase) in which the direction of the change reverses (i.e., reinforcement of being out-of-seat instead of in-seat). 14

Role-playing. Performance of a sequence of responses to simulate the action of another individual or the same individual under other circumstances. A method of *behavioral rehearsal*. 17

Rule-governed behavior. Behavior under the control of such S^Ds as rules and instructions, rather than behavior shaped by reinforcing or aversive consequences. 17, 21

S^+. A stimulus designated to become a discriminative stimulus. 15

S⁻. A stimulus not to function as an Sᴰ, but as an Sᴬ or Sᴰ⁻. 15

Satiation. The reduction in performance or in reinforcer effectiveness that occurs after a large amount of that type of reinforcer has been delivered (usually within a short time period) following the behavior. 10

Schedule of reinforcement. The response requirements that determine when reinforcement will be delivered. *See also* Interval validity, Fixed and Variable time, Ratio schedules of reinforcement, Limited hold, Differential reinforcement of high rates (DRH), and Adjusting schedules. 11

Sᴰ. *See* Discriminative stimuli. 15

Sᴰ⁻. *See* Discriminative stimuli. 16, 25

S delta (Sᴬ). *See* Discriminative stimuli. 15

Sᴱ. *See* Establishing stimulus. 16

Seclusion. *See* Timeout. 26

Secondary reinforcer. *See* Conditioned reinforcer. 9

Self-control. Choosing a larger more delayed reinforcer over a smaller more immediate reinforcer. (Examples are completing a work assignment instead of watching TV, allowing time to visit friends on the weekend, or avoiding the pressure of a last-minute rush.) Sometimes referred to as *self-management*. 8, 30

Self-instruction. Guiding one's own learning, usually by reciting a sequence of verbal prompts or using other prompting, fading, and reinforcement strategies. 8, 30

Self-management. A procedure in which individuals change some aspect of their own behavior. One or more of four major components are generally involved: (1) Self-selection of goals; (2) monitoring one's own behavior; (3) selection of procedures; and (4) implementation of procedures. 8

Self-modeling. A form of modeling in which trainees are shown videotaped segments of the best samples of their own behavior; external prompts and flawed examples are edited out. Self-modeling is designed to prompt imitation of one's own exemplary performance. 17

Sequence analysis. A description of an individual's behaviors and the events observed to precede and follow those behaviors. Used to provide clues about the possible functional properties of various antecedent and consequential stimuli. 2

Sequence effects. A situation in which one experimental treatment phase *within the experiment* influences subsequent performance during another treatment phase. 22

Sequential withdrawal design. An experimental design in which first one element of the treatment is withdrawn, then a second, and so on, until all elements have been withdrawn; particularly well suited to assessing behavior for maintenance. 22

Setting events. Stimulus events (or contexts), including complex antecedent conditions, events and stimulus-response interactions, that exert general control over other stimulus-response interactions. Setting events may precede and/or overlap with other discrete stimulus-response (Sᴰ — R) relationships (e.g., noisy surroundings could influence adversely the interaction between a work assignment and a student's performance). 15

Shaping. Teaching new behaviors by systematically reinforcing *successive approximations* toward the behavioral objective. Sometimes PSI or individualized instruction is referred to as *shaping*. 19

"Show" procedure. *See* Modeling procedure. 17

Simultaneous treatment design. *See* Alternating treatment design. 22

Single-case designs. *See* Within-subject experimental designs. 14

Skills analysis. *See* Task analysis. 4

Slot machine game. A game of chance in which participants receive reinforcers as prizes. Several cups are placed upside down, concealing paper slips on which the names of reinforcing items or events are written. Each selected participating student or staff member selects one cup, receiving access to the indicated reinforcer. 10

Social reinforcer. An interpersonal act that serves a reinforcing function. Praise (e.g., "That's a good job") usually functions as a social reinforcer. 10

Social validity. A feature of measured results that includes (1) the social significance or importance of the goals, (2) the social appropriateness of the procedures, and (3) the social importance of the effects. 22

Specific praise. The delivery of praise paired with the rationale or reason for its delivery. For example, rather than just saying, "I like that," the change agent would say, "I like that because you kept your eyes on your work." This technique may both reinforce a given behavior *and* assist the learner to discriminate the conditions under which the response is to be emitted. Often called *labeled* or *qualitative praise*. 10

Spontaneous recovery. The reappearance of a response that had not occurred for an extended time interval during extinction conditions. Robert Epstein (personal communication) prefers the term *resurgence* because the phenomenon is not random but controlled by the state of the organism's conditioning history and current circumstances, as are all forms of operant responding. 23

Sʳ. *See* Conditioned reinforcer; Positive reinforcer; Reinforcement. 9

Sᴿ. *See* Unconditioned reinforcer (Sᴿ). 9

Step size. The number of new responses in a subset,

or the extensiveness of the change in topography that constitutes a *successive approximation* in a specific shaping procedure. For example, the step size for teaching one youngster to use a swing on a playground might consist of approaching, touching, sitting down, and following verbal instructions to pump; for another child, pumping might have to be broken down into smaller steps including physical guidance, modeling, and so on.

Stimulus. A physical object or event that has an effect on the behavior of an individual. Stimuli may be internal (e.g., pressure, pain, covert statements) or external to the person. Stimuli that frequently are arranged in behavior analysis programs include reinforcing stimuli, aversive stimuli, and discriminative stimuli. 7

Stimulus change. The presentation or removal of functional discriminative stimuli. 16

Stimulus change decrement. A decrease in response as a function of a change in stimuli, probably due to fewer common stimuli or S^Ds being present. 29

Stimulus control. Systematic influence of an antecedent stimulus (or set of stimuli) on the probability of occurrence of a response. The response form or frequency differs from under one controlling stimulus, or set of stimuli, to another. These controlling stimuli are referred to as *discriminative stimuli.* See also Discriminative stimuli. Section III, 15

Stimulus control, complete. A phenomenon described by a very high probability of behaviors occurring (or not occurring) in the presence of particular antecedent stimuli, and a very low (or higher) probability of occurring in their absence. 16

Stimulus control, incomplete. A phenomenon, inferred by observing, that the antecedent stimulus does not consistently regulate the behavior (i.e., the behavior does not reliably occur or fail to occur, respectively, in response to the presence or absence of the stimulus). 16

Stimulus delay procedure. *See* Delayed prompting and Time delay procedure. 18

Stimulus equalization. Temporarily eliminating the irrelevant dimensions of complex stimuli, leaving only the critical dimensions in order to facilitate discrimination. 18

Stimulus equivalence. Classes of stimuli characterized by reflexivity, symmetry and transitivity among members. 15, 21

Stimulus fading. *See* fading.

Stimulus generalization. *See* Generalization, stimulus. 15

Stimulus property. An attribute or parameter of the stimulus such as topography, texture, volume, size, color, position, and intensity. *See also* Parameter. 23

Subset of behavior. The group of simpler response components that may combine to form a more complex behavior.

Successive approximations. Behavioral elements or subsets, each of which more closely resembles the specified terminal behavior. 19

Supplementary reinforcers. Reinforcers used in addition to the natural reinforcers. 11

Systematic replication. To repeat or duplicate experimental findings despite varying a number of conditions, such as task, setting or other parameters of the basic procedures. 22

Tangible reinforcers. Tangible items (magazines, jewelry, toys, cars, and so on) the contingent delivery of which increases or maintains a behavior. 10

Target behavior. The behavior to be changed. In this book the term often is used interchangeably with *pinpoint, dependent variable,* or *wanted* or *unwanted behavior.* 2

Task analysis. Breaking down a complex skill, job or behavioral chain into its component behaviors, subskills, or subtasks. Each component is stated in its order of occurrence and should set the occasion for the occurrence of the next behavior. Task analyses are particularly useful in planning specific stimulus control and chaining procedures. Two types of task analyses are rational and empirical. The rational is derived from studying the subject matter and specifying the process or procedure that is presumed to be involved in doing the task. The empirical task analysis is based on systematically observing performers in action. 4, 20

Tell procedure. An instructional or stimulus control procedure that uses oral or written instructions or rules to prompt a response under appropriate conditions so that reinforcement may be delivered. 17

Terminal behavior. The behavior that ultimately is to be achieved at the end of a behavior analysis program. The terminal behavior is described according to all its relevant behavioral dimensions or parameters; usually it is assigned a criterion by which an acceptable level of performance is to be judged. Often used interchangeably with *behavioral* or *instructional objective, goal behavior,* and *target behavior;* occasionally denoted by the noun *pinpoint.* 7

Three-term contingency. A phrase used to describe the interrelation among antecedents, behavior and consequences: A-B-C's. When a behavior (B) occurs under specific stimulus conditions (the antecedents—A), it is reinforced (the consequences—C). 15

Time delay prompting. A procedure, sometimes called *progressive delay* or *delayed prompting,* designed to teach a behavior by interposing a time delay between the presentation of the natural and an artificial discriminative stimulus. Initially, the natural discriminative stimulus is presented concurrently with a currently effective artificial S^D or prompt to evoke and reinforce a response. Then, systematically, on successive trials, the time gradually is increased between presentation of the natural S^D and the artificial prompt, until eventually the responder "anticipates"—that is, expresses the response before the prompt is given. 18

Timeout. A procedure in which access to varied sources of reinforcement is removed or reduced for a particular time period contingent on a response. The opportunity to receive reinforcement is contingently removed for a specified time. Either the behaving individual is contingently removed from the reinforcing environment, or the reinforcing environment is contingently removed for some stipulated duration.

Several levels of timeout have been described: *Seclusion* or *isolation*, in which the client is located in a separate room or behind a physical barrier, with "locked timeout" being the most restrictive; and *exclusionary*, considered the next most intrusive form, in which the client is moved to another part of the room or area. Nonexclusionary methods are the least restrictive, such as *contingent observation* and the *timeout ribbon*. 26

Timeout ribbon. A relatively benign form of timeout. A ribbon serves as a necktie. Contingent on misbehavior, the ribbon is removed for 3 minutes, or longer, if necessary, until the misbehavior stops. Treats and praise are delivered every few minutes only to those who are wearing their ribbons. 26

Timeout room. A physical space that is arranged to minimize the reinforcement that an individual is apt to receive during a given time period. Sometimes referred to as timeout booth or quiet place. Procedures for using such facilities must conform to ethical and legal standards. 26

Time-sampling. A direct observational procedure in which the presence or absence of specific behaviors is recorded within short uniform time intervals. (E.g., an observer observes for 10 seconds and records the occurrence or nonoccurrence of a behavior during the following 5 seconds.) This procedure may continue for a specific 30-minute period each day. Time-sampling variations include: (1) Whole-interval time-sampling, (2) partial-interval time-sampling, and (3) momentary time-sampling. 5

Token economy. A contingency package. Tokens (exchangeable reinforcers) are given as soon as possible following the emission of a target response. The recipient later exchanges the tokens for a reinforcing object or event. 13

Token reinforcer. A symbol or object (i.e., check marks, poker chips) that can be exchanged at a later time for a functional reinforcer, an item or activity; an

exchangeable reinforcer (e.g., money). The extent to which tokens serve as reinforcers depends on the individual's experience with them and on the back-up items available. 10

Topography of response. The configuration, form, or shape of a response. The correct topography of a behavior can be determined by photographing an expert performing the behavior. 4

Total task method of chaining. *See* Concurrent task method of teaching. 20

Transfer of stimulus control. A process by which a new antecedent stimulus begins to evoke a response instead of a previous antecedent stimulus. In applied behavior analysis this is often deliberately arranged by using *fading* or *delayed prompting*. 18

Transitory behavior. A behavior that does not leave an enduring product (e.g., smiling, paying attention, or teasing). Such a behavior needs to be observed and recorded as it occurs or preserved by recording it on film, audiotape, or videotape. 5

Treasure box. Toys, games, and arts and crafts materials are contained in colorful boxes and used as reinforcers for young people. Boxes are exchanged periodically among classrooms to increase novelty. 10

Treatment. The behavioral procedures, intervention, program, or independent variable(s) being applied. May be referred to as a *treatment* or *contingency package* when specific behavioral procedures are combined into a unitary treatment. 7

Treatment phase. The period of time during which the intervention is in effect. 1

Treatment utility of assessment. The degree to which assessment is demonstrated to contribute to desired or beneficial treatment outcomes. 4

Unconditioned aversive stimulus (S^P). A stimulus, object, or event, such as a painful electric shock, a bee sting, or a sudden loud noise, that functions aversively in the absence of any prior learning history (i.e., its contingent occurrence is punishing). 9, 27

Unconditioned reinforcer (S^R). A stimulus, such as food, water, or sexual activity, that usually is reinforcing in the absence of any prior learning history; often used interchangeably with *primary reinforcer*. 9

Validity. The extent to which measures actually measure what they are purported to measure. 5

Variable(s). Any behavior or condition in the individual's internal or external environment that may assume any one of a set of values. *See also* Dependent variable; Independent variable. 1

Variable interval (VI) schedule. *See* Interval schedules of reinforcement. 31

Variable ratio (VR) schedule of reinforcement. *See* Ratio schedules of reinforcement. 32

Variable time schedule. A schedule in which reinforcement is delivered contingent on the passage of a variable time interval, not upon the occurrence of a particular response. 31

Verbal behavior. Behavior reinforced through the mediation of other persons. It includes any verbal or nonverbal form of communication that helps people get what they want and avoid what they don't want faster and more efficiently. Included under the rubric of verbal behavior are speaking, gestures, writing, typing, touching, and so on. Verbal behavior, then, refers to antecedent stimuli that set the occasion for others, or ourselves, to provide us with reinforcement. 21

Verbal stimuli. Words, gestures, and other symbolic stimuli. 21

Voluntarily. The degree to which an individual agrees to pursue a behavioral goal or program in the absence of coercion. Voluntariness is assumed when the individual chooses and/or initiates action toward a goal in the absence of strong threats or highly intrusive, unusually powerful, incentives. 3

Weak stimulus control. See Stimulus control, incomplete. 15

Whole-interval DRO. See Differential reinforcement of other behaviors (DRO). 24

Whole-interval time-sampling. A time-sampling procedure, often referred to simply as interval recording, that requires the response to be emitted throughout the entire interval for its presence to be scored. See also Time-sampling. 5

Whole task. See Concurrent task method of teaching. 20

Withdrawal design. An experimental design that involves the removal of the intervention in order to test its effect. For example, one frequently used withdrawal design involves: (1) Obtaining a base rate of the target behavior; (2) repeatedly applying the intervention or procedure; (3) withdrawing the intervention for a time, so conditions are the same as those that were in effect during the baseline period; and (4) reapplying the intervention. This design is used to determine whether the effect of the intervention can be reproduced. (Often abbreviated as ABAB design.) 14

Within-subject experimental designs. Behavioral research designs based on repeated measurement of a behavior under the same and under different conditions of the independent variable (phases). During each phase, sufficient data are collected to depict a convincingly valid representation of the behavior under that condition. Sometimes referred to as *intensive designs*. Used to evaluate unambiguously the effects of the independent variable on the behavior of a single organism. See also Experimental design; Alternating treatment design; Multiple baseline design; Reversal design; Withdrawal design. 14

X-axis. See Abscissa. 6

Y-axis. See Ordinate. 6

Zone system. An observational system similar to partial-interval time-sampling in which not time but space—such as the school yard—is divided into specific predesignated areas. Each area, or zone, is relatively small and provides equivalent opportunities for the target behavior to occur in it. The observer watches and counts all the presence or absence of the behavior or results within a particular area. One or more instances of the targeted behavior recorded within that zone during the observational interval (e.g., 10 seconds, a day) indicate the occurrence of the behavior or result. The observer may score behavior within 1 zone over several time intervals before moving on to the next. 6

References

Abramowitz, A. J., O'Leary, S. B., & Futtersak, M. W. (1988). The relative impact of long and short reprimands on children's off-task behavior in the classroom. *Behavior Therapy, 19,* 243–247.

Acker, M. M., & O'Leary, S. G. (1988). Effects of consistent and inconsistent feedback on inappropriate child behavior. *Behavior Therapy, 19,* 619–624.

Adams, J. (1972). The contribution of the psychological evaluation to psychiatric diagnosis. *Journal of Personality Assessment, 36,* 561–566.

Alabiso, F. (1975). Operant control of attention behavior: A treatment for hyperactivity. *Behavior Therapy, 6,* 39–42.

Alavosius, M. P., & Sulzer-Azaroff, B. (1985). An on-the-job method to evaluate patient lifting technique. *Applied Ergonomics, 16,* 307–311.

Alavosius, M. P., & Sulzer-Azaroff, B. (1986). The effects of performance feedback on the safety of client lifting and transfer. *Journal of Applied Behavior Analysis, 19,* 261–267.

Alavosius, M. P., & Sulzer-Azaroff, B. (1990). Acquisition and maintenance of health-care routines as a function of feedback density. *Journal of Applied Behavior Analysis, 23,* 151–162.

Alevizos, K. J., & Alevizos, P. N. (1975). The effects of verbalizing contingencies in time-out procedures. *Journal of Behavior Therapy and Experimental Psychiatry, 6,* 253–255.

Alford, G. S., Morin, C., Atkins, M., & Schoen, L. (1987). Masturbatory extinction of deviant sexual arousal: A case study. *Behavior Therapy, 18,* 265–271.

Allen, K. D., & Stokes, T. F. (1987). Use of escape and reward in the management of young children during dental treatment. *Journal of Applied Behavior Analysis, 20,* 381–390.

Allen, K. E., Hart, B. M., Buell, J. S., Harris, F. R., & Wolf, M. M. (1964). Effects of social reinforcement on isolate behavior of a nursey school child. *Child Development, 35,* 511–518.

Allen, K. E., Henke, L. B., Harris, F. R., Baer, D. M., & Reynolds, N. J. (1967). Control of hyperactivity by social reinforcement of attending behavior. *Journal of Educational Psychology, 58,* 231–237.

Allen, L. C., Gottselig, M., & Boylan, S. (1982). A practical mechanism for using free time as a reinforcer in classrooms. *Education and Treatment of Children, 5,* 347–353.

Allison, A. G., & Ayllon, T. (1980). Behavioral coaching in the development of skills in football, gymnastics, and tennis. *Journal of Applied Behavior Analysis, 13,* 297–314.

Altman, K., Haavik, S., & Cook, J. (1978). Punishment of self-injurious behavior in natural settings using aromatic ammonia. *Behaviour Research and Therapy, 16,* 85–96.

American Psychological Association. (1973). *Ethical principles in the conduct of research with human participants.* Washington, D.C.: Author.

American Psychological Association. (1981). Ethical principles of psychologists (revised). *American Psychologist, 36,* 633–638.

American Psychological Association. (1982). *Ethical principles in the conduct of research with human participants.* Washington, D.C.: Author.

Anderson, C. A., & Anderson, D. C. (1984). Ambient temperature and violent crime: Tests of the linear and curvilinear hypotheses. *Journal of Personality and Social Psychology, 46,* 91–97.

Anderson, D. C., Crowell, C. R., Hantula, D. A., & Siroky, L. M. (1988). Task clarification and individual performance posting for improving cleaning in a student-managed university bar. *Journal of Organizational Behavior Management, 9,* 73–90.

Anderson, M. A. (1985). Cooperative group tasks and their relationship to peer acceptance and cooperation. *Journal of Learning Disabilities, 18,* 83–86.

Anderson, R. C. (1967). Educational psychology. *Annual Review of Psychology, 18,* 129–164.

Anderson, R. C., & Faust, G. W. (1973). *Educational psychology.* New York: Dodd, Mead.

Apolloni, T., Cooke, S. A., & Cooke, T. P. (1976). Establishing a normal peer as a behavioral model for developmentally delayed toddlers. *Perceptual and Motor Skills, 43,* 1155–1165.

Arrington, R. E. (1943). Time-sampling in studies of social behavior: A critical review of techniques and results with research suggestions. *Psychological Bulletin, 40,* 81–124.

Ary, D. (1984). Mathematical explanation of error in duration recording using partial interval, whole interval, and momentary time sampling. *Behavioral Assessment, 6,* 221–228.

Association for the Advancement of Behavior Therapy. (1977). Ethical issues for human services. *Behavior Therapy, 8,* 763–764.

Association for Advancement of Behavior Therapy Task Force

Report. (1982). The treatment of self-injurious behavior. *Behavior Therapy, 13*, 529–554.

Atthowe, J. M. (1973). Token economies come of age. *Behavior Therapy, 4*, 646–654.

Atwater, J. B., & Morris, E. K. (1988). Teachers' instructions and children's compliance in preschool classrooms: A descriptive analysis. *Journal of Applied Behavior Analysis, 21*, 157–167.

Axelrod, S. (1973). Comparison of individual and group contingencies in two special classes. *Behavior therapy, 4*, 83–90.

Axelrod, S. (1983). *Behavior modification for the classroom teacher.* (2nd Ed.). New York: Academic Press.

Axelrod, S. (1987). Book review: Doing it without arrows: A review of Lavigna and Donnellan's *Alternatives to punishment: Solving behavior problems with non-aversive strategies. The Behavior Analyst, 10*, 243–251.

Axelrod, S., & Apsche, J. (1983). *The effects of punishment on human behavior.* New York: Plenum.

Ayer, W. A. (1976). Massed practice exercises for the elimination of tooth-grinding habits. *Behaviour Research and Therapy, 14*, 163–164.

Ayllon, T., & Azrin, N. H. (1965). The measurement and reinforcement of behavior of psychotics. *Journal of the Experimental Analysis of Behavior, 8*, 357–383.

Ayllon, T., & Azrin, N. (1968). *The token economy: A motivational system for therapy and rehabilitation.* New York: Appleton.

Ayllon, T., & Kelly, K. (1972). Effects of reinforcement on standardized test performance. *Journal of Applied Behavior Analysis, 5*, 477–484.

Ayllon, T., Layman, D., & Kandel, H. J. (1975). A behavioral-educational alternative to drug control of hyperactive children. *Journal of Applied Behavior Analysis, 8*, 421–433.

Ayllon, T., & Roberts, M. (1974). Eliminating discipline problems by strengthening academic performance. *Journal of Applied Behavior Analysis, 7*, 71–76.

Azrin, N. H. (1956). Effects of two intermittent schedules of immediate and non-immediate punishment. *Journal of Psychology, 42*, 3–21.

Azrin, N. H. (1960). Effects of punishment intensity during variable-interval reinforcement. *Journal of the Experimental Analysis of Behavior, 3*, 128–142.

Azrin, N. H. (1964, April). *Aggressive responses of paired animals.* Paper presented at the symposium on Medical Aspects of Stress, Walter Reed Institute of Research, Washington, D.C.

Azrin, N. H., & Armstrong, P. M. (1973). The "mini-meal": A method for teaching eating skills to the profoundly retarded. *Mental Retardation, 2*, 9–13.

Azrin, N. H., & Foxx, R. M. (1971). A rapid method of toilet training the institutional retarded. *Journal of Applied Behavior Analysis, 4*, 89–99.

Azrin, N. H., Hake, D. G., Holz, W. C., & Hutchinson, R. R. (1965). Motivational aspects of escape from punishment. *Journal of the Experimental Analysis of Behavior, 8*, 31–44.

Azrin, N. H., & Holz, W. C. (1961). Punishment during fixed-interval reinforcement. *Journal of the Experimental Analysis of Behavior, 4*, 343–347.

Azrin, N. H., & Holz, W. C. (1966). Punishment. In W. A. Honig (Ed.), *Operant behavior: Areas of research and application* (pp. 380–447). New York: Appleton.

Azrin, N. H., Holz, W. C., & Hake, D. F. (1963). Fixed-ratio punishment. *Journal of the Experimental Analysis of Behavior, 6*, 141–148.

Azrin, N. H., Holz, W. C., & Hake, D. F. (1962). Intermittent reinforcement by removal of a conditioned aversive stimulus. *Science, 136*, 781–782.

Azrin, N. H., Hutchinson, R. R., & Hake, D. F. (1963). Pain-induced fighting in the squirrel monkey. *Journal of the Experimental Analysis of Behavior, 6*, 620.

Azrin, N. H., Hutchinson, R. R., & Hake, D. J. (1966). Extinction-induced aggression. *Journal of the Experimental Analysis of Behavior, 9*, 191–204.

Azrin, N. H., & Lindsley, O. R. (1956). The reinforcement of cooperation between children. *Journal of Abnormal and Social Psychology, 52*, 100–102.

Azrin, N. H., & Peterson, A. L. (1989). Reduction of an eye tic by controlled blinking. *Behavior Therapy, 20*, 467–473.

Azrin, N. H., Shaeffer, R. M., & Wesolowski, M. D. (1976). A rapid method of teaching profoundly retarded persons to dress by a reinforcement-guidance method. *Mental Retardation, 14*, 29–33.

Azrin, N. H., & Wesolowski, M. D. (1974). Theft reversal: An overcorrection procedure for eliminating stealing by retarded persons. *Journal of Applied Behavior Analysis, 7*, 577–581.

Azrin, N. H., & Wesolowski, M. D. (1975). Eliminating habitual vomiting in a retarded adult by positive practice and self correction. *Journal of Behavior Therapy and Experimental Psychiatry, 6*, 145–148.

Azrin, R. D., & Hayes, S. C. (1984). The discrimination of interest within a heterosexual interaction: Training, generalization, and effects on social skills. *Behavior Therapy, 15*, 173–184.

Babcock, R., Sulzer-Azaroff, B., & Sanderson, M. (1989). *Increasing staff use of HIV-related infection precautions in a head injury treatment center.* Paper presented at the annual convention of the Association for Behavior Analysis, Milwaukee, WI.

Bachrach, A. J. (Ed.). (1962). *Experimental foundations of clinical psychology.* New York: Basic Books.

Bacon-Prue, A., Blount, R., Pickering, D., & Drabman, R. (1980). An evaluation of three litter control procedures: Trash receptacles, paid workers, and the marked item technique. *Journal of Applied Behavior Analysis, 13*, 165–170.

Baer, D. M. (1970). A case for the selective reinforcement of punishment. In C. Neuringer and J. L. Michael (Eds.), *Behavior modification in clinical psychology.* New York: Appleton.

Baer, D. M. (1982). Applied behavior analysis. In G. T. Wilson & Franks (Eds.), *Contemporary behavior therapy: Conceptual and empirical foundations* (pp. 277–309). New York: Guilford Press.

Baer, D. M., & Bushell, D. (1981). The future of behavior analysis in the schools: Consider its recent past, then ask a different question. *School Psychology Review, 10,* 259–270.

Baer, D. M., & Guess, D. (1971). Receptive training of adjectival inflections in mental retardates. *Journal of Applied Behavior Analysis, 4,* 129–139.

Baer, D. M., Peterson, R. F., & Sherman, J. A. (1967). The development of imitation by reinforcing behavior of similarity to a model. *Journal of the Experimental Analysis of Behavior, 10,* 405–416.

Baer, D. M., & Stokes, T.F. (1977). Discriminating a generalization technology. In P. Mittler (Ed.) *Research to Practice in mental retardation. Vol. II. Education and training.* University Park Press, Baltimore pp. 331–336.

Baer, D. M., & Wolf, M. M. (1970). The entry into natural communities of reinforcement. In R. Ulrich, T. Stachnek, & J. Mabry (Eds.), *Control of human behavior* (Vol. 2) (pp. 319–324). Glenview, IL: Scott Foresman.

Baer, D. M., Wolf, M. M., & Risley, T. R. (1968). Some current dimensions of applied behavior analysis. *Journal of Applied Behavior Analysis, 1,* 91–97.

Baer, D. M., Wolf, M. M., & Risley, T. R. (1987). Some still-current dimensions of applied behavior analysis. *Journal of Applied Behavior Analysis, 20,* 313–327.

Baer, R. A., Detrich, R., & Weninger, J. M. (1988). On the functional role of the verbalization in correspondence training procedures. *Journal of Applied Behavior Analysis, 21,* 345–356.

Baer, R. A., Williams, J. A., Osnes, P. G., & Stokes, T. F. (1985). Generalized verbal control and correspondence training. *Behavior Modification, 9,* 477–489.

Bailey, J. S., Shook, G. L., Iwata, B. A., Reid, D. H., & Repp, A. C. (1987). *Behavior analysis in developmental disabilities, 1968–1985.* Reprint series, Vol. 1, by the Society for the Experimental Analysis of Behavior, Inc., Lawrence, Kansas.

Bailey, J. S., Timbers, G. D., Phillips, E. L., & Wolf, M. M. (1971). Modification of articulation errors of pre-delinquents by their peers. *Journal of Applied Behavior Analysis, 4,* 265–281.

Bailey, J. S., Wolf, M. M., & Phillips, E. L. (1970). Home-based reinforcement and the modification of pre-delinquents classroom behavior. *Journal of Applied Behavior Analysis, 3,* 223–233.

Balcazar, F., Hopkins, B. L., & Suarez, Y. (1985–86). A critical, objective review of performance feedback. *Journal of Organizational Behavior Management, 7,* 65–89.

Ballard, K. D., & Glynn, T. (1975). Behavioral self-management in story writing with elementary school children. *Journal of Applied Behavior Analysis, 8,* 387–398.

Bandura, A. (1965a). Various processes: A case of no-trial learning. In L. Berkowitz (Ed.), *Advance in experimental social psychology.* Vol. 2. New York: Academic Press, pp. 1–55.

Bandura, A. (1965b). Influence of models' reinforcement con-

tingencies of the acquisition of imitative responses. *Journal of Personality and Social Psychology, 1,* 589–595.

Bandura, A. (1965c). Behavioral modification through modeling procedures. In L. Krasner & L. P. Ullman (Eds.), *Research in behavior modification* (pp. 310–340). New York: Holt, Rinehart & Winston.

Bandura, A. (1968). Social-learning theory of identification processes. In D. A. Goslin & D. C. Glass (Eds.), *Handbook of socialization theory and research.* Chicago: Rand McNally.

Bandura, A. (1969). *Principles of behavior modification.* New York: Holt, Rinehart & Winston.

Bandura, A. (1977). *Social learning theory.* Englewood Cliffs, NJ: Prentice-Hall.

Bandura, A. (1986). *Social foundations of thought and action: A social cognitive theory.* Englewood Cliffs, NJ: Prentice-Hall.

Bandura, A., Grusec, J., & Menlove, F. (1967). Some social determinants of self-monitoring reinforcement systems. *Journal of Personality and Social Psychology, 5,* 449–455.

Bandura, A., & Kupers, C. J. (1964). Transmission of patterns of self-reinforcement through modeling. *Journal of Abnormal and Social Psychology, 69,* 1–19.

Bandura, A., & Menlove, F. L. (1968). Factors determining vicarious extinction of avoidance behavior through symbolic modeling. *Journal of Personality and Social Psychology, 8,* 99–108.

Bandura, A., Ross, D., & Ross, S. (1963a). Vicarious reinforcement and imitative learning. *Journal of Abnormal and Social Psychology, 67,* 601–607.

Bandura, A., Ross, D., & Ross, S. A. (1963b). Imitation of film-mediated aggressive models. *Journal of Abnormal and Social Psychology, 66,* 3–11.

Bandura, A., & Walters, R. H. (1963). *Social learning and personality development.* New York: Holt, Rinehart & Winston.

Barlow, D., Agras, W. S., Leitenberg, H., & Wincze, J. P. (1970). Experimental analysis of the effectiveness of "shaping" in reducing maladaptive avoidance behavior: An anlogue study. *Behavior Research and therapy, 8,* 165–173.

Barlow, D. H., & Hayes S. C. (1979). Alternating treatments design: One strategy for comparing the effects of two treatments in a single subject. *Journal of Applied Behavior Analysis, 12,* 199–210.

Barlow, D. H., Hayes, S. C., & Nelson, R. O. (1984). *The scientist practitioner: Research and accountability in clinical and educational settings.* New York, NY: Pergamon.

Barlow, D. H., & Hersen, M. (1984). *Single case experimental designs: Strategies for studying behavior change* (2nd ed.). New York: Pergamon Press.

Barlow, D. H., & Hersen, M. (1984). *Single case experimental designs: Strategies for studying behavior change in the individual* (2nd ed.). Elmsford, NY: Pergamon Press.

Barlow, D. H., Reynolds, J., & Agras, W. S. (1973). Gender identity change in a transexual. *Archives of General Psychiatry, 28,* 569–576.

Barnard, J. D., Christophersen E. R., Altman, K., & Wolf, M.

M. (1974, August). Parent mediated treatment of self-injurious behavior using overcorrection. Paper presented at the meeting of the American Psychological Association, New Orleans.

Baron, A., & Galizio, M. (1983). Instructional control of human operant behavior. *The Psychological Record, 33,* 495–520.

Barrera, R. D., Lobato-Barrera, D., & Sulzer-Azaroff, B. (1980). A simultaneous treatment comparison of three expressive language training programs with a mute autistic child. *Journal of Autism and Developmental Disorders, 10,* 21–37.

Barrera, R. D., & Sulzer-Azaroff, B. (1983). An alternating treatment comparison of oral and total communication training programs with echolalic autistic children. *Journal of Applied Behavior Analysis, 16,* 379–394.

Barrett, R. P., McGonigle, J. J., Ackles, P. K., & Burkhart, J. E. (1987). Behavioral treatment of chronic aerophagia. *American Journal of Mental Deficiency, 91,* 620–625.

Barrett, R. P., & Sisson, L. A. (1987). Use of the alternating treatments design as a strategy for empirically determining language training approaches with mentally retarded children. *Research in Developmental Disabilities, 8,* 401–412.

Barrish, H. H., Saunders, M., & Wolf, M. M. (1969). Good Behavior Game: Effects of individual contingencies for group consequences on disruptive behavior in a classroom. *Journal of Applied Behavior Analysis, 2,* 119–124.

Barry, N. J., & Overman, P. B. (1977). Comparison of the effectiveness of adult and peer models with EMR children. *American Journal of Mental Deficiency, 82,* 33–36.

Barton, E. J. (1981). Developing sharing: An analysis of modeling and other behavioral techniques. *Journal of Abnormal and Social Psychology, 66,* 3–11.

Barton, E. J., & Bevirt, J. (1981). Generalization of sharing across groups: Assessment of group composition with preschool children. *Behavior Modification, 5,* 503–522.

Barton, E. J., & Osborn, J. G. (1978). The development of sharing by a teacher using positive practice. *Behavior Modification, 2,* 231–250.

Barton, L. E., Brulle, A. R., & Repp, A. C. (1986). Maintenance of therapeutic change by momentary DRO. *Journal of Applied Behavior Analysis, 19,* 277–282.

Bass, R. F. (1987). Computer-assisted observer training. *Journal of Applied Behavior Analysis, 20,* 83–88.

Bates, P., Renzaglia, A., & Wehman, P. (1981). Characteristics of an appropriate education for severely and profoundly handicapped students. *Education and Training of the Mentally Retarded, 16,* 142–149.

Bauman, K. E., & Iwata, B. A. (1977). Maintenance of independent housekeeping skills. *Behavior therapy, 8,* 554–560.

Baumeister, A. A., & Baumeister, A. A. (1978). Suppression of repetitive self-injurious behavior by contingent inhalation of aromatic ammonia. *Journal of Autism and Childhood Schizophrenia, 8,* 71–77.

Beaman, A. L., Stoffer, G. R., Woods, A., & Stoffer, J. E. (1983). The importance of reinforcement schedules in the development and maintenance of altruistic behaviors. *Academic Psychology Bulletin, 5,* 309–317.

Bebko, J. M., & Lennox, C. (1988). Teaching the control of diurnal bruxism to two children with autism using a simple cuing procedure. *Behavior Therapy, 19,* 249–255.

Beck, A. T., & Emery, G. (1985). *Anxiety disorders and phobias: A cognitive perspective.* New York: Basic Books.

Becker, J. V., Turner, S. M., & Sajwaj, T. E. (1978). Multiple behavioral effects of the use of lemon juice with a ruminating toddler-age child. *Behavior Modification, 2,* 267–278.

Becker, W. C., & Carnine, D. W. (1981). Direct instruction: A behavior theory model of comprehensive educational intervention with the disadvantaged. In S. W. Bijou & R. Ruiz (Eds.), *Behavior modification: Contributions to education* (pp. 145–210). Hillsdale, NJ: Lawrence Erlbaum Associates.

Becker, W. C., Engelmann, S., & Thomas, D. R. (1975). *Teaching 2: Cognitive learning and instruction.* Chicago: SRA.

Becker, W. C., Madsen, D. H., Arnold, C. R., & Thomas, D. R. (1967). The contingent use of teacher attention and praise in reducing classroom behavior problems. *Journal of Special Education, 1,* 287–307.

Belcastro, F. P. (1985). Gifted students and behavior modification. *Behavior Modification, 9,* 155–164.

Bellamy, G. T., Horner, R. H., & Inman, D. P. (1979). *Vocational habilitation of severely retarded adults.* Austin, TX: Pro-Ed.

Benoit, B. (1972). *The Learning Analyst Newsletter, 1,* 6–7.

Benoit, R. B., & Mayer, G. R. (1975). Timeout: Guidelines for its selection and use. *The personnel and Guidance Journal, 53,* 501–506.

Bentall R. P., & Lowe, C. F. (1987). The role of verbal behavior in human learning: III. Instructional effects in children. *Journal of the Experimental Analysis of Behavior, 47,* 177–190.

Berg, W. K., & Wacker, D. P. (1989). Evaluation of tactile prompts with a student who is deaf, blind, and mentally retarded. *Journal of Applied Behavior Analysis, 22,* 93–99.

Berkowitz, L. (1983). Aversively stimulated aggression: Some parallels and differences in research with animals and humans. *American Psychologist, 38,* 1135–1144.

Berkowitz, L., Cochran, S. T., & Embree, M. C. (1981). Physical pain and the goal of aversively stimulated aggression. *Journal of Personality & Social Psychology, 40,* 687–700.

Bernal, G., Hilpert, P., Johnson, K., Peters, J., Ramey, G., Siedentop, D., Souweine, J., & Sulzer-Azaroff, B. (1976, December). *Behavior analysis-task analysis: Optimizing reviewer skills.* Paper presented at the meeting of the Association for the Advancement of Behavior Therapy, New York.

Bernal, M. E., Gibson, D. M., Williams, D. E., & Pesses, D. I. (1971). A device for automatic audio tape recording. *Journal of Applied Behavior Analysis, 4,* 151–156.

Bernhardt, A. J., & Forehand, R. (1975). The effects of labeled and unlabeled praise upon lower and middle class children. *Journal of Experimental Child Psychology, 19,* 536–543.

Bernstein, D. A., & Borkovec, T. D. (1973). *Progressive relaxation training: A manual for the helping professions.* Champaign, IL: Research Press.

Bijou, S. W., & Baer, D. M. (1960). The laboratory-experimental study of child behavior. In P. H. Mussen (Ed.), *Handbook of research methods in child development*. New York: Wiley. pp. 140–197.

Bijou, S. W., Birnbrauer, J. S., Kidder, J. D., & Tague, C. (1967). Programmed instruction as an approach to teaching of reading, writing, and arithmetic to retarded children. In S. W. Bijou & D. M. Baer (Eds.), *Child development: Readings in experimental analysis*. New York: Appleton.

Bijou, S. W., & Orlando, R. (1961). Rapid development of multiple-schedule performances with retarded children. *Journal of the Experimental Analysis of Behavior, 4*, 7–16.

Bilsky, L., & Heal, L. W. (1969). Cue novelty and training level in the discrimination shift performance of retardates. *Journal of Experimental Child Psychology, 8*, 503–511.

Birnbrauer, J. S., Wolf, M. M., Kidder, J. D., & Tague, C. (1965). Classroom behavior of retarded pupils with token reinforcement. *Journal of Experimental Child Psychology, 2*, 219–235.

Bitgood, S. C., Crowe, M. J., Suarez, Y., & Peters, R. D. (1980). Immobilization: Effects and side effects on stereotyped behavior in children. *Behavior Modification, 4*, 187–208.

Bitgood, S. C., Peters, R. D., Jones, M. L., & Hathorn, N. (1982). Reducing out-of-seat behavior in developmentally disabled children through brief immobilization. *Education and Treatment of Children, 5*, 249–260.

Bitter, G. G. (1987). Computer-assisted mathematics—A model approach. *Computers in the Schools, 4*, 37–47.

Bittle, R., & Hake, D. F. (1977). A multielement design model for component analysis and cross-setting assessment of a treatment package. *Behavior Therapy, 8*, 906–914.

Blakely, E., & Schlinger, H. (1987). Rules: Function-altering contingency-specifying stimuli. *The Behavior Analyst, 10*, 183–187.

Blew, P. A., Schwartz, I. S., & Luce S. C. (1985). Teaching functional community skills to autistic children using nonhandicapped peer tutors. *Journal of Applied Behavior Analysis, 18*, 337–342.

Blom, D. E., & Zimmerman, B. J. (1981). Enhancing the social skills of an unpopular girl: A social learning intervention. *Journal of School Psychology, 19*, 295–303.

Bloom, B. S. (1980). The new direction in educational research: Alterable variables. *Phi Delta Kappan, 61*, 382–385.

Bloom, B. S. (1984). The 2 sigma problem: The search for methods of group instruction as effective as one-to-one tutoring. *Educational Researcher, June/July*, 4–16.

Bloomfield, H. H. (1973). Assertive training in an outpatient group of chronic schizophrenics: A preliminary report. *Behavior Therapy, 4*, 277–281.

Blount, R. L., Drabman, R. S., Wilson, N., & Stewart, D. (1982). Reducing severe diurnal bruxism in two profoundly retarded females. *Journal of Applied Behavior Analysis, 15*, 565–571.

Boe, E. E., & Church, R. M. (1967). Permanent effects of punishment during extinction. *Journal of Comparative and Physiological Psychology, 63*, 486–492.

Boe, R. B. (1977). Economical procedures for the reduction of aggression in a residential setting. *Mental Retardation, 15*, 25–28.

Bondy, A. S. (1982). Effects of prompting and reinforcement of one response pattern upon imitation of a different modeled pattern. *Journal of the Experimental Analysis of Behavior, 37*, 135–141.

Boren, J. (1956). Response rate and resistance to extinction as functions of the fixed ratio. *Dissertation Abstracts, 14*, 1261.

Boren, J. J., & Colman, A. D. (1970). Some experiments on reinforcement principles within a psychiatric ward for delinquent soldiers. *Journal of Applied Behavior Analysis, 3*, 223–233.

Borg, W. R. (1979). Teacher coverage of academic content and pupil achievement. *Journal of Educational Psychology, 71*, 635–645.

Bornstein, M. R., Bellack, A. S., & Hersen, M. (1977). Social-skills training for unassertive children: A multiple baseline analysis. *Journal of Applied Behavior Analysis, 10*, 183–195.

Bornstein, P. H. (1985). Self-instructional training: A commentary and state-of-the-art. *Journal of Applied Behavior Analysis, 18*, 69–72.

Bornstein, P.H., Balleweg, B. J., McLellarn, R. W., Wilson, G. L., Sturm, C. A., Andre, J. C., & Van Den Pol, R. A. (1983). The "Bathroom Game": A systematic program for the elimination of encopretic behavior. *Journal of Behavior Therapy and Experimental Psychiatry, 14*, 67–71.

Bornstein, P. H., & Quevillon, R. P. (1976). The effect of a self-instructional package on overactive preschool boys. *Journal of Applied Behavior Analysis, 9*, 179–188.

Bostow, D. E., & Bailey, J. B. (1969). Modification of severe disruptive and aggressive behavior using brief timeout and reinforcement procedures. *Journal of Applied Behavior Analysis, 2*, 31–37.

Bradley-Johnson, S., Graham, D.P., & Johnson, C. M. (1986). Token reinforcement on WISC-R performance for white, low-socio-economic, upper and lower elementary-school-age-students. *Journal of School Psychology, 24*, 73–79.

Bradley-Johnson, S., Sunderman, P., & Johnson, C. M. (1983). Comparison of delayed prompting and fading for teaching preschoolers easily confused letters and numbers. *Journal of School Psychology, 21*, 327–335.

Brakman, C. (1985). A human rights committee in a public school for severely and profoundly retarded students. *Education and Training of the Mentally Retarded, 20*, 139–147.

Brantner, J. P., & Doherty, M. A. (1983). A review of timeout: A conceptual and methodological analysis. In S. Axelrod & J. Apsche (Eds.), *The effects of punishment on human behavior* (pp. 87–132). New York: Academic Press.

Braukmann, C. J., Fixsen, K. L., Kirgin, K., Phillips D., Phillips K., & Wolf, M. M. (1975). Achievement Place: The training and certification of teaching parents. In W. S. Wood (Ed.),

Issues in evaluating behavior modification. Champaign, IL: Research Press.

Braukmann, C. J., Maloney, D. M., Fixsen, D. L., Phillips, E. L., & Wolf, M. M. (1974). An analysis of a selection interview training package for predelinquents at achievement place. *Criminal Justice and Behavior, 1,* 30–42.

Brechner, K. C., Linder, D. E., Meyerson, L., & Hays, V. L. (1974). A brief report on a device for unobtrusive visual recording. *Journal of Applied Behavior Analysis, 7,* 499–500.

Brehm, J. W., & Cohen, A. R. (1962). *Explorations in cognitive dissonance.* New York: Wiley.

Breyer, N. L., & Allen, C. (1975). Effects of implementing a token economy on teacher attending behavior. *Journal of Applied Behavior analysis, 8,* 373–380.

Brigham, T. A., Finfrock, S. R., Breuning, M. K., & Bushell, D. (1972). The use of programmed materials in the analysis of academic contingencies. *Journal of Applied Behavior Analysis, 5,* 177–182.

Brigham, T. A., Graubard, P. S., & Stans, A. (1972). An analysis of the effects of sequential reinforcement contingencies on aspects of composition. *Journal of Applied Behavior Analysis, 5,* 421–429.

Brockman, M. P., & Leibowitz, J. M. (1982). Effectiveness of various omission training procedures as a function of reinforcement history. *Psychological Reports, 50,* 927–941.

Broden, M., Beasley, A., & Hall, R. V. (1978). In-class spelling performance: Effects of home tutoring by a parent. *Behavior Modification, 2,* 511–530.

Broden, M., Bruce, C., Mitchel, M. A., Carter, V., & Hall, R. V. (1970). Effects of teacher attention on attending behavior of two boys in adjacent desks. *Journal of Applied Behavior Analysis, 3,* 199–203.

Broden, M., Hall, R. V., & Mitts, B. (1971). The effect of self-recording on the classroom behavior of two eighth-grade students. *Journal of Applied Behavior Analysis, 4,* 191–199.

Brody, G. H., & Brody, J. A. (1976). Vicarious language instruction with bilingual children through self-modeling. *Contemporary Educational Psychology, 1,* 138–145.

Brody, G. H., Lahey, B. B., & Combs, M. L. (1978). Effects of intermittent modelling on observational learning. *Journal of Applied Behavior Analysis, 11,* 87–90.

Brooks, B. D. (1974). Contingency contracts with truants. *The Personnel and Guidance Journal, 52,* 316–320.

Browder, D. M., Morris, W. W., & Snell, M. E. (1981). The sue of time delay to teach manual signs to a severely retarded student. *Education and Training of the Mentally Retarded, 16,* 252–258.

Brown, B. S., Wienckowski, L. A., & Stolz, S. B. (1975). *Behavior modification: Perspective on a current issue.* Washington, D.C.: U.S. Department of Health, Education and Welfare, National Institute of Mental Health.

Brown, L., Branstron, M. B., Hamre-Nietupski, S., Pumpian, I., Certo, N., & Gruenewald, L. (1979). A strategy for developing chronological-age-appropriate and functional curricular content for severely handicapped adolescents and young adults. *Journal of Special Education, 13,* 81–90.

Brown, P., & Elliott, R. (1965). Control of aggression in a nursery school class. *Journal of Experimental Child Psychology, 2,* 103–107.

Brown, W. H., Fox J. J., & Brady, M. P. (1987). Effects of spatial density on 3- and 4-year-old children's socially directed behavior during freeplay: An investigation of a setting factor. *Education and Treatment of Children, 10,* 247–258.

Brownell, K. D., & Jeffery, R. W. (1987). Improving long-term weight loss: Pushing the limits of treatment. *Behavior Therapy, 18,* 353–374.

Brownell, K. D., Marlatt, G. A., Lichtenstein, E., & Wilson, G. T. (1986). Understanding and preventing relapse. *American Psychologist, 41,* 765–782.

Brownstein, A. J., & Shull, R. L. (1985). On terms: A rule for the use of the term, "rule-governed behavior." *The Behavior Analyst, 8,* 265–267.

Bruder, M. B. (1986). Acquisition and generalization of teaching techniques: A study with parents of toddlers. *Behavior Modification, 10,* 391–414.

Bruno, J. E. (1987). Using computers for instructional delivery and diagnosis of student learning in elementary schools. *Computers in the Schools, 4,* 117–134.

Bucher, B., & Hawkins, J. (1971, September). *Comparison of response cost and token reinforcement systems in a class for academic underachievers.* Paper presented at the meeting of the Association of the Advancement of Behavior Therapy, Washington, D.C.

Bucher, B., & Lovaas, O. I. (1968). Use of aversive stimulation in behavior modification. In M. R. Jones (Ed.), *Miami symposium on the prediction of behavior: Aversive stimulation.* Coral Gables: University of Miami Press.

Bucher, B., & Reaume, J. (1979). Generalization of reinforcement effects in a token program in the home. *Behavior Modification, 3,* 63–72.

Budd, K., & Baer, D. M. (1976, Summer). Behavior modification and the law: Implications of recent judicial decisions. *The Journal of Psychiatry & Law;* a special reprint, 171–274.

Budd, K. S., Leibowitz, M., Riner, L. S., Mindell, C., & Goldfarb, A. L. (1981). Home-based treatment of severe disruptive behaviors. A reinforcement package for preschool and kindergarten children. *Behavior Modification, 5,* 273–298.

Budd, K. S., Madison, L. S., Itzkowitz, J. S., George, C. H., & Prince, H. A. (1986). Parents and therapists as allies in behavioral treatment of children's stuttering. *Behavior Therapy, 17,* 538–553.

Buehler, R. E., Patterson, G. R., & Furniss, J. M. (1966). The reinforcement of behavior in institutional settings. *Behaviour Research and Therapy, 4,* 157–167.

Burchard, J. D., & Barrera, F. (1972). An analysis of timeout and response cost in a programmed environment. *Journal of Applied Behavior Analysis, 5,* 271–282.

Bunck, T. J., & Iwata, B. A. (1978). Increasing senior citizen participation in a community-based nutritious meal program. *Journal of Applied Behavior Analysis, 11,* 75–86.

Burgio, L. D., Page, T. J., & Capriotti, R. M. (1985). Clinical behavioral pharmacology: Methods for evaluating medications and contingency management. *Journal of Applied Behavior Analysis, 18,* 45–59.

Burton, T. A. (1981). Deciding what to teach the severely/profoundly retarded student: A teacher responsibility. *Education and Training of the Mentally Retarded, 16,* 74–79.

Buskist, W. F., & Miller, H. L. (1986). Interaction between rules and contingencies in the control of human fixed-interval performance. *The Psychological record, 36,* 109–116.

Buskist, W. F., Morgan, A. B., & Rossi, M. (1984). Competitive fixed interval performance in humans: Role of "orienting" instructions. *The Psychological Record, 34,* 241–257.

Buskist, W. F., & Morgan, D. (1987). Competitive fixed-interval performance in humans. *Journal of the Experimental Analysis of Behavior, 47,* 145–158.

Butterworth, T. W., & Vogler, J. D. (1975). The use of a good behavior game with multiple contingencies to improve the behavior of a total class of fifth-grade students. *Los Angeles County Division of Program Evaluation, Research and Pupil Services Newsletter.*

Butz, R. A., & Hasazi, J. E. (1973). Developing verbal imitative behavior in a profoundly retarded girl. *Journal of Behavior Therapy and Experimental Psychiatry, 4,* 389–393.

Byrne, B. (1969). Attitudes and attraction. In L. Berkowitz (Ed.), *Advances in experimental social psychology.* Vol. 4. New York: Academic Press.

Byrne, B., & Griffitt, W. (1969). Similarity and awareness of similarity of personality characteristics as determinants of attraction. *Journal of Experimental Research in Personality, 3,* 179–186.

Calpin, J. P., Edelstein, B., & Redmon, W. K. (1988). Performance feedback and goal setting to improve mental health center staff productivity. *Journal of Organizational Behavior Management, 9,* 35–58.

Campbell, A., & Sulzer, B. (1971, February). *Naturally available reinforcers as motivators towards reading and spelling achievement by educable mentally handicapped students.* Paper presented at the meeting of the American Educational Research Association, New York.

Campbell, C. R., & Stremel-Campbell, K. (1982). Programing "loose training" as a strategy to facilitate language generalization. *Journal of Applied Behavior Analysis, 15,* 295–301.

Cantor, J. H., & Cantor, G. N. (1964). Observing behavior in children as a function of stimulus novelty. *Child Development, 35,* 119–128.

Carden Smith, L. K., & Fowler, S. A. (1984). Positive peer pressure: The effects of peer monitoring on children's disruptive behavior. *Journal of Applied Behavior Analysis, 17,* 213–227.

Carey, R. G., & Bucher, B. D. (1981). Identifying the educative and suppressive effects of positive practice and restitutional overcorrection. *Journal of Applied Behavior Analysis, 14,* 71–80.

Carey, R. G., & Bucher, B. D. (1983). Positive practice overcorrection: The effects of duration of positive practice on acquisition and response reduction. *Journal of Applied Behavior Analysis, 16,* 101–109.

Carey, R. G., & Bucher, B. D. (1986). Positive practice overcorrection: Effects of reinforcing correct performance. *Behavior Modification, 10,* 73–92.

Carlson, C. S., Arnold, C. R., Becker, W. C., & Madsen, G. H. (1968). The elimination of tantrum behavior of a child in an elementary classroom. *Behavior Research and Therapy, 6,* 117–120.

Carlson, J. D., & Mayer, G. R. (1971). Fading: A behavioral procedure to increase independent behavior. *The School Counselor, 18,* 193–197.

Carnine, D. W. (1976). Effects of two teacher-presentation rates on off-task behavior, answering correctly, and participation. *Journal of Applied Behavior Analysis, 9,* 199–206.

Carnine, D. W. (1981). High and low implementation of direct instruction teaching techniques. *Education and Treatment of Children, 4,* 43–51.

Carr, E. G., Binkoff, J. A., Kologinsky, E., & Eddy, M. (1978). Acquisition of sign language by autistic children. I: Expressive labelling. *Journal of Applied Behavior Analysis, 11,* 489–501.

Carr, E. G., & Durand, V. M. (1985a). Reducing behavior problems through functional communication training. *Journal of Applied Behavior Analysis, 18,* 111–126.

Carr, E. G., & Durand, V. M. (1985b). The social-communicative basis of severe behavior problems in children. In S. Reiss & R. Bootzin (Eds.), *Theoretical issues in behavior therapy.* (pp. 219–254), New York: Academic Press.

Carr, E. G., & Kologinsky, E. (1983). Acquisition of sign language by autistic children II: Spontaneity and generalization effects. *Journal of Applied Behavior Analysis, 16,* 297–314.

Carr, E. G., & McDowell, J. J. (1980). Social control of self-injurious behavior of organic etiology. *Behavior Therapy, 11,* 402–409.

Carr, E. G., & Newsom, C. D. (1985). Demand-related tantrums: Conceptualization and treatment. *Behavior Modification, 9,* 403–426.

Carr, E. G., Newsom, C. D., & Binkoff, J. A. (1976). Stimulus control of self-destructive behavior in a psychotic child. *Journal of Abnormal Child Psychology, 4,* 139–153.

Carr, E. G., Newsom, C. D., & Binkoff, J. A. (1980). Escape as a factor in the aggressive behavior of two retarded children. *Journal of Applied Behavior Analysis, 13,* 101–117.

Carta, J. J., Greenwood, C. R., Dinwiddie, G., Kohler, F., & Delquadri, J. (1987). *The Juniper Gardens classwide peer tutoring programs for spelling, reading, and math: Teacher's manual.* The Juniper Gardens Children's Project, Bureau of Child Research, University of Kansas, 1614 Washington Boulevard, Kansas City, Kansas 66102.

Catania, A. C. (1968). *Contemporary research in operant behavior.* Glenview, IL: Scott, Foresman.

Catania, A. C. (1984). *Learning.* (2nd Ed.). Englewood Cliffs, NJ: Prentice-Hall.

Catania, A. C., Matthews, B. A., & Shimoff, E. (1982). Instructed versus shaped behavior: Interactions with nonverbal responding. *Journal of the Experimental Analysis of Behavior, 38,* 233–248.

Catania, A. C., Sagvolden, T., & Keller, K. J. (1988). Reinforcement schedules: Retroactive and proactive effects of reinforcers inserted into fixed-interval performances. *Journal of the Experimental Analysis of Behavior, 49,* 49–73.

Caudill, B. D., & Lipscomb, T. R. (1980). Modeling influences on alcoholics' rates of alcohol consumption. *Journal of Applied Behavior Analysis, 13,* 355–365.

Cautela, J. R., & Groden, J. (1978). *Relaxation: A comprehensive manual for adults, children, and children with special need.* Champaign, IL: Research Press.

Cautela, J. R., & Kastenbaum, R. A. (1968). A reinforcement survey schedule for use in therapy, training, and research. *Psychological Reports, 20,* 1115–1130.

Certo, N. (1983). Characteristics of educational services. In M. E. Snell (Ed.), *Systematic instruction of the moderately and severely handicapped* (pp. 2–15). Columbus, OH: Merrill.

Chappell, L. R., & Leibowitz, J. M. (1982). Effectiveness of differential reinforcement as a function of past reinforcement and present schedule. *Psychological Reports, 51,* 647–659.

Charlop, M. H. (1983). The effects of echolalia on acquisition and generalization of receptive labeling in autistic children. *Journal of Applied Behavior Analysis, 16,* 111–126.

Charlop, M. H., Burgio, L. D., Iwata, B. A., & Ivancic, M. T. (1988). Stimulus variation as a means of enhancing punishment effects. *Journal of Applied Behavior Analysis, 21,* 89–95.

Charlop, M. H., Schreibman, L., & Thibodeau, M. G. (1985). Increasing spontaneous verbal responding in autistic children using a time delay procedure. *Journal of Applied Behavior Analysis, 18,* 155–166.

Charlop, M. H., & Walsh, M. E. (1986). Increasing autistic children's spontaneous verbalizations of affection: An assessment of time delay and peer modeling procedures. *Journal of Applied Behavior Analysis, 19,* 307–314.

Chase, P. N., Johnson, K. R., & Sulzer-Azaroff, B. (1985). Verbal relations within instruction: Are there subclasses of the intraverbal? *Journal of the Experimental Analysis of Behavior, 43,* 301–313.

Christy, P. R. (1975). Does use of tangible rewards with individual children affect peer observers? *Journal of Applied Behavior Analysis, 8,* 187–196.

Church, R, M. (1963). The varied effects of punishment on behavior. *Psychological Review, 70,* 369–402.

Claerhout, S., & Lutzker, J. R. (1981). Increasing children's self-initiated compliance to dental regimens. *Behavior Therapy, 12,* 165–176.

Clark, H. B., Brandon, F. G., Macrae, J. W., McNees, M. R., Davis, F. L., & Risley, T. R. (1977). A parent advice package for family shopping trips: development and evaluation. *Journal of Applied Behavior Analysis, 10,* 605–624.

Clark, H. B., Northrop, J. T., & Barkshire, C. T. (1988). The effects of contingent thank-you notes on case managers' visiting residential clients. *Education and Treatment of Children, 11,* 45–51.

Clark, H. B., Rowbury, T., Baer, A. M., & Baer, D. M. (1973). Timeout as a punishing stimulus in continuous and intermittent schedules. *Journal of Applied Behavior Analysis, 6,* 443–455.

Clark, H. B., & Sherman, J. A. (1975). Teaching generative use of sentence answers to three forms of questions. *Journal of Applied Behavior Analysis, 8,* 321–330.

Clarke, S., Remington, B., & Light, P. (1986). An evaluation of the relationship between receptive speech skills and expressive signing. *Journal of Applied Behavior Analysis, 19,* 231–239.

Cohen, H. L., & Filipczak, J. (1971). *A new learning environment.* San Francisco: Josse-Bass.

Cohen, P. A., Kulik, J. A., & Kulik, C. C. (1982). Educational outcomes of teaching. *American Educational Research Journal, 19,* 237–248.

Coleman, R. (1970). A conditioning technique applicable to elementary school classrooms. *Journal of Applied Behavior Analysis, 3,* 293–297.

Colter, S. B., Applegate, G., King, L. W., & Kristal, S. (1972). Establishing a token economy program in a state hospital classroom: A lesson in training student and teacher. *Behavior Therapy, 3,* 209–222.

Connecticut Civil Liberties Newsletter (1974).

Cook, T. D., & Campbell, D. T. (1979). *Quasi-experimentation: Design & analysis issues for field settings.* Chicago: Rand McNally College Publishing Company.

Cooke, T. P., & Apolloni, T. (1976). Developing positive social-emotive behaviors: A study of training and generalization effects. *Journal of Applied Behavior Analysis, 9,* 65–78.

Coon, M. E., Vogelsberg, R. T., & Williams, W. (1981). Effects of classroom public transportation instruction on generalization to the natural environment. *Journal of the Association for the Severely Handicapped, 6,* 46–53.

Cooper, J. O., Heron, T. E., & Heward, W. L. (1987). *Applied behavior analysis.* Columbus, OH: Merrill Publishing Company.

Cooper, M. L., Thomson, C. L., & Baer, D. M. (1970). The experimental modification of teacher attending behavior. *Journal of Applied Behavior Analysis, 3,* 153–157.

Corey, J. R., & Shamow, J. (1972). The effects of fading on the acquisition and attention of oral fading. *Journal of Applied Behavior Analysis, 5,* 311–315.

Correa, V. I., Poulson, C. L., & Salzberg, C. L. (1984). Training and generalization of reach-grasp behavior in blind, retarded young children. *Journal of Applied Behavior Analysis, 17,* 57–69.

Cossairt, A., Hall, R. V., & Hopkins, B. L. (1973). The effects of experimenter's instructions, feedback, and praise on teacher praise and student attending behavior. *Journal of Applied Behavior Analysis, 6,* 89–100.

Cotton, J. L., Vollrath, D. A., Froggatt, A. L., Lengnick-Hall, M. L., & Jennings, K. R. (1988). Employee participation: Diverse forms and different outcomes. *Academy of Management Review, 13*, 8–22.

Craig, A., & Andrews, G. (1985). The prediction and prevention of relapse in stuttering: The value of self-control techniques and locus of control measures. *Behavior Modification, 9*, 427–442.

Craig, H. B., & Holland, A. L. (1970). Reinforcement of visual attending in classrooms for deaf children. *Journal of Applied Behavior Analysis, 3*, 97–109.

Craighead, W. E., Kazdin, A. E., & Mahoney, M. J. (1981). *Behavior modification: Principles, issues, and applications.* Boston: Houghton Mifflin.

Craighead, W. E., Mercatoris, M., & Bellack, B. (1974). A brief report on mentally retarded residents as behavioral observers. *Journal of Applied Behavior Analysis, 7*, 333–340.

Croner, M. D., & Willis, R. H. (1961). Perceived differences in task competency and asymmetry of dyadic influence. *Journal of Abnormal Psychology, 31*, 68–95.

Cronin, K. A., & Cuvo, A. G. (1979). Teaching mending skills to mentally retarded adolescents. *Journal of Applied Behavior Analysis, 12*, 401–406.

Cross, S. M., Dickson, A. L., & Sisemore, D. A. (1978). A comparison of three response-elimination procedures following training with institutionalized, moderately retarded individuals. *Psychological Record, 28*, 589–594.

Crowell, C. R., Anderson, D. C., Abel, D. M., & Sergio, J. P. (1988). Task clarification, performance feedback, and social praise: Procedures for improving the customer service of bank tellers. *Journal of Applied Behavior Analysis, 21*, 65–71.

Cullen, R. (1988). Computer-assisted composition: A case study of six developmental writers. *Collegiate Microcomputer, 6*, 202–212.

Cunningham, C. E., & Linscheid, T. R. (1976). Elimination of chronic infant ruminating by electric shock. *Behavior Therapy, 7*, 231–234.

Cuvo, A. J. (1978). Validating task analyses of community living skills. *Vocational Evaluation and Work Adjustment Bulletin, 11*, 13–21.

D'Angelo, J. (1988). Computers for art teachers. *Art Education, 41*, 41–44, 47–48.

Daniels, A. C. (1989). *Performance management.* Tucker, GA: Performance Management Publications.

Dardig, J. C., & Heward, W. L. (1976). *Sign here: A contracting book for children and their parents.* Kalamazoo, MI: Behaviordelia.

Davidson, H. R., & Lang, G. (1960). Children's perception of their teachers feelings toward them related to self-perception, school achievement, and behavior. *Journal of Experimental Education, 29*, 107–188.

Davidson, N. A., & Osborne, J. G. (1974). Fixed ratio and fixed interval schedule control of matching-to-sample errors by children. *Journal of the Experimental Analysis of Behavior, 21*, 27–36.

de Noronha, Z. E., & de Noronha, M. (1984). Integrate or segregate? *School Psychology International, 5*, 161–165.

Deckner, C. W., Deckner, P. O., & Blanton, R. L. (1982). Sustained responding under intermittent reinforcement in psychotic children. *Journal of Abnormal Child Psychology, 10*, 203–213.

Deitz, S. M., & Malone, L. W. (1985). Stimulus control terminology. *The Behavior Analyst, 8*, 259–264.

Deitz, S. M., & Repp, A. C. (1973). Decreasing classroom misbehavior through the use of DRL schedules of reinforcement. *Journal of Applied Behavior Analysis, 6*, 457–463.

Deitz, S. M., & Repp, A. C. (1974). Differentially reinforcing low rates of misbehavior with normal elementary school children. *Journal of Applied Behavior Analysis, 7*, 622.

Deitz, S. M., Slack, D. J., Schwarzmueller, E. B., Wilander, A. P., Weatherly, T. J., & Hilliard, G. (1978). Reducing inappropriate behavior in special classrooms by reinforcing average interresponse times: Interval DRL. *Behavior Therapy, 9*, 37–46.

Delquadri, J., Greenwood, C. R., Stretton, K., & Hall, R. V. (1983). The peer tutoring game: A Classroom procedure for increasing opportunity to respond and spelling performance. *Education and Treatment of Children, 6*, 225–239.

Delquadri, J., Greenwood, C. R., Whorton, D., Carta, J. J., & Hall, R. V. (1986). Classwide peer tutoring. *Exceptional Children, 52*, 535–542.

DeLuca, R. V., & Holborn, S. W. (1985). Effects of a fixed-interval schedule of token reinforcement on exercise with obese and non-obese boys. *The Psychological Record, 35*, 525–533.

Demana, F., & Waits, B. (1987). Problem solving using microcomputers. *College Mathematics Journal, 18*, 236–241.

Demetral, F. D., & Lutzker, J. R. (1980). The parameters of facial screening in treating self-injurious behavior. *Behavior Research of Severe Developmental Disabilities, 1*, 261–277.

Depaulis, A. (1983). A microcomputer method for behavioural data acquisition and subsequent analysis. *Pharmacology, Biochemistry, and Behavior, 19*, 729–732.

DeRicco, D. A., & Niemann, J. E. (1980). In vivo effects of peer modeling on drinking rate. *Journal of Applied Behavior Analysis, 13*, 149–152.

Deur, J. L., & Parke, R. D. (1970). The effects of inconsistent punishment on aggression in children. *Developmental Psychology, 2*, 403–411.

Devany, J. M., Hayes, S. C., & Nelson, R. (1986). Equivalence class formation in language-able and language-disabled children. *Journal of the Experimental Analysis of Behavior, 46*, 243–257.

Dickinson, A. M. (1989). The detrimental effects of extrinsic reinforcement on "Intrisic Motivation." *The Behavior Analyst, 12*, 1–15.

Dineen, J. P., Clark, H. B., & Risley, T. R. (1977). Peer tutoring among elementary students: Educational benefits to the tutor. *Journal of Applied Behavior Analysis, 10*, 231–238.

Dingman, L. A. (1978). How well-managed organizations develop their executives. *Organizational Dynamics*, Autumn, 63–77.

Dinsmoor, J. A., & Campbell, S. L. (1956). Escape-from-shock-training following exposure to inescapable shock. *Psychological Reports, 2*, 43–49.

Dinwiddie, G. (1986). *An assessment of the functional relationship between classwide peer tutoring and students' academic performance*. Doctoral Dissertation. Department of Human Development and Family Life, University of Kansas.

DiRisi, W. J., & Butz, G. (1975). *Writing behavioral contracts*. Champaign, IL: Research Press.

Dixon, L. S. (1981). A functional analysis of photo-object matching skills of severely retarded adolescents. *Journal of Applied Behavior Analysis, 14*, 465–478.

Dixon, M. (1976). Teaching conceptual classes with receptive label training. *Acta Symbolica, 7*, 17–35.

Dixon, M. J., Helsel, W. J., Rojahn, J., Cipollone, R., & Lubetsky, M. J. (1989). Aversive conditioning of visual screening with aromatic ammonia for treating aggressive and disruptive behavior in a developmentally disabled child. *Behavior Modification, 13*, 91–107.

Dodge, K. A., Schlundt, D. C., Schocken, I., & Delugach, J. D. (1983). Social competence and children's sociometric status: The role of peer group entry strategies. *Merrill-Palmer Quarterly, 29*, 309–336.

Doe v. Koger, 480 F. Supp. 225, N.S. Ind. 1979.

Doke, L. A., & Risley, T. R. (1972). The organization of daycare environments: Required versus optional activities. *Journal of Applied Behavior Analysis, 5*, 405–420.

Doke, L. A., Wolery, M., & Sumberg, C. (1983). Treating chronic aggression: Effects and side effects of response-contingent ammonia sprits. *Behavior Modification, 7*, 531–556.

Doleys, D. M., Wells, K. C., Hobbs, S. A., Roberts, M. W., & Cartelli, L. M. (1976). The effects of social punishment on noncompliance: A comparison with timeout and positive practice. *Journal of applied Behavior Analysis, 9*, 471–482.

Donnerstein, E., & Wilson, D. W. (1976). Effects of noise and perceived control on ongoing and subsequent aggressive behavior. *Journal of Personality and Social Psychology, 34*, 774–781.

Dorsel, T. N. (1977). Implementation of variable schedules of self-reinforcement procedures. *Behavior Therapy, 8*, 489–491.

Dorsel, T. N., Anderson, M. L., & Moore, E. M. (1980). A further simplification of variable schedule self-reinforcement procedures. *Journal of Behavior Therapy and Experimental Psychiatry, 11*, 35–36.

Dorsey, B. L., Nelson, R. O., & Hayes, S. C. (1986). The effects of code complexity and of behavioral frequency on observer accuracy and interobserver agreement. *Behavioral Assessment, 8*, 349–363.

Dorsey, M. F., Iwata, B. A., Ong, P., & McSween, T. E. (1980). Treatment of self-injurious behavior using a water mist: Initial response suppression and generalization. *Journal of Applied Behavior Analysis, 13*, 343–353.

Dorsey, M. F., Iwata, B. A., Reid, D. H., & Davis, P. A. (1982). Protective equipment: Continuous and contingent application in the treatment of self-injurious behavior. *Journal of Applied Behavior Analysis, 15*, 217–230.

Doty, D. W., McInnis, T., & Paul, G. L. (1974). Remediation of negative side effects of an on-going response-cost system with chronic mental patients. *Journal of Applied Behavior Analysis, 7*, 191–198.

Dougan, J. D., McSweeney, F. K., & Farmer, V. A. (1985). Some parameters of behavioral contrast and allocation of interim behavior in rats. *Journal of the Experimental Analysis of Behavior, 44*, 325–335.

Dougherty, B. S., Fowler, S. A., & Paine, S. C. (1985). The use of peer monitors to reduce negative interactions during recess. *Journal of Applied Behavior Analysis, 18*, 141–153.

Downs, A. F. D., Rosenthal, T. L., & Lichstein, K. L. (1988). Modeling therapies reduce avoidance of bath-time by the institutionalized elderly. *Behavior Therapy, 19*, 359–368.

Dowrick, P. W., & Dove, D. (1980). The use of self-modeling to improve the swimming performance of spina bifida children. *Journal of Applied Behavior Analysis, 13*, 51–56.

Drabman, R. S., Hammer, D., & Rosenbaum, M. S. (1979). Assessing generalization in behavior modification with children: The generalization map. *Behavioral Assessment 1*, 203–219.

Drew, C. J., & Hardman, M. L. (1985). *Designing and conducting behavioral research*. Elmsford, NY: Pergamon Press.

Dube, W. V., McIlvane, W. J., Mackay, H. A., & Stoddard, L. T. (1987). Stimulus class membership established via stimulus-reinforcer relations. *Journal of the Experimental Analysis of Behavior, 47*, 159–175.

Dunlap, G., & Johnson, J. (1985). Increasing the independent responding of autistic children with unpredictable supervision. *Journal of Applied Behavior Analysis, 18*, 227–256.

Dunlap, G., & Koegel, R. L. (1980). Motivating autistic children through stimulus variation. *Journal of Applied Behavior Analysis, 13*, 619–627.

Dunlap, K. (1928). A revision of the fundamental law of habit formation. *Science, 67*, 360–362.

Dunlap, K. (1930). Repetition in breaking of habits. *The Scientific Monthly, 30*, 66–70.

Durand, V. M. (1985). Employee absenteeism: A selective review of antecedents and consequences. *Journal of Organizational Behavior Management, 7*, 135–167.

Durand, V. M. (in press). The Motivation Assessment Scale. In M. Hersen & A. S. Bellack (Eds.). *Dictionary of behavioral assessment techniques*. New York: Pergamon Press.

Durand, V. M., & Carr, E. G. (1987). Social influences on "self-stimulatory" behavior: Analysis and treatment application. *Journal of Applied Behavior Analysis, 20*, 119–132.

Durand, V. M., & Crimmins, D. B. (1988). Identifying the variables maintaining self-injurious behavior. *Journal of Autism and Developmental Disorders, 18*, 99–117.

Durand, V. M., & Kishi, G. (1987). Reducing severe behavior

problems among persons with dual sensory impairments: An evaluation of a technical assistance model. *Journal of the Association for Persons with Severe Handicaps, 12,* 2–10.

Dustin, R. (1974). Training for institutional change. *The Personnel and Guidance Journal, 52,* 422–427.

Dyer, K., Christian, W. P., & Luce, S. C. (1982). The role of response delay in improving the discrimination performance of autistic children. *Journal of Applied Behavior Analysis, 15,* 231–240.

Dyer, K., Santarcangelo, S., & Luce, S. C. (1987). Developmental influences in teaching language forms to individuals with developmental disabilities. *Journal of Speech and Hearing Disorders, 52,* 335–347.

Eagen, P., Luce, S. C., & Hall, R. V. (1988). Use of a concurrent treatment design to analyze the effects of a peer review system in a residential setting. *Behavior Modification, 12,* 35–56.

Eaton, M. D., Gentry, N. D., Haring, N. B., & Lovitt, T. C. (1972, October). *Applying experimental analysis of behavior to investigating curriculum and making instructional decisions.* Paper presented at Southern California Fourth Annual Conference of Behavior Modification, Los Angeles.

Edgar, R., & Clement, P. (1980). Teacher-controlled and self-controlled reinforcement with underachieving black children. *Child Behavior Therapy, 2,* 33–56.

Egan, P., Luce, S. C., & Hall, R. V. (1988). Use of a concurrent treatment design to analyze the effects of a peer review system in a residential setting. *Behavior Modification, 12,* 35–56.

Egel, A. L., Richman, G. S., & Koegel, R. L. (1981). Normal peer models and autistic children's learning. *Journal of Applied Behavior Analysis, 14,* 3–12.

Eggelston, D., & Mayer G. R. (1976). *The effects of reinforcement contingencies upon attending behavior and academic achievement of high school students.* Unpublished manuscript. California State University, Los Angeles.

Elliott, S. N. (1988). Acceptability of behavioral treatments: Review of variables that influence treatment selection. *Professional Psychology: Research and Practice, 19,* 68–80.

Elliott, S. N., Witt, J. C., Galvin, G. A., & Peterson, R. (1984). Acceptability of positive and reductive behavioral interventions: Factors that influence teachers' decisions. *Journal of School Psychology, 22,* 353–360.

Elliott, S. N., Witt, J. C., Peterson, R., & Galvin, G. A. (1983). *Acceptability of behavioral interventions: Factors that influence teachers' decisions.* Unpublished manuscript.

Ennis, B. J., & Friedman, P. R. (Eds.). (1973). *Legal rights of the mentally handicapped.* Vols. 1–2. Practicing Law Institute, The Mental Health Law Project, Washington, D.C.

Epstein, L. H., Doke, L. A., Sajwaj, T. E., Sorrell, S., & Rimmer, B. (1974). Generality and side effects of overcorrection. *Journal of Applied Behavior Analysis, 7,* 385–390.

Epstein, L. H., Wing, R. R., Koeske, R., Ossip, D., & Beck, S. (1982). A comparison of lifestyle change and programmed aerobic exercise on weight and fitness changes in obese children. *Behavior Therapy, 13,* 651–665.

Epstein, R. (1983). Resurgence of previously reinforced behavior during extinction. *Behavior Analysis Letters, 3,* 391–397.

Epstein, R., & Goss, C. M. (1978). A self-control procedure for the maintenance of nondisruptive behavior in an elementary school child. *Behavior Therapy, 9,* 109–117.

Epstein, R., Lanza, R. P., & Skinner, B. F. (1980). Symbolic communication between two pigeons. (*Columba livia domestica*). *Science, 207,* 543–545.

Epstein, R., & Skinner, B. F. (1980). Resurgence of responding after the cessation of response-independence reinforcement. *Proceedings of the National Academy of Sciences, U.S.A., 77,* 6251–6253.

Erken, N., & Henderson, H. (1976). *Practice skills mastery program.* Logan, UT: Mastery Programs, Ltd.

Eron, L. D. (1982). Parent-child interaction, television violence, and aggression of children. *American Psychologist, 37,* 197–211.

Eron, L. D. (1987). The development of aggressive behavior from the perspective of a developing behaviorism. *American Psychologist, 42,* 435–442.

Espin, C. A., & Deno, S. L. (1989). The effects of modeling and prompting feedback strategies on sight reading of students labeled learning disabled. *Education and Treatment of Children, 12,* 219–231.

Etzel, B. C. (1969). *The difference between some and different.* Paper presented at the Society for Research in Child Development, Santa Monica.

Eubanks, J. L., O'Driscoll, M. P., Hayward, G. B., Daniels, J. A., & Connors, S. H. (1990). Behavioral competency requirements for organizational development consultants. *Journal of Organizational Behavior Management, 11,* 77–97.

Evans, G. W. (1979). Behavioral and physiological consequences of crowding in humans. *Journal of Applied Social Psychology, 9,* 27–46.

Everett, P. B., Studer, R. G., & Douglas, T. J. (1978). Gaming simulation to pretest operant-based community interventions: An urban transportation example. *American Journal of Community Psychology, 6,* 327–338.

Executive Committee and Behavior Modification Special Interest Group of Division 33 (Mental Retardation and Developmental Disabilities) of the American Psychological Association (1989). *Psychology in Mental Retardation and Developmental Disabilities, 14,* 3–4.

Fairbank, J. A., & Prue, D. M. (1982). Developing performance feedback systems. In L. W. Frederiksen (Ed.). *Handbook of organizational behavior management.* New York: Wiley.

Fantuzzo, J. W., & Clement, P. W. (1981). Generalization of the effects of teacher- and self-administered token reinforcers to nontreated students. *Journal of Applied Behavior Analysis, 14,* 435–447.

Fantz, R. L. (1964). Visual experience in infants: Decreased attention to familiar patterns relative to novel ones. *Science, 146,* 668–670.

Farber, H., & Mayer, G. R. (1972). Behavior consultation in

a barrio high school. *The Personnel and Guidance Journal, 51,* 273–279.

Farmer-Dugan, V. (1987). *The childrens interactional behavior scale.* Unpublished paper. Amherst, MA: University of Massachusetts, Walden Learning Center.

Farnum, M., & Brigham, T. A. (1978). The use and evaluation of study guides with middle school students. *Journal of Applied Behavior Analysis, 11,* 137–144.

Fauke, J., Burnett, J., Powers, M. A., & Sulzer, B. (1973). Improvement of handwriting and letter recognition skills: A behavior modification procedure. *Journal of Learning Disabilities, 6,* 296–300.

Favell, J. E., Azrin, N. H., Baumeister, A. A., Carr, E. G., Dorsey, M. F., Forehand, R., Foxx, R. M., Lovaas, O. I., Rincover, A., Risley, T. R., Romanczyk, R. G., Russo, D. C., Schroeder, S. R., & Solnick, J. V. (1982). The treatment of self-injurious behavior. *Behavior Therapy, 13,* 529–554.

Favell, J. E., McGimsey, J. F., & Jones, M. L. (1978). The use of physical restraint in the treatment of self-injury and as positive reinforcement. *Journal of Applied Behavior Analysis, 11,* 225–241.

Feldman, R. F. (1985). *Social psychology,* New York: McGraw-Hill.

Feldman, R. S. (1990). *Understanding psychology.* (2nd Ed.). New York: McGraw-Hill.

Feldman, R. B., & Werry, J. S. (1966). An unsuccessful attempt to treat a tiqueur by massed practice. *Behaviour Research and Therapy, 4,* 111–117.

Fellner, D. J., & Sulzer-Azaroff, B. (1984). A behavioral analysis of goal-setting. *Journal of Organizational Behavior Management, 6,* 33–51.

Fellner, D. J., & Sulzer-Azaroff, B. (1985). Occupational safety: Assessing the impact of adding assigned or participative goal setting. *Journal of Organizational Behavior Management, 7,* 3–24.

Ferritor, D. E., Buckhold, D., Hamblin, R. L., & Smith, L. (1972). The noneffects of contingent reinforcement for attending behavior on work accomplished. *Journal of Applied Behavior Analysis, 5,* 7–17.

Ferster, C. B., & Skinner, B. F. (1957). *Schedules of reinforcement.* New York: Appleton.

Finley, W. W., Rainwater, A. J., & Johnson III, G. (1982). Effect of varying alarm schedules on acquisition and relapse parameters in the conditioning treatment of enuresis. *Behaviour Research and Therapy, 20,* 69–80.

Finley, W. W., & Wansley, R. A. (1976). *Journal of Pediatric Psychology, 4* (1), 24–27.

Fischer, J., & Nehs, R. (1978). Use of commonly available chores to reduce a boy's rate of swearing. *Journal of Behavior Therapy and Experimental Psychiatry, 9,* 81–83.

Fishbein, J. E., & Wasik, B. H. (1981). Effect of the good behavior game on disruptive library behavior. *Journal of Applied Behavior Analysis, 14,* 89–93.

Fisher, E. B. Jr. (1979). Overjustification effects in token economies. *Journal of Applied Behavior Analysis, 12,* 407–415.

Fitterling, J. M., & Ayllon, T. (1983). Behavioral coaching in classical ballet. *Behavior Modification, 7,* 345–368.

Fixsen, D. L., Phillips, E. L., & Wolf, M. M. (1972). Achievement Place: The reliability of self-reporting and peer-reporting and their effects on behavior. *Journal of Applied Behavior Analysis, 5,* 19–30.

Fixsen, D. L., Phillips, E. L., & Wolf, M. M. (1973). Achievement Place: Experiments in self-government with pre-delinquents. *Journal of Applied Behavior Analysis, 6,* 31–47.

Fjellstedt, N., & Sulzer-Azaroff, B. (1973). Reducing latency of responding to adult instruction by means of a token system. *Journal of Applied Behavior Analysis, 6,* 125–130.

Flanagan, S., Adams, H. E., & Forehand, R. (1979). A comparison of four instructional techniques for teaching parents to use time-out. *Behavior Therapy, 10,* 94–102.

Flanders, N. A. (1965). *Teacher influence, pupil attitudes, and achievement.* Cooperative Research Monograph, No. 12.

Fleming, R. K. & Sulzer-Azaroff, B. (1989). Enhancing quality of teaching by direct care staff through performance feedback. *Behavioral Residential Treatment, 4,* 377–395.

Fleming, R. K., & Sulzer-Azaroff, B. (1990, May). *Peer training. effects on staff teaching performance.* Paper presented at the International Association for Behavior Analysis, Nashville, TN.

Ford, J. D., McClure, G., & Haring-McClure P. (1979). A token is not a token. . . . : Interactive effects of intrinsic and extrinsic reinforcement with children. *Behavior Therapy, 10,* 295–297.

Forehand, R., & Baumeister, A. A. (1976). Deceleration of aberrant behavior among retarded individuals. In M. Hersen, R. M. Eisler, & P. M. Miller (Eds.), *Progress in behavior modification (Vol. 2).* New York: Academic Press.

Forehand, R., & King, H. E. (1977). Noncompliant children: Effects of parent training on behavior and attitude change. *Behavior Modification, 1,* 93–108.

Forehand, R., Roberts, M. W., Doleys, D. M., Hobbs, S. A., & Resick, P. A. (1976). An examination of disciplinary procedures with children. *Journal of Experimental Child Psychology, 21,* 109–120.

Forman, S. G. (1980). A comparison of cognitive training and response cost procedures in modifying aggressive behavior of elementary school children. *Behavior Therapy, 11,* 594–600.

Foster, C. D., Billionis, C. S., & Lent, J. R. (1976). *Using a sanitary napkin.* Northbrook, IL: Hubbard.

Foster, C. D., & Keilitz, I. (1983). Empirical bases for program revisions of task analysis. *Journal of Special Education Technology, 6*(3), 13–12.

Fowler, S. A., Baer, D. M., & Stloz, S. B. (Eds.). (1984). *Analysis and intervention in developmental disabilities: Special Issue: Self management tactics for the developmentally disabled, 4.* New York: Pergamon.

Fowler, S. A., Dougherty, B. S., Kirby, K. C., & Kohler, F. W. (1986). Role reversals: An analysis of therapeutic effects achieved with disruptive boys during their appointments as peer monitors. *Journal of Applied Behavior Analysis, 19,* 437–444.

Fowler, S. A., Rowbury, T. G., Nordyke, N. S., & Baer, D. M. (1976). Color-matching technique to train children in the correct use of stairs. *Physical Therapy, 56*, 903–910.

Fox, C. F., & Sulzer-Azaroff, B. (1989). The effectiveness of two different sources of feedback on staff teaching of fire evacuation skills. *Journal of Organizational Behavior Management, 10*, 19–35.

Fox, C. J., & Sulzer-Azaroff, B. (1982). *A program to supervise geographically dispersed foster parents' teaching of retarded youth.* Unpublished manuscript.

Fox, C. J., & Sulzer-Azaroff, B. (1987). Increasing completion of accident reports. *Journal of Safety Research, 18*, 65–71.

Fox, C. J., & Sulzer-Azaroff, B. (1989). The effectiveness of two different sources of feedback on staff teaching of fire evacuation skills. *Journal of Organizational Behavior Management,* 19–35.

Fox, D. K., Hopkins, B. L., & Anger, W. K. (1987). The long-term effects of a token economy on safety performance in open-pit mining. *Journal of Applied Behavior Analysis, 20*, 215–224.

Foxx, R. M. (1982). *Decreasing behaviors of severely retarded and autistic persons.* Champaign, IL: Research Press.

Foxx, C. L., Foxx, R. M., Jones, J. R., & Kiely, D. (1980). Twenty-four hour social isolation: A program for reducing the aggressive behavior of a psychotic-like retarded adult. *Behavior Modification, 4*, 130–144.

Foxx, R. M., & Azrin, N. H. (1972). Restitution : A method of eliminating aggressive-disruptive behavior of retarded and brain damaged patients. *Behaviour Research and Therapy, 10*, 15–27.

Foxx, R. M., & Azrin, N. H. (1973). The elimination of autistic self-stimulatory behavior by overcorrection. *Journal of Applied Behavior Analysis, 6*, 1–14.

Foxx, R. M., & Bechtel, D. R. (1982). Overcorrection. *Progress in Behavior Modification, 13*, 227–228.

Foxx, R. M., Bittle, R. G., Bechtel D. R., & Livesay, J. R. (1986). Behavioral treatment of the sexually deviant behavior of mentally retarded individuals. *International Review of Research in Mental Retardation, 14*, 291–317.

Foxx, R. M., & Jones, J. R. (1978). A remediation program for increasing the spelling achievement of elementary and junior high school students. *Behavior Modification, 2*, 211–230.

Foxx, R. M., & Livesay, J. (1984). Maintenance of response suppression following overcorrection: A 10-year retrospective of eight cases. *Analysis and Intervention in Developmental Disabilities, 4*, 65–79.

Foxx, R. M., & Martin, P. L. (1971). A useful portable timer. *Journal of Applied Behavior Analysis, 4*, 60.

Foxx, R. M., & McMorrow, M. J. (1985). Teaching social skills to mentally retarded adults: Follow-up results from three studies. *The Behavior Therapist, 8*, 77–78.

Foxx, R. M., McMorrow, M. J., Bittle, R. G., & Bechtel, D. R. (1986a). The successful treatment of a dually-diagnosed deaf man's aggression with a program that included contingent electric shock. *Behavior Therapy, 17*, 170–186.

Foxx, R. M., McMorrow, M. J., Bittle, R. G., & Ness J., (1986). An analysis of social skills generalization in two natural settings. *Journal of Applied Behavior Analysis, 19*, 299–305.

Foxx, R. M., McMorrow, M. J., Faw, G. D., Kyle, M. S., & Bittle, R. G. (1987). Cues-pause-point language training: Structuring trainer statements to provide students with correct answers to questions. *Behavioral Residential Treatment, 2*, 103–115.

Foxx, R. M., McMorrow, M. J., Hernandez, M., Kyle, M., & Bittle, R. J. (1987). Teaching soical skills to emotionally disturbed adolescent inpatients. *Behavior Residential Treatment, 2*, 77–88.

Foxx, R. M., McMorrow, M. J., Rendleman, C., & Bittle, R. G. (1986b). Increasing staff accountability in shock programs: Simple and inexpensive shock device modifications. *Behavior Therapy, 17*, 187–189.

Foxx, R. M., Plaska, T. G., & Bittle, R. G. (1986c). Guidelines for the use of contingent electric shock to treat aberrant behavior. In M. Hersen, R. M. Eisler, & P. M. Miller (Eds.), *Progress in behavior modification* (pp. 1–34). New York: Academic Press.

Foxx, R. M., & Rubinoff, A. (1979). Behavioral treatment of caffeinism: Reducing excessive coffee drinking. *Journal of Applied Behavior Analysis, 12*, 335–344.

Foxx, R. M., & Shapiro, S. T. (1978). The timeout ribbon: A nonexclusionary timeout procedure. *Journal of Applied Behavior Analysis, 11*, 125–136.

Frank, A. R., Wacker, D. P., Berg, W. K., & McMahon, C. M. (1985). Teaching selected microcomputer skills to retarded students via picture prompts. *Journal of Applied Behavior Analysis, 18*, 179–185.

Frankowsky, R. J., & Sulzer-Azaroff, B. (1975, December). *Individual and group contingencies and collateral social behaviors.* Paper presented at the meeting of the Association for the Advancement of Behavior Therapy, San Francisco.

Frankowsky, R. J., & Sulzer-Azaroff, B. (1978). Individual and group contingencies and collatoral social behaviors. *Behavior Therapy, 9*, 313–327.

Freagon, S., & Rotatori A. F. (1982). Comparing natural and artificial environments in training self-care skills to group home residents. *The Journal of the Association for the Severely Handicapped, 7*(3), 73–86.

Frentz, C., & Kelley, M. L. (1986). Parents' acceptance of reductive treatment methods: The influence of problem severity and perception of child behavior. *Behavior Therapy, 17*, 75–81.

Frisch, M. B., & Higgins, R. L. (1986). Instructional demand effects and the correspondence among role-play, self-report, and naturalistic measures of social skill. *Behavioral Assessment, 8*, 221–236.

Frisch, S. A., & Schumaker, J. B. (1974). Training generalized receptive prepositions in retarded children. *Journal of Applied Behavior Analysis, 7*, 611–621.

Gaetani, J. J., Hoxeng, D. D., & Austin, J. T. (1985). Engineering compensation systems: Effects of commissioned versus wage payment. *Journal of Organizational Behavior Management*, 7, 51–63.

Gagnon, J. H., & Davison, G. C. (1976). Asylums, the token economy, and the metrics of mental life. *Behavior Therapy*, 7, 528–534.

Galizio, M. (1979). Contingency-shaped and rule-governed behavior: Instructional control of human loss avoidance. *Journal of the Experimental Analysis of Behavior*, 31, 53–70.

Garcia, E. E., Bullet, J., & Rust, F. P. (1977). An experimental analysis of language training generalization across classroom and home. *Behavior Modification*, 1, 531–550.

Garcia, E. E., & DeHaven, F. (1974). Use of operant techniques in the establishment and generalization of language: A review and analysis. *American Journal of Mental Deficiency*, 79, 169–178.

Garrett, N., & Hart, R. S. (1988). Foreign language teaching and the computer. *Foreign Language Annals*, 21, 359–362.

Gast, D. L., & Nelson, C. M. (1977). Legal and ethical considerations for the use of timeout in special education settings. *The Journal of Special Education*, 11, 457–467.

Gast, D. L., Van Biervliet, A., & Spradlin, J. E. (1979). Teaching number-word equivalences: A study of transfer. *American Journal of Mental deficiency*, 83, 524–527.

Gaul, K., Nietupski, J., & Certo, N. (1985). Teaching supermarket shopping skills using an adaptive shopping list. *Education and Training of the Mentally Retarded*, 20, 53–59.

Gelfand, D. M. (1962). The influence of self-esteem on rate of verbal conditioning and social matching behavior. *Journal of Abnormal and Social Psychology*, 65, 259–265.

Gelfand, D. M., & Hartmann, D. P. (1984). *Child behavior analysis and therapy, 2nd (Ed.),* New York: Pergamon Press.

Gelfand, D. M., Hartmann, D. P., Lamb, A. K., Smith, C. L., Mahan, M. A., & Paul, S. C. (1974). The effects of adult models and described alternatives on children's choice of behavior management techniques. *Child Development*, 45, 585–593.

Geller, E. S., Winett, R. A., & Everett, P. B. (1982). *Preserving the environment: New strategies for behavior change.* New York: Pergamon Press.

George, J. T., & Hopkins, B. L. (1989). Multiple effects of performance-contingent pay for waitpersons. *Journal of Applied Behavior Analysis*, 22, 131–141.

Gettinger, M. (1986). Issues and trends in academic engaged time of students. *Special Services in the Schools*, 2, 1–17.

Giangreco, M. F. (1983). Teaching basic photography skills to a severely handicapped young adult using simulated materials. *The Journal of the Association for the Severely Handicapped*, 8, 43–49.

Gillat, A., & Sulzer-Azaroff, B. (1990). *Involving school principals in the implementation of goal setting and feedback with teachers and students.* Paper presented at the International Association for Behavior Analysis, Nashville TN.

Gladstone, B. W., & Sherman, J. A. (1975). Developing generalized behavior modification skills in high school students working with retarded children. *Journal of Applied Behavior Analysis*, 8, 169–180.

Glaros, A. G., & Rao, S. M. (1977). Bruxism: A critical review. *Psychological Bulletin*, 84, 767–781.

Glover, J., & Gary, A. L. (1976). Procedures to increase some aspects of creativity. *Journal of Applied Behavior Analysis*, 9, 79–84.

Glover, J. A., Zimmer, J. W., Filbeck, R. W., & Plake, B. S. (1980). Effects of training students to identify the semantic base of prose materials. *Journal of Applied Behavior Analysis*, 13, 655–667.

Glynn, E. L., Thomas, T. D., & Shee, S. M. (1973). Behavioral self-control of on-task behavior in an elementary classroom. *Journal of Applied Behavior Analysis*, 6, 105–113.

Goetz, E. M., Ayala, J. M., Hatfield, V. L., Marshall, A. M., & Etzel, B. C. (1983). Training independence in preschoolers with an auditory stimulus management technique. *Education & Treatment of Children*, 6, 251–261.

Goetz, E. M., & Salmonson, M. M. (1972). The effect of general and descriptive reinforcement on "creativity" in easel painting. In G. Semb (Ed.), *Behavior analysis and education.* Lawrence: University of Kansas.

Goldiamond, I. (1974). Toward a constructional approach to social problems: Ethical and constitutional issues raised by applied behavior analysis. *Behaviorism*, 2, 1–85.

Goldstein, A. P., Sprafkin, R. P., Gershaw, N. J., & Klein, P. (1980). *Skillstreaming the adolescent.* Champaign, IL: Research Press.

Goldstein, G., & Wickstrom, S. (1986). Peer intervention effects on communicative interaction among handicapped and nonhandicapped preschoolers. *Journal of Applied Behavior Analysis*, 19, 209–214.

Goldstein, H., & Brown, W. H. (1989). Observational learning of receptive and expressive language by handicapped preschool children. *Education and Treatment of Children*, 12, 5–37.

Goldstein, R. S., Minkin, B. L., Minkin, N., & Baer, D. M. (1978). Finders, keepers?: An analysis and validation of a free-found-ad policy. *Journal of Applied Behavior Analysis*, 11, 465–473.

Goodwin, D. L. (1969). Consulting with the classroom teacher. In J. D. Krumboltz & C. E. Thoresen (Eds.), *Behavioral counseling cases and techniques.* New York: Holt, Rinehart & Winston.

Gottman, J., Gonso, J., & Rasmussen, B. (1975). Social interaction, social competence, and friendship in children. *Child Development*, 46, 709–718.

Grabe, M. (1988). Technological enhancement of study behavior: On-line activities to produce more effective learning. *Collegiate Microcomputer*, 6, 253–259.

Granger, R. G., Porter, J. H., & Christoph, N. L. (1984). Schedule induced behavior in children as a function of inter-reinforcement interval length. *Physiology and Behavior*, 33, 153–157.

Graubard, P. S., Rosenberg, H., & Miller, M. B. (1971). Student applications of behavior modification to teachers and environments or ecological approaches to social deviancy. In E. A. Ramp & B. L. Hopkins (Eds.), *A new direction for education: Behavior analysis*. Lawrence: University of Kansas. pp. 80–101.

Green, C. W., Reid, D. H., McCarn, J. E., Schepis, M. M., Phillips, J. F., & Parsons, M. B. (1986). Naturalistic observations of classrooms serving severely handicapped persons: Establishing evaluative norms. *Applied Research in Mental Retardation, 7*, 37–50.

Green, C. W., Reid, D. H., White, L. K., Halford, R. C., Brittain, D. P., & Gardner, S. M. (1988). Identifying reinforcers for persons with profound handicaps: Staff opinion versus systematic assessment of preferences. *Journal of Applied Behavior Analysis, 21*, 31–43.

Green, G. R., Linsk, N. L., & Pinkston, E. M. (1986). Modification of verbal behavior of the mentally impaired elderly by their spouses. *Journal of Applied Behavior Analysis, 19*, 329–336.

Green, R. B., Hardison, W. L., & Greene, B. F. (1984). Turning the table on advice programs for parents: Using placemats to enhance family interaction at restaurants. *Journal of Applied Behavior Analysis, 17*, 497–508.

Greene, B. F., Winett, R. A., Van Houten, R., Geller, E. S., & Iwata, B. A. (1987). *Behavior analysis in the community, 1968–1986*. Reprint series, Volume 2, by the Society for the Experimental Analysis of Behavior, Inc. Lawrence, Kansas.

Greene, D., & Lepper, M. R. (1974). Intrinsic motivation: How to turn play into work. *Psychology Today, 8*, 49–54.

Greene, R. J., & Hoats, D. L. (1971). Aversive tickling: A simple conditioning technique. *Behavior Therapy, 2*, 389–393.

Greenwood, C. R., Baskin, A., & Sloane, H. N. (1974). Training elementary aged peer behavior managers to control small group programmed mathematics. *Journal of Applied Behavior Analysis, 7*, 103–114.

Greenwood, C. R., Carta, J. J., & Hall, V. H. (1988). The use of peer tutoring strategies in classroom management and educational instruction. *School Psychology Review, 17*, 258–275.

Greenwood, C. R., Delquadri, J. C., & Hall, R. V. (1984). Opportunity to respond and student academic performance. In W. L. Heward, T. E. Heron, J. Trap-Porter, & D. S. Hill (Eds.), *Focus on behavior analysis in education* (pp. 55–88). Columbus, OH: Charles Merrill.

Greenwood, C. R., Delquadri, J. C., Stanley, S. O., Terry, B., & Hall, R. V. (1985). Assessment of Eco-behavioral interaction in school settings. *Behavioral Assessment, 7*, 331–347.

Greenwood, C. R., Dinwiddie, G., Bailey, B., Carta, J. J., Dorsey, D., Kohler, F. W., Nelson, C., Rotholz, D., & Schulte, D. (1987). Field replication of classwide peer tutoring. *Journal of Applied Behavior Analysis, 20*, 151–160.

Greenwood, C. R., Dinwiddie, G., Terry, B., Wade, L., Stanley, S., Thibadeau, S., & Delquadri, J. (1984). Teacher-versus peer-mediated instruction: An eco-behavioral analysis of achievement outcomes. *Journal of Applied Behavior Analysis, 17*, 521–538.

Greenwood, C. R., Hops, H., Delquardi, J., & Guild, J. (1974). Group contingencies for group consequences in classroom management: A further analysis. *Journal of Applied Behavior Analysis, 7*, 413–425.

Greenwood, C. R., Hops, H., Walker, H. M., Guild, J. J., Stokes, J., Young, K. R., Keleman, K. S., & Willardson, M. (1979). Standardized classroom management program: Social validation and replication studies in Utah and Oregon. *Journal of Applied Behavior Analysis, 12*, 235–253.

Greer, C. R., & Labig, C. E. (1987). Employee reactions to disciplinary action. *Human Relations, 40*, 507–524.

Greer, R. D. (1980). *Design for music learning*. New York: Teachers College Press.

Greer, R. D. (1981). An operant approach to motivation and affect: Ten years of research in music learning. In *Documentary report of the Ann Arbor Symposimu: Applications of pspychology to the teaching and learning of music* (pp. 102–121). Music Educators National Conference, Reston, VA.

Greer, R. D., & Polirstok, S. R. (1982). Collateral gains and short-term maintenance in reading and on-task responses by some inner-city adolescents as a function of their use of social reinforcement while tutoring. *Journal of Applied Behavior analysis, 15*, 123–139.

Groden, G. (1989). A Guide for conducting a comprehensive behavioral analysis of a target behavior. *Journal of Behavior Therapy and Experimental Psychiatry, 20*, 163–170.

Gross, A. M., Farrar, M. J., & Liner, D. (1982). Reduction of trichotillomania in a retarded cerebral palsied child using overcorrection, facial screening, and differential reinforcement of other behavior. *Education and Treatment of Children, 5*, 133–140.

Gross, A. M., Heimann, L., Shapiro, R., & Schultz, R. M. (1983). Children with diabetes: Social skills training and hemoglobin A1c levels. *Behavior Modification, 7*, 151–164.

Gruber, B., Reeser, R., & Reid, D. H. (1979). Providing a less restrictive environment for profoundly retarded persons by teaching independent walking skills. *Journal of Applied Behavior Analysis, 12*, 285–297.

Guess, D., & Baer, D. M. (1973). An analysis of individual differences in generalization between receptive and productive language in retarded children. *Journal of Applied Behavior Analysis, 6*, 311–329.

Guess, D., Helmstetter, E., Turnbull, H. R., & Knowlton, S. (1987). Use of aversive procedures with persons who are disabled: An historical review and critical analysis. *Monograph of the Association for Persons with Severe Handicaps*.

Guess, D., Sailor, W., Rutherford, G., & Baer, D. M. (1968). An experimental analysis of linguistic development: The productive use of the plural morpheme. *Journal of Applied Behavior Analysis, 1*, 297–306.

Guevremont, D. C., Osnes, P. G., & Stokes, T. F. (1986). Programming maintenance after correspondence training interventions with children. *Journal of Applied Behavior Analysis, 19*, 215–219.

Gustafson, C., Hotte, E., & Carsky, M. (1976). *Everyday living skills*. Unpublished manuscript, Mansfield Training School, Mansfield Depot, CT.

Hagen, R. L., Craighead, W. E., & Paul, G. L. (1975). Staff reactivity to evaluative behavioral observations. *Behavior Therapy, 6,* 201–205.

Hake, D. F., Donaldson, T., & Hyten, C. (1983). Analysis of discriminative control by social behavioral stimuli. *Journal of the Experimental Analysis of Behavior, 39,* 7–23.

Hake, D. F., & Laws, D. R. (1967). Social facilitation of responses during a stimulus paired with electric shock. *Journal of the Experimental Analysis of Behavior, 10,* 387–392.

Hall, C., Sheldon-Wildgen, J., & Sherman, J. A. (1980). Teaching job interview skills to retarded clients. *Journal of Applied Behavior Analysis, 13,* 433–442.

Hall, L. J., & Sulzer-Azaroff, B. (1987). Promoting program implementation by parents: A case exploration of the use of time management and self-administered reward. *Journal of Child and Adolescent Psychology, 6,* 29–30.

Hall, L. J., & Sulzer-Azaroff, B. (1988). The effects of time management with a parent training program. Paper presented at the annual meeting of the Association for Behavior Analysis, Philadelphia.

Hall, L. J., & Sulzer-Azaroff, B. (1991). *Study guide to accompany Behavior Analysis for Lasting Change.* Fort Worth, TX: Holt, Rinehart & Winston.

Hall, R. V. (1971a). *Managing behavior: Behavior modification: The measurement of behavior. No. 1.* Lawrence, KS: H & H Enterprises.

Hall, R. V. (1971b). *Managing behavior: Behavior modification: Applications in school and home, No. 3.* Lawrence, KS: H & H Enterprises.

Hall, R. V., Axelrod, S., Tyler, L., Grief, E., Jones, F. C., & Robertson, R. (1972). Modification of behavior problems in the home with a parent as observer and experimenter. *Journal of Applied Behavior Analysis, 5,* 53–64.

Hall, R. V., Delquadri, J., Greenwood, C. R., & Thurston, L. (1982). The importance of opportunity to respond in children's academic success (pp. 107–149). In E. D. Edgar, N. Haring, J. R. Jenkins, & C. Pious (Eds.), *Serving young handicapped children: Issues and research.* Austin, TX: Pro-Ed.

Hall, R. V., Lund, D., & Jackson, D. (1968). Effects of teacher attention on study behaviors. *Journal of Applied Behavior Analysis, 1,* 1–12.

Hallahan, K. P., Marshall, K. J., & Lloyd, J. (1981). Self-recording during group instruction: Effects on attention-to-task. *Learning Disability Quarterly, 4,* 407–413.

Halle, J. W., Baer, D. M., & Spradlin, J. E. (1981). Teachers' generalized use of delay as a stimulus control procedure to increase language use in handicapped children. *Journal of Applied Behavior Analysis, 14,* 389–409.

Halle, J. W., Marshall, G. M., & Spradlin, J. E. (1979). Time delay: A technique to increase language usage and facilitate generalization in retarded children. *Journal of Applied Behavior Analysis, 12,* 431–439.

Hamblin, R. L., Hathaway, C., & Wodarski, J. (1974). Group contingencies, peer tutoring, and accelerating academic achievement: Experiment 1. In E. Ramp & B. L. Hopkins

(Eds.), *A new direction for education: Behavior analysis* (pp. 41–53). Lawrence: University of Kansas.

Handen, B. L., & Zane, T. (1987). Delayed prompting: A review of procedural variations and results. *Research in Developmental Disabilities, 8,* 307–330.

Handleman, J. S. (1979). Generalization by autistic-type children of verbal responses across settings. *Journal of Applied Behavior Analysis, 12,* 273–282.

Haney, J. I., & Jones, R. T. (1982). Programming maintenance as a major component of a community-centered preventative effort: Escape from fire. *Behavior Therapy, 13,* 47–62.

Hanley, E. M., Perelman, P. F., & Homan, C. I. (1979). Parental management of a child's self-stimulation behavior through the use of timeout and DRO. *Education and Treatment of Children, 2,* 305–310.

Hannum, J. S., Thoresen, C. E., & Hubbard, D. R. (1974). A behavioral study of self-esteem with elementary teachers. In M. J. Mahoney & C. E. Thoresen (Eds.), *Self-control: Power to the person.* Monterey, CA: Brooks/Cole.

Hansen, D. J., Tisdelle, D. A., & O'Dell, S. L. (1985). Audio recorded and directly observed parent-child interactions: A comparison of observation methods. *Behavioral Assessment, 7,* 389–399.

Hansen, G. D. (1979). Enuresis control through fading, escape, and avoidance training. *Journal of Applied Behavior Analysis, 12,* 303–307.

Hardiman, S. A., Goetz, E. M., Reuter, K. E., & LeBlanc, J. M. (1975). Primis, contingent attention and training: Effects on a child's motor behavior. *Journal of Applied Behavior Analysis, 8,* 399–409.

Haring, N. G. (1988). *Generalization for students with severe handicaps.* Seattle: Washington University Press.

Haring, T. G. (1985). Teaching between-class generalization of toy play behavior to handicapped children. *Journal of Applied Behavior Analysis, 18,* 127–139.

Haring, T. G., & Kennedy, C. H. (1988). Units of analysis in task-analytic research. *Journal of Applied Behavior Analysis, 21,* 207–215.

Haring, T. G., Kennedy, C. H., Adams, M. J., & Pitts-Conway, V. (1987). Teaching generalization of purchasing skills across community settings to autistic youth using videotape modeling. *Journal of Applied Behavior Analysis, 20,* 89–96.

Haring, T. G., Roger, B., Lee, M., Breen, C., & Gaylord-Ross, R. (1986). Teaching social language to moderately handicapped students. *Journal of Applied Behavior Analysis, 19,* 159–171.

Harmatz, M. G., & Lapuc, P. (1968). Behavior modification of overeating in a psychiatric population. *Journal of Consulting and Clinical Psychology, 32,* 583–587.

Harmon, T. M., Nelson, R. O., & Hayes, S. C. (1980). The differential effects of self-monitoring mood versus activity in depressed patients. *Journal of Consulting and Clinical Psychology, 48,* 30–38.

Harris, F. R., Wolf, M. M., & Baer, D. M. (1967). Effects of adult social reinforcement on child behavior. In S. W. Bijou

& D. M. Baer (Eds.), *Child development: Readings in experimental analysis*. New York: Appleton.

Harris, S. L., & Ersner-Hershfield, R. (1978). Behavioral suppression of seriously disruptive behavior in psychotic and retarded patients: A review of punishment and its alternatives. *Psychological Bulletin, 85,* 1352–1375.

Harris, S. L., Hershfield, R. E., Kaffashan, L. C., & Romanczyk, R. G. (1974). The portable time-out room. *Behavior Therapy, 5,* 687–688.

Harris, S. L., & Wolchik, S. A. (1979). Suppression of self-stimulation: Three alternative strategies. *Journal of Applied Behavior Analysis, 12,* 185–198.

Harris, V. W., Bushell, D., Sherman, J. A., & Kane, J. F. (1975). Instructions, feedback, praise, bonus payments, and teacher behavior. *Journal of Applied Behavior Analysis, 8,* 462.

Harris, V. W., & Sherman, J. A. (1973a). Effects of peer tutoring and consequences on the math performance of elementary classroom students. *Journal of Applied Behavior Analysis, 6,* 587–597.

Harris V. W., & Sherman, J. A. (1973b). A use and analysis of the "good behavior game" to reduce disruptive classroom behavior. *Journal of Applied Behavior Analysis, 6,* 405–417.

Hart, B. M., Allen, K. E., Buell, J. S., Harris, F. R., & Wolf, M. M. (1964). Effects of social reinforcement on operant crying. *Journal of Experimental Child Psychology, 1,* 145–153.

Hart, B. M., & Risley, T. R. (1968). Establishing use of descriptive adjectives in the spontaneous speech of disadvantaged preschool children. *Journal of Applied Behavior Analysis, 1,* 109–120.

Hart, B., & Risley, T. R. (1974). Using preschool materials to modify the language of disadvantaged children. *Journal of Applied Behavior Analysis, 7,* 243–256.

Hart, B., & Risley, T. R. (1975). Incidental teaching of language in the preschool. *Journal of Applied Behavior Analysis, 8,* 411–420.

Hart, B., & Risley, T. R. (1980). In vivo language intervention: Unanticipated general effects. *Journal of Applied Behavior Analysis, 13,* 407–432.

Hartmann, D. P. (1977). Considerations in the choice of interobserver reliability estimates. *Journal of Applied Behavior Analysis, 10,* 103–116.

Hartmann, D. P., Gottman, J. M., Jones, R. R., Gardner, W., Kazdin, A. E., & Vaught, R. (1980). Interrupted time-series analysis and its application to behavioral data. *Journal of Applied Behavior Analysis, 13,* 543–559.

Haskett, G. J., & Lenfestey, W. (1974). Reading-related behavior in an open classroom: Effects of novelty and modelling on preschoolers. *Journal of Applied Behavior Analysis, 7,* 233–241.

Hatch, J. P. (1980). The effects of operant reinforcement schedules on the modification of human heart rate. *Psychophysiology, 17,* 559–567.

Haupt, E. J., Van Kirk, M. J., & Terraciano, T. (1975). An inexpensive fading procedure to decrease error and increase retention of number facts. In E. Ramp & G. Semb (Eds.),

Behavior analysis: Areas of research and application (pp. 225–232). Englewood Cliffs, NJ: Prentice-Hall.

Hawkins, R. P. (1985). Comment: On Woolfolk and Richardson. *American Psychologist, 40,* 1138–1139.

Hawkins, R. P. (1986). Selection of target behaviors. In R. O. Nelson & S. C. Hayes (Eds.), *Conceptional foundations of behavioral assessment* (pp. 331–385). New York: Guilford.

Hawkins, R. P., & Dotson, V. A. (1975). Reliability scores that delude: An Alice in Wonderland trip through the misleading characteristics of inter-observer agreement scores in interval recording. In E. Ramp & G. Semp (Eds.), *Behavior analysis: Areas of research and application* (pp. 359–376). Englewood Cliffs, NJ: Prentice-Hall.

Hayes, L. J., Tilley, K., & Hayes, S. C. (1988). Extending equivalence class membership to gustatory stimuli. *The Psychological Record, 38,* 473–482.

Hayes, S. C. (Ed.). (1989). *Rule-governed behavior: Cognition, contingencies, and instructional control*. New York: Plenum.

Hayes, S. C., & Hayes, L. J. (1989). The verbal action of the listener as a basis for rule-governace. In S. C. Hayes (Ed.), *Rule-governed behavior: Cognition, contingencies, and instructional control*. New York: Plenum.

Hayes, S. C., Munt, E. D., Korn, Z., Wulfert, E., Rosenfarb, I., & Zettle, R. D. (1988). The effect of feedback and self-reinforcement instructions on studying performance. *The Psychological Record, 36,* 27–37.

Hayes, S. C., Nelson, R. O., & Jarrett, R. B. (1987). The treatment utility of assessment. A functional approach to evaluating assessment quality. *American Psychologist, 42,* 963–974.

Hayes, S. C., Rosenfarb, I., Wulfert, E., Munt E. D., Korn, Z., & Zettle, R. D. (1985). Self-reinforcement effects: An artifact of social standard setting? *Journal of Applied Behavior Analysis, 18,* 201–214.

Hayes, S. C., & Wolf, M. (1984). Cues, consequences, and therapeutic talk: Effects of social context and coping statements on pain. *Behaviour Research and Therapy, 22,* 385–392.

Haynes, S. N. (1978). *Principles of behavioral assessment*. New York: Gardner Press.

Haynes, S. N., & Geddy, P. (1973). Suppression of psychotic hallucinations through time-out. *Behavior Therapy, 4,* 123–127.

Haynes, S. N., & Horn, W. F. (1982). Reactivity in behavioral observation: A review. *Behavioral Assessment, 4,* 369–385.

Haynes, S. N., & Wilson, C. C. (1979). *Behavioral assessment: Recent advances in concepts, methods, and outcomes*. San Francisco: Jossey-Bass.

Heal, I. W., Colson, L. E., & Gross, J. C. (1984). A true experiment evaluating adult skill training for severely mentally retarded secondary students. *American Journal of Mental Deficiency, 89,* 146–155.

Heffer, R. W., & Kelley, M. L. (1987). Mothers' acceptance of behavioral interventions for children: The influence of parent race and income. *Behavior Therapy, 18,* 153–163.

Heffernan, T., & Richards, C. S. (1981). Self-control of study behavior: Identification and evaluation of natural methods. *Journal of Counseling Psychology, 28,* 361–364.

Heiby, E. M. (1983). Toward the prediction of mood change. *Behavior Therapy, 14,* 110–115.

Heifetz, L. J. (1977). Behavioral training for parents of retarded children: Alternative formats based on instructional manuals. *American Journal of Mental disorders, 82,* 194–203.

Heins, E. D., Lloyd, J. W., & Hallahan, D. P. (1986). Cued and noncued self-recording of attention to task. *Behavior Modification, 10,* 235–254.

Heller, M. C., & White, M. A. (1975). Rates of teacher verbal approval and disapproval to higher and lower ability classes. *Journal of Educational Psychology, 67,* 796–800.

Heller, R. F., & Forgione, A. G. (1975). An evaluation of bruxism control: Massed negative practice and automated relaxation training. *Journal of Dental Research, 54,* 1120–1123.

Henderson, H. S., Jenson, W. R., & Erken, N. F. (1986). Using variable interval schedules to improve on-task behavior in the classroom. *Education and Treatment of Children, 9,* 250–263.

Hendrickson, J. M., Strain, P. S., Tremblay, A., & Shores, R. E. (1982). Interactions of behaviorally handicapped children: Functional effects of peer social initiations. *Behavior Modification, 6,* 323–353.

Herbert, E. W., & Baer, D. M. (1972). Training parents as behavior modifiers: Self-recording of contingent attention. *Journal of Applied Behavior Analysis, 5,* 139–149.

Heron, T. E., Heward, W. L., Cooke, N. L., & Hill, D. S. (1983). Evaluation of classwide peer tutoring systems: First graders teach other sight words. *Education and Treatment of Children, 6,* 137–152.

Herrnstein, R. J. (1964). Aperiodicity as a factor in choice. *Journal of the Experimental Analysis of Behavior, 7,* 179–182.

Herrnstein, R. J. (1970). On the law of effect. *Journal of the Experimental Analysis of Behavior, 13,* 243–266.

Herrnstein, R. J. (1989). IQ and falling birth rates. *The Atalantic Monthly, 263,* 73–79.

Hersen, M. H., & Barlow, P. H. (1976). *Single case experimental designs.* New York: Pergamon.

Heward, W. L., & Eachus, H. T. (1979). Acquisition of adjectives and adverbs in sentences written by hearing impaired and aphasic children. *Journal of Applied Behavior Analysis, 12,* 391–400.

Heward, W. L., Heron, T. E., Ellis, D. E., & Cooke, N. L. (1986). Teaching first grade peer tutors to use verbal praise on an intermittent schedule. *Education and Treatment of Children, 9,* 5–15.

Hewitt, F. M. (1965). Training speech to an autistic child through operant conditioning. *American Journal of Orthopsychiatry, 35,* 927–936.

Hicks, D. J. (1965). Imitation and retention of film-mediated aggressive peer and adult models. *Journal of Personality and Social Psychology, 2,* 97–100.

Higgins Hains, A., & Baer, D. M. (1989). Interaction effects in multielement designs: Inevitable, desirable, and ignorable. *Journal of Applied Behavior Analysis, 22,* 57–69.

Hineline, P. N. (1981). The several roles of stimuli in negative reinforcement. In P. Harzem and M. D. Zeiler (Eds.), *Predictability, correlation, and contiguity* (pp. 203–246). New York: Wiley.

Hineline, P. N. (1984). Aversive control: A separate domain? *Journal of the Experimental Analysis of Behavior, 42,* 495–509.

Hively, W. (1962). Programming stimuli in matching to sample. *Journal of the Experimental Analysis of Beahvior, 5,* 279–298.

Hobbs, S. A., & Forehand, R. (1975). Effects of differential release from timeout on children's deviant behavior. *Journal of Behavior Therapy and Experimental Psychiatry, 6,* 256–257.

Hobbs, S. A., Forehand, R., & Murray, R. G. (1978). Effects of various durations of timeout on noncompliant behavior of children. *Behavior Therapy, 9,* 652–656.

Hodgson, J. M. (1988). Teaching engineering design using computer workstations. *European Journal of Engineering Education, 13,* 213–221.

Hogan, W. A., & Johnson, D. P. (1985). Elimination of response cost in a token economy program and improvement in behavior of emotionally disturbed youth. *Behavior Therapy, 16,* 87–98.

Hoko, J. A., & LeBlanc, J. M. (1988). Stimulus equalization: Temporary reduction of stimulus complexity to facilitate discrimination learning. *Research in Developmental Disabilities, 9,* 255–275.

Holland, J. G., & Skinner, B. F. (1961). *The analysis of behavior.* New York: McGraw-Hill.

Hollandsworth, J. G., Galzeski, R. C., & Dressel M. E. (1978). Use of social-skills training in the treatment of extreme anxiety and deficient verbal skills in the job-interview setting. *Journal of Applied Behavior Analysis, 11,* 259–269.

Holz, W. C., & Azrin, N. H. (1961). Discriminative properties of punishment. *Journal of the Experimental Analysis of Behavior, 6,* 399–406.

Holz, W. C., Azrin, N. H., & Allyon, T. (1963). Elimination of behavior of mental patients by response produced extinction. *Journal of the Experimental Analysis of Behavior, 6,* 407–412.

Homer, A. L., & Peterson, L. (1980). Differential reinforcement of other behavior: A preferred response elimination procedure. *Behavior Therapy, 11,* 449–471.

Homme, L., Csanyi, A. P., Gonzales, M. A., & Rechs, J. R. (1970). *How to use contingency contracting in the classroom.* Champaign, IL: Research Press.

Homme, L. E., deBaca, P. C., Devine, J. V., Steinhorst, R., & Rickert, E. J. (1963). Use of the Premack Principle in controlling the behavior of nursery school children. *Journal of the Experimental Analysis of Behavior, 6,* 544–548.

Hoogeveen, F. R., Smeets, P. M., & Lancioni, G. E. (1989). Teaching moderately mentally retarded children basic reading skills. *Research in Developmental Disabilities, 10,* 1–18.

Hopkins, B. L. (1968). Effects of candy, social reinforcement, instructions, and reinforcement schedule leaning on the modification and maintenance of smiling. *Journal of Applied Behavior Analysis, 1,* 121–129.

Hopkins, B. L. (1987). Comments of the future of applied behavior analysis. *Journal of Applied Behavior Analysis, 20,* 339–346.

Hopkins, B. L., Connard, R. J., Dangel, R. F., Fitch, H. G., Smith, J. J., & Anger, W. K. (1986). Behavioral Technology for reducing occupational exposures to styrene. *Journal of Applied Behavior Analysis, 19,* 3–11.

Hopkins, B. L., Schutte, R. C., & Garton, K. L. (1971). The effects of access to a playroom on the rate and quality of printing and writing of first and second grade students. *Journal of Applied Behavior Analysis, 4,* 77–87.

Horner, R. D., & Baer, D. M. (1978). Multiple-probe technique: A variation of the multiple baseline. *Journal of Applied Behavior Analysis, 11,* 189–196.

Horner, R. D., & Budd, C. M. (1985). Acquisition of manual sign use: Collateral reduction of maladaptive behavior and factors limiting generalization. *Education and Training of the Mentally Retarded, 20,* 39–47.

Horner, R. D., & Keilitz, I. (1975). Training mentally retarded adolescents to brush their teeth. *Journal of Applied Behavior Analysis, 8,* 301–309.

Horton, S. B. (1987). Reduction of disruptive mealtime behavior by facial screening. A case study of a mentally retarded girl with long-term follow-up. *Behavior Modification, 11,* 53–64.

Hosford, R. E. (1980). Self-as-a-model: A cognitive social learning technique. *The Counseling Psychologist, 9,* 45–61.

Hosford, R. E., Moss, R. E., & Morrell, G. (1976). Developing law abiding behavior. The-self-as-a-model technique: Helping prison inmates change. In J. D. Krumboltz and C. E. Thoresen (Eds.) *Counseling methods.* (pp. 487–495). New York: Holt, Rinehart & Winston.

Howie, P. M., & Woods, C. L. (1982). Token reinforcement during the instatement and shaping of fluency in the treatment of stuttering. *Journal of Applied Behavior Analysis, 15,* 55–64.

Hughes, C. A., & Hendrickson, J. M. (1987). Self-monitoring with at-risk students in the regular class setting. *Education and Treatment of Children, 10,* 225–236.

Hutchinson, R. R. (1977). By-products of aversive control. In W. K. Honig & J. E. R. Staddon (Eds.), *Handbook of operant behavior,* Englewood Cliffs, NJ: Prentice Hall, 415–431.

Hutchinson, R. R. & Azrin, N. H. (1961). Conditioning of mental hospital patients to fixed-ratio schedules of reinforcement. *Journal of the Experimental Analysis of Behavior, 4,* 87–95.

Hutchinson, R. R., Azrin, N. H., & Hunt, G. M. (1968). Attack produced by intermittent reinforcement of a concurrent operant response. *Journal of the Experimental Analysis of Behavior, 11,* 489–495.

Hutt, C. (1975). Degrees of novelty and their effects on children's attention and preference. *British Journal of Psychology, 66,* 487–492.

Irvin, L. K., & Singer, G. S. (1984). *Human rights review manual.* Eugene, OR: Oregon Research Institute.

Irvin, L. K., & Singer, G. S. (1985). *Informed consent for intrusive behavioral treatments.* Eugene, OR: Oregon Research Institute.

Israel, A. C. (1978). Some thoughts on correspondence between saying and doing. *Journal of Applied Behavior Analysis, 11,* 271–276.

Israel, A. C., & Brown, M. S. (1977). Correspondence training, prior verbal training, and control of non-verbal behavior via control of verbal behavior. *Journal of Applied Behavior Analysis, 10,* 333–338.

Israel, A. C., & O'Leary, K. D. (1973). Developing correspondence between children's words and deeds. *Child Development, 44,* 575–581.

Iwata, B. A. (1987). Negative reinforcement in applied behavior analysis: An emerging technology. *Journal of Applied Behavior Analysis, 20,* 361–378.

Iwata, B. A., & Bailey, J. S. (1974). Reward versus cost token systems: An analysis of the effects on students and teachers. *Journal of Applied Behavior Analysis, 7,* 567–576.

Iwata, B. A., Dorsey, M. F., Slifer, K. J., Bauman, K. E., & Richman, G. S. (1982). Toward a functional analysis of self-injury. *Analysis and Intervention in Developmental Disabilities, 3,* 1–20.

Iwata, B. A., & Lorentzson, A. M. (1976). Operant control of seizure-like behavior in an institutionalized retarded adult. *Behavior Therapy, 7,* 247–251.

Iwata, B. A., Pace, G. M., Kalsher, M. J., Cowdery, G. E., & Cataldo, M. F. (1990). Experimental analysis and extinction of self-injurious escape behavior. *Journal of Applied Behavior Analysis, 23,* 11–27.

Jackson, A. (1974). Fostering a positive classroom atmosphere by teaching kids to reinforce kids. *The Learning Analyst Newsletter, 2,* 3.

Jackson, D. A., & Wallace, R. F. (1974). The modification and generalization of voice loudness in a fifteen-year-old retarded girl. *Journal of Applied Behavior Analysis, 7,* 461–471.

Jacob, R. G., Fortmann, S. P., Kraemer, H. C., Farquhar, J. W., & Agras, W. S. (1985). Combining behavioral treatment to reduce blood pressure. *Behavior Modification, 9,* 32–54.

Jacobs, H. E., Fairbanks, D., Poche, C. E., & Bailey, J. S. (1982). Multiple incentives in encouraging car pool formation on a university campus. *Journal of Applied Behavior Analysis, 15,* 141–149.

James, S. D., & Egel, A. L. (1986). A direct prompting strategy for increasing reciprocal interactions between handicapped and nonhandicapped siblings. *Journal of Applied Behavior Analysis, 19,* 173–186.

James, W. (1890). *The principles of psychology.* New York: Holt, Rinehart & Winston.

Jason, L. A. (1985). Using a token-actuated timer to reduce

television viewing. *Journal of Applied Behavior Analysis, 18,* 269–272.

Jenson, W. R. (1980). The individual point card: Incorporating fixed and variable ratio schedules of reinforcement. *Child Behavior Therapy, 2,* 65–67.

Jenson, W. R., Neville, M., Sloane, H. N., & Morgan, D. (1982). *Child & Family Behavior Therapy, 4,* 81–85.

Jenson, W. R., Rovner, L., Cameron, S., Petersen, B. P., & Kesler, J. (1985). Reduction of self-injurious behavior using a water mist: Initial response suppression and generalization. *Journal of Behavior Therapy and Experimental Psychiatry, 16,* 77–80.

Johnson, C. A., & Katz, R. C. (1973). Using parents as change agents for their children: A review. *Journal of Child Psychology and Psychiatry and Allied Disciplines, 14,* 181–200.

Johnson, D. W., & Johnson, R. T. (1975). *Learning together and alone: cooperation, competition, and individualization.* Englewood Cliffs, NJ: Prentice Hall.

Johnson, D. W., & Johnson, R. T. (1983). Effects of cooperative, competitive, and individualistic learning experience on social development. *Exceptional Children, 49,* 323–329.

Johnson, D. W., Johnson, R. T., Warring, D., & Maruyama, G. (1986). Different cooperative learning procedures and cross-handicap relationships. *Exceptional Children, 53,* 247–252.

Johnson, D. W., Maruyama, G., Johnson, R., Nelson, D., & Skon, L. (1981). Effects of cooperative, competitive, and individualistic goal structures on achievement: A meta-analysis. *Psychological Bulletin, 89,* 47–62.

Johnson, K. R., & Ruskin, R. S. (1977). *Behavior instruction: An instructive review.* Washington, D.C.: American Psychological Association.

Johnson, K., & Sulzer-Azaroff, B. (1977). *An experimental analysis of proctor prompting behavior in a personalized instruction course.* Paper presented at the meeting of the American Educational Research Association, New York.

Johnson, K. R., Sulzer-Azaroff, B., Dean, M., & Freyman, D. (1976, August). *An experimental analysis of proctor quiz scoring accuracy in personalized instruction courses.* Paper presented at the meeting of the American Psychological Association, Washington, D.C.

Johnson, M. S., & Bailey, J. S. (1977). The modification of leisure behavior in a half-way house for retarded women. *Journal of Applied Behavior Analysis, 10,* 273–282.

Johnson, S. M., & Bolstad, O. D. (1973). Methodological issues in naturalistic observation: Some problems and solutions for field research. In L. A. Hamerlynck, J. Handy & D. A. Mash (Eds.), *Behavior change: Methodology, concepts, and practice* (pp. 7–67). Champaign, IL: Research Press.

Johnson, S. M., & Bolstad, O. D. (1975). Reactivity to home observation: A comparison of audio recorded behavior with observers present or absent. *Journal of Applied Behavior Analysis, 8,* 181–185.

Johnson, S., & Brown, R. (1969). Producing behavior change in parents of disturbed children. *Journal of Child Psychology and Psychiatry, 10,* 107–121.

Johnston, J. M., & Pennypacker, H. S. (1980). *Strategies and tactics of human behavioral research,* Hillsdale, NJ: Lawrence Erlbaum Associates.

Jones, F. H., & Eimers, R. C. (1975). Role playing to train elementary teachers to use classroom management "skill package." *Journal of Applied Behavior Analysis, 8,* 421–433.

Jones, F. H., Fremouw, W., & Carples, S. (1977). Pyramid training of elementary school teachers to use a class-room management "skill package." *Journal of Applied Behavior Analysis, 10,* 239–253.

Jones, F. H., Simmons, J. Q., & Frankel, F. (1974). An extinction procedure for eliminating self-destructive behavior in a 9-year-old autistic girl. *Journal of Autism and Childhood Schizophrenia, 4,* 241–250.

Jones, R. T., & Kazdin, A. E. (1975). Programming response maintenance after withdrawing token reinforcement. *Behavior Therapy, 6,* 153–164.

Jones, R. T., Nelson, R. E., & Kazdin, A. E. (1977). The role of external variables in self-reinforcement. A review. *Behavior Modification, 1,* 147–178.

Jones, R. T., Ollendick, T. H., & Shinske, F. K. (1989). The role of behavioral versus cognitive variables in skill acquisition. *Behavior Therapy, 20,* 293–302.

Jones, R. T., Van Hasselt, V. B., & Sisson, L. A. (1984). Emergency fire-safety skills: A study with blind adolescents. *Behavior Modification, 8,* 59–78.

Kagan, N. (1972). *Influencing human interaction.* East Lansing: Michigan State University, Instructional Media Center.

Kagel, J., & Winkler, R. (1972). Behavioral economies: Areas of cooperative research between economies and applied behavior analysis. *Journal of Applied Behavior Analysis, 5,* 335–342.

Kale, R. J., Kaye, J. H., Whelan, P. A., & Hopkins, B. L. (1968). The effects of reinforcement on the modification, maintenance, and generalization of social responses of mental patients. *Journal of Applied Behavior Analysis, 1,* 307–314.

Kaloupek, D. G., Peterson, D. A., Boyd, T. L., & Levis D. J. (1981). The effects of exposure to a spatial ordered fear stimulus: A study of generalization of extinction effects. *Behavior Therapy, 12,* 130–137.

Kanareff, V., & Lanzetta, J. T. (1960). Effects of success-failure experiences, and probability of reinforcement upon acquisition and extinction of an imitative response. *Psychological Reports, 7,* 151–166.

Kapust, J. A., & Nelson, R. O. (1984). Effects of the rate and spatial separation of target behaviors on observer accuracy and interobserver agreement. *Behavioral Assessment, 6,* 253–262.

Karoly, P., & Dirks, M. J. (1977). Developing self-control in preschool children through correspondence training. *Behavior Therapy, 8,* 398–405.

Katz, R. C. (1973). A procedure for currently measuring elapsed time and response frequency. *Journal of Applied Behavior Analysis, 6,* 719–720.

Katz, R. C., & Singh, N. N. (1986). Comprehensive fire safety training for adult mentally retarded persons. *Journal of Mental Deficiency Research, 30,* 59–69.

Kaufman, A., Baron, A., & Kopp, R. E. (1966). Some effects of instructions on human operant behavior. *Psychonomic Monograph Supplements, 1,* 243–250.

Kazdin, A. E. (1972). Response Cost: The removal of conditioned reinforcers for therapeutic change. *Behavior Therapy, 3,* 533–546.

Kazdin, A. E. (1973a). The effect of vicarious reinforcement on attentive behavior in the classroom. *Journal of Applied Behavior Analysis, 6,* 71–78.

Kazdin, A. E. (1973b). A methodological and assessment considerations in evaluating reinforcement in applied settings. *Journal of Applied Behavior Analysis, 6,* 517–531.

Kazdin, A. E. (1973c). The effect of response cost and aversive stimulation in suppressing punished and nonpunished speech disfluencies. *Behavior Therapy, 4,* 73–82.

Kazdin, A. E. (1974a). Self-monitoring and behavior change. In M. J. Mahoney & C. E. Thoresen (Eds.), *Self-control: Power to the person* (pp. 218–246). Monterey: Brooks/Cole.

Kazdin, A. E. (1974b). Covert modeling, model similarity, and reduction of avoidance behavior. *Behavior Therapy, 5,* 325–340.

Kazdin, A. E. (1975). Recent advances in token economy research. In M. Hersen, R. M. Eisler, & P. M. Miller (Eds.), *Progress in behavior modification,* Vol. 1 (pp. 233–274). New York: Academic Press.

Kazdin, A. E. (1976). Statistical analyses for single-case experimental designs. In M. Hersen & D. H. Barlow (Eds.), *Single case experimental designs: Strategies for studying behavior change* (pp. 265–316). New York: Pergamon.

Kazdin, A. E. (1977). Assessing the clinical or applied significance of behavior change through social validation. *Behavior Modification, 1,* 427–452.

Kazdin, A. E. (1980a). Acceptability of alternative treatments for deviant child behavior. *Journal of Applied Behavior Analysis, 13,* 259–273.

Kazdin, A. E. (1980b). Acceptability of time-out from reinforcement procedures for disruptive child behavior. *Behavior Therapy, 11,* 329–344.

Kazdin, A. E. (1981). Acceptability of child treatment techniques: The influence of treatment efficacy and adverse side effects. *Behavior Therapy, 12,* 493–506.

Kazdin, A. E. (1984). Acceptability of aversive procedures and medication as treatment alternatives for deviant child behavior. *Journal of Abnormal Child Psychology, 2,* 289–302.

Kazdin, A. E., & Bootzin, R. R. (1972). The token economy: An evaluative review. *Journal of Applied Behavior Analysis, 5,* 343–372.

Kazdin, A. E., & Erickson, L. M. (1975). Developing responsiveness to instructions in severely and profoundly retarded residents. *Journal of Behavior Therapy and Experimental Psychiatry, 6,* 17–21.

Kazdin, A. E., French, N. H., & Sherick, R. B. (1981). Acceptability of alternative treatments for children: Evaluation of inpatient children, parents, and staff. *Journal of Consulting and Clinical Psychology, 49,* 900–907.

Kazdin, A. E., & Geesey, S. (1977). Simultaneous-treatment design comparison of the effects of earning reinforcers for one's peers versus for oneself. *Behavior Therapy, 8,* 682–693.

Kazdin, A. E., & Hartmann, D. P. (1978). The simultaneous treatment design. *Behavior Therapy, 9,* 912–922.

Kazdin, A. E., & Klock, J. (1973). The effect of nonverbal teacher approval on student attentive behavior. *Journal of Applied Behavior Analysis, 6,* 643–654.

Kazdin, A. E., & Mascitelli, S. (1980). The opportunity to earn oneself off a token system as a reinforcer for attentive behavior. *Behavior Therapy, 11,* 68–78.

Kazdin, A. E., & Polster, R. (1973). Intermittent token reinforcement and response maintenance in extinction. *Behavior Therapy, 4,* 386–392.

Kazdin, A. E., Silverman, N. A., & Sittler, J. L. (1975). The use of prompts to enhance vicarious effects of nonverbal approval. *Journal of Applied Behavior Analysis, 8,* 279–286.

Kazdin, A. E., & Wilson, G. T. (1978). *Evaluation of behavior therapy: Issues, evidence, and research strategies.* Cambridge: Ballinger.

Keirsey, D. W. (1965). *Transactional casework: A technology for inducing behavior change.* Paper presented at the meeting of the California Association of School Psychologists and Psychometrists, San Francisco.

Keller, F. S. (1968). Goodbye, teacher. . . . *Journal of Applied Behavior Analysis, 1,* 79–90.

Keller, F. S., & Schoenfeld, W. N. (1950). *Principles of psychology.* New York: Appleton.

Kelley, H. H. (1950). The warm-cold variable in first impressions of persons. *Journal of Personality, 18,* 431–439.

Kelly, J. F. (1969). Extinction induced aggression in humans. Unpublished master's thesis, Southern Illinois University.

Kendall, P. C., & Hollon, S. D. (Eds.). (1979). *Cognitive-behavioral interventions: Theory, research, and procedures.* NY: Academic Press.

Kendall, P. C., Nay, W. R., & Jeffers, J. (1975). Timeout duration and contrast effects: a systematic evaluation of a successive treatments design. *Behavior Therapy, 6,* 609–615.

Kennedy, D. A., & Thompson, I. (1967). Use of reinforcement technique with a first grade boy. *The Personnel and Guidance Journal, 46,* 366–370.

Kent, R. N., Kanowitz, J., O'Leary, K. D., & Cheiken, M. (1977). Observer reliability as a function of circumstances of assessment. *Journal of Applied Behavior Analysis, 10,* 317–324.

Kidd, T. A., & Sandargas, R. A. (1988). Positive and negative consequences in contingency contracts: Their relative effectiveness on arithmetic performance. *Education and Treatment of Children. 11,* 118–126.

Kincaid, M. S., & Weisberg, P. (1978). Alphabet letters as tokens: Training preschool children in letter recognition and labeling during a token exchange period. *Journal of Applied Behavior Analysis, 11,* 199.

King, G. R., & Logue, A. W. (1987). Choice in a self-control paradigm with human subjects: Effects of changeover delay duration. *Learning and Motivation, 18,* 421–438.

Kirby, F., & Shields, F. (1972). Modification of arithmetic response rate and attending behavior in a seventh grade student. *Journal of Applied Behavior Analysis, 5,* 79–84.

Kirby, K. C., & Holborn, S. W. (1986). Trained, generalized, and collateral behavior changes of preschool children receiving gross-motor skills training. *Journal of Applied Behavior Analysis, 19,* 283–288.

Kirby, K. C., Holborn, S. W., & Bushby, H. T. (1981). Word game bingo: A behavioral treatment package for improving textual responding to sight words. *Journal of Applied Behavior Analysis, 14,* 317–326.

Kirigin, K. A., Braukmann, C. J., Atwater, J. D., & Wolf, M. M. (1982). An evaluation of Teaching-Family (Achievement Place) group homes for juvenile offenders. *Journal of Applied Behavior Analysis, 15,* 1–16.

Kirsch, I., Wolpin, M., & Knutson, L. N. (1975). A comparison of *in vivo* methods for rapid reduction of "stage fright" in the college classroom: A field experiment. *Behavior Therapy, 6,* 165–171.

Kissel, R. C., Whitman, T. L., & Reid, D. H. (1983). An institutional staff training and self-management program for developing multiple self-care skills in severely/profoundly retarded individuals. *Journal of Applied Behavior Analysis, 16,* 395–415.

Kistner, J., Hammer, D., Wolfe, D., Rothblum, E., & Drabman, R. S. (1982). Teacher popularity and contrast effects in a classroom token economy. *Journal of Applied Behavior Analysis, 15,* 85–96.

Kleitsch, E. C., Whitman, T. L., & Santos, J. (1983). Increasing verbal interaction among elderly socially isolated mentally retarded adults: A group language training procedure. *Journal of Applied Behavior Analysis, 16,* 217–233.

Kluwin, T. N., & Moores, D. F. (1985). The effects of integration on the mathematics achievement of hearing impaired adolescents. *Exceptional Children, 52,* 153–160.

Knight, M. F., & McKenzie, H. S. (1974). Elimination of bedtime thumbsucking in home setting through contingent reading. *Journal of Applied Behavior Analysis, 7,* 33–38.

Kniveton, B. H. (1986a). Peer models and classroom violence: An experimental study. *Educational Research, 28,* 111–116.

Kniveton, B. H. (1986b). Peer modelling of classroom violence and family structure: An experimental study. *Educational Studies, 12,* 87–94.

Koegel, R. L., Dunlap, G., & Dyer, K. (1980). Intertrial interval duration and learning in autistic children. *Journal of Applied Behavior Analysis, 13,* 91–99.

Koegel, R. L., Dyer, K., & Bell, L. K. (1987). The influence of child-preferred activities on autistic children's social behavior. *Journal of Applied Behavior Analysis, 20,* 243–252.

Koegel, R. L., & Rincover, A. (1976). Some detrimental effects of using extra stimuli to guide learning in normal and autistic children. *Journal of Abnormal Child Psychology, 4,* 59–71.

Koegel, R. L., & Rincover, A. (1977). Research on the difference between generalization and maintenance in extra-therapy responding. *Journal of Applied Behavior Analysis, 10,* 1–12.

Koegel, R. L., Schreibman, L., Britten, K., & Laitinen, R. (1979). The effects of schedule of reinforcement on stimulus overselectivity in autistic children. *Journal of Autism and Developmental Disorders, 9,* 383–397.

Kohlenberg, R. J. (1970). The punishment of persistent vomiting: A case study. *Journal of Applied Behavior Analysis, 3,* 241–245.

Kohlenberg, R., Phillips, T., & Proctor, W. (1976). A behavior analysis of peaking in residential electrical-energy consumers. *Journal of Applied Behavior Analysis, 9,* 13–18.

Kohler, F. W. (1986). *Classwide peer tutoring: Examining natural contingencies of peer reinforcement.* Doctoral Dissertation. Department of Human Development and Family Life, University of Kansas.

Kohler, F. W. (1987, May). *Peer-mediation in the integrated classroom: A presentation of research at the LEAP preschool.* Symposium presented at the Thirteenth Annual Convention of the Association for Behavior Analysis, Nashville, TN.

Kohler, F. W., & Fowler, S. A. (1985). Training prosocial behaviors to young children: An analysis of reciprocity with untrained peers. *Journal of Applied Behavior Analysis, 18,* 187–200.

Kohler, F. W., & Greenwood, C. R. (1986). Toward a technology of generalization: The identification of natural contingencies of reinforcement. *The Behavior Analyst, 9,* 19–26.

Kohler, F. W., Greenwood, C. R., & Baer, D. M. (1985). Assessing the peer tutoring process: The identification of natural communities of social reinforcement. Paper presented at the annual meetings of the Association for Behavior Analysis, Columbus, OH.

Komaki, J. (1982). Why we don't reinforce: The issues. *Journal of Organizational Behavior Management, 4,* 97–100.

Komaki, J. L., Desselles, M. L., & Bowman, E. D. (1988). Definitely not a breeze: Extending an operant model of effective supervision to teams. *Journal of Applied Psychology, 74,* 522–529.

Komaki, J., & Dore-Boyce, K. (1978). Self-recording: Its effects on individuals high and low in motivation. *Behavior Therapy, 9,* 65–72.

Konarski, E. A. Jr., Johnson, M. R., Crowell, C. R., & Whitman, T. L. (1980). Response deprivation and reinforcement in applied settings: A preliminary analysis. *Journal of Applied Behavior Analysis, 13,* 595–609.

Konarski, E. A. Jr., Johnson, M. R., Crowell, C. R., & Whitman, T. L. (1981). An alternative approach to reinforcement for applied researchers: Response deprivation. *Behavior Therapy, 12,* 653–666.

Konarski, E. A. Jr., Krowell, C. R., & Duggan, L. M. (1985). The use of response deprivation to increase the academic performance of EMR students. *Applied Research in Mental Retardation*, 6, 15–31.

Koorland, M. A., & Martin, M. B. (1975). *Principles and procedures of the standard behavior chart*. Gainesville, FL: Learning Environments.

Korchin, S. J., & Schuldberg, D. (1981). The future of clinical assessment. *American Psychologist*, 36, 1147–1158.

Kornhaber, R., & Schroeder, H. (1975). Importance of model similarity and extinction of avoidance behavior in children. *Journal of Clinical and Consulting Psychology*, 43, 601–607.

Krumboltz, J. D. (1966). *Revolution in counseling: Implications of behavioral science*. Boston: Houghton Mifflin.

Krumboltz, J. D., & Hosford, R. (1967). Behavioral counseling in the elementary school. *Elementary School Guidance and Counseling*, 1, 27–40.

Krumboltz, J. D., & Krumboltz, H. B. (1972). *Changing children's behavior*. Englewood Cliffs, NJ: Prentice-Hall.

Krumboltz, J. D., & Thoresen, C. E. (1964). The effects of behavioral counseling in groups and individual settings on information seeking behavior. *Journal of Counseling Psychology*, 11, 324–333.

Krumboltz, J. D., & Thoresen, C. E. (Eds.). (1969). *Behavioral counseling cases and techniques*. New York: Holt, Rinehart & Winston.

Kubany, E. S., & Sloggett, B. B. (1973). Coding procedure for teachers. *Journal of Applied Behavior Analysis*, 6, 339–344.

Lafleur, N. K., & Johnson, R. G. (1972). Separate effects of social modeling and reinforcement in counseling adolescents. *Journal of Counseling Psychology*, 19, 291–295.

Lagomarcino, A., Reid, D. H., Ivancic, M. T., & Faw, G. D. (1984). Leisure-dance instructions for severely and profoundly retarded persons: Teaching an intermediate community living skill. *Journal of Applied Behavior Analysis*, 17, 71–84.

Lahey, B. (1971). Modification of the frequency of descriptive adjectives in the speech of head start children through modeling without reinforcement. *Journal of Applied Behavior Analysis*, 4, 19–22.

Lahey, B. B., & Drabman, R. S. (1974). Facilitation of the acquisition and retention of sight-word vocabulary through token reinforcement. *Journal of Applied Behavior Analysis*, 7, 307–312.

Lahey, B. B., Gendrich, J. G., Gendrich, S. I., Schnelle, J. F., Gant, D. S., & McNees, M. P. (1977). An evaluation of daily report cards with minimal teacher and parent contacts as an efficient method of classroom intervention. *Behavior Modification*, 1, 381–394.

Lahey, B. B., McNees, M. P., & McNees, M. C. (1973). Control of an obscene "verbal tic" through timeout in an elementary school classroom. *Journal of Applied Behavior Analysis*, 6, 101–104.

Lamal, P. A. (1978). Reinforcement schedule and children's preference for working versus freeloading. *Psychological Reports*, 42, 143–149.

Lancioni, G. E., Smeets, P. M., & Oliva, D. (1987). Introducing

EMR children to arithmetical operations: A program involving pictorial problems and distinctive-feature prompts. *Research in Developmental Disabilities*, 8, 467–485.

Larzelere, R. E. (1986). Moderate spanking: Model or deterrent of children's aggression in the family? *Journal of Family Violence*, 1, 27–36.

Latham, G. P., & Baldes, J. J. (1975). The 'practical significance' of Locke's theory of goal setting. *Journal of Applied Psychology*, 60, 122–124.

Latham, G. P., & Dossett, D. L. (1978). Designing incentive plans for unionized employees: A comparison of continuous and variable ratio reinforcement schedules. *Personnel Psychology*, 3, 47–61.

Lavigna, G., & Donnellan, A. (1986). *Alternatives to punishment: Solving problems with non-aversive strategies*. New York: Irvington Publishers.

Lawler, E. E., III, & Hackman, J. R. (1969). Impact of employee participation in the development of pay incentive plans: A field experiment. *Journal of Applied Psychology*, 53, 467–471.

LeBlanc, J. M., & Ruggles, T. R. (1982). Instructional strategies for individual and group teaching. *Analysis and Intervention in Developmental Disabilities*, 2, 129–137.

Lehner, P. N. (1979). *Handbook of ethological methods*, New York: Garland STPM Press.

Leitenberg, H. (1973). The use of single case methodology in psychotherapy research. *Journal of Abnormal Psychology*, 82, 87–101.

Leitenberg, H., Burchard, J. D., Burchard, S. N., Fuller, E. J., & Lysaght, T. V. (1977). Using positive reinforcement to suppress behaviors: Some experimental comparisons with sibling conflict. *Behavior Therapy*, 8, 168–182.

LeLaurin, K., & Risley, T. R. (1972). The organization of daycare environments: "Zone" versus "man-to-man" staff assignments. *Journal of Applied Behavior Analysis*, 5, 225–232.

Lemanek, K. L., Williamson, D. A., Gresham, F. M., & Jensen, B. J. (1986). Social skills training with hearing-impaired children and adolescents. *Behavior Modification*, 10, 55–71.

Lennox, D. B., Miltenberger, R. G., & Donnelly, D. R. (1987). Response interruption and DRL for the reduction of rapid eating. *Journal of Applied Behavior Analysis*, 20, 279–284.

Levin, H., Glass, G., & Meister, G. (1984). *Cost-effectiveness of four educational interventions*. (Report No. 84-A11). Institute for Research in educational Finance and Governance (IFG), Stanford University, Stanford, CA.

Levy, E. A., McClinton, B. S., Rabinowitz, F. M., & Wolkin, J. R. (1974). Effects of vicarious consequences on imitation and recall: some developmental findings. *Journal of Experimental Child Psychology*, 17, 115–132.

Lewis, F. D., Nelson, J., Nelson, C., & Reusink, P. (1988). Effects of three feedback contingencies on the socially inappropriate talk of a brain-injured adult. *Behavior Therapy*, 19, 203–211.

Liberman, R. P., Teigen, J., Patterson, R., & Baker, V. (1973).

Reducing delusional speech in chronic, paranoid schizophrenics. *Journal of Applied Behavior Analysis, 6,* 57–64.

Liebert, R. B., & Poulos, R. W. (1973). *Educational psychology: A contemporary view.* Del Mar, CA: CRM Books.

Lifter, K., & Bloom, L. (1989). Object knowledge and the emergence of language. *Infant Behavior and Development, 12,* 395–413.

Lifter, K., Sulzer-Azaroff, B., Anderson, S. R., & Edwards, G. (1989, May). *Utility of teaching developmentally based play activities to children with developmental delays.* Paper presented at the 15th Annual Convention of the Association for Behavior Analysis. Milwaukee, WI.

Lindsley, O. R. (1968). A reliable wrist counter for recording behavior rates. *Journal of Applied Behavior Analysis, 1,* 77–78.

Ling, P. A., & Thomas, D. R. (1986). Imitation of television aggression among Maori and European boys and girls. *New Zealand Journal of Psychology, 15,* 47–53.

Lipinski, P., & Nelson, R. (1974). Problems in the use of naturalistic observation as a means of behavioral assessment. *Behavior Therapy, 5,* 341–351.

Lippman, L. G., & Meyer, M. E. (1967). Fixed-interval performance as related to instructions and to subject's verbalizations of the contingency. *Psychonomic Science, 8,* 135–136.

Litow, L., & Pumroy, D. K. (1975). A brief review of classroom group-oriented contingencies. *Journal of Applied Behavior Analysis, 8,* 341–347.

Lloyd, K. E., Garlington, W. K., Lowry, D., Burgess, H., Euler, H. A., & Knowlton, W. R. (1972). A note on some reinforcing properties of university lectures. *Journal of Applied Behavior Analysis, 5,* 151–155.

Loberg, D. E. (1980). *Department of developmental services standards for aversive or restrictive behavior intervention procedures.* Department of Developmental Services, Health & Welfare Agency, State of California.

Logue, A. W., Pena-Correal, T. E., Rodriguez, M. L., & Kabela E. (1986). Self-control in adult humans: Variation in positive reinforcer amount and delay. *Journal of the Experimental Analysis of Behavior, 46,* 159–173.

London, P. (1974, April). Behavior technology and social control—Turning the tables. *APA Monitor,* p. 2.

Long, E. R. (1962). Additional techniques for producing multiple- schedule control in children. *Journal of the Experimental Analysis of Behavior, 5,* 443–455.

Long, E. R. (1963). Chained and tandem scheduling with children. *Journal of the Experimental Analysis of Behavior, 6,* 459–472.

Long, J. D., & Williams, R. L. (1973). The comparative effectiveness of group and individually contingent free time with inner-city junior high school students. *Journal of Applied Behavior Analysis, 6,* 465–474.

Lovaas, O. I. (1964). Cue properties of words: The control of operant responding by rate and content of verbal operants. *Child Development, 35,* 245–246.

Lovaas, O. I., Berberich, J. P., Perloff, B. F., & Schaeffer, B. (1966). Acquisition of imitative speech in schizophrenic children. *Science, 151,* 705–707.

Lovaas, O. I., & Favell, J. E. (1987). Protection for clients undergoing aversive/restrictive interventions. *Education and Treatment of Children, 10,* 311–325.

Lovaas, O. I., Freitag, G., Gold, V. J., & Kassorla, I. C. (1965). Experimental studies in childhood schizophrenia: Analysis of self-destructive behavior. *Journal of Experimental Child Psychology, 2,* 67–84.

Lovaas, O. I., Litrownik, A., & Mann, R. (1971). Response latencies to auditory stimuli in autistic children engaged in self-stimulatory behavior. *Journal of Abnormal Psychology, 7,* 39–49.

Lovaas, O. I., Schreibman, L., Koegel, R. L., & Rehm, R. (1971). Selective responding by autistic children to multiple sensory input. *Journal of Abnormal Psychology, 77,* 211–222.

Lovitt, T. C. (1969). *Self-management projects with children.* Unpublished manuscript, University of Washington.

Lovitt, T. C., & Curtiss, K. (1969). Academic response rate as a function of teacher- and self-imposed contingencies. *Journal of Applied Behavior Analysis, 2,* 49–53.

Lowe, C. F., Beastay, A., & Bentall, R. P. (1983). The role of verbal behavior in human learning: Infant performance on fixed interval schedules. *Journal of the Experimental Analysis of Behavior, 39,* 157–164.

Lowe, C. F., Harzem, P., & Bagshaw, M. (1978). Species differences in temporal control of behavior II: Human performance. *Journal of the Experimental Analysis of Behavior, 29,* 351–361.

Lowe, K., & Lutzker, J. R. (1979). Increasing compliance to a medical regimen with a juvenile diabetic. *Behavior Therapy, 10,* 57–64.

Lowitz, G. H., & Suib, M. R. (1978). Generalized control of persistent thumbsucking by differential reinforcement of other behaviors. *Journal of Behavior Therapy & Experimental Psychiatry, 9,* 343–346.

Luce, S. C., Christian, W. P., Lipsker, L. E., & Hall, R. V. (1981). Response cost: A case for specificity. *The Behavior Analyst, 4,* 75–80.

Luce, S. C., Delquadri, J., & Hall, R. V. (1980). Contingent Exercise: A mild but powerful procedure for suppressing inappropriate verbal and aggressive behavior. *Journal of Applied Behavior Analysis, 13,* 583–594.

Luce, S. C., & Hall, R. V. (1981). Contingent exercise: A procedure used with differential reinforcement to reduce bizarre verbal behavior. *Education and Treatment of Children, 4,* 309–327.

Ludwig, D. J., & Maehr, M. L. (1967). Changes in self concept and stated behavioral preferences. *Child Development, 38,* 453–467.

Luiselli, J. K. (1980). Controlling disruptive behaviors of an autistic child: Parent-mediated contingency management in the home setting. *Education and Treatment of Children, 3,* 195–203.

Luiselli, J. K., & Donellon, S. (1980). Use of a visual stimulus fading procedure to teach color naming to an autistic child. *Journal of Behavior Therapy and Experimental Psychiatry, 11,* 73–76.

Luiselli, J. K., Helfen, C. S., Pemberton, B. W., & Reisman, J. (1977). The elimination of a child's in-class masturbation by overcorrection and reinforcement. *Journal of Behavior Therapy and Experimental Psychiatry, 8,* 201–204.

Luiselli, J. K., & Reisman, J. (1980). Some variations in the use of differential reinforcement procedures with mentally retarded children in specialized treatment settings. *Applied Research in Mental Retardation, 1,* 277–288.

Lutzker, J. R. (1978). Reducing self-injurious behavior by facial screening. *American Journal of Mental Deficiency, 82,* 510–513.

Lutzker, J. R., & Sherman, J. A. (1974). Producing generative sentence usage by imitation and reinforcement procedures. *Journal of Applied Behavior Analysis, 7,* 447–460.

Luyben, P. D. (1980). Effects of informational prompts on energy conservation in college classrooms. *Journal of Applied Behavior Analysis, 13,* 611–617.

Luyben, P. D., Funk, D. M., Morgan, J. K., Clark, K. A., & Delulio, D. W. (1986). Team sports for the severely retarded: Training a side-of-the-foot soccer pass using a maximum-to-minimum prompt reduction strategy. *Journal of Applied Behavior Analysis, 19,* 431–436.

Mace, F. C., Hock, M. L., Lalli, J. S., West, B. J., Belfiore, P., Pinter, E., & Brown, D. K. (1988). Behavioral momentum in the treatment of noncompliance. *Journal of Applied Behavior Analysis, 21,* 123–141.

Mace, F. C., & Kratochwill, T. R. (1985). Theories of reactivity in self-monitoring: A comparison of congitive-behavioral and operant models. *Behavior Modification, 9,* 323–343.

Mace, F. C., Page, T. J., Ivancic, M. T., & O'Brien, S. (1986). Effectiveness of brief time-out with and without contingent delay: A comparative analysis. *Journal of Applied Behavior Analysis, 19,* 79–86.

Mackay, H. A., & Sidman, M. (1984). Teaching new behavior via equivalence relations. In P. H. Brooks, R. Sperber, and C. McCauley (Eds.), *Learning and cognition in the mentally retarded* (pp. 293–513). Hillsdale, NJ: Lawrence Erlbaum Associates.

Madsen, C. H., Madsen, C. K., & Thompson, F. (1974). Increasing rural Head Start children's consumption of middle-class meals. *Journal of Applied Behavior Analysis, 7,* 257–262.

Mager, R. F. (1962). *Preparing instructional objectives.* Palo Alto: Fearon.

Mager, R. F. (1972). *Goal analysis.* Palo Alto: Fearon.

Maheady, L., & Harper, G. (1987). A classwide peer tutoring program to improve the spelling test performance of low-income, third- and fourth- grade students. *Education and Treatment of children, 10,* 120–133.

Maheady, L., Sacca, M. K., & Harper, G. F. (1988). Classwide peer tutoring with mildly handicapped high school students. *Exceptional Children, 55,* 52–59

Maheady, L., & Sainato, D. (1985). The effects of peer tutoring upon the social status and social interaction patterns of high and low status elementary students. *Education and Treatment of Children, 8,* 51–65.

Maher, C. A. (1981/1982). Performance feedback to improve the planning and evaluation of instructional programs. *Journal of Organizational Behavior Management, 3,* 33–40.

Maher, C. A. (1982). Improving teacher instructional behavior: Evaluation of a time management training program. *Journal of Organizational Behavior Management, 4,* 27–36.

Mahoney, K. (1974). Count on it: A simple self-monitoring device. *Behavior Therapy, 5,* 701–703.

Mahoney, M. J. (1974). *Cognition and behavior modification.* Cambridge, MA: Ballinger.

Maier, S. F., Seligman, M. E. P., & Solomon, R. L. (1969). Pavlovian fear conditioning and learned helplessness: Effects on escape and avoidance behavior of (a) the CS-US contingency and (b) the independence of the US and voluntary responding. In B. A. Campbell and R. M. Church (Eds.), *Punishment and aversive behavior.* New York: Appleton Century Crofts.

Maloney, K. B., & Hopkins, B. L. (1973). The modification of sentence structure and its relationship to subjective judgements of creativity in writing. *Journal of Applied Behavior Analysis, 6,* 425–433.

Malott, R. W., & Garcia, M. E. (1987). A goal-directed model for the design of human performance systems. *Journal of Organizational Behavior Management, 9,* 125–159.

Mandelker, A. B., Brigham, T. A., & Bushell, D. Jr. (1970). The effects of token procedures on a teacher's social contacts with her students. *Journal of Applied Behavior Analysis, 3,* 169–174.

Mann, P. H. (Ed.) (1975). *Mainstream special education: Issues and perspectives in urban centers.* (USOE Project No. CEG-0–72-3999 [609].) Reston, Va: Council for Exceptional Children.

Mann, R. A., & Baer, D. M. (1971). The effects of receptive language training on articulation. *Journal of Applied Behavior Analysis, 4,* 291–298.

Manos, M. J. (1983). Effects of verbal elaborations and social reinforcement on children's discrimination learning. *Education and Treatment of Children, 6,* 263–275.

Marholin, D., O'Toole, K. M., Touchette, P. E., Berger, P. L., & Doyle, D. A. (1979). "I'll have a Big Mac, large fries, large coke, and apple pie . . ." or teaching adaptive community skills. *Behavior Therapy, 10,* 236–248.

Marlatt, G. A., & Gordon, J. R. (Eds.). (1985). *Relapse prevention: Maintenance strategies in addictive behavior change.* New York: Guilford.

Marshall, H. H. (1965). The effect of punishment on children: A review of the literature and a suggested hypothesis. *The Journal of Genetic Psychology, 106,* 23–33,

Martin, J. A. (1974, August). *Children's task preferences: Effects of reinforcement and punishment.* Paper presented at the meeting of the American Psychological Association, New Orleans.

Martin, J. A. (1975). Generalizing the use of descriptive adjectives through modelling. *Journal of Applied Behavior Analysis, 8,* 203–209.

Martin, J. E., & Rusch, F. R. (1987). Use of the partial-withdrawal design to assess maintenance of mentally retarded adults' acquired meal preparation skills. *Research in Developmental Disabilities, 8,* 389–399.

Martin, J. E., Rusch, F. R., James, L., Decker, P. J., & Trtol, K. A. (1982). The use of picture cues to establish self-control in the preparation of complex meals by mentally retarded adults. *Applied Research in Mental Retardation, 3,* 105–119.

Martin, R. (1974). *Legal challenges to behavior modification.* Champaign, IL: Research Press.

Mash, E. J. (1987). Behavioral assessment of child and family disorders: Contemporary approaches. *Behavioral Assessment, 9,* 201–205.

Mash, E. J., & McElwee, J. D. (1974). Situational effects on observer accuracy: Behavioral predictability, prior experience, and complexity of coding categories. *Child Development, 45,* 367–377.

Mason, S. A., McGee, G. G., Farmer-Dougan, V., & Risley, T. R. (1989). A practical strategy for ongoing reinforcer assessment. *Journal of Applied Behavior Analysis, 22,* 171–179.

Mathews, B., Catania, A. C., & Shimoff, E. (1985). Effects of uninstructed verbal behavior on nonverbal responding: Contingency descriptions versus performance descriptions. *Journal of the Experimental Analysis of Behavior, 43,* 155–164.

Mathews, J. R., Friman, P. C., Barone, V. J., Ross, L. V., & Christophersen, E. R. (1987). Decreasing dangerous infant behaviors through parent instruction. *Journal of Applied Behavior Analysis, 20,* 165–169.

Matson, J. L. (1981). Use of independence training to teach shopping skills to mildly mentally retarded adults. *American Journal of Mental Deficiency, 86,* 178–183.

Matson, J. L., Horne, A. M., Ollendick, D. G., & Ollendick, T. H. (1979). Overcorrection: A further evaluation of restitution and positive practice. *Journal of Behavior Therapy and Experimental Psychiatry, 10,* 295–298.

Matson, J. L., Stephens, R. M., & Horne, A. M. (1978). Overcorrection and extinction-reinforcement as rapid methods of eliminating the disruptive behaviors of relatively normal children. *Behavioral Engineering, 4,* 89–94.

Matson, J. L., & Taras, M. E. (1989). A 20 year review of punishment and alternative methods to treat problem behaviors in developmentally delayed persons. *Research in Developmental Disabilities, 10,* 85–104.

Matthews, B. A., Shimoff, E., & Catania, A. C. (1987). Saying and doing: A contingency-space analysis. *Journal of Applied Behavior Analysis, 20,* 69–74.

Matthews, B. A., Shimoff, E., Catania, A. C., & Sagvolden, T. (1977). Uninstructed human responding: Sensitivity to ratio and interval contingencies. *Journal of Experimental Analysis of Behavior, 27,* 453–467.

Mausner, B. (1954). The effect of prior reinforcement in the interaction of observer pairs. *Journal of Abnormal and Social Psychology, 49,* 65–68.

Mausner, B., & Block, B. L. (1957). A study of the additivity of variables affecting social interaction. *Journal of Abnormal and Social Psychology, 54,* 250–256.

Mawhinney, B. T., Bostow, D. E., Laws, O. R., Blumenfeld, G. T., & Hopkins, B. L. (1971). A comparison of students' studying behavior produced by daily, weekly, and three-week testing schedules. *Journal of Applied Behavior Analysis, 4,* 257–264.

May, J. G., Risley, T. R., Twardosz, S., Friedman, P., Bijou, S., Wexler, D., et al. *Guidelines for the use of behavioral procedures in state programs for retarded persons.* NARC Monograph, *MR Research,* 1976, Arlington, TX.

Mayer, G. R., & Butterworth, T. (1979). A preventive approach to school violence and vandalism: An experimental study. *The Personnel and Guidance Journal, 57,* 436–441.

Mayer, G. R., & Butterworth, T. (1981). Evaluating a preventive approach to reducing school vandalism. *Phi Delta Kappan, 62,* 498–499.

Mayer, G. R., Butterworth, T., Nafpaktitis, M., & Sulzer-Azaroff, B. (1983). Preventing school vandalism and improving discipline: A three-year study. *Journal of Applied Behavior Analysis, 16,* 355–369.

Mayer, G. R., & Kahn, J. (1976). *A behavioral framework for group counseling with school children.* Unpublished manuscript. California State University at Los Angeles.

Mayer, G. R., Nafpaktitis, M., Butterworth, T., & Hollingsworth, P. (1987). A search for the elusive setting events of school vandalisms: A correlational study. *Education and Treatment of Children, 10,* 259–270.

Mayer, G. R., Rohen, T. H., & Whitley, A. D. (1969). Group counseling with children: A cognitive-behavioral approach. *Journal of Counseling Psychology, 16,* 142–149.

Mayer, G. R., & Sulzer-Azaroff, B. (1990). Interventions for vandalism. In G. Stoner, M. K. Shinn, & H. M. Walker (Eds.), *Interventions for achievement and behavior problems.* National Association of School Psychologists Monograph: Washington, D.C.

Mayhew, G., & Harris, F. (1979). Decreasing self-injurious behavior: Punishment with citric acid and reinforcement of alternative behavior. *Behavior Modification, 3,* 322–336.

McAfee, J. K. (1987). Classroom density and the aggressive behavior of handicapped children. *Education and Treatment of Children, 10,* 134–145.

McAllister, L. W., Stachowiak, J. G., Baer, D. M., & Conderman, L. (1969). The application of operant conditioning techniques in a secondary school classroom. *Journal of Applied Behavior Analysis, 2,* 277–285.

McCandless, B. R. (1967). *Children, behavior and development.* Hinsdale, IL: Dryden.

McCullagh, P. (1987). Model similarity effects on motor performance. *Journal of Sport Psychology, 9,* 249–260.

McDonnell, J. J. (1987). The effects of time delay and increasing prompt hierarchy strategies on the acquisition of purchasing skills by students with severe handicaps. *The Journal of the Association for Persons with Severe Handicaps, 12,* 227–236.

McDonnell, J., & Ferguson, B. (1989). A comparison of time delay and decreasing prompt hierarchy strategies in teaching banking skills to students with moderate handicaps. *Journal of Applied Behavior Analysis, 22*, 85–91.

McDonnell, J., & McFarland, S. (1988). A comparison of forward and concurrent chaining strategies in teaching laundromat skills to students with severe handicaps. *Research in Developmental Disabilities, 9*, 177–194.

McDowell, E. E. (1968). A programmed method of reading instruction for use with kindergarten children. *Psychological Record, 18*, 233–239.

McDowell, E. E., Nunn, L. K., & McCutcheon, B. A. (1969). Comparison of a programmed method of beginning reading instruction with the look-and-say method. *Psychological Record, 19*, 319–327.

McEvoy, M. A., & Brady, M. P. (1988). Contingent access to play materials as an academic motivator for autistic and behavior disordered children. *Education and Treatment of Children, 11*, 5–18.

McEvoy, M. A., Nordquist, V. M., Twardosz, S., Heckaman, K. A., Wehby, J. H., & Denny, R. K. (1988). Promoting autistic children's peer interaction in an integrated early childhood setting using affection activities. *Journal of Applied Behavior Analysis, 21*, 193–200.

McFall, R. M. (1970). Effects of self-monitoring on normal smoking behavior. *Journal of Consulting and Clinical Psychology, 35*, 135–142.

McGee, G. G., Almelda, M. C., Sulzer-Azaroff, B., & Feldman, R. S. (1990). *Increasing recipiccal interactions via peer-mediated teaching*. Unpublished manuscript, University of Massachusetts, Dept. of Psychology, Amherst.

McGee, G. G., Krantz, P. J., Mason, D., & McClannahan, L. E. (1983). A modified incidental-teaching procedure for autistic youth: Acquisition and generalization of receptive object labels. *Journal of Applied Behavior Analysis, 16*, 329–338.

McGee, G. G., Krantz, P.J., & McClannahan, L.E. (1985). The facilitative effects of incidental teaching on preposition use by autistic children. *Journal of Applied Behavior Analysis, 18*, 17–31.

McGonigle, J. J., Duncan, D. V., Cordisco, L., & Barrett, R. P. (1982). Visual screening: An alternative method for reducing stereotypic behavior. *Journal of Applied Behavior Analysis, 15*, 461–467.

McGookin, R., Mayer, G. R., Bibelheimer, M., Byrne, M. J., Thompson, L., Jackson, G. M. (1974). *Guidance objectives and learner success*. Fountain Valley School District, CA.

McGreevy, P. (1983). *Teaching and learning in plain English*. Kansas City, MO: Plain English Publications.

McKenzie, T. L., & Rushall, B. S. (1974). Effects of self-recording on attendance and performance in a competitive swimming training environment. *Journal of Applied Behavior Analysis, 7*, 199–206.

McLaughlin, T. F. (1981). An analysis of token reinforcement: A control group comparison with special education youth employing measures of clinical significance. *Child Behavior Therapy, 3*, 43–50.

McLaughlin, T. F., & Malaby, J. E. (1975a). Elementary school children as behavioral engineers. In E. Ramp & G. Semp (Eds.), *Behavior analysis: Areas of research and application* (pp. 319–328). Englewood Cliffs, NJ: Prentice-Hall.

McLaughlin, T. F., & Malaby, J. E. (1975b). The effects of various token reinforcement contingencies on assignment completion and accuracy during variable and fixed token exchange schedules. *Canadian Journal of Behavioral Science, 7*, 411–419.

McMahon, R. S. (1987). Some current issues in the behavioral assessment of conduct disordered children and their families. *Behavioral Assessment, 9*, 235–252.

McMorrow, M. J., Foxx, R. M., Faw, G. D., & Bittle, R. G. (1987). Cues-pause-point language training: Teaching echolalics functional use of their verbal labeling repertoires. *Journal of Applied Behavior Analysis, 20*, 11–22.

McReynolds, L. V. (1969). Application of timeout from positive reinforcement for increasing the efficiency of speech training. *Journal of Applied Behavior Analysis, 2*, 199–205.

McReynolds, W. T., & Church, A. (1973). Self-control, study skills development and counseling approaches to the improvement of study behavior. *Behaviour Research and Therapy, 11*, 233–235.

McSweeny, A. J. (1978). Effects of response cost on the behavior of a million persons: Charging for directory assistance in Cincinnati. *Journal of Applied Behavior Analysis, 11*, 47–51.

McSweeney, F. K. (1982). Positive and negative contrast as a function of component duration for key pecking and treadle pressing. *Journal of Experimental Analysis of Behavior, 37*, 281–293.

McSweeney, F. K. (1983). Positive behavioral contrast when pigeons press treadles during multiple schedules. *Journal of Experimental Analysis of Behavior, 39*, 149–156.

Meichenbaum, D. (1974). *Cognitive behavior modification*. Morristown, NJ: General Learning Press.

Meichenbaum, D. H., & Goodman, J. (1971). Training impulsive children to talk to themselves: A means of developing self-control. *Journal of Abnormal Psychology, 77*, 115–126.

Melin, L., & Gotestam, K. G. (1981). The effects of rearranging ward routines on communication and eating behaviors of psychogeriatric patients. *Journal of Applied Behavior Analysis, 14*, 47–51.

Merbaum, M. (1973). The modification of self-destructive behavior by a mother-therapist using aversive stimulation. *Behavior Therapy, 4*, 442–447.

Mercatoris, M., & Craighead, W. E. (1974). The effects of non-participant observation on teacher-pupil classroom behavior. *Journal of Educational Psychology, 66*, 512–519.

Michael, J. (1974). Statistical inference for individual organism research: Mixed blessing or curse? *Journal of Applied Behavior Analysis, 7*, 647–653.

Michael, J. (1980). On terms: The discriminative stimulus or S^D. *The Behavior Analyst, 3*, 47–49.

Michael, J. (1982). Distinguishing between discriminative and motivational functions of stimuli. *Journal of the Experimental Analysis of Behavior, 37,* 149–155.

Michael, J. (1985, March). *Stimulus change decrement.* Paper presented at the meeting of the Northern California Association of Behavior Analysis, San Mateo, CA.

Michelson, L., Dilorenzo, T. M., Calpin, J. P., & Williamson, D. A. (1981). Modifying excessive lunchroom noise: Omission training with audio feedback and group contingent reinforcement. *Behavior Modification, 5,* 553–564.

Millenson, J. R. (1967). *Principles of behavior analysis.* New York: Macmillan.

Miller, A. J., & Kratochwill, T. R. (1979). Reduction of frequent stomachache complaints by time out. *Behavior Therapy, 10,* 211–218.

Miller, L. K., & Feallock, R. A. (1975). A behavior system for group living. In E. Ramp & G. Semb (Eds.), *Behavior analysis: Areas of research and application* (pp. 73–96). Englewood Cliffs, NJ: Prentice-Hall.

Miltenberger, R. G., & Fuqua, R. W. (1981). Overcorrection: A review and critical analysis. *The Behavior Analyst, 4,* 123–141.

Miltenberger, R. G., & Fuqua, R. W. (1983). Effects of token reinforcement schedules on work rate: A case study. *American Journal on Mental Deficiency, 88,* 229–232.

Minkin, N., Braukmann, C. J., Minkin, B. L., Timbers, G. D., Timbers, B. J., Fixsen, D. L., Phillips, E. L., & Wolf, M. M. (1976). The social validation and training of conversational skills. *Journal of Applied Behavior Analysis, 9,* 127–139.

Mischel, W., & Grusec, J. E. (1966). Determinants of the rehearsal and transmission of neutral and aversive behaviors. *Journal of Personality and Social Psychology, 3,* 197–205.

Mithaug, D. E., & Wolfe, M. S. (1976). Employing task arrangements and verbal contingencies to promote verbalizations between retarded children. *Journal of Applied Behavior Analysis, 9,* 301–314.

Morales v. Turman. 364 F. Supp. 166 (E.D. Texas 1973).

Morris, E. K., & Redd, W. H. (1975). Children's performance and social preference for positive, negative, and mixed adult-child interactions. *Child Development, 46,* 525–531.

Morris, E. K., & Rosen, H. S. (1982). The role of interobserver reliability in the evaluation of graphed data. *Behavioral Assessment,* 387–399.

Morse, W. H., & Kelleher, R. T. (1977). Determinants of reinforcement and punishment. In W. K. Honig & J. E. R. Staddon (Eds.), *Handbook of operant behavior* (pp. 174–200). Englewood Cliffs, NJ: Prentice Hall.

Moussorgsky (1874). *Boris Godonov.* Angle Records.

Muir, K. A., & Milan, M. A. (1982). Parent reinforcement for child achievement: The use of a lottery to maximize parent training effects. *Journal of Applied Behavior Analysis, 15,* 455–460.

Mulick, J., Hoyt, R., Rojahn, J., & Schroeder, S. (1978). Reduction of a "nervous habit" in a profoundly retarded youth by increasing toy play: A case study. *Journal of Behavior Therapy and Experimental Psychiatry, 9,* 381–385.

Mullins, M., & Rincover, A. (1985). Comparing autistic and normal children along the dimensions of reinforcement maximization, stimulus sampling, and responsiveness to extinction. *Journal of Experimental Child Psychology, 40,* 350–374.

Munger, G. F., Snell, M. E., & Loyd, B. H. (1989). A study of the effects of frequency of probe data collection and graph characteristics on teachers' visual analysis. *Research in Developmental Disabilities, 10,* 109–127.

Murdock, J. Y., Garcia, E. E., & Hardman, M. L. (1977). Generalizing articulation training with trainable mentally retarded subjects. *Journal of Applied Behavior Analysis, 10,* 717–733.

Murph, D., & McCormick, S. (1985). Evaluation of an instructional program designed to teach minimally literate juvenile delinquents to read road signs. *Education & Treatment of Children, 8,* 133–151.

Murphy, H. A., Hutchinson, J. M., & Bailey, J. S. (1983). Behavioral school psychology goes outdoors: The effect of organized games on playground aggression. *Journal of Applied Behavior Analysis, 16,* 29–36.

Murphy, R. J., Ruprecht, M., & Nunes, D. L. (1979). Elimination of self-injurious behavior in a profoundly retarded adolescent using intermittent time-out, restraint, and blindfold procedures. *AAESPH Review, 4,* 334–345.

Nation, J. R., & Boyajian, L. G. (1980). Continuous before partial reinforcement: Effect on persistence training and resistence to extinction in humans. *American Journal of Psychology, 93,* 697–710.

Nelson, C. M., & Rutherford, R. B. (1983). Timeout revisited: Guidelines for its use in special education. *Exceptional Education Quarterly, 3,* 56–67.

Nelson, G. L., & Cone, J. D. (1979). Multiple-baseline analysis of a token economy for psychiatric inpatients. *Journal of Applied Behavior Analysis, 12,* 255–271.

Nelson, R. O. (1983). Behavioral assessment: Past, present, and future. *Behavioral Assessment, 5,* 195–206.

Nelson, R. O., & Hayes, S. C. (1979). Some current dimensions of behavioral assessment. *Behavioral Assessment, 1,* 1–16.

Neville, K. G., & Shemberg, K. M. (1978). Establishing the use of color-noun combinations in the spontaneous speech of disadvantaged children. *Behavior Therapy, 9,* 235–242.

Nevin, J. A. (1988). Behavioral momentum and the partial reinforcement effect. *Psychological Bulletin, 103,* 44–56.

Newby, T. J., & Robinson, P. W. (1983). Effects of grouped and individual feedback and reinforcement on retail employee performances. *Journal of Organizational Behavior Management, 5,* 51–68.

Newsom, C., Favell, J., & Rincover, A. (1983). The side effects of punishment. In S. Axelrod & J. Apsche (Eds.), *The effects of punishment on human behavior* (pp. 285–316). New York: Academic Press.

New York State Association for the Retarded Children v. Rock-efeller, 357 F. Supp. (E.D. N.Y. 1973).

Nunes, D. L., Murphy, R. J., & Ruprecht, M. L. (1977). Reducing self-injurious behavior of severely retarded individuals through withdrawal of reinforcement procedures. *Behavior Modification, 1,* 499–516.

Nyborg, K. F., & Nevid, J. S. (1986). Couples who smoke: A comparison of couples training versus individual training for smoking cessation. *Behavior Therapy, 17,* 620–625.

O'Brien, F., Azrin, N. H., & Bugle, C. (1972). Training profoundly retarded children to stop crawling. *Journal of Applied Behavior Analysis, 2,* 131–137.

O'Brien, R. M., & Simek, T. C. (1978, August). *A comparison of behavioral and traditional methods of teaching golf.* Paper presented at the annual convention of the American Psychological Association, Toronto.

O'Conner, R. D. (1972). Relative efficacy of modeling, shaping, and the combined procedures for modification of social withdrawal. *Journal of Abnormal Psychology, 79,* 327–334.

Odom, S. L., Hoyson, M., Jamieson, B., & Strain, P. S. (1985). Increasing handicapped preschoolers' peer social interactions: Cross-setting and component analysis. *Journal of Applied Behavior Analysis, 18,* 3–16.

Odom, S. L., & Strain, P. S. (1986). A comparison of peer-initiation and teacher-antecedent interventions for promoting reciprocal social interaction of autistic preschoolers. *Journal of Applied Behavior Analysis, 19,* 59–71.

O'Leary, K. D., & Becker, W. C. (1967). Behavior modification of an adjustment class: A token reinforcement program. *Exceptional Children, 33,* 637–642.

O'Leary, K. D., Becker, W. C., Evans, M. B., & Saudargas, R. A. (1969). A token reinforcement program in a public school: A replication and systematic analysis. *Journal of Applied Behavior Analysis, 2,* 3–13.

O'Leary, K. D., Kaufman, K. F., Kass, R. E., & Drabman, R. (1970). The effect of loud and soft reprimands on the behavior of disruptive students. *Exceptional Children, 37,* 145–155.

O'Leary, K. D., & Kent, R. N. (1973). Behavior modification for social action: Research tactics and problems. In L. A. Hamerlynk, P. O. Davidson, and L. E. Acker (Eds.), *Critical issues in research and practice.* Champaign, IL: Research Press.

O'Leary, K. D., Kent, R. N., & Kanowitz, J. (1975). Shaping data collection congruent with experimental hypotheses. *Journal of Applied Behavior Analysis, 8,* 43–51.

Olenick, D. L., & Pear, J. J. (1980). Differential reinforcement of correct responses to probes and prompts in picture-name training with severely retarded children. *Journal of Applied Behavior Analysis, 13,* 77–89.

Oliver, S. D., West, R. C., & Sloane, H. N., Jr. (1974). Some effects on human behavior of aversive events. *Behavior Therapy, 5,* 481–493.

Ollendick, T. H., Dailey, D., & Shapiro, E. S. (1983). Vicarious reinforcement: Expected and unexpected effects. *Journal of Applied Behavior Analysis, 16,* 485–491.

Ollendick, T. H., Matson, J. L., Esveldt-Dawson, K., & Shap-

iro, E. S. (1980). Increasing spelling achievement: An analysis of treatment procedures utilizing an alternating treatments design. *Journal of Applied Behavior Analysis, 13,* 645–654.

Olson, R. L., & Roberts, M. W. (1987). Alternative treatments for sibling aggression. *Behavior Therapy, 18,* 243–250.

Ono, K. (1987). Superstitious behavior in humans. *Journal of the Experimental Analysis of Behavior, 47,* 261–271.

Ordione, G. S. (1965). *Management by objectives.* Belmont, CA: Fearon-Pitman Publishers.

Pace, G. M., Iwata, B. A., Edwards, G. L., & McCosh, K. C. (1986). Stimulus fading and transfer in the treatment of self-restraint and self-injurious behavior. *Journal of Applied Behavior Analysis, 19,* 381–389.

Paniagua, F., & Baer, D. M. (1982). The analysis of correspondence training as a chain reinforceable at any point. *Child Development, 53,* 786–798.

Panyan, M., Boozer, H., & Morris, N. (1970). Feeedback to attendants as a reinforcer for applying operant techniques. *Journal of Applied Behavior Analysis, 3,* 1–4.

Parke, R. D. (1969). Effectiveness of punishment as an interaction of intensity, timing, agent nurturance, and cognitive structuring. *Child Development, 40,* 213–235.

Parsons, J., & Davey, G. C. L. (1978). Imitation training with a 4-year old retarded person: The relative efficiency of time-out and extinction in conjunction with positive reinforcement. *Mental Retardation, 16,* 241–245.

Paschalis, A. P. (1987). Tokens and their economy: The greeks had a use for them. *Journal of Applied Behavior Analysis, 20,* 427.

Patterson, G. R. (1965). An application of conditioning techniques to the control of a hyperactive child. In L. P. Ullman & L. Krasner (Eds.), *Case studies in behavior modification* (pp. 370–375). New York: Holt, Rinehart & Winston.

Patterson, G. R. (1979). A performance theory for coercive family interaction. In R. B. Cairns (Ed.), *The analysis of social interactions: Methods, issues and illustrations* (pp. 119–163). Hillsdale, NJ: Lawrence Erlbaum.

Patterson, G. R. (1982). *Coercive family process.* Eugene OR: Castlia Publishing Company.

Patterson, G. R., & Gullian, M. E. (1968). *A guide for the professional for use with living with children: New methods for parents and teachers* (Rev. ed.). Champaign, IL: Research Press.

Patterson, G. R., Jones, R., Whittier, J., & Wright, M. A. (1965). A behavior modification technique for the hyperactive child. *Behavior Research and Therapy, 2,* 217–226.

Paul, G. L. (1966). *Insight vs. desensitization in psychotherapy.* Stanford: Stanford University Press.

Paul, G. L., & Lentz, R. J. (1977). *Psychological treatment for chronic mental patients: Milieu versus social-learning programs.* Massachusetts: Harvard Univ. Press. Pp. 528.

Paulus, P. B. (1980). *Psychology of group influence.* Hinsdale, NJ: Erlbaum.

Paulus, P. B., & Matthews, R. W. (1980). When density affects task performance. *Personality and Social Psychology Bulletin, 6,* 119–124.

Pavlov, I. P. (1927). *Conditioned reflexes: An investigation of the physiological activity of the cerebral cortex* (W. H. Grant, Trans.). London: Oxford University Press.

Pawlicki, R. E. & Morey, T. M. (1976). A low cost instrument for "thinning" self-directed schedules of reinforcement, *Behavior Therapy, 7,* 120–122.

Peck, C. A., Killen, C. C., & Baumgart, D. (1989). Increasing implementation of special education instruction in mainstream preschools: Direct and generalized effects of nondirective consultation. *Journal of Applied Behavior Analysis, 22,* 197–210.

Pendergrass, V. E. (1972). Timeout from positive reinforcement following persistent, high-rate behavior in retardates. *Journal of Applied Behavior Analysis, 5,* 85–91.

Perri, M. G., & Richards, C. S. (1977). An investigation of naturally occurring episodes of self-controlled behaviors. *Journal of Counseling Psychology, 24,* 178–183.

Perri, M. G., Richards, C. S., & Schultheis, K. R. (1977). Behavioral self-control and smoking reduction: A study of self-initiated attempts to reduce smoking. *Behavior Therapy, 8,* 360–365.

Perri, M. G., Shapiro, R. M., Ludwig, W. W., Twentyman, C. T., & McAdoo, W. G. (1984). Maintenance strategies for the treatment of obesity: An evaluation of relapse prevention training and posttreatment contact by mail and telephone. *Journal of Consulting and Clinical Psychology, 52,* 404–413.

Peters, T. J., & Austin, N. (1985). *A passion for excellence.* New York: Random House.

Peterson, L. (1984). The "safe at home" game: Training comprehensive prevention skills in latchkey children. *Behavior Modification, 8,* 474–494.

Peterson, L., Homer, A. L., & Wonderlich, S. A. (1982). The integrity of independent variables in behavior analysis. *Journal of Applied Behavior Analysis, 15,* 477–492.

Pfiffner, L. J., & O'Leary, S. G. (1987). The efficacy of all-positive management as a function of the prior use of negative consequences. *Journal of Applied Behavior Analysis, 20,* 265–271.

Phillips, E. L. (1968). Achievement Place: Token reinforcement procedures in a home-style rehabilitation setting for "pre-delinquent" boys. *Journal of Applied Behavior Analysis, 1,* 213–223.

Phillips, E. L., Phillips, E. A., Fixsen, D., & Wolf, M. M. (1971). Achievement place: Modification of behavior of pre-delinquent boys within a token economy. *Journal of Applied Behavior Analysis, 4,* 45–61.

Phillips, E. L., Phillips, E. A., Fixsen, D., & Wolf, M. M. (1972). *The teaching family handbook.* Lawrence: University of Kansas, Department of Human Development.

Phillips, E. L., Phillips, E. A., Wolf, M. M., & Fixsen, D. L. (1973). Achievement Place: Development of the elected manager system. *Journal of Applied Behavior Analysis, 6,* 541–561.

Pierce, C. H., & Risley, T. R. (1974). Recreation as a rein-

forcer: Increasing membership and decreasing disruptions in an urban recreation center. *Journal of Applied Behavior Analysis, 7,* 403–411.

Pigott, H. E., Fantuzzo, J. W., & Clement, P. W. (1986). The effects of reciprocal peer tutoring and group contingencies on the academic performance of elementary school children. *Journal of Applied Behavior Analysis, 19,* 93–98.

Pigott, H. E., Fantuzzo, J. W., Heggie, D. L., & Clement, P. W. (1984). A student-administered group-oriented contingency intervention: Its efficacy in a regular classroom. *Child and Family Behavior Therapy, 6,* 41–55.

Platt, J. S., Harris, J. W., & Clements, J. E. (1980). The effects of individually designed reinforcement schedules on attending and academic performance with behaviorally disordered adolescents. *Behavioral Disorders, 5,* 197–205.

Poche, C., Brouwer, R., & Swearingen, M. (1981). Teaching self-protection to young children. *Journal of Applied Behavior Analysis, 14,* 169–176.

Podsakoff, P. M. (1982). Effects of schedule changes on human performance: An empirical test of the contrasting predictions of the law of effect, the probability-differential model, and the response-deprivation approach. *Organizational Behavior and Human Performance, 29,* 322–351.

Polirstok, S. R., & Greer, R. D. (1977). Remediation of mutually aversive interactions between a problem student and four teachers by training the student in reinforcement techniques. *Journal of Applied Behavior Analysis, 10,* 707–716.

Polirstok, S. R., & Greer, R. D. (1986). A replication of collateral effects and a component analysis of a successful tutoring package for inner-city adolescents. *Education and Treatment of Children, 9,* 101–121.

Pollack, M. J., Fleming, R. K., & Sulzer-Azaroff, B. (1990, May). *Patterns of professional goal setting and achievement within a performance management system.* Paper presented at the International Association for Behavior Analysis, Nashville, TN.

Pollack, M. J., & Sulzer-Azaroff, B. (1981). Protecting the educational rights of the handicapped child. In J. Hanna, H. B. Clark, & W. P. Christian (Eds.), *Preservation of client rights* (pp.61–82). New York: The Free Press.

Polvinale, R. A., & Lutzker, J. R. (1980). Elimination of assaultive and inappropriate sexual behavior by reinforcement and social restitution. *Mental Retardation, 18,* 27–30.

Pomerleau, O. F. (1979). Behavioral medicine: The contribution of the experimental analysis of behavior to medical care. *American Psychologist, 34,* 654–663.

Pomerleau, O. F., & Pomerleau, C. S. (1984). Neuroregulators and the reinforcement of smoking: Towards a biobehavioral explanation. *Neuroscience and Biobehavioral Reviews, 8,* 503–513.

Pomerleau, O. F., & Rodin, J. (1986). Behavioral medicine and health psychology. In S. L. Garfield & A. E. Bergin (Eds.), *Handbook of psychotherapy and behavior change.* New York: Wiley.

Porterfield, J. K., Herbert-Jackson, E., & Risley, T. R. (1976).

Contingent observation: An effective and acceptable procedure for reducing disruptive behavior of young children in a group setting. *Journal of Applied Behavior Analysis, 9,* 55–64.

Powell, J., Martindale, A., & Kulp, S. (1975). An evaluation of time-sample measures of behavior. *Journal of Applied Behavior Analysis, 8,* 463–469.

Powell, L., Felce, D., Jenkins, J., & Lunt, B. (1979). Increasing engagement in a home for the elderly by providing an indoor gardening activity. *Behaviour Research and Therapy, 17,* 127–135.

Praderas, K., & MacDonald, M. L. (1986). Telephone conversational skills training with socially isolated, impaired nursing home residents. *Journal of Applied Behavior Analysis, 19,* 337–348.

Premack, D. (1959). Toward empirical behavior laws: I. Positive reinforcement. *Psychological Review, 66,* 219–233.

Pruitt, D. G. (1971). Choice shifts in group discussion: An introductory review. *Journal of Personality and Social Psychology, 20,* 339–360.

Quattrochi-Tubin, S., & Jason, L. A. (1980). Enhancing social interactions and activity among the elderly through stimulus control. *Journal of Applied Behavior Analysis, 13,* 159–163.

Ramey, G., & Sulzer-Azaroff, B. (1979, September). *Generalization effects of involving behaviorally disordered children as teachers.* Paper presented at the annual meeting of the American Psychological Association, New York.

Rapport, M. D., Murphy, H. A., & Bailey, J. S. (1982). Ritalin vs. response cost in the control of hyperactive children: A within-subject comparison. *Journal of Applied Behavior Analysis, 15,* 205–216.

Rauer, S. A., Cooke, T. P., & Apolloni, T. (1978). Developing nonretarded toddlers as verbal models for retarded classmates. *Child Study Journal, 8,* 1–8.

Ray, B. M. (1985). Measuring the social position of the mainstreamed handicapped child. *Exceptional Children, 52,* 57–62.

Redd, W. H. (1969). Effects of mixed reinforcement contingencies on adults' control of children's behavior. *Journal of Applied Behavior Analysis, 2,* 249–254.

Redd, W. H., Morris, E. K., & Martin, J. A. (1975). Effects of positive and negative adult-child interactions on children's social preference. *Journal of Experimental Child Psychology, 19,* 153–164.

Redmon. W. K., & Farris, H. E. (1987). Application of basic research to the treatment of children with autistic and severely handicapped repertoires. *Education and Treatment of Children, 10,* 326–337.

Redmon, W. K., & Lockwood, K. (1986). The matching law and organizational behavior. *Journal of Organizational Behavior Management, 8,* 57–72.

Reese, E. P. (1966). *The analysis of human operant behavior.* Dubuque, IA: Wm. C. Brown.

Reese, E. P. (1971). Skills training for the special child. Behavioral Films, 202 West St., Granby, MA, 01033.

Reese, E. P., Howard, J. S., & Reese, T. W. (1977). *Human behavior: An experimental analysis and its applications.* Dubuque, IA: Wm. C. Brown.

Reese, E. P., Howard, J., & Rosenberger, P. (August, 1974). *A comparison of three reinforcement procedures in assessing visual capacities of profoundly retarded individuals.* Paper presented at the meeting of the American Psychological Association, New Orleans.

Reese, E. P., & Werden, D. A. (1970). *A fading technique for teaching number concepts to severely retarded children.* Paper presented at the meeting of the Eastern Psychological Association, Atlantic City.

Reid, D. H., Parsons, M. B., McCarn, J. E., Green, C. W., Phillips, J. F., & Schepis, M. M. (1985). Providing a more appropriate education for severely handicapped persons: Increasing and validating functional classroom tasks. *Journal of Applied Behavior Analysis, 18,* 289–301.

Reid, J. B. (1970). Reliability assessment of observation data: A possible methodological problem. *Child Development, 41,* 1143–1150.

Reiser, R. A. (1984). Reducing student procrastination in a personalized system of instruction course. *Educational Communication & Technology Journal, 32,* 41–49.

Reitz, A. L. (1984). Teaching community skills to formerly institutionalized adults: Eating nutritionally balanced diets. *Analysis and Intervention in Developmental Disabilities, 4,* 229–312.

Remington, B., & Clarke, S. (1983). Acquisition of expressive signing by autistic children: An evaluation of the relative effects of simultaneous communication and sign-alone training. *Journal of Applied Behavior Analysis, 16,* 315–328.

Renne, C. M., & Creer, T. L. (1976). Training children with asthma to use inhalation therapy equipment. *Journal of Applied Behavior Analysis, 9,* 1–11.

Repp, A. C., Barton, L. E., & Brulle, A. R. (1983). A comparison of two procedures for programming the differential reinforcement of other behaviors. *Journal of Applied Behavior Analysis, 16,* 435–445.

Repp, A. C., & Dietz, S. M. (1974). Reducing aggressive and self-injurious behavior of institutionalized retarded children through reinforcement of other behaviors. *Journal of Applied Behavior Analysis, 7,* 313–325.

Repp, A. C., Felce, D., & Barton, L. E. (1988). Basing the treatment of stereotypic and self-injurious behaviors on hypotheses of their causes. *Journal of Applied Behavior Analysis, 21,* 281–289.

Repp, A. C., Harman, M. L., Felce, D., Van Acker, R., & Karsh, K. G. (1989). Conducting behavioral assessments on computer-collected data. *Behavioral Assessment, 11,* 249–268.

Resnick, L. B., & Ford, W. W. (1978). Analysis of tasks for instruction: An information processing approach. In A. C. Catania & T. A. Brigham (Eds.). *Handbook of applied behavior analysis: Social and instructional processes* (pp. 378–409). New York: Irvington Publishers.

Reynolds, G. S. (1961). Behavioral contrast. *Journal of the Experimental Analysis of Behavior, 4,* 57–71.

Reynolds, G. S. (1968). *A primer of operant conditioning.* Glenview, IL: Scott, Foresman.

Reynolds, J. (1973, August). *Aspects of child advocacy practice.* Paper presented for workshop symposium, Counseling and Advocacy, at the annual meeting of the American Psychological Association, Montreal.

Reynolds, N. J., & Risley, T. R. (1968). The role of social and material reinforcers in increasing talking of a disadvantaged preschool child. *Journal of Applied Behavior Analysis, 1,* 253–262.

Richards, B. F. (1987). Use of low-cost 3-D images in teaching gross anatomy. *Medical Teacher, 9,* 305–308.

Richards, C. S. (1981). Improving college students' study behaviors through self-control techniques: A brief review. *Behavioral Counseling Quarterly, 1,* 159–175.

Richardson, W. K., & Warzak, W. J. (1981). Stimulus stringing by pigeons. *Journal of the Experimental Analysis of Behavior, 36,* 267–276.

Rickard, H. C., Melvin, K. B., Creel, J., & Creel, L. (1973). The effects of bonus tokens upon productivity in a remedial classroom for behaviorally disturbed children. *Behavior Therapy, 4,* 378–385.

Rickert, V. I., Sottolano, D. C., Parrish, J. M., Riley, A. W., Hunt, F. M., & Pelco, L. E. (1988). Training parents to become better behavior managers. *Behavior Modification, 12,* 475–496.

Riddle, K. D., & Rapoport, J. L. (1976). A 2-year follow-up of 72 hyperactive boys. Classroom behavior and peer acceptance. *Journal of Nervous and Mental Disease, 162,* 126–134.

Ridley, L. L. (1986). Effects of self-recording on the maintenance of appropriate eating behaviors by a moderately retarded six-year-old boy. *Education and Treatment of Children, 9,* 232–238.

Rilling, M. (1977). Stimulus control and inhibitory processes. In W. K. Honig & J. E. R. Staddon (Eds.), *Handbook of operant behavior* (pp. 432–480). Englewood Cliffs, NJ: Prentice-Hall.

Riordan, M. M., Iwata, B. A., Finney, J. W., Wohl, M. K., & Stanley, A. E. (1984). Behavioral assessment and treatment of chronic food refusal in handicapped children. *Journal of Applied Behavior Analysis, 17,* 327–341.

Risley, R. R. (1975). Certify procedures not people. In S. Wood (Ed.), *Issues in evaluating behavior modification.* Champaign, IL: Research Press.

Risley, R. R., & Cataldo, M. F. (1973). *Planned activity check: Materials for training observers.* Lawrence, KS: Center for Applied Behavior Analysis.

Risley, R. R., & Cuvo, A. J. (1980). Training mentally retarded adults to make emergency phone calls. *Behavior Modification, 4,* 513–525.

Risley, R. R., & Sheldon-Wildgen, J. (1982). Invited peer review: The AABT experience. *Professional Psychology, 13,* 125–131.

Risley, R. R., & Twardosz, S. (January, 1974). *Florida guidelines for the use of behavioral procedures in state programs for the retarded.* Tallahasee: State of Florida Department of Health and Rehabilitation Services, Division of Retardation.

Risley, T. R. (1968). The effects and side effects of punishing the autistic behaviors of a deviant child. *Journal of Applied Behavior Analysis, 1,* 21–35.

Risley, T. R. (1970). Behavior modification: An experimental-therapeutic endeavor. In L. A. Hamerlynck, P. O. Davidson & L. E. Acker (Eds.), *Behavior Modification and Ideal Mental Health Services* (pp. 103–127). Calgary: University of Calgary Press.

Risley, T. R., & Hart, B. M. (1968). Developing correspondence between the nonverbal and verbal behvior of preschool children. *Journal of Applied Behavior Analysis, 1,* 267–281.

Risley, T. R., & Reynolds, N. J. (1970). Emphasis as a prompt for verbal imitation. *Journal of Applied Behavior Analysis, 3,* 185–190.

Roberts, M. W. (1984). An attempt to reduce timeout resistance in young children. *Behavior Therapy, 15,* 210–216.

Roberts, M. W. (1988). Enforcing chair timeouts with room timeouts. *Behavior Modification, 12,* 353–370.

Roberts, M. W., Halzenbuehler, L. C., & Bean, A. W. (1981). The effects of differential attention and time out on child noncompliance. *Behavior Therapy, 12,* 93–99.

Roberts, M. W., McMahon, R. J., Forehand, R., & Humphreys, L. (1978). The effect of parental instruction-giving on child compliance. *Behavior Therapy, 9,* 793–798.

Roberts, R. R., & Renzaglia, G. A. (1965). The influence of tape recording on counseling. *Journal of Counseling Psychology, 12,* 10–16.

Robertson, S. J., DeReus, D. M., & Drabman, R. S. (1976). Peer and college-student tutoring as reinforcement in a token economy. *Journal of Applied Behavior Analysis, 9,* 169–177.

Robinson, P. W., Newby, T. J., & Ganzell, S. L. (1981). A token system for a class of underachieving hyperactive children. *Journal of Applied Behavior Analysis, 14,* 307–315.

Roffers, T., Cooper, B. A. B., & Sultanoff, S. M. (1988). Can counselor trainees apply their skills in actual client interviews? *Journal of Counseling and Development, 66,* 385–388.

Rogers, R. W., Rogers, J. S., Bailey, J. S., Runkle, W., & Moore, B. (1988). Promoting safety belt use among state employees: The effects of promting and a stimulus-control intervention. *Journal of Applied Behavior Analysis, 21,* 263–269.

Rogers-Warren, A. K. (1984). Ecobehavioral analysis. *Education and Treatment of Children, 7,* 283–303.

Rogers-Warren, A. K., & Baer, D. M. (1976). Correspondence between saying and doing: Teaching children to share and praise. *Journal of Applied Behavior Analysis, 9,* 335–354.

Rogers-Warren, A. K., & Warren, S. F. (1977). The developing ecobehavioral psychology. In A. Rogers-Warren & S. F. Warren (Eds.), *Ecological perspective in behavior analysis* (pp. 3–8). Baltimore, MD: University Park Press.

Rogers-Warren, A. K., Warren, S. F., & Baer, D. M. (1977). A component analysis: Modeling, self-reporting, and reinforcement of self-reporting in the development of sharing. *Behavior Modification, 1*, 307–322.

Rojahn, J., McGonigle, J. J., Curcio, C., & Dixon, M. J. (1987). Suppression of pica by water mist and aromatic ammonia: A comparative analysis. *Behavior Modification, 11*, 65–74.

Rolider, A., & Van Houten, R. (1984). The effects of DRO alone and DRO plus reprimands on the undesirable behavior of three children in home settings. *Education and Treatment of Children, 7*, 17–31.

Rolider, A., & Van Houten, R. (1985a). Movement suppression time-out for undesirable behavior in psychotic and severely developmentally delayed children. *Journal of Applied Behavior Analysis, 18*, 275–288.

Rolider, A., & Van Houten, R. (1985b). Suppressing tantrum behavior in public places through the use of delayed punishment mediated by audio recording. *Behavior Therapy, 16*, 181–194.

Romanczyk, R. G., Kent, R. N., Diament, C., & O'Leary, D. O. (1973). Measuring the reliability of observational data. A reactive process. *Journal of Applied Behavior Analysis, 6*, 175–184.

Roos, P. (1972). Reconciling behavior modification procedures with the normalization principle. In W. Wolfensberger (Ed.), *The principle of normalization in human services*. Toronto: National Institute on Mental Retardation.

Rosekrans, M. A. (1967). Imitation in children as a function of perceived similarity to a social model and vicarious reinforcers. *Journal of Personality and Social Psychology, 7*, 307–315.

Rosen, H. S., & Rosen, L. A. (1983). Eliminating stealing: Use of stimulus control with an elementary student. *Behavior Modification, 7*, 56–63.

Rosen J. C., Saltzberg, E., & Srebnik, D. (1989). Cognitive behavior therapy for negative body image. *Behavior Therapy, 20*, 393–404.

Rosenbaum, M. E., Chalmers, D. K., & Horne, W. C. (1962). Effects of success and failure and the competence of the model on the acquisition and rehearsal of matching behavior. *Journal of Psychology, 54*, 251–258.

Rosenfarb, I. S., & Hayes, S. C. (1984). Social standard setting: The Achilles' heel of informational accounts of therapeutic change. *Behavior Therapy, 15*, 515–528.

Rosenfarb, I. S., Hayes, S. C., & Linehan, M. M. (in press). Instructions and experiential feedback in the treatment of social skills deficits in adults. *Psychotherapy: Theory, Research, and Practice*.

Rosenfeld, P., Lambert, N., & Black, A. (1985). Desk arrangement effects on people/classroom behavior. *Journal of Educational Psychology, 77*, 101–108.

Rosenshine, B., & Stevens, R. (1986). Teaching functions. In M. C. Wittrock (Ed.), *Handbook of research on teaching* (pp. 376–391). NY: Macmillan.

Rosenthal, T. L., & Bandura, A. (1978). Psychological modeling: Theory and practice. In S. L. Garfield & A. E. Bergin (Eds.), *Handbook of psychotherapy and behavior change* (pp. 621–658). New York: Wiley.

Rosenthal, T. L., & Downs, A. (1985). Cognitive aids in teaching and treating. *Advances in Behaviour Research and Therapy, 7*, 1–53.

Ross, A. O. (1977). *Learning disability: The unrealized potential*. New York: McGraw-Hill.

Ross, P. C. (1982). Training: Behavior change and the improvement of business performance. In L. W. Frederiksen (Ed.), *Handbook of organizational behavior management* (pp. 181–217). New York: Wiley.

Roth, D., Bielski, R., Jones, M., Parker, W., & Osborn, G. (1982). A comparison of self-control therapy and combined self-control therapy and antidepressant medication in the treatment of depression. *Behavior Therapy, 13*, 133–144.

Rotter, J. B. (1966). Generalized expectancies for internal versus external control of reinforcement. *Psychological Monographs, 80*, 1–28.

Rourke, D., Dorsey, M., Geren, M., Barry, G., & Kimball, J. (1990). *MAS: A failure to replicate*. Unpublished manuscript.

Rubin, B. K., & Stolz, S. B. (1974). Generalization of self-referent speech established in a retarded adolescent by operant procedures. *Behavior Therapy, 5*, 93–106.

Rusch, F. R., & Kazdin, A. E. (1981). Toward a methodology of withdrawal designs for the assessment of response maintenance. *Journal of Applied Behavior Analysis, 14*, 131–140.

Ruskin, R. S., & Maley, R. F. (1972). Item preference in a token economy ward store. *Journal of Applied Behavior Analysis, 5*, 373–378.

Russell, B. (1955). Science and human life. In J. R. Newman (Ed.), *What is science* (pp. 6–17). New York: Simon and Schuster

Rutter, M. (1978). Developmental issues and prognosis. In M. Rutter & E. Schopler (Eds.), *Autism: A reappraisal of concepts and treatment* (pp. 497–505). New York: Plenum.

Ryan, B. A. (1974). *PSI. Keller's personalized system of instruction: An appraisal*. American Psychological Association, Washington. D.C.

Sabornie, E. J. (1985). Social mainstreaming of handicapped students: Facing an unpleasant reality. *Remedial and Special Education, 6*(2), 12–16.

Sackett, G. (Ed.). (1978). *Observing behavior, Vol. 2, Data collection and analysis methods*. Baltimore: University Park Press.

Saigh, P. A., & Umar, A. M. (1983). The effects of a good behavior game on the disruptive behavior of Sudanese elementary school students. *Journal of Applied Behavior Analysis, 16*, 339–344.

Sainato, D. M., Maheady, L., & Shook, G. L. (1986). The effects of a classroom manager role on the social interaction patterns and social status of withdrawn kindergarten students. *Journal of Applied Behavior Analysis, 19*, 187–195.

Salend, S. J., & Sonnenschein, P. (1989). Validating the effectiveness of a cooperative learning strategy through direct observation. *Journal of School Psychology, 27*, 47–58.

Salmon, D. J., Pear, J. J., & Kuhn, B. A. (1986). Generalization of object naming after training with picture cards and with objects. *Journal of Applied Behavior Analysis, 19,* 53–58.

Sanders, M. R., & Parr J. M. (1989). Training developmentally disabled adults in independent meal preparation. *Behavior Modification, 13,* 168–191.

Sanders, R. M., Hopkins, B. W., & Walker, M. B. (1969). An inexpensive method for making data records of complex behaviors. *Journal of Applied Behavior Analysis, 2,* 221.

Sanok, R. L., & Striefel, S. (1979). Elective mutism: Generalization of verbal responding across people and settings. *Behavior Therapy, 10,* 357–371.

Sasso, G. M., & Rude, H. A. (1987). Unprogrammed effects of training high-status peers to interact with severely handicapped children. *Journal of Applied Behavior Analysis, 20,* 35–44.

Saudergas, R. W., Madsen, C. H., & Scott, J. W. (1977). Differential effects of fixed- and variable-time on production rates of elementary school children. *Journal of Applied Behavior Analysis, 10,* 673–678.

Sawin, D. B., & Parke, R. D. (1979). Inconsistent discipline of aggression in young boys. *Journal of experimental Child Psychology, 28,* 525–538.

Scarboro, M. E., & Forehand, R. (1975). Effects of two types of response-contingent time-out on compliance and oppositional behavior of children. *Journal of Experimental Child Psychology, 19,* 252–264.

Schaefer, H. H., & Martin, P. L. (1969). *Behavior therapy.* New York: McGraw-Hill.

Schaeffer, R. W. (1979). Human preferences for time-dependent and response-dependent reinforcement schedules. *Bulletin of the Psychonomic Society, 14,* 293–296.

Scheflen, K. C., Lawler, E. E., III, & Hackman, J. R. (1971). Long-term impact of employee participation in the development of pay incentive plans: A field experiment revisited. *Journal of Applied Psychology, 55,* 182–186.

Scheirer, M. A., & Kraut, R. E. (1979). Increasing educational achievement via self-concept change. *Review of Educational Research, 49,* 131–150.

Schepis, M. M., Reid, D. H., Fitzgerald, J. R., Faw, G. D., van den Pol, R. A., & Welty, P. A. (1982). A program for increasing manual signing by autistic and profoundly retarded youth within the daily environment. *Journal of Applied Behavior Analysis, 15,* 363–379.

Schilmoeller, G. L., Schilmoeller, K. J., Etzel, B. C., & LeBlanc, J. M. (1979). Conditional discrimination after errorless and trial-and-error training. *Journal of the Experimental Analysis of Behavior, 31,* 405–420.

Schilmoeller, K. J., & Etzel, B. C. (1977). An experimental analysis of criterion and non-criterion-related cues in "errorless" stimulus control procedures. In B. C. Etzel, J. M. LeBlanc, & D. M. Baer (Eds.), *New developments in behavioral research: Theory, method and application.* Hinsdale, NJ: Lawrence Erlbaum Associates.

Schinke, S.P., Gilchrist, L.D., Smith, T.E., & Wong, S.E.

(1979). Group interpersonal skills training in a natural setting: An experimental study. *Behaviour Research and Therapy, 17,* 149–154.

Schleien, S. J., Wehman, P., & Kiernan, J. (1981). Teaching leisure skills to severely handicapped adults: An age-appropriate darts game. *Journal of Applied Behavior Analysis, 14,* 513–519.

Schloss, C. N., Schloss, P. J., & Smith, M. A. (1988). Enhancement of employment interview skills using self-monitoring with communicatively impaired youths. *Education and Treatment of Children, 11,* 19–28.

Schmidt, G. W., & Ulrich, K. E. (1969). Effects of group contingent events upon classroom noise. *Journal of Applied Behavior Analysis, 2,* 171–179.

Schmidt, J. A. (1974). Research techniques for counselors: The multiple baseline. *The Personnel and Guidance Journal, 53,* 200–206.

Schnake, M. E. (1986). Vicarious punishment in a work setting *Journal of Applied Psychology, 71,* 343–345.

Schoen, S. F. (1986). Assistance procedures to facilitate the transfer of stimulus control: Review and analysis. *Education and Training of the Mentally Retarded, 21,* 62–74.

Schram, H., & Sulzer-Azaroff, B. (1972). *A "normal" peer as a language tutor for a language delayed child.* Unpublished paper, Southern Illinois University, Carbondale, IL.

Schreibman, L. (1975). Effects of within-stimulus and extra-stimulus prompting on discrimination learning in autistic children. *Journal of Applied Behavior Analysis, 8,* 91–112.

Schreibman, L., Koegel, R. L., & Craig, M. S. (1977). Reducing stimulus overselectivity in autistic children. *Journal of Abnormal Child Psychology, 5,* 425–436.

Schreibman, L., Koegel, R. L., Mills, J. I., & Burke, J. C. (1981). Social validation of behavior therapy with autistic children. *Behavior Therapy, 12,* 610–624.

Schumaker, J. B., Hovell, M. F., & Sherman, J. A. (1977a). An analysis of daily report cards and parent-managed privileges in the improvement of adolescents' classroom performance. *Journal of Applied Behavior Analysis, 10,* 449–464.

Schumaker, J. B., Hovell, M. F., & Sherman, J. A. (1977b). *Managing behavior. A home-based school achievement system.* Lawrence, KS: Excel Enterprises, Inc.

Schumaker, J., & Sherman, J. A. (1970). Training generative verb usage by imitation and reinforcement procedures. *Journal of Applied Behavior Analysis, 3,* 273–287.

Schunk, D. H. (1987). Peer models and children's behavioral change. *Review of Educational Research, 57,* 149–174.

Schuster, J. W., Gast, D. L., Wolery, M., & Guiltinan, S. (1988). The effectiveness of a constant time-delay procedure to teach chained responses to adolescents with mental retardation. *Journal of Applied Behavior Analysis, 21,* 169–178.

Schwartz, G. J. (1977). College students as contingency managers for adolescents in a program to develop reading skills. *Journal of Applied Behavior Analysis, 10,* 645–655.

Schweitzer, J. B., & Sulzer-Azaroff, B. (1988). Self control:

Teaching tolerance for delay in impulsive children. *Journal of the Experimental Analysis of Behavior, 50*, 173–186.

Schwitzgebel, R. K. (1971). *Development and legal regulation of coercive behavior modification techniques with offenders.* (Rockville, Md.: DHEW Publication, No. (HSM) 73–9015.

Scott, P. M., Burton, R. B., & Yarrow, M. R. (1967). Social reinforcement under natural conditions. *Child Development, 38*, 53–63.

Secan, K. E., & Egel, A. L. (1986). The effects of a negative practice procedure on the self-stimulatory behavior of developmentally disabled students. *Education and Treatment of Children, 9*, 30–39.

Seigel, F. S. (1988). *Let's stop fighting . . . Let's start playing.* St. Paul: Social Skills Press.

Siegel, G. M., Lenske, J., & Broen, P. (1969). Suppression of normal speech disfluencies through response cost. *Journal of Applied Behavior Analysis, 2*, 265–276.

Seligman, M. E. P. (1975). *Helplessness: On depression development and death.* San Francisco: Freeman.

Semb, G., Hopkins, B. L., & Hursh, D. E. (1973). The effects of study questions and grades on student test performance in a college course. *Journal of Applied Behavior Analysis, 6*, 631–642.

Seymour, F. W., & Stokes, T. F. (1976). Self-recording in training girls to increase work and evoke staff praise in an institution for offenders. *Journal of Applied Behavior Analysis, 9*, 41–54.

Shapiro, E. S., & Goldberg, R. (1986). A comparison of group contingencies for increasing spelling performance among sixth grade students. *School Psychology Review, 15*, 546–557.

Shapiro, E. S., & Klein, R. D. (1980). Self-management of classroom behavior with retarded/disturbed children. *Behavior Modification, 4*, 83–97.

Shapiro, E. S., & Lentz, F. E. (1985). A survey of school psychologists use of behavior modification procedures. *Journal of School Psychology, 23*, 327–336.

Shapiro, E. S., & Shapiro, S. (1985). Behavioral coaching in the development of skills in track. *Behavior Modification, 9*, 211–224.

Sharan, S. (1980). Cooperative learning in small groups: Recent methods and effects on achievement attitudes and ethnic relations. *Review of Educational Research, 50*, 241–271.

Sherman, T. M., & Cormier, W. H. (1974). An investigation of the influence of student behavior on teacher behavior. *Journal of Applied Behavior Analysis, 7*, 11–21.

Sherry v. N.Y. State Education Dept., 479f Supp. 1328 W.D., NY, 1979

Shimoff, E., Catania, A. C., & Matthews, B. A. (1981). Uninstructed human responding: Sensitivity of low-rate performance to schedule contingencies. *Journal of the Experimental Analysis of Behavior, 36*, 207–220.

Sidman, B. (1960). *Tactics of scientific research.* New York: Basic Books.

Sidman, M. (1953). Avoidance conditioning with brief shock and no exteroceptive warning signal. *Science, 18*, 157–158.

Sidman, M. (1969). Generalized gradients and stimulus control in delayed matching to sample. *Journal of the Experimental Analysis of Behavior, 12*, 745–757.

Sidman, M. (1971). The behavioral analysis of aphasia. *Journal of Psychiatric Research, 8*, 413–422.

Sidman, M. (1977). Teaching some basic prerequisites for reading. In P. Mittler (Ed.), *Research to practice in mental retardation: Vol. 2. Education and training* (pp. 353–360). Baltimore, MD: University Park Press.

Sidman, M. (1987). Two choices are not enough. *Behavior Analysis, 22*, 11–18.

Sidman, M. (1989). *Coercion and its fallout.* Boston: Authors Cooperative, Inc.

Sidman, M., & Cresson, O., Jr. (1973). Reading and cross-modal transfer of stimulus equivalences in severe retardation. *American Journal of Mental Deficiency, 77*, 515–523.

Sidman, M., Cresson, O., Jr., & Willson-Morris, M. (1974). Acquisition of matching to sample via mediated transfer. *Journal of the Experimental Analysis of Behavior, 22*, 261–273.

Sidman, M., Kirk, B., & Willson-Morris, M. (1985). Six-member stimulus classes generated by conditional-discrimination procedures. *Journal of the Experimental Analysis of Behavior, 43*, 21–42.

Sidman, M., & Stoddard, L. T. (1967). The effectiveness of fading in programming a simultaneous from discrimination for retarded children. *Journal of the Experimental Analysis of Behavior, 10*, 3–16.

Sidman, M., & Tailby, W. (1982). Conditional descrimination vs. matching to sample: An expansion of the testing paradigm. *Journal of the Experimental Analysis of Behavior, 37*, 5–22.

Sidman, M., Wynne, C. K., Maguire, R. W., & Barnes, T. (1989). Functional classes and equivalence relations. *Journal of the Experimental Analysis of Behavior, 52*, 261–274.

Siegel, G. M., Lenske, J., & Broen, P. (1969). Suppression of normal speech disfluencies through response cost. *Journal of Applied Behavior Analysis, 2*, 265–276.

Simon, S. J., Ayllon, T., & Milan, M. A. (1982). Behavioral compensation: Contrast-like effects in the classroom. *Behavior Modification, 6*, 407–420.

Singer, F. L., Pasnak, R., Drash, P. W., & Baer, R. (1978). Rapid reduction of lengthy pausing during vocal responding by nonverbal retarded children. *Behavior Therapy, 9*, 669–670.

Singer, G. S., & Irvin, L. K. (1987). Human rights review of intrusive behavioral treatments for students with severe handicaps. *Exceptional Children, 54*, 46–52.

Singh, N. N. (1980). The effects of facial screening on infant self-injury. *Journal of Behavior Therapy and Experimental Psychiatry, 11*, 131–134.

Singh, N. N. (1987). Overcorrection of oral reading errors. A comparison of individual and group-training formats. *Behavior Modification, 11*, 165–181.

Singh, N. N., Beale, I. L., & Dawson, M. J. (1981). Duration of facial screening and suppression of self-injurious behavior: Analysis using an alternating treatments design. *Behavioral Assessment, 3*, 411–420.

Singh, N. N., & Katz, R. C. (1985). On the modification of acceptability ratings for alternative child treatments. *Behavior Modification, 9*, 375–386.

Singh, N. N., & Millichamp, C. J. (1987). Independent and social play among profoundly mentally retarded adults: Training, maintenance, generalization, and long-term follow-up. *Journal of Applied Behavior Analysis, 20*, 23–34.

Singh, N. N., & Singh, J. (1984). Antecedent control of oral reading errors and self-corrections by mentally retarded children. *Journal of Applied Behavior Analysis, 17*, 111–119.

Singh, N. N., & Singh, J. (1986). Increasing oral reading proficiency. A comparative analysis of drill and positive practice overcorrection procedures. *Behavior Modification, 10*, 115–130.

Singh, N. N., Singh, J., & Winton, A. S. W. (1984). Positive practice overcorrection of oral reading errors. *Behavior Modification, 8*, 23–37.

Singh, N. N., Watson, J. E., & Winton, A. S. W. (1986). Treating self-injury: Water mist spray versus facial screening or forced arm exercise. *Journal of Applied Behavior Analysis, 19*, 403–410.

Singh, N. N., Winton, A. S., & Dawson, M. J. (1982). The suppression of antisocial behavior by facial screening using multiple baseline and alternating treatment designs. *Behavior Therapy, 13*, 511–520.

Siqueland, E. R., & Lipsitt, L. P. (1966). Conditioned head-turning in human newborns. *Journal of Experimental Child Psychology, 3*, 356–376.

Sisson, L. A., & Barrett, R. P. (1984). An alternating treatments comparison of oral and total communication training with minimally verbal retarded children. *Journal of Applied Behavior Analysis, 17*, 559–566.

Sisson, L. A., Kilwein, M. L., & Van Hasselt, V. B. (1988). A graduated guidance procedure for teaching self-dressing skills to multihandicapped children. *Research in Developmental Disabilities, 9*, 419–432.

Skidgell, A., & Bryant, R. (1975). *The Mansfield training program in dining skills*. Mansfield Depot, Conn.: Mansfield Training School, Psychology Department.

Skinner, B. F. (1938). *The behavior of organisms*. New York: Appleton.

Skinner, B. F. (1948). *Walden two*. New York: Macmillan.

Skinner, B. F. (1953). *Science and human behavior*. New York: Macmillan.

Skinner, B. F. (1957). *Verbal behavior*. New York: Appleton-Century-Crofts.

Skinner, B. F. (1958). Teaching machines. *Science, 128*, 969–977.

Skinner, B. F. (1961). *Cumulative record*. (Enl. ed.) New York: Appleton.

Skinner, B. F. (1966). Operant behavior. In W. K. Honig (Ed.), *Operant behavior: Areas of research and application* (pp. 12–32). New York: Appleton-Century-Crofts.

Skinner, B. F. (1968). *Technology of teaching*. New York: Appleton.

Skinner, B. F. (1969). *Contingencies of reinforcement: A theoretical analysis*. New York: Appleton-Century-Crofts.

Skinner, B. F. (1971). *Beyond freedom and dignity*. New York: Knopf.

Skinner, B. F. (1974). *About behaviorism*. New York: Knopf.

Skinner, B. F. (1983). *Notebooks*. Englewood Cliffs, NJ: Prentice Hall.

Skinner, B. F., & Krakower, S. A. (1968). *Handwriting with write and see*. Chicago: Lyons & Carnahan.

Skinner, B. F., & Vaughan, M. E. (1983). *Enjoy old age*. New York: W.W. Norton & Company.

Slavin, R. E., (1983). When does cooperative learning increase student achievement? *Psychological bulletin, 94*, 429–445.

Slavin, R. E., Madden, N. A., & Leavey, M. (1984). Effects of team assisted individualization on the mathematics achievement of academically handicapped and nonhandicapped students. *Journal of Educational Psychology, 76*, 813–819.

Smeets, P. M., Lancioni, G. E., & Striefel, S. (1987). Stimulus manipulation versus delayed feedback for teaching missing minuend problems to difficult-to-teach students. *Research in Developmental Disabilities, 8*, 261–282.

Smith, B. M., Schumaker, J. B., Schaeffer, J., & Sherman, J. A. (1982). Increasing participation and improving the quality of discussions in seventh-grade social studies classes. *Journal of Applied Behavior Analysis, 15*, 97–110.

Smith, E. V., & Mayer, G. R. (1978, September). The secret pal game: Students praising students. *The Guidance Clinic*, pp. 3–6.

Smith, L. K. C., & Fowler, S. A. (1984). Positive peer pressure: The effects of peer monitoring on children's disruptive behavior. *Journal of Applied Behavior Analysis, 17*, 213–227.

Smith, N. C. (1970). Replication studies: A neglected aspect of psychological research. *American Psychologist, 25*, 970–975.

Snell, M. E. (1982). Teaching bedmaking to severely retarded adults through time delay. *Analysis of Intervention in Developmental Disabilities, 2*, 139–155.

Snell, M. E., & Browder, D. M. (1986). Community-referenced instruction: Research and issues. *Journal of the Association for the Severely Handicapped, 11*, 1–11.

Snyder, G. (1989). "How do you reinforce a neurosurgeon?": Performance managing the medical profession. *Performance Management Magazine, 7*, 17–25.

Solnick, J. V., Rincover, A., & Peterson, C. R. (1977). Some determinates of the reinforcing and punishing effects of time-out. *Journal of Applied Behavior Analysis, 10*, 415–424.

Solomon, R, L. (1964). Punishment. *American Psychologist, 19*, 239–253.

Solomon, R. W., & Wahler, R. G. (1973). Peer reinforcement

control of classroom problem behavior. *Journal of Applied Behavior Analysis, 6*, 49–56.

Speidel, G. R., & Tharp, R. G. (1980). What does self-reinforcement reinforce: An empirical analysis of the contingencies in self-determined reinforcement. *Child Behavior Therapy, 2*, 1–22.

Speltz, M. L., Shimamura, J. W., & McReynolds, W. T. (1982). Procedural variations in group contingencies: Effects on children's academic and social behaviors. *Journal of Applied Behavior Analysis, 15*, 533–544.

Spetch, M. L., & Dunn, R. (1987). Choice between reliable and unreliable outcomes: Mixed percentage-reinforcement in concurrent chains. *Journal of the Experimental Analysis of Behavior, 47*, 57–72.

Spooner, F., Weber, L. H., & Spooner, D. (1983). The effects of backward chaining and total task presentation in the acquisition of complex tasks by severely retarded adolescents and adults. *Education and Treatment of Children, 6*, 401–420.

Spradlin, J. E., & Dixon, M. H. (1976). Establishing conditional discriminations without direct training. *American Journal of Mental Deficiency, 80*, 555–561.

Staats, A., Staats, C. K., Schutz, R. E., & Wolf, M. M. (1962). The conditioning of reading responses utilizing "extrinsic" reinforcers. *Journal of the Experimental Analysis of Behavior, 5*, 33–40.

Staines, J. W. (1958). The self-picture as a factor in the classroom. *British Journal of Educational Psychology, 28*, 97–111.

Stamps, L. W. (1973). The effects of intervention techniques on children's fear of failure behavior. *Journal of Genetic Psychology, 123*, 85–97.

Stansberry, P. (1973). The treasure box. *The Learning Analyst Newsletter, 1*, 4.

Statland, E., Zander, A., & Natsoulas, T. (1961). The generalization of interpersonal similarity. *Journal of Abnormal and Social Psychology, 62*, 250–256.

Stedry, A. C., & Kay, E. (1966). The effects of goal difficulty on performance: A field experiment. *Behavior Science, 11*, 459–470.

Steege, M. W., Wacker, D. P., & McMahon, C. M. (1987). Evaluation of the effectiveness and efficiency of two stimulus prompt strategies with severely handicapped students. *Journal of Applied Behavior Analysis, 20*, 293–299.

Steeves, J. M., Martin, G. L., & Pear, J. J. (1970). Self-imposed time-out by autistic children during an operant training program. *Behavior Therapy, 1*, 371–381.

Stein, N. (1980). Innoculation against learned helplessness. *Psychological Reports, 47*, 1143–1151.

Stephens, C. E., Pear, J. J., Wray, L. D., & Jackson, G. C. (1975). Some effects of reinforcement schedules in teaching picture names to retarded children. *Journal of Applied Behavior Analysis, 8*, 435–447.

Stephenson, G. R., & Roberts, T. W. (1977). The SSR System: A general encoding system with computerized transcription. *Behavior Research Methods & Instrumentation, 9*, 434–441.

Stern, G. W., Fowler, S. A., & Kohler, F. W. (1988). A comparison of two intervention roles: Peer monitor and point earner. *Journal of Applied behavior Analysis, 21*, 103–109.

Stevens-Long, J., & Rasmussen, M. (1974). The acquisition of simple and compound sentence structure in an autistic child. *Journal of Applied Behavior Analysis, 7*, 473–479.

Stevens-Long, J., Schwarz, J. L., & Bliss, D. (1976). The acquisition and generalization of compound sentence structure in an autistic child. *Behavior Therapy, 7*, 397–404.

Stevenson, H. C., & Fantuzzo, J. R. (1984). Application of the "Generalization Map" to a self-control intervention with school-aged children. *Journal of Applied Behavior Analysis, 17*, 203–212.

Stewart, C. A., & Singh, N. N. (1986). Overcorrection of spelling deficits in mentally retarded persons. *Behavior Modification, 10*, 355–365.

Stewart, N. R. (1969). Exploring and processing information about educational and vocational opportunities in groups. In J. D. Krumboltz & C. E. Thoresen (Ed.), *Behavioral counseling: Cases and techniques* (pp. 213–234). New York: Holt, Rinehart & Winston.

Stitzer, M. L., Rand, C. S., Bigelow, G. E., & Mead, A. M. (1986). Contingent payment procedures for smoking reduction and cessation. *Journal of Applied Behavior Analysis, 19*, 197–202.

Stokes, T. F., & Baer, D. M. (1976). Preschool peers as mutual generalization-facilitating agents. *Behavior Therapy, 7*, 549–556.

Stokes, T. F., & Baer, D. M (1977). An implicit technology of generalization. *Journal of Applied Behavior Analysis, 10*, 349–367.

Stokes, T. F., & Kennedy, S. H. (1980). Reducing child uncooperative behavior during dental treatment through modeling and reinforcement. *Journal of Applied Behavior Analysis, 13*, 41–49.

Stokes, T. F., & Osnes, P. G. (1989). An operant pursuit of generalization. *Behavior Therapy, 20*, 337–355.

Stolz, S. B. (1976). Ethics of social and educational interventions: Historical context and a behavior analysis. In T. A. Brigham & A. C. Catania (Eds.), *Analysis of behavior: Social and educational processes*. New York: Irving-Neiburg Wiley.

Stotland, E., & Hillmer, M. L., Jr. (1962). Identification, authoritarian defensiveness, and self-esteem. *Journal of Abnormal and Social Psychology, 64*, 334–342.

Stouthamer-Loeber, M., & Peters, R. D. (1984). A prior classification system of observation data: The eye of the beholder. *Behavioral Assessment, 6*, 275–282.

Strain, P. S. (1981). Modification of sociometric status and social interactions with mainstreamed mild developmentally disabled children. *Analysis and Intervention in Developmental Disabilities, 1*, 157–169.

Strain, P. S. (1983). Identification of social skill curriculum targets for severely handicapped children in mainstreamed preschools. *Applied Research in Mental Retardation, 4*, 369–382.

Strain, P. S., Cooke, T. P., & Apolloni, T. (1976). *Teaching exceptional children: Assessing and modifying social behavior.* New York: Academic.

Strain, P. S., & Fox, J. E. (1981). Peers as therapeutic agents for isolate classmates. In A. E. Kazdin (Eds.), *Advances in clinical child psychology* (Vol. 4, pp. 167–197). New York: Plenum.

Strain, P. S., Kerr, M. M., & Ragland, E. U. (1981). The use of peer social initiations in the treatment of social withdrawal. In P. Strain (Ed.), *The utilization of classroom peers as behavior change agents* (pp. 101–128). NY: Plenum.

Strain, P. S., Odom, S. L., & McConnell, S. (1984). Promoting social reciprocity of exceptional children: Identification, target behavior selection, and intervention. *Remedial and Special Education, 5,* 21–28.

Strang, H. R. (1988). A microcomputer-based laboratory experience to assist undergraduate students in learning basic concepts in human memory and retention. *Collegiate Microcomputer, 6,* 184–188.

Striefel, S., Bryan, K. S., & Aikins, D. A. (1974). Transfer of stimulus control from motor to verbal stimuli. *Journal of Applied Behavior Analysis, 7,* 123–135.

Striefel, S., & Owens, C. R. (1980). Transfer of stimulus control procedures: Applications to language acquisition training with the developmentally handicapped. *Behavior Research of Severe Developmental Disabilities, 1,* 307–331.

Striefel, S., & Wetherby, B. (1973). Instruction-following behavior of a retarded child and its controlling stimuli. *Journal of Applied Behavior Analysis, 6,* 663–670.

Stuart v. Nappi, 443 F. Supp. 1235, D. CT, 1978.

Sullivan Associates Program. (1965). *Programmed reading book.* C. D. Buchanan (Ed.), New York: McGraw-Hill.

Sulzer, B., Hunt, S., Ashby, E., Koniarski, C., & Krams, M. (1971). Increasing rate and percentage correct in reading and spelling in a class of slow readers by means of a token system. In E. A. Ramp & B. L. Hopkins (Eds.), *New directions in education: Behavior analysis* (pp. 5–28). Lawrence: University of Kansas, Department of Human Development.

Sulzer, B., Mayer, G. R., & Cody, J. J. (1968). Assisting teachers with managing classroom behavioral problems. *Elementary School Guidance and Counseling, 3,* 40–48.

Sulzer, E. (1962). Reinforcement and the therapeutic contract. *Journal of Counseling Psychology, 9,* 271–276.

Sulzer-Azaroff, B. (1982). Behavioral approaches to occupational safety and health. In L. Frederiksen (Ed.), *Handbook of organizational behavior management* (pp. 505–538). New York, Wiley.

Sulzer-Azaroff, B. (1985). Feedback and safety: Involving workers. Unpublished raw data.

Sulzer-Azaroff, B. (1987). The modification of occupational safety behavior. *The Journal of Occupational Accidents, 9,* 177–197.

Sulzer-Azaroff, B. (1989). *Job Safety: Broadscale replication in organizational settings.* Invited address. American Psychological Association Annual Convention. New Orleans.

Sulzer-Azaroff, B., Drabman, R. S., Greer, R. D., Hall, R. V., & O'Leary, K. D. (1988). *Behavior analysis in education.* Reprint series 3, by the Society for the Experimental Analysis of Behavior, Inc., Lawrence, KS.

Sulzer-Azaroff, B., & Fellner, D. J. (1984). Searching for performance targets in the behavior analysis of occupational safety: An assessment strategy. *Journal of Organizational Behavior Management, 6,* 53–65.

Sulzer-Azaroff, B., Fox, C., Moss, S. M., & Davis, J. M. (1990). Feedback and safety: Involving workers. Unpublished manuscript, University of Mass.

Sulzer-Azaroff, B., Hunt, S., & Loving, A. (1972, April). *Increasing rate and accuracy of academic performance through the application of naturally available reinforcers.* Paper presented at the meeting of the American Educational Research Association, Chicago.

Sulzer-Azaroff, B., Johnson, K., Dean, M., & Freyman, D. (1976, August). *Experimental analysis of proctor quiz scoring accuracy in personalized instruction.* Paper presented at the meeting of the American Psychological Association, Washington, D.C.

Sulzer-Azaroff, B., Loafman, B., Merante, R. J., & Hlavacek, A. C. (1990). Improving occupational safety in a large industrial plant: A systematic replication. *Journal of Organizational Behavior Management, 11,* 99–120.

Sulzer-Azaroff, B., & Mayer, G. R. (1972). *Behavior modification pprocedures for school personnel.* New York: Dryden Press.

Sulzer-Azaroff, B., & Mayer, G. R. (1977). *Applying behavior analysis procedures with children and youth.* New York: Holt, Rinehart & WInston.

Sulzer-Azaroff, B., & Mayer, G. R. (1986). *Achieving educational excellence using behavioral strategies.* New York: Holt, Rinehart & Winston.

Sulzer-Azaroff, B., & Reese, E.P. (1982). *Applying behavior analysis. A program for developing professional competence.* New York: Holt, Rinehart & Winston.

Sulzer-Azaroff, B., Thaw, J., & Thomas, C. (1975). Behavioral competencies for the evaluation of behavior modifiers. In S. Wood (Ed.), *Issues in evaluating behavior modification* (pp. 47–98). Champaign, IL: Research Press.

Sundberg, M. L. (1987). *Teaching language to the developmentally disabled: A course manual.* Prince George, B.C. College of New Caledonia.

Switzer, E. B., Deal, T. E., & Bailey, J. S. (1977). The reduction of stealing in second graders using a group contingency. *Journal of Applied Behavior Analysis, 10,* 267–272.

Szykula, S. A., Saudargas, R. A., & Wahler, R. G. (1981). The generality of self-control procedures following a change in the classroom teacher. *Education and Treatment of Children, 4,* 253–263.

S-1 v. Turlington, 635 F. 2nd 342, 1981.

Taber, J. I., Glaser, R., & Schaefer, H. (1965). *Learning and programmed instruction.* Reading, MA: Addison-Wesley.

Taggart, A. C., Taggart, J., & Siedentop, D. (1986). Effects of a home-based activity program: A study with low fitness elementary school children. *Behavior Modification, 10,* 487–507.

Tanner, B. A., & Zeiler, M. (1975). Punishment of self-injurious behavior using aromatic ammonia as the aversive stimulus. *Journal of Applied Behavior Analysis, 8,* 53–57.

Tate, B. G., & Baroff, G. S. (1966). Aversive conditioning of self-injurious behavior in a psychotic boy. *Behavior Research and Therapy, 4,* 281–287.

Tawney, J. W. (1972). Training letter discrimination in four-year-old children. *Journal of Applied Behavior Analysis, 5,* 455–465.

Terrace, H. S. (1963). Discriminative learning with and without errors. *Journal of Experimental Analysis of Behavior, 6,* 1–27.

Terrace, H. S. (1966). Stimulus control. In W. K. Honig (Ed.), *Operant behavior: Areas of research and application* (pp. 271–344). New York: Appleton.

Tharp, R. G., & Wetzel, R. J. (1969). *Behavior modification in the natural environment.* New York: Academic Press.

Theobald, D, E., & Paul, G. I. (1976). Reinforcing value of praise for chronic mental patients as a function of historical pairing with tangible reinforcers. *Behavior therapy, 7,* 192–197.

Thomas, C. M., Sulzer-Azaroff, B., Lukeris, S., & Palmer, M. (1977). Teaching daily self-help skills for "long-term" maintenance. In B. Etzel, J. LeBlanc, & D. Baer (Eds.), *New developments in behavioral research: Theory, method and application.* Hillsdale, NJ: Erlbaum Associates.

Thomas, D. R., Becker, W. C., & Armstrong, M. (1968). Production and elimination of disruptive classroom behavior by systematically varying teacher's behavior. *Journal of Applied Behavior Analysis, 1,* 35–45.

Thomas, D. R., Nielsen, L. J., Kuypers, D. S., & Becker, W. C. (1969). *Contributions of social reinforcement and remedial instruction in the elimination of a classroom behavior problem.* Unpublished manuscript, University of Illinois.

Thomas, G. V., Faulkner, H., & Bolt, E. G. (1988). Some effects of combining reinforcers in operant training with mentally handicapped persons. *Behavior Modification, 12,* 525–548.

Thomas, J. D. (1976). Accuracy of self-assessment of on-task behavior by elementary school children. *Journal of Applied Behavior Analysis, 9,* 209–210.

Thomas, J. H., Due, K. M., & Wigger, D. M. (1987). Effects of the competence and sex of peer models on children's imitative behavior. *Journal of Genetic Psychology, 148,* 325–332.

Thomas, J. K., Presland, I. E., Grant, M. D., & Glynn, T. (1978). Natural rates of teacher approval and disapproval in grade-7 classrooms. *Journal of Applied Behavior Analysis, 11,* 91–94.

Thompson, T. J., Braam, S. J., & Fuqua, R. W. (1982). Training and generalization of laundry skills: A multiple probe evaluation with handicapped persons. *Journal of Applied Behavior Analysis, 15,* 177–182.

Thoresen, C. E., & Anton, J. L. (1974). Intensive experimental research in counseling. *Journal of Counseling Psychology, 21,* 553–559.

Thoresen, C. E., & Mahoney, M. J. (1974). *Behavioral self-control.* New York: Holt, Rinehart & Winston.

Thorndike E. L. (1932). *The fundamentals of learning.* New York: Teachers College.

Thyer, B. A., & Geller, E. S. (1987). The "buckle-up" dashboard sticker: An effective environmental intervention for safety belt promotion. *Environment & Behavior, 19,* 484–494.

Timberlake, W., & Allison, J. (1974). Response deprivation: An empirical approach to instrumental performance. *Psychological Review, 81,* 146–164.

Tosi, D. J., Upshaw, K., Lande, A., & Waldron, M. A. (1971). Group counseling with nonverbalizing elementary students: Differential effects of Premack and social reinforcement techniques. *Journal of Counseling Psychology, 18,* 437–440.

Touchette, P. E. (1971). Transfer of stimulus control: Measuring the moment of transfer. *Journal of the Experimental Analysis of Behavior, 15,* 347–354.

Touchette, P. E., & Howard, J. S. (1984). Errorless learning: Reinforcement contingencies and stimulus control transfer in delayed prompting. *Journal of Applied Behavior Analysis, 17,* 175–188.

Touchette, P. E., MacDonald, R. F., & Langer, S. N. (1985). A scatter plot for identifying stimulus control of problem behavior. *Journal of Applied Behavior Analysis, 18,* 343–351.

Trent, J. T. (1983). Role of reinforcement and response cost in discrimination learning. *Psychological Reports, 53,* 207–211.

Troutner, J. (1988). Computers and writers: Software and other resources (instructional materials). *English Journal, 77,* 92–94.

Trovato, J., & Bucher, B. (1980). Peer tutoring with or without home-based reinforcement for reading remediation. *Journal of Applied Behavior Analysis, 13,* 129–141.

Truax, C. B. (1966). Reinforcement and nonreinforcement in Rogerian psychotherapy. *Journal of Abnormal Psychology, 71,* 1–9.

Trudel, G., Boisvert, J., Maruca, T., & Loroux, P. (1974). Unprogrammed reinforcement of patients behaviors in wards with and without token economy. *Behavior Therapy and Experimental Psychiatry, 5,* 147–149.

Tryon, W. W. (1982). A simplified time-series analysis for evaluating treatment interventions. *Journal of Applied Behavior Analysis, 15,* 423–429.

Tucci, V. (1987, May). *The competent learner model.* Paper presented at the annual meeting of the Association for Behavior Analysis, Nashville.

Tucker, D. J., & Berry, G. W. (1980). Teaching severely multihandicapped students to put on their own hearing aids. *Journal of Applied Behavior Analysis, 13,* 65–75.

Twardosz, S., & Baer, D. M. (1973). Training two severely retarded adolescents to ask questions. *Journal of Applied Behavior Analysis, 6,* 655–661.

Twardosz, S., Cataldo, M. F., & Risley, T. R. (1974). Open

environment design for infant and toddler day care. *Journal of Applied Behavior Analysis, 7,* 529–549.

Tyler, V. O., Jr. (Sept., 1965). *Exploring the use of operant techniques in the rehabilitation of delinquent boys.* Paper presented at the meeting of the American Psychological Association, Chicago.

Tyler, V. O., & Brown, G. D. (1967). The use of swift, brief isolation as a group control device for institutionalized delinquents. *Behavior Research and Therapy, 5,* 1–9.

Tyron, W. W. (1984). Principles and methods of mechanically measuring motor activity. *Behavioral Assessment, 6,* 129–139.

Ulman, J. D., & Sulzer-Azaroff, B. (1975). Multielement baseline design in educational research. In E. Ramp & G. Semb (Eds.), *Behavior analysis: Areas of research and application* (pp. 377–391). Englewood Cliffs, NJ: Prentice-Hall.

Ulrich, R. E., & Azrin, N. H. (1962). Reflexive fighting in response to aversive stimulation. *Journal of the Experimental Analysis of Behavior, 5,* 233–237.

Upper, D. (1973). A "ticket" system for reducing ward rules violations in a token economy program. *Behavior Therapy and Experimental Psychiatry, 4,* 137–140.

Upshur, C. (1982). Respite care for mentally retarded and other disabled populations: Program models and family needs. *Mental Retardation, 20,* 2–6.

U. S. Dept. of Health, Education and Welfare. (1971). *Institutional guide to DHEW policy on protection of human subjects.* Bethesda: Author. [DHEW Publication No. (NIH) 72–102].

Van den Pol, R. A., Iwata, B. A., Ivancic, M. T., Page, T. J., Neef, N. A., & Whitley, F. P. (1981). Teaching the handicapped to eat in public places: Acquisition, generalization and maintenance of restaurant skills. *Journal of Applied Behavior Analysis, 14,* 61–69.

Van Der Kooy, D., & Webster, C. D. (1975). A rapidly effective behavior modification program for an electively mute child. *Journal of Behavior Therapy and Experimental Psychiatry, 6,* 149–152.

Van Hasselt, V. B., Hersen, M., Egan, B. S., McKelvey, J. L., & Sisson, L. A. (1989). Increasing social interactions in deafblind severely handicapped young adults. *Behavior Modification, 13,* 257–272.

Van Houten, R. (1983). Punishment: From the animal laboratory to the applied setting. In S. Axelrod & J. Apsche (Eds.), *The effects of punishment on human behavior* (pp. 13–44). New York: Academic Press.

Van Houten, R. (1987). Comparing treatment techniques: A cautionary note. *Journal of Applied Behavior Analysis, 20,* 109–110.

Van Houten, R., Axelrod, S., Bailey, J. S., Favell, J. E., Foxx, R. M., Iwata, B. A., & Lovaas, O. I. (1988a). The right to effective behavioral treatment. *Journal of Applied Behavior Analysis, 21,* 381–384.

Van Houten, R., Axelrod, S., Bailey, J. S., Favell, J. E. Foxx, R. M., Iwata, B. A., & Lovaas, O. I. (1988b). The right to effective behavioral treatment. *The Behavior Analyst, 11,* 111–114.

Van Houten, R., & Doleys, D. M. (1983). Are social reprimands effective? In S. Axelrod & J. Apsche (Eds.), *The effects of punishment on human behavior* (pp. 45–70). New York: Academic Press.

Van Houten, R., & Nau, P. A. (1980). A comparison of the effects of fixed and variable ratio schedules of reinforcement on the behavior of deaf children. *Journal of Applied Behavior Analysis, 13,* 13–21.

Van Houten, R., Nau, P. A., MacKenzie-Keating, S. E., Sameoto, D., & Colavecchia, B. (1982). An analysis of some variables influencing the effectiveness of reprimands. *Journal of Applied Behavior Analysis, 15,* 65–83.

Van Houten, R., & Rolider, A. (1984). The use of response prevention to eliminate nocturnal thumbsucking. *Journal of Applied Behavior Analysis, 17,* 509–520.

Van Houten, R., & Rolider, A. (1988). Recreating the scene: An effective way to provide delayed punishment for inappropriate motor behavior. *Journal of Applied Behavior Analysis, 21,* 187–192.

Van Houten, R., & Van Houten, J. (1977). The performance feedback system in a special education classroom: An analysis of public posting and peer comments. *Behavior Therapy, 8,* 366–376.

Van Houten, V., Malenfant, L., & Rolider, A. (1985). Increasing driver yielding and pedestrian signaling with prompting, feedback, and enforcement. *Journal of Applied Behavior Analysis, 18,* 103–110.

Vargas, J. S. (1972). *Writing worthwhile behavioral objectives.* New York: Harper & Row.

Vasta, R., & Wortman, H. A. (1988). Nocturnal bruxism treated by massed negative practice: A case study. *Behavior Modification, 12,* 618–626.

Vaughan, M. E. (1985). Repeated acquisition in the analysis of rule-governed behavior. *Journal of the Experimental Analysis of Behavior, 44,* 175–184.

Voeltz, L. M., & Evans, I. M. (1983). Educational validity: Procedures to evaluate outcomes in programs for severely handicapped learners. *TASH Journal, 8,* 3–14.

Volpe, J. S., King, G. R., & Logue, A. W. (1988). *Choice in a self-control paradigm with human subjects: Effects of a distractor.* Paper presented at the Fourteenth Annual Convention of the Association for Behavior Analysis, Philadelphia, PA.

Von Brock, M. B., & Elliott, S. N. (1987). Influence of treatment effectiveness information on the acceptability of classroom interventions. *Journal of School Psychology, 25,* 131–144.

Vukelich, R., & Hake, D. F. (1971). Reduction of dangerously aggressive behavior in a severely retarded resident through a combination of positive reinforcement procedures. *Journal of Applied Behavior Analysis, 4,* 215–225.

Vyse, S., Mulick, J., & Thayer, B. (1984). An ecobehavioral assessment of a special education classroom. *Applied Research in Mental Retardation, 5,* 395–408.

Waas, G. A. (1987). Aggressive rejected children: Implications for school psychologists. *Journal of School Psychology, 25,* 383–388.

Wacker, D. P., Berg, W. K., Perrie, P., & Swatta, P. (1985). Generalization and maintenance of complex skills by severely handicapped adolescents following picture prompt training. *Journal of Applied Behavior Analysis, 18,* 329–336.

Wahler, R. G. (1969). Setting generality: Some specific and general effects of child behavior therapy. *Journal of Applied Behavior Analysis, 2,* 239–246.

Wahler, R. G. (1980). The insular mother: Her problems in parent-child treatment. *Journal of Applied Behavior Analysis, 13,* 207–219.

Wahler, R. G., & Fox, J. J. (1980). Solitary toy play and time out: A family treatment package for children with aggressive and oppositional behavior. *Journal of Applied Behavior Analysis, 13,* 23–39.

Wahler, R. G., & Fox, J. J. (1981). Setting events in applied behavior analysis: Toward a conceptual and methodological expansion. *Journal of Applied Behavior Analysis, 14,* 327–338.

Walder, L. O., Cohen, S. I., & Daston, P. G. (1967). *Teaching parents and others principles of behavior control for modifying the behavior of children* (Progress report No. 32-31-7515-5024). Washington, D.C.: U.S. Office of Education.

Walker, D. (1985). *Peer-mediated instruction between autistic students: Tutor training and tutor effectiveness.* Unpublished Masters Thesis, Department of Human Development and Family Life, University of Kansas.

Walker, H. M., & Buckley, N. K. (1972). Programming generalization and maintenance of treatment effects across time and settings. *Journal of Applied Behavior Analysis, 5,* 209–224.

Walker, H. M., & Buckley, N. K. (1975). *Token reinforcement techniques: Classroom application for the hard to teach child.* Champaign, IL: Research Press.

Walker, H. M., & Hops, H. (1979). The CLASS program for acting out children: R & D procedures, program outcomes and implementation issues. *School Psychology Digest, 8,* 370–381.

Walker, H. M., Hops, H., & Johnson, S. M. (1975). Generalization and maintenance of classroom treatment effects. *Behavior Therapy, 6,* 188–200.

Walker, H. M., Retana, G. F., & Gersten, R. (1988). Replication of the CLASS program in Costa Rica. *Behavior Modification, 12,* 133–154.

Wallach, M. A., Kogan, N., & Burt, R. B. (1967). Group risk taking and field dependence-independence of group members. *Sociometry, 30,* 323–338.

Wallander, J. L., Conger, A. J., & Conger, J. C. (1985). Development and evaluation of a behaviorally referenced rating system for heterosocial skills. *Behavioral Assessment, 7,* 137–153.

Walls, R. T., Haught, P., & Dowler, D. L. (1982). Moments of transfer of stimulus control in practical assembly tasks. *American Journal of Mental Deficiency, 87,* 309–315.

Walls, R. T., Zane, T., & Ellis, W. D. (1981). Forward and backward chaining, and whole task methods. *Behavior Modification, 5,* 61–74.

Walls, R. T., Zane, T., & Thvedt, J. E. (1980). Trainer's personal methods compared to two structured training strategies. *American Journal of Mental Deficiency, 84,* 495–507.

Walz, G. R., & Johnson, J. A. (1963). Counselors look at themselves on videotape. *Journal of Counseling Psychology, 10,* 232–236.

Warner, R. W., & Swisher, J. D. (1976). Drug-abuse prevention: Reinforcement of alternatives. In J. D. Krumboltz & C. E. Thoresen (Eds.), *Counseling methods* (pp. 510–517). New York: Holt, Rinehart & Winston.

Warren, S. & Rogers-Warren, A. (1983). A longitudinal analysis of language generalization among adolescents with severely handicapped conditions. *Journal of the Association for the Severely Handicapped, 8,* 18–32.

Watson, J. B. (1924). *Behaviorism.* New York: Norton.

Watson, J. B., & Rayner, R. (1920). Conditioned emotional reactions. *Journal of Experimental Psychology, 3,* 1–14.

Watson-Perczel, M., Lutzker, J. R., Green, B. F., & McGimpsey, B. J. (1988). Assessment and modification of home cleanliness among families adjudicated for child neglect. *Behavior Modification, 12,* 57–81.

Watt, M. E., Watt, A. (1987). A tape-based system of interactive video for computerized self-instruction. *Medical Teacher, 9,* 309–315.

Wattenberg, W. W., & Clifford, C. (1964). Relation of self-concepts to beginning achievement in reading. *Child Development, 35,* 461–467.

Webster, D., & Azrin, N. H. (1973). Required relaxation: A method of inhibiting agitative-disruptive behavior of retardates. *Behavior Research and Therapy, 11,* 67–78.

Wedel, J. W., & Fowler, S. A. (1984). "Read me a story, mom": A home-tutoring program to teach prereading skills to language-delayed children. *Behavior Modification, 8,* 245–266.

Weeks, M., & Gaylord-Ross, R. (1981). Task difficulty and aberrant behavior in severely handicapped students. *Journal of Applied Behavior Analysis, 14,* 449–463.

Weiner, H. (1964a). Response cost effects during extinction following fixed interval reinforcement with humans. *Journal of the Experimental Analysis of Behavior, 7,* 333–335.

Weiner, H. (1964b). Conditioning history and fixed-interval performance. *Journal of the Experimental Analysis of Behavior, 7,* 383–385.

Weiner, H. (1969). Controlling human fixed-interval's performance. *Journal of the Experimental Analysis of Behavior, 12,* 349–373.

Weiner, H. (1970). Human behavioral persistence. *Psychological Record, 20,* 445–456.

Weiner, H. (1979). Some observations on apathetic operant responding of chronic schizophrenics. *Perceptual and Motor Skills, 48,* 1083–1090.

Weiner, H. (1980). Response rates and choices of schizophrenics under fixed-ratio schedules of reinforcement. *Perceptual and Motor Skills, 51,* 1239–1243.

Weiner, H. (1981a). Effects of schedule information on the

slowed fixed ratio responding of schizophrenics. *Perceptual and Motor Skills, 52*, 452–454.

Weiner, H. (1981b). Increasing slowed operant responding of schizophrenics under a fixed-ratio schedule of reinforcement. *Perceptual and Motor Skills, 53*, 579–582.

Weiner, H. (1982). Histories of response omission and human operant behavior under a fixed-ratio schedule of reinforcement. *The Psychological Record, 32*, 409–434.

Weiner, H. (1983). Some thoughts on discrepant human-animal performances under schedules of reinforcement. *The Psychological Record, 33*, 521–532.

Weinrott, M. R., Garrett, B., & Todd, N. (1978). The influence of observer presence on classroom behavior. *Behavior Therapy, 9*, 900–911.

Weinstein, N. D., Grubb, P. D., & Vautier, J. S. (1986). Increasing automobile seat belt use: An intervention emphasizing risk susceptibility. *Journal of Applied Psychology, 71*, 285–290.

Weisberg, P., & Waldrop, P. B. (1972). Fixed interval work habits of Congress. *Journal of the Experimental Analysis of Behavior, 5*, 93–97.

Weiss, G., Kruger, E., Danielson, U., & Elman, M. (1975). Effect of long-term treatment of hyperactive children with methylphenidate. *Canadian Medical Association Journal, 112*, 159–165.

Welch, S. J., & Pear, J. J. (1980). Generalization of naming responses to objects in the natural environment as a function of training stimulus modality with retarded children. *Journal of Applied Behavior Analysis, 13*, 629–643.

Wells, K. C., Forehand, R., Hickey, K., & Green, K. D. (1977). Effects of a procedure derived from the overcorrection principle on manipulated and nonmanipulated behaviors. *Journal of Applied Behavior Analysis, 10*, 679–687.

Welsch v. Likins, 373 F. Supp. 487 (D. Minn., 1974).

Wendel, J. W., & Fowler, S. A. (1984). "Read me a story, mom": A home-tutoring program to teach prereading skills to language-delayed children. *Behavior Modification, 8*, 245–266.

Wepner, S. B., & Kramer, S. (1987). Organizing computers for reading instruction. *Computers in the Schools, 4*, 53–66.

West, R. R., & Sloane, H. N. (1986). Teacher presentation rate and point delivery rate: Effects on classroom disruption, performance accuracy, and response rate. *Behavior Modification, 10*, 267–286.

Wexler, D. B. (1973). Token and taboo: Behavior modification, token economies and the law. *California Law Review, 61*, 81–109.

Wexley, K. N., & Yukl, G. A. (1984). *Organizational behavior and personnel psychology* (rev. ed.). Homewood, IL: Richard D. Irwin, Inc.

Wheeler, A. H., & Fox, W. L. (1972). *Managing behavior, Part 5: A teacher's guide to writing instructional objectives.* Lawrence, KS: H and H Enterprises.

Wheeler, A. J., Miller, R. A., Springer, B. M., Poteet, N. K., Thornhill, C. A., & Myers, A. M. (1987). The Murdoch Center program library; 2nd Ed. Butner NC. Murdoch Center Foundation, Inc.

Wheeler, A.J., & Sulzer, B. (1970). Operant training and generalization of a verbal response form in a speech-deficient child. *Journal of Applied Behavior Analysis, 3*, 139–147.

White, G. D. (1973). *Effects of observer presence on mother child behavior.* Paper presented at the meeting of the Western Psychological Association, Anaheim, CA.

White, G. D., Nielsen, G., & Johnson, S. M. (1972). Timeout duration and the suppression of deviant behavior in children. *Journal of applied Behavior Analysis, 5*, 111–120.

White, M. A. (1975). Natural rates of teacher approval and disapproval in the classroom. *Journal of applied Behavior Analysis, 8*, 367–372.

White, O. R. (1971). *A glossary of behavioral terminology.* Champaign, IL: Research Press.

Whitehurst, G. J. (1971). Generalized labeling on the basis of structural response classes by two young children. *Journal of Experimental Child Psychology, 12*, 59–71.

Whorton, D., Walker, D., Locke, P., Delquadri, J., & Hall, R. V. (1987). *A comparison of one-to-one instruction by peers, one-to-one instruction by adults, and small group instruction with children with autism.* Juniper Gardens Children's Project, Bureau of Child Research, University of Kansas: Kansas City, KS.

Wiggins, J. S. (1973). *Personality and prediction: Principles of personality assessment.* Reading, MA: Addison-Wesley.

Wikoff, M., Anderson, D. C., & Crowell, C. R. (1982). Behavior management in a factory setting: Increasing work efficiency. *Journal of Organizational Behavior Management, 4*, 97–127.

Wilcox, J., Sbardellati, E., & Nevin, A. (1987). Cooperative learning groups aid integration. *Teaching Exceptional Children, 20*, 61–63.

Wilczenski, F. L., Sulzer-Azaroff, B., Feldman, R. S., & Fajardo, D. E. (1987). Feedback to teachers on student performance as a tool for effective mainstreaming. *Professional School Psychology, 2*, 161–172.

Williams, J. A., & Stokes, T. F. (1982). Some parameters of correspondence training and generalized verbal control. *Child and family Behavior Therapy, 4*, 11–312.

Willis, S. E., & Nelson, R. O. (1982). The effects of valence and nature of target behavior on the accuracy and reactivity of self-monitoring. *Behavioral Assessment, 4*, 401–412.

Wilson, C. C., Robertson, S. J., Herlong, L. H., & Haynes, S. N. (1979). Vicarious effects of time-out in the modification of aggression in the classroom. *Behavior Modification, 3*, 97–111.

Wilson, C. W., & Hopkins, B. L. (1973). The effects of contingent music on the intensity of noise in junior high home economics classes. *Journal of Applied Behavior Analysis, 6*, 269–275.

Wilson, F. E., & Evans, I. M. (1983). The reliability of target-behavior selection in behavior assessment. *Behavioral Assessment, 5*, 15–32.

Wilson, G. T., & O'Leary, K. D. (1980). *Principles of behavior therapy.* Englewood Cliffs, NJ: Prentice-Hall.

Wilson, P. G., Reid, D. H., Phillips, J. G., & Burgio, L. D. (1984). Normalization of institutional mealtimes for profoundly retarded persons: Effects and noneffects of teaching family-style dining. *Journal of Applied Behavior Analysis, 17,* 189–201.

Winett, R. A., & Winkler, R. C. (1972). Current behavior modification in the classroom: Be still, be quiet, be docile. *Journal of Applied Behavior Analysis, 5,* 499–504.

Wing, L. K. (1976). *Early childhood autism.* Oxford: Pergamon.

Winkler, R. C. (1970). Management of chronic psychiatric patients by a token reinforcement system. *Journal of Applied Behavior Analysis, 3,* 47–55.

Winkler, R. C. (1971). Reinforcement schedules for individual patients in a token economy. *Behavior Therapy, 2,* 534–537.

Winett, R. A., Kramer, K. D., Walker, W. B., Malone, S. W., & Lane, M. K. (1988). Modifying food purchases in supermarkets with modeling, feedback, and goal-setting procedures. *Journal of Applied Behavior Analysis, 21,* 73–80.

Winston, A. S., Singh, N. N., & Dawson, M. J. (1984). Effects of facial screening and blindfold on self-injurious behavior. *Applied Research in Mental Retardation, 5,* 29–42.

Wisocki, P. A. (1973). A covert reinforcement program for the treatment of test anxiety: Brief report. *Behavior Therapy, 4,* 264–266.

Witt, J. C., & Adams R. M. (1980). Direct and observed reinforcement in the classroom. *Behavior Modification, 4,* 321–336.

Wolf, M. M. (1978). Social validity: The case for subjective measurement, *or how applied behavior analysis is finding its heart. Journal of Applied Behavior Analysis, 11,* 203–214.

Wolf, M. M., Braukmann, C. J., & Ramp, K. A. (1987). Serious delinquent behavior as part of a significantly handicapping condition: Cures and supportive environments. *Journal of Applied Behavior Analysis, 20,* 347–359.

Wolf, M. M., Giles, D. K., & Hall, V. R. (1968). Experiments with token reinforcement in a remedial classroom. *Behavior Research and Therapy, 6,* 305–312.

Wolf, M. M., Risley, T. R., Johnson, M., Harris, F., & Allen, E. (1967). Application of operant conditioning procedures to the behavior problems of an autistic child, a follow-up extension. *Behaviour Research and Therapy, 5,* 103–112.

Wolf, M. M., Risley, T. R., & Mees, H. (1964). Application of operant conditioning procedures to the behavior problems of an autistic child. *Behavior Research and Therapy, 1,* 305–312.

Wolfe, J. A., Fantuzzo, J. W., & Wolfe, P. K. (1986). The effects of reciprocal peer management and group contingencies of the arithmetic proficiency of underachieving students. *Behavior Therapy, 17,* 253–265.

Wolfe, J. A., Fantuzzo, J., & Wolter, C. (1984). Student-administered group-oriented contingencies: A method of combining group-oriented contingencies and self-directed behavior to increase academic productivity. *Child & Family Behavior Therapy, 6,* 45–60.

Wolfe, V. V., Boyd, L. A., & Wolfe, D. A. (1983). Teaching cooperative play to behavior-problem preschool children. *Education and Treatment of Children, 6,* 1–9.

Wolter, C., Pigott, H. E., Fantuzzo, J. W., & Clement, P. W. (1984). Student-administered group-oriented contingencies: The application of self-regulation techniques in the context of a group to increase academic productivity. *Techniques: A Journal for Counseling and Remedial Education, 1,* 14–22.

Wong, S. E., Terranova, M. D., Bowen, L., Zarate, R., Massel, H. K., & Liberman, R. P. (1987). Providing independent recreational activities to reduce stereotypic vocalizations in chronic schizophrenics. *Journal of Applied Behavior Analysis, 20,* 77–81.

Wood, R., & Flynn, J. M. (1978). A self-evaluation token system versus an external evaluation token system alone in a residential setting with predelinquent youth. *Journal of Applied Behavior Analysis, 11,* 503–512.

Woodward, J., Carnine, D., & Collins, M. (1988). Closing the performance gap: CAI and secondary education for the mildly handicapped. *Journal of Educational Computing Research, 4,* 265–286.

Wright, L. (1973). Aversive conditioning of self induced seizures. *Behavior Therapy, 4,* 712–713.

Wulfert, E., & Hayes, S. C. (1988). The transfer of conditional control through conditional equivalence classes. *Journal of the Experimental Analysis of Behavior, 50,* 125–144.

Wyatt v. Stickney. (1972). 344 F. Supp. 373; 344 F. Supp. 387 (M.D. Alabama).

Yamamoto, J., & Mochizuki, A. (1988). Acquisition and functional analysis of manding with autistic students. *Journal of Applied Behavior Analysis, 21,* 57–64.

Yates, A. J. (1958). Symptoms and symptom substitution. *Psychological Review, 65,* 371–374.

Yates, B. T. (1985). Cost-effectiveness analysis and cost-benefit analysis: An introduction. *Behavioral Assessment, 7,* 207–234.

Young, C. C. (1981). Children as instructional agents for handicapped peers: A review and analysis. In P. Strain (Ed.), *The utilization of classroom peers as behavior change agents* (pp. 305–326). NY: Plenum.

Young, J. A., & Wincze, J. P. (1974). The effects of the reinforcement of compatible and incompatible alternative behaviors on the self-injurious and related behaviors of a profoundly retarded female adult. *Behavior Therapy, 5,* 614–623.

Young, K. R., & West, R. P. (1983, May). *Training elementary students to conduct therapy sessions with autistic children.* Paper presented at the Association for Behavior Analysis Ninth annual Convention, Milwaukee, WI.

Young, K. R., West, R. P., Howard, V. F., & Whitney, R. (1986). Acquisition, fluency training, generalization, and maintenance of dressing skills of two developmentally disabled children. *Education & Treatment of Children, 9,* 16–29.

Young, R. M., Bradley-Johnson, S., & Johnson, C. C., (1982). Immediate and direct reinforcement on WISC-R performance of retarded students. *Applied Research in Mental Retardation, 3,* 13–20.

Yukl, G. A., & Latham, G. P. (1975). Consequences of reinforcement schedules and incentive magnitudes for employee performance: Problems encountered in an industrial setting. *Journal of Applied Psychology, 60,* 294–298.

Yukl, G. A., Latham, G. P., Pursell, E. D. (1976). The effectiveness of performance incentives under continuous and variable ratio schedules of reinforcement. *Personnel Psychology, 29,* 221–231.

Yukl, G. A., Wexley, K. N., & Seymour, J. D. (1972). The effectiveness of pay incentives under variable ratio and continuous reinforcement schedules. *Journal of Applied Psychology, 56,* 19–23.

Zane, T., Walls, R. T., & Thvedt, J. E. (1981). Prompting and fading guidance procedures: Their effect on chaining and whole task teaching strategies. *Education and Training of the Mentally Retarded, 16,* 125–135.

Zegiob, L. E., Alford, G. S., & House, A. (1978). Response suppressive and generalization effects of facial screening on multiple self-injurious behavior in a retarded boy. *Behavior Therapy, 9,* 688.

Zegiob, L. E., Jenkins, J., Becker, J., & Bristow, A. (1976). Facial screening: Effects on appropriate and inappropriate behaviors. *Journal of Behavior Therapy and Experimental Psychiatry, 7,* 355–357.

Zeilberger, J., Sampen, S. E., & Sloane, H. N. (1968). Modification of a child's problem behaviors in the home with the mother as a therapist. *Journal of Applied Behavior Analysis, 1,* 47–54.

Zeiler, M. (1977). Schedules of reinforcement: The controlling variables. In W. K. Honig and J. E. R. Staddon (Eds.), *Handbook of operant behavior.* Englewood Cliffs, NJ: Prentice-Hall.

Zettle, R. D., & Hayes, S. C. (1982). Rule-governed behavior: A potential theoretical framework for congitive behavior therapy. In P. C. Kendall (Ed.), *Advances in congitive behavioral research and therapy (vol. 1)* (pp. 73–118). New York: Academic Press.

Zimmerman, E. H., & Zimmerman, J. (1962). The alteration of behavior in a classroom situation. *Journal of the Experimental Analysis of Behavior, 5,* 59–60.

Zimmerman, J., & Baydan, N. T. (1963). Punishment of S^{Δ} responding of humans in conditional matching-to-sample by timeout. *Journal of the Experimental Analysis of Behavior, 6,* 589–597.

Zimmerman, J., & Ferster, C. B. (1963). Intermittent punishment of S^{Δ} responding in matching-to-sample. *Journal of the experimental Analysis of Behavior, 6,* 349–356.

Zimmerman, B. J., & Rosenthal, T. L. (1974). Observational learning of rule-governed behavior by children. *Psychological Bulletin, 81,* 29–42.

Zohar, D., Cohen, A., & Azar, N. (1980). Promoting increased use of ear protectors in noise through information feedback. *Human Factors, 22,* 69–79.

Author Index

Abel, D., 165
Abramowitz, A., 477
Acker, M., 475, 477
Ackles, P., 409
Adams, H., 294
Adams, J., 45
Adams, M., 509
Adams, R., 424
Agras, W., 39, 326, 530
Aikins, D., 307
Alabiso, F., 551
Alavosius, M., 51, 53, 173, 275, 343, 349, 391, 504, 508, 521
Alevizos, K., 461
Alevizos, P., 461
Alford, G., 406, 419, 458
Allen, C., 216, 532
Allen, E., 451
Allen, K., 143, 419
Allen, L., 425
Allison, A., 159, 459, 473
Almeida, 199
Altman, K., 161, 470, 495
Anderson, C., 127, 268
Anderson, D., 127, 165, 268, 328
Anderson, M., 199
Anderson, R., 51, 317
Anderson, S., 378
Andrews, G., 530
Anger, W., 207
Anton, J., 228
Apolloni, T., 190, 297, 325
Applegate, G., 451
Apsche, J., 403
Arington, R., 71
Armstrong, P., 153, 180, 406
Arnold, C., 406, 424
Ary, D., 73
Ashby, E., 208
Atkins, M., 406
Atthowe, J., 211, 220
Atwater, J., 255, 520
Austin, J., 165
Austin, N., 545
Axelrod, S., 51, 192, 403, 426
Ayala, J., 253
Ayer, W., 472
Ayllon, T., 26, 33, 104, 134, 158, 166, 181, 207, 208, 220, 235, 325, 335, 421, 459, 473, 567
Azar, N., 548
Azrin, N., 104, 142, 151, 153, 158, 166, 180, 181, 207, 208, 220, 232, 256, 313, 314, 325, 437, 440, 458, 462, 469, 470, 471, 472, 473, 474, 475, 476, 477, 478, 482, 483, 484, 485, 486, 487, 489, 493, 495, 554, 555, 556
Azrin, R., 368, 408

Babcock, R., 234
Bachrach, A., 57
Bacon-Prue, A., 16
Baer, A., 454
Baer, D., 3, 5, 25, 30, 35, 46, 50, 63, 98, 103, 104, 122, 127, 129, 164, 185, 198, 210, 231, 235, 237, 280, 295, 298, 306, 307, 326, 360, 361, 362, 366, 367, 377, 380, 383, 384, 386, 389, 437, 453, 454, 492, 501, 503, 505, 507, 508, 510, 513, 524, 584
Baer, R., 365, 367, 511
Bagshaw, M., 541
Bailey, J., 16, 125, 128, 207, 255, 257, 288, 359, 426, 437, 439, 451, 454, 460, 462
Baker, V., 364
Balcazar, F., 165, 183, 290
Baldes, J., 31
Ballard, K., 79, 126
Bandura, A., 127, 198, 294, 296, 297, 298, 299, 409, 484, 488, 489
Barkshire, C., 155
Barlow, D., 35, 39, 227, 228, 229, 326, 381, 384, 386
Barnard, J., 495
Barnes, T., 262, 360
Baroff, G., 107
Baron, A., 546
Barone, V., 451
Barrera, F., 438, 440, 441, 461
Barrera, R., 295, 297, 301, 363, 378, 381, 382
Barrett, R., 363, 378, 409, 458
Barrish, H., 432, 548
Barry, N., 178, 296, 297
Barton, E., 298, 299, 484
Barton, L., 429, 460
Baskin, A., 192
Bass, R., 83
Bates, P., 33
Bauman, K., 288
Baumeister, A., 470, 482
Baumgart, D., 242
Baydan, N., 460, 461
Beale, I., 458
Beaman, A., 557, 558
Bean, A., 451
Beasley, A., 39
Beasty, A., 541
Bebko, J., 240
Bechtel, D., 402, 472, 484, 494, 495
Beck, A., 364
Beck, S., 530
Becker, J., 458, 470
Becker, W., 249, 311, 406, 424, 523
Belcastro, F., 16
Bell, L., 140
Bellack, A., 420
Bellack, S., 79
Bellamy, G., 53
Benoit, R., 345, 462
Bentall, R., 541, 547
Berberich, J., 295
Berg, W., 279, 280
Berger, P., 288
Berkowitz, L., 486

Bernal, G., 53
Bernal, M., 81, 82
Bernhardt, A., 165
Bernstein, D., 302
Berry, G., 51, 310
Bevirt, J., 298
Bielski, R., 530
Bigelow, G., 134
Bijou, S., 208, 231, 554
Billionis, C., 51
Bilsky, L., 277
Binkoff, J., 140
Birnbrauer, J., 208, 439
Bitgood, S., 452, 473
Bitter, G., 331
Bittle, R., 280, 319, 325, 381, 402, 491
Black, A., 19
Blakely, E., 292
Blanton, R., 562
Blew, P., 298
Blis, D., 361
Block, B., 297
Blom, D., 420
Bloom, B., 36, 199, 200
Bloomfield, H., 325
Blount, R., 16, 470
Boe, E., 127, 476
Bolstad, O., 82
Bolt, E., 146, 153
Bondy, A., 302
Bootzin, R., 222
Boozer, H., 164
Boren, J., 439, 555
Borg, W., 200
Borkovec, T., 302
Bornstein, M., 420
Bornstein, P., 134, 514, 532, 559, 562
Bostow, D., 426, 454, 460, 463
Bowman, E., 164
Boyajiana L., 558
Boyd, L., 208
Boyd, T., 406
Boylan, S., 425
Braam, S., 53
Bradley-Johnson, S., 26, 307
Brady, M., 128, 156
Brakman, C., 456
Brantner, J., 454, 456
Braukmann, C., 59, 215, 298, 520
Brechner, K., 61
Breen, C., 361
Brehm, J., 489
Breuning, M., 360
Breyer, N., 216, 532
Brigham, T., 216, 238, 360, 361
Bristow, A., 458
Britten, K., 285
Brockman, M., 432
Broden, M., 39, 79, 161
Brody, G., 294
Brody, J., 294
Broen, P., 365
Brooks, B., 40, 110
Brouwer, R., 16
Browder, L., 33, 307
Brown, B., 116, 131, 168
Brown, G., 451
Brown, L., 33
Brown, M., 367
Brown, P., 406
Brown, R., 294
Brown, W., 128, 294

Brownell, K., 134, 533
Brownstein, A., 355
Bruder, M., 506
Brulle, A., 429
Bruno, J., 331
Bryan, K., 307
Bryant, R., 335
Bucher, B., 107, 190, 212, 440, 484, 496
Buckley, N., 191, 208, 513
Budd, K., 35, 103, 122, 125, 210, 402, 453, 454, 492, 505
Buehler, R., 519, 520
Bugle, C., 325
Bullet, J., 506
Bunck, T., 271
Burchard, J., 426, 438, 440, 441, 461
Burchard, S., 426
Burgio, L., 53, 380, 476
Burke, J., 391
Burkhart, J., 409
Burnett, J., 280
Burt, R., 290
Burton, T., 33, 406
Bushby, H., 360
Bushell, D., 104, 134, 216, 360
Buskist, W., 540, 541, 546, 548
Butterworth, T., 255, 432, 486
Butz, G., 40
Butz, R., 360
Byrne, B., 296, 298

Calpin, J., 191, 239, 328
Cameron, S., 470
Campbell, A., 151, 217, 218, 220
Campbell, C., 361
Campbell, D., 373, 390
Campbell, S., 474
Cantor, G., 277
Cantor, J., 277
Capriotti, R., 380
Carden Smith, L., 207, 208, 215
Carey, R., 484, 496
Carlson, C., 406
Carlson, J., 312
Carnine, D., 200, 255, 293, 331, 523
Carples, S., 296
Carr, E., 20, 32, 100, 140, 326, 335, 363, 401, 402, 406, 409, 410, 423, 452, 460, 486
Carsky, M., 65, 341, 342
Carta, J., 192, 200, 203
Cartelli, L., 453
Carter, V.,
Cataldo, M., 20, 86, 127, 357
Catania, A., 139, 254, 324, 340, 346, 356, 367, 436, 501, 538, 541, 547, 566
Caudill, B., 294
Cautela, J., 100, 154, 302
Certo, N., 33, 309
Chalmers, D., 296
Chappell, L., 555, 561

Charlop, M., 307, 360, 476
Chase, P., 509
Cheiken, M., 62
Christian, W., 319, 436
Christoph, N., 544
Christophersen, E., 451, 495
Christy, P., 169, 190
Church, R., 127, 185, 469, 476
Cipollone, R., 403
Claerhout, S., 208, 212
Clark, H., 155, 196, 347, 360, 442, 454, 460, 462
Clark, K., 279
Clarke, S., 293, 301, 356, 363
Clement, P., 127, 185, 197, 199, 207
Clements, J., 561
Clifford, C., 489
Cochran, S., 486
Cohen, A., 489, 548
Cohen, H., 208
Cohen, P., 199
Cohen, S., 31
Colavecchia, B., 479
Coleman, R., 151
Collins, M., 331
Colman, A., 439
Colson, L., 288
Colter, S., 451
Combs, M., 294
Cone, J., 207, 208, 215
Conger, A., 59, 60
Conger, J., 59, 60
Cook, J., 470
Cook, T., 373, 390
Cooke, N., 199
Cooke, S., 297
Cooke, T., 190, 297, 325
Coon, M., 288
Cooper, B., 104
Cooper, J., 342
Cooper, M., 164
Cordisco, L., 458
Corey, J., 313, 359
Cormier, W., 168
Correa, V., 309, 310
Cossairt, A., 104, 165, 183, 238
Cotton, J., 290
Cowdery, G., 20, 357
Craig, A., 285, 530
Craig, H., 151
Craighead, W., 79, 82, 85, 364
Creel, J., 220
Creel, L., 220
Creer, T., 133, 140, 166, 338, 346, 389
Cresson, O., 261, 283
Crimmins, D., 409
Croner, M., 296
Cronin, K., 53, 347
Cross, S., 417
Crowe, M., 473
Crowell, C., 159, 160, 165, 328
Crucio, C., 470
Csanyi, A., 40
Cullen, R., 331
Cunningham, C., 483
Curtiss, K., 108
Cuvo, A., 53, 288, 343, 347

Dailey, D., 300
D'Angelo, J., 331
Daniels, A., 32, 100, 101, 489, 556
Danielson, U., 438
Dardig, J., 40
Daston, P., 31
Davey, G., 456
Davidson, H., 489
Davidson, N., 542, 554, 563
Davis, J., 63, 532
Davis, P., 460
Davison, G., 221
Dawson, M., 458
de Noronha, M., 106
de Noronha, Z., 106
Deal, T., 437
Decker, P., 280
Deckner, C., 562
Deckner, P., 562
DeHaven, F., 425
Deitz, S., 311, 426, 428, 430, 431
Delquadri, J., 199, 200, 202, 203, 471, 526
DeLuca, A., 539
Delugach, J., 507
Deluilo, D., 279
Demana, F., 331
Demetral, F., 458
Deno, S., 302
Depaulis, A., 82
DeReus, D., 134, 174
DeRicco, D., 294, 298
Desselles, M., 164
Detrich, R., 367
Deur, J., 477
Devany, J., 262
Diament, C., 62
Dickinson, A., 176, 179
Dickson, A., 427
Dilorenzo, T., 191
Dineen, J., 196, 513
Dingman, L., 335
Dinsmoor, J., 474
Dinwiddie, G., 199, 203
DiRisi, J., 40
Dirks, M., 367
Dixon, L., 318
Dixon, M., 262, 403, 470, 477
Dodge, K., 507
Doherty, M., 454, 456
Doke, L., 19, 127, 470, 471
Doleys, D., 453, 469, 479
Donaldson, T., 295, 547
Donellon, S., 360
Donnellan, A., 403
Donnelly, D., 430
Donnerstein, E., 268
Dore-Boyce, K., 126
Dorsel, T., 561
Dorsey, B., 62, 87, 178
Dorsey, M., 460, 470
Dory, D., 441
Dossett, D., 555, 561
Dotson, V., 73
Doty, D., 440
Dougan, J., 541
Dougherty, B., 192, 443
Douglas, T., 555
Dove, D., 296
Dowler, D., 307
Downs, A., 294, 297
Dowrick, P., 296
Doyle, D., 288

Drabman, R., 16, 49, 134, 142, 174, 207, 360, 470, 504
Drash, P., 365
Dressel, M., 294
Drew, C., 277
Dube, W., 318
Due, K., 296
Duggan, L., 160
Duncan, D., 458
Dunlap, G., 293, 476
Dunlap, K., 472
Durand, V., 32, 100, 140, 178, 255, 401, 402, 409, 410, 423
Dustin, R., 183
Dyer, K., 36, 140, 293, 319, 378, 380

Eachus, H., 294, 364
Eagen, P., 378
Eaton, M., 231
Eddy, M., 363
Edelstein, B., 239
Edgar, R., 127, 185
Edwards, G., 268, 378
Egan, P., 164, 310
Egel, A., 192, 297, 473, 493
Eggleston, D., 421
Eimers, R., 134
Elliott, R., 406, 420, 490
Elliott, S., 6, 439
Ellis, D., 199, 344
Elman, M., 438
Embree, M., 486
Emery, G., 364
Englemann, S., 249
Ennis, B., 453, 454
Epstein, L., 408, 471, 530, 533
Epstein, R., 127, 295, 597
Erken, N., 551
Erickson, L., 253, 292
Eron, L., 268, 486, 488
Ersner-Hershfield, R., 462
Espin, C., 302
Esveldt-Dawson, K., 379
Etzel, B., 253, 273, 293, 316, 317
Eubanks, J., 104
Evans, G., 268
Evans, I., 31, 343, 391
Everett, P., 16, 555

Fairbank, J., 183
Fairbanks, D., 207
Fajardo, D., 19
Fantuzzo, J., 184, 197, 199, 207
Fantz, R., 277
Farber, H., 80
Farmer, V., 541
Farmer-Dugan, V., 84, 154
Farnum, M., 238
Farquhar, J., 530
Farrar, M., 428, 458
Farris, H., 160, 549
Fauke, J., 280
Faulkner, H., 146, 153
Faust, G., 51
Favell, J., 106, 107, 122, 268, 459, 460, 470, 475, 484, 493
Faw, G., 280, 319, 512
Feallock, R., 215
Felce, D., 82, 460, 507, 525
Feldman, R. B., 472, 547
Feldman, R. F., 199
Feldman, R. S., 2, 19
Fellner, D., 85, 86, 290, 327
Ferguson, B., 307, 360
Ferritor, D., 33, 421
Ferster, C., 429, 449, 453, 460, 475, 538, 541, 543, 554

Filberk, R., 359
Filipczak, J., 208
Finfrock, S., 360
Finley, W., 559
Fischer, J., 471
Fishbein, J., 433
Fisher, E., 224
Fitterling, J., 325, 335
Fixsen, D., 79, 85, 108, 127, 155, 208, 298
Fixsen, K., 195
Fjellstedt, N., 69, 292
Flanagan, S., 294, 462
Flanders, N., 489
Fleming, R., 66, 192, 296, 309, 328, 347, 532
Flynn, J., 207, 208, 218, 219
Ford, J., 213, 341, 343
Forehand, R., 165, 294, 449, 451, 463, 479, 482, 484
Forgione, A., 472
Forman, S., 437
Fortmann, S., 530
Foster, C., 51, 53
Fowler, S., 127, 134, 185, 192, 195, 196, 207, 208, 215, 280, 326, 423, 443, 527
Fox, C., 63, 134, 184, 212, 232, 254, 288, 438, 461, 479, 532
Fox, D., 207, 208, 220, 223
Fox, J., 128, 192, 200, 452
Fox, W., 50
Foxx, C., 462
Foxx, R., 80, 280, 313, 319, 325, 335, 375, 376, 402, 420, 425, 458, 462, 471, 473, 483, 484, 487, 489, 491, 494, 495
Frank, A., 279
Frankel, F., 486
Frankowsky, R., 192, 527
Freagon, S., 310
Freitag, G., 107
Fremouw, W., 296
French, N., 420
Frentz, C., 439
Friedman, P., 453, 454
Friman, P., 451
Frisch, M., 62
Frisch, S., 361
Fuller, E., 426
Funk, D., 279
Fuqua, R., 53, 472, 484, 557
Furniss, J., 519
Futtersak, M., 477

Gaetani, J., 165
Gagnon, J., 221
Galizio, M., 355, 546
Galvin, G., 420, 439
Ganzell, 207
Garcia, E., 288, 365, 425, 506
Garrett, B., 383
Garrett, K., 331
Garton, A., 159
Gary, A., 275, 276, 360
Gast, D., 262, 344, 455, 461
Gaul, K., 309, 310
Gaylord-Ross, R., 140, 361
Geddy, P., 450
Geesey, S., 191, 378
Gelfand, D., 230, 297, 488
Geller, E., 16, 257
Gentry, N., 231
George, C.,
George, J., 242
Geren, 178
Gersham, F., 335
Gershaw, N., 420

Gersten, R., 392
Gettinger, M., 69
Giangreco, M., 310
Gilchrist, I., 502
Giles, D., 208
Gladstone, B., 18, 211
Glaros, A., 472
Glaser, R., 282
Glass, G., 199
Glazeski, R., 294
Glover, J., 275, 276, 359, 360
Glynn, E., 531
Glynn, T., 79, 126, 489
Goetz, E., 253, 324, 479
Gold, V., 107
Goldberg, R., 190
Goldiamond, I., 32
Goldstein, A., 420
Goldstein, G., 192, 198
Goldstein, H., 294
Goldstein, R., 437
Gonso, J., 533
Gonzales, M., 40
Goodwin, D., 101
Gordon, J., 533
Goss, C., 127
Gotestam, K., 268
Gottman, J., 420
Gottslig, M., 425
Grabe, M., 331
Graham, D., 26
Granger, R., 544
Grant, M., 489
Grass, J., 288
Graubard, P., 168, 212, 361
Green, C., 177
Green, G., 33, 364
Green, K., 484
Green, R., 168, 250
Greene, B., 16, 208, 250
Greene, D., 167, 179
Greene, R., 470
Greenwood, C., 87, 192, 199, 200, 202, 203, 273, 391, 524, 526, 527
Greer, C., 494
Greer, R., 199, 202, 215, 312, 513
Griffitt, W., 296, 298
Groden, G., 401
Groden, J., 302
Gross, A., 325, 428, 458
Grubb, P., 257
Gruber, B., 344, 345
Grusec, J., 488, 489
Guess, D., 347, 361, 482, 485
Guevremont, D., 528
Guild, J., 526
Guiltnan, S., 344
Gullivan, M., 129
Gustafson, C., 65, 341, 342, 347
Gustavson, C., 221

Haavik, S., 470
Hackman, J., 108
Hagen, D., 82
Hake, D., 295, 381, 408, 428, 456, 472, 474, 486, 489, 547
Hall, C., 294
Hall, L., 84, 511, 529, 531
Hall, R., 39, 79, 104, 164, 183, 199, 200, 375, 377, 378, 406, 428, 436, 471
Hall, V., 192, 208
Hallahan, K., 129, 531
Halle, J., 307, 308, 309, 360
Halzenbuehler, L., 451
Hamblin, R., 191, 192
Hammer, D., 49, 207
Handen, B., 307, 308, 309
Handleman, J., 360
Haney, J., 288
Hanley, E., 459

Hannum, J., 127, 185
Hansen, D., 65
Hansen, G., 312
Hantula, D., 328
Hardiman, S., 324, 325, 335
Hardison, W., 250
Hardman, M., 365
Haring, N., 231
Haring, T., 66, 361, 404, 503, 507, 509, 514
Haring-McClure, P., 214
Harman, M., 525
Harmatz, M., 439
Harmon, T., 79
Harper, G., 199
Harris, F., 326, 451, 470
Harris, J., 561
Harris, S., 425, 428, 455, 459, 462
Harris, V., 134, 381, 432
Hart, B., 127, 331, 361, 362, 367, 406, 511
Hartman, M., 299
Hartmann, D., 73, 230, 381, 390
Harzem, P., 541
Hasazi, J., 360
Haskett, G., 293, 294
Hatch, J., 555
Hatfield, V., 253
Hathaway, G., 191
Hathorn, N.,
Haught, P., 307
Haupt, E., 313
Hawkins, J., 440
Hawkins, R., 31, 32, 33, 34, 35, 36, 37, 73
Hayes, L., 186, 262, 356
Hayes, S., 35, 36, 45, 62, 79, 175, 229, 262, 353, 356, 358, 365, 368, 381, 443
Haynes, S., 60, 61, 450
Heal, J., 288
Heal, L., 277
Heffernan, T., 185
Heggie, D., 197
Heiby, E., 567
Heifetz, L., 326
Heimann, L., 325
Heins, E., 531
Helfen, C., 493
Heller, M., 472, 489
Helmstetter, E., 482
Helsel, W., 403
Henderson, H., 551
Hendrickson, J., 127, 129, 190
Herbert, E., 129
Herlong, L., 450
Hernandez, M., 325
Heron, T., 199, 342
Herrnstein, R., 173, 566
Hersen, M., 227, 228, 229, 310, 381, 384, 386, 420
Hershfield, R., 455
Heward, W., 40, 199, 202, 294, 342, 364
Hewitt, R., 469
Hickey, K., 484
Hicks, D., 296
Higgins Hains, A., 380, 383, 384
Higgins, R., 62
Hill, D., 199
Hineline, P., 139, 470, 482
Hively, W., 311
Hlavacek, A., 288, 289
Hoats, D., 470
Hobbs, S., 453, 463
Hodgson, J., 331
Hogan, W., 218, 220, 221, 439, 441
Hoko, J., 318
Holborn, S., 360, 506, 539
Holland, A., 151
Holland, J., 407
Hollandsworth, J., 294
Holz, W., 142, 181, 437,

440, 456, 469, 470, 472, 474, 476, 477, 478, 482, 489, 493
Homan, C., 459
Homer, A., 129, 403, 425
Homme, L., 40, 158, 159
Hopkins, B., 59, 61, 104, 120, 121, 159, 160, 165, 183, 207, 242, 364, 383, 406, 483, 527
Hops, H., 392, 513, 526
Horn, W., 60, 61
Horne, W., 296, 484
Horner, R., 53, 237, 343, 377, 402
Horton, S., 458
Hosford, R., 79, 296, 406
Hotte, E., 65, 341, 342
House, A., 458
Hovell, M., 125
Howard, J., 26, 278, 307, 308, 407
Howard, V., 314
Howie, P., 207, 221, 326
Hoxeng, D., 165
Hoyson, M., 208
Hoyt, R., 268
Hubbard, D., 127
Humphreys, L., 451
Hunt, G., 408, 556
Hursh, D., 383
Hurt, S., 208, 217
Hutchinson, J., 128, 451
Hutchinson, R., 408, 468, 474, 485, 486, 489, 554, 555, 556
Hutt, C., 277
Hyten, C., 295, 547

Inman, D., 53
Irvin, L., 453, 454, 455, 456
Isreal, A., 367, 514
Ivancic, M., 385, 386, 476, 512
Iwata, B., 20, 140, 268, 271, 288, 357, 409, 410, 426, 437, 439, 452, 460, 470, 476

Jackson, A., 194
Jackson, D., 365, 406
Jacob, M., 530
Jacobs, H., 207, 208, 215
James, L., 280
James, S., 192
Jamieson, B., 208
Jarrett, R., 45
Jason, L., 207, 215, 268
Jeffers, J., 461
Jeffery, R., 134
Jenkins, J., 458, 507
Jenson, W., 470, 562
Johnson, C., 26, 101, 307
Johnson, D., 37, 190, 191, 199, 218, 220, 221, 439, 441
Johnson, J., 79, 476
Johnson, K., 85, 86, 312, 330, 509
Johnson, M., 159, 160, 288, 451
Johnson, R., 37, 190, 199, 299
Johnson, S., 82, 294, 460, 513
Johnston, J., 64, 227, 229, 242, 450
Jones, F., 134, 296, 297, 486, 513
Jones, J., 484
Jones, M., 452, 470, 530
Jones, R., 185, 223, 288, 325, 380, 386, 425, 462

Kabela, E., 174

Kaffashan, L., 455
Kagan, N., 79
Kagel, J., 220
Kahn, J., 296, 297
Kale, R., 364
Kaloupek, D., 406, 419
Kalsher, M., 20, 357
Kanareff, V., 296
Kandel, H., 134
Kane, J., 134
Kanowitz, J., 62
Kapust, J., 66, 84
Karoly, P., 367
Karsh, K., 82, 525
Kass, R., 142
Kassorla, I., 107
Kastenbaum, R., 100, 154
Katz, R., 69, 101, 288, 420
Kaufman, A., 355
Kay, E., 31
Kaye, J., 364
Kazdin, A., 6, 79, 127, 161, 185, 191, 219, 222, 223, 227, 232, 239, 253, 292, 296, 364, 378, 380, 381, 389, 390, 420, 424, 437, 439, 455, 479, 482, 490
Keilitz, I., 51, 53, 343
Kelleher, R., 471
Keller, F., 200, 236, 330, 594
Keller, K., 346
Kelley, H., 44
Kelley, M., 439
Kelly, J., 408
Kelly, K., 26
Kendall, P., 364, 461
Kennedy, C., 66, 404, 509
Kennedy, D., 161, 502
Kennedy, S., 294
Kent, R., 62
Kerr, M., 200
Kesler, J., 470
Kidd, T., 110
Kidder, J., 208
Kiely, D., 462
Kiernan, J., 53
Killen, C., 242
Kilwein, M., 314
Kimball, 178
Kincaid, M., 212
King, G., 174
King, H., 451
King, L., 451
Kirby, K., 192, 360, 506, 556
Kirigen, K., 520
Kirk, B., 262
Kirsch, I., 326
Kishi, G., 402
Kissel, R., 127
Kistner, J., 207, 208, 216
Klein, P., 420
Klein, R., 127, 185
Kleitsch, E., 361
Klock, J., 161, 479
Kluwin, T., 106
Knight, M., 134
Kniverton, b., 488
Knowlton, S., 482
Knutson, L., 326
Koegel, R., 140, 190, 277, 285, 293, 316, 391, 513, 560
Koeske, R., 530
Kogan, N., 290
Kohlenberg, R., 16, 483
Kohler, F., 134, 192, 195, 196, 199, 203, 524, 527
Kologinsky, E., 363
Komaki, J., 126, 161, 164
Komarski, C., 208
Konarski, E., 159, 160
Koorland, M., 88
Korchin, S., 45

Kornhaber, R., 296
Kraemer, H., 530
Krakower, S., 325, 336
Kramer, K., 294
Kramer, S., 331
Krams, M., 208
Krantz, P., 360, 511
Kratochwill, T., 79, 451
Kraut, R., 33
Kristal, S., 451
Kruger, E., 438
Krumboltz, H., 167, 299, 306, 320, 475
Krumboltz, J., 35, 40, 167, 306, 320, 406, 475
Kubany, E., 80
Kuhn, B., 360
Kulic, C., 199
Kulik, J., 199
Kulps, S., 70
Kupers, C., 299
Kuypers, D., 406
Kyle, M., 280, 325

Labig, C., 494
Lafleur, N., 299
Lagomarcino, A., 512
Lahey, B., 125, 294, 360, 451
Laitinen, R., 285
Lamal, P., 555
Lambert, N., 19
Lancioni, G., 280
Lane, M., 294
Lang, G., 489
Langer, S., 46
Lanza, R., 295
Lanzetta, J., 296
Lapuc, P., 439
Larzelere, R., 494
Latham, G., 31, 555, 561
Lavigna, G., 403
Lawler, E., 108
Laws, D., 547
Layman, D., 134
Lazelere, R.,
LeBlanc, J., 267, 293, 317, 318, 324
Lee, M., 361
Lehner, P., 82
Leibowitz, J., 432, 555, 556
Leitenberg, H., 326, 381, 426
LeLaurin, K., 19, 127
Lemanek, K., 335
Lenfestey, W., 293, 294
Lennox, C., 240
Lennox, D., 430
Lenske, J., 365
Lent, J., 51
Lentz, F., 104, 207, 208, 506
Lepper, M., 167, 179
Levin, H., 199
Levis, D., 406
Levy, E., 299
Lewis, F., 364
Liberman, R., 364
Lichstein, K., 294
Lichtenstein, E., 533
Liebert, R., 522
Lifter, K., 36, 378, 380
Light, P., 293, 356
Linehan, M., 368
Lindsley, O., 65, 151
Liner, D., 428, 458
Ling, P., 488
Linscheid, T., 483
Linsk, N., 364
Lipinski, P., 61
Lippman, L., 541
Lipscomb, T., 294
Lipsett, L., 151
Lipsker, L., 436
Litow, L., 190
Litrownik, A., 401
Livesay, J., 483, 490
Lloyd, J., 129, 382, 531
Loafman, B., 288, 289
Lobato-Barrera, D., 295

Loberg, D., 455
Locke, P., 199
Lockwood, K., 255
Logue, A., 174
Long, J., 240
Lorentzson, A., 426, 452
Lovaas, O., 106, 107, 122, 285, 295, 366, 401, 459, 460, 493
Loving, A., 217
Lovitt, T., 108, 231
Lowe, C., 541, 546, 547
Lowe, K., 208
Lowitz, G., 426, 428
Loyd, B., 378
Lubstsky, M., 403
Luce, S., 36, 164, 298, 319, 378, 428, 436, 471
Ludwig, D., 161, 414, 489
Luiselli, J., 360, 425, 428, 493
Lukeris, S., 208, 507
Lutzker, J., 156, 208, 212, 347, 361, 458, 484
Luyben, P., 279, 312, 313
Lysaght, T., 426

MacDonald, R., 46, 364
Mace, F., 79, 175, 186, 255, 385, 386, 463
Mackay, H., 262, 318, 356, 361
MacKenzie-Keating, S., 479
Madsen, C. H., 134, 539
Madsen, C. K., 134, 539
Madsen, D., 406, 424
Maehr, M., 161, 529
Mager, A., 47, 49, 50, 51, 485
Maguire, R., 262, 318, 360
Maheady, L., 198, 199
Maher, C., 104, 529
Mahoney, M., 66, 79, 83, 126, 212, 364
Maier, S., 354, 487
Malaby, J., 79, 563
Malenfant, L., 257
Maley, R., 219, 220
Malone, S., 294, 311
Maloney, D., 298
Maloney, K., 59
Malott, R., 288
Mandelker, A., 216
Mann, R., 297, 360, 401
Manos, M., 207, 208
Marholin, D., 288
Marlatt, G., 533
Marshall, A., 253
Marshall, G., 307
Marshall, H., 484
Marshall, K., 129
Martin, G., 452
Martin, J., 38, 41, 103, 280, 288, 361, 380, 486, 489
Martin, M., 88
Martin, R., 268
Martindale, A., 70
Maruyama, G., 190, 199
Mascitelli, S., 219
Mash, E., 45, 62
Mason, D., 360
Mason, S., 154, 177
Mathews, A., 451
Matson, J., 288, 379, 482, 483, 484, 485, 491
Matthews, B., 356, 366, 367, 541, 547
Matthews, R., 268
Mausner, B., 297
Mawhinney, B., 542, 543
Mayer, G., 16, 35, 51, 72, 80, 86, 123, 185, 194, 255, 296, 297, 298, 312, 421, 462, 486, 541

Mayhew, G., 470
McAfee, J., 127
McAllister, L., 237
McCandless, B., 315
McClannahan, L., 360, 511
McClinton, B., 299
McClure, G., 214
McConnell, S., 291
McCormick, S., 276
McCosh, K., 268
McCullagh, P., 298
McCutcheon, B., 316
McDonnell, J., 307, 320, 344, 345, 452
McDowell, J., 316
McElwee, J., 62
McEvoy, M., 156, 193
McFall, R., 411, 426
McFarland, S., 344, 345
McGee, G., 154, 199, 202, 360, 511
McGimpsey, B., 156
McGimsey, J., 208, 470
McGonigle, J., 409, 458, 470
McGonigle, R., 110, 158
McGookin, R., 110, 158
McGreevy, P., 333
McInnis, T., 460
McIlvane, W., 318
McKelvey, J., 310
McKenzie, T., 134
McLaughlin, T., 79, 556, 563
McMahon, R., 44, 45, 280, 309, 451
McMorrow, M., 280, 319, 325, 360, 402, 491
McNees, M. C., 451
McReynolds, W., 127, 185, 191, 207, 457
McSween, T., 470
McSweeney, F., 541, 548
McSweeny, A., 437
Mead, A., 134
Mees, H., 107, 451, 454
Meister, D., 199
Melin, L., 268
Melvin, K., 220
Menlove, F., 294, 489
Merante, R., 288, 289
Merbaum, M., 487
Mercatoris, M., 79, 82
Meyerson, L.,
Michael, J., 134, 152, 180, 231, 256, 390, 512
Michelson, L., 191
Milan, M., 207, 208, 215, 567
Millenson, J., 180, 407, 408
Miller, A., 451
Miller, H., 540, 546
Miller, L., 215
Miller, M., 168
Millichamp, C., 314
Mills, J., 391
Miltenberger, R., 430, 472, 484, 557
Minkin, B., 437
Minkin, N., 325, 359, 437
Mischel, W., 488
Mithaug, D., 467
Mitts, B., 79
Mochizuki, A., 360
Moore, E., 106, 257
Morey, T., 561
Morgan, A., 541, 548
Morgan, D., 562
Morgan, J., 279
Morin, C., 406
Morrell, D., 279
Morris, E., 73, 75, 255, 486
Morris, N., 164
Morris, W., 307
Morse, W., 471
Moss, S., 63, 79, 532
Moussorgsky, 479

Muir, K., 207, 208, 215
Mulick, J., 268, 504
Mullins, M., 566
Munger, G., 378
Murdock, J., 365
Murph, D., 276
Murphy, H., 128, 255, 451
Murphy, R., 458, 460
Murray, R., 463

Nafpaktitis, M., 255, 486
Nation, J., 558
Natsoulas, T., 296
Nau, P., 207, 208, 479, 557
Nay, W., 461
Nehs, R., 471
Nelson, C., 44, 364, 455, 457, 461
Nelson, D., 190
Nelson, G., 207, 208, 215, 460
Nelson, J., 364
Nelson, R., 35, 36, 45, 61, 62, 66, 79, 80, 84, 185, 229, 262
Ness, J., 325
Nevid, J., 532
Neville, K., 360
Neville, M., 562
Nevin, A., 199
Newby, T., 133, 140, 207
Newsom, C., 20, 140, 423, 460, 484, 486, 487
Nielsen, L., 406
Niemann, J., 294, 298
Nietupski, J., 309
Nordyke, N., 280
Northrop, J., 155
Nunes, D., 458, 460
Nunn, L., 316
Nyborg, K., 532

O'Brien, F., 325, 335
O'Brien, R., 277
O'Brien, S., 385, 386
O'Conner, C., 294
O'Dell, S., 65
Odom, S., 208, 291
O'Leary, D., 62
O'Leary, K., 30, 31, 62, 142, 367, 406, 410, 514
O'Leary, S., 475, 477, 484
Olenick, D., 360
Oliva, D., 280
Oliver, S., 453, 486
Ollendick, T., 300, 379, 380, 381, 382, 484
Olson, R., 450
Ong, P., 470
Ono, K., 539
Ordione, G., 50
Orlando, R., 554
Osborn, G., 530
Osborn, J., 484
Osborne, J., 542, 554, 563
Osnes, P., 505, 511
Ossip, D., 530
O'Toole, K., 288
Overman, P., 296, 297
Owens, C., 308

Pace, G., 20, 268, 312, 357
Page, T., 380, 385, 386
Paine, S., 443
Palmer, M., 208
Panyan, M., 164
Parke, R., 477, 494
Parker, W., 530
Parr, J., 288, 310
Parsons, A., 456
Paschalis, A., 207
Pasnak, R., 365
Patterson, G., 46, 129, 410, 425, 519

Paul, G., 82, 207, 208, 302, 384, 440
Paulus, P., 127, 268
Pavlov, I., 3, 251
Pawlicki, R., 561
Pear, J., 360, 452
Peck, C., 242
Pemberton, B., 493
Pena-Correal, T., 174
Pendergrass, V., 456
Pennypacker, H., 64, 227, 229, 242, 450
Perelman, P., 459
Perloff, B., 295
Perri, M., 126, 185, 280, 534
Peters, R., 63, 452, 473
Peters, T., 545
Petersen, B., 470
Peterson, A., 232, 235
Peterson, C., 459
Peterson, D., 406
Peterson, L., 129, 325, 403, 425
Peterson, R., 235, 364, 420, 439
Pfiffner, L., 484
Phillips, E. A., 155, 195, 208
Phillips, E. L., 79, 108, 125, 127, 155, 195, 208, 214, 222, 298, 359, 436, 437
Phillips, J., 53
Phillips, T., 16
Pickering, D., 16
Pierce, C., 134, 140
Pigott, H., 197, 199, 202
Pinkston, E., 364
Pitts-Conway, V., 509
Plake, B., 359
Plaska, T., 491
Platt, J., 561
Poche, C., 16, 207, 298
Podsakoff, P., 160
Polirstok, S., 168, 199, 202, 215, 513
Pollack, M., 38, 328
Polster, R., 223
Polvinale, R., 484
Pomerleau, C., 409
Pomerleau, O., 16, 409, 519
Porter, J., 544
Porterfield, J., 457
Poulos, R., 522
Poulson, C., 309
Powell, J., 70, 72
Powell, L., 507
Powers, M., 280
Praderas, K., 364
Premack, D., 158, 159, 160
Presland, J., 489
Prince, H.,
Proctor, W., 16
Prue, D., 183
Pumroy, D., 190
Pursell, E., 555

Quattrochi-Tubin, S., 268
Quevillon, R., 134

Rabinowitz, F., 299
Ragland, D., 200
Ramey, G., 200, 201, 202
Ramp, K., 215
Rand, C., 134
Raos, S., 472
Rapport, M., 255, 438
Rasmussen, M., 361, 437
Rauer, S., 297
Ray, B., 106
Rayner, R., 487
Reaume, J., 212
Rechs, J., 40
Redd, W., 382, 383, 486
Redmon, W., 160, 239, 255, 549

Reese, E., 9, 26, 40, 83, 100, 104, 110, 111, 112, 131, 141, 154, 315, 316, 336, 341, 344, 407, 449, 530
Reese, T., 26
Rehm, R., 285
Reid, D., 33, 53, 62, 127, 344, 460, 512
Reisman, J., 425, 493
Reiser, R., 8, 440
Reitz, A., 288
Remington, B., 293, 356, 363
Rendelman, C., 491
Renne, C., 133, 140, 166, 338, 346, 389
Renzaglia, A., 33, 82
Repp, A., 82, 426, 428, 429, 430, 431, 460, 525
Resnick, L., 341, 343
Retana, G., 392
Reuter, K., 324
Reynolds, F., 173, 182, 259
Reynolds, G., 324, 427, 543, 550, 556, 558
Reynolds, J., 39, 40
Reynolds, N., 359, 360
Richards, B., 331
Richards, C., 126, 185
Richardson, W., 339
Richman, G., 190
Rickard, H., 220
Rickert, V., 300
Riddle, K., 438
Ridley, L., 531
Rilling, M., 311, 512
Rimmer, B., 471
Rincover, A., 316, 459, 484, 513, 566
Riordan, M., 151
Risley, R., 21, 86, 104, 121, 151, 160
Risley, T., 3, 5, 19, 25, 107, 127, 134, 140, 154, 196, 359, 360, 361, 362, 367, 389, 390, 451, 454, 487, 511
Roberts, M., 33, 421, 450, 451, 453, 458, 461, 462
Roberts, R., 82, 288
Roberts, T., 82
Robertson, S., 134, 140, 166, 174, 450
Robinson, P., 133, 140, 207, 212
Rodin, J., 519
Rodriquez, M., 174
Roffers, T., 104
Roger, B., 361
Rogers, J., 257
Rogers, R., 257
Rogers-Warren, A., 34, 36, 46, 100, 281, 298, 301, 366, 367, 504
Rohen, T., 298
Rojahn, J., 268, 403, 470
Rolider, A., 257, 313, 428, 459, 460, 475
Romanczyk, R., 62, 85, 455
Roos, P., 107
Rosekrans, M., 296
Rosen, H., 73, 75, 428
Rosen, S., 428
Rosenbaum, M., 49, 296
Rosenberg, H., 168
Rosenbergen, P., 407
Rosenfarb, I., 365, 368, 443
Rosenfeld, P., 19
Rosenshine, B., 200
Rosenthal, T., 294, 297, 298, 299
Ross, A., 277
Ross, D., 127, 198
Ross, L., 451

Ross, P., 341
Ross, S., 127, 198
Rossi, M., 548
Rotatori, A., 310
Roth, D., 530
Rothblum, E., 207
Rotter, J., 530
Rourke, 178
Rovner, L., 470
Rowbury, T., 280, 454
Rubin, B., 361
Rubinoff, A., 375, 376
Rude, H., 198
Ruggles, T., 267, 293
Runkle, 257
Ruprecht, M., 458, 460
Rusch, F., 232, 280, 380, 381
Rushall, B., 134
Ruskin, R., 85, 219, 220, 330
Russell, B., 3
Rust, F., 506
Rutherford, R., 457
Rutter, M., 193
Ryan, B., 85

Sabornie, E., 106
Sacca, M., 199
Sackett, G.,
Sagvolden, T., 346, 356
Saigh, P., 207. 208
Sainato, D., 198, 199
Sajwaj, T., 470, 471
Salend, S., 191
Salmon, D., 360
Salmonson, M., 479
Salzberg, C., 309
Sameoto, D., 479
Samper, S., 451
Sandargas, R., 110
Sanders, M., 288, 310, 432
Sanders, R., 61
Sanderson, M.234
Santarcangelo, S., 36
Santos, J., 361
Sasso, G., 198
Saudergas, R., 184, 539
Sawin, D., 477
Sbardellati, E., 199
Scarborro, M., 449
Schaefer, H., 208, 282
Schaeffer, B., 295, 314, 564
Schaeffer, J., 360
Scheflen, K., 108
Scheirer, M., 33
Schepis, M., 363
Schilmoeller, G., 317, 318
Schilmoeller, K., 316, 317
Schinke, S., 502, 504
Schleien, S., 53
Schlinger, H., 292
Schloss, C., 294
Schloss, P., 294
Schlundt, D., 507
Schmidt, G., 191
Schmidt, J., 237
Schnake, M., 438, 440
Schocken, I., 507
Schoen, L., 406
Schoen, S., 267, 306, 309
Schoenfeld, W., 236
Schram, H., 232, 234
Schreibman, L., 280, 281, 285, 360, 391
Schroeder, S., 268, 296
Schuldberg, D., 45
Schultheis, K., 185
Schultz, R., 325
Schumaker, J., 125, 360, 361
Schunk, D., 297
Schuster, J., 344, 347, 348
Schutte, R., 159
Schwartz, G., 359
Schwartz, I., 298

Schwartz, J., 361
Schweitzer, J., 174, 526
Schwitzgebel, R., 41, 103
Scott, J., 539
Scott, P., 406
Secan, K., 473
Seigel, F., 326
Seigel, G., 365
Seligman, M., 354, 414
Semb, G., 383
Sergio, J., 165
Seymour, F., 126
Seymour, J., 555
Shamow, J., 313, 359
Shapiro, E., 104, 127, 185, 190, 294, 300, 379, 506
Shapiro, R., 325
Shapiro, S., 294, 458
Sharan, S., 199
Sheldon-Wildgen, J., 121, 294
Shemberg, K., 360
Sherick, R., 420
Sherman, J., 125, 134, 168, 211, 235, 294, 347, 360, 361, 381, 432
Sherman, T., 18
Shields, F., 556
Shimamura, J., 191, 207
Shimoff, E., 356, 367, 541, 547
Shinske, D., 380
Shook, G., 198
Shores, R., 190
Shull, R., 355
Sidman, B., 5, 381, 382, 392
Sidman, M., 254, 261, 262, 283, 318, 319, 356, 360, 361, 403, 476, 590
Siedentop, D., 134
Siegel, G., 439, 440
Silverman, N., 424
Simek, T., 277
Simmons, J., 486
Simon, S., 567
Singer, F., 365, 453, 454
Singer, G., 455, 456
Singh, J., 361, 484
Singh, N., 288, 314, 361, 420, 458, 484
Siqueland, E., 151
Siroky, L., 328
Sisemore, D., 427
Sisson, L., 310, 314, 325, 363, 378
Sittler, J., 424
Skidgell, A., 335
Skinner, B., 3, 114, 173, 282, 295, 325, 328, 336, 353, 355, 407, 408, 429, 443, 449, 453, 467, 468, 501, 532, 538, 541, 543, 554, 555
Skon, L., 190
Slavin, R., 191, 197, 200
Sloane, H., 192, 255, 293, 451, 453, 486, 562
Sloggett, B., 80
Smeets, P., 280
Smith, B., 360
Smith, E., 194
Smith, L., 195, 196
Smith, M., 294
Smith, N., 5
Smith, T., 502
Snell, M., 293, 307, 339, 344, 345, 347, 348, 378
Snyder, G., 249
Solnick, J., 459, 460
Solomon, R., 190, 354, 410, 469
Sorrell, S., 471
Speidel, G., 186

Speltz, M., 191, 192, 207, 208, 217
Spooner, D., 345
Spooner, F., 345, 347
Sonnenschein, P., 191
Spradlin, J., 262, 307, 308
Sprafkin, R., 420
Staats, A., 220
Staines, J., 489
Stamps, L., 127, 185
Stans, A., 361
Stansberry, P., 158
Stanland, E., 296
Stedry, A., 31
Steege, M., 309, 310
Steeves, J., 452
Stein, N., 560
Stephens, C., 360, 484, 555, 556
Stephenson, G., 82
Stern, G., 196
Stevens, R., 200
Stevens-Long, 361
Stevenson, H., 184
Stewart, C., 484
Stewart, D., 470
Stewart, N., 299
Stitzer, M., 134
Stoddard, L., 318, 319
Stoffer, G., 557
Stoffer, J., 557
Stokes, T., 126, 143, 294, 306, 362, 366, 501, 503, 505, 507, 508, 510, 511, 513
Stolz, S., 116, 127, 185, 361, 401
Stouthamer-Loeber, M., 63
Strain, P., 190, 192, 195, 198, 200, 208, 291
Strang, H., 331
Stremel-Campbell, K., 361
Stretton, K., 200
Striefel, S., 301, 307, 308, 440
Studer, R., 555
Suarez, Y., 165, 183, 473
Suib, M., 426, 428
Sultanoff, S., 104
Sulzer, B., 33, 151, 208, 217, 218, 220, 222, 236, 280, 329, 347, 361, 421, 437, 509
Sulzer, E., 40
Sulzer-Azaroff, B., 9, 16, 19, 35, 38, 40, 51, 53, 55, 63, 66, 69, 72, 79, 83, 84, 85, 86, 100, 104, 110, 111, 112, 123, 131, 134, 154, 173, 174, 184, 191, 192, 199, 200, 201, 202, 208, 217, 218, 232, 233, 234, 255, 275, 288, 290, 292, 295, 296, 301, 309, 312, 327, 328, 341, 343, 347, 349, 363, 375, 378, 381, 382, 393, 391, 392, 393, 475, 479, 483, 486, 504, 508, 509, 511, 521, 526, 527, 529, 530, 531, 532
Sumberg, C., 470
Sundberg, M., 353
Sunderman, P.,307
Swatta, P., 280
Swearingen, M., 16
Swisher, J., 297
Switzer, E., 437
Szykula, S., 184, 186

Taber, J., 282, 595
Taggart, A., 134
Taggart, J., 134

Tague, C., 208
Tailby, W., 254, 262
Tanner, B., 470
Taras, M., 482, 483, 484, 485, 491
Tate, B., 107
Tawney, J., 360
Teigen, J., 364
Terrace, H., 315, 317, 319, 320
Terraciano, T., 313
Tharp, R., 99, 167, 186
Thaw, J., 79
Thayer, B., 504
Theobald, D., 384
Thibodeau, M., 360
Thomas, C., 79, 208, 214, 215, 222, 314, 335
Thomas, D., 249, 406, 424, 488
Thomas, G., 146, 153
Thomas, J., 79, 296, 297, 298, 489
Thomas, T., 531
Thompson, F., 134
Thompson, I., 161, 502
Thompson, T., 53, 378, 379
Thomson, C., 79, 83, 126, 127
Thoresen, C., 35, 212, 228, 299
Thorndike, E., 3
Thurston, L., 199
Thvedt, J., 267
Thyer, B., 257
Tilley, K., 262
Timberlake, W., 159
Timbers, G., 359
Tisdelle, D., 65
Todd, N., 383
Tosi, D., 161
Touchette, P., 46, 278, 281, 282, 283, 288, 307, 308, 504
Tremblay, A., 190
Trent, J., 438
Troutner, J., 331
Trovato, J., 190
Trtol, K., 280
Truax, C., 8
Trudel, G., 216
Tucci, V., 16
Tucker, D., 51, 310
Turnbull, GH., 482
Turner, S., 470
Twardosz, S., 21, 127, 454, 460
Tyler, V., 451, 460
Tyron, W., 82, 390

Ulman, J., 191, 217, 378, 381, 382, 383
Ulrich, R., 99, 191, 256
Umar, A., 207, 208
Upper, D., 221
Upshur, C., 503

Van den Pol, R., 505
Van Der Kooy, D., 333, 334
Van Hasselt, V., 310, 314, 325
Van Houten, J., 192
Van Houten, R., 192, 207, 208, 313, 395, 402, 425, 428, 459, 460, 469, 473, 475, 479, 485, 491, 557
Van Houten, V., 257
Van Kirk, M., 313
VanAcker, R., 525
VanBiervliert, A., 262
Vargas, J., 50
Vasta, R., 473
Vaughan, M., 541
Vautier, J., 257
Voeltz, L., 343, 391
Vogelsberg, R., 288
Volger, J., 432
Volpe, J., 174

Von Brock, M., 490
Vukelich, R., 428, 456
Vyse, S., 504

Waas, G., 488
Wacker, D., 279, 280, 309
Wahler, R., 46, 184, 254, 410, 451, 452
Waits, B., 331
Walder, L., 31
Waldrup, P., 542
Walker, D., 199
Walker, H., 191, 208, 392, 513
Walker, M., 61
Walker, W., 294
Wallace, R., 365
Wallach, M., 290
Wallander, J., 59, 60
Walls, R., 267, 307, 320, 344, 345
Walsh, M., 307
Walters, R., 409, 488
Walz, G., 79
Wansley, R., 559
Warak, W., 339
Warner, R., 297
Warren, S., 36, 100, 298, 504
Warring, D., 199
Wasik, B., 433
Watson, J., 3, 458, 487
Watson-Perczel, M., 156, 208, 215
Watt, A., 331
Watt, M., 331
Wattenberg, W., 489
Weber, L., 345
Webster, D., 333, 334, 458, 484
Wedel, J., 326
Weeks, M., 140
Wehman, P., 33, 53
Weiner, H., 355, 437, 438, 523, 540, 541, 546, 547, 555, 559, 561
Weinrott. M., 383
Weinstein, N., 257
Weisberg, P., 212, 542
Weiss, G., 438
Welch, S., 360
Wells, K., 453, 484
Weninger, J., 367
Wepner, S., 331
Werden, D., 315
Werry, J., 472
Wesolowski, M., 314, 462, 472, 493
West, R., 202, 255, 293, 314, 453, 484
Wetherby, B., 301
Wetzel, R., 99, 167
Wexler, D., 41, 103
Wexley, K., 339, 340, 341, 344, 555
Whaler, R., 190
Wheeler, A., 50. 53, 151, 236, 347, 361, 509
Whelan, P., 364
White, G., 82, 460
White, M., 489
White, O., 259
Whitehurst, G., 347
Whitley, A., 298
Whitman, T., 127, 159, 160, 361
Whitney, R., 314
Whitt, J., 420
Whittier, J., 425
Whorton, D., 199, 200, 201
Wickstrom, S., 192, 198
Wienczowski, L., 116
Wigger, D., 296
Wiggins, J., 82
Wikoff, M., 165
Wilander, A.,
Wilcox, J., 199

Wilczenski, F., 19, 86, 89
Williams, J., 366, 511
Williams, R., 240
Williams, W., 288
Williamson, D., 191, 335
Willis, R., 296
Willis, S., 79, 80
Wilson, C., 61, 406, 450
Wilson, D., 268
Wilson, F., 31
Wilson, G., 30, 31, 227, 482, 533
Wilson, N., 470
Wilson, P., 53, 344
Wilson-Morris, M., 261, 262
Wincze, J., 326, 421, 428
Wing, L., 193
Wing, R., 530
Winkler, R., 31, 32, 220, 437, 449
Winett, R., 16, 31, 32, 294
Winston, A., 458
Winton, A., 458, 484
Wisocki, P., 161, 414
Witt, J., 424, 439
Wodarski, J., 191
Wolchik, S., 425, 428, 459
Wolery, M., 344, 470
Wolf, M., 3, 5, 6, 25, 79, 107, 108, 125, 127, 155, 195, 198, 208, 215, 223, 229, 298, 326, 359, 389, 391, 406, 432, 451, 454, 460, 495, 520
Wolfe, D., 207, 208
Wolfe, J., 197, 199
Wolfe, J., 197, 199
Wilfe, M., 361, 365
Wolfe, P., 197
Wolfe, V., 208, 223
Wolkin, J., 299
Wolpin, M., 326
Wolter, C., 197
Wonderlick, S., 129
Wong, S., 364, 502
Wood, R., 207, 208, 218, 219
Woods, C., 207, 221, 326, 557
Woodward, J., 331
Wortman, H., 473
Wray, L., 360
Wright, L., 483
Wright, M., 425
Wulfert, E., 262
Wynne, C., 262, 360

Yamamoto, J., 360
Yarrow, M., 406
Yates, B., 45, 391, 392, 472
Young, C., 199, 202
Young, J., 421, 428
Young, K., 202, 314, 523, 555
Young, R., 26
Yukl, G., 339, 340, 341, 344, 555

Zander, A., 296
Zane, T., 267, 307, 308, 309, 344
Zarcone, 410
Zegiob, L., 458
Zeilberger, J., 451
Zeiler, M., 470, 538
Zettle, R., 358, 365
Zimmer, J., 359
Zimmerman, B., 298, 299, 420
Zimmerman, E., 406
Zimmerman, J., 406, 460, 461, 475
Zohar, D., 548

Subject Index

"ABAB" designs. *See* Withdrawal

Abacus for recording, f68

A-B-C analysis, 26, 182, 243, 583. *See also* Sequence analysis

Abscissa, 88, 175, 583

Accountability: in applied behavioral analysis, 6, 7, 58, 122–3; defined, 583; in single case design, 228, 229

Accuracy, 583; behavioral dimension, 49; in recording, 85; of observer, 62

Achievement Place program, 21, 125, 155, 214–15, 217, 218, 220

Acquired behaviors, 91

Across-behavior multiple-baseline design, 583

Across-individuals multiple-baseline design, 583

Across-situations multiple-baseline design, 583

Activity reinforcers, 155–8, 583; listed, 156–7; "treasure box," 158

Activity table, 583

Adaptation phase, 61, 79, 89–91, 476, 583

Adjusting schedule, 583

Advocacy, 39–40, 106, 211, 482, 494, 583. *See also* Legal decisions affecting applied behavioral analysis

Aggressive behavior: illustration of, 4, 5, 16–17, 21, 24, 44, 49, 57, 282–3; modeled by powerful person, 488; as negative reinforcement, 14; occasioned by extinction, 408, 576; occasioned by punishment, 468, 486, 571, 579; occasioned by response cost, 439, 577; occasioned by timeout, 430, 486, 578; restraints for, 473, 477

Alt-R (differential reinforcement of alternative): as benign procedure, 420; combined with other procedures, 423; combined with punishment example, 493; disadvantages, 421; distinguished from DRI, 419; illustration with other procedures, 423; lasting change, 420; mixed evidence of effectiveness, 421; reinforcing incompatible behavior, 421; selecting behavior already occurring, 422; selecting behavior with same function, 422; with "Good Behavior Game," 432; with modeling, 423

Alternating treatment, 583; advantages and disadvantages, 323; comparison of techiques, 382; defined, 381; for comparison, 384; multielement designs, 381; pairing distinctive S^d's, 381 designs, 381–6, 583

American Psychological Association (APA): ethical code of, 39, 41, 103, 104, 492; statement concerning restrictiveness, 454

Antecedent control: response delay, 319

Antecedent prompting strategies: choosing, 302

Antecedent stimulus, 269–70, 270, 271, 280, 584; complexity, 256; effect on newly acquired behavior, 525; emphasizing or enhancing, 276–7; for applying behavioral procedures, 267; role in stimulus control, 243; to set the occasion, 249; to deter behavior, 268; with abstract properties, 258

Antecedent stimulus properties, 276

Antecedents: combined with responses, 256; defined, 98; evoke responses, 257

Applied behavior analysis (ABA): alterations sought in, 5–6; compared with experimental, 3; defined, 3–4, 98, 584; different roles, 9; essence of, 3; as experiment, 231; features of, 4–5; highest priority of, 13; illustrated, 3; importance of reading literature of, 498; key roles, 18; literature sources, 20; measuring success of, 6; methods of analysis, 5; model for, 10–11; performance based, 4; practical considerations of program, 23; preliminary steps, 13–28; problem prevention, 16; procedures for treatment, 5, 97; professional aspects of, 7; program flowchart, 131; program steps outlined, 10; promoting generality and durability, 497; scientific method in, 7, 30, 31, 50; socially important, 5; strategies for generalization, 33; technological aspect of, 7; use of precision, 24

Applied behavioral analysis program: client's willingness to participate in, 20; controls over in federally sponsored programs, 40; costs of, 22; designing of, 24, 44–5; necessity of, 16–18; persons involved in, 18–19; possibilities of success of, 20–1; prior consultations over, 19–20

Applied behavioral analyst. *See* Behavioral analyst

Applied research, 584

Artificial discriminative stimulus, 584

Artificial reinforcer, 584

Association for Advancement of Behavior Therapy (AABT): ethical questions, 105; peer review process, 121–2

Association for Behavior Analysis (ABA): ethics, 103

Association for Behabior Analysis Task Force, 491

Association for Persons with Severe Handicaps, 482

Association for Retarded Citizens, 482

Aubrey Daniels and Associates, 100

Audio cuing tape, 80

Autism: ABAB design, 234; engagement in activities, 414; overselectivity, 285; peers as models, 297; tantrums reduced with timeout, 451, 459; teaching compound sentences, 361; training affection, 193; using a rapid rate of instruction, 293

Automated Recording Systems, 81–3

Aversive procedures: activities, 471–4; combining with other procedures, 477–8; concurrent contingencies, 477–8; contextual factors, 478–9; contrasted with positive procedure, 106–8, 110, 121, 402; cost of, managing, 490; density, 476; difficulty in selecting activities, 490; extending duration, 495; immobilization example, 473; intensity, 476–7; keeping performance consistent, 495; opportunity to escape, 474; overcorrection—contingent exertion, 396; quality, 474–5; reinforced positive practice, 496; restitutive training, 471; schedule and delay, 475–6; selecting those relevant to misbehavior,

494; the "freeze" technique, 473; variables influencing effectiveness, 474–9. *See also* Punishment

Aversive stimuli: adaptation, 476; advantages of, 482–5; as consequence, 139; avoiding habituation, 476; conditioned, 470–1; considerations in using, 490–4, 571; defined, 139, 469, 584; disadvantages of, 485–90; effective use of, 494–6; extrinsic and intrinsic, 471, 590, 592; intensity, 476; intrusiveness or restrictiveness, 474; mild, 478; paired with unconditioned punishment, 477; positive versus negative reinforcers, 139–43; quality, 474; schedule, 47; unconditioned, 469–70, 599; unnecessary in extinction, 407. *See also* Electric shock therapy; Punishment

Avoidance, 139, 142, 584; signaled, 443, 571, 579. *See also* Escape behavior

Back-up reinforcers, 166, 208–9, 218, 219, 220, 525, 584

Backward chaining procedure, 345–6; 584

Baseline: brief baseline phase, 234–5; data, 92; defined, 584; determination of, 91; intervention phases as, 234; 379–80; multiple baseline designs, 237–42; use of in measuring, 91–3; phase, 91, 230, 234–5; with reinforcement not contingent on dependent variable, 232–4

Baselines: lengths, 92; strength of demonstration, 374

Behavior: defined, 584; examples of dramatic changes, 134; scientific study of, 2–3; principles of, 5

Behavior analysis procedures, 97–8; defined, 97; effectiveness, 104; factors to consider, 14; limitations, 116

Behavior change, 7–11, 23–4; ask for, 20; broader implications of, 46; monitoring, 13–14; tables of procedures for, 570–82; ways of accomplishing, 19–20; voluntary, 41

Behavior modification, 584. *See* Applied behavioral analysis

Behavior of organisms, 2

Behavior-recording techniques. *See* Recording data

Behavior Therapy, 478

Behavior Therapy and Experimental Psychiatry, 478

Behavioral analysis: defined, 3, 584; enabling new discoveries, 231; ongoing evaluation, 227

Behavioral analyst, 19, 30, 584; competence of, 20–1, 22, 104–6; and concern for client, 36

Behavioral anchored rating scale (BARS), 66, 68, 585

Behavioral approach: constructional and functional, 32–3; direct and indirect, 33–4; and foundational skills, 34; mission of, 36–7; priorities in 22–3; setting goals, 24–5

Behavioral assessment: clinical significance, 390; concerning target selection, 31; defined, 44, 584; for individuals, 44; four aspects listed, 45; functional evaluation, 45; justification

for, 45; multidimensional approach, 44–5; selecting measures, 50–9; treatment utility, 45. *See also* Ecobehavioral assessment

Behavioral chains: composition of, 339–41; forging, 341–9; formation of, 338–9

Behavioral community psychology, 16

Behavioral contract, 40–1, 108, 585; alteration of, 124; daily report card, 125–6; guidelines for, 123–4; samples, 109–13

Behavioral contrast, 585; defined, 427; effect on ratio schedules, 567; negative and positive, 548; with punishment, 487

Behavioral dimensions, 47–50; terms defined, 48, 585

Behavioral goals. *See* Goal selection

Behavioral intervention: necessity of, 16–18, 21, 22

Behavioral laws, 393, 585

Behavioral objectives, 31; assessment of, 44–7; context, 49; defined, 47, 585; reviewing for generalization, 33; samples of, 50; specifying, 47–50

Behavioral principles: applicability, 116; defined, 98, 585

Behavioral procedures, 32, 142

Behavioral program, 9, 102, 129

Behavioral recording staff, 79–81

Behavioral recording techniques, 63–74

Behavioral rehearsal, 585

Behavioral repertoires, 23–4, 139

Behavioral technicians, 18–19, 79, 585

Behaviorally anchored rating scale (BARS), 66, 68

Behavior Research and Therapy, 478

Beyond Freedom and Dignity, B. F. Skinner (1971), 114

Biological model, 2–3

Bonus response cost, 442

Bonus tokens, 220

Bottom-line measures, 64

Bribery, 167–8

BRISS component behaviors, 60

Bruxism, rates of, 240–1, 470

Chain, 585

Chaining procedure, 244, 575; backward chaining, 344–6, 584; combining responses, 244; combining with fading, 348; combining with shaping, 348, 349; composition of chains, 339–41; concurrent or simultaneous method, 344; defined, 338, 585; and discriminative stimuli, 346–8; example of stimulus components, 340; forging of behavioral chains, 341–9; formation of behavioral chains, 338–9; forward method, 344; illustration, 339; starting, 344; strengthening response chains, 349; successive approximations, 347; supplemental reinforcers in, 346; in teaching correspondence, 367, 527–8; terminal behavior, 341; total task method, 346; using task analyses, 341; validating task analyses, 342–3; whole task method, 344

Chains: complexity, 339; composition, 339; formation, 338; length, 339

Change agent, 18

Changing criterion design, 374–6; con-

trol of reinforcement, 377; defined, 374, 585; illustrations, 375; multiple probes, 376; reducing caffeine intake, 376; selecting criterion levels, 375
Checklists: as starting point, 99
Children's game: "Secret Pal Game," 194. *See also* Games
CLASS: program, 392
Classroom: attendance as Alt-R, 419; back-up reinforcer use, 218; contextual stimuli, 255; for "handicapped"—generalization problems, 513; fuzzy-gram examples, 194; "Good Behavior-Game," 432; having enough materials, 19; illustrations of imitative S^ds, 299; peers as social reinforcers, 527; *Practice Skills Mastery Program*, 551; studies with tokens, 217; teachers as models, 297; time management program, 529; use of "compliment meter," 194; use of "zones," 19
Client: approval of punishment procedure, 106, 108, 494; defined, 18, 585; endangered from timeout procedure, 459–60; and physical guidance, 301–2; and selection of procedures, 108; and selection of targeted behavior, 30–1, 35–6; and self-directed reinforcement, 184–5; and self-management of procedure, 126–7; self-modeling procedure, 296–7; and self-recording of data, 79–80, 126; and token economy, 210–11; willingness to participate, 20. *See also* Advocacy; Voluntariness
Clinical significance, 585
Coded interval-recording sheet, 70, 71, 585
Coercion, 41, 114, 126, 586
Cognitive behavior modification, 364
Collateral behavior, 586
Collateral measures: defined, 50, 57, 586
Communicative behavior: acquisition of manual communicative skills, 363; defined, 353, 586; maladaptations, 357, 363–5; problems in, 357–9, 365; promoting generalization, 361; and rule governance, 354–6, 357–9, 365–8; shaped by verbal community, 353–4; shaping illustrated, 353
and speech topographics, 357, 365; and stimulus equivalence, 356–7; teaching, 359–63
Communicative disorders, 357
Communicatives skills: teaching, 359–63
Community: applied behavioral analysis in, 16; input, 21; least restrictiveness, 403; problems in rule formulation, 358; support, 121; task analyses to aid functioning, 344
Comparison group, 18
Complex behavior, 575; defined, 586; avoiding use of rules, 368; difficulty of measuring, 62; specifying stimulus properties, 275
Compliment meter, 194
Comprehension: described by stimulus control 260
Computer assisted instruction (CAI): defined, 586; with shaping, 330–1
Concept, 258, 586
Concurrent task method of teaching, 586
Conditional discriminations, 586
Conditional aversive stimulus, 586
Conditioned reinforcer: defined, 144, 586; establishing, 145–6
Conditions: for reinforcer discrimination, 175
Confounding variables, 227, 586
Consequences: defined, 98; general, 102
Consistency: in token delivery, 217
Constructional approach: to goal selection, 32
Consumer satisfaction: use of data in measurement, 59; and validity, 59; with training, 391

Constructional approach, 32, 586
Context: influence on behavior, 254; specifying,47
Contextual conditions, 26
Contextual stimuli: setting events, 254
Contextual variables: with sign language, 363
Contingencies: affecting relapse, 518; analyses, 100–101, 586; analysis chart, 102; competing, 181–2; controlling, 101–3, 586; defined, 98–9, 586; four-term, 254; identification of, 99; management, 102; natural, 98; naturally supportive, 182; of reinforcement—rules, 355; sensitivity to changes, 356; supplemental, 186; three-term, 251
Contingency delay, 462, 586
Contingency managers, 104–6, 586; defined, 18; peers as, 192–8; as recorder, 80; and selection of procedures, 108; withdrawal designs, 236
Contingency-shaped behavior, 586
Contingency-shaped group, 356
Contingency-specifying stimuli, 355
Contingent exercise, 586–7
Contingent exertion, 471, 586
Contingent observation, 457–8, 587
Contingent reinforcement loss. *See* Response cost
Contingent relation, 587
Continuous behavior, 587
Continuous reinforcement schedule (CRF), 182–3, 543, 587
Contracting: clarifying terms, 124; from high school student, 112; goal completion card, 113; guidelines illustrated, 123; option to withdraw, 124; sample with client, 110; selecting contingencies, 109; selecting procedures, 123; with institution, 111
Contractual arrangements, 123–7; as signals for reinforcers, 175
Contrast phenomenon, 548–9, 587
Contrived prompts: example with auditory stimuli, 280
Contrived reinforcers, 166–70
Control, 587
Cooperative learning, 190, 587
Correspondence: defined, 366; reinforcing, 366–7, 367–8; teaching, 366–7, 527–8, 575, 580, 587
Correspondence training: defined, 366; for maintenance, 527; for mediating generalization, 511, 514; functional equivalence, 367; social importance, 366; using modeling and chaining, 367
Cost and benefits of programs, 124
Cost effectiveness, 35, 45, 124, 391–2, 490
Counselling: and behavior change, 20
Countercontrol, 114–15, 168–9, 436, 587
Co-workers: peer training, 199
CRF. *See* Continuous reinforcement schedule
Criterion: defined, 49, 587; for program steps, 334; level selected, 50; specifying for behavioral objectives, 49–50, 185; observer, 84, 587; with accuracy dimension, 50
Critical features of stimuli: defined, 587; emphasizing, 281; learned through prompts, 279; magnifying, 285; of stimuli, 256
Cuing: irrelevant, 284. *See also* Prompting
Cumulative numbers: graphing of, 89, 90, 92, 542

Daily report card: defined, 587; for nonsoiling, 558; with children, 125
Data: as feedback, 129; change due to functional relations, 229; demonstration of small improvements, 128; ongoing systems, 64; pitfalls in analyzing, 66

Delayed prompting: advantages and disadvantages, 308; defined, 307, 587; examples of success, 307; graduated, 306; illustrated, 308; in complex teaching programs, 309; moment of transfer, 307
Delinquency: selecting functional goals, 36; use of timeout, 452
Delphi method, 587
Dependent group contingency: advantages and disadvantages, 192; defined, 191, 587; functional relations, 229
Dependent variable, 232–4; defined, 57, 587
Deprivation of reinforcers, 176, 588
Developmentally disabled: advocacy, 40; controversy over aversives, 482; fading of soccer skills, 312; Public Law 94-142, 402; selecting age appropriate goals, 36; selecting peer tutors, 202; teaching community living skills, 288; use of aversive stimuli, 476; use of negative practice, 473; use of physical guidance, 301; using match-to-sample method, 283
Differential reinforcement: advantages, 420; applied effectively, 277; avoids aversive stimuli, 396; defined, 252–3, 588; elements of, 253–4; essential to success, 274; establishing operation, 255; examples, 419; illustrated, 258; implementing procedure, 274–8, 572; in goal-setting, 290–1; in imitation games, 294; reversal, 235–6; stimulus equivalence, 262; with several stimuli, 258
Differential reinforcement of diminishing rates (DRD): advantages, 430–1; defined, 430, 588; disadvantages, 431; effective use of, 431–3
Differential reinforcement of high rates (DRH), 564–5, 582, 588
Differential reinforcement of incompatible behavior (DRI), 419, 576, 588
Differential reinforcement of low rates (DRL): advantages, 430–1; defined, 429, 588; DRD as variation, 430; disadvantages, 431; effective use of, 431–3, 577
Differential reinforcement of zero rates of the behavior (DRO): advantages, 425–6; as primary procedure, 425; attention to the negative, 426; combined with other procedures, 428, 429; combined with timeout, 452; comparison of whole interval and momentary, 428; defined, 424–5, 588; disadvantages, 426–7; durable effects, 425; effective use of, 427–8, 577; graduated omission training, 427; illustrated, 425; momentary DRO, 428–9, 592; whole-interval versus momentary DRO, 429
Direct approach, 33
Direct contingencies, 359
Direct instruction, 523, 588
Direct observation, 99
Discomfort, 116
Discrete behavior: defined, 65, 588; measuring, 65
Discrete events, 65
Discriminated operant, 588
Discrimination: antidote to generalization, 249–50; between presence or absence of stimulus, 257; between two or more antecedent stimuli, 257–9; between two or more responses, 260; of contextual factors, 174–5; defined, 588; developing imitative prompts as, 294–5; developing instructions as, 292–4; learning by response sound, 261; discriminative properties: of facial expression, 261; use of prompts, 280
Discriminative stimulus: as link in chain, 339; combined to occasion generalization, 512; combining with shaping,

334–6; defined, 250–1, 588; detecting those mysterious, 281; effects of removing, 269; establishing discriminative control, 251; example, 250; fading, 318; for aversive consequences, 29; as reason for relapse to unwanted behavior, 520; as reinforcer on interval schedule, 546–8; rules with response cost, 443; to occasion telephone answering, 259; use in reducing behavior, 444–5; used in behavioral chains, 346–8; used to inhibit illustrated, 444
Doe v. Koger, 453
DRD. *See* Differential reinforcement of diminishing rates
DRH. *See* Differential reinforcement of high rates
DRL. *See* Differential reinforcement of low rates
Duration, 48, 589
Duration recording, 48, 69, 74, 589

Echolalia, 47
Ecobehavioral assessment, 87, 100; analyses, 102; defined, 45–7, 589
Edible reinforcers, 151–3, 589
Electric shock therapy, 483, 491–2
Elicit, 589
Emit, 589
Employee absenteeism, 254
Enabling skills. *See* Foundational skills
Environment: in applied behavioral analysis, 19–20, 45–7, 186–7, 193; enriching for timeout effectiveness, 459; establishing change, 152, 532–3; home support, 125; preparation of, 127–8; reinforcing, 186–7; Epilepsy: self-inflicted, 483
Equivalence classes, 261–2, 589
Errorless learning, 314–16, 317, 319, 320, 573, 589
Escape behavior, 139, 142, 571, 576, 577, 578, 579, 589. *See also* Avoidance
Establishing operations: being punished, 468; defined, 152, 180, 589; described, 255; effect of generalization, 504; example, 255; impact of punishment, 478; influence of behaviors, 256
Establishing stimulus, 256, 589
Ethical considerations, 589; AABT questions, 105; APA code, 41, 104, 492; in applied behavioral analysis, 7, 24, 30, 31, 35, 101, 103–5; and behavioral contracts, 40–1; exploitation in behavior modification, 9–10; in use of punishment, 485; use of reinforcers, 168. *See also* Legal decisions affecting applied behavioral analysis
Evaluation of procedures experimentally: group designs, 227–8
Evaluation of treatment programs, 98; alternating treatment (multielement) design, 381–6; changing-criterion design, 374–6; effects of procedural interventions, 393; functional analysis of acquired skills, 374; generality of findings, 392–3; multiple probes, 376–8; preliminary considerations, 373–4; significance of demonstrated functional relation, 389–92; single-subject design, 386–9; within-subjects comparative designs, 378–9
Event recording, 65–6, 68, 74, 589
Exchangeable reinforcers, 166
Exemplars, 508–10, 580, 589
Experimental behavior analysis, 3, 231, 589
Experimental design, 386, 387–7, 589
Experimental significance, 590
Exploitation, 9
External reinforcement, 178
External validity, 590
Extinction burst, 590
Extinction differential, 141
Extinction-induced aggression, 590
Extinction procedure, 402, 576; advan-

tages, 406–7; as management tool, 405; clearly specifying conditions, 412; combined with R+ of incompatible behavior, 407; combined with reinforcement, 406; combining with other procedures, 413–14; compared to planned ignoring, 457; continuation for sufficient time, 413; deciding when appropriate, 414; defined, 405–6, 590; delayed effects, 409; diagrammed, 449; disadvantages, 409; effective use of, 409–14; examples of effectiveness, 406; extinction bursts, 408, 409, 576; gradual effect, 407–8; imitation of inappropriate behavior, 409; increases in rate and intensity of response, 408; inducing aggression, 408, 409; long-lasting effect, 407; peer reactions, 409; positive scanning, 411; properties of, 407–9; reinforcement, 409–12; responding during, 543–4; response maintenance, 543; solving the dilemma, 410; spontaneous recovery, 408–9; to avoid aversive stimuli, 396; uncontrollable reinforcers, 409; when using timeout, 456; with other procedures, 413; withholding all reinforcers, 410

Facial screening, 458, 590
Fading, 311–12; combining with chaining, 348; combining with shaping, 335–6; defined, 311, 590; effectiveness of, 312–14, 574; and errorless learning, 314–16, 317, 320, 573, 589; focusing on critical stimuli, 316–17; graduated guidance, 313; illustrated, 312; in counseling, 312; of irrelevant stimulus features, 315; of physical prompts, 313; removing irrelevant stimuli, 318; response delay, 319–20; steps with prompts, 280; stimulus equalization, 318; versus delayed prompting, 320
Families: Project 12-Ways, 156; study comparing Alt-R and DRO, 426; time management, 531; tokens used when shopping, 442
Feedback, 62–3, 133–4, 590; and recording bias, 63; as a reinforcer, 164–5, 184, 217; from self-recordings, 164; "I Spy" activity, 196; staff training, 164; to nurses, 234; with tokens, 215. See also Punishment; Reinforcement
Fixed-interval scallops, 541–2
Fixed-interval (FI) schedule: adding limited-hold schedules, 549–50, 581; advantages and disadvantages, 544–5; compared to fixed-time interval, 538–9; compared to variable-interval schedule, 539–40, 550, 581; compared with limited hold, 550; consistency of performance under, 541–2; defined, 538, 590; error patterns, 542; fixed-interval scallops, 541–2; promoting preferred rates of responding under, 543–50; sponding during extinction, 543–4; response rates, 540–1; of study behavior, 543; in work environments, 545
Fixed-ratio (VR) schedule: characteristics of, 554; compared with variable-ratio schedule, 555–7, 582; compared with interval schedules, 557–60, 582; defined, 554, 590; illustrated, 554; responding during extinction, 557; variability of performance, 556
Fixed-time (FT) schedule: compared to fixed-interval schedule, 538–9; compared with variable-time schedule, 539–40; defined, 538, 590
Flexibility, 123
Forward chaining, 590
Foundational skills, 34
Four-term contingency, 254, 590
Frames, 329
Freeze technique, 590

Frequency of behavior, 590; measuring, 62
Frustration, 2, 31
Functional analysis: of acquired skills, 374; designs, 387–8; determining significance of, 389–90
Functional equivalence, 261–2, 590
Functional movement training, 472
Functional reinforcers, 32
Functional relations, 228, 229, 378, 590; determining significance of, 389–92; in withdrawal designs, 232, 236; using differential reinforcers, 236
Functional skill, 590
"Fuzzy-Gram," 194

Games, 155, 158, 187, 194–5, 197, 295, 423, 433, 548, 591, 599
Generalization of response: advantages and disadvantages, 501–2; asking for, 506; assessing for, 504–5; assessment during multiple baseline, 241; by correspondence training, 514; caution in multiple baseline, 240; combined with cognitive behavior sequentially, 506; of communicative behavior, 360; defined, 6, 500–501, 590; evaluation of, 392–3; fluency, 504, 522–4; lack of trained behavior, 504; modifying behaviors sequentially, 506–7; modifying maladaptive consequences, 508; programmed, 503–4, 505; punishment promotes inappropriate, 486–7; response induction, 501; reviewing and refining objectives, 505–6; shaping, 502; teaching, 514–15; training sufficient exemplars, 500, 508–10, 580, 588; training loosely, 510–11, 580, 591; training to naturally supportive conditions, 507–8, 575; unprogrammed, 502–3; using indiscriminable antecedent and consequential contingencies, 511–12
Generalization of stimulus: advantages and disadvantages, 501; defined, 249, 500, 590–1; generalization map, 49; programming common stimuli, 512–14; programming techniques, 506; stimulus change decrement, 512; strategies, 515. See also Transferring stimulus control
Generalized imitation, 295, 591
Generalized reinforcer, 165, 176, 591
Genetics, 23
Gifted students, 16
Goal Analysis, Mager (1972), 49
Goal conflicts, 37; advocacy, 39–40; behavior analyst role in, 38–9; and behavioral contracts, 40–1; client involvement, 38; institutional review committees, 40; other concerned individuals, 39; parental involvement, 39; responsible, 30
Goal outcome, 591
Goal process, 591
Goal selection, 13–16, 27–8; alternative, 30, 31; attainable, 21–2, 31; behavioral approach, 24–5; constructional and functional, 32, 33, 35–6, 47; compatible with mission, 36; cooperative, competitiveness, and individualist, 37; cost/benefit analysis, 35; direct and indirect, 33–4; explicit immediate and long-term, 34–6, 41; general rule for, 35–6; guided by concern for client, 36; guidelines for, 30–42; high priority, 42; initial considerations, 28; involving parents, 39; justification of, 34–5; mission-oriented, 36–7; questions for, 41–2; respecified as behavioral objectives, 54; scientific process, 41; as scientific question, 31; unchallenging, 31; unrealistic, 17, 31, 38; using behavioral contracts, 41
Goal-setting: choosing among different antecedent prompting strategies, 302;

defined, 288, 591; as discriminative stimuli, 290; effectiveness of, 290–1; illustrated, 288; instructional prompts (the "tell" procedure), 291–4; prompting with physical guidance, 175, 301–2; providing a model (the "show" procedure), 294–301
Goals: achievable, 328; as discriminative stimuli, 290; as full behavioral objectives, 290, as task hierarchies, 34; attainment through shaping, 328; competitive, 37; cooperative, 37; defined, 30; described, 24; expanding or constraining options, 33; percentage achieved, 329; potentially controversial, 35; reasonable yet challenging, 31; responsible selection, 9; short- and long-term benefits, 34; to objectives-flowchart, 54; unrealistic, 17; use of behavioral assessment systems, 25; verbal descriptions or numerical values, 29; what individuals do, not say, 25; with general utility listed, 33
"Good Behavior Game," 432, 433, 548, 591
"Grab Bag Game," 155
Graduated guidance, 314
Graduated prompting, 309, 310
Graphing, 10, 327, 494; demonstrating progress, 128; depicting intervals, 91; described, 87–9; steady state versus acquisition data, 92–3
Group: assessment for comparison, 18; contingencies for peer support, 527; dependent contingencies, 191; design or single-subject design, 386; ecobehavioral assessment, 87; experimental designs, 227; "Good Behavior Game," 433; independent contingencies, 190; interdependent contingencies, 190; member diversity, 296; observational recording, 86; the power of the tests, 229; programs with fixed time schedules, 539; selecting step size, 334; social faciliation, 547; token programs, 216; use of shaping, 327
Group reinforcement: comparative effects of different group contingencies, 191–2, 591; dependent group contingencies, 191; independent group contingencies, 190; interdependent group contingencies, 190–1. See also Peer reinforcement
Groups: observer behavior of, 86–7

Habituation. See Adaptation
Handicapped children: peers programs, 198; sign language training, 356
Health practices, 16
Heterogeneous: links in chain, 339
Hints. See Prompting
History: historical information about contingencies, 100. See also Learning history of behavioral problem
Homogeneous: links in chain, 339
Human rights committee, 107, 121, 455

Identification of problems, 17–18
Imitation, 576, 591; from modeling, 298; generalized, 295; underdeveloped skills, 295. See also Modeling
Imitative prompts, 294
Immobilization, 473
Incidental teaching, 361–3, 511, 591
Incompatible behavior, 591
Increasing behavior: table for procedures, 570–1
Independent group contingency, 190, 591
Independent variable: defined, 50, 97, 591; functional relations, 229; or intervention, 57
Indexes of agreement, 85
Individual: ability to change, 22
Informed consent: as safeguard, 107; defined, 591; for aversive procedures,

492, 494; for timeout, 455; right to withdraw, 40; with token economies, 210. See also Client
Institutional review: as U.S. government requirement, 40
Instructional programs: effective teaching, 331; forms listed, 329; reinforcing properties, 40
Instructional prompts: influence of, 62, 175, 291–301, 591
Instructions: combined with modeling, 298; developing discriminative stimuli, 292; illustrations from literature, 291; influence of interval schedules, 546; prompts, 278, 291; the "Tell" procedure, 291; using a rapid presentation rate, 293
Intensity, 592
Interdependent group contingencies: classroom example, 191; defined, 190; with tokens, 217
Intermittent reinforcement: fading token system, 183; schedule, 182–3, 581, 592; thinning reinforcement, 592; with extinction, 407
Interobserver agreement: formula, 65–6; formula for events, 68; how calculated, 69; indexes, 63, 592; score sheet, 68; when broad categories are used, 63; with event recording, 66
Interpersonal skills: using peers, 198
Interval schedules of reinforcement: adding limited-hold schedules, 549–50; advantages and disadvantages, 544–5; arranging competition, 548; capitalizing on behavioral contrast, 548–9; characteristics of interval-schedule performance, 540–4; choosing between fixed and variable schedules, 550–1; consistency of performance, 541–2; defined, 538, 592; effects of self-statements, 547; error patterns, 542; fixed-interval (FI), 538; fixed-time (FT), 538–9; maintaing high rate patterns, 546; modifying rates of responding, 547; promoting preferred rates of responding under, 545–50; providing appropriate history, 545–6; rate-building illustration, 545; reducing length of interval, 545; responding during extinction, 543–4; response maintenance, 543; response rates, 540–1, 545; selecting by response rates, 540; size of interval, 545; thinning reinforcement under, 551; using discriminative stimuli, 546–8; variable-interval (VI), 539–40; variable-time (VT), 539; with verbal stimuli, 546
Interval time-sample, 69–73, 74, 80, 81
Intervention, 393
Intervention phase, 92, 97; as baseline, 234, 379; stability, 230
Intrinsic motivation, 592
"I-Spy" activity, 195, 196

"Job Jar," 181
Journal of Applied Behavior Analysis: articles of significance, 390
Judges: evaluating social validity, 391

Labeled praise. See Specific praise
Language: development by shaping, 326; expanding complex repertoires, 361; inappropriate, 357; influence on behavior, 353
Latency, 69, 592
Laws: natural, 7; token economies, 210
Leadership and supervisory effectiveness: feedback, 164
Learning, 592
Learning history: and conditioned reinforcers, 146; effect of aversive stimuli, 473; effect on interval schedules, 545; effect on maintenance, 525; effect on response cost, 438; effect on timeout, 460; effects on punishment, 477; ef-

fects on variable ratio schedules, 559; differential treatment, 169; gathering information about, 100, 185; of individual, 185; reinforcement schedules necessary, 561; and rule governed behavior, 292; sensitivity to schedules, 566; stimulus control, 258

Learning Together and Alone, Johnson and Johnson (1975), 37

Least restrictive environment: philosophy, 402; policy, 454

Legal decisions affecting applied behavioral analysis, 103, 485; *Doe v. Koger*, 453; *Morales v. Turman*, 453; *New York State Association for Retarded Children v. Rockefeller*, 453; in reducing behavior, 402; *S-1 v. Turlington*, 453; *Sherry v. New York State Education Department*, 453; *Stuart v. Nappi*, 453; in a token economy, 209–10; in timeout procedure, 453–5, 578; *Welsch v. Likins*, 453; *Wyatt v. Stickney*, 103, 106, 108, 122, 453, 492. *See also* Advocacy; Behavioral contract; Ethical considerations

Limited hold, 592; examples 550; illustrated, 549; to increase response rates, 550

Links: defined, 592; discriminative features, 340; dual stimulus function, 339; interdependence, 340; point to begin fading, 349; subskills, 338; use those in repertoire, 344

Locus of control scale: relapse prevention, 530

Long-term benefits, 34, 41

Maintaining behavior, 8–9, 534, 575, 580; by time management, 530; capitalizing on natural reinforcers, 525; challenges to, 519; changing one's lifestyle, 533; collecting follow-up data, 498; evoking social reinforcement, 533; factors impeding, 518–20; factors promoting programming contingencies for maintenance, 521–2, 592; identifying natural antecedents, 525; minimize errors during acquisition, 522; peer punishment as problem, 520; punishment of change, 520; Relapse Prevention Model, 434; strategies for preventing relapse, 522–35; table for procedures for, 580–2; tendency to relapse, 519; tightening reinforcement criteria, 526; unplanned reinforcement, 521; unprogrammed maintenance, 520–1; with correspondence training, 527

Mangers: effective use of response cost, 437; use of praise, 165

Marketing: novel token economies, 220

Masochism: and aversive procedure, 478

Matching law, 592

Match-to-sample method, 574; defined, 283, 592; delayed, 258; errorless teaching of discrimination, 284; example, 259; for communicative skills, 361; illustration, 315; phases of training, 317; simultaneous, 258

Maximum-to-minimum prompts: fading, 313

Measurement: accuracy of, 57–8; collateral, 57; implementing procedures flowchart, 93; objective, 593; selecting valid methods of, 58–9, 63; wrist abacus, 68. *See also* Evaluation of treatment programs; Recording data

Modeling (the "show" procedure), 293, 570, 592; as adjunct to chaining, 348; choosing over vocal prompts, 302; combined with shaping, 334; combining with shaping, 334–5; defined, 293; encouraging rehearsal, 298, 573; facilitation of responses, 298; imitation, 294–5, 298–301; influence of multiple models, 298; model competence, 296;

participant, 297; prompting imitation, 298; punishment, 487–8; selection of, 295–8; the "Show" procedure, 293; in teaching correspondence, 367; using simple behavior, 299; with Alt-R, 424; with instructions and rules, 298

Models: selecting prestige, 297; similarity, 298

Momentary DRO, 428

Momentary time-sampling: defined, 70, 74, 592; invalid estimations, 72; for persistent behaviors, 70; PLA-Check, 86

Monitoring of procedures, 126–9, 494

Monitoring of reinforcement, 185–6

Morales v. Turman, 453

Motivation Assessment Scale (MAS), 178

Movement suppression timeout, 459, 592–3

Multielement designs: advantages, 383; comparatives purposes of, 384; defined, 381; disadvantages, 384. *See also* Single-case experimental designs

Multiple-baseline designs: across behaviors, 237–8; across individuals, 238–9; across settings, 239, 240; across situations, 239–41; assess for generalization, 241–2; defined, 237, 593; illustration with individuals, 239; selection considerations, 238; unplanned generalization, 238; with reversal design, 386; withdrawing elements, 38. *See also* Single-case experimental designs

Multiple probes, 376–9, 593

Multiple schedule design. *See* Alternative treatment design

Multiple treatment interference, 593

Narrative recording: defined, 26, 593

Natural discriminative stimulus, 593

Natural reinforcers, 32, 138, 179–80, 186, 218, 221–2, 524–5, 570, 593

Needs assessment, 593

Negative contingencies. *See* Aversive stimuli; "Good Behavior Game"; Overcorrection; Punishment; Response cost procedure; Timeout

Negative practice, 472, 473, 593

Negative punishment. *See* Response cost

Negative reinforcement: combined with positive, 143; differential definition, 141; effective uses, 140; for social avoidance, 140; habit development, 141; procedure defined, 140, 593; when to apply, 142

Negative reinforcer, 593. *See also* Aversive stimuli

New York State Association for Retarded Children v. Rockefeller, 453

Noncontingent restraint, 473

Nonverbal behavior, 25, 282

Norm. *See* Baseline

Objective. *See* Behavioral objectives

Objective measures, 58

Objectives: intermediate or enabling, 288; shaping, 331

Objectivity: in measurements, 58

Observation and measurement, 57–63

Observational method: choices of, 72–3, 74

Observational recording: zone system, 86

Observational system: for applied behavior analysis programs, 10; if unreliable, 63

Observational training: on site, 83

Observer drift, 84

Observer independence, 85

Occasioning behavior, 243–5, 259; defined, 249, 570, 593; table for procedures, 572–5

Omission training, 424–34

Operant behavior, 593

Operant level, 593

Operation, 25

Operational definition: applied to target behavior, 25, 63; defined, 25, 593

Operationizing: target behaviors, 63; vague terms, 4

Operational statement, 593

Ordinate, 87, 175, 593

Organizational management: expression of appreciation, 193; reinforcement bombardment, 195; who controls reinforcers?, 184

Organizational policies: conditions of aversive consequences, 494

Outcomes, evaluating. *See* Evaluation of treatment programs

Outcome variables, 593

Overcorrection, 402, 495, 578, 594; examples of educative aspect, 484; for reducing self-stimulation, 483; positive practice component, 471; with "low functioning" people, 483

Overgeneralization, 250, 594

Over selectivity: correcting, 285

Parameters, 594. *See also* Behavioral dimensions

Parents: approval of procedure, 210, 494; and choosing goals, 39; observations, 102; and recording data, 79, 101; and selection of measurements, 59; and selecting procedures, 108; and training to implement procedure, 494; use of activity reinforcers, 155; using daily report cards, 125

Partial-interval time-sampling, 74; defined, 70, 74, 594; overestimates occurences, 72; score sheet, 71; system illustration, 70

A Passion for Excellence, Peters and Austin (1985), 545

Peer management: use of extinction, 410

Peer-mediated strategies, 192, 199

Peer reinforcement: peer feedback, 217; peers as contingency managers, 195–8; peers as tutors and trainers, 198–203, 494; in modeling, 297, 573; punishment as instructive to peers, 484–5; strategy for, 192–3; support for maintaining changed behavior, 491, 527, 580; training for, 193–5

Peer review of procedures, 121–2, 491, 594

Peer training, 199

Peer tutoring: checklist, 201; cost effective, 199; examples, 199; of handicapped children, 202; organizing a program, 200; program steps, 205; progress evaluation, 205; to increase generalization, 513; selection and training, 200; successful programs, 202

Peers, direct involvement, 192–203; as positive reinforcers, 532; imitation of punished behavior, 485; positive practice model, 484; reasons for program involvement, 195; support, 527

Penalties. *See* Response cost procedure; Timeout

Performance: as feature of applied behavior analysis, 4–5, 33; match with report, 25; measuring of, 57–9; as result of treatment program, 374

Permanent product: recording can minimize reactivity, 64; to measure performance, 64

Personalized system of instruction (PSI), 85, 330, 563, 594; peer tutors, 199; use of dense intervals, 541

Physical guidance, 495; combining with chaining, 347; combining with shaping, 335; defined, 301, 594; prompting with, 175, 301–2

Planned activity check (PLA-Check): defined, 86, 594

Planned ignoring, 457, 594

Plateau, 334

Positive feedback, 216

Positive practice: compared with/without reinforcement, 496; illustrated, 472

Positive reductive procedures, 434

Positive reinforcement procedures: contrasted with aversive procedures, 106–8, 110, 139–43, 570, 571, 574, 575, 594

Positive reinforcer, 570, 594; as consequences, 139; illustrated, 140; to increase behavior, 138

Positive scanning, 411–12, 594; by modeling with Alt-R, 424

Post-reinforcement pauses, 541

Praise. *See* Specific praise

Precise behavioral measurement, 594

Premack principle, 158–9, 160, 595

Preparing the Environment, 127-8

Preschool children, 367

Primary reinforcer. *See* Unconditioned reinforcer

Principles of behavior: immediacy, 173; generated by single-subject designs, 392; derived scientifically, 5; of effective shaping in PSI, 330; to govern behavior, 23

Privileges, 169

Probe, 595

Procedural package, 97

Procedural selection: aversiveness, 106–8; chart outlining, 117; and community support, 121; contracting for, 109–10, 123–4; countercontrol, 114–15; evidence of effectiveness, 104; flexibility, 123; implementing, 131; inventories and interviews, 99; involving key people, 108; peer review of, 121–2; phase, 97; positiveness, 106; preparing environment, 127–8; procedural package, 97; required resources, 120–1; restrictiveness, 106; revising unsuccessful procedures, 129; stimulus, 97–8; strategies, 101; terminating successful procedures, 129–30; treatment, 99

Procedural strategies: selection, 102-16

Procedures: behavioral, 142; defined, 5; demonstrated effective, 20; examples of various effects, 404; factors to consider, 14; founded on laws, 5; monitoring, 128; parametric values, 403; reinforcing to the user, 120; replication of, 5; revising if unsuccessful, 129; selecting most constructive, 402; selection flowchart, 118; selection of, 25; shaping, 324; tables for altering behavior, 570-82

Procrastination: illustration of, 4, 5

Proctor, 330

Programmed instruction, 282, 328–9, 595

Program packages: as alternative to supervised training, 104

Project 12-Ways, 156

Prompting: defined, 278, 595; delayed, 307–9, 320–1, 573; fading of, 311–15, 320–1, 572, 573; graduated, 309–11, 573, 591; illustration, 278; imitative, 591; modeling (the "show" procedure), 294–301, 314; physical guidance, 301–2, 313–14, 572; the process, 279; samples as, 283–4; selecting, 278–80; size and intensity, 316; the "tell" procedure, 291–4, 314; time delay, 598–9; unnecessary, 306; with auditory prompts, 317

Prompting strategies, 278, 279

Prompts: color, 280; contrived, 278; defined, 278, 595; extra-stimulus, 278; instructional, 291; language example, 281; mathematical, 281; within-stimulus, 278

PSI. *See* Personalized system of instruction

Public Law 94-142: client involvement, 38; rules for expulsion, 453

Punisher, 595

Punishment, 32, 249; administered consistently and immediately, 475; advantages of, 482–5; promotes aggression, 486, 579; applied too frequently, 467; behavioral contrast example, 487; caution concerning consistent use, 475; clearly communicating conditions, 479; combined with Alt-R, 493; combined with extinction, 477; compared with response cost, 440; considerations in using, 490–4; convenience to managers, 485; course of reactions described, 485; defined, 469, 595; delayed, 475; detrimental effects, 482; diagrammed, 450; differential definition, 141; disadvantages of, 485–90; difficulty selecting relevant kinds, 490; effective use of, 494–6, 579; effects of discriminative stimuli, 478; electric shock therapy, 491–2; examples of Sᵈ, 479; facilitating adaptive behavior, 484; history, 274; in schools, 467; influence of agent, 479; inform about conditions, 494; issues of restrictiveness, 396; and "learned helplessness," 487; mild, 467; modeling, 487–8; of modified behavior as reason for relapse, 519–20; overuse, 489–90; paired with non-reinforcement, 470; person as conditioned aversive stimuli, 488; prevalence of, 468; procedures, 106–8, 141–2, 467–9; programming generalization and maintenance, 494; promotes inappropriate generalization, 486–7, 579; promotes negative "self-esteem," 488–9, 579; public antipathy, 490; recidivism rates, 477; reinforceable alternatives as prevention, 489; risk of stimulus generalization, 486; suppresses responses, 486; unnecessary prompting seen as, 306; provokes withdrawal, 485–6, 579. See also Ethical considerations

Rate, 48, 595
Ratio schedules of reinforcement: adjusting schedule, 556; advantages, 559–60; changes in reinforcement density, 567; characteristics of performance under, 554–9; compared with interval schedules, 565–8; consistency of performance, 556–7; continued responding in extinction, 557–8; defined, 554, 595; disadvantages of, 563–4; effective use of, 561–3; effect of size, 555; factors influencing responding rates, 560; fixed-ratio (FR) schedule, 554; high rates of responding, 555–6; ratio strain in, 555–6, 595; reinforcement density, 558–9; variable-ratio (VR) schedule, 554
Ratio strain, 217, 555, 562
Reactivity: defined, 59–61, 595; distinguished from adaptation, 90–1; in observational recording, 60; influence upon the data, 62; may compromise validity, 59; problems with automated recording systems, 82; reduction of, 61–2
Recalibrate: observers, 84
Recorders of data: automated systems, 81–3; calibration of, 84–5, 595; contingency managers, 80–1; daily report cards, 125–6; observer drift, 84, 593; parents, 79; self-recording, 62, 79–80, 83, 126–7, 175, 185–6, 530–1; training, 83–4. See also Recording data
Recording data: coded interval-recording sheet, 70–1; cues for timing, 80–1; duration, 69, 74; event, 65, 74; from groups, 86; guide for selecting, 74; independent collection of, 85; interobserver agreement assessment (IOA), 64–5, 66–9; interval time-sample, 69–73, 74, 80; permanent product, 64, 74, 594; PLA-Check, 86–7; in a token

economy, 211; transitory, 63, 65; variables, 87; zone system, 86. See also Measurement; Recorders of data; Reliability
Recording systems: automated, 79; computerized, 82
Records: as starting point, 99; clients, 26; for token program, 211
Recovery, 141, 595
Reducing behavior (Chapters, 23, 24, 25, 26, 27), 6; comparison of positive reduction procedures, 434, 595; decision to target, 401–3; extinction, 405–14; Good Behavior Game, 432, 433; procedures for, 403–5; selecting procedure for, 496; table of defined and illustrated procedures, 397–8, 576–9. See also Differential reinforcement; Response cost procedure; Stimulus control
Reinforcers, 32, 33, 596; activity, 155–8, 583; appropriateness of, 143, 176–80, 217–18, 570; arranging competition, 548; artificial, 179; back-up, 15, 166, 208–9, 216, 218, 219, 220, 525; check, 177; choice of, 108; concerns and suggestions, 166; conditioned, 144–6, 251, 586; delivery of, 183–7, 215; discrimination, 174; edible, 151–3, 589; exchangeable, 166; extrinsic, 166–7, 178–9; feedback, 164–5, 184; functional, 32, 410; generalized, 165–6, 176, 184; group, 197; hierarchy, 100; identification, 176; intrinsic, 340–1; learned, 144; matching with individuals, 146, 169, 177, 218–20; menu, 178, 596; natural, 32, 138, 179–80, 186, 218, 221–2, 524–5, 570, 593; neutral, 144, 146; novelty, 180–1; planned, 138; positive versus negative, 139–43, 570, 594; preferences, 177; and the Premack principle, 158–9, 160; quality, 176; removing during timeout, 457; as reserve in response cost, 440; rewards, 179, 187; sampling, 181, 570, 596; self-selection, 177; social, 160–4, 597; specific and labeled praise, 165, 216–17; supplementary, 173–4, 346, 598; survey, 154, 596; tangible, 153–5, 219, 598; tokens, 210, 212–14, 525–6, 599; unconditioned average stimuli, 144; unconditioned positive, 144, 599; used contingently in chaining, 345; variety, 180; vary, 177; when traditional rewards fail, 167; who dispenses, 184; withhold, 576. See also Aversive stimuli
Reinforcement, 10, 133–4; absence of, 274; activities, 186; adequate amount, 176; adjustment for maintenance, 525; availability under limit-hold, 549; available for alternative behaviors, 477; of behavioral chain, 349; bribery, 167; cessation as cause of relapse, 518–19; change in schedule of, 549; characteristics of interval schedules, 540; combined with extinction, 406; component of developing expertise, 243; consistency, 183, 277; continued reinforcement of unwanted behavior as reason for relapse, 519; in correspondence, 367–8, 527–8; defined, 138, 141, 595; delayed with preschoolers, 526; density, 595; determining quantity, 176; differential, 251, 290–1; effect of response deprivation, 160; establishing behavioral chains, 338; external monitoring, 186; in fixed interval schedules, 538; group, 190–2, 548; histories, 46; identifying natural contingencies, 138, 524; immediate versus delayed, 124, 173, 214–15, 526; individual preference, 144; maintaining stimulus control, 321; management of contingencies, 135; maximizing in environ-

ment, 223; of modeled behavior, 299; and "natural leaders," 138, 139; natural use with token economy, 223; peer, 192–203, 527; planned, 138; postponement under schedules, 551; procedure, 139, 595; reserve, 445, 596; selection, 143; self-directed, 184–5, 531–2; supportive environment, 186–7, 193; supportive schedules of, 182–3, 574; survey, 178; thinning, 183; token economies, 207; waiting, 174; withdrawal with timeout and response cost, 396; withholding, 169–70, 576, 578. See also Token economies
Reinforcement conditions: communicated clearly, 17
Reinforcing alternative and incompatible behaviors, 419–20; advantages, 420–1; differential reinforcement of zero rates of behavior (DRO), 424–9; differential reinforcing low and diminishing rates of behavior (DRL and DRD), 429–34; disadvantages, 421; effective use of, 423–4; selecting replacement behavior, 421–3
Reinforcing stimuli, 139
Relapse prevention: arranging environmental stimuli for, 532; by self recording, 530; formal strategies, 522; model for substance abusers, 533–5; opposing powerful discrimination, 520; reinforcers withdrawn abruptly, 518; self-management strategies, 528
Reliability in measurements, 58, 62, 63, 73–5, 85–6, 596
Repertoires, 8, 32–3, 53; absence of response from, 272–3; behavior, 139, 574; and behavioral assessment, 44; expansion of, 32, 39; for replacement behavior, 422; shaping, 324; using links in creating behavioral chains, 343–4, 348; verbal, 357, 360, 361
Replication of procedure, 21, 596; across individuals, 228; as scientific responsibility, 5; defined, 5; direct, 392; to assure natural support, 524; to establish generality, 392; using changing-criterion design, 375
Representative judges: for assessing validity, 59
Required relaxation, 458–9, 596
Respondent behavior, 596
Response, 576, 596; delay, 319–20, 574, 596; fluency, 596; suppressed by punishment, 486
Response cost procedure, 402; advantages, 437–9; bonus response cost systems, 442; caution, 441; combining with other procedures, 443; communicating the rules, 442; compared with punishment, 436; convenience, 439; defined, 436–7, 596; diagrammed, 436; disadvantages, 439–40; effective use of, 440–3, 537; emotional reactions, 441; example, 441; illustrated, 437; illustration with stimulus control, 444; long-lasting effects of, 439; minimizing the magnitude, 441; promotes discrimination, 438; with other procedures, 443
Response delay, 319–20
Response deprivation hypothesis (RDH), 159–60, 596
Response fluency, 522–3
Response generalization, 324
Response induction, 324, 501, 502
Responses: imitative, 294
Restitutional overcorrection, 495
Restrictiveness, 106, 402–3
Resurgence. See Spontaneous recovery
Reversal design, 596
Rewards: defined, 140; "extrinsic" and "intrinsic," 179. See also Reinforcement
Role-playing, 596

Rule govern, 291–2
Rule-governed behavior: breaking overdependence, 368; defined, 354–5, 596; control by rules, 355–6, 573, 575; how generalized, 292; problems in, 357–9; and sensitivity to contingencies in effect, 356; teaching, 365
Rules: as control, 291; difficulty in specification, 359; discrimination control, 355; failure to follow, 358; influence on interval schedules, 547

Sᵈs, 268; advantages of developing, 444; defined, 259; disadvantages, 445
S⁺, 596
S⁻, 597
S-1 v. Turlington, 453
Safeguards: for exclusionary timeout, 455; for intense, aversive or unusual procedures, 107; for use of aversive procedures, 492; through measurement, 129
Safety: at level of subgoals, 289; reducing accidents, 288; specialists as source, 184; timeout to prevent home accidents, 451
Satiation: defined, 152–3, 596; avoiding, 154–5, 158, 209
Scatter plot, 46, 182, 281–3
Schedules of reinforcement, 597; influence of schedule, 566; influence of laboratory, 498; interactions, 565; untangling interacting, 567. See also Continuous reinforcement schedule; Intermittent reinforcement schedule; Interval schedules of reinforcement; Ratio schedules of reinforcement
Schizophrenia, 364
Scientific method: selecting variables, 7
Seclusion: compared with timeout, 454
Secondary reinforcer. See Conditioned reinforcer
"Secret Pal Game," 194–5
Selecting discriminative stimuli: illustrations, 271
Selecting procedures: contracting, 123
Self-concept: as improved performance, 33
Self-control, 597
Self-injurious behavior: as high priority, 21; effective use of timeout, 459; effects of punishment, 483; fading restraints, 312; management of antecedents, 268; reduced by contingent exercise, 472; restraint as positive reinforcement, 475; use of electric shock, 491; uses of facial screening, 458; using movement suppression, 459
Self-management, 597; accuracy, 127; basic components, 126; by staff, 127; literature examples, 127; programs, 126; reinforcer delivery, 185; reinforcing one's own behavior, 531; relapse prevention, 528; self reinforcement schedules, 567; self-recording, 126
Self-modeling: as imitative prompt, 296; defined, 296
Self-monitoring: confounds, 83; defined, 185, 597. See also Self-management
Self-recording, 62, 79–80, 83, 126–7, 175, 185–6, 530–1
Self-reinforcement: factors in success, 185; quality assurance, 186
Self-rule formulation: problems, 358
Self-statements: private or public, 365
Sequence analysis, 57, 597; sample of, 26–8
Sequence effects, 26, 597
Sequence of steps, 333
Sequential withdrawal design, 597
Setting events: defined, 254, 597
Shaping procedure, 10, 244, 574, 597; combined with chaining, 348; combined with discriminative stimuli, 334–6; combined with fading, 335; combined with modeling illustrated, 335;

combined with other procedures, 325–7; combined with physical guidance, 335; and computer assisted instruction, 330–1; defined, 324; effectively used, 331–6; illustrated, 324; with groups, 327–8; and personalized system of instruction, 330; procedure to reduce social problems, 326; and programmed instruction, 328–9; reserving reinforcer delivery, 244; selecting step size, 333; strengthening newly acquired behavior, 336; successive approximations, 324; when used, 324

Sheltered workshop: adding self-monitoring, 175

Sherry v. New York State Education Department, 453

"Show" procedure, 294–301, 314, 597

Significance: social, personal or clinical, 390–1, 585; educational, 391, 589; experimental, 389, 590; in single-subject designs, 389

Simultaneous treatment design: or group design, 386. *See also* Alternating treatment design

Single-case experimental designs, 228; accountability, 229; advantages, 228; controlling extraneous variables, 228, 230; demonstrating functional relations, 229–30, 389; enabling new discoveries, 231; selecting appropriate design, 386–9; stability of data points, 229; use of inferential statistics, 385; yielding general findings, 230–1

Single-case research: enables new discoveries, 231; yields general findings, 230

Situational analysis: test scores, records, etc., 25; narrative recording, 26–8

Slot machine game, 158, 597

Social facilitation: of rates of responding, 547

Social feedback: increased with token delivery, 21

Social reinforcers, 160–4, 597

Social responsiveness: enhanced by punishment, 484

Social skills, 34; defined, 60

Social validity: three factors, 391

Specific praise, 165, 597

Speech Topography, 357, 365

Spontaneous recovery, 407, 408–9, 597

Staff training: competence and supervision, 183; reinforcing substeps, 347; token programs, 211

Standardized tests, 25–6

Steady state behavior, 91

Step size, 574, 597–8

Stereotypy: decreased through DRI, 420

Stimulus: acquiring reinforcing properties, 144; complexity, 256, 260–1; defined, 97–8, 598; discriminating presence or absence, 256; enhanced examples, 276; equalization, 318; equivalence, 261–2, 356–7, 360–1, 598; establishing, 256, 575; generalization, 249; mysterious, 280–3; overdependence, 284; overselectivity, 284–5; property, 598; relevant, 282; terminology, 252; used for discrimination, 249, 319; using familiar, 293. *See also* Antecedent stimulus; Discriminative stimulus

Stimulus change, 267–9; as adjunct, 270; advantages of using, 269–70; with aggressive behavior, 282; defined, 267, 598; disadvantages of using, 270; effectively using, 271–2, 572; failure of, 272–4; illustrated, 268; with other procedures, 271

Stimulus control, 10; absence of, 273; absence of reinforcement, 274; aiding extinction, 413; antecedent and response combinations, 256; and aversion procedures, 493; complete, 267, 598; complex, 260; contingent reinforcement, 274; critical to societal survival, 243; defined, 243, 249, 598; developing multiple, 260; development of, 253; discriminative operants, 243, 250; discrimination, 318; examples, 249; illustrations, 267; incomplete, 273; interfering stimuli, 273; maintenance of, 320–1; management of S^ds, 270; reducing behavior, 443–5; reducing errors, 261; shaping and chaining procedures, 244; sensory deficits as problem, 274; simplest instance, 251; timing of stimulus to response, 249; transferring, 306–21; with two or more stimuli, 259

Stimulus generalization: defined, 249; described, 500; possible problems, 501

Stuart v. Nappi, 453

Students: cooperative learning approach, 191

Subgoals: for shaping, 331

Successive approximations: defined, 324, 574, 598; reinforcing, 328; steps of shaping, 333. *See also* Shaping procedure

"Success-O-Gram," 195, 196

Supervision: of aversive procedures, 106

Supplementary reinforcers, 173–4, 346, 598

Support for application of procedures, 120-3

Support groups, 21, 22

Systematic replication: illustrations, 392

Tables for procedures for behavior change, 570–82

Tangible reinforcers, 153–5, 598

Tangible rewards: avoiding satiation, 154

Tape recorder, 69, 81

Target behavior, 30; defined, 24, 598; diminished by punishment, 482; in direct and indirect approach, 33–4; identified, 44; measurement of, 50; for reduction, 401; reinforced with DRL, 430; relapse prevention, 518; selection of, 30–1; to be identified, 24; in a token economy, 208–9; when to target reduction, 396

Task analysis: in behavioral chain, 342–3; check list, 51–2; defined, 51, 598; generation of, 53; of lifting and transfer, 343; literature, 53; measuring, 65–7; peer tutor training, 202; "rational" and "empirical," 344; synonyms,51; validating, 342; of washing hair at sink, 342; with event recording, 65; with feedback to teachers, 67; with rule governed behavior, 365; for safe transfer of patients, 52

"Tell" Procedure (instructional prompts), 291–4, 598

Terminal behavior, 598. *See also* Goal

Tests: for response in repertoire, 272

Test scores and records, 25–6

"Thank You Board," 195, 197

Three-term contingency, 251, 598

Time delay prompting. *See* Delayed prompting

Time management: burnout caution, 530; described, 528; programs, 529

Timeout, 402; advantages, 450–2; combined with DRO, 452; combined with other procedures, 451–2, 456, 578; communicating conditions, 461; compared with extinction, 449; compared with punishment, 450; contingent delay, 462; contingent observation,454, 457; defined, 449–50, 599; diagrammed, 449; disadvantages, 452–6; duration of, 460; effective use of, 456–63, 495, 578; example, 449; exclusionary, 454; facial screening, 458; importance of consistency, 461; legal restrictions on, 453–5, 578; movement suppression method, 458; as non-constructive contingency, 452; overcoming resistance, 462; paired with reinforcement, 456; potential for abuse, 455; public concern over, 455–6; removing reinforcers illustrated, 456; ribbon, 599; risk for abuse, 455; room, 599; seclusion, 453; selecting, 463; skills needed to apply, 462; suppression of other behaviors, 456; time-in, 459; varients, 457–9; versus seclusion, 454; *Welsch v. Likins*, 453

Time sampling system of recording, 86–7, 599. *See also* Interval time-sample

Token economies: administrative approval, 210; cuing praise, 216; defined, 207, 599; definition to measure cleanliness, 219; designing a system, 209–12; essential aspects, 208; examples from literature, 208; implementation, 15-33, 212–20; maintain behavior changed in, 33, 221–4; obtaining approval, 209; parental approval, 210; passing out token system, 222–3; phasing out, 222; populations where applied, 207; providing appropriate amount, 217; reducing behavior in, 220–1; as reponse cost, 439; specifying conditions, 218; steps before implementing, 209; tiered or level systems, 222; token exchange, 222; when to use?, 207

Token reinforcer, 599

Tokens: absence and maintenance, 223; bonus-point system, 214; collective system, 217; delivery and positive feedback, 216; for bonus response cost, 442; logistical and instructional, 212; minimal delay in administering, 214; multiple functions, 213; suggestions, 166; teaching non-verbal clients, 215; with extinction program, 411; with response cost, 437

Token systems: avoidance of ratio strain, 218; from artificial to natural, 221; individualizing, 218; introducing delay of delivery, 222; marketing, 219; point booklet, 213; "price tags" for disabled clients, 214; shifting to natural reinforcers, 224

Topography: communication problems, 365; teaching geometry, 317

Topography of response, 599

Total communication approaches, 363

Training: contingency managers, 104; recorders of data, 83–4, 106; sites, 83–4; staff for a token economy, 211–12

Transferring stimulus control, 306; delayed prompting, 307–9; defined, 599; fading, 311–21; graduated prompting, 309–11; moment of transfer, 307, 573

Transitory behavior, 63, 65, 81, 599

Treasure box, 158, 599

Treatment: phase, 97, 599; utility of assessment, 45, 599

Unconditioned aversive stimulus, 144, 469–70, 599

Unconditioned positive reinforcers, 144

Unconditioned reinforcer, 144, 599

U.S. Department of Health, Education and Welfare: informed consent, 41

Validity, 599; baseline data, 92; described, 229; educational and social, 391, 597; externally and internally in treatment programs, 373, 592; of internal recording, 72; in measurements, 58

Vandalism: in a school system, 128; rates in schools due to punishment, 486

Variable-interval (VI) schedules: adding limited-hold schedules, 549–50, 581; advantages and disadvantages, 544–5; compared to variable-time interval, 538–9; compared to fixed-interval schedule, 539–40, 550, 581; consistency of performance under, 541–2; defined, 538; described, 539; error patterns, 542; promoting preferred rates of responding under, 543–50; responding during extinction, 543–4; response rates, 540–1; scallop, 541–2; when to choose, 551

Variable-ratio (VR) schedules: characteristics of, 554; compared with fixed-ratio schedule, 555–7, 582; compared with interval schedules, 557–60, 582; defined, 554; diagrammed, 557; examples of self-reinforcement, 561; with DRH, 565

Variable-time (VT) schedules: compared to fixed-interval schedule, 538–9; compared with fixed-time schedule, 539–40; defined, 538, 599–600; example, 539

Variables: confounding, 227; contextual, 254; defined, 4, 599; dependent, 57, 232–4; distinguishing perspective, 404; extraneous, 230; impact on performance, 4; independent, 50, 97; influenced by context, 6; outcome, 593; recording, 87; socially important, 4

Verbal behavior, 353, 600; and stimulus equivalence, 357-67; possible problems, 357. *See also* Communicative behavior

Verbal repertoire: inadequacies, 357

Verbal stimuli, 600. *See also* Instructional prompts

Video recorder, 81

Videotape, 84, 509

Voluntariness, 41, 109, 110, 114–17, 573, 600

Waiting, 174

Walden Two, Skinner (1948), 467

Welsch v. Likins, 453

Whole-interval time-sampling: defined, 70, 74, 600; underestimates occurrence, 72

Withdrawal: punishment provokes, 485–6

Withdrawal designs: advantages and disadvantages, 236–7; assessing for maintenance, 380; comparisons, 380–1; defined, 232, 600; described, 232; examples, 232; of eye tics, 235; of feedback, 233; sequential-withdrawal design, 380; variations, 232-6; of verbal responses, 234

Within-subject experimental design, 600

Wrist abacus: illustrated, 68

Wyatt v. Stickney, 103, 106, 108, 122, 170, 453, 492

X axis, 88

Y axis, 87

Zone system, 86, 600